AUSTRALIAN DICTIONARY
OF BIOGRAPHY
SUPPLEMENT 1580–1980

AUSTRALIAN DICTIONARY OF BIOGRAPHY

SUPPLEMENT 1580–1980

With a name index to the *Australian Dictionary of Biography* to 1980

Edited by
CHRISTOPHER CUNNEEN
with
JILL ROE, BEVERLEY KINGSTON *and* STEPHEN GARTON

MELBOURNE UNIVERSITY PRESS

MELBOURNE UNIVERSITY PRESS
An imprint of Melbourne University Publishing Ltd
187 Grattan Street, Carlton, Victoria 3053, Australia
mup-info@unimelb.edu.au
www.mup.com.au

First published 2005
Reprinted 2006

Text © Australian National University 2005
Design and typography © Melbourne University Publishing Ltd 2005

Typeset in Malaysia by Syarikat Seng Teik Sdn. Bhd.
Printed in Australia by BPA Print Group

National Library of Australia Cataloguing-in-Publication entry

Australian dictionary of biography. Supplement 1580-1980.
  ISBN 0 522 84236 4 (set).
  ISBN 0 522 85214 9 (supplement 1580-1980).
  1. Biography. 2. Australia—Biography—Dictionaries.
  I. Cunneen, Christopher, 1940-.
920.094

WORKING PARTIES

Armed Services
Peter Burness, C. D. Clark, John Coates, Peter Dennis, Alec Hill, David Horner (chair), John McCarthy, Perditta McCarthy, Philip Mulcare, Anthony Staunton, Alan Stephens, D. Stevens, A. J. Sweeting

Commonwealth
Nicholas Brown (chair), David Carment, Patricia Clarke, John Farquharson, Bill Gammage, Tom Griffiths (retired), Robert Hyslop, John Nethercote, Graeme Powell, Libby Robin, John Thompson, Jill Waterhouse

New South Wales
John Carmody, Chris Cunneen, Ross Curnow, Frank Farrell*, Stephen Garton, Bridget Griffen-Foley, Murray Goot, Warwick Hirst, Beverley Kingston (chair), J. K. McLaughlin, Andrew Moore, Bede Nairn, Heather Radi (retired), Jill Roe, Dagmar Schmidmaier, Alan Ventress

Queensland
Pat Buckridge (chair), M. D. Cross, Kay Ferres, Richard Fotheringham, M. W. French, Jennifer Harrison, I. F. Jobling, Lorna McDonald, Belinda McKay, Dawn May, Olivia Robinson, S. J. Routh, Joanne Scott, C. G. Sheehan

South Australia
Margaret Allen, R. André, J. Bannon, Joyce Gibberd, R. M. Gibbs, David Hilliard, P. A. Howell (chair), Helen Jones, J. H. Love, Judith Raftery, Jenny Tilby Stock, Patricia Stretton

Tasmania
G. P. R. Chapman, Shirley Eldershaw, Margaret Glover-Scott, Elizabeth McLeod, S. Petrow, Anne Rand, O. M. Roe (chair), J. A. Taylor

Victoria
J. Arnold, G. R. Brown, Mimi Colligan, B. J. Costar, Jim Davidson, D. Dunstan, Charles Fahey, F. J. Kendall, J. F. Lack (chair), P. Love, Janet McCalman, D. T. Merrett, R. A. Murray, J. R. Poynter, Carolyn Rasmussen, J. D. Rickard, Judith Smart, F. Strahan*

Western Australia
Wendy Birman, David Black, G. C. Bolton (chair), Michal Bosworth, Dorothy Erickson, Charles Fox, Sue Graham-Taylor, Jenny Gregory, Lenore Layman, John McIlwraith, Jenny Mills, Jill Milroy, Clement Mulcahy, Jan Ryan, Tom Stannage

Indigenous
Nicholas Brown, Dawn Casey, Ann Curthoys, Ann McGrath, Margo Neale, Frances Peters-Little (chair), Kaye Price, Peter Read, Tim Rowse

* deceased

vi

PREFACE

Since the inception in 1962 of the *Australian Dictionary of Biography* (*ADB*), sixteen volumes of the nation's premier dictionary of historical biography have appeared in print. Contributors to these volumes have researched and written biographies of more than 10 000 individuals of significance in Australian history who died by 1980. Further volumes covering the period 1981–2000 are in preparation. This volume is a supplement to Volumes 1–16, adding more than 500 new biographies to the coverage of the series to date, and including men and women who range in time from Dirk Hartog, born in 1580, to John McKeddie, who died in 1980.

From the outset the *ADB* has served as an essential work of reference for scholars in the humanities and the social sciences, and as an authoritative source of biographical information available to all Australians. Nonetheless many of the volumes, particularly the early ones, were published before the explosion in Australian historical research in the 1970s and 1980s.

As a supplement to the series, this volume seeks to both capture and advance biographical knowledge brought to light by research and scholarship in recent times. Newer fields, such as women's history, Indigenous history and social and cultural history, have highlighted many names of significant individuals little known at the time earlier volumes were produced, for example, the artist Mickey of Ulladulla and the entrepreneur Maria Lord. Likewise new names of significance have been uncovered in well-established fields such as convict history, as happened when the journals of First Fleet diarist Jacob Nagle were discovered in the 1990s. Ongoing research in established fields has also made possible reassessments of individuals passed over for earlier volumes but now seen as more significant for understanding Australia's past, such as the Aboriginal warriors Pemulwuy and Tarenorerer and the temperance advocate Jessie Ackermann. In a few instances, important individuals, such as James Matra, the proponent of a convict colony at Botany Bay, Sir George Davis, the manufacturer of Davis Gelatine, and Edwin Street, who founded Streets Ice Cream, were inadvertently overlooked. In addition, some well-known names, such as the Dutch navigator Dirk Hartog and the shipwreck victim Eliza Fraser, who were previously considered outside the criteria for inclusion in earlier volumes, have been further researched.

The production of a supplementary volume is a major initiative of the editorial board of the *ADB*. The idea dates from 1996, when the possibility of a 'missing persons' volume was first raised at the board. The next step was to canvas opinion from a wider group involved in producing the *Dictionary*. In 1998 the supplement idea was referred for comment to the working parties, which received it enthusiastically. Thus, in 2000 the board formally endorsed the proposal for a supplementary volume. It was, however, evident that such a volume, although necessary, could not be accommodated within the *Dictionary*'s publication schedule for a number of years, and that an alternative source of funding had to be found if the proposal was to proceed.

It was decided that applying for an Australian Research Council grant offered the best opportunity to obtain the funding required for such an ambitious project. Jill Roe, chair of the editorial board, persuaded the board that a cross-university research team, preferably based in one city to ensure the effective management of the project, would be a sound basis on which to develop a grant application. The board endorsed this approach, and she then invited fellow board members Beverley Kingston, from the University of New South Wales, and Stephen Garton, from the University of Sydney, to join her as Chief Investigators in a grant application, which proved successful. Keys to this success were the appointment of former deputy general editor of the *ADB*, Chris Cunneen, as senior research associate and project manager, together with the readiness of the Department of Modern History at Macquarie University to host the project.

The volume has been five years in the making. Because its focus is on identifying notable Australians worthy of addition to the current published series, it does not attempt to cover a broad cross-section of society, as do other volumes. With, for instance, 161 women and 49 Aborigines, a far higher proportion than in earlier volumes, the entries here focus on Australians of significance previously missed, regardless of their representativeness. This also explains the lack of long entries. Early volumes have provided a comprehensive and authoritative coverage of the most notable Australians, from prime ministers to criminals: politicians, for example, warranted substantial entries of up to 6000 words. Here, the largest entries are just more than 1000 words; the smallest is 426 words.

As has generally been the practice for the *ADB*, entries and authors were chosen by working parties. The steering committee is grateful for the sterling work of these committees and their chairs. This volume contains 142 entries selected by the New South Wales working party, 103 by the Victorian, 76 by the South Australian, 54 by the Queensland, 43 by the Tasmanian, 39 by the West Australian and 6 by the Commonwealth. The steering committee, consisting of Chris Cunneen and the three Chief Investigators, added 41 others.

The *ADB* headquarters is at the Australian National University. The support and input of the general editor Dr Diane Langmore and staff, and previously of Professor John Ritchie, is gratefully acknowledged elsewhere, but particular mention must be made here of essential assistance in verifying birth, death and marriage details. Because project funding was limited, however, there has been less cross-checking of information included in entries than is usual in the *ADB* itself. It has therefore been necessary to rely more heavily upon individual authors for accuracy.

The 399 contributors have given unstinting support. Most of them have written a single article; however, fifty-two wrote two articles each, twelve wrote three entries, seven wrote four and three (including the *Dictionary*'s most prolific author Gerry Walsh) provided five. David Dunstan contributed six entries, Beverley Kingston and John Lack seven each, and the top-scorer for this volume, Wendy Birman, wrote eight. Five authors, Greg Curnow, Frank Farrell, Philippa Fletcher, Joan Kerr and John D. Kerr, died after submitting their articles. We deeply regret their deaths. The steering committee is very grateful to all contributors for the free contribution of their time and research.

At the end of this book there is an index of names that appear in the *Supplement* and in the sixteen volumes of the *ADB* published to date. This will assist readers quickly and easily to find the appropriate volume and page number for the men and women, now approaching 11 000, who died before 1981 whose biographies are included in the series as a whole. This also means that those who appear in this volume end up where they rightly belong, in the mainstream.

ACKNOWLEDGMENTS

This supplementary volume to the *Australian Dictionary of Biography* (*ADB*) was funded by a large grant from the Australian Research Council. The headquarters of the project was in the Department of Modern History, Division of Humanities, at Macquarie University, Sydney. Chief investigators represented that university as well as the University of Sydney and the University of New South Wales. From the beginning, generous support and help was provided by Professor John Ritchie and Dr Diane Langmore, successively general editors of the *ADB*, and their staff, based in the Research School of Social Sciences at the Australian National University in Canberra. Darryl Bennet, Jolyon Horner, Anthea Bundock, Edna Kauffman, Brian Wimborne, Gail Clements and Karen Ciuffetelli provided invaluable help, as did the *ADB*'s interstate research assistants, in particular Joyce Gibberd, Rachel Grahame, Jennifer Harrison, Anne Rand and Kim Torney. However, gratitude is due to all the *ADB* staff in Canberra.

Heartfelt thanks are due to Robyn Arrowsmith, the *Supplement*'s hard-working administrative officer, and to Martha Campbell and Christine Fernon whose assistance with each entry in the supplement was indispensable. Wendy Birman was indefatigable in helping with research in Perth. In the compilation of the name index, a debt is due to Hilary Kent, who edited the index to volumes 1 to 12 of the *ADB* (1991), which has been heavily relied upon for the name index in this volume.

Section editors and working parties are also thanked for their generous assistance, not only in choosing names, authors and word lengths, but also for general help with other inquiries. All gave their time freely and willingly. For particular advice the supplement owes much to friends such as Rob Anderson, Ivan Barko, David Carment, John Carmody, Jan Critchett, Ambrose Chong, Ross Curnow, Mel Davies, Ed Duyker, Warwick Eather, Vicki Grieves, Bridget Griffen-Foley, Ian Hancock, Matthew Higgins, Leonard Janiszewski, Carol Liston, Lorine Marsh, Tim Moroney, Heather Radi, Kerry Regan, Mark Richmond, Sue Rosen, Spencer Routh, F. B. Smith, Alan Ventress, Ellen Warne and Wendy Sutherland.

Within Australia the *Supplement* is indebted to many librarians and archivists; particular thanks are due to the National Library of Australia, the Australian War Memorial, the Australian Institute of Aboriginal and Torres Strait Islander Studies, ScreenSound Australia and the National Archives of Australia, all in Canberra; to the State Library of New South Wales, Sydney, the State Library of South Australia, Adelaide, the Library of Western Australia, Perth, the State Library of Queensland, Brisbane; and to the Melbourne Club, the State Library of Victoria, the Royal Humane Society of Australasia and the University of Melbourne Archives, Melbourne. Generous assistance was also provided by John Shields and the Biographical Register of the Australian Labour Movement.

Essential help in verifying birth, death, marriage and probate details has been provided by the co-operation of registrars in New South Wales, Queensland, South Australia, Tasmania, Victoria, Western Australia, the Northern Territory and the Australian Capital Territory; by the General Register offices in London and Edinburgh; by the Register General, Northern Ireland, and the registrars of probate in Adelaide and Melbourne.

ACKNOWLEDGMENTS

For other assistance overseas, thanks are due to Judith Farrington and Pamela Ayshford, London; Betty Iggo, Edinburgh; William Murphy, Dublin; and Roger Joslyn, New York; to the universities of Cambridge and Oxford, and the London Metropolitan Archives, England; the universities of Edinburgh and Glasgow, Scotland; and the University of Vienna and the Technical University of Vienna, Austria. We are grateful, too, to Dr Elisabeth Lebensaft of the *Austrian Dictionary of Biography*, Vienna; Dr Makariusová of the *Czech Biographical Dictionary*; and to other individuals and institutions who have co-operated with the supplement project.

AUTHORS

AITKEN, Richard:
  Cole, T. C.
ALBRECHT, Paul:
  Tjalkabota
ALLEN, Margaret:
  Day
ANDERSON, Douglas:
  Jolly
ANDRÉ, Roger:
  Smith, R.
ANEMAAT, Louise:
  Radecki
ANGUS, Beverley M.:
  Pound
ARKLEY, Lindsey:
  Sievwright
ARNOLD, John:
  Kennedy; Kirtley
ARROWSMITH, Robyn:
  Wallace
ATTWOOD, Bain:
  Cameron, E.

BACH, Joanne:
  Moffatt; Morgan, A.
BAIN, Jim:
  Mullens
BANNERMAN, Colin:
  Abbott
BANNON, J. C.:
  Griffiths
BARRETT-LENNARD, R. J. S.:
  McClemans
BARWICK, Laura:
  Briggs
BATE, Weston:
  Dendy; Hart, E.
BEAUMONT, Joan:
  Waugh
BEGGS SUNTER, Anne:
  Seekamp
BEILHARZ, Peter:
  Tripp
BELL, Peter:
  Watson, J.
BENTLEY, Philip:
  Hodgson
BERTRAND, Ina:
  Howarde; Morgan, V.
BETTISON, Margaret:
  Hodge; Ling; Martel
BIDDINGTON, Judith:
  Russell, D.
BIRMAN, Wendy:
  Barr; Booty; Braine; Forster; Hayman; Mayrhofer; Perkins; Wolff

BLACK, David:
  Sampson
BLADES, Genevieve:
  Samuels
BLAINEY, Anna E.:
  Lloyd
BLAIR, Sandy:
  Howe
BOLTON, G. C.:
  Cameron, R.; Grave; Hughes, T.; McClemans; Marshall, T.
BONGIORNO, Frank:
  Fryer; Kroemer
BOSWORTH, Michal:
  Nicolay
BRADSHAW, Richard:
  Merlin
BRANAGAN, D. F.:
  Campbell, Joseph; Thompson
BREEN, Shayne:
  Beeton
BROOME, Richard:
  Meekin
BROWN, Elaine:
  Fraser; Pettigrew
BROWN-MAY, Andrew:
  Cahill, E.; Henderson, D.
BROWNE, Geoff:
  Costello; Girdlestone; Kyte; Martin, W.
BROWNRIGG, Jeff:
  Forde
BRUMBY, Michael:
  Hall
BUCKRIDGE, Patrick:
  Moynihan
BURGMANN, Verity:
  Waite
BURLEY, Stephanie:
  Adams, S.
BUSH, Janine:
  Zichy-Woinarski
BUTCHER, Mike:
  Knight
BUTTERFIELD, Annette:
  Steffanoni
BYGOTT, Ursula:
  Barff; King; MacCallum
BYRNE, Geraldine:
  Grave

CAIN, Frank:
  Wood, W.
CAMPBELL, Keith O.:
  Broughton
CANNON, Michael:
  Grover

xi

CAPPER, Betty:
  McLeod
CARDEN-COYNE, Ana:
  Lindsay
CARMODY, John:
  Giorza; Lowin
CHANT, Barry:
  Hetherington
CHITTLEBOROUGH, Jon:
  Horrocks
CLARK, Laurel:
  Baillière
CLARKE, Patricia:
  Barton; Mowle
CLARSEN, Georgine:
  Anderson, A.
CLUNE, David:
  Colbourne
COLEBATCH, Hal G. P.:
  Gibson, F.
COLLIGAN, Mimi:
  Edwards, M.; Hennings; Kreitmayer; Lewis
CONNORS, Libby:
  Dundalli
CONOLE, Peter:
  Smith, Matthew
COOKE, Simon:
  Candler
COSSINS, Geoffrey:
  Wilson
CRITCHETT, Jan:
  Hood; Kaawirn Kuunawarn; Mobourne
CRITTENDEN, Victor:
  Yates
CROSS, Manfred:
  Barney
CROWLEY, Bill:
  Pugliese
CUNNEEN, Chris:
  Bethel; Caesar; Cashin; Hughes, J.; Rogers
CUNNINGHAM, Jackie:
  Costello
CURNOW, Greg*:
  West
CUSHING, Nancy:
  Baker

DALY, John A.:
  Leschen
DARIAN-SMITH, Kate:
  Buntine
DARRAGH, Thomas A.:
  Harris; Müller; Proeschel
DAVIES, Lynn:
  Keen
DE ARAUGO, Tess:
  Pepper
DE JABRUN, Mary d'Eimar:
  Culpin
DE SERVILLE, Paul:
  Austin, E.
DEWAR, Mickey:
  Dhakiyarr
* deceased

DICKENSON, Mary:
  Nowland
DICKEY, Brian:
  Farr, J.; Willuson
DIEHM, Ian:
  Henry
DOWLING, Peter A.:
  Grosse
DOWNS, Stephen:
  Baker
DUNCAN, Beth:
  Thomas
DUNSTAN, David:
  Akehurst; Curtain; Deschamps; Jamieson; Knight; Trouette
DURDIN, Joan:
  Sweetapple
DUYKER, Edward:
  Girardin; Huon De Kermadec; Marion Dufresne; Siebenhaar
DYSTER, Barrie:
  Ross, J. & T.

EASTGATE, Marianne:
  North
EASTON, Arthur:
  Nagle
EDWARDS, Ken:
  Samuels
ELLEM, Bradon:
  O'Neill
ELLIS, Julie-Ann:
  Green, Anne
ERICKSON, Dorothy:
  Dorrington; Lazenby; Rossi
ERICKSON, Rica:
  Adams, J.
EVANS, Julie:
  Adamson

FAHEY, Charles:
  Russell, E.
FARRELL, Frank*:
  Judd
FENCAK, Mary M.:
  Hays
FERRES, Kay:
  Forrest
FINN, Rosslyn:
  Packham
FLANNERY, Nancy Robinson:
  Mawson
FLETCHER, B. H.:
  Austin, C.; Bladen
FLETCHER, Philippa L.*:
  Milne
FLOREANI, Carmel:
  Del Fabbro
FORSYTH, Sue:
  McGahey
FOSTER, Robert:
  Logic; Poltpalingada

* deceased

JONES, Helen:
  Colton; Corbin; Forsyth; Lake
JONES, Philip:
  Cubadgee; Unaipon
JORDENS, Ann-Mari:
  Harwood

KEENE, Judith:
  Bull, J.
KELLY, Farley:
  Alexander
KENNY, Robert:
  Stähle
KERR, Anthea:
  Bluett, A.
KERR, Joan*:
  Horseman
KERR, John D.*:
  Easterby
KEVIN, Catherine:
  Melocco
KING, Norma:
  Corlis
KINGSTON, Beverley:
  Gowing; Maclurcan; Muskett; Parry; Pyke; Richardson; Wicken
KITSON, W. S.:
  Warner
KLAASSEN, Nic:
  Nuyts
KLEINERT, Sylvia:
  Bull, E.
KNEEBONE, Heidi:
  Teichelmann
KOCH, Christopher:
  Koch
KOHEN, J. L.:
  Pemulwuy
KOWALD, Margaret:
  Duncan
KRAEHENBUEHL, Darrell N.:
  Tepper

LACK, John:
  Allen; Buley; Carroll; Clement; Gibson, J.; Hardie; Ross, C.
LALOR, Norm:
  South
LASTER, Kathy:
  Knorr
LAUGHREN, Pat:
  Mobsby
LAWSON, Valerie:
  Bloch
LEE, Christopher:
  Crist
LEWI, Hannah:
  Beasley
LEWIS, Miles:
  Barnet
LIGHTFOOT, Mary Louise:
  Lightfoot

* deceased

LONDEY, Peter:
  Nimmo
LONGHURST, Robert I.:
  Drew, W.
LOVE, J. H.:
  Hamilton, G.
LOVE, Peter:
  Robertson
LOW, John:
  Simos
LUPTON, Roger:
  Maclean
LYDON, Jane:
  Way Kee

McCARTHY, Greg:
  Crooks
MacCULLOCH, J.:
  Levvy
McEWIN, Emma:
  Mawson
McFARLANE, Ian:
  Dalrymple
MacFIE, Peter:
  Crooke
MacGILLIVRAY, Leith G.:
  Smith, C.; Stevenson
MACILWAIN, Margaret:
  Cooke
McILWRAITH, John:
  Troup
MACINTYRE, Rosemary:
  Orr
McKAY, Belinda:
  Coungeau
McKERN, H. H. G.:
  Hamlet
MACKINNON, Alison:
  Benham
McKINNON, Ross:
  Hill
McLAREN, Glen:
  Austin, R.
McLEOD, E. A.:
  Irvine
McMAHON, J. F.:
  Douglas
MACNAB, K. K.:
  Green, Alexander
McQUEEN, Humphrey:
  Wimble
McQUILTON, John:
  Morgan, D.
MANSFIELD, Joan:
  Goodlet
MARENDY, Michael:
  Brydon; Walker
MARKEY, Ray:
  Stanley
MARTIN, John Stanley:
  Lyng
MARTIN, Megan:
  Lorenzini; Miller; Smith, Maria

MASSY, Charles:
  Collins
MATSON-GREEN, Vicki maikutena:
  Tarenorerer
MAWER, Granville Allen:
  Doolan
MAXWELL-STEWART, Hamish:
  Herbert
MEDCALF, M.:
  Wood, M.
MENGHETTI, Diane:
  Fraire
MERCER, D. R.:
  Morwood
MILLS, Jenny:
  Hamilton, C.
MITCHELL, Bruce:
  Webster
MOORE, Andrew:
  De Groot
MOORE, Clive R.:
  Tonga
MORGAN, Kevin:
  Ross, C.
MORRIS, Barry:
  Moseley
MORRIS, Deirdre:
  Weigel
MOSS, Prim:
  Corrie
MULCAHY, Clement:
  Torres
MULVANEY, D. J.:
  Erlikilyika; Tulaba

NELSON, Judy:
  Kerr
NEVILLE, Richard:
  Backler
NEWBIGIN, Nerida:
  May
NOONAN, Gerard:
  Horsfall
NORMAN, Anthony:
  McMahon
NUGENT, Maria:
  Timbery
NUNN, Jean M.:
  Bates
NURSEY-BRAY, Paul:
  Fantin

O'CALLAGHAN, Jennifer:
  Grace
O'DONNELL, Ruan:
  Dwyer
OPPENHEIMER, Melanie:
  Goward

PAGE, Vilma:
  Lucas; Morrice
PAISLEY, Fiona:
  Fernando; Jones, E.

PALMER, Sheridan:
  Nuttall
PARK, Margaret:
  Blue
PARRY, Naomi:
  Lock; Musquito
PEARCE, Vicki:
  Petersen
PENNAY, Bruce:
  Mott
PENNEY, Jan:
  Edwards, A.
PEOPLES, Jo:
  Serena
PERKINS, John:
  Lowe
PETROW, Stefan:
  Coulter; Ewing
PHILLIPS, Margaret:
  Crooks
PHILLIPS, Murray G.:
  Springfield
PHILLIPS, Walter:
  Johnston, K.
PINK, Kerry:
  Bell
PLAYFORD, Phillip, E.:
  Hartog
POPE, Brian:
  Cuper
POYNTER, J. R.:
  Campbell, C.
PRESS, Margaret M.:
  Leigh
PRICE, Barry:
  Watson, A.

QUARTLY, Marian:
  Lightfoot

RADCLIFFE, John C.:
  Kenny; Marshall, R.
RADI, Heather:
  Makin; Ridgeway
RAMSAY, Mary S.:
  Forlong
RAMSLAND, John:
  Nott
RASMUSSEN, Amanda:
  Lambrick
RASMUSSEN, Carolyn:
  Johnston F.; Walcott
RAY, Andrew J.:
  Sennitt; Wertheim
REECE, R. H. W.:
  MacNamara
REGAN, Kerry:
  Cahill, T.; Peyser
REIGER, Kerreen M.:
  Primrose
REYNOLDS, H.:
  Arthur
REYNOLDS, Peter:
  Jolly

TONKIN, John:
Mercer
TORNEY, Kim:
Rogers
TRACEY, Sue:
Anderson, S.; Francis; Seery
TRANTER, Deborah:
Bolton
TREMBATH, Richard:
Ansell; Coventry
TURNER, Bernadette:
Mayne
TYRRELL, Ian:
Ackermann

VALENTINE, Barbara:
Munro
VAN DEN HOORN, Rob:
Chinner
VAN DE VEN, Anne-Marie:
Broadhurst
VELTRI, Damian:
Kitchen

WADE, John:
Dick; Hogarth
WALKER, D. R.
Hingston
WALL, Barbara:
Congreve
WALSH, G. P.:
Inglis; McGillivray; Mowbray; Narelle;
Zöllner
WALSH, Robin:
Jarvis
WARBURTON, Elizabeth:
Dobbie
WATERHOUSE, Jean:
Joyner
WATERSON, D. B.:
Coffill; MacDonald
WATSON, Al:
Hyde

WATSON, Don:
Marks
WATSON, Joanne:
Curry
WATSON, Tom:
Berry
WEATHERBURN, Hilary:
Gordon
WEBB, Gwenda M.:
Sutton
WHIMPRESS, Bernard:
Marsh
WILKEY, Don:
Richards
WILLIAMS, Lesley:
Greenham
WILLINGHAM, Allan F.:
Buck; Ginn
WILSON, Jacqueline Zara:
Kelly, E.
WINTER, Gillian:
Koch; Wintle
WOODFORDE, Peter:
Fraire
WOODS, Martin:
Birks
WOOLLACOTT, Angela:
Quong
WOOLLEY, Colleen:
Connor
WOTHERSPOON, Garry C.:
Foy
WRIGHT, R.:
Wallis

YOUNG, David:
Blundstone
YOUNG, John:
Sullivan

ZONGOLLOWICZ, Bogumila:
Wroblewski

A NOTE ON SOME PROCEDURES

Differences of opinion exist among our authors, readers and the editorial board as to whether certain information should normally be included—such as cause of death, burial or cremation details, and value of estate. In this volume our practices have been as follows:

Cause of death: usually included, except in the case of those aged over 70.

Burial/cremation: included when details available.

Value of estate: included where possible for categories such as businessmen, and if the amount is unusually high or low. In recent years, when the practice developed of distributing assets early to avoid estate and probate duties, the sum is not always meaningful; moreover, at times it is impossible to ascertain full details. Hence we have resorted to discretionary use.

Some other procedures require explanation:

Measurements: as the least unsatisfactory solution we have used imperial system measurements (as historically appropriate), followed by the metric equivalent in brackets.

Money: we have retained £ (for pounds) for references prior to 14 February 1966 (when the conversion rate was A£1 = A$2).

Religion: stated whenever information is available, but there is often no good evidence of actual practice; for example, the information is confined to marriage and funeral rites.

[q.v.]: the particular volume is given for those included in volumes 1-16, but not for those in this volume. Note that the cross-reference [q.v.] now accompanies the names of all who have separate articles in the *ADB*. In volumes 1-6 it was not shown for royal visitors, governors, lieutenant-governors and those Colonial Office officials who were included.

Small capitals: used for relations and others when they are of substantial importance, though do not have an entry in their own right; these people are also accompanied by a q.v.

Floruit and 'date of death': for the period 1788 to 1939, the placing of subjects in volumes 1 to 12 was determined by when they flourished; in contrast, volumes 13 to 16 (for the period 1940 to 1980) include only people who died in those years.

CORRIGENDA

Every effort is made to check every detail in every article, but a work of the *ADB*'s size and complexity is bound to contain some errors.

Corrigenda have been published with each volume. A consolidated list, including corrections made after the publication of volume 12 (1990), forms part of the index to volumes 1 to 12 (1991). A list of corrigenda compiled since 2000 accompanied volume 16. The next corrigenda will appear with volume 17.

Only corrections are shown; additional information is not included; nor is any reinterpretation attempted. The exception to this procedure occurs when new details about parents, births, marriages and deaths becomes available.

Documented corrections are welcomed. Additional information, with sources, is also invited, and will be placed in the appropriate files for future use. In both cases, readers should write to:

> The General Editor
> Australian Dictionary of Biography
> Research School of Social Sciences
> Coombs Building, No 9
> Australian National University
> CANBERRA ACT 0200
> Australia

The following and other standard works of reference have been widely used, though not usually acknowledged in individual biographies:

Australian Encyclopaedia, 1-2 (Syd, 1925), 1-10 (1958), 1-12 (1983)

Biographical registers for various Australian parliaments: (A. W. Martin & P. Wardle *and* H. Radi, P. Spearritt & E. Hinton *and* C. N. Connolly—New South Wales; D. Black & G. Bolton—Western Australia; K. Thomson & G. Serle *and* G. Browne—Victoria; D. B. Waterson *and* D. B. Waterson & J. Arnold—Queensland; H. Coxon, J. Playford & R. Reid—South Australia; S. & B. Bennett—Tasmania; and J. Rydon—Commonwealth)

O'M. Creagh and E. M. Humphris (eds), *The V.C. and D.S.O.: A Complete Record ...* 1-3 (Lond, 1934)

Dictionary of National Biography (Lond, 1885-1990)

C. A. Hughes and B. D. Graham, *A Handbook of Australian Government and Politics 1890-1964* (Canb, 1968) and 1965-1974 (1977); *Voting for the Australian House of Representatives 1901-1964*, with corrigenda (Canb, 1975), *Queensland Legislative Assembly 1890-1964* (Canb, 1974), *New South Wales* (1975), *Victoria* (1975), and *South Australian, Western Australian and Tasmanian Lower Houses* (1976), D. Black, *An Index to Parliamentary Candidates in Western Australian Elections 1890-1989* (Perth, 1989)

J. Thomas (ed.), *South Australians 1836-1885*, 1-2 (Adel, 1990), J. Statton (ed.), *Biographical Index of South Australians 1836-1885*, 1-4 (Adel, 1986)

F. Johns, *Johns's Notable Australians* (Melb, 1906), *Fred Johns's Annual* (Lond, 1914); *An Australian Biographical Dictionary* (Melb, 1934); P. Serle, *Dictionary of Australian Biography*, 1-2 (Syd, 1949); D. Carment et al (eds), *Northern Territory Dictionary of Biography*, 1 (Darwin, 1990), 2 (Darwin, 1992), 3 (Darwin, 1996); D. Horton (ed.), *The Encyclopaedia of Aboriginal Australia*, 1-2 (Canb, 1994)

S. Sadie (ed.), *The New Grove Dictionary of Music and Musicians*, 1-20 (Lond, 1980); W. Bebbington (ed.), *The Oxford Companion to Australian Music* (Melb, 1997); P. Parsons (ed.), *Companion to Theatre in Australia* (Syd, 1995)

W. Moore, *The Story of Australian Art*, 1-2 (Syd, 1934), (Syd, 1980); A. McCulloch, *Encyclopedia of Australian Art* (Lond, 1968), 1-2 (Melb, 1984), revised S. McCulloch (Syd, 1994)

E. M. Miller, *Australian Literature . . . to 1935* (Melb, 1940), extended to 1950 by F. T. Macartney (Syd, 1956); H. M. Green, *A History of Australian Literature*, 1-2 (Syd, 1961, 2nd edn 1971), revised by D. Green (Syd, 1984-85); W. H. Wilde, J. Hooton & B. Andrews, *The Oxford Companion to Australian Literature* (Melb, 1985), 2nd edn (1994)

Who's Who (Lond) and *Who's Who in Australia* (Syd, Melb), present and past edns

Jobson's Year Book of Public Companies (Syd, Melb), present and past edns

ABBREVIATIONS USED IN BIBLIOGRAPHIES

ABC	Australian Broadcasting Commission/Corporation	Hist	History/Historical
ACT	Australian Capital Territory	HO	Home Office
ADB	Australian Dictionary of Biography	Hob	Hobart
		HR	House of Representatives
Adel	Adelaide	*HRA*	*Historical Records of Australia*
ADFA	Australian Defence Force Academy	*HRNSW*	*Historical Records of New South Wales*
AIF	Australian Imperial Force	Inc	Incorporated
AJCP	Australian Joint Copying Project	Inst	Institute, Institution
ALP	Australian Labor Party	intro	introduction, introduced by
ANU	Australian National University		
ANZAAS	Australian and New Zealand Association for the Advancement of Science	*J/Jnl*	*Journal*
		JCU	James Cook University, Townsville
A'sia/n	Australasia/n	JOL	John Oxley Library, Brisbane
Assn	Association		
Aust/n	Australia/n	L/Lib	Library
AWM	Australian War Memorial, Canb	LA	Legislative Assembly
		LaTL	La Trobe Library, Melb
Bd	Board	Launc	Launceston
BHP	Broken Hill Proprietary Co. Ltd	LC	Legislative Council
bib	bibliography	Lond	London
biog	biography, biographical		
BL	J. S. Battye Library of West Australian History, Perth	*Mag*	*Magazine*
		Melb	Melbourne
Brisb	Brisbane	mfm	microfilm
		MJA	*Medical Journal of Australia*
c	circa	ML	Mitchell Library, Syd
CAE	College of Advanced Education	ms/s	manuscript/s
Canb	Canberra		
CO	Colonial Office, London	NAA	National Archives of Australia
co	company	nd	date of publication unknown
comp	compiler	NLA	National Library of Australia, Canb
Corp/s	Corporation/s		
CSD	Chief Secretary's Department	no	number
CSIRO	Commonwealth Scientific and Industrial Research Organisation	NSW	New South Wales
		NT	Northern Territory
		NY	New York
CSO	Colonial Secretary's Office	NZ	New Zealand
cte	committee		
Cwlth	Commonwealth	OD	Outward Dispatches
		ODNB	*Oxford Dictionary of National Biography*
Dept	Department		
ed/s	editor/s	p, pp	page, pages
Edinb	Edinburgh	*PD*	*Parliamentary Debates*
edn	edition	PNG	Papua New Guinea
Eng	England	*PP*	*Parliamentary Papers*
		PRO	Public Record Office
Fr	Father (priest)	*Procs*	*Proceedings*
		pt/s	part/s
Geog	Geographical		
Govt	Government	Qld	Queensland
		QSA	Queensland State Archives
HA	House of Assembly	*Qtrly*	*Quarterly*

RMIT	Royal Melbourne Institute of Technology	Tas	Tasmania/n
		T&CJ	*Australian Town and Country Journal*
SA	South Australia/n	*Trans*	*Transactions*
Sel	Select	ts	typescript/transcript
SLNSW	State Library of New South Wales	TSA	Tasmanian State Archives
SLQ	State Library of Queensland	UK	United Kingdom
SLSA	State Library of South Australia	UNE	University of New England
SLT	State Library of Tasmania	Univ	University
SLV	State Library of Victoria	UNSW	University of New South Wales
SLWA	State Library of Western Australia	UPNG	University of Papua New Guinea
		USA	United States of America
SMH	*Sydney Morning Herald*	UWA	University of Western Australia
Soc	Society		
SRNSW	State Records Authority of New South Wales	V&P	Votes and Proceedings
		Vic	Victoria/n
SRSA	State Records of South Australia	vol/s	volume/s
SRWA	State Records Office of Western Australia	WA	Western Australia/n
Supp	Supplement		
Syd	Sydney	* deceased	

A

ABBOTT, EDWARD (1801-1869), politician and 'aristologist', was born on 25 February 1801 in Sydney, eldest son of Edward Abbott [q.v.1], a Canadian-born army officer, and his wife Louisa. Arriving in Hobart Town in February 1815, when Edward senior took up the post of deputy judge-advocate, in 1818 young Edward became clerk to his father. He continued to work in the Lieutenant Governor's Court until 1824, then became a pastoralist, having received land grants of 1100 acres (445 ha) on the Derwent River in 1823. In 1828 he was made a justice of the peace.

In 1839 Abbott founded the *Hobart Town Advertiser* and was its editor and publisher until 1842. He was appointed a police magistrate in 1848 at Kangaroo Point. At his residence there, on 25 April 1853, he married Ann Johnson; the minister of the Independent Chapel officiated. On 15 September 1856 Abbott was elected to the first House of Assembly as member for Clarence, retaining the seat until 27 January 1864, when he was elected unopposed to the Legislative Council for Cambridge. In 1867 he retired to become usher of the Black Rod. He was warden of Clarence municipality from its inauguration in 1860 until 1868.

Rarely speaking at length on the substance of legislation, Abbott was renowned for his knowledge of procedure and readiness to take issue on points of order. From about 1839 he took over his family's relentless pursuit of a claim against the government over the ownership of 210 acres (85 ha) of land known as the Launceston swamp. After virtually exhausting his financial resources he succeeded in 1860 in obtaining substantial compensation, though less than he had sought. His landmark publication, *The English and Australian Cookery Book. Cookery for the many, as well as for the "upper ten thousand"* (London, 1864), was probably an attempt to recover his fortunes.

Although published pseudonymously, by 'an Australian Aristologist', the book was known to be Abbott's work. It was a gastronomic miscellany of 'the modern cookery of the mother country and the colonies', and of Continental and Hebrew cookery. Recipes included 'Roast Beef of Old England', 'kangaroo steamer' and 'slippery bob'—a dish of battered kangaroo brains fried in emu fat. In scope and style the book was somewhat idiosyncratic, as in its use of the arcane expression 'aristology' (coined by Thomas Walker in London in 1835 to describe the art of dining) and its extensive selection of 'appropriate quotations and racy extracts'.

Abbott was noted for his hospitality and his excellent *cuisine*. Friends praised his integrity in official duties, while acknowledging his eccentricities. Said to be 'the first to counsel the settling of disputes in legal matters, and to prevent litigation', he hardly demonstrated such qualities in pursuit of his own claims. To his successors at the *Advertiser* he was 'a thoroughly high principled, and truthful politician'. The *Mercury* saw him as 'but a very moderately educated man, a violent partisan with nothing of experience, but that which the limited circle of his colonial intercourse has given him'. He occasionally gave way to violent passion, as when he assaulted the attorney-general (Sir) Francis (Villeneuve) Smith [q.v.6], for which he was fined £5 and bound over to keep the peace, or was unruly and abusive during a parliamentary debate and ordered to leave the House.

Survived by his wife and two sons, Abbott died of prostate disease on 4 April 1869 at Bellerive and was buried in old St Mark's Anglican chapel where an impressive monument was erected. As author of possibly the first substantial cookery manual by an Australian, he made an important contribution to Australian culinary literature.

HRA, 3, pt iv, pp 158 & 556, pt vii, p 442; E. Morris Miller, *Pressmen and Governors* (Syd, 1952); T. Walker, *Aristology, or, The Art of Dining* (Cambridge, UK, 1965); *Tas Ancestry*, 20, no 3, Dec 1999, p 151; *Hob Town Advertiser*, 11 Jan 1864; *Examiner* (Lond), 20 Aug 1864, p 538; *Mercury* (Hob), 5 May 1856, p 2, 4 Feb 1858, p 2, 31 July 1858, p 1, 2 Aug 1858, p 2, 2 Sept 1858, p 3, 21 Dec 1868, p 2, 5 April 1869, p 1; *Tas Times*, 5 Apr 1869; C. Bannerman, Print Media and the Development of an Australian Culture of Food and Eating c.1850 to c.1920 (Ph.D. thesis, Univ Canb, 2001).   COLIN BANNERMAN

ABDULLAH, MULLAH (c.1855-1915), camel-driver and Islamic priest, was born probably in Afghanistan or a nearby region of India (Pakistan), as he was literate in Dari, the formal language of Afghanistan. He may have come from a family of mullahs, a profession generally handed from father to son, the title was conferred after training in Islamic spiritual teachings and law at a *madrasa* school, usually within a mosque. Arriving in South Australia about 1890, from about 1899 he worked at Broken Hill, New South Wales, probably as a camel-driver and certainly as mullah to the Afghans at the local 'Ghantown'.

As spiritual head of a group of cameleers, he led the daily prayers, presided at burials and killed animals *al halal* for food consumption. A sanitary inspector twice prosecuted him for killing meat illegally and for not belonging to the butchers' union. By 1915 Abdullah was a grey-bearded zealot, fiery when insulted.

Also in Broken Hill was GOOL BADSHA MAHOMED (c.1875-1915), camel-driver, soldier and labourer. He had been born near the North-West Frontier of India, in the mountainous Tirah region of Afghanistan, an area that operated under local tribal law and was never governed by the powers of Kabul. An Afridi tribesman, whose characteristics were fieriness and feuding, he spoke Pushtu. Gool came to Australia in his youth and probably worked as a cameleer before going home to enlist in the Turkish Army. After fighting in four campaigns under Sultan Abdul Mohammed Rasheed, he returned to Australia about 1912, but the camel carrying-business was beginning to decline. After working in the silver-mines at Broken Hill he was retrenched. He became an ice-cream vendor, pushing his cart around the streets. In World War I his religious and nationalistic fervour increased as he became incensed by the conflict and by the many unemployed miners enlisting in the services. He and Abdullah smoked marihuana together as they discussed their mutual grievances and intentions.

On the morning of 1 January 1915 the two men raised the Turkish flag on the ice-cream cart and, using the cart to carry their weapons, set out on a terrorist-suicide mission: an attack on a train carrying holiday-makers to Silverton for the annual Manchester Unity Order of Oddfellows picnic. Gool (fighting for the Turks against the British allies) and Abdullah (avenging his malice against the butchers' union sanitary inspector and his honour as Islamic priest) opened fire on the moving, open carriages. Four citizens were killed and seven others severely wounded. The sanitary inspector, though on the train, was not among the victims. The two Afghans then moved to higher ground where, after a lengthy exchange of fire, a posse of local rifle-club members, civilians and police rushed them. Abdullah was shot dead. Gool, wounded, was taken to the Broken Hill hospital where he died of gunshot wounds. A letter bearing the seal of the sultan, honouring his services to the Turkish Army, was found in his waist-belt. In suicide notes left at the scene of the battle, found three days later, they had written of their grievances and stated that they acted alone. Gool was illiterate; his letter, written by the mullah, was in a mixture of Dari and simple Urdu.

On the night of New Year's Day the two bodies were buried secretly and hurriedly below the floor of a public building used for storing mine explosives. Police employed an Aboriginal tracker to dig the graves; the townspeople, wanting their own revenge, had refused to bury the Afghans.

P. Rajkowski, *In the Tracks of the Camel-men* (Syd, 1987); C. Stevens, *Tin Mosques & Ghantowns* (Melb, 1989); *Barrier Miner*, 1, 2, 4, 5, 12 Jan 1915; Mr B. Carlton, correspondence, 30 Sept 1979, Broken Hill L archives (NSW).

CHRISTINE STEVENS

ACKERMANN, JESSIE A. (1857?-1951), traveller, journalist and social reformer, was born possibly on 4 July 1857 in Frankfort, Illinois, United States of America, daughter of Charles Ackerman(n), and his wife Amanda, née French. Jessie supplied these details in old age, but in the 1890s she claimed to have been born in 1860 in Boston, Massachusetts. She grew up in Chicago and then moved to California, where in 1880 she studied at the University of California, Berkeley, but did not graduate. In 1881 she began working as a temperance organizer for the Independent Order of Good Templars in California. She moved to the Woman's Christian Temperance Union in 1888, undertaking a mission to British Columbia and Alaska.

In 1889 Ackermann was appointed round the world missionary for the American-based World's W.C.T.U. (founded 1884), and travelled via New Zealand to South Australia. Here she spent three months, during which she galvanized the recently founded local W.C.T.U. branch, before moving on to China. Next year she returned to Australia. Building on small, existing unions, she organized W.C.T.U. affiliates in all colonies and became in 1891 inaugural president of the federated Australasian W.C.T.U., Australia's largest women's reform group.

Using lantern-slide techniques, Ackermann lectured widely in cities and outback towns, speaking on travel and temperance, and advocating equal political, legal and property rights for women. 'The true dignity of labor is being taught to girls', she wrote in 1894, 'and the world is beginning to look with discredit upon women who hang helplessly on men, instead of doing their own work, and, if necessary, earning their own living'. She won a devoted following. Her message constantly emphasized the need for women to obtain the vote and use it wisely, and she has been described as 'a major voice in the Australian suffrage movement'.

Ackermann visited South East Asia about September 1892, came back to Australia in 1893, then left for southern Africa in early 1894. Ill from tropical fever, by October next year she had returned to Chicago, where she became an assistant pastor in a Baptist church in 1896. After 1900 she resumed her travels, this time to Europe, where she lived in London, and became world's president of the Girl's Realm Guild of Service, a Church of England organization. For this body she returned to Australia in May 1907. After five months she moved on to Wellington, New Zealand, in October before proceeding to England.

In May 1910 Ackermann was back in Australia. On this visit she worked as political organizer in Western Australia for the Australian Women's National League. Tirelessly moving about the State, she set up A.W.N.L. branches and urged women to exercise their right to vote. Despite her efforts on behalf of the Liberal government of Frank Wilson, the Labor leader John Scaddan [qq.v.12,11] won the election in October 1911. Ackermann resigned and left Australia for the last time in December. During the preceding twenty-two years she had spent some five years in the country and by her own count written 420 newspaper articles and 5949 letters, distributed 60 000 leaflets and delivered more than 2500 speeches.

Ackermann also gave many newspaper interviews, and wrote *The World through a Woman's Eyes* (1896) and *What Women Have Done with the Vote* (1913). Her most important book, *Australia from a Woman's Point of View* (1913), recorded her forthright impressions of her Australian W.C.T.U. work and travels, and was a significant commentary on the position of women in Australia in the early twentieth century. By the time she moved to Johnson City, Tennessee, in the 1920s she claimed she had circumnavigated the globe eight times. In the 1930s she lived mostly at Los Angeles, California.

Tall, vigorous and, by her own admission 'good-looking', Ackermann never married but in 1902 was engaged to a Russian count who died in a snowstorm; close female admirers corresponded with her. A strong supporter of world peace and the anti-opium agitation, she had been world's superintendent of the W.C.T.U.'s anti-opium department in 1893-95. She also served the World Order of Rechabites and in 1906 was made a fellow of the Royal Scottish Geographical Society. Ackermann died on 31 March 1951 at Sierra Lodge Sanitarium, Pomona, California, and was cremated. She was honoured in 1962 by being made a memorial member of the World's W.C.T.U. Devotedly Christian in her youth, she suffered (both financially and emotionally) at the hands of a Christian confidence man in the late 1920s but still claimed at the end of her life that her 'business' was 'religion'.

E. H. Cherrington (ed), *Standard Encyclopedia of the Alcohol Problem*, 1 (Westerville, US, 1925); I. Tyrrell, *Woman's World Woman's Empire* (North Carolina, USA, 1991); Audrey Oldfield, *Woman Suffrage in Australia* (Melb, 1992); Kirsten Lees, *Votes for Women, the Australian Story* (Syd, 1995); *Pacific Ensign* (San Francisco), 13 Oct 1892, p 2; *White Ribbon Signal*, 1 Nov 1894, p 7, 1 Dec 1894, p 5; J. Ackermann papers (Sherrod Collection, East Tennessee State Univ, Johnson City, Tennessee, USA); Woman's Christian Temperance Union (A'sia), convention reports, 1891, 1894, 1897 (held ML).

IAN TYRRELL

ADAMS, JANE SWAIN (1851-1934), farmer, was born on 28 February 1851 at Toodyay, Western Australia, second of four children of Charles Glass, a Scottish-born farmer and later an innkeeper, and his wife Jane Mary, née Cameron. On 6 November 1868 in Wicklow Hills schoolroom, Toodyay, with Presbyterian forms young Jane married Charles Frederick Adams. A cobbler by trade, he was working as a shepherd in arid country over a hundred miles (160 km) to the east, at Yarragin. Here her first child was born in April 1869. In the next twenty-two years she gave birth to eleven more.

In 1875 the family moved ten miles (16 km) away to Mangowine, where they built a stone and mud brick home with a roof of reeds across gimlet pole rafters. A friendly relationship was established with local Aborigines; Jane trusted the women as nursemaids, to help with housework and tend the vegetable garden. Twice yearly in summer Charles took the wagon, loaded with wool and sandalwood, to Guildford or Toodyay and traded for stores. About every second year Jane went too, to visit her mother. In 1881 Charles became a special police constable, and was often away on patrol or shifting sheep, leaving Jane alone with her children. Water was a dominant concern, only being found at soaks at the bases of granite outcrops. Once, with two children, she walked to Yarragin for water; another time she sent the two eldest girls with a washtub to Yarragin to fetch it. Adams purchased a 100-acre (40 ha) block at Barbalin, to secure water rights.

In 1887 Jane began recording weather data for the government meteorological office, a task she continued until her death. The rush to the Yilgarn goldfield in 1888 ended her isolation. Charles built an inn at the homestead to cater for prospectors trekking past. It was licensed in 1889. Jane provided food and lodgings until 1893 when a new railway line from Northam to Southern Cross bypassed Mangowine and the inn closed. Charles died of a heart attack in 1895. With nine children still at home, Jane managed the property: running sheep, growing vegetables for the family and the railway workers, and cropping the wheat-fields. Having survived typhoid in 1896, next year she won a tender for the mail run, with her 15-year-old son Charles as the mailman.

After 1900 land in the vicinity was opened up and inexperienced farmers struggling to survive looked to Granny Adams for help and advice. Nearby Nungarin grew into a township. Her sons Charles and Thomas served in World War I, Charles dying in France in 1917. In 1929 Jane was guest of honour at ceremonies opening the Barbalin Water Scheme, for which her block had been resumed. She died on 9 November 1934 at Mangowine and was buried in Nungarin cemetery with Congregational rites. Four daughters and two sons survived her. Memorial gates in her honour were erected at Nungarin and in 1968 Mangowine homestead became a National Trust property.

D. Popham (ed), *Reflections: Profiles of 150 Women Who Have Helped Make Western Australia's History* (Perth, 1978); R. Erickson, 'Jane Adams of Mangowine', WA Hist Soc, *Early Days*, 7, pt 6, 1974, p 7.   RICA ERICKSON

ADAMS, SOPHIA CHARLOTTE LOUISA (1832-1891), Dominican prioress known as Mother Rose Columba, was born on 21 March 1832 at Tower House, Woodchester, Gloucestershire, England, daughter of wealthy Anglican parents James Smith Adams (d.1860), indigo manufacturer, and his second wife Elizabeth Emma, née McTaggert. Sophie was educated both at home and at school. In 1851 she converted to Catholicism, despite parental disapproval, and in 1856 entered the Dominican convent at Stone, Staffordshire. She was professed on 26 May 1857, taking the religious name of Rose Columba. In 1866-83 she was in charge of St Mary's convent (later priory) at St Mary Church, Torquay, Devon.

Mother Rose Columba led a group of six professed sisters and two postulants who left Tilbury in July 1883 in the *Orient*. They were responding to a request—under the auspices of Bishop Christopher Reynolds [q.v.6]— from Elizabeth Baker [q.v.] and her mother Isabella for Dominican sisters to nurse the sick in Adelaide. The nuns disembarked at Largs Bay, South Australia, six weeks later. Their leader's journal provided vivid descriptions of the voyage.

Expecting that they would care for women, Mother Rose Columba realized on arrival that they were to nurse men as well, which their order's constitution forbade. The dilemma was resolved by her decision to manage the hospital temporarily and open a select school at Strangways Terrace, later in Molesworth Street, North Adelaide, to teach Catholic, Protestant and Jewish pupils. The sisters also embroidered vestments, painted pottery and illuminated documents. The prioress was committed to the Dominican spiritual tradition of contemplation, in the form of Perpetual Adoration (prayer in the presence of the Blessed Sacrament). She perceived the sisters' involvement in the public sphere as a necessity to survive, but her ambition was to provide the spiritual atmosphere that the colony seemed to lack. This was to attract an increasing number of women to the community.

In 1887 many of the sisters' dowries were forwarded from England, and Mother Rose Columba determined that they would be used to build an appropriate chapel at the Molesworth Street convent. She designed the building and its furnishings, but did not live to see its completion. She died from kidney failure on 30 December 1891 at the convent and was buried in West Terrace cemetery, Adelaide. Her own considerable dowry, amounting to £6250, was used to complete the chapel of the Holy Spirit, one of the best examples of Gothic architecture in Adelaide.

The sisters' spiritual and social contributions to the Adelaide church were shaped significantly by the first prioress. She was fervent, zealous and meticulous about her spiritual obligations, despite frequent ill health. To her community an inspiration and a model, she attracted outsiders and corresponded with the male clerical hierarchy as an equal. She was creative and artistic, although her biographer reported that singing was 'a great trial to her'. She showed strong sympathies, but also strong antipathies, was self-righteous periodically, and occasionally made harsh judgements. Her life reflected the responsibilities, concerns, isolation and irritations of a female religious pioneer.

St Dominic's Priory North Adelaide: Souvenir of Golden Jubilee (Adel, 1933); W. R. Brownlow, *Memoir of Mother Mary Rose Columba Adams, O.P.* (Lond, 1895); M. R. MacGinley, *A Dynamic of Hope* (Syd, 1996); H. Northey, *Living the Truth* (Adel, 1999); Dominican Sisters archives (Stone, UK, and North Adel).   STEPHANIE BURLEY

ADAMSON, DAVID BEVERIDGE (1823-1891), wheelwright, carpenter and astronomer, was born on 22 March 1823 at Scaw Mill, Hawick, Roxburghshire, Scotland, second son of James Adamson, carpenter, and his wife Elizabeth, née Beveridge. The family later moved to Edinburgh, then to Crossgates, near Dunfermline. On 19 September 1839 James, Elizabeth and their seven surviving children arrived in South Australia in the *Recovery*; David, his father and brother Adam (1821-1898) were described as carpenters and wheelwrights.

In 1840 James established an agricultural implement manufacturing business in Adelaide. About 1855 it became Adamson Brothers, with David, Adam, John Beveridge (1827-1915) and James Hazel (1829-1902) as principals; branches were established at Kapunda, Auburn and Laura. The brothers retired from business about 1882. Their wheat harvesters and strippers (based on John Ridley's [q.v.2] invention) had won a high reputation—'Adamson's machines', it was said, 'never gave the country blacksmith a living for repairs'. On 6 November 1849 at Tenterden Cottage, Adelaide, with Congregational rites David had married 18-year-old Emma Golding La Vence from England. Following her death in 1880 he married 26-year-old, native-born Mary Ann Humphris at Stow [q.v.2] Memorial Church on 7 December 1882.

Adamson had attended school at Dunfermline but thereafter was self-educated in a wide field of knowledge, with an insatiable interest in science and mechanics. He built furniture and musical instruments, claiming (in 1876) to have made the first violin in the colony in 1841. Known locally as a mechanical genius, he designed and built a valuable collection of scientific instruments, mechanical appliances and toys used to illustrate his public lectures and demonstrations. He was an ardent student of astronomy: pre-eminent among his constructions were a Gregorian and a Newtonian telescope, a beautifully produced orrery (made about 1870, now held by the Royal Astronomical Society of South Australia) and a Foucault's gyroscope. Elected a fellow of the Philosophical Society (later Royal Society) of South Australia in 1867, Adamson was a council member from 1879 until his death. He published three papers in the society's *Transactions and Proceedings*.

A founding member of Chalmers Church, Adamson was later a member of Stow Memorial Church. He became a supporter of societies for improvement such as the Young Men's Christian Association. David's siblings shared the strong commitment of their parents to church and community. Adam was an office-bearer or promoter of such public bodies as the Chamber of Manufactures and the Destitute Board. James, an artist and photographer as well as machinery maker and inventor, tried—ultimately unsuccessfully —to establish a harvester machinery business in California, United States of America.

Survived by his second wife, and by thirteen of the fifteen children of his first marriage, David Adamson died of rheumatic heart disease on 23 June 1891 at his residence in Adelaide and was buried in West Terrace cemetery. He was an important member of a small group who helped to influence Adelaide's social and intellectual life before the establishment of the university. The family holds a painting of him from about 1850, probably by his brother James.

R. Adamson and B. Evans, *Dunfermline to Down Under* (Adel, 1994); Roy Soc of SA, *Annual Report*, 1891; *SA Register*, 13 May 1879; *Chronicle* (Adel), 24 June 1882, 9 Oct 1886; *Observer* (Adel), 27 June 1891, p 31.
                                                   JULIE EVANS

AGNEW, MARY ANN ELIZA (1857-1940), kindergarten teacher, was born on 6 November 1857 at Openshaw, near Manchester, England, daughter of Hugh Agnew, chain maker, and his wife Eliza, née Byrom. Beginning her career as a pupil-teacher in November 1870, Mary attended Liverpool Training College from January 1876 to December 1877 and was headmistress of St Francis' Girls School, West Gorton, Manchester, from 1878. She arrived in Queensland in August 1890 and joined the Department of Public Instruction as a teacher at Ipswich North Girls' and Infants' School on 22 September 1890, though suffering a bout of typhoid fever that year.

On 10 August 1891 Agnew was appointed kindergarten instructor and began to introduce the methods of Friedrich Froebel to female teachers in Brisbane and suburbs. The lessons included a series of teaching sessions involving young children with the teachers observing. Her letters to the inspector-general David Ewart [q.v.4] raised issues such as which Froebelian 'gifts' should be used, the extent to which kindergarten should form part of the curriculum of infants' schools, the amount of time to be spent on it and the introduction of kindergarten techniques to other schools. She stressed that young children could not spend long periods of time each day engaged in 'dry intellectual work'. Due partly to financial constraints during the depression, however, the number of children undertaking kindergarten work was reduced and Agnew's position was abolished from 1 July 1893, when she returned to classroom duties at Brisbane South Girls' and Infants' School, although the department continued to call on her advice generally. In 1903 she was appointed part-time kindergarten inspector. Her reports indicated that the kindergarten work then being undertaken was based on a fundamentalist interpretation of Froebel's ideas. It was not until the appointment of R. H. Roe [q.v.11] as inspector-general in 1909 that further efforts were made to bring the infants' schools up to a suitable standard. Agnew was granted extended leave in 1909-10 to visit kindergartens in Europe.

On her return, concerned about the antiquated methods and equipment in Queensland's infants' schools, she recommended and was appointed to a committee to investigate infant education. After a conference in July 1911, the committee's report, which she wrote, influenced departmental policy on infants and kindergarten work for the next few years. Though restricted to larger schools, use of kindergarten methods increased during and after World War I. From 1910 Agnew was stationed at Dutton Park Girls' and Infants' School as head teacher. She retired in 1920 and thereafter lived at Ingleston, Wynnum South.

Miss Agnew died at Mater Misericordiae Hospital, South Brisbane, on 14 June 1940 and was buried with Catholic rites in Nudgee cemetery. Despite her efforts, kindergarten method had remained fundamentalist in her first twenty years in Queensland and it was only in the last years of her career that her pioneering work in pre-school education began to be implemented.

34th Report of the Secretary for Public Instruction for the Year 1909, *PP* (Qld), 1910, vol 2; *Links*, no 4, 1982, p 14; S. Grieshaber, 'Preschool Pioneer', in G. Logan and T. Watson (eds), *Soldiers of the Service*, 1 (Qld, 1992), p 72; *Unicorn*, 20, no 2, June 1994, p 73; Memo, General Inspector David Ewart to Undersecretary J. G. Anderson, 10 March 1903, A/15943 *and* Register of Teachers (female), 1860-1903, EDU/V21 (QA).   SUSAN GRIESHABER

AKEHURST, ARTHUR PURSSELL (1836-1902), public servant and magistrate, was born on 13 September 1836 at Pimlico, London, eldest son of William Vialls Akehurst, surveyor, and his wife Anne Purssell, née Stone. Arthur was educated at Taunton Grammar School, Somersetshire, and migrated to Geelong, Victoria, about 1850. He started work as a law clerk, intent on obtaining articles, but in November 1852 Lieutenant-Governor La Trobe [q.v.2] appointed him clerk of the bench and registrar of the small debt court at Buninyong, where his father was now postmaster. In 1853 he was transferred to Ballarat.

The young man enlisted as a special constable and with the militia took part in the bloody suppression of the Eureka stockade. On 3 December 1854 a digger named Henry Powell, who had not been in the stockade, received sabre and bullet wounds while standing at his tent. Troopers then galloped over the injured man and he died soon afterwards, but not before he had implicated Akehurst. An inquest's verdict was that Akehurst had killed him. This Akehurst denied; he was charged with murder but the case was dismissed when Powell's dying deposition was ruled inadmissible. Raffaello Carboni [q.v.3] was among those who believed Akehurst got

off on a technicality. He remained a popular villain, his career in positions of authority and matching personal style in no way diminishing his reputation. He was provoked to defend himself in writing when, in 1874, the firebrand radical Francis Longmore [q.v.5] accused him in parliament of being 'a magistrate who had got his position by murdering people on the gold-fields'.

His midlife career was less eventful. Transferred to petty sessions at Geelong in 1855 and thence to Beechworth, in 1865 Akehurst was appointed police magistrate, warden and coroner at Wood's Point, then a gold-mining centre. He went to 'the Irish colony' of Kilmore in 1866 and in 1873 was one of five law officers directed to report on the courts of the colony. From Kilmore he was appointed relieving police magistrate at Melbourne in 1876. A victim of (Sir) Graham Berry's [q.v.3] 'Black Wednesday' in 1878, only with 'great difficulty' was he restored to the public service.

He was a surprising non-medical choice in 1884 as chairman of the Central Board of Health, following the forced resignation of Dr Richard Youl [q.v.6]. Responding to mounting public and professional concern at the incidence of infectious disease, Akehurst came to the view that the local authorities were at fault. Through new legislation he proposed, initially, to discipline and then to bypass them altogether with a full department of health with increased powers under a responsible minister. As a member of the royal commission into the sanitary conditions of the metropolis of 1889 he influenced its recommendation to create a department of health. Political opposition, marshalled by the City of Melbourne's town clerk Edmund FitzGibbon [q.v.4], transformed the outcome and required Akehurst's removal. The following year he was made secretary of the Crown Law Department. Subsequently, he served on the locomotive branch inquiry, the Synnott inquiry board and the retrenchment committee, which was the government's pruning knife during the 1890s depression.

Akehurst's career was varied and controversial. To Premier Sir George Turner [q.v.12], whose political parsimony he implemented, he was 'an honest conscientious man, but certainly a very hard man, who was determined that the public servants under him should strictly do their duty'. Of average height and slender, Akehurst wore a greying beard in old age and became 'grave but courteous', adopting 'the characteristics of an English gentleman' who was 'loyal to his church and state'. His nephew A. W. H. Akehurst remembered him as a martinet (like his father before him), 'a terror to evil doers' as a police magistrate and warden, and that as a department head 'it was known he would dismiss the inefficient (and unlucky)'.

Baptized a nonconformist, Akehurst became an Anglican after he married, on 5 April 1856 at Christ Church, Geelong, Irish-born Charlotte Mary Armstrong. He died of bronchitis on 27 June 1902 in his residence at St Kilda and was buried in the local cemetery with Anglican rites. His wife and their son and daughter survived him. His estate was sworn for probate at £8273. Akehurst had outlived most of his gold generation contemporaries, with whose radical and aspirant democratic values he had little natural sympathy.

R. Carboni, *The Eureka Stockade* (Melb, 1855); *Men of the Time in Australia: Victorian Series* (Melb, 1878); D. Dunstan, *Governing the Metropolis* (Melb, 1984); *PD* (Vic), 23 June 1874, p 461, 13 Aug 1874, p 910, 6 Oct 1887, p 1527; *A'sian Medical Gazette*, Aug 1884, p 264; *Table Talk*, 17 Apr 1896, p 4; Clerk of Courts (Vic), *Chronicle*, 22, no 3, Sept 1982, p 13, no 4, Dec 1982, p 13; *Argus*, 14 Dec 1854, p 6, 15 Dec 1854, p 5; *Ballarat Courier*, 29 Aug 1890, p 3; papers held by and information from Mr C. Akehurst, Windsor, Melb.   DAVID DUNSTAN

ALEXANDER, LILIAN HELEN (1861-1934), medical practitioner, was born on 15 March 1861 at St Kilda, Melbourne, second daughter of Thomas Alexander, an English-born printer and bookseller, later a public servant, and his Irish-born wife Jane, née Furnell. From the 1870s to the mid-1890s her mother ran a small, private 'ladies' college', Lawn House, latterly in Murphy Street, South Yarra. Lilian, who remained single, was to live in this street all her life. Educated at Lawn House and at Presbyterian Ladies' College for a matriculation honours year, in 1883 she entered the University of Melbourne (B.A., 1886; M.A., 1888) as one of a tiny group of women enrolled in arts. Alexander Leeper [q.v.10] accepted her as the first female student at Trinity College 'against considerable opposition'; more women followed. In 1888 she proposed an 'autonomous, non-denominational and state-funded' women's college, but the hostel, now named Janet Clarke [q.v.3] Hall, developed on Leeper's model. After graduating, Lilian taught at Ruyton Girls' School.

Through her maternal uncle, surgeon-general in Madras, India, Alexander had a medical connexion. In January 1887 she and Helen Sexton wrote a letter to the *Age* asking women who were interested in studying medicine at the University of Melbourne to contact them. This was audacious: an assault on those who believed women would be 'unsexed' by medical knowledge and a challenge to the profession. Five women replied, and the university council decided to admit them. Alexander took out her M.B. in 1893 and her B.Ch. in 1901. She was inaugural secretary of the Victorian Women's Medical Association in 1895, and later its president. Her first appointment was at the Women's Hospital in Carlton, but she was soon involved with other recent female graduates in a new venture: a hospital for women run by women doctors, for which a small clinic had previously demonstrated a real demand. A statewide 'shilling fund' to mark the monarch's diamond jubilee in 1897 raised sufficient money to establish the Queen Victoria Hospital for Women and Children. Alexander was one of the original staff members. Despite her late start she specialized in surgery.

When her sister Constance Cudmore's four sons were orphaned in 1913, they made a home with their aunt. In 1917 she visited her nephews, then serving overseas in World War I. After the war she resigned from the honorary medical staff of the 'Queen Vic', but retained the title of honorary consultant. In 1921 the *Bulletin* described her as a 'magnificent, silver-haired presence' at V.W.M.A. meetings. She was listed as practising privately until 1928.

Alexander died on 18 October 1934 at South Yarra and was buried in the new Melbourne general cemetery at Fawkner. Her estate, sworn for probate at £5891, was divided among her three surviving nephews. In 1936 they honoured her memory with the gift to the University of Melbourne of a substantial sculpture, 'The Wheel of Life', by C. Web Gilbert [q.v.9].

K. Fitzpatrick, *PLC Melbourne* (Melb, 1975); M. Theobald, *Ruyton Remembers 1878-1978* (Melb, 1978) and *Knowing Women* (Melb, 1996); M. Hutton Neve, *'This Mad Folly!'* (Syd, 1980); F. Kelly, *Degrees of Liberation* (Melb, 1985) *and* The 'Woman Question' in Melbourne (Ph.D. thesis, Monash Univ, 1983); L. Gardiner, *Janet Clarke Hall 1886-1986* (Melb, 1986); *Home Beautiful* (Syd), 1 Feb 1936; *Age* (Melb), 19 Oct 1934, 6 Apr 1936; *Argus*, 20 Oct 1934; Southern Health, MMC Hist Collection (Univ Melb Archives).   FARLEY KELLY

ALLEN, ALFRED WEAVER (1870-1925), manufacturing confectioner, was born on 18 June 1870 at Emerald Hill, Victoria, seventh and youngest child of English-born parents Joseph Weaver Allen (d.1886), a photographer, formerly a publican and councillor for the municipality of Sandridge, and his wife Rebecca Martha, née Cox. The family lived at Dunedin, New Zealand, where Joseph had a portrait and general photographic business, until returning to Melbourne about 1885. Employed by the confectioner (Sir) Macpherson Robertson [q.v.11] from the age of 17, Alf gained repute as 'a tiger for work'. He was injured in a fall at MacRobertson's; after he entered the confectionery business on his own account in 1891 he was severely scalded.

Allen made sweets at the rear of his Fitzroy confectionery shop, supplied a brother's North Fitzroy shop and Eastern Market stall and, prospering, took over the premises of two North Melbourne confectionery manufacturers in 1896-99. He married Bridget Mary Dunn, a dressmaker, at St Jude's Church of England, Carlton, on 2 September 1897. They had three daughters; later a son was stillborn.

In 1903 Allen took A. J. Burroughs as a partner, and by 1909 theirs was the third largest confectionery business in Melbourne, after those of MacRobertson and Abel Hoadley [q.v.9]. In 1911 Allen and Burroughs travelled to Britain and Europe, inspected modern processes and plant, and returned with machinery for milk-chocolate making. The outbreak of World War I disrupted imports and placed them in a position to enlarge their market share. Allen induced eight established confectionery makers and a dentist, including Long & Smith, Clark Luke Pty Ltd, Tuckett Obbinson & Co. Pty Ltd, Amazon Confectionery Co. and National Candy Co., to amalgamate in 1917 as A. W. Allen Pty Ltd. Holding the major, although not a controlling, interest, Allen became chairman and managing director. The company concentrated production in North Melbourne, then moved to the city, and finally transferred to South Melbourne where, launched as a public company in 1922, A. W. Allen Ltd acquired a site across the Yarra River from Flinders Street Station. Allen also held shares in and directorships of Maize Products Pty Ltd and Federal Milk Pty Ltd. In November 1922 he visited the United States of America, inspecting factories and ordering new machinery. 'Cure-'Em Quick' and 'Irish Moss Gum Jubes' were then among the firm's popular products.

A keen cyclist in his youth, Allen was an early member of the Automobile Club. Photographs of him in middle age showed him as moustached, with a sturdy figure and a full head of hair. An oil portrait (1909) by F. E. Bawden captured his astuteness. He was an employer representative on the Confectioners Wages Board in 1904-17. In 1918 he bought a mansion at Brighton Beach, and in 1924 he took his family to Europe. Allen died on 5 October 1925 in St Andrew's Private Hospital, Brighton, following surgery for acute appendicitis, and was buried with Anglican rites in Brighton cemetery. His wife and their three daughters survived him, inheriting an estate valued for probate at £41 142.

About the time of Allen's illness and death the company's fortunes declined and, reducing production, it abandoned chocolate making. During and after World War II, however, A. W. Allen Ltd flourished as one of Australia's biggest manufacturers and distributors of confectionery. In 1985 the firm was sold to overseas interests. Two years later the spectacular Allen's Sweets neon sign, Melbourne's largest, was dismantled.

H. Knight, *Photography in New Zealand* (Dunedin, NZ, 1971); E. Downard, *The Sweetest of Them All: The History of the Allen's Neon Sign* (Melb, 1987); R. Fitzgerald, *Rowntree and the Marketing Revolution, 1862-1969* (Cambridge, UK, 1995); *A'sian Confectioner and Soda Fountain Jnl*, 24 Oct 1925, p 14, 24 Nov 1925, p 82; *Sun News-Pictorial*, 22 Nov 1922, p 21; *Argus*, 6 Oct 1925, p 10; *Herald* (Melb), 1 Aug 1972, p 17; *Age*, 28 June 1985, p 21; information from Mrs J. Hartley, Hawthorn, Mrs G. O'Brien, Black Rock, Melb, and Mr R. F. Tate, Alexandra, Vic.   JOHN LACK

ANDERSON, ALICE ELIZABETH FOLEY (1897-1926), garage proprietor, was born on 8 June 1897 in Melbourne, third of five children of Irish-born parents Joshua Thomas Noble Anderson (Anderton), engineer, and his wife Ellen Mary, née White-Spunner. Joshua, sometime partner of (Sir) John Monash [q.v.10], was an inept businessman. Alice's childhood was spent in relative poverty in the family's bush house near Narbethong, outside Melbourne. Hers was an unconventional upbringing for a middle-class girl. She wore utilitarian clothing such as bloomers and men's boots, was an excellent horsewoman, became skilled at hunting and fishing and learned to drive and repair charabancs at the local co-operative bus service. After five terms as a day pupil at the Church of England Girls' Grammar School (Merton Hall), Melbourne, she left in 1914, family finances preventing her finishing secondary school or entering university.

Instead, Anderson developed her own business in the newly emerging field of motor-vehicle service and repair. She began part time, as an 18-year-old clerical worker with one touring car, and soon developed an after-hours business taking parties on picnics into the Dandenong Ranges. By 1918 she was working full time from the backyard of a house in Kew. By next year she had raised the finance for a block of land in Cotham Road, and had a brick garage built to her own design. The Alice Anderson Motor Service offered everything then expected from motor garages—petrol sales, vehicle repairs, a driving school, a 24-hour chauffeur service, either with the garage's cars or the client's vehicles stored on the premises—and organized chauffeured tourist parties on interstate trips. It also provided services to educate women in the new technology. Driving classes included mechanical instruction on demonstration engines; for an extra fee women could work alongside mechanics on their own cars;

a programme enabled women to work as pupil-mechanics to learn the mechanical side of motoring.

Anderson was a member of the Lyceum Club, Melbourne. Her all-women business, though it struggled financially, became famous throughout the city's eastern suburbs and employed as many as eight khaki-uniformed chauffeusses and mechanics in the early 1920s. Short and energetic, with shingled hair, Anderson usually dressed in uniform and peaked cap. Press articles were written about her and she contributed motoring columns to *Woman's World*. Attempting to build on ideas of female independence expressed during World War I, she declared that her ambition was to turn garage work into a profession suitable for women. That ambition was not to be tested. In August 1926 she visited Alice Springs with her friend Jessie Webb [q.v.12]. On their return Anderson died of a gunshot wound to the forehead on 17 September in hospital at Kew after having accidentally injured herself while cleaning firearms. She was buried in Boroondara cemetery with Anglican rites. Her estate was sworn for probate at £5195.

The garage continued with her friend Ethel, sister of Freda Bage [q.v.7], as the new manager, though with less success. It was still operating in 1942 when the last of the staff left to join the women's services in World War II. Anderson was part of a generation who conceived of women's advancement in terms of economic and professional equality. Long before organized feminists took up the slogan, she had chosen to 'give a girl a spanner'.

M. Lake and F. Kelly (eds), *Double Time* (Melb, 1985); H. Radi (ed), *200 Australian Women* (Syd, 1988); *Aust Motorist*, 2 June, 1 Dec 1919; *Home* (Syd), Dec 1920, p 74; *Adam and Eve*, June 1926; *Herald* (Melb), 6 Aug, 17, 18 Sept 1926; *Argus*, 18 Sept 1926, p 41.   GEORGINE CLARSEN

ANDERSON, SELINA SARAH ELIZABETH (1878-1964), parliamentary candidate, trade unionist and photographic retoucher, was born on 12 May 1878 at Tambaroora Road, near Hill End, New South Wales, only child of Irish-born James Charters (d.1879), an elderly, illiterate labourer, and his 19-year-old, English-born wife Sarah Charlotte, née Lawrence. The widowed Sarah married Jerome Anderson in 1880 and 'Senie' took his surname. In 1892 she was attending Tambaroora Public School, where she 'sulked and refused to answer when in class'. She worked in Sydney as an artist and photographic retoucher in 1903-06, living at Mrs Margaret Cahill's boarding-house in Elizabeth Street.

Anderson was the first woman to contest an election for the Australian House of Represen-

tatives, in December 1903, the first Federal election in which women were entitled to stand for parliament. Supported by trade unionists, she was one of two Protectionist candidates for Dalley, polling 17.74 per cent, saving her £25 deposit. From 1904 until 1907 she wrote letters to the press, addressed meetings, supported the rights of women to become doctors and promoted better conditions for tramway employees. She campaigned against the importation of domestic servants and opposed Chinese immigration and industry, becoming secretary of the Anti-Chinese and Asiatic League in May 1904. In June (with the encouragement of her stepfather) she sued a Hill End shopkeeper for defamation, alleging that he had described her as a woman of 'libidinous and licentious nature and disposition'. She maintained that these remarks had prevented her standing for the Senate, but the case was unsuccessful.

By November 1904 Anderson was a member of the organizing committee of the Sydney Labor Council of New South Wales and active in the Pyrmont Labor League and the Labor Women's League. She helped to set up the Cardboard Box Makers' Union, of which she became secretary. Later, as a delegate from the Shop Assistants' Union, she was a member of the anti-sweating committee of the labor council. In February 1906 she became the only woman member of the council's executive and its organizing committee. As a member of that committee she pursued an award for laundresses, assisting W. A. Holman [q.v.9] at the hearing. By 1906 she was one of seven women, including Catherine Dwyer [q.v.8] and Edith Bethel [q.v.], on the State executive of the Australian Labor Party. Anderson had intended to recontest Labor pre-selection for Dalley; but by September 1906 her goal became East Sydney, for which she unsuccessfully sought labor council endorsement. Undeterred, she campaigned in 1907 for numerous Labor candidates, including J. J. Morrish in Mudgee. One onlooker later remembered her: 'with a ribbon band across her chest ... this red headed woman of medium build speaking so well'.

On 1 January 1908 at St John the Baptist Church of England, Wellington, she married an Irish-born widower Christopher Hewitt Siggins, a publican and former alderman. They sailed for Dunedin, New Zealand, in December 1909, spent some time at Auckland and by 1915 were back at Dunedin where Christopher was acting gaoler at Otago gaol. They had returned to Australia by April 1918, when Selina was one of the first two women to stand for the South Australian parliament, contesting the seat of Adelaide as an Independent. Her manifesto included compulsory voting, proportional representation, benefits for returned servicemen and their families, bonuses for families of more than five children and price controls for food. During the campaign, she attacked both the Labor Party and socialism. She polled 2.06 per cent.

Moving back to Wellington, New South Wales, in 1922, Selina became the first woman delegate to the Farmers and Settlers' Association. That year, in December, she stood unsuccessfully as a second Country Party candidate for the Federal seat of Calare, polling 1.72 per cent. By 1928 she and her husband were living near Canterbury racecourse, Sydney, where they had stables and a couple of racehorses. Predeceased by her husband, Selina Siggins died on 30 November 1964 at Ashbury and was buried in Field of Mars cemetery with Anglican rites. She had no children. Her estate was sworn for probate at more than £5000. An individualist, with a reputation for meanness in later life, Selina Siggins was articulate and vigorous. She earned a significant place in Australian political history.

E. Ryan, *Two-thirds of a Man* (Syd, 1984); H. Jones, *In Her Own Name* (Adel, 1994); R. Cooper, *Making the New South Wales Union Movement?* (Syd, 1996); *Women's Budget* (Syd), 6 Feb 1906, p 18, 20 Feb 1906, p 18; *Catholic Press* (Syd), 26 Nov 1903; *SMH*, 7 Dec 1903, p 8, 19 May 1904, p 8, 17 June 1904, p 4, 18 June 1904, p 11, 2 June 1905, p 8, 13 Sept 1906, p 7, 4 Dec 1906, p 4; *Worker* (Syd), 16 Jan 1904, p 5, 4 Mar 1905, p 5, 19 July 1906, p 6; *Wellington Times*, 26 July 1906, p 4; *Western Post* (Mudgee, NSW), 4, 8, 11, 15, 22, 29 July 1907, 1, 8 Aug 1907, 2, 5, 16 Sept 1907; *Land* (Syd), 25 Aug 1922, p 12; Labor Council (NSW), Minutes, 9 Nov 1906, p 576, 5 Apr 1906, 1 Nov 1906 (ML); Edna Ryan papers (ML); Tambaroora Public School records (NSWA).   SUE TRACEY

ANSELL, ERIC NORMAN (1878?-1952), rubber goods manufacturer, was born in London, son of Michael Ansell, a commercial traveller, and his wife Martha, née Solomon. Eric worked in the rubber industry in England before becoming assistant purser in the *Omrah*. According to family tradition, he met Mildred Daisy 'Dai' Jones, who was returning to her native Geelong from England, in 1902. He jumped ship to marry her, with Free Christian Church forms, on 14 October at Queen Street, Melbourne. They were to have two sons, (Eric) Lloyd (1903-1978) and Harvey Neil (1905-1984).

Ansell worked briefly as a traveller then as a mechanic at the Dunlop Pneumatic Tyre Co. of Australasia Ltd works at Montague, Melbourne. In 1905 he set up his own business, manufacturing condoms. He remained discreet about this product for the rest of his life. In 1912-19 he worked at the Zenith Rubber Co., while continuing to manufacture prophylactics, but thereafter devoted himself exclusively to his own company. Harvey joined the firm in 1922, Lloyd in 1925: in 1929 the business was registered as E. N. Ansell & Sons Pty Ltd, the name changing to the Ansell Rubber Co. Pty Ltd in 1934. The range of products expanded as the sons' chemical and mechanical skills took effect. In 1919 they began manufacturing balloons and by 1925 were producing household and surgical gloves.

Tariff protection in Australia under the Lyons [q.v.10] government assisted the enterprise in the Depression. Ansell's importation of liquid latex in 1929 was crucial to future developments; the firm became one of the first Australian organizations to move away from the use of rubber in a solid form. In the 1930s Ansell kept abreast of developments abroad, travelling with family members to the United States of America and Europe to study new techniques.

The company prospered during World War II. An 'essential industry', the business overcame difficulties in importing raw product after the Japanese seized Malaya's rubber plantations. Ansell acquired lucrative government contracts for the production of gas masks, surgical gloves and the ubiquitous condom. After the war ended, a long-planned move to larger premises in River Street, Richmond, took place. In 1946 Ansell and his sons automated the glove-making process, with other products being automated by 1952. That year the company was ready to launch a national advertising campaign that would result in many Australian homes using the pink household glove with silver lining. Hot water bottles were another popular product.

Inside the factory Ansell was an autocrat. Within his family circle he was more relaxed. He died on 1 May 1952 in the Mercy Hospital, East Melbourne, and was cremated. Survived by his wife and by his sons, on whom the company devolved, Ansell left a personal estate of £15 154 and realty worth £7500. The lack of fuss and absence of public obituaries were indicative of a hard-working, carefully innovative man who was devoted to the interests of his family and his company. He left remarkably few public records, eschewing entries in *Who's Who in Australia* or industrial gazetteers. At his death the company was wholly family owned. In 1969 Dunlop Rubber Australia Ltd bought it and in 2002 Pacific-Dunlop Ltd changed its name to Ansell Ltd.

G. Blainey, *Jumping Over the Wheel* (Syd, 1993); M. Johnston and J. Wippell, *Ansell* (Melb, 1990); *Argus* (Melb), 3 May 1952.   RICHARD TREMBATH

ARTHUR, WALTER GEORGE (c.1820-1861), Aboriginal leader, was the son of Rolepa, known to Europeans as 'King George', a senior man of the Ben Lomond tribe in north-eastern Tasmania. There is some dispute about Walter's mother but the leading authority, N. J. B. Plomley, has named her as Mary Anne who he believes was 'a half-caste'. The boy, separated from his kin and taken from his country in unknown circumstances, appears to have learned little of his people's language, culture and traditions. He lived for several years at Launceston where, known as 'Friday', he engaged in pickpocketing and petty theft on behalf of European criminals.

In February 1832 Friday was taken into the care of G. A. Robinson [q.v.2] and went with him to Wybalenna, the Aboriginal settlement on Flinders Island, living there until November when he was sent to the Boys' Orphan School at New Town on the northern outskirts of Hobart. There he learned to read and write with reasonable facility. In May 1835 he returned to Flinders Island where he taught reading and writing, assisted in church services and wrote articles for the small settlement's newspaper. He was renamed in honour of the governor (Sir) George Arthur [q.v.1] in January 1836. Next year a visiting school inspector recorded that Walter Arthur possessed considerable intellect and could read the Bible with a perfect English idiom. In 1837 he began a relationship with a fellow teacher at the school, Mary Anne Cochrane, daughter of Tarenootairer. The young couple were found in bed together and Arthur was punished with a four-day sentence in the settlement prison. Robinson and other officials arranged a marriage on 16 March 1838. The ceremony, conducted by the Presbyterian minister Rev. Thomas Dove, was accompanied by Aboriginal dancing. For nine months Walter and Mary Anne lived on small islands off the shore of Flinders Island shepherding the settlement's flock. In March 1839 they accompanied Robinson and his family to Port Phillip, where Robinson took up the position of chief protector of Aborigines. Between August and December Walter travelled with Europeans overlanding cattle to South Australia. On his return he worked on a property acquired by the Robinson family on the Goulburn River. The couple had no children.

In August 1842 Walter and Mary Anne returned to Flinders Island where they came into conflict with the superintendent Dr Henry Jeanneret [q.v.4 C. E. Jeanneret], who though replaced in February 1844 was subsequently reinstated. On hearing news of his imminent return Walter, Mary Anne and a group of friends began to agitate for his dismissal. Their most significant action was to prepare a petition to Queen Victoria, complaining about Jeanneret's behaviour and arbitrary use of power. Dated 17 February 1846, it was signed by 'Walter G. Arthur, Chief of the Ben Lomond

tribe', and seven other men. An inquiry by Matthew Friend [q.v.1], harbourmaster at George Town, established that while the petitioners sought the assistance of several Europeans it was largely their own work. Both Walter and Mary Anne wrote subsequent letters to the governor seeking his support for their rights.

After the small surviving Aboriginal community was transferred to Oyster Cove, twenty-five miles (40 km) south of Hobart, in October 1847, the Arthurs played a prominent role in demanding improved conditions. Walter farmed nearby land and attempted unsuccessfully to obtain a convict assistant. From September 1859 to January 1861 he was a crewmember on a whaling voyage in the Hobart-based 361-ton barque *Sussex*. Returning by rowing boat to Oyster Cove from Hobart on 11 May 1861, possibly inebriated, he fell overboard; his body was not recovered.

N. J. B. Plomley (ed), *Weep in Silence* (Hob, 1987); H. Reynolds, *Fate of a Free People* (Melb, 1995); S. Dammery, *Walter George Arthur* (Melb, 2001).
H. REYNOLDS

ATKINSON, CHARLOTTE; *see* BARTON

AUSTIN, CHARLOTTE ELIZABETH (1878-1933), community leader, was born on 4 June 1878 at Dubbo, New South Wales, fourth surviving child of Sydney-born parents George Fullerton, commissioner of crown lands, and his wife Georgiana Sarah, née Clarke. Educated at Rivière College, Woollahra, Lottie graduated with first-class honours in history and second-class in English from the University of Sydney (B.A., 1902; M.A., 1905). Her supervisor was G. A. Wood [q.v.12] and, like many of her fellow history honours students, she made her mark in Australia.

At university, partly through their membership of the Australasian Student Christian Union, Lottie met Alfred Herbert Austin, a former South Australian National Bank employee who came to Sydney to study for the Congregational ministry. He was ordained in December 1902 and next year graduated with honours in philosophy. The two were married on 21 March 1903 in the Presbyterian Church, Randwick, and departed for South Australia where Alfred was Congregational minister at Gawler. They were to remain childless.

In 1905 the couple returned to Sydney where Alfred became pastor of Mosman Congregational Church. In 1916-17 he ministered as senior chaplain in troopships and was then called to the church at Ipswich, Queensland. He and Lottie went overseas in 1924 and from

1926 until Alfred's death on 30 December 1930 served at Hunters Hill, Sydney.

Lottie taught at schools in Sydney and Queensland and she was also active in parish work, conducting reading circles and Bible-study groups and counselling young people. Her interests, like those of her husband, were far from parochial. Prominent in the London Missionary Society she was president of the New South Wales ladies auxiliary in 1911-17 and secretary in 1928. While in Queensland she became commissioner in the Western Moreton district for the Girl Guides' Association. She was involved with the Congregational Women's Guild and with women's meetings at the annual assemblies of the Congregational Union.

She also played a prominent role in the Young Women's Christian Association, a branch of which her husband had established at Gawler. A charter member of the national body, formed in 1907, Mrs Austin joined its board and in 1919 and 1922 presided over national Y.W.C.A. conventions. In 1913 she wrote an *Outline Sketch of the Young Women's Christian Associations in Australasia*. In 1916 she gained temporary release from the national board to take over as general secretary of the Sydney branch. This position she relinquished after her husband returned from the war, but while at Ipswich she became vice-president of the Brisbane association and chair of the finance committee. She resigned from the national board to again become general secretary of the Sydney branch in August 1928, after visiting North America to learn more about the functioning of the association. A devout Christian whose high intellectual qualities and talents as an organizer and public speaker were used to spread the gospel and assist young women, she died of myocardial infarction on 21 November 1933 in St Lawrence Private Hospital, Chatswood. She was buried in the Congregational section of the Field of Mars cemetery.

B. H. Fletcher, *History and Achievement* (Syd, 1999); *SMH*, 22 Nov 1933, p 21, 23 Nov 1933, p 13; G. L. Lockley, The Foundation, Development and Influence of Congregationalism in Australia with Emphasis on the Nineteenth Century (Ph.D. thesis, Univ Qld, 1966); Uniting Church archives, Parramatta.   B. H. FLETCHER

AUSTIN, ELIZABETH PHILLIPS (1821-1910), philanthropist, was born on 14 August 1821 at Middle Chinnock, Somerset, England, fourth daughter of Robert Harding, yeoman farmer, and his wife Mary, née Phillips. Elizabeth sailed for Port Phillip in the *Ward Chapman* in 1841 with her brother William. As a squatter, he took up land at Winchelsea,

in the Western District of what became Victoria. One of the few women to venture inland in the early 1840s, Elizabeth married a neighbour, also from Somerset, Thomas Austin [q.v.1] on 14 August 1845 at St James's Church, Melbourne. Three of her eleven children died young; the other eight married into pastoral or city families.

The Austin family, later a notable pastoral dynasty, held many runs, Thomas's headquarters being at Barwon Park, where he and his wife entertained the Duke of Edinburgh [q.v.4] in 1867. Allegedly mortified at having to receive the Duke in an undistinguished homestead and 'consumed with jealousy by the sight of her sister-in-law [Rebecca Austin] queening it at the Abbey House, Glastonbury', Elizabeth persuaded Thomas to build a substantial, bluestone mansion, designed by Davidson & Henderson. Begun in 1869, it was finished in 1871; six months later Thomas unexpectedly died.

In her first years of widowhood, according to Margaret Kiddle's [q.v.15] informants, Elizabeth withdrew from society and lived at Barwon Park, 'disappointed and domineering'. In contrast, two grandchildren recalled a shrewd, determined woman—one called her 'zestful'—who drove out every afternoon with her companion, Miss Maides, in her brougham, the coachman dressed in full livery. She was known among the family as 'Aunt Tom'.

By 1880 Mrs Austin had quietly begun a second career, as a philanthropist. Her family believed that her interest in those struck down by incurable disease derived from a case among her staff. When an appeal was made to found a hospital for incurables in Melbourne, through an intermediary she offered a substantial amount (£6000) to launch the scheme. Her example prompted others to donate money and on her birthday in 1882 the Austin Hospital for Incurables was opened. She gave further donations towards its maintenance, corresponded regularly with the secretary, and in 1898 paid for the establishment of a children's ward. She reportedly visited the place she called with some justification 'my hospital' monthly. Continuing the family connection, three of her granddaughters served on the hospital committee until the 1960s.

Her other principal benefaction was the Austin Homes for Women at South Geelong, built to commemorate Queen Victoria's jubilee in 1887. Mrs Austin also supported the Servants' Training Institute, St Thomas's Church, Winchelsea, the Ladies' Benevolent Society and local charities. By 1892 her name was described by Philip Mennell [q.v.10] as 'a household word throughout the colony'. She died on 2 September 1910 at Winchelsea and was buried in Geelong cemetery with

Anglican rites; the funeral was a civic event. Her personal estate was sworn for probate at £1607. Elizabeth Austin was the most prominent woman philanthropist of her generation and a pioneer of female benefaction in Victoria.

P. Mennell, *Dictionary of Australasian Biography* (Lond, 1892); A. Henderson, *Early Pioneer Families of Victoria and Riverina* (Melb, 1936); M. Kiddle, *Men of Yesterday* (Melb, 1961); E. W. Gault and A. Lucas, *A Century of Compassion* (Melb, 1982); *Geelong Advertiser*, 3 Sept 1910, p 3, 6 Sept 1910, p 3.

PAUL DE SERVILLE

AUSTIN, ROBERT (1825-1905), explorer, surveyor and engineer, was born on 31 December 1825 at Wanstead House, Epping Forest, Essex, England, son of James Gardner Austin, architect, and his wife Mary Ann, née Pole. With his parents and brother James, Robert arrived at Australind, Western Australia, in the *Island Queen* in December 1840. Joining the Surveyor-General's Department in 1847, over the next fifteen years Austin carried out extensive fieldwork. He surveyed the Toodyay-Northam areas and was included in a number of expeditions—such as that of B. F. Helpman [q.v.1]—but was remembered primarily for his exploration of the Murchison and Gascoyne regions.

Starting out from Northam on 10 July 1854, the party he led was dogged by disaster. On 21 August several horses ate poisonous native plants and died in agony in ensuing days; more were found dead a week later. Austin was compelled to discard much equipment and press on partly unmounted in an unforgiving environment. One of the men, Charles Farmer, accidentally shot himself on 19 September and died eight days later. Subsequently, the remainder battled dangerous salt marshes and poor feed for the horses. With temperatures rising rapidly, meagre surface water supplies were evaporating by the day.

Eventually, on 29 October, when approximately a hundred miles (160 km) from the mouth of the Gascoyne River, they came to a standstill. The horses had not drunk for two days. On his return from a reconnoitre Austin found, as he reported:

the whole of the party stripped and buried in the sand under the shade of their blankets thrown over a bush, and our horses standing up with their heads under their masters' blankets, too thirsty to feed ... *the men were drinking their own and the horses' urine*, and a native I captured and kept to find water, as he knew the country, did the same, saying we should all die if I persisted in pushing on.

Austin had no option but to retreat some thirty-seven miles (59 km) to the last waterhole and then to return to Port Gregory, arriving on 25 November. In the course of the journey he had found and named Mount Magnet. He also reported indications of gold in the Murchison region, but his claim for recognition of its discovery was never acknowledged.

A month after resigning in April 1860, Austin was appointed surveyor, second class, in the Queensland Surveyor-General's Department. He was promoted to surveyor first class in January 1861. Eight months later he became a commissioner of crown lands and in May 1862 secured the position of engineer of roads for the southern district. On 22 October 1862 at St John's Church of England, North Brisbane, he married Sophia Catherine Douglas; they were to have ten children. By the late 1880s he appears to have transferred entirely to metropolitan civil engineering and surveying operations. In June 1891 he was appointed sergeant-at-arms to the Legislative Assembly. Due to economic depression, he was dismissed in August 1893. Austin died alone in bed on 24 February 1905 at Thornborough, Queensland, and was buried in the local cemetery. His wife, four daughters and two sons survived him. Lake Austin, Western Australia, was named after him.

J. S. Battye (ed), *The History of the North West of Australia* (Perth, 1915); *West Australian*, 8 June 1896, p 5; WA Dept of Lands, exploration diaries, PR5441, v 4, pp 347-50, *and* Austin papers (BL).

GLEN McLAREN

B

BACKLER, JOSEPH (1813?-1895), convict artist and portrait painter, was born probably in 1813 in London, son of Joseph Backler, painter on glass, and his wife Jane, née Cowie. Convicted in 1831 for uttering forged cheques, the 18-year-old, who seemed to *The Times* 'a highly respectable young man', was sentenced to death, later commuted to transportation for life.

Backler arrived in Sydney in the *Portland* on 25 May 1832. Indents described him as being able to read and write and by profession a landscape painter. He was assigned to the Surveyor-General's Department but, suspected of being involved in further crimes, he was sent in May 1833 to Port Macquarie. Here Backler was continually in trouble. All told he received 150 lashes, a year in irons and twenty-three days in cells. At some point, however, he also painted at least six landscape oils of the settlement—either there or soon after his return to Sydney in January 1843. Two of these views were of St Thomas's Church of England, Port Macquarie, where he married Margaret Magner on 7 May 1842.

In February 1842 he had been granted a ticket-of-leave and from 1843 was assigned to Messrs Cetta & Hughes, frame makers and carvers in Sydney. He was granted a conditional pardon in 1847. In 1843 Backler advertised his services as a 'Portrait, Miniature and Landscape Painter, in oils and watercolours'. It was as a portrait painter in oils, however, that he made his name. In August 1845 he visited Goulburn, advertising his availability for portrait painting. During the 1840s he visited Yass, Bathurst (where he also painted a townscape), Newcastle and Maitland despite complaining, during an 1849 insolvency hearing, that itinerant portrait painting was not profitable. Creditors claimed that in two months at Newcastle he made more than £100.

Backler rarely involved himself with the small, Sydney art world. He contributed to a commercial art union in 1850, recklessly claiming as an original design an entry which was spotted immediately as a copy after Titian. His wife died in November 1852, yet in June 1853 a 'Mrs Backler' had a son who did not survive long. In the early 1860s he travelled north. He was at Tenterfield in 1860 (returning in 1878), painting a number of portraits and at least two landscapes, and in Brisbane by 1863. By 1869 he had moved to Gympie where he remained for a time. By 1882 he was back in Sydney. His style was now based on photographs and more sophisticated because of it. Survived by his second wife Sarah Vincer, Backler died on 22 October 1895 at Liverpool Street, Sydney, and was buried in Waverley cemetery.

With few exceptions, his client base had been drawn from the upper working and lower middle classes: publicans, builders, millers, ship-owners, shop-owners, and farmers—people who had done well in the colonies. His portraits were conventionally posed, using well-established stylistic devices, such as background columns and drapery. The most distinctive feature of his work was his careful delineation of his subjects' faces. The apparent literalness of his portraits could be startling, and rarely flattering (which explained why few middle-class families employed him). Despite this, Backler was probably the most prolific of all oil painters in early colonial Australia. More than 120 of his works have survived; the Mitchell [q.v.5] Library holds an extensive collection of them.

E. Buscombe, *Artists in Early Australia and their Portraits* (Syd, 1978); J. Kerr (ed), *The Dictionary of Australian Artists* (Melb, 1992); R. Neville, *Backler & Friends in the Picture Gallery* (Syd, 1999); R. Neville, 'Joseph Backler. Portrait Painter to the Not Particularly Rich or Famous', *Aust Antique Collector*, July-Dec 1993; *The Times* (Lond), 4 July 1831, p 4; *SMH*, 13 May 1843, p 3; *Bell's Life in Sydney*, 29 June 1850; insolvency files, 2/8855, no 1901 (NSWA).

RICHARD NEVILLE

BADHAM, CHARLES (1884-1943), medical practitioner and public health officer, was born on 15 March 1884 at Armidale, New South Wales, son of English-born parents Charles Lennard Cobet Badham, clerk of petty sessions, and his wife Wilhelmina, née Baynes, and grandson of Professor Charles Badham [q.v.3]. After his schooling, young Charles spent some time in commerce before studying pharmacy at the University of Sydney. Having gained his diploma in 1907, with the gold medal of the Pharmacy Board, he enrolled in science, graduating (B.Sc., 1913) with first-class honours and the university medal in biology and becoming the John Coutts postgraduate scholar in zoology. On 22 January 1914 at St Stephen's Presbyterian Church, Sydney, he married Kate Miriam 'Birdie' Brodziak, a demonstrator in zoology.

Badham then studied medicine (M.B., Ch.M., 1917). As an undergraduate he demonstrated in biology and zoology and lectured in veterinary pharmacy at the university and in botany at Sydney Technical College. Graduating with honours, he served as a resident medical officer at Royal Prince Alfred Hospital. On 15 February 1918 he was appointed captain, Australian Army Medical Corps, Australian Imperial Force. He served with the 5th Field Ambulance in France and after the Armistice made further studies of biology at University College, London, and elsewhere in England.

In September 1919 Badham returned to Australia where his A.I.F. appointment terminated on 9 October. He practised at Kendall and Laurieton on the north coast of New South Wales where for a time he travelled by horse and buggy. While there he wrote up descriptions of two parasitic worms in children. In 1921 he joined the microbiological laboratory of the Department of Public Health and two years later became the first medical officer for industrial hygiene, a position established at the request of the Arbitration Court. In 1926 the university granted him a diploma in public health. With H. B. Taylor [q.v.16], assistant government analyst, he showed that there was normally some lead excretion in the urine of Sydney residents and established the level. Lead was then the main industrial poison and Badham worked for regulations for its control, which were gazetted in 1928. He also reported on a sugar dust explosion, occupational dermatitis in rubber works and ventilation in wine cellars.

Badham's most significant research was on dust diseases of the lungs of workers in coal-mines and in sandstone tunnels, for which he received international recognition. He developed methods of dust sampling and did pathology examinations of miners' lungs and also animal experiments on the effect of injected and inhaled dusts. He and Taylor developed a method of analysis of lung tissue for silica and carbon, and he distinguished between coal workers' pneumoconiosis and the differing, but frequently associated, silicosis. Badham played an important role in introducing compensation for workers with dusted lungs in New South Wales. He was associate editor of the *Journal of Industrial Hygiene and Toxicology*.

Enthusiastic about his work, Badham was respected and trusted by workers and employers. Early in World War II he gave evidence in support of some Australians who, he felt, had been unjustly interned. He had an extensive literary knowledge and an interest in art. In his later years he suffered from a cardiac complaint but, apart from taking leave in 1942, remained working. He died of chronic nephritis on 6 August 1943 in hospital at North Sydney and was cremated. As he was an atheist there was no religious service. His wife and son survived him.

MJA, 2 Oct 1943, p 287; information from Dr C. D. Badham, Paddington, Syd.

ROBERT A. B. HOLLAND

BAILLIÈRE, FERDINAND FRANÇOIS (1838-1881), bookseller and publisher, was born on 11 July 1838 in London, youngest son of Hippolyte Baillière and his wife Karanaputch, née Hagon. Ferdinand's formal education is not known but it is likely he had experience in the book trade from an early age. His uncle Jean-Baptiste Baillière founded a bookselling and publishing company in Paris. Ferdinand's father, who owned a bookshop in Regent Street, London, also became a publisher, running the business until his death in 1870. The business, later Baillière, Tindall & Cox, became prominent in medical publishing; in 2005 the multinational Harcourt company was still publishing under the Baillière name. Two of Ferdinand's brothers went to New York in the nineteenth century and entered bookselling and publishing.

Ferdinand left England in 1860 and reached Melbourne on 30 October, commissioned to purchase works on Australian exploration and history for the British Museum. His first address was Temple Court. The business was then at 85 Collins Street East and from 1865 at 104 Collins Street, where it remained until he died. Little is known of his bookselling activities, although he issued three catalogues and sold books to the Public Library, Museums and National Gallery of Victoria and the University of Melbourne. His shop was described by the *Bulletin* as 'the constant resort of many of the literary and medical celebrities of the city'. At Christ Church, St Kilda, on 21 December 1861, Baillière married with Anglican rites London-born Sophia Frederica Medex.

In 1862 Baillière issued the *Journal of Landsborough's Expedition from Carpentaria, in search of Burke & Wills*. The imprint of this book and all subsequent publications listed Melbourne, London, Paris, New York and Madrid. A further work, *J. M'Douall Stuart's explorations across the continent of Australia* (1863), announced on the title page that Baillière was 'Publisher in Ordinary to the Victorian Government', a claim difficult to substantiate. He brought out fiction as well as verse, but was best known for his gazetteers for Victoria, New South Wales, South Australia, Tasmania and Queensland and post office directories for Melbourne and Queensland, issued from 1865 until 1880.

Ever the entrepreneur, Baillière published more than fifty-five works, including books by notable colonists such as Marcus Clarke, (Sir) Thomas a'Beckett [qq v.3], (Sir) John O'Shanassy, Richard Daintree and R. Brough Smyth [qq.v.5,4,6]. Baillière also produced his own journal, the *Medical & Surgical Review (Australasia)*, in 1863-71, and sold medical instruments. He was associated with the charlatan James George Beaney [q.v.3], issuing ten of his books. Having obtained, possibly improperly, an official commission for Beaney to use when he travelled to England, in a celebrated court case in 1880 he sued the doctor for failure to pay for his services, thus airing the scandal. But he lost the case. In July he became insolvent.

Baillière was killed when the Brighton express train to Melbourne was derailed on 30 August 1881. Beaney attended the accident and pronounced his adversary dead. Baillière was buried in St Kilda cemetery with Anglican rites. His wife, daughter and son survived him.

The Medical Embassy to England: Being a Report of the Trial Baillière v. Beaney (Melb, 1880); *Australasian*, 31 July 1880, p 147; 3 Sept 1881, supp, p 4; *Argus*, 1 Sept 1881, p 5; L. Clark, Aspects of Melbourne Book Trade History: Innovation and Specialisation in the Careers of F. F. Baillière and Margareta Webber (M.A. thesis, Monash Univ, 1997).

LAUREL CLARK

BAKER, DAVID (1861-1942), steelworks manager, was born on 30 May 1861 at East Boston, Massachusetts, United States of America, son of Reuben Rich Baker, mariner, and his wife Mary Cobb, née Atwood. David was educated at the grammar and high schools at Newton, and at the Massachusetts Institute of Technology, graduating as a mining engineer and metallurgist in 1885. He married Katherine Miller and they had two children.

Baker worked as a blast furnace superintendent with the Pennsylvania Steel Co. at Steelton, Pennsylvania, and from 1887 oversaw the establishment of new steelworks at Sparrows Point. He disseminated his ideas about reducing labour costs through articles such as 'The Rock-drill Applied to Opening the Tapping Hole of a Blast-Furnace' in the *Transactions of the American Institute of Mining Engineers* (1892). In 1898 he moved to the Illinois Steel Co. From 1901 to 1904 he was general superintendent at Dominion Steel in Nova Scotia, Canada, then a consulting metallurgical engineer based in Philadelphia, U.S.A. Later he formed a partnership with James B. Ladd to work on projects such as the planning of the new Bethlehem steelworks. Inventions including the Baker and Neumann distributor tap, the Baker top controller and the Ladd and Baker pig breaker established him as an innovator in the industry.

In 1912 Baker was selected by Guillaume Delprat [q.v.8], general manager of Broken Hill Pty Co. Ltd, as a 'tiptop' man to advise on establishing steel-making in Australia. Travelling with his daughter, Baker spent several months investigating B.H.P.'s position and concluded that steel could be produced at a profit by carrying iron ore from South Australia to company-owned land near the New-castle coalfields in New South Wales and by focusing on producing steel rails. In 1913 he was engaged to oversee construction and management of the steelworks. With his wife and son, he settled at Newcastle and began the transformation of the water-soaked site.

Baker was one of a series of American experts employed by B.H.P. both in mining and steel-making. He brought with him the latest knowledge and had connexions in the U.S.A. that ensured a continuing flow of materials, technology and skilled workers, including his son David, as overseers in the works. Baker maintained his network through membership of the British Iron and Steel and the American Iron and Steel institutes, the American Society of Mining Engineers and the Geological Society of the United States.

The coincidence of the opening of the Newcastle steelworks with World War I created unexpected pressures and opportunities, leading to the addition of a second blast furnace in 1918 and a third in 1921. Baker presided over his thousands of workers with a quiet dignity. Energetic and capable of making decisions rapidly, he expected a high level of commitment and rewarded loyalty, but was frustrated when what he thought fair treatment failed to prevent strikes. His anti-union attitudes were consistent with those that then prevailed at B.H.P. and, despite strikes and shut downs, he persisted with policies such as seven-day working weeks for waged employees.

Baker and his wife engaged with the local community: he belonged to the Newcastle Club and organized wartime fund-raising concerts. He was a member of the Society of Friends. As B.H.P. was the principal industry in the city, the couple frequently entertained official visitors, from the Prince of Wales to members of service groups. Overnight guests were accommodated in the large works' manager's house, built in 1920 for the Bakers. Photographs showed him with a moustache and goatee beard. He believed in the power of an orderly environment: one of his last public statements at Newcastle was advice on the beautification of the historic centre of the city.

Ailing by 1920, Baker was ready to return to his homeland. After six months of ill health, and a restorative visit to the U.S.A. in 1921, he oversaw the upgrading of the steelworks during the closure from April 1922 to February 1923 and began to groom Leslie Bradford [q.v.13] as his successor. Baker departed permanently in March 1925, but remained active for the next decade as an adviser based at Philadelphia. In 1935-36 his reminiscences were published in the *B.H.P. Review*. Predeceased by his wife in 1936, Baker died on 12 December 1942 at Wellfleet, Massachusetts, and was buried in West Laurel Hill cemetery, Philadelphia. The main road through the Newcastle steelworks site was named after him. Baker's son succeeded him as adviser and retired in 1946. The steelworks closed in 1999.

H. Hughes, *The Australian Iron and Steel Industry 1848-1962* (Melb, 1964); A. Trengrove, *What's Good for Australia* (Syd, 1975); G. Blainey, *The Steel Master* (Melb, 1981); D. Sawer, *Australians in Company* (Melb, 1985); E. M. Johnston-Liik et al, *A Measure of Greatness* (Melb, 1998); *BHP Review: Jubilee Number*, June 1935; *BHP Review*, 20, no 2, March 1943, p 7; *BHP Jnl*, no 2, 1979, p 30; *Newcastle Morning Herald*, 25 Jan 1921, p 5, 24 Aug 1923, p 4, 6 Mar 1925, p 5, 9 Mar 1925, p 4, 18 Dec 1942, p 2; Baker file (BHP Billiton archives, Melb).

NANCY CUSHING

BAKER, ELIZABETH ANSTICE (1849-1914), intellectual and social activist, was born on 24 September 1849 at the family mansion, Morialta, at Magill, South Australia, sixth of eight surviving children of John Baker [q.v.3], an English-born pastoralist and politician, and his wife Isabella Morrison, née Allan, from Scotland. Bessie's older brother was (Sir) Richard Chaffey Baker [q.v.7]. She was educated at home and in 1860-63 in Paris. Back in Adelaide she joined in Church of England services with her family, played the organ and taught Sunday School classes. Independently wealthy after her father's death in 1872 she returned to Europe with her mother and sisters in 1876.

In Paris in December 1877 Baker was received into the Catholic Church. In the final stage of an intense period of study and reflection she was instructed by Etienne Le Vigoureux, a French Dominican priest, who remained her spiritual guide. Another adviser was fellow convert Englishman Robert Hugh Benson. Baker returned to Adelaide in 1879 and visited Europe again in 1881, by which time her mother had also become a Catholic.

Thereafter Baker concentrated on a variety of social causes. From early adulthood she had been committed to the alleviation of poverty, both material and spiritual. She either provided or found accommodation, counselling and financial support for many women in need. Baker initiated the migration to Adelaide in 1883 of English Dominican sisters, led by Mother Rose Columba (Sophia) Adams [q.v.]. That year, with financial support from her mother, Baker established Adelaide's first Catholic hospital, in Stangways Terrace, and managed it and its successful school of nursing from 1884.

Moving to England in 1901, Baker was the author of *A Modern Pilgrim's Progress*, published in London in 1906. A 'psychological history' of her beliefs, it was widely reviewed and ran to several editions. The book detailed her conversion from an unsatisfying Anglicanism to a devout Roman Catholicism, by way of a struggle with modern philosophical and religious ideas. She was impressed by Kant's insistence that both religion and morality be grounded in reason. Charles Darwin [q.v.1] strengthened her belief in God as immanent in creation as well as transcendent, and suggested to her that God is also present in the evolution of the church and its doctrines. Conscious that she was self-educated in philosophy, theology and science, Baker inclined to realism and often appealed to common sense and her own experience. Her engagement with the ideas of many renowned thinkers nonetheless revealed a capable, inquisitive, independent and logical mind; her criticisms of Herbert Spencer's social Darwinism, for example, were penetrating and persuasive.

Baker maintained broad, intellectual interests throughout her life, read widely and wrote journal articles on a range of topics, especially the reconciliation of religion and science, seeking to promote modern ideas. She actively supported women's suffrage, both in Australia and England. In her mature years, as a voluntary helper of the Catholic Missionary Society, she worked to spread the message of the Church in England and Wales. With other members of the Catholic Women's League, she gave aid to refugees from the war in Belgium.

Small in stature, with fine features and expressive, dark eyes, Baker was elegantly simple in hairstyle and dress. After contracting influenza, she died of pneumonia on 16 October 1914 at her home in Kensington, London. She was buried in the churchyard of St Thomas, Fulham.

C. C. Martindale, *The Life of Monsignor Robert Hugh Benson*, 2 (Lond, 1917); M. Press, *Three Women of Faith* (Adel, 2000); *Catholic Monthly* (Adel), 2 May 1889; *Observer* (Adel), 20 Oct 1883; *Southern Cross* (Adel), 30 Oct 1914.

STEPHEN DOWNS

BARCLAY, AUBREY COLVILLE HENRI DE RUNE (1880-1950), journalist and conservative campaigner, was born on 20 January 1880 in County Down, Ireland, youngest of six sons and brother of three daughters of William Malo de Rune Barclay, army officer, and his wife Harriet Jane, née Leslie. In 1881 the family moved to Tauranga, New Zealand, where William took a position with the Department of Lands and Bridges. Aubrey attended Woodcote House School, Wellington, where he won the first form mathematics prize. About 1903 he joined the *Evening Post*, Wellington; from 1905 he worked with the

Southland Times, Invercargill, of which he became acting editor. He also contributed to the *Australasian Accountant and Businessman's Journal* (1906) and produced satirical magazines, the *Tickler* and the *Rag*. His early writing included poetry, social commentary and an essay on 'The Literaryness of [Henry] James'.

On 17 September 1903 at St Paul's Church, Thorndon, he married Alice Anne, daughter of Sir Edward Osborne Gibbes. Barclay worked with the *Daily Telegraph* in Sydney from 1913, and then became editor-in-chief of Hugh D. McIntosh's [q.v.10] *Sunday Times* and *Referee*. About 1921 he quarrelled with McIntosh and resigned. In 1923 he established *Pacific*, a short-lived magazine devoted to regional current affairs and lifestyle. He contributed prose and verse to the *Bulletin* as 'Inver G.'.

Increasingly concerned at the threat posed by international communism, Barclay founded the Sane Democracy League in 1925. As full-time secretary he organized and participated in public speeches and radio broadcasts, placed newspaper advertisements and edited the journal *Sane Democracy*. He maintained contact with right-wing groups, including the British Economic League. Also targeting J. T. Lang [q.v.9], the S.D.L. was active in the 1932 State election. Distressed by the Depression, having met unemployed or underemployed 'good men', Barclay made efforts to find work for them and felt that capitalism was fighting a rear-guard action. In the 1930s he developed an interest in fascism, maintaining an amicable—though not entirely credulous —correspondence with Chicago-based anti-Semite Harry Curran Wilbur and contact with the All for Australia and the Australian Unity leagues.

Ambivalent about the Spanish Civil War, Barclay was opposed to Italian aims in North Africa, outspoken against the Japanese annexation of Manchuria, concerned by the aggression of Nazi Germany and critical of the 'ourselves alone' policy of the United States of America. He worried at rumours of Sydneysiders greeting each other with Nazi salutes and questioned the patriotism of some on the political right. He was most unsettled by a visit from Adolf Mills, publisher of the *Angle* and *National Socialist*, whom Barclay thought to be a Nazi agent. In conjunction with other members of the S.D.L., Barclay began a 'Crusade for Democracy' culminating in the formation of the National Defence League, of which he was acting honorary secretary.

Despite Australia's alliance with the Soviet Union, Barclay reminded listeners in radio broadcasts of Australian communists' complicity in the Nazi-Soviet non-aggression pact. Towards the end of World War II his attention broadened to include the likely extension of

wartime planning to peacetime governance. In 1945 his efforts attracted retaliation from the Federal parliamentarian D. A. Mountjoy who, under parliamentary privilege, accused Barclay of running a propaganda campaign against the Labor Party. Finance allegedly came from companies such as Commonwealth Steel Pty Ltd and the Colonial Sugar Refining Co. Ltd, solicited by senior military intelligence personnel through a 'select house of assignation'. This was denied in the press and in parliament and was never substantiated.

Athletic and wiry, known as 'Barc' to his friends, he was an active member of Manly Golf Club and tended the family vegetable garden but grew no flowers. He would rise at 5 a.m. to buy a copy of the *Sydney Morning Herald*, make tea for the household and eat yeast extract on toast. In the evening he repaired to the Royal Prince Alfred Yacht Club or the Neutral Bay Club, where he enjoyed a drink, a pipe and conversation. Brought up within a strict Protestant household, he sent his children to Sunday School but encouraged them to be independent thinkers. He did not attend church but studied the Bible closely.

Barclay's son Captain Aubrey Geoffrey de Rune (Peter) was killed in action on the Kokoda Track, Papua, on 23 October 1942. Barclay died of cancer on 4 March 1950 in Royal North Shore Hospital and was cremated with Methodist forms. His wife and their daughter (who had married Russell, the son of F. M. Gellatly [q.v.8]) survived him. The Sane Democracy League did not long outlast him.

Sane Democracy League, *Sane Democracy* (Syd, 1926); A. Moore, *The Right Road?* (Melb, 1995); *PD* (Cwlth), 181, Mar 1945, pp 612, 620, 720, 760, 772, 776; *J of Aust Studies*, no 1, June 1977, p 70; *SMH*, 6 June 1932, p 8; 13 Dec 1932, p 8, 1 Feb 1933, p 17, 17 Mar 1945, p 5, 5 Mar 1950, p 1, 6 Mar 1950, p 3; *Truth* (Syd), 25 Mar 1945; C. Priday, Sane Democracy in New South Wales 1920 to 1940 (B.A. Hons thesis, Macquarie Univ, 1975); papers held by Mrs B. Gellatly, Frenchs Forest, Syd.

RICHARD M. STRAUSS

BARFF, JANE FOSS (1863-1937), educationist, was born on 24 October 1863 at Sydney Observatory, daughter of Henry Chamberlain Russell [q.v.6], astronomer, and his wife Emily Jane, née Foss. Educated by a Miss Hooper, in 1878 Jane passed the junior public examination and in 1881 the senior, each time sharing the Fairfax [q.v.4] prize for the best pass gained by a female. Matriculating in 1883, she joined the second group of women to enrol at the University of Sydney (B.A., 1886; M.A., 1889).

Although few girls were taught science at school, Jane in her first year obtained first-class honours in chemistry, experimental physics and classics, and second-class in mathematics. She graduated with first-class honours in classics and second-class in mathematics, then travelled to England and Europe, spending time at Cambridge visiting Girton and Newnham women's colleges. Returning to Sydney in 1887, she taught mathematics at Ascham, later teaching at Mlle Soubeiran's [q.v.12] Kambala and privately. Her M.A. was the first in Sydney for a woman.

Jane promoted the cause of female graduates and undergraduates. Involved in early fund-raising for the university's Women's College, she was elected to its first council and served continuously until 1937. In May 1892 she and Louisa Macdonald [q.v.10] formed the Sydney University Women's Association; Jane succeeded Louisa as president in 1893. Though she was by nature and position more conservative in her views than Louisa, there was a lasting friendship between them. In 1891 Jane had been a founding member of the Sydney University Women's Society. Members worked at Newington asylum for aged women, the Woolloomooloo girls' club and at Harrington Street night school for girls, where in 1891-96 classes were under Jane's supervision.

Succeeding Helen Phillips, in 1892 Miss Russell was appointed tutor to female students at the university, the sole female post on the teaching staff, at an annual salary of £250. Possessing high ideals and strong principles, she enjoyed a good relationship with students and staff. What she saw as unseemly behaviour would earn the student a sharp reprimand, even if it occurred on the tennis court. She resigned to marry Henry Ebenezer Barff [q.v.7], the university registrar and librarian, on 6 September 1899 at Holy Trinity Church, Sydney. They had two children.

Macdonald described her dignified friend at an evening entertainment in 1900, where Jane wore 'a handsome black brocaded satin trimmed with jet'. Mrs Barff was involved in moves which led in 1913 to the Sydney University Women's Settlement; she was president in 1914-15 and 1919-24. Also interested in public affairs, she was a member of the National Council of Women and a proxy convener of the standing committee on emigration and immigration, subjects on which she wrote a comprehensive report for the 1914 quinquennial conference in Rome. A deeply committed Anglican, she was a council member of the Mothers' Union and of St Catherine's Church of England School for Girls and a strong advocate of religious education for young people.

After her husband's death in 1925 Mrs Barff continued her public activities. She died at her Rose Bay home on 10 June 1937 and was buried in Waverley cemetery, survived by her daughter. Her Women's College friends instituted a prize in her memory.

W. V. Hole and A. H. Treweeke, *The History of the Women's College Within the University of Sydney* (Syd, 1953); U. Bygott and K. J. Cable, *Pioneer Women Graduates of the University of Sydney 1881-1921* (Syd, 1985); R. Williams, *The Settlement* (Syd, 1988); C. Turney, U. Bygott and P. Chippendale, *Australia's First: A History of the University of Sydney*, 1 (Syd, 1991); R. Annable (ed), *Biographical Register: The Women's College Within the University of Sydney*, 1, 1892-1939 (Syd, 1995); J. Beaumont and W. V. Hole, *Letters from Louisa* (Syd, 1996); Univ Syd Archives, *Record*, 4, no 1, May 1976, p 3; *Daily Telegraph* (Syd), 14 Apr 1915, p 6.

URSULA BYGOTT

BARNET, NAHUM (1855-1931), architect and journalist, was born on 16 August 1855 at Swanston Street, Melbourne, son of Isaac Barnet, Polish-born pawnbroker, jeweller and tobacconist, and his London-born wife Flora, née Abrahams. Nahum attended Scotch College, and is said to have begun his career as an insurance clerk. He matriculated at the University of Melbourne, wrote on architectural subjects in the press and the *Victorian Review* and in 1876-79 was articled at a relatively advanced age to (Leonard) Terry & (Percy) Oakden [qq.v.6,5].

By February 1879 Barnet was calling tenders in his own right. A letter to the *Argus* in 1880 expressed his views on the unsuitability of English Gothic for local conditions; stucco, 'Melbourne's great architectural curse', should be abandoned in favour of a colourful, new style using terracotta, faience and tiles. A member of the Victorian Institute of Architects from 1884, he had some success in competitions, winning, among others, that for the Working Men's College (Royal Melbourne Institute of Technology), with Terry & Oakden. The college in La Trobe Street (1884-86) proceeded to his design and was one of his major early works, as was the Alexandra Theatre (1885-86) for Jules Joubert [q.v.4] in Exhibition Street, remodelled in 1903 to become Her Majesty's Theatre.

In March 1880 Barnet was elected secretary of the Anglo-Jewish Association. By 1882 he was honorary architect to the Jewish Philanthropic Society and doing work at the Jewish almshouses (later Montefiore homes). He was to develop an extensive Jewish clientele, designing many houses and a number of tobacco warehouses and factories. In 1887 he failed to obtain a commission for an extension of St Kilda Synagogue (but succeeded in 1903-04). With John Grainger, Barnet designed the Fergusson & Mitchell (Robur) building (1887-88) on difficult, filled ground south of the Yarra and in 1890 the Austral Building in

Collins Street for Alex McKinley [q.v.5], for whom he had previously designed a printery. He weathered the depression better than most architects, with some small shops, Northcote fire station (1894), the London Tavern, off Collins Street (1895-96), a warehouse, a factory and work for his tobacco patrons.

Some of his buildings had an explicitly Eastern if not necessarily Jewish character, as in the house, Rosaville (1882-83, now part of Medley Hall), for Abraham Harris. In commercial work Barnet often used a version of the American-Romanesque, with Art Nouveau overtones, as in D. Bernard's Swiss portrait studios, Bourke Street (1900); the F. J. Dodge Building, Elizabeth Street (1902), B. H. Altson's building, Elizabeth and Collins streets (1903) and the Paton building, Elizabeth Street (1905). His warehouse (1909) for Barnet Glass [q.v.9], now Legacy House, Swanston Street, was in a more austere form of redbrick Romanesque. Otherwise he favoured 'a glorious fluorescent Italian style'.

His theatres included the rebuilding of Queens Hall to become a cinema; the Variety Theatre, Bourke Street (1911, in conjunction with Eaton & Bates of Sydney); Tait's [q.v.12] Auditorium (1913), Collins Street; and the Britannia (cinema) (1912) in Bourke Street. He was also responsible for the (new) London Hotel in Elizabeth Street (1911); the Young Women's Christian Association clubrooms in Russell Street (1913); and an early motor garage (1913) in Franklin Street for the Connibere brothers [q.v.8]. His work during and after World War I is imprecisely documented, but included a number of second-ranking city buildings.

Late in life Barnet was a member of the council of the British Empire League, and he appears to have been an Anglophile. His first and only overseas trip, in the 1920s, was principally a visit to England. It is said to have changed his previous perception that synagogues all over the world were basically the same, but the Synagogue in Toorak Road (1928-30), his last major work, was conventionally classical in a Corinthian Baroque style, with a dominating dome (though richly treated internally).

On 16 June 1885 in the Great Synagogue, Sydney, Barnet had married Ada Rose Marks. He was a friend of the sculptor Sir Bertram Mackennal and the writer Isaac Selby [qq.v.10,16]. Predeceased by his wife and survived by four daughters, Barnet died on 1 September 1931 at his residence in St Kilda, and was buried in St Kilda cemetery. His estate was sworn for probate at £5879. It was claimed by Selby that Barnet had designed a building in every street in Melbourne proper.

I. Selby, *The Old Pioneers' Memorial History of Melbourne* (Melb, 1925); *Argus*, 29 July 1880, p 3, 2 Sept 1931, pp 5 & 6; N. Lewis, Biographical Study of Nahum Barnet (B.Arch. essay, Univ Melb. 1974); M. Lewis, *Australian Architectural Index* (mf, Melb, 1987). MILES LEWIS

BARNEY, ELISE (1810-1883), postmistress, was born on 21 October 1810 in Lisbon, Portugal, eldest daughter of Captain James Rivers and his wife Mary, née Martin. On 6 November 1833 at St Mary's Cathedral, New Ross, Ireland, she married John Edward Barney, army officer. His regiment was transferred in July 1839 to St Helena, where he had responsibility for the tomb of Napoleon Bonaparte until the Emperor's remains were removed to Paris in 1840. After Barney's service in South Africa in the Kaffir war the family returned to England in 1846.

Next year John's brother Lieutenant-Colonel George Barney [q.v.1] was appointed superintendent of a proposed convict colony of North Australia and offered John an appointment. The latter sold his commission and the family embarked for Sydney in the *Ganges*, arriving on 1 September 1847. By then North Australia had been abandoned, but the pastoral industry offered opportunities. He applied for the lease of Kogan Creek station, north-west of the Darling Downs. Attack by Aborigines caused the family to return to Moreton Bay, where Barney was appointed commissioner of crown lands on 28 October 1849 and a magistrate on 30 January 1850.

With the commencement of direct immigration to Moreton Bay and the expansion of pastoral settlement, Barney was appointed postmaster on 1 March 1852. Brisbane was the focus of the postal service in what became Queensland. It was the only centre with a full-time postmaster, a letter-carrier and town delivery. Under Captain Barney the number of offices increased from nine to eleven. He died on 25 November 1855. His wife, who had assisted him when his health began to decline, succeeded him on the following day. By December 1859, when Queensland was separated from New South Wales, there were fifteen post offices; she received a generous testimonial from the secretary of the General Post Office, Sydney. It was obvious that a postal inspector was needed and Thomas Lodge Murray-Prior [q.v.5] was appointed on 6 November 1860; he became postmaster-general on 4 January 1862. The Brisbane G.P.O. now served twenty-five offices. Elise's salary increased to £350. She and Murray-Prior became incompatible after he forced her son (Edward) Whiston to resign from his position as her clerk in 1863.

She remained postmistress until 2 April 1864 when she was transferred to the money order branch. There, however, her principal assistant proved to be dishonest, and a deficiency of £648 was identified in December. A public service investigation found that lack of proper supervision rested on both Murray-Prior and Mrs Barney. Each was directed to contribute half the loss and Mrs Barney was to be retired. However, (Sir) Robert Mackenzie [q.v.5], formerly minister in charge of the postal department, moved in the Legislative Assembly for a select committee into the organization and management of the post office. This found that neither Mrs Barney nor Murray-Prior should be held responsible for the defalcations and drew attention to the inadequate accommodation and shortage of trained staff. On 31 December 1864 Mrs Barney retired, with a gratuity of £2000, to her house in Gipps Street, Fortitude Valley. There, survived by her son and daughter, she died of diphtheria on 5 July 1883; she was buried in Toowong cemetery with Anglican rites. The *Brisbane Courier* acknowledged her role as 'giving entire satisfaction, and making many friends by her lady-like demeanour and the kindliness of her disposition'. During her time as postmistress the postal service had expanded to serve forty-five offices.

H. Radi, *200 Australian Women* (Syd, 1988); K. Jobst, *The Barneys 1835-1865* (Brisb, 1997); *V&P* (LA, Qld), 1865, p 1035; Hist Soc of Qld, *J*, 1, no 2, Feb 1916, p 76; *Moreton Bay Courier*, 26 Nov 1855, p 1; *Brisb Courier*, 7 July 1883, p 4.

MANFRED CROSS

BARR, ANDREW (1855-1939), farmer, inventor and dreamer, was born on 12 July 1855 at Halfmerkland Farm, Scorrieholm, Lesmahagow, Lanarkshire, Scotland, son of Robert Barr, leasehold farmer, and his wife Isabella, née Wilson. Leaving school at 13, he worked as a farmhand until the family migrated to South Australia. A staunch Presbyterian, Andrew married a Congregationalist, Rosetta Almedia Gilbert, on 27 September 1877 at Pinkerton Downs; of their fourteen children, eight survived infancy. Barr worked as a woodcutter and farmhand before acquiring Balaklava farm at Wild Horse Plains. In 1880 he won a prize for his invention of a stump-jump, disc plough, although the prior claims of Richard Bowyer and Clarence Herbert Smith [qq.v.] were later recognized. Barr prospered until struck in the 1890s by drought and by the bankruptcy of James Martin, agent for his plough. Reduced to living in a tent at Mount Remarkable, in 1897 the family sailed for Western Australia, while two sons overlanded stock and machinery.

Next year, when the sixty-acre (24 ha) wheat crop on his original selection at Doodlakine failed, Barr moved towards Minda-booka and pioneered the Bruce Rock district. He built a homestead of local stone and mud mortar near a spring on a 2034-acre (823.2-ha) leasehold at Quorncutting. His isolated family lived rough, often eating kangaroo and wallaby. An occasional Bible-reading with distant neighbours was the main social activity. Following the stillbirth of her fourteenth child, Rosetta died of septicaemia in June 1901. She was buried at Nunagin Rock. Delegating specific indoor and outside duties to each child, Barr continued to gather sandalwood, grow wheat and raise sheep and cattle. He exhibited at the first Doodlakine cattle sale in 1911. Yet his daughter Rose recalled that he was often absorbed 'with wild thoughts and vain preoccupations'.

In June 1903 Barr sent a working model of an aeronautical appliance, designed 'to convey people in the air as on a ship at sea', to the Department of Defence. The aluminium apparatus supported by steel bearings would feature inverted wings to prevent air rush. He volunteered to build a prototype within three months for £6 a week with a final payment of one million pounds. The specifications were rejected by Major General Sir Edward Hutton and Sir John Forrest [qq.v.9,8], minister for defence. Undaunted, he formed the Barr flying machine syndicate with the investor W. E. Hearman and mining entrepreneur T. H. Brimage. Together in London they experienced strong competition and rejection from the Imperial government. At home E. G. 'Dryblower' Murphy [q.v.10] lampooned him as 'Poor busted Barr of Doodlekine'. Barr married Anna Dickie Smith Thomson, nursing matron, on 26 August 1904 at St George's Church, Bloomsbury, London, and returned to Western Australia.

His inventions patented between 1901 and 1933 included an improved method of conveying passengers over rough country, a power digging-machine, a mechanism for destroying wire entanglements (offered to the War Office in 1915), a solar machine, a mallee eradicator and an improved stump-jump eradicator. Although used by farmers, none of Barr's inventions brought him wealth. A tall, straight man, wearing heavy moustaches, he was an entertaining raconteur and excelled at draughts and bridge. He died on 9 February 1939 at Bendering and was buried at Kondinin with Presbyterian forms.

E. G. Murphy, *Jarrahland Jingles* (Perth, 1908); H. Clift, *A Clouded Vision* (Lesmurdie, 1994); *Rock Review*, no 494, 30 June 1988; *Tarmac Topics* (Perth), 7, no 4, 1993; *Merredin Mercury*, 23 Feb 1939; *West Australian*, 3, 4 June 1903; *Western Mail* (Perth), 8 June 1922, 9 July 1931, 29 July 1937, 19 July 1951, 5 April 2003; *Sunday Times*, 17, 28 Nov 1929, 19 Nov 1936, 7 Sept 1944; Barr papers, MN 1533 ACC 4817A (BL).

WENDY BIRMAN

BARTON, CHARLOTTE (1796-1867), governess, feminist and author, was christened on 13 March 1796 at St Mary's, Marylebone, London, third daughter of Albert Waring, barrister, and his wife Elizabeth, née Turner. When Charlotte was less than 2 her mother died. Reputedly a child prodigy, from the age of 10 she attended a school in Kent where she was instructed in the 'general branches of polite female education' including music, drawing and French. She studied painting under John Glover [q.v.1]. On leaving school, aged about 15, she was engaged as a governess but was allowed to continue her education. About 1815 she took a position in Lancashire where she was in charge of five children. Two years later she resigned because of ill health.

Charlotte sailed for Sydney in the *Cumberland* in 1826, employed to teach the children of Hannibal Macarthur [q.v.2] at the high salary of £100 a year. On the voyage she became engaged to James Atkinson [q.v.1], who was returning to his property, Oldbury, at Sutton Forest. She took up her position with the Macarthurs but left to marry Atkinson at St Paul's Church of England, Cobbity, on 29 September 1827. Her first child, Charlotte, was born in 1828; (Jane) Emily in 1830; James in 1832; and (Caroline) Louisa [q.v.3 Atkinson] in 1834. The death of her husband that year left his widow to manage a large holding, run far-flung outstations, control convict labour in a district beset by bushranging gangs and care for her children.

On 3 March 1836 at All Saints' chapel, Sutton Forest, Charlotte married George Bruce Barton, superintendent at Oldbury. Her remarriage changed her legal position from being custodian of Oldbury to merely the lessor's wife. The executors of Atkinson's will, John Coghill and Alexander Berry [q.v.1], leased the property to Barton, who proved to be violent, unpredictable, a drunkard and mentally disturbed. In 1839 Charlotte fled from him with her children down the precipitous Meryla Pass through the wild gorges of the Shoalhaven River to a coastal outstation at Budgong where she continued their education, particularly inculcating a love of nature. In 1840 the family moved to Sydney and Charlotte applied for legal protection from Barton. Her relations with the executors deteriorated, Berry referring to her as 'a notable she-dragon'. She became involved in long-running legal battles, *Atkinson* v. *Barton and Others*, in which she fought to retain custody of her children. At one stage the master in equity determined that they should be taken from her and educated in boarding schools but this decision was overturned.

At a time when she was receiving no money from the Atkinson estate, Charlotte published *A Mother's Offering to Her Children* (1841).

The first children's book to be published in Australia, it was a collection of instructional stories arranged in the form of a dialogue between a mother and her four children. The anonymous author was 'A Lady Long Resident in New South Wales', but a contemporary review in the *Sydney Gazette*, where the book was printed, identified her.

Despite the disruption of continuing legal cases, Charlotte maintained a close-knit family life in an atmosphere of learning and scholarship. In 1846 the family returned to Oldbury. There, and later in Sydney and at Kurrajong, she particularly fostered the talents of her youngest daughter Louisa. Survived by a son and two daughters, Charlotte died at Oldbury on 10 October 1867 and was buried in the family vault at All Saints' graveyard, where her first husband was interred. She was a small woman, 5 ft 1½ ins (156 cm) tall, of 'particularly handsome and brilliant' appearance with 'full large black eyes, black hair which curled naturally and fine features', well educated, with artistic talent and a great interest in natural history. Fiercely independent, though an abused wife and sole parent she succeeded in challenging the male-dominated legal system.

P. Clarke, *Pioneer Writer* (Syd, 1990) and for bib.
PATRICIA CLARKE

BATES, GEORGE (1800?-1895), sealer and trader, was born possibly on 13 April 1800 at Cheapside, London, son of a militiaman. After attending the Marine Society's school George proceeded to a school-ship at Deptford. He began life at sea in the man-of-war H.M.S. *Warrior* when aged 11 and saw Bombay, the Persian Gulf and the Cape of Good Hope on naval service. In 1823 in the crew of the convict ship *Commodore Hayes* he reached Hobart Town, where he joined the sealing vessel *Nereus*, which operated in Bass Strait and beyond. While anchored in one of Kangaroo Island's sheltered bays in January 1824, he and a mate stole ashore and hid in the scrub.

At first Bates planned to return to England, but soon joined other renegades and remained on the island. His impressive figure, red hair and beard earned him the nickname 'Fireball'. Many of the fugitives, including Bates, abducted Aboriginal women from Van Diemen's Land and the mainland. Using their traditional skills, these captive women helped islanders to gather seal, kangaroo and wallaby skins and salt from the lagoons. Islanders bartered this produce with crews of vessels from Port Jackson and Hobart Town for subsistence requirements, including rum and tobacco, enabling the men to survive in relative ease.

Bates relished his independence and roamed far and wide, living by his own rules. On one excursion to the mainland he glimpsed Lake Alexandrina, passed on the information and inadvertently contributed to growing interest in South Australia. In July 1836 he shared the dismay of other unofficial settlers as the South Australian Co.'s official colonists disembarked from the *Duke of York*. William Light [q.v.2] hired Bates and his women. The islanders' uncivilized appearance alarmed the newcomers who, to survive, eventually adapted some of their unconventional companions' skills. Bates chose to retain his independence and bypass authority. He retreated to Hog Bay (Penneshaw) where he continued to live by trading. In the 1840s he loaded ships on Port Adelaide wharves. Sometimes he helped those in authority, such as Alexander Tolmer [q.v.6], to pursue lawbreakers but his sympathies were with the fugitives, whom he also assisted.

On 7 August 1848 at Holy Trinity Church of England, Adelaide, Bates married illiterate, English-born Elizabeth Mainstone. In the 1850s he joined in the rush to the Victorian goldfields but had little success and returned to island life. Building a stone cottage at Hog Bay he settled into a degree of conformity. By 1870 he was unable to support his wife; neighbours arranged for the frail couple to receive government assistance. Aged 87, Bates was an honoured 'Old Colonist' at the Jubilee Exhibition in Adelaide, where his reminiscences of the lawless years entertained the staid citizens. An interviewer in 1895 reported that the old man's 'intellect is clear, his hearing fair, and his speech good'; he liked reading history, geography and travel books but 'did not care for ... love novels'. Predeceased by his wife, Bates died in the Destitute Asylum, Adelaide, on 8 September 1895. His remains were buried in the hilltop cemetery above his former dwelling at Penneshaw.

A. Tolmer, *Reminiscences of an Adventurous and Chequered Career at Home and at the Antipodes* (Lond, 1882); J. S. Cumpston, *Kangaroo Island 1800-1836* (Canb, 1970); J. M. Nunn, *This Southern Land* (Adel, 1989); *Advertiser* (Adel), 27 Dec 1886, p 6; *Observer* (Adel), 2 Feb 1895, p 16, 14 Sept 1895, p 16; *Register* (Adel), 9 Sept 1895, p 7; *Chronicle* (Adel), 2 Mar 1933; Woodforde family papers (SLSA).

JEAN M. NUNN

BEASLEY, HILLSON (1855-1936), architect, was born on 30 April 1855 at Canterbury, Kent, England, son of Edward Beasley, dyer, and his wife Caroline, née Saunders. Educated at Wesley College, Sheffield, he was articled to an architect in Dover, then practised in London, Carlisle and Oxford. He married Fanny Clarke on 22 December 1877 at the parish church, Great Missenden, Buckinghamshire. They were childless. Moving to Cape Colony, South Africa, he was employed by the Public Works Department for three years. The couple arrived in Melbourne in 1886 and Beasley opened his own practice. Early built works included the Presbyterian (Uniting) Church, St Kilda (1887), featuring polychromatic brickwork, and a competition entry for public buildings at Fern Tree Gully described as American Romanesque in red brick, stone, slate and terracotta.

Beasley promoted academic discussion on architecture and taught at the Working Men's College and the University of Melbourne in 1893. Among lectures reproduced in professional journals was a series on 'Greek and Roman Architecture' in *The Australian Builders Contractors News*, 1893. In 'The Value of Technical Education to Artisans' (*Building and Engineering Journal* 1893), he advocated the teaching of trades and crafts through manual training and apprenticeship, as opposed to theoretical education. 'The Sanitation of Dwellings' in the same journal emphasized proficiency of knowledge in sanitation, drainage and ventilation.

Moving to Perth in 1896, Beasley continued to work within the palette of contrasting stone and red brick. He joined the Public Works Department as a draftsman under the direction of George Temple Poole [q.v.11], and in 1897 became chief draftsman and assistant to John Grainger, who succeeded Poole. A loyal lieutenant, Beasley in turn was chief architect from 1905 until June 1917. He was a conservative practitioner, knowledgeable in the eclectic architectural languages of the late nineteenth century, and believing that the style of buildings should fit their purpose, be well mannered and appropriately decorated only to enrich their type. Decoration was typically derived from local masonry materials and sometimes patterned in the striated manner of the 'blood and bandages' style of Federation architecture.

Due to the gold rushes, population increase and the need for new building types with the coming of responsible government in 1891, Beasley oversaw a great number of new government works and additions in Perth, Fremantle and towns along the railway to the eastern goldfields. He designed or was responsible for Government House ballroom, Perth (1899), the competition-winning Western Australian Parliament House (1900), Claremont Teacher Training College (1902), Perth Modern School (1909-11), additions to the Western Australian Art Gallery and Library (1899-1911), Midland Courthouse (1907), Fremantle Post Office (1907) and Fremantle Technical College annexe (1910).

In retirement, Beasley lectured at the University of Western Australia in 1920-21, then visited England. A prominent member of Trinity Congregational Church, Perth, sometime chairman of the Congregational Union, he was later connected with Scots Church, Albany, where he was choir conductor and an elder. Survived by his wife, he died on 7 October 1936 at Albany and was buried in the local Presbyterian cemetery.

The Cyclopedia of Western Australia, 1 (Perth, 1913); M. Pitt Morison and J. White (eds), *Western Towns and Buildings* (Perth, 1979); C. T. Stannage (ed), *A New History of Western Australia* (Perth, 1981); H. Lewi et al, *Visualising the Architecture of Federation* (CD-Rom, Perth, 2001); *Building & Engineering J of Aust & NZ*, 12, no 290, 20 Jan 1894, p 21; *Albany Advertiser*, 17 Oct 1936.

HANNAH LEWI

BEETON, LUCY (1829-1886), Aboriginal teacher and businesswoman, was born on 14 May 1829 on Gun Carriage (Vansittart) Island, eastern Bass Strait, daughter of Thomas (John) Beeton (also known as Beedon, Baden or Beadon), from a Jewish family of jewellers in London, and Emmerenna ('Bet Smith'), a Tasmanian Aborigine from Cape Portland. Beeton had been a sailor in the British navy, transported for seven years in 1817 for mutiny. His sentence completed, he voluntarily moved to Bass Strait in 1824, became an independent sealer and was paid a 'handsome allowance' by his family.

In 1831 Lucy's childhood was disrupted when G. A. Robinson [q.v.2] arrived with authority to remove resident sealers and establish a settlement for Aborigines. Beeton was evicted from the island. Lucy and her pregnant mother remained, as inmates in Robinson's 'settlement', until Lieutenant Governor (Sir) George Arthur [q.v.1] agreed to Thomas's request that he be reunited with his family. When in October Robinson moved the settlement to Flinders Island, the Beetons returned to Gun Carriage Island. Lucy was educated by private tutors in either George Town or Launceston, and her father taught her skills in business and sailing.

In 1850 the government rejected a petition to appoint a catechist-teacher, financed from the Land Fund, so Lucy became a teacher herself, apparently at Gun Carriage Island. Bishop F. R. Nixon [q.v.2] noted in 1854 that each day she gathered local children to impart 'secular and religious knowledge'. Some time between 1855 and 1860 the family moved west to Badger Island. Nursing her father during his final years, she ceased teaching and took over the family business when he died in 1862. That year, following approaches from Lucy, Archdeacon Thomas Reibey [q.v.6] proposed to the government that a school be established to educate the sixty-six children

then living on the islands. The government agreed to provide £250 if public subscription provided the same, an amount the islanders did not have. Lucy responded by appointing two teachers from Melbourne. In 1871, frustrated with continued lack of government support, she established a school in a tent on Badger Island. Next year the government relented and appointed a schoolteacher. For her efforts to 'instruct and civilise' the islanders, Lucy was rewarded with a lifetime lease to Badger Island, at a yearly rent of £24.

A prominent member of the wider Bass Strait community, Lucy was regarded by many as the 'Queen of the Isles'. Her physical size enhanced her status: when 25 years old she weighed about 23 stone (146 kg). For much of her adult life she controlled trading operations, earning herself the nickname 'the commodore' from her practice of sailing to Launceston with a fleet of boats laden with produce, including mutton birds, their eggs, feathers, fat and oil. With her father and others, she was active in islanders' efforts from the 1850s to gain land, especially mutton-bird rookeries, as compensation for Aboriginal dispossession in Tasmania.

Nixon described Lucy as good-humoured, a kind-hearted friend to everyone on the islands, high-minded and earnest in her Christian profession. Sharing the Beeton homestead with her two brothers and their families, she never married and was close to her brothers' children, especially her niece Isabella, whose friends knew Lucy as 'Miss Bella'. Later relations and community members called her 'Aunty Lucy'. In 1872 she offered Truganini [q.v.6 Trugernanner] a home on Badger Island, but the offer was not taken up.

From 1872 Lucy was friendly with M. B. Brownrigg [q.v.3], a Church of England canon at Launceston. In February 1882 she helped him to organize a temperance meeting at Long Beach on Cape Barren Island. Abhorring the practice of White traders offering rum and other intoxicating drinks as payment for produce, Beeton was distressed that 'her people' were wronged and robbed, and complained bitterly about the absence of police protection. She used her relationship with influential clergy to advance the interests of indigenous Tasmanians, and articulated the view that Europeans had 'dispossessed "her people" of their land, and banished them to die on Flinders Island'.

Lucy 'Beadon' died of congestion of the lung on 7 July 1886 at Badger Island and was buried on the island's east coast.

J. Bonwick, *Last of the Tasmanians* (Lond, 1870); B. Mollison and C. Everitt, *The Tasmanian Aborigines and Their Descendants* (Hob, 1978); S. Murray-Smith (ed), *Mission to the Islands* (Hob, 1979);

I. West, *Pride Against Prejudice* (Canb, 1987); T. Reibey, Letter from the Venerable Archdeacon Reibey on the Subject of the Half-caste Islanders in the Straits, *Journals* (LC, Tas), 1862, paper no 17; T. Reibey, Half-caste Islanders in Bass's Straits: Report of the Venerable Archdeacon Reibey, *Journals* (LC, Tas), 1863, paper no 48.

SHAYNE BREEN

BELL, GEORGE RENISON (1840-1915), prospector and mine-manager, was born on 21 November 1840 at Bothwell, Van Diemen's Land, youngest of three children of George Bell (d.1852), a schoolmaster from Scotland, and his English-born wife Sarah, née Danby. Young Bell was educated at the Society of Friends' (Quaker) school in Hobart. In 1857 he joined his mother and sister at Dunedin, New Zealand, where he worked on a station, then joined the rush to the South Island gold diggings in 1861, beginning his lifelong passion for prospecting and mining.

Bell visited Tasmania for six months in 1864 and trekked around the island, including the unmapped west coast. Returning again in 1866 he prospected and panned for gold in the Mathinna area for three years. After consulting James 'Philosopher' Smith [q.v.6] at Mount Bischoff, in 1874 Bell discovered payable alluvial tin at Boobyalla, which led to the tin-mining industry around Derby, Gladstone and Weldborough.

A student at the Ballarat School of Mines, Victoria, in 1876-77, he prospected on Wilsons Promontory in 1880, returning in 1882 to north-eastern Tasmania where he assisted with the development of several mines. In 1890 Bell was employed by a Launceston syndicate to prospect in western Tasmania. During six months of lone exploration he found and pegged a half square mile (1.3 sq km) mineralized zone north of Zeehan, which later became the Renison Bell tin-field. By 1893 he was in Queensland where he developed and managed the Tate River tin-mine west of the Atherton Tablelands, and he managed gold leases in Western Australia in 1895-98 before returning to Tasmania to prepare a comprehensive report on the Renison Bell tin-field.

On 13 June 1877 Bell had married Phoebe Cox, daughter of a pardoned convict; both staunch Quakers, George and Phoebe exchanged vows at the monthly meeting of the Society of Friends in Hobart. According to descendants, Bell was a domineering father and not always a good provider. During his long absences, the quiet but resourceful Phoebe often relied on support from fellow Quakers.

Bell had self-doubts. An 1893 diary entry reads: 'I wish to be more humble and contented, and not aspiring in all things to be better than others'. In 1898 he wrote: 'I see no improvement in my spiritual nature for it is still dominated by carnal desire and came very near to leading me into some serious scrapes'. He eventually left the Society of Friends but remained a devout Christian.

From 1900 Bell prospected for the Mt Lyell Mining & Railway Co. Ltd, retiring in 1908. In 1907 the State government had belatedly granted him an annual pension of £100 in recognition of his mineral deposits discovery. He was a handsome, neatly bearded man, nicknamed 'Little' because of his short stature. Bell died on 2 September 1915 at Devonport and was buried in Mersey Bluff cemetery. Two daughters and five sons, including John Renison Bell [q.v.13], survived him.

A number of companies and syndicates worked leases on the Renison Bell tin-field in the early years, but profitable recovery of metal from the complex low-grade ores was almost impossible with the metallurgical technology of those times. It was not until 1965, when multinational Consolidated Goldfields Australia Ltd acquired the Renison field, that deep drilling proved an immense ore reserve. With multimillion dollar investment on underground mining and surface treatment mills, Renison Ltd became Australia's biggest tin producer. Bell's headstone was re-erected at the Renison Bell mine in 1973.

K. Pink and P. Crawford, *Renison* (Zeehan, Tas, 1996); *Advocate* (Burnie), 29 Dec 1973, p 10; 5 Jan 1974, p 10, 12 Jan 1974, p 10; Bell's diaries (held by Ms J. Cole, Devonport, Ms P. Crawford, St Marys, and the author).   KERRY PINK

BENHAM, AGNES MARY MATILDA (1850-1932), socialist and advocate of sex reform, was born on 3 December 1850 in Adelaide, second daughter of Edward Planta Nesbit, schoolmaster, and his first wife Ann, née Pariss. Agnes grew up in a literary and reform-minded milieu: her father was deeply religious and wrote poetry. Her mother died after bearing a fifth child, (Edward) Paris(s) Nesbit [q.v.11], later a notorious lawyer. The family had radical connexions, particularly through their English cousin Edith Nesbit, writer of children's fiction and wife of Hubert Bland, a founder of the Fabian Society. Agnes was part of a small, freethinking circle in Adelaide, one familiar with the works of Charlotte Perkins Gilman, the Fabian socialists and the American idealists. They shared a faith in evolution towards human perfectability.

On 21 April 1870 at her father's house in North Adelaide Agnes married John James Benham (1835-1919), an English-born land-broker. The couple had three children; their daughter ROSAMUND AGNES (1874-1923)

became an early medical graduate of the University of Adelaide (M.B., B.S., 1902) and like her mother an advocate of sexual reform. In 1893 only the decrepit state of the ship *Royal Tar* was said to have dissuaded the Benhams from moving to New Australia in Paraguay. Agnes was a frequent speaker at the Adelaide Democratic Club. Her first forays into print in the 1890s were in regular articles for the labour paper, the *Weekly Herald* (*Herald*), under the pen name 'Garde'. Later she wrote for the *Morning* (renamed *Century* in 1901), founded and edited by her brother. In this weekly journal she developed a series of articles on relations between the sexes, which were to be the basis of her book *Love's Way to Perfect Humanhood* (Adelaide, 1904).

Benham's central concern was 'the right relations of the sexes and the propagation of children that may be truly called well-born'. Containing elements of transcendentalist, evolutionary and early psychological thinking, the book presented a challenge to patriarchy and a rationale for women's improved education and political rights as well as control of their sexuality. She deplored the contempt accorded those who gave birth outside wedlock, advocated divorce where love had departed (a loveless marriage was 'legalized prostitution') and insisted upon a woman's right to sexual passion, through which partners could achieve a finer spiritual union. The child conceived through love and nurtured prenatally by the mother—the 'soul gardener' —would strengthen the race and invest the mother with greater prestige. In this, Benham was of her time as well as ahead of it, as anxieties about racial degeneration were then pervasive. But within the constraints of available reform philosophies she was an original thinker. Her commitment both to social reform and to the reform of relations between the sexes was rare.

Mrs Benham was a foundation board member of the South Australian Co-operative Clothing Co., opened in February 1902. In November, inspired by Tom Mann [q.v.10], she helped to form the Clarion Fellowship of Socialists. Rosamund married Thomas Gilbert Taylor, secretary of the Western Australian Social Democratic Federation, in 1903. They had two children before separating, when Rosamund and her children resumed her maiden name. In addition to practising medicine, she wrote poetry and had some verse published in the Sydney *Bulletin*. She worked in Queensland in 1908-18 and later at Sunbury and Kew asylums, Melbourne, until her death from chronic nephritis on 11 December 1923. Her mother, too, seems to have spent some time in Queensland, as well as in Western Australia. In the last decades of her life Agnes lived in Melbourne. Survived by a son, she died on 7 March 1932 at Queen Victoria Hospital and was buried in Brighton cemetery.

R. Chivers, *The Benham Family in Australia* (Adel, 1970); V. Burgmann, *'In our time'* (Syd, 1985); *JHSSA*, no 15, 1987, p 110; A. Mackinnon and C. Bacchi, 'Sex, Resistance and Power: Sex Reform in South Australia c.1905', *Aust Hist Studies*, 23, no 90, Apr 1988, p 60.   ALISON MACKINNON

BENJAFIELD, HARRY (1845-1917), medical practitioner and entrepreneur, was born on 8 March 1845 at Silton, Wiltshire, England, son of Charles Benjafield, yeoman, and his wife Mary Ann, née Cross. Harry grew up on the family farm, himself working on it as a youth. Interest in medicine impelled him to study first at University College, London, then at the University of Edinburgh (M.B., Ch.M., 1871)—always having to earn his livelihood. On 8 February 1873 at Zion Chapel, Stockport, he married Amelia Pywell, daughter of the presiding Baptist minister. Fulfilling Harry's long-indulged dreams of sunny Australia, the couple immediately sailed for Hobart. There he succeeded to the practice of Dr Ebenezer Atherton, said to be the city's first homoeopathic practitioner. In 1874 the tyro gave several public lectures on medical matters; lucid and informed, they perhaps offered most interest when following H. F. Maudsley on psychological issues. 'Nearly all our actions are animated by emotions in the shape of *desire*', went one dictum (in his 'Lecture on "The Mind"'). While the mainstream profession spurned homoeopathy, the industrious and dynamic Benjafield enjoyed remarkable success.

Claiming to own but £20 on arrival, by 1879 he was building a splendid home, The Willows, later Mimosa, reputedly costing £5000. There he raised five sons and five daughters. One son died in infancy. Several of the children helped their father's business ventures. The paterfamilias insisted that women could have no fulfilment but marriage.

Benjafield remained in active practice virtually life-long, stories telling of his skill and readiness to serve the destitute without fee. He sought greater effectiveness of vaccination against smallpox by using calf (rather than human) lymph, and sent the product throughout Australia. In 1882 Benjafield contested the Hobart General Hospital's refusal to allow a homoeopathic ward, and later moved to establish a homoeopathic hospital (St John's, 1899). The man's most enduring enthusiasms were for the health-giving quality of pure air, clean water, ample sunshine and fresh food. He proposed an outdoor camp in bush Tasmania as a cure-resort for consumptives, such ideas running counter to the waxing popularity of supervised bed-rest as the best treatment. In disputing plans for a tuberculosis sanatorium in Hobart, Benjafield showed himself a bitter controversialist. He served as medical officer for various local government agencies.

Benjafield proved an entrepreneur. Buying a property, Derwent Park (later Albert Park, its homestead Dorset House), in Hobart's northern exurbia in 1881, he planned large-scale dairying. Labour costs impaired the operation. In 1891-92 scandal hovered as he sold the property to the government and then rebought it for less. The doctor and some relations, brought to Hobart for this purpose, remained interested in dairying, this story entailing tragedy in 1896 as the kin's business became the channel for fatal diphtheria. When inspected, Benjafield's own dairy was found but moderately clean. From around 1883 he had developed orchards at Albert Park and on a property at Nubeena, Tasman Peninsula. In time they prospered, and Benjafield was a major figure in the history of Tasmania's fruit industry. Building extensive cool-sheds and otherwise attending to market presentation, he exported much high-quality produce. The propagation of the Tasma (later Democrat) apple and the introduction of many pome varieties were claimed for him, and the Royal Horticultural Society recognized his work. Sale for suburban development of part of Albert Park gave another bonus. The Benjafields moved to semi-retirement and Albert Park around 1905.

Since early days in Hobart, Benjafield preached and wrote in gospel/moralist style, and he did much to establish the city's formal Baptist Church. One complement was his support of the Friends' High School. Back in 1879, Benjafield had joined a Protestant reformist move in municipal politics, and he was later active on the Mount Stuart town board, which he chaired in 1896-99. In 1895 he argued for bimetallism in a radical way; later words contemned 'political labourites', but on his death the leftist *Daily Post* was to eulogize 'A Life of Usefulness'.

In various British journals, as in 'The Tasmanian'—his autobiography written in 1914—Benjafield proclaimed the glorious beauty of Tasmania. Whereas his lectures of 1874 hinted that he found Tasmanians often dirty and shiftless, he now applauded their virtue, notably in surmounting the convict legacy. The veteran found neither desire nor time to return to Britain. Vigorous to the end, he died of a heart attack on 13 June 1917 at his home, his estate to be valued for probate at more than £31 000. His wife and nine children survived him.

L. F. Rowston, *One Hundred Years of Witness* (Hob, 1984); A. Alexander, *Glenorchy 1804-1964* (Glenorchy, Tas, 1986); M. Roe, *Life Over Death* (Hob, 1999); L. Gannell, *Inasmuch: St John's Hospital, Hobart: 1899-1999* (Sandy Bay, Tas, 1999); Dr Benjafield and the Derwent Park Estate, *J&PP* (Tas), paper no 108, vol 26, 1892; Diphtheria in Hobart and Neighbourhood, *J&PP* (Tas), paper no 21, vol 35, 1896; *Cold*, 7, 1916, p 87; *Tasman Peninsula Chronicle*, no 8, Apr 1998; *Mercury* (Hob), 29 Apr 1879, p 3; 14 June 1917, p 6; NS 677/1 and AD960/38 (TA).   MICHAEL ROE

BENTLEY, MARY ANN MOORE; *see* LING

BERRY, MARGARET (1832-1918), educationist, was born on 24 August 1832 at Naas, Kildare, Ireland, daughter of Terence Berry, clerk, and his wife Margaret, née Allen. After six months training in 1851 at Marlborough Street Training College, Dublin, she taught in Ireland then migrated to New South Wales in 1856 to teach at the Catholic school at Bathurst. She was at the National School, William Street, Sydney, in 1857-60. In August 1860 the newly appointed Queensland inspector Randal MacDonnell [q.v.5] selected her for the key post of headmistress and teacher trainer at Brisbane National Girls' School and from 1862 at Brisbane Girls' Normal (Central) School.

She became 'the indomitable Margaret Berry' because of her bold stand for female teachers in evidence to the royal commission into education in 1874, at which she was their sole representative. Others had declined to appear. Berry criticized MacDonnell for usurping her authority over the teaching of music and the appointment of an assistant teacher. She also complained about the lower salaries for women following the abolition of school fees in 1870, and stressed her faith in the ability of senior girls to tackle advanced scientific subjects.

Serving wholly as a teacher in the heart of a rapidly expanding Brisbane, Berry faced serious over-crowding in inadequate classrooms, in hat-rooms and on verandahs. Other problems included the erection of new or extended buildings; noise and pollution from nearby factories; exposure to curious carters and pedestrians; and regular bouts of sickness affecting both staff and students, especially in winter. The water supply, stored in a metal tank, caused additional health risks: one mother wrote that her daughter tasted 'Something dead in it'. Summer brought stifling heat, which she tried to counter by planting bamboos; after the establishment of Arbor Day in 1890 she attempted to grow other shade trees in the stony surface of the playground, but had to admit defeat.

Yet successive district inspectors commended her as a skilled administrator in conditions that sometimes caused her self-confessed physical and mental exhaustion.

They reported: 'The discipline and tone are excellent; the children shew a becoming demeanour and lively interest in their work' (1870); and 'V. efficient; an excellent disciplinarian, exercises complete control and thorough supervision over her subordinates' (1884). Advancing years made her more formulaic but she retained her zest, as evidenced in this report given in her seventy-second year: 'The methods are often suitable, but sometimes very mechanical and are applied with very fair skill and much energy' (1903).

Her training of pupil-teachers did not receive such complimentary assessments, due to the heavy professional burdens placed upon her, one of which was to examine teachers' needlework. Yet she always regarded their training and welfare as part of her duty and she expected the highest standards. When two young teachers played tricks on their pupils one April Fools Day she felt bound to report them. Many such girls had few career options except as lowly paid teachers and through them her influence spread to all parts of Queensland.

Berry retired in 1905. During her long career she had the strong support of other family members, especially her younger sister Eliza, who became the headmistress of Kangaroo Point Girls' and Infants' School, Brisbane. Margaret also adopted an orphaned niece, May Mulligan, whom she trained as a pupil-teacher. Berry died on 3 November 1918 at New Farm and was buried with Catholic rites in a family grave in Toowong cemetery. A plaque on the former site of the Normal School commemorates 'the work of Margaret Berry, first head mistress of the girls' normal school for forty-three years (1862-1905), and that of her successor Elizabeth Large (1905-1921). Their contribution to the education of girls in this city was outstanding.'

T. Watson, 'There was a Spirit in the Place: the Brisbane Normal School', in G. Logan and T. Watson (eds), *Soldiers of the Service* (Brisb, 1992); Royal Commission into Education, *V&P* (Qld), 1875, 2, p 83; Bd of General Education (Qld), *Annual Report*, 1860-75; Minister of Public Instruction (Qld), *Annual Report*, 1876-1905; *Unicorn*, 17, no 4, Nov 1991, p 243; Brisb Normal School file, and Female Teachers' Register (QA).   TOM WATSON

BETHEL, EDITH (1871-1929), political organizer, was born on 1 March 1871 at Bowen, Queensland, second daughter of William Clarke, an Irish-born accountant, sometime mayor, and his English-born wife Mary Sophia, née Edkins. By 1882 the family was in Sydney, where Edith was tutored by J. Dobbie, B.A. A musician and an English and French scholar, she acquired 'a good mental grasp of economic questions in the school of experience and sympathy', being an active member of the Pitt Street Congregational Church as a girl and a visitor to the mission in Sussex Street. Interested in the welfare of women and children and the insanitary and comfortless housing of the poor, she gravitated towards Labor politics. About 1882 she formed a relationship with WALTER EDMUND BETHEL (1863-1941), a public servant. In 1894 she gave birth to a daughter who was fostered to another family.

Born on 14 April 1863 at Ashfield, Sydney, Walter was the son of George Henry Bethel, printer, and his wife Christina Straith, née Matheson. He was educated at Fort Street Model School and entered the Department of Public Instruction in August 1878. On 22 September 1882 in Sydney with Presbyterian forms he had married Eva Louisa Brierly; they had two sons and a daughter before being divorced in June 1895. Walter married Edith on 5 July that year at Mosman Congregational Church. In 1902 he and Edith took a delegation of Australian teachers to South Africa. He was clerk-in-charge Norfolk Island affairs, Chief Secretary's Department, from 1904, returning to the Department of Public Instruction in 1906. After touring the Gilbert Islands in 1908 he wrote a series of press articles.

In response to the founding of the conservative Women's Liberal and Reform League, Edith was one of the small group which formed the Women's Central Organising Committee of the Political Labor League of New South Wales. At the inaugural W.C.O.C. meeting, attended by some 300 women in the Trades Hall on 1 September 1904, she became secretary. She attended Labor's annual conference in February 1905, the first to admit women, as a delegate for St Leonards, won election to the party's executive and was re-elected in 1906-08. In August 1906 she became president of a women's branch formed at North Sydney. For her efforts in helping to win Hartley for Labor in 1907 she was presented with a 'fighting' trophy in the shape of a silver belt. Described by a reporter as 'a tall and willowy blonde ... bright, vivacious and enthusiastic', she was a good public speaker, a willing worker in Labor's electoral campaigns from Murwillumbah in the north to Eden on the south coast and a contributor to the press.

Forced by ill health to relinquish all her activities in September 1908, she was presented with an oak-framed illuminated address and went to the South Sea islands for rest and recuperation. By 1913 she was again active in Labor's State and Federal electoral campaigns and an alternate delegate to the party conference. During World War I, however, with its competing strains of patriotism and party loyalty, Mrs Bethel was prominent in the cause of conscription. Again she traversed the

State, this time urging a 'yes' vote in the referendum campaign of 1916. Her tour of the Inverell district was so successful that local committees asked that she remain there until polling day. Following the divisive defeat of the referendum proposal, most of the party's leaders were expelled and Mrs Bethel went with them. She helped to found the Women's National Movement in November 1916 and was a member of the Nationalist Association Council in 1917-23. About 1917 she left her husband and moved to Randwick. They were divorced in June 1919.

Walter had been chief clerk in the Department of Education from 1916 and in 1922 he became president of the State Children's Relief Board. Having been influential in child welfare policy from about 1905, in 1923 he was appointed secretary of the Child Welfare Department, which replaced the board and was organized upon lines he had recommended. Later inquiries into complaints of unsatisfactory accounting and ill-treatment of boys made no direct finding against Bethel personally, but his belief in institutional discipline represented a retreat from the progressive probation, outdoor relief and cottage home regime of Sir Charles Mackellar [q.v.10]. On 29 April 1924 at Pitt Street Congregational Church Bethel married a widowed public servant, Berta Sarah Marguerite Humphreys, née Alpen. Retiring in February 1929, Walter wrote historical articles for the Sydney press. He was an enthusiastic swimmer and was interested in artistic matters. Photographs showed him with a trim moustache and slightly hooded eyes. He died at Neutral Bay on 8 September 1941.

After the divorce Edith had shifted to Petersham. She was appointed a justice of the peace in October 1923. Later she lived at Chatswood. Leaving an estate sworn for probate at £197, she died of a cerebral haemorrhage on 21 December 1929 in a private hospital at Mosman and was cremated with Anglican rites; her daughter survived her. Mrs Bethel had been one of the most prominent women of her generation in public life in New South Wales. A peripheral casualty of Australia's conscription crisis, like many of the Labor leaders whom she followed into the front ranks of her former opponents, she was never at home again.

Worker (Syd), 10 Sept 1904, p 6, 26 Nov 1904, p 4, 28 Jan 1905, p 4, 3 Sept 1908, p 21, 1 Oct 1908, p 23, 30 Jan 1913, p 16; *Daily Telegraph* (Syd), 24 Mar 1915, p 6, 20 Oct 1916, p 12, 18 Nov 1916, p 18, 4 Oct 1923, p 6, *Fighting Line* (Syd), 21 July 1917, p 18, 24 Jan 1921, p 17; *SMH*, 15 Feb 1922, p 13, 13 Dec 1923, p 8, 7 Mar 1929, p 5, 9 Sept 1941, p 7; information from Ms S. Tracey, Randwick, and Mrs K. O'Hagan, Frenchs Forest, Syd.

CHRIS CUNNEEN

BEVINGTON, WILLIAM FAULKNER (1871-1944), school inspector and promoter of special education, was born on 10 June 1871 in Brisbane, eldest son of William Joseph Bevington, a compositor from England, and his Dublin-born wife Jane Mary Margaret, née Faulkner. Bevington senior entered the Queensland teaching service in May 1875; Jane Bevington also taught as an untrained, unclassified assistant to her husband, at Glamorgan Vale in 1875 and at Hemmant in 1879.

Aged 12, young Bevington became a pupil-teacher under his father at Sandgate State School on 15 February 1884 and remained there until he became a classified teacher in 1890. He had to repeat the first and second years—he was younger than most pupil-teachers—but his final assessment described him as 'a moderate student and a fairly successful teacher during his pupilage'.

On 14 November 1891 at the bride's mother's residence, Sandgate, Bevington married Mary Hudson Macfarlane with Presbyterian forms. Next year he commenced on the promotion trail, first in one-teacher schools at Alfred (1892) and Fernvale (1894) and then Mulgrave (1911), Goodna (1913) and Wooloowin (1914-20), where he was responsible for the introduction of domestic science classes and began a long professional and personal association with Kathleen Eileen Sheehy (1892-1981). Inspectors' reports on Bevington while at Wooloowin described his organizing power as excellent. He was appointed acting district inspector of schools in March 1920 and in August district inspector.

Bevington was as assiduous in his inspecting duties as he was in his teaching and administration. Initially he relieved inspectors on leave. He was then responsible for the districts of Northern, Western and Southern Downs, with Toowoomba as his base, and eventually South-East Moreton, which included all schools south of the Brisbane River to the State border. Using rail travel where it existed, a hired car if available and sometimes horse and buggy or just a horse, Bevington always covered his assigned area.

In 1922 with two colleagues he represented Queensland at the Australasian Conference of Inspectors of Schools in Melbourne. *En route* and during the conference, at the behest of the minister 'Honest John' Huxham [q.v.9], Bevington investigated the provision of education for the 'mentally defective' in other States and consulted innovators such as Lorna Hodgkinson [q.v.14] in Sydney. The minister readily accepted his report and gave him the task of organizing the classes. In addition to his inspector's duties, Bevington tested and selected children for the special classes, one of the earliest extensive uses of the 1916

Stanford-Binet test of intelligence. He was assisted in this by Miss Sheehy but failed to acknowledge her contribution.

During 1923 Bevington organized classes at South Brisbane, New Farm and Fortitude Valley and at Ipswich, Rockampton, Townsville and Toowoomba. The 'Backward Classes' became the 'Opportunity Classes' in 1926 at the suggestion of Sheehy. Next year further classes were established at Petrie Terrace and two for boys described by the minister as 'subnormal in mental power' and by Bevington as having an IQ below 50. He closely supervised the classes, found and supported suitable teachers and provided detailed annual reports. In 1933 he was appointed chief inspector and the work of organizing was left to local inspectors. Following Bevington's retirement in December 1937, the outbreak of World War II in 1939 and staff shortages, the classes lost their well-defined identity and became the repository for severely handicapped children. Some classes disappeared.

While chief inspector, Bevington had chaired a syllabus committee and with a group of teachers produced three resource books: *Our Birds* (1932), *Our Plants* (1933) and *Our Insects* (1934). After retiring, under a grant from the Carnegie Corporation of New York he became education liaison officer at the Queensland Museum. Pleasant and avuncular, he was quick to establish rapport with children. His wife died in 1936. Survived by his daughter and son, Bevington died on 10 January 1944 at the Mater Misericordiae Hospital, South Brisbane, and was cremated with Anglican rites.

Dept of Public Instruction (Qld), Annual Report, in *PP* (Qld), 1923-37; G. Swan, 'Pioneers in Education, William Faulkner Bevington', *Educational Historian*, no 2, 1988, *and* 'Pioneers in Education, Kathleen Sheehy', no 1, 1995, *and* Opportunity Classes—Alternatives (M.Ed. thesis, Univ Qld, 1978), *and* From Segregation to Integration: The Development of Special Education in Queensland (Ph.D. thesis, Univ Qld, 1996); Bevington personal file *and* Dept of Public Instruction (Qld) files, A/16032, A/16033, A/16035 (QA).

GEOFFREY SWAN

BIDENCOPE, JOSEPH (1837-1915), tailor and mercer, was born in 1837 in Poland, son of David Bidencope, tailor, and his wife Caroline. He lived for a short time with a sister in Paris before going to London in 1846. In 1857 he signed as crew in the *Trade Wind* and sailed for Tasmania. During the voyage he was flogged by the first mate but was defended by the carpenter, who was greatly praised by the passengers.

Arriving in Hobart Town in February 1858, Bidencope was employed as a tailor by Henry Cook in Elizabeth Street. Soon he opened his own business in Collins Street, moving in 1860 to new premises in the same street. At St David's Cathedral on 15 January 1861 he married with Anglican rites English born Emma Jane Booker. She died in 1892. On 21 March 1894 in the Wesleyan Church, South Yarra, Melbourne, Joseph married Somerset-born Emily Maggs.

By 1862 the firm had become a well-known fashion house, with naval and military uniforms a continuing feature. In 1869 Bidencope established new premises in Murray Street, Hobart. That year hats were added to the business and in 1874 £3000 worth were manufactured and sold in Tasmania and Sydney. At first felt was imported from England. Later, hats were made at a Battery Point factory, where rabbit skins, purchased in hundreds of thousands, were made into felt. Orphaned boys were taken on as apprentices.

The fashionable and the fastidious shopped exclusively at Bidencopes. In 1874 the family moved to Barton Vale, Salvator Road, close to the foothills of Mount Wellington, where the garden became a showpiece, visited by many prominent Hobart residents. Bidencope's hats gained medals, awards and compliments for samples he sent to exhibitions at Philadelphia, United States of America, in 1876 and in Sydney in 1877. Duties imposed by other colonies forced him to close the hat factory before Federation.

In 1878 the firm had tendered to the Tasmanian government to make 470 scarlet patrol jackets, leggings and caps for the Volunteer Rifle Regiment, at a price of £2 per suit. Bidencope continued to prosper with government tenders for uniforms for the police, rail and tramway workers and for miners. Two sons of his first marriage worked in the company: Joseph Zelly (1866-1940) and Richard Booker (1868-1942), both educated at the Hutchins School, Hobart, and Horton College, Ross.

The Hobart store was modernized in 1924 and a ladies department established. During World War II the firm made uniforms as it had in the Boer War and World War I. Joseph's grandsons sold the business in 1977. Its founder had been one of the best-known and respected businessmen in Hobart. A Freemason, sometime worshipful master of the Tasmanian Operative Lodge and an office-holder in the Grand Lodge of Tasmania, he was appointed a justice of the peace in 1902. Survived by two sons and two daughters of his first marriage and by his wife and their son and three daughters, Bidencope died in North Hobart on 19 February 1915, after his usual day at business in Murray Street.

P. Quarry (comp), *Trade Wind Voyage 1858* (Hob, 1992); I. Schaffer, 'Joseph Bidencope: Founder of a

Hobart Clothing Business', *PTHRA*, 45, no 2, June 1998, p 63; *Mercury* (Hob), 8 Jan 1868, 20 Feb 1915, 21 July 1956, 9 Aug 1977; Colonial Secretary (Tas) Dispatches, CSD10/61/1437 (TA).

IRENE SCHAFFER

BIGGS, ALFRED BARRETT (1825-1900), teacher, bank officer, astronomer and inventor, was born on 10 April 1825 in London, eldest son of Abraham Biggs, carpenter, and his wife Eliza, née Coleman. In 1833 the family moved to Van Diemen's Land. Abraham's involvement in Methodism and eventually in the teaching profession was to have a strong influence on Alfred, who took up a tutoring position at Bothwell in 1845. Three years later he became a bank clerk in Hobart Town, but left for Melbourne in 1852, continuing in banking then returning to teaching. On 22 February 1855 at Melville Street Wesleyan Chapel, Hobart, Biggs married Harriet Burville. In 1858 he became headmaster of the Hoddle Street School, Melbourne. The family returned in 1864 to Tasmania, where Biggs again took a teaching post at Bothwell. In 1872 they moved to Campbell Town. There he taught in the public school and befriended Dr William Valentine. Both men were fascinated by astronomy and in 1874 a rare astronomical event occurred: the transit of Venus. Valentine had invited an American expedition to view the transit from his home. Biggs assisted with the observations and the Americans gave him a building they had used in making their observations.

In 1877 Biggs learned of the invention of the telephone. He then constructed a pair of telephones and had them connected between Launceston and Campbell Town, successfully transmitting sounds between the two locations. It has been claimed that this was the first telephone connection in Australia. About 1879 he moved to Launceston and took a position as accountant and ledger-keeper with the Launceston Bank for Savings. His continuing interest in astronomy led to the construction of an observatory in the western part of the city. Despite the small size of his telescopes— his instruments were then a 2-inch (51-mm) and a 3-inch (76-mm) refractor—Biggs was a diligent and pedantic observer, becoming known as Launceston's 'Astronomer Royal'. He contributed reports to the local newspaper and from 1884 papers to the Royal Society of Tasmania, of which he was that year elected a fellow. He made observations and measurements of comets, double stars, eclipses and transits of Mercury and Venus (another transit of Venus occurred in 1882). In 1885 he came into possession of an 8½-inch (216-mm) diameter reflecting telescope, originally owned by Valentine.

Biggs had a reputation as an inventor and instrument maker. He constructed a microscope—grinding the lenses himself— and both a vertical and a horizontal seismometer; his interest in seismology was likely to have been aroused by Launceston's small earth tremors about 1880. Other devices he made included an observatory clock driven by a float and micrometers to measure angular separations, such as the apparent distance between double stars, through the telescope. For the detection of counterfeit coins he invented a coin tester.

His devotion to religious activities was lifelong. At St Andrew's Presbyterian Church, Launceston, Biggs played the organ and conducted the choir; he composed at least three hymns. He saw no conflict between religion and science. When he was a teacher, he had some difficult times with the Board of Education. However, his thin, bearded face was suggestive of a man with a sense of humour. A frequent writer of letters to the press, he was a committee member and sometime president and treasurer of the Launceston Mechanics' Institute. Predeceased by his wife, Biggs died on 19 December 1900 at his residence above the bank and was buried in the general cemetery. Six of his eight children survived him. A 1935 memorial to Biggs stands in Royal Park, Launceston, near the former site of his observatory.

M. Giordano, *Watcher of the Skies* (Launc, Tas, 1995); Roy Soc of Tas, *Papers and Procs*, 1933; *Records of the Queen Vic Museum Launc*, no 89, 1985; *Examiner* (Launc), 29 Sept 1886, p 2, 20 Dec 1900, p 7; Biggs family papers (TSA); information from Mr R. A. Biggs, Tas.

MARTIN GEORGE

BIRD, ANN; *see* HOWE

BIRKS, ROSETTA JANE (1856-1911), suffragist and philanthropist, was born on 12 March 1856 in Adelaide, one of nine children of English-born parents William Kyffin Thomas [q.v.6], newspaper proprietor, and his wife Mary Jane, née Good. The granddaughter of Mary Thomas [q.v.], Rose grew up in a family that strongly supported public affairs and philanthropic and religious causes. She was a lifelong member of the evangelical Flinders Street Baptist Church, co-founded by her father. On 8 March 1879 at Glenelg Rosetta married with Baptist forms her sister's widower CHARLES NAPIER BIRKS (1844-1924), a draper, and became stepmother to his six children.

Charles had been born on 13 February 1844 at Chorlton, Manchester, England, fourth son of George Vause Birks, druggist, and his wife Hannah, née Napier. The family reached Adelaide about 1853 and George opened a shop at Angaston, later run by his widow. Charles first worked for his uncle John McKirdy, a seedsman, and from 1864, with David Robin, ran a drapery shop in Hindley Street. The partnership was dissolved in 1876 and Charles opened a store in Rundle Street. On 13 September 1866 he married Rose's eldest sister Mary Maria (d.1878). His brother George Napier Birks had married a third Thomas sister (Helen).

Charles and Rose lived for a time in England after their marriage, returning to Adelaide in 1886 when the Commercial Bank of South Australia collapsed due to defalcations by Alexander Crooks [q.v.]. Charles resumed management of what became one of the best-known department stores in Adelaide. An enlightened employer, he improved working conditions for his staff and set up an employees' trust fund.

As Mrs Charles Birks, Rose presided over several Baptist women's associations, including a mothers' union, her devout service culminating in the formation (1909) of a women's guild, whose purpose was to bring her church's women workers in touch with each other. In 1882 she had joined the Ladies' Social Purity Society and worked energetically as treasurer of that and many philanthropic organizations. When in 1888 the society gave rise to the Women's Suffrage League, she capably and generously managed its finances until the vote was achieved in 1894.

Regular meetings held at Knutsford, the Birks's home at Glenelg, won much support for women's suffrage in social circles. The W.S.L. was dissolved in 1895 and Rose became treasurer of the short-lived, idealistic and educational Woman's League. When Charles's brother George died at New Australia, Paraguay, in 1895, Rose and Charles provided support until Helen and her children returned to Adelaide two years later. Rose became a board member of the Adelaide Hospital in 1896. In 1902 she helped to found and became vice-president of the South Australian branch of the National Council of Women, and was appointed to the board of the Queen's (maternity) Home.

The high point of her work among girls was within the Young Women's Christian Association and she was credited with the modernization of the Australasian movement. In South Australia it had long shared concerns for protection of young women, temperance and social purity with the Woman's Christian Temperance Union and the Social Purity Society. Rose was elected president of the South Australian branch of the Y.W.C.A. in 1902. In 1903 Adelaide's was the first branch to introduce junior membership, enabling club activities to draw girls as young as 10 to moral and religious instruction. Other innovations were child-rearing lectures and an expanded Bible studies programme. Birks believed that 'the ideal is to work towards a healthful, efficient feminine Christian womanhood'. During her oversight of significant building extensions in Hindmarsh Square in Adelaide (1907) membership reached record levels. She pioneered Y.W.C.A. work among nurses and university women and her presidency was marked by inclusion of classes promoting development of womanhood 'science'.

In London and Paris in 1906 and Berlin in 1910 Mrs Birks attended international conferences as member for Australasia of the world's committee. Adelaide was the first branch to launch the *Young Women's Evangel* in Australia. She was a central figure both in the formation of the National Y.W.C.A. of Australasia, confirmed at the fourth National Conference, Sydney, 1907, and in revising the association's secretarial training methods. In 1911 she launched a Y.W.C.A. Travellers' Aid Society linked to government-assisted immigration, particularly for girls intended as domestic servants. She ensured support for charitable causes, notably the Babies' Aid Society, of which Lucy, wife of Charles's son Napier Kyffin Birks, was president, and for which Rose secured Y.W.C.A. sponsorship and clothing prepared at Charles Birks & Co.

Dignified and self-assured, she enjoyed the luxuries of wealth and travel but believed in service for others. Photographs show her wearing a pince-nez and with her hair swept into a knot on top of her head. Mrs Birks collapsed and died of myocarditis while addressing a meeting of the College Park Congregational Church on 3 October 1911. Her estate was sworn for probate at £7000.

Charles married Alice May Hone, twenty-two years his junior, on 11 September 1913 and soon retired, transferring his interest to his son Napier. Survived by his wife and by four daughters and one son of his first marriage, Charles died on 29 April 1924 in Adelaide. His estate was sworn for probate at £29 180. Napier died on 22 August 1953, leaving an estate valued at £209 360. The Rundle Street store merged with David Jones [q.v.2] Ltd in 1954. Birks Chemists, founded by Charles's brothers George and William and still in Adelaide, no longer has any link with the family.

L. E. Austin, *Outline Sketch of the Young Women's Christian Associations in Australasia* (Syd, 1913); R. M. Gibbs, *Bulls, Bears and Wildcats* (Adel, 1988); J. K. Willington (ed), *Maisie* (Adel, 1992); H. Jones, *In Her Own Name* (Adel, 1994); R. Woods, *History of the Birks Family and Family Tree* (Adel, 1994); Women's Suffrage League of SA, *Report*, 24 July 1894 (ML); YWCA (SA), *Annual Report*, 1910-11; *Southern Baptist*, 19 Oct 1911; *JHSSA*, 21, 1993, p 72; *Observer* (Adel), 28 Mar 1896, p 16, 7 Oct 1911, p 39; *Register* (Adel), 6 Oct 1911, p 8, 30 Apr 1924, p 10; *Advertiser* (Adel), 24 Aug 1953, p 2; M. Woods, Towards a Civil Society: Voluntary Community Service and Womanhood in South Australia, 1836-1936 (Ph.D. thesis, Flinders Univ, 2000).

MARTIN WOODS

BLACKBURN, DAVID (1753-1795), naval officer, was born on 1 January 1753 at Newbury, Berkshire, England, eldest son of Rev. John Blackburn and his wife Elizabeth, née Martineau. After John's death in 1762 the family moved to Norwich. On 5 May 1779 David entered the navy, joining H.M.S. *Victory*. Promoted midshipman on 14 July he transferred to H.M.S. *Rattlesnake* on 7 October and ten days later returned to the *Victory* as acting quartermaster.

By April 1785 Blackburn was serving as master of H.M.S. *Flora* in the West Indies. A period of unemployment followed until April 1787 when, at short notice, he was appointed master of the armed tender *Supply* bound for Botany Bay with the First Fleet. His captain was Lieutenant Henry Lidgbird Ball [q.v.1] with whom he had served in the *Victory*. Initially Blackburn was reluctant to take up the posting as he had hoped to be appointed to the sloop *Bulldog*, but as refusal would have adversely affected his career he accepted. On 19 April he wrote to his sister 'my dislike to the voyage begins gradually to wear off'.

The *Supply* arrived in Botany Bay on 18 January 1788, two days ahead of most of the fleet. On 21 January Blackburn accompanied Governor Arthur Phillip [q.v.2] and a small party to explore Port Jackson, which proved to be a far superior site for settlement. Blackburn sailed in the *Supply* on 14 February to set up another colony on Norfolk Island. During the return voyage Ball charted Lord Howe Island, which had been sighted on the journey out, and named a small offshore island Blackburn Isle. Blackburn returned to Norfolk Island in September 1788 in command of the transport *Golden Grove* with provisions and additional convicts.

In March 1790 he sailed again for Norfolk Island on the *Supply* in company with H.M.S. *Sirius*. The *Sirius* was wrecked while attempting to land supplies and, on arriving back at Port Jackson, the *Supply* was ordered to Batavia for provisions in her place. While there Ball fell ill with fever and, on returning to Port Jackson, Blackburn was given command of the *Supply* for two further voyages to Norfolk Island. In a dispatch to England Phillip commended him for his 'very officer-like conduct'.

Ball resumed command in November 1791 when the *Supply* sailed for England. During his four years in New South Wales Blackburn had formed an unflattering opinion of the place. 'It certainly is a very poor country', he wrote to his sister. 'The best that can be said of the country is the healthiness of the climate and the excellent harbours it affords.' He dismissed the indigenous inhabitants as 'certainly the lowest class of human beings'.

Reaching England in May 1792, Blackburn was discharged from the *Supply* and received no appointment until September the next year when he joined H.M.S. *Dictator*. He died in Haslar Naval Hospital, Portsmouth, on 10 January 1795, probably of a consumptive complaint. His letters, especially those to his family and sister Margaret, reveal him to have been an uncomplicated, conscientious man, and throw light on early European life at Port Jackson.

HRNSW, 1, pt 2; D. Neville, *Blackburn's Isle* (Lavenham, UK, 1975); M. Gillen, *The Founders of Australia* (Syd, 1989); Blackburn letters (ML).

WARWICK HIRST

BLADEN, FRANK MURCOTT (1858-1912), librarian and historian, was born on 22 December 1858 at Hanley, Staffordshire, England, son of Thomas Bladen, boiler plate roller, and his wife Amy, née Murcott. The family reached New South Wales in 1863 and settled at Mittagong. Educated at the local public school, in 1876 Frank won an essay competition at the Sydney Juvenile Exhibition. His interest in astronomy had led to his appointment on 8 March 1875 to the Sydney Observatory where he became a map compiler in 1878. In 1881 he matriculated at the University of Sydney and, exempted from lectures, enrolled in arts. He won a gold medal for English verse in 1882 and the Rosebery [q.v.5 Primrose] medal (1885) for an essay on Anglo-Australian relations (published in 1886), but did not graduate. In 1886 he was appointed clerk in the Government Printing Office. Having read law, he was called to the Bar on 6 June 1891.

Bladen's literary knowledge and skill in composition had prompted Charles Potter, the government printer, to enlist his services in revising the *Official History of New South Wales* for the 1888 centenary celebrations. Bladen's hopes of becoming editor were dashed by the successive appointment of journalists G. B. Barton [q.v.3] and Alexander Britton. When the latter died in 1892, Bladen assumed duties on what had become a multi-volumed *History of New South Wales from the Records*. The plan was abandoned after volume 2 and he was then made editor of the *Historical Records of New South Wales*. Transferred in 1896 to the Public Library of New South Wales, he worked on the *Records* until

1899 when he took charge of the library's lending branch. After seven volumes appeared, the *Records* project ceased in 1902 for financial reasons.

On 25 August 1897 at St Andrew's Cathedral, Sydney, Bladen had married with Anglican rites Sydney-born Madeline Schiller Fitz Stubbs, from a family of musicians. They were to have no children. From 1 January 1907 Bladen was appointed principal librarian at the public library. A lifetime of overwork affected his health, however, producing habits of drinking that resulted in slipshod administration. He served from 1905 as chairman of the New South Wales Geographical Board and was a member of the Commonwealth Literary Fund board from 1907.

A founder of the (Royal) Australian Historical Society in 1901, Bladen became a fellow of the Royal Historical and of the Royal Geographical societies, London. In 1902 he was delegated by the Commonwealth government to attend the Congress on Historical Sciences in Rome and to enquire into the possibility of establishing a Commonwealth archive. His report (published 1903) surveyed overseas developments and recommended a plan for Australia. One of the earliest Australians to appreciate the need for an empirical approach to history, he believed that access to original documents was essential if history was to rest on a scientific basis. Several of his writings were published, but all were overshadowed by the *Historical Records*, which made possible original research on the colony's early years.

Bladen retired from the library in January 1912 because of ill health and died of nephritis on 20 September at his home at Mosman. He was buried with Congregational forms in Gore Hill cemetery. His wife survived him.

B. H. Fletcher, *The 1888 Centenary Celebrations and New Developments in the Writing of Australian History* (Syd, 1988) and *Australian History in New South Wales 1888 to 1938* (Syd, 1993); *T&CJ*, 25 Sept 1912, p 29; *SMH*, 21 Sept 1912, p 18; D. J. Jones, W. H. Ifould and the Development of Library Services in New South Wales 1912-1942 (Ph.D. thesis, Univ of NSW, 1993); items 1/34-5, 2/1264, 20/13002.2 (SRNSW); Bladen papers (ML).

B. H. FLETCHER

BLAUBAUM, ELIAS (1847-1904), minister of religion and editor, was born on 19 November 1847 at Rotenburg in the German landgraviate of Hesse-Kassel, son of Orthodox Jewish parents Aaron Blaubaum, drapery merchant, and his wife Marianne (Miriam), née Nussbaum. About 1870 Elias graduated from the Royal Provincial College of Kassel, where he had specialized in education, and became assistant minister and Hebrew teacher to the Jewish community of Gudensberg. Although never a qualified rabbi, he had received a thorough grounding in Jewish law and lore. In 1873 he arrived in Melbourne to assume the position of inaugural minister of the St Kilda Hebrew congregation, founded mainly by Jews of German origin. His outlook reflected that of his fellow German Rabbi Samson Raphael Hirsch, a founder of neo-Orthodoxy.

At the time of his arrival the St Kilda congregation, under lay leadership, had made changes to time-honoured Jewish liturgy and ritual. Blaubaum tolerated these, but made his traditionalist approach clear; although he went on to introduce minor innovations he stalwartly opposed more radical steps. During the thirty-one years of his ministry he proved an implacable foe of Reform Judaism, of the continuing use of Yiddish in Australia, and of political Zionism—although at the end of his life, with the 1903 pogrom at Kishinev as the probable catalyst, he had a change of heart.

On 17 January 1877 at Malvern Blaubaum had married Agnes Rebecca Cohen (d.1892), who had been born in New South Wales. He was naturalized in 1885. A man of restless energy and dogged determination, he had a marked pedagogic bent. His membership of the three-man Victorian Beth Din (rabbinical court) and presidency of the United Jewish Education Board lent him an authority that extended beyond the confines of his synagogue. But his chief significance lay in his editorship, from its foundation in 1879 until his death, of the *Jewish Herald* (Melbourne). At first a monthly, later a weekly, it circulated throughout Australia, and set the benchmark for Australian Jewish journalism. Through his robust editorials and learned essays on a variety of relevant subjects, it aimed to arouse its readers to their responsibilities as Jews and as citizens. The newspaper campaigned vigorously against anti-Semitism whenever and wherever that occurred in Australia. This, and his personal combativeness and tenacity when confronted with anti-Jewish prejudice, made him the nearest approximation to a nationwide, communal spokesman that Australian Jewry possessed.

At the same time, Blaubaum fostered positive relations with the wider Australian community, writing articles in mainstream journals —such as 'Judaism' for the *Melbourne Review* in January 1883—and teaching Hebrew at Melbourne's Congregational College. He also wrote pamphlets on religious themes, including *On the Mountains* (Melbourne, 1892). He had attempted to persuade the South Australian government to allow the establishment of an agricultural colony of persecuted Russian Jews, and was thereby obliged to resign from the outraged Melbourne branch of the Anglo-Jewish Association, which later reinstated him. Despite his doctrinal conservatism, he held progressive social views, championing the secular rights of women and deploring the White Australia policy.

Blaubaum died of cancer on 21 April 1904 at Dr Moore's private hospital, Melbourne, and was buried in St Kilda cemetery. Two daughters and five sons survived him.

H. L. Rubinstein, *The Jews in Australia*, 1 (Melb, 1991) and 'Rev. Elias Blaubaum (1847-1904): Minister, Editor and Scholar', *Aust Jewish Hist Soc J*, 9, pt 8, 1985, p 567; St Kilda Hebrew Congregation archives; Aust Jewish Hist Soc (Vic) archives (SLV).

HILARY L. RUBINSTEIN

BLOCH, JACOB SIMON (1898-1961), shoemaker, was born on 14 May 1898 at Plunge, Telsas Apsketes, Lithuania (then part of Russia), and named Yaacov Shimon (known in Lithuanian as Simonas Jankelis), son of Lozer Blochas, painter and cobbler, and his wife Chaja. Apprenticed to a shoemaker at the age of 11, the youngster also studied dance until he was 15, when he moved to Varniai, to work as a cobbler. There in 1919 he married Zise Sandler, a bootmaker's daughter.

The couple's social life revolved around local theatre and folk dancing, at which Yaacov excelled. They had five children, including a son and a daughter who died in childhood. Zise's sister Polly and her British husband had migrated to Australia in the late 1920s. They sent the necessary papers to allow Yaacov to migrate as well and he arrived in Sydney in 1930, determined to find enough work to allow his family to follow him.

Known in Australia as Jacob (or Jack) Bloch, he charmed potential employers when he went from shop to shop, seeking work as a cobbler. At one city store, a display of ballet shoes inspired him to establish his own business. He rented a small shop in Oxford Street, Paddington, where he made dance shoes to order. For the students of Sydney's ballet schools, Bloch made flat ballet slippers, *pointe* shoes, tap shoes and national character dance shoes—including Russian Cossack boots and Irish and Scottish dance shoes. In 1933 his wife and three children joined him.

In 1936 Bloch expanded to a second floor workshop at Taylor Square, Darlinghurst. Many ballet troupes came to Australia in the 1930s, among them the Dandréa-Levitoff company in 1934 and Colonel de Basil's Ballets Russes de Monte Carlo, which toured in 1936, 1938 and 1939. Dancers who bought and wore his shoes in Australia included the ballerinas Olga Spessivtseva, Irina Baronova, Tamara Toumanova, Tatiana Riabouchinska and Tamara Tchinarova and the premier danseur David Lichine.

While visiting English dancers usually preferred lighter shoes, made in England, Bloch always boasted that his *pointe* shoes were strong and long lasting. When Russian-speaking dance companies came to Sydney, he visited the dancers backstage, acting as an interpreter and taking orders for his shoes. Accompanying him was his daughter Betty, who loved to watch the dancers from the wings. Bloch was naturalized on 26 June 1940, when he was described as 5 ft 9 ins (175.3 cm) tall, with dark hair and grey eyes.

His business grew in a modest way, and by 1950 he was making about fifty pairs of ballet shoes each week. Despite his output, Bloch was more craftsman than businessman. Sometimes his orders would be finished on time, often not. He was not ambitious, he was not compelled to meet deadlines and he never became wealthy. In 1950 he opened a small factory at Botany. It was not a success, as the damp sea air affected the drying time of his glue-stiffened *pointe* shoes. With another factory at Zetland, in 1959 he opened a shop in the city, in the Piccadilly Arcade. Outgoing, gregarious and popular, 'Jack' Bloch loved parties and cards—gin rummy most of all. When the European community of Sydney met at the Russian Club or at private parties, he often led the dancing.

A heavy smoker all his life, Bloch died of myocardial infarction on 12 April 1961 at his home in Bronte Road, Waverley. He was buried in the Jewish cemetery at Rookwood. His wife and their two sons and one daughter survived him.

SMH, 24 Sept 1950, p 7; ST1233, item N6609 (NAA, Syd); information from and family papers held by Mrs B. Wilkenfeld, Rose Bay, Syd.

VALERIE LAWSON

BLUE, WILLIAM (c.1767?-1834), convict, settler and ferryman, was born possibly in Jamaica, West Indies. As he later claimed to have served with the British army in the American war of independence, he may have been a freed African-American slave from colonial New York. By 1796, however, he was living at Deptford, London, and working as a chocolate-maker and a lumper (labourer) in ships in the River Thames. On 4 October that year at Maidstone, Kent, Blue was convicted of stealing raw sugar—presumably intended for confectionery making—and sentenced to seven years' transportation. After over four years in convict hulks, he was transported to Botany Bay in the *Minorca*. He was described in convict records as 'a Jamaican Negro sailor', aged 29 in 1796.

Reaching Sydney on 14 December 1801, Blue had less than two years of his sentence to serve. By July 1804 he was living at The Rocks with Elizabeth Williams, a 30-year-old,

English-born convict, who had arrived from Hampshire the previous month. They married on 27 April 1805 at St Philip's Church of England and were to have six children. Billy worked as a waterman and collected and sold oysters and other items. He found favour with both government officials and the public, to whom he endeared himself with his whimsical style and banter.

In 1808 his name was included in a list of citizens who supported the arrest of Governor Bligh [q.v.1]. Blue was appointed harbour watchman and constable by Governor Macquarie [q.v.2] in 1811. These titles enabled him to acquire a new home overlooking Sydney Harbour, which became a local landmark known as 'Billy Blue's Cottage'. Macquarie was a regular user of the ferry services; he reported in his diary in 1817 that his wife and son were taken up the river to Parramatta in Blue's boat. That year Blue was granted a farm of eighty acres (32.4 ha), which he called Northampton, at the southernmost tip of the north shore of Port Jackson. The headland became known as Billy Blue's Point. As a landowner on the north side of the harbour, he saw the potential for operating a boat service to the site and quickly built up a 'fleet of ferries'. Macquarie light-heartedly dubbed him 'Commodore'; Blue became known as 'The Old Commodore'.

The location and business offered opportunities to participate in smuggling. In October 1818, arrested for possessing two casks of rum, he claimed that he had found them floating and lashed them to his boat to return them to the shore. Encouraged by Deputy-Judge-Advocate Wylde [q.v.2] to plead guilty and name his accomplices, Blue refused, lost his position as harbour watchman and constable and was imprisoned for a year.

In 1823 Edward Wollstonecraft and William Gore [qq.v.2,1], both landholders on the north shore with vested interests in harbour trade, attempted to oust Blue from his land and ferrying service, alleging that he was a law-breaker who regularly smuggled goods and harboured escaped prisoners. In response Blue petitioned Sir Thomas Brisbane [q.v.1] that, in view of his long and trusted service for the government, he should be granted 'in his old age the peaceable enjoyment of his premises and ferry'. The governor found in his favour, authorizing him to 'have the Use and Occupation of his ferry, which he formerly occupied between his farm in Northampton and Sydney'.

Elizabeth died in 1824. In the 1828 census Blue gave his age as 80. Described by (Sir) James Dowling [q.v.1] as 'an eccentric, loquacious character', he took to donning a travesty of a naval uniform, with a top hat, and would board newly berthed vessels as 'commodore'

to welcome the officers to Sydney. Brushes with the law continued. He was found guilty of harbouring an escaped convict and of manslaughter—when he threw a stone at a boy who was tormenting him and the youth later died—but avoided prison. By 1833 he and his family were reported as keeping a ferryboat and cultivating vegetables and fruit for the Sydney market.

Blue died on 7 May 1834 at his North Sydney home. His will, which he signed with a mark, left his property to his surviving three sons, including William junior, and two daughters. Streets in North Sydney were named after him and the site of his northern ferry terminus remained known as Blues Point. The Mitchell [q.v.5] Library, Sydney, holds several portraits of him, including an etching by Charles Rodius [q.v.2], a lithograph of 'The Old Commodore' by John Carmichael and an oil painting by J. B. East.

M. Swords, *Billy Blue, the Old Commodore* (Syd, 1979); I. Duffield and J. Bradley, *Representing Convicts* (Lond, 1997); *Hist Today*, Feb 1987, p 43; *J of Popular Culture*, 33, no 1, Summer 1999, p 7; *Sydney Gazette*, 2 Aug 1807, p 2, 31 Oct 1833, 10 May 1834, p 2; W. Blue petition (ML); research notes (Stanton Lib, North Syd).
                                                    MARGARET PARK

BLUETT, ALBERT ROBERT (1879-1944), local government official and solicitor, was born on 17 November 1879 at Wagga Wagga, New South Wales, fifth surviving son of Francis William Anstruther Bluett (d.1889), a pound keeper from Jersey in the Channel Islands, and his Adelaide-born wife Jessie, née Wallace. Educated at Bathurst and at Fort Street Model School, Sydney, Albert served his articles in the securities department of the Savings Bank of New South Wales and was admitted as a solicitor on 9 March 1907. On 30 November 1904 he had married Maude Alice Wayland (d.1936) at St Peter's Church of England, St Peters, Sydney. They were to have a daughter and two sons. Bluett was appointed secretary and solicitor of the Local Government Association of New South Wales in 1910 and of the Shires Association of New South Wales in 1922.

His older brother EDWARD CAMPBELL BLUETT (1874-1958) had been born on 10 October 1874 at Wagga Wagga and after attending school there entered Fort Street Training College, Sydney. Edward married Ruby Florence Blair on 26 March 1902 at St Philip's Church of England, Sydney. Following a posting to a one-teacher school at Wolumla, in 1909 he returned to Sydney and, encouraged by Albert, left the Department of Public Instruction to become secretary of the newly formed Local Government Clerks' Association. In this role he helped to formulate the revenue basis on which all town and shire clerks' salaries were paid.

Albert (often known as 'A.R.'), the acknowledged expert in local government law, was closely involved in drafting the Local Government Act (1919). Next year he was invited to join a conference rewriting building ordinances: he was co-author of *Regulations & Law as to Erection of Buildings in New South Wales* (1922). In August 1941 he compiled a report for the committee considering a scheme to create a 'Greater Sydney' council. His submission to the annual conference of the Local Government Association in August 1943 argued that Australia had the 'feeblest and most restricted form of local government that is known to the English speaking world'. Suggesting that greater local powers would enhance democracy, he advocated the formation of regional councils that would undertake a broader role such as providing health and social services.

A member of the Sydney Press Club, he wrote a weekly column for the *Sydney Morning Herald* for some twenty years and provided syndicated leaders for the country press. He edited the *Shire and Municipal Record* for thirty-six years from its first publication in 1908. With R. J. Browning he wrote legal textbooks, including *A Digest of Australian Cases relating to Local Government* (1919) and *Local Government Law and Practice: New South Wales* (1929). Bluett also compiled *The Law and Procedure at Meetings of Councils* (1924). Perhaps his greatest legacy is the *Local Government Handbook*, which was first published in 1920 and in 2002 was in its fourteenth edition.

He had a photographic memory and was prolific in opinions, reports and articles, estimating that he had furnished more than 80 000 opinions on local government law during his career. To *Smith's Weekly* his only possible weakness was that he had too many friends, being 'one of those extraordinary busy men who always has time to see anyone'. His recreations included reading, bridge, fishing and watching cricket.

On 31 January 1940 he married Margaret Reilly at St Mary's Catholic Cathedral, Sydney. He retired in 1943. Bluett died of pulmonary tuberculosis on 21 April 1944 at his Lindfield home and was cremated with Anglican rites. His wife and the children of his first marriage survived him. In 1945 the A. R. Bluett memorial awards were established; presented annually to an urban and a rural council, they recognize outstanding progress in services to the community. The Mitchell Library holds a caricature of him, by R. W. Coulter, which was printed in the *Bulletin* in September 1924. It shows a thin, slightly harrowed man with a prominent forehead.

While Albert was the secretary of the employers' organization, Edward represented the employees. As the clerks' association could not afford to pay him a full salary, he also established the Shire and Municipal Supply Co. Determining which products individual councils would require, from disinfectant to water-carts, he liaised between manufacturers and councils to procure them. A keg of beer in the corner of his office in O'Connell Street, Sydney, was kept to entertain visiting town clerks. He retired from the L.G.C.A. in 1939.

In 1915 Edward had established the Local Government Coaching College to give candidates a grounding in local government before they sat the examination to qualify as a town or shire clerk. The college was a success: at one time 80 per cent of the State's town and shire clerks had qualified there. It operated until the 1960s when the Sydney Technical College took over the role. 'E.C.' was a tall, well-built man who was popular within local government circles. He died on 22 May 1958 at Ulladulla and was buried with Anglican rites at Milton, survived by his wife and two sons, one of whom, Roger Blair Bluett (1905-1990), was also prominent in local government.

Shire and Municipal Record, 28 June 1939, p 73, 28 July 1939, p 131, 28 Apr 1944, pp 1, 3, 28 May 1944, p 31, 28 July 1944, p 78; *Bulletin*, 4 Sept 1924, p 20; *Smith's Weekly*, 11 Oct 1924, p 2; *SMH*, 22 Apr 1944, p 3; D. J. A. Moloney, A Great Many Interests in Common: A History of the Local Government and Shires Associations of New South Wales (M. Letters paper, Univ Sydney, 1996); information from Mr B. Bluett, Mosman, Syd.   ANTHEA KERR

BLUETT, FREDERICK GEORGE (1876-1942), vaudevillian, and AUGUSTUS FREDERICK (1902-1936), comedian, were father and son. Fred was born on 20 January 1876 at Marylebone, London, son of Frederick William Goodwin, letter carrier, and his wife Elizabeth Sarah, née Dell. His grandfather and father—the latter as William 'Bluett'—were on the stage, and Fred reputedly made his début at the age of 3. In 1892 he was sent to Melbourne to learn the boot trade with a brother-in-law. Interested in boxing and amateur theatricals, he appeared as a vocalist at smoke concerts before returning to Britain. Stranded at Dunedin, New Zealand, when Ada Juneen's company folded in 1899, he sang comic songs at smoke concerts and amused (Sir) Benjamin Fuller [q.v.8] who gave him an eighteen-month contract in 1900.

On 20 April 1901 Bluett appeared for the Fullers at the Empire Theatre, Sydney. By the following April he had joined Harry Rickards's [q.v.11] New Tivoli Vaudeville Company, and he was to work the Tivoli circuit for ten years. As he strutted the stage with 'red nose, baggy pants and huge flapping boots', clowning and singing comic songs in an exaggerated Cockney accent, Bluett 'could literally roll an audience in the aisles'. He had an 'extra-ordinary talent for wisecracks not in the script'. Backstage, he enraged (understand-ably) his fellow thespians with practical jokes —such as inserting pins in sticks of grease paint or nailing stage shoes to the floor. Weighing sixteen stone (101 kg), he was 'vir-tually immune from physical attack' and ignored verbal abuse.

Bluett had married Catherine McKechnie, a dressmaker, on 1 April 1901 at her father's house at Dunedin, New Zealand; thenceforth Kate was always with him, either at home or at the theatre as his dresser. Their only son Gus was born on 23 April 1902 at Prahran, Melbourne; he always travelled with his parents, had very little regular schooling and learned his stagecraft from his father.

At the Tivoli, Sydney, in May 1910 Fred pre-sented 'a joyous burlesque of the Boy Scout inanity', with himself as scoutmaster and a line of scouts ranging from Gus to a 16-year-old, which 'tickled the city almost into con-vulsions'. About 1912 the Bluetts, including their daughter Belle (b.1909), went to South Africa for six months, then to Britain, where Fred worked in music halls. In London, he appeared in a revue with Fred Kitchen, in which Gus got his first speaking part, as a pageboy. The youngster studied black-and-white art in London and regarded his younger sister Kitty, born during a Zeppelin raid in 1916, as his special responsibility.

By March 1917 the family was back in Australia and Fred was playing at the Tivoli, Melbourne. He spent eighteen months (c.1920-21) in Brisbane and bowed to popular demand to revive the Boy Scouts burlesque. In December 1922 he was the Dame in the pantomime *Cinderella* at the Theatre Royal, Sydney; Gus was Buttons. Throughout the 1920s Fred continued to play in vaudeville and created his famous role as a pirate. He per-formed in the pantomime *Aladdin* with Roy Rene [q.v.11] in 1926.

Gus had begun to get small parts in J. C. Williamson [q.v.6] Ltd's productions such as *Hello, Everybody* from 1918. Following his success with Ada Reeve in the pantomime *Aladdin* (1924), Williamsons engaged him for a straight part, the title role in *Kempy*. The same year he played Adrian van Piffel in *The Cousin from Nowhere* and Gabrielle in *Wild-flower*. He quipped that the Firm gave him the 'love-sick parts ... I live and love in vain'.

More versatile than his father, Gus capti-vated Australian audiences in musical comedy roles such as Reggie in *The Five O'Clock Girl*

(1929). He 'had only to put his face round the corner and blink across the footlights, and the house was in a roar'. In 1930 he played a sea-son of revivals with Gladys Moncrieff [q.v.10], including *The Maid of the Mountains*. He supported Madge Elliott and Cyril Ritchard [qq.v.14] in 1932-33 in *Our Miss Gibbs* and other musicals. Their 1934 season ended with *Blue Mountain Melody*, in which Bluett played 'Dynamite Danny Duffy, the role specially written for him' by James Bancks [q.v.7]. A 'man of infinite wit and charm', Gus lived exuberantly and refused to follow his doctors' advice to slow down. He did not marry. Early in March 1936 he finished the Melbourne run of *Yes, Madam?* and returned to the family home, established by Fred and Kate at Double Bay, Sydney. Gus died of haemorrhaging gastric ulcers on 14 March in Sydney Hospital and was cremated without religious rites.

In 1934 Fred had taken up radio work, using his fruity voice to good effect in comedy, drama, musicals and children's productions. He made a comfortable living. According to Claude McKay [q.v.15], he had 'unction, an elastic face and great comic gusto' and looked 'well-nourished and dapper, with just that sartorial jauntiness' one associated with a vaudeville artist. Bluett chaired the Australian Broadcasting Commission's series 'Music Hall Memories' in 1938. On 3 December 1942 he left the A.B.C. studios after playing Albert, the Cockney air-raid warden, in 'Searchlights over London' for the fortieth time, and died of coronary vascular disease in his sleep at his home; he was cremated with Presbyterian forms. His wife and daughters survived him. Belle had married the variety star Jimmy Jewell. Kitty became a popular radio actress and in 1948 went to England where she achieved stardom.

Bulletin, 5 May 1910, 19 May 1910, p 8; *Theatre, Society and Home*, 1 Jan 1925, p 26; *Table Talk*, 23 Dec 1926, p 12; *Wireless Weekly*, 5 Aug 1938, p vi; *ABC Weekly*, 19 Dec 1942, p 26; *Parade* (Melb), Apr 1960, p 14; *Otago Witness* (Dunedin, NZ), 5 Sept 1900, p 55, 27 Mar 1901, p 55, 8 May 1901, p 57; *SMH*, 20 Apr 1901, p 14, 22 Apr 1901, p 3, 12 Apr 1902, p 10, 22 Dec 1919, p 12, 6 Oct 1934, p 10, 16 Mar 1936, p 11, 17 Mar 1936, p 12, 5 Dec 1942, p 11; *Star* (Melb), 21 Mar 1936; *Smith's Weekly*, 21 June 1941, p 12; *Herald* (Melb), 1 Sept 1955, p 11; *Daily Mirror* (Syd), 12 Nov 1973, p 30.

MARTHA RUTLEDGE

BLUNDSTONE, JOHN (c.1831-1895), boot-maker, was born at Derby, England, son of William Blundstone, a jeweller. On 11 May 1853 at Friargate Presbyterian Chapel, Derby, aged 22 and described as a coach-body maker, John married 19-year-old Eliza Martin. In 1855 he and Eliza migrated to Van Diemen's

Land, arriving on 14 October. John began in business in Hobart as a coachbuilder, but in 1870 set up as an importer of boots and shoes. By 1878 he had opened his own bootmaking firm. The enterprise grew rapidly and in 1882 John was in a position to purchase his rented Collins Street factory.

The Blundstone family also expanded, six boys and four girls being born between 1856 and 1873. In 1883 the eldest surviving son Sylvanus (1858-1915) joined his father in the firm, renamed John Blundstone & Son. In addition to boot manufacture and wholesale importing, the company sold a wide range of leather and rubber goods as well as boots and shoes. By 1891 a subsidiary retail business, W. H. Blundstone & Co., was created under the management of William Henry (1864-1918), the second son. To finance this expansion, John took out a mortgage of £900 in 1887 and one of £300 in 1891. He also built a new factory at 126 Collins Street. In 1894 both companies displayed their wares at the Tasmanian International Exhibition, W. H. Blundstone & Co. winning a second-class and John Blundstone & Son a first-class certificate.

A respected and active member of the Hobart community, from 1879 Blundstone acted as a trustee of the Mechanics Hall. Some time after his arrival in Tasmania he changed his religious affiliation from Church of England to Wesleyan and for a number of years was an office-bearer of the Melville Street Wesleyan Church. In 1891 he was appointed a justice of the peace and for a time was a judge of vehicles for the Southern Tasmanian Agricultural and Pastoral Association. Blundstone died of pleurisy on 24 September 1895 at his residence in Campbell Street, Hobart, and was buried in Cornelian Bay cemetery. He was survived by his wife and eight children.

His sons continued to run the two businesses. Both appeared successful, but by 1900 neither of the mortgages taken out by Blundstone had been reduced and the companies had incurred further debts. In February 1901 Sylvanus filed for the bankruptcy of John Blundstone & Son and in May Henry Cane, a Hobart hardware merchant, acquired the firm. The retailer, Blundstone & Co., filed for bankruptcy in 1909. From that date, no member of the original family had any connexion with the Tasmanian-based footwear company although subsequent owners have retained the name Blundstone. By the 1990s the brown, elastic-sided work-boots had become an internationally known brand name, sometimes abbreviated to 'Blunnies', and featured in the Australian stage entertainment *Tapdogs*.

Tasmanian International Exhibition Souvenir (Launc, 1896); *Mercury* (Hob), 15 Oct 1855, p 2, 27 Sept 1895, p 2, 31 Jan 1983, p 4, 22 Feb 1996, p 6, 24 Nov 1997, p 3; CB7/17/2, SC84/23, SC342/1 (TA).

DAVID YOUNG

BOAG, JAMES (c.1822-1890) and JAMES (1854-1919), brewers, were father and son. Born at Paisley, Scotland, son of William Boag, manufacturer, and his wife Martha, née Henderson, James senior married Janet Swan on 22 August 1844 at St James Chapel. They had four children before migrating to Victoria in May 1853.

The family spent a few months on the goldfields, then moved to Van Diemen's Land and settled at Launceston, where young James was born in 1854, followed by five more children. Boag soon joined John Fawns's Cornwall Brewery as manager and chief brewer. At first living in a cottage owned by Fawns in Frankland Street, he later purchased his own home in Goodwin Street and another property in George Street. After education at the Collegiate Institute, a day school, James junior joined his father at the Cornwall Brewery in 1870. James senior retired in 1878 and returned to Scotland for a year. Back in Tasmania, a widower, on 20 February 1882 at Cameron Street, Launceston, he married with Presbyterian forms Janet Muir, a widow and the daughter of another Scottish brewer.

On 24 November 1880 at Holy Trinity Church, Launceston, James junior had married Elizabeth Edwards. They were to have nine children. In 1879 he formed a partnership with J. T. Glenwright at the Cataract Brewery. J. Boag & Son was established in February 1883, the company buying the Esk cordial manufactory and brewery, which had been set up by Charles S. Button two years earlier. The brewery was a creditable piece of Queen Anne style architecture, on the busy artery of William Street. In 1887 a new malt-house was erected and Boag's soon became the dominant beer in the northern half of Tasmania, while Cascade ruled the south. A freemason, Boag senior was a member of the Loyal Cornwall Lodge and of Manchester Unity Independent Order of Odd Fellows. Having retired again in 1887 he died on 9 November 1890, while visiting his daughter in Melbourne, and was buried with Presbyterian forms in Launceston cemetery. His wife and son, and four daughters of his first marriage, survived him

Young James took a keen interest in the Launceston Artillery, earning the long-service medal. He was a generous supporter of the Newnham Racing, North Esk Rowing, A.B.C. Bowling and the North Launceston Football clubs. The Caledonian Society also attracted his attention. He topped the poll for election as warden of the Launceston Marine Board in

December 1903, but was defeated in December 1912. J. Boag & Sons was restructured in 1911. Like his father, Boag was visiting Melbourne when he died, of cancer, on 6 February 1919, and was also buried in Launceston cemetery with Presbyterian forms. His wife, four sons and four daughters survived him. His son James (1881-1944), trained as a brewer with Tooth [qq.v.6] & Co. in Sydney, was an all-round sportsman and ran the company, except for some years in the 1920s when he lived in England. He was an alderman on Launceston City Council in 1937-40. After his death, J. Boag & Son experienced changes of ownership and fortune until acquired by the Philippine-based San Miguel Corporation in June 2000.

T. W. H. Leavitt, *The Jubilee History of Tasmania*, 2 (Melb, 1887); *Cyclopedia of Tasmania*, 2 (Hob, 1900); M. Bingham, *Cascade* (Hob, 1992); J. W. W. Ison, *A Review of Some Events and Personalities in Launceston* (Launceston, 2001); *Examiner* (Launc), 10 Nov 1890, p 4, 7 Feb 1919, p 6, 5 Aug 1944, p 4, 18 Nov 1985, supplement, p 10, 10 May 2000, p 17.

ROSS SMITH

BOLTON, WILLIAM ROBERT FOSSEY (1905-1973), transport operator and philanthropist, was born on 24 May 1905 at Taringa, Queensland, second of five children and eldest son of Henry Fossey Bolton, an Irish-born telegraphist of Scottish ancestry, and his Queensland-born wife Flora Grace, née MacKay. Bolton's first name was registered as Willie; later he used William and was known as Bill. His primary education took place in Brisbane and at Charleville, Stanthorpe and Toowoomba as his father was regularly transferred by the Post Office. Henry committed suicide in his Toowoomba home in 1918 and was found by his 12-year-old son. The family's financial situation became difficult, but (with a scholarship) Bolton was able to commence his secondary education at Toowoomba Grammar School, becoming a boarder in 1918 when his mother returned to her family at Chinchilla. Having obtained a public service pass in the 1920 junior examination, he joined the Lands Department in Brisbane as a junior clerk and studied accountancy part time, qualifying in 1928.

He returned to Toowoomba in 1935 to establish his own accountancy practice and on 1 June at Sandgate, with Presbyterian forms, married Marion Isabel Salisbury. When he enlisted in the Australian Imperial Force at Rockhampton on 5 June 1941 he was 5 ft 7 ins (175 cm) tall, with brown hair and brown eyes. He served with the 2nd/15th Battalion in the Middle East and New Guinea and was discharged on 20 November 1944. With Percy

Redman as partner, Bolton had purchased a transport business, registered as Redmans Transport on 24 June 1943. The enterprise proved successful, largely due to lucrative contracts with Paul's Dairy Co.

A fervent nationalist who admired the values of Australia's bush pioneers, in 1948 Bolton renamed his business Cobb & Co. Redman Transport after Australia's legendary coaching firm founded by Freeman Cobb [q.v.3]. Although the original company had gone into liquidation in 1929, Gordon Studdert, its last secretary, retained the name and threatened legal action. A settlement was reached in 1954 with Bolton acquiring the name, which was later also used on his extensive motor coach service operating throughout the eastern States.

In Queensland, the end of World War II provided unparalleled opportunities for road transport, while the railways were burdened with ageing rolling stock and strikes. Between 1948 and 1950 Bolton and Redman bought new, larger trucks and registered several subsidiary transport companies to serve southern Queensland. Conflict ensued, with the Nicklin [q.v.15] government determined to re-establish a viable rail transport system. In 1957 Bolton purchased two transport companies in New South Wales and began border hopping to circumvent payment of new licensing fees using Section 92 of the Australian Constitution. The government reacted by cancelling the licence of Downs Transport, a Cobb & Co. subsidiary. The battle between Bolton and (Sir) Gordon Chalk, minister for transport, was fierce and personal. Protracted legal and political conflict was finally resolved in the Queensland government's favour by the Privy Council in 1966. That year Bolton was appointed M.B.E. His challenge to the right of the States to collect excise in licence fees eventually made possible a successful 1997 New South Wales case against State tobacco licence fees, which added to the need to introduce a goods and services tax in 2000 to replace such revenue.

Never forgetting the charity his family received, Bolton was generous in his support of others. He provided bursaries to country children to attend private schools, funds to establish the Blue Nursing Service at Toowoomba and an oval at Toowoomba Grammar School. He greatly admired Rev. John Flynn [q.v.8] and was a life member of the Royal Flying Doctor Service. In 1963 he raised £26 000 for the service, organizing and funding a three-month Cobb & Co. coach journey from Port Douglas to Melbourne along original coaching routes. He lured fast bowler Ray Lindwall north to play cricket by a job with Cobb & Co.

Bolton was an associate of the Chartered Institute of Secretaries, the Australian Association of Accountants and the Institute of Transport. With his shock of pure white hair, his tattered cardigans, his Mackay clan woollen tartan ties, nicotine-stained fingers and characteristic growl he was easily recognized. He became a foundation member of the Queensland branch of the Society of St Andrew of Scotland, and corresponded with the Scottish poet Will Ogilvie [q.v.11]. After the poet's death in 1963 the family sent Bolton the whip and tail from the horse that Ogilvie had ridden while droving in Australia.

Possessing an encyclopaedic knowledge of Australian history, art and literature, Bolton developed extensive collections of each. With the support of the Lindsay [q.v.10] family he established the Lionel Lindsay Art Gallery and Library in Toowoomba, opened by the prime minister (Sir) Robert Menzies [q.v.15] in 1959. Bolton's Australiana Museum and Garden of Remembrance, including his collection of twenty-eight original, horse-drawn vehicles available for fund-raising, was opened in 1965.

The strain of the conflict with the State government and the decision to award costs against Cobb & Co. Ltd affected Bolton's health. He suffered a stroke in 1968 and was forced to retire from business. He died on 3 August 1973 at Toowoomba, survived by his wife, two of their three sons and two daughters, and was cremated with Presbyterian forms. His collections were donated to public institutions and are displayed in the Cobb & Co. Museum and the Toowoomba Regional Art Gallery.

C. Hazlehurst, *Gordon Chalk* (Toowoomba, Qld, 1987); D. Tranter, *Cobb & Co.* (Brisb, 1990); *The Lionel Lindsay Collection*, exhibition cat (Brisb, 1991); D. Tranter and J. Powell, *Cobb & Co. Museum* (Brisb, 1992); B. MacAuley, *Celebrating Bill Bolton's Vision of Australia* (Toowoomba, Qld, 2001); M. French, *Bill Bolton's Toowoomba* (Toowoomba, Qld, 2001); *Toowoomba Chronicle*, 22 Oct 1960, p 3, 17 Apr 1965, p 4, 6 Aug 1973, 6 June 1983; Bolton papers (Cobb & Co. Museum, Toowoomba, Qld); information from Mr J. Tattam, California, USA.

DEBORAH TRANTER

BOOTY, FREDERICK FRANCIS (1879?-1914), caricaturist, was born probably on 15 March 1879 in Sydney, fourth child of English-born Phillip Galloway Booty, law clerk, and his native-born wife Mary, née Grattan. He was descended from a long line of artists and lithographers. With his mother and five other siblings, he arrived at Fremantle, Western Australia, in 1896 aboard the *Rockton* to join his father and three older brothers who had preceded them. Fred supported himself by designing advertisements for the *Umpire*

(Fremantle); in the evening he attended drawing and painting classes. He also sent cartoons and illustrations to the local newspapers.

The colony was booming and the press, on the verge of its 'inky golden years', attracted an influx of well-regarded journalists and visual artists from the economically depressed east. These pioneers provided Booty's inspiration for his caricature series, the 'Press Gang' and 'Brother Brushes' in the *Sunday Times* (Perth) and the *Sun* (Kalgoorlie). Although a youngster among such peers, Booty was deft with his pen and looked, listened and learned. His mentors were Ben Strange [q.v.12] and Dick Hartley, between whose sketches his own contributions were periodically interspersed in the weekly papers. Doing the rounds of the public houses, he rubbed shoulders with literati such as Frederick Vosper, Andrée Hayward, 'Bluebush' (J. P. Bourke) and 'Dryblower' (E. G. Murphy) [qq.v.12,9,7,10]. Booty's caricatures supported Dryblower's popular lampoon column 'Verse or Worse' in the *Sunday Times*.

Booty thought public figures and current events fair game. He often devoted a series of sketches to a particular topic, for example Sir John (Forrest) [q.v.8] 'at home'; 'abroad'; dealing with Federation; with women's franchise; and his cabinet as 'a musical melange'. His favourite targets were politicians and the newspaper fraternity. Booty's most poignant illustrations complemented 'With the Bushmen', Bert Toy's South African war series in the *Morning Herald*. Naturally industrious, he had a prodigious output yet his whimsical wit and sure strokes remained distinctive. 'The Story of Chanticleer', in the 1901 Christmas edition of the *Western Mail*, was described as 'brightly written and made much brighter by the pretty work of the promising young artist'. Booty reputedly made the first line block print for the Perth Printing Works in April 1901.

He enjoyed undertaking decorative work for memorials or manuscripts or preparing theatre programmes. Slight of build, with a shock of dark hair, he was an engaging young man with an eye for the girls and a taste for the nightlife around the town. His consuming passion for the theatre ranged from vaudeville to oratorio. Grown restive by 1904, he returned to Sydney and applied for a job with the Victorian Stamp Co. Next year he joined a lithography partnership in London until the theatre lured him to the United States of America to work as a stage designer and caricaturist. Booty died of pneumonia on 13 January 1914 at Peter Bent Brigham hospital, Boston, and was cremated. He was married but the details are unknown.

The Booty Caricatures of WA Personalities at the Turn of the Century, exhibition cat (Perth, 1993).

WENDY BIRMAN

BOSWELL, ANNABELLA ALEXANDRINA CAMPBELL (1826-1914), diarist and gentlewoman, was born on 16 September 1826 at Yarrows, Bathurst Plains, New South Wales, elder daughter of George Innes, a landholder, and his wife Georgianna Lorn Moorshead, neé Campbell, both Scottish born. In 1834 Annabella's parents moved sixty miles (97 km) north to a cattle station, Glen Alice, at Capertee, while she attended Mrs Evans's boarding school in Bridge Street, Sydney. After twelve months she rejoined her family to be tutored by governesses. Tall and handsome, she was a bright pupil and a prolific reader with a preference for European history and Sir Walter Scott's Waverley novels. To Annabella's regret, her mother banned the works of Shakespeare as 'unsuitable'.

In 1839, hoping to improve his health, her father took his family to stay at Port Macquarie with his brother Major Archibald Innes [q.v.2]. Four months later George died. Mrs Innes and her daughters returned to Capertee, sold Glen Alice and, after two years at Parramatta, rejoined their relations at Port Macquarie in 1843. Already a prolific diarist, Annabella found much to write about at Lake Innes House and the nearby settlement. Remote though they were, the family borrowed regularly from the Australian Subscription Library, Sydney. The house was noted for its hospitality, aided by liveried footmen, maids, stable hands and a piper. Foremost among the many guests was Governor FitzRoy [q.v.1] with his entourage. Lively reports of events, fashions worn, foods consumed and visitors' personal quirks duly appeared in Annabella's journal.

A knowledgeable gardener and horsewoman, Annabella was proficient in most of the domestic skills required of a countrywoman. Quick to learn, she could crack a whip as well as any stockman or churn butter. She was also a fine water-colourist and pianist. In March 1843 a giant comet appeared, terrifying local people, who were convinced it presaged the end of the world. Annabella described it as 'magnificent—the tail is beautiful, springing upwards from the star like an aigrette of light'.

By 1848, without convict staff to maintain it, Lake Innes was no longer viable. Major Innes was appointed police magistrate at Newcastle, where in 1849 Annabella met Patrick Charles Douglas Boswell. A free settler from Ayrshire, Scotland, who was related to James Boswell, the biographer, Patrick was employed by the Bank of New South Wales as accountant, later becoming manager. On 17 June 1856 Annabella married Boswell at Christ Church Cathedral with Anglican rites. She bore one son and three daughters before their departure in 1865 for Scotland, where Patrick had inherited the family estate. In 1867 Annabella's last child was born at their home, Garrallan,

Old Cumnock, Ayrshire. She continued to live the life of a gentlewoman. Patrick died in 1892.

Annabella expressed nostalgia for her birthplace by publishing three books based on her diaries. Her pamphlet, *Recollections of Some Australian Blacks*, was written in 1890. *Some Recollections of My Early Days* (1908) was republished as *Annabella Boswell's Journal* (Sydney, 1965 and reprinted 1981 and 1993). Her vivid account of colonial life, *Further Recollections of My Early Days in Australia* (1911), was republished as *Annabella Boswell's Other Journal* (Canberra, 1992). She had died at Garrallan on 25 October 1914. One son and three daughters survived her.

V. Crittenden, introduction to *Annabella Boswell's Other Journal 1848-1851* (Canb, 1992); *SMH*, 30 Aug 1911, p 5; Innes papers (ML); information from Mrs G. Griffin, Hastings District Family History Society and Port Macquarie History Society.

NGAIRE M. SOUTER

BOWEN, DIAMANTINA (1833-1893), governor's wife, was born in 1833 on the island of Zante (Zakinthos), Greece, tenth of eleven children of Conte Giorgio-Candiano Roma and his wife Contessa Orsola, née di Balsamo. The family—originally named Regolo and with origins in thirteenth-century Rome—included notable men in the Venetian occupation of Corfu, the Peloponnese and Crete, and some distinguished personages in newly independent Greece. Belonging to the small aristocracy of the Ionian Islands, Diamantina enjoyed a privileged life during the British rule (1815-64). Her father was president of the Corfiot Senate and titular head of the Ionian Islands Republic. Queen Victoria appointed him the islands' poet laureate.

On 28 April 1856 in the Palace of St Michael and St George, Corfu, Contessa Diamantina Roma married (Sir) George Ferguson Bowen [q.v.3], government secretary of the islands. He was appointed first governor of Queensland in 1859 and Lady Bowen accompanied him to Brisbane with their daughter, arriving on 10 December. She ably fulfilled the ceremonial role of governor's wife. In 1864, with a silver spade and a cedar wheelbarrow, she turned the sod for Queensland's first railwayline, at Ipswich. An exemplary hostess at Government House and a tireless worker for charity, she gave birth to three children while in Brisbane and helped to found the Lady Bowen Lying-In Hospital in 1866. In January 1868 she and Sir George proceeded to New Zealand on his appointment as governorgeneral. Here their last child was born. They returned to Australia in March 1873 when Bowen was sworn in as governor of Victoria.

By then Diamantina had acquired some of the characteristics of a *grande dame*, and was an elegant and fascinating figure evoking popular respect. To a gossip columnist she was 'as exotic as a bird of paradise, still a beauty, with black dazzling eyes, a flawless cream complexion and a figure that, even in the dresses of the period, was the envy of many younger matrons'. Mrs Campbell Praed [q.v.11] had described Lady Bowen's 'soft foreign accent'; in private conversation with Sir George she normally spoke Italian. Active in charitable causes and cultural events, she was dignified but also unconventional: on one occasion she went roller-skating. Attacked by a deranged woman (Esther Gray) in Collins Street in 1876, she suffered only slight injury. In February 1879 a large assemblage at a Melbourne banquet heard Marcus Clarke's [q.v.3] poem, 'Farewell to Lady Bowen', set to music by Alfred Plumpton. Sir George was governor of Mauritius until 1882 and of Hong Kong in 1882-86.

His wife was a woman of poised serenity and kindness, with a degree of reserve. Self-disciplined, compassionate, dutiful, she was interested in garden plants, music and *objets d'art*, and was a fine pianist and singer. On Sir George's retirement they and their two unmarried daughters settled in London, where she worshipped at the Greek Orthodox Church in Moscow Road. She died of acute bronchitis on 17 November 1893 in Cadogan Square, and was buried in the Bowen family grave at Kensall Green. Her husband and their five children survived her.

Among many place names commemorating her are the town of Roma and the Diamantina River in Queensland. In 1953 her many letters, long preserved in a villa on Zakinthos, were destroyed after earthquakes in the Ionian Islands.

U. G. Prentice, *Diamantina, Lady Bowen, Queensland's First Lady* (Brisb, 1984); H. Gilchrist, *Australians and Greeks*, 1 (Syd, 1992), and for bib; M. Hancock, *Colonial Consorts* (Melb, 2001).

HUGH GILCHRIST

BOYCE, BENJAMIN (c.1820-1847), ordinary seaman and labourer, was born at Scrane End, a hamlet near Freiston, Lincolnshire, England, son of Samuel Boyce, a beer-house keeper. Benjamin was one of the thirty-six crew of the *Moffatt*, which sailed from the Thames in August 1839 with about 200 emigrants for the new colony of South Australia. He appears not to have known of its destination, nor to have had any intention of being himself a migrant. During the voyage he was ill, twenty-eight settlers died and two were drowned. The vessel arrived in December,

by which time Boyce had developed a close relationship with Louisa Thomson, who was accompanying her family from Sussex. With their co-operation, Boyce and two others jumped ship on Boxing Day. He lived a fugitive existence in the sandhills, with a reward of £2 for his capture, until the departure of the *Moffatt*, then found employment in a dairy looking after twenty cows, after which he cut hay on government land in Adelaide.

Competition drove him out to the Adelaide Hills. Here he set up in partnership with William Holland, an ex-convict who, by remarkable coincidence, came from Boyce's village in Lincolnshire and had served fourteen years in Van Diemen's Land. They worked at tree-cutting and erecting rough houses and fences in the hills. In nine months Boyce was able to save the extraordinary sum of £40 and then took work in a grog shop; he bought a pony and cart and harness for £20 and was owed £28 by an employer. On 26 September 1843 in St John's Church of England, Adelaide, he married Louisa; she signed with a mark. A son Thomas had been born in April. They lived at Walkerville, Benjamin working as a shearer in the bush for George Anstey [q.v.1 Thomas Anstey], averaging sixty to seventy sheep a day, he claimed.

Boyce became known to posterity from three of his remarkable letters written to his parents in England—graphic accounts of an unofficial immigrant in South Australia as it passed through depression and into recovery in 1842-46. In semi-phonetic prose, he described vividly his reactions to shipboard life, local Aborigines, employment, prospects, marriage, and his feelings about home and the colony. He urged anyone unsuccessful in England to migrate to South Australia. He did not expect ever to see England again. There was a bravado in his words and he declared that he was 'not a fraid to go from the smoke of my mothers chimney'.

He exulted that 'I ... bean making muny as fast as I cud count it ... I uest to spend it faster than I earnt it'. His luck ran out in August 1846 when he fell from a tree. After much medical treatment he died on 1 December 1847 at Walkerville. He had been a member of the Albion Lodge of the South Australian Independent Order of Oddfellows, which, for his subscriptions amounting to £4 14s. 2d., had provided free medical support, sixteen months sick pay and funeral expenses, a total of some £85.

E. Richards, 'Immigrant Lives, 1836-1986' in E. Richards (ed), *The Flinders History of South Australia: Social History* (Adel, 1986); *South Australian*, 7 Dec 1847, p 3; Boyce letters, D 4308/1-3(L) *and* Robert Thomson letter, D 7703(L) (SLSA); *Moffatt* manifest book, GRG 41/8, item GAG 41/8, v 2, p 88 (SRSA).   ERIC RICHARDS

BRAINE, HENRY EDWARD (1884-1957), company manager and wheat industry administrator, was born on 3 January 1884 at Buckhurst Hill, Chigwell, Essex, England, only son of Harry Brain, bricklayer and builder, and his wife Martha, née Huddlestone. Henry was educated at a school in Buckhurst Hill. Employed as a clerk by a silk indent agent, in 1909 he travelled to Japan on the trans-Siberian railway. Two years later he arrived in Western Australia and leased an orchard at Yornup, south of Bridgetown. He married his sweetheart Rosaline Florence Webster on 5 January 1914 at the register office, West Ham, London, giving his surname as Braine.

Returning to Bridgetown, he joined Westralian Farmers Ltd's fruit department and was briefly in the potato section at Bunbury before being transferred to the wheat division in Perth. By 1918 the firm was sole agent for the Australian Wheat Board. Braine energetically addressed problems of receival, storage and shipment. As a company officer uninvolved in political wrangling, he expedited the transition from the State Wheat Board to a voluntary wheat pool, which retained Westralian Farmers as its agent. Promoted wheat inspector in 1925, Braine succeeded John Thomson as the company's wheat manager and secretary to the Co-operative Wheat Pool of Western Australia. An acknowledged authority and able organizer, from 1934 he was managing director of Co-operative Bulk Handling Ltd, overseeing most of the construction of the silos which ended the need to bag grain for transport. He retired in 1951 to become manager of the trustees of the wheat (later grain) pool. On overseas trips (England 1929; China and Japan 1939), he had generated interest in Western Australian wheat. In 1950 he published three monographs on the sale of wheat under the fair average quality system.

During World War II Braine had served in the Volunteer Defence Corps. From 1942 until 1953 he was also a volunteer ambulance officer for the St John Ambulance Perth Water Supply Division. Tall, athletic and ascetic, Braine spent weekends on his farm at Chittering breeding sheep and cattle and experimenting with agricultural techniques. He maintained a close association with the Western Australian Institute of Agriculture, whose postwar soil fertility research programme he persuaded the wheat pool to sponsor. He also successfully lobbied the State government to legislate for a research subvention for wheat-farmers.

Braine could not abide small talk or chatty social gatherings, although he proved a genial host to Dame Sybil Thorndike and Sir Lewis Casson at a bush-barbecue in 1955. Passionate about the theatre, opera and ballet, he gained support for the Adult Education Board's community arts programmes and the Western Australian Ballet Company. He was dubbed 'a fairy godfather' for negotiating a partnership between the Westralian Wheat Buildings Pty Ltd and entrepreneurs Eric Edgley [q.v.14] and Clem Dawe, resulting in the post-war revitalization of His Majesty's Theatre, Perth, as a theatrical venue.

In 1954 Braine was a foundation member of the Australian Elizabethan Theatre Trust. He also belonged to the British Overseas Settlers' Association. Survived by his wife and their two daughters, Braine died on 15 March 1957 at Royal Perth Hospital and was cremated with Anglican rites. His estate was sworn at £34 546. Rosaline Braine had served in the women's auxiliary services during World War II and was active in the Perth Repertory Club and as a charity worker.

F. R. Mercer, *On Farmers' Service* (Perth, 1955); *Co-operative Bulk Handling* (Perth, 1965); G. H. Burvill (ed), *Agriculture in Western Australia 1829-1979* (Perth, 1979); W. K. P. Smith, *A Bunch of Pirates* (Perth, 1984); G. C. Bolton, *A Fine Country to Starve In* (Perth, 1994); R. Goldfinch, *Legends of the Grain Game* (Perth, 2003); *Wesfarmers News*, 21 Mar 1957; Dept of Agriculture (WA), *Bulletin*, Mar 1984; *West Australian*, 5 Jan 1933, p 50, 16 Mar 1957, p 2, 11 May 1957, p 7, 16 July 1968, p 7; *Sunday Mail* (Adel), 26 June 1954, p 9; *Countryman* (Perth), 21 Mar 1957, p 3; Wesfarmers records (BL); information from Mrs B. Coppin, Porongurup, and Mr J. R. Luyer, Cottesloe, WA.   WENDY BIRMAN

BRENAN, JOHN O'NEILL (1856-1940), public servant, was born on 27 March 1856 at Garryowen, Balmain, Sydney, eldest son of nine children of John O'Neill Brenan, an Irish-born barrister, and his second wife Mary Elizabeth, née Fitzgerald, and grandson of John Ryan Brenan [q.v.1]. Educated under Professor W. J. Stephens [q.v.6] at Sydney Grammar School until his father's death in 1869 young John entered the Queensland Public Service on 17 June 1872 as a junior clerk in the Government Savings Bank.

On 22 April 1879 at St Thomas's Church of England, Toowong, Brisbane, he married Gertrude Georgina (Ina), daughter of William Leworthy Drew [q.v.]; they were to have six children. Brenan worked for the Stamp Office, in Treasury and with the curator of intestate estates before his appointment as chief clerk in the immigration office in December 1884. Given additional responsibility as Pacific Islanders inspector in 1890, after he learned pidgin he heard many tragic recruitment stories. By August 1893 Brenan was immigration agent and in charge of the government labour bureau and relief, as well as the Pacific Island labour branch. Three years later he was for several months the first inspector under the Factories and Shops Act of 1896. Courteous, compassionate and wary of red-tape inflexibility, he handled difficult situations diplomatically, making lifelong friends from among the thousands he assisted on their arrival.

In 1906 Prime Minister Alfred Deakin [q.v.8] took charge of the Pacific Island Labour Department and promised Brenan a free hand to conduct the deportation of over 6000 Islanders, and direct access through the permanent secretary of the Department of External Affairs Atlee Hunt [q.v.9]. Although doubts were harboured whether 'Jack o' the Islands' was sufficiently tough for the acrimonious job, later he was glowingly commended for the trouble-free evictions. With an understanding of the Islanders and trust in his own officers, he urged empathetic exemptions and efficiently achieved the desired result. By 1908 the deportations were completed and he returned to the State civil service.

As Brenan had charge of admissions to Dunwich Benevolent Society, he also administered the indigents' allowance and later supervised the introduction of old age pensions. Despite seeking promotion in other branches, he continued as immigration agent and at the labour bureau until his retirement in March 1923, by which time the Commonwealth had assumed the main responsibilities for immigration. He then was appointed on a yearly basis as a temporary clerk in his old department until seconded as secretary of the New Settlers' League on 22 April 1929. He retired on 31 December 1929.

As a young man Brenan had excelled at amateur athletics, long-distance running and football. He was a lifelong naturalist and accurate observer, writing many newspaper articles on Queensland birds. Brenan died on 12 March 1940 in Brisbane and was cremated. His wife, three sons and two daughters survived him.

Qld Naturalist, Nov 1922, p 120; *Courier-Mail*, 13 Mar 1923, 29 Mar 1923, p 6, 13 Mar 1940, p 6; Immigration Dept, register of officers, IMM/258 and Public Service Board file, A/53979, file 75 (QA); information from Mr and Mrs W. Brenan, North Tamborine, Qld.   JENNIFER HARRISON

BRIGGS, LOUISA (1836-1925), Aboriginal leader, dormitory matron and nurse, was born on 14 November 1836 on Preservation Island, Bass Strait, daughter of John Strugnell, a sealer, and Mary (Polly) Munro. Strugnell, as a 17-year-old London chimney sweep, had been transported in 1818. Polly was probably the daughter of James Munro [q.v.], another sealer, and Doog-by-er-um-bor-oke (Margery

Munro), a Woirorung woman kidnapped from Port Phillip.

Louisa was an attractive woman with blue eyes and dark, wavy hair with a distinctive white streak. In 1853 she married John Briggs, the son of a Tasmanian Aboriginal woman and a sealer. Briggs was formerly married to Louisa's aunt Ann Munro. He and Louisa joined the gold rush in Victoria and worked as shepherds in the Beaufort district and for a squatter near Violet Town until the late 1860s. Between 1853 and 1871 they had nine children. Work was scarce and in 1871 the destitute family joined Coranderrk Aboriginal station, near Healesville.

Next year a dispute with the Board for the Protection of the Aborigines, which managed the station, over the board's failure to pay a cash wage to all the workers resulted in John being expelled after seeking paid work elsewhere. In 1874 the family returned, in great need, to Coranderrk. There Louisa acted as a nurse and dormitory matron and was appointed a salaried staff member in 1876.

The board's policy over Coranderrk's income and the inclusion of newcomers, who were not related to the Kulin clan inhabitants, caused resentment among the residents. Rebellion ensued. Louisa's leadership and hereditary right made her a spokesperson. She had learned to read, but not to write, so her children acted as scribes for her numerous letters of protest. When the popular manager was replaced, Louisa fought the plans to sell Coranderrk and to relocate its residents. To this end she gave evidence in August 1876 at an inquiry into the running of the station. Widowed in 1878, after further protests Louisa was forced off the reserve, seeking asylum at Ebenezer Aboriginal station, Lake Hindmarsh, where she again acted as a matron. Conditions there were poor and she wrote to the board to complain of the lack of food in 1878 and again in 1881. Following another inquiry into Coranderrk, Louisa returned to the station in 1882 and was left briefly in charge of the dormitory.

Legislation in 1886 forced 'half-castes' under the age of 35 off the reserves and Louisa's family was again exiled from Coranderrk; they sought refuge at Maloga mission in New South Wales. She pleaded to return to Coranderrk but the board claimed that the family was Tasmanian and refused re-entry. In 1889 Louisa and her children moved to Cumeroogunga reserve, on the New South Wales side of the Murray River, opposite Barmah. She again requested to return to Coranderrk in 1892 and was denied. In 1895 'half-castes' were excluded from Cumeroogunga, forcing the family to settle in a makeshift camp at Barmah. In 1903, at the age of 67, Louisa asked for the rations to which she was entitled by age and ancestry. Again the board refused 'for the reason she is a half caste of Tasmania'. She later returned to Cumeroogunga, where she died on 6 September 1925. Out of affection, local children covered her coffin with violets. A church going Presbyterian, Louisa was strong minded, hardworking, known for her kindness and love of children and for her humour, audacity and courage.

R. B. Smyth, *The Aborigines of Victoria* (Melb, 1878); D. E. Barwick et al, *Metaphors of Interpretation* (Canb, 1985); H. Radi (ed), *200 Australian Women* (Syd, 1988); D. E. Barwick, *Rebellion at Coranderrk* (Canb, 1998); album of 156 photos by Frederick Kruger, 1876-78 (National Museum of Vic).   LAURA BARWICK

BRIGHT, ANNIE (1840-1913), journalist and spiritualist, was born on 14 July 1840 at Mount Hooton, Nottingham, England, and registered as Anna, daughter of William Wright, book-keeper, later silk merchant, and his wife Charlotte, née Hooton. Although her father was a freethinker, Annie was educated at Anglican schools, becoming a good linguist with an especial interest in literature and music. Discontented with the life expected of her as a young lady, she spent much of her time helping factory girls, teaching them in the large Sunday School held in the local Unitarian chapel. Aspiring suitors held no attraction until Rev. James Pillars, a Unitarian minister, encouraged her to leave home and accompany him to Australia. They were married on 6 July 1864 in the High Pavement Unitarian Chapel, Nottingham, and migrated shortly afterwards to Sydney, where he took up his position as minister of a freethought church.

Pillars was acknowledged as an excellent preacher, but his advanced ideas split the congregation, delaying the completion of a new church building. A decline in subscriptions caused financial hardship and, in an effort to alleviate this as well as to further her own abilities, Annie began a small school with the help of her husband, teaching the daughters of their friends. On 31 July 1875 she was left to do this alone when Pillars, while on a Sunday School excursion, fell from a cliff, was swept off the rocks at Bondi and presumably drowned. A monument was erected at Tamarama Beach.

This tragedy reunited the differing church elements, but Annie, disillusioned by previous unkindness, refused to join them. She continued her school, building up the numbers as her pupils proved their achievement, while also looking after her young family of two sons (another had died in infancy) and two daughters. Although she had considered herself a materialist, she was persuaded to try using the planchette as a possible means of contact with her late husband. This led to the receipt of messages through a medium and, eventually, to Annie's attendance at a lecture given by Charles Bright [q.v.3], a divorced former Melbourne journalist who was a convert to spiritualism. They became friends and on 23 April 1883 were married by a Unitarian minister at Stanmore, Sydney.

Charles and Annie remained active in Sydney's volatile freethought circles, and in 1884 she lectured in New Zealand on 'The Emancipating Influence of Spiritualism'. She also wrote articles on various topics for local journals. From 1894 to 1896 she was editor of *Cosmos Magazine*. Both Annie and Charles were ordained Unitarian ministers in Sydney in 1902. After Bright's death in 1903, Annie was invited to become editor of the *Harbinger of Light*. She moved to Melbourne to take up this position in 1905, writing much of the journal herself, while maintaining her dependence on unseen spiritual helpers. Her autobiographical novel, *A Soul's Pilgrimage*, was published in Melbourne in 1907. She wrote *What Life in the Spiritualist World Really Is* in 1912 by 'transmission' from W. T. Stead, the crusading editor who went down with the *Titanic*.

Although a convinced spiritualist, Annie refused to label herself as such, believing that words and definitions were inadequate to describe spiritualist experience as well as being divisive. Strong-minded and resolute, she always believed in the rightness of her own destiny. She died at her home in East Melbourne on 21 June 1913 and was buried in Brighton cemetery. A son and daughter of her first marriage survived her.

J. Roe, *Beyond Belief: Theosophy in Australia* (Syd, 1986); A. G. Gabay, *Message From Beyond* (Melb, 2001); *Harbinger of Light*, 1 Nov 1904; *The Liberal*, 12 May 1883.   LURLINE STUART

BRITTON, THEODOSIA; *see* WALLACE

BROADHURST, FLORENCE MAUD (1899-1977), designer, businesswoman, singer and banjolele player, was born on 28 July 1899 at Mungy Station, near Mount Perry, Queensland, fourth surviving child of Queensland-born parents William Broadhurst, stockman, later a grazier and hotelier, and his wife Margaret Ann, née Crawford. After winning prizes in local eisteddfods, Florence joined 'the Diggers' and sang at the Princess Theatre, Toowoomba, in 1918. On 4 December 1922 she left Australia to perform with a musical comedy sextet, the 'Globe Trotters', in South

East Asia and China under the stage name 'Miss Bobby'. She also performed with the 'Broadcasters', 'Carlton Follies' and 'Carlton Sparklers', received favourable reviews for her singing and Charleston dancing and was photographed for the English-language newspapers—including the *Eastern Mail* (Delhi) and the *South China Morning Post*. In 1926 she established the Broadhurst Academy in Shanghai, offering tuition in violin, pianoforte, voice production, banjolele playing (taught by Florence), modern ballroom dancing, classical dancing, musical culture and journalism.

Returning to Queensland in July 1927, Broadhurst was involved in a car accident before travelling in October to England in the *Orvieto*. On 22 June 1929 at the Brompton Oratory, South Kensington, she married with Catholic rites Percy Walter Gladstone Kann, a stockbroker. In the early 1930s the two were co-directors (and she designer and dress consultant for) Pellier Ltd, Robes & Modes, in New Bond Street, Mayfair. But Kann soon departed and she and her second husband Leonard Lloyd Lewis, a diesel engineer, lived at Banstead, Surrey, from 1939. During World War II she joined the Australian Women's Voluntary Services, offering hospitality to Australian soldiers. In 1945 the Lewises moved to Worthing, Sussex, where Florence obtained fishing and passenger boat licences. She became honorary secretary of the Art Women's Movement Against Socialisation.

In 1949 she came back to Australia with Lewis and their son. Taking up painting, she drove around northern and central Australia, reportedly producing some 114 works in two years. Solo exhibitions of her 'Paintings of Australia' were held in 1954 at David Jones's [q.v.2] art gallery, Sydney, and next year at Finney's gallery, Brisbane, and at the Art Society of Canberra gallery. She also participated in group showings, including the All Nations Club's Ten Guineas and Under exhibition at David Jones. Florence became a foundation member of the Art Gallery Society of New South Wales and a member of the Society of Interior Designers of Australia.

In the 1950s, as Mrs Lewis, she became involved in charitable and fund-raising activities. But by 1961 Leonard had moved to Queensland, leaving Florence and her son to run a motor-sales business at St Leonards, Sydney. She continued her charity work, designing the festoon decorations for the 1964 *Die Fledermaus* Opera House Ball and acting as vice-president and honorary organizer for the United Nations Association of Australia international ball committee in 1966. In the 1970s she was connected with the Royal Art Society, the Sydney Opera House appeal and the Australian Red Cross Society.

In 1959 Broadhurst had established Australian (Hand Printed) Wallpapers Pty Ltd, in premises behind the motor business. With a small staff, she designed, manufactured and marketed locally produced, high-quality, handcrafted wallpapers in luxurious, oversized patterns with vivid combinations of colours, inspired by an eclectic range of sources. Brightly coloured peacocks were a feature, as were bold geometrical, striped and floral designs. Innovations included printing onto metallic surfaces, the development of a washable, vinyl-coating finish and a drying rack system that allowed her wallpapers to be produced in large quantities. Moving to Paddington in July 1969, the company became known as Florence Broadhurst Wallpapers Pty Ltd, advertised as 'the only studio of its kind in the world' and exporting to North America, England, Hawaii, Kuwait, Peru, Norway and Paris. In 1972 the Australia News and Information Bureau issued a press release claiming an international reputation for the designer. By then her wallpapers reportedly contained around 800 designs in eighty different colour ways.

A striking-looking woman, Broadhurst was renowned for her flamboyant clothes, antique jewellery and coiffed, hennaed hair. In 1973 with her eyesight and hearing failing, she flew to Britain to attend a cell therapy clinic in the hope of improving her health and rejuvenating her body. Back in Sydney, she was brutally murdered on 15 October 1977 at her Paddington premises; the killer has never been identified. Survived by her son, Florence was cremated. The Powerhouse Museum, Sydney, holds a collection of her work. The Broadhurst collection was acquired by Signature Prints Pty Ltd, and in 2005 many of her boldest wallpaper designs were still available, some reinterpreted as fabric prints by Akira Isogawa, Nicole Zimmermann and other leading Australian fashion designers.

S. O'Brien, *A Life by Design* (Syd, 2004); *People*, 16 Jan 1963, p 54; *Aust House and Garden*, Apr 1965, p 101, May 1977, p 22, Oct 1979, p 17; *Vogue Living*, 11 Feb-11 May 1972, p 103, 15 June-14 Aug 1975, p 10; *Harper's Bazaar*, Oct 1984, p 132; *Shanghai Daily Times*, 27 Dec 1925; *Sun-Herald* (Syd), 16 Nov 1969, p 140; *Australian*, 17 Oct 1977, p 1; *SMH*, 18 Oct 1977, p 2, 5 June 1999, 'Good Weekend', p 34; Aust News and Information Bureau, press release, November 1971, Q980.106/18(ML); Broadhurst papers (ML and Powerhouse Museum).

ANNE-MARIE VAN DE VEN

BROGER (BROGHER); *see* BROUGHTON

BROOKS, WILLIAM THOMAS (1889-1943), policeman, was born on 28 April 1889 in Port Melbourne, second of seven surviving children of John Thomas Brooks, an English-born gas-stoker, and his native-born wife Catherine, née Postlethwaite. After working as a gas-stoker with the Metropolitan Gas Co., West Melbourne, William joined the Victoria Police on 28 September 1911 and soon after transferred to Dimboola for duty as a mounted constable, where he served for one year, resigning on 28 February 1913. Nine months later he rejoined as a foot constable and was stationed for relatively short periods at Russell Street, Melbourne, and at Seymour and Prahran, before being appointed on 3 March 1916 to South Yarra. Here he was employed mainly on liquor licensing duty. Commended twice, he was described by his superintendent as 'efficient, energetic and well conducted'. On 11 December 1915 at St Thomas's Church of England, Essendon, he had married Mary Ethel Booth, a farmer's daughter from Hay, New South Wales. They were to have seven children.

In October 1921 Brooks transferred to the licensing branch where he was commended for his part in 846 licensing prosecutions and sly-grog cases. Despite this, he was one of seventeen licensing police ordered back to beat duty in a purge by the chief commissioner Alexander Nicholson in February 1923. Aggrieved, Brooks circulated a petition headed 'Comrades and Fellow Workers' among metropolitan police. Signed by almost 700 men, its bold tone established him as unofficial leader of those police agitating for improved work conditions. Nicholson responded by transferring him away from his Prahran home to Geelong 'for special work' and thence, even more remotely, to Colac for licensing duty—which he refused to perform. Suspended and charged for this refusal of duty, he called Nicholson to give evidence at a much-publicized discipline hearing held in the Melbourne City Court during May 1923. The charge was dismissed and on reinstatement to the force an embittered Brooks promised to 'cause a lot more trouble'. And he did.

On the night of 31 October 1923 Brooks led twenty-eight other constables at Russell Street station out on strike, refusing to parade for night-shift beat duty until a covert system of special supervisors (who spied on police) was discontinued. In the days that followed Brooks toured suburban police stations rallying men to strike. The absence of patrolling police unleashed a wave of violence across Melbourne. Mobs of looters rampaged through city shops and 636 police were discharged for refusing duty. Brooks was dismissed from the force on 1 November 1923 for organizing and leading Australia's only police strike. He was not called to give evidence at the subsequent royal commission appointed to inquire into its causes.

After the strike he moved to Hay, where he worked as a water-boring contractor, then for many years as a night watchman. In July 1943 he became caretaker at St Patrick's College, Ballarat, Victoria. Brooks died of myocardial infarction on 15 November 1943 in hospital at Ballarat and was buried with Catholic rites in the local cemetery. His wife and three daughters survived him.

R. Haldane, *The People's Force* (Melb 1986); G. Brown and R. Haldane, *Days of Violence* (Melb, 1998); Report of the Royal Commission on the Victorian Police Force, *PP* (Vic), 1925, vol 2, p 853; *Argus*, 29 May 1923, p 7; personal file, nos 5697 and 5944 (Vic Police archives, Melb); information from Mrs I. Hutchings, Essendon, Melb.

ROBERT HALDANE

BROUGHTON (c.1798-c.1850), Aboriginal guide, tracker and constable, and **BROGER** (**BROGHER**) (c.1800-1830), Aboriginal tribesman, were close relations, probably siblings, born at Boon-ga-ree—known in 1822-88 as Broughton Creek and subsequently as Berry—in the Shoalhaven area of New South Wales. The brothers responded in different ways to the challenges posed by the influx of Europeans. Broughton, whose Aboriginal name was rendered as Toodwick, Toodood or Toodwit, accepted and strove to adapt to the new society introduced by the colonists. By 1818 he was working for Dr Charles Throsby [q.v.2] of Liverpool, who probably named him after William Broughton [q.v.1]. The trusted Aboriginal served as a guide and translator on several of Throsby's explorations to the south and at least once for John Oxley [q.v.2]. In 1822 Broughton started work for Alexander Berry [q.v.1], whose grant incorporated Boon-ga-ree, setting up Berry's farm, Coolangatta, recruiting Aboriginal labour, keeping the peace, capturing bushrangers, droving cattle and providing his own labour. He became a favourite of Berry's, who called him 'my Landsman' and later 'my oldest surviving Black friend' and who presented him with a rectangular breastplate inscribed 'Broughton Native Constable of Shoalhaven. 1822'.

Broger was less accepting of European ways and values, though he could speak English. To Broughton's distress, he refused to undertake regular labour for Berry, preferring instead the company of his wife and at least three children in the forest at Boon-ga-ree. On 6 February 1829, with his Aboriginal friend George Murphy (probably a close relative), he took two sawyers, John Rivett and James Hicks, into the bush in Kangaroo Valley to show them some fine cedar. Here, Broger killed Rivett. Broughton, because of his reputation as a skilled tracker, was recruited to hunt down his brother but led the search party on a wild goose chase. Captured in May, when taken on board ship, Broger stole the keys to his irons from a sleeping guard, jumped overboard and fled. Recaptured in October 1829, he was committed for trial by magistrates Berry and Charles Windeyer [q.v.2].

It emerged that Broger, Murphy, Rivett and Hicks knew each other. Sawyers of the district, Rivett in particular, had a bad reputation for their dealings with Aborigines. A few days before his death, Rivett had cheated Broger and Murphy in an exchange of flour for bush turkey eggs. Further, it was rumoured that Rivett had seduced Murphy's wife. If this were true, then Broger may have been obliged to assist Murphy in securing redress under Aboriginal law. Perhaps, too, Broger resented the effects being wrought by sawyers on the stands of timber in the area, for he was known to refer possessively to Boon-ga-ree as 'his own place'. At his trial at Campbelltown on 20 August 1830 before Chief Justice (Sir) Francis Forbes [q.v.1], witnesses noted his claims that Rivett had attacked him first and he had acted in self-defence. However, he was not allowed to speak in his own defence. He was found guilty and sentenced to death. On 30 August Broger was publicly executed by Alexander Green [q.v.].

As his knowledge and skills lost their value, Broughton was gradually forced to the margin of European society in the Shoalhaven. His problems within his own society multiplied. He was mocked by his relatives for his devotion to a foreign work ethic, which made him appear to them like a convict worker. Broughton had three wives in all. The first two were Mary, from Kangaroo Valley, and Charlotte. Both were unfaithful to him, and Charlotte died from a beating he gave her. He later took another wife. At least two of the four children of his wives were part-European. An 8-year-old daughter was raped by convicts. His earlier devotion to Berry had earned him an entitlement to regular rations from the Coolangatta store, but records show that he claimed them less frequently over time, indicating perhaps that he spent more time with his family and friends in the bush. He died about 1850.

The names of the brothers survive in several physical features and localities in the Shoalhaven. Brogers Creek is named after the one. After the other there is Broughton Creek, Broughton's Head, Broughton Vale, Broughton Village and Broughton Mill Creek. A sketch of Broughton (called Broton), by Jacques Arago, the artist with the French scientific expedition, in 1819, shows a thoughtful, even intense, young man with a lightly whiskered face and medium length hair in free-flowing curls.

Berry papers, vol 111, appendix B (ML); CGS 898 [9/2743], CGS 13696 [5/1161, COD 294B], CGS 13477 [T 146], CGS 905 [4/2023, 29/2013] (SRNSW).   KEITH O. CAMPBELL

BROWNE, FRANK STYANT (1854-1938), pharmacist and photographer, and EMMA ANN (1857-1941), philanthropist, were husband and wife. Frank was born on 10 July 1854 at Norwich, Norfolk, England, son of George Browne, bookseller, and his wife Ann, née Styant. Educated at King Edward VI School, Norwich, Derby Grammar School and Westminster College of Pharmacy, Frank was apprenticed to a chemist and also studied at the Derby School of Art in the 1870s. He lived in London for a short time before marrying Emma Ann Elmes in the parish church, Wimborne, Dorset, on 22 June 1882.

Born on 24 February 1857 at Wareham, Dorset, daughter of John Clifford Elmes, journeyman coachbuilder, and his wife Matilda, née Warland, Emma had been educated at a private school. The couple arrived in Hobart in November 1882. After working with H. T. Gould, a friend and fellow college student, next year Browne established a homoeopathic pharmacy in Elizabeth Street, in association with Dr Harry Benjafield [q.v.]. Later in 1883 he moved to Launceston, where he operated a homoeopathic pharmacy in Elizabeth Street, then in Fergusons Block, Brisbane Street, and from about 1887 until his retirement in 1932 at 112 Brisbane Street.

Browne's enthusiasm for photography led to the formation in 1889 of the Northern Tasmanian Camera Club. At the first meeting, held in his pharmacy, he was elected honorary secretary, a position he held for some twenty years. In June 1891 he photographed some of the first Australian demonstrations of sound recording on wax cylinders. Obtaining an X-ray plant in June 1896, in September he became the first in Tasmania to demonstrate X-ray photography successfully. A year later he demonstrated examples of three-colour photography to the N.T.C.C., in 1901 gave the earliest known Australian demonstration of a home movie projector and in 1905 took colour photographs, probably among the first to be produced in Australia. He won many photographic awards within Australia and overseas.

In 1890 Styant Browne (as he was generally known) had been elected to the northern council of the Pharmaceutical Council. President of the Pharmaceutical Society of Tasmania in 1906-07, he was a board member for many years and an examiner in botany. He was appointed a justice of the peace on 21 December 1916. With the decline of impressionism in photography, he increasingly turned to painting as a spare time pursuit. For several years he was president of the Launceston Art Society.

Browne had helped to found the Homoeopathic Cottage Hospital, which opened at Launceston in 1900. He was honorary secretary until 1929, while Emma was a board member from its inception to the time of her resignation in 1924. An untiring philanthropic worker, she was a founder of the Queen Victoria Maternity Hospital at Launceston, a life member of the Victoria League, a member of the Shakespearian Society, a reciter of Shakespearian plays and a writer of essays on ethical and political subjects. She was also one of the earliest members of the National Council of Women, sometime honorary secretary, vice-president and finally president for northern Tasmania.

The Brownes had one daughter and six sons; four sons served in World War I, one having also served in the Boer War. Frank died on 17 April 1938 at his home at Launceston and Emma on 24 October 1941. Their children survived them, including a son Frank who was also a photographer. The Queen Victoria Museum and Art Gallery, Launceston, holds a collection of Styant Browne's work.

M. McArthur (ed), *Prominent Tasmanians* (Hob, 1924); *Salute to the X-ray Pioneers of Australia* (Syd, 1946); C. Long, *Tasmanian Photographers 1840-1940* (Hob, 1995); P. A. C. Richards, 'A Brisbane street homoeopath: Frank Styant Browne, dispenser of medicines', Tas Hist Research Assn, *Papers and Procs*, 44, no 4, Dec 1997, p 261; *Examiner* (Launc), 18 Apr 1938, p 6.   PAUL A. C. RICHARDS

BRUCE, ROBERT (c.1836-1908), pastoralist and writer, was born at Mitcham, Surrey, England, son of James Bruce, a native of Scotland. Robert received a sound education in the Scottish tradition, but his first place of employment was an English shipyard. An interest in ships and nautical travel was to remain with him. In 1853 he worked his passage in the *Gypsy* to South Australia, finding work as a locker in a bond-store at Port Adelaide. Following his elder brother Douglas, in 1858 Robert travelled to the Northern Flinders Ranges, where he was appointed overseer at Arkaba station. Soon he was managing the north-western part of the property, which was practically stripped bare by locusts. Bruce spent months in the saddle in a desperate attempt to keep the stock alive. After good rains in 1860 he went to Adelaide to recuperate; then he and his brother took up Wallelberdina, adjoining the eastern shore of Lake Torrens.

On 30 January 1872 at Pendibacowie Robert married with Bible Christian forms Mary, the 17-year-old daughter of a neighbour, John O'Keefe. After his brother was killed in a horse riding accident in 1873, Robert sold Wallelberdina and entered into partnership with James Moseley who was developing Coondambo station, some 200 miles (322 km) west of Port Augusta. Eventually Bruce became the sole proprietor.

Even as a young man Bruce had given thought to the best ways of handling and training stock-horses, the most efficient procedures for pasturing sheep and cattle and the least harmful methods of exploiting the countryside. He enclosed Coondambo with a vermin-proof fence, one of the first in South Australia's north-west. This was expensive, but the country benefited and the cost was soon recouped. He lived on the station for most of his remaining years; towards the end he purchased a home in Adelaide and called it Coondambo. He revisited England in the 1860s and in 1878.

Bruce achieved temporary fame as a writer, being the author of a novel, *Benbonuna* (Adelaide, 1900), an autobiography, *Reminiscences of an Old Squatter* (Adelaide, 1902, republished 1973) and four volumes of poetry, all published in Adelaide—*The Dingoes: and Other Tales* (1875), *A Voice from the Australian Bush* (1877), *Echoes from Coondambo* (1893) and *Re-echoes from Coondambo* (1902). In addition, he wrote two plays and the music and lyrics for several songs. The plays were published in England, as were several of his songs. His poetry has rhyme and rhythm but lacks true poetic force. His prose cannot be compared with that of his contemporary fellow-pastoralist and writer Simpson Newland [q.v.11]. To Paul Depasquale, 'Bruce can be absurdly pretentious but he also frequently writes of the crude realities of outback life in unsubtle verse whose primary function is to inform as it entertains'.

In 1901 Bruce stood unsuccessfully as a Liberal for the State seat of Flinders. He died on 4 November 1908 at North Adelaide and was buried in the Catholic section of West Terrace cemetery, survived by his wife and their four daughters; two sons had died in infancy. His estate was sworn for probate at £22 100. An obituarist recalled Bruce's tall figure and 'arrow-like straightness', clear, kindly eyes and gentle spirit.

N. A. Richardson, *The Pioneers of the North-West of South Australia* (Adel, 1925); R. Cockburn, *Pastoral Pioneers of South Australia*, 2 (Adel, 1927); P. Depasquale, *A Critical History of South Australian Literature 1836-1930* (Adel, 1978); H. Mincham, *The Hub of the Flinders* (Hawker, SA, 1980); *Register* (Adel), 6 November 1908, p 5; L. H. Rye, South Australian Verse (M.A. thesis, Univ Qld, 1936).
                                                          G. K. JENKIN

BRYDON, MARIANNE HELENA (1864-1941), educationist, was born on 19 May 1864 at Tynan, County Armagh, Ireland, eldest daughter of Rev. James Carson, Presbyterian minister, and his wife Marianna, née Coey. The family came to Queensland about 1868.

At 13 Marianne began training as a pupil-teacher at Charters Towers State School, resigning in February 1878 to take up a state scholarship at Brisbane Girls' Grammar School. Having passed the University of Sydney junior (1879) and senior (1881) public examinations—on both occasions winning the Fairfax [q.v.4] prize—in 1882 she began teaching at Miss Jardine's school in Wickham Terrace. She became a form mistress at Brisbane Girls' Grammar School in 1883. On 2 April 1885, at her father's house in South Brisbane, she married with Presbyterian forms Scottish-born shipping agent John McKenzie Brydon and left teaching.

Following her husband's death in July 1895, with five children to support, Mrs Brydon opened the South Brisbane High School and Kindergarten, a private school for girls. Appointed secretary and teacher of mathematics and science at South Brisbane Technical College in October 1903, within three years she was promoted to principal. She moved to the newly formed Central Technical College in Ann Street in 1909 as teacher of English, physics and French. From July 1912 supervisor of commercial and domestic science day classes, next year she became the first supervisor of the domestic science department, which in 1914 was transferred to a new building in George Street. The new facility prompted the establishment of a full-time domestic science day school, offering instruction for girls in cookery theory and practice, laundry-work and housewifery, ambulance and home nursing, domestic science, English and arithmetic. She was supervisor of women's work from 1916 and inspector of women's work from 1919.

Although the number of schools was steadily increasing it was difficult to provide domestic science classes in Queensland's remote areas. Brydon was convinced that this could be overcome with the use of domestic science railway carriages. Plans were drawn up in 1920 and in October 1923 the first car arrived at Roma Street. Two carriages served the northern part of the State. Shunted to a railway siding, each remained for up to seven weeks, with girls attending classes in cookery, dressmaking, housewifery, laundry-work and needlework.

Brydon influenced other developments in domestic science education in her time. Syllabuses were revised in the early 1920s, new textbooks adopted, salaries increased and the first domestic science junior examination was held at the school. In 1924 she visited institutions in Sydney and Melbourne which offered instruction in housecraft subjects. Two years later Queensland introduced a three-year domestic science and art diploma.

In addition to her professional commitments, Brydon was a committee member of the Brisbane School of Arts from 1911 to 1927. She was the first vice-president of the Brisbane Girls' Grammar School Old Girls' Association and served as treasurer for eleven years on the standing committee of the Women's College, University of Queensland. Due to health problems, she took extended leave on full pay in March 1928 and spent time in Britain and Canada. After retiring in 1932 she lived at Redcliffe and participated in philanthropic and church affairs. Two sons and a daughter served in World War I: the elder, Kenneth, was killed in Flanders in 1917; the daughter Jean was appointed associate, Royal Red Cross (1919). Marianne Brydon died in Brisbane Hospital on 17 November 1941 and was cremated with Presbyterian forms. Her three daughters and one son survived her.

G. Logan, *A Centenary History of Home Economics Education in Queensland 1881-1981* (Brisb, 1982); *Educational Historian*, 3, 1988, p 3; *Queenslander*, 20 Oct 1923, p 6; *Brisb Courier*, 27 Aug 1932, p 22; *Telegraph* (Brisb), 17 Nov 1941; student file (Brisb Girls' Grammar School archives).

MICHAEL MARENDY

BUCK, HENRY (1860-1933), clothing manufacturer and retailer, was born on 26 November 1860 at Clerkenwell, London, second child of Thomas Buck (1819-1886), master electroplater, later a corn factor, and his wife Ann, née Swinburn. Henry grew up at Bridge House, Danby, Yorkshire, and entered the soft goods trade in Milk Lane, London, in May 1873. Suffering from tuberculosis, he migrated to New South Wales in 1887 and worked at Manfred, a sheep-raising property near Euston. Here his health improved. His fiancée Laura Jane Rose joined him, but was repelled by life on the remote station and they moved to Melbourne. On 25 June 1887 at Armadale the couple married with Presbyterian forms.

Buck worked as a bookbinder's assistant, losing his job in 1890 after rashly demanding an increase in salary. He sought a job with a friend, who had borrowed £50 from him to set up a shirt store, but found that he had been duped. Rather than take legal action, Buck assumed control of the deserted shop and Laura took over as book-keeper. With the assistance of two machinists, Henry learned the trade of shirt cutting and opened a new retail store on 25 August 1890 in the fashionable Queens Walk, off Swanston Street.

Although he struggled in the depression, within a decade Buck had won repute as an exclusive maker of made-to-measure shirts, using the finest English cloth. In the early 1900s he diversified into warehousing and wholesaling, and founded Wallace Buck & Goodes Pty Ltd, the London Tie Co. Pty Ltd and Beaucaire Knitting Mills. At 35 Rockley Road, South Yarra, in 1910 he had built, from designs by architects H. W. & F. B. Tompkins, a two-storey house, Danby. The Bucks lived there until 1926.

Henry and Laura had four children, three of whom had died by 1912. On 26 August 1919 their surviving child Elsie Maude married Frederick William Dennett, an English concert pianist, then on a world tour with Jack Waller's company. Their working honeymoon ended at Bombay, India, when Dennett accepted Buck's cabled offer to join the firm; in 1921 he became a director of Henry Buck & Co. Pty Ltd. About the same time Buck formed Eyelets Pty Ltd, with his enthusiastic and talented son-in-law as the principal partner.

Tall and handsome, Buck was a respected figure in Melbourne—where he belonged to the Commercial Travellers' Association, the Royal Automobile Club of Victoria, the Melbourne Cricket Club and the Master Drapers' Association of Victoria—as well as in London, where he was a member of the Portland Club. He was an authority on bridge and solo and belonged to the Melbourne Philharmonic Society. Buck discreetly supported many charitable institutions including the Australian division of the British Red Cross Society. In 1915 he set up and directed the latter's Volunteer Motor Corps, providing transport for returned servicemen and nurses after disembarkation and health trips for invalids. He was appointed O.B.E. on 19 October 1920.

In Buck's later years he left the management of the business to the Dennetts and with his wife made fourteen visits to their homeland. Henry died on 7 May 1933 at Marylebone, London, and was cremated, survived by his wife and daughter. His family inherited most of his estate, sworn for probate at £100 054, but his will also provided for several loyal employees, as well as a £3000 scholarship in his name at the University of Melbourne and a £2500 bequest to the Children's Hospital. Laura died in 1960, and the firm moved in 1963 to the new Colonial Mutual Building, Collins Street, where the plush atmosphere of the old store was re-created. Therein, the life of the founder, a celebrated figure in the Australian clothing industry, was commemorated in a display of photographs and memorabilia.

Table Talk, 28 Aug 1919, pp 1, 5; *Draper of A'sia*, 31 May 1933, p 27; *Aust Storekeepers and Traders' J*, 31 May 1933; *Herald* (Melb), 8 May 1933, p 7; *Argus* (Melb), 9 May 1933, p 6; A. Willingham, Residence (formerly Danby) 35 Rockley Road South Yarra 3141: A Cultural History (ts, 1998, held by author); Henry Buck Pty Ltd records, Collins Street, Melb; information from Mrs S. Cecil, Toorak, Melb.

ALLAN F. WILLINGHAM

BULEY, ERNEST CHARLES (1869-1933), journalist and author, was born on 4 July 1869 at Ballarat West, Victoria, youngest of nine children of English-born parents James Buley, builder, and his wife Susannah Eliza, née Crook. Ernest was educated at Grenville College, Ballarat, where his brother Arthur was later headmaster. Ernest's school friend Bernard O'Dowd [q.v.11] remembered him as 'a brilliant, wayward youth who took life lightly', who was familiar with the Ballarat demimonde and given to witty and penetrating comments on local politics. Moving to Melbourne, in 1885 Buley became a junior assistant in the Public Library, museums and National Gallery of Victoria, transferring to the imperial service in 1889 as a junior clerk in the local branch of the Royal Mint. On 11 September 1891 at West Melbourne Presbyterian Church he married Olga Amelia Ernst, a German-born teacher.

Keen from his youth on horse racing, Buley contributed as a tipster to the column 'The Quick and the Dead' in H. H. Champion's [q.v.7] 1895-97 weekly the *Champion*, but was unsuccessful as a punter. He was promoted senior clerk in 1895 at the Mint, where he was entrusted with handling the worn silver purchased from the banks for smelting, and the receipt and issue of gold bullion. His annual salary of £285, however, apparently proved inadequate for his life at fashionable North Brighton and his interest in racehorses. When a hundred sovereigns and £125 in silver went missing in May 1897, Buley was charged on two counts of 'larceny as a public servant' after detectives watched him betting heavily in the paddock at Flemington. He admitted two thefts and was convicted for these, although the superintendent of the Mint calculated that his defalcations amounted to £2259. The prison record described him as being almost 5 ft 9 ins (175 cm) tall, weighing 11 st. 11 lb. (75 kg), with a sallow complexion, grey hair and brown eyes. His religious affiliation was Church of England. Set free from Pentridge gaol in September 1898, he left for England in April 1900 with Olga and two children—a son had died weeks before. Champion wrote, 'he has starved since [his release]. But he really is a "white man", in spite of this indiscretion and will make his way in London if he gets a chance.'

Another daughter was born in England. Somehow Buley established himself as a writer, producing for George Newnes Ltd the well-received *Australian Life in Town and Country* (1905) and for Andrew Melrose, publisher for the Sunday School Union and founder of the Boys' Empire League, *Into the Polar Seas: The Story of Sir John Franklin* and *The Hero of India: The Story of Lord Clive* (both published in 1909). Working as a journalist and by 1908 living at Dulwich, London, he wrote and edited for publications including the *Sunday Dispatch*, *Reynolds*, the *British-Australasian* and Alfred Harmsworth's *Daily Mirror*. He set a killing pace, producing as many as 35 000 words a week for weeks on end. Two volumes on the physical geography and natural resources of Brazil followed in 1914 for Sir Isaac Pitman & Sons but, with the outbreak of war, Buley discovered a new and more lucrative vein. *The Real Kaiser* (1915), published anonymously so as not to embarrass his German relatives, was praised by *The Times* and lauded by the *Times Literary Supplement* as the best book on the subject. It quickly went through three editions.

He followed in June 1915 with *The Dardanelles: Their Story and their Significance in the Great War*, which was reprinted twice within weeks, and substantially enlarged in October, by which time Melrose had also released his *Glorious Deeds of Australasians in the Great War*. Buley had interviewed scores of Australians in hospital in London, fashioning their narratives—'delivered with a modesty which I have not sought to reproduce'—into an account of Gallipoli up to early autumn. Hailed as 'the first Anzac book', *Glorious Deeds* was reprinted three times before the end of the year and issued in an enlarged edition within weeks of the Gallipoli evacuation. The *Bulletin* praised it as a 'record of a valiant adventure undertaken by a new sort of soldier'. Next year Buley's *Child's History of Anzac* appeared. Subsequently he turned his hand to popular fiction, between 1919 and 1933 writing ten romances, often with boxing and horseracing themes, that he wryly described as belonging to 'the posthumous works of Nat Gould' [q.v.9]; at least six went into second editions.

Photographs of Buley in his fifties showed keen eyes beneath prominent eyebrows, his bald head balanced by a neat George V moustache and spade beard. Predeceased by his wife in 1923, he died of cardiac failure on 10 April 1933 at Dulwich. At least two children survived him, a son Ernest Bernhardt, who published popular fiction as 'Bernard Buley', and daughter Olga, who in 1939 was to edit the women's page for the *Daily Independent*. *The Times* announced: 'No mourning, at his request'. To the *British Australian and New Zealander* Buley was one of the most competent and versatile Australian journalists in England, an excellent editor and 'a writer of wonderful industry, with vivid imagination, rather sardonic humour, a wide range of knowledge, and great technical skill'.

F. A. Marteau, *Who's Who in Press, Publicity, Printing* (Lond, 1939); V. Kennedy and N. Palmer, *Bernard O'Dowd* (Melb, 1954); *Age* (Melb), 10 May 1897, p 5; *Argus* (Melb), 10 May 1897, p 5, 15 May 1897, p 9, 6 Aug 1915, p 4; *Herald* (Melb), 14 May 1897, p 5; *Brighton Southern Cross*, 15 May 1897; *British-Australasian*, 14 Dec 1905, p 18, 2 Dec 1915, p 29; *Times Literary Supplement*, 17 June 1915, p 208, 4 Nov 1915, p 395, 11 Nov 1915, p 398, 14 Dec 1916, p 612; *The Times* (London), 11 Apr 1933, p 1; *British Australasian and New Zealander*, 27 Apr 1933, p 15; VPRS 30/P, unit 1105, VPRS 5151, unit 51, VPRS 10858, unit 10 (PRO, Vic); information from Mrs L. Andel, Balwyn, Melb, and Dr F. Bongiorno, Armidale, NSW.   JOHN LACK

BULL, ELLIOTT RONALD (1942-1979), Aboriginal artist, was born on 22 August 1942 at Lake Tyers Mission Station, Victoria, son of Alfred Marshall Bull and his wife Agnes, née Moore, who had had moved from Cumeroogunga Aboriginal Station, New South Wales, in the late 1930s. Alfred, originally from the Victor Harbor region, South Australia, worked as a general labourer, and Agnes, from Swan Hill, Victoria, gained renown for her feather flowers. They had twenty-one children, seventeen surviving to adulthood. Ronald was removed from his family as an infant and again as a young boy, when he joined several of his brothers at Tally Ho Boys' Training Farm, a Methodist Church institution in Burwood, Melbourne. Here he was provided with painting materials and publications on art. At 15 he was placed in foster care at Lilydale.

Bull's artistic talent was evident at an early age. Combining his Aboriginal concern for country with a European landscape tradition, he studied the landscapes of English and Australian artists John Constable, J. M. W. Turner, Arthur Streeton and Hans Heysen [qq.v.12,9] whose work he saw in the National Gallery of Victoria and in reproductions. Living in Melbourne, Bull studied informally with a leading representational painter, Ernest Buckmaster [q.v.13]. He also corresponded with and visited Heysen. Like the Arrernte artist Albert Namatjira [q.v.15], with whom he was often compared, Bull gained considerable public recognition, but his work was not included in institutional collections such as State art galleries. Following his first showing at Morwell in 1965, he participated in a number of solo and group exhibitions: in 1966-67 with Keith Namatjira, fourth son of Albert, and in 1976 with Lin Onus. Bull's most important surviving artwork is the mural which he painted in 1960 during one of several gaol terms he spent in Pentridge prison. This powerful work, depicting a classic tribal scene, has been restored and preserved at the former penitentiary as part of Aboriginal cultural heritage. A prolific painter, producing some 2000 works, Bull is also represented in the collection of the Koorie Heritage Trust, Melbourne.

Of medium build with a gentle and reserved disposition, he had an irrepressible sense of humour. In 'To White Families Who Take Children for Holidays', published in *Smoke Signals* in June 1966, and in an Australian Broadcasting Commission television programme in March 1976, he reflected upon the trauma and confusion he suffered as a result of his childhood experiences. Bull died of hypertensive cardiovascular disease on 8 September 1979 at his home at Mont Albert, Melbourne. Buried by choice with Anglican rites in Emerald cemetery, Macclesfield, he was survived by his wife and their three children, by a former wife Lynette Davies and their daughter, and by a daughter from his relationship with Betty Williams.

Bull's talent and tenacity ensured that, against all odds, he achieved success as an artist. Once relegated to obscurity, he is now considered a significant figure in the regional history of Aboriginal Australia, a parallel in the south-east for Namatjira and a precursor to a later Koori art movement in Melbourne.

Smoke Signals, 6, no 1, Feb-Mar 1967, p 12; S. Kleinert, 'Aboriginal Landscapes', in G. Levitus (ed), *Lying about the Landscape* (Syd, 1997), *and* 'Bull, Ronald', in S. Kleinert and M. Neale (eds), *The Oxford Companion to Aboriginal Art and Culture* (Melb, 2000), *and* '"Blood from a Stone": Ronald Bull's Mural in Pentridge Prison', *Aust J of Art*, 14, no 2, 1999, p 93 *and* 'Jacky Jacky was a Smart Young Fella': Art and Aboriginality in South East Australia 1900-1980 (Ph.D. thesis, ANU, 1994); information from Ms S. Smith, Museum Vic, Mr Murray Bull, Sale, Vic, and Mr Timothy Lee, Melb.

SYLVIA KLEINERT

BULL, JOSEPH NUGENT PALMER (1908-1940), undertaker and 'bridegroom of death', was born on 3 April 1908 at Newtown, Sydney, fourth son and youngest child of native-born William Nugent Bull, undertaker, and his Dublin-born wife Mary, née Palmer. Educated at the Marist Brothers' High School, Darlinghurst, and St Joseph's College, Hunters Hill, young Nugent was strongly influenced by Brother Gerard, a Marist teacher prominent in Sydney Catholic intellectual circles. An extrovert at school, Nugent was an excellent cricketer. After matriculating in 1926 he joined the family firm W. N. Bull Pty Ltd at Newtown. Later he worked in the accounts department at Luna Park and for the Mansion Hotel group. He remained active in St Joseph's literary and debating society, Newtown, the Campion Society and St Joseph's College Old Boys' Union and often attended the Domain, supporting Catholic speakers and heckling socialists.

Some Australian Catholics had a long attachment to Spain. From 1931 they followed closely the establishment of the second Spanish republic; the dismantling of church schools there was critically reported in the *Catholic Freeman's Journal* and similar newspapers. Determined to defend his faith and volunteer with General Franco's forces, Bull resigned his job in July 1937, travelled to Spain via the Vatican and enlisted in the Spanish Foreign Legion on 16 October at Talavera de la Reina.

Bull was the only Australian to fight for the Nationalists during the Spanish Civil War. Knowing no Spanish, he was placed with French volunteers in the Joan of Arc *bandera* where he drew on his schoolboy French. The legion's hymn, 'We are the Bridegrooms of Death', was sung each day on the parade ground. Bull was wounded in the battle for Teruel at the end of 1937 when both sides slogged through heavy snow and sub-zero temperatures. Having sustained a serious knee injury and no longer fit for infantry duty, he transferred to the transport division, where he drove the trucks which maintained supply lines to the front. After Franco's victory, Bull was demobilized on 17 July 1939 and made his way, via Lourdes in France, to London.

On the outbreak of World War II as Nugent Joseph Bull he enlisted in the Royal Air Force and was posted to No.149 Squadron. Trained as an air-gunner, Sergeant Bull flew what he described in letters home as 'cracker' raids over Germany, bombing factories that had provided arms for Franco's forces. On 9 September 1940, soon after midnight and having just left the English coast for Boulogne Harbour, his aircraft was struck by a severe electrical storm and, with an engine in flames, was abandoned. One pilot managed to reach the English coast safely and the bodies of two of the crew were later recovered from the sea. Despite several false alarms, which raised the family's hopes that he had been seen in a French prisoner-of-war camp, Bull was eventually declared missing, presumed dead.

J. Keene, *Fighting for Franco* (NY, 2001) and 'An Antipodean Bridegroom of Death: An Australian with Franco's Forces in the Spanish Civil War', *JRAHS*, 70, no 4, Apr 1985, p 251; family papers (held by W. N. Bull Pty Ltd, Syd).   JUDITH KEENE

BUNTINE, AGNES (c.1822-1896), pastoralist and bullocky, was born at Glasgow, Scotland, eldest of six children of John Davidson, crofter, and his wife Sarah, née Wallace. The family left Scotland in December 1839, probably at the urging of brick and tile maker Hugh Buntine (1803-1867), a former neighbour at Little Netheraith, Ayrshire, who had emigrated in 1838 with his wife Mary and five children. Mary had died of typhoid in Sydney quarantine station and Hugh had moved to Melbourne, purchasing farming land on the Richmond Flats. In April 1840, when the Davidsons arrived in the barque *Glenhuntly*, Buntine arranged employment for the parents. Agnes worked locally as a dairymaid then married Hugh on 30 October in Melbourne with Presbyterian forms.

The Buntines established a dairy farm on Merri Creek then, attracted by the prospect of fertile land in Gippsland, they built a hut near Port Albert in July 1841. In September Agnes gave birth to Albert, thought to be the first white child born in Gippsland. After running cattle and a small inn at Morris Creek, outside Tarraville, by 1845 the couple established Bruthen Creek station—almost 8000 acres (3240 ha). Five more children were born between 1843 and 1855. To supplement their income, Hugh opened a slab-and-bark public house, the Bush Inn, on land adjoining the road to Sale. Agnes acquired a bullock team and began to transport stores. In 1851 she carried a load of butter and cheese from Port Albert across the mountains to Forest Creek on the Sandhurst (Bendigo) goldfields. She opened a store there, and later at the McIvor diggings, returning in 1853 to Bruthen Creek. By 1858 they had moved to a farm at Flynns Creek, near Rosedale. Hugh was ill; Agnes supported her family through the bullocky business, eventually carrying goods from Melbourne throughout Gippsland, though unwilling to undertake long trips. When gold was discovered at Walhalla in 1862 she was the first to transport supplies to the township over difficult terrain, and the next day slaughtered a bullock to feed the miners.

After Hugh's death, 'Mother' Buntine continued to operate her bullock teams and the property. On 17 February 1873 at Sale, with Presbyterian forms, she married 29-year-old Michael Dawe Hallett, an English-born farmer, and retired as a bullocky, the couple continuing to farm at Flynns Creek. Known as an intrepid rider, bushwoman and farmworker in her youth, Agnes was described in later years as a 'big rough looking woman', eccentrically dressed in short skirts, long leather leggings, thick blucher boots, and a loose jumper adorned by a bright neckerchief. She smoked an old, black, plug pipe. While contemporaries stressed her modesty and kindness, they also commented (admiringly) on her liberal use of a stockwhip on local Aborigines and insolent or drunk white men. Through an unconventional role for a woman, she exemplified the colonial drive for social and economic mobility, working hard to secure a better future for her descendants, and by extension for Gippsland settlers.

Agnes died on 29 February 1896 in Gippsland Hospital, Sale, survived by her husband and by one son and three daughters of her first marriage. She was buried alongside her first husband in the Presbyterian section of Rosedale cemetery. Many of her children and stepchildren settled as small landowners around south Gippsland; William Buntine, known as 'Talone Ordell' [q.v.11], actor and writer, was a grandson.

G. Dunderdale, *The Book of the Bush* (Lond, 1870); L. Braden, *Bullockies* (Adel, 1968); *Morwell Advertiser*, 6 Mar 1896, p 2; J. D. Buntine, Hugh Buntine of Gippsland: A Brief Family Survey (ms, 1979, held RHSV); W. J. Pickard, Agnes Buntine (ms, 1990, held by The King's School, Syd).

KATE DARIAN-SMITH

BURKINSHAW, MABEL; *see* FORREST

C

CADOGAN, ROSE; *see* SUMMERFIELD

CAESAR, JOHN 'BLACK' (c.1763-1796), convict and bushranger of unknown African parentage, may have been born on Madagascar. He was a servant living in the parish of St Paul, Deptford, England, in 1786. On 13 March that year at Maidstone, Kent, charged with the theft of some £12 from a dwelling house, he was sentenced to transportation for seven years and sent to the hulk *Ceres*. He embarked on 6 January 1787 in the *Alexander*, which reached Botany Bay with the First Fleet on 19 January next year. Popularly known as 'Black Caesar', he became known in the colony as a hard worker and a conscientious labourer.

Nevertheless, on 29 April 1789 he was once more tried for theft at the Criminal Court and sentenced to a second term of transportation, this time for life. Fourteen days later he stole arms and escaped into the bush, only to be apprehended on 6 June and sent to work in chains at Garden Island. David Collins [q.v.1] declared him at this time to be:

Incorrigibly stubborn ... his frame was muscular and well calculated for hard labour; but in his intellects he did not very widely differ from a brute; his appetite was ravenous, for he could in any one day devour the full ration for two days ... He declared while in confinement, that if he should be hanged, he would create a laugh before he was turned off, by playing off some trick upon the executioner.

Later allowed to work without chains, on 22 December Caesar escaped in a stolen canoe, again taking a gun. His efforts to survive in the bush—by robbing settlers' gardens, threatening encamped Aborigines and taking their food—were fruitless, and on 31 January 1790 he returned to camp, having been speared by local Aborigines.

On 4 March Governor Phillip [q.v.2] sent Caesar in the *Supply* to Norfolk Island. There he gained a measure of independence. By 1 July 1791 he was supporting himself on a lot at Queenborough and was issued with a hog. In January next year he was given one acre (0.4 ha) and ordered to work three days a week. His daughter by Ann(e) Power, a convict who had arrived in the *Lady Juliana* in 1790, was born on 4 March 1792. Caesar returned to Port Jackson in the *Kitty* twelve months later, leaving behind Ann (who died in 1796) and his daughter. He decamped in July 1794 but was soon back in custody. After severe punishment, he declared exultantly and with contempt (according to Collins): 'all that would not make him better'.

Late in 1795 he was with a party at Botany Bay that was attacked by Aboriginal warriors led by Pemulwuy [q.v.], whom Caesar wounded. The convict escaped from custody for the last time in December 1795 and led a gang of absconders and vagabonds in the Port Jackson area—becoming Australia's first bushranger. Collins noted that 'every theft that was committed was ascribed to him'. Settlers were warned against supplying him with ammunition and on 29 January 1796 Governor Hunter [q.v.1] offered a reward of five gallons of spirits for his capture. On 15 February Caesar was shot by John Wimbow at Liberty Plains (Strathfield) and died after being carried to Thomas Rose's hut. Caesar's daughter, baptized as Mary Ann Fisher Power in 1806, went to Van Diemen's Land in 1813.

D. Collins, *An Account of the English Colony in New South Wales* (Lond, 1798-1802); M. Gillen, *The Founders of Australia* (Syd, 1989); *History Today*, Feb 1987, p 44; *Sun* (Syd), 5 Apr 1978, p 49.

MOLLIE GILLEN
CHRIS CUNNEEN

CAHILL, ELLEN (c.1863-1934), street singer, familiar to a generation of Melburnians as 'Killarney Kate', was born at Castlecomer, Kilkenny, Ireland, probably the daughter of a Patrick Cahill. She came to Melbourne in the early 1870s with her parents, who ran a hotel in Lonsdale Street. Though she was described by Alan Marshall in 1952 as 'once better known in Melbourne than Flinders Street Station', only a sketchy outline of her life can be extracted from obituaries embroidered by rumour, the stark record of her petty criminal career, and the nostalgic memories of those who encountered her in their youth.

Said to have trained in Ireland as a singer, young Ellen sang at charity concerts in Melbourne and at her parents' hotel. An unhappy romance was presumed to be the cause of her later street career, and she was known at least by the 1910s as a perambulating singer. Her repertoire featured Irish ballads—her favourite, *Killarney's Lakes*, provided her sobriquet. She often sang on trams, had an unofficial free tram pass and was known to stand in the middle of the tramlines and not budge until she had finished her song. Her city pitches included the Town Hall corner, the *Argus* building in La Trobe Street, Queen Victoria Market and the Homoeopathic Hospital, where she would perform from the gardens for patients on the verandahs.

Cahill was renowned for her beautiful singing voice and, though well spoken, her coarse language, which could often offend. Seemingly a poor and pathetic figure with a blackthorn stick, purple hat and a passion for horse racing, she was reputed either to have been comfortably off or to depend on the charity of Melbourne's Irish Catholic establishment. She took a prominent part in Irish demonstrations and festivities, including St Patrick's Day parades.

Her petty criminal record spanned almost two decades, from her first conviction in 1909 for stealing from a Collins Street residence, where she had been employed as a domestic servant, to regular sentences for having insufficient means of support, offensive behaviour and drunkenness. Prison registers reported her as: single, in domestic service, born in Ireland, arrived in Australia in the ship *Markara*, 5 ft 6 ins (168 cm) tall, over the years her hair turning from brown to grey, her complexion from fresh to sallow.

Cahill's persistent presence in the city streets could be both an affront to middle-class respectability and a challenge to homogeneous notions of public space, as well as a source of amusement, comfort and public entertainment. She died of myocarditis on 3 January 1934 in Melbourne and was buried with Catholic rites following a procession of some three hundred people from the (Royal) Melbourne Hospital to Fawkner cemetery. To avoid a pauper's burial, the funeral was arranged by a prominent theatrical personality. A rare image of 'Killarney Kate', with portraits of contemporaneous street personalities including 'Starlight', 'Anzac' and 'Bible Jo', is included in a State Library of Victoria collection of photographs of 1920s and 1930s street personalities.

B. Wannan (comp), *Australian Folklore* (Melb, 1970); J. Cranston, *The Melbourne Cable Trams 1885-1940* (Melb, 1988); *Argus*, 21 Nov 1923, p 10, 30 May 1952, 'supplement', p 8; *Herald* (Melb), 3 Jan 1934, p 4, 4 Jan 1934, p 4; *Age* (Melb), 4 Jan 1934, p 8; *Sun News-Pictorial*, 4 Jan 1934, p 11; VPRS 516, unit 13, p 225, prisoner record—Ellen Cahill, 7138 and VPRS 30/P, unit 1513, criminal case file, 274 (PRO, Vic).
ANDREW BROWN-MAY

CAHILL, TERESA GERTRUDE (1896-1979), confectioner and company director, was born on 26 January 1896 at Newtown, Sydney, third child of John Thomas Cahill, a draughtsman born at Parramatta, and his wife Jessie Frances, née Graf, from Victoria. After attending a Catholic school at Enmore, Teresa was employed as a clerk by George Witham, agent for Indian and Henderson motorcycles.

Her brother REGINALD HENRY (1890-1955) had been born on 7 November 1890 at Enmore. A motor mechanic, he enlisted in the Australian Imperial Force on 3 January 1916, was allotted to the 1st Mining Corps, Engineers, as a sapper and was wounded in action in France. Later he served with the Australian Motor Transport Service in England. Corporal Cahill returned to Australia in November 1917 and was discharged medically unfit on 19 February 1918.

About 1919 Teresa travelled to the United States of America and obtained a position as an advertising manager for the Peerless Motor Co. at Los Angeles. Within months she was promoted superintendent of the tuning and testing section. During her three-year stay at Los Angeles she took confectionery classes at night. Though she hoped to open her own motor business back in Australia, insufficient funds stopped her from realizing her dream. She had enough, however, to invest with her brother in a small sundae and confectionery shop, which opened in Pitt Street, Sydney, in 1922. This was the beginning of a successful business partnership.

Reg managed the production of confectionery; Teresa was responsible for marketing. By 1927 they had formed a company, Cahills Holdings, controlling a factory at Alexandria and five shops in the city to retail their products. Other confectionery outlets followed in Melbourne, Adelaide and Brisbane, including refreshment concessions in new theatres. With an eye for selling and a deft hand in decoration, Teresa influenced retail expansion. Opened at 51 Castlereagh Street in 1933, the Italian Coffee Shop was criticized by the *Australasian Confectioner*: 'it would be difficult to conceive of anything less attractive as a shop name to the average Sydneysider'. In 1937, with shops and restaurants established in the city and suburbs, they opened their most ambitious venture. Taking up four floors in Pitt Street, with a refrigeration and air-conditioning unit in the basement, the building had a ground floor café with a soda fountain, a high-class restaurant on the first floor and a banqueting or dance room on the second.

On 4 October 1928 at St Mary's Cathedral, Sydney, Reg married Mary Florence Hickey; his brother Cyril, a Redemptorist priest, officiated. Teresa had a practical approach to the business; aunts who lived with her at Centennial Park were employed to run cash registers at the restaurants. Reg was kept busy with the interstate ventures and a refrigeration enterprise, and worked in the business until he died of cerebral thrombosis, on 12 September 1955. In 1961 the company listed on the Sydney Stock Exchange as Cahills' Holdings Ltd. Teresa and two of Reg's children were among the directors, with Edgar

Swain chairman. At their peak there were twenty-five themed restaurants, 'tricked out in gewgaws from the South Sea Islands, or Holland, or Tudor England', or African 'Safariland' or Bavaria.

The family remained on the board until Nestlé Australia Ltd bought a controlling interest in 1970; the multinational corporation made a complete takeover in 1977. Though Nestlé announced plans for expansion, the restaurants never regained their former glory.

Described as 'a fantastic woman' by former staff, Miss Cahill oversaw a special service to patrons. Still she had time to indulge her other interest: motoring. Her first car was a powerful, six-cylinder Chrysler, which she drove around the city in the 1920s. She was said to have driven one of the first electric model motorcycles in Sydney. In her garage she had Buicks and Packards, although her favourites were Daimlers. She was, as well, an avid reader.

A devout Catholic and charity worker, Teresa raised money for the missions, and helped to spread the teachings of the Church especially after the second Vatican Council. By the 1960s she lived at Darling Point. She died on 9 September 1979 at the Sacred Heart hospice, Darlinghurst, and was buried in the Catholic section of Waverley cemetery. The restaurants that Teresa and Reginald established were part of Sydney's social scene for over forty years—'for romantic trysts, family gatherings and girls' nights out'. They were also good places for women dining alone. Cahills' restaurants were known for ice-cream cakes and waffles, but the fondest memories were for their caramel sauce—which could be purchased in waxed paper tubs to take home.

Smith's Weekly, 5 Sept 1925, p 16; *A'asian Confectioner*, 24 Sept 1925, p 90, 24 Aug 1927, p 58, 24 July 1928, p 85, 23 Feb 1929, p 82, 22 Apr 1933, p 64, 24 Mar 1937, p 17; *Catholic Weekly* (Syd), 7 Oct 1979, p 22; *SMH*, 6 Sept 1961, p 20, 11 Dec 1970, p 19, 22 Sept 1971, p 3, 14 Feb 1983, p 16, 23 July 2001, p 12.   KERRY REGAN

CALYUTE, (*fl.*1833-1840), Aboriginal resistance leader, also known as Kalyute, Galyute or Wongir, was a man of the Pinjareb group, then known as the Murray River tribe, about 60 miles (100 km) south of Perth. Nothing is known of him before 1833. His brothers Woodan (also known as Jungil) and Yanmar are recorded and he had at least two wives, Mindup and Yamup, and two sons Ninia and Monang.

In December 1833 a dispute between the Murray people and those of the Swan River district was resolved at a corroboree that restored to the former a right of access for ceremonies and kinship visits. These visits, beginning in February 1834, led to conflict with British settlers when the visiting Aborigines' dogs killed stock. In one stand-off, a soldier held a musket to the tall, imposing Calyute's side while the latter's spear was pressed to the soldier's chest. Such incidents renewed the rift between the Aborigines of the two regions, forcing a duel between Calyute and a Swan River man Yaloot in which both were wounded.

On 24 April 1834 some twenty to thirty Murray men and women, led by Calyute, besieged a flour mill within sight of Perth, threatened the miller George Shenton [q.v.2], and stole a large quantity of flour. Swan River men identified Calyute, Yedong, Monang, Wamba and Gummol as the leaders of the raid, the reasons for which are unknown. Although Calyute's territory fell partially within the 250 000 acres (101 000 ha) granted to entrepreneur Thomas Peel [q.v.], the traditional owners had not yet been physically dispossessed by settlers and their stock, and were able to hunt, gather and fish with little interference.

Several days later, Captain T. T. Ellis, the superintendent of the mounted police, and a detachment of troopers captured Calyute, Yedong and Monang. During the struggle Calyute was bayoneted and the others wounded by gunfire. They were taken to Perth where, despite their injuries, they were flogged in the main street, Calyute receiving sixty lashes. As the raiders' ringleader, he was confined at Fremantle prison until 10 June 1834. His organization of Aboriginal resistance to white settlers, however, continued.

Next month he, Yedong and seventeen others killed Private Hugh Nesbitt and wounded a former sergeant, Edward Barron, in an ambush at Peel's property in the Murray district. Settlers' concerns at the increase in hostilities in the region led to the decision by the governor Sir James Stirling [q.v.2] to punish Calyute's clan. With the surveyor-general J. S. Roe [q.v.2], Stirling assembled an armed party of twenty-five, including soldiers of the 21st Regiment, mounted police and civilians, at Mandurah on 27 October. Next morning, at about 8 a.m., the Murray camp—with an estimated eighty men, women and children—was found on the west bank of the Murray River, south of the present town of Pinjarra. Stirling and fourteen others lined the east bank. Armed men commanded the fords above and below the position. Ellis, Captain Norcott and three troopers rode into the camp looking for the wanted men. In the *melée* that followed at least five Aborigines were killed and the others—men, women and children—retreated to the river, then about 100 ft (30 m) wide, with sloping wooded banks, where they came under gunfire. In the 'Battle of Pinjarra', a soldier was speared in the arm and Ellis was mortally injured; he died on 11 November. The Aboriginal dead were never counted and estimates vary between eleven and fifty. The official report by Stirling put the toll at fourteen. Calyute and Yedong escaped, but Calyute's son Ninia was killed and his younger wife Yamup, her leg shattered by a shot, died soon after.

The survivors retreated south-west to Lake Clifton. Calyute's name did not appear on the census conducted by Francis Armstrong in 1837, but was recorded again in May 1840 when, with others from the Murray, he attacked an Aboriginal camp near Perth, spearing five people. Yedong was accidentally shot at the Murray in 1838 but there is no record of Calyute after 1840 or of his death, although he reputedly survived into old age.

H. Bunbury, *Early Days in Western Australia* (Lond, 1930); A. Hasluck, *Thomas Peel of Swan River* (Melb, 1965); R. Richards, *The Murray District of Western Australia* (Mandurah, WA, 1978); N. Green, *Broken Spears* (Perth, 1984); S. Hallam and L. Tilbrook (comps), *Aborigines of the Southwest Region 1829-1840* (Perth, 1990); F. Armstrong census, CRS 58.158-163/1836, and J. S. Roe, Field book no 3, 1834-1839, Acc 629/2, and Despatches to Colonial Office, Sir J. Stirling to E. G. Stanley, 1 Nov 1834, 14 Sept-6 Dec 1938, letter no 14(SRWA).

NEVILLE GREEN

CAMERON, ALEXANDER (1810-1881), overlander and pastoralist, was born on 18 August 1810 at Lochaber, Inverness-shire, Scotland, fourth of nine children of John Cameron, sawmiller, and his wife Margaret, née Fraser. Alexander attended school at Inverroy, near Ben Nevis, and worked as a shepherd before obtaining an assisted passage in the *Boyne* to Sydney. The healthy, literate, six feet (183 cm) tall, Highland Catholic stepped ashore on 2 January 1839 with 101 other enterprising Camerons. He immediately embarked on an epic, clan trek organized by his uncles—droving sheep to Port Phillip, following the wheel-ruts of (Sir) Thomas Mitchell's [q.v.2] wagons three years earlier. One uncle, Duncan Cameron (1800-1860), settled on the Glenroy run, now a Melbourne suburb, while another, Alexander 'Black Sandy' Cameron (1791-1858), advanced into Australia Felix to pioneer Mount Sturgeon Plains, near Dunkeld.

On 27 June 1843 Cameron married Margaret MacKillop in St Francis's Catholic Church, Melbourne. They were to have ten children. He continued to overland his sheep westwards to new pastures in South Australia where he was the first to apply, on 19 December 1845, for the forty-eight square-mile (18.53-km²) occupation licence surrounding the future site of Penola. This frontier venture, subsequently in partnership with his uncle 'Black Sandy', prospered, as did a lucrative sideline—shipping remounts to the Indian cavalry, prepared by a local horsebreaker and poet Adam Lindsay Gordon [q.v.4], who 'received the greatest kindness' from Cameron while recovering from a violent kick to the groin.

Having built the original Royal Oak Hotel by 1848, Cameron encouraged his station tradesmen to establish their own businesses by purchasing eighty acres (32 ha) freehold on 4 April 1850, which he subdivided to found the private township of Penola. In 1852 he initiated the Penola races, renowned for their Highland balls, and would drive through the township to the racecourse, once 'with a piper in full blast and ribbons flying' to the great astonishment and excitement of his nostalgic kinsmen. Full-bearded, handsome and commanding in stature, but with a curiously falsetto voice and a strong Highland accent, he was remembered as 'a sterling fellow ... like the Highland chief both in person and hospitality'.

The Camerons' 18-year-old niece Mary MacKillop [q.v.5] joined the growing family as governess in 1860. In 1863 Cameron's wife Margaret died, as did his eldest daughter in childbirth. Selling Penola station next year, he expanded his pastoral holdings on Mount Sturgeon Plains, in Victoria, and at Avoca Forest, near St Arnaud. On 14 February 1867 at Duck Ponds, Geelong, with Catholic rites, he married 23-year-old Ellen Keogh; they lived in Melbourne at Moreland Hall, Coburg. Cameron died there on 2 September 1881 and was buried in Melbourne general cemetery. His wife, their three daughters and four of their five sons, and one son and five daughters of his first marriage survived him. He left a net estate of £72 000 that included over 22 000 freehold acres (9000 ha) and 53 000 sheep. Known to his contemporaries as 'King' Cameron, he has been commemorated as the founder of Penola by a life-sized bronze statue by John Dowie, erected by public subscription in the main street beside his Royal Oak Hotel.

R. Cockburn, *Pastoral Pioneers of South Australia*, 1 (Adel, 1925); V. Feehan, *Alexander Cameron— King of Penola—A Biographical Sketch* (Melb, 1980); P. Rymill, *The Founders* (Penola, SA, 1995); W. Milne, Notes of a Journey from Adelaide to South Eastern District of SA, January 1863 (ms, SLSA).

PETER RYMILL

CAMERON, ELIZABETH (BESSY) (c.1851-1895), Aboriginal teacher, was born at King Georges Sound, Western Australia, second of four children of a Nyungar couple, John and Mary Flower, who worked for the government resident Henry Camfield and his wife Anne.

The Flowers allowed their children to be raised in a Church of England home and school, Annesfield, run by Anne Camfield at Albany. Bessy became devoted to the Camfields and acquired a love of music and reading. When aged about 13, she was awarded a certificate of proficiency. In 1864-65 she attended a Church of England model school in Sydney, where pupils learned English, history, geography and arithmetic, took optional subjects such as drawing, music and dancing, and were trained as teachers. She also learned to play chess. In 1866 she returned to Albany to become Camfield's assistant and also organist at St John's Church.

Next year Bessy accepted an offer to be the teacher at Ramahyuck mission station in Gippsland, Victoria, for two years. However, the Moravian superintendent Rev. F. A. Hagenauer [q.v.4] was more intent on securing her and four other Annesfield girls as wives for his converts. Shy, anxious and homesick, Bessy tried to please but found Ramahyuck's regime austere and Hagenauer a demanding and autocratic taskmaster. On 4 November 1868 at the chapel at Ramahyuck, aged 17, she married with both Presbyterian and indigenous forms Adolph Donald Cameron, a young 'half-caste' man from Wimmera.

Bessy was replaced by a male teacher. She and Donald were given the responsibility of managing the mission's boarding school and she began to bear and raise her eight children. She also gave religious instruction and accompanied church services but soon found her domestic roles onerous and unrewarding. In 1872 the Camerons resigned but continued living on the mission where they were relatively secure and well off.

Over the next few years Bessy, increasingly bored by her domestic tasks, lost confidence and became depressed. Two of her children died, as did her younger sister Ada. The missionaries rebuked Bessy for neglecting her housework and failing to be a role model for other Aborigines. Donald became Hagenauer's overseer before he, too, erred by having an adulterous relationship. Bessy sought to leave Ramahyuck but Hagenauer opposed her keeping custody of her children.

In 1882 she and Donald were reconciled, but they no longer wished to live on a mission station and their relations with Hagenauer broke down again. They also clashed with the Victorian Board for the Protection of Aborigines as Bessy sought permission for moves between Gippsland and the Western District and a return to a mission station. After draconian legislation was passed in 1886, which required 'able-bodied half-castes' to leave the stations, she and Donald were forced into the settler community, where they encountered racism and struggled to get work. Although they were allowed to return to Ramahyuck, two of their daughters were forcibly indentured as domestic servants, became pregnant and had illegitimate children.

From 1892 the Camerons were separated for long periods. Bessy lived at Ramahyuck from time to time, trying to help her children and other Aboriginal women to keep their families together. They sought the assistance of the Aborigines' Board at the same time as they resisted its attempts to remove their children. In this struggle for survival, Bessy manipulated government authorities as best she could but fell foul of Hagenauer, now the board's secretary. These events took a mounting physical and psychological toll. She died of peritonitis on 14 January 1895 at Bairnsdale and was buried in the cemetery there. Her husband, three daughters and two sons survived her.

National Assn in Aid of the Moravian Mission to the Aborigines of Australia, *Facts Relating to the Moravian Mission* (Melb, 1860-67); B. Attwood, *The Making of the Aborigines* (Syd, 1989), *and* '"In the Name of all My Coloured Brethren and Sisters ...": A Biography of Bessy Cameron', *Hecate*, 12, nos 1-2, 1986, p 9.   BAIN ATTWOOD

CAMERON, ROBERT GEORGE (1886-1960), educationist, was born on 26 September 1886 at Macdonaldtown, Sydney, eldest child of Scottish-born parents George Cameron, bootmaker, and his wife Jessie Peter, née Forbes. Robert was admitted to Teachers' College in 1906 and, after four years as a pupil-teacher and three in public secondary schools, joined the staff of Teachers' College in 1912 under Alexander Mackie [q.v.10]. On 10 April that year at St Stephen's Anglican Church, Newtown, Cameron married Stella Howe, a milliner.

In 1908 Cameron had matriculated to the University of Sydney (B.A. 1912; M.A. 1917) where he was an evening student and from 1917 an evening lecturer. His understanding of modern educational theory was fortified by a visit to Europe in 1923. He specialized in rural education and was an early advocate of psychological testing of intelligence.

When the University of Western Australia sought an appointee to the joint position of foundation professor of education and principal of the established Teachers' Training College at Claremont in 1927, Cameron applied. Vice-chancellor Hubert Whitfeld telegraphed Professor G. A. Wood [qq.v.12]: 'Can you inform whether applicant is a scholar and a man of university spirit?' In reply, Wood described a 'man of enthusiasm energy excellent administrator organiser speaker', but added, 'his scholarship and culture seem rather limited and specialised'. Cameron was appointed, in the process separating from his wife, who was later confined to an asylum and whom he subsequently divorced.

To many, Cameron seemed 'a breath of fresh air in Western Australian education', who 'opened up the awareness ... that there was a world of educational thought beyond Rottnest Island'. His pugnaciously modern-minded zeal found critics, including his deputy T. J. Milligan, a union stalwart. The old guard fought unavailingly Cameron's creation of a graduate diploma of education at the University of Western Australia in 1929. His future clouded when the State government closed the Teachers' College as an economy measure in 1931, but skilful lobbying ensured State funding to permit his retention as professor on a reduced salary. In 1933 the Carnegie Corporation invited him to visit the United States of America. The college reopened in 1934. When it was taken over by the armed forces in 1942-45, its operations moved to the university campus. Here Cameron remained as full-time professor of education, although in 1945 another principal was appointed when the college moved back to Claremont.

Square-jawed and personable, and in later life rubicund, Cameron became well known in Perth as a freemason and Rotarian, and in 1934 founded the Twenty Club, a dining and discussion group linking town and gown, still active in 2005. In demand as a public speaker and broadcaster, he was disappointed not to become Western Australia's first representative on the Australian Broadcasting Commission. After 1945 he concentrated on administration, serving as dean of arts in 1945-47 and foundation dean of the education faculty established in 1950. He oversaw the introduction of physical education in 1952 and after extended tenure retired in June 1954. On 30 April 1947 in Perth he had married with Methodist forms Catherine Wallace Miller Small, principal of St Hilda's Anglican School for Girls. Cameron died on 4 September 1960 in hospital in Perth and was cremated. His wife survived him. The faculty of education at the university holds a portrait of Cameron by Ella Fry.

F. Alexander, *Campus at Crawley* (Melb, 1963); G. Bolton and G. Byrne, *The Campus that Never Stood Still* (Perth, 2002); *West Australian*, 5 Sept 1960, p 12; Cameron personal file (Univ WA Archives); personal information.   G. C. BOLTON

CAMPBELL, CHARLES (1840-1905), merchant and pastoralist, was born on 14 January 1840 at Aberdeen, Scotland, son of Duncan Campbell, cattle driver, and his wife Catherine, née McLean. Charles migrated to the Victorian goldfields in 1858, working at Woodend as agent for a firm of carriers before moving to New Zealand, where he became a successful flour-miller at Dunedin. Returning to Melbourne in the late 1860s he entered the lime business, and prospered. On 5 June 1861 in Wesley Church, Lonsdale Street, Melbourne, he had married Mary Ellen Smith, who had been born at Berwick-upon-Tweed, England. They were to have four sons and six daughters.

In 1872 Campbell was approached by the farrier James Cuming [q.v.8], an Aberdonian friend of his youth, to join in buying an acid works at Yarraville formerly managed by Cuming's brother-in-law George Smith. Campbell put up £3300 of the £4000 required, and as senior partner of Cuming, Smith & Co. led the new firm's diversification into fertilizers in 1875. In 1872 he had skilfully negotiated agreements to protect the market when customers Alfred Felton and F. S. Grimwade [qq.v.4], wholesale druggists, built an acid works in competition; later Campbell and Cuming worked with Felton and Grimwade setting up an acid works in New Zealand (which Smith ran from 1880) and forming in 1882 the Adelaide Chemical Works Co. Excellent managers, the partners reinvested profits, eschewed speculation and easily survived the 1890s depression. By 1897, when Felton Grimwade merged their acid works in a reconstructed Cuming, Smith & Co., the firms were a major force in Australia's chemical and fertilizer industries.

Campbell was also a founder of the successful Apollo Stearine Candle Co, and in 1888 joined Grimwade in founding the Royal Bank, the only Melbourne bank not to suspend payments in 1893. With James Service [q.v.6], C. E. Miller and others he established the Port Melbourne Sugar Co., which later merged with Colonial Sugar Refining Co., a major survivor when the sugar boom faltered. Becoming, like many Melbourne merchants, a pastoralist, he invested in the Malvern Hills Pastoral Co. of Queensland, and in 1884 formed an equal partnership with Felton to purchase Murray Downs, a station of some 97 000 acres (39 255 ha) near Swan Hill. The partners spent heavily on improvements, spreading much superphosphate—presumably of their own manufacture—and establishing the largest irrigated area of the time on the Murray. In 1889 the station sent 327 bales of wool down river to the railhead at Echuca, but wool prices fell in the 1890s and drought was a recurrent problem. Campbell helped to set up the Pastoralists' Association of Victoria and Southern Riverina, became its treasurer, and was thanked by its council for services (unspecified) during the great strike of 1891.

In 1885 Campbell had joined Felton in supporting Rev. Charles Strong [q.v.6], the charismatic preacher expelled from Scots Church, encouraging him to found another. Described by Felton as 'the ablest practical head that the confraternity can claim', Campbell helped to build Strong's new Australian Church, and in 1897 was one of four 'proprietors' who cleared the building of debt and rented it back to the Church. By then he had joined Scots Church, where a window was later installed in his memory.

In maturity Campbell was bearded, bald and genial, but keen-eyed; Felton always admired his 'stubborn strength'. His family was established in Wollahra, a mansion in East Melbourne, but spent much time at Murray Downs; one daughter married the station manager and in 1895 his son Alec drowned there, on his twenty-first birthday, a few months after the death of Cameron's eldest daughter.

In 1897 Campbell and Felton bought, for £85 300, another large property, Langi Kal Kal, near Beaufort. When Felton died in January 1904, Campbell bought out his share in both stations. Campbell died of pneumonia on 13 September 1905 at Wollahra. He was buried in Boroondara cemetery, Kew; in its obituary, the *Pastoralists' Review* called him 'one of the ablest business men in Melbourne'. His estate, sworn for probate at £233 000 in Victoria, £115 672 in New South Wales and £24 080 in South Australia, was left in trust for his widow, surviving children and grandchildren.

A. Croft, *History of Murray Downs Station* (Swan Hill, Vic, 1965); J. R. Poynter, *Russell Grimwade* (Melb, 1967) and *Mr Felton's Bequests* (Melb, 2003); *James Cuming: An Autobiography*, edited by J. Lack after M. A. Cuming (Melb, 1987); J. Lack, *A History of Footscray* (Melb, 1991); *Pastoralists' Review*, 16 Oct 1905, p 627; *Argus*, 14 Sept 1905, p 5; *Australasian*, 16 Sept 1905; Felton Grimwade papers and Cuming Smith papers (Melb Univ Archives); Felton Bequest papers (LaTL).   J. R. POYNTER

CAMPBELL, JOHN WILLIAM WALLACE (1906-1979), refrigeration mechanic and anti-Catholic journalist, was born on 27 November 1906 at Johannesburg, South Africa, son of John William Wallace Campbell, an Australian labourer who had served in the South African War, and his wife Antonette Cholette, née Bleckmann. 'Wal' came to Australia with his mother and siblings as an infant, and was christened in the Presbyterian Church. He was a telegram delivery boy, drover and shearer before becoming a refrigeration mechanic. When he enlisted in the Australian Imperial Force on 31 May 1940 he was 5ft 10½ ins (179 cm) tall, with blue eyes, fair complexion and fair hair. After serving in the Middle East and Papua with the 2nd/4th Field

Company, Royal Australian Engineers, he was invalided home in August 1943 with malaria. Sergeant Campbell was discharged on 23 October 1945.

Meanwhile, he had been set on his life's mission when he observed a man signalling from a monastery window in Syria, which he took to be Syrian Catholic priests betraying the Allied forces. Unable to convince the army of Catholic 'fifth column' activities, Campbell collected a portfolio of material, including observations in New Guinea, which he thought to have his brother William, a printer, publish. Instead, absorbing the more spectacular approach of American wartime papers, he cashed in his deferred pay and in January 1945 turned the book project into a 'brash eight page tabloid', the *Rock*.

The weekly publication appealed to the Protestant political lobby after the war. Recognizing 'no censor but the truth', Campbell mixed traditional anti-Catholic polemics with sensationalist stories of corruption, convent sex-scandals and political intrigue in the Catholic hierarchy. After his relationship with his brother dissolved in 1948 in a bitter libel case, Campbell lifted circulation to some 30 000 in the 1950s, although the number of effective subscribers was much less—perhaps 1000. Running little advertising and supported by an ageing donor base, the paper was always marginal. He blamed later declining circulation on apathy and indifference among Protestants. He also ran a printery that specialized in anti-Catholic tracts, posters, handbills and books.

The *Rock* had its last hurrah during the debates over public funding of private schools and 'the Split' in the Australian Labor Party. When Pope John Paul I died in 1978, Campbell was not alone in assuming a conspiracy. In later years there was talk of his declining mental state (evidenced by his arrest in 1978 after a fracas at Royal Prince Alfred Hospital, Sydney). It is a matter of opinion, however, as to how much of this was mere ascription, due to his old-fashioned polemics seeming increasingly paranoid in a world which was redefining what was reasonable. Evicted from his rented, shopfront printery at Glebe in 1976, by the end of the 1970s he had moved to Calvert, Queensland, where he was provided with free accommodation and use of a press; the weekly became a monthly.

Campbell was easy to dismiss as a mere crank or as the essence of intolerance. Those close to him described him as a 'tender hearted and compassionate man ... motivated by a burning hatred of injustice, [and] cruelty and [by] a love for the liberty and freedom of the Gospel of Christ'. A lifelong smoker, he died on 4 July 1979 at Grandchester, Queensland, and was cremated with the forms of the Reformed Presbyterian Church. He was unmarried; a sister survived him. The *Rock* was left to slow extinction, in 1995.

M. C. Hogan, *The Catholic Campaign for State Aid* (Syd, 1978) and *The Sectarian Strand* (Melb, 1987); D. C. Shelton (ed), *The Campbell File* (Syd, 1981); *People*, 21 Nov 1951, p 36; *SMH*, 12 July 1979, p 8, 27 Aug 1982, p 7.   MARK HUTCHINSON

CAMPBELL, JOSEPH (1856-1933), clergyman and scientist, was born on 13 September 1856 at St Marys, New South Wales, second son of London-born parents William Branch Campbell, storekeeper, and his wife Elizabeth Anne, née Jackson. The family lived at Lane Cove, near Sydney, and Joseph was educated at a private school and by a tutor. After several years as a schoolteacher on a family property near Prospect, he matriculated in 1877. He studied mathematics, natural science and divinity at the University of Sydney (B.A., 1880; M.A., 1882), gaining the Belmore [q.v.3] scholarship for geology and agricultural chemistry. On 7 January 1882 at St Michael's Church, Surry Hills, Campbell married Eliza Marian Holt. Of independent means, she was the daughter of the late William Holt and a medallist in French at the junior and senior public examinations. During the leave of John Smith [q.v.6] in 1882-83, Campbell was acting professor of experimental physics.

From a Presbyterian background, Campbell was made a Church of England deacon in December 1880 and ordained priest on 21 June 1882. A fine preacher, he served in Sydney (1881-83), at rural Glen Innes (1883-86) and, in Sydney again, at Randwick (1889-90) and Coogee (1890-97). His wife's financial support enabled Campbell to undertake scientific and technical activities independent of his clerical stipend, and his church employment was interspersed with periods of leave when he travelled and experimented with the treatment of ores.

Beginning in 1876 Campbell wrote a number of booklets covering geography, practical photography, religion and science. First published in 1885, his *Simple Tests for Minerals, or Everyman his own Analyst* ran to four editions and numerous reprints until 1936; 'Campbell's Prospector's Box', to carry out the tests, accompanied it. Appointed a commissioner for the Colonial and Indian Exhibition, London (1886), he and his family spent three years in Britain, where he preached. He was elected a fellow of the Geological Society of London, the Linnean Society of London and the Royal Institute of Chemistry. Back in Sydney, in 1893 he founded and became principal of St Nicolas's College, Randwick, for 'the proper training of mining experts', and published another successful booklet, *Gold, and how to get it* (1894). Following a visit to

England and North America, in 1897 the family moved to New Zealand, where Campbell held a general licence in the diocese of Auckland, while he managed a company attempting to treat refractory gold ores on Hauraki Peninsula. The work ceased in 1900 and, returning to church duties, he became vicar at St Paul's, Papanui.

Leaving New Zealand in 1903, Campbell was archdeacon and rector at Cairns, Queensland, from 1904 until 1909. In addition, he gave courses in mineralogy and mineral exploration and began active research on tropical agriculture. His wife had died in England in 1901. On 9 October 1909 at St Michael's Church, Sydney, giving his occupation as cotton planter, he married Ellen Kate Male, an 18-year-old typist from Cooktown, Queensland. Resigning his ministry, he travelled overseas to form a company to develop large-scale cotton farming, returning to Cairns in 1912. The war interfered with his cotton plans, however, and he turned to sugar cane, to paper production from pandanus and to the manufacture of native dyes, and opened a small laboratory and museum of science. In 1919, during a shipping strike and influenza epidemic, he converted his paper pulp machine to crush maize, producing much-needed flour for the district.

Campbell came back to Sydney in the 1920s and set up an advisory scientific bureau. A man of restless energy, he was perhaps by this time behaving somewhat eccentrically. From 1926, through his friend Bishop L. B. Radford [q.v.11], Campbell had a series of relieving positions in churches in southern New South Wales. He died on 17 October 1933 at Barmedman and was buried in the local cemetery with Anglican rites. His wife, their three children, and the two daughters from his first marriage survived him.

D. Jones, *Trinity Phoenix* (Cairns, Qld, 1976); D. F. Branagan, 'Then Look Not Coldly on Science. Joseph Campbell, M.A. Journeyman Cleric', Roy Soc NSW, *J and Procs*, 131, pts 1-2, 1998, p 19; *Aust Mining Standard*, 15 July 1897, p 2031, 26 Nov 1903, p 724; list of references to Campbell in the *Cairns Post* (Cairns L, Qld).   D. F. BRANAGAN

CANDLER, SAMUEL CURTIS (1827-1911), coroner, was born in October 1827 in Norfolk, England, son of Samuel Candler, miller, and his wife Harriet, née Datelle. Curtis began a medical education and became a licentiate of the Society of Apothecaries, but did not take his diploma because of ill health, instead migrating to Van Diemen's Land about 1850, then to the Victorian goldfields. While a digger at Avoca, Candler was a regular conservative contributor to the *Melbourne Morning Herald* on political subjects under the pseudonym 'Scrutator'. He secured a number of government appointments: coroner in Korong district (1853), district surgeon, public vaccinator (1855). In 1856 he stood unsuccessfully for the Loddon District in the first elections for the Legislative Assembly.

Next year Candler was appointed coroner for the County of Bourke. His duties took him across Melbourne's suburbs (although not the city), hearing inquests on a miserable catalogue of fatalities. Occasionally, inquests provoked larger questions—such as the adequacy of the diet in the colony's insane asylums and the detention and restraint of lunatics in the city's gaols. Candler took evidence on these matters, which were subsequently pursued at a parliamentary inquiry in 1860-61. In 1897 he succeeded to the post of city coroner, held for the previous forty years by his friend Richard Youl [q.v.6]. Youl and Candler exercised medical authority over inquests, a practice that would be replaced by legal expertise in the twentieth century. Although reluctant to comment on inquests outside his court, Candler published speculative essays, in the *Argus* and in book form, on matters relating to public health, including dysentery, measles and tuberculosis. He retired on 1 January 1908, one of the last of a generation of public servants who emigrated during the gold rushes and were influential in Australia throughout the nineteenth century.

Candler had joined the Melbourne Club in 1856. Its secretary in 1857-59, he lived there from 1857 to 1911 and bequeathed to it his copy of *The Memoirs of Casanova*. While enjoying the exclusively masculine surrounds of the club, he also took pleasure in the entertainments of wealthy Melbourne society. He was a founding member of the Yorick Club. His diaries reveal an avid gossip and prurient recorder of sexual innuendo and intrigue. On 19 May 1882 at Glebe Point, Sydney, Candler had married with Presbyterian forms Laura Ellen Kennedy, who had earlier given birth to four children: Laura Mary (b. and d.1872), George Curtis (1873), Laura Mabel (1875) and Alice Marian (1877). He did not acknowledge paternity, or his marriage, publicly.

Described as 'a man of unusual reserve' who 'lived within himself', Candler was exacting and austere in the execution of his duties. Yet, in private, he delighted in jokes and storytelling. Possessing an athletic bearing into old age, he took only a single meal each day. For rescuing a boy from the river Yarra he was awarded the Royal Humane Society medal. Candler died on 5 June 1911 in a Melbourne private hospital and was buried in Boroondara cemetery. The Melbourne Club, which was astonished to receive a letter from his widow in Rhodesia thanking it for its kindness to her husband, holds his portrait by J. C. Waite [q.v.6].

M. and B. Beavis, *Avoca* (Warrnambool, Vic, 1986); P. de Serville, *Pounds and Pedigrees* (Melb, 1991); P. Russell, *A Wish of Distinction* (Melb, 1994); *Australasian*, 29 Aug 1891, p 427, 10 June 1911, p 1487; *Argus* (Melb), 6 June 1911, p 7; *Herald* (Melb), 6 June 1911, p 8; C. Candler, Notes about Melbourne, and diaries (ms, VSL).

SIMON COOKE

CARPENTER, GEORGE LYNDON (1872-1948), Salvation Army general, and MINNIE LINDSAY (1873-1960), Salvationist author, were husband and wife. George was born on 20 June 1872 at Millers Forest, New South Wales, only son among six children of Tristan de Acunha Carpenter, a farmer born at sea *en route* to Sydney, and his wife Hannah, née Worboys, from England. George trained as a pupil-teacher, then became apprenticed to a printer on the *Gloucester Gazette* and by 1891 was a compositor on the *Blue Mountains Express* at Katoomba. From a Methodist family, with a Salvationist mother, he was a rebellious teenager but at 19 was converted. He entered the Salvation Army's training garrison in Melbourne in 1892.

Most of Carpenter's early work involved editing and publishing journals, such as the *War Cry*. In this work he met Minnie Lindsay Rowell, who had been born on 12 December 1873 at Bombira, near Mudgee, New South Wales, fifth child of Nicholas Rowell, a native-born farmer, and his wife Sarah, née Peters, from England. The family was Salvationist and after training in Melbourne in 1892, Minnie worked in Victoria and in Western Australia; by 1893 she commanded the Perth corps, with crowds of 1000 or more at her services. In 1896 she was transferred to the editorial staff in Melbourne. George and Minnie were married on 21 June 1899 in Melbourne by Herbert Booth [q.v.7].

George was involved in travelling evangelical groups and making the film *Soldiers of the Cross*. In addition to editing the *Young Soldier* and other papers, Minnie helped to found the League of Mercy and visited those in need, especially prisoners and hospital patients. Three children were born between 1901 and 1908. Their experience in editorial work led to the Carpenters' transfer in 1911 to London, where Minnie wrote the biographies of early Salvationist heroes, including *The Angel Adjutant* and a children's life of William Booth. In 1914 George, promoted colonel, became confidential literary secretary to General Bramwell Booth and the confidant of many Salvation Army leaders. He developed a wide circle of acquaintances but was never charged with partisanship.

By 1927 the ageing Bramwell Booth was causing anguish to many of his subordinates by his autocratic methods. Carpenter tried to help but his intervention was not welcomed and he found himself back in Australia, 'sent to the freezer' as editor of the Sydney *War Cry*. After Edward Higgins became general in 1929, Carpenter was again appointed to important leadership positions, including chief secretary in New South Wales and Queensland (1929) and territorial commander in South America East (1933), based in Buenos Aires, and in Canada (1937). In these appointments, both Carpenters established new ventures. George was vice-president of the High Council meeting held in London in 1934.

On 24 August 1939 he was elected international leader of the Salvation Army, although he had supported the election of a younger man. His term as fifth Salvationist general commenced on 31 October. World War II placed great demands on the leadership of a world-wide organization, but normal control was replaced by delegated authority. Carpenter relied on the local leadership, even in countries at war with Britain, and Salvationists the world over knew they could trust him. Although the leader's usual international visits were impossible, Carpenter worked hard from his headquarters in London to maintain contact, often through intermediaries in neutral countries. His facility with the pen proved its worth in his weekly bulletins in the *War Cry*, some later published in book form.

Each Christmas, Carpenter prepared a gift for Salvationists serving in the forces: books designed to fit into a battle dress pocket so as to be available for reading at all times. The first, *New Battlegrounds*, was adopted as a handbook for all Protestants in the United States of America's forces, with printings totalling one and a half million. Minnie exercised a pastoral ministry, and was world president of the Home League. One of her initiatives was a fellowship group for nurses. In addition she continued to write, publishing some sixteen books in all. The Carpenters revisited Australia in 1945.

In the aftermath of the war Carpenter began the work of reconstruction, particularly in shattered Europe. Because of the difficulties of assembling electors for the High Council, his term was extended until April 1946. Upon the appointment of his successor, he and his wife and daughter retired to Sydney, arriving in June. Carpenter died on 9 April 1948 at Earlwood. Following a Salvation Army service he was buried in Rookwood cemetery. Minnie Carpenter died on 23 November 1960 at Undercliffe, Sydney, and was also buried in Rookwood cemetery. The Carpenters' daughter and their son George, who became known as the teacher of the British prime minister Harold Wilson, survived them.

M. Richards, *One of the Gang* (Lond, 1955); A. J. Gilliard, *All the Days* (Lond, 195?); S. Carpenter, *A Man of Peace in a World at War* (Montville, Qld, 1993); *SMH*, 25 Aug 1939, p 12, 10 Apr 1948, p 3, 27 Mar 1976, p 19; *Smith's Weekly*, 9 Sept 1939, p 6; records held at Salvation Army Heritage Centre, Syd.

GEORGE HAZELL

CARROLL, THOMAS (1888-1968), mechanical engineer, was born on 12 April 1888 at Bullengarook, near Gisborne, Victoria, eldest of five children of Victorian-born parents Michael John Carroll, farmer, and his wife Mary Elizabeth, née Fitzgerald. Tom's education to eighth grade at the local state school was frequently interrupted. From about the age of 10 he drove the family's horse-drawn binder, and ran the steam engine and threshing machine whenever the visiting German contractor got drunk. Tom learned the fundamentals of blacksmithing from his father, picked up carpentry and bricklaying from local tradesmen, drove a sawmill traction engine, and became fascinated by mechanics while repairing neighbours' implements and machinery. Although he attended night school, and later took a two-year correspondence course in mechanical engineering from the United States of America, he remained essentially self-taught.

At the age of 16 Carroll began working for the Buckeye Harvester Co. in Melbourne, assisting farmers to set up their American binders and mowers. Supervising their tillage implement business acquainted him with foundry and moulding practices and machine shop operations. As an expert with J. Mitchell & Co.'s stripper harvesters from 1909, he soon encountered Massey-Harris of Toronto's reaper-thresher; it had been developed by Australians Matt H. East and J. S. Charlton employing the North American header principle in order to dodge the stiff tariff on imported copies of the Australian stripper-harvester. The Canadians' South American distributor engaged Carroll in 1911 to assemble and test run reaper-threshers for farmers in Argentina. Revelling in life on the pampas, and soon fluent in Spanish, he entered the direct employment of Massey-Harris in 1917, the year he married Thomasine Laidlaw of Toronto, Canada. She often travelled with him, and their life became virtually one continuous summer spent on the Argentine pampas, the Canadian prairies or the Australian plains. He estimated that in fifty years he experienced only four winters.

After Carroll's reaper-thresher took clear honours in the field trial at Bahia Bianca, Argentina, in the summer of 1919-20, he was appointed chief field engineer, and by 1924-25 his machine was harvesting extensively in North and South America. He was a good listener, ever alert to farmers' needs. In the

Argentine, Italian farmers were experimenting with self-propelled harvesters. The attempt of H. V. McKay [q.v.10] Pty Ltd to supply the Americas with Headlie Taylor's [q.v.12] brilliant but expensive auto-header from a plant at Waterloo, Ontario, failed spectacularly in the droughts and Depression of the early 1930s. When times improved, the initiative had passed to Massey-Harris, who gave Carroll the responsibility of developing a self-propelled combine. His successful No.20 of 1937 was followed three years after by a version light and cheap enough to command a wide market. The No.21 went into volume production in 1940, just in time to answer an acute wartime rural labour shortage. By 1955, when Carroll was promoted chief combine engineer for the Western Hemisphere, self-propelled machines were working grain fields across the globe, and in 1963 the company held the largest slice of a world combine market that had eluded the Australians.

In 1954 H. V. McKay's heirs sold their business to Massey-Harris, Headlie Taylor retired, and Tom Carroll came home to supervise over three seasons (1956-58) the design of a new self-propelled header for Australian conditions, the successful Massey-Ferguson 585. In 1958 he became the first non-American to be awarded the American Society of Agricultural Engineers' Cyrus Hall McCormick medal for his outstanding contribution to world agriculture.

Although he had become a Canadian citizen, Carroll always remained an Australian at heart. His wife died about 1954; they had no children. Carroll retired in 1962. He died after a short illness on 22 February 1968 in Bethlehem Private Hospital, Caulfield, Melbourne. After a requiem mass, he was buried in the family grave at Gisborne. In Australia and Canada, Massey-Ferguson and the press properly hailed him as the pioneer of modern harvesting, who had designed the 'world's first commercial self-propelled combine'.

M. Denison, *Harvest Triumphant* (Toronto, Canada, 1948); E. P. Neufeld, *A Global Corporation* (Toronto, Canada, 1969); G. R. Quick and W. F. Buchele, *The Grain Harvesters* (Michigan, USA, 1978); *Agricultural Engineering*, 29, no 3, Mar 1948, p 101; *Canadian Farm Implements*, Nov 1961, p 12; *Massey-Ferguson Review*, June 1964; J. Lack and C. Fahey, 'Harvester Wars: The Global Struggle between H. V. McKay, Massey-Harris and International Harvester', *Ontario Hist*, 96, no 1, 2004, p 9; *Family Herald* (Toronto, Canada) 16 Aug 1962; *Telegram* (Toronto, Canada), 16 Mar 1967; *Weekly Times*, 6 Mar 1968, p 6; T. Carroll papers in Massey-Ferguson collection (Univ of Guelph, Ontario, Canada); information from Mr T. Brown, Goderich, Ontario, Canada, Fr J. Carroll, Fern Tree Gully, Vic, Mrs J. Deany, Toorak, Melb, and the Gisborne and Mount Macedon Districts Historical Society.

JOHN LACK

CASHIN, ALICE ALANNA (1870-1939), army nurse, was born on 26 March 1870 at Londsdale Street, Melbourne, daughter of Richard Cashin, a boot and shoe manufacturer from Sydney, and his Melbourne-born, second wife Catherine, née Meehan, who died in 1871. By 1880, with Alice and her older half-brother, Richard had moved to Sydney, and that year he remarried; the family, which soon included two more daughters, lived at Redfern.

Educated at a 'ladies private college' in Sydney, Alice trained for three years from October 1893 at St Vincent's Hospital, Darlinghurst, and stayed on as a certificated nurse to January 1897, then entered private nursing. She lived at the nurses' home, Dowling Street, Moore Park, and on 30 July 1901 joined the Australasian Trained Nurses' Association. Nurse Cashin left Australia in 1909 for London, where she studied massage and obtained a diploma of the International School of Therapeutic Massage. She intended to return home in 1914 but in the early months of World War I nursed in the general hospital at Calais, France. As Alice Eleanor Cashin she joined Queen Alexandra's Imperial Military Nursing Service Reserve on 19 July 1915. She took charge of a large surgical ward in the general hospital at Ras-el-din in Egypt.

Twice mentioned in dispatches, including a special mention from Sir Archibald Murray, commander-in-chief of the Egyptian Expeditionary Force, in January 1917 Sister Cashin was awarded the Royal Red Cross. From June 1916 she was matron of the hospital ship *Gloucester Castle*, which was torpedoed without warning by a German U-boat in the English Channel on 30 March 1917. In her later account, now held by the Australian War Memorial, Canberra, she described how, having 'secured my crucifix, prayerbook and the cape that had been given me by Her Majesty Queen Alexandra', she had checked that all her sisters and the wounded were safe before she took to the boats. She was awarded a bar to the R.R.C., becoming the first Australian to receive this honour. A commendation noted that she 'showed an example of coolness & devotion to duty, and rendered invaluable service'. She also received the French Croix de Guerre. From 7 May 1917 Matron Cashin had charge of the 400-bed military hospital at Whittington barracks, Lichfield, England, where she was much loved by the patients. On leaving in July 1919 she was showered with daisies gathered by 'her boys'. She embarked to return to Australia in the *Morea* on 18 October.

Although Cashin was a much-decorated Australian nurse, because her service was with the Q.A.I.M.N.S. the details of her career were little known. Photographs of her displaying her medals, in uniform with a starched, matron's veil, showed a cheerful face, slightly hooded eyes and hair rolled up on her head. She described herself as 'a heavy woman'.

Back in Sydney, Cashin wrote 'The torpedoing of H.M.H.S. *Gloucester Castle*' for the *Australasian Nurses' Journal* (March 1920). She nursed her aged father, then worked as a saleswoman. Miss Cashin died of chronic nephritis on 4 November 1939 in her home at Marrickville and was buried in Woronora cemetery after a requiem mass at St Bridget's Catholic Church, Marrickville.

R. Goodman, *Our War Nurses* (Brisb, 1988); *Australasian Nurses' Journal*, 15 June 1917, p 226, Feb 1920, p 38; *Times* (Lond), 2 Jan 1917, p 2; 14 Apr 1917, p 6; 7 Sept 1918, p 4; *Freeman's J* (Syd), 9 Aug 1917, p 22, 15 May 1919, p 18; *SMH*, 28 Feb 1920, p 9; personal file, WO399/1386 (National Archives, London); MT1487/1, item CASHIN AE (NAA, Melb); A2489, item 1920/1515 (NAA, Canb); Australasian Trained Nurses' Association Register, 1907 (ML).

CHRIS CUNNEEN

CHINNER, JOHN HENRY (1865-1933), cartoonist and insurance manager, was born on 30 June 1865 at Brighton, Adelaide, son of George William Chinner, company manager, and his wife Mary, née Edwards. After attending Prince Alfred College, John undertook a course in life-drawing at the Adelaide School of Design under H. P. Gill [q.v.9]. Art was, however, a part-time career, and never his main source of income. He worked for some years with an Adelaide insurance agent and broker L. A. Jessop. In 1895 Chinner became manager of the Atlas Assurance Co., where he remained until retiring in 1925.

On 11 September 1889 he had married Harriet Agnes Wallace at the Wesleyan church, Parkside, where he was active all his life; they had five children. Chinner wrote several hymns and was a much-liked Sunday School superintendent. A genial, energetic man of average height, he often wore a flower in his buttonhole. He was a member of and office-holder in the Parkside Literary Society, won prizes for his short stories and regularly gave talks on a wide range of topics. From 1899 to 1902 he was a councillor for Fullarton Ward, Unley City Council, and was twice mayor of Unley. His favourite sport was lawn bowls, which he excelled at, representing South Australia several times.

Chinner's first paid position as a cartoonist was with the satirical weekly the *Lantern* in the late 1880s. By 1889 the rival journal *Quiz*, which became *Quiz and the Lantern* (1890-1900), had appointed him as its regular cartoonist. Soon his work approached the technical quality and creative standards of the English illustrator John Tenniel, an early influence, and 'Hop' [q.v.4 L. Hopkins]. For the next forty years Chinner worked for almost every major newspaper in Adelaide, the Sydney *Bulletin* and London *Punch*. At times he was producing one full-page cartoon and up to six caricatures a week for *Quiz*— no mean feat for a man with other, full-time employment.

The 1890s offered him plenty of raw material. With his nimble mind and ability to get to the nub of complicated issues quickly, Chinner provided a gently mocking commentary on South Australian politics. Many of his cartoons presupposed a degree of understanding of the classics, Shakespeare and English history. He drew for, and was of, the middle classes; his cartoons and caricatures were a distillation of middle-class South Australians' view of the world. During his years with *Quiz* and the *Critic* he provided weekly caricatures of well-known personalities in regular segments such as 'Round the Town' or 'Federationists'. In the 1920s he produced a long-running series, 'Notable Citizens', in *Saturday's Journal*, published by the *Register*. The caricatures provided a marvellous collection of character studies of Adelaide's leaders during the 1890s and 1920s and showed his keen political insight and wit as well as a controlled, meticulous line.

Chinner's work also appeared in church and bowling club publications; he illustrated several books, designed invitations for mayoral functions, created personal Christmas and greeting cards, painted water-colour landscapes and designed lead-light windows for Parkside church. He died of a coronary occlusion on 15 December 1933 at Parkside. His wife, two sons and two daughters survived him, inheriting an estate sworn for probate at £12 618. The Art Gallery of South Australia holds an indexed collection of 212 original printer's proofs of Chinner's 'Notable Citizens', also available in the South Australian Archives, and Unley Museum has two framed panels of his original caricatures.

H. T. Burgess (ed), *The Cyclopedia of South Australia*, 1 (Adel, 1907); M. Mahood, *The Loaded Line* (Melb, 1973); *Literary Societies' J* (SA), 10 Aug 1907; *A'sian Insurance and Banking Record*, 21 Feb 1925, p 157; *Unley Citizen*, 14 Sept 1906; *Register* (Adel), 29 Oct 1928, p 11; *Christian Commonwealth*, 25 Nov 1932; *Advertiser* (Adel), 16 Dec 1933, p 14; *Chronicle* (Adel), 21 Dec 1933, p 16.

ROB VAN DEN HOORN

CLAYTON, WILLIAM (1833-1933), sawyer, was born on 9 April 1833 at Manchester, England, son of Benjamin Clayton, a Catholic

hand-sawyer from Yorkshire, and his Protestant wife Ellen, née Jubb. Aged 7, William
began as an errand boy for a fishmonger at
one shilling a week plus his dinners; he then
assisted a pastry-cook before being employed
in a dye works. In 1844 his father was killed in
a log fall at work; his employer paid his funeral
expenses and gave the widow £1 a week for
three months, reducing to ten shillings a
week. At 11 William was taken on at a weaving
factory, working from 5.30 a.m. to 7 p.m. on
weekdays and from 7 until 4 on Saturdays. In
his memoirs, written seventy years later, he
spoke of the plight of even younger children
in the cotton and silk factories; the 5-year-old
chimney-sweeps were even worse off. At 15
Clayton was apprenticed to his father's former
employer, making packing cases and trunks.
He later recalled belonging to a union that
campaigned against Saturday afternoon work,
a strike in 1847 and the appearance of
Chartists at Manchester that decade.

At 16 Clayton thought of migrating to the
United States of America but became ill with
smallpox. On 26 June 1854 at Manchester he
married Mary Ann Court, a cotton-winder.
The disruption of the cotton trade during the
Crimean War caused them to seek an assisted
passage to Australia. Mary gave birth to twins
en route and the family reached Port Adelaide
in the *Grand Trianon* in March 1855. William
had earned £2 as a steward during the
voyage. Unable to find employment, his family destitute, Clayton accepted charity. Eventually he worked as a sawyer in Port Adelaide,
taking on extra labour filling railway trucks
until fatigue, heat and flies curtailed his
regime. In 1856, through a Manchester connexion, he accepted work at Gawler, cutting
timber for railway sleepers. Clayton's mobile
ways continued and he took to the road as a
sawyer and digger between Adelaide and
Mount Gambier and as far as the Snowy River,
New South Wales, before settling at Robe
about 1860 on an acre (0.4 ha) of land with a
two-roomed slab house and a four-roomed
storehouse.

In 1864 the couple, with four children, sold
up and returned to England. It was an unfortunate homecoming: he could not find
work in his old trade as case-maker. At a reunion at Selby, Yorkshire, family relationships
fell apart and all was soured. William and
Mary resolved to go back to Australia and the
emigration commissioners approved a second
assisted passage, with the proviso that it be
the last. The Claytons arrived in South Australia in the *Trevalyan* in March 1866 and
William was soon sawing at Victoria Creek,
sometimes working on his own account, still
tramping for employment. After a job in a
Melbourne hotel he based himself at Mount
Gambier, where he constructed telegraph
lines and worked for Adam Lindsay Gordon

[q.v.4]. The peripatetic sawyer never accumulated savings. His wife died in 1912.

At 80 Clayton penned his remarkable
memoirs in semi-literate prose. Held in the
Mortlock Library, Adelaide, they cover in
vivid and candid detail the career of a working
man from the 1840s to the Depression of 1929
and provide documentation of life in the for-
mative years of colonial development. Clayton
died on 13 August 1933 at Glen Osmond.
Three daughters survived him.

Eric Richards, 'Immigrant Lives, 1836-1986' in
E. Richards (ed), *The Flinders History of South
Australia: Social History* (Adel, 1986); *Advertiser*
(Adel), 14 Aug 1933, p 10.   ERIC RICHARDS

CLEMENT, MARGARET (1881-1952?),
missing person, was born on 8 March 1881 at
Prospect, Victoria, third of six children of
Peter Clement, a grazier from Perthshire,
Scotland, and his Victorian-born wife Jane,
née Thomson. Margaret's father had worked
as a bullocky, invested in quartz mining and
was a large shareholder in the rich Long
Tunnel mine. He bought Prospect station in
1886, but died in 1890 leaving a young widow
with five children under 12, another on the
way and reputedly a fortune of £50 000.

The family moved to Melbourne, entertained lavishly and toured Britain and Europe.
After their two sisters married, Margaret and
Jeanie travelled in Europe and the Far East. In
1907 with their brother Peter's assistance they
bought Tullaree at Tarwin Lower, Gippsland,
a difficult property that had been selected,
developed in 1884-93 and then abandoned
by Francis Longmore [q.v.5]. Whether they
attempted to farm seriously or (as journalists
later alleged) simply aped high society, the
sisters depended on hired help when Peter
left after marrying in 1912. Personal extravagance, poor judgement, employee chicanery
and expensive litigation compounded their
problems. By the early 1920s the Clements
were in serious financial trouble and Tullaree
was heavily mortgaged, only a timely caveat
on the title in 1926 preventing their eviction.
Impoverished, dependent on relations for
food and clothing, Margaret and Jeanie sank
into near destitution and became reclusive.

Their situation came to public notice on the
death of Jeanie in 1950, when police waded
through miles of swamp to retrieve her body
from a crumbling mansion lacking basic
amenities such as tank water and surrounded
by dense scrub, house-high blackberries and
piles of rusting food tins. Newspapermen
interviewed Margaret and fashioned the
story of the 'Lady of the Swamp', an eccentric
gentlewoman with only a dog as her companion, who carried provisions home in a

sugar bag, read detective stories by kerosene lamp, and lived on memories of past social glories. When she disappeared towards the end of May 1952 and a week of extensive searches in appalling conditions failed to find her, Margaret became the central figure in a media-sensationalized 'whodunit'. The police could uncover no motive for foul play, but the press, dismissing prosaic explanations, fashioned a Gothic tale of fallen splendour, buried stolen gold, skulduggery, abduction and murder. Suspicion fell on neighbours Stanley and Esme Livingstone who had befriended Clement, promised her life-tenancy of an onsite cottage and in 1951 bought Tullaree, which they improved and sold twelve years later at a handsome profit. Accusations and counter accusations flew when Margaret's nephew Clement Carnaghan, whom she had disinherited in 1951, unsuccessfully contested her will in 1955.

The mystery became a staple of press features and popular magazines, especially when human remains were discovered in the district. Police reopened the case when the buried skeleton of an elderly woman was found at Venus Bay in 1978. Ten years earlier a hammer and a spade had been discovered near the site, and a woman's handbag and shawl were unearthed in 1979. Experts at the 1980 inquest could not agree whether the remains were Aboriginal or European. The coroner returned an open verdict, noting the unsatisfactory nature of evidence given by the Livingstones, who in 1986 issued a press statement alleging Clement's abduction by her nephew, who had died in 1982. In 1997 the Melbourne coroner described the case as 'one of the great unsolved mysteries, but not one beyond resolution'. Although she was declared legally dead in 1954, the fate of Margaret Clement, more certainly the victim of media frenzy than of any murderer, remains one of Australia's most baffling missing person cases.

R. Shears, *The Lady of the Swamp* (Melb, 1981); *Gippsland Times*, 27 July 1950, p 1; *Sun News-Pictorial*, 28 July 1950, p 1, 31 Dec 1985, p 3, 1 Jan 1986, p 6, 21 May 1988, p 14; *Argus* (Melb), 26 May 1952, p 1, 27 May 1952, p 1, 28 May 1952, p 1, 29 May 1952, p 1, 30 May 1952, p 1, 31 May 1952, p 1, 2 June 1952, p 7; *Truth* (Melb), 31 May 1952, p 1; *People*, 30 July 1952, p 14; *Herald* (Melb), 9 Aug 1980, p 4; *Age* (Melb), 18 Feb 1985; *Herald-Sun* (Melb), 30 Mar 1997, p 76, 6 Apr 1997, p 22; VPRS 24/P1, unit 317, file 801699 (PRO Vic).

JOHN LACK

CLEMENTS, HUBERT INGHAM (1886-1969), engineer, was born on 8 June 1886 at Burwood, Sydney, eldest son of Australian-born parents Ingham Suttor Clements, surveyor, and his wife Mary Bell, née Pinhey. After attending Fort Street Model School and in 1900-03 Sydney Grammar School, Hubert was apprenticed to a mechanical engineer. In January 1906 he obtained a diploma in mechanical drawing with honours from the Sydney School of Mechanical Drawing.

Fascinated by the internal combustion engine, by 1906 Clements had constructed a functional automobile. He established his own engineering business at Strathfield in 1908, manufacturing both marine and land-based petrol engines; a motorcycle bearing his name appeared in 1910. During World War I he was contracted to the Australian defence forces, servicing and repairing motor lorries. The business flourished with the increasing popularity of the motorcar; spare parts being hard to obtain, his workshop was able to fabricate replacements and improve the reliability of the original designs. Quality machines were his specialty, including some of the great marques of the period, such as Duesenberg, Minerva and Thames. Clements was sometime vice-president of the Institute of Automotive Mechanical Engineers. On 2 April 1914 he married a nurse, Annie Grace McQueen, at St Thomas's Church of England, Enfield. They were to have four children.

Probably through the many doctors among his clientele Clements became interested in medical equipment, especially anaesthesia apparatus. As early as 1917, in collaboration with Dr Mark Lidwill, he designed and manufactured an ether vaporiser, incorporating an electrically powered source of compressed air. From the 1920s Clements devoted himself increasingly to improving ether apparatus and manufacturing portable suction machines for use in hospital operating theatres. The latter machines were to earn an unrivalled reputation for reliability; many remained in service more than thirty years after their date of production. Among their ingenious features was the use of fractional electric motors of commercial origin (many had been destined for vacuum cleaners). An innovation was the pump and its unique lubrication system, which made the device almost immune to abuse by the technically ignorant.

Clements's other successful projects included centralized vacuum systems, breast pumps and laboratory centrifuges used in blood banks throughout Australia. Expanding business necessitated several moves—from Rushcutters Bay to Crows Nest, then to St Leonards and finally to Ryde. His son William, a science graduate, brought useful academic skills to the business, which became H. I. Clements & Son, but he died prematurely (of cancer). When Hubert was disabled by two strokes the company was sold in 1967 for $52 500; by the late 1980s the new owners had achieved a turnover of $60 million.

Clements died on 29 June 1969 in a private hospital at Chatswood and was cremated. His wife, a son and two daughters survived him. Beautiful examples of his youthful drawings are in the Powerhouse Museum, Sydney. The Australian Society of Anaesthetists holds a collection of his apparatus and one of Harold Cazneaux's [q.v.7] photographic portraits of a doctor with a Clements Ether Vaporiser.

Clements records, 95/256/1 (Powerhouse Museum, Syd); information from Messrs J. Boorne, AO, Robert Gregg, Robert Stern and R. Goss, Sydney, and Dr Richard Bailey, former curator of the Harry Daly Museum, Society of Anaesthetists, Edgecliff; family records held by Mrs Nyree Phillips, Turramurra, Syd.   ROSS HOLLAND

COFFILL, JOSEPH TAYLOR (1841-1919), teamster, livery stable proprietor and funeral director, was born on 15 May 1841 at Kensington, London, son of Joseph Coffill, a farmer of French Huguenot descent, and his wife Margaret, née Taylor from Edinburgh. After working as a porter at Covent Garden markets and a mortar-man on building sites, young Joe took his Irish workmate's advice, abandoned his shovel for a skillet, and became a seaman-cook in the clipper *Golden City*.

Arriving in Moreton Bay, Queensland, on 3 January 1865, he drew his pay, acquired a horse and cart and began transporting goods to and from the ports, first to the pastoral districts and then to the goldfields of Ravenswood and Charters Towers. He set up a carrying business based on Townsville, Rockhampton and Charters Towers, with a break when he mined for copper at Cloncurry. On some eight occasions he drove mobs of horses from Queensland to Sydney for sale. Coffill was twice insolvent but had a wonderful affinity with horses and eventually prospered as a teamster. Alone, except for his dogs, in 1878 he moved to Sydney, where he constructed expensive livery stables at Ultimo. That year on 12 February at St Andrew's Cathedral he married native-born Elizabeth Ann Bates, a farmer's daughter; he gave his occupation as drover.

Coffill's business flourished. His drags, carriages, hearses and sociables were the most opulent and lucrative in Sydney, attracting vice-regal patronage. Superb horses drew his elegant conveyances—some imported, others beautifully crafted at his own workshop. As the business of 'undertaking' evolved into 'funeral directing', Coffill branched out into a logical extension of his activities and added a funeral department to the livery stables in 1899, concentrating on 'reform funerals', with service and volume replacing more expensive Victorian display and solemnity. His master-

piece, however, was the processional funeral car, the 'Car of Death'. Designed in Italian Renaissance style, this unique hearse featured angels, the Messiah rising above the clouds and coloured wood carvings by Oscar Guinand. In 1912 Coffill merged with A. C. J. Wood to form the largest funeral-directing enterprise in Sydney. Caskets, corpses and carriages made a winning combination: Coffill received £20 000 in cash and 20 000 £1 shares on the firm's formation.

In 1879, following childbirth, his wife had died of pneumonia. On 30 July 1881 at St Peter's Church, Richmond, with Episcopalian church rites, he married Anne Ivory. She died in 1894. His third marriage was on 29 July 1897 at Christ Church, Sydney, to a widowed hotelkeeper Ada Hannah Ambler, née Morris, said to have been one of the first local female embalmers. He made two overseas tours (1909 and 1910), wryly noting after visiting the Ford plant in Detroit that 'he felt some pangs for the future of the horse'. Like many funeral directors he was a prominent Freemason, and was grand pursuivant (1890) of the United Grand Lodge, Sydney, and president (1901-04) and mainstay of the Masonic Board of Benevolence. Coffill was a director of the Royal Hospital for Women, the Renwick [q.v.6] Hospital for Children and the New South Wales Benevolent Society. Proud of his mother's Scots ancestry, he was vice-president of the Highland Society of New South Wales.

Coffill was fond of moral aphorisms such as 'man has a big part in his own building up and he should ever be on the alert not to botch the structure'. He was a full-bearded, handsome, square-jawed, laconic man with commanding eyes and an aquiline nose who had financially surpassed his Cockney origins. Coffill died on 8 April 1919 at his residence, Curraweena, Homebush, and was buried in Rookwood cemetery with Anglican rites. His wife, the son of his first marriage, four sons and five daughters of his second and a daughter of his third survived him. The name Wood, Coffill survives as a Sydney funeral business in 2005 in other, albeit Australian, hands.

Australian Men of Mark, vol 2, version 3 (Syd, 1889), p 348; *Coffill and Company, an Australian Advance* (Syd, 1905); *Procs of the United Grand Lodge of NSW*, 1919, p 225; *Gavel*, 26 Mar 1898, p 3; *NSW Masonic Herald*, 17 Dec 1906, p 265; *Brisb Courier*, 5 Jan 1865, p 2, 6 Jan 1865, p 2; *SMH*, 9 Apr 1919, pp 4, 12; *Daily Telegraph* (Syd), 9 Apr 1919, p 5; Col/A62, 1865/3444 (QA); information from Mr N. T. Coffill, Rhodes, Syd.   D. B. WATERSON

COLBOURNE, WILLIAM REGIS (1895-1979), political organizer, was born on 16 December 1895 at Ultimo, Sydney, eleventh of fourteen children of Irish-born parents Richard Colbourne, labourer, and his wife Mary Ann, née Dinan. Educated at St Benedict's convent school, Chippendale, Colbourne first worked as a commercial traveller. He followed family tradition by joining the Phillip branch of the Political Labor League (Labor Party), which his father had helped to found in the 1890s. The family moved to Petersham in the 1920s and Bill became secretary of the party's local branch. Rising rapidly, he became president of both the State and Federal electorate councils and a regular and active delegate at the party's annual conferences. He was a delegate to the Federal executive of the Australian Labor Party and conference in 1929-36.

In early years a stand-up comedian in travelling shows, he met Hyacinthe Mary Burgess, a violinist, when they shared a bill; they were married with Catholic rites in St Mary's Cathedral, Sydney, on 27 April 1936. When J. T. Lang [q.v.9] split Labor in 1931, Colbourne had become secretary of the newly established New South Wales (Federal) branch. Faced with a lack of supporters and resources and even the threat of physical violence, he fought to keep the minority party alive. Following the achievement of a precarious unity in February 1936, a condition was that Colbourne be employed as an organizer. Lang reneged and Colbourne found himself out of a job. He finally found work as a life insurance agent. Establishing the Industrial Life Assurance Agents' Union, he was its first federal secretary in 1940-51. In 1952 he became a research officer with the Federated Ironworkers' Union and next year an industrial officer with the Federated Clerks' Union.

Regaining prominence in the A.L.P., Colbourne was an alderman on Leichhardt Municipal Council in 1941-44 and 1948-50 and became a member of the State executive in 1946. His strong anti-Communism and deeply held Catholic faith meant he supported the industrial groups. When they took control of the State branch in 1952, Colbourne became president and in 1954 salaried secretary. That year he was the unsuccessful industrial group ('grouper') candidate for federal secretary, instead becoming junior vice-president.

At the 1955 Federal conference Colbourne participated in the boycott by New South Wales delegates when the 'anti-grouper' Victorian delegation was admitted. Nevertheless, he took a moderate position in the subsequent split. His fundamental loyalties were to the A.L.P. more than to the groups and B. A. Santamaria's Catholic Social Studies Movement, and he adopted the pragmatic approach that the Federal executive would always triumph over any breakaway. Colbourne's personal experiences of the consequences of disunity also meant that he strongly opposed a new schism. His position was that a compromise could be reached that would enable the groups to preserve much of their existing power base by remaining within the party.

Colbourne accepted the decision of the Federal authorities to disband the New South Wales executive in June 1956. The 'stay in and fight' line largely prevailed and there was no major split in the State. He retained his position as State secretary when a new, 'balanced' executive was set up. It had an anti-group majority but moderates, centred on the party officers, held the balance of power. Although all the other office-holders were group opponents, Colbourne was soon working closely with his new colleagues to preserve the fragile consensus.

By the early 1960s former 'groupers' and anti-group moderates had merged into a controlling right faction, personified by the partnership of Colbourne and the Australian Workers' Union secretary C. T. Oliver, A.L.P. president since 1959. Colbourne astutely kept the right-wing unions in a supportive but not interventionist role. He was Federal president of the party for twelve months from July 1961, then reverted to senior vice-president until 1971. In April 1969 he retired as State secretary after a record term. In 1970 Colbourne thwarted the readmission of Lang to the A.L.P. but reluctantly relented the next year. He was appointed C.B.E. in 1977.

Of diminutive stature and unquestioned integrity, Colbourne was described by Graham Freudenberg as 'a sturdy, obstinate, persevering cock-sparrow of a man'. He had a dour and taciturn official manner but could be charming and amusing in private company. Although a teetotaller he was a keen punter. Colbourne suffered a heart attack and died during an A.L.P. life-membership presentation ceremony at Broken Hill on 19 November 1979. Predeceased by his wife and daughter and survived by two sons, both priests of the Franciscan Capuchin order, he was buried in Rookwood cemetery after a funeral at St Fiacre's Catholic Church, Leichhardt.

L. F. Crisp, *Ben Chifley* (Melb, 1961); R. Murray, *The Split* (Melb, 1970); J. Warhurst (ed), *Machine Politics in the Australian Labor Party* (Syd, 1983); B. Nairn, *The 'Big Fella'* (Melb, 1986); G. Freudenberg, *Cause for Power* (Syd, 1991); B. Duncan, *Crusade or Conspiracy?* (Syd, 2001); *SMH*, 9 June 1952, p 1, 15 June 1971, p 1, 21 Nov 1979, p 12; biog of W. R. Colbourne (ts, 1970, held ML); information from Fr P. Colbourne, Leichhardt, Mr J. Johnson, Maroubra, Syd, and Fr D. Colbourne, Melb.

DAVID CLUNE

COLE, JOHN THOMAS (1854-1927), dairy farmer and stud-breeder, was born on 2 November 1854 at Jamberoo, New South Wales, second son and one of eight children of William Cole (d.1867), emancipist farmer, and his wife Annabella, née Mackenzie (d.1889). From about 1876 Tom and his elder brother JAMES WILLIAM (1852-1919), who was born on 2 November 1852, were showing stock as Cole Brothers and favouring deep-milking Shorthorn strains. Early devotees of milking records to improve herds, they came second in the Kiama show society's first notable production competition in 1879-80. Tom owed much of his later confidence in public affairs to a Jamberoo debating society.

James more often let his cattle speak for him. He married with Presbyterian forms Margaret Thorburn on 6 November 1882 at Jasper's Mount, Shoalhaven. Over the next quarter of a century James bought out much of the family-held land and increasingly showed stock under his own name. He followed a circuit of Illawarra shows—his Major V and Gold of Coleville were renowned show and stud cattle. A younger brother Ebenezer (1858-1930) was also a dairy farmer as well as a horse-breeder and served on Kiama Municipal Council.

Tom married Agnes Dixon Lamond on 6 March 1889 at Shoalhaven with Presbyterian forms. They were to have one daughter. He had progressively taken on local public offices, being an alderman on Kiama Municipal Council in 1882-90 and founding president of Jamberoo School of Arts in 1890, but was unsuccessful when he stood for Kiama as a free trader in elections in 1889 and 1895. Moving to Nowra in 1895 and later to Sydney, he continued some farming interests, but travelled widely with C. E. D. Meares [q.v.10], promoting dairy industry co-operation generally and the South Coast and West Camden Co-operative Co. specifically.

In 1899 Tom Cole became manager of the Scottish Australian Investment Co.'s dairying operations at Bolaro, near Adaminaby. He and Frank McCaffrey upgraded the stock with Illawarra dairy strains, including Cole's bull, Banker. Cole's expertise, and his transfer in 1907-08 to the more benign climate and well-watered land of Darbalara, near Gundagai, led the cattleman George Grey to write that the herd had 'the biggest dairy cows I have ever seen'.

For about three decades dairy stud breeding was bedevilled by contention between Milking Shorthorn and Illawarra Dairy Cattle breeders. Illogicalities abounded. J. T. Cole was president (from 1908) and standard-bearer of the Milking Shorthorn party; Darbalara cattle won almost all champion awards for the breed in Sydney between 1910 and 1926, with the bull, Emblem of Darbalara, and a series of cows from the Melba line outstanding. Through cattle such as Banker, Heather and Madame, his line breeding continually drew on decades of the Coles's favoured Major strains.

In 1912 the Darbalara herd was the first stud herd to be regularly tested by the Department of Agriculture, and was enthusiastically publicized at home and abroad, particularly when in 1924 Melba XV—'the world's champion butter-fat cow'—for the second time broke world production records. In 1925 Cole received the New South Wales Chamber of Agriculture award for 'eminent service to the cause of agriculture'.

The Darbalara herd was dispersed in 1926. Abstemious, with a gaunt face but neat beard, Tom Cole was lauded by veteran employees and share-farmers for his knowledge, judgement and considerate oversight. The brothers all retired to Sydney. James had died on 24 November 1919. John Thomas died on 13 May 1927 at Glebe and was buried in Rookwood cemetery. His wife and daughter survived him. In 1930 rival cattlemen resolved their differences and the official name of the locally developed breed, to which the Cole brothers had been such major contributors, became the Australian Illawarra Shorthorn.

The Milking Shorthorn Cattle Herd Book of New South Wales, 1 (Syd, 1906); F. McCaffrey, *The History of Illawarra and its Pioneers* (revised edn Syd, 1924); G. F. Finlay (ed), *Cattle Breeding* (Edinburgh, Scotland, 1925); *Australian Illawarra Shorthorn Society: Golden Jubilee Souvenir 1980* (Kiama, NSW, 1980); D. O'Keefe, *'Gone But Not Forgotten'* (Jamberoo, NSW, 1983?); J. Cole, *A History of the Cole Family in Australia* (Syd, 1992); A. Cousins, *The Garden of New South Wales* (Wollongong, NSW, 1994); *R. A. S. Annual*, 1907, p 113; *Agricultural Gazette* (NSW), 2 Oct 1914, p 889, 1 July 1924, p 489; *Sydney Mail*, 14 Feb 1880, p 328; *Gundagai Times*, 1 Nov 1910, p 1; *Kiama Independent*, 26 Nov 1919, p 2; *Gundagai Independent*, 27 May 1926, p 1; *Daily Telegraph*, 3 Sept 1926, p 4; *SMH*, 16 May 1927, p 12.

S. J. ROUTH

COLE, THOMAS CORNELIUS (1810-1889), horticulturist and nursery proprietor, was born in 1810 at Sudbury, Middlesex, England, son of Guy Cole, market gardener, and his wife Elizabeth, née Nutt. In 1837 at nearby Harrow Thomas married Elizabeth Whitmore. Accompanied by her, their three children and his brother George (1822-1868), Cole reached Melbourne in February 1842—a son had died on the voyage. Thomas, George and a cousin, John Cole (1816-1894), who had preceded them in 1839, established nurseries, orchards and market gardens on the Merri Creek.

In 1847 Thomas purchased land with a Yarra River frontage at Burnley where he established an orchard and nursery. According to E. E. Pescott [q.v.11], Cole issued his first catalogue from the Richmond Nursery in 1850, making it one of the earliest produced in Victoria. He took a keen interest in the horticultural progress of the colony and was a prime mover behind the establishment of the Horticultural Society of Victoria's experimental garden at Burnley.

Cole purchased 38 acres (15 ha) of land with a frontage to Tooronga Road, Upper Hawthorn, in 1853. By 1860 he had established another orchard and nursery and erected a large, brick house on this estate, named Twyford. He drew on his long horticultural experience—then unparalleled among fellow colonists—in his book *Cole's Gardening in Victoria* (1860). Besides monthly notes on the kitchen, fruit and flower garden, Cole included authoritative remarks 'On Selecting Fruit Trees' and much of interest regarding garden design. He recognized the futility of large expanses of lawn in oppressive Australian summers but was generally little concerned with questions of garden styles. He was careful and cautious, even conservative, in outlook and in the pages of the *Yeoman and Australian Acclimatiser* he clashed during 1863 with the progressive agriculturist Josiah Mitchell over the question of exhaustion of soils.

In 1862 Cole leased the Richmond Nursery to his son John Charles (1838-1891), who specialized in fruit trees and vines and supplemented the rapidly urbanized site in the mid-1880s with a generous land selection at Fern Tree Gully (Belgrave), which he named Glen Harrow. Another of Thomas's sons, Rev. Thomas Cornelius junior (1836-1879), was also active in Melbourne horticultural circles. In 1864 Thomas senior purchased a further 37 acres (15 ha), adjoining the Twyford estate, and leased it to his son Henry Ungerford (1843-1904), who established the Shorland orchard and nursery. Like his father and brother, with whom he worked closely, Henry was noted for his work as a pomological hybridist and as a judge of fruit at horticultural shows

Thomas Cole's wife died in 1879. On 5 July 1881 at Christ Church, Hawthorn, he married with Anglican rites Catherine Mary Josephine Mathers. He died on 31 July 1889 at Twyford and was buried in Melbourne general cemetery, survived by his wife, and by two sons and three daughters of his first marriage. His estate was valued at £85 100. Henry Cole's Shorland Nursery carried on in the early decades of the twentieth century; by the 1930s Twyford had been demolished and subdivided for residential purposes. Thomas Cole was a pioneer of Victorian horticulture and his outstanding work in the raising of seedling fruits and vegetables produced varieties for Australian conditions vastly superior to their predecessors.

R. Aitken and M. Looker (eds), *The Oxford Companion to Australian Gardens* (South Melb, 2002); V. Cole, A Fruitful Tree: The Cole Family, Horticultural Pioneers in the Port Phillip District of New South Wales (ms, 1994, held by Mrs V. Cole, Tyabb, Vic).

RICHARD AITKEN

COLLINS, ARTHUR LEONARD (1896-1969), pastoralist and sheep breeder, was born on 3 May 1896 at Mount Bryan, South Australia, seventh of nine children of John Collins (1859-1932), stud merino breeder, and his wife Catherine, née Simpson. Art's grandfather Henry Collings (Collins) (1833-1929) had purchased land (Lucerndale) in 1859 at Mount Bryan where he farmed wheat and lucerne and from 1884 bred merino sheep. In 1889 Art's father bought a 50 000-acre (20 243 ha) station in the colony's mid-north, across Goyder's [q.v.4] line, which he named Collinsville; here in 1895 he founded a stud with ewes purchased from Koonoona. Art grew up in this dry, harsh environment where, with an eight-inch (200 mm) annual rainfall, sheep had to be tough to survive on saltbush.

Educated at home by a governess and as a boarder at Prince Alfred College, Adelaide (1912-15), he took over from his father and brother Melvin as stud-master in 1916. While remaining in partnership with his brothers Lindsay and Newton for many years, in 1924 he assumed management control of John Collins & Sons. He had enormous vigour, acute powers of observation, excellent management skills and an innate ability with stock. Despite financial difficulties in the Depression, by the mid-1930s Collins, by trial and error and by rigorous selection, had developed a strain that combined size and early maturity with a superior wool quality and density. He deliberately exposed his breeding ewes to harsh conditions. His new sheep type—the Collinsville—was a blend of the large, hardy but coarser-woolled South Australian strain with the finer-woolled Peppin [q.v.5] variety from New South Wales. Within a few years Collinsville had emerged as a major merino stud, selling its bloodlines to pastoralists in all Australian States, particularly to those in the harsher environments.

After World War II the property comprised over 200 000 acres (80 972 ha) of dry country near Mount Hay and 6000 acres (2429 ha) in the rich, wetter region near Rooboruwle and Mount Bryan. Ram sales soared, reaching over 3000 annually in the 1960s. Many of these went to other studs, which in turn disseminated Collinsville blood.

On 9 January 1926 at Malvern Methodist Church Collins had married Ellen Lang, a farmer's daughter from Narridy. They had three daughters. He was a strict but loving father and loyal husband, with a vibrant sense of humour, although shy and reserved. A long-time asthmatic, he was gifted musically, capable at tennis and passionate about cricket, captaining his local team, Mount Bryan, until into his sixties. He loved a flutter on the horses. To outsiders, he was dominating but not domineering. A big, well-built man, he had a powerful presence; in later life receding, grey hair and bushy, dark eyebrows reinforced his patrician air. He was of that old school who were never seen without a tie, even at work.

Collins died on 5 February 1969 in hospital in Adelaide and was buried in Burra cemetery. He was survived by his wife and daughters. His estate was sworn for probate at $84 720. At its peak, Collinsville was one of Australia's largest and most famous merino studs; by the late 1980s it was estimated to have a genetic influence in 30 per cent of the national merino flock of over 100 million sheep.

M. Richards, *Hallett: A History of Town & District* (Adel, 1977); C. Massy, *The Australian Merino* (Melb, 1990), and for bib; *Australian Stud Merino Flock Register, 1925-1990; Adel Stock & Station J,* 18 Aug 1964.   CHARLES MASSY

COLTON, MARY (1822-1898), philanthropist and suffragist, was born on 6 December 1822 in London, eldest of three children of Samuel Cutting, bootmaker, and his wife Hannah. In 1839 Mary accompanied her widowed father, her brother and sister to Adelaide. On 3 December 1844 at Trinity Church she married (Sir) John Colton [q.v.3], saddler and hardware merchant. Committed Methodists, they attended Gawler Place Wesleyan Chapel and from 1851 its Pirie Street successor. Mary was one of Adelaide's earliest Sunday School teachers, continuing her classes for girls and young women for over fifty years. Devoted to her 'dear girls', she often walked to visit and help them if they were ill. In some homes she saw poverty and despair: her lifelong philanthropy, based on her ideals of Christian service, emerged from these experiences. She began with the church's Dorcas Society, the South Adelaide Wesleyan Ladies' Working Society (secretary from 1844) and later the Nursing Sisters' Association, which cared for needy mothers after childbirth.

At ease alike with those of exalted station and poor cottage-dwellers, she acknowledged no social barriers. As her husband's business, civic and political career flourished—he was premier in 1876-77 and 1884-85—the couple entertained generously in their Hackney home, Alma House, on the city's perimeter.

Mary was energetic, serene, 'sunshiny' and hospitable, even as 'shoals' came to her door for help. She had nine children; several died in infancy and after her last child was born in 1865 she devoted herself to good causes. In 1870 and in 1872 she joined deputations that included Caroline Clark and Catherine Helen Spence [qq.v.3,6] pressing the government to end institutional care and to introduce boarding-out for state children. After they succeeded in 1872, Mary worked on the Boarding-out Society's committee, then from 1885 on the pioneering State Children's Council, which was responsible for children cared for by licensed foster parents, in reformatories or in industrial schools.

In particular she helped women. From the late 1860s she served on the ladies' committee that managed the practical affairs of the Servants' Home, a facility for newly arrived female immigrants and servants awaiting employment. By 1867 she had joined the ladies' committee of the Female Refuge, which sheltered single pregnant girls, reformed prostitutes, deserted wives and victims of violence. She befriended and counselled inmates. In 1883 she became treasurer and then president of the new ladies' division of the Social Purity Society, campaigning to have the age of consent raised from 12. In the House of Assembly John had introduced relevant enabling legislation that eventually passed in 1885. Mary became convinced, like her co-worker Mary Lee [q.v.10], that women needed the parliamentary suffrage to right further injustices.

In 1876 she was a founder of Adelaide Children's Hospital (opened 1879) when she accepted Allan Campbell's [q.v.7] request to form a women's advisory planning committee and subsequently joined the board of management, advising and visiting for the rest of her life. Renowned for her public work, she was also a friend to many whom she helped privately. She actively served some twenty-two causes, including the Home for Incurables; blind, deaf and dumb institutions; cottage homes organizations; the Maternity Relief Association; and the Strangers' Friend Society. In the 1880s and 1890s, as president of the Adelaide Female Reformatory, she visited prisoners and assisted them on discharge.

The welfare of her senior Sunday School girls with no family home deeply concerned her. In 1884 she co-founded a club with a Christian focus for working girls; in December that year it became a branch of the Young Women's Christian Association, of which she remained president all her life. In 1893 (by then Lady Colton) she helped to found and presided over the Wesleyan Ladies' Missionary Auxiliary.

Her accumulated experience became politically important during the women's suffrage campaign. Although she was abroad when the Women's Suffrage League began, in May 1892 she succeeded (Sir) Edward Stirling [q.v.6] as its president. Distinguished yet unassuming, she represented the contemporary ideal of womanhood. She spoke simply, briefly and to the point at public meetings and strengthened the league, guiding it 'through all difficulties and discouragements'. The secretary Mary Lee recorded that Lady Colton 'never once failed ... in wise counsel'. She was applauded warmly when the league met triumphantly to dissolve itself after the suffrage legislation was gazetted in March 1895.

Lady Colton continued her strenuous activities at the expense of her health during the hot 1897-98 summer. She died at her home on 30 July 1898 and was buried in West Terrace cemetery. Her husband, one daughter and four sons survived her. Colton Ward at the Children's Hospital and the Lady Colton Hall in a new Y.W.C.A. building (1900) were named after her.

C. H. Spence, *State Children in Australia* (Adel, 1907); H. Jones, *In Her Own Name* (Adel, 1994); *Christian Weekly and Methodist J*, 12 Aug 1898, p 4; *Observer* (Adel), 6 Dec 1884, p 25; *SA Register*, 1 Aug 1898, p 4; *Advertiser* (Adel), 1 Aug 1898, p 4; Methodist Church (Adel), Ladies Wesleyan Missionary Auxiliary, Central Committee Minutes, 1893-98, and Women's Suffrage League of SA, Report, 1894 (SLSA); information from the late Mr J. Colton, Adel.　　　　HELEN JONES

CONGREVE, HENRY JOHN (1829-1918), adventurer, journalist and preacher, was born on 31 March 1829 in London, eldest of four sons of Henry Congreve, a chemist with some medical experience, and his second wife Elizabeth Ann, née Jacob. Henry senior, whose lineage included the playwright William Congreve, lost money in speculations and the impoverished family was forced to emigrate. Young Harry, who had medical training, and his next brother William preceded their parents, two sisters and two brothers to South Australia, reaching Port Adelaide in January 1849.

Attracted by bush life and the possibility of adventure, Harry went to Port Lincoln where he worked among the Aborigines, became acquainted with their traditions, learned several of their dialects and acted as their doctor. Later he drove bullocks at Burra and loaded wool at Pekina but set off on foot for the Victorian diggings when gold was discovered in 1851. He prospected for twelve years near Inglewood, settling there in 1863 as a journalist and editor of the *Inglewood Advertiser*. On 14 December 1865 at Inglewood, with Congregational forms, he married 18-year-old Jane Marshall Kirkwood, a domestic servant

from Glasgow, Scotland. They had ten children, four dying in infancy. Congreve became secretary of the Inglewood district hospital and school board, manager of the Jersey Reef Mining Co. and a land and insurance agent. He was a contributor to Thomas Howard's *History of the Inglewood Reefs* (Inglewood, 1883).

In 1880 Congreve and his family left for South Australia, where his sister Matilda Evans [q.v.4] lived. Settled at Gawler as editor of the *Standard* and from 1885 of the *Bunyip* (after those two weeklies merged), he wrote novels for and contributed articles to these papers and to the *Observer*, Adelaide. Active in many areas of Gawler society, particularly as a member of the Presbyterian Church, in 1882 —although not ordained—he was asked to supply the pulpit at the church at Smithfield and in 1885 at Golden Grove. He applied for ordination but failed to satisfy the Church's requirements. The heavy work-load and exigencies of travelling long distances to give services telling on his health, he resigned from the *Bunyip* in July 1890 and moved to Semaphore—where he was known as 'Rev. Congreve'. In 1894 he moved to Hackney and later to East Adelaide. He joined Chalmers Church, and was an elder in 1899-1916 and active as a preacher and church visitor.

Congreve died on 10 July 1918 at his home, Stretton, in East Adelaide, survived by his wife, a daughter and five sons, and was buried in Payneham cemetery. His estate was sworn for probate at £960. All his sons served either in the Boer War or World War I. Congreve's versatility, energy, public spirit and strong faith made him respected and admired wherever he lived. Photographs showed him beetle-browed, with a full, untidy beard. Some fifty of his stories of Aborigines, pioneering life and the diggings survive in the newspapers for which he wrote.

E. H. Coombe (comp), *History of Gawler 1837 to 1908* (Adel, 1910); B. Wall, *Our Own Matilda* (Adel, 1994) and 'A Grand Old Pioneer: Henry John Congreve 1829-1918', *J of the Hist Soc of SA*, no 24, 1996, p 58; *Presbyterian Banner*, Aug 1918, p 5; *Bunyip* (Gawler, Adel), 29 Oct 1886, p 3, 19 July 1918, p 2; *Register* (Adel), 31 Mar 1909, p 8; *Observer* (Adel), 20 July 1918, p 18.　　　　BARBARA WALL

CONNOR, MADGE IRENE (1874?-1952), policewoman, was born possibly on 14 November 1874 at Waterford, Ireland, only child of John Edward Howard McCarthy, master mariner, and his wife Mary, née Barron. By the time she retired, however, Madge had eight recorded variations of her name and four dates of birth. She claimed that after her father was lost at sea, when she was aged 2, she went with her grandmother and mother to England, then the United States of America where they stayed for two and a half years before moving to New Zealand. Her mother died when Madge was 7, leaving her upbringing to an aunt. Aged 16, Madge eloped to Australia. Life in Melbourne with her husband Edward Connor (O'Connor), an English-born labourer, and two children was difficult.

Edward died suddenly in 1916, and it is possible that the police constable informant for Edward's death registration brought Madge to the attention of detectives. She started working undercover for the Victoria Police later that year: by her account obtaining evidence against 'many subtle craft people and illegal bettors' and taking up residence in a boarding house with a hardened criminal and 'his woman' in order to obtain evidence against him.

This work stood her in good stead when, following campaigns by women's groups, the Victorian government appointed female police agents. Connor was the first of two, selected in July 1917, on half the pay of a policeman, with no powers of arrest or rights to a pension. They did not wear uniforms. In 1922 she helped in undercover surveillance of a witness in the case against Colin Campbell Ross [q.v.]. Quickly accumulating commendations for her work, she was stationed at Russell Street and Fitzroy for most of her career. As early as 1920 Connor led deputations of female police and watch-house matrons to the chief secretary, arguing for an increase in their salaries. She described the often distasteful duties they had to undertake for seventeen shillings and sixpence per week. Successful in obtaining a small increase, Connor made further representations in 1923. Unrelenting in pursuit of equality, she wrote several reports, insisting that a 'stroke of the pen' would solve all problems.

Connor proved correct. On 12 November 1924 the by then four policewomen were sworn in, becoming the first women to obtain equal pay, nearly half a century ahead of women in other occupations in Australia. Then 5 ft 6 ins (167 cm) tall, with grey eyes, light brown hair and a fair complexion, Connor gave her religion as Church of England. Because of a technicality in the police seniority system, she lost her place as 'senior in service', becoming 'junior in number'. She continued to bring petty criminals, fortune-tellers and bookmakers before the courts until she was forced to retire on 14 November 1929.

Ineligible for a police pension, having not completed the necessary fifteen years as a sworn officer, Connor operated as a private detective. She died on 12 October 1952 at St Vincent's Hospital, Fitzroy, and after a Catholic service was buried in Boroondara cemetery, Kew, survived by her daughters.

C. A. Woolley, *Arresting Women* (Melb, 1997), and for bib.   COLLEEN WOOLLEY

COOKE, CONSTANCE MARY TERNENT (1882-1967), Aboriginal rights advocate and social reformer, was born on 9 February 1882 at Kent Town, Adelaide, fifth of eight surviving children of Percival Edward Hoare, accountant and collector of antiquities, and his wife Susette, née Gameau. Constance and her five sisters were educated at home. In 1898-1902 she was assistant at Somersal House preparatory school, Stepney, conducted by her second cousin Constance Mary, sister of Edward Warner Benham [q.v.13]. On 21 August 1907, at the chapel of the Collegiate School of St Peter, Constance Hoare married Dr William Ternent Cooke, of the department of chemistry at the University of Adelaide; they were to have two children.

An executive member (president 1924-27) of South Australia's Women's Non-Party Association, said to be the first women's organization to make the cause of the Aborigines part of its platform, from 1928 Mrs Cooke was convenor of the association's Aborigines' welfare committee. Her determination to work for the interests of Aboriginal people was confirmed on a visit to view first hand what she described as 'the disgraceful condition of the Federal Home for half-caste children at Alice Springs'. In line with its principle to put women on public boards, the W.N.P.A. secured the appointment of two women to the Advisory Council of Aborigines: Ida McKay in 1927 and Constance in 1929. It was through the persistence of the association, and her advocacy, that legislation for the protection of indigenous women and girls was included in the 1939 Aborigines Act.

In 1927 Cooke (sometimes referred to as Ternent-Cooke) was a member of the Australian delegation to the British Commonwealth League's conference in London. From then, as a result of contacts with like-minded people, she was able to advertise overseas the plight of Australia's indigenous people. She represented the Australian Federation of Women Voters at the second Pan-Pacific Women's Conference at Honolulu in 1930. In 1926 she had been a foundation member of the Aborigines Protection League, whose aims included the creation of self-determining 'Native States'. A vice-president of the league for twenty years, by 1939 she was its advocate on 'fully detribalised' Aborigines and 'half-castes'. She believed the emphasis should be on better living conditions and improved economic status with the aim of 'self-development and self-respect'.

Appointed to the newly constituted Aborigines' Protection Board in 1939, with Alice, the wife of Thomas Harvey Johnston [q.v.9], for over twenty years as a board member Cooke stressed the importance of the material welfare of the Aboriginal people. It was officially minuted that the female members consistently urged improvements to both the Colebrook Home for children, Eden Hills, and the Sussex Street Women's Home, North Adelaide. Their warnings were ignored until the homes became 'entirely unsatisfactory'. In 1956 she wrote: 'we are not required to carry out our duty to the original inhabitants of this country in the cheapest way possible … Neither have we been charged with the assimilation of the aborigines into our white community within an unreasonable time'. She urged that 'the pastoral portion of the North West Reserve should be used for the sole benefit of our native people' and that pastoral companies should not be allowed to 'open up' the country.

A justice of the peace from 1927, Cooke was appointed M.B.E. in 1964 for her work for Aboriginal protection and welfare. Her other achievements were as commissioner of the State branch of the Girl Guides' Association, transport driver for the Australian Red Cross Society during World War II, first president of the Women Justices' Association of South Australia and member of the special panel of justices for the Children's Court. Photographs revealed her to have been a handsome and fashionably dressed woman. Determined and resourceful, she was afraid neither of expressing her opinions nor of motoring long distances over rough, dirt tracks to Aboriginal camps and missions. Following her husband's death in 1957, she moved to be near family in Sydney. Constance Cooke died on 2 April 1967 at Turramurra, survived by her son and daughter, and was cremated with Anglican rites.

R. R. Chivers, *The Benham Family in Australia* (Adel, 1970) and *The Hoare Family* (Adel, 1971-74); *Daylight* (Adel), 31 July 1928; *Advertiser* (Adel), 16 June 1939, p 29, 13 June 1964, p 3, 7 Apr 1967, p 18; V. Szekeres, A History of the League of Women Voters in South Australia, 1909-1976 (B.A. Hons thesis, Univ Adel, 1976); Dept Aboriginal Affairs (SA), letter, 12 Jan 1956, and minute, 5 Sept 1956, GRG 52/1/74/1955 (SRSA); Women's Non-Party Assn papers, misc photos, newsletters (SLSA).

MARGARET MACILWAIN

COOMBE, SIR THOMAS MELROSE (1873-1959), businessman, film exhibitor and philanthropist, was born on 3 December 1873 at Melrose, South Australia, eldest of seven surviving children of Thomas Coombe (1847-1925), a Cornish-born timber and iron merchant, and his first wife Sarah, née Beddome. Coombe senior had begun in business at Port Pirie, and by 1886 was a storekeeper at Broken Hill, New South Wales, where he was mayor in 1890. In 1895 the gold rush drew him to Western Australia; he flourished anew as a supplier of building materials and was mayor of South Perth for two years (1906-07).

Young Tommy was educated at Thomas Caterer's school, Norwood, at Hahndorf College, and finally until 1891 at Prince Alfred College, Adelaide, where he was an all-round sportsman. Following his family westward in 1898, he began working for his father. On 14 February 1900 at Christ Church, North Sydney, he married with Anglican rites Alice Senior, of Mosman. He set up as an importer of sporting materials about 1904, represented Western Australia at cricket in 1905-06, and prospered.

In 1910 he teamed up with T. J. West, the British exhibitor who had the largest cinema circuit in Australia. At first Coombe provided the venues only, beginning with the simple Melrose Gardens, at a prime location in Murray Street, Perth, which in December 1911 gave way to the barn-like Melrose Theatre and in 1922 to the elegant Prince of Wales. He built the Princess Theatre at Fremantle in 1912 and controlled several others in Perth for varying periods. When West merged with his competitors in 1913 Coombe became a partner and the local managing director of Union Theatres Ltd. In 1928 he financed the ornate, 'atmospheric' Ambassadors Theatre in central Hay Street.

As president of the Theatrical Managers' Association, Coombe raised large sums for charities. In World War I he was active on the Federal War Loan Committee and later promoted the welfare of ex-servicemen and their families. He also chaired and generously supported the Boy Scouts' Association of Western Australia. In 1921 he donated £5000 to found the Coombe scholarships, enabling six schoolboys per year to continue to upper secondary education. He also encouraged the pianist Eileen Joyce. Rumoured to have financially supported the government of Sir James Mitchell [q.v.10], Coombe was knighted while on a visit to Britain in 1924.

In July 1928 he retired from a managerial role but continued as a director of Union Theatres. His business suffered from the effects of the Depression and particularly from a sharp decline in cinema attendances, and in 1931 he was prosecuted and fined £100 for income tax evasion, an offence he blamed on his over-expenditure in building the Ambassadors in the lavish style demanded by American film suppliers. After Union Theatres collapsed that year, effective leadership in film exhibition passed to the rival Hoyts chain. One by one, he sold or relinquished control of his theatres.

Coombe's marriage ended in divorce in 1932 and on 11 January 1933 at St Andrew's Presbyterian Church, Carlton, Melbourne, he married 29-year-old Frances Smith, of Perth. A few years later the couple moved to Glenelg, Adelaide, although he retained ownership of the Ambassadors and other property in Perth. Sir Thomas invested in real estate, continued his interest in sport and travelled. In his last years he and his wife made lengthy visits to England, where three of his children resided. He died on 22 July 1959 in a nursing home at Epsom, Surrey, England, and was cremated. His estate in South Australia and Western Australia was sworn for probate at £53 418. He also had assets in England. Coombe was survived by his wife and their two sons, and by the son and three daughters of his first marriage. His youngest daughter Gwennyth (1911-1966) had settled in London in 1930, and pursued a successful career in theatre, film and television under the name of 'Carol' Coombe.

R. Butler, *A College in the Wattles* (Adel, 1989) p 285; *SA Genealogist*, 15, no 4, Oct 1988, p 5; *Kino Cinema Q*, no 34, Dec 1990, p 12; no 79, Autumn 2002, p 30, no 80, Winter 2002, p 46, no 81, Spring 2002, p 36; *Western Mail*, 15 Sept 1921, 2 Aug 1928; *West Australian*, 3 June 1924, p 18; *Advertiser* (Adel), 4 June 1924, p 9; *Observer* (Adel), 21 June 1924, p 36; *SMH*, 22 Dec 1931, p 9; information from Dr A. M. Coombe, Glengowrie, SA.

J. H. M. HONNIBALL

CORBIN, LAURA MARY LOUISA (1841-1906), crèche founder, was born on 26 April 1841 in Adelaide, daughter of Alfred Hardy, town surveyor, and his wife Mary Louisa, née Newenham. Educated at home by her mother, Laura was a constant reader 'with a sweet disposition'. On 16 June 1869 at St Michael's Church, Mitcham, she married Thomas Wilson Corbin, a medical practitioner; Bishop Augustus Short [q.v.6] celebrated the marriage. The Corbins visited England in 1872 and next year settled in King William Street, South Adelaide, where Thomas practised near the city's poorest quarter. 'Very beautiful', Laura bore six daughters and four sons. Continuing her family's charitable traditions, in 1876 she joined Mary Colton [q.v.] and others on the foundation ladies' advisory committee planning what became Adelaide's children's hospital. She became deeply concerned at the plight of poor mothers, often widows, forced to leave children at home alone, sometimes with tragic consequences, while they worked at charring, laundering or office cleaning. In June 1880 an unnamed

lady, possibly Mrs Corbin, advertised and opened a short-lived English style 'crèche or day nursery' near Victoria Square.

In May 1887 Laura founded the South Adelaide Day Nursery. Designed, like its predecessor, for 'taking care of the children of women who go out to work by the day', it opened with four children in a rented room. Laura visited city missions to publicize the service. Admissions, staff and facilities gradually increased: by 1889 weekly attendance averaged forty-one. Babies and children under 6, admitted for twopence per day between 7 a.m. and 6 p.m., were washed, freshly clothed and given good food and care by carefully chosen staff. Health and hygiene were paramount considerations and the 'sleeping decoctions' some mothers administered were banned. With her family's backing, Laura devoted herself to every aspect of management; she presided over both general and house committees, whose pioneering rules were adopted by crèches in other colonies. Despite 'disappointments and discouragements', she persevered, encouraged by the children's wellbeing and mothers' gratitude. The crèche became a colony-wide cause: many, like Port Elliot's needlewomen, giving essential money and gifts in kind. Governors' wives were patrons.

The name became South Adelaide Crèche after Laura found in 1891 in London that, apart from having a playground, it operated similarly to the Whitechapel 'mother crèche'. During the 1893 depression admissions temporarily plummeted. Laura inaugurated a soup kitchen and founded a Women's Distress Relief Fund, working indefatigably with Augusta Zadow and Mary Lee [qq.v.12,10] to organize and distribute necessities to impoverished families. In reporting this work the *Register*, unusually, published modest Laura's own three initials, not her husband's.

In August 1896, in a ceremony watched by thousands, she laid the foundation stone of a distinctive new crèche building, reminiscent of a doll's house, in Gouger Street, using generous donations from the popular children's Sunbeam Society. In 1897, having seen 37 000 admissions, she resigned from her presidency and 'labor of love', taking her last opportunity to protest against employers' long hours for working women. She died of pneumonia on 24 October 1906 at Woodville and was buried in Mitcham cemetery. The crèche closed in the late 1930s; its building was finally demolished in 1996 after a heritage controversy.

F. Cuming, *'Claremont' Glen Osmond* (Adel, 1982); S. Marsden, P. Stark and P. Sumerling (eds), *Heritage of the City of Adelaide* (Adel, 1990); SA Day Nursery or Creche, *Annual Report*, 1889-97; *Register* (Adel), 3, 10 July 1880, 25 Sept 1893, 13 June, 20 July, 8, 10 Aug, 18 Dec 1896; *Observer* (Adel), 20 June 1878, 8 July 1893, pp 29, 30, 15 Aug 1896, 27 Oct

1906, p 38, 24 Aug 1918, p 19; *Evening Standard*, 21 June 1878; information from Corbin family members and the late Dr J. Tregenza.   HELEN JONES

CORLIS, MARGARET AMELIA (c.1840-1925), medical practitioner, was born at Townsend, Ontario, Canada, daughter of Adam Walker, a farmer. Margaret attended Villa Nova public school and became a teacher. In 1862 at Villa Nova she married JOSIAH CORLIS (1841-1922), also from Townsend. He became a Baptist minister but soon moved to Montreal where he enrolled in medicine at McGill University (M.D., Ch.M., 1868) while his wife supported him by taking in medical students as boarders. Josiah practised at St Thomas's Hospital, Ontario, and also had a chemist shop there. The couple had three sons and a daughter, whose death from diphtheria may have been the reason for Margaret's decision to study medicine. Despite her age and her child-rearing responsibilities, in 1881 she installed a housekeeper and enrolled in the medical school at Queens University, Kingston, Ontario (M.D., Ch.M., 1885), becoming one of the first five female graduates of the school.

The Corlises migrated to Sydney in 1891, their eldest son staying behind to complete his studies in veterinary science before joining them. The two younger boys arrived with their parents and, like them, became doctors. On 11 May 1892 Margaret registered in New South Wales and opened a practice in Elizabeth Street, Sydney. Afterwards, she and her husband set up a joint practice at Bellingen.

Josiah moved to Southern Cross, Western Australia, in 1894 and then to Coolgardie to help during a typhoid epidemic. Margaret joined him in 1895 and practised at Coolgardie. By November that year Josiah had been appointed surgeon and physician of the hospital and miners' institute, Menzies. Soon Margaret was also working there: in May 1897 *T'Othersider* reported that the hospital (a canvas building) had 'the benefit of two doctors for the price of one ... Mrs Corlis is probably the only she-physician in W.A.' Margaret was parted from her husband for up to a week at a time, attending out-patients and travelling long distances, often on camels. According to a descendant, she 'had her own Afghan camel attendant with one particularly good bull camel of uncertain temperament. She had scars where this animal bit her in several places.'

Returning to New South Wales in December 1903, the Corlises then went to Canada for the first of two holidays. Although retired, Josiah was a ship's doctor on passenger steamers in the Pacific islands and Asia, and Margaret accompanied him. In later years they sometimes worked as *locum tenens* for their sons and other doctors in New South Wales. Barely 5 ft (152 cm) tall, Margaret had good health all her enterprising life. After unsuccessful operations for cataracts she became blind but still successfully delivered a baby in an emergency, with the help of a neighbour. Following Josiah's death on 8 July 1922, she lived with her son Charles at Bangalow. She died on 6 January 1925 at Grafton and was buried in Bangalow cemetery with Presbyterian forms. Her sons survived her.

C. Hacker, *The Indomitable Lady Doctors* (Toronto, 1974); N. King, *Daughters of Midas* (Perth, 1988); RAHS, *History*, no 25, Oct 1992, p 8; *SMH*, 13 Jan 1925, p 8.   NORMA KING

CORNISH, ELSIE MARION (1870-1946), landscape gardener, was born on 7 January 1870 at Glenelg, South Australia, daughter of Samuel Cornish, ironmonger, and his wife Agnes Maria, née Kirkpatrick. Educated in North Adelaide and self-trained in landscape design, Elsie began her career in the 1910s, progressively attracting a supportive group of clients. Her family residence, which also served as her plant nursery, was in Palmer Place, North Adelaide, and she inherited the property, which had once been occupied by architects Henry Stuckey and Edmund Wright [q.v.]. She drew on the ideas of Gertrude Jekyll and on Mediterranean traditions, including the use of cottage and northern Italian plants, sunken rock gardens, entry porches and walls, which she often planned, built and planted for clients. Major elements included a sense of formality and symmetry, features such as statues, terraces and water, and a predilection for circular shapes.

Following contemporary English practices, her work displayed a respect for the local environment, similar to the ideas of Jocelyn Brown [q.v.13, A.J.Brown] and Edna Walling [q.v.16], and attracted the patronage of the architect Walter Bagot [q.v.7] and the friendship of Zara, Lady Hore-Ruthven [q.v.9 Gowrie]. Cornish's projects in Adelaide included entries in the annual Adelaide Royal Show model garden competition (1929-36); the grounds of Christ Church, North Adelaide (where she was a communicant); and the gardens of Isabel, wife of Sir Sidney Kidman, Sir George Brookman [qq.v.9,7], Sidney Wilcox, and the Darling [q.v.4 John Darling junior], Darian Smith and Reid families. She also advised Eva Waite on her Jekyll-inspired Broadlees garden at Crafers and helped to develop the garden at Stangate House, Aldgate, for her sister-in-law Gwenyth Cornish.

Miss Cornish's two significant commissions were the University of Adelaide escarpment (1934-46) and the Pioneer Women's Garden (1938-40). The exposed, sunny, northerly aspect and poor soils of the former prompted her to plant it with a mixture of tough but flowering succulents and Italian hillside species resulting in 'a blaze of color ... a real adornment not only to the University but also to Adelaide'. Despite protracted disputes with the city council about Cornish's design and folkloric plant selections for the women's garden, Adelaide Miethke [q.v.10], who chaired the centenary council, doggedly supported her proposal, claiming 'it is probably the lack of a perfectly free hand, or trying to work in other peoples' ideas which has detracted from the garden ... in the eyes of the Council. All this must be said in fairness to Miss Cornish whose reputation as a Landscape Gardener stands high in the community.' Cornish also contributed 'Her Garden' to *A Book of South Australia* (1936).

She died on 20 October 1946 at her home in North Adelaide and was buried beside her family at St Jude's Church of England cemetery, Brighton. Her estate was sworn for probate at £19 991. Cornish was regarded as 'one of Adelaide's best known landscape gardeners, and was responsible for the design and care of many of the city's most beautiful gardens'.

Fifth Australian Urban History/Planning History Conference (Adel, 2000); D. S. Jones, 'Pioneer of University Landscape', *Adelaidean*, 7 Oct 1996, p 6, *and* '20th Century Landscape Design in Adelaide', *J of the Hist Soc of SA*, no 25, 1997, p 35, *and* 'Elsie Marion Cornish (1887-1946)', *Landscape Aust*, 20, no 1, 1998, p 92; *Advertiser* (Adel), 8 Oct 1938, 23 Oct 1946, p 12; staff file, D63/1934 (Univ Adel Archives); file no 1788 (City of Adel Archives).

DAVID S. JONES

CORRIE, SOPHIA (1832-1913), farmer, orchardist and writer, was born on 26 November 1832 at Hunter Street, Sydney, daughter of John Wheeler, dealer, and his wife Elizabeth, née Brumby. Sophie's parents had been orchardists at Curl Curl Lagoon where the Wheeler pear was evolved by the budding process. She attended a dame's school in Phillip Street. On 20 October 1855 in Sydney she married with Wesleyan forms William Christian McDona, a Dublin-born surgeon. He died of heart and lung disease in 1857, aged 29. On 25 January 1862 at Surry Hills, again in a Wesleyan service, she married Charles Pitman Corrie, an ironmonger from the Isle of Wight. They had seven children between 1863 and 1876.

Following the death of her second husband in 1875, to give her children healthy fruit, milk, vegetables and fresh air Sophie settled at Bargo Brush (Colo Vale), near Mittagong, where a 'slab and bark hut in an uncleared paddock was her first home'. Purchasing 40 acres (16 ha) and free selecting some 600 acres (240 ha), she cleared the selected land, helped with the burning off and fencing, and planted and attended to every fruit tree until her children were old enough to help.

For some sixteen years Mrs Corrie was a constant exhibitor and sometime judge at local country shows and for ten years at the Sydney Royal Show, where she was a frequent prize-winner. In all she claimed to have won over 700 prizes with 500 firsts—including the local Royal Agricultural Society's 1893 national prize of ten guineas for the best method of utilizing surplus fruit and vegetables. She also collected two silver medals for candied dried fruits, pickles and condiments.

Corrie needed to be independent, as Bargo Brush had bad roads, no schools or police and was a bushranging area. She encouraged self-sufficiency in her book *The Art of Canning, Bottling and Preserving Fruits*, published in Sydney in 1892 and reprinted six times by 1913. Aimed at housewives making their own preserves, it was notable for an emphasis on technique. For preserving fruits she preferred cans to the more popular bottles and claimed that it was the exclusion of air, rather than the presence of sugar, that prevented fermentation. Her book was full of common-sense advice:

There is no need to call a tinsmith to solder lids on preserves. The housewife can accomplish the task herself with little difficulty. Do it yourself.

In April 1906 Corrie travelled in the *Ventura* (Miles Franklin [q.v.8] was a fellow passenger) to the United States of America, then on to Europe and Britain, visiting friends and relations and attending the opening of parliament in London. On her return to Sydney in 1908, she was the first woman to be appointed to a seat on the council of the New South Wales Chamber of Agriculture.

While attending her son Arthur's wedding in Brisbane in 1913, Corrie caught a chill, and died at Bowen Hills on 27 September. She was buried in the family vault in the Methodist section of Rookwood cemetery, Sydney. Two sons and two daughters survived her.

C. Bannerman, *A Friend in the Kitchen* (Syd, 1996); *Station, Farm and Dairy*, 26 Apr 1906, p 1826; *Town and Country J*, 28 Oct 1908, p 39; *SMH*, 1 Oct 1913, p 7, 8 Oct 1913, p 7, 15 Oct 1913, p 7; letter, Corrie to Lady Windeyer, 25 Oct 1892 (ML).

PRIM MOSS

COSTELLO, PATRICK (1824-1896), publican, contractor and politician, was born on

18 March 1824 in County Leitrim, Ireland, the son of a farmer and his wife Jane, née Maxwell. An assisted migrant, Patrick arrived with his sister Mary in Melbourne in the *William Metcalf* on 27 August 1841. Establishing himself as a builder and contractor, by 1849 he was licensee of two city hotels. On 15 June 1847 at St Francis's Catholic Church, Melbourne, he married Irish-born Catherine Donovan. Costello's fortunes flourished with the gold rush. In 1852-55 he dealt in property and built a substantial home at Carlton.

Elected to the Melbourne City Council in 1855, Costello contested the Legislative Assembly seat of North Melbourne in 1859 and 1861, winning it at his second attempt. A protectionist, he opposed the Masters and Servants Act, saying, 'No such word as "master" ought to be used in a free country'. He favoured a 'general, liberal and entirely secular' education system—a bold stance for a Catholic.

Sworn in on 31 August 1861, Costello was already facing charges arising out of the poll for the seat of Mornington, which had taken place only days after his own election. He had organized a steamer trip during which a number of men were asked to personate deceased or absent Mornington electors. Found guilty, Costello was sentenced to twelve months imprisonment; before his sentence had been passed he was expelled from the Victorian parliament on 1 November 1861.

The blatancy of the offence indicated a limited sense of wrongdoing on Costello's part, and there were suggestions that he was acting on behalf of others. Personation, common practice in Victorian elections at that time, was part of a broader unacknowledged pattern of political corruption, the scope of which would not be revealed until the expulsion of Hugh Glass [q.v.4] in 1869. Costello's sentence aroused considerable public sympathy. Several petitions were presented to the governor, seeking mitigation of his sentence: one was signed by thirty-seven parliamentarians from both sides of the assembly, including James Service [q.v.6], mover of the expulsion motion against him. Costello was released on 31 March 1862, having first resigned from the Melbourne City Council.

His business interests suffered severely during his trial and imprisonment, and legal bills worsened his situation. Declared insolvent in 1863, Costello endured the death of his wife in 1866. Described as being of medium height and build, with a 'high forehead, thin nose, fair hair and complexion, of good address and gentlemanly appearance', he was resilient. He continued to work as a contractor and briefly as a coach trimmer. By 1882 he was again an owner of property in North Melbourne. Although not released from insolvency until 1891, he was elected to the North

Melbourne City Council in the same year and was mayor in 1892-93. Costello died on 17 October 1896 at his Canning Street home, and was buried in Melbourne general cemetery. His estate was valued at £998. Predeceased by three children, he was survived by two daughters and four sons; a great-great grandson, Peter Costello, became Federal treasurer in 1996.

D. Dunstan, *Governing the Metropolis* (Melb, 1984); T. Costello, *Tips From a Travelling Soul-Searcher* (Syd, 1999); family information.

GEOFF BROWNE
JACKIE CUNNINGHAM

COULTER, JAMES (1832-1907), municipal police superintendent, was born on 6 September 1832 at Kincon, and baptized in the Church of Ireland parish of Ballysakeery, County Mayo, Ireland, son of Robert Coulter, police officer, and his wife Elizabeth. After 'a good, useful, practical education', James joined the Royal Irish Constabulary on 12 July 1852 and was described as 5 ft 8¼ ins (173 cm) in height. He served in County Cork as correspondent and finance clerk until October 1857 when he resigned, with testimonials praising his intelligence, sobriety, diligence and trustworthiness, and left for Victoria. Soon he moved to Launceston, Tasmania, where he became sub-inspector of police in March 1858. In 1861 he was appointed bench clerk, gaining an intimate knowledge of the criminal laws. He was also first lieutenant of the Volunteer Rifle Corps, distinguishing himself by his thorough knowledge of military drill and 'firm, quiet and gentlemanly demeanour'.

Praised for his exemplary conduct, in June 1866 Coulter became superintendent of the Launceston Municipal Police. He assumed an independent stand, brooking no interference in his legal duty and proceeding against aldermen if necessary. In 1874 he enforced payment of an unpopular railway rate levied by the central government. On 4 and 5 February crowds protested and vandalized property. Although seriously injured, Coulter ordered his men to enforce the law 'without favour or affection, and to the best of their ability, skill, and knowledge'. Sensitive to community opinion on moral issues, he generally resisted heavy-handed law enforcement against publicans and prostitutes. Before the 1886 select committee on police centralization, he staunchly defended municipal policemen, asserting that they were superior to the territorial police controlled by the colonial government.

Although a disciplinarian, Coulter safeguarded his men's interests by drafting a police superannuation scheme in 1877. He became special auditor under the Launceston Police Provident Fund Act (1878), which entitled policemen with fifteen years of service to retire at 60 on an annuity for life. Provision was made for mental and physical infirmity and for families if a policeman died. Deductions were made from the pay of each man and increased according to his age. In 1895 he persuaded the council to extend superannuation to all employees. He resigned in 1896 with an annual allowance of £304; aldermen commended his zeal, integrity and fidelity. In June Coulter was appointed a justice of the peace, his knowledge of court procedure making him one of Launceston's most capable.

On 5 July 1867 he had married with Church of Scotland forms Christina Dean at her father's house in Launceston. There were seven children of the marriage. Coulter helped to set up the Equitable Building Society in 1870. Its first actuary, he framed the actuarial tables and served ten years as unpaid director. He was a founder and director of the Mutual Fire Insurance Co.

Coulter helped to form the Launceston Bowling Club and for forty years was a member of the Launceston Mechanics' Institute's board of management (vice-president, 1900, and secretary, 1901-06). A respected member of the Episcopal Church, he made an outstanding contribution to the municipal, legal, financial, religious and social life of Launceston. Coulter died on 6 April 1907 at his home and, escorted by a large and representative cortège, was buried in the Anglican cemetery, Elphin. His wife, two sons and two daughters survived him.

S. Petrow, *Going to the Mechanics* (Launc, Tas, 1998), and 'Tolerant Town, Model Force: The Launceston Municipal Police, 1858-1898', *Univ Tas Law Review*, 16, no 2, 1997, p 235, and 'Turbulent Tasmanians: Anti-railway Rate and Sectarian Riots and Police Reform in the 1870s', *Aust J of Legal Hist*, 3, no 1, 1997, p 73; Police Committee: Progress Report and Evidence, *J & PP* (Tas), 1880, vol 39; Report of the Select Committee on the Centralisation of the Police, *J & PP* (Tas), 1886, vol 9; *Examiner* (Launc), 11 Feb 1896, p 7, 8 Apr 1907, p 6; *Daily Telegraph* (Launc), 8 Apr 1907, p 5; *Tas Mail*, 13 Apr 1907, pp 13, 19; Coulter papers (SLT).

STEFAN PETROW

COUNGEAU, EMILY (1860?-1936), poet, was born probably on 3 May 1860 in Essex, England, youngest of twelve children of William Howard, head gardener at St Osyth's Priory, and his wife Ann, née Hester. Educated at a village school in Essex, Emily when a young girl became a ladies' companion, travelling extensively in the Mediterranean and becoming fluent in five languages. In 1887 she migrated to Australia, following three of her brothers, the nurseryman Amos William Howard [q.v.9], the headmaster Canon Walter Henry Howard and the music teacher Albert Edward Howard, who all became well known in South Australia.

On 21 February 1889 at the registry office, Richmond, Melbourne, giving her occupation as parlourmaid, Emily married Albanian-born restaurant keeper Naoum (Norman) Coungeau, whom she had met on Lesbos. The couple immediately moved to Brisbane, where they operated a wine saloon in Petrie Bight, opposite the Customs House. Here they served light wines, a continental-style luncheon with fruit and confectionery, and a renowned *café au lait*. Bernice May recalled that the saloon in 1916 was 'a picturesque place which was crowded with soldiers, the walls decorated with grapes and Bacchantes in purple and gold and red and wine shades'. Business prospered and the Coungeaus eventually owned two city buildings. In 1919 they retired to a gracious, Queenslander-style home on Bribie Island, where Naoum created a tropical garden filled with palms and pawpaws.

From 1913 Emily published poems in the Brisbane *Courier*, the Sydney *Bulletin* and the *Australian Woman's Mirror*, and produced four books of verse: *Stella Australis* (Brisbane, 1914), *Rustling Leaves* (Sydney, 1920), *Palm Fronds* (Brisbane, 1927) and *Fern Leaves* (Brisbane, 1934). Her 'romantic poetical drama' *Princess Mona* (Sydney, 1916), a fantasy of the birth and development of Australia, became the libretto for an opera entitled *Auster*, with a score by Alfred Hill [q.v.9]. Described by Thorold Waters as 'more promising for the development of a real Australian opera than anything that has yet been done', *Auster* was performed in a concert version in Sydney in 1922, and staged in Melbourne in 1935. Coungeau saw herself as a public poet whose role was to uphold the values of the British Empire and contribute to 'Australia's national hymn of progress' through celebrating the arrival of Celtic and Saxon kin in an empty land. Her best work exemplified the emergence of a female, cosmopolitan aesthetic in Australian writing.

Diminutive and birdlike, Coungeau was a gracious hostess and a noted philanthropist. She was a patron of artist Vida Lahey [q.v.9] and a supporter of women's associations such as the Lyceum Club and the Women's College within the University of Queensland. She and her husband also made generous donations to the Church of England. In 1935 she was awarded King George V's silver jubilee medal and was also elected to life membership of the Society of British Authors, Composers & Arrangers. She died on 26 July 1936 in Brisbane and was cremated with Anglican rites.

Her husband died five weeks later; they had no children.

Bulletin, 7 Sept 1922, p 42, 3 Apr 1935, p 16; *Aust Woman's Mirror*, 3 Apr 1928, p 11; *Aust Musical News*, 1 Apr 1935, p 4; *SMH*, 1 Sept 1922, p 10; *Courier-Mail*, 14 Sept 1922, p 12, 23 Nov 1926, p 11, 1 Mar 1935, p 19, 27 July 1936, p 14; *Daily Telegraph* (Brisb), 27 July 1936, p 18, 2 Aug 1936, p 23, 7 Sept 1936, p 13; *Sunday Mail*, 2 Aug 1936, p 23; Coungeau papers (OL and Fryer L, Brisb); information from, and family papers held by, Mrs E. Gobolos, Dulwich, Adel.   BELINDA McKAY

COVENTRY, SYDNEY ALFRED (1899-1976) and GORDON RICHARD JAMES (1901-1968), Australian Rules footballers, were born on 13 June 1899 at Greensborough, and on 25 September 1901 at Diamond Creek, Victoria, seventh and eighth children of Victorian-born parents Henry Coventry, carter later orchardist, and his wife Jane Henrietta, née Spencer.

Both Syd and Gordon were educated at Diamond Creek State School and played their early football for Diamond Creek in the Heidelberg League. Gordon worked in his father's orchard. Syd was a miner at Queenstown, Tasmania, when the Victorian Football League club, St Kilda, signed him in 1921. Collingwood claimed him, however, and he joined that club in 1922 after sitting out a season; he quickly established a permanent position with the 'Magpies'. He was a gas company employee when he married Gladys Eileen Trevaskis on 8 October 1921 at St Mary's Church of England, North Melbourne; that year he joined the Melbourne and Metropolitan Board of Works.

Syd was 5 ft 11 ins (180 cm) tall, with a vigorous playing style, alternating between ruck and defence. In 1927 he won the Brownlow medal for fairest and best player; as captain in 1927-34, he led Collingwood to the still unequalled record of four successive premierships between 1927 and 1930 and played 227 games for the club. He represented Victoria twenty-seven times from 1922 to 1933 and was sometime captain.

In 1935-36 Syd coached Footscray unsuccessfully. He enjoyed a long administrative career at Collingwood, being vice-president (1939-49) and president (1950-63). Although he was a poor chairman, with a weak grasp of meeting procedure, his geniality and warmth made up for these deficiencies. He retired from the board of works in 1964. Syd died on 10 November 1976 at his son's home at Fairfield and was cremated. His wife and four sons—two of whom, Hugh in 1941 and Sydney in 1954, had brief careers with Collingwood—survived him.

Gordon was one of Australian Rules football's greatest full-forwards, his scoring feats sometimes seeming to overshadow his brother's role as captain. In 306 games for Collingwood, from 1920 to 1937, he scored 1299 goals, a record not surpassed until 1999 (by Tony Lockett). Gordon played in five premiership-winning sides, headed the league annual goal-kicking totals on six occasions and represented Victoria twenty-five times. In 1930 he was the first man to kick 100 goals in a V.F.L. season and scored seventeen goals in a match, the then individual record. Nicknamed 'Nuts' (probably because his family considered that as a child he had a big head), he was a superb mark and a strong, rather than a fast, forward. He was 5 ft 11½ ins (182 cm) tall and in 1928 weighed 13 st. 2 lb. (83.5 kg). A mild-mannered player, the favourite of Collingwood patron John Wren [q.v.12], he was suspended only once, in 1936, when he retaliated after being struck on boils on the back of his neck.

On 28 February 1925 in Melbourne Gordon had married with Unitarian forms Christabel Violet Lawry. He was a boiler-worker in a yeast factory then became a foreman. After his retirement he also worked as a football columnist on the Melbourne *Sporting Globe*. He died of heart disease on 7 November 1968 at his property at Diamond Creek and was buried in the local cemetery. His wife, two sons and two daughters survived him.

R. Stremski, *Kill for Collingwood* (Syd, 1986); M. Roberts, *A Century of the Best* (Melb, 1991); R. Holmesby and J. Main, *The Encyclopedia of AFL Footballers* (Melb, 1998); *Table Talk*, 30 Aug 1928, p 17; *Age* (Melb), 8 Nov 1968, p 28, 12 Nov 1976, p 27; Collingwood Football Club archives; information from Mr G. Coventry, Templestowe, Melb.   RICHARD TREMBATH

COWPER, ROBINA FORDYCE (1866-1948), church worker and women's rights advocate, was born on 18 August 1866 at Sandridge (Port Melbourne), eldest of twelve children of Scottish-born parents John William Inglis, Presbyterian minister, and his wife Mary, née Fordyce. Educated at Clarendon College, Ballarat, Robina trained as a teacher. On 10 December 1890 at St Andrew's manse, Parramatta, New South Wales, with her father officiating, she married Charles William Cowper, a ship-owner from Melbourne. The Cowpers were stalwarts of the Augustine Congregational Church, Hawthorn, where she became a member. A daughter, born in 1892, died in 1895; Robina and Charles had no other children.

A member of the Collins Street Independent Church by 1901, from 1912 Mrs

Cowper was one of its delegates to the Congregational Union of Victoria. In 1913 she was elected to the union's home mission committee and the women's home mission committee executive. Her gifts were soon put to use as a speaker and as editor of the committee's journal, the *Clarion*. At the Congregational Union of Australia meeting in Adelaide in 1914 she gave a paper on home mission work, which work she maintained until 1921. She preached extensively in Victoria and in Congregational churches in New South Wales when she visited her parents.

In all her activities she advocated women's rights. She was the first woman on the Congregational Union executive committee (1922-25) and a founding member of the executive of the Congregational Women's Association in 1923. From 1921 she spent most of her time on the union's public questions committee as secretary and convenor. With delegates from other churches she lobbied the government on social justice issues such as the need for more women in the police force, protection of children, and temperance. As a representative of her church she was the only woman on the united social services committee. She thought Congregationalists were to the fore in the representation of women, whereas some of the other denominations were 'pickled in sex as to their ideas'. She continued to preach and speak. A paper she presented at the union meeting in 1924 on 'The State and the Child Criminal' was published in the *Woman* (December 1924) and reprinted by the *Honorary Magistrate*, official organ of the justices of South Australia.

Cowper's temperance work began when she became an organizer for the Woman's Christian Temperance Union in August 1923. After a few months, funding for the post was cut, and she was superintendent of the women's department of the Anti-Liquor (Prohibition) League until 1929. At the league's annual conference in 1926 it was reported that 'in a vigorous campaign amongst women and girls in factories', she had addressed '225 audiences as well as many church organisations'. In 1928 she was appointed a special magistrate of the Children's Court in Melbourne. Later that year she declined re-election as convenor of her church's public questions committee.

In an era before women were ordained or admitted to church governance, Mrs Cowper was elected to pioneer leadership roles in the Congregational Union of Victoria, excelling as preacher and administrator as she put her Christian faith into action. After her husband died in 1936 she moved to New South Wales to live with her sister. Robina Cowper died on 3 August 1948 at Parramatta and was cremated.

Victorian Congregational Year Book, 1925; *Victorian Independent*, 1 Sept 1914, 1 Dec 1921, p 229, 1 Apr 1925, p 71, 1 June 1925, p 104, 1 June 1929, p 105; Congregational Union (Vic), records (SLV); WCTU records (Melb Univ Archives); St Michael's Uniting Church archives, Melb; Clarendon College archives, Ballarat, Vic

ALISON HEAD

CRAMP, WILLIAM THOMAS (1849-1935), coachbuilder and fishing administrator, was born on 21 March 1849 in Hobart Town, second son of Richard James Cramp, an English-born clerk, and his wife Eliza, née Sadler. The family lived at Geelong, Victoria, from 1853. Returning to Hobart in 1862, William was apprenticed to the coachbuilder and wheelwright E. C. A. Nichols. In the next twenty-seven years he progressed to manager of the firm.

About 1880 his youngest brother Richard James was taken on as an apprentice and in 1892 they established their own business, which quickly won repute as a manufacturer of first-class coaches and carriages. In the 1920s Cramp Bros mastered the transition to motorcars, buses and trucks by importing engines and chassis from overseas then building the bodies and finishing the vehicles. Ford, Austin, Studebaker and Fiat were just some of the makes that rolled out of the Harrington Street works. In 2005 the business still operated at its original site, although it had been sold by the family in the 1940s.

On 1 June 1871 at Brighton Cramp had married Henrietta Jane Ludbey (d.1918) with rites of the Independent Church. They had five children. Active in the Memorial Congregational Church in Hobart, for fifty-nine years he was a prominent member of the Independent Order of Rechabites. His philanthropic interests also included the Friendly Society movement.

About 1895 Cramp took up trout fishing. Soon he began to assist Michael Jones to strip eggs from trout at the salmon ponds at Plenty and developed a passion for pisciculture. His brother Richard shared this interest until he drowned in 1907 while fishing in Lake Crescent. In 1910 William stocked the Hobart Rivulet with trout supplied by Jones and delivered in milk cans. Cramp carried the fish to the stream in his sulky. Except for a brief period, laymen such as Cramp managed Tasmanian fisheries until the 1940s. Most were anglers with a single-minded interest in developing salmonid fishing. After 1895 this honorary body, the Commissioners of Fisheries, relied on anglers' licence fees to finance its activities.

As a member—later vice-president and life member—of the Southern Tasmanian Licensed Anglers' Association, Cramp took a close interest in the trout fishery in Lake Sorell, established in 1909. In July 1919 he led a deputation from the association offering to build and run a hatchery there if the commissioners gave approval and technical support. His offer was accepted and the government granted £50 to assist in construction. In 1920, 100 000 trout fry were produced and production grew steadily over the next three years. Named the W. T. Cramp Hatchery, it operated until the 1940s. Said to have unrivalled knowledge of the State's lakes and streams, he visited the hatchery every winter for almost twenty years to supervise the collection of brown trout eggs.

In 1921 Cramp was appointed a commissioner of fisheries and continued after 1927 when the government amended the Fisheries Act to create a Sea Fisheries Board but left responsibility for inland fisheries with the renamed Salmon and Fresh Water Fisheries Commission. He retired in 1931 and was replaced on the board by his second son Harold. Predeceased by his wife in 1918, Cramp died on 30 July 1935 at his residence in Hobart and was buried at Cornelian Bay cemetery. He was survived by four sons and a daughter. In 1934 the S.T.L.A.A. had erected an obelisk to him at Interlaken.

His eldest son Harry Wilfred (1875-1962), secretary of the S.T.L.A.A. and chairman of the fisheries commission until 1948, was commemorated by memorial gates erected in 1952 at the Plenty salmon ponds. In the 1950s Harry's nephew George Chatfield Cramp (1904-1987) was also a fisheries commissioner. William, the founder of this dynasty, has been called the 'father of fishing' in Tasmania.

J. Clements, *Salmon at the Antipodes* (Melb, 1988); STLAA, *Annual Report*, 1955-56; *Mercury* (Hob), 31 July 1935, p 2; *Saturday Evening Mercury* (Hob), 6 Oct 1979, p 19.   A. J. HARRISON

CRAWFORD, JAMES (1908-1973), journalist and playwright, was born on 6 February 1908 at Manchester, England, and registered as John Oakden, youngest of four children of John Oakden Potter, a mechanical engineer of part-Scottish extraction, and his wife Janet Kerr, née Crawford, from the island of Arran. Young John's mother died when he was about 11.

Leaving grammar school at 16, Potter came to Australia as an assisted immigrant in 1924, disembarking in Brisbane. He worked in the Gulf Country and the Northern Territory as a stockman, station hand, ringer and boundary-rider, tried gold fossicking, then tramped around New Zealand in 1929-32. Back in Australia, he joined the ranks of the itinerant unemployed and exchanged a sustenance ticket with Bob Norman, whose name he assumed. In 1932 he was active in the Unemployed Workers' Movement and was involved in protests at evictions at Cairns, Queensland, and in the 'riots' of the unemployed at Mackay. Next year at the 'bagman's' camp, Victoria Park, Brisbane, he gave lectures on Shakespeare to his fellow unemployed. In 1934 he joined the Communist Party of Australia. He also founded the Roving Reds Revue Company, a short-lived theatrical group.

Travelling widely on his bicycle and expounding the need for proletarian revolution, he worked among cotton farmers of the Callide Valley, Queensland, cut cordwood for bakers' ovens in New South Wales, milked cows on dairy farms and packed tomatoes. He also went to Adelaide. Arriving in Melbourne in 1936 he became active in the Left Book Club, the Workers' Art Club and the Unity (Melbourne New) Theatre. On 8 August 1939 at the government statist's office, Melbourne, as Oakden Potter he married Ursula Mary Hill. He had previously joined the editorial staff of the *Workers' Voice* (*Victorian Guardian*), for which he wrote a weekly column as 'Jim Crawford': in 1940 he adopted that name by deed poll. When the Communist Party was declared illegal that year and the *Victorian Guardian* became a proscribed paper, he went underground with it until the Soviet Union entered the war.

Crawford enlisted in the militia on 21 January 1942 and served with the Australian Army Medical Corps. Discharged on 26 September, he joined the Royal Australian Naval Reserve two days later as a stoker. He was described as 5 ft 10 ins (178 cm) tall, with a dark complexion, blue eyes and light brown hair. Suffering from a duodenal ulcer, he was invalided out of the navy in Melbourne in January 1945 with a pension. He returned to work, freelancing for the *Sporting Globe* and other large newspapers, and rejoined the Melbourne *Guardian*. After the production in 1946 of his one-act play, *Welcome Home*, dealing with the effects of Melbourne's housing shortage on returning ex-servicemen, Jim devoted more time to the theatre. He was divorced in 1946 and in 1948 moved to Brisbane to work with the *Queensland Guardian*. On 22 December 1949 in Brisbane he married with Presbyterian forms Pamela Mary Seeman, an artist, and they settled at Mount Tamborine.

Crawford wrote at least seventeen plays. *Rocket Range* (1947), showing the impact of capitalism on Aboriginal society, was praised for presentation and acting but thrown out of the British Drama League festival as 'ideological propaganda'. Other dramas included *Refugee* (1949), about anti-Semitism, and *The*

Governor's Stables (1955), a plea for a national people's theatre, which won first prize in the Theatre Council of West Australia's 1951 competition. He wrote many skits and sketches for May Day, and contributed to both the Victorian and Queensland *Guardian*. Crawford was a playwright of the working class—intensely human, kind and tolerant to workers but intolerant of cant and hypocrisy. His great good humour was aimed as a barb at the enemies of the workers. He died of myocardial infarction on 11 November 1973 in Greenslopes Repatriation Hospital and was cremated. Childless, he was survived by his wife.

C. Healy, *Defiance: Political Theatre in Brisbane 1930-1962* (Brisb, 2000), and for bib; *Spa* (Syd), 11 Nov 1973, p 7; *Courier-Mail*, 11 Nov 1973, p 7; family information.   CONNIE HEALY

CRIST, ALICE GUERIN (1876-1941), author and journalist, was born on 6 February 1876 at Clare Castle, Clare, Ireland, daughter of Patrick Guerin, chapel master, and his wife Winifred, née Roughan. Alice migrated with her family to Queensland at the age of 2. As her father was a teacher, she spent her childhood at small, south-eastern rural schools where he supervised her education and her work as a pupil-teacher. In 1896 she was appointed to Blackhall Range State School near Landsborough but, after a transfer to West Haldon next year, she was unfairly dismissed when an inspector found her *en route* to a wedding to retrieve truant students. She returned to her family at Douglas on the Darling Downs. On 4 October 1902 at St Patrick's Catholic Church, Toowoomba, she married a German immigrant farmer, Joseph Christ, who later changed the name to Crist. The couple moved to an isolated property at Rosenberg near Bundaberg in 1910 but returned to Toowoomba in 1913 when Jo began a fuel supply business there.

Alice pursued an active literary career despite significant periods when she had to concentrate on farm work and the care of her five children. A prolific writer of verse and short fiction, she published widely in the Australian secular and religious press, including the *Bulletin* (Sydney), *Worker*, *Steele Rudd's Magazine*, *Home Budget*, *Toowoomba Chronicle*, *Catholic Advocate* and *Catholic Press*. Her devout Irish Catholicism was at first associated with democratic politics and in 1902 she joined the Social Democratic Vanguard. She also became friendly with another poet and schoolteacher (Dame) Mary Gilmore [q.v.9], who published her work in the women's page of the *Australian Worker*. Crist wrote about her rural and domestic experiences, frequently celebrating the beauty of the bush and the virtues and struggles of Irish-Australian pioneers. A marked Celtic influence is discernible in poems about the homesickness of immigrants and in the sprites and faeries of her nature verse and poems for children.

Crist was a long-term member and vice-president of the Toowoomba Ladies' Literary Society, which played an important role promoting the culture of the Darling Downs. In 1917 her youngest brother Felician was killed at Passchendaele, Belgium; for many years she contributed Anzac Day poems to the *Toowoomba Chronicle*. She published *When Rody Came to Ironbark and Other Verses* (Sydney, 1927) and *Eucharist Lilies and Other Verses* (Sydney, 1928).

From 1927 the Brisbane *Catholic Advocate* began to pay Crist for rural and religious poems, short stories and a serial celebrating the contribution of the Christian Brothers to Catholic education, which resulted in the novel, *"Go It! Brothers!!"* (Sydney, 1928). In 1930 she became 'Betty Bluegum', editor of the children's page, and used the versatility of this outlet to stimulate Queensland's Catholic children. Crist's page, like her verse, was an inventive mix of Catholic Irish-Australian nationalism, domestic virtue and appreciation of nature, and she encouraged young correspondents.

In 1935 she was awarded King George V's jubilee medal and in 1937 King George VI's coronation medal. Crist died of tuberculosis on 13 June 1941 in hospital at Toowoomba and was buried in Toowoomba cemetery. Her husband, three daughters and two sons survived her. In September 1953 a wing of the Holy Spirit Hospital, Brisbane, was dedicated in her name.

J. Duhig, 'foreword' in A. G. Crist, *Eucharist Lilies* (Brisb, 1929); H. A. Kellow, *Queensland Poets* (Lond, 1930); D. Dornan, *Alice With Eyes A-Shine* (Brisb, 1998); family papers (held by Mrs D. Dornan, The Gap, Brisb).   CHRISTOPHER LEE

CROMER, VICTOR EUGENE; *see* KROEMER

CROOKE, WILLIAM GEORGE (1846-1920), schoolteacher, conservationist, journalist and social reformer, was born on 13 October 1846 at Saltwater River probation station, Tasman Peninsula, Van Diemen's Land, son of Rev. Robert Crook[e], a station catechist from Dublin, and his wife Caroline Jane, née Drew. The family moved to Franklin, in the Huon district, in 1853. Following a scandal when Robert sued for libel but lost the case, the Crookes left for Melbourne in 1858.

William worked as a monitor in his parents' Emerald Hill school, South Melbourne, then taught in Victorian suburban and rural schools. On 20 December 1872 at the Independent Church, Maryborough, he married London-born Ellen Alston. Soon the couple went to Costerfield, a mining town near Heathcote. When Crooke expressed concern in a local newspaper at the effect of smelting fumes on his pupils he was reprimanded. He opposed corporal punishment. A school inspector criticized him for being disorganized, but another observed his 'considerable intelligence'.

Transferred to Wodonga in 1885, Crooke became secretary of the Athenaeum and Free Library Society, and developed a strong interest in fisheries, wildlife and the environment. After moving to the coastal town of Portland, he indulged his passion for angling. On 13 July 1894, suffering poor health, he was superannuated but began the most productive period of his life. He was an outspoken advocate for the Victorian Fish Protection and Anglers' Society and drew attention to diminishing fish numbers caused by industrial pollution and over-fishing. Dismayed by the lack of policing powers of the Victorian Fisheries Act of 1890, Crooke became the society's delegate on the Fisheries Board, drafting recommendations for an 1893 select committee.

In 1892 and 1894 Crooke visited Tasmania as a delegate of the Australian Natives' Association, discussing Federation issues. A democrat, he supported the proposal for a convention, urged that it be 'BIG—6 or 700' strong and criticized the lack of full male and female suffrage for the election of delegates. In 1894 he returned to Tasmania to live in Hobart, briefly operating a small, private school at Battery Point. He joined organizations, attended meetings and wrote innumerable letters to newspapers on a range of issues. Through the Southern Tasmanian Railway League he urged the line's extension into timbered rural areas. In 1903 he was a founding member of the Southern Tasmanian Licensed Anglers' Association, whose members included the urban intellectuals who were to make early conservation moves successful.

Crooke was initially drawn to the Workers' Political League, writing in the pro-labour newspaper, the *Clipper*, ridiculing the National Association and members such as G. P. Fitzgerald [q.v.4]. He argued for the right to strike and the arbitration system and praised industrial legislation that guaranteed wages. Attracted to the Citizens' Moral and Reform League and the politics of Bishop J. E. Mercer

[q.v.10], he challenged the Church's support of workers. By March 1906 he had rejected unionism and lost to W. A. Woods [q.v.12] in an election to the House of Assembly. In May 1915 he unsuccessfully contested Legislative Council elections as a Liberal.

From 1904 Crooke was fishing correspondent for the Hobart *Mercury* under the pseudonym 'Jollytail', using the column to air environmental issues. He was influenced by park models in Africa and the United States of America, declared that 'rivers should be national property' and argued for control over all forms of fishing. Quoting the philosophies of Henry Thoreau and Walt Whitman and the poetry of Henry Kendall [q.v.5], Crooke applied an international vision to local issues. In 1906 he promoted the concept of land reservation for the Mount Wellington and Queen's Domain parks, Hobart, and of wildlife reserves including bird sanctuaries. In 1916 he gave evidence to the royal commission conducted by T. T. Flynn [q.v.8] on Tasmanian fisheries. Critical of Flynn's refusal to publish the evidence, he printed extracts in his newspaper column.

Crooke died after a long illness on 27 August 1920 in hospital in Hobart. Survived by his wife and a son, he was buried in Queenborough cemetery. He was remembered by the *Mercury* for his 'flashes of witty merriment which set many a table in a roar', although he was a teetotaller. At the dedication of an obelisk to him at Mount Field National Park in 1924, he was described as 'years ahead of current thought' and 'intensely patriotic, wonderfully progressive, courageous & tenacious'.

R. Crooke, *The Convict* (Hob, 1958); *Report From the Select Committee upon the Fisheries' Act Together with the Proceedings of the Committee and Minutes of Evidence* (Melb, 1862); *Mercury* (Hob), 29 Aug 1903, p 8, 4 Jan 1906, p 6, 26 Mar 1906, p 4, 28 Aug 1920, p 6, 18 Feb 1995, p 4; *Tasmanian Mail*, 2 Sept 1920, p 22; *Weekly Courier* (Launc), 2 Sept 1920, p 33; *Weekly Courier* (Launc), 2 Sept 1920, p 33; P. H. MacFie, 'One Spot Secure From Change'—William Crooke the 'Father' of Mt Field (ts, 1994, copy held by author); VPS 795/3295, item 19/1/1873, VPS 40/41, item 22/9/1885 (PRO, Vic); W. Crooke, Victorian Department of School Education, personal file (copy held by author, Dulcott, Tas).

PETER MacFIE

CROOKS, ALEXANDER (1847-1943), bank manager, cricketer and embezzler, was born on 23 September 1847 at Leith, Midlothian, Scotland, youngest of seven children of William Crooks, printer, and his wife Ann, née Thompson. The family sailed in the *Coloomey* and reached Port Adelaide on 7 December 1852. In the 1860s Alexander was employed as a bank clerk at Angaston, returning to Adelaide in 1872. On 18 September 1873 at the Wesleyan Church, Kent Town, he married Emily Hannah Birks; his sister Jemima had married Emily's brother Walter Richard. In 1874 Crooks gained a moment of cricketing fame when, representing the colony at Adelaide Oval, he took a spectacular boundary catch to dismiss the legendary W. G. Grace (for 6 runs). Crooks's cricketing skills brought him into contact with an elite fraternity, including Sir Henry Ayers and C. C. Kingston [qq.v.3,9], and in 1874-85 he was treasurer of the South Australian Cricket Association. In October 1885 he became chairman of the association but resigned at the December meeting, shortly before he was engulfed by scandal.

In 1879 Crooks had been employed as an accountant in the newly established Commercial Bank of South Australia; within a year he was manager. With one son and three daughters (a son had died in infancy), the family lived in North Adelaide. The bank grew rapidly, its balance sheet rising from £221 130 in 1879 to £1 909 537 by 1886, with twenty-six branches in South Australia, including Palmerston (Darwin), and offices in Melbourne, Perth and London. On 24 February 1886, to the shock of the Adelaide business community, the bank suspended trading. Three days later Crooks was arrested and charged with fraud. It soon emerged that lending and accounting practices in the bank were lax, with Crooks engaging in speculative lending to prominent businessmen and supplementing his income from the till.

The collapse of the bank created an atmosphere of recrimination against the managers and directors; at an Adelaide Town Hall meeting there was a call to lynch Crooks. He was charged with embezzling £5000. Kingston defended him at the trial, held on 6 April 1886, where he pleaded guilty. In passing a sentence of eight years' hard labour at the Stockade, Yatala, the judge commented that Crooks had probably misappropriated some £20 000 to £30 000 and had made advances to customers without approval from the directors to an extent of £278 000. The bank went into liquidation—a fate that the South Australian Cricket Association managed to avoid through astute management and a secret loan from the brewer (Sir) Edwin Smith [q.v.6].

In detention Crooks, a model prisoner, was placed in charge of the dispensary. He was granted early release on 11 October 1890 and in 1899 sought a new life in Western Australia, where he became a manager of a mining company, Gray & Sons, at Norseman. He left Western Australia in 1916, returned to Adelaide about 1923 and retired to Brighton. Predeceased by his wife in 1932, Crooks died on 29 August 1943 at Brighton and was buried in St Jude's Church of England cemetery. A son and two daughters survived him.

G. Blainey, *Gold and Paper* (Melb, 1958); S. J. Butlin, *The Australian Monetary System 1851 to 1914* (Syd, 1986); R. M. Gibbs, *Bulls, Bears and Wildcats* (Adel, 1988); T. Sykes, *Two Centuries of Panic* (Syd, 1988); *A'sian Insurance and Banking Record*, 15 Mar 1886, pp 116, 123, 15 Apr 1886, p 196; 13 May 1886, p 252; *Advertiser* (Adel), 26 Feb 1886, pp 4, 5, 27 Feb 1886, p 4; 1 Mar 1886, p 5, 5 Mar 1886, p 5; *Sun* (Syd), 3 Mar 1977, p 28.

GREG MCCARTHY
MARGARET PHILLIPS

CROW, AGNES; *see* EDWARDS

CUBADGEE, DICK (1870-1889), Aboriginal guide and cultural broker, was born in 1870 near Tennant Creek, South Australia (Northern Territory), second son of a ceremonial leader of the Warumungu people, known to Europeans as 'King Tapanunga'. The names Tapanunga and Cubadgee would be rendered today as Japanangka and Jappaljarri. Cubadgee—whose name has also been recorded as Kubadji—held primary ritual responsibility for Jurnkurakurr waterhole, a 'Carpet Snake' dreaming site on Tennant Creek. He grew up in the vicinity of the newly established telegraph station, becoming familiar with English and European ways and acquiring his first name, Dick. By April 1886, when he met the explorers David Lindsay [q.v.10] and his brother George at Eva Downs near Anthony Lagoon, he was initiated and was probably familiar with the extent of Warumungu country.

Becoming 'a first rate camel man', Cubadgee assisted Lindsay in surveying new pastoral leases verging on Warumungu territory and then accompanied the party to the Gulf of Carpentaria. The Lindsays embarked for Adelaide by ship. Cubadgee and the Afghan cameleer took the party's camels and horses overland to Hergott Springs (Marree) without loss, an epic 1250-mile (c.2000 km) journey accomplished in four weeks.

On Cubadgee's arrival in Adelaide by train he became David Lindsay's coachman and lodged with Lindsay's father-in-law, who was director of the Destitute Asylum. Cubadgee met influential Adelaide figures, including Chief Justice (Sir) Samuel Way [q.v.12], a noted ethnographic collector. When Lindsay contributed an exhibit to the Adelaide International Exhibition of 1887, combining Aboriginal artefacts with prospecting charts and samples of 'rubies' from Harts Range, Cubadgee became its centre-piece, as 'King of the Warramanga'. He used the opportunity to tell visitors of his country.

Cubadgee stood 6 ft 6 ins (198 cm) tall. His slim physique and striking looks, confident demeanour and ready sense of humour made him a popular figure and attracted the attention of medical anthropologists and scientists. He threw boomerangs on Adelaide Oval and demonstrated the rotary drill fire-making method with his own fire-sticks in the Exhibition Building and for select groups at Government House. Not simply 'Lindsay's boy', he was aware of the increasing pressure which European pastoralism imposed upon his people; his southern experiences gave him confidence to seek a different outcome.

After appearing at the Melbourne Centennial Exhibition, Cubadgee returned to Central Australia with the Lindsays in late 1888 and assisted in their ruby prospecting. Learning that his elder brother had been murdered, he considered taking revenge, but his time there was cut short by illness. Lindsay arranged his admission to Adelaide Hospital on 19 April 1889 and the surgeon Archibald Watson [q.v.12] performed a successful operation on a neck tumour. During Cubadgee's long convalescence he informed his hospital visitors that, although Europeans were established in his country, they should pay with cattle for usurping tribal land, so as to enable his people to have a viable future. Five months after his operation, Cubadgee succumbed to a secondary infection and died of 'tubercular meningitis' on 15 September 1889, aged just 19.

Watson and the South Australian Museum director (Sir) Edward Stirling [q.v.6], who had become Cubadgee's friends, regarded him as an 'outstanding specimen of his race'. They persuaded the Lindsays to allow them to preserve his skeleton for science. Following a service at Holy Trinity Church of England on 19 September 1889 his remains were buried in West Terrace cemetery. The mounted skeleton was displayed in the South Australian Museum until the 1950s. On 4 June 1991, after consultation with the Warumungu community, Cubadgee's skeleton was buried in a moving ceremony in his ancestral country, at Jurnkurakurr.

P. G. Jones, *Ochre and Rust* (Adel, 2002), and 'A Tracker Comes Home: The Story of Dick Kubadji', *Adelaide Review*, Sept 1991; Roy Geographical Soc of A'sia (SA), *Procs*, 1952-53, p 35; *Land Rights News*, July 1991, p 14; *Observer* (Adel), 21 Sept 1889, p 30; *Mail* (Adel), 2 July 1927; information from Mr J. S. Rattray, Syd.   PHILIP JONES

CULPIN, MILLAIS (1874-1952), schoolteacher, medical practitioner and psychologist, was born on 6 January 1874 at Ware, Hertfordshire, England, second of six children of Millice Culpin (1847-1941), leather-seller, later a medical practitioner, and his wife Hannah Louisa, née Munsey. Millais spent his early years at Stoke Newington, where he attended school; later he attended the Grocers' Company (Hackney Downs) School. Joining a group of amateur naturalists, he also developed a lifelong passion for entomology. In 1891 he matriculated at the University of London, but that year the family left in the *Ruapehu* for Melbourne. In search of a healthier climate, his father settled in Brisbane as a general practitioner and in 1903-06 was Labor member for Brisbane in the House of Representatives. The Nonconformist Culpins conveyed to their children the virtues of rational thought, self-reliance and hard work.

In 1891 Millais was briefly an assistant teacher at a private boarding school at Nundah. Following three unprofitable months on the Gympie goldfields, in August 1892 he accepted a post in a one-teacher, provisional school at Laura in the State's far north. His salary was £120, of which the local community contributed £20. At this time he described himself as a Methodist. Inspectors reported that he worked hard with indifferent students, was a good disciplinarian and showed 'very considerable skill as a teacher'. Sober and frugal, he spent weekends and holidays exploring the countryside and gathering insects, some of which he mounted for the school museum. He also sent samples to English colleagues, noting that 'ants, lepisma, white ants, roaches and the wet season combined are enough to ruin anything here'. His illuminating letters (published in 1987) offered rare insights into life in the tropics, where Culpin enjoyed bush carpentry, fishing, riding and shooting.

His request to remain at Laura being unsuccessful, in July 1896 Culpin was promoted to assistant teacher at Ross Island, Townsville. On 20 June next year he resigned and went back to London to study medicine at the London Hospital (member, Royal College of Surgeons, and licentiate, Royal College of Physicians, 1902). After a year in his father's Brisbane practice, he resumed study at the University of London (M.B., B.S., 1905; M.D., 1919). He continued to work at the London Hospital, specializing in surgery, and became a F.R.C.S. in 1907. That year he went to Shanghai, where in 1913 he married Ethel Maude Bennett, matron of the British hospital, at which he was senior surgeon. Their honeymoon included a visit to Australia and a trip to Laura. Millais also worked as a *locum tenens* around the country. A daughter was born at Young, New South Wales, in 1914, before the family sailed for England.

During World War I Culpin served in the Royal Army Medical Corps. As a military surgeon at Portsmouth and in France his experiences with shell-shocked soldiers led to an interest in war neuroses and its varied psychological manifestations. He published his research findings for his doctoral thesis as *Psychoneuroses of War and Peace* (Cambridge, 1920). In the 1920s he devoted his time to medical psychology, researched industrial health and lectured part time at the University of London. An eclectic thinker, with interests in psychoanalysis, temperament and abnormality, he was captive of no school, a loner, although well respected. In 1931 Culpin was appointed professor in industrial and medical psychology at the London School of Health and Tropical Medicine. Among his publications was a 1935 article for the *Practitioner*, 'Neurasthenia in the Tropics', which argued that white people could inhabit the tropics without ill effects.

Retiring in 1939, Culpin was president of the British Psychological Society in 1944. His pastimes included playing bridge and he was adept at the more learned crosswords. He died on 14 September 1952 at St Albans, Hertfordshire, survived by his wife and daughter.

F. Mackeith (ed), *Letters from Laura* (Townsville, Qld, 1987); Dept of Public Instruction (Qld), Annual Report, *PP* (Qld), 1892-97; *British Medical J*, 27 Sept 1952, p 727; *Lancet*, 27 Sept 1952, p 643; M. de Jabrun, Environmental Factors Affecting Teaching and Learning in North Queensland 1875-1905 (Ph.D. thesis, Univ Qld, 1999); Register of teachers, male (QA).   MARY D'EIMAR DE JABRUN

CUPER, MARY ELLEN (1847-1877), Aboriginal postmistress and telegraphist, was born in 1847 at Bunbury, Western Australia, daughter of Yanjipp, an Aboriginal woman, and William Ramsey (Ramsay), a European. Known as Pangieran, in 1862 Mary (Maria) Ellen was sent to Bishop Salvado's [q.v.2] Benedictine mission at New Norcia, where she was educated. She married Peter Nhawer on 8 December that year. Her husband died soon after their marriage and Mary Ellen married Benedict Cuper, son of an English-born father and an Aboriginal mother, on 6 April 1863. It was Benedict's second marriage. They had one child, who died in infancy. The Cupers took up 15 acres (6 ha) of mission land and made it into a successful farming operation, often shown to important visitors as an example of what could be achieved.

A post office, known officially as Victoria Plains, was opened, probably at New Norcia, in April 1857. The approval of a telegraph line to Geraldton via New Norcia in the early 1870s meant that a full-time telegraphist would be required and Salvado personally trained Mary Ellen for this work. When the position of postmistress at Victoria Plains became vacant un-

expectedly in May 1873, the superintendent of telegraphs, James Fleming, reported that Salvado had 'an applicant in a female aboriginal who is perfectly familiar with the telegraph Code, and manipulation of the Key, and can read and write smartly; but I fear the lady would prove inconstant and it will be necessary to appoint someone to whom the quarters and a small salary will suffice'. But Salvado strongly supported Mary Ellen's application and, despite Fleming's gloomy prognostication, she took over as postmistress in August 1873. She was formally appointed in January 1874 with an annual salary of £30, and shown as H(elen) Cuper in the postal records from this time.

New Norcia became a post and telegraph office in March 1874 and the Cupers took up residence next to the office. When Helen contracted tuberculosis and her health started to deteriorate towards the end of 1875, she trained Sarah Ninak, another Aboriginal woman, as a telegraphist. Sarah took over much of the postal and telegraphic work. In 1876 Governor (Sir) William Robinson [q.v.6] visited New Norcia at a time when Sarah was temporarily in charge and was so impressed that he sent her photograph and a very complimentary dispatch to London. Helen Cuper died on 12 January 1877 and was buried in New Norcia cemetery with Catholic rites. She was survived by her husband, who subsequently remarried. For reasons unknown, Sarah Ninak did not continue in the post and telegraph office.

N. Green and L. Tilbrooks (comps), *Aborigines of New Norcia 1845-1914* (Perth, 1989); B. Pope, Postal Services in Western Australia, 1826-1901: The Growth of an Organisation (M.Phil. thesis, Murdoch Univ, 1989); Colonial Secretary's Office records, Acc 36, 758, 148 (SRWA).   BRIAN POPE

CURRY, ROBERT HENRY (1885-1930), superintendent of Palm Island Aboriginal reserve, was born on 7 August 1885 in South Brisbane, second son of Queensland-born parents George Adam Curry, compositor, and his wife Alice Amelia, née Willson. Then a stockman at Malanda, Bob enlisted in the Australian Imperial Force on 19 October 1915. He served in the Middle East with the 2nd Australian Remounts Unit from April to October 1916, and was discharged in Brisbane on 13 December with a 'mildly crushed foot' and a wasted left forearm.

Joining the Department of Native Affairs, Curry was appointed assistant superintendent at Barambah in June 1917 and on 5 July, at St Andrew's Presbyterian Church, Brisbane, he married a widow, Agnes Mathers, née Dries. When a cyclone demolished Hull River settlement in March 1918, Curry was given the task of establishing a reserve on nearby Palm Island. Agnes was to follow as matron.

Curry slept in a tent on the beach while supervising the construction of the settlement. In response to challenges to white authority on the mainland, Palm Island soon became a punitive reception centre for those sentenced by courts or banished by mainland institutions. By the 1920s Curry had a reputation as a 'benevolent dictator' and a diligent worker. His efforts to establish a football team, movie theatre, brass band and weekly corroborees were widely appreciated by inmates. Yet others felt the force of his domination, with lengthy imprisonments, public humiliations and floggings of those he perceived as threatening his control. His ultimate punishment was to exile individuals to nearby Eclipse Island with only bread and water.

At 5 ft 9 ins (175 cm), Curry had a lean and suntanned figure, blue eyes and light brown hair; his constant patrols of the island were usually accompanied by Native Police. A crack shot, he would fire his revolver at wildlife, including whales, and at midnight each New Year's Eve. By the close of his twelve-year reign he had become driven and ill-tempered, with an unhealthy attachment to the reserve. Despite chronic shortage of funds and widespread ill health, the population of the island had reached 1000 by 1930. Feuds among the staff became the subject of official inquiries; relations between the reserve's doctor C. M. Pattison and the superintendent were bitter, and Curry was found to have twice assaulted colleagues. The home secretary's office report concluded that the consumption of alcohol 'was at the bottom of the trouble'.

In April 1929 Curry was officially reprimanded for breaching regulations by severely flogging a female inmate. In November his wife died in childbirth. By December Curry was grief-stricken, fearful of losing his position, drinking heavily and withdrawing from novocaine—Pattison's treatment for 'neuralgia of the cranial nerve'. The doctor and his patient had ceased to communicate. In this context the home secretary's office began investigations into accusations by inmates that Curry had interfered with Aboriginal girls on the island. The subsequent report found that there was no truth to the allegations, that the reserve functioned in 'a high state of efficiency' and that the management reflected the 'greatest credit on all concerned'.

In the early hours of 3 February 1930, however, the superintendent had run amok, clad in a bathing suit and armed with dynamite, petrol and revolvers. He drugged his 11-year-old son Robbie and 19-year-old stepdaughter Edna and dynamited the family home in which they slept, shot and injured the doctor and

his wife, set fire to the homes of other staff and blew up the reserve's main buildings. Drinking from a bottle, and with bouts of 'maniacal laughter', he took the launch *Rita* to nearby islands. Returning to Palm Island in the afternoon, Curry marched up the beach —as if to 'frame his own execution'. He was ambushed by a group of inmates, on the instruction of white officials, and died from bullet wounds at 6.15 p.m. Curry, his son and his stepdaughter were buried in the new cemetery, Townsville. The tragedy provided the basis for Thea Astley's novel *The Multiple Effects of Rainshadow* (1996).

Report on the Operations of Certain Sub-departments for 1930, *PP* (Qld), vol 1, 1931; *North Qld Register*, 8 April 1918, p 34, 18 Mar 1918, p 20, 15 Feb 1930, p 21, 22 Feb 1930, p 44; *Truth* (Brisb), 16 Feb 1930, p 15; *Daily Standard* (Brisb), 17 Feb 1930, p 1; J. Watson, Becoming Bwgcolman (Ph.D. thesis, Univ Qld, 1993); POL/J21, 413m *and* JUS/N 907, 260, 413m *and* HOM/J712 *and* R. v. *Pryor*, A/18421, 1930, 65 a, b, c (QA).   JOANNE WATSON

CURTAIN, JOHN (1835?-1905), publican, politician and entrepreneur, was born at Grange, Limerick, Ireland, son of Timothy Curtain, farmer, and his wife Susan, née Goggin. Reaching Melbourne, probably in the *Queen of the Seas* in September 1854, John travelled to the Ovens, Lachlan and Murray regions, where he worked as a teamster and goldfields carrier. He returned to Melbourne in 1860, settled at Carlton and opened a hotel. On 7 April 1861 at St Francis's Catholic Church he married Catherine Mary Josephine Peacocke, also from Limerick. They had eight children.

He built Curtain's hotel, in Elgin Street, in 1863 and other buildings, including Curtain Terrace. In 1870 Curtain was elected to Melbourne City Council as an inaugural councillor of Victoria Ward, created to represent the rapid growth of North Carlton. He was elected to the Legislative Assembly in April 1871 for North Melbourne and held the seat until 1877 when the constituency was divided. Standing for Carlton, he was beaten by James Munro [q.v.5] in a celebrated contest—the publican had a predictably testy relationship with the rising temperance leader. Curtain failed to win Carlton again in 1879 and 1883 and Melbourne in 1897. His municipal career had a similar pattern. Defeated for Albert Ward in 1876, he was returned for Gipps Ward, narrowly losing the mayoralty that year to James Paterson [q.v.5]. Kate died in 1879. On 23 December 1882 at Carlton with Catholic rites Curtain married Ballarat-born Mary Wood. He was a justice of the peace, and remained a Melbourne city councillor until 1887.

Curtain was a speculator in suburban property, a director of several companies, chairman of the Licensed Victuallers' Brewing Co. and co-proprietor of the Melbourne *Herald*. In partnership with the expatriate Frenchman, town planner and winemaker Ludovic Maric, in 1875 he acquired a distillery on the south bank of the Yarra. In 1885 Curtain purchased 550-acres (222.5 ha), including about 25 acres (10 ha) of vines, on the northern slopes of Mount Saddleback in north-eastern Victoria, in which he had been a minority shareholder from 1881 with L. L. Smith, George Coppin [qq.v.6,3] and Marie. Expanding plantings, he brought it into line with the largest vineyard holdings in the region and sold his Yarrabank distillery for £60 000, intending to relocate brandy production to the now renamed Chateau Dookie. A grand, Italianate mansion, large winery and well-equipped distillery were built, and he employed many hands, including a Swiss vineyard manager. But Curtain and the turbulent Marie fell out and in 1887 were embroiled in legal conflict.

Following the collapse of the wine industry in the 1890s depression, Chateau Dookie was not sustainable; Curtain was ruined, but not apparently bankrupted, in 1892. In 1896 the Bank of Victoria appointed François de Castella [q.v.13] as manager. Curtain claimed to have planted 700 acres (283.3 ha) of vines at Chateau Dookie; de Castella's more sober assessment of 497 acres (201.1 ha) still makes it an astonishing figure by world standards at the time. The winery buildings were destroyed by fire in 1907.

Ambitious, gregarious and flamboyant, Curtain embodied the aspirant values of Melbourne's inner-suburban, gold-generation immigrants. He was essentially a speculator and entrepreneur, and his later business and political associates included mavericks such as Smith and (Sir) Thomas Bent [q.v.3]. His ambitions, like those of many of his generation who gambled on their luck and further prosperous times, crashed when the tide turned. He spoke with a rich brogue but believed the Irish had integrated in Victoria. While his Irish Catholicism, local interests and liquor trade associations provided a network, they also guaranteed opposition. An old age pensioner, he died of chronic bronchitis on 22 October 1905 in Melbourne Hospital, and was buried in Melbourne cemetery, survived by four daughters and four sons from his two marriages. Curtain Street, Carlton, is named after him.

D. Dunstan, *Better Than Pommard!* (Melb, 1994); *Men of the Time in Australia: Victorian Series* (Melb, 1878); *Leader* (Melb), supp, 6 June 1874; 28 Oct 1905; *Age* and *Argus* (Melb), 24 Oct 1905, p 5.

DAVID DUNSTAN

CURTIS, HARRY ARTHUR (1882-1933), engineer, was born on 6 June 1882 at Lyttelton, New Zealand, son of English-born parents Charles Evin Curtis, coal merchant, and his wife Eliza, née Westgate. Educated at Christchurch, Harry was an apprentice with the government railways from 1898, obtaining a certificate of competency as an engineer, 3rd class. He also attended evening classes in the school of engineering and technical science at Canterbury College, University of New Zealand, and passed elementary descriptive geometry in 1899. From 1903 he was a ship's engineer plying to and from England, Europe, Africa and the United States of America. Returning to New Zealand in 1912, he worked for Lyttelton Harbour Board and Christchurch City Council before joining the New Zealand Board of Works on the construction of a hydro-electric scheme at Lake Coleridge. Here he met (Sir) John Butters [q.v.7] who visited the site as a consultant. On 20 August 1913 at St Saviour's Church, Lyttelton, Curtis married Agnes Brown.

Butters offered him a position at the Waddamana power station in the centre of Tasmania and, moving there with his wife, Curtis became superintendent on 1 January 1916. In July he was appointed chief operator of the Hydro Electric Department and in 1919, when new machinery needed to be installed to extend the plant capacity, he also became engineer in charge of electrical construction. In 1921 he took responsibility for all plant and construction work at Waddamana, Miena, Liawenee and Arthurs Lake, as well as the transmission line construction, on the completion of which he was appointed engineer for electrical design while retaining his operating duties. Assistant chief engineer from 1924, Curtis was given a five-year contract as general manager of the H.E.D. next year, when Butters departed for Canberra. On 18 January 1930 he became the first commissioner of the new Hydro-Electric Commission Tasmania.

A member of the Institution of Engineers, Australia, in 1927 Curtis had been elected chairman of the Tasmanian division. He was a member of the Hobart Technical College council and the Engineering Board of Management, and sometime chairman of the faculty of engineering at the University of Tasmania. A devotee of tennis, he also belonged to Hobart Rotary and Kingston Golf clubs and was a member of the Tasmanian Amateur Jockey and Tasmanian Racing clubs. 'Tod' Curtis, as he was often called, was short, stocky and rather dour, described as 'a character ... bald as an egg ... short in his remarks to junior staff'. Much of his time and energy was spent extending the power grid to the farthest corners of the island to produce a truly State-wide system. In 1929 there was severe flooding in the north and the commissioner gained considerable publicity for standing in a small boat in the middle of the raging South Esk River to make emergency repairs to an overhead power line.

Curtis died on 20 May 1933 following an operation in St John's hospital, Hobart. He was buried in Cornelian Bay cemetery, survived by his wife and son William Robert, who spent his working life, apart from war service in the Royal Australian Navy, with the operations branch of the H.E.C.

R. Lupton, *Lifeblood* (Syd, 2000?); Hydro-Electric Commission, *Report*, 1932-33, p 2; *Mercury* (Hob), 22 May 1933, p 7; HEC personal file, 14/5/11/20, film R9 (Hydro Tasmania, Hob); family information from Mrs M. Curtis, Hob.   H. DE V. GILBERT

D

DALRYMPLE, DOLLY (c.1808-1864), Aboriginal matriarch, was born in the Furneaux Islands in Bass Strait, daughter of George Briggs, a sealer from Bedfordshire, England, and Woretemoeteyenner (also known as Pung or Margaret), who was the daughter of Mannarlargenna, a chieftain from the northeast of Van Diemen's Land. One of two Aboriginal women abducted by Briggs, she bore him three children before he sold her to another sealer, John Thomas, for a guinea. Three of her daughters, including Dolly, were adopted by European couples on the mainland, and her younger son John remained in the islands to be cared for by James Munro [q.v.], another sealer.

Dolly's foster parents Jacob Mountgarrett (1773-1828), the surgeon at Port Dalrymple, and his wife Bridget had her baptized Dalrymple on 18 March 1814. The author Charles Jeffreys [q.v.2] referred to her in 1820 as 'Miss Dalrymple' and James Bonwick [q.v.3] as Dolly Dalrymple, the name by which she has become known. Jacob Mountgarrett was in continual conflict with the authorities and notorious as a bad debtor, suspected of cattle stealing and misappropriating stores and medicines. His adopted daughter, however, was taught all the necessary domestic skills, as well as reading and writing, and was quick to learn. About 1825 she left the Mountgarretts, to live with a convict stockman Thomas Johnson (1801-1867), who worked at Dairy Plains near Deloraine. Born in Cambridgeshire, England, he had been convicted of burglary in December 1822 and sentenced to death, later commuted to transportation for life.

On 24 September 1830 G. A. Robinson [q.v.2] visited the family, which then included two girls aged 6 and 2. Informed by a local stock-keeper that many Aborigines had recently been killed in the district, Robinson also recorded that Dalrymple had lived for a time with the notorious murderer Cubitt and had assisted him in the killing of Aborigines. On 22 May 1831, perhaps in response to earlier grievances, a group of Aborigines mounted an attack on the Johnsons' hut while the mother was alone with her children. Armed with a musket, she held off the attack for six hours until help arrived. As a reward, the government granted her twenty acres (8 ha) of land at nearby Perth, where Johnson erected a dwelling.

Dalrymple married Thomas Johnson on 29 October 1831 with Anglican rites. In August 1836, only recently pardoned, Johnson received a further seven-year prison sentence for receiving stolen wheat. With four children to support, his wife displayed great resourcefulness and tenacity in holding her family together. In October she petitioned Governor Arthur [q.v.1], asking that her husband be assigned to her as a servant, but the request was refused. By 1841, with Johnson out of gaol, conditions began to improve and Dalrymple requested that her mother, then at Wybalenna, on Flinders Island, be permitted to live with her. The petition was granted and Woretemoeteyenner came to Perth to live with her daughter and seven grandchildren.

The family moved to the Mersey region in 1845 and Johnson, pardoned again, took over the tenancy of the Frogmore estate. Prospering in the new district, he purchased 500 acres (202.3 ha) south-west of Frogmore, where he built the family home, Sherwood Hall. He became the owner of two hotels (the Native Youth Inn at Sherwood and the Dalrymple Inn at Ballahoo), a coalmine (the Alfred colliery) and a timber exporting business. The family became one of the largest landholders in the district and was well respected. Dalrymple was said to be devoutly religious. She died on 1 December 1864 at Latrobe aged 56, survived by her husband and ten of her thirteen children. In 1865 the widower married a younger woman, Marie Emma Bourne. He died on 3 December 1867.

J. West, *The History of Tasmania*, A. G. L. Shaw ed (Syd, 1971); B. C. Mollison, *Tasmanian Aboriginal Genealogies*, 3 (Hob, 1977); C. Ramsay, *With the Pioneers* (Hob, 1979); R. M. Fowler, *The Furneaux Group, Bass Strait* (Canb, 1980); L. Robson, *A History of Tasmania*, 1 (Melb, 1983); N. J. B. Plomley, *Weep in Silence* (Hob, 1987); H. Felton, *On Being Aboriginal*, book 1 (Hob, 1984); N. J. B. Plomley and K. A. Henley, *The Sealers of Bass Strait and the Cape Barren Island Community* (Hob, 1990); CSO 1/886/18804 (TA).   IAN MCFARLANE

DAVIS, SIR GEORGE FRANCIS (1883-1947), industrialist, was born on 22 November 1883 at New Lynn, Auckland, New Zealand, third and youngest son of Charles George Davis, from Worcestershire, England, and his American-born wife Lillian Edwedinah, née Ball, whose father operated a glue factory at Leeds in partnership with one of the Davis family. Charles had migrated to New Zealand in 1879, intending to farm but instead used his small, inherited income to establish a modest glue factory at New Lynn in 1881. Acquiring a site at Onehunga on Manukau Harbour, in 1888 Charles built a new factory there. In 1892 his eldest son Charles Christopher (Chris) began to work in the factory. The second son, Maurice, went to sea as a marine engineer when he was old enough (and stayed away until 1915). In 1899 Charles formed the New Zealand Glue Co. Ltd, in which he held one third of the shares, and Chris became manager.

After schooling at King's College, Remuera, Auckland, in 1895-97, George went to sea under sail for four years. In 1901 he joined Chris in the factory, while their father went to England. Returning in 1903, Charles bought out the other shareholders and gave George and Chris shares equal to his own. The Davis family expanded the glue manufactory after 1903 and in 1909 bought its major rival at Woolston, Christchurch, where George became manager.

When Davis senior died in April 1913, his sons decided to diversify into gelatine, which was not made on any scale in Australasia at that time. To learn the craft, George went to London to a plant run by B. Young & Co., largely owned by his mother's family. J. G. V. 'Jack' Ball, George's cousin, educated him in the intricacies of gelatine production.

Plant for the manufacture of gelatine was erected at Woolston in 1913, catering for the whole of New Zealand and soon for Australia and Canada as well. His brother Maurice joined George at Woolston in 1915. After a share issue in 1916, the New Zealand Glue Co. expanded to Australia, establishing a gelatine factory in New South Wales. George was chosen to go to Sydney, where he arrived on 27 October 1917, accompanied by a Woolston colleague, an Auckland architect and Elizabeth Eileen Schischka, the Auckland-born daughter of a friend of George's mother.

Davis acted decisively. He purchased twenty acres (8 ha) of sand-hill country close to Botany Bay, formed Davis Gelatine Co. Ltd and married Eileen at St James's Church of England, Sydney, all on the day of arrival. In December 1917 the foundations of the new factory were laid and on 6 January 1919 the first commercial gelatine was produced.

The Davis family bought out possible competition in New South Wales, demolishing two existing factories, while Botany expanded. To reflect the new position of Davis gelatine in world markets, the company structure was progressively changed. In 1921 the Botany concern became Davis Gelatine (Australia) Pty Ltd, the principal holding company for the family; next year Davis Gelatine (Africa) Pty Ltd was formed in Cape Town to sell gelatine from both Botany and Woolston to African markets; in 1925 Davis Gelatine (Canada) Ltd was created; in 1926 the old New Zealand Glue Co. Ltd was restructured as Davis Gelatine (NZ) Ltd, a subsidiary of the Australian company; and in 1929 Davis Gelatine Pty Ltd was created in Victoria, with a factory in Melbourne to make glue and stock foods. Davis's cousin Jack Ball migrated from England to become works manager at Botany in 1924 and a director of the company.

Davis created a model environment at Botany, surrounding the gelatine plant with extensive landscaping: in the 1930s an industrial expert commented that with 'well kept lawn and park-like approaches, beautiful flower beds, tennis courts and bowling green, it does not look like a factory at all'. The remains were described in 2000 as 'the best surviving example in NSW of a factory garden inspired by the Garden City Movement'.

The company progressively diversified: first into limestone mining at Mount Frome near Mudgee after 1923, with a processing plant in Sydney at St Peters in the 1930s; then into diatomaceous earth at Bugaldie used for clarifying the gelatine at Botany. In 1933 George and some colleagues independently took over the lease of Cockatoo Island Dockyard in Sydney from the Commonwealth government, forming a new company, Cockatoo Docks & Engineering Co. Ltd, which revitalized the ailing facility and benefited from the challenges of World War II, employing 3500 workers at its peak, ten times the workforce inherited from the Commonwealth in 1933.

Fear of war in the 1930s also prompted the Federal government to consider the need to have a local source of oil and petrol, using the rich deposits of oil shale in New South Wales that had been exploited since 1865. The mines at Newnes had closed in 1922, but the shale seam in the Capertee Valley was still viable. The minister of development, Senator A. J. McLachlan [q.v.10], persuaded George and Chris Davis to form a subsidiary of Davis Gelatine—National Oil Pty Ltd, consolidated by Acts of both the Federal and New South Wales parliaments in 1937. The Davises put up a quarter of the initial capital, the State government another quarter and the Commonwealth the remainder.

George gave up most of his other business activities to lead the new enterprise. He travelled widely, especially in Scotland, the home of the oil-shale industry, in Estonia and in the United States of America to inspect retorts and other equipment. The new industrial complex in the Capertee Valley was named Glen Davis after George, the great vertical retorts were in operation by 1939, the oil refinery started pumping petrol in 1941 and the grandly planned township grew rapidly. In recognition, Davis was knighted in January 1941, but the new Curtin [q.v.13] government took control of National Oil Pty Ltd in December and new directors were appointed. For the rest of World War II, Davis was largely preoccupied with Cockatoo Dockyard and with the Australian gelatine business.

Davis's business activities were his life: from 1917 he had lived next to the gelatine works in Spring Street, Botany, moving to Vaucluse only in 1930. He had no children. His hobbies were gardening, motoring and travel; deafness made him reticent in company. *Smith's Weekly* described him in 1940 as 'quiet and purposeful' in manner, and in appearance 'short and stubby, rather fat-cheeked, wearing a sound box just over his right lapel'. Davis died of cardiovascular disease on 13 July 1947 at his home and was cremated with Anglican rites. His wife survived him. The Cockatoo Dockyard & Engineering Co. Ltd was acquired by Vickers in 1947, while the gelatine companies expanded worldwide in a number of combinations with other food firms. The Davis Botany plant was closed in 1990, and the company's interests were merged in Goodman Fielders and in Leiner Davis Gelatin Ltd, which in 1995 opened the successor plant to Botany at Beaudesert in Queensland.

R. G. Parker, *Cockatoo Island* (Melb, 1977); *The History of Glen Davis* (Syd, nd); *Heritage NSW*, 7, no 3, Winter 2000, p 8; *Smith's Weekly*, 28 June 1924, p 2, 7 Sept 1940, p 5; *SMH*, 6 July 1940, p 15, 1 Jan 1941, p 5, 1 Nov 1941, p 3, 14 July 1947, p 3; H. E. Morgan, Cockatoo Dockyard, Oldest in Australia (ts, 1958, ML); M. C. Davis, Davis Gelatine: An Outline History (ts, 1993, Mascot Library, Botany Bay, Syd) *and* A Few Notes Concerning Davis Gelatine and Some of its People (ts, 1996, Mascot Library, Botany Bay, Syd); M. Barrow, A Report on the Archives of Davis Gelatine (Australia) Ltd (1997, placement report for MIM (Archives), Univ NSW).   R. IAN JACK

DAVIS, WILLIAM (1821-1910), pastoralist and sportsman, was born on 13 November 1821 at Bloxham, Tiverton, Devonshire, England, fourth of eleven children of William Davis and his wife Jane Elizabeth, née Weston. Young William was educated at the Blue Coat School, London. His elder brother John and sister Mary travelled to Australia with a family friend, Bishop William Broughton [q.v.1]. William arrived in Sydney in the *Alfred* on 31 December 1837; his parents and other siblings migrated in 1842.

Employed as a clerk with the Commercial Banking Co. of Sydney, Davis later took charge of the Goulburn branch. His first pastoral experience was with Charles Campbell [q.v.1], as overseer of Duntroon at Limestone Plains (Canberra). With his brother Henry, Davis overlanded cattle to Adelaide in 1847. He then established a cattle station in Gippsland, Victoria, for G. T. Palmer [q.v.2]. Returning to New South Wales about 1849, Davis managed Ginninderra for Palmer, whose daughter Susan Adriana he married on 11 April 1850 at the Church of St John the Baptist, Canberra.

In 1854 Susan inherited the estate and Davis, its trustee and manager, became known as 'the Squire of Ginninderra'. Writing in the *Golden Age* (Queanbeyan) in 1863, James Wood commended him for the best-ordered establishment he had seen in the colony: 'everything seems to work by clockwork … and the people of the estate seem to partake of the order around them'. In 1865 Davis grew an excellent wheat crop from the seed of a newly introduced, rust-resistant strain from Adelaide. He owned successful racehorses and hunters and judged blood horses at important shows. A crack shot and renowned prizewinner, he won the Goulburn Gun Club's trophy in the 1890s when he was well over 70.

Davis's greatest local fame sprang from his passion for cricket, a game he introduced to the district in the early 1850s. His almost unbeaten team included three Aborigines —Jimmy and Johnny Taylor and Bobby Hamilton—justly regarded as the star players. In 1864 the Ginninderra eleven played the combined Queanbeyan and Bungendore elevens and still won. Davis added to the excitement of the matches and public occasions with dinners, balls, brass bands and fireworks. In 1851-77 he was a warden of St John's. Largely due to his efforts, St Paul's combined church and school, Ginninderra, was built in 1862. That year Davis built a new home, not far from Ginninderra, naming it Gungahline.

A generous and considerate employer, in 1857 Davis had established a school in a room in old Ginninderra on the estate and about two years later introduced a weekly half-day holiday for his employees, championing the introduction of such a holiday throughout the district. A justice of the peace, he sat on the Queanbeyan Bench of Magistrates. Davis had no children. His nephew Henry William Ernest Palmer, whom he had virtually adopted, was killed in 1877 and the Davises soon moved to Woodhouselee near Goulburn. His wife died in 1902. In his last years William was living with his niece May McKay whom he regarded as his adopted daughter. He died on 13 July 1910 at Brisbane Grove and was buried with Anglican rites in St Saviour's Cathedral's cemetery, Goulburn.

L. Gillespie, *Ginninderra, Forerunner to Canberra* (Canb, 1992); *Pastoralists' Review*, 15 Aug 1910, p 626; *Golden Age* (Queanbeyan, NSW), 12 Mar 1863, p 2; *Goulburn Evening Penny Post*, 14 July 1910, p 2; *Canb Times*, 31 May 1980, p 13, 16 Jan 1982, p 15; information from Mr J. Jauncey, Mollymook, Mrs J. Palmer, Wagga Wagga, Mr D. Dowland, Callala Bay, and the late Mr W. Brook Forbes.
                                              LYALL GILLESPIE

DAY, JOHN MEDWAY (1838-1905), journalist and minister of religion, was born on 24 February 1838 at Bedford, England, son of Samuel Day, carver and gilder, and his wife Elizabeth, née Stamford. After schooling at Bedford, John worked in a local solicitor's office, was secretary of the young men's improvement class at Bunyan Baptist Church and studied for the ministry in 1861-65 at Regent's Park College, London.

Day (often referred to as Medway Day) migrated to South Australia in the *Octavia* in 1866 and served at Mount Gambier Baptist Church; from 1869 he was at Kapunda. Active in community life, he was a popular lecturer and a member of local institute committees. From 1868 he regularly contributed to the Baptist publication *Truth and Progress*, of which he became editor in 1874. He chaired the South Australian Baptist Association in 1870-71.

Feeling constrained by his position as a clergyman, in 1875 Day left his ministry and became leader writer for the *Register* in Adelaide. When acting editor in 1883-84, he was criticized for using his position to advance his 'extreme' views on land nationalization. He so strongly championed the co-operative village settlements on the Murray that the *Bulletin* could say they were 'largely of his making'. Representing country institutes on the board of the Public Library, Museum and Art Gallery from 1886, he was chairman in 1889-90. On 12 August 1886 at Southwark he married with Anglican rites Ellen Sandland.

Day left the *Register* in March 1892 and became editor of the Single Tax League's paper, the *Pioneer*. In December 1892 he launched a weekly, the *Voice*, styled as 'In the Cause of Humanity'. He wrote much of the copy, seeking to 'stimulate enquiry, to consolidate and give voice to the public feeling on [current] social and political questions'. Day spoke frequently on land reform, effective voting, political economy, women's suffrage, unionism and other reform topics: between May and December 1893 he delivered fifty-six lectures in Adelaide and country areas. Some of his lectures were published, including *Political Economy in a Nutshell for Young Men and Women* (Adelaide, 1893) and *Idlers in the Marketplace* (Sydney, 1896). In 1893 he failed to win the House of Assembly seat of Gumeracha. He organized a reform convention in September 1893 and was acknowledged as 'leader of the Forward Movement', a loose coalition of trade unionists, democrats, single taxers, feminists, Christian sociologists and socialists.

In 1894 Day went to Sydney as the first professional editor of the *Australian Worker*, the paper of the bush unions that were to amalgamate to form the Australian Workers' Union

in 1895. Following a brief, financially disastrous move from a weekly to a daily paper in 1894, he was closely questioned at the initial A.W.U. conference in February 1895 and again in 1896, but gained overwhelming support from the rank and file. When also manager of the *Worker* in 1896, he used his own savings to advance wages, but the paper ceased publication in February 1897. He became manager of the Trades' Council Co-operative Store in Sydney and promoted the co-operative movement. In May 1895 he had contested Labor preselection for Grenfell but was defeated by W. A. Holman [q.v.9]. Preselected for Gundagai instead, Day lost.

When his wife died in April 1894 he described her as having been an 'earnest co-worker in the cause of humanity'. Day married Marcella Mary Carr, née Blake, a widow, on 8 September 1897 in St Patrick's Catholic Church vestry, Sydney. He continued to lecture on social questions and strongly advocated unification rather than Federation. Appointed editor of the *Tasmanian Mail*, in 1904 he moved to Hobart. Day died of an intestinal obstruction on 8 July 1905 at Hobart. Childless, he was survived by his wife.

With commanding presence and a large leonine head, opinionated and egotistical, he was referred to by fellow journalists as 'Judgement Day'. A man of integrity and marked ability, while favouring land reform and Henry George's [q.v.4] ideas, he refused to be known as a single taxer. He reputedly belonged to the Social Democratic Federation but, curiously, a conservative Hobart obituarist asserted: 'With socialists he had no affinity'. According to the *Worker*, however, a 'kindly thought' was due to his memory, as 'one who steered the ship for a while when many of the rocks in the course were uncharted'.

H. V. Evatt, *Australian Labour Leader* (Syd, 1942); L. F. Crisp, 'John Medway Day: A South Australian Who in 1893 Went East, Not West', *JHSSA*, no 9, 1981, p 111; *Daily Telegraph* (Syd), 15 Jan 1897, p 6; *Mercury* (Hob), 10 July 1905, p 5; *Clipper* (Hob), 15 July 1905, p 8; *Observer* (Adel), 15 July 1905, p 24; *Worker* (Syd), 15 July 1905, p 4; *Bulletin*, 9 April 1892, p 10, 17 Aug 1905, p 15; W. J. Sowden, Our Pioneer Press (ts, 1926, SLSA).

MARGARET ALLEN

DE GROOT, FRANCIS EDWARD (1888-1969), antique dealer and member of the New Guard, was born on 24 October 1888 at 23 Upper Liffey Street, Dublin, youngest son of Cornelius De Groot, a sculptor of Dutch Huguenot descent, and his wife Mary, née Butler, from a Clonmel family of Norman Irish background. After a pre-emptory and unhappy schooling at Blackrock and Belvedere colleges, Frank joined the merchant navy, aged 13. He completed a five-year apprenticeship to his uncle Michael Butler, an antique dealer, before migrating to Australia in 1910.

When the booksellers George Robertson and Fred Wymark [qq.v.11,12] opened a city art gallery that also sold antiquities, De Groot's knowledge and connections with the trade in Dublin and London proved invaluable. He claimed to have been advanced £10 000 by Robertson to purchase antiques for resale in Sydney and quickly became a minor celebrity as a purveyor of fine, antique furniture.

Soldiering was De Groot's other passion. In 1907 he had joined the South of Ireland Imperial Yeomanry and in 1909 spent six months in barracks with the 5th Dragoon Guards. In 1914 he was in Ireland, where he enlisted in the 15th Hussars. He served with distinction on the Western Front, later transferring to the 15th Tank Battalion with the rank of acting captain. His commanding officer described him as an 'Excellent disciplinarian and leader of men, a very determined officer with plenty of dash'. There is some evidence that early in April 1919 he volunteered to serve in Russia to fight Bolsheviks. On 25 October at the Star of the Sea Catholic Church, Donnybrook, Dublin, he married Mary Elizabeth (Bessie) Byrne of Portumna, Galway.

The couple came to Sydney in May 1920. De Groot enhanced his reputation when, specializing in Queensland maple, he opened a business designing, manufacturing and marketing reproduction furniture of the highest quality. This was his most profound contribution to the city of Sydney. By 1927 he claimed to employ a staff of 200 artisans at his factory at Rushcutters Bay. Major commissions included a lavish refit of the retailer David Jones [q.v.2] Ltd's department stores.

De Groot's politics were conservative. While he claimed sympathy with the conservative Irish nationalism of John Redmond [q.v.6], in essence he was an ardent Empire loyalist. As the Depression hit Australia, he became increasingly concerned about the depredations of the Labor premier J. T. Lang [q.v.9] and communists, and joined the proto-fascist New Guard of Eric Campbell [q.v.7] in September 1931. By February 1932 he was a zone commander, a senior member of the council of action and a veteran of many street mêlées. Campbell regarded him as a trusted intermediary in dealing with the Commonwealth attorney-general (Sir) John Latham [q.v.10].

On 19 March 1932 De Groot became the unofficial central actor at the ceremonial opening of Sydney Harbour Bridge, which Campbell had vowed that Lang would not perform. Either to prevent his leader from losing face or to deflect him or others from more militant action, De Groot insinuated himself into the vice-regal entourage. Mounted on horseback, at the crucial moment he slashed the opening ribbon with his sword, declaring the bridge open 'in the name of the decent and respectable people of New South Wales'. Dragged from his horse by irate police, he was escorted to the Darlinghurst reception centre, where he survived the suggestion that he was insane. Though convicted of offensive behaviour, De Groot served a writ on the New South Wales police alleging wrongful arrest, ultimately securing a tidy out of court settlement.

In a polarized society De Groot basked in both public adulation and condemnation. Poems and songs eulogized his 'gesture of contempt, with a humorous flavour'. The minutiae of the incident, irregularities in his uniform and the choice of horse (an apparently inelegant steed) commanded obsessive attention, while the presence of a Cinesound news camera in close proximity helped the event to secure an enduring niche in Australian folklore. Pranksters 'doing a De Groot' became a frequent accompaniment to the opening of roads and bridges in New South Wales. Despite his legendary position in the New Guard, De Groot possibly provided information to Military Intelligence. In November 1932 he broke with Campbell and considered linking 'a considerable number of men' with the Melbourne-based League of National Security, having already maintained high-level contact with that secret organization's leaders.

A compact, trim, dapper man, De Groot returned to his manufacturing business, which flourished. As well as furnishing the extension of the New Australia Hotel, in 1935 De Groot provided for Sir Isaac Isaacs [q.v.9] a suite of furniture that included an elegant ceremonial chair, later acquired by the Mitchell [q.v.5] Library, Sydney. During World War II, assisted by the patronage of Major-General Gordon Bennett [q.v.13], Major De Groot held postings with the Citizen Military Forces and the Australian Imperial Force. In 1942-43 he was commandant at Greta army camp, where his 'fascist' past became the subject of controversy. Further stints with the army at Tamworth and at the Sydney showground in charge of courts of inquiry into escapes from detention preceded a six-month attachment to the United States Army in the South Pacific Area Command. He was placed on the Retired List in January 1944.

In 1950 De Groot and his wife returned to Dublin, where he dabbled in antiques and was active in the Irish Australian Society. He died on 1 April 1969 in a Dublin nursing home. Childless, he was survived by his wife. The bridge opening remained a talking point among Sydneysiders. In 2005, sections of the ribbon were in private hands, in the Mitchell

Library and in the Australasian Pioneers Club, and De Groot's sword was held privately in Sydney.

K. Amos, *The New Guard Movement 1931-1935* (Melb, 1976); A. Barker, *George Robertson* (Brisb, 1982); A. Atkinson (ed), *Footnote People in Australian History* (Syd, 1987); A. Moore, *The Secret Army and the Premier* (Syd, 1989) and 'Another Wild Colonial Boy' in *Aust J of Irish Studies*, 2, 2002, p 135; *Australiana*, 22, no 1, Feb 2000, p 19; *SMH*, 21 Mar 1932, 24 Mar 1992, p 1, 7 Aug 2000, p 5, 1 May 2004, p 3; MP742/1, item D/2/306 (NAA, Melb); De Groot papers and autobiography (ML); information from Mr M. Hardwick, Gordon, and Mr S. O'Connor, Cheltenham, Syd.   ANDREW MOORE

DEL FABBRO, UMBERTO PRIMO (ALBERT)

DEL FABBRO, UMBERTO PRIMO (ALBERT) (1899-1978), terrazzo contractor, businessman and Fascist, was born on 2 December 1899 at Segnacco, Friuli, Italy, one of nine children of Giacomo Del Fabbro and his wife Teonilla, née Di Giusto. Umberto was named after the reigning king of Italy, which may have influenced his enduring national pride. After elementary school he attended trade school, where he acquired expertise in terrazzo paving, a specialty of the region. Following his father to Australia, he arrived in Sydney in the *Osterley* on 28 January 1915 and found work on the construction of Burrinjuck Dam.

When Italy entered World War I with the Allies, Del Fabbro was repatriated to serve with the Italian army in 1918. He was employed in reconstruction work undertaken by the military near his home town and formally discharged in 1920. Having returned to Sydney in 1921, next year he joined his brother Amedeo in Melbourne and, with another Italian, formed Zoz-Del Fabbro, a mosaic and terrazzo business employing some twenty tradesmen. Now known as Albert, he moved to Adelaide in 1925, set up a factory at Kent Town and began to promote the use of terrazzo as an attractive building material. His business grew as he gained important contracts, and the premises of Albert Del Fabbro Ltd moved to Flinders Street, in the city, in 1935.

A 6 feet (183 cm) tall, imposing figure, with dark hair and piercing, blue eyes, Del Fabbro was then one of the most successful and influential Italians in South Australia. He had married Victorian-born Bessie Jane Jewkes on 5 February 1927 in the Maughan [q.v.5] Methodist Church vestry, Pitt Street, Adelaide; they were to have two daughters. In 1930 Albert became a naturalized British subject, assimilating well into the community. Nevertheless, he was an active member of the State branch of the Fascist Party from its inception in 1926 and administrative secretary in 1930-40. While many Italians joined to maintain their culture, Del Fabbro's commitment was political; he recruited members, had a mosaic portrait of Mussolini in his office and retained a fierce loyalty to Italy. In 1937 he wrote to the *Advertiser* protesting about racial prejudice against Southern European 'foreigners'. When Italy joined the war in June 1940 Del Fabbro was interned at Hay, New South Wales; he was later at Loveday, South Australia. His naturalization was revoked in 1943 on the grounds of disloyalty and his wife wrote begging him to 'give up worrying about and discussing world affairs'.

Released in 1944, Del Fabbro rebuilt his business and by the 1960s had 120 employees. He sponsored the migration of Italian tradesmen, helping them with fares and accommodation. His generosity and enterprise were acknowledged with a gold medal from the Chamber of Commerce of Udine, Italy, and his appointment as cavaliere of the Order of Merit by the Italian government in 1964. Active in the Lions Club and the Liberal Country League and a director of several companies, he was an instigator and foundation member of the Italian Club of South Australia, established in 1967 to encourage cultural activities for all Italians and to foster integration into the Australian community. In retirement he lived at Mitcham, continued to enjoy playing bocce with his compatriots and returned to Italy often. Predeceased by his wife, Del Fabbro died on 7 July 1978 in St Andrew's hospital, Adelaide, and was cremated after a service at St Paul's Monastery. His daughters survived him.

D. O'Connor, *No Need to be Afraid* (Adel, 1996); *Advertiser* (Adel), 6 Sept 1937, p 22, 12 June 1940, p 18; D1915, items SA2367 and SA2452, AP501/2, items 1, 3, 9 and 10, A463, item 1963/1399, and A1838, item 1535/18/35 (NAA); information from Mrs F. Del Fabbro, St Georges, SA.

CARMEL FLOREANI

DENDY, HENRY

DENDY, HENRY (1800-1881), special survey proprietor, was born on 24 May 1800 at Abinger, Surrey, England, only son of Samuel Dendy, farmer, of Great Millfields and other property in Sussex and Surrey, and his wife Sarah, née Hampshire, who died when Henry was aged 3. When his father died in 1838, Henry was a brewer at nearby Dorking, which may help to explain why he sold the farms in 1840 and paid £1 an acre for a special survey of 5120 acres (2048 ha) at Port Phillip. He arrived in Melbourne on 5 February 1841 with his wife Sarah, née Weller, whom he had married at Capel, Surrey, on 6 January 1835, and their 5-year-old son Henry.

Dendy's behaviour was extraordinary, especially his attempt to establish a manorial estate in the pastoral colony. Inadvertently, though, he almost made a fortune. If applied to urban land, his order was thought to be worth £100 000. Melbourne's capitalists were agog, and Superintendant La Trobe [q.v.2], alarmed by the unexpected situation, appealed to Governor Gipps [q.v.1], who withdrew from sale land within five miles (8 km) of towns.

Astonished by his potential windfall, Dendy accepted advice from the forceful merchant J. B. Were [q.v.2], who was his agent when the land order was presented to La Trobe on 8 February. Defiantly, they claimed urban land before accepting two miles (3.2 km) of bay frontage at the Melbourne five-mile limit. Their Brighton Estate was surveyed in May 1841.

The ambitious plan, a pace-setter for Melbourne, offered delightful foreshore sites, a township with crescents and an inland village among seventy-eight-acre (33 ha) farms. Dendy built a two-storey 'manor house' and made his seventy-four-acre (32 ha) seafront home, Brighton Park, a show place. In partnership with Were, he played the role of founder, implemented a grant of ten acres (4 ha) to the Church of England and hosted a picnic match between the Brighton and Melbourne cricket clubs. His prosperity seemed assured, although the original manorial dream had been amended. Unable to employ the twenty-nine families and twenty-two single workers he had sponsored under the land regulations, he helped them to settle. They left names like Carpenter, Lindsay, Male and Hampton on Brighton streets; a street was also named after Dendy.

When depression hit the colony in 1843, land sales ceased and bad debts accumulated. Dendy suffered severely but kept afloat until required to honour his guarantee of £1500 on a bank loan to Were. In April 1845 he was declared insolvent, a fate softened by his wife's ownership (as her dowry) of Brighton Park. While Were was sustained by his brother in England, Dendy attempted to recover by brewing at Geelong in 1846-48, but could not keep the Brighton property. When it was sold in 1848, he tried squatting at Christmas Hills in 1849-53 and Upper Moira in 1853-55. The former was miserable, but the latter, near Nathalia, carried 8000 sheep when gold-rush demand for meat was strong. Its sale enabled him to visit England, apparently for several years.

Dendy, the dignified rolling stone, returned to a sheep property near Werribee, then to a flour mill at Eltham, where Sarah died in 1861. He sold the mill in 1867 to go to Gippsland, where he was a director of the Thomson River copper mine. It devoured his capital. Growing old, Henry lived with his son, who drove the engine at the Long Tunnel gold-mine, Walhalla. Pathetically, seeking independence,

Dendy asked the friend who had built Brighton Park for materials to do up an old hut in the bush. On 11 February 1881 Dendy died at Walhalla, where he was buried. An epitaph might be the comment of his former servant John Booker: 'a good, honourable, kind master, but no businessman'.

W. Bate, *A History of Brighton* (Melb, 1962); L. A. Schumer, *Henry Dendy and his Emigrants* (Melb, 1975); Dendy file (Brighton Historical Society, Melb).   WESTON BATE

DESCHAMPS, VICTOR JOSEPH CLEMENT (1812-1878), vigneron, was born in 1812 at Cressier, Neuchâtel, Switzerland, son of Antoine Marie Deschamps, a Protestant vigneron who had migrated from Saint Pierre-Le-Vieux in southern Burgundy, France, and his wife Marie Anne, née Corbet. Joseph managed a large vineyard estate at Peseux and had a small, 3-acre (1.2 ha) vineyard outside the town. In 1835 he married Susanne Catherine Duvoisin (1813-1897), by whom he had three sons.

According to family sources, Lieutenant-Governor La Trobe [q.v.2], who had known Joseph at school in Switzerland, encouraged him to come to Victoria. After he arrived in January 1854 in the *Kerin Hasselaar* with his sons Louis Auguste (1838-1900), known as Auguste, and Jean Louis (1842-1884), known as Louis, they stayed with La Trobe at his home, Jolimont, in Melbourne. Catherine and the youngest boy Joseph Clement (1844-1887), known as Clement, came two years later. Intent on vine growing, Joseph toured the Geelong and upper Yarra valley districts, rejecting the soils of the latter as too fertile. He then secured 100 acres (40.5 ha) at Kyneton in 1854, 15 acres (6.1 ha) of which he planted with vines. This experience was a disaster. Frost destroyed his infant plants and bushfires the property. Their meagre savings gone, the family settled at Lilydale where they contracted to work for Paul de Castella [q.v.3], another Swiss immigrant who had been known to Joseph at Neuchâtel. Deschamps senior was naturalized in 1857, Louis in 1862.

At the first Lilydale land sales in 1860, Joseph purchased 90 acres (36.5 ha) on both sides of the village, which his sons cleared and transformed into three vineyard holdings. Auguste had Lilydale and Pine Grove vineyards, 35 acres (14.2 ha), now known as Deschamps Hill, Louis the Olinda vineyard of 18 acres (7.3 ha) and Clement the Market Street vineyard of 30 acres (12.1 ha). Having settled his sons, Joseph then purchased a smaller allotment on Mont Albert Road, Boroondara, on the outskirts of Melbourne, planted a small vineyard and eventually retired.

The Deschamps made excellent wine, winning prizes both at home and abroad. A base wine grown and made by the family into Champagne-method sparkling wine for the entrepreneur L. L. Smith [q.v.6] was a success at the Melbourne International Exhibition of 1880-81. Melbourne and Geelong cafés took the bulk of the 6000 to 8000 gallons produced annually by the brothers. Brandy was also made at Clement's vineyard (1500 gallons in 1877), and the family ran a cellar for sales in Melbourne. They established a business for splitting vine stakes and fencing posts for vignerons and a cooperage. In 1872 Louis was a member of the first Lilydale Shire Council.

For touring parties Lilydale became a picturesque stopping point and a gateway to the vineyards and hills beyond. A wine hall built by Louis in 1878 included a skittle alley and was itself a local attraction. For one excursionist, J. S. James [q.v.4] in 1885, the vineyards 'planted right down the slopes into the town', the sloping hills, valley vistas, cool atmosphere and clear sky reminded him of Bavaria. Joseph died on 2 March 1878 at Boroondara and was buried in Lilydale cemetery.

Additional migrants from Switzerland followed the Deschamps example, working for vignerons and then branching out. De Castella's brother Hubert [q.v.3] reflected that it was the immigrant workingmen and their families, not the aspirant Swiss *grandees*, who succeeded as viticulturists and winemakers in the new land. To him, the Deschamps were exemplars of the Australian story. Hard work and expertise saw them prosper. The Yarra Valley never experienced the devastation caused by Grape Phylloxera, but the collapse of the industry in the 1890s depression saw the Deschamps family wine enterprises wither as did larger concerns. The last surviving was the Olinda Vineyard, which closed in 1913. The three brothers all left descendants.

E. Parkinson, *Warburton Ways* (Melb, 1984); H. de Castella, *John Bull's Vineyard* (Melb, 1886); D. Dunstan, *Better than Pommard!* (Melb, 1994); information from Mr N Deschamps, South Yarra, Vic.   DAVID DUNSTAN

DHAKIYARR WIRRPANDA (c.1900-1934?), Aboriginal leader, was born near Blue Mud (Caledon) Bay, in north-eastern Arnhem Land, northern Australia, and had a traditional education among the Dhayyi-speaking people; his name was also spelt as Tuckiar, Takia, Tarkiera and Dagier. He had three wives, of whom only Djaparri (Japari, Yapparti) has been identified in the written records.

Following the killing of a Japanese trepang crew at Caledon Bay in September 1932, a party of investigating police, led by Mounted Constable Ted Morey, came across a group of Aboriginal women on Woodah Island on 1 August 1933. Constable Stewart McColl and the women, including Djaparri, became separated from the others. Dhakiyarr, who was hidden nearby, attempted to make contact with Djaparri. Seeing him and believing him a threat, McColl shot at him. The pistol misfired and Dhakiyarr threw a spear, which killed McColl.

It was suggested at the subsequent trial that McColl had been engaged in sexual intercourse with Djaparri, but this has been disputed in an oral account collected by Ted Egan during an interview with Djaparri in 1976. A contributing motive for McColl's murder was possibly that Dhakiyarr believed that McColl had come to Woodah because of the murders of William Fagan and Frank Traynor. These two 'beachcombers' had arrived there in the dry season of 1933 and had negotiated with Dhakiyarr's group for firewood and the sexual use of Djaparri and her mother Wamirapu. One morning Dhakiyarr and another man had swum out to their boat, killed the two men and thrown their bodies overboard.

In April 1934 he and others accused of the killing of McColl and the Japanese trepangers were brought to Darwin by Rev. A. J. Dyer and a Church Missionary Society 'Peace Expedition' to stand trial. Procedural irregularities occurred at every step: Dhakiyarr's lawyer implied in a statement to the court that Dhakiyarr had admitted guilt; few witnesses were called and the accused were not permitted to testify; the police tracker also acted as the interpreter. The proceedings were a miscarriage of justice, but on 5 August Judge T. A. Wells [q.v.16] sentenced 'Tuckiar' to death for the murder of McColl. An appeal to the High Court of Australia, heard between 29 October and 8 November 1934, resulted in the quashing of the conviction. Dhakiyarr was freed from Fannie Bay Gaol, where he had been held for seven months, and taken to the Kahlin compound in Darwin on 12 November. Dyer had arranged to meet him at the cinema, but Dhakiyarr did not appear and was never seen again.

There have been many explanations for his disappearance, including that he was the victim of a vendetta or had absconded. The oral tradition in Darwin is that friends of McColl had murdered Dhakiyarr and disposed of the body in the harbour. His family in Arnhem Land, including at least one son, survived him. In 2004 a documentary film was made about Dhakiyarr and a ceremony of reconciliation held at the Supreme Court, Darwin, where a memorial was dedicated to him and to McColl.

V. C. Hall, *Dreamtime Justice* (Adel, 1962); M. Dewar, *The 'Black War' in Arnhem Land* (Darwin,

1992), *and* 'Death in the Gulf: A Look at the Motives Behind the Caledon Bay and Woodah Island Killings', *Jnl of NT Hist*, no 4, 1993, p 1 *and* Strange Bedfellows: Europeans and Aborigines in Arnhem Land Before World War II (M.A. thesis, UNE, 1989); T. Egan, *Justice All Their Own* (Melb, 1996); *Cwlth Law Reports*, 52, 1934, p 335; *SMH*, 10 May 2004, p 9; Tuckiar vs the King and Territory (Hindsight, ABC Radio National, 2 June 2002).

MICKEY DEWAR

DICK, ALEXANDER (c.1791-1843), silversmith, was born in Scotland, one of at least seven children and possibly related to an Edinburgh silversmith with the firms Dick & Robertson or Dick & McPherson. Alexander arrived as a free settler in Sydney from Leith on 16 October 1824 in the *Portland*. At first he may have worked for James Robertson, who had come from Scotland in 1822, but by April 1826 Dick was advertising his already-established business at 104 Pitt Street. He married Charlotte, daughter of William Hutchinson [q.v.1], on 2 June at the Scots Church.

Business prospered, the 1828 census showing that he employed two silversmiths, two jewellers and a servant girl. He soon moved to new premises at 6 Williams Place, George Street, where he employed up to six other craftsmen. In January 1829, smarting from a flogging of twenty-five lashes instigated by Dick, his assigned convict Alexander Robertson accused him of receiving twelve silver dessertspoons stolen from the home of Alexander McLeay [q.v.2], the colonial secretary. Charged with receiving stolen goods, Dick was tried on 26 May, found guilty and sentenced to seven years imprisonment on Norfolk Island. The merchant Samuel Terry [q.v.2], watchmaker James Robertson and engraver Samuel Clayton were among those who testified to his good character. Forty leading citizens, including a reluctant McLeay, signed a memorial to Governor Darling [q.v.1] on behalf of Mrs Dick. On 1 February 1833 Governor Bourke [q.v.1] pardoned Dick, stating that 'some favourable circumstances have been represented to me on his behalf'.

The pardon described Dick: 'Height 5 ft 7 ins [170 cm]—Complexion fair ruddy and a little pock pitted—Hair sandy brown—Eyes grey—Remarks less a front tooth in Upper Jaw, Mole right side of Chin, Nose broad and broken'. Returning to Sydney, he resumed business. He was praised as the maker of the eighty-four ounce (2381 g) silver Sydney Subscription Cup (now lost), ornamented with a gold horse finial and gold horse-heads, for a race-meeting in 1834. That year, the Polish explorer John Lhotsky [q.v.2] claimed to have found the first gold in Australia on the Monaro Plains and took it to Dick, who heated the samples in a crucible and poured out a small button of molten gold.

In February 1835 and October 1836 Dick advertised for more craftsmen, moving in February 1837 to bigger premises in the most fashionable area, opposite the barracks gate on the eastern side of George Street. The *Charlotte*, arriving in January 1840, brought from Scotland sixteen bounty immigrants sponsored by Dick, including two jewellers, a silversmith-clockmaker and a watchmaker. He bought land, built The Hermitage at Vaucluse and went on family picnics around the harbour. He and Charlotte had four sons and four daughters.

His works were spare, Classical Revival in style, and derivative, often with elaborate and florid embossed scenes. Extant silver pieces include communion plate for the Scots Church, Sydney; a dog collar presented in 1834 to the publican Michael Farrell's dog Tiger for killing twenty rats in two minutes two seconds; the forty-four-ounce (1247 g) bell-shaped Cavan Challenge Cup won by Lieutenant Waddy's horse Frederick at the Yass plains races in 1836; a foundation trowel for the Royal Exchange, Sydney, 1840; the Anniversary Day Regatta Cup, 1840 (held by the Art Gallery of South Australia); tankards, pap boats, christening mugs and many pieces of cutlery. The 1835 silver snuff box (held by the Powerhouse Museum, Sydney) presented to Captain T. B. Daniel, with a crudely embossed view of Sydney Harbour, emu, kangaroo and Aborigine under a palm tree, has been attributed to his workman Joseph Forrester. Imported clocks, watches, plate and jewellery rather than his local manufactures, however, were the backbone of his business.

Dick announced in the *Australian* in August 1841 that he intended to retire due to ill health; in September he lost two sons from scarlet fever. His firm continued to trade until his death, after a long illness, on 15 February 1843 at his George Street residence; he was buried in the Presbyterian section of the Devonshire Street cemetery and left an estate of nearly £9000. His wife and six children survived him. In 1846 his widow sold up and in 1848 married her neighbour Francis Ellard, the music-shop owner, singer and composer, with her eldest son Alexander (1827-1867) as witness.

J. B. Hawkins, *Nineteenth Century Australian Silver*, 1 (Suffolk, Eng, 1990); *Australiana*, 9, no 4, Nov 1987, p 110, 23, no 4, Nov 2001, p 111; *Australian*, 21 Oct 1824, p 3, 6 June 1827, p 3, 30 May 1829, p 3, 25 April 1834, p 3, 28 Jan 1840, p 2, 26 June 1841, p 2, 21 Aug 1841, p 3; *Sydney Gazette*, 15 Apr 1826, p 3, 28 May 1829, p 2, 17 Feb 1835, p 1, 14 Nov 1835, p 2, 1 Dec 1835, p 2, 7 June 1936; *Sydney Herald*, 21 Dec 1835, p 2, 24 Dec 1835, p 2.

JOHN WADE

DITTER, OTTO KURT (1889-1967), fruit and nut merchant, was born on 17 April 1889 at Chemnitz, near Dresden, Germany, third son and fourth child of Otto Wilhelm Ditter, hotel proprietor, and his second wife Martha. Young Otto worked on the King of Saxony's estate in summer and attended horticultural college in winter. After qualifying he moved to Nice on the French Riviera and worked for an export florist, and then in flower shops in Paris and at Leipzig, Germany. At the age of 21 he migrated to South Australia.

Disembarking in Adelaide from the *Konigin Luise* on 5 March 1910, Ditter travelled to Port Pirie where his brother Johannes (Hans) was a metallurgist. After a few months in the smelters Otto returned to Adelaide, worked for two years for the printing firm Basedow Eimer & Co. and then taught in a Lutheran school. In August 1914 he was naturalized. He married Clara Magdalena Louise Remien on 15 July 1916 in Adelaide.

The forced closure of Lutheran schools in 1916, as a result of anti-German feeling during World War I, led to his return to horticultural work. Ditter spent a year at E. F. Lipsham's market garden, then he and Lipsham opened a stall at the East End market to sell vegetables and almonds. They transferred to the Adelaide Central Market and added roasted peanuts—possibly the first time they had been sold in Adelaide—to their products. When Lipsham withdrew from the business Ditter specialized in nuts. In 1927 he moved to a shop in nearby Pirie Street, and Ditters Ltd was incorporated in 1928. He pioneered the retailing of almond meal, marzipan, crystallized fruits, angelica and ginger and their acceptance as gourmet foods. By 1963 he had three shops, a factory at Clarence Gardens and fifty employees in peak times.

Always conservative in business, Ditter was meticulous both in dress and in the presentation of his produce. He revisited Germany and was active in the German Club (president 1928-29). In 1933 he sought appointment as honorary consul for Germany, but the consul-general in Sydney considered him unsuitable. A police report in 1939 described him as 5 ft 7 ins (170 cm) tall, with fair complexion, grey hair, blue eyes and a small moustache. Ditter's two sons served with the Australian Imperial Force in World War II. Despite being reported for allegedly unpatriotic statements, he became an Air Raid Precautions warden at Edwardstown. An indication of his acceptance into the community was the Federal government's grant to him of the entire South Australian allocation of raw peanuts, an important replacement food for nursing mothers during rationing. He also developed an export line of glacé fruits that locals could send to their British relations. These 'overseas parcels' became so famous that on a visit to Adelaide

in 1945 the Duchess of Gloucester ordered three.

By the late 1940s all the children and a son-in-law had joined Ditters Ltd. Otto Ditter died on 22 May 1967 at Tusmore and was cremated. He was survived by his wife and their two sons and two daughters. In 1969-70 the company made major additions to its range, such as 'gourmet cakes' (popularly called 'stained-glass window cakes' because they were at least eighty per cent glacé fruit) and chocolate-dipped candied fruits and ginger. In April 1985 the business was sold to Bennett & Fisher Ltd, but the remaining Ditters' store in 2003 was run by one of Otto's grandsons.

Advertiser (Adel), 23 May 1967, p 3; D1915, item SA 15131 (NAA, Adel); information from Mr C. Ditter, Adel.   KERRIE ROUND

DOBBIE, ALEXANDER WILLIAMSON (1843-1912), brassfounder, merchant and inventor, was born on 12 November 1843 at Glasgow, Scotland, one of at least three sons of William Dobbie, an engraver, and his wife, 'a descendant of the Campbells'. With his parents and brothers, Alexander arrived in South Australia from Melbourne in the *Slains Castle* on 22 February 1851. Educated at James Bath's school in Adelaide, he was apprenticed to G. E. Schwann, a brassfounder, started his own business at the age of 19 and developed a successful foundry and retail shop. On 6 June 1865 in Adelaide he married with Wesleyan Methodist forms Esther Catherine Elizabeth Wallis. They were to have ten children.

A visit to the Philadelphia International Exhibition, United States of America, while on a world tour in 1876, was a revelation to Dobbie. He gained useful importing agencies for sewing machines, bicycles, milking separators and washing machines, and ever afterwards he was inventing and reproducing machinery for farm and home. With drawings in the *Scientific American* as guides, he made an early workable telephone, a phonograph and microphone. It was a joke in Adelaide that he could go to bed with a new idea in his mind and wake up with a claim for a patent.

A photographer, pianist, optician, astronomer and gardener, Dobbie was also a writer of direct, individual style. His *Rough Notes of a Traveller* was published in 1877. He gave lectures on electro-metallurgy, the microphone, phonograph and mesmerism; visitors to the city were taken to meet him, as to a living marvel. The Dobbie home at College Park was crowded with his inventions and items brought back from his travels, and his garden was a spectacle for passers-by as well as callers. He demonstrated his first scientific wonder—an electric pen which marked paper 'so that an immense number of impressions can be printed off'—in April 1878. In August friends and neighbours were invited to his own scientific exhibition. Some guests were sent to the greenhouse, where they listened on telephones to the rest of the party talking and singing. Subsequently Dobbie played a role in the development of Adelaide's telephone system. Believed to be able to ease pain by hypnosis, he was often visited by those about to go to the dentist. At home he arranged séances and other clairvoyant experiments.

Dobbie was involved in the Chamber of Manufactures and the Agricultural and Horticultural Society of South Australia, and was a foundation member of the Philosophical Society (later the Royal Society of South Australia). He was an active Methodist layman and for many years was a Sunday School teacher (sometime superintendent). In 1889 he went overseas again and published another book entitled *Rough Notes of a Traveller* (1890) about that journey. He had mining interests in Western Australia in the 1890s and at Broken Hill.

Describing him in 1889, a Methodist journal noted 'the strong-built sinewy frame; the restless, energetic, driving movements; the swart and gipsy-like complexion; the black hair and beard'. Another writer called him 'the champion absent-minded man of this city ... known to tie his buggy and pair up in front of the G.P.O. and go home without them'. Dobbie died of chronic nephritis on 18 July 1912 at College Park, and was buried in West Terrace cemetery. His wife, three sons and three daughters survived him.

W. F. Morrison, *The Aldine History of South Australia* (Syd, 1890); E. Warburton, *St. Peters, a Suburban Town* (Adel, 1983); D. A. Cumming and G. C. Moxham, *They Built South Australia* (Adel, 1986); *SA Chronicle*, 30 May 1868; *Christian Weekly and Methodist J*, 25 Feb 1876, 7 June 1889, p 1; *Quiz* (Adel), 16 Dec 1904, p 56; *Register* (Adel), 23 Feb 1878, p 14; *Observer* (Adel), 24 June 1889, p 17; *PD* (SA) 16 Aug 1881, p 586.

ELIZABETH WARBURTON

DOOLAN, JOHN (1856-1882+), bushranger, was born on 28 April 1856 in Castlemaine, Victoria, second son and one of of at least six children of William Dooling and his wife Ann, née Burke, Irish ex-convicts who had left Van Diemen's Land for the Victorian goldfields in the 1850s. By 1867 the family was at Sandhurst (Bendigo) where William, an unsuccessful miner, ran an eating-house. When John was 12 he was apprenticed to a shoemaker.

The local magistrates already knew the boy for a scamp but in January 1869 he stabbed a fellow apprentice during an altercation at work. Committed for trial in the circuit court —under the name 'Doolan'—on a charge of grievous bodily harm, the boy was sentenced by Chief Justice Sir William Stawell [q.v.6] to a year in the reformatory ship *Sir Harry Smith*. There he met Edward James Donnelly, who was serving five years for horse stealing. John was released in February 1870; Ned absconded three months later.

In December 1871 the two went bushranging together. They stole men's clothing at Huntly, and a horse at Axedale and at pistol point robbed Bridget Foley, a widow, of her loose change, some fowls and a couple of billycans. Their crime wave peaked on 9 January 1872. At first light they bailed up Patrick Hallinan's farm on the Campaspe River and stole his spring cart. Trooper Davidson overtook the boys and arrested them opposite the Robin Hood Hotel, White Hills. Although armed with a revolver, the youths, dubbed 'larrikin bushrangers' by the local press, did not resist.

On 19 February 1872 at Bendigo Ned and John (wrongly charged as James) were tried and convicted for robbery under arms. Justice (Sir) Edward Eyre Williams [q.v.6], believing deterrent sentences to be appropriate, gave them seventeen and fourteen years hard labour respectively. In 1870 Harry Power [q.v.5], then Victoria's most notorious bushranger, had been given only fifteen. Doolan's mother became distraught and disrupted court proceedings with 'a piercing lamentation', crying repeatedly 'my poor boy!' The local press reacted by criticizing the severity of the sentences and a petition was circulated seeking consideration of the boys' ages. It failed, but remission reduced Doolan's term to ten and a half years, served mainly in Pentridge gaol, Melbourne. On admission, he was described as 5 ft 1 ins (155 cm) tall, weighing 7 st. 12½ lb. (48.1 kg), buck-toothed, sallow complexioned, with brown hair and eyes and a freckled face. He was released in August 1882 and vanished from official records, whereas Ned, released in 1885, married, worked as a railway labourer and died at Richmond in 1923.

'Jack Doolan' is the name of the bushranger described in the song *Wild Colonial Boy*, which also states that he was born in Castlemaine. A number of incidents in the ballad can be indirectly related to the story of John Doolan, but others appear to have been drawn from the careers of Power and 'Bold' Jack Donohoe [q.v.1]. The earliest documented performance of the song was in June 1880, when it was sung for the Kelly [q.v.5] gang at Glenrowan.

R. Edwards, *Australian Folk Songs* (Kuranda, Qld, 1994); *Bendigo Evening News*, 8, 13, 19 Jan 1869, 13, 15 Feb 1869, 16, 18 Jan 1872; *Bendigo Advertiser*, 10,

11 Jan 1872, 20, 26 Feb 1872; VPRS 515/14, no 9556 (PRO, Vic); Children's Register of State Wards, old series, vol 5, folio 243 (Dept Health and Community Services, Vic); G. A. Mawer, *The Life and Legend of Jack Doolan* (Canb, 2004).

GRANVILLE ALLEN MAWER

DORRINGTON, ANNIE (1866-1926), artist, was born on 19 March 1866 at Litchfield Ashe, Southampton, England, second of nine children of Richard Whistler, farmer, and his wife Sarah Mills, née Vines; Richard was a distant relation of the artist James McNeil Whistler. When Annie was aged 4 her father became a tenant farmer at Winkfield, Berkshire. The children led an idyllic childhood near the Thames, riding ponies, painting and skating. Annie was pretty and petite, later only about 5 ft 2 ins (160 cm) tall, with dark, curly hair. Her father died in 1887 and, with her mother and siblings, she migrated to Victoria in the *Britannia* in 1890. Also on the ship was Charles Dorrington, the bailiff who had come to manage the farm after her father's death.

Charles and Annie married in St Alban's Church of England, Armadale, Melbourne, on 18 April 1892. The couple moved to Western Australia in 1895. They lived at Fremantle in 1897, and moved to Perth next year. Until 1914 Charles was the manager of the Swan River Shipping Co. With no children, Annie's life focussed on her art. She had begun to paint wildflowers and by 1901 had completed fifty-four, which she offered to sell to Bernard Woodward [q.v.12], director of the Western Australian Museum and Art Gallery. Her friend Alice Moore had picked many of the flowers in Kings Park and was given paintings in return. Annie taught painting privately from her home in 1902-06.

Adept at capturing the unusual local wildflowers, Dorrington exhibited watercolours in the Western Australian pavilion at the Paris (1900) and Glasgow (1902) international exhibitions. She also showed at the St Louis International Exposition (1904) in Missouri, United States of America, and some fifty of her paintings were included in the Franco-British Exhibition, London (1908).

Under the name 'Ahasuerus'—a pet name for her husband—in 1901 Annie entered an international competition to design an Australian flag. When the prime minister (Sir) Edmund Barton [q.v.7] announced the joint winners of the prize of £200, she was the first named of the five whose designs were similar, all featuring the Southern Cross. The other winners were I. W. Evans [q.v.14], L. J. Hawkins, E. J. Nuttall and William Stevens. The new flag was first raised on 3 September over the Exhibition Building in Melbourne.

Suffering bouts of depression, in 1908 Annie was admitted to the Claremont Mental Hospital for a few months treatment. In 1914 the couple moved to Serpentine where Charles farmed and grew fruit until 1922. He was also shire clerk of the Serpentine Jarrahdale Roads Board at Mundijong. In 1918 Annie had again been admitted to Claremont hospital. She died there of cancer on 21 April 1926 and was buried with Anglican rites in an unmarked grave in Karrakatta cemetery. Charles died in 1935 and next year 124 of Annie's works were given to the Art Gallery of Western Australia. Her paintings were displayed in a 1991 survey exhibition there and published in the resulting book. In 1999 the National Flag Association erected a memorial on her grave.

J. Gooding, *Wildflowers in Art* (Perth, 1991); *Review of Reviews for Australasia*, 20 Sept 1901, p 241; *Berkshire Family History Society*, 25, no 4, June 2002; *West Australian*, 26 Oct 1998, p 10; *Australian*, 30 Dec 1998, p 7; information from Mrs T. Prestwood, Dianella, Perth, and Dorothy Cooper, Nicholson, Vic.   DOROTHY ERICKSON

DOUGHARTY, HELEN ELIZABETH (1886-1968), community worker, was born on 6 September 1886 at Launceston, Tasmania, and registered as Elizabeth Helen, one of five children of Alexander Evans, manufacturer, and his wife Elizabeth Grace, née Groom. Nellie was educated by a governess. On 8 December 1915 at St John's Church, Launceston, she married Frederick George Dougharty, a bank officer from Victoria. In 1918 he was killed in action at Ypres, France. Nellie's involvement in returned soldiers' projects started later that year when she was appointed as organizer of a committee to raise money for the erection and maintenance of Launceston Anzac Hostel and War Veterans' Home.

In 1920 Mrs Dougharty was one of four responsible for the distribution of money and food to distressed diggers and families. She also ran, for two years, a soup kitchen and food depot at Launceston. In 1925 she visited Queensland to adopt a daughter. An inaugural member of the board of management of Broadland House Church of England Girls' Grammar School, Launceston, Nellie was secretary and literature officer of the Mothers' Union from 1928. From 1929 to the 1930s she was a stalwart of the Australian Women's National League. While an executive member of the Country Women's Association she was responsible for planning exhibitions and festivals. She formed the Launceston branch of the Women's League of Remembrance in the late 1940s.

Dougharty was a committee member of the Launceston 50000 League and it was her suggestion that trees should be planted along the Midland Highway between Launceston and Hobart and dedicated to Tasmanian pioneers;

the first of the 8500 trees donated by W. A. G. Walker [q.v.16] was planted in April 1935. She also proposed the formation of the Tasmanian Society to preserve historic buildings, organized the erection of the Paterson [q.v.2] memorial at George Town, and in the 1940s produced two spectacular plays involving 300 children. The balls Nellie devised for adults and children at the Albert Hall became a Launceston institution.

During World War II she was involved with the Elphin Camp canteen and was a leader of the Australian Comforts Fund in Tasmania. She started Friday stalls at the Anzac Hostel and a Custom House canteen for service recruits, was a committee member of the A.C.F. leave club and was convenor of the Australian Imperial Force ball. A member of the emergency service of the Australian Red Cross Society, she became an official of the Red Cross executive in 1940. She also formed the Church of England Club for Servicemen in Northern Tasmania and the Voluntary War Widows' Salvage Committee. Appointed Launceston City Council delegate to the State Evacuation Committee in 1942, she was a member of the Civil Defence Legion. Dougharty organized A.I.F. luncheons at the Albert Hall and comfort coin collections.

Petite and pretty, quietly efficient, forceful in action yet reluctant to accept praise, she was 'one of the foremost women organisers in Northern Tasmania'—though she managed mostly on a pension. She enjoyed gardening and sewing. In 1955 she moved to Hobart and in April 1968 to Brisbane, where her daughter then lived. Nellie Dougharty died on 8 August 1968 in Greenslopes Repatriation Hospital, Brisbane, and was buried in Pinnaroo lawn cemetery, Aspley, with Anglican rites. Her daughter survived her.

J. Roelvink, *Small Feet Walking* (Hob, 2002); *Tas Hist Studies*, 7, no 1, 2000, p 81; *Examiner* (Launc), 9 Aug 1968, p 9; *Mercury* (Hob), 9 Aug 1968, p 6; family papers held by author; information from Mr G. Ashton-Jones, Hob.   JEANETTE ROELVINK

DOUGLAS, SHOLTO (1795-1838), army officer, was born on 14 December 1795, at Dinsworth, Chichester Supra, West Sussex, England, son of Major James Sholto Douglas and his wife Sarah, née Dawes. Lieutenant General (Sir) James Douglas was Sholto's brother and their sister Sarah married a family connexion, the 7th Marquess of Queensberry. In September 1811 Sholto was commissioned, by purchase, ensign in the 50th Regiment of Foot. He served in Portugal, Spain and France in 1812-14, purchasing promotion to lieutenant in July 1813. From December 1814 he was thrice on half-pay. In 1819 representations by his brother succeeded in cancelling Douglas's appointment to a regiment in the unhealthy West Indies. Paying £166 1s., in 1820 he returned to full time duty with the 63rd Regiment. By 1827 he had purchased his majority and in 1826-28 he served in Portugal.

Departing from England in June 1828 for Van Diemen's Land, he administered command of the 63rd until superseded in March 1830. Apart from guarding convicts, the regiment engaged in anti-guerrilla operations in the 'Black War' against Tasmanian Aborigines. In October-November 1830 Douglas led over 1000 soldiers and armed civilians in the 'Black Line' sweep of the colony from north to south, to drive warlike tribes into Tasman Peninsula. The operation was planned and commanded by the lieutenant-governor George Arthur [q.v.1] and not, as some historians have claimed, by Douglas.

Douglas was also chairman of magistrates for Oatlands and Campbell Town. On 25 March 1830 at St David's Church of England, Hobart, he married Henrietta Patricia, second daughter of the colonial secretary John Burnett and granddaughter of Sir Henry Browne Hayes [qq.v.1]. Returning to England with his family in November 1831, Douglas retired from the army the following November. Although he disliked Van Diemen's Land, by next year the family was back in Hobart Town. Arthur offered him a minor post, which he declined in expectation of the appointment of sheriff. This did not materialize and in January 1835 he settled on a developed property of 160 acres (64.75 ha) at New Norfolk. In April he sold up and in November returned to England with his son, but was back in the colony by early 1837 and appointed ordnance storekeeper. Now in ill health, he soon again returned to England, where his wife joined him in December 1838.

His voluminous correspondence with Arthur revealed Douglas as not particularly efficient, feeling his honour was at stake whenever criticized. He demanded an inquiry 'before a competent tribunal' when Arthur pointed out an uneven distribution of troops and a lack of vigilance in one of Douglas's subunits. He also had deficiencies in handling subordinates and lacked attention to his soldiers' wellbeing. According to Arthur, prior to departing for England in November 1831, Douglas had '*taken to his bottles* and behaved exceeding ill'. On his return, Arthur noted: 'Unfortunately he soon lapsed into gross intemperance, associating with the lowest Company, by whom he was made a complete Tool'. Douglas, in turn, complained to Arthur of his 'oppression' and 'persecution of power' in his treatment of those who fell from favour. He was shamed and infuriated when the local press reported in 1837 that his application to be placed on the jury list was refused by the lieutenant-governor Sir John Franklin [q.v.1], because his employment as ordnance store-keeper was only of warrant officer status. As the proud young officer and gentleman with ready access to patronage faded, it seems that Douglas failed.

He died on 24 December 1838 on the Isle of Man and was buried in Fifeshire, possibly on a property of his sister, the Marchioness of Queensberry. His wife, who remarried in 1844, survived him, as did his only son Edward Sholto (1831-1853), who served in the Royal Navy.

P. L. Brown (ed), *Clyde Company Papers* (Lond, 1941); P. Chapman (ed), *The Diaries and Letters of C. T. W. B. Boyes*, 1 (Melb, 1985); Tas Hist Research Assn, *Papers & Procs*, 48, no 1, Mar 2001, p 65; J. F. McMahon, The British Army and the Counter-insurgency Campaign in Van Diemen's Land with Particular Reference to the Black Line (M.Humanities thesis, Univ Tas, 1995); AJCP microfilm, PRO 6808, WO25/797, p 167, WO31/377, WO31/494, WO31/515 and WO31/607 (PRO, Lond); GO 33/21, p 785, CSO 19/1, pp 352-3, CSO 1/324/7578 (TA).

J. F. McMAHON

DREW, ANN (1822?-1907), welfare worker, was born probably on 4 May 1822 at Ashton, Devon, England, daughter of John Cornish, a yeoman farmer, and his wife Sarah, née Smalridge. On 21 December 1848 at St James's Church, Exeter, Ann married RICHARD LANGLER DREW (1823-1869). He had been born on 9 October 1823 at Highweek, near Newton Abbot, Devon, son of Richard Langler Drew, yeoman farmer, and his wife Mary Frances, née Evans.

In 1851 the younger Drews were living at Totnes, Devon, Richard a clerk in a railway company. Reputed to have served in the Royal Navy during the Chinese War, he migrated with Ann to Victoria in about 1858 and after three years they moved to Queensland. Briefly a customs agent, then shipping master, in July 1862 Drew was appointed, at £300 a year, shipping master and secretary to the Marine Board—in effect chief clerk. W. L. G. Drew [q.v.], possibly a relation, was under-secretary of the Queensland Treasury, the supervising department.

Richard Drew in 1862 bought and sub-divided land on the outskirts of Brisbane, setting up a signboard: 'This is the village of Toowong'. Described as the 'spirit which began and leavened nearly all the movements both religious and secular in early Toowong', Drew donated land for the first Church of St Thomas the Apostle, and was one of its original trustees.

Childless, Ann (who also signed as 'Anne') used her connections to advocate and help administer an array of welfare institutions for four decades, more visibly after her husband's death from a ruptured aortic aneurysm on 8 October 1869 in Brisbane. She was, for example, secretary (1870-79) of the committee of the Lady Bowen [q.v.] Hospital, which met weekly. Most notably, she founded the Female Refuge and Infants' Home ('Mrs Drew's Home') in April 1871 for 'those who having lost their character are desirous of reforming'. After fifteen months, during which she and her friends funded the home, she successfully sought government help, but as 'Lady Superintendent' also obtained many donations in money or kind, and effectively managed investment and some income from the residents' work. A public meeting on 13 May 1885 led to the establishment of Lady Musgrave Lodge as a hostel and training place for immigrants and other 'friendless' girls: as lady president of the Social Purity Society, Ann Drew was a prominent participant. She also took part in agitation to repeal the Contagious Diseases Act of 1868.

In September 1885 she returned to England for eighteen months. Prior to her departure the premier (Sir) Samuel Griffith [q.v.9] thanked her on behalf of the government and her fellow-colonists for her 'many and great services', and offered travel funds. By early 1887 she was back in charge.

In October 1900 F. E. Hare reported to the government that, with Ann Drew's increasing age and dominance in administration, her methods had 'perhaps become somewhat out of touch with modern ideas'. Hare acknowledged, however, 'the good will and gratitude of very numerous [past] inmates' towards her. The government subsidy was withdrawn from the refuge, whose finances, nevertheless, continued sound. After a series of reforms, in 1906 Mrs Drew retired as 'Foundress and Superintendent'.

The Drews' friend J. B. Fewings described R. L. Drew as 'timid, modest, and retiring', yet unobtrusively successful in realizing his plans; by comparison, Ann Drew's talents were much more evident and varied; he emphasized particularly her 'great practicable ability'. Ann Drew died at Sandgate, near Brisbane, on 5 August 1907. The Drews are buried in Toowong cemetery. Ann left an estate valued at about £2000 to her adopted daughter Fanny Elizabeth Parke.

H. Gregory, *A Church for its Times* (Toowong, Qld, 1977); K. Daniels and M. Murnane (eds), *Uphill all the Way* (Brisb, 1980); H. Gregory (ed), *Arcadian Simplicity: J. B. Fewings Memoirs of Toowong* (Brisb, 1990); *Qld Heritage*, 2, no 10, May 1974, p 27, 3, no 1, Nov 1974, p 21; *Queenslander*, 16 Oct 1869, p 2; *Brisb Courier*, 15 Aug 1884, p 6, 7 Aug 1907, p 7; R. L. Evans, Charitable Institutions of the Queensland Government to 1919 (M.A. thesis, Univ Qld, 1970); PRV 8779/1/2, PRV9294 and SRS5253/1/426/letter3543 (QA).

S. J. ROUTH

DREW, WILLIAM LEWORTHY GOODE (1826-1898), naval officer and public servant, was born on 14 October 1826 at Broadstairs, Kent, England, son of Captain George Drew, R.N., and his wife Caroline Fulford, née Goode. George, who had served during the Napoleonic wars, was later superintendent of the invalid convict station at Impression Bay, Van Diemen's Land. William acquired an interest in figures at the King Charles Mathematical Foundation at Christ's Hospital, London (the Blue Coat School), where he was said to have calculated 'how many hidings went to the week before he'd been there a month'. He joined the Royal Navy at 16, eventually becoming paymaster on the Australian and New Zealand Station, Sydney, in 1853.

On 30 January 1855 at St Thomas's Church, North Sydney, Drew married Gertrude Jane, daughter of Frederick Augustus Hely [q.v.1]. Gertrude and William were to have twelve children. Paid off with the rank of fleet paymaster in 1856, Drew was appointed clerk in the Railway Department in February 1857 and within five months became secretary of the Steam Navigation Board. By 1858 he had joined the staff of the Union Bank. In 1862, following a scandal which led to the dismissal of the incumbent Arthur Edward Dodwell, Drew was appointed under-secretary of the Queensland Treasury. For fifteen years he served a succession of ministries, gaining an enviable reputation for efficiency, leadership and tact. He also made determined efforts to weaken the influence of the Audit Office and F. O. Darvall, his successful rival for the post of auditor-general in 1869. Upon Darvall's resignation in 1877, Drew was appointed his successor and surprised many by quickly asserting the independence of the office and by criticizing government financial policy when he saw fit. He also set high standards for his staff at a time when the pressure of work was multiplying and employee numbers remained static. According to R. S. Browne [q.v.7], Drew 'had no use for an audit officer who was not capable, fearless in duty, and absolutely appreciative of his duty to the public'.

His term in office coincided with a massive growth in Queensland's public debt, especially under the first McIlwraith [q.v.5] ministry (1879-83). By 1883 the colony's loans had reached £13 125 826 and Drew's growing concern led to his ordering a raid on Treasury books in July. His subsequent report, tabled in the Legislative Assembly, assisted the election of (Sir) Samuel Griffith [q.v.9] in November 1883. Some suspected Drew of partisanship, and certainly his relationship with the Griffith ministry proved far more amicable. The government made no efforts to reduce the level of public debt but raised his annual salary to £1000.

Drew retired as auditor-general in 1889, when he was appointed C.M.G. and became chairman of the new Civil Service Board. For many years he was a prominent Anglican layman, particularly involved with St Thomas's Church of England, Toowong, close to his riverside estate, Minto. In later years he served as a diocesan synodsman and treasurer. Photographs show a determined face, clean-shaven but with mutton-chop sidelevers. Drew died on 14 July 1898 at Toowong and was buried in the local cemetery. His wife, four daughters (one of whom married John O'Neil Brenan [q.v.]) and four sons survived him. Obituarists, mindful of the financial collapse of the early 1890s, praised Drew as one of the few not to be 'blinded by the dazzle of boom time ... he steadily and independently warned the Government that the reckless financing then in vogue must lead to eventual ruin'.

S. Brown, *A Journalist's Memories* (Brisb, 1927); R. B. Joyce, *Samuel Walker Griffith* (Brisb, 1984); H. Gregory (ed), *Arcadian Simplicity* (Brisb, 1990); R. Longhurst, *The Plain Truth* (Brisb, 1995); *Queenslander*, 19 June 1897, p 1355; *Brisb Courier*, 15 July 1898, p 6; *Sydney Mail*, 20 Aug 1898, p 455.

ROBERT I. LONGHURST

DUNCAN, LAURA (1875-1955), pastoralist and charity worker, was born on 25 August 1875 at Balmain, Sydney, fourth child of Charles Davis, a solicitor from London, and his Sydney-born wife Maria Finch, née Heney. Laura spent her early years at the family home, Llewellyn, on the Parramatta River. In the late 1890s, while living with her sister Millicent and the latter's husband Allen Alexander at Daroo station, near Birdsville, Queensland, Laura met William Duncan, who had arrived in Australia from Midlothian, Scotland, in 1876 and was the manager of Mooraberrie station, a cattle property in the Channel Country of south-west Queensland. Laura married William on 28 April 1898 at Daroo. They had four children and purchased Mooraberrie in 1906. Following William's death on 16 February 1907, from consumption complicated by a fall from a horse, Laura managed the station.

In her fight to retain and improve the property and its cattle, Mrs Duncan aimed at building up a first-class Shorthorn herd and helped to pioneer the 'baby-beef trade' in south-west Queensland. Slightly built, quiet, kindly, but efficient and determined, she advocated the right of pastoralists to market their stock where they chose. In 1917 she contested the compulsory seizure by the T. J. Ryan [q.v.11] government of some 500 Mooraberrie cattle under the Sugar Acquisition Act of 1915, which had sweeping powers over livestock as well as raw sugar. The Mooraberrie Cattle Case

(*Duncan* v. *Queensland, Duncan* v. *Theodore*) challenged the power of the Queensland government to overrule section 92 of the Constitution, guaranteeing the freedom of interstate trade. Although backed by the Graziers' Association and the Commonwealth government, she lost in the Queensland Supreme Court and won in the High Court of Australia, but in 1919 the Privy Council decided against her.

A stickler for justice and a generous supporter of good causes, Duncan gave her Brisbane residence, Lynne Grove, at Corinda, as a home for the orphaned and destitute children of World War I soldiers. She travelled widely in her Ford motorcar during World War I to aid the Australian Red Cross Society and other patriotic causes. A splendid horsewoman, she was a capable educator of her three daughters; her only son had died of croup in childhood. Duncan respected Aboriginal people and observed their laws and rights to the land.

On 13 September 1920 at St Aidan's Church of England, Marden, Adelaide, she married John McKenzie, a contractor. He died in 1922. In 1940 she passed the management of Mooraberrie to her daughter Laura Lothian Duncan (1903-1988)—the property was managed continuously by the two women for some eighty years. Her other daughters, Alice Monkton Duncan-Kemp (1901-1988), who was the author of several books, and Beatrice Margaret Galagher (1904-1995), had both married graziers. Duncan retired to her home at Kangaroo Point, Brisbane, where she died on 20 June 1955. She was cremated with Anglican rites.

E. Pownall, *Mary of Maranoa* (Melb, 1964); D. J. Murphy, *T. J. Ryan* (Brisb, 1975); P. L. Watson, *Frontier Lands and Pioneer Legends* (Syd, 1998); *Cwlth Law Reports*, 22, 1916-17, p 556, 23, 1916-17, p 510, 26, 1918-19, p 276; *Qld Country Life*, 4 Aug 1955, p 22; *Pastoral Review*, 16 Aug 1955, p 1015; information from Mr D. S. Duncan-Kemp, Oakey, Qld.   MARGARET KOWALD

DUNDALLI (c.1820-1855), Aboriginal leader, was born in the mountains (Blackall Range), north-west of Moreton Bay (Queensland). He probably came from the Dalambara clan of the Dalla language group. His name meant wonga pigeon. In August 1841 he was part of a delegation of Dalla who met German missionaries J. P. Niqué and A. T. W. Hartenstein [qq.v.2 Schmidt] on their journey north from Brisbane. From the mid-1840s he lived on Bribie Island, whose traditional owners, the Djindubari people, had adopted him.

Accused of involvement in the spearing of a shepherd on the Archer brothers' [q.v.1] Durundur station in 1843, Dundalli eluded capture. In 1845 a German missionary testified that he heard Dundalli issuing instructions to Aborigines engaged in robbing and then burning his hut. A mass attack on Andrew Gregor's station on the Pine River in October 1846, which resulted in the death of Gregor and his pregnant female servant, cemented Dundalli's growing reputation and triggered a series of reprisals and counter-reprisals. Evidence, often confused and based on rumour, allegedly linked Dundalli to the Gregor crime, an attack on three sawyers in September 1847 in which William Boller lost his life, the killing of a fisherman, Charles Gray, in 1849, the theft from the hut of a settler named Cash in 1852 and an attack on a shepherd named Halloran. Circumstantial evidence pointed to him, however, as an indigenous leader who was determined to repay violence with violence and to defend the honour and dignity of his people.

In a wave of frontier police actions, three of Dundalli's companions, including his brother Oumulli, were captured and killed, others were arrested or questioned and the death penalty was imposed and later remitted on another supporter, Mickaloe. A legend grew up around Dundalli as he evaded capture over a fourteen-year period and the whites sought to connect him with almost every act of violence committed on the northern side of the Brisbane River. The indigenous community was divided between those who supported and attempted to protect him and the traditional enemies of the Djindubari, who feared him and were prepared to inform the police of his whereabouts. One reason for his mystique was his size. His trial judge later wrote that Dundalli 'was the largest man I ever looked upon', well over six feet (183 cm) tall.

From May 1853 in Moreton Bay he worked for twelve months in their boat of William Wilson, a European and his name exchange 'brother'. Captured at Fortitude Valley in May next year, Dundalli was tried before (Sir) Roger Therry [q.v.2] at the Brisbane Circuit Court in November. In his *Reminiscences* (London, 1863), Therry described how the prisoner brazenly attempted to bribe him, for sixpence, and on another occasion offered to row the judge to Sydney if he would release him. Dundalli was sentenced to death for the murders of Andrew Gregor and William Boller. The gallows were erected on the Queen Street footpath in front of Brisbane Gaol.

A crowd gathered to witness the execution on 5 January 1855, and the town constabulary and a detachment of native police surrounded the gallows to prevent any attempt at escape or rescue. As Dundalli mounted the scaffold he called out to a large number of indigenous people, who were gathered in the brushes that lined the Wickham Terrace hill, overlooking the scene, to avenge his death. They let out a loud cry when his body dropped. Alexander Green [q.v.], the executioner sent from Sydney, bungled the hanging. Dundalli's feet fell upon his coffin, forcing Green to bend and drag on the hanged man's long legs until he died. This was the last official public execution in Queensland.

Dundalli was married, so it is likely that he had children. A sketch by Silvester Diggles, reproduced for the *Illustrated Sydney News*, shows Dundalli dressed in the open, smock shirt of a workingman of the 1850s, with wavy, black hair and neatly trimmed beard cut in the European style.

C. Campbell Petrie, *Tom Petrie's Reminiscences of Early Queensland* (Brisb, 1904); L. Connors, 'The Theatre of Justice', in R. Fisher (ed), *Brisbane: The Aboriginal Presence 1824-1860* (Brisb, 1992); *Moreton Bay Courier*, 27 May 1854, p 2, 25 Nov 1854, p 2, 6 Jan 1855, p 2, 13 Jan 1855, p 2; *Illustrated Sydney News*, 16 Dec 1854; *Brisb Courier*, 18 Jan 1919; *R v Dundalli*, 9/6386 (SRNSW).

LIBBY CONNNORS

DWYER, MICHAEL (1772?-1825), Irish revolutionary and political exile, was the eldest of seven children of John and Mary Dwyer of Camera, Wicklow, Ireland. The family moved to a mountainous twenty-four-acre (9.7 ha) farm at Eadestown, Glen of Imaal, in 1784. Schooled at Bushfield, then Ballyhubbock, Michael worked as an ostler for the Morris family and helped his father to tend sheep.

In the spring of 1797, with scores of relations and friends, he joined the Society of United Irishmen. Rebellion broke out in Wicklow on 23 May. After fighting at the battle of Arklow, he was promoted 'captain' on 24 June. Dwyer killed at least one Welsh cavalryman in an ambush at Ballyellis on 30 June. In mid-July, as the rebellion waned, he joined the militant rump commanded by Joseph Holt, which rejected amnesty terms, hoping for military assistance from France. Actions later in 1797 established Dwyer's reputation as a dynamic rebel leader. A core group attached to him kept fighting after Holt surrendered in November 1798.

On 16 October that year Dwyer had married Mary Doyle, of Cullentragh. He supported the conspiracy by Robert Emmet for an attempted *coup d'etat* in July 1803. After severe measures against the rebels were introduced in November his extended family was facing transportation and, to alleviate their situation and save other comrades from execution, Dwyer surrendered on 14 December 1803, anticipating migration to the United States of America. Instead, he was gaoled at Kilmainham pending deportation to New South Wales as an unsentenced exile.

With his wife and the two eldest of their six children, Dwyer reached Port Jackson in the *Tellicherry* on 14 February 1806; the other children were left with relations in Dublin. He was allocated 100 acres (40.5 ha) of uncleared land fronting Cabramatta Creek, adjacent to grants to his comrades Hugh 'Vesty' Byrne, John Mernagh, Arthur Devlin and Martin Burke. In February 1807 Governor Bligh [q.v.1] arrested several of the group and on 11 May Dwyer was tried for sedition. Although acquitted, he was ordered to be sent to Norfolk Island, an act of injustice that aggrieved elements in the New South Wales Corps. In January 1808 he was moved to the Derwent settlement, Van Diemen's Land, where he spent a year before being allowed back to Cabramatta by the anti-Bligh clique. Governor Macquarie [q.v.2] confirmed favourable decisions extended to Dwyer by William Paterson [q.v.2] in 1809, paving the way for his full integration into colonial society in 1810. In August Dwyer became constable of the Georges River district and in December 1812 poundkeeper.

Active in the colony's Catholic community, in 1821, having amassed 610 acres (246.9 ha), he contributed £10 to St Mary's church building fund. He was appointed chief constable of Liverpool in May 1820 but was dismissed in October for drunken conduct and mislaying important documents. In December 1822 he was sued for aggrandizing his farm with Ann Stroud's. This spurred a major debtor, Daniel Cooper [q.v.1], to demand restitution of some £2000 invested in Dwyer's popular Harrow Inn. Bankrupted, he was forced to sell off most of his assets, although this did not save him from several weeks incarceration in the Sydney debtors' prison in May 1825. Here he evidently contracted dysentery, to which he succumbed on 23 August 1825.

Originally interred at Liverpool, his remains were reburied in the Devonshire Street cemetery, Sydney, in 1878 by his grandson John Dwyer, dean of St Mary's Cathedral. In May 1898 the coincidence of the planned closure of the cemetery and centenary celebrations for the 1798 rebellion suggested the second reinterment of Dwyer and his wife in Waverley cemetery, where a substantial memorial was erected in 1900. The massive crowds attending Dwyer's burial and the subsequent unveiling of the monument testified to the unique esteem in which Irish-Australians held the former Wicklow hero.

C. Dickson, *The Life of Michael Dwyer* (Dublin, 1944); G. Cargeeg, *The Rebel of Glenmalure* (Perth, 1988); K. Sheedy, *Upon the Mercy of Government* (Dublin, 1988); R. O'Donnell, *The Rebellion in Wicklow, 1798* (Dublin, 1998) and *Aftermath: Postrebellion Insurgency in Wicklow, 1799-1803* (Dublin, 2000) and 'Michael Dwyer: The Wicklow Chief', in B. Reece (ed), *Irish Convict Lives* (Syd, 1993).

RUAN O'DONNELL

E

EASTERBY, HARRY TINNISWOOD (1867-1932), sugar chemist and administrator, was born on 10 October 1867 at Echuca, Victoria, son of English-born parents Richard Tinniswood Easterby, journalist, and his wife Jane, née Bould. Harry became a shorthand writer and on 8 April 1890 at St Paul's Church of England, Sale, married Alice Marriott Watson. He later worked in Australia's only sugar beet factory at Maffra, Victoria, and in 1899 was recruited by Angus Gibson [q.v.4] to be head chemist at Bingera sugar mill and plantation near Bundaberg, Queensland. Walter Maxwell [q.v.10], the first director of the Bureau of Sugar Experiment Stations, appointed Easterby assistant director on 24 July 1901 and placed him in charge of the station at Mackay.

Easterby carried out the experimental programme at Mackay effectively. Maxwell left in 1909 and the industry's campaign to control the bureau was thwarted when the minister for agriculture added the duties of director to those of the under-secretary E. G. E. Scriven. Easterby remained assistant director, thus saving the director's salary. In 1910, however, he resigned and became manager of the Maffra refinery. A new position, general superintendent of the bureau, was created for Gibson's son Arthur. Easterby replaced him two years later, and moved the headquarters to Brisbane, still under Scriven's control. Responsible for the experimental and scientific programme, Easterby recruited staff more qualified than he, allowing them scope to pursue scientific investigations, including plant growth, varietal selection, disease and entomological studies. The decision to acquire a new station at Bundaberg was taken by Scriven, but Easterby selected the site. He also oversaw the expansion of work to South Johnstone and Meringa stations in the far north.

Easterby's detailed knowledge of the industry was recognized by his appointment to the 1915 royal commission into the working of Central Sugar Mills at Mackay, the 1916 board of enquiry into overproduction and the establishment of additional sugar mills and the 1922 royal commission into suitable locations for new sugar mills. He complained forcefully when departmental misdirection in 1922 proved 'liable to puzzle the officers in charge and weaken my control' and later that year was eventually appointed director. The most far-reaching change to the bureau came from the suggestion of the chief justice, T. W. McCawley [q.v.10], that surplus funds paid by the sugar industry be used to award three-year scholarships to three young graduates—A. F. Bell, N. Bennett [qq.v.13] and H. W. Kerr

—to enable them to study overseas and return to work for the bureau. Easterby applauded the scheme and gave the recipients the opportunity to implement their ideas.

Although he was an amiable gentleman, Easterby 'had no place for agitators in his domain' and moved the abrasive Bennett to Mackay in the minister's electorate, thus solving a problem and earning kudos. He continued to undertake onerous field trips despite years of heart trouble. It was on such a visit shortly before his planned retirement that he died of a cerebral haemorrhage on 28 September 1932 at Cairns; his wife and their daughter and son survived him. He was buried with Anglican rites in Cairns cemetery. He had written *The Queensland Sugar Industry*, which was published from his manuscript in 1933 and became the most quoted general historical reference on the subject.

PD (Qld), 86, 1900, p 2325; Bureau of Sugar Experiment Stations (Qld), *Annual Report*, 1901-32; *Bundaberg Mail*, 12 June 1899; *Aust Sugar J*, 67, no 7, Oct 1975, p 363; *Gympie Times*, 26 July 1910; 38/20524, AGS/N72 and 3626, A/53973-54451 (QA); H. W. Kerr, memoirs (c.1990).   JOHN D. KERR*

EATOCK, LUCY HARRIET (1874-1950), political activist, was born on 7 June 1874 at Springsure, Queensland, and registered as the ninth child of Scottish-born parents Alexander Wakenshaw, a bushman and later pastoralist, and his wife Jane Lindsay, née Cousins. On 18 November 1895 at Springsure Lucy married with Presbyterian forms William Eatock (1869-1943), an Aboriginal stockman; they had nine children.

By 1908 Bill was working in the abattoirs at Brewarrina, New South Wales. Finding living with a large family in tents and humpies too onerous, Lucy and Bill later separated. Two sons stayed with their father while Lucy brought one daughter and the younger children to Sydney. With work difficult to obtain, Lucy took a series of domestic positions in rural districts and boarded the children out —principally at Bowral where, the children were later to claim, they went to school with (Sir) Donald Bradman.

Lucy was able to gather her children together and live for a few years in relative comfort in the 1920s, with her sons Richard Alexander (Alec), William Donald (Don) and Adam labouring in brickyards at St Peters, Sydney, Roderick (Dick) apprenticed to an electrician, and daughter Lindsay at a nearby umbrella factory. The young Eatocks became active unionists and, with Lucy, members of the Communist Party of Australia. In 1929 the party adopted an ultra-left line and regularly clashed with police in street demonstrations, which Lucy attended—large and stately, impeccably dressed as a suburban matron, wearing a hat and gloves and often carrying an umbrella. This respectable attire did not save her from a public whipping by a police inspector in St John's Road, Glebe, on 27 October 1932, when a gathering of the unemployed, protesting against harsh dole regulations, was broken up. 'Old Mum Eatock' became known for delivering mutton or blackberry pies to families of the unemployed.

Earlier that October Alec had been sentenced to two-and-a-half years imprisonment for his part in resisting the eviction of a group of communists and unemployed men occupying a sandbagged house in Brancourt Avenue, Bankstown, in June 1931. He received by far the harshest sentence for this clash. After an affray between police and unemployed outside Glebe Town Hall, which left a police sergeant badly injured, Lucy's youngest son Noel (aged 20) and Thomas Sharpe, a former soldier who had been wounded in World War I, were tried for assault in 1933. Despite stronger evidence against Sharpe and testimony of witnesses that Noel was not present at the incident, Sharpe was acquitted and Noel convicted and sentenced to two-and-a-half years gaol. Both Alec and Noel had young families and served nineteen months of their sentences.

In the course of these trials, Lucy became convinced that the Communist Party leaders did not commit enough resources to her boys' defence; her anger was compounded when these same leaders denied material help to the families of the imprisoned men. Left-wing communists at Glebe and Balmain shared her disillusionment (especially over the case of Noel) and this was a major contributing factor in their split with the C.P.A. and the formation of a Trotskyist group in Sydney. Embittered by his time in gaol, Noel left Sydney soon after his release. His family never heard from him again. Adam was killed in a bicycle accident in January 1935.

In the following years Lucy lived with various of her children. Predeceased by her husband, she died on 12 February 1950 in Brisbane Hospital and was cremated with Presbyterian forms. Two daughters and three sons survived her. With the exception of Lindsay, who remained a communist to the end of her days, they retired from politics. When, in a time of reawakened pride for indigenous Australians, Lucy's grandchildren and great-grandchildren reclaimed their Aboriginality, they also suggested that Lucy's mother had been Kitty, an Aboriginal woman employed by the Wakenshaws. Neither Lucy nor any of her children is known to have made such an assertion.

A. Johnson, *Bread & Roses* (Syd, 1990); H. Greenland, *Red Hot: The Life and Times of Nick Origlass* (Syd, 1998); J. de Cressac, *Delusions of Grandeur* (Alice Springs, 2003); *SMH*, 10 Nov 1931, p 6, 13 Nov 1931, p 6; N. Wheatley, The Unemployed Who Kicked, (M.A. thesis, Macquarie Univ, 1975); L. Mountjoy, My Life (ms, 1982, held by Mr K. Lowe, NSW Board of Studies, Syd).   HALL GREENLAND

EATON, GEORGE BURNETT (1886-1954), teacher, actor and producer, was born on 8 November 1886 at Govan, Glasgow, Scotland, third child of William Eaton, master mariner, and his wife Isabella, née Walker. Soon after, William migrated to Australia. Isabella and their children followed him, reaching Brisbane in the *Jumna* in December 1889. A fourth child was born in 1891. Educated in Brisbane, on 1 March 1901 George became a pupil-teacher at West End Boys' School. He taught at Brisbane South School for Boys, from 1910 at Kelvin Grove Road Boys' School and from 1911 at Taringa. Described as 5 ft 5¼ ins (165.7 cm) tall, with ruddy complexion, grey eyes and dark brown hair, he enlisted in the Australian Imperial Force on 20 September 1915, served with the 1st Australian Field Ambulance in France, and was promoted corporal. He was discharged on 9 March 1920.

Back in Brisbane, on 12 July Eaton was appointed to the Central Technical College, where he taught languages. On 20 December 1930 at the Methodist Church, Torwood, he married Kathleen Ada Elledge, a London-born dressmaker. That year he had been transferred to the Industrial High School, where he became officer-in-charge in 1945 and principal in 1947, receiving awards for excellence in teaching in 1948 and 1950. He introduced special classes for students and organized a timetable adapted to the abilities of the less able pupils, whose parents mended his 1928 Whippet motorcar in gratitude. Eaton retired on 31 December 1952.

His military experiences had given Eaton an implacable hatred of war and his sojourn in France set him on the path of internationalism. Gregarious, egalitarian and a bit of a show-off, with a firm streak of moral rectitude, he claimed to be an agnostic. He taught singing and gave recitals, often entertained visiting ballet companies, including the Ballets Russes de Monte Carlo and Borovansky's [q.v.13], and organized social gatherings in their honour in his house, Segovia. Fluent in French and active in the Civil Liberties League, he taught English to Russian emigrés through a French interpreter.

From its inception in 1929 until 1941, Eaton produced and acted in plays for the Workers' Educational Association dramatic society, coached many of its actors and was a play adjudicator. Described by John Manifold as a brilliant conversationalist, he was well read and forward thinking; this was reflected in the dramatic society's repertoire, which included works by Sean O'Casey, Elmer Rice and Eugene O'Neill. Eaton made many friends in the theatrical and artistic world, such as Vance and Nettie Palmer [qq.v.11]. Both were interested in presenting Australian drama on stage, and Vance acted as adjudicator in the 1932 one-act play competition organized by the W.E.A. Eaton's diverse interests included writing radio programmes for children; in the 1940s and 1950s he became the voice of 'Dr Day' who gave advice on medical problems and hygiene.

In 1953 Eaton went to England in the *Orcades* for an extended holiday. He died of myocardial infarction on 8 August 1954 at a private hospital in South Brisbane and was cremated with Methodist forms. His wife and two sons survived him. Mel Haysom reputedly painted his portrait but its whereabouts is unknown.

Connie Healy, *Defiance* (Brisb, 2000); *Courier-Mail*, 9 Aug 1954, p 6; information from Mr D. N. Eaton, Witta, Qld.   CONNIE HEALY

EDWARDS, AGNES (c.1873-1928), Aboriginal craftworker, was born at Mellool Station, near Swan Hill, Victoria, only child of Jim and Sarah Crow, of the Wati Wati people from the Edwards River region in New South Wales. Her father worked for many years at the station, which had a large, well-paid, Aboriginal workforce. About 1890 'Black Aggie', as she was sometimes known, married Harry Edwards, a much older Muti Muti man, probably through traditional marriage arrangements. She became widely known in the district as 'Queen Aggie' after 1897 when she was introduced to the governor Lord Hopetoun [q.v.9] at the local show. For this occasion Mrs Reeves, a Swan Hill dressmaker friend, made a black silk dress for Agnes, which showed her tall, slim figure and striking manner to perfection.

Following the death of her parents in 1898, Agnes and Harry moved to a campsite on the Edwards River, some twenty-five miles (40 km) north of Swan Hill, to join other Aboriginal friends who operated a depot for changing horses on the Cobb [q.v.3] & Co. route to Balranald. After Harry died about 1912 she remained in the area, which became known as Aggie's Swamp. She lived alone, near four or five older inhabitants until only she and Bob Nicholls were left. They each had separate, substantial, bark-walled homes with brick chimneys, but were known as a couple.

Edwards used her people's traditional skills to earn her living. Her ability to adapt old knowledge to a new market and her appearance, enterprise and character made a lasting impact. She and Nicholls fished, netted or trapped and sold fish, freshwater crayfish and mussels, wild duck, rabbits and other game as well as eggs. She excelled, however, in creating hand-made craft articles, especially her very fashionable feather flowers. These reflected her sense of style and design, and her ability to blend colours: from the delicate rose pink and pale grey of the galah to the flamboyant greens, yellows and reds of the various parrots. Her creations enlivened many a bureau or overmantel in homes on the Murray River; the Museum of Victoria, Melbourne, holds seven such arrangements from this district, probably made by Aggie. In addition, she trapped water rats and turned their skins into drawstring purses. She also made reed mats, to protect polished furniture, and feather lures for fishermen and wove baskets.

Photographs of her camp show that she lived a comfortable life. On Saturday mornings she travelled in her buggy to Swan Hill to sell her craftwork, buy supplies, visit friends and, as she grew older, to collect her government rations. Agnes Edwards died on 17 November 1928 at her home and was buried in Swan Hill cemetery with Church of Christ forms. She had been a popular figure in the wider community, and the local Australian Natives' Association erected a tombstone in her memory.

A. Feldtmann, *Swan Hill* (Adel, 1973); J. P. Penney, 'Queen Aggie: The Last of Her Tribe', in M. Lake and F. Kelly (eds), *Double Time* (Melb, 1985) and The Death of Queen Aggie: Culture Contact in the Mid-Murray Region (B.A. Hons thesis, La Trobe Univ, 1977); *Australasian*, 6 May 1922, p 821; *Swan Hill Guardian*, 3 Feb 1965, p 5; series B313 and B332 (NAA, Melb); G. Walker, Pioneering Days at Swan Hill (1922), ms, 1922, *and* A. Feldtmann papers *and* photos taken in 1911 (Swan Hill L); H. Booth, letters (held by Mrs A. Whelan, Kilmore, Vic).

JAN PENNEY

EDWARDS, MARION ('BILL') (1874-1956), transsexual barman, pony trainer and bookmaker, was born on 19 March 1874 at Murchison, Victoria, fourth child of John Edwards, a Welsh-born blacksmith, and his wife Margaret, née McKay, from Scotland. Marion claimed to have been born in Wales and brought to Australia by her parents at the age of 4, but it is probable that she used her father as a model for her male persona.

According to her fanciful memoir, *Life and Adventures of Marion-Bill-Edwards* (Melbourne, 1907?), she worked on her uncle's farm on the Goulburn River and as a waitress, refused offers of marriage and 'made hot love' to women. About 1896 she decided to dress and live as a man, claiming that this earned her more money. Edwards later purported to have appeared as a female impersonator entertaining troops in Africa during the Boer War and to have delivered horses to India.

As William Ernest Edwards, on New Year's Day 1900 at St Francis's Catholic Church, Melbourne, Marion went through a form of marriage with a 30-year-old widow Lucy Minihan, née Repacholi, a lodging-house proprietor. In her memoir, Edwards claimed that the marriage was one of convenience. They soon separated. In April 1905, arrested for burglary when found in a hotel at 3 a.m., Marion explained her presence by saying she was trying to catch a prowler. Fearful that her gender would be discovered, she absconded to Queensland. Her 'wife', who had put up bail of £50, was sentenced to one month's gaol for Bill's default. After a second arrest in Brisbane in October 1906, Edwards returned to Melbourne, a celebrity once her masquerade was revealed. Taking advantage of the publicity, she performed as a sharpshooter in an exhibition between film shows at the Fitzroy Cyclorama. She also appeared at Kreitmayer's [q.v.] Bourke Street waxworks, billed as 'The Far-famed Male Impersonator'. At her trial on 1 November 1906 she was found not guilty. About this time her memoir was published, illustrated with photographs of her posing in male and female garb. Interviewed by *Lone Hand* in 1908, she was described as a modern Mademoiselle de Maupin, from the novel dealing with bisexuality.

Although there are references to Edwards in *Truth* and police records on 'sly-grog' matters, nothing was proven. A newspaper article in 1927 referred to her as a pony trainer at Port Melbourne. Living in West Melbourne from 1930, her lesbian notoriety forgotten, but still in male attire, she worked in hotels, iron foundries and factories, and as a starting price bookmaker. Electoral rolls gave her occupation as dyer. Neighbours knew she was female but described her later as an 'old gentleman'. Bill preferred to appear as a male. Nevertheless, near the end of her life the Mount Royal Geriatric Home forced her to dress in women's clothes. She died on 22 March 1956 at the Royal Melbourne Hospital and was buried in Fawkner cemetery. Her death certificate stated wrongly that she was Sarah Isobel, known as Marion Edwards, an actress, and gave incorrect details of her parents. In 1984 she was the subject of a play, *In Male Attire*, performed at St Martin's Theatre, Melbourne.

Lone Hand, 1 Jan 1908, p 305; *Refractory Girl*, no 5, Summer 1974, p 21; *Brisb Courier*, 5 Oct 1906, p 5; *Argus* (Melb), 16 Oct 1906, p 5, 23 Oct 1906, p 7, 7 Nov 1906, p 12; *Truth* (Melb), 14 Oct 1916, p 2, 21 Nov 1953, p 3, 7 Apr 1956, p 1; *Smith's Weekly*, 3 Sept 1927, p 3; VPRS 30/P, unit 1434, item 425, VPRS 807, unit 332, item C2048 (PRO, Vic); information from the late Mr W. Power.

MIMI COLLIGAN

EGGE, JOHN (c.1830-1901), Chinese riverboat captain, was born in Shanghai, China, and came to Australia in 1852 in the *Queen of Sheba*, owned by Francis Cadell [q.v.3]. When Cadell opened the Murray River trade with paddle steamers, John, on the books as 'John Bull', served as cook in each new ship as it was launched. In 1856 he assumed by deed poll his Scandinavian surname. While establishing a piggery on Hindmarsh Island in Lake Alexandrina, South Australia, he met a Devon girl, Mary Perring, whom he courted by swimming the river to visit her, his clothes piled on his head.

John and Mary married on 8 April 1857 at St Jude's Church of England, Port Elliot, and were to have eleven children. In 1859 the couple worked their passages up the Murray to Wentworth, New South Wales, where they set up a business hawking pies and pasties that they baked in camp ovens. By 1863 they owned a bakery and butchery, were general dealers and kept a boarding-house to cater for the many single men in the area. About 1867 Egge chartered the *Teviot* to trade on the river as a floating shop. Next he chartered the *Moira* to carry cargo and in 1868 bought the *Endeavour* to ply the upper Murray between Echuca and Albury.

By the 1870s Egge was one of the biggest traders on the river, operating from his large store near the wharf at Wentworth. He was said to pay up to £1000 a month in customs duties. The *Murrumbidgee* was his most elaborate boat, fitted with polished counters and mahogany showcases. For years he advocated Federation, foreseeing that it would end the poll tax he repeatedly had to pay—despite becoming a naturalized British subject in 1868—when he berthed his boat in the different colonies through which the Darling and Murray rivers flowed. One flamboyant exhibition increased his reputation: during a particularly high flood, he brought the *Prince Alfred* out of the river and down the main street of Wentworth.

Wentworth's citizens presented Egge with a testimonial and a gold ring set with diamonds when the family left in 1888 to live for a time in Adelaide, where their children went to school. Often in court suing or being sued for non-payment of bills, he put a value on apologies: 'I'm ten pounds sorry', he would say. 'How sorry are you?' He was generous to religious and social groups, making his boats freely available for dances and river picnics. Many a hard-up shed hand or station hand got a free ride. During the shearing strike of 1891, angry mobs held up riverboats that tried to carry strikebreakers, but picketing shearers cheered his boats from bend to bend.

The drought of the 1890s forced him to cease operations on the river. Egge died at Wentworth on 11 September 1901 and was buried with Wesleyan rites in the local cemetery. Four sons and three daughters survived him. In the 'White Australia' of the first half of the twentieth century, his family conveniently lost knowledge of him as a Chinese. That would not have upset him, as he always maintained that he was not an alien. In the 1970s, however, his descendants rediscovered his true character.

P. Howell, *South Australia and Federation* (Adel, 2002); *Hemisphere*, 28, no 1, July/Aug 1983, p 35; *Northern Territory Times*, 25 June 1887, p 3; *Observer* (Adel), 10 Mar 1888, p 31, 21 Sept 1901, p 33.

ERIC ROLLS

EISDELL, CATHERINE; *see* PARKER, KATHARINE

ELLERY, TORRINGTON GEORGE (1872-1923), town clerk, was born on 23 June 1872 at Mount Gambier, South Australia, eldest son of James Albert Ellery (1844-1905), publican, and his wife Julia Anna, née Moore. Educated at Norwood Grammar School and Whinham College, where he won the headmaster's silver medal in 1885 for proficiency in the classics, Torrington joined Adelaide City Council in 1890 as assistant to the town clerk Thomas Worsnop [q.v.6]. On 10 September 1896 at Kent Town Wesleyan Church, Ellery married Mabel Alice Wood. He became chief clerk following Worsnop's death in 1898, then town clerk next year after Worsnop's successor (Adam Wright) was dismissed for embezzlement.

Ellery embarked on a programme of reform intended to place the city 'well abreast of modern ideas in municipalisation', especially in regard to public health and sanitation. To combat the outbreak and spread of major infectious diseases, such as pulmonary tuberculosis, a refuse destructor was installed for incinerating household garbage, previously dumped on the park lands; a steam disinfector station was opened for disinfecting the belongings of infectious disease sufferers; a central authority was established to control the quality of Adelaide's milk supplies; and the council's health department was expanded with a trained nurse employed to educate citizens about good hygiene.

More important was the enforced closure of the city's numerous, and notoriously unhygienic, privately owned slaughterhouses, replaced in 1913 by modern public abattoirs, erected and managed jointly by the city and suburban councils. Acclaimed at the time as being 'the greatest civic enterprise in Australasia', the new abattoirs were a triumph for Ellery's pragmatic idealism; he was appointed first secretary, treasurer and general manager of the Municipal Abattoirs Board, which represented the participating councils.

A leading exponent of the Greater Cities movement, Ellery campaigned to amalgamate the city council with the surrounding local government bodies. This, he insisted, would result in improved economy, efficiency and uniformity of action in local government. Overcoming the parochial interests of the metropolitan councils, however, proved insurmountable and his vision never materialized.

In 1901 Ellery was offered the post of town clerk of Sydney but, suffering from insomnia, declined. In 1915 he became town clerk of Melbourne, where he facilitated improvements in the system of milk and fish supplies, control of markets and rat destruction. Again he advocated municipal unification to overcome divided control of public utilities such as the tramways and electricity supply. He also confronted such issues as noxious trades and the congestion and overcrowding in inner city areas—a cause pursued in a paper he contributed to the Australian Town Planning Conference in Adelaide in October 1917.

Shrewd, stoic, stern-faced, Ellery was the epitome of civic officialdom. His son later described his father as 'combative, ambitious, largely self-educated and of iconoclastic frame of mind'. An omnivorous reader, he spent most of his leisure in his private library, which included numerous works on municipal law and administration and practical sanitary science. He was vice-president of the Institute of Hygiene and Bacteriology and a fellow of the Royal Sanitary Institute, London, and lectured and wrote widely about public sanitation. Though highly regarded by most councillors, he had a despotic style of management, which won him few friends among subordinates. Reprimands, salary reductions, demotions and instant dismissals were endured by many who worked under him.

Nonetheless, Ellery's zeal and dedication made him a leader in local government in Australia for a quarter of a century. He was widely acknowledged as being one of the ablest, best informed and most progressive municipal administrators of his time. The Adelaide *Observer* remarked that his 'work is his hobby, and he is never so happy as when engaged upon it'. Ellery's passion for his work was also thought to have contributed to his untimely death: 'the work he had done night after night hastened his illness ... he was a slave to the council', was how the lord mayor of Melbourne, Sir John Swanson [q.v.12], summed up Ellery's career.

Ellery died of cancer on 16 October 1923 at his home at Elsternwick, and was buried in Brighton cemetery with Anglican rites. His wife, daughter and son Reginald Spencer [q.v.14], who became a prominent psychiatrist in Melbourne, survived him.

H. Burgess (ed), *The Cyclopedia of South Australia*, 1 (Adel, 1907); R. S. Ellery, *The Cow Jumped Over the Moon* (Melb, 1956); B. Dickey (ed), *William Shakespeare's Adelaide 1860-1930* (Adel, 1992); P. Morton, *After Light* (Adel, 1996); *Observer* (Adel), 27 May 1899, p 16, 20 Oct 1923; Town Clerk's Dept records, 1890-1915 (Adel City Council Archives).   ROBERT THORNTON

ERLIKILYIKA (c.1865-c.1930), Aboriginal sculptor, artist and anthropological interpreter, was born into the southern Arrernte language group, Central Australia. As *erlia* signified emu, his totemic name may relate to an emu ritual region near Charlotte Waters telegraph station at Adnyultultera waterhole. The station attracted Aborigines, a few of whom gained employment. As he also spoke Kaytetye, the language around Barrow Creek, he probably worked along the Overland Telegraph line.

A sympathetic Charlotte Waters stationmaster, P. M. Byrne, appreciated his abilities, recommending him as 'a first class black boy' to (Sir) Baldwin Spencer and F. J. Gillen [qq.v.12,9] for their 1901-02 cross-continental anthropological expedition. They recruited him and Parunda (Warwick), also a southern Arrernte man, in March 1901. Both proved indispensable as guides, rounding up and harnessing horses, providing game and in various camp duties. Erlikilyika, known to Europeans as Jim Kite or Kyte, often drove the supply wagon, also riding long distances delivering or collecting mail at repeater stations. As the sole expedition member who spoke Kaytetye, for several weeks at Barrow Creek he was virtually a research assistant. Spencer's patronizing journal entry (11 June 1901) praised 'a splendid blackfellow with us—Jim by name ... he helps us much and acts as an interpreter. He is by way of being an artist and is very fond of drawing on bits of paper so we give him a sheet ... and a pencil and he makes what he calls notes when asking [informants] questions'. His markings (probably traditional message stick signs) were successive stages in stories, which were recorded by Spencer in more literary form. After the party reached Borroloola in November 1901, the Aborigines departed for home on horseback, armed with revolvers. Two packhorses and cached food ensured supplies. Following their nearly 700-mile (1127 km) trek across unrelated tribal lands, Byrne received their horses and equipment in good order, four months later.

As well as expedition guide and interpreter, Erlikilyika showed remarkable artistic aptitude. Invited to sketch on one blank page in a journal, to Gillen's surprise he enthusiastically filled all the blank pages with eleven sketches. Three weeks later Gillen provided a book in which the artist drew twenty-seven original drawings for Gillen's sons. He was also celebrated for sculpting or carving items from wood or kaolinite, the latter quarried near Charlotte Waters. Popular tourist items included kaolin meerschaum pipes, grasshoppers, cicadas and scorpions, or slabs engraved with scenes of Aboriginal activity. The whiteness of the clay heightened the visual impression, although some objects retain ochre traces. Wooden boomerangs and spear throwers made by him have finely tooled lizards and animals.

Erlikilyika exhibited his work while on a visit to Adelaide in 1913, receiving favourable press comment. Herbert Basedow [q.v.7] purchased many items (now in the National Museum of Australia, as are the sketches for Gillen's sons). Observers noted his simple tools: penknife, wire, shearing blade gripped with rag and gum. Probably during this visit, he produced twenty-four botanical drawings, annotated with Arrernte and scientific names, for the South Australian Museum.

Returning to Charlotte Waters, he sold items to passing travellers until the 1920s. Bypassed by the railway, by 1930 the telegraph station had closed. Erlikilyika may already have died. He had participated in ceremonies in 1923, but his presence was not recorded in 1935, when his brother Jack Kite was involved ritually.

Gillen nicknamed Erlikilyika 'the subdued', reflecting his quiet, agreeable and reliable character. The anthropological assistance and his long, productive artistic career suggest a stable man, adapted to cultural challenges. So does the suited, watch-chained, moustached figure photographed during his Adelaide visit. He evidently retained traditional beliefs, while producing artworks suiting European taste. His motifs, however, like those of Albert Namatjira [q.v.15], reflected an entirely Aboriginal universe.

A. Sayers, *Aboriginal Artists of the Nineteenth Century* (Melb, 1994); H. Morphy, *Aboriginal Art* (Lond, 1998); J. Mulvaney, *From the Frontier* (Syd, 2000), and 'Erlikilyika' in A. Anderson, I. Lilley and S. O'Connor (eds), *Histories of Old Ages* (Canb, 2001); *Register* (Adel), 18 July 1913, p 7.
                                        D. J. MULVANEY

EUMARRAH (c.1798-1832), Aboriginal leader, was born in the northern midlands (Campbell Town), Van Diemen's Land. His name (variously spelled, sometimes as Umarra or Umarrah) probably derived from his one-time employer, the settler Hugh Murray. Alternative names were Kanneherlargenner and Moleteheerlaggenner. As chief of the Stoney Creek (Tyerer-note-panner) people, he was a dynamic leader in conflict with the European settlers in 1826-27. One of Lieutenant-Governor (Sir) George Arthur's roving parties, led by Gilbert Robertson [qq.v.1,2], captured Eumarrah and his wife Laoninneloonner late in 1828. The *Hobart Town Courier* on 22 November reported that the 'King, named Eumarrah ... declares it his determined purpose ... to destroy all the whites he possibly can, which he considers a patriotic duty'. Yet, before the Executive Council on 19 November the captives had denied any killing. Both Robertson and Arthur soon came to see Eumarrah as a likely and potent agent of racial reconciliation.

After a year in Richmond gaol, the Aboriginal leader joined G. A. Robinson's [q.v.2] 'friendly mission' through the south-west in early 1830. Eumarrah impressed Robinson, but never subordinated himself, and in May he decamped. Showing mighty bushcraft (and an island-wide reach), he trekked from near Trial Harbour to his homeland region. In October he presented himself to the Launceston authorities and, at Arthur's request, immediately joined the 'Black Line' operation, as it sought to corral the remaining Aborigines. To Arthur's chagrin, Eumarrah soon left the line and began harassing settlers in the Tamar and Esk valleys and in the northeast. Robinson was then working there and on 29 August 1831 the two met again. 'How I rejoiced to hear that this man was in being', wrote Robinson, who promised that if the Aborigines stopped hostilities they might remain on the land.

With other Aborigines, Eumarrah accompanied Robinson's mission to the Big River people from October 1831 to January 1832, shaping it to their own purposes—both helping and hindering the search. At night Eumarrah sang hour-long stories of 'amorous adventures, exploits in war &c'. The idyll ended as Robinson took the party to Hobart Town. Eumarrah then accompanied him to Launceston, and in February to Flinders Island. Back at Launceston, Eumarrah became ill with dysentery. He died on 24 March 1832 in hospital there and was buried in St John's graveyard with some formality, European and Aboriginal.

Eumarrah's first wife had been killed in an inter-Aboriginal dispute in 1831. His second wife was Woolaytoopinneya, who died in May 1832. He had several siblings, or at least band-

associates, of interest. His reputed sister Planobeena (Fanny) became the wife of PEEVAY (c.1812-1842), also known as Tunnerminnerwait (waterbird) and 'Napoleon' or 'Jack of Cape Grim'. Probably the son of Keeghernewboyheener, of Robbins Island, Peevay had met Robinson at Robbins Island in June 1830, when he began a long and complex relationship with the 'friendly mission'. Robinson spoke of him as 'an exceeding willing and industrious young man', who was 'stout and well made, of good temper, and performed his work equal to any white man'.

Perhaps Peevay was more deliberate than Eumarrah in his hopes of using the association to outwit Robinson and the colonizers generally. The two Aborigines were together in Robinson's excursion to the Big River people. In October 1835 Peevay went with Robinson to Flinders Island, where his tie with Fanny firmed. Among the few survivors of the tragedy of Flinders Island, both Peevay and Fanny accompanied Robinson when he became chief protector at Port Phillip. Their apparent closeness with Robinson continued until winter 1841, but in September Peevay, Fanny and three others, including Trugernanner [q.v.6] and Timme, formed a band which attacked Europeans in much the same style as had earlier prevailed in Van Diemen's Land. Consequently the Supreme Court found Peevay ('Jack Napoleon Tarraparrura') and Timme ('Robert Timmy Jimmy Small-boy') guilty of the murder of two whalers. Peevay was reported as saying that 'after his death he would join his father in Van Diemen's Land and hunt kangaroo; he also said that he had three heads, one for the scaffold, one for the grave, and one for V. D. Land'. The convicted men were hanged on 20 January 1842, the first offenders to be executed at Port Phillip.

Eumarrah had possessed remarkable personal qualities, and his experience, like that of Peevay, illustrated how British settlement offered indigenes a mix of challenge, opportunity, confusion and disaster. He evidently felt some attraction to the colonists and hoped to use their presence to his own advantage. Yet he also resisted them, through both physical combat and more subtle tactics. In mirror image, colonists viewed Eumarrah with mingled hostility, admiration and hope that he would serve their ends.

Van Diemen's Land: Copies of All Correspondence Between Lieutenant-Governor Arthur and His Majesty's Secretary of State for the Colonies, on the Subject of the Military Operations Lately Carried on Against the Aboriginal Inhabitants of Van Diemen's Land, A. G. L. Shaw introd (Hob, 1971); N. J. B. Plomley (ed), *Friendly Mission* (Hob, 1966) and *Weep in Silence* (Hob, 1987); H. Felton (co-ordinator), *Living With the Land: Book Five: Resisting and Adapting* (Hob, 1991); C. Pybus, *Community of Thieves* (Melb, 1991); I. MacFarlane, 'Pevay: A

Casualty of War', Tas Historical Research Assn, *Papers and Procs*, 48, no 4, Dec 2001, p 280; *Port Phillip Herald*, 26 Nov 1841, p 2, 24 Dec 1841, p 2, 21 Jan 1842, p 2.   MICHAEL ROE

EVANS, WILLIAM MEIRION (1826-1883), Wesleyan minister and editor, was born on 12 August 1826 at Isallt Fawr, parish of Llanfihangel-y-Pennant, Carnarvonshire, Wales, son of Edmund Evans, farmer, and his wife Mary, née Williams. William spent most of his early life in Llanfrothen, Merionethshire, an area he regarded as his native locality. Raised as a devout Welsh Calvinistic Methodist, he was self-taught and largely acquired his education from the local Sunday School. As a youth he went to work in the Ffestiniog slate-mines and also became a Sunday School teacher.

Attracted by news of economic opportunities, Evans reached Adelaide on 19 May 1849. He was employed in smelting works at Yatala and Apoinga and in the Willunga slate quarries. At Burra, where he worked in the copper-mine, he held Welsh-language religious services and about 1850 preached the first recorded Welsh-language sermon in Australia. In 1852 he went to the gold-mines at Bendigo, Victoria. Returning to Wales in 1853, he migrated with his parents and other family members to Illinois, United States of America. There, on 9 June 1855 he married Mary Jane Hughes. They were to have two children who died young. By June 1861 William had been ordained as a minister with the Welsh Calvinistic Methodist Church in Columbus, Wisconsin.

Evans arrived back in Victoria on 6 March 1863; his wife joined him in 1865. At first a miner and part-time preacher in the Ballarat area, he gave up mining in 1864 on being appointed minister of the Welsh Calvinistic Methodist churches at Ballarat, Sebastopol and Cambrian Hill. His wife died in 1869. On 7 November 1870 at his Ballarat residence he married Ellen Jones, née Roberts, a widow. In April 1871 the Welsh Calvinistic Methodist General Association of Victoria transferred Evans to take charge of the Welsh Church in Melbourne. He was also given full powers to oversee the building of the new La Trobe Street church, which opened on 31 December 1871.

An enterprising, kind and considerate man, Evans had a reputation for doing good deeds for their own sake. His energy and determination invigorated Welsh, and especially Welsh-language, religious and cultural activities in the colony, and he became a respected community leader. The driving force behind the only two Welsh-language periodicals to be published in Australia in the nineteenth century, he served variously as joint or sole editor of the *Yr Australydd* [the *Australian*], published in 1866-72, and *Yr Ymwelydd* [the *Visitor*], which appeared in 1874-76. He contributed many articles to Welsh journals in Wales and the U.S.A. as well as to his own, where his editorials urged Welsh immigrants to maintain their native language. Retaining their nationality, he argued, was compatible with loyalty to their adopted country. In 1872 he was one of the founders of the Cambrian Society of Victoria.

Following his retirement, Evans opened a bookshop in Bourke Street, Melbourne, and later at Ballarat, though he continued to preach at services in both places. After a long illness he died on 4 August 1883 at Ballarat, survived by his second wife and their three daughters. He was buried in Ballarat cemetery.

The Dictionary of Welsh Biography Down to 1940 (Lond, 1959); M. Williams, *Cymry Australia* (Llandybie, Wales, 1983); L. Lloyd, *Australians from Wales* (Caernarfon, Wales, 1988); *Cylchgrawn Hanes y Methodistiaid Calfinaidd*, 7, 1983, p 43; B. Jones, 'Welsh Identity in Colonial Ballarat', in W. Prest and G. Tulloch (eds), *Scatterlings of Empire* (Brisb, 2001); *Ballarat Star*, 6 Aug 1883; memoir of the Rev. W. M. Evans, ms (Welsh Church, Melb, and National L of Wales).   BILL JONES

EVENDEN, JOHN EDWIN (c.1819-1890), convict, constable and caretaker, was born at St Leonards, Sussex, England, son of a builder. While employed as a brewer and clerk in London, John was sentenced to fourteen years transportation for stealing letters containing £2 10s. 4d. He arrived in Hobart Town in the *Hindostan* on 19 January 1841 and was sent to Port Arthur, where his exemplary conduct soon brought rewards.

Employed as a schoolmaster during his period of probation, Evenden became a constable and, according to his own account, gave invaluable service to the authorities. The bushranger Martin Cash [q.v.1] supported his claims of efficiency: 'my own case affording a melancholy proof'. In 1870 Marcus Clarke [q.v.3] was told of 'the acuteness of Mr John Evenden'. On 2 March 1851 at Tasman Peninsula he had married Margaret Louisa Flora MacDonald. They were to have nine children. When the constabulary was reduced in 1861, Evenden leased the former government farm at Saltwater River but, just over a year later, suffered financially when the property was resumed.

An appointment as policeman at New Norfolk in 1863 was timely but ultimately unfortunate. Evenden's wife had long suffered from mental illness and was often a patient at the New Norfolk Asylum. With a large family and sick wife, in 1871 Evenden was charged with misappropriating £140 in road trust monies and sentenced to eighteen months imprisonment, the presiding judge noting the similarity to his original offence.

Freed after fifteen months, Evenden remained at Port Arthur and, as he had done some thirty years earlier, became a constable. He also acted as wharfinger, coxswain, semaphore repairer, and telegraph operator. With the closure of the settlement looming, he was appointed caretaker at five shillings per day and also acted as guide to the tourists who came to the previously restricted area. He remained on the payroll until 1881, when his duties were taken over by the police constable. Given a half pension, but refused a full pension or a position with light duties, he remained on Tasman Peninsula, where he owned a small amount of land. In 1884 he wrote his memoirs so that they could be used as an authoritative account of the settlement. Enlivened by personal experience but marred by inaccuracy, his account was nevertheless used by Port Arthur guides until at least 1954.

Evenden died at the General Hospital, Hobart, on 30 May 1890, survived by his wife, five daughters and two sons. He was buried in Cornelian Bay cemetery and his death noted on his convict record.

Martin Cash, the Bushranger of Van Diemen's Land in 1843-4 (Hob, 1870); B. Wannan (ed), *A Marcus Clarke Reader* (Melb, 1963); *Mercury* (Hob), 13 Sept 1871, p 3, 2 June 1890, p 3; W. N. Hurst papers (Roy Soc of Tas, Hob); Convict Dept records, Colonial Secretary's Office records, Chief Secretary's Dept records and Port Arthur Scenic Reserve Board records, and file nos CSD10/6/95, CSD16/26/344 and AA610/2 (TA).

MARGARET GLOVER

EWING, ROBERT KIRKWOOD (c. 1823-1899), minister of religion and controversialist, was born at Glasgow, Scotland, son of John Ewing, merchant, and his wife Elizabeth, née Young. Robert arrived in Sydney in 1839 and worked as a teacher. On 2 January 1841 at St James's Church he married Letitia Blakemore, a widow. A Presbyterian, Ewing turned to Congregationalism after hearing the preaching of Dr Robert Ross [q.v.2] and secured a position with the Colonial Missionary Society in Van Diemen's Land. After his ordination in February 1847 he was Congregational minister at Green Ponds. Failing in health and aggrieved by his inadequate pay, in July 1848 he was inducted into the Presbyterian Church at the old kirk in Charles Street, Launceston. His preaching attracted a growing congregation and he threw himself into fund-raising. Within eighteen months £4000 had been collected for the new St Andrew's Church.

His tenure at St Andrew's was marked by charges of immorality, frequent unrest and clashes of opinion, resulting in intervention from the Presbyterian Church. Nevertheless, his congregation made 'remarkable progress', with the Sunday School and Young Men's Association especially strong. Critics thought Ewing too worldly, spending too much time on 'pursuits unconnected with his sacred calling' and neglecting 'his own flock'. Ewing argued that a clergyman who took a narrow view of his calling lost in 'practical humanity and adaptation to the wants and characteristics of the age'. His interests included membership of St Andrew's Club, a benefit society promoting co-operation within the Scottish community. He was president of the Launceston Philharmonic Society and formed St Andrew's Teetotal Society. For five years he was president of Launceston Mechanics' Institute, where he taught elocution, gave lectures and helped to raise funds for a new building. Ewing was a Freemason and became provincial grand master in 1858. His achievements were tainted by his inclination to take and give offence. In a dispute with the Hobart lodge that year he was accused of abandoning his wife. He was elected moderator of the Presbyterian Church in 1863.

After losing his voice, Ewing retired in April 1868 with a presbyterial certificate and a pension worth £74 11s. 9d. He moved to Melbourne and, regaining his voice, assumed control of Scott's Private College. Eleven days after his wife's death in Tasmania, he married 28-year-old Frances Sanden on 13 January 1863 at South Yarra. By 1874 Ewing was at Beechworth where in 1877 he again became embroiled in controversy, when accused of acting as a mining company manager and speculating in mining shares. Although his congregation supported him, the charges were found to be true and his admission to the Presbyterian Church of Victoria was prevented. Ewing thereupon joined the Church of England and served at Inverell, New South Wales. In 1896 he became a canon and rural dean.

A man of 'marked ability and unbounded energy', Ewing was a brilliant conversationalist and an effective orator. Among his publications were *A Lecture Replying to Objections Against Phrenology* (Launceston, 1852), *Moses and Colenso* (Hobart, 1864), *Sunday Evening Lectures on Larrikinism* (Inverell, 1888) and a book of poems, *Filings of Time* (Launceston, 1860?). Photographs showed him to be prophet-like, with a shaggy white beard and wispy hair, but his eyes belied his mild appearance and hinted at a volcanic temper. Ewing died on 10 April 1899 in the vicarage at Lismore and was buried in the local cemetery. His wife, son and two daughters survived him.

Cyclopedia of Tasmania, 2 (Hob, 1900); J. Heyer, *The Presbyterian Pioneers of Van Diemen's Land* (Launc, Tas, 1935); S. Petrow, *Going to the Mechanics* (Launc, 1998); *V&P* (LA, NSW), 1887, 5, p 974, 1892-3, 5, p 1433; *Examiner* (Launc), 8 July 1848, p 440, 2 Aug 1848, p 496, 3 July 1858, p 2, 20 July 1858, p 3, 21 Nov 1867, p 5, 12 Apr 1899, pp 5, 10; *Cornwall Chronicle*, 16 Feb 1859, p 4; *Australasian*, 28 Nov 1874, p 694, 19 May 1877, supp, p 1, Colonial Missionary Society correspondence, 1847-48, non state 586/13 and Presbyterian Church records, non state 435/4/5 (TA).   STEFAN PETROW

EYRE, JOYCE EILEEN (1909-1950), teacher and academic, was born on 4 April 1909 at Sandy Bay, Hobart, eldest child of English-born parents Matthew Henry Eyre, carpenter, and his wife Annie Elizabeth, née Metcalfe. Joyce was educated at primary schools in Hobart and at Launceston, the State High School, Launceston, and the University of Tasmania (B.A., 1932; M.A., 1940). After teaching at the State High School, Hobart, in 1929-32 she worked as a lecturer and school principal with the Seventh Day Adventist Church in New South Wales and New Zealand. Following extensive overseas travel in 1938, she returned to Hobart, completed her master's degree in Tasmanian history, on Sir John Franklin's dispute with John Montagu [qq.v.1,2], and lectured in English and history at Hobart Teachers' College from 1940 to 1945.

Appointed lecturer in the English department at the University of Tasmania in 1946, Eyre introduced a course on Australian literature and founded in 1947 the Glebe Theatre Players, a drama school within the department. Her Australian literature course was an optional unit, representing one-third of the final year's English programme, and was the most extensive university course of its kind taught in Australia at the time. It comprised twenty-seven lectures and seminars and examined the works of some fifteen prose writers and poets, giving particular attention to writers of the 1930s and 1940s. This work attracted national attention and was publicized in journals such as *Poetry* and *Southerly*; the editor of the former congratulated the university 'for making an innovation long desired by lovers of our own literature'.

With E. Morris Miller [q.v.10], Louis Triebel and the historians Basil Rait and John Reynolds, Eyre founded the Tasmanian branch of the Fellowship of Australian Writers in 1947 and applauded the work of local authors such as Roy and Hilda Bridges, Marie Bjelke-Petersen and Catherine Shepherd [qq.v.7,16]. As corresponding secretary for the branch, Eyre was in regular contact with writers, and hosted visiting lecturers, including Vance and Nettie Palmer, James Devaney [qq.v.11,18,13], 'Furnley Maurice' [q.v.12 Wilmot] and Arthur Phillips, often entertaining them at her home at Battery Point. She encouraged all students of English to participate in regular public readings and stage productions of plays prescribed in the English syllabus. She was active in the Workers' Educational Association and the Tasmanian branch of the League of Nations Union, co-editing its journal *World Review* for some years.

Eyre was 'tall, fair, blue-eyed and confident'. On 9 April 1949 at Davey Street Congregational Church she married Norman Edwin Phillips (1902-1972), a Scottish-born bank clerk and former naval officer who helped with her work in drama. She was invited to present a series of Commonwealth Literary Fund lectures in Perth in 1951, but died from complications arising from pregnancy on 9 October 1950 in the Alexandra Hospital, Hobart. Her husband survived her. Joyce Phillips's premature death cut short a promising career as academic, writer and critic. Her students' admiration for her skills as a teacher and enthusiastic commitment to Australian literature was shared by her colleagues. Miller had 'cherished great hopes that she would develop into an important writer and literary leader', and Nettie Palmer described her as 'one of the best informed as well as the most attractive lecturers on our literature anywhere', predicting that in time 'she would have made her own contribution ... as critic and literary historian'.

L. Dale, *The English Men* (Canb, 1977); J. Reynolds and M. Giordano, *Countries of the Mind* (Hob, 1985); *Poetry*, no 20, 30 Sept 1946, p 34; Fellowship of Aust Writers, *Fellowship*, June 1947, p 4; *Meanjin*, 10, no 1, Autumn 1951, p 68; *Southerly*, 12, no 2, 1951, p 111; *Togatus*, 8 Aug 1949, 4 May 1951, p 2; *Mercury* (Hob), 11 Oct 1951, p 6; Eyre staff file and K. Dallas papers (Univ Tas Archives); Fellowship of Australian Writers (Tas) papers and League of Nations Union (Tas) papers (TA).

                                         RALPH SPAULDING

F

FAIRTHORNE, FREDERICK KIRK (1846-1919), pharmacist and entrepreneur, was born on 9 December 1846 at Longford, Van Diemen's Land, elder son of LANDON FAIRTHORNE (1823-1890), chemist, and his wife Maria Emily, née Cooper, formerly Gellard. Born on 13 February 1823 in London, Fairthorne senior arrived in South Australia in 1839 and moved in 1842 to Tasmania, where he qualified to practise as a chemist by examination in 1844. Landon then opened in business at Longford before setting up as a chemist and druggist at Launceston. Intercolonial shipping and gold- and tin-mining ventures were other interests, and he was mayor of Launceston in 1884-85. Landon died on 17 August 1890. His success had given his son a good start in colonial life.

Frederick was educated at Horton College, Ross, and at Launceston Church Grammar School in 1861. After a few years on the mainland in shipping and wheat-broking, he was articled to his father, qualified as a chemist in 1871 and was soon taken into partnership. L. Fairthorne & Son expanded into a large wholesale as well as retail and dispensing pharmacy. Frederick was a founding member and sometime president of the Pharmaceutical Society of Tasmania.

On 27 July 1884 at St John's Church, Launceston, he married Louisa Letitia Hardman. They were to have three sons and two daughters. Appointed a justice of the peace in 1893, in December 1897 Fairthorne was elected an alderman of the city of Launceston and was mayor in 1900-02. He resigned from the council in 1908. Closely identified with the Tasmanian Defence Force, for some years he was adjutant of the Launceston Rifle Regiment, holding the rank of captain on his retirement. He shared his father's interest in mining. In 1890 Frederick was appointed director of the Mount Bischoff Tin Mining Co. and was subsequently chairman. He was also chairman of the Royal George Co. and personally owned and worked several small mining ventures with more or less success. His interests extended to both the north-east and the west coast of Tasmania, where silver, lead and zinc were being mined very profitably in the late nineteenth century.

Fairthorne was involved in several good causes at Launceston. He was governor and honorary treasurer of the Girls' Industrial School and director of Launceston Savings Bank. He was also on the local directorate of the New Zealand Insurance Co. Respected by his colleagues and the citizens of Launceston,

he was often encouraged to stand for parliament, but declined to take an active role in party politics. The Reform League, however, which argued for level State expenditure and taxation in post-Federation Tasmania, won his firm support. After a long illness, Fairthorne died at his home at Launceston on 14 November 1919 and was buried in Carr Villa cemetery. He was survived by his wife and two daughters, and by two sons who carried on the business. Fairthorne Road, at Trevallyn, Launceston, was probably named after the younger son, Frederick Falkener Fairthorne (1887-1963), athlete and pharmacist, who served in the Australian Imperial Force in World War I. The firm had become Drug Houses of Australia Ltd (Tasmania) some years before his death.

Cyclopedia of Tasmania, 2 (Hob, 1900); B. W. Rait, *The Story of the Launceston Church Grammar School* (Launc, Tas, 1946); *Landon Fairthorne* (Launc, Tas, 1946); J. and D. Morris, *History in Our Streets* (Launc, Tas, 1988); M. Roe, *The State of Tasmania* (Hob, 2001); *Examiner* (Launc), 15 Nov 1919, p 11; *Mercury* (Hob), 15 Nov 1919, p 7, 21 May 1962, p 5, 7 October 1963, p 14.

PAUL A. C. RICHARDS

FALLENI, EUGENIA (c.1875-1938), convicted murderer, was born reputedly in Florence, Italy, and moved with her family to New Zealand about 1877. According to later medical reports, she had frequently run away as a child, seeking jobs in brickyards and other places where she dressed as a boy. In her teens Falleni found employment aboard a ship that plied the south seas. At some point during her voyages, her sex was discovered and she became pregnant. About 1898 Falleni disembarked at Newcastle, New South Wales, friendless, with a baby girl. It is possible that she was the unmarried Lena Falleni, born at Livorno, Italy, who gave birth to a daughter Josephine in Sydney in 1898. The child was put into a Sydney woman's care and Falleni proceeded to present herself to the world as 'Harry Leo Crawford'.

Crawford worked in Sydney for employers who thought nothing of the gruff, taciturn man's bearing He held a series of manual jobs—in a meat factory, hotels, laundries, a rubber company and in private service. By 1912 he was a yardman and driver for Dr G. R. C. Clarke of Wahroonga, where he met Annie Birkett. A widow with a 9-year-old son, Annie was a general domestic with the Clarkes but had saved a nest egg. Harry took mother and son on sulky rides and to visit the circus. The courting pair resolved to leave service and set up a confectionery shop in Balmain. Claiming to be a widower aged 38, son of a master mariner, also named Harry Leo Crawford, Harry went through a marriage ceremony with Annie on 19 February 1913 at the Methodist Parsonage, Balmain South, and embarked on a brief, stormy family life. It remains unclear whether Annie realized that her husband was not a man. Neighbours later reported that the pair quarrelled frequently, particularly after Falleni's daughter Josephine reappeared.

While young Harry Birkett was away from home, the Crawfords celebrated the Eight-Hour Day holiday in 1917 with a picnic at Chatswood. Mrs Crawford did not return. On 2 October a woman's body was discovered, charred beyond recognition and apparently battered. Crawford did not report his wife missing; rather he claimed that she had left him. Josephine moved out and, selling the household goods, Crawford moved to inner Sydney with his stepson. On 29 September 1919 at Canterbury registry office Harry Leo Crawford, a widower and a mechanical engineer, married Elizabeth King Allison. The groom's parents were given as Harry Crawford, ship-owner, and Elizabeth Falleni. By 1920 the body at Chatswood had been identified as Annie Crawford and police tracked down her husband. Arrested on suspicion of murder on 5 July, Crawford asked to be held in the women's cells.

The press relished the revelation. Sydney's 'man-woman' created a sensation. At his preliminary hearing in July 1920 the defendant appeared in men's clothes. At the trial for murder in October, however, the accused sat in the dock dressed as a woman. The Crown argued that Falleni had perpetrated 'sex fraud' and had killed to cover her deception. The defence countered that she was innocent and merely a 'congenital invert'. Falleni was convicted and condemned to death, but her sentence was commuted. Released from Long Bay prison in February 1931 she assumed the name 'Jean Ford' and worked as a landlady. She was living at Paddington when she was struck by a motorcar in Oxford Street on 9 June 1938. Falleni died of her injuries the following day in Sydney Hospital and was buried with Anglican rites in Rookwood cemetery.

Speculation about Falleni's identity and guilt did not stop with her death. At her 1920 trial her daughter had testified: 'My mother has always gone about dressed as a man'. Since then doctors, psychiatrists, journalists, endocrinologists, feminists, playwrights, film makers and historians have tried to make sense of Falleni. They have labelled her variously as a sexual hermaphrodite, a homo-sexualist, a masquerader, a person with misplaced atoms, a sex pervert, a passing woman, a transgendered man, and as gender dysphoric. Falleni proclaimed her innocence of the murder but never explained what induced her to live as a man.

H. M. Moran, *Viewless Winds* (Lond, 1939); S. Falkiner, *Eugenia* (Syd, 1988); L. Parry, *Eugenia* (Wellington, NZ, 1996); *Gender & History*, 12, no 1, Apr 2000, p 158; *Daily Telegraph* (Syd), 6 July 1920, p 4, 7 July 1920, pp 5 & 9, 8 July 1920, p 5, 20 Aug 1920, p 9, 7 Oct 1920, p 4, 13 June 1938, p 2; *Truth* (Syd), 22 Aug 1920, p 11, 10 Oct 1920, p 10, 16 Mar 1930, p 1, 22 Feb 1931, p 1; *Smith's Weekly*, 16 Oct 1920, pp 11 & 17; *People*, 21 Oct 1953, p 32; N. Haire, Sex Education: Sex and the Individual, Norman Haire Collection, file 2.1 (Univ Syd special collections); R v. Eugene Falleni, depositions, 9/7250, and trial transcripts, 6/1007 (SRNSW).

CAROLYN STRANGE

FANTIN, FRANCESCO GIOVANNI (1901-1942), labourer and anti-fascist, was born on 20 January 1901 at San Vito di Leguzzano, Vicenza, Italy, one of five children of Giovanni (Battista) Fantin, textile worker, and his wife Catarina, née Manea. After a brief formal education Francesco adopted his father's trade. Against a backdrop of conflicting social forces that were to engender both fascism and the Italian Communist Party, he became active as a trade unionist and political militant, with anarchism as his political creed.

Reaching Melbourne on 27 December 1924 in the *Re d'Italia*, Fantin was employed mainly as an agricultural labourer and cane cutter in Queensland, where his brothers Luigi and Alfonse had a cane farm at Sawmill Pocket, Edmonton. At Mourilyan (1924-28) Francesco joined the Australian Workers' Union. In 1931-32 and 1939-40 he worked at the Federal Woollen Mill at Geelong, Victoria. Known as Frank or 'Chico', he was active in the labour and anti-fascist movements, attracting the unfavourable attention of the Italian consular authorities. In 1939 he was involved with Frank Carmagnola in opening the anti-fascist Matteotti Club in Melbourne, and was a correspondent for the anti-fascist newspaper *La Riscossa*.

In 1940 Fantin was denounced to the Australian authorities as a fascist, possibly the result of confusion with his brother Luigi; paradoxically, Frank was also accused of spreading communist propaganda among the cane workers. He was arrested on 14 February 1942. In his appeal against his detention he gave his religion as atheist, and stated that he was married to Maria, née Zamon, a textile worker, living at San Vito, Italy. On 20 March Fantin was moved to Loveday Internment Camp 14A at Barmera, South Australia. A peculiarity of the internment system was that inmates were segregated by nationality rather than by political affiliation. The result in Camp 14A, where the Italians were interned, was a forced integration of anti-fascists with fascists and a consequent politicization of camp life. Taking a leading role in opposing the fascists, Fantin was abused, threatened and assaulted.

Matters came to a head late in 1942. At 6.30 p.m. on 16 November he was drinking alone from a water tap when he was approached by Giovanni Bruno Casotti, a known fascist. There are two versions of subsequent events. The fascist version suggested that, after an altercation, Casotti pushed Fantin who fell, hitting his head on the tap support. Anti-fascists argued that Casotti struck him with a piece of wood and kicked him in the body after his fall. Fantin died from his injuries later that day in the military hospital.

In the Supreme Court, Adelaide, in December Casotti pleaded guilty to manslaughter. Moves to change the charge to murder were opposed by the government, the army and the Commonwealth Security Service, since a charge of murder would have further fuelled the public outcry at Fantin's death and the internment policy. Casotti was sentenced to two years imprisonment. Public pressure, however, brought about changes in the policy: increasingly, anti-fascists were released if they could satisfy the authorities that they posed no threat. Fantin's death made him a martyr, and a symbol of the fight against fascism waged by a substantial proportion of the Australian Italian migrant community.

Internment in South Australia: History of Loveday (Adel, 1946); G. Cresciani, *Fascism, Anti-Fascism and Italians in Australia 1922-1945* (Canb, 1980); *Radio Times* (Melb), 23 Jan 1943; P. Nursey-Bray, 'Anti-fascism and Internment: The Case of Francesco Fantin', *JIISSA*, no 17, 1989; *North Qld Guardian*, 15 Jan 1943; *Advertiser* (Adel), 17 Mar 1943, p 6; BP242/1, item Q30084, CRS A373, Box 21:10913, AP80/1, item P2565, MP742, item 255/12/12 (NAA).

PAUL NURSEY-BRAY

FARR, CLINTON COLERIDGE (1866-1943), physicist, was born on 22 May 1866 in Adelaide, last of seven children of George Henry Farr [q.v.4], headmaster of the Collegiate School of St Peter, and his wife Julia Warren, née Ord [q.v. Farr]. Beginning in 1884 at the University of Adelaide (B.Sc., 1888; D.Sc., 1902), Coleridge (known to his family as 'Cole') failed first-year science in 1885. His studies blossomed, however, with the arrival of (Sir) William Henry Bragg [q.v.7] to teach mathematics and physics: Farr graduated with second-class honours in both subjects. That year (1888) he was the first recipient of the Angas [q.v.3] engineering exhibition, and

next year won the Angas engineering scholarship for three years work in Britain.

Farr enrolled at University College, London, but serious illness caused him to return to Australia in 1890. His health recovered and he continued his scholarship at the University of Sydney in 1891-93, studying electrical engineering under (Sir) Richard Threlfall [q.v.12]. Farr was appointed clerk of works for the distribution of electricity through Redfern. Threlfall also involved him in research into magnetism. Several publications resulted, although the diamagnetism of bismuth proved intractable. Farr tutored at St Paul's College, within the university, until 1894 when he went back to the University of Adelaide as lecturer in electrical engineering. In 1895-96 he renewed his tutorship at St Paul's, in the vain hope of finding employment with Threlfall.

Late in 1896 Farr was appointed lecturer in mathematics and physics at Lincoln Agricultural College, Christchurch, New Zealand. He sought the assistance of Pietro Baracchi [q.v.7], acting government astronomer for Victoria, to extend the contemporary magnetic survey of the globe to the neighbourhood of New Zealand, and Baracchi secured a loan of instruments from Kew Observatory and the Royal Society, London. With the backing of the Australasian Association for the Advancement of Science, Farr persuaded the New Zealand government to fund a comprehensive survey of the islands and a magnetic observatory at Christchurch, with Farr as director, a position he occupied in 1899-1903. In 1902 he was awarded the University of Adelaide's first doctorate of science for his thesis on the early New Zealand magnetic survey. He published a comprehensive report on the project in 1916.

On 22 April 1903 Farr married Maud Ellen Haydon at St Paul's Church, Papanui. Next year he became lecturer in electricity and surveying at Canterbury College, Christchurch, being appointed professor of physics in 1911 when a chair was created. His teaching was effective and stimulating, his manner idiosyncratic and absent-minded, his support for original research strong. He had a colourful personality, a keen sense of humour and wide human interests. In the early 1920s the case of his wife's confinement for many years to mental institutions in Sydney and New Zealand came to the attention of the Lunacy Reform League and in part led to a wide-ranging royal commission on the lunacy laws in New South Wales. The league's claim that Mrs Farr was wrongfully confined was completely rejected by the commission.

Farr's later research included work on the properties of liquid sulphur, the radioactivity of New Zealand artesian waters and igneous rocks, and the breakdown of insulators on electrical transmission lines. He became a fellow of the New Zealand Institute (Royal Society of New Zealand) in 1919, winner of its Hector medal and prize in 1922, and its president in 1929-30. In 1928 he was elected a fellow of the Royal Society of London. He retired in 1936. During World War II he taught at St Peter's College, Adelaide. Farr died on 27 January 1943 at Christchurch and was cremated with Anglican rites. His wife and son survived him.

R. W. Home, *Physics in Australia to 1945* (Melb, 1990); *The Dictionary of New Zealand Biography*, 4, (Auckland, NZ, 1998), p 167; *Trans and Procs of the Roy Soc of NZ*, 73, 1943-44, p xlv; *Obituary Notices of Fellows of the Roy Soc*, Lond, 13, no 4, 1944, p 503; *JHSSA*, no 12, 1984, p 76; *Hist Records of Aust Science*, 6, no 3, 1986, p 333; *Australian Historical Studies*, vol 24, no 97, Oct 1991, p 340; *NZ Science Review*, 58, no 2, 2001, p 71; *SMH*, 20 April 1921, p 8, 4 May 1921, p 8; Melb Observatory, outward letter books (PRO, Vic); archives of St Peter's College, Adel, Univ Adel and Univ Syd; royal commission into lunacy laws and administration 12/1398 (SRNSW); Farr (Sharp) family papers, MSS 1826 K22137 (ML).

JOHN JENKIN
R. W. HOME

FARR, JULIA WARREN (1824-1914), charity worker, was born on 14 August 1824 at Greensted Hall, Essex, England, one of seven children of Sir Robert Hutchinson Ord, of the Royal Artillery, and his wife Elizabeth, neé Blagrave. Julia, orphaned at 16, and her siblings were cared for at Woolwich by their uncle Harry, father of Sir Harry Ord [q.v.5]. She had a genteel education and became competent in singing and the French language. On 5 February 1846 at Woolwich parish church Julia married George Henry Farr [q.v.4], an Anglican clergyman serving in Cornwall. Her Christian Brethren brother and other family members had opposed the marriage.

The Farrs' first child Eleanora was born in Cornwall in 1848. However, consumption was judged to threaten her life, prompting migration to the dry Adelaide climate in 1854, where George became headmaster of the Collegiate School of St Peter. Julia bore six more children, the youngest being Clinton Coleridge Farr [q.v.]. While principally concerned with family affairs, she was active in the school, and at times was in control of the boarding-house. She sang in the school choir and maintained cultural interests dating from her schooldays, notably in French literary classics. Her children depicted her as 'naturally gifted, with a quick, clear brain and a power of terse expression'.

The creation and conduct of Adelaide's orphan home for parentless girls was Julia Farr's major life work. Gathering a group of like-minded men and women, all Anglicans, and with the support of Bishop Augustus Short [q.v.6], she convened meetings in 1860 to establish the institution, which was located until 1907 in Carrington Street, and subsequently at Mitcham. She remained the driving force until shortly before her death. For many years she chaired the organizing committee, solicited donations from among her expanding circle of middle-class friends, supervised the matrons as a regular monthly visitor, and arranged the subsequent placement of the teenage girls—mainly as domestic servants with her acquaintances around Adelaide.

Farr watched over the careers of the approximately 300 girls admitted in 1860-1912, annotating the registers regularly with news of their lives, being especially pleased when they 'married respectably'. The children were not required to pass a religious test, but the Book of Common Prayer and the regular visits of a chaplain governed the daily life of the home, while the bishop was the legal visitor. Farr's Anglicanism and her husband's Anglo-Catholicism ensured such a denominational and indeed sacramental outcome. It eventually meant the subsumption of the Orphan Home, known since 1934 as Farr House, into the welfare services of the synod of the diocese of Adelaide.

In 1878 Mrs Farr's social conscience had been aroused at the fate of people confined in the Destitute Asylum with incurable diseases. Supported by Dr William Gosse, father of W. C. Gosse [q.v.4], she rallied medical and philanthropic friends to establish at Fullarton the non-denominational Home for Incurables (in 1981 named the Julia Farr Centre).

On leaving St Peter's in 1878 Julia was rector's wife at Semaphore, Mitcham and Whitmore Square, Adelaide. George died in 1904. Leaving an estate sworn for probate at £7000, Julia died on 21 April 1914 at North Adelaide and was buried beside her husband in North Road cemetery. Three daughters and a son survived her. Orphan home 'old girls' wrote in tribute: 'It was to her we owed our upbringing, our education, our home, and our spiritual teaching, and many a day will pass before we forget the lessons she loved to teach us, and with her example before us may we strive to be "Christ's faithful Soldiers and Servants unto our lives' end"'.

Early Days at St Peter's College, Adelaide 1854-1878 (Adel, 1936); C. Kerr, *The Home for Incurables* (Adel, 1979); J. Tregenza, *Collegiate School of St Peter, Adelaide* (Adel, 1996); J. Healey (ed), *S.A.'s Greats* (Adel, 2001); B. Dickey, *Giving a Hand: A History of Anglicare SA 1860-2001* (Adel, 2003); Orphan Home records (SLSA and Anglican Archives, Adel); information from, and papers held by, Miss J. Clift, Walkerville, Adel.

BRIAN DICKEY

FARRELL, JAMES (1803-1869), clergyman, was born on 26 November 1803 at Longford, Ireland, son of Rev. James Farrell, of the United Church of England and Ireland. Educated at home by his father, in 1818 young James entered Trinity College, Dublin (B.A., 1823; M.A., 1832), where he imbibed Tory political views and mixed in evangelical circles. The bishop of Killala ordained him deacon in 1826 and priest in 1827. Farrell was curate of Kilfree, County Sligo, before leaving his homeland in 1832 in search of a secure living. After two years in Paris, where he was private chaplain to a wealthy American, he served in rural parishes in Guernsey and at Studley, Worcestershire, England. In March 1840 he was accepted by the Society for the Propagation of the Gospel as a missionary to South Australia.

Reaching the province in the *Lysander* on 6 September 1840, Farrell was appointed to Adelaide's second Anglican church, St John's, Halifax Street. In July 1843 he succeeded C. B. Howard [q.v.1] as colonial chaplain and incumbent of Trinity Church. Until 1846 Farrell was the only Church of England clergyman in South Australia. His business acumen assisted Trinity Church to eliminate its oppressive debt. Privately, he invested successfully in real estate and lent substantial sums on mortgage.

Farrell's reputation slipped in February 1845 when he was prosecuted for indecent assault of his landlady's 14-year-old female servant. Sympathetic magistrates dismissed the case, but the whiff of scandal hung around for several years. On 12 November 1845 at St Mary's-on-the-Sturt, near Adelaide, Farrell was married—by a Church of Scotland minister —to Grace Montgomery Howard, née Neville, widow of his predecessor; he became stepfather to her four young daughters.

Farrell taught a 'simple manly religion' and took a close interest in the education of the young. After the arrival in 1847 of Bishop Augustus Short [q.v.6], Farrell's influence was clipped. Despite their theological differences, however, Short valued Farrell's shrewd advice and in 1849 appointed him first dean of Adelaide. Although state aid to religion in South Australia was abolished in 1851, Farrell retained the position, and salary, of colonial chaplain. His combative evangelicalism mellowed and he became more tolerant of the religious views of others, 'if in them he saw the love of God really shed abroad in their hearts', so that his social circle eventually embraced prominent Unitarians. In 1854-56, travelling alone, he visited Britain and the Holy Land, with a side-trip to the Crimea to observe the war. In 1856 he was elected first chairman of the board of governors of the South Australian Institute.

Farrell's active ministry ended in May 1866 when, instead of medicine, he accidentally drank a lotion that probably contained arsenic. His health deteriorated. In a desperate search for medical treatment, at the end of 1868 he sailed to England. While taking the 'water cure' at Malvern, Worcestershire, he died of 'malignant ulceration' of the stomach on 26 April 1869 and was buried in Malvern cemetery. After small annuities to his widow (d.1870) and other family members, he left his residual estate, valued at £15 700, to the Collegiate School of St Peter, Adelaide. This bequest, and that of his friend Benjamin Mendes da Costa [q.v.5], ensured the school's prosperity. There are two portraits in oils by unknown artists, one (c.1855) at St Peter's College and another (c.1860) at the Anglican Church Office, Adelaide.

D. Pike, *Paradise of Dissent* (Melb, 1957); D. Hilliard, *Godliness and Good Order* (Adel, 1986); B. Dickey, *Holy Trinity Adelaide 1836-1988* (Adel, 1988); B. Dickey (ed.), *The Australian Dictionary of Evangelical Biography* (Syd, 1994); J. Tregenza, *Collegiate School of St Peter Adelaide* (Adel, 1996); A. Laube, *A Lady at Sea* (Adel, 2001); *SA Mag*, 1, no 7, Jan 1842, p 241; *Register* (Adel), 1 Mar 1845, p 1, 8 June 1869, p 2; *Observer* (Adel), 19 June 1869, p 5; Grace Montgomery Marryat diaries (SLSA).

DAVID HILLIARD

FELL, HELEN WILSON (1849-1935), diarist and philanthropist, was born on 27 July 1849 at Hawick, Roxburghshire, Scotland, one of four children of Rev. Adam Thomson [q.v.6], Presbyterian clergyman, and his first wife Helen Ritchie, née Wilson. When young Helen's mother died her father remarried and there were two more children. In 1861 the family came to Australia.

In 1868 Helen started her diary, mostly recording her social life. On 9 June 1870 in Sydney, with her father as celebrant, she married James Walter Fell, a Glasgow-born engineer and businessman. The couple and their three children were *en route* to Britain in 1882 when James died, leaving her well provided for. That year she resumed her diary, the entries written as letters for her family to read. She continued the practice until 1927, providing an evocative record of her growth in personal autonomy, her love for her extended family and church, her Scottish-Australian identity and her gradual turning to public activities as an active, enfranchised citizen.

From 1885 Helen made their home, called Branxholme, in North Sydney. Presbyterianism was central to her life. An ardent teetotaller and strict Sabbatarian, she taught Sunday School at her local church, St Peter's, attended choir and prayer meetings, collected subscriptions for church organizations and, with the clergyman's wife, visited the sick. She also read the Bible to patients at the North Shore Cottage (Royal North Shore) Hospital. The church was an important training field for her public activities, especially through her membership of its literary and relief societies, and she helped to raise large sums of money for it and for missions.

Devastated when her 18-year-old son, a talented university student, died in 1891, she and her daughters lived for a time in Scotland, but she was back by 1896, actively involved with charities, working mainly for women and children. She was on the board of Crown Street Women's Hospital and was a member of the Kindergarten Union of New South Wales, the Young Women's Christian Association and the women's auxiliary of the Association for the Protection of Native Races. Her interest in women's rights was reflected in her membership of the board of the National Council of Women. After women's suffrage was achieved, Fell joined the executive of the Women's Liberal League. She supported the Dunmore Hostel for Girls, St Andrew's Settlement House, the Presbyterian Social Services Committee and Burnside Homes. Founding treasurer of the Presbyterian Women's Missionary Association, she inaugurated its children's groups and with D. Symonds in 1941 compiled its early history.

Her remarkable diaries showed her as a courageous, compassionate and determined reformer. She rarely condemned and regularly helped on an individual basis. One entry read: 'Did not feel well but after visiting a poor woman who seems to be dying of consumption and who has 8 children the youngest a baby two months old *I was cured* ... I felt I need never complain again'. She had no time for the trade unions' campaign against Chinese labour: 'Talk of tyranny' she wrote, 'I have great sympathy for the working classes but when they band together to become tyrants there my sympathy ends'. Her kindly nature was revealed in her excellent relations with her servants and ex-servants. The diaries revealed her commitment to Australia, yet Britain remained 'Home'. Her photographs showed an attractive woman, dressed in the plain style of a widow, with a kindly but determined expression. Predeceased by her son and in 1927 by a daughter, Fell died on 13 April 1935 in North Sydney and was cremated with Presbyterian forms. A daughter survived her.

NSW Presbyterian, 20 Sept 1928, p 44, 8 May 1935, p 277; J. Godden, 'Portrait of a Lady: A Decade in the Life of Helen Fell', in M. Bevege et al (eds), *Worth Her Salt* (Syd, 1982), p 33, *and* 'Containment and Control: Presbyterian Women and the Missionary Impulse in New South Wales 1891-1914', *Women's History Review*, 6, no 1, 1997, p 75, *and* Philanthrophy and the Women's Sphere (Ph.D. thesis, Macquarie Univ, 1983); Fell diaries (ML).

JUDITH GODDEN

FENNESCEY, JOHN (1866-1948) and **MARY JANE** (1878-1946), church benefactors, were husband and wife. John was born on 13 April 1866 at Wallaroo, South Australia, fourth child of Irish migrants Patrick Fennescey (d.1913) and his wife Mary Ann, née Dunn(e). Settled in South Australia by 1856, Patrick was a labourer, first at Port Adelaide and then at the Yorke Peninsula copper-mines where, from an early age, his six sons were also employed. In 1887 Mary, 'ruling the family with a rod of iron', persuaded Patrick to lease, in partnership with an established farmer, 1918 acres (776.2 ha) at Tiparra, south-east of Wallaroo, at an annual rental of a penny an acre.

With his father and brothers, John cleared the stony scrub, earning sustenance by working for neighbours. When able to afford their own horses and machinery, the family purchased the partner's interest and later the freehold title to the property. Collectively and individually they acquired and cleared additional land, and built homesteads. Before the government grasped that the peninsula was the best place in the world for growing malting barley, it was selling freeholds at from ten to twenty shillings an acre. By the 1910s each of the surviving Fennesceys had farms averaging over 2000 acres; they found that, in the good seasons that ran from 1902 to 1913, profits from the first harvest of barley on each property were more than sufficient to recoup its purchase price. Devout but thrifty Catholics, they used draught horses to draw their buggies the eight miles (13 km) to Sunday Mass at Arthurton.

John was tall, with handsome features and a neat moustache but already going bald when on 12 April 1904 at St Agatha's Church, Arthurton, he married Mary Jane Hanrahan, a large-eyed beauty. She was born on 27 March 1878 at Maitland, South Australia, eldest of six children of Daniel Hanrahan, farmer, and his wife Mary, née Kenny. In 1902 young Mary began purchasing commercial properties at Arthurton, where she was already 'loved and respected' for her 'gentle charity'. She also assisted the Catholic orphanages at Goodwood and Largs Bay and, later, the Little Sisters of the Poor home for the aged at Myrtle Bank. Just as John's mother had pushed her sons from wage earners to gentlemen farmers, his wife taught him that wealth entailed responsibility. Mary encouraged him to join community organizations and to share her interests in helping the needy and beautifying the sanctuaries of country churches. She also introduced him to the delights of motoring —they became one of the earliest two-car couples in the State—and encouraged diversification into mortgages and urban property.

John long outlived all his brothers. As sole or surviving executor of their wills, he ran their farms, in some cases for more than twenty years, for the benefit of their widows and children. Ultimately, where it emerged that the heirs had no interest in farming, he purchased the land at fair prices and his income grew rapidly.

Despite William Leigh's [q.v.] endowments in the 1840s, the Catholic Church in South Australia had remained relatively impoverished. John and Mary Fennescey began remedying that situation on realizing they would have no children of their own. In the 1920s they sold nearly all their country properties at the top of the market and retired to Glenelg; they helped to build for that suburb the grandest parish church erected in South Australia in the twentieth century. They also enabled Archbishop Spence [q.v.12] to complete (1926) most of St Francis Xavier's Cathedral, Adelaide, and gave Calvary Hospital £10 000 for a maternity wing and £8000 to buy adjoining land. In 1939 they gave £30 000 for the purchase of the half-acre (0.2 ha) containing all the properties between the cathedral and Victoria Square. Their long-term aim was to prevent the cathedral being overshadowed by a big commercial building. In the short run the donation provided church office space and warehouses that were let at good rents. In 1976 the sites were sold to the Dunstan government, which turned them into parkland, much enhancing the cathedral.

In 1940-42 the Fennesceys largely met the cost of twelve acres [4.9 ha] at Rostrevor for a diocesan seminary and the construction of its first building. They also enabled the contemplative Carmelites to enclose their Glen Osmond convent with a high masonry wall, after the sisters had rejected Archbishop Killian's [q.v.9] view that a barbed-wire fence would do. In 1943 Mary persuaded Archbishop Beovich to accept their gift of £8000 to buy the mansion, Ennis, at Medindie, for an episcopal residence. In 1945-46, they paid for half an acre of land east of the cathedral and for a large building to house the Catholic Education Office, Newman Institute and Catholic Library. Beovich named it Fennescey House as a memorial to their generosity. Meanwhile they were handsomely but, as usual, anonymously, contributing to the funds for the Boys' Town orphanage at Brooklyn Park and Aquinas College within the University of Adelaide.

Mary died on 23 April 1946 in Calvary Hospital, North Adelaide, where John died on 2 June 1948. Both were buried in the Catholic cemetery, Kadina. In December 1846 he had been awarded the papal medal 'Pro Ecclesia et Pontifice'. As residual beneficiary under John's will, the archbishop received a further £50 000 for educational and charitable purposes. In Beovich's words, the Fennesceys 'did in their life-time what many charitable people of substance defer till their death. They gave with princely generosity to the cause of religion, and no charitable work appealed to them in vain. Nor did they forget their kin before they began their munificent benefactions.'

M. Press, *Colour and Shadow* (Adel, 1991); *Southern Cross* (Adel), 11, 18 Apr 1941, 3 May 1946, 27 Dec 1946, 11 June 1948; Fennescey file and Beovich papers (Catholic Archives, Adel); Lands Titles Office (SA), records; Crown lease books, GRG 59, *and* miscellaneous lease books, GRS 3567 (SRSA); information from Mrs M. Keneally, Warradale, Mrs E. Meegan, Somerton Park, Adel, and the late Archbishop James Gleeson.   P. A. HOWELL

FERNANDO, ANTHONY MARTIN (1864-1949), Aboriginal activist and toymaker, was by his own account born on 6 April 1864 at Woolloomooloo, Sydney, son of an Aboriginal woman, probably of the Dharug people. He may have been descended from John Martin, an African-American convict in the First Fleet who had children with Dharug women. Separated from his clan as a child, Anthony worked as an engine driver in Sydney. By the time he returned to his people, his mother had died. The thought of her, he was to assert, was 'the guiding star' of his life. In 1887 he witnessed the murder of an Aborigine by two white men, but was refused the opportunity to give evidence; the murderers were acquitted.

Disgusted with Australia, from about 1890 he publicized the Aboriginal cause overseas. In the following decades he travelled through Asia to Europe, working as a welder, toymaker, jewellery-maker, trader and servant. He lived for a time in Italy where, out of respect for the Italian people, he adopted what he described as a plain, Italian workingman's name. By 1910 'Fernando' was in Austria. British authorities repeatedly denied his claims to be a British subject. Interned in Austria during World War I, in June 1916, stating that he had been born in Australia, he requested prison relief through the consul for the United States of America in Vienna. The British Foreign Office, describing him as 'a negro', referred the matter to the Australian government, which found no evidence of his birth, and his appeal was rejected.

After the war Fernando settled in Milan, Italy, where he worked in an engineering workshop. According to surveillance reports, he attempted to present a private petition to the Pope, interviewed members of the League of Nations in Geneva and protested in a German newspaper against Australian injustice towards Aborigines. Returning to Italy, he was arrested for distributing pamphlets declaring that the British race was exterminating his people. In 1923 he was deported to Britain.

Fernando became the servant of an English barrister who offered him a stipend to settle down and write his life story; but he preferred his independence and travelled again in Europe. By 1928 he was back in London where he continued his crusade by picketing Australia House, 'his long grey beard damp with mist, his frail elderly frame wrapped in a large overcoat'. Pinned to his coat were scores of small, white, toy skeletons and he wore a placard proclaiming: 'This is all Australia has left of my people'. He also spoke at Hyde Park. In January 1929, described as a toy hawker, he appeared at the Old Bailey, charged with drawing a revolver in response to a racial taunt. After some resistance on his part, Fernando spoke to Mary Bennett [q.v.7], who visited his cell while he was awaiting trial. She reported a small man with a gentle demeanour, self-educated, well spoken, with a command of many languages and a good knowledge of the Bible. Bennett found him to be sane, intelligent yet driven. The prison doctor agreed, reporting that 'although he held strong views about his race, there was no indication of any delusions', and no reason to commit him to an asylum. When Fernando appeared in court, he received a sympathetic hearing. He accused Whites of murdering and ill-treating Aborigines, adding, 'I have been boycotted everywhere ... It is tommyrot to say that we are all savages. Whites have shot, slowly starved and hanged us.' Given a gaol sentence, suspended on two years probation, he briefly worked as a cook in the barrister's employment, then continued his agitations.

In January 1938 Fernando was back before the courts, accused of assaulting a fellow lodger. Unrepentant, once more he protested at the treatment of his people. He was sentenced to three months imprisonment. Later Fernando retired to an old men's home. He died on 9 January 1949 at Ilford, Essex.

M. Bennett, *The Australian Aboriginal as a Human Being* (Lond, 1930); M. Brown, 'Fernando: The story of an Aboriginal Prophet', *Aboriginal Welfare Bulletin*, vol 4, no 1, 1964, p 7; *Aboriginal Law Bulletin*, 2, no 33, 1988, p 4; F. Paisley, 'An education in white brutality', in A. Coombes (ed), *Making History Memorable* (Manchester, England, forthcoming); *SMH*, 2 Feb 1929, p 17, 21 Mar 1929, p 11, 7 Feb 1938, p 8; GRG 52/32/31 (SRSA); A11803/1, 14/89/475 (NAA, Canb); D1915/0, SA608 (NAA, Adel); H. Goodall, Anthony Martin Fernando: angry ambassador (ms 1989 held by authors).

ALISON HOLLAND
FIONA PAISLEY

FLOWER, SARA ELIZABETH (c.1823-1865), opera singer and teacher of singing, was born at Grays, Essex, England, daughter of William Lewis Flower. Sara studied with Gaetano Crivelli at the Royal Academy of Music, London. After a successful career as a concert singer in London, she took up the suggestion of the composer Stephen Marsh and came to Australia in 1850, making her concert début in Melbourne. Considered to be the most talented singer then to come to Australia, she was hailed by the Melbourne press as 'the modern Sappho', 'the Queen of song' and 'the Australian Nightingale'.

Moving to Sydney, where the existence of an opera company performing on a regular basis offered more scope, Flower made her Australian opera début at the Royal Victoria Theatre, on 1 May 1851, as the heroine in an English adaptation of Rossini's *La Cenerentola*. On 20 December that year at St James's Church of England, Sydney, she married Samuel Howard Taylor, an actor known as Sam Howard; the prima donna Marie Carandini [q.v.3] was a witness.

Roles premièred by Flower in Australia included the title role in *The Enchantress* (by Michael Balfe), Bertha in *The Night Dancers* (Edward Loder)—the operatic version of the ballet *Giselle*—and most importantly, and curiously, since she was a contralto, the title role in Bellini's *Norma* on 16 February 1852. A shortage of tenors on the Australian colonial operatic stage often meant that women had to perform male roles, and Flower sang Edgardo in the first Australian performance of Donizetti's *Lucia di Lammermoor* on 13 February 1855. She also made appearances with *ad hoc* companies formed by visiting stars and local impresarios. Opposite the Norma of Catherine Hayes in Sydney in 1855, she sang the role of Adalgisa and in the second performance, when Hayes was unable to finish, took over the title role for the last scene.

In Melbourne shortly afterwards, another tenor problem caused Carandini and Flower to take the tenor roles in Hayes's opera season. Flower sang Edgardo in *Lucia* again, Pollione in *Norma* and, in her proper vocal range, the travesty role of Maffeo Orsini in the Australian première of Donizetti's *Lucrezia Borgia*. With the English soprano Anna Bishop in Melbourne in 1857, her performances included the baritone role of Don Carlo in Verdi's *Ernani*.

In 1859—in her proper vocal range—she was a distinguished Azucena in the first hearing in Sydney of Verdi's *Il Trovatore*. Thereafter her appearances were mainly restricted to concerts. She had taken part in the major choral festival to inaugurate the Great Hall at the University of Sydney in 1854, when Handel's *Messiah* and Haydn's *Creation* were performed.

As a teacher, Flower advertised herself as a graduate of the Royal Academy of Music and the principal musical societies of Milan, offering tuition 'according to the approved systems of Masters Crivelli and Mazzucato'. She was red-haired, large framed and not particularly good looking, although her expression became transfigured by the music on the concert platform or stage and she radiated great emotional power. On tours of the goldfields where she was, like many others, showered with nuggets by appreciative miners, she was said to be fond of porter with the boys.

Reputedly, Flower converted to Catholicism about 1863, regularly attending St Benedict's Church, Sydney. She was poor in her later years. Sara Elizabeth Flower Howard died of rheumatism on 20 August 1865 at her home at Woolloomooloo and was buried in the Catholic section of the Devonshire Street cemetery. Her remains were removed in 1902 to La Perouse where a memorial was erected.

F. C. Brewer, *The Drama and Music in New South Wales* (Syd, 1982); K. Brisbane (ed), *Entertaining Australia* (Syd, 1991); A. Gyger, *Civilising the Colonies* (Syd, 1999); *Bulletin* (Syd), 25 Jan 1902, p 13; *Freeman's J*, 1 Feb 1902, pp 24, 29; *Aust Star*, 19 Apr 1902, p 3; *Daily Telegraph* (Syd), 7 Apr 1923, p 13; *Sun* (Syd), 25 Aug 1958.   ALISON GYGER

FORBES, ELIZABETH MARY; *see* GOODLET

FORDE, FLORRIE (1875-1940), music hall artist, was born on 16 August 1875 at Fitzroy, Melbourne, and registered as Flora, sixth of eight children of Lott Flannagan, an Irish-born stonemason, and his wife Phoebe, née Simmons. Possibly Jewish, Phoebe had been born in either London or the United States of America, and had two children from a previous marriage to Daniel James Cahill. Florrie's father later ran the United Service Hotel, Fitzroy; her parents' marriage ended about 1878. In 1888 Phoebe Cahill, claiming to be a widow, married Thomas Henry Snelling Ford, a Melbourne theatrical costumier, by whom she had six children (some prenuptial) before she died in 1892, aged 46. Florrie and some of her numerous siblings were put into a convent for a time, then she ran away with her sister Nan, seeking shelter with an aunt in Sydney. According to a later report, she was an under housemaid at Government House.

Adapting her stepfather's name as her stage name, 'Florrie Forde' first appeared as a singer in a vaudeville programme at the Polytechnic Music Hall in the Imperial Arcade, Pitt Street, on 1 February 1892, performing popular and comical songs. At the Mariner's Church, Sydney, on 2 January 1893, purportedly with her father's written consent, she married with Congregational forms Walter Emanuel Bew, a 31-year-old water police constable from England and a widower.

Forde's long and illustrious career in pantomime began when she played Jack in George Rignold's [q.v.6 Rignall] *The House that Jack Built* in 1894 in Sydney. She also took dramatic parts in plays such as *The Work Girl*, but preferred singing and the lively exchanges with music hall audiences. She toured with Harry Rickards's [q.v.11] variety company and in March 1897 appeared at the Theatre Royal, Adelaide, for one week, during which time the programme was adapted to become a special concert for the members of the Australasian Federal Convention, then meeting. She sang *She Wore a Little Safety Pin, Behind*, which the *Adelaide Advertiser*'s reviewer thought *risqué*, but which appealed to the 'boys in the gallery'. Encouraged by the visiting vaudevillian G. H. Chirgwin, and with an invitation to tour with him in Britain, Florrie determined that she would establish a career abroad for herself, without his assistance.

On August Bank Holiday 1897, she made her first appearances in London at three music halls—the South London Palace, the Pavilion and the Oxford—in the one evening, singing *You Know and I Know*. Immediately booked for three years on the Moss and Thorton circuit, she never looked back. With clear diction, and a commanding stage presence, she had the ability to select songs with catchy choruses and to lead an audience in singing them. Her early successes included *Down at the Old Bull and Bush* in 1904, which became a music hall anthem. Other numbers that she made popular and recorded included *Pack Up Your Troubles, It's a Long Way to Tipperary, Oh! Oh! Antonio, Hold Your Hand Out Naughty Boy, Goodbye-ee* and *Has Anybody Here Seen Kelly*.

Florrie was a regular star in pantomime all her life, continuing to play principal boys in costumes designed to flatter 'leggy' girls and not the portly matron she became—by 1922 she weighed 16 st. 10 lb. (106 kg). Once settled into a routine of performing and recording, she released an avalanche of songs on cylinders and discs, making 700 individual recordings between 1903 and 1936. In 1906 she introduced another Australian, Billy Williams, to the Edison Bell recording studios. Forde was known for her generosity, particularly helping other performers who were down on their luck, and for her enduring sense of Australian-ness, evident in recordings of her broad, nasal vowels, which she retained to the end of her career.

On 22 November 1905 at the register office, Paddington, London, as Flora Augusta Flanagan, spinster, she married Laurence Barnett (d.1934), an art dealer. They made their home at Shoreham, Sussex. She appeared in a royal command performance in 1912 and in World War I was at the height of her fame. During the 1920s she helped to establish the duo of Chesney Allen and Bud Winthrop, bringing them together in a show she called 'Flo and Co'. Winthrop used Florrie's maiden name, thus creating the celebrated team of 'Flanagan' and Allen. In the 1930s Forde appeared in small parts in several films and continued as 'queen' of the hippodromes and music halls. After entertaining patients in a naval hospital, she died of a cerebral haemorrhage on 18 April 1940 at Aberdeen, Scotland. The Anglo-Irish poet Louis MacNeice left a tribute to her in a poem, 'Death of An Actress', recalling how:

With an elephantine shimmy and a sugared wink
She threw a trellis of Dorothy Perkins roses
Around an audience come from slum and suburb
And weary of the tea-leaves in the sink.

P. Gammond, *Your Own, Your Very Own! A Music Scrapbook* (Lond, 1971); R. Busby, *British Music Hall* (Lond, 1976); P. Parsons (ed), *Companion to Theatre in Australia* (Syd, 1995); J. Brownrigg, 'Has Anybody Seen Florrie?', in G. Osborne and D. Jenkin, *Australian Communication Lives* (Canb, 1999) and '"A Gaudy Posy for the Popular Soul": Recovering Australia's Early Popular Recording Stars', *J of Popular Culture*, 33, no 1, Summer 1999, p 105; *Referee* (Syd), 23 Jan 1895, p 7; *Theatre Mag* (Syd), 10, no 2, 1 Feb 1922, pp 1, 6; *Smith's Weekly*, 23 Feb 1929, p 17; *Victorian Arts Centre Magazine*, May 1987, p 21; *Call Boy* (Lond), 29, no 2, Summer 1992, p 9; F. Forde memorabilia (NL, Performing Arts Museum, Melb, ScreenSound, Canb).

JEFF BROWNRIGG

FORLONG (FORLONGE), ELIZA (1784-1859), pastoralist, was baptized as Betty on 21 October 1784 at Glasgow, Scotland, daughter of Alexander Jack, teacher, and his wife Jean, née Mackinnon. On 26 November 1804 Eliza married John Forlonge (Forlong or Furlong), a Glasgow merchant. Although she bore at least six children, by the mid-1820s consumption had reduced the family to two sons William [q.v.1] and Andrew. Farming in a warmer climate appeared desirable.

Aware that fine wool from merino sheep in the German kingdom of Saxony was bringing the highest prices, the Forlongs went to Leipzig to study methods of sheep rearing and wool preparation. Their expertise was enhanced by the use of an instrument to measure wool. In 1828-30 Eliza walked through Saxony buying sheep. She identified each animal for later collection and drove them to Hamburg for shipping to Britain. She selected the sheep that came to Australia with William in the *Clansman* in 1829 as well as those accompanying the Templeton [q.v.6 William] and Forlonge families in the *Czar* in 1831. Eliza also visited Rambouillet in France.

In January 1831 Eliza, John and Andrew joined William in Van Diemen's Land at Kenilworth, near Campbell Town. They built sheep houses in the Saxon style, wells, a farmhouse and outbuildings. Never content with the size and situation of their land grants, the family conducted an 'epistolary war' with colonial officials, and in April 1834, in an attempt to influence English authorities, Eliza, her husband and younger son went back in the *Norval* to Britain. John died there in November 1834.

Mrs Forlonge soon returned to Van Diemen's Land where she found that William planned a move to the Port Phillip District. They sold Kenilworth and part of their flock in 1838 to the Taylor [q.v.2] family. Eliza made further voyages to Scotland (in 1840 and 1844) and assisted bounty emigrants. After some years squatting, Andrew moved to the United States of America. Eliza lived with William and his family at Woodstock, Merri Creek, near Whittlesea. They moved to Euroa in 1853 and eventually settled at Seven Creeks station. Eliza ran the house and managed station affairs in the frequent absences of William and his wife.

William Howitt [q.v.4] described her as 'one of the pleasantest and most energetic ladies I have ever met with', but Nancy Adams portrayed her unfavourably in the novel *Saxon Sheep* (Melbourne, 1961). Sally Wilde claimed that her actions suggested 'a strong willed, not to say positively eccentric, woman'. Although Eliza's pioneering and managerial skills were outstanding, it was her ability to select sheep that was special. David Taylor of Winton and T. and S. Learmonth [q.v.2] of Ercildoun(e), Victoria, founded their studs on the Forlonges' Saxon merinos, which were greatly sought after by breeders of fine-woolled sheep.

Eliza died on 5 August 1859. A memorial, in the shape of a wool bale, stands near her grave at Euroa. Other memorials include a sundial at the new Kenilworth house and a mural by Tom Thompson at TAFE Sydney Institute, Ultimo.

W. Howitt, *Land, Labour and Gold* (Melb, 1855); C. McIvor, *The History and Development of Sheep*

Farming (Syd, 1893); F. Clune, *Search for the Golden Fleece* (Syd, 1965); C. Massy, *The Australian Merino* (Melb, 1990); S. Wilde, *Eliza Forlonge* (Euroa, Vic, 1994); *Argus* (Melb), 11 Aug 1859, p 4; Forlonge files (Euroa Historical Society, Vic, and TA); CSO 1/516/11259-60 (TA); information from Mrs M. Higgins, St Ives, Syd.   MARY S. RAMSAY

FORREST, MABEL (1872-1935), writer, was born on 6 March 1872 near Yandilla, Darling Downs, Queensland, and registered as Helena Mabel, second of three children of James Checkley Mills, station manager, and his English-born wife Margaret Nelson, née Haxell. The family lived on stations near Dalby, Stanthorpe and Goondiwindi, border towns that appeared in her fiction as 'Brolga'. Except for one year of schooling at Parramatta, New South Wales, she was taught by her mother, 'who spoke several languages fluently and had been to school in France and Germany'. Mabel's sister Ethel also became a writer, publishing stories and poems in the Sydney *Bulletin*.

On 5 July 1893 at Callandoon, near Goondiwindi, Mabel married with Anglican rites John Frederick Burkinshaw, a selector. A daughter was born in 1894 at Tulloona station in northern New South Wales. The marriage was unhappy. With her husband unable to support his family, Mabel contributed by taking in sewing, and began to write and publish her work. The couple separated when Burkinshaw went to Perth in 1896 to look for work. They were divorced on the grounds of his 'adultery, desertion and cruelty' in April 1902. On 22 July that year in Brisbane she married with Wesleyan forms John Forrest (d.1921), a railway surveyor. In public accounts of her life, she expunged her first marriage, but the experience informed many of her most powerful lyric poems.

She made her living as a writer—'the most industrious versifier in the Commonwealth'. Publishing in the *Australasian*, the *Bulletin*, *Smith's Weekly*, the *Triad* and the *Lone Hand*, she signed herself 'M. Forrest', 'Reca' or 'M. Burkinshaw'. Her stories from the *Australasian* were collected as *The Rose of Forgiveness* (1904). Her first volume of poems, *Alpha Centauri*, was published in 1909. She regularly won literary competitions, and her works appeared in the *Pall Mall Gazette* and the *Spectator* (London), and in the United States of America.

Forrest's most successful work was *The Wild Moth* (London, 1924), filmed by Charles Chauvel [q.v.7] as *The Moth of Moonbi*. Scenes from her novels were performed in public, and her play, *The Highwayman*, was staged at the Cremorne Theatre. Fidelity and betrayal in love were recurrent themes in her fiction. Her narratives of Australian bush life invited comparison with Rosa Praed [q.v.11], but she also documented the coming of modernity, taking up issues such as city planning, and describing the growth of suburbs (*Streets and Gardens*, 1922). Her characters were as likely to ride on trains and trams as on horses and in sulkies. Some poems were recited on civic occasions: 'The City Hall' was read at the building's 1930 opening in Brisbane and later etched on a commemorative marble tablet there.

A member of the Society of Authors, London, and the Fellowship of Australian Writers, Forrest was a life member of the Queensland Press Institute. Her last poem, 'Waning Moon', appeared in the *Australasian* on 16 March 1935. She died of pneumonia two days later in hospital at Goodna and was cremated with Presbyterian forms, survived by her daughter. A short manuscript autobiography in the John Oxley [q.v.2] Library and the depositions from the divorce case are unreliable remnants of her life.

Contemporaries were critical of Forrest's writing, H. M. Green [q.v.14] calling it 'overfacile', Nettie Palmer [q.v.11] 'fluent and ornate'. Her children's verse, however, was praised as attractive and technically dextrous. She acknowledged debts to Scott, Melville, Browning, Adam Lindsay Gordon [q.v.4] and Edith Wharton. Although Forrest's contemporaries saw her work in a tradition of colonial writing, it could also stand alongside that of Cross, Lesbia Harford [q.v.9], Gwen Harwood, Eleanor Dark and Dymphna Cusack, as the work of a modernist, sharing their interests in psychology and sexuality.

N. Palmer, *Modern Australian Literature* (Melb, 1924); H. M. Green, *An Outline of Australian Literature* (Syd, 1930); H. A. Kellow, *Queensland Poets* (Lond, 1930); D. Adelaide, *Australian Women Writers* (Syd, 1988); *Aust National Review*, 2, no 12, Dec 1937, p 89; *Qld Review*, 8, no 1, May 2001, p 31; *Courier-Mail*, 15 Oct 1927, p 22; *Argus*, 6 Apr 1935, p 6; G. Fox, Mabel Forrest: Early Life and Works (B.A. Hons thesis, Univ Qld, 1984) *and* Writing for Bread: The Professional Life of Mabel Forrest 1902-1935 (M.A. thesis, Univ Qld, 1986).   KAY FERRES

FORSTER, WILLIAM FREAR (1857-1932), newspaper editor, was born on 11 March 1857 at Parkend, Northumberland, England, son of John Forster, agricultural labourer, and his wife Mary, née Makepiece. William trained as a journalist on the *Daily Chronicle*, Newcastle-upon-Tyne. At Christ Church, Gateshead, Durham, on 3 January 1884 he married Ann Handcock with Anglican rites. The couple migrated to Western Australia in 1886, the same year as Forster's future partner L. V. De Hamel [q.v.8]. Forster was sporting editor for the *West Australian* until 1888 when he and

De Hamel set up the *Australian* (later *Albany*) *Advertiser*. He was editor for the next twelve years and sole owner after De Hamel's departure in 1891.

Outspoken, inclined to bluntness, but loyal and considerate to young cadets, Forster developed a passionate interest in Albany and its affairs. He later said, 'it is in my nature to speak out and hit straight and in writing of the political affairs of Albany, I had need to do so'. Soon a recognized voice in the community, he promoted an Albany-Fremantle rivalry that haunted the district long after his departure. Ambitious to produce a leading provincial newspaper, he published a progressive, tri-weekly, penny paper to serve Albany residents, settlers in the region and travellers in the visiting mail steamers. Although providing an admirable range of local, colonial, national and international news, it had no literary content. His printing company published several editions of *Alluring Albany: Handbook for the Port and Back Country and Guide to the Chief West Australian Health Resort*.

Forster supported female suffrage; his wife Ann was active on numerous women's committees. An ardent separationist, during the Federation debate he questioned the validity of Western Australia being controlled by other territories. He clashed with the local politician A. Y. Hassell, supported younger aspirants such as George Leake junior and was critical of Sir John Forrest's [qq.v.4,10,8] government for directing funds away from Albany for Fremantle harbour development and the 'quixotic' Coolgardie pipeline. Forster declared that Albany suffered through the lack of improved railways, higher education or support for trade, through disproportionate customs' tariffs, the offloading of ballast at Frenchmans Bay and lack of interest in an Admiralty plan to extend the Princess Royal Harbour. He was particularly dispirited when he lost a strenuous fight to retain the mail steamer service for Albany.

Initially suspected of being over-solicitous in support of De Hamel's mining ventures and bid for the mayoralty and for his 'inquisitiveness', Forster had a genuine concern for the community. Even an old adversary, who once thought him 'poisonous', changed his opinion. A keen golfer and founding member of the Albany Bowling Club, Forster was well informed about sport in general. In September 1900 he left for Perth to edit the *Morning Herald*. Two years later, he moved to Melbourne as sports editor for the *Age*.

After a stint in Auckland on the *New Zealand Herald*, from 1908 to 1932 Forster was sub-editor on the Hobart *Mercury*, and played a prominent part in the steady growth of the paper, enjoying the 'esteem and confidence of the proprietors and his colleagues'. A keen bowler, he represented the State against mainland teams. He was also interested in football, cricket and rowing. His son William, editor of the *Sporting Globe* in Melbourne, predeceased him. Forster died on 21 December 1932 in hospital in Hobart, survived by his wife, two sons and a daughter.

D. S. Garden, *Albany* (Melb, 1977); *Albany Advertiser*, 21 Jan 1899, p 2, 26 Jan 1899, p 2, 28 Jan 1899, p 2, 18 Sept 1900, p 3, 3 Jan 1933, p 4; *Mercury* (Hob), 22 Dec 1932, p 6; information from Albany public library, WA.   WENDY BIRMAN

FORSYTH, IDA MURIEL (1884-1953), nurse and community worker, was born on 17 August 1884 at Kooringa, South Australia, daughter of Robert Brummitt, an English-born medical practitioner, and his wife Jane, née Roach, who was native-born. Ida's parents were public-spirited Methodists, and her education, especially at Tormore House school under Caroline Jacob [q.v.9], reinforced her family tradition of intellectual enquiry and Christian service. She trained as a nurse at Adelaide Children's Hospital in 1909-12 before accompanying her father on a tour of Fijian Methodist missions.

On 20 November 1915 Ida Brummitt joined the Australian Army Nursing Service. Discharged in June next year because of 'sickness at home', she re-enlisted as a staff nurse in February 1918. At this time she was 5 ft 3½ ins (161 cm) tall, weighed 8 st. 9¾ lb. (55.2 kg) and had a clear complexion, grey eyes and light brown hair. In November she was appointed to the Australian Imperial Force. After serving in India, she fell dangerously ill with enteric fever. She returned to Adelaide where her appointment terminated in February 1920.

On 29 March 1923 at her father's residence, Medindie, Ida married Samuel Forsyth [q.v.8], a Methodist minister and widower with two children; they were to have one son. Ida devoted herself to her family and to supporting her husband. She contributed to the Methodist Ministers' Wives Circle and was active in the Maughan [q.v.5] Church branch of the Women's Auxiliary of Overseas Methodist Missions until 1951 (president 1929-37). With Samuel she visited British city central missions in 1929. Practical and adaptable, Ida helped the Sisters of the People in the Adelaide Central Methodist Mission's social welfare and relief work and was a fearless publicist for the poor and the unemployed. She attracted support by her calm, warm manner and skills in speaking and writing. In 1929-52 she led the mission's mothers' meetings. A crèche freed tired mothers to enjoy their weekly 'Bright Hour' with singing, talks, a thrift club, afternoon teas and parties at Christmas. From 1936 the Forsyths lived next to the Magill Methodist Children's Homes; Ida befriended the children and helped the staff.

In 1930 Samuel founded Kuitpo (pronounced 'Kypo') Industrial Colony, in the southern Mount Lofty ranges, to provide training for unemployed men, and Mrs Forsyth became a standard-bearer. Her logical, heartfelt articles and pamphlets warned that neglecting young unemployed men could make them 'idle spongers': Kuitpo's training could 'stem this waste'. As vice-president of the Kuitpo Helpers' Association from 1932 she publicized the colony. The association supported her proposal to invite 'people of ability and influence' to join in large-scale fundraising. The resulting undenominational Central Mission Aid Society, almost continuously under her presidency in 1932-52, collected substantial sums for Kuitpo and mission relief work, especially through annual, two-day galas in Adelaide's Exhibition Building when women from nearly all the churches and the Jewish Women's Guild worked together. In 1936 Ida conceived an ingenious 'Pioneer Ships' competition: she organized twelve young women from pioneer families to compete for penny votes, raising over £1000. She believed that because Kuitpo lacked official Methodist sanction, help came from 'every section of the community'.

In 1944 Ida broadcast bi-weekly talks on the mission's radio stations 5KA and 5AU. 'Between Ourselves' offered lonely people 'something else to think about'. She and Samuel visited missions and churches overseas in 1950. He retired in 1952 and Ida wrote his biography, *He Came from Ireland* (Adelaide, 1954), in which, characteristically, she barely figured. Survived by her husband, son and stepson, Ida died of a cerebrovascular accident on 24 October 1953 in hospital in North Adelaide and was buried in Payneham cemetery. Her estate was sworn for probate at £10 427.

R. Brummitt, *A Winter Holiday in Fiji* (Lond, 1914); *SA Methodist*, 30 Oct 1953; Central Methodist Mission (SA), *Annual Report*, 1929-52; Maughan Church branch, Women's Assn of Overseas Methodist Missions, Minutes, 1929-51 (Adel Central Mission archives); B2455, item Brummitt, I. (NAA, Canb); Forsyth papers *and* Tormore House school, Old Scholars Assn records (SLSA); information from Prof E. C. Forsyth, Melb.   HELEN JONES

FORTUNE, MARY HELENA (c.1833-c.1910), author, was born at Belfast, Ireland, daughter of George Wilson, a civil engineer of Scottish ancestry, and his wife Eleanor, née Atkinson. Mary later wrote that she 'never knew either mother or sister or brother'. With her father, she moved to Montreal, Canada, which she considered her home. Her schooling is unknown but, adept at written English, she sometimes wrote in an educated, copperplate hand and her works were sprinkled with Gallicisms and Latin tags. On 25 March 1851 at Melbourne, Canada, she married Joseph Fortune, a surveyor, son of Colonel Joseph Fortune, of Pointe-Fortune. The couple had one son. Mary's father then migrated to the Australian goldfields, where he worked as a storekeeper. After a brief time in Britain, she and her son joined him, arriving in Melbourne on 3 October 1855.

In November 1856 at Buninyong she gave birth to a second son, later a habitual criminal. She claimed Joseph Fortune as the father, although no record has been found of him in Australia. He died in Canada in 1861. With her father and her sons, she moved about the goldfields. The elder boy died in January 1858. On 25 October at Dunolly, Mary married with Anglican rites Percy Rollo Brett, a mounted constable and the son of a clergyman from Wexford, Ireland. On the certificate she described herself as a widow. Percy left the police force that year but the marriage soon failed and he moved to New South Wales, where he married Mary Ann Leek at St John's Church, Corowa, on 26 June 1866, apparently without a divorce from his previous wife.

Mary Fortune's writing career began in 1855 with pseudonymous contributions, including radical poetry, to goldfields newspapers. The *Mount Alexander Mail* offered her a sub-editor's position, but it was withdrawn upon revelation of her gender. In late 1865 as 'Waif Wander', a self-description, she began to contribute to the newly founded *Australian Journal* in Melbourne. Beginning in that year she and James Skipp Borlase jointly wrote one of the first Australian detective series. He later reprinted her 'Mystery and Murder' under his own name. In 1866 Mary wrote 'Bertha's Legacy' for the magazine, the first of six serialized novels, which ranged from tales of contemporary life to gothic melodrama. She also wrote lively journalism until 1875.

Fortune's major work was the police procedural series 'The Detective's Album'. It appeared in the *Australian Journal* under her pseudonym of 'W. W.' from 1868 (when she moved to Melbourne) to 1908. She was among the earliest female detective writers in the world, and certainly the first to specialize in the field in Australia. Some of her crime writing appeared as *The Detective's Album* (Melbourne, 1871), the first book of detective fiction published in Australia. She also wrote 'Twenty-Six Years Ago; or, the Diggings from '55', a vivid if unreliable memoir, later republished in *The Fortunes of Mary Fortune* (Melbourne, 1989).

Despite her long career, Fortune remained anonymous to her reading public. Failing eyesight ended her writing and she was in financial difficulties, suffering from alcoholism. Even in the 1870s she had been locked up by the police for drunkenness and vagrancy. The *Australian Journal* supported her with an annuity from about 1909. The place and date of Fortune's death are unknown. It was not until the 1950s that the book collector J. K. Moir [q.v.15] revealed the name behind the pseudonyms.

D. Adelaide, *A Bright and Fiery Troop* (Melb, 1988); L. Sussex and E. Gibson, *Mary Helena Fortune* (Brisb, 1998); L. Sussex, 'The Mystery of Mary Fortune, a Nineteenth-Century Canadian-Australian Detective Writer', *Epilogue* (Canada), 12, no 1, 1997, p 23; L. Sussex and J. Burrows, 'Whodunit? Literary Forensics and the Crime Writing of James Skipp Borlase and Mary Fortune', Bibliographical Soc of Aust and NZ, *Bulletin*, 21, no 2, 1997, p 73; Moir papers (SLV).   L. SUSSEX

FOY, HARRY SIDNEY (1901-1942), barman and female impersonator, was born on 7 November 1901 at Waterloo, Sydney, sixth of eight children of Sydney-born parents Henry Foy (d.1936), a horse-trainer, and his wife Elizabeth Anne, née McKinnon. The family later moved to Kensington. By 1942 Harry worked as a barman at the Surrey Club Hotel, Cleveland Street, Redfern, where he also lived. By night he was an accomplished nightclub entertainer. He danced cleverly and sang well. In addition, he was Sydney's best-known female impersonator, having supplanted the recently deceased 'Lea Sonia'.

Foy had carved out his own world, one of theatricality and glamour, and over the previous fifteen years had appeared at various clubs and restaurants in Sydney, as well as in vaudeville at the Empire Theatre. He was 'popular and well-billed wherever he appeared'. His lifestyle gave him access to a variety of worlds not usually open to Waterloo boys, and he probably drank at such city hotels as the Australia, Ushers, the Carlton, or any of the working-class pubs that tolerated homosexuals, particularly the so-called 'salt-meat alley'—hotels in George Street.

The Ziegfeld Club, in King Street, a well-known venue for drag acts, was his favoured haunt. He was not paid for his performances there. The club's manager told *Truth* he received 'kentuckies': when guests were pleased they would throw him money. A 'man who became a real woman while he did his act', he had 'a very natural woman's charm and the voice, walk and actions were those of a female when facing the spotlight'.

On the night of 22 December 1942 he appeared at the Ziegfeld Club. Dressed in a mixture of men's and women's clothing, with his face painted with rouge, powder and lipstick, and wearing earrings, he performed and flirted with many of the men there, as was his habit. *Truth* reported a witness as saying that Foy 'appeared to be a fairy' and that he thought Foy was 'queer'. One of the patrons, a sailor from the United States of America, whom he tried to kiss, took offence and struck him in the mouth. Foy fell heavily on the floor on his back.

He never recovered consciousness. Foy died on 23 December in Sydney Hospital, the coroner reported, 'from the effects of a fractured skull feloniously inflicted upon him at the Ziegfeld Café, Number 88 King Street, Sydney ... by one John Tyler Williams'. Williams was committed for trial on the charge of manslaughter, released on £40 bail and handed over to a United States shore patrol, after which he disappeared from Australia's legal records. Foy was buried in the Anglican section of Botany cemetery. His mother, one brother and five sisters survived him.

G. Wotherspoon, 'Comrades-in-arms: World War II and Male Homosexuality in Australia', in J. Damousi and M. Lake (eds), *Gender and War* (Cambridge, UK, 1995); *Daily Telegraph* (Syd), 25 Dec 1942, p 5; *Truth* (Syd), 3 Jan 1943, p 7; *Sunday Telegraph* (Syd), 3 Jan 1943, p 18; H. S. Foy inquest, 19/3691 (SRNSW).   GARRY C. WOTHERSPOON

FRAIRE, CHIAFFREDO VENERANO (1852-1931), merchant and immigration agent, was born on 22 October 1852 at Envie, Piedmont, Italy, eldest son of Chiaffredo Venerano Fraire, farmer, and his wife Giovanna Maria, née Bovo. Young Chiaffredo was educated to secondary level, probably at Cuneo. At the age of 20 he exchanged his interest in the family estate for cash in order to travel to Australia.

With sixteen priests and a number of other middle-class Italian men, he was attracted to Queensland by Bishop James Quinn [q.v.5.]. Fraire travelled with the bishop in the *Silver Eagle*, reaching Brisbane on 24 May 1872; the sculptor Achille Simonetti [q.v.6] was also in the party. Fraire began work as a draper's apprentice but next year rushed to the new goldfield on the Palmer River. His career as a miner was short lived, however, and he became a clerk in a tent-store in the diggings, before leaving for Townsville within a year.

Fraire was then employed by the draper (Sir) James Burns, whose secretary (Sir) Robert Philp [qq.v.7,11] took over the Townsville branch in 1876 when Burns moved to Sydney. Philp and Fraire shared a house in these years. Burns, Philp & Co. prospered and Fraire, who was naturalized in 1878 (the year he took up Freemasonry), was despatched to England as a buyer in 1879. He also spent some months in Italy. On his return he married Brisbane-born Sarah Ann Shekelton with Anglican rites on 27 July 1880 at Townsville. They had four children between 1881 and 1886. In partnership with a fellow Quinn recruit, the pharmacist Pio Vico Armati, in 1880 he opened a drapery in a former Burns, Philp warehouse. In 1887 he sold out and again visited Italy.

Back at Townsville next year Fraire set up his own drapery and was appointed a justice of the peace. He also lobbied planters to support his scheme to recruit northern Italian agricultural labourers for the sugar industry. Philp had entered politics and with his support Fraire was despatched in 1891 to recruit his Piedmontese labourers. Despite some objections from the Italian government, 331 northern Italians arrived at Townsville in the *Jumna* on 2 December 1891. These workers formed the nucleus of what was to become in the 1920s a mass Italian migration into the north Queensland sugar industry.

In the following years Fraire speculated, not always successfully, in land and was declared bankrupt at Townsville in June 1899. After brief spells in Brisbane, and at Maryborough and Cairns, and the death of his wife in 1906, he settled at Rockhampton where he focused his enormous energy and enthusiasm on theosophy (which he had taken up around 1900) and Freemasonry. He established the Theosophical Hall (opened 1919) and wrote a regular theosophy column, under the pen-name 'Vigour', for the Rockhampton *Bulletin*.

In the 1890s Fraire was slight and dark-haired, and sported a neat beard. In later years he wore a moustache but later still was clean-shaven. An early twentieth-century photograph showed him in fancy dress as Garibaldi. He was a passionate vegetarian. 'Padre' Fraire died at Rockhampton on 5 January 1931 and was buried in North Rockhampton cemetery with Anglican rites. His son and three daughters survived him. A later biographer—Dr J. W. B. Bean, the brother of C. E. W. Bean [q.v.7]—wrote:

No one could have been humbler, more single-hearted, or less self-conscious than Fraire ... His will-power was amazing, and to his own weaknesses and physical failings he was ruthless, but always tender and considerate towards others.

F. Galassi, *Sotto La Croce del Sud: Under the Southern Cross* (Townsville, Qld, 1991); W. A. Douglass, *From Italy to Ingham* (Brisb, 1995); P. M. Armati, *Pio Vico Armati* (Syd, 1997); J. W. Bean, biography of C. V. Fraire (ms, James Cook Univ, Qld).

DIANE MENGHETTI
PETER WOODFORDE

FRANCIS, SUSAN (1877-1946), midwife and political activist, was born on 14 October 1877 at Kelvin Grove, Brisbane, fifth child of English migrants William Radford, labourer, and his wife Selina, née Stapleton. Susan described herself as a housekeeper when, on 20 February 1897 in South Brisbane, she married with Baptist forms Arthur Rawlins, known as 'Francis'. He was a widower and a seaman from Plymouth, England. About 1911 Susan came to Sydney with the two surviving of their three children. Between 1915 and 1917 she assumed the name 'Tarrant' while living at Ultimo.

From the early 1920s Nurse Francis advertised her services as a midwife and attended many births in Pyrmont, Ultimo, Redfern and Waterloo—often without payment. Legislation in 1924 required nurses to be registered by December 1925. She was reported for operating as an unregistered midwife in 1927 and 1930 and was the subject of two inquiries before the Nurses' Registration Board, which did not result in prosecution. In 1929 she was unsuccessful in an N.R.B. examination. Although she never qualified, she continued to describe herself as a nurse.

Francis was active in the Pyrmont branch of the Australian Labor Party until 1926, then joined the Bondi branch and stood for that State seat in 1927, obtaining 3278 votes (22.79 per cent). That year she was appointed a justice of the peace. President and then secretary of the Labor Women's Organising Committee in 1928-35, she led delegations to ministers, organized public meetings, campaigned for candidates and was a delegate to the State Labor annual conference. She was one of three New South Wales delegates to the Interstate Women's Conference, 1930, and was president of the Blind Workers' Union in 1931. Francis stood unsuccessfully for Waverley Municipal Council as a (J. T.) Lang [q.v.9] Labor candidate in 1932. In early 1931 she had been appointed as an employment relief inspector, raising parliamentary scrutiny of her *bona fides*. During this debate it was revealed that Francis had a conviction for witnessing false enrolment cards in Bondi prior to the 1930 election; the successful candidate, Abraham Landa, defended her.

During the Depression Francis was secretary of a Labor women's committee that raised money to set up the Hostel for Homeless Women and Girls, which opened in October 1931. The government provided premises at 28 Elizabeth Street, but the committee raised all other funds to equip and run the hostel for forty unemployed females. In 1935 Francis became matron of a hostel for women and girls at 45 Argyle Street.

Plump and short, Nurse Francis was much loved in the labour movement. When she announced in early 1936 her forthcoming (second) marriage, a presentation committee was set up (with Kate Dwyer [q.v.8] as a vice-president) to organize a huge function in Mark Foy's [qq.v.4,8] Empress Rooms. Tributes were paid to her work during the influenza epidemic of 1918-19 and her tireless help for the poor. There was even a pause at that year's party conference to allow Lang to make a presentation to her. On 18 April 1936 at St Mary's Catholic Cathedral, Sydney, describing herself as a widow, aged 52, she married 44-year-old John Laurence Wilkes, a widower and a council employee. From then she was known as Nurse Francis-Wilkes, and she and her husband appear to have lived at the Argyle Street hostel.

Francis-Wilkes was still active and secretary of the Darling Harbour Labor Party branch at the time of her death from myocardial infarct and diabetes on 22 April 1946 at Argyle Street, Sydney. She was buried in Botany cemetery with Catholic rites. Her husband and a son and daughter of her first marriage survived her.

The Australian Labor Year Book, 1934-35; *Golden Jubilee Souvenir of the Labor Women's Central Organising Committee 1904-1954* (Syd, 1954); *PD* (NSW), 3 June 1931, p 3125; *Labor Daily* (Syd), 4 Feb 1926, p 7, 19 Sept 1931, p 7, 12 Oct 1931, p 7, 24 Oct 1931, p 8, 2 Nov 1931, 7 Dec 1931, p 7, 12 May 1933, p 16, 10 July 1933, p 7, 22 Apr 1935, p 9, 5 Mar 1936, p 9, 23 Mar 1936, p 9, 8 Apr 1936, p 13, 20 Apr 1936, p 9; *SMH*, 15 Sept 1927, pp 12 & 14, 5 Jan 1932, p 10, 24 Apr 1946, p 20; NSW Nurses' Registration Board, NSR/AGY/6, (SRNSW).   SUE TRACEY

FRANK THE POET; *see* MACNAMARA

FRASER, ELIZA ANNE (c.1798-1858?), shipwreck victim and source of myth and legend, was born perhaps in Derbyshire, England. Her maiden name was Slack and she was literate. Sometime before 1821 she married James Fraser, a mariner. In 1835, leaving their 14-year-old daughter and two sons in the care of the Presbyterian minister at Stromness, in the Orkney Islands, she accompanied her ailing, 56-year-old husband, captain of the brig *Stirling Castle*, to Australia.

The ship left London on 22 October and, after a successful voyage with passengers and cargo to Hobart Town and then to Sydney, sailed north for Singapore. On the night of 21 May 1836 the vessel hit a coral reef and foundered off the north-eastern coast of Australia. Taking to the lifeboats, the survivors headed south, hoping to reach the convict settlement at Moreton Bay. A few days after leaving the wreck, Eliza gave birth to a baby, who died. The two lifeboats lost contact; the faster, mistakenly by-passing Moreton Bay,

came ashore at the Tweed River; six seamen died and a survivor was rescued at the Macleay.

Meanwhile, the leaking longboat reached the northern tip of Great Sandy Island—later to be renamed after Captain Fraser. Trading goods with local Aborigines for fish, the castaways repaired the boat. When six seamen defiantly took guns, however, and set off to walk south along the beach, the Frasers and four others were obliged to follow. Along the way Aborigines stripped the party of clothes, blankets and possessions. At the southern tip of the island a strait barred their way. The Aborigines divided the men among family groups to assist with hunting, fishing and gathering firewood. Aboriginal women cleansed Eliza's sunburned body with sand, rubbed it with charcoal and grease and decorated it with colour and feathers. She was required to nurse their children, dig fern roots and rob bees' nests, but was so inept and resentful that the women tormented her. She witnessed the death of her husband, after he was speared. His first mate also died and two seamen drowned attempting to swim the strait. Fed on scraps and taken by canoe to the mainland, but not permitted to contact the other castaways, Eliza felt herself a slave.

Three crewmen crossed to the mainland and moved south with Aboriginal groups until, at Bribie Island, they encountered Lieutenant Charles Otter of the Moreton Bay garrison. Commandant Foster Fyans [q.v.1] immediately organized a rescue party of volunteer soldiers and convicts, led by Otter and guided by a convict absconder John Graham [q.v.1]. Graham rescued two *Stirling Castle* seamen from the western shore of Lake Cooroibah (near Noosa). From a camp at Double Island Point he proceeded north to Fraser Island and returned the next day with the second mate John Baxter. Graham then located Mrs Fraser near the northern end of Lake Cootharaba. Assisted by his Aboriginal 'relatives', he took her to the beach to meet Otter and his soldiers. The rescue party returned to Brisbane on 21 August 1836.

The survivors recovered from their ordeal at Moreton Bay and then returned to Sydney, where newspapers published exaggerated accounts of their experiences. Eliza stayed at the home of the colonial secretary, was feted in Sydney society and received a large sum of money raised by public subscription. On 3 February 1837 at St Andrew's Presbyterian Church, with Rev. John McGarvie [q.v.2] officiating, she married Captain Alexander John Greene. They sailed in his ship, *Mediterranean Packet*, for Liverpool. To the authorities there and in London, Eliza purported to be a penniless widow. The lord mayor of London held a public inquiry and opened an appeal. After it was revealed that she had remarried and had already received recompense, the lord mayor's fund was mostly allocated to the Fraser children, and Greene took Eliza back to Stromness to be reunited with them.

Eliza's character was variously described by people who knew her. To the seaman Harry Youlden, she was 'a most profane, artful wicked woman'. But the journalist John Curtis portrayed her sympathetically, believing she suffered from 'aberration of the mind' as a result of her experiences. In 1842 a runaway convict David Bracewell [q.v.1] claimed that he had helped to rescue Eliza, adding to the conflicting traditions. Fraser descendants believed that the Greenes eventually moved to Auckland, New Zealand, and that Eliza died in Melbourne in a carriage accident in 1858.

As early as 1841 Charlotte Barton [q.v.] included a synthesised account of the events in her book, *A Mother's Offering to her Children*. The recounting of the tale had negative effects on Aboriginal-settler relations in Australia and the questions surrounding her rescue and its aftermath led to lasting controversy. Descendants of the Aborigines resented the way their ancestors' attempts to help the castaways were misrepresented. In the twentieth century historians re-examined her story. The painter (Sir) Sidney Nolan, novelist Patrick White and composer Peter Sculthorpe based significant works on her legend, a feature film was produced in 1976 and academics began to study the complex mythologies that her legacy had created.

J. Curtis, *Shipwreck of the Stirling Castle* (Lond, 1838); H. S. Russell, *The Genesis of Queensland* (Syd, 1888); R. Gibbings, *John Graham, Convict 1824* (Lond, 1937); M. Alexander, *Mrs. Fraser on the Fatal Shore* (Lond, 1971); C. C. Petrie, *Tom Petrie's Reminiscences of Early Queensland* (Melb, 1975); B. Dwyer and N. Buchanan, *The Rescue of Eliza Fraser* (Noosa, Qld, 1986); K. Schaffer, *In the Wake of First Contact* (Cambridge, UK, 1995); I. J. McNiven, L. Russell and K. Schaffer, *Constructions of Colonialism* (Lond, 1998); E. Brown, *Cooloola Coast* (Brisb, 2000).   ELAINE BROWN

FRIDAY; *see* ARTHUR, WALTER GEORGE

FROST, LILLIAN MARY (1870-1953), organist, was born on 4 September 1870, at Launceston, Tasmania, second of seven children of John Frost, a draper and amateur musician, and his wife Amelia Annie, née Sage. Lillian was baptized at St John's Church of England. Identifying her musical talents, her parents took her to London in 1879 for three years of tuition, the final year at the Guildhall School of Music.

From mid-1886 Frost performed and taught at Launceston. Soon appointed organist at the Christ Church Congregational Church, she performed at the opening of the local Albert Hall in May 1891 and at the New South Wales–Launceston Tasmanian Exhibition of 1891-92. She also accompanied touring musical groups, including the Kowalski-Poussard company from Sydney. This led to an invitation to perform in Sydney, which in turn resulted in Frost's appointment as organist at Pitt Street Congregational Church in September 1895. According to the Tasmanian press, the young musician exhibited both musical maturity and physical stamina. Her dramatic style suited the emphasis on individual expression favoured by the Romantic composers.

Frost's career at the church in Sydney proved long and difficult. A new organ took nearly ten years to come and led to court action against the church in 1909. The case turned into an attack on Frost, whom church and a range of musical experts combined to defend. Friction also arose over the next three decades between Frost and a succession of male choirmasters, who objected when she asserted her musical authority. Frost was underpaid for most of this period. Her position changed in 1925 when a new pastor, Rev. T. E. Ruth [q.v.11], proclaimed her work a musical ministry, giving her greater autonomy as musical director and higher pay. In September 1945 a 'Festival of Music' drew church, civic and musical circles together in celebration of Frost's jubilee as church organist.

From her arrival in Sydney in 1895, Frost was active in the secular musical world. She gave a successful series of recitals at Sydney Town Hall in 1896. Photographs showed the massive city organ dwarfing her petite figure. As accompanist, she toured with a range of international musicians in 1898-1904; in 1903 she was one of two women invited to a reception for the English organist Edwin Lemare. Frost travelled to Britain and Europe in 1912, when she studied with Sir Walter Alcock and Charles-Marie Widor, and again in 1927, when she also visited the United States of America. In Sydney she gave lessons and collaborated with the wider musical community to encourage promising pupils and to raise musical taste. With conservatorium staff and other organists and teachers she served on the organizing committee of the first Australian Music Week in 1930. She also conceived and promoted the idea of 'Music Sunday' to draw the churches into Music Week activities.

Combining her professional, teaching and religious roles, Frost had launched a series of musical recitals in 1913. Held in the Pitt Street Church, they featured a range of local and visiting musicians and a diverse selection of old and modern music, the Wednesday recitals became an institution. A sign of their sacred and secular significance was the scale of congratulation that greeted Frost's 1000th recital on 13 November 1940.

Although hindered by the onset of Alzheimer's disease and a hip injury in 1947, Frost continued her ministry to December 1948. She lived the remainder of her years with her sister at Launceston. Miss Frost died on 22 December 1953 at St Luke's hospital.

G. D. Rushworth, *Historic Organs of New South Wales* (Syd, 1988); *Canon* (Syd), 7, no 7, Feb 1954, p 294; *Examiner* (Launc), 23 Dec 1953, p 4; Pitt Street Congregational Church papers, MSS 2093 (ML).

JANE E. HUNT

FRYER, JANE (1832-1917), political and religious radical, was born on 14 October 1832 at Taunton, Somerset, England, daughter of Leonard Trump, a baker of Dutch extraction, and his wife Ruth, née Dewelley. Jane left her strict Wesleyan home aged 15 and went to live at Bristol. She was a servant when she married Welsh-born John Robbins Fryer (1826-1912), carpenter, at the register office, Clifton, on 27 October 1853. Jane was an independent-minded woman who refused 'to wear a wedding-ring, on the grounds that it symbolised servitude to her spouse'; a grandson remembered John as a gentle soul with 'a permanent twinkle in his dark eyes'. They were to have ten children, although three died in infancy and another in childhood. Jane would act as a foster-mother to six more.

Associated with the Chartist, ragged schools and feminist movements in England, Jane was 'as ready as her husband to support anything she deemed progressive'. Following John's brother Jethro, who was already at Ballarat, the couple came to Victoria in 1854. After a brief career as a digger, John turned to building houses to provide for his family, who later moved to Melbourne. When his sight began to fail John, prompted by his wife, opened the Carlton Boot Palace at 183 Lygon Street, Melbourne, in the late 1870s.

In Victoria Jane and John were initially involved in Methodism but they soon gravitated to the Society of Friends. They were also members of the rationalist Sunday Free Discussion Society, which was formed in 1870, and early in the 1880s they joined the committee of the newly formed Australasian Secular Association. One of their sons, J. N. Fryer, became full-time secretary, and two other sons and three daughters were members. Jane became a 'Leader' of the Melbourne Progressive Lyceum, a Sunday School that included both spiritualists and secularists, and she was also a teacher in the Melbourne Secular Lyceum, which was conducted by her husband. She joined the editorial committee of the *Australasian Secular Association Lyceum Tutor* (1888), an anthology edited by Bernard O'Dowd [q.v.11], to which she contributed poetry. The Fryers all took an enthusiastic part in the work of the Lyceum, but the secular association disintegrated in 1888 over conflict arising from the conduct of its authoritarian president Joseph Symes [q.v.6]. The Fryer family were prominent opponents of Symes in this dispute, and found themselves unjustly accused of anarchism and financial dishonesty.

The Fryers' daughter Evangeline married O'Dowd in 1889. He described Jane at this time as 'a fine woman, the finest indeed I have ever seen'. She was kind, practical, very fond of her children and yet capable of suppressing 'all emotion' when necessary. 'She is free from most of the shams that modern society stinks with', O'Dowd commented, '& in consequence of this & of the care she has taken of herself she looks more in the "twenties" than in the "fifties"'.

After John's boot business failed in the depression of the early 1890s, the O'Dowds and the Fryers moved to Glenroy, on Melbourne's outer northern fringe, where the Fryers owned a block of land acquired during the land boom. The two families lived under the one roof for about three years. These domestic arrangements caused considerable unhappiness, with the forceful personality of Jane apparently the main cause—a grandson recalled her as 'generous, humane and forgiving' but also 'an uncompromising disciplinarian'. The unhappy arrangement ended when the O'Dowds moved closer to town.

In Melbourne, Jane joined the spiritualist, eight-hour day and early-closing movements, and was associated with the Theosophical Society. She was also involved in the women's suffrage movement and the Women's Political and Social Crusade. A member of the Prahran branch of the Political Labor Council, from 1906 she belonged to the Victorian Socialist Party. Described as a woman of great mental and physical energy, during World War I, although in weak health, she attended a Women's Anti-Conscription Procession and made an impression with an impromptu address. Jane Fryer died on 16 June 1917 at Moonee Ponds and was buried in Melbourne general cemetery, without religious rites. Two sons and three daughters survived her. Except perhaps in her sex, Jane was typical of those described by F. B. Smith as 'honest doubters', who were the mainstay of religious unorthodoxy and political radicalism in eastern Australia between the gold rushes and World War I.

V. Kennedy and N. Palmer, *Bernard O'Dowd* (Melb, 1954); Royal Commission on Employees in Shops, Report, *PP* (LA Vic), 1883, vol 2, paper no 16,

Q. 1724-45, p 62; *Labour History*, no 5, Nov 1963, p 26; *Overland*, no 39, Aug 1968, p 17; Aust Society for the Study of Labour History (Melb), *Recorder*, no 81, Apr 1976, p 10; *Socialist*, 22 June 1917, p 2, 27 July 1917, p 3; F. B. Smith, Religion and Free-thought in Melbourne, 1870-1890 (M.A. thesis, Univ Melb, 1960); Hugh Anderson's transcript of Bernard O'Dowd's diary, 1888-89 (H. Anderson collection of B. O'Dowd materials, H. Ransom Humanities Research Center, Univ of Texas at Austin).

FRANK BONGIORNO

FURNEAUX, TOBIAS (1735-1781), navigator, was born on 21 August 1735 at the family estate, Swilly, near Plymouth, Devon, England, son of William Furneaux—believed to have been descended from a progenitor who accompanied William of Normandy in 1066—and his wife Susanna, née Willcocks. Tobias was christened at St Andrew's Church, Stoke Damerel, Devonport. Joining the Royal Navy, in February 1755 he became a midshipman in H.M.S. *Marlborough*. He was stationed for a time in the West Indies in the Seven Years War and was promoted lieutenant in November 1759 for good behaviour in action. In 1760 he returned to England.

Serving in the frigate *Melampe* from October 1762, Furneaux was second lieutenant in H.M.S. *Dolphin*, under Samuel Wallis, which sailed from the Nore in July 1766, under Admiralty instructions 'to discover and obtain a complete knowledge of the Land or Islands supposed to be situated in the Southern Hemisphere'. Passing through the Strait of Magellan, Wallis reached Otaheite (Tahiti) on 19 June 1767. During the protracted Pacific voyage, when Wallis and his first lieutenant suffered sickness Furneaux often assumed command. Thus, on 25 June, he took possession of Tahiti, declaring it to be 'King George's Island'. After one month the *Dolphin* continued westwards, reaching the Thames estuary in March 1768. Furneaux was paid off on 24 June.

Furneaux was third lieutenant in H.M.S. *Trident* in December 1770 and, from 30 December, in H.M.S. *Torbay*, later becoming second lieutenant. On 29 November next year he was promoted commander and appointed captain of H.M.S. *Adventure* under James Cook's [q.v.1] overall command in H.M.S. *Resolution*. The expedition sailed from Plymouth in July 1772, called at Cape Town in November, and headed south and east. On 8 February 1773 the ships were separated in fog, and *Adventure* made for the agreed rendezvous, Queen Charlotte Sound, New Zealand. *En route* Furneaux directed his course for Van Diemen's Land, sighting South West Cape on 9 March, becoming the first English vessel to retrace Tasman's [q.v.2] 1642 discoveries. *Adventure* lay off Bruny Island from 11 March

1773 'wooding and watering' in this haven, which Furneaux called Adventure Bay. Other features in the region he named were the Mewstone, the Friars, Fluted Cape and Penguin Island.

Sailing north on 15 March, Furneaux named St Patrick's Head, St Helen's Point, Bay of Fires and Eddystone Point, all on 17 March. Next day he noted 'the land trenches away to the westward, which I believe forms a deep bay'; it was, in fact, the entrance to Banks Strait. On this day islands were sighted, the land high and rocky, and the south-eastern point was named Cape Barren. He considered investigating whether a strait lay westward but decided to rejoin his commander, and on 19 March the vessel 'haul'd up for New Zealand'. Furneaux later declared that 'it is my opinion that there is no strait between New Holland and Van Diemen's Land', a view he persuaded Cook to accept. *Adventure* and *Resolution* were united in New Zealand in May 1773 and in August Furneaux re-visited Tahiti where the Tahitian Omai was taken on board. The vessels were again separated in October and Furneaux returned to England, arriving at Spithead in July 1774.

During the American War of Independence, in August 1775, he took command of the 28-gun frigate *Syren*. The ship was sunk in Narragansett Bay in November 1777 and her crew imprisoned. Released next April, Furneaux was acquitted by court martial of any misconduct. He acted as a volunteer in H.M.S. *Isis* in July 1778, but had no further naval service, being resident at Swilly in September 1779 when he applied to be entered on the half-pay list. He died, unmarried, on 18 September 1781, and was interred in Stoke Damerel church.

An experienced, if somewhat unimaginative, navigator, who twice circumnavigated the globe, Furneaux had solid achievements in two lengthy Pacific voyages. George Robertson, master of the *Dolphin*, described him as 'a Gentele Agreeable well behaved Good man and very humain to all the Ships company'. The Furneaux islands in Bass Strait, named by Cook, commemorate him. His portrait in oils by James Northcote is held by Lady Juliet Townsend of Banbury, England, and a copy is in Parliament House, Canberra.

R. W. Giblin, *The Early History of Tasmania*, 1 (Lond, 1928); G. Robertson, *The Discovery of Tahiti* (Lond, 1948); J. C. Beaglehole (ed), *The Journals of Captain James Cook on his Voyages of Discovery* (Cambridge, UK, 1955-74); R. Furneaux, *Tobias Furneaux, Circumnavigator* (Lond, 1960); A. David (ed), *The Charts and Coastal Views of Captain Cook's Voyages* (Lond, 1992); Captains' Logs, Adventure, T. Furneaux 1772-74 (AJCP reels 1550-1); Captains' letters, T. Furneaux 1768-77 (AJCP reel 3270); Furneaux's Narrative (British L).   DAN SPROD

G

GETHER, SUSANNE VILHELMINE (1857-1911+), woodcarver, was born on 14 September 1857 at Neksø, Bornholm, Denmark, sixth and last child of Jens Johan Gether, judge and sometime mayor, and his wife Barbara Petrea, née Jespersen. Susanne learned woodcarving in Switzerland. In Denmark she acquired further skills and worked in woodcarving, leatherwork and pyrography (pokerwork), later asserting that the Danish recognized such skills as proper for the 'highest lady in the land'.

Gether travelled from Copenhagen to Dunedin, New Zealand, in 1890 and within a year had a number of 'lady students'. In 1892 she became a teacher at the Dunedin Technical Classes Association; the vocational woodcarving class was cancelled, however, due to lack of support. When offered again in 1893 it attracted nine pupils. That year her name was included among the colony's first female electors. At the Otago Jubilee Industrial Exhibition (1898), in the home industries court, she exhibited work that included carved animals regarded as the 'best of the collection'.

In 1899 some Sydney women on holiday at Dunedin—including Lena, the wife of Geoffrey Fairfax, and Mabel, the wife of (Sir) James O. Fairfax [q.v.8]—admired the work of Gether's pupils and arranged for her to move to Sydney and hold classes in the Queen Victoria building. In August she exhibited her craft at a bazaar. The two Mrs Fairfaxes were among her first students, as was the philanthropist (Dame) Eadith Walker [q.v.12]. Woodcarving became a popular craft among middle-class women in Sydney. Gether pointed to their achievements in 1908: 'There are hands, brains, energy, and understanding for it all, for ... women of this country do not care to be classed as unemployed'. That year she launched a campaign to teach weaving. This involved developing original designs and the creative and skilful use of old handlooms.

The Society of Arts and Crafts of New South Wales was set up by amateur craft workers—men and women—at Mosman in 1906. Gether quickly joined, and from December the society held meetings at her studio, now in St James's Chambers, King Street. She also served on the New South Wales organizing committee for the Exhibition of Women's Work (Melbourne, 1907) initiated by Lady Northcote, the wife of the governor-general [q.v.11]. For the exhibition Gether designed a carved rosewood table and six chairs, which sixty-two pupils and members of the arts and crafts society executed. The suite was then shown at the Franco-British Exhibition, London (1908).

When numerous new, non-practising members joined the society, the founding members, including Gether, resigned. New groups of non-practitioners, linked to the social circles in which Lena and Mabel Fairfax moved and apparently loyal to Gether, commandeered the leadership of the society in 1910. She accepted the office of vice-president in April that year, but had resigned again by the end of June.

After Gether left Sydney in March 1911, the Sydney Club and Depot of Arts and Domestic Economy (Women's Handicrafts Association) was established, 'for the purpose of continuing the work initiated by Miss Gether'. By focusing increasingly on social aims and on activities such as needlework and cooking, however, the W.H.A. missed the point of her campaign to expand the pastimes of women. Details of Gether's later life are unknown. The Art Gallery of New South Wales holds two of her weavings.

Official Record of the Otago Jubilee Industrial Exhibition, 1898; Australian Exhibition of Women's Work, *List of Prizes* (Melb, 1907); *Official Souvenir Catalogue: First Australian Exhibition of Women's Work, 1907* (Melb, 1907); Sydney Club and Depot of Arts and Domestic Economy, *Objects, Notice and Rules* (copy in Women's Handicrafts Assn, PAM FILE 745.06/W, ML); J. Kerr (ed), *Heritage: The National Women's Art Book* (Syd, 1995); *Art & Architecture*, 5, no 2, Mar-Apr 1908, p 50; J. E. Hunt, Cultivating the Arts: Sydney Women Culturists 1900-50 (Ph.D. thesis, Macquarie Univ, 2001).

JANE E. HUNT

GIBSON, SIR FRANK ERNEST (1878-1965), pharmacist and politician, was born on 11 July 1878 at Egerton, Victoria, eighth son of Alexander Gibson, an Irish-born policeman, and his wife Louisa, née Herring, from London. Frank was educated at Grenville College and at the School of Mines, Ballarat, then qualified in pharmacy and moved to Western Australia, where he managed a shop at Cue. He bought premises at Leonora in 1909.

On 10 August 1911 at the district registrar's office, Kalgoorlie, he married Jean Rodger Dunkley, née Ella, a widow with two young sons. There were to be twins of the marriage. Gibson became mayor of Leonora in 1912. He moved to Fremantle in 1914, where he was mayor for some twenty-nine years, from 1919 to 1923 and from 1926 to 1952. Appointed a justice of the peace in 1916, he won the seat of Fremantle in the Legislative Assembly as a Nationalist in 1921 but was defeated in 1924. He stood unsuccessfully against John Curtin [q.v.13] for Federal parliament in 1928 and was member of the Legislative Council for the Metropolitan-Suburban Province in 1942-50 and for Suburban Province from 1950 to 1956.

Fremantle was strongly Labor, but Gibson held office over a long period as a conservative on a personal vote. When he retired from the Legislative Council, Labor won his former seat. For many years he was the district's best-known identity. It was said that during World War II, when the port was a major naval as well as commercial base, he visited every ship that called, and worked to help the morale of visiting servicemen and a civilian population which—with the fall of Singapore —feared bombing and invasion. Radiating cheerfulness and optimism, which he was privately often far from feeling, he did much to establish Fremantle as a haven for war-weary seamen and soldiers. In the process he accumulated a huge collection of mementoes presented by ships' companies.

In 1945 Gibson was a foundation member of the Liberal Party. His son-in-law was Sir Hal Pateshall Colebatch [q.v.8], a former Western Australian premier and senator. Gibson had friends in all parties, however, including his onetime opponent Curtin, with whom he worked closely during the war. Gibson's integrity, public service and freedom from sectarianism won him universal respect. He was a commander of the Order of St John of Jerusalem and sat on the executives of many organizations, including the Milk Board, Lotteries Commission and Fire Brigades Board, and pharmaceutical professional and examining boards. He was knighted in 1948.

From about 1929 Gibson played an influential part in creating Monument Hill, overlooking Fremantle, as a war memorial. He supported establishing a naval base on the west coast. With his friend and successor as mayor (Sir) Frederick Samson [q.v.16], he began the campaign to preserve Fremantle's historic buildings and precincts before such conservation became fashionable. He unsuccessfully advocated keeping Fremantle's trams.

Active in many charities, such as the crippled children's home at Point Peron, he also put his philosophy of public-spiritedness into practice by personally sweeping the footpath and street in front of his High Street chemist shop before opening every morning. He quietly helped many individuals in trouble and among his possessions was a gold watch presented to him by a grateful ex-convict, with a letter assuring him that the money that paid for it had been honestly earned. As a very old man he was known to intervene and break up fights on the wharves on more than one occasion.

Late in life Gibson and his wife lived at the Orient Hotel, Fremantle. Both loved literature and poetry. A tall, handsome man, with white hair from an early age, he was a keen golfer and rifle-shot and remained very active until the last weeks of his life. Lady Gibson died in 1955. Sir Frank died on 31 December 1965 in hospital at Shenton Park, and was cremated with Anglican rites. His son and daughter and two stepsons survived him.

D. Black and G. Bolton, *Biographical Register of Members of the Parliament of Western Australia*, 1 (Perth, 1990); *West Australian*, 14 Mar 1921, pp 6 & 7, 1 Jan 1966, pp 2 & 7; family papers, held by author, Nedlands WA; personal information.

HAL G. P. COLEBATCH

GIBSON, JULIA (1872-1953), fortune-teller, was born Julia Glushkova on 7 February 1872, in Odessa, Russia, daughter of Nikita Glushkov, army officer, and his wife Mary, née Morrison. According to Julia's later account, the family became drawn into revolutionary activities and at 16 she was arrested for bomb throwing. Her death sentence was commuted to life imprisonment but she fled to England. On 23 May 1890 in the parish church of St Mary the Virgin, Cardiff, Wales, she married Christian Olsen, an illiterate Norwegian seaman. They had two children. After leaving him she ran a temperance hotel; Olsen stabbed her and died in gaol while serving his sentence.

In 1903 in Warsaw Julia married Henry Gibson, an Australian-born vaudeville artist and circus performer, possibly of Russian extraction, known as 'Zakaree Ermakov'. Julia later claimed that, working for the British Secret Service, she travelled extensively on missions through the Continent and into central Asia and that, although carrying a Cossack bullet in her body, she had the satisfaction of killing a son of the corrupt General Kuropatkin. Her estranged husband was to write to the press in 1922, however, that this was 'all bunkum', he having accidentally shot her during a circus performance in Russia. The Gibsons toured Europe, Russia, central Asia and Turkestan, Julia working as a fortune-teller by day and as Henry's stage assistant by night. They returned to England in 1912, sailed for South Africa in 1916 and arrived in Australia in 1917. After the couple separated, Julia took responsibility for their three children.

Early in 1918 she established herself in Melbourne's Eastern Arcade as a costumier.

Operating also as 'Madame Ghurka, phrenologist' she built a sizeable clientele among the gullible and the desperate, anxious to have their fortunes told. Gibson appears to have disliked wine saloon licensee Colin Ross [q v] for lowering the tone of the arcade with his criminal and streetwalker patrons. In November 1921 Ross sacked Ivy Matthews, who rented a flat from Gibson and was encouraged by her to testify against Ross. As a result, he was charged with the murder of a child, Alma Tirtschke. During the trial, Crown witnesses were under police protection at Gibson's house, and after Ross was convicted and hanged, she shared the rewards distributed by the government and the *Herald* newspaper.

In July 1922, giving evidence in a divorce case involving her son, and speaking with a heavy accent underlined by gestures, she displayed an agile mind, but Judge (Sir) William McArthur [q.v.10] described her as 'the sort of woman who would say a thing if it was true or untrue' and as 'a bitter, vengeful woman'. Stung by the barrister T. C. Brennan's [q.v.7] criticism of the Crown case against Ross and of her role in fabricating it, she replied by publishing *The Murder of Alma Tirtschke* (1923). In 1925, when Melbourne *Truth* journalists wrote that she had not been called as a witness in the Ross case for fear of discrediting the Crown's case, she sued for libel and was awarded £100 damages. She also won £100 for being slandered in 1932.

Her business suffered from the continuing controversy. Advertising as a phrenologist, character reader and business adviser, Gibson took the precaution of having clients sign statements that she did not engage in fortune telling or palmistry. Yet in August 1929 she was fined on two charges of having 'by subtle craft, including palmistry, imposed upon and deceived' two plain-clothed policewomen, and in September she failed in her appeal against police refusal to renew the registration of her revolver. In 1933 she was convicted again and fined £20, and in 1937 another charge was dismissed. In 1951 she sued the Herald and Weekly Times Ltd for defamation after the *Herald* described her as 'the notorious fortune teller'. Despite her reputation and earlier convictions, the jury awarded her £1000 damages.

Gibson was a widow with four living sons when she died on 14 September 1953 at North Carlton. After a service at the Russian Orthodox Church, Fitzroy, she was buried in Fawkner cemetery. *Truth*, which since 1925 had cautiously described her as 'a character reader', now hailed 'Madame Ghurka' as the 'Queen of fortune tellers'.

T. C. Brennan, *The Gun Alley Tragedy* (Melb, 1922); N. Ghurka, *Graft* (Melb, 1930?); *Argus*

(Melb), 24 Feb 1922, p 7, 20 July 1922, p 8, 29 July 1922, p 23, 7 Aug 1929, p 15, 24 Feb 1932, p 5, 11 May 1951, p 5; *Herald* (Melb), 6 Aug 1929, p 4, 8 May 1951, p 3, 10 May 1951, p 3, 11 May 1951, p 7, 16 Sept 1953, p 10; *Smith's Weekly*, 15 July 1922, p 10; *Age* (Melb), 8 Aug 1929, p 11; *Sun News-Pictorial*, 9 May 1951, p 8; *Truth* (Melb), 22 July 1922, p 3, 5 Aug 1922, p 2, 6 June 1925, p 7, 20 June 1925, p 9, 21 Nov 1925, p 10, 27 Feb 1932, p 14, 30 July 1932, p 4, 12 May 1951, p 8, 19 Sept 1953, p 3; B741/3, item V/74 (NAA, Canb).

JOHN LACK

GINN (GHINN), HENRY (1818-1892), architect, company secretary and pastoralist, was born late in 1818 at Bexhill, Sussex, England, and christened at St Peter's Church, Hamsey, on 31 January 1819, third of five children of Benjamin Ginn, a clerk of works with the Royal Engineers, and his wife Mary, née Guy (d.1822). Henry worked for a London-based builder, gaining experience on the architect William Cubitt's housing estates and residential squares, before visiting Europe. Reaching Sydney in the *Meanwell* on 26 January 1840, under the patronage of George Barney [q.v.1], a family friend, Ginn was engaged as architect for the Holy Trinity (Garrison) Church, Millers Point. Subsequently appointed clerk of works with the Royal Engineers, in 1841 he was sent back to London to organize labour and materials for several local projects.

Returning to Sydney in June 1842, Ginn overlayed his original modern Gothick design for Holy Trinity with fashionable mediaeval details, in an attempt to erect the first 'correct Early Victorian parish church in Australia'. In private practice from 1843, he won commissions to design the Australian Subscription Library and the Royal Exchange, Sydney, St Andrew's Church, Stockton, and a bridge at Bathurst. On 12 November 1844 at Christ Church St Laurence, Sydney, he married with Anglican rites Jane, daughter of William Grant Balmain. They had seven children. Encouraged by Mortimer Lewis [q.v.2], the colonial architect, Ginn applied for the position of clerk of works at Port Phillip. When his appointment was approved at a salary of £200, he cancelled plans to return to England and with his young family moved to Melbourne on 4 May 1846.

Soon acquiring a 26-acre (10.5 ha) lot at Richmond, Ginn designed and erected a Colonial Regency style residence, and subdivided the block into residential allotments, which he later sold at great profit. He encountered increasing conflict with his subordinates, difficulties with a distant administration and intransigent local contractors. Nevertheless, he oversaw the erection of major public works such as the Lunatic Asylum at Yarra Bend. He also designed buildings for Williamstown,

Geelong and Portland, including the lighthouse at Williamstown (1848) and the equally rugged Colonial Georgian style Custom House at Portland (1849-50)—both rare surviving examples of his work. In 1847 his brother-in-law James Balmain came to Port Phillip to join Ginn's office.

As secretary to the (Royal) Botanic Gardens committee, Ginn prepared designs for the layout of the gardens in the Domain, Melbourne. He was appointed auditor of the Victorian Horticultural Society on its formation in November 1848 and next year succeeded John Pascoe Fawkner [q.v.1] as secretary, establishing a reputation as an exhibitor then judge. In November he became a building referee under the Melbourne Building Act (1849) and in 1851 was elected first president of the short-lived Victorian Association of Architects.

With effect from the separation of Victoria on 1 July 1851, Ginn was promoted to colonial architect. His department was soon paralysed by the gold rushes—key staff deserted and calls for tenders went unanswered. Ginn opposed the day labour system and advocated his return to London to seek both labour and prefabricated buildings and materials for urgent public works. However, a bitter dispute arose over the merits of his depleted department preparing plans for both the new Legislative Council chambers and Government House. The decision of the Legislative Council to conduct a public architectural competition riled Ginn. He then lost his influence on the Tender Board and fell into open dispute with the administration over the funding of public works in the goldfields districts. On 11 April 1853 he resigned; responsibility for the Colonial Architect's Office was handed to Balmain.

Ginn then became a director and secretary of the Melbourne, Mount Alexander & Murray River Railway Co. He declined a requisition to stand for election to the Legislative Council. After overseeing the commencement of building of the general central terminus in Spencer Street, Ginn, then managing director, was sent to Britain to raise £1 000 000 in share capital, leaving with Jane and their children on 4 December 1853.

In London Ginn received news that the Victorian government had bought out the railway company. He became secretary of the Commercial Union Assurance Co. at Cornhill. Jane died in 1858. On 23 November 1859, having changed the spelling of his surname, Henry Ghinn married Sophia Hyslop at All Souls, Langham Place, Marylebone. Their only child, a son, was born in 1861; Sophia died early next year.

Ghinn, long held to be a man of plain, manly and straightforward disposition, became general manager of the London and Australian Agency Corporation in the late 1860s and was subsequently posted to Melbourne to investigate the company's affairs, arriving with his children in December 1869. He recommended winding up the company and became the sole liquidator. Later he acquired Ballandry station, in the Riverina, New South Wales. He continued to support charities, including the Indian Famine Relief and the Prince Consort Memorial funds. Predeceased by his eldest and youngest sons, Ghinn died on 23 January 1892 at Risca, Regent Street, Elsternwick, Melbourne. He was buried in St Kilda cemetery. Four daughters and two sons of his first marriage survived him.

J. M. Freeland, *The Making of a Profession* (Syd, 1971); J. Kerr and J. Broadbent, *Gothick Taste in the Colony of New South Wales* (Syd, 1980); G. Tibbits and A. Roennfeldt, *Port Phillip Colonial 1801-1851* (Melb, 1989); *Argus* (Melb), 18 Apr, 1853, p 5, 5 Dec 1853, p 4, 25 Jan 1892, p 5; *Age* (Melb), 25 Jan 1892, p 1; D. Kennedy, Henry Ginn 1817-1892: His Work and Life (B.Arch. thesis, Univ NSW, 1986); A. Roennfeldt, Public Buildings in the Port Phillip District 1836-1851 (research report, Dept Architecture and Building, Univ Melb, 1987).

ALLAN F. WILLINGHAM

GIORZA, PAOLO (1832-1914), musician, was born on 11 November 1832 in Milan, Italy, son of Luigi Giorza, baritone, organist and itinerant painter. Having studied first with his father and Enrico La Croix, at the age of 10 Paolo won a scholarship to the Royal Conservatory of Music, Milan; Luigi's political activities, however, forced the family to move to nearby Desio. Eventually Paolo heard Rossini's *Mosé* at La Scala, Milan, and his destiny was determined. The first of Giorza's more than sixty ballets, *Il Giucatore*, was performed at Canobbiana theatre in 1853. His next ballet, *Un Fallo*, opened at La Scala, in September 1854. He later worked in Venice, Vienna, London and Paris.

In a concert in late December 1858 Giorza's polka-song *La Bella Gigogin* had its première in Milan: it had eight curtain calls. Recognizing its political significance, the Austrian rulers banned performances of the song, but it became the rallying cry for Lombardian liberation and was played when Napoléon III and Victor Emanuel II entered Milan in 1859. Garibaldi sought battle music from Giorza and the King appointed him cavaliere, as did King Carlos of Portugal.

Although Giorza's first opera, *Corrado, Console di Milano*, performed at La Scala in March 1860, was 'an unmitigated disaster', he remained devoted to music drama as composer and conductor and was a professional associate of Rossini, Auber, Meyerbeer, Verdi and Gounod. Giorza's opera *La Capanna dello Zio Tom* (*Uncle Tom's Cabin*) played in Milan in the mid-1860s. In 1867, as conductor of an Italian company, he travelled to central and North America. His proposed directorship of the Mexican Opera was thwarted by the execution of Emperor Maximilian; Giorza went to the United States of America. There he wrote a suite of incidental music for the soprano Adelaide Ristori's 1867 season of Giacometti's *Marie Antoinette.*

In 1871 Giorza arrived in Australia as music director of a small opera ensemble, the Agathe States group, which gave performances in Sydney in December and at the Princess Theatre, Melbourne, in February 1872. He remained in Australia, employed by W. S. Lyster [q.v.5] and then the Lyster-Cagli company. Later he worked with J. C. Williamson's [q.v.6] English Opera Company and the Pompei-Lazar and Lazar Royal Italian companies. His broad repertoire encompassed Verdi and Gilbert and Sullivan; contemporary reviewers praised his versatility and the fluidity of his direction. Described as Australia's then 'leading score doctor', he frequently wrote songs for interpolation into performances. All this time he was teaching (including the organ in Adelaide), composing (especially religious music) and directing music (at St Francis's Church, Melbourne, in 1873-74 and later at St Patrick's, Sydney).

In Sydney in late 1874 his Catholic connexions developed, especially with (Sir) Patrick Jennings [q.v.4]. Giorza rejoined forces with Ristori and directed the orchestra for Ilma di Mirska's concerts in the mid-1870s. Several of his masses were performed, and in 1875 he conducted the Sydney première of Verdi's *Requiem* and his own *Cantata* for the Daniel O'Connell centenary celebrations, in the presence of Ristori and Archbishop Polding [q.v.2]. Jennings, a passionate music-lover, chose Giorza as director of music for the Sydney International Exhibition of 1879-80. The appointment generated protest, especially from Sydney's resident professionals who feared, needlessly, exclusion from the musical programme. They also resented that Giorza (with Henry Kendall [q.v.5] providing the text) was commissioned to compose the grand celebratory opening cantata. This he did with great success. It was scored for a large chorus and children's choir, a demi-chorus, soloists and a full orchestra, 'comprising every musician of note in the city', which incorporated the organ and eight pianists, one of them the composer's wife Luiga.

During the exhibition, Giorza also provided daily concerts, some of them grand orchestral and choral occasions, with Handel's oratorios prominent as well as band and chamber music and piano recitals. Frequently, Giorza was the soloist, especially on the second-

hand, 'asthmatic, little' English organ that had been purchased for the Garden Palace, although he failed to play one hour per day as stipulated in his contract, which Jennings threatened to terminate. Giorza survived to perform at the closing ceremony in April; during the interminable presentations, he improvised on the national songs of the participant nations—with the conspicuous omission of Austria.

In July 1883 Giorza invited Sir Henry Parkes [q.v.5] to a farewell concert, after which he departed for Europe. There he published his book of dance music, *Souvenir d'Australia* (Milan, 1884), and secured some performances, including his last ballet, *Rodope,* which opened at La Scala on 5 January 1892. Then, presumably for financial reasons, he returned to the U.S.A. A report in the *American Catholic Standard* in March 1902 mentioned that he was in Philadelphia for a performance of the first of his nine masses but in 1906, having lost most of his scores in the fires which followed the San Francisco earthquake, he moved to Seattle, where he continued to teach but became impoverished. An obituarist described him as 'a sturdy figure of a quaint old man with a splendid halo of white hair'. He died on 4 May 1914 in a boarding-house at Seattle. After a service at St Benedict's Catholic Church, he was buried in Calvary cemetery, the grave and funeral costs being paid by Ambrose Chiappa.

Although he was an internationalist, Giorza's career illustrates the richness of Australian intellectual and cultural life before Federation. He was, with Isaac Nathan [q.v.2], the most significant musician to work in Australia during the nineteenth century.

F. Savio, *Enciclopedia dello Spettacolo,* 5 (Rome, 1958); A. Gyger, *Civilising the Colonies* (Syd, 1999); *Dizionario biografico degli Italiani* (Rome, 2000); P. Proudfoot, R. Maguire, R. Freestone (eds), *Colonial City, Global City* (Syd, 2000); *SMH,* 26 Dec 1878, p 5, 29 Mar 1879, p 6, 13 May 1879, p 5, 20 May 1879, p 5, 23 May 1879, p 7, 24 May 1879, p 3, 21 Apr 1880, pp 9, 10; *Post-Intelligencer* (Seattle), 5 May 1914, p 1; *Seattle Times,* 30 Mar 1961, p 30; Giorza music collection (Veech Library, Catholic Inst of Syd); newspaper cuttings, vols 188-89 *and* concert programmes, Sydney International Exhibition, 1879-80 (ML).

JOHN CARMODY

GIRARDIN, MARIE-LOUISE VICTOIRE (1754-1794), ship's steward and cross-dresser, was born on 29 June 1754 in the parish of Saint-Louis, Versailles, France, daughter of Jean Girardin, a former royal gardener turned wine merchant, and his wife Angélique Benoise, née Hanet. Marie-Louise was one of nine children. In 1776 she married 26-year-old Etienne Lesserteur, a café proprietor at

Versailles. On 14 April 1778 her 11-month-old son Jean died, and on 14 July 1781 she was widowed.

In the early days of the revolution, Girardin fled disgrace and paternal wrath after giving birth to an illegitimate child. Small, plain and very youthful in appearance, she disguised herself as a man and journeyed to Brest with a letter of introduction to the widowed sister of Jean-Michel Huon de Kermadec [q.v.], Mme Le Fournier d'Yauville. In the busy port of Brest, Huon de Kermadec helped her to find a post as a *commis* (steward), under the name of Louis Girardin, on board the 74-gun ship *Deux Frères*, commanded by Le Jar Du Clesmeur. When the crew threatened mutiny, Huon de Kermadec helped her to transfer to *La Recherche*, which was about to leave in search of La Pérouse [q.v.2]. The vessel sailed from Brest in September 1791 under the command of Bruny d'Entrecasteaux [q.v.1].

As a steward, Girardin was exempt from medical examination and enjoyed a small, separate cabin. On 23 April 1792 the expedition reached Recherche Bay in Van Diemen's Land, and Girardin became probably the first European woman to visit the island. The French ships left for New Caledonia on 28 May 1792. Girardin was with them when they visited the south-western coast of New Holland (Western Australia) between 9 and 17 December 1792 and when they were back in Van Diemen's Land between 21 January and 27 February 1793. During this second stay, there was much curiosity on the part of the indigenous inhabitants regarding the gender of crewmembers and the apparent lack of women among the ranks of the expedition. Jacques-Malo La Motte du Portail, an officer in *L'Espérance*, commented in a letter that had the Aborigines examined the steward of *La Recherche* 'they would have come across what they wished to find'.

The expedition also visited Tenerife, the Cape of Good Hope, New Ireland, the Admiralty Islands, Ambon, Tongatapu, and Balade (New Caledonia) before disintegrating on royalist and republican lines in the Dutch East Indies on receipt of news of the execution of King Louis XVI. Although her shipmates suspected that she was female, Girardin maintained her assumed identity with dogged determination. With operatic dash, she was even slashed on the arm in a duel with an impertinent assistant-pilot whom she had challenged. There is evidence, in the La Motte du Portail journal, that she may eventually have formed a relationship with Mérite, a young ensign in *La Recherche*. Both died of dysentery, within a day of the other—Mérite at Batavia and Marie-Louise in the Dutch transport *Dordrecht* on 18 December 1794. The ship's surgeon then revealed her true gender.

M. Dupont, *D'Entrecasteaux: Rien que la Mer un Peu de Gloire* (Paris, 1983); E. and M. Duyker (eds and translators), *Bruny d'Entrecasteaux: Voyage to Australia and the Pacific 1791-1793* (Melb, 2001); E. Duyker, *Citizen Labillardière* (Melb, 2003); *Connaître les Yvelines: Historie et Archéologie dans les Yvelines*, no 9, Oct 1981; papers held by Mr P. Huon de Kermadec, Versailles, and Dr P. Huon de Kermadec, Landerneau, France.

EDWARD DUYKER

GIRDLESTONE, THARP MOUNTAIN (c.1823-1899), surgeon, politician and sanitary reformer, was born in Norfolk, England, youngest of six children of Rev. Theophilus Girdlestone and his wife Mary, née Gay. Tharp undertook medical training at Norwich, and at St Bartholomew's and York-road Lying-in hospitals, London, later becoming a house surgeon at St Bartholomew's. A member of the Royal College of Surgeons from 1845, he was made a fellow in 1849. He was an active boxer and rower.

On 1 March 1850 Girdlestone reached Victoria in the *Lord Stanley*. At Christ's Church, Geelong, on 18 February 1853 he married Irish-born Mary Green with Anglican rites. Registered with the Medical Board of Victoria in 1854, he moved about the gold-rush districts for three years. He was resident surgeon at Castlemaine and coroner at Alma, Maryborough and Ararat, where he bought property in 1858 and became founding chairman of the improvement association. Girdlestone displayed 'energy and determination' and did not shirk public argument. A trustee and committee member of the local hospital from 1859, he was appointed honorary surgeon in 1860 but resigned next year. Elected chairman of the town council in November 1861, he stood down in April 1862 upon election to the Legislative Assembly for Ararat. An 'abrupt' but 'earnest' speaker, and a supporter of liberal views, he advocated reform of the Upper House. He was defeated at elections in January 1866.

Although Girdlestone again contested Ararat in 1875, he remained in Melbourne, where he had maintained a Collins Street practice since 1862, gaining a reputation as 'probably the best surgeon in Melbourne'. 'Slow and safe', he pioneered the use of kangaroo tendon as suture material, investigated cures for snake bite, published medical papers and embraced the new, antiseptic surgery. A member of the Melbourne Hospital committee in 1866-70 and 1879-82 and a founding member of the Alfred Hospital executive committee in 1868, he was a dedicated hospital practitioner. He served as an honorary surgeon and as chairman of the medical staff at the Alfred from 1871, but resigned in 1876, believing that management was ignoring the opinions of medical staff.

Girdlestone was president (1867) and treasurer (1878-83) of the Medical Society of Victoria. In 1873 he was provisionally appointed lecturer in surgery at the University of Melbourne, deposing Edward Barker, who appealed and was restored to his post. Girdlestone eventually replaced Barker in December 1880. His membership of the Melbourne Hospital committee did not prevent his campaigning against the hospital during 1868-69, on account of its offensive drainage. He was acting in his capacity as part-time medical officer to the City of Melbourne, an appointment he held in 1868-85 and discharged with 'skill, earnestness and energy'. In November 1876 he had become assistant honorary surgeon at the Melbourne Hospital, and was a surgeon there in 1883-87, but lost the post when defeated at the election by subscribers. He spoke out against the practice of trenching nightsoil in public parks and argued persistently that the Yan Yean reservoir, the principal water supply system for Melbourne, was polluted at its source. A member of the 1888 royal commission into the sanitary condition of Melbourne, in 1892 he gave evidence on the unsatisfactory condition of the Melbourne Hospital to the royal commission on charitable institutions.

Girdlestone suffered heavy losses in the 1890s depression. In failing health, he returned to England in 1895 and died at his brother's house at Sunningdale, Berkshire, on 6 July 1899. His wife, who had remained in Victoria, survived him. Their only child, a son, had died in China in 1873. Described as 'a little man with a massive head', Girdlestone had a forthright character that compelled one obituarist to point out that 'he was a much pleasanter man than was generally supposed'.

K. F. Russell, *The Royal Melbourne Hospital and its Early Surgeons, 1841-1900* (Melb, 1948) and *The Melbourne Medical School 1862-1962* (Melb, 1977); K. S. Inglis, *Hospital and Community* (Melb, 1958); A. M. Mitchell, *The Hospital South of the Yarra* (Melb, 1977); D. Dunstan, *Governing the Metropolis* (Melb, 1984); H. Love, *James Edward Neild* (Melb, 1989); *Intercolonial Medical J*, 20 Aug 1899, p 426; Royal Melb Hospital archives.   GEOFF BROWNE

GISBORNE, FREDERIC AUGUSTUS WINGFIELD (1860-1934), conservative ideologue, was born on 23 July 1860 in Ceylon (Sri Lanka), of unknown parentage and possibly mixed race. Apparently Frederic had some education at an English superior school before migrating to Australia about 1880. He later spoke of being an outback worker in Queensland, before settling in Tasmania. From 1889 he taught in the colony's education depart-

ment, and on 9 July 1891 at St Paul's Church of England, East Devonport, married Eva Grace Young. The marriage was childless. Gisborne rose to become headmaster of Castle Forbes Bay school from July 1899. He found but little satisfaction in teaching, and developed interests in orcharding, mining and writing. Mining led to ownership of a property in the Forth valley, still known (especially to bushwalkers) as 'Gisborne's'.

Having resigned from the education service in 1907, he established a poultry farm at New Town, Hobart. Gisborne had already published in respected journals: perhaps his most impressive essays were written by 1912, on various aspects of economic activity in Tasmania. A steadier and probably more congenial outlet came to be the London journal *Empire Review*. By May 1910 the *Review* tagged Gisborne as 'our Special Correspondent to the Commonwealth', and in that guise he wrote many essays over following years. Bewailing especially the strength of trade unions and the Labor Party, and the general effect of Federation, they presented Australia in bleak mode. Britain, too, Gisborne saw as undermined by 'welfareism' and the liberal radicalism sustained by Celtic nationalists rather than true-blue Britons. He offered a general critique of democracy, seeing hope for the future only in eugenic improvement of the race. His eugenics had the relative novelty of including advocacy of euthanasia. Another of his proposals for countering democracy's evils was that all aspirant politicians undergo academic training in political science.

Gisborne at first welcomed World War I as promising renovation of the Australian spirit, but then became ever more rancorous towards anti-conscription Labor and more distressed by the impoverishment of rural industry—to him the sole source of true national wealth. The 1920s victories of the Nationalists and, still more, the Country parties would seem to have promised to please Gisborne, but his pessimism went too deep. In these years, however, he published across a remarkably wide field: for the *Australasian Journal of Psychology and Philosophy* and *Australian Quarterly* at home; for the *Edinburgh Review*, *National Review*, *English Review* and *Quarterly Review* in Britain. His thrust remained much as in earlier years, if with more extreme touches—'a kind of Imperial Fascisti movement' was one of his prescriptions, working in accord with 'a race of super-men'. In 1928 Longmans Green published his *Democracy on Trial*, a collection of characteristic essays, including support for Bacon over Shakespeare as author of the plays.

All the while Gisborne continued on his poultry farm, while also an orchardist on Bruny Island. He upheld Tasmania's case for secession from the Commonwealth, associating in this with the publicist Leslie Norman. In 1929 he retired to St Helen's, on Tasmania's east coast, publishing until near his death on 24 July 1934. His wife survived him.

M. Roe, 'F. A. W. Gisborne (1860-1934) Global Conservative, Tasmanian Resident', *Tas Hist Research Assn, Papers and Procs*, 47, no 3, 2000, p 141; T. Rowse, *Australian Liberalism and National Character* (Melb, 1978).   MICHAEL ROE

GOODLET, ANN ALISON (c.1824-1903) and ELIZABETH MARY (1854-1926), church workers and philanthropists, were the first and second wives of John Hay Goodlet [q.v.4], a wealthy Sydney merchant. Ann was born in Edinburgh, eldest daughter of William Panton. She was a governess when she married John Dickson, a bank clerk, on 20 June 1853 at St Cuthbert's Episcopal Church, Edinburgh. In 1855 they came to Sydney, where Dickson died of phthisis in 1859. His widow married Goodlet on 3 May 1860 at Redfern with Presbyterian forms.

The couple supported hospitals, schools and charitable institutions, and were active in the Presbyterian Church at Ashfield. Ann was president of the first Australian branch of the Young Women's Christian Association from 1880 to 1903, and served on the State Children Relief Board and the boards of the Benevolent Society, the New South Wales Institution for the Deaf and Dumb and the Blind, the Queen's Jubilee Fund and the Sydney Female Refuge Society—where 'unfortunate females' were sheltered and 'where washing and needlework are done for the public on very reasonable terms'. She was sometime secretary of this refuge and also president of the ladies' auxiliary of the Young Men's Christian Association.

Her other great interest was the mission work of the Presbyterian Church of New South Wales. Ann Goodlet was one of a small band of women who established in 1867 a ladies' association to support the Church's New Hebrides Mission. She was its first and only president until 1891 when it was amalgamated with the new Presbyterian Women's Missionary Association, established to support the Zenana mission work of the Church of Scotland at Madras, India. This provided education for girls and women of different castes, in schools or in their homes. Ann became the W.M.A.'s first president, and continued in that role until her death. A small photograph of her showed a strong but gentle face in harmony with the descriptions of her wisdom and kindness. She had no children. She died on 3 January 1903 at Canterbury and was buried in Rookwood cemetery with Presbyterian forms.

On 3 February 1904 at Ashfield the widower married Elizabeth Mary Forbes. She had been born in 1854 at Singleton, daughter of Alexander Leith Forbes, inspector of schools, formerly a Free Church minister in Scotland, and his wife Jean, née Clark. In 1877 the Forbes family moved from Richmond to Ashfield, and Elizabeth became an enthusiastic and loyal member of the Presbyterian Church there. She later recalled that her parents had dedicated her as a baby to God, and that as a child she prayed that God would carry on his work in her even though it should be by suffering. This memory motivated her in her philanthropic interests. She was a Sunday School teacher for many years and was interested in all aspects of the Church's work, particularly foreign missions.

When the W.M.A. was formed in 1891 under the presidency of Ann Goodlet, Elizabeth Forbes was elected honorary secretary, a position she occupied until 1912. She fulfilled the role with enormous drive, for some years travelling to found branches in congregations throughout New South Wales. By 1902 there were fifty branches, and the annual report declared that the original aim of helping foreign missions 'has developed into our being the organization authorized by the General Assembly for collecting the revenue both for its Home and its Foreign Missions'. One of her initiatives was the formation of Young People's Mission Bands, which had a long life in many Presbyterian congregations. Overseas trips in 1894 brought her personal contact with the Aberdeen W.M.A. in Scotland and with American mission work in Cairo, and in 1910 she attended the World Missionary Conference in Edinburgh.

After their marriage in 1904, Elizabeth and her husband provided funds to build a hospital at Sholingur, India, and she developed a detailed knowledge of mission work and contact with missionaries by a voluminous correspondence and hospitality during their furloughs. Her personal interest was reflected in her report of 1894 of the stimulus the W.M.A. provided for women to bestir themselves in the Church's work. In 1912 she was elected president of the W.M.A., which she led with characteristic energy and enthusiasm. She was also active in the support of the Institution for the Deaf and Dumb and the Blind, Y.W.C.A., Queen Victoria Homes for Consumptives, Sydney Female Refuge and the British and Foreign Bible Society.

Following John's death in 1914 his widow continued his financial support of charities and of the Presbyterian Church. She had no children. Elizabeth died on 26 July 1926 at Goodlet Street, Canterbury, and was buried in Rookwood cemetery. The serious face and determined chin shown in a photograph confirmed the words of an obituarist: 'Naturally of a shy and retiring disposition, she conquered all feelings of reserve when it was necessary to show a firm front for whatever she thought was right'. Memorial windows to both Mrs Goodlets are in the Presbyterian Church, Ashfield.

James Cameron, *Centenary History of the Presbyterian Church in NSW* (Syd 1905), pp 111-14; B. Dickey (ed), *Australian Dictionary of Evangelical Biography* (Syd, 1994); *Woollahra Messenger,* January 1893, p 168; *The Messenger,* 16 January 1903, p 346; *Ministering Women* (magazine of the NSW Women's Missionary Association) Jan 1898, p 1, Apr 1903, p 4, July 1912, p 2, Aug 1926, pp 1-3; *NSW Presbyterian,* 2 Sept 1926, p 10, 10 Oct 1929, p 82; Minutes of the General Assembly of the Presbyterian Church of NSW 1894, p 65, 1902, p 84.   JOAN MANSFIELD

GOOSEBERRY, CORA (c.1777-1852), Aboriginal woman known as 'Queen Gooseberry', was probably from the Cammeray clan, north of Sydney Harbour, daughter of a koradji or clever man. For twenty years after the death in 1830 of her husband Bungaree [q.v.1], the Broken Bay chief, she was a Sydney identity, with her trademarks a government issue blanket and headscarf and a clay pipe which she habitually smoked. When he first saw her at Brisbane Water in 1841, explorer John F. Mann [q.v.5] noted that 'she had little on beyond an old straw bonnet', but in an 1844 pencil portrait by Charles Rodius [q.v.2], she wore a modest Mother Hubbard dress. Gooseberry's mob, including Ricketty Dick, Jacky Jacky and Bowen Bungaree, camped in the street outside Sydney hotels or in the Domain, where they gave exhibitions of boomerang throwing. Her name also appears in magistrates' blanket lists in Sydney as 'Lady Bongary' or 'Mrs Gooseberry'. Boio or 'Long Dick', of the Walkeloa (Brisbane Water clan), claimed to be her son by King Bungaree.

In July 1844 the *Australian* reported that Gooseberry attended a levee at Government House, wearing her straw hat, a 'new pink robe of very curious workmanship' with 'the order of her tribe in the form of a crescent, suspended by a brass chain from her ebon neck'. She could spin a yarn as convincingly as Bungaree, telling the artist George French Angas [q.v.1] that Bungaree ruled the Sydney Aborigines at the time of the First Fleet in 1788—when he was probably a 10-year-old boy. In July 1845, in exchange for flour and tobacco, Gooseberry took Angas and the police commissioner W. A. Miles [q.v.2] on a tour of Aboriginal rock carvings at North Head and told them 'all that she had heard her father say' about the places where 'dibble dibble walk about', an inference that he had been a koradji from that region.

On 30 July 1852 Gooseberry was found dead at the Sydney Arms Hotel in Castlereagh Street, where according to press reports she had been drinking in the kitchen the previous night. The coroner returned a verdict of death from natural causes. The publican E. Borton (or Berton) paid for her burial and headstone in the Presbyterian section of the Sandhills cemetery (Central Railway). The stone was later removed to the pioneers cemetery at Botany; the epitaph has now faded, but was recorded by Mrs A. G. Foster in 1901. There are portraits of Gooseberry by Rodius, William Fernyhough, Eugène Delessert and James S. Bray. Angas's water-colour, 'Old Queen Gooseberry, Widow of Bungaree', which he had exhibited at the Egyptian Hall, London, in 1846, is held by the South Australian Museum, Adelaide. Her rum mug and a brass gorget or breastplate inscribed 'Cora Gooseberry Freeman Bungaree Queen of Sydney and Botany' are among relics in the Mitchell Library, Sydney. Another gorget, engraved 'GOOSEBERRY Queen of Sydney to South Head', is held by the Australian Museum, Sydney.

G. F. Angas, *Savage Life and Scenes in Australia and New Zealand* (Lond, 1847); A. G. Foster, *The Epitaph Book* (Syd, 1901); K. V. Smith, *King Bungaree* (Syd, 1992); Geog Soc of A'sia (NSW & Vic), *Procs,* 1883-84, p 27; *Australian* (Syd), 27 May 1844, p 299; *SMH,* 2 Aug 1852, p 3, 22 June 1900; *Truth* (Syd), 28 Aug 1910; Return of Natives, Syd, 1833-1836 (SRNSW).   KEITH VINCENT SMITH

GORDON, ANN (c.1795-1868), female factory superintendent, was born at Portsmouth, England, daughter of James King, government courier, and his wife Ann, née Ovey. Young Ann probably received some schooling. Her sister Martha married a Limerick militiaman in 1812, and on 2 May that year at St Mary's Church, Portsea, Hampshire, Ann married Robert Gordon of the 26th Limerick Militia.

After returning to Ireland Robert enlisted as a private in the 48th Regiment in June 1816. In August next year he, his wife and their two daughters arrived in Sydney. Ann's daughter Letitia, born prior to her marriage, remained in Ireland. Robert was sent to the Newcastle garrison where Ann gave birth to two children between 1820 and 1822. Following the departure of the regiment for India in 1824, the Gordons remained in the colony as settlers. Land apparently granted to them in the Burragorang Valley in 1825 was rapidly disposed of, and by 1828 Robert was employed as a storekeeper with the commissariat.

In October 1827 Ann was appointed superintendent and matron of the Female Factory at Parramatta, a place of supervision for transported women who were not assigned as servants to settlers. Also the colony's principal female penitentiary, it played an important role in the provision of medical care for the wider female convict community and was the means of enforcing moral and social standards upon both convict and destitute free women. Mrs Gordon's appointment was surprising: eight months earlier, Governor Darling [q.v.1] had requested a competent replacement from Britain for the then incumbent (Elizabeth Fulloon, later Raine) because he saw 'no chance' of finding a suitable local. Possibly Gordon had experience in handling female convicts at Newcastle. At a salary of £150 per annum, including quarters, fuel and light, she received less than her predecessor's £200, although throughout her time there she had a larger—not always cooperative—staff of two or three assistant matrons, a storekeeper, a clerk, a porteress and a gatekeeper cum constable. By 1835 there was also a midwife and several monitoresses chosen from the best-behaved women.

Gordon's administration (1827-36) coincided with the terms of governors Darling and Bourke [q.v.1]. Concerned by reports of mismanagement, Darling sought to place the institution on a firmer administrative footing and overcome problems created by inadequate resources and Colonial Office demands to economize. Gordon tried to implement policies designed to achieve the smooth running of an institution that was both a place of punishment and asylum, to maintain the health and welfare of the women, alleviate overcrowding where possible, provide some employment and encourage moral improvement. Darling commended her superintendency.

Under Bourke the numbers in the factory (later dubbed 'Gordon Villo' by the Sydney Gazette) increased alarmingly and conditions worsened. By the mid-1830s discipline had deteriorated, and reports reached London about immoral conduct by members of the matron's family, including her husband. Bourke's disabled son was rumoured to be the father of Mrs Gordon's daughter's children. In September 1836 Bourke informed his superiors that he had instituted major reforms: the factory was re-established on a prison footing and the services of Mrs Gordon terminated, although 'no blame was attached to her' and she was given a year's wages.

The Gordons remained at Parramatta. Robert held a publican's licence for 1837. Next year Ann sought unsuccessfully reappointment as matron of the factory. By the early 1840s the family had moved to Maitland. In July 1848 Ann applied for but failed to obtain the post of matron of Tarban Creek (Gladesville) Asylum. Robert died in 1863 and Ann on 6 June 1868 at East Maitland, where she was buried with Anglican rites. She was survived by three daughters and by her son Henry (1820-1910), who had attended The King's School as a day pupil (1832-36) and was later a police magistrate.

A. Salt, *These Outcast Women* (Syd, 1984); H. Weatherburn, 'The Female Factory', in J. Mackinolty and H. Radi (eds), *In Pursuit of Justice* (Syd, 1979), and The Female Factory, Parramatta 1804-1848 (B.A. Hons thesis, Univ Syd, 1978).

HILARY WEATHERBURN

GOWARD, RAYMOND SPENCER (1891-1979), chartered accountant and Australian Comforts Fund commissioner, was born on 15 February 1891 at Ashfield, Sydney, youngest of three sons of George Goward, an English-born stationer, later a dispenser, and his Australian-born wife Mary, née Mason. By 1914 Raymond was chief clerk in the Sydney accounting firm Smith, Johnson & Co.

Claiming to have 'volunteered for active service' in World War I, instead Goward became in September 1915 an honorary commissioner with the War Chests Fund (Australian Comforts Fund), a national federated philanthropic organization that provided a range of comforts, including refreshments, recreational equipment and budget accommodation, for soldiers both in the front line and on leave in Egypt, London and later France. His youth and financial skills were both beneficial to the A.C.F. After working from October 1915 in London, in September 1916 he took charge in Egypt, including Gaza and Beersheba, with the honorary rank of major from July 1918. In hospital with malaria for two months from September that year, which effectively ended his war service, he returned to Sydney in March 1919. Next year he was appointed M.B.E. for his voluntary war work.

After the war he set up his own accountancy firm with fellow A.C.F. commissioner W. F. A. Larcombe, also a public accountant. Goward married Ruby Violette Connochie at St Stephen's Presbyterian Church, Phillip Street, on 26 April 1923. Their infant son died in 1926, and Ruby died in 1932. On 12 April 1935, at the new St Stephen's Church, Macquarie Street, Goward married Daisy Louise Scott, née Methven, a divorcee.

On the outbreak of World War II, in September 1939 Goward resigned from his directorships and volunteered once more to work in an unpaid capacity for the A.C.F. His experience and expertise in the previous war was invaluable. Appointed the first A.C.F. commissioner and promoted honorary lieutenant-colonel, he sailed with the Australian Imperial Force to the Middle East in January 1940. Following eighteen months co-ordinating the efforts of the organization, he came back to Australia in July 1941, when he retired briefly from the A.C.F. He was then co-opted onto the executive in an advisory capacity, working closely with (Sir) Roy McKerihan [q.v.15]. Goward was appointed chief commissioner of the A.C.F. in Australia and the Pacific in March 1942, and spent the remainder of the war co-ordinating supplies and personnel in northern Australia, New Guinea and the south-west Pacific. Recommending him for an honour in 1942, General Sir Thomas Blamey [q.v.13] described him as a person of 'unremitting energy, even temperament and cheerful disposition'. Goward was mentioned in dispatches in October 1942 and appointed C.B.E. on 7 June 1951. A rather quiet, unassuming man who did not enjoy public speaking, he was at home behind the scenes. His recreations were golf, bridge and fishing.

In April 1943 Goward had been appointed a director of Intercolonial Investment Land & Building Co. Ltd. Later he joined the board of Australian Metropolitan Life Assurance Co. Ltd. He lived at Double Bay. Goward died on 12 June 1979 in St Luke's Hospital, Darlinghurst, and was cremated. He was survived by his wife and by a stepson and stepdaughter.

S. H. Bowden, *The History of the Australian Comforts Fund* (Syd, 1922); *SMH*, 1 Jan 1918, p 4, 21 Dec 1939, p 8, 7 June 1951, p 1; M. Oppenheimer, Volunteers in Action: Voluntary Work in Australia, 1939-1945 (Ph.D. thesis, Macquarie Univ, 1997); A663, item O150/3/10, A816/1, item 66/301/15, A2908, item H15 (NAA, Canb).   MELANIE OPPENHEIMER

GOWING, JOHN ELLIS SYMONDS (1835-1908), retailer, was born in 1835 at Cranley Hall, Eye, Suffolk, England, eldest son and one of ten children of Ellis Symonds Gowing, gentleman farmer, and his wife Charlotte, née Lanchester. With the future of farming bleak in the aftermath of the repeal of the Corn Laws, John Ellis sailed for Sydney in 1857 with £400, in an American ship, the *Commonwealth*, arriving on 25 December intending to buy farming land. His parents and siblings followed him in 1858. Although they prospered, it was not as farmers.

Gowing found work in a warehouse on the harbour front, then in retailing with David Jones [q.v.2], becoming head of the mercery department, living on the premises as retail staff did, sitting at the head of the table and carving the joint at the staff evening meal. In 1863 he opened his own drapery business in Crown Street, East Sydney. He entered into partnership on 4 November 1868 with his brother Preston Robert (1839-1900), who had been working as a storekeeper in Victoria. They set up the Mercery and Glove Depot, at 318 George Street, which John managed for £200 per annum plus half the profits of the business. A year later a new mercery warehouse, Edinburgh House, was opened at 344 George Street. On 3 May 1874 at St Peter's Church, St Peters, John married Elizabeth Andrews, a milliner from Cambridgeshire.

Two years later Preston married Mary McClelland and in 1878 he gave up his job as manager of another outfitters to work with John. When they opened a second store, at 498 George Street, opposite the Central Police Court, their youngest brother Charles Mac (1854-1932) joined them as 'dog walloper'— chasing dogs to prevent them from fouling the pavement. Gradually ladies' gloves and silk umbrellas became less important and Gowings became known as a high-class, gentlemen's outfitter. John believed in listening to his customers, treating them as he would his friends and stocking the best quality goods he could sell.

During the depression of the 1890s Gowing Bros began to advertise as a cash business, while still trying to maintain their reputation for class. In supporting local manufacture and their 'advocacy of the Australian article', they also appealed to rising nationalist sentiment. The store hoarding in 1896 described them as 'Austral clothiers, mercers, hatters'. 'Australian wool for Australian people' became one of their slogans. Mail order country customers were offered Marrickville tweeds from John Vicars [qq.v.6,12] & Co. and 'bosker' rugs manufactured expressly for Gowings in their Austral workrooms. With his full, unruly beard Gowing himself looked not unlike a typical swaggie.

Preston died on 5 January 1900 at Leura. In 1907 John arranged the transfer of the business to Preston's son Robert Preston and his own sons Preston Lanchester and Reginald Mack. John died quietly at his home, Lyndhurst, in Middleton Street, Stanmore, on 2 October 1908, survived by his wife, three daughters and five sons. After a service at All Saints', Petersham, he was buried in the Anglican section at Rookwood cemetery, where in addition to the graveside rites an 'impressive masonic service' was conducted by the worshipful master, Brother J. Rickard of the Prince Alfred Masonic Lodge, Petersham, which Gowing had helped to found.

S. Gowing, *Gone to Gowings* (Syd, 1993); *Gowings a Pictorial Review* (Syd, 2001); *SMH*, 3 Oct 1908, p 12, 6 Oct 1908, p 6.   BEVERLEY KINGSTON

GRACE, HENRY ALBERT (1885-1966), electrician and bird enthusiast, was born on 28 June 1885 at Moree, New South Wales, eldest of five children of native-born parents Albert Henry Grace, solicitor, and his wife Catherine Ruth, née Muirson. Henry worked as an electrician on shift work for the New South Wales Government Railways and Tramways for forty-five years. In 1910, however, he was in England, for on 2 August that year in the parish church at Erdington, Warwickshire, he married Deborah Watling Carter, from Norfolk. Next year he worked as an electrical switchboard attendant at Wolverhampton. Back in Sydney the family lived at Willoughby; after World War II they moved to Jannali.

Grace had first taken up his hobby of bird watching in 1917. With an old police bicycle (given to him by his father in 1896), he took the steam train south from Sydney to the (Royal) National Park, where he was an honorary ranger for twenty-seven years. During his working life he maintained a love for the bush and nature. After retiring, he devoted himself to bird watching or more precisely bird listening, for which purpose he designed his own whistles so that he might 'talk with the birds'.

From his backyard workshop, Grace painstakingly constructed a series of extraordinary instruments, fashioned from old brass tubing, wire and rubber bands. In the National Park he would test the whistles in the wild, using his own birdcall notation (said to be a cross between Morse code and shorthand) to record the songs he heard in reply. He could imitate some sixty native species with his whistles, often with such perfection that he would fool the birds themselves— they would imitate each other. Sometimes he ranged further afield, catching the train to Otford or Thirroul loaded with bicycle, whistles, firewood and supplies, and then riding into the bushland, often camping out overnight. His favourite sound was the dawn chorus: 'First the yellow robin, then the coachwhip, the currawongs, and the kookaburras. Finally the wonga-wonga and bronze-wing pigeons and orioles would join in ... The chorus only lasts about 20 minutes, but it was worth camping out all night to hear,' he said.

When his hearing became impaired, Grace built himself metal ear trumpets, which enabled him to hear the sounds he had cherished throughout his lifetime. As he aged and his memory became rusty, he would increasingly refer to his exercise books full of birdcall notation, to remind himself of the calls.

Grace visited the Minimurra falls regularly until his eightieth year, travelling by train to Wollongong, then pushing his bike thirty miles (48 km) to the reserve. He died on 4 July 1966 in hospital at Caringbah and was cremated with Anglican rites. His wife, four daughters and one son survived him. In 1999 Grace's whistles, notebooks, bicycle and a 16-mm film of him in the Royal National Park featured in an exhibition at the State Library of New South Wales, 'Sydney Eccentrics: A Celebration of Individuals in Society'.

J. Carter, *Stout Hearts and Leathery Hands* (Adel, 1968); State Library of NSW, *Sydney Eccentrics*, exhibition catalogue (Syd, 1999); *Sun-Herald* (Syd), 1 Sept 1968, p 70; *St. George and Sutherland Shire Leader*, 10 June 1999, p 11; H. Grace papers, photos, film, bird whistles, amplifiers and hearing aids (ML); Grace bicycle (Powerhouse Museum, Syd); correspondence files (ML and Powerhouse Museum L).

JENNIFER O'CALLAGHAN

GRAVE, JAMES (1848-1906), investor, was born on 15 April 1848 in London, son of William George Grave, sailmaker, and his wife Elizabeth, née Wade. The family came to Port Phillip a few months later. Educated at Scotch College and Melbourne Church of England Grammar School, James went, aged 16, to the Hokatika goldfields in New Zealand. After a period in charge of the Gippsland Steam Navigation Co. at Clydebank, Victoria, he returned to New Zealand. By the time he moved to Western Australia in 1878 he had married Irish-born Annie Ward.

Accumulating capital during the 1880s as senior partner in the firm of Grave & Smith, James invested unsuccessfully in the Yilgarn gold rush of 1888, but profited substantially from Perth suburban land during the boom of the 1890s. His partners included (Sir) Stephen Henry Parker [q.v.11] and Henry Anstey, who claimed credit for discovering the Yilgarn goldfield. They subdivided much of the future suburb of Bassendean as well as part of Claremont bordering Peppermint Grove. In 1894 Grave built Perth's finest hotel on a cliff top at Claremont. The Osborne was surmounted by a tower and turrets with panoramic views of ocean and river and surrounded by two acres (5 ha) of beautifully landscaped gardens, watered from supplies deep under the limestone cliffs and raised by a powerful electric pump.

The owner of Perth's first significant electricity generator, Grave for a time supplied neighbouring properties without charge in order to popularize the area. He also developed a waterworks and was elected to the Claremont Roads Board. Having invested in coal, timber and lime, he found himself financially embarrassed by 1898 and had to sell the Osborne Hotel and the waterworks to William Dalgety Moore [q.v.5]. Grave remained as manager until the sale of the hotel in 1901 to the Loreto Sisters as a school. Bedridden with illness for several years, he died on 4 June 1906 at Cottesloe, Perth, and was buried in the Catholic section of Karrakatta cemetery. He was survived by his wife, six sons and three daughters, two of whom entered religious orders.

His youngest daughter OCTAVIA (1890-1974), a pioneer physiotherapist, was born on 10 July 1890 in Perth and gained her certificate as a masseuse while visiting Britain during World War I. Returning to Perth she set up practice in the city in 1920, bringing an increased professionalism to the handful of established practitioners. During the next forty years she established herself as the doyen of the profession, winning the confidence of leading physicians. She was recognized by the award of the first life membership of the State branch of the Australian Physiotherapy Association. After the death of her mother in 1932 she indulged a passion for world travel. Of above average height and somewhat stooped in later life, with untidy, long hair tied back, fussy in her manner and always losing things, she was compared to 'Aunty Mame'. While travelling she would have twenty suitcases and three hatboxes and always insisted on sitting at the captain's table. She was an effervescent conversationalist who knew everyone in Perth, dropped names and talked irreverently about specialists.

A devout Catholic, Octavia was a daily communicant. Fortified by the rites of the Church, she died on 4 December 1974 and was buried in Karrakatta cemetery.

W. B. Kimberly (comp), *History of West Australia* (Melb, 1897); J. Carter, *Bassendean: A Social History 1829-1979* (Perth, 1986); G. Bolton and J. Gregory, *Claremont: A History* (Perth, 1999); *Aust J of Physiotherapy*, 21, no 1, Mar 1975, p 30; *Morning Herald* (Perth), 5 June 1906, p 5; information from Mr Justice E. Heenan.   G. C. BOLTON
                                    GERALDINE BYRNE

GRAY, ROBERT (1839-1931), military officer and pastoralist, was born on 4 February 1839 at Hughenden Manor, West Wycombe, Buckinghamshire, England, eldest of eight children of Charles Gray, clerk, later clergyman, and his wife Agnes, née Norris. Educated at Marlborough and at Brighton College, Robert joined the 97th Regiment of Foot in April 1857 as an ensign. Embarking for India, he served with the force commanded by Brigadier-General (Sir) Thomas Franks, which routed mutinous sepoys in Oudh before joining in the final recapture of Lucknow in March 1858. Gray fought in the taking of the Kaiser Bagh there. He was later adjutant of the 4th Sikh Cavalry and the 7th Bengal Cavalry. Granted six months leave, he visited Sydney in 1862. On 19 November at St Mark's Church of England, Alexandria, he married Charlotte Grayson, daughter of Rev. Wiliam Sowerby [q.v.6]. Next year Gray resigned his commission and the couple returned to Sydney.

With his cousin Ernest Henry [q.v.4], Robert sailed to Port Denison (Bowen), Queensland, then travelled inland to a cattle station that Henry had near Mount McConnel and the Burdekin River. Gray bought 1800 sheep, and entered into partnership with Henry. They then took up land in the Flinders River region, naming their station Hughenden. Lottie Gray was the first woman of British descent in the region. Over-extended financially, Henry sold his share of Hughenden to Robert's brother Charles in 1865. Charles and his first wife Lucy were at Hughenden or Glendower, an outstation principally used for cattle, most of the time from 1868 to 1876. Lucy was an energetic rider, and also left vivacious descriptions of outback travel and station life. Another brother Mowat participated in the enterprise for some years. From late 1874 to 1876 Robert took Lottie on a visit to Sydney, Goulburn and on to England.

There was a preliminary survey for a township at Hughenden in 1877. When the railway reached there in 1887 it became easier to move both wool and livestock to market. In 1891 Gray shore 80 000 sheep. Described as still 'of smart build, and of quiet, cheerful disposition' late in his Australian career, he sold out in 1911. 'Of my contemporaries in the Hughenden district none remain there', he wrote.

Robert and Lottie retired to live in England in 1912, and his *Reminiscences of India and North Queensland 1857-1912* were published next year. In them he described, almost imperturbably, battles in India; times as his own shepherd when workers found isolation and Aborigines too frightening; 'fever and ague'; lack of meat markets until the Cape River (1867) and later mineral strikes; droughts and cyclones. He was not as successful as his neighbour Robert Christison [q.v.3] in relations with Aborigines, but did for a time use South Sea Islanders as shepherds. The detail of the *Reminiscences* petered out when he reached the mid-1870s, but the book adds an extra dimension to the story of the occupation of the Flinders region.

Lottie died in February 1921; they had had no children. On 3 August that year at St Dominic's Catholic Church, St Pancras, London, the widower married 41-year old Jane McBreen. Robert Gray died on 24 March 1931 at Kensington, London. The funeral took place at Godmanchester, Huntingdonshire. His estate was sworn for probate at £14 235.

G. B. Malleson (ed), *Kaye's and Malleson's History of the Indian Mutiny of 1857-8* (Lond, 1888-89); J. B. Burke, *A Genealogical and Heraldic History of the Colonial Gentry*, 2 (Lond, 1895); J. Black, *North Queensland Pioneers* (Townsville, Qld, 1932?); D. F. and J. Erricker (comps), *Official Souvenir of the Centenary of Settlement in Hughenden and District 1863-1963* (Hughenden, Qld, 1963); A. Allingham, *Taming the Wilderness*, 2nd ed (Townsville, Qld, 1978); *Pastoralists' Review*, Nov 1906, p 755, Dec 1906, p 837; *Cummins and Campbell's Monthly Mag,*

Oct 1934, p 83; *Qld Heritage*, 1, no 1, Nov 1964, p 11; 1, no 2, May 1965, p 17; *The Times* (Lond), 26 Mar 1931, p 16.   S. J. ROUTH

GREEN, ALEXANDER (c.1802-1855+), flogger and public executioner, was born in the Netherlands, son of a travelling circus performer. At Shrewsbury Quarter Sessions on 16 January 1824 he was sentenced to be 'transported for the term of his natural life' for stealing a 'piece of brown stuff from a shop'. His indent read: 'Native Place: Holland; Calling: Tumbler; Age: 22; Height: 5 ft 4½ ins [163.8 cm]; Complexion: Pale, pitted; Hair: Flax; Eyes: Lt Blue'. He reached Sydney in the *Countess of Harcourt* on 12 July 1824.

Lodged in Hyde Park barracks, Green was assigned briefly to William Hutchinson, then Samuel Marsden [q.v.2]. He received a conditional pardon in May 1825, worked intermittently as an official scourger at the barracks and Sydney gaol, as a labourer and honorary constable at Port Stephens, and eventually as assistant to Harry Stain, the hangman. When Stain died in January 1828 Green became public executioner of Sydney Town and the colony of New South Wales at £15 14s. 2d. per annum plus accommodation within Sydney gaol.

Over the next twenty-seven years Green officiated at the public execution of almost 490 people, including six women. More than 70 per cent of these were carried out in his first ten years, when harsh penal policies prevailed: under Governor Darling he hanged 170 people in 3 years 10 months, under Bourke 183 in 6 years. But under Gipps it was 10 in 8 years and under FitzRoy [qq.v.1] 27 in 8 years 6 months. The last, shortly after Denison [q.v.4] arrived in January 1855, was the first under the Act banning public executions.

Most of Green's hangings were carried out at the rear of Sydney gaol, on a high, wooden platform visible to crowds in the Rocks. On thirty-seven occasions, almost all before 1840, four or more prisoners were executed together, the largest group being eleven men in October 1828. Other notable executions were of ten bushrangers in Bathurst in November 1830, thirteen convict mutineers over two days on Norfolk Island in September 1834, seven stockmen hanged in December 1838 for the Myall Creek massacre and the Aborigines Broger and Dundalli [qq.v.].

In classic 'Bloody Code' tradition, thirty-two of those executed by Green had their bodies 'given over for dissection', to be 'anatomised' by the surgeons. The bodies of two men executed at Goulburn Plains in November 1831 were 'hung in chains', until Bourke ordered their burial in 1833. Despite several 'botched' executions, 'the finisher of the law'

appears to have been a competent hangman. He was strong, and skilled with ropes and mechanical drops and at assessing his victims. Notwithstanding occasional reports that prisoners 'died hard', or that Green swaggered and strutted, most executions went off routinely.

Green associated with warders, criminals, ex-convicts and the lower orders generally. He had several minor brushes with the law, some of which involved incidents with women, but apparently he never married. He was instantly recognizable, having a livid scar down the side of his face, the result of an axe attack by a prisoner in December 1830. On 26 January 1831, his original sentence having been commuted to seven years, he became free. With the opening of Darlinghurst gaol in July 1841, Green moved into a small tenement on ground later known as Green Park, though whether it was named after him or an alderman is not clear. Most executions were now outside the main gate, the most famous being that of John Knatchbull [q.v.2] in February 1844.

From the mid-1840s Green, by now earning just over £60 a year, was in growing disfavour with the authorities for intoxication, insolence and mental instability. In early May 1855 the colonial secretary (Sir) Edward Deas Thomson [q.v.2] ordered him committed to the Tarban Creek Lunatic Asylum. Nothing further is known; the relevant records are missing.

P. N. Grabosky, *Sydney in Ferment* (Canb, 1977); R. and R. Beckett, *Hangman: The Life and Times of Alexander Green, Public Executioner to the Colony of New South Wales* (Melb, 1980); M. Sturma, *Vice in a Vicious Society* (Brisb, 1983); New South Wales Death Sentence Register, Nov. 1839-Nov. 1968 (NSW Dept of Prisons, nd), Dept of Corrective Services Archives, Long Bay, NSW; *Australian*, 13 June 1828, 21, 28 Apr, 26 June, 30 Sept, 21, 31 Oct 1829, 15 July, 18 Nov 1831, 15 Feb 1844 and 26 Apr 1845; New South Wales Capital Punishment Database 1788-1955 (created and held by author, Univ Syd).
          K. K. MACNAB

GREEN, ANNE SYRETT (1858-1936), welfare worker and evangelist, was born on 2 December 1858 at Brunswick, Melbourne, sixth child of London-born parents Henry Green, butcher, and his wife Emma Rebecca, née Syrett. Annie was educated at the Presbyterian Common School and attended Brunswick Baptist Church.

In 1877 the family moved to South Australia, where she worshipped at Stepney Christian Church. She became a volunteer with the Adelaide City Mission, an interdenominational, Protestant institution, offered English lessons to the Chinese community and assisted working-class mothers at the mission hall in Light Square. In 1881 Green was appointed to a staff position at the A.C.M. She was innovative and charismatic, recruiting other women as volunteer helpers and organizing new activities such as nightly 'rescue work' among prostitutes, a 'flower mission' at the Adelaide Hospital and a Dorcas Society to provide clothing for the poor. She also proved to be hard to control and intolerant of close supervision.

Green was briefly given general oversight of the whole mission, and ran it with the help of 'twelve lady volunteers' in 1887. When another missionary was employed in 1888, Green resigned to take up work as the secretary of the Young Women's Christian Association. Without her, the mission languished and volunteers fell away. She rejoined the mission late in 1890, but resigned again next year to tour rural South Australia for the Bible Christian Church, with Ruth Nesbit (later McDowell), half-sister of Edward Paris Nesbit [q.v.11] and formerly a city missionary with the Baptist Church. The Wesleyan Methodist Conference engaged Annie and Ruth as travelling evangelists in 1894.

In 1897 Green set up a branch of the A.C.M. in Sussex Street, a working-class area of North Adelaide. She established Bible classes, savings clubs, mothers' meetings, clubs for boys and girls, and basketball and cricket clubs, and held regular evangelistic services. In addition she gave direct help following house-to-house visits, including counselling, emergency assistance and finding employment. From 1905, when she presented a well-received paper to the first interstate conference of city missions, she began to establish a wider reputation for welfare work. She was appointed a justice of the peace in February 1916.

Tensions with the A.C.M. committee remained. Green was impatient of formal accounting procedures and of any supervision (especially from the male superintendent), which she saw as 'dictatorship'. The committee was reluctant to pay her more than a minimal salary. In 1911 and 1917 she resigned; each time she was persuaded to return, on the promise of 'a free hand' in running Sussex Street. In 1921, unable to find a male missionary for the work in Light Square, the A.C.M. decided to hand responsibility for much of the programme there to the Salvation Army. Anonymous correspondents in the daily press, probably close associates of Green's, condemned this move, and noted the 'magnificent work' carried on by her, in contrast to the 'decadent' parent mission.

Miss Green was appointed superintendent of the entire mission in 1923. The arrangement with the Salvation Army was terminated, and she moved back to Light Square, instituting various clubs and offering services to the factory workers nearby. The Sussex Street premises became an A.C.M. hostel for Aboriginal women and children visiting Adelaide.

As the Depression began to bite, Green was approached by the premier (Sir) Richard Layton Butler [q.v.7] to assist with accommodation for homeless men in winter and for general discussion of welfare needs. She oversaw extensive relief work, some in co-operation with the government. Also approached by the Welfare Department to run some of their services, she refused after 1930 because she felt that government control would impair the mission's independence.

Tall and erect, Green dressed with elegant severity and was an impressive figure. She died on 14 April 1936 at her home at Kingswood and was buried in Mitcham cemetery.

E. Green, *Evergreen Annie* (Adel, 1988); Adelaide City Mission records (SLSA).   JULIE-ANN ELLIS

GREENHAM, ELEANOR CONSTANCE (1874-1957), medical practitioner, was born on 15 April 1874 at Ipswich, Queensland, second child and only daughter of John Greenham, an English-born draper, and his wife Eleanor, née Johnstone, from Ireland. John later established a general store, Greenhams Pty Ltd, in the business centre at Ipswich. Ella attended Ipswich Central Girls' and Infants' School then Brisbane Girls' Grammar School, where she won the English and the natural history prizes. On 1 February 1892 she was the first pupil to be enrolled at Ipswich Girls' Grammar School. There she won the silver medal for the top girl in science and four other prizes. Passing the senior public examination next year and winning six more prizes, she proceeded to advanced studies for university entrance.

In 1895 Greenham went to Women's College within the University of Sydney (M.B., Ch.M., 1901), entering the faculty of arts as a necessary preliminary to her medical studies. She was the first Queensland-born woman to graduate in medicine. Registered to practise in Brisbane on 2 May 1901 as medical practitioner no.711, she began work as resident medical officer at the Lady Bowen [q.v.] Hospital, Brisbane, probably becoming the first woman to receive a residential position in a Queensland hospital. Choosing to work in private practice, in 1903 she took rooms in City Chambers, Queen and Edward Streets, Brisbane, moving in 1907 to 284 Edward Street. Although she met opposition from some male colleagues, her bright personality and attentive care gradually attracted patients and she built up a successful practice.

Greenham was dedicated to her profession and, like many early medical women, she did not marry. She was an accomplished pianist, enjoyed attending the theatre and visiting flower shows, and was described as 'a large lady, fond of flowing, floral garments'; at the lady mayoress's 'At Home' in 1904 she wore an Assam silk gown and a hat of blue chiffon. One of the earliest female car-owners in Queensland, she drove a Darracq in 1907 and later a Hupmobile. Indeed, she became a shareholder in the Hupmobile agency, Evers Motor Co. Ltd, Brisbane. She also became chairman of directors of Greenhams Pty Ltd.

In 1945 the Queensland Medical Women's Society elected her to honorary membership for her contribution to women's health and in 1953 she was made honorary member of the British Medical Association (Queensland Branch) for fifty years uninterrupted membership. In her eightieth year she retired to 85 Oxlade Drive, New Farm, but she continued to treat her old patients.

Greenham was a pioneer and a skilful, caring doctor. By her persistence and expertise, she swept away difficulties and opposition, helping to shape the future for women in medicine in Queensland. She died on 31 December 1957 at New Farm and was cremated with Anglican rites.

L. M. Williams, 'A Pioneer not a Traditionalist: The Life and Work of Dr Eleanor Greenham', *RHSQJ*, 15, no 1, Feb 1993, p 26; *Courier-Mail*, 13 Dec 1890, p 5, 11 Mar 1904, p 6; Ipswich Girls' Grammar School archives, Women's College, Univ Syd Archives, Qld Medical Women's Society Archives, AMA Archives, Brisb.   LESLEY WILLIAMS

GRIFFITH, MARY HARRIETT (1849-1930), philanthropist, was born on 4 November 1849 at Portishead, Somerset, England, third of five children of Rev. Edward Griffith, Congregational minister, and his wife Mary, née Walker, and older sister of (Sir) Samuel Griffith [q.v.9]. After Edward accepted a call from the Colonial Missionary Society to found a Congregational Church at Ipswich, New South Wales (Queensland), the family reached Moreton Bay on 6 March 1854. In a pioneer region, they endured harsh conditions.

Life was hardly easier at West Maitland, where Griffith was appointed in 1857. Their home was flooded three times—on one occasion Mary and her father narrowly escaped drowning. In 1860 he was called to Wharf Street Congregational Church, Brisbane. The family home was Weymouth, opposite the church, where Mary was a Sunday School teacher for over fifty years. She was, as well, a life deaconess.

At first educated by their aunt Lydia Walker, after her return to England in 1865 Mary and two younger sisters attended the Misses Rhodes' School. The eldest daughter,

Mary did not marry but cared for her parents. In 1885 she accompanied them on a year-long trip to Britain. Their health failing, they and she moved to Strathmore at New Farm, a Brisbane river suburb. Edward died in September 1891 and his wife the following April.

Mary immersed herself in good works. She joined the Woman's Christian Temperance Union and became founding secretary of the Brisbane Benevolent Society, which helped people in distress following floods in south-east Queensland in 1893. She was honorary secretary (vice-president 1912-28) of the committee of Lady Musgrave Lodge, a home for nurses and single female immigrants. As Queensland representative for the Travellers' Aid Society, she maintained contact with the British Women's Emigration League. She served on the ladies' management committee of the Hospital for Sick Children in 1894-1924.

In 1899 the Young Women's Christian Association of Brisbane was re-formed; Mary was president (1902-12), honorary president to 1921, then honorary life president. She was vice-president of the Queensland division of the British (Australian) Red Cross Society during World War I and in 1921 patroness of St David's Welsh Society of Queensland—Sir Samuel had been founding patron in 1918. Other organizations to which she contributed her intelligence and energy were the National Council of Women, the Brisbane City Mission, the Queensland auxiliary of the London Missionary Society, the British and Foreign Bible Society, the Queensland Women's Electoral League, the Protestant Federation, the United Sudan Mission and the Charity Organisation Society. In 1911 she was appointed a lady of grace of the Order of the Hospital of St John of Jerusalem and was invested at Government House, Brisbane.

Miss Griffith was a well-known figure in Brisbane, walking to engagements dressed in a long, black gown, with sleeves to her wrists, wearing a bonnet tied with ribbons under her chin, long out of fashion. Her hair was rolled into a neat bun. 'She was never idle. Whether in public or on short train journeys, or in private, she was always knitting or sewing.' A small woman, she appeared frail, but pursued her ideals with determination and strength. She was a gifted writer who contributed articles to church magazines, often anonymously, and compiled a tribute to her father, *Memorials of the Rev. Edward Griffith* (Brisbane, 1892). She disapproved of the worldly ways of her brother.

In 1922 Mary moved into the Aged Christian Women's Home, at New Farm, which she had helped to establish. In 1927 she laid the foundation stone for the new hall at Wharf Street Congregational Church. She had been healthy all her life and only complained of feeling unwell shortly before she died on 27 July 1930 at New Farm. She was buried with Congregational forms in Toowong cemetery.

R. B. Joyce, *Samuel Walker Griffith* (Brisb, 1984); A. Gillespie, *Widening Horizons: The YWCA in Queensland 1888-1988* (Brisb, 1995); *Brisb Courier*, 13 Dec 1911, p 11, 10 July 1925, p 17, 2 May 1927, p 14, 29 July 1930, p 18; C. Lassell, Miss Mary Griffith (ms, 1950, copy in ADB file); L. Cazalar, The Other Griffith—Mary Harriett (ms, nd, copy in ADB file); Griffith family papers (OL).

ALINE GILLESPIE

GRIFFITHS, WALTER (1867-1900), mining investor and politician, was born on 4 July 1867 at Kent Town, Adelaide, son of Frederick Griffiths, a well-to-do ironmonger, and his wife Helen, née Giles. After attending St Aloysius College, Sevenhills, and the Collegiate School of Saint Peter, Adelaide, at 15 Walter joined his uncle William K. Griffiths, a storekeeper with interests in mining, at Yam Creek in the Northern Territory. Walter was a protégé of mining investor and importer V. L. Solomon [q.v.12], becoming his partner in mining ventures in the territory and in the Kimberley, Kalgoorlie and Coolgardie goldfields, Western Australia. They owned the *Northern Territory Times* and he helped Solomon to produce an influential *Guide to the W.A. Goldfields*, becoming a prominent member of the Kalgoorlie Chamber of Mines.

On his uncle's death in 1892, Walter took over the business, retaining his association with Solomon, who in 1890 had become one of the two members for the Northern Territory in the South Australian House of Assembly. In 1893 Griffiths successfully stood with Solomon, at the age of 25 becoming the youngest member. He held the seat until his death. As member for the Territory he was famous for his travels, twice overlanding from the railhead at Marree to Palmerston, and visiting other remote areas by camel and horse. He also travelled to Hong Kong and Japan and published a pamphlet, *The Empires of the East* (Adelaide, 1895).

Griffiths achieved a moment of national fame in the Federation cause following the agitation on the goldfields for Western Australia to join the Commonwealth. He worked with South Australian Federationists, including P. M. Glynn, C. C. Kingston and (Sir) Josiah Symon [qq.v.9,12], to advise and encourage the Eastern Goldfields Reform League, formed in December 1899 following the Western Australian government's refusal to hold a referendum. The league gathered signatures for a giant petition to be presented to Queen Victoria seeking 'separation for federation'—the creation of a State, 'Auralia', which would join the federation. Griffiths was elected to the league's executive and chosen to take the petition to London in early 1900, to support the Australian delegates and lobby the British government to either agree to separation or force Western Australia to join.

Although the British colonial secretary Joseph Chamberlain refused to see him, Griffiths generated a persistent and strongly worded correspondence claiming that the petitioners were 'justly incensed' at being prevented from presenting their case. (Sir) Edmund Barton, Alfred Deakin [qq.v.7,8] and Kingston publicly expressed their gratitude for the support he gave to their efforts to prevent the British government from amending the Commonwealth of Australia Constitution bill. Kingston congratulated him 'on the courageous and tactful manner in which you represented the interest of Westralian Federationists and Separationists'. Griffiths left London only after Chamberlain had advised him that Sir John Forrest [q.v.8] had conceded and Western Australians would vote on the question of entry into the Commonwealth. While in Britain he had also made representations to the War Office on fortifications at Darwin and military horse-breeding opportunities in the Territory.

Arriving home in late June, Griffiths reported that 'the petition of separation had achieved all that was desired'. But a few weeks after his return he was diagnosed with typhoid fever. He was in Wakefield Hospital for some weeks during the parliamentary sittings, and although described as having great 'strength and splendid physique', a shocked House was told on 4 September 1900 that he had died that day. A bachelor and an active and convivial member, he was praised by obituarists for his 'genial character' and 'true patriotism'. There were many dignitaries at his funeral and representatives from the Darwin-Adelaide overland telegraph operators and the Stragglers Cricket Club, for whom he had played.

J. L. Parsons (ed), *History of Adelaide and Vicinity* (Adel, 1901); H. Coxon et. al., *The Biographical Register of the South Australian Parliament 1857-1957* (Adel, 1985); *PD* (HA, SA), 5 Sept 1900, p 449; *Register* (Adel), 23 June 1900, 5 Sept 1900, p 6; *Advertiser* (Adel), 5 Sept 1900, p 6; *Observer* (Adel), 8 Sept 1900, p 16; *Western Argus*, 13 Sept 1900, p 37.

J. C. BANNON

GRIFFITHS LLOYD, JESSIE MARY; *see* LLOYD

GRIMSTONE, MARY LEMAN (1796?-1869), author and feminist, was born either in England or in the German city-state of Hamburg, one of at least five children of Leman Thomas Rede, bibliographer of early Americana. Two of Mary's brothers—Leman

Thomas Tertius Rede (1799-1832) and William Leman Rede (1802-1847)—won esteem on the London stage, and two sisters—Lucy and Louisa—shared some of her literary skill. Mary published verse of fair quality from about 1815 and her first novel, *The Beauty of the British Alps*, in 1825. By then she had married a man named Grimstone, who probably died soon afterwards. Perhaps this episode heightened the nervous stress that recurrently beset her. Late in 1825 she embarked for Hobart Town, accompanying her sister Lucy and the latter's husband Stephen Adey [q.v.1], an official with the Van Diemen's Land Co. It seems likely that during the voyage and immediately after she composed her second novel, *Louisa Egerton: A Tale of Real Life* (London, 1829). If so, this appears to have been the first such work of Australian provenance.

Mary continued to write—good verse prompted by the local scene, an essay (which gained some local notoriety) bemoaning the colony's lack of cultural and social amenity and *Woman's Love*, traditionally joined with Henry Savery's [q.v.2] *Quintus Servinton* as the first Australian novels. In 1829 Mary returned to Britain. *Woman's Love* was published in 1832, with a postscript which advanced feminist ideas in much the same terms as had Mary Wollstonecraft. Grimstone's best novels were *Character: Or Jew and Gentile* (1833), in which a protagonist appears to be modelled on the author in physique and feminist-radical ideology, and *Cleone: A Tale of Married Life* (1834). Only a few Tasmanian references appear throughout these novels.

About 1836 Mary married William Gillies, a wealthy corn merchant; but this marriage did not flourish. 'Mrs Gillies' appeared in Leigh Hunt's poem 'Blue-Stocking Revels' (1837), in terms suggesting that Hunt found her didacticism tedious. Among her associates within London's radical intelligentsia were Caroline Norton, Robert Owen, W. J. Linton and Elizabeth Gaskell, and Mary may have been the model for Alfred (Lord) Tennyson's Lady Psyche in *The Princess* (London, 1847). Her essays and verse continued to appear in various magazines, such as the Unitarian *Monthly Repository*, whose editor W. J. Fox ranked Mary with Jane Austen.

Mary retained an interest in Australia, her pen sometimes espousing colonial sympathies and loyalties. To some degree she presented colonial experience in terms of nationalist concepts as currently expounded by Mazzini and others. In 1832 her sister Louisa had married Alexander Goldie [q.v.1], then an employee of the Van Diemen's Land Co., and subsequently spent thirty years in Tasmania and thirty more in Victoria. Adela Lucy Leman, second daughter of the Adeys, who returned to Britain in 1837, married the eminent physician (Sir) William Jenner. The Jenners retained ties with Mary as she entered an apparently poor and sad older age. Predeceased by her husband, Mary Gillies died, after swallowing disinfectant, on 4 November 1869 at Paddington, London.

E. M. Miller, *Pressmen and Governors* (Syd, 1952); P. Clarke, *Pen Portraits* (Syd, 1988); M. Roe, 'Mary Leman Grimstone (1800-1850?): For Women's Rights and Tasmanian Patriotism', Tas Hist Research Assn, *Papers and Procs*, 36, no 1, Mar 1989, p 9, and 'Mary Leman Grimstone and her Sisters', Tas Hist Research Assn, *Papers and Procs*, 42, no 1, Mar 1995, p 36.   MICHAEL ROE

GROSSE, FREDERICK (1828-1894), engraver and vigneron, was born in February 1828 at Aschersleben, Prussia, son of Tibertus Andrew Arristoft Grosse, founder, and his wife Dorothea, née Hensher. Frederick arrived in Adelaide in January 1854, departing a few days later for Victoria. After a year on the Sandhurst (Bendigo) goldfields he set up business in Melbourne as a designer and woodengraver. At his home in Flinders Lane on 6 November 1856 he married with Lutheran rites Caterina Sophia Henriette Hachmann, née Hanstein, a German-born widow. They were to have four children, three of whom died in childhood.

Grosse had mixed success in business, mainly producing woodblocks for illustrated periodicals that rarely ran for long. His earliest recorded work was in the first issue of *Melbourne Punch* on 2 August 1855, after which he engraved illustrations for the *Newsletter of Australasia*, the *Illustrated Melbourne News* and the *Illustrated Australian Mail*. Yet he was optimistic concerning the future of graphic journalism in the young colony, being a partner with the publisher William Detmold and the artist-illustrator Nicholas Chevalier [q.v.3] as proprietors of the *Illustrated Melbourne News*, which ran for six weeks at the beginning of 1858. The most likely cause of failure was a lack of capital, compounded by an ambitious weekly publication schedule given Victoria's small, decentralized population.

Engaged to engrave the punches for two series of Victorian postage stamps, Grosse produced the Beaded Ovals series (1860) and the Laureated series (1863-67). Also at this time, he and Rudolph Jenny, possibly an employee, developed what seems to have been a woodblock stereotype process known as 'Bismuthography'. This was patented on 16 February 1861 but there were no commercial applications. In 1862-68 Grosse's engraving work for illustrated periodicals expanded with the launching of the *Illustrated Melbourne Post* and the *Illustrated Australian News*. His monogram appeared on many illustrations in both these monthly papers. A new prosperity was reflected by his 1864 purchase of Tooronga Vineyard on Emu Creek, Strathfieldsaye, near Bendigo, after having sold a vineyard he had planted in 1857 at Thomastown.

On 11 June 1868 Grosse was appointed supernumerary wood-engraver to the Government Printing Office. He subsequently produced hundreds of engravings for government publications, most notably R. B. Smyth's [q.v.6] *The Goldfields and Mineral Districts of Victoria* (1869) and *The Aborigines of Victoria* (1878). Grosse was given a permanent appointment on 1 July 1877, but lost his position six months later in the Berry [q.v.3] government's 'Black Wednesday' dismissal of sections of the public service.

Grosse then became a full-time vigneron. In May 1881 he expanded upon his operation by opening Bendigo Wine Cellars in Melbourne. His wines won prizes at colonial, intercolonial and international wine shows, and he displayed further entrepreneurial flair in 1889 when he engaged a German-trained wine-maker Maurice Steiner, from Hungary, to manage his vineyard. In the early 1890s Grosse bought the adjoining Emu Vineyard, giving him a total holding of sixty-eight acres (27.5 ha) under vine; he became the largest grape grower in the Bendigo district.

His wife died in 1887. In December 1893 he found *Phylloxera vasatrix* in his vineyard, the first discovery of the disease in the district; his vines were uprooted in early 1894. The experience told heavily and, after a short illness, Grosse died of influenza and pneumonia on 4 October that year at St Kilda and was buried in St Kilda cemetery. One daughter survived him.

M. Mahood, *The Loaded Line* (Melb, 1973); G. Kellow, *The Stamps of Victoria* (Melb, 1990); J. Kerr (ed), *The Dictionary of Australian Artists* (Melb, 1992); D. Dunstan, *Better than Pommard!* (Melb, 1994); *Aust Vigneron and Fruit-Growers' Journal*, no 4, 1893, p 124, no 7, 1894, p 110; *Advertiser* (Bendigo), 8 Oct 1894, p 3; P. A. Dowling, Chronicles of Progress: The Illustrated Newspapers of Colonial Australia, 1853-1896 (Ph.D. thesis, Monash Univ, 1997).   PETER A. DOWLING

GROVER, JESSIE (1843-1906), journalist and sericulturist, was born on 9 June 1843 in Melbourne, youngest of four children of William McGuire, innkeeper, and his wife Elizabeth Jane, née Price. William's father Peter John had been a marine sergeant transported to Van Diemen's Land for highway robbery. When William died in 1844 the freehold and licence of the Red Lion Inn in Lonsdale Street, Melbourne, passed to his widow. She leased the inn in 1848, but continued to

conduct a boarding-house. Jessie was sent to live with an uncle, Patrick McGuire, who operated the Emu Inn and McGuire's punt (Shepparton) at the Goulburn River. It was probably there that she met Harry Ehret Grover, an Eton-educated Englishman, who had migrated in 1851 and had been a police trooper at Shepparton. Harry and Jessie married on 28 January 1869 in St James's Church of England, Melbourne.

In 1873 Jessie and her friend Mrs Sara Florentia Bladen-Neill decided that congenial work could be provided for women if a silk production industry was established. They formed the Victorian Ladies' Sericultural Co. Ltd, with Jessie as managing director. The company articles specified that 'No person but a woman shall be eligible as a Director'. Prominent Melbourne women took up most of the £4 shares. The government made a grant of 600 acres (242.8 ha) of hilly land at Harcourt, near the Mount Alexander diggings, where bluestone buildings were erected and thousands of mulberry trees planted. The surveyor had fixed on the wrong location, however, and the enterprise collapsed after several years of intensive effort.

Jessie's mother died in 1879, leaving most of her estate to her daughters. Jessie and Harry were now able to buy a large house at St Kilda and live mainly from their investments. Harry contributed humorous items to *Melbourne Punch*. Jessie was social editor of the *Melbourne Bulletin* in 1880-86 and Australian correspondent for the *Queen* (London). She covered events at Government House, garden parties, charity bazaars and a few scandals in a human and personal style, later to become the hallmark of her son Montague's [q.v.9] mass-circulation newspapers. She wrote under various pseudonyms such as 'Gladys', 'Iris', 'Humming Bee' and 'Queen Bee'. A photograph of her in the 1880s showed her to be plump and forceful. Harry bought a racehorse, named it Jessie, but failed in an attempt to win the Melbourne Cup.

The Grovers lost most of their assets in the bank crash of 1893 and were forced to move into hotel rooms. Jessie spent much time in charitable work: cooking cheap food for penniless families living in shanties on the St Kilda foreshore and collecting clothing for them. She died of cancer on 17 March 1906 at St Kilda and was buried in Melbourne general cemetery, survived by her son. Several of his descendants continued the connection with journalism. The bluestone ruins of the silk enterprise have been nominated for inclusion in the Register of the National Estate.

M. Cannon (ed), *Hold Page One* (Main Ridge, Vic, 1993); *Age* (Melb), 19 Nov 1873; *Sun* (Syd), 13 Feb 1911, 2 Apr 1911, 27 Aug 1911; Montague Grover papers (NLA).   MICHAEL CANNON

GUEST, THOMAS BIBBY (1830-1908), biscuit manufacturer, was born on 15 November 1830 at Chester, Cheshire, England, fifth of eleven children of William Sellar Guest, tanner, and his wife Ann, née Bibby. In May 1852 Thomas and his father reached Sydney in the *Salacia*. They began making biscuits and after a few years moved to Melbourne. In William Street from 1856 Barnes, Guest & Co. manufactured biscuits, using steam power and employing six people. The firm was T. B. Guest & Co. from 1858. On 15 November 1861 at St Mary's Church of England, North Melbourne, Thomas married London-born Jemima Campbell. They had thirteen children.

From the 1870s the business, with others in the family involved, expanded and won awards at international exhibitions in London, at Philadelphia, United States of America, and in Melbourne. By 1883 Guest employed ninety men working under nine hours a day and produced £30 000 worth of biscuits a year. With the increase of demand in Melbourne, the firm had little export trade and Guest resented the duty on imported machinery; the local engineering industry could not meet his requirements. The costs of automated equipment slowed growth for a time, but profitability was so high that he soon enlarged the William Street premises. In 1897 Guest took advantage of lower land prices to buy a site at North Melbourne on which he built a factory, enlarged in 1907 to a five-storeyed building. T. B. Guest & Co. Pty Ltd was incorporated in Victoria in 1898, Thomas having purchased the undertaking from the family partners for £79 995. The family firm needed massive injections of capital.

Thomas Guest had exceptional business ability; he found little to interest him outside biscuit making and the organization of the company. Remaining actively associated with the firm until his death, he refused all entreaties to enter public life. In Melbourne he lived at Cestria, Glenferrie Road, Hawthorn. He also owned Bona Vista farm at Warragul, where the horses for the company's travellers' buggies and wagons were raised and rested. He gave generously but inconspicuously to charities. Guest died on 3 April 1908 at his home and was buried in Melbourne general cemetery with Anglican rites, leaving an estate sworn for probate at £64 722. His wife and three sons and four daughters survived him.

For many years associated with Sulina Sutherland's [q.v.6] philanthropic work, Jemima Guest (d.1925) was sometime president of the Sutherland Homes for Orphaned Neglected and Destitute Children and of the Hawthorn Ladies' Benevolent Society. She was also a committee member of the Hawthorn branch of St Martin's Boys' Home. Guest's sons Thomas Bibby junior (1866-1933) and Edgar Leopold (1854-1936) continued the business, then a grandson, Edgar Leopold Gordon (Leo) Guest (1903-1963), became chairman. The company merged with William Arnott [q.v.3] (Holdings) Pty Ltd in November 1962, with Guest family members continuing to serve on the board of the extended company. It was by then a pale imitation of the great Australian companies that had flourished in the late nineteenth century.

Victoria and Its Metropolis, 2 (Melb, 1888); V. Burgmann and J. Lee (eds), *Making a Life* (Melb, 1988); Tariff: Report of the Royal Commission, *PP* (LA, Vic) vol 4, paper no 50; *Age* (Melb), 4 Apr 1908, p 13, 4 Sept 1963, p 3; *Argus* (Melb), 4 Apr 1908, p 17, 1 Sept 1925, p 10, 23 Oct 1933, p 8; T. G. Parsons, Some Aspects of the Development of Manufacturing in Melbourne, 1870-1890, Ph.D. thesis, Monash Univ, 1970; T. B. Guest & Co. papers (Univ Melb Archives).   J. ANN HONE

H

HALL, GEORGE FREDERICK EMANUEL (1891-1972), engineer, was born on 19 October 1891 at Charters Towers, Queensland, third of six children of George Hall, an African West Indian from Tobago who worked on the goldfields as a carter, and his English-born wife Annie Elizabeth, née Collett. Young George attended Richmond Hill State School and received a state bursary to attend Townsville Grammar School, where he was cricket captain, senior gymnast, an outstanding footballer, shooter and swimmer and athletics champion three years in a row. He was also head prefect and the school's best scholar. When Hall was presented with the governor's cup for good service and 'honourable powers of leadership', the headmaster Percy Rowland [q.v.11] commented, 'He has triumphed over prejudice by sheer merit; whatever will be his future, he can always look back on his years with us as years of uninterrupted success'. Hall won a bursary to the Charters Towers School of Mines but instead became North Queensland's first Rhodes scholar in 1910. A public subscription raised funds for his passage to Britain and a purse of sovereigns.

Taking up residence in Lincoln College, Oxford (B.A., 1913), to read medicine, Hall changed to engineering science and graduated with second-class honours. Finding employment with the Scottish firm of Andrew Barclay & Sons, which manufactured industrial locomotives, he remained there for most of World War I. He enlisted in the Royal Air Force on 10 May 1918. When the war ended he was at a flying training depot and was repatriated to Australia in April 1919 as a second lieutenant.

After working with the New South Wales Cement, Lime & Coal Co. at Kandos, about 1926 Hall moved to Sydney to begin a thirty-year working association with the Main Roads Board of New South Wales (Department of Main Roads). He began as an assistant engineer and was promoted acting class 2 engineer in the construction branch in 1928. In 1935-37 he worked in various country divisions before returning to Sydney to work in the design branch of the metropolitan division. In 1951 Hall was promoted supervising engineer. With six engineers under him, he was involved in main roads expenditure in thirty-one local government councils comprising metropolitan Sydney as well as the maintenance of roads directly cared for by the department.

Hall's engineering reports and exceptional command of English made colleagues believe his academic background was in letters, not engineering. His fondness for sport continued for most of his life: at the age of 40 he lined up for the professional officers' tug-of-war team at their annual picnic. At 48 he was a renowned 'demon' bowler in the Moore Park A grade cricket competition.

Yet covert racism was evident in Hall's sluggish promotion through the engineering ranks at the department, despite his colleagues believing him capable of greater things. He was a handsome man, of medium height, but he told workmates that, because his 'ancestry would be a barrier', he decided never to marry. After retiring as supervising engineer in 1957 he lived at Homebush. He died on 15 July 1972 at Parramatta District Hospital and was cremated with Anglican rites.

A. McKay, *Percy Fritz Rowland* (Townsville, Qld, 1974); *A Register of Rhodes Scholars, 1903-1981* (Oxford, 1981); K. Allen, *History of the Townsville Grammar School* (Townsville, Qld, 1990); *Evening Telegraph* (Charters Towers, Qld), 5 Mar 1910, 9 July 1910, p 5; *Nth Qld Register*, 8 March 1910, p 5, 11 July 1910.
MICHAEL BRUMBY

HAM, NATHANIEL BURNETT ('BERTIE') (1865-1954), physician and public health administrator, was born on 13 June 1865 at Smythesdale, Victoria, fifth of nine children of David Ham, an English-born sharebroker and member of the Legislative Council, and his wife Mary, née Jones, from Ireland. 'Bertie', as he was known from childhood, was educated at Grenville College, Ballarat, and Wesley College, Melbourne. After studying arts at the University of Melbourne in 1887-88, he was apprenticed to Cornell & King, chemists of Ballarat, and registered as a pharmacist in 1890. He then enrolled in medicine at Melbourne, completed his studies at Guy's Hospital, London, and qualified as a member of the Royal College of Surgeons and licentiate of the Royal College of Physicians in 1896. That year Guy's medical school awarded him the Golding-Bird gold medal for sanitary science. In 1900 he was awarded an M.D., with distinction, at the Université Libre de Bruxelles, Belgium.

Ham was a good cricketer, playing for Ballarat against Lord Sheffield's English team and later for Guy's Hospital. On 26 April 1897 at the Zion Chapel, Llandudno, North Wales, he married with Baptist forms Margaret Roberts. In 1899 he published a *Handbook of Sanitary Law for the Use of Candidates for*

Public Health Qualifications, which eventually went to twelve editions.

Appointed Queensland's first commissioner of public health from January 1901, Ham tackled the problems of bubonic plague, food adulteration, sanitation and infectious diseases. His *Report on Plague in Queensland, 1900-07* (Brisbane, 1907) received worldwide recognition. At a time when the role of fleas in transmitting plague to humans was being evaluated, he made several vital observations on the survival of the insects after leaving their host rat and their increased activity with suitable environmental conditions. In the area of food adulteration, his initiatives led to Queensland's being the first Australian State to draw up food standards laws; he also called for uniformity in food standards throughout Australia. Ham introduced compulsory notification of diseases, including tuberculosis and hookworm. He was, as well, founding president of the Queensland branch of the Life Saving Society of London (Royal Life Saving Society) in 1905.

In 1909 Ham was appointed permanent head of the Department of Public Health, chairman of the Board of Public Health and administrator of sanatoria for Victoria. His enlightened, non-moralistic attitude set the direction for venereal disease legislation, which was adopted almost Australia-wide during World War I, establishing principles that are followed today. He wrote prolifically, published widely in Australian medical journals and provided reports on public health issues for the governments of Queensland and Victoria.

Following differences of opinion with the minister for health W. H. Edgar, in May 1913 Ham resigned and returned to England. On the outbreak of World War I in 1914 he joined the Royal Army Medical Corps as medical officer in the Irish Guards. At the end of the war he became deputy commissioner of medical services to the Ministry of National Services and Pensions in London. Thereafter he was in private practice in London. He investigated allergy, pioneered inhalation therapy for chest diseases and published books on skin diseases, nervous disease and psychotherapy. As Bertie Burnett-Ham he died on 28 March 1954 in Orpington Hospital, Bromley, Kent. A daughter survived him.

J. R. Winders, *Surf Life Saving in Queensland* (Brisb, 1970); R. Patrick, *A History of Health and Medicine in Queensland 1824-1960* (Brisb, 1987); M. J. Thearle, 'Dr B. Burnett Ham: Father of Queensland's Department of Health', *MJA*, 161, 4 July 1994, p 55, *and* Crisis or Consideration: Public Health Measures in Queensland Following the Appointment of Dr B. Burnett Ham as the First Commissioner of Public Health 1901-1909 (B.A. Hons thesis, Univ Qld, 1994). M. JOHN THEARLE

HAMILTON, CHARLES GREENLAW (1874-1967), educationist, critic and naturalist, was born on 16 January 1874 at Guntawang, near Gulgong, New South Wales, eldest of four children of Alexander Greenlaw Hamilton [q.v.9], a schoolteacher and naturalist from Ireland, and his native-born wife Emma, née Thacker. The family was steeped in the love and study of nature: Charles's brother Harold Wynne (1875-1933) was a founder and honorary secretary of the Gould [q.v.1] League of Bird Lovers of New South Wales. Another brother, Edgar Alexander, built up the extensive collection of native orchids begun by his father.

In 1897 Charles joined the Education Department of Western Australia as an advisory teacher in art and nature study. The work entailed widespread travelling. Carrying a sketchbook, soft pencil and penknife to note the wildlife, he developed a special knowledge of the plants and animals of the southwest and goldfields. His drawing ability enabled him to captivate children in outback schools with blackboard depictions of nature, 'humorously interspersed with sketches of himself'.

Hamilton married Nina Helen Leslie on 26 September 1912 at St Matthew's Church of England, Boulder. After serving as headmaster at Como State School, in 1934 he took charge of East Claremont Practising School. Close to the influential R. G. Cameron [q.v.], Hamilton tried out new education systems at the school while working with colleagues at Claremont Teachers' Training College, where he was also a well-liked lecturer. He 'strongly advocated a more enlightened and free method of teaching'.

After retiring in 1938 Hamilton taught several subjects at Hale [q.v.4] School where he was also sports master during World War II. He finally left teaching in 1954. A tall man, in his later years slightly stooped with a thick mop of white hair, he had a wide range of friends, from painters, academics and sportsmen to goldfields engineers with whom he was keen to discuss precious metals. He exhibited paintings with the West Australian Society of Arts and the Perth Society of Artists and was founding secretary and life member of the West Australian Naturalists' Club. He was also associated with the Patch Theatre. A member of the West Australian Cricket Association, he was 'an accomplished all rounder, a graceful left hander and a wily slow bowler'. At 72 he achieved a hat-trick bowling against the Hale School XI. He was also a good shot, a billiards player and a member of Mount Lawley bowling club.

As 'C.G.', Hamilton was an esteemed art critic for the *West Australian* newspaper in 1946-64, and was a foundation and honorary life member of the Australian division of the International Association of Art Critics. He endeavoured to help young artists but was sometimes paternalistic in tone. While grounded in realism he was discerning in his admiration for such artists as Guy Grey Smith and Howard Taylor. He recorded thoughts about art and life and comments (not always flattering) on local artists, in small Croxley notebooks. These were probably also used for the philosophical and educational articles that he wrote for the Royal Perth Hospital journal. In 1962 Hamilton was appointed M.B.E. Predeceased by his wife, he died on 29 August 1967 in Royal Perth Hospital. (The day before, he had played a good game of billiards.) Survived by his three sons, he was cremated with Anglican rites. Both the Western Australian Society of Arts and the Perth Society of Artists honoured him with a memorial exhibition after his death.

Naturalist News, Oct 1967, p 5; *WA Naturalist*, 11, no 1, Oct 1968, p 22; *West Australian*, 30 Aug 1967, p 17, 6 Apr 1974, p 32; C. Hamilton biog file (Art Gallery of WA).   JENNY MILLS

HAMILTON, GEORGE (1812-1883), police commissioner, was born on 12 March 1812, probably in Hertfordshire, England, one of at least eight children of Charles Hamilton. Following education at Harrow School in 1823-26, George served in the navy as a midshipman. He reached Sydney before 1837, when he overlanded sheep to Australia Felix. In 1839, following Charles Bonney's [q.v.3] southern route, he drove cattle to Adelaide.

He began mixed farming in partnership with Arthur Hardy [q.v.4], while venturing, with scant success, into commerce and lithography, and visiting Melbourne in 1846. Next year he helped to organize the first exhibition of South Australian artists' works, including some of his own. A founding member of the South Australian Society of Arts in 1856, he won and gave prizes, and later acted as a judge, at its exhibitions. He contributed some of the illustrations for published journals of exploration by (Sir) George Grey and E. J. Eyre [qq.v.1].

Hamilton became a clerk in the South Australian Treasury in 1848 and inspector of mounted police in 1853. His duty took him on a journey in 1859 to the far north with the governor Sir Richard MacDonnell [q.v.5], whom he considered a blustering humbug. Hamilton had to do the work of the police commissioner P. E. Warburton [q.v.6], as well as his own, while the latter was away on exploring expeditions, and organized the fitting out of the last two expeditions of John McDouall Stuart [q.v.6]. In 1867 Warburton was removed from office and Hamilton became commissioner, surviving public criticism and two parliamentary inquiries. His prudent management during financial stringency led to expansion later, including the re-establishment of a detective unit and the use of camels in the far north.

As an active member of the Acclimatization Society (later Royal Zoological Society of South Australia), he was invited in 1881 to advise a parliamentary committee on sparrows, which were causing financial loss to farmers. He favoured a bounty on sparrows and their eggs to reduce their numbers and, incidentally, give an outlet for the 'larrikin instinct' of boys.

From 1848 Hamilton had contributed stories, verse and topical essays to Adelaide periodicals. His reminiscences, originally serialized, were published in 1879 as *Experiences of a Colonist Forty Years ago, and A Journey from Port Phillip to South Australia in 1839, by 'An Old Hand'*, and reprinted the following year with *A Voyage from Port Phillip to Adelaide in 1846*. Hamilton's most ambitious poem, of about fifty pages, published in 1868, was *Pscycos and Phrenia, or the World before Man's Advent*, giving a romantic account of evolution to the point where 'Man' suddenly makes his appearance. In 1864-77 he published three booklets on horses, denouncing the cruel methods commonly used for breaking them in and advocating improved methods of shoeing and stabling. His books were illustrated with lithographs and photographic prints from his own drawings.

Hamilton's writings contain vivid descriptive passages and whimsical comments on human foibles. His pictures capture the horse in all its moods and, like his narratives, include valuable historical information. He is not among the first ranks of Australian painters, poets or authors, but is better than most of his amateur contemporaries in all these fields.

Energetic, ambitious and a strict but fair disciplinarian, Hamilton was nonetheless noted for his genial nature, while some of his poetry was quite sentimental. His expert knowledge of horses enabled him to raise the standard of the mounted police so that it became an attractive occupation for 'well-bred young men'. He helped to organize hunt meets and was a principal founder of the Adelaide Club, which became his home. He did not marry. Hamilton retired in 1882 and died on 2 August 1883 at Burnside. His estate was sworn for probate at £6500. A lake on Eyre Peninsula and a creek and a hill in the far north were named after him. Pictures by him are held by the State Libraries of New South Wales and South Australia, the National Library of Australia and the Art Gallery of South Australia, which also holds a portrait of him by John Upton.

P. Depasquale, *A Critical History of South Australian Literature* (Adel, 1978); A. Carroll, *Graven Images in the Promised Land* (Adel, 1981); R. Clyne, *Colonial Blue* (Adel, 1987); R. Holden, *Photography in Colonial Australia* (Syd, 1988); J. Kerr (ed), *The Dictionary of Australian Artists* (Melb, 1992); *Frearson's Weekly*, 5 May 1883, supp, 4 Aug 1883, p 409; *Observer* (Adel), 4 Aug 1883, p 32; Colonial Secretary's Office correspondence (SRSA); letter from Hamilton to his sister, 24 Sept 1860 (SLSA); information from Rita M. Gibbs, Harrow School archivist.   J. H. LOVE

HAMLET, WILLIAM MOGFORD (1850-1931), chemist and bushwalker, was born on 20 August 1850, at Southsea, near Portsmouth, England, elder son of William Hamlett, stay maker, and his wife Rebecca, née Mogford. Young William modified both his middle and surnames. Intended for a commercial career, he was apprenticed to a Bristol shipping firm but early developed an interest in science. He attended evening classes in chemistry and physics at the Bristol Trade and Mining Schools (Polytechnic), then trained at the Royal College of Chemistry, London, under Sir Edward Frankland, F.R.S., obtaining in 1873 first-class honours in inorganic chemistry and winning the Queen's medal.

Next year, with his widowed mother and brother, Hamlet moved to King's Lynn, Norfolk, where he was an analytical and consulting chemist. In 1875 he was elected a fellow of the Chemical Society, London. His appointment as borough analyst in 1877 led to commissions in the fields of water, foodstuffs, drugs and forensic work. A mounting interest in the microbiological researches of Louis Pasteur and Robert Koch inspired him in 1880 to take up a research appointment in chemical microbiology in London with the brewing and distilling firm Watney & Co. In 1881 he became a chemist with the Sara Creek Gold Mining Co. Ltd in the Dutch colony of Suriname in tropical South America. Bouts of malaria forced him to return to England late in 1882. Ill health persisted and, advised to seek a warm, drier climate, he left London, reaching Sydney in the *Commonwealth* on 14 February 1884.

Hamlet speedily found employment as a lecturer in chemistry for the New South Wales Board of Technical Education. On 1 January 1885 he succeeded E. H. Rennie [q.v.11] as assistant to the government analyst within the Department of Health. Hamlet was government analyst of New South Wales from 1887 to 1915. His major responsibilities were the policing of legislative standards for foodstuffs, water, drugs and medicinal preparations. It was his forensic work in criminal cases, how-

ever, as well as his public lectures on diet, that led to his becoming a public figure. He lectured also for the University Extension Board.

A member of the government's Anthrax Board, Hamlet was a scientific witness and participant in experiments on anthrax in sheep at Junee in 1888. In 1892 he was a member of a board of enquiry into lead poisoning at Broken Hill. He had been elected to the Royal Society of New South Wales in 1887, and served on its council in 1891-1915; he was president in 1899-1900 and 1908-09. In 1888 he had been elected a fellow of the Institute of Chemistry of Great Britain and Ireland. He strongly supported the foundation in 1889 of the Australasian Association for the Advancement of Science, to which he contributed papers; at the 1892 meeting in Hobart he was president of section B (chemistry and mineralogy), and at the 1898 Sydney meeting he was a member of the council as well as section B secretary.

On 19 April 1887 at St Thomas's Church of England, North Sydney, Hamlet married English-born Ada Murray. They had five children. The family lived at Mosman; later William and Ada moved to Glenbrook in the lower Blue Mountains. From Glenbrook he travelled daily to the city where in 1919 he established a practice as an analytical and consulting chemist.

Hamlet promoted walking for exercise and mental recreation, a leisure-time activity he had long practised during his years in Britain, in the tradition of the European Romantic movement. In 1895 he was a co-founder of the Warragamba Walking Club, of which his friend Professor John Le Gay Brereton [q.v.7] was also a member. Another walking companion was Henry J. Tompkins, a colleague from the Department of Health, who was first secretary of the club and author of the walking handbook *With Swag and Billy* (1906). Hamlet and his companions largely used roads or tracks—then undisturbed by motor traffic. On long rambles, each day's march was planned to reach overnight accommodation by evening. He walked twice from Brisbane to Sydney (1907 and 1913) and in 1912, with Tompkins, from Sydney to Melbourne along the Princes Highway, covering some 750 miles (1200 km) in thirty-three days: on one day Hamlet, then 62, and Tompkins walked thirty-six miles (58 km).

Hamlet was of small stature, with a moustache and short beard. Precise and cultivated in speech, he was a lover of good English, widely read and an accomplished organist. He was politically conservative, an active Anglican and a loyal monarchist. He died on 18 November 1931 at Glenbrook and was cremated with Anglican rites. His wife, two daughters and a son survived him.

H. McKern, *William Mogford Hamlet 1850-1931* (Syd, 1995), and for bib; Hamlet papers (ML); personal knowledge.   H. H. G. McKern

HARDIE, JAMES (1851-1920), businessman, was born on 27 July 1851, at Linlithgow, Scotland, second of five children and eldest of three sons of Alexander Hardie, master tanner, and his wife Margaret, née Duncan. Jim learned the trade with his father, was office manager and bookkeeper, and became a partner in Alexander Hardie & Sons several years before he left for Melbourne, perhaps attracted by the milder climate and better business prospects.

Armed with testimonials to his personal and business character, Hardie arrived early in 1887 and established an office for importing and supplying machinery and chemicals to Melbourne's tanneries. He applied himself assiduously to 'working up what with care may develop into a very good business', as he described his prospects in 1891 to Andrew Reid (1867-1939), a Linlithgow acquaintance who was about to migrate to Australia.

Hardie soon enjoyed the confidence of Melbourne's leading tanners. He was honorary secretary (1890-1901) of the revived Master Tanners' and Curriers' (Master Tanners' and Leather Manufacturers') Association of Victoria, which held its meetings in his Flinders Lane office. From 1890 to 1894 he campaigned among butchers and woolbrokers to improve the flaying and branding of hides, and he initiated the 1900 intercolonial conference of Australian tanners that framed tariff recommendations for the industry. Hardie's disagreement with some of the recommendations caused his resignation as association secretary, but he joined its executive and was later honorary treasurer.

His business survived the 1890s depression and prospered, partly because in 1892 he recruited Reid as his salesman. Junior partner from 1896 and owner of a half share from 1899, Reid set up the Sydney office in 1900. In February 1902 Hardie opened enlarged Melbourne premises with a traditional Scottish 'shop-warming'. His company was described that year as importers, shippers, and leather and bark factors.

Hardie had married with Wesleyan forms Clara Evelyn, daughter of John Buncle [q.v.3], on 11 January 1893 at her father's home at West Brunswick. They had four children. In 1903, convalescing from illness, he took his wife on a seven-month trip through Britain, Europe and North America, where he inspected tanneries with Melbourne businessmen Squire Kennon and Herbert Burgess. Having secured new agencies for advanced American machinery, chemicals and dye-

stuffs, he returned with his health restored and with a trial shipment of a new type of roofing and lining slate, made by the French Fibro-Ciment Co.

Despite its fragility, fibro-cement sheeting (made from cement and asbestos) proved popular because of its resistance to heat extremes, ants and termites. Hardie & Co. was soon the sole Australasian and Pacific agent for the product. Among the firm's earliest Melbourne customers was the Victorian Railways, which built linesmen's huts and roofed the new Spencer Street Railway Station—a 'temporary solution' that lasted until the 1960s—with fibro-cement.

Bald, with a neat, ginger beard, Hardie had a rather severe appearance. The family's homes, successively at Ascot Vale, Hawthorn, Brighton and East Malvern, were named Lithgae or Lithca, diminutives of Linlithgow, his birthplace, which he again visited in 1910 during a second world trip with Clara. In 1912 he sold his interest in James Hardie & Co. to Reid for £17 000. In retirement he continued as honorary treasurer of the master tanners' association, which honoured him with a life membership in 1913. At Brighton Beach Hardie was a prominent supporter of St Leonard's Presbyterian Church and the progress association, and his wife was active in the Red Cross Society. Hardie died of arteriosclerotic heart disease on 20 November 1920 while visiting Pine Farm, which he had established for his son at Poowong North, Gippsland. He was buried in Brighton cemetery and left an estate valued for probate at £18 809. His wife, two daughters and one son survived him. The daughters erected a memorial window to James and Clara (d.1948) in the Ewing Memorial Church, East Malvern.

None of James Hardie's children had issue, but his name survived. Reid, who had initiated the Australian manufacture of 'Fibrolite' in 1917, retained the founder's name when he floated a public company in 1920. After his death, his sons Andrew Thyne Reid [q.v.16] and (Sir) John ran the business.

J. Smith, *Cyclopedia of Victoria*, 1 (Melb, 1903) p 503; B. Carroll, *'A Very Good Business': One Hundred Years of James Hardie Industries Limited 1888-1988* (Syd, 1987); *Austn Leather Jnl*, Oct 1899, p 652, June 1900, p 67, Aug 1900, p 160, Oct 1901, p 337, Mar 1902, p 729, Oct 1903, p 387, 15 Dec 1903, p 536, 15 Sept 1906, p 337, 15 Feb 1907, p 694, 16 Sept 1907, p 331, 15 Jan 1910, p 507, 15 Mar 1910, p 621, 15 Dec 1910, pp 432 & 434, 15 Mar 1911, p 616, 15 June 1911, p 74, 15 Feb 1913, p 648, 15 Dec 1920, p 730; *Scientific Australian*, 20 Sept 1904, pp 5 & 6; *Brighton Southern Cross*, 23 March 1918, p 2; *Argus* (Melb), 22 Nov 1920, p 6; note [MSB 401] from James Hardie to his wife, on the occasion of their visiting his old family home in Linlithgow, 18 Sept 1910, in Annie Vanstone papers, MS 11284 (SLV); James Hardie Industries records (ML).

JOHN LACK

HARRIS, WILLIAM JOHN (1886-1957), school principal and palaeontologist, was born on 10 December 1886 at Sandhurst (Bendigo), Victoria, third child of William John Harris, a farmer from Cornwall, England, and his Melbourne-born wife Eugenie Elizabeth, née Hooper. Young William was educated at Naring West, Numurkah and Shepparton state schools before joining the Education Department in 1902. He entered Melbourne Teachers' College in 1907, received his Dip.Ed. in 1911 and continued to study at the University of Melbourne (B.A., 1914).

First appointed to Kevington State School near Woods Point, Harris then taught at Strathkeller in the Western District. On 17 July 1916 at Wesley Church, Melbourne, he married Edith Garner Tilley (d.1937), a teacher. They had two children. He later transferred to the high school system, taught at Castlemaine and Kyneton and was head-master at Echuca in 1923-43. In 1944 he moved to Warragul High School where he remained until his retirement in December 1951. He married Frances Marie Braithwaite on 19 May 1945 at St John's Church of England, Malvern.

Teaching in the country enabled Harris to pursue an interest in the palaeontology of central Victoria and from 1912 he spent his spare time mapping the fossil content of Ordovician rocks. Of his thirty-seven papers, the first—published in 1916 with encouragement from T. S. Hall [q.v.9]—was on the palaeontological sequence of the Castlemaine district, building on the pioneering work of Hall in the same area. Following Hall's death, (Sir) Baldwin Spencer [q.v.12] suggested to the secretary for mines that Harris should be asked to carry out graptolite identifications formerly undertaken by Hall. This suggestion was taken up, and from 1916 Harris maintained a close association with the Department of Mines. In December 1934 he was awarded a D.Sc. from the university; his thesis was a collection of nine of his published papers.

When D. E. Thomas [q.v.16] was appointed to the staff of the Department of Mines, he and Harris collaborated in a series of twenty-four papers. Of particular significance was their 1938 article in the *Mining and Geological Journal* in which they completely revised the classification and correlation of the Ordovician rocks, building on Harris's work on the graptolite succession of Bendigo East and his investigations of the *Isograptus* series. Their zonal scheme was subsequently applied throughout large sections of the globe, particularly in New Zealand, North America and Asia, in the elucidation of the sequence of Ordovician rocks. Harris's field-work with Thomas was carried out during the summer vacation, some of it in the mountains of Gippsland, accessible only by packhorse, where both combined a love of trout fishing with geology.

A respected schoolteacher, well liked by staff and students alike, Harris had been given civic functions at Echuca on receipt of his D.Sc. and on the occasion of his transfer. He was, as well, one of the most significant Australian palaeontologists and stratigraphers of the twentieth century. Harris died of cancer on 26 June 1957 at his home at Beaumaris and was cremated. His wife and the son and daughter of his first marriage survived him.

Mining and Geological J, 6, no 2, 1957/58, pp 21 & 64; *VHJ*, 69, no 1, June 1998, p 40; *Riverine Herald*, 15 Oct 1934, p 2, 15 Dec 1943, p 5, 1 July 1957, p 4; *Warragul Guardian*, 4 Dec 1951, 2 July 1957.

THOMAS A. DARRAGH

HART, EADY (1848-1931), dyemaker, was born on 28 December 1848 at Wolverhampton, Staffordshire, England, second daughter of Isaac Booth, hatter, and his wife Catherine Elvin, late Payne, née Rainals. Eady's paternal grandfather (Isaac) was a governor of the Bank of England and an uncle, Abraham Booth, a distinguished chemist. Lured by gold, her family migrated to Victoria, probably arriving in the *Francis Henty* in May 1854. Eady became a dressmaker. On 14 December 1876 at Wycliff Church of England, Learmonth, she married English-born William Hart, later an engineer with the Ballarat Gas Co. They had four sons and four daughters before he deserted her.

After her children had grown up, Eady augmented her pension with sewing and millinery and by fostering four girls and two boys; they thought this tiny, gifted woman 'one in a million'. Thriftily, using potatoes, she created a blancmange-like breakfast food. She moved often at Ballarat, working also as a taxidermist. Creative, energetic and well organized, she found time to work for the war effort during World War I, in which two of her sons were severely wounded. Experimenting with natural products, Eady made firelighters from the pulverized trunks of grass trees ('*Xanthorrhoea australis*, then known as 'black-boys'). The children hawked them, snowball size, in packs of a dozen. But her great success came from experimenting with natural dyes. Grass trees, when boiled with washing soda and lime, produced a brilliant gold dye, while the various parts of other indigenous plants added a great range of colours.

From 1914 to 1919 Eady struggled with the formalities involved in patenting her natural processes—others used poisonous chemicals. She hoped to provide employment at Ballarat, especially for returned soldiers, but was frustrated when a supporter, who had joined herself to the patent application, foiled attempts to form a company. Meanwhile, on her kitchen stove Eady perfected Hart's Royal Dyes and in October 1921 mounted a sensational public display of soft greys, glowing yellows, a strong black and a wonderful henna. Articles in *Work and Energy* (England) and the London *Daily Express* attracted attention. By then, patents had been achieved in Australia, England, India and the United States of America. When entrepreneurs approached her about floating a company, and Ballarat identities offered support, Eady mortgaged her house, formed a syndicate and built a substantial laboratory at Canadian Gully to demonstrate the practicality of her process. Hart's Australian Dyes was incorporated late in 1921, and a big demand for shares followed a display on many fabrics of colours more natural and flower-like than those of rivals. Later, on Mair Street, a factory was built with the hope of reducing German dominance of the Australian market.

Despite technical success, the company failed. Although Eady won awards at the British Empire Exhibition, London, in 1924, she was ruined. An earlier fear that she would end up in a charitable institution, like many inventors, proved accurate. She died on 28 February 1931 at Ballarat District Hospital and was buried in the new Ballarat cemetery. Her eight children and six foster children survived her.

W. Bate, *Lucky City* (Melb, 1978); *Ballarat Courier*, 26 Oct 1921, p 2, 21 Nov 1921, p 2, 17 Dec 1921, p 2, 22 Dec 1921, p 2, 10 July 1922, p 2, 13 July 1922, p 2, 15 July 1922, p 2, 18 July 1922, p 2, 27 July 1922, p 2; E. Hart's specimens and scrapbooks (Gold Museum, Sovereign Hill, Vic); family information.   WESTON BATE

HART, HELEN (1842-1908), feminist preacher and lecturer, was born on 6 March 1842 at Birmingham, England, sixth child and fourth daughter of Henry Hart, gunmaker, and his first wife Elizabeth, née Birch. In her childhood Helen became involved with anti-slavery and temperance movements, and began open-air preaching from the age of 19. She was in London by the 1860s, working as a lecturer and possibly a journalist. In 1876 she was on the executive committee of the National Society for Women's Suffrage and on the provisional executive committee of the Association to Promote Women's Knowledge of the Law. As such she was known to many of the leaders of the women's movement.

In 1879, carrying references from leading English clergymen, Hart sailed to New Zealand, as matron in a migrant ship. Failing to find employment, she returned to the lecture stage and travelled the South Island, speaking on a number of topics, including women's rights. A year later she arrived in Melbourne and preached at Dr John Singleton's [q.v.6] Mission Hall at Collingwood in December 1880. This was followed by gospel addresses in the Fitzroy and Flagstaff gardens over the next few months. She spoke on a wide range of subjects, including public health, temperance, politics and women's rights, in many city and suburban venues.

For the rest of her life, Hart continued to lecture and preach, and sell her portraits and poems, in almost every city and country town in Victoria and numerous others in New South Wales and South Australia. In many areas the first woman to speak publicly on the subject of women's rights, she was subjected to physical assault, practical jokes—such as having fireworks thrown at her—derision and even sexual harassment. The press was at times hostile, and some public servants deliberately insulted her; she expected them to help her, but as she got older and more pathetic she was treated more like a servant than the lady she presumed to be. Hart responded in the only way she could. She wrote letters to newspapers, complained to government ministers and parliamentarians, threatened and sometimes took court action, and in one case attempted to horsewhip an impudent country editor. Although she considered herself a leader of the women's suffrage movement, others did not acknowledge her as such.

Described as a 'rebel and unorthodox ... clever and eloquent', 'buxom', 'raw-boned' and 'angular', Hart was resourceful, self-reliant and self-confident in her prime. Her manner changed in the mid-1890s, however, probably the result of being stalked over a number of years and after a dispute with a sergeant of police and the inaction of the government to rectify the matter. Hart's mental capabilities deteriorated, she became paranoid and her behaviour and claims became noticeably erratic. She continued her activities but, increasingly isolated, appealed unsuccessfully for funds to return to England. Radical to the end, she planned to join the militant suffragettes in London.

Hart never married. She died of pneumonia on 16 July 1908 in a boarding-house at South Yarra, Melbourne, and was buried in an unmarked grave in Kew cemetery with Anglican rites.

H. Harris, 'Helen Hart—Pioneer Suffragist', *Central Highlands Historical J*, 2, 1994, p 9, *and* In Search of Miss Helen Hart (M.A. thesis, Monash Univ, 2001).   HELEN D. HARRIS

HARTNETT, PATRICK JOSEPH (1876-1944), bushman, was born on 11 November 1876 at Westbury, Tasmania, one of fourteen children of Irish-born parents Patrick Hartnett, schoolteacher, and his wife Mary, née Collins. Young Paddy was literate, but his formal education ended when, aged 12, he became a bush labourer in New Zealand, as did about forty other boys from his district. Returning to Tasmania two years later, he carried supplies to the Corinna goldfields, where a bottle of whisky won in a rowing contest began his undoing. Red-haired, blue-eyed and sturdy, a fine axeman and rower, by 1900 he was hunting around the Great Western Tiers. On 23 August 1915 at Deloraine Hartnett married with Catholic rites Lucy Hanson, of Waratah. They would struggle to support eight children, initially managing the Liena general store, a highland staging post.

Hartnett helped to open Tasmania's alpine country. When tramping was a novelty, he, Bob Quaile (a Wilmot farmer) and Gustav Weindorfer [q.v.12] conducted guided overnight tours in the Cradle Mountain-Lake St Clair area. On the trips, Paddy—distinguished by his 'hard-hitter' or bowler hat—was guide, bearer, hunter, cook, waiter and raconteur. He loved the bush, which was also for him a refuge from alcoholism, but was frustrated by lack of opportunity. A superb bushman and King-Billy-pine carpenter, he was charismatic when sober but an easy dupe when drunk. He never swore, although he often muttered 'Jerusalem the golden', perhaps after a favourite snaring-ground, the Walls of Jerusalem; this region was the setting for Roger Scholes's movie, *The Tale of Ruby Rose*, inspired by pioneers such as the Hartnetts.

Paddy's seasonal regime in the spectacular Mersey and Forth valleys involved burning off in spring, and guiding and prospecting as far south as Lake St Clair in summer. In winter he caught Bennett's wallabies in the relatively merciful 'necker' snare. To safeguard the drying skins, his wife and son Billy joined the circuit of Paddy's Du Cane, Mount Ossa (Pelion East), Kia Ora and other huts, braving snowstorms and primitive conditions.

While farming at Lorinna on the upper Forth in 1916, Hartnett established a sporadically worked wolfram mine. In the 1920s he sought mining work in Tasmania's rugged west, washed osmiridium at Adamsfield and prospected for gold at the Jane River. His family scraped by in Hobart. Gradually alcoholism consumed him. A drunken fall damaged an eye, which Paddy covered with a black patch. Mining, hunting and farm work at remote Gordon Vale sustained him until he suffered a stroke in 1938. Delirium tremens followed. He died of cancer on 26 September 1944 in a Hobart hospital and was buried in Cornelian Bay cemetery. His wife, two sons and five daughters, one named Marion St Clair after neighbouring highland lakes, survived him. Geographical features named after him—the mountain Paddys Nut, Hartnett Rivulet and Hartnett Falls—reflected his love of highland Tasmania. Given reserve status in 1922, the areas that he had helped to make accessible became a national park in 1947.

R. and K. Gowlland, *Trampled Wilderness* (Devonport, Tas, 1976); F. Perrin, Account of a Trip to Barn Bluff via the Forth Valley in January 1920 (ts, copy held by author, Perth, Tas); NS573/1/11 (TA); L. Hartnett, The Beginning of a Life as a Mother (ts, c.1962, held by Mrs N. Williams) and information from Mrs N. Williams, Hobart.

NIC HAYGARTH

HARTOG, DIRK (1580-1621), mariner, was baptized on 30 October 1580 in the Oude Kerk (Old Church), Amsterdam, the Netherlands, second son and one of at least four children of Hartych Krynen, mariner, and his wife Griet Jans. On 20 February 1611, in the Old Church, Dirk married with Calvinist forms 18-year-old Meynsgen Abels. They are not known to have had children. At a time when Dutch spellings were not standardized, his name was variously spelled, including Hartogszoon, Hartogsz, Hartoogs, Hatichs and Hertoghsz as his surname, and Dirck or Dirick as his first name. He signed his name (in several extant documents) as Dyrck Hartoochz. In Australian history, however, he has become known as Dirk Hartog.

By 1615 Hartog had engaged on voyages to various European ports as the owner and skipper of a small trading vessel, the *Dolphyn* (Dolphin). In 1616 he was appointed to the Vereenigde Oost-Indische Compagnie (United East India Co.) as skipper of the *Eendracht* (Concord) on its maiden voyage to the East Indies (Indonesia). It sailed from Texel on 23 January, carrying ten money chests containing 80 000 reals (pieces-of-eight), valued at about 200 000 guilders. The weather was bitterly cold, and immediately before sailing twenty-one crewmembers and eight soldiers deserted by walking ashore over sea ice.

The *Eendracht* reached the Cape of Good Hope on 5 August 1616 and left on 27 August, following the newly adopted 'Brouwer' route, which directed V.O.C. ships to sail east across the Indian Ocean for a thousand Dutch miles (c.7400 km), before heading north to the Sunda Strait. Longitude could then be estimated only very approximately, however, and it was inevitable that a V.O.C. navigator would eventually sail too far east and come upon the west coast of Australia. Hartog was the first to do so. On 25 October 1616 members of the

Eendracht's crew landed at the north end of what is now known as Cape Inscription on Dirk Hartog Island. They left a record of their visit inscribed on a flattened pewter plate, nailed to an oak post and placed upright in a fissure on the cliff top. The inscription on the plate may be translated as:

1616, 25 October, is here arrived the ship the Eendracht of Amsterdam, the upper-merchant Gillis Miebais of Liege, skipper Dirck Hatichs of Amsterdam; the 27th ditto set sail again for Bantam, the under-merchant Jan Stins, the uppersteersman Pieter Dookes van Bill, Anno 1616.

On 14 December the *Eendracht* reached Macassar (Ujung Pandang), where a confrontation with local inhabitants resulted in the deaths of fifteen of its men. Hartog then visited other trading centres in the East Indies, delivering chests of money. Still under his command, the *Eendracht* left Bantam (Banten) on 17 December 1617, carrying a rich cargo of benzoin (an aromatic wax used for medicinal purposes), silk and other goods. The ship reached Zeeland in the Netherlands on 16 October 1618.

Leaving V.O.C. employment, Hartog skippered the *Geluckige Leeu* (Lucky Lion) on voyages to European ports. He died in 1621, in Amsterdam, and was buried on 11 October in the grounds of the Nieuwe Kerk (New Church). His remains were later removed to a communal grave field outside the city.

The *Eendracht* plate remained where it had been placed until 2 February 1697, when men of Willem de Vlamingh's [q.v.2] expedition found it lying beside a decayed post. Vlamingh replaced it with another flattened pewter plate, inscribed with a copy of the text on the old plate and a record of his own visit, and nailed it to a new post. He took the *Eendracht* plate to Batavia (Jakarta); from there it was transferred to the V.O.C.'s archives in the Netherlands and later to the Rijksmuseum, Amsterdam. It is the oldest known record of a landing by Europeans in Australia.

Hartog's discovery had a major impact on world cartography. Although Willem Jansz [q.v.2] had charted the west coast of Cape York Peninsula some ten years earlier, that land was generally regarded as an extension of New Guinea. After Hartog's discovery, the mythical continent known as Terra Australis Incognita (the Unknown South Land) was replaced on maps by a major landmass called 't Landt van de Eendracht (the Land of the *Eendracht*). Later discoveries extended charts of its coastline, and the continent was later renamed Hollandia Nova (New Holland) by the Dutch and Australia by the British.

J. E. Heeres, *The Part Borne by the Dutch in the Discovery of Australia 1606-1765* (Lond, 1899);

G. Schilder, *Australia Unveiled* (Amsterdam, 1976); J. P. Sigmond and L. H. Zuiderbaan, *Nederlanders ontdekken Australie* (Bussum, Netherlands, 1976) and *Dutch Discoveries of Australia* (Syd, 1979); G. Schilder (ed), *Voyage to the Great South Land, Willlem de Vlamingh 1696-1697* (Syd, 1985); J van der Veen, *Australië: Het Onbekende Zuidland Nuderbij* (Groningen, Netherlands, 1988); P. E. Playford, *Carpet of Silver* (Perth, 1996) and *Voyage of Discovery to Terra Australis* (Perth, 1998); information from Mr C. Boer and Ms G. Bouma, Groningen, and Mr J. van der Veen, Amsterdam, from the National Archives, the Hague, and the Municipal Archives, Amsterdam.

PHILLIP E. PLAYFORD

HARWOOD, MARIAN FLEMING (1846-1934), scholar, pacifist and philanthropist, was born on 9 March 1846 at Greenock, Scotland, daughter of Henry Reid, merchant, and his wife Catherine, née Barnett. Brought up in Belfast, Ireland, and taught French by her mother and at the Belfast Academy, Marian was also fluent in German. She studied Romance philology at the University of Zurich, Switzerland, and counted Matthew Arnold among her friends.

On 2 December 1885 at Newtownbreda Presbyterian Church, County Down, she married Septimus Harwood, an English-born medical practitioner, and next year they came to New South Wales for his health. He died in 1889; they had no children and Marian returned to Ireland. After her mother's death, she came back to Australia and in March 1896, granted admission *ad eundum* from the Royal University of Ireland, enrolled at the University of Sydney (B.A., 1897). Harwood then attended the school of English and German, University of Melbourne (M.A., 1900). Her book, *The Shakespeare Cult in Germany from the Sixteenth Century to the Present Time*, was published in Sydney in 1907.

Involved that year with Rose Scott [q.v.11] in the founding of the Peace Society, New South Wales branch, Mrs Septimus Harwood became a vice-president in 1909, and thereafter played an important part in its activities. She represented the peace societies of Sydney and Melbourne at the eighteenth Peace Congress in Stockholm in 1910, and spoke on the Australian peace movement at the University of Freiburg, Germany, and at a conference at Coventry, England, where she met leaders of the international movement. She observed sympathetically the troubles of the suffragettes, writing to Scott, 'it is hard to be calm and patient when tried and treated as they have been for nearly 50 years'. While in Europe, she also spoke about Australia as a representative of the National Council of Women at a conference of women held in conjunction with the Exposition Internationale, Brussels.

Returning to Sydney in 1912 Harwood founded and edited the journal *Pax*. She also established a library of peace literature at her rooms in Sydney, where she taught languages. Eye problems forced her to resign from the N.C.W. in 1914 and as editor of *Pax* in 1916. During World War I the peace society quietly continued its meetings. She later wrote that pacifists (she preferred the word 'peacemakers') 'were often cut by old acquaintances, and cold-shouldered sometimes even by old friends: our private letters ... ruthlessly opened by officious censors'.

A member of the Teachers' Association of New South Wales, in 1912 Harwood instituted a series of talks in Sydney that aimed at 'familiarising the sound of foreign languages to the ears of British people'. In 1917 the lectures were taken over by the Modern Language Association, of which she remained a member. In her pamphlet *The Neglect of the Study of Modern Languages in Australia*, she advocated compulsory oral examinations and the teaching of foreign languages from kindergarten level. She disapproved of Esperanto. Her publications included an article on the Australian women's movement in *Christian Commonwealth*, monographs about the peace movement and reminiscences of Rose Scott. Harwood corresponded extensively with overseas pacifist and feminist organizations.

Although supporting the League of Nations, in the 1920s Harwood regarded it as 'only one of many efforts peacewards' and disdained Australian members of the League of Nations Union as imperialists and non-pacifists who joined because of the annual fancy-dress balls. She considered protection 'one of the causes of war' and free trade as 'one of the Forces that would make for Peace'. Although she was a Christian, she observed that while clergymen 'always *pray* "Give peace in our time, O' lord,"' as a rule they refrain from *preaching* much about it, and during the War left the "Sermon on the Mount" severely alone'.

With boundless intellectual and physical energy, Harwood still swam regularly at 82, was forthright in her opinions and was sometimes harsh in her judgements of people. Amelia Lambrick [q.v.] described her as 'exceedingly hard to get on with' and 'most exacting'. Independently wealthy, Harwood practised public and private philanthropy, endowing a children's peace prize and beds in many children's homes and hospitals and in each of the Queen Victoria homes for consumptives. She lived all her life in boardinghouses, for many years at 129 Macquarie Street, where she first went to reside in 1909. Marian Harwood died on 29 July 1934 at Quambaar, Bellevue Hill, and was cremated with Congregational forms. Her estate was sworn for probate at £282 511 in New South Wales and £267 122 in England.

A-M. Jordens, 'Against the Tide: The Growth and Decline of a Liberal Anti-War Movement in Australia, 1905-1918', *Historical Studies*, 22, no 88, Apr 1987, p 373, *and* 'Marian Harwood', in H. Radi (ed), *200 Australian Women* (Syd, 1988), p 47, *and* 'Anti-war Organisations in a Society at War, 1914-18', *Journal of Aust Studies*, no 26, May 1990, p 78; J. A. Allen, *Rose Scott* (Melb, 1994); Peace Society (NSW), *Annual Report*, 1910, p 6, 1911, p 5, 1912, p 4, 1916, p 4; *Pax* (Syd), no 1, July 1912, p 6, no 35, July 1915, p 21, no 44-45, May-June 1916, p 35; *Sun* (Syd), 2 Apr 1911, p 19; *SMH*, 7 July 1925, p 13, 1 Aug 1934, p 19; Women's International League for Peace & Freedom, papers (Univ Melb L).

ANN-MARI JORDENS

HASSALL, ELIZA MARSDEN (1834-1917), clergyman's daughter and philanthropist, was born on 2 November 1834 at Denbigh, Cobbity, New South Wales, seventh of eight children of Rev. Thomas Hassall [q.v.1], colonial chaplain, and his wife Ann, eldest daughter of Rev. Samuel Marsden [q.v.2]. Eliza was educated at home, by a governess and by her brothers' tutors. She assisted with the Sunday schools at Heber Chapel (built by Thomas for the Denbigh estate workers) and St Paul's Church, Cobbity (1842). Intensely interested in her extended family, with whom she corresponded, Eliza practised both domestic and estate management—even learning to make table and fortified wines. She also ministered to the families of the estate's skilled tradesmen and tenants. Her older sisters married. She did not, devoting her life to helping her father and her eldest brother Rev. James Hassall, caring for her widowed mother and finally promoting overseas missions.

In 1855 her father wrote of her taking up 'so earnestly' the work of the British and Foreign Bible Society. Through him, she acquired a farm at Bowral, sold in 1866 for £450. After he died in 1868, she and her mother moved to Parramatta. In time Eliza became pietistic and didactic, exhorting one niece to break off an engagement 'whatever you may suffer' since 'he does not have a good character', and telling a sister-in law that one of 'the lessons affliction is sent to teach us is to be more sympathetic and forgiving to others'. In July 1880 she helped to found the New South Wales branch of the Young People's Scripture Union, of which she became secretary. Her mother died in June 1885.

In July 1892 the Church Missionary Association of New South Wales was formed, reflecting unprecedented interest in evangelical missions. It set its own policies and recruited its own missionaries, although the parent committee retained ultimate control over their placement. About 1893 Eliza bought Cluden, on the corner of Frederick and Church streets, Ashfield, close to the church of St John the Baptist. In response to a request from the C.M.A., here she established Marsden House (the Marsden Training Home for Women Missionaries). Its first recruit, her niece Amy Isabel Oxley, went to China in 1896.

The training home's curriculum comprised Bible studies and missionary geography. Eliza was voluntary superintendent and president of the ladies' fund-raising committee. In 1898 the home expanded into further leased premises and the following year held a successful missionary exhibition. Eliza was made an honorary life member of the Church Missionary Society, London. She retired in 1903 and moved to a cottage in Charlotte Street, Ashfield, which she also called Cluden. The Deaconess Institute at Redfern took over the training of female missionaries.

Eliza died on 26 December 1917 at Coogee and was buried in the churchyard of St Paul's, Cobbity. Almost three-quarters of Australian missionaries overseas in her time were women. She had contributed significantly to their recruitment in Sydney.

K. Cole, *A History of the Church Missionary Society of Australia* (Melb, 1971); H. Radi (ed), *200 Australian Women* (Syd, 1988); B. Dickey (ed), *The Australian Dictionary of Evangelical Biography* (Syd, 1994); *SMH*, 27 Dec 1917, p 4, 9 Jan 1918, p 7; Hassall papers (ML).   RUTH TEALE

HAYMAN, WILLIAM GEORGE INGLIS (1897-1968), electrical engineer and educationist, was born on 1 July 1897 at Norwich, England, son of George Samuel Thomas Hayman, timber merchant's foreman, and his wife Annie Frances, née Leman. Young Hayman, known as George, attended school at Great Yarmouth until the family migrated to Western Australia (about 1911). After further education in Perth, he joined the staff of Perth Technical School (College) in 1915 as senior cadet (technical assistant) in the physics laboratory while studying part-time; in 1918 he became assistant lecturer in physics.

Hayman's education, which straddled the gap between technical training and academic studies, profoundly influenced his educational philosophy. Starting as an evening student at the technical school, he gained diplomas in mechanical and electrical engineering and graduated from the University of Western Australia (B.Sc., 1922; B.E. with first-class honours, 1925). He married Ruth Lynette Coleman on 17 January 1923 at Claremont Congregational Church. A (Sir John) Hackett [q.v.9] research scholarship enabled him to study wireless technology abroad. Attached to the British radio research station at Slough,

England, in 1930, he was inspired by the inventor of radar, Sir Robert Watson-Watt. Back in Perth, he progressed in 1939 to head of the engineering department at Perth Technical College.

Throughout World War II Hayman led an experimental, secret Ultra High Frequency station, based in the university's engineering school. He was an amateur radio enthusiast and the respected patron of the State division of the Wireless Institute of Australia. Under his call signal YK6GH, from 1946 he reached a wide network of amateur broadcasters.

In April 1948 Hayman succeeded L. W. Phillips [q.v.15] as superintendent (later director) of technical education. Concurrently he was regional director of industrial training for the Commonwealth Department of Labour and National Service. Already an experienced negotiator with the Commonwealth Reconstruction Training Scheme, the building industry and the State's Arbitration Court on apprenticeship regulations, he helped to design courses that embraced technological developments appropriate for ex-service personnel, a burgeoning multicultural population and industry's unprecedented demand for a skilled workforce. His administrative responsibilities included co-ordinating building specifications and resolving manifold organizational problems, not least the establishment of outlying suburban and country centres suitable for diverse aspects of technical education. Appointed deputy director-general of education in 1960 he retired in February 1962.

Although initially dismissed as 'guess work, half truths and conjecture', Hayman's proposal in 1948 to establish an institute of technology was reconsidered in 1952. He was then briefed to assess the Collier pine plantation at Bentley as a possible site. The 1966 enabling legislation for the establishment of the Western Australian Institute of Technology (later Curtin [q.v.13] University) was described as 'one of the greatest milestones in the educational history of this State'.

Hayman was of slightly below medium stature, with receding dark hair and a full face; he wore heavy spectacles and was an amiable, no-nonsense man, popular with students and respected by colleagues. A member of Perth Rotary Club and several professional associations, he was a Freemason and belonged to Westralia Preceptory No.167 and University Lodge No.154. His wife died in July 1968 and he on 16 September that year in hospital at Shenton Park, survived by their daughter and son. He was cremated.

M. White, *The Community and Post-school Education in Western Australia* (Perth, 1981), and *WAIT to Curtin* (Perth, 1996), and *Thomas Logan Robertson 1901-1969* (Perth, 1999); *Education Circular* (Perth), 65, no 3, 1964, p 65; *Technical*

Topics (Perth), no 19, Nov 1967, no 21, Nov 1968; *West Australian*, 18 Sept 1968, p 9; EDF 034/15, and W. G. Hayman, ACC1022A (PRO, WA).

WENDY BIRMAN

HAYS, WILLIAM BENNETT (1814-c.1887), civil engineer and architect, was christened on 15 December 1814 at St Mary's, Lewisham, London, son of Thomas Hays, wharfinger, and his wife Elizabeth. William, whose surname was sometimes recorded as Hayes, was an associate of the Institute of Civil Engineers and worked with Walker & Burgess on projects in England and Ireland. On 20 June 1839 at the parish church of St Mary Newington, Surrey, he married Elizabeth Hays.

Arriving in South Australia on 4 November 1849 in the *Navarino*, he was appointed surveyor of main roads in January 1850, later became clerk of works and architect, and in January 1852 was promoted to the new position of colonial architect and superintendent of works in the colonial engineer's department. A widower, on 3 October 1850 at Holy Trinity Church, Adelaide, he married Harriet Gilbert, from Essex. A daughter was born in 1853.

In 1851 Hays won a competition for a building for the enlarged Legislative Council in Victoria Square, but the exodus to Victoria's goldfields prevented commencement. The prospect of parliamentary government led in 1853 to abandonment of the earlier scheme. Instead, Hays drew plans for a limestone and redbrick House of Assembly building in North Terrace to adjoin the existing council chamber, and for enlargement of the latter. The outcome, completed in 1855, was his best-known surviving building, now the Constitutional Museum. Hays was criticized because its cost (£17 550) was double his estimate. Nevertheless, the legislature approved his design for a bridge over the Torrens, providing direct access from King William Street to North Adelaide. Widened in 1877, it withstood many floods before being replaced in 1920.

In 1853 Hays had been a founding member of the Adelaide Philosophical Society. That year he was nominated to the Board of Undertakers for the construction of the Adelaide to Port Adelaide railway line. W. Giles, manager of the South Australian Co., made a complaint against him for enticing workmen to the railway project. Hays also worked on plans for a harbour at Port Elliot for the export of wool brought down the River Murray to Goolwa. Abandoning his scheme for a canal, he supervised, instead, the building of a tramway from Goolwa to Port Elliot. On its completion Hays requested a bonus. This was denied and he was criticized for 'lack of intelligence and zeal' in carrying out government works.

His several disagreements with the government partly arose from his creative streak. Among his inventions was a system for making charcoal; he went to Poonindie on Eyre Peninsula to supervise the use of his apparatus. He also applied for a patent for the construction of iron jetties and prepared specifications for an electric telegraph from the city of Adelaide to Port Adelaide.

Late in 1853 Hays applied for a year's leave of absence to return to England. While there he supervised the purchase of material for the Glenelg jetty, also offering his services to purchase material for the Adelaide to Gawler railway. Before leaving, he had prepared plans for the extension of the Port Willunga jetty using a special T head for the breakwater, which he had designed. He charged the contractor £76 extra for his design, without the knowledge of the government. An investigation was instituted when the contractor asked for reimbursement from the department. Hays, in Britain, maintained that the patent had been registered in London and that he was legally entitled to charge for its use. The colonial secretary was scathing in reply, saying that Hays's behaviour was 'most inexcusable and highly unbecoming an officer in his position', and suggesting underhand conduct. It was decided that his behaviour merited dismissal and his services were terminated in January 1856.

Hays's book *Engineering in South Australia* was published in London that year and reprinted as a facsimile in 1965. He did not return to South Australia and in 1881 was living at Wimbledon, Surrey, with his wife and their three daughters. His date of death is unknown, although he had predeceased his wife by her death in October 1887. Hays's parliamentary buildings, Adelaide Armory and adjacent former police buildings have been preserved, as has the Glen Osmond house, Wooton Lea, now part of Seymour College. His depots for female immigrants and extensions to the lunatic asylum have been demolished.

E. J. R. Morgan and S. H. Gilbert, *Early Adelaide Architecture 1836 to 1886* (Melb, 1969); D. A. Cumming and G. C. Moxham, *They Built South Australia* (Adel, 1986); M. Page, *Sculptors in Space* (Adel, 1986); G. H. Manning, *The Tragic Shore* (Adel, 1988); P. Stretton, *The Life and Times of Old Parliament House* (Adel, 1988); S. Marsden et al, *Heritage of the City of Adelaide* (Adel, 1990); Colonial Secretary's Office, GRG 24/6 (SRSA).

MARY M. FENCAK

HEALY, FRANCIS VINCENT (1834-1925), hardware merchant and community worker, was baptized on 5 December 1834 in Dublin, fourth son of John Healy, hairdresser, and his wife Susan, née Head. Francis saw the flood of refugees into Dublin after the 'great famine' of 1845-49, when Catholic laymen formed conferences (local groups) of the Society of St Vincent de Paul (founded in Paris in 1833) to alleviate suffering. In 1854 Healy helped to set up a conference at the parish of St Paul's, Arrans Quay, and took a leading role in following decades.

About the same year he began working for an uncle in the Tolka Ironworks, with a city store and iron yard at Arrans Quay. By the 1860s Healy was the proprietor. On 27 September 1864 at St Michan's Chapel, Dublin, he married Ann Carton. His business was ruined following an explosion in 1878 that destroyed the city premises and a flood in 1879 that washed away the ironworks. In 1882 Healy migrated to Melbourne with two children. By the time his wife and remaining five children joined him in 1885 he had a hardware business at 100 Elizabeth Street. At first he sold locally made items, but from about 1889 he indented, representing British and American manufacturers.

About 1883 Healy suggested to the Jesuits in his Richmond parish of St Ignatius that a Vincentian conference be started. As a branch of the Friendly Brothers Society already existed there, the proposal was rejected, but his perception of the need for assistance for the poor was correct and Catholic charities were relatively few. In late 1883 he helped to organize a men's conference of the St Vincent de Paul society at St Patrick's Cathedral, reviving a short-lived group set up in 1854. Members visited homes, provided relief, sought funds and promoted spirituality. A night shelter for destitute men was established at Fitzroy. By 1886 Healy sometimes presided over meetings. He became vice-president next year and president in 1888.

That year the society's Paris headquarters directed that a governing body (Particular Council) be established in Melbourne and Healy was elected founding president. Under him the organization was consolidated and expanded, surmounting such crises as the 1890s depression—when bank suspensions left it without funds for the night shelter and poor relief. After bushfires in Gippsland in 1898 the society distributed clothing and bedding. Healy was particularly interested in setting up a home for destitute children. A boys' club, a night school for city boys and a seamen's mission were also established. When a conference was started at Richmond, he became its president. In addition to his management role, he visited the poor.

His long leadership led some to regard Healy as autocratic. Reporting his resignation in 1907 the Particular Council described him as having 'for many years ruled the Society in this state'. Healy nominated his replacement but deferred to Archbishop Carr [q.v.7] who wanted a different candidate. Healy was deprived of all offices after the Sydney-based Superior Council reported him to Paris for lack of 'deference and submission to the clergy'. An appeal, however, led to the Council General's statement that It had not intended to deprive him of membership and that it hoped that he would remain active.

Despite this controversy, Healy's supporters celebrated his retirement with a function to acknowledge his work as founder of the society in Melbourne and his fifty years of service to the poor there and in Dublin. He died on 19 August 1925 in hospital at Fitzroy and was buried in Boroondara cemetery. Two daughters and five sons survived him.

E. M. Bond, *Society of St Vincent de Paul Victoria* (Melb, 1980); *A'sian Hardware and Machinery*, 24, no 10, Sept 1909, p 294; Superior Council, Society of St Vincent de Paul in A'sia, *Report*, 1907; *Advocate* (Melb), 6 May 1893, p 16, 12 Nov 1898, p 16, 27 Aug 1925, p 20; St Patrick's Cathedral, Minute Book, 1895-1907 *and* Particular Council, Society of St Vincent de Paul in A'sia, Minute Book, 1905-19 (St Vincent de Paul archives, Melb).   PAULINE RULE

HENDERSON, DANIEL (c.1834-1892), newspaper vendor, orator and commission agent, was born in Kingston, Jamaica, son of Thomas Henderson, cabinet-maker, and his wife Elizabeth, née Ross. Of African ancestry, Daniel possibly sojourned in England and acquired an education there before migrating to Melbourne about 1865. He came to notice with the publication of his pamphlet *Our Imbroglio: (the crisis) and the way out of it* (1868). Citing extensive imperial and Victorian precedents and recommending ultimate arbitration by the governor in the matter of appropriation bills, it was a response to the blocking of supply by the Legislative Council in 1865 and three times in 1867. The pamphlet's preface included a studio photograph of the elegantly attired author.

He was most famous, however, for his role as 'Henderson Africanus' during the political crisis a decade later. The council had again blocked supply in 1877, resulting in the dismissal of public servants, judges and magistrates on 8 January 1878, 'Black Wednesday'. In an attempt to resolve the deadlock, a deputation comprising Charles Pearson and (Sir) Graham Berry [qq.v.5,3] went to London late in 1878 to petition the British government to reform the Victorian Constitution. As a political joke, Berry's opponents proposed Henderson as the third ambassador, and his nomination furnished Melbourne with one of its most celebrated episodes of political burlesque. Henderson took the joke more seriously than his sponsors; it was reported that he attempted to secure an interview with the governor, who was unfortunately stag-hunting at Werribee. Recounting the episode in 1939, A. B. Paterson [q.v.11] suggested that Henderson had embarked for England but was intercepted 'somewhere in America'; there is no evidence, however, that Henderson ever went.

At public meetings, by letters to the press —under his own name or under the pseudonym 'Snowball'—and as a Yarra bank orator, Henderson continued to publicize his political views opposing free trade. He worked by serving summonses for the city court or selling newspapers in Bourke Street near the Eastern Market. On 3 July 1880 at the registry office, Fitzroy, giving his occupation as commission agent, he married Aphra ('Affy') Emily Lightbourne, née Odell, an English-born widow. It was her fourth marriage.

Henderson customarily wore 'a very tall white hat' and was 'remarkably shabby in appearance'. He had a habit of writing to the police on matters as diverse as the social evils of prostitution, the behaviour of his step-daughter, the ruses of rival news vendors, or thefts from his household. His letters included a complaint accusing the local butcher of stealing his spaniel Hector, which he had been training to save human life. To his critics, Henderson was a windbag, 'intermeddler' and buffoon. As an educated, independent and opinionated man of colour, however, he was a contradiction in a colonial society. He died of peritonitis on 24 December 1892 in Melbourne Hospital and was buried in the Anglican section of the new cemetery, survived by his wife.

Argus (Melb), 23 Dec 1878, p 4, 27 Dec 1892, p 5; *Age* (Melb), 24 Dec 1878, p 5; *Herald* (Melb), 3 Jan 1879, p 3, 16 July 1879, p 3; *Australasian* (Melb), 31 Dec 1892, p 1284; *SMH*, 4 Mar 1939, p 21; VPRS 3181, unit 852, 1889/1073, VPRS 937, units 298, 311, bundles 1 & 3, 314, bundle 1, 320, bundle 4, 321, bundles 1 & 3, 325, bundles 3 & 4, 330, bundle 7, & 337, bundle 6 (PRO, Vic)   ANDREW BROWN-MAY

HENDERSON, GILBERT DOWLING (1890-1977), dentist, was born on 7 July 1890 at Hawthorn, Melbourne, third child and elder identical twin son of Victorian-born parents Edgar Henderson, architect, and his wife Mary, née O'Neill. In the 1890s the family (there were to be five surviving children) moved to Western Australia, where Gilbert's father designed their home in McCourt Street, Leederville, as well as a Catholic primary school and the first buildings for St John of God Hospital, Subiaco.

The boys were educated at the nuns' school and Christian Brothers' College, Perth. Gilbert studied dentistry in the practice of Dr Bennett

and Dr Nathan and was registered by the Dental Board on 4 October 1915. He served at the training camp at Blackboy Hill during World War I. On 27 November 1918 at St Mary's Catholic Cathedral, Perth, he married Frances Josephine Dennehy, a nurse. They had five children. Beginning general dental practice, he became enthusiastically involved in the struggle of the profession to raise dentistry standards. In 1922 he was a founding member of the State branch of the Australian Dental Association, on which he served for many years.

Henderson was the first chairman of the Perth Dental Hospital in 1926 and of the board of management of the associated Western Australian College of Dental Science in 1936. He was both a clinical teacher and an administrator. In the 1930s he also represented Western Australia on the dental committee of the Council for Scientific and Industrial Research.

Resigning as dean of the college, Henderson began full-time duty on 27 April 1942 as captain, Australian Army Medical Corps (Dental). Described as 5 ft 5 ins (165 cm) tall, with brown hair and brown eyes, he served at the 118th General Hospital at Northam and was promoted major in October. In January 1943 he was posted to the 115th Military Hospital, Heidelberg, Victoria, where he served as a specialist, designing mechanical aids for repairing fractured facial bones, and fine prosthetic shields to restore soft tissue loss, especially for ears, noses and eyes. He was best known for building a prosthetic hand, activated by rods inserted in the arm muscles. His sensitivity to patients' morale was especially appreciated and remembered. On 26 November 1945 his appointment terminated in Perth.

Henderson practised as a specialist in oral surgery and radiology and resumed his role as dean of the dental science college (later the University of Western Australia's faculty of dental science); next year he became an original member of the advisory board to the faculty. In 1948 he was vice-president of the Perth congress of the Australian Dental Association. Appointed C.B.E. in 1950 he was also elected a fellow of dental surgery of the Royal College of Surgeons, Edinburgh, and fellow of the International College of Dentistry. At the 1964 dental congress in Perth the opening address was the 'Gilbert Henderson Oration', delivered by Professor K. J. G. Sutherland

Particularly concerned about the dental needs of people living in remote places, Henderson taught one pastoralist's wife how to provide emergency sedative dressings for decayed teeth and a Kimberly-based police sergeant Athol Monck—later police commissioner—to extract teeth painlessly, ensuring the dental board knew and approved of his para-dental training. Henderson's was a dedicated life and many of his kindnesses were private. Regarding community service as an obligation, he served simultaneously as honorary oral surgeon to Royal Perth and Fremantle hospitals and to the Princess Margaret Hospital for Children—a heavy workload in addition to his practice.

Henderson's wife died in 1951. He retired in 1965 but did not finally leave the university faculty until April 1970. The latter established a Gilbert Henderson prize in oral surgery and conferred on him a doctorate of dental science, the first award of such a degree by the university. He died on 19 October 1977 in St John of God Hospital, Subiaco, and was buried in Karrakatta cemetery. Three sons and a daughter survived him.

Dental Bulletin, 14, no 10, Nov 1977, p 4; *West Australian*, 25 Oct 1977, p 8; R. F. Stockwell papers (BL); B883 item WX36383 (NAA); Aust Dental Assn, Perth Dental Hospital, WA College of Dental Science, WA Dental Bd, records; information from Dr E. A. Adler, Mt Lawley; family information.

R. F. STOCKWELL

HENNINGS, JOHN (1835?-1898), scenic artist, was born probably on 6 July 1835 at Bremen, in the German Kingdom of Hanover, and named Johann Friederich, son of Danish-born parents Johann Hennings, merchant, and his wife Caroline, née Schutze. At 15 young Johann was apprenticed to a house decorator and studied briefly at the Dusseldorf Academy of Art. He then travelled widely in Europe.

Attracted by the Australian gold rush, Hennings followed a brother to Australia, reaching Melbourne in July 1855. He found work as a scenic artist at Geelong and, in Melbourne, at Cremorne Gardens and George Coppin's [q.v.3] Olympic Theatre. Generally known in Australia as John, he also worked at the Theatre Royal, the Princess and, from 1862, the Haymarket theatres, under the managers G. V. Brooke, J. Simmons and Barry Sullivan [qq.v.3,2,6]. In 1866 he joined W. S. Lyster's [q.v.5] opera company in Sydney. From 1867 to 1882 his success as scene designer made him welcome as a partner in various lesseeships of the Theatre Royal, Melbourne, with Coppin and others. With Coppin and J. R. Greville, he also leased the Queen's Theatre, Sydney, in 1880. His most popular work was the annual Christmas pantomime with its topical moving panorama, a type of early newsreel.

After J. C. Williamson, George Musgrove [qq.v.6,5] and Arthur Garner took over Melbourne's Theatre Royal in 1882, Hennings remained scenic artist until 1887 when he suffered from temporary blindness and was unable to work for two years. He returned in 1889 with a triumphant contribution to sets for *Antony and Cleopatra* at the Melbourne Opera House. His last notable work was *The Cyclorama of Early Melbourne*, commissioned by the Exhibition Trustees in 1892, for which he was paid five hundred guineas.

A handsome man, with long hair and a bushy moustache, Hennings formed a long relationship with Ellen Targett, an English-born ballet dancer, who had arrived in Melbourne in October 1857. With strong links to the small but influential German community, he was associated with the Melbourne Deutsche Turnverein and the Liedertafel. From 1870 he was a foundation member of the Victoria Academy of Arts, and it is likely that he sent paintings back to Germany for exhibition. He was also a member of the Yorick Club.

For nearly thirty years Hennings dominated stage design in Melbourne. The departure of his competitors W. J. Wilson and Alexander Habbe to Sydney in the early 1860s had left the field clear for him. His skill in architectural perspective and careful accuracy of historical detail, at a time when scenery and production were at least as important as acting, was often praised by reviewers James Smith and J. E. Neild [qq.v.6,5]) as the highlight of the production. Harold Love referred to his 'brilliant sky effects ... perfectly rendered romantic images of trailing foliage ... and masterful use of shadow'. His fellow scenic artist George Gordon compared him favourably with London contemporaries, expressing surprise at finding 'such a fine artist in the colonies'.

Hennings died of chronic pneumonia on 13 October 1898 at Middle Park, Melbourne, and was buried in Melbourne cemetery. His wife Ellen and two daughters survived him as did his one son, John Henry (1867-1959), also a scenic artist, by his mistress Elizabeth Collins (d.1888). In November a benefit performance for his family was held at the Princess Theatre, 'with all theatres participating'. There was also a 'free distribution of ... magnificent Oil Paintings and Water Colors by the late artist'. Although none of his stage scenery has survived, in 1956 the State Library of Victoria acquired his 1892 cyclorama, and a descendant holds his paintings.

H. Love, *The Golden Age of Australian Opera* (Syd, 1981); H. M. Humphreys (comp), *Men of the Time in Australia: Victorian Series* (Melb, 1882); J. Kerr (ed), *The Dictionary of Australian Artists* (Melb, 1992); M. Colligan, 'Full Circle', *La Trobe Library J*, 13, no 50, Spring 1992, p 1; *SMH*, 27 Dec 1880, p 2; *Lorgnette*, 23 Feb 1889, p 6; *Table Talk*, 22 Mar 1889, p 6, 15 Nov 1889, p 5; *Age* (Melb),

14 Oct 1898, p 5; *Argus* (Melb), 23 Nov 1898, p 5, 14 Oct 1898, p 6; information from Mr G. Morris, Glenroy, Vic.   MIMI COLLIGAN

HENRY, ALBERT (c.1880-1909), Aboriginal cricketer, was born at Lowood, Queensland. His parents were possibly Jagara or Jukambe people. At the age of 18 he moved from Nanango, in the Kingaroy district, to the Deebing Creek reserve, near Ipswich. Albert was a talented sprinter. He began his cricket career with the Deebing Creek Aboriginal team and by 1901 was playing for Bundamba in the Queensland Cricket Association competition. Tall, lithe and lean, he developed express pace as a right-arm fast bowler. His speed to the wicket came from his foot running, and his athleticism contributed to his brilliant fielding. Photographs of him showed a good-looking, elegant man with a fashionable moustache.

There was tremendous interest in Henry's selection for country against metropolitan Brisbane. His blistering speed—which forced the wicket-keeper to stand some sixty-six feet (20 m) behind the stumps—and figures of 3 for 61 ensured his selection for the match against New South Wales in March 1902. He was probably the first Aborigine to play first-class cricket for Queensland. On his début, Henry broke through early, then ran out a batsman when he diverted a drive onto the stumps at the bowler's end. Henry bowled his Aboriginal counterpart Jack Marsh [q.v.] who in turn dismissed him.

With his great speed, Henry was usually able to effect an early breakthrough. Most of his victims were clean bowled—the slip fielders were unable to hold on to catches from his bowling. He took part in all three matches for Queensland in the 1902-03 season, including a visit to Sydney, and in November 1903 represented the State against (Sir) Pelham Warner's England team. Henry's raw pace shocked the England opener Len Braund, who was caught off the last ball of Henry's first over and later claimed that it was the fastest bowling he had ever faced. During this season he was brought to live in South Brisbane to qualify for that electorate cricket team. The club secured the premiership; Henry made an important contribution to its success. In one match, however, the umpire Albert Cossart no-balled him for throwing, then reported him for dissent. The fiery cricketer was suspended for one month and missed Queensland's final game of the season.

Sent back to the Deebing Creek reserve, Henry resumed playing for Ipswich and competed in professional sprint races there and in Brisbane. He was omitted from the Queens-

land cricket team's southern tour to Melbourne and Sydney but was recalled in April 1905 for what proved to be his last match for the State. In seven first-class matches, Henry claimed 21 wickets at an average of 32.04 and scored 36 runs at 6.

Back at Deebing Creek, Henry was again under the strict control of the Queensland government, which treated any defiance as criminal behaviour. About 1908 he was removed to Barambah (Cherbourg), where he was imprisoned for one month 'for loafing, malingering and defying authority'. From there, he was sent to Yarrabah in northern Queensland, where he died of tuberculosis in March 1909 after a long stay in hospital.

E. H. Hutcheon, *A History of Queensland Cricket* (Brisb, 194?); R. Webster, *First-Class Cricket in Australia*, 1 (Melb, 1991); R. Cashman (ed), *The Oxford Companion to Australian Cricket* (Melb, 1996); B. Whimpress, *Passport to Nowhere* (Syd, 1999); I. Diehm, *Green Hills to the Gabba* (Syd, 2000); G. A. Blades, Australian Aborigines, Cricket and Pedestrianism 1880-1910 (B. Human Movement Hons thesis, Univ Qld, 1985).   IAN DIEHM

HENSCHKE, ALBERT JULIUS (1888-1955), stonemason, monumental mason and sculptor, was born on 22 August 1888 at North Rhine (later Keyneton), upper Barossa Valley, South Australia, sixth child of Paul Gotthard Henschke, farmer and winemaker, and his wife Johanne Mathilde, née Schulz. Paul's father Johann Christian had arrived from Prussia in 1841.

Julius attended the North Rhine Lutheran school then trained as a monumental mason at Tanunda. He married Alfrida Amalia Klein on 12 September 1913 at the Lutheran Parsonage, Wakefield Street, Adelaide, and in the 1920s opened his own business at Tanunda. Many gravestones in Barossa Valley cemeteries carry his trade name—'Henschke Tanunda'. In addition, he probably carved the fonts in a number of churches. He moved to Adelaide in 1926 to become master mason in the South Australian Monumental Works.

In 1926 the architect Louis Laybourne Smith [q.v.11] commissioned the sculptural elements of the National War Memorial in Adelaide from George Rayner Hoff [q.v.9], who made one-quarter-size plaster models in his Sydney studio. Henschke scaled up the models and carved the Angaston-marble reliefs of angels *in situ* as the memorial was constructed—a labour which lasted from 1927 to 1931 and was his major achievement.

Hoff also commissioned Henschke to carve two independent statues from his plaster models: the portrait of Len Lye, which won the Wynne Prize in 1927, and 'Australian

Venus' (1932), which is in the Art Gallery of New South Wales. Henschke never received acknowlegement for this work. He carved war memorials at Tanunda (1920) and Freeling (1923) and the Tanunda monument to E. H. Coombe [q.v.8], who had defended Barossa Valley people 'of German extraction' during World War I. Henschke was one of these. Although a patriotic, third-generation Australian, he was refused the commission for the Gawler South war memorial in 1920 solely because of his German name.

More than a skilled monumental mason, Henschke painted many signs and illuminated addresses, the interior decoration of the church at Gnadenburg in the Barossa Valley (later obliterated) and 'The Good Shepherd' in Alawoona Lutheran church. According to local tradition, he sculpted a life-size female nude, which remains in the garden of his former home at Tanunda, but this cannot be confirmed from records.

Henschke carved the Corinthian capitals and other architectural features on Parliament House, Adelaide (c.1938), the Australian Mutual Provident Society building (1936) and the Art Gallery of South Australia (1937), and the emblem of the Savings Bank of South Australia on its King William Street building (1941). One of his last works was the base of Maurice Lambert's equestrian statue of King George V, in Angas Gardens, Adelaide, which was unveiled in 1956.

With an attractive and convivial personality, Henschke was a skilled player of the euphonium, a long-serving member of the Tanunda Brass Band and its deputy leader about 1925. He died of cerebrovascular disease on 30 April 1955 in Royal Adelaide Hospital, survived by his wife and their two daughters. The vigneron Cyril Henschke [q.v.14] was his nephew.

Henschke Heritage (Adel, 1995); D. Richardson, *Julius Henschke* (Mount Barker, SA, 2000).

DONALD RICHARDSON

HERBERT, DANIEL (1802-1868), convict and stonemason, was baptized on 17 February 1802 in the Paul Street Independent Chapel, Taunton, Somerset, England, son of Daniel Herbert, a corporal in the 6th (Inniskillen) Dragoons, and his wife Mary. Daniel later moved with his mother to Leeds, where he worked as a signboard writer and stonemason. Later he lived in his parents' native town of Manchester. In March 1827, with James Camble and John Lynch, he was charged before the North Eastern circuit assizes with four counts of highway robbery and with putting 'in bodily fear and danger'. Herbert had already served part of a seven-year sentence for stealing in a dwelling house; he and

his co-accused pleaded guilty and were sentenced to death on 7 April. Reprieved on condition of transportation for life, Herbert was shipped aboard the *Asia*, arriving in Hobart Town in December 1827.

As a stonemason, he was placed in the Engineer's Department and for the next seven years was employed on government projects in Hobart, including the new female factory at Cascade. In the late 1820s and early 1830s Herbert made a number of appearances before the magistrates' bench, charged with being absent from the works and drinking. By 1835 he was employed as overseer of stonemasons on the construction of the new customs house, a service for which he was paid one shilling a day. When Josiah Spode [q.v.2], principal superintendent of convicts, was asked to recommend two stonemasons to be transferred to Ross to oversee the completion of a replacement bridge across the Macquarie River, Herbert was one.

Despite being promised a conditional pardon for successfully completing the task, Herbert asked to be allowed to remain three weeks longer in Hobart to marry Mary Witherington. In the event, they married at Ross on 1 July 1835. The bridge was completed in July 1836. It contained 186 keystones or voussoirs carved by Herbert, or completed under his supervision, in fifty-six weeks between May 1835 and July 1836. Various interpretations of their curious motifs have been put forward, including claims that the many carved heads were portraits of Herbert and his wife, Jorgen Jorgenson, Lieutenant-Governor (Sir) George Arthur [qq.v.2,1] and other colonial officials and local personalities.

Herbert was granted a free pardon in February 1842 and continued to live at Ross, where he worked as an ornamental stonemason. He was credited with carving a number of motifs for other buildings in Tasmania, including St Luke's Presbyterian Church, Bothwell. Daniel Herbert died of bronchitis on 28 February 1868 at Campbell Town, survived by his wife; they had three children. Reputedly, he designed and carved his own tomb in the old burial ground at Ross. In 2005 his bridge there was still in use.

L. Greener and N. Laird, *Ross Bridge and the Sculpture of Daniel Herbert* (Hob, 1971); Offence registers, Con 31/19, Colonial Secretaries' correspondence, CSO1/311/7501, and Herbert correspondence file (TA).

HAMISH MAXWELL-STEWART

HETHERINGTON, ISABELLA (c.1870-1946), missionary to Aborigines, was born in Ireland, daughter of William Hetherington, property holder, and his wife Rebecca, née White, who died when Isabella was 11. Her father and only brother also died of consumption. A nurse, she migrated on medical advice to Melbourne from Liverpool, England, arriving in the *Persic* in December 1903. Settling at Ballarat, she worked as a governess but had a deep desire, she later wrote, 'to go and succour others', especially the Australian Aborigines, about whose privations she had heard while still in Ireland.

Inducted in the Baptist Church, Dulwich Hill, Sydney, after two years working in an Aboriginal camp on the banks of the Murray River, Hetherington joined the Australian (United) Aborigines' Mission early in 1906 and served for the next three years in a community located 'beyond the rubbish tip', near Wellington. A pleasant faced, demure and 'extremely short-sighted' woman with small, round glasses, she demonstrated compassion, generosity, hard work (she cycled around the area), mystical devotion to Christ, a willingness to serve with all denominations and a love for children. At Wellington she adopted a 3-year-old, orphaned Aboriginal child NELLIE HETHERINGTON (1903-1940), whose parents had died of tuberculosis.

The strenuous work took a toll on Isabella's health and in 1910 she spent four weeks in hospital being treated for pleurisy. Late that year, given twelve months leave, she travelled with Nellie through Victoria, where she met the Pentecostal matriarch Sarah Jane Lancaster (1858-1934). Isabella and Nellie visited mission homes at Sunshine and Bunyip and the leper colony at Peel Island, Queensland. About 1912 Hetherington settled for a term at Manunka near Point Macleay, South Australia. By January 1913 she was stationed at the U.A.M.'s base at La Perouse, New South Wales, where, early in March, there was an unusual occurrence of charismatic expressions of worship, including glossolalia. These phenomena were too controversial for the mission leaders, and Hetherington withdrew. She and Nellie again engaged in itinerant work. By 1928 they were at Maryborough, Queensland. Hetherington published a booklet, *Aboriginal Queen of Sacred Song* (Melbourne, 1929), to raise funds for Nellie, a talented singer and pianist, who performed at Methodist mission functions and for wider audiences. Nellie also played the organ, guitar and ukulele, recited poetry and was an accomplished embroiderer; she died on 1 February 1940 at Barambah (Cherbourg) reserve.

About 1930 Hetherington had pioneered Pentecostal mission work among the Aborigines at Mossman, in northern Queensland. She set up a 'Faith Mission' in the Gorge reserve, where she and Ethel Vale (b.1871) laboured together. Initially, they lived in a humpy and undertook the heavy manual work of clearing dense scrub, planting gardens and establishing a school. Hetherington was often without funds, but carried out ministerial duties including conducting funerals, tending the sick and washing the feet of her Aboriginal charges. On occasion, she intervened to prevent spear fights between the men.

In 1933 she was recognized as an Assemblies of God missionary to the Aborigines, and a small church and school building was opened in 1938. When the government policy of removing children with a non-Aboriginal father from their families accelerated in the 1930s, Hetherington opposed the practice, although not publicly. From 1933 she seems to have received a pension. She died on 31 August 1946 at Mossman and was buried with Methodist forms in the local cemetery.

B. Chant, *Heart of Fire* (Adel, 1973), and The Spirit of Pentecost: Origins and Development of the Pentecostal Movement in Australia, 1870-1939 (Ph.D. thesis, Macquarie Univ, 1999); S. Hunt, *The Assemblies of God Queensland Conference* (Brisb, 1978); J. Harris, *One Blood* (Syd, 1990); R. Guy, *Baptised Among Crocodiles* (Mossman, Qld, 1999); Assemblies of God, *Australian Evangel*, vol 10, no 1, 1940, p 7, vol 11, no 7, 1941, p 9, vol 11, no 11, 1945, p 3.   BARRY CHANT

HILL, WALTER (1819-1904), horticulturist, was born on 31 December 1819, at Scotsdyke, Dumfriesshire, Scotland, one of twin sons and nine children of David Hill, tollsman, and his wife Elizabeth, née Beattie. When not yet 16, Walter was apprenticed to his brother David, then head gardener at Balloch Castle, Dumbarton, later working at Dickson's Nursery, Edinburgh, and as foreman at Minto House, Roxburghshire. He then accepted a position in the Royal Botanic Garden, Edinburgh, under William McNab, on whose recommendation he went in 1843 to the Royal Botanic Gardens, Kew, London, where he subsequently became foreman of the propagation and new plant departments. On 16 September 1849 at Holy Trinity Church, Brompton, Middlesex, he married Jane Smith.

The couple reached Sydney in the *Maitland* in February 1852. Hill worked for six months on the Turon gold diggings with indifferent success, then visited Beechworth, Sandhurst (Bendigo) and other Victorian goldfields. In 1854 with F. Strange and others he set out from Sydney on an expedition to explore from Keppel Bay to Cape York. On Percy Island the party separated to collect specimens. When Hill returned to the boat he found that Aborigines had killed the entire group, except an Aboriginal. The two managed to sail to Moreton Bay.

On 21 February 1855 the government of New South Wales chose Hill as first superintendent of the Botanic Gardens, Brisbane. He was allotted nine acres (3.64 ha) and £500 to purchase rare plants, and, when Queensland became a separate colony in 1859, was appointed colonial botanist. Provided with a house and garden within the reserve, he lived there until his retirement. Also placed in charge of forest reserves in Queensland, Hill introduced and acclimatized numerous trees and plants of economic importance from all over the world. He was credited with the introduction of the mango, pawpaw, ginger, poinciana and jacaranda (1864); he also established the first commercially grown macadamia, which he brought from the Queensland bush to the Botanic Gardens in 1858, and in the same year introduced tamarind and mahogany trees into the colony.

Perhaps Hill's greatest economic achievement was on 25 April 1862 when, with a planter from Barbados, John Buchot, he granulated the first sugar in Queensland and Australia by 'crushing the canes with a lever and boiling the juice in a saucepan. No one was allowed to witness the tremendous experiment (carried out in the dead of night) which was to settle the problem of whether the juice of Queensland sugar cane would granulate.' A cairn marking the site of the first sugar cane grown in Queensland was later erected in the centre of the city gardens, Brisbane. He also planted (1858-67) the fine avenue of bunya pines *Araucaria bidwillii*, named in honour of J. C. Bidwill [q.v.1], on the river bank that forms a boundary for the botanic gardens. A complete avenue still stood in 2003.

Hill acted as a botanist on a number of voyages of exploration up the Queensland coast and into its interior. The expedition to the north-eastern coast in 1873 under the leadership of G. E. Dalrymple [q.v.4] led Hill to report: 'Half-a-million acres of good land, 300 000 of that fit for sugar'. Hill thought the area they explored, around the Johnstone River south of Cairns, 'the most valuable discovery in Australia'.

During his term as superintendent, Hill arranged for Queensland's flora and fauna to be exhibited at international exhibitions throughout the world, and in return received numerous rare specimens for Queensland's benefit. He published several impressive reports and catalogues (later prized by botanists). Many species of plants were named after him. Hill's association with the public service ended, however, on a sour note. Following a comment in parliament that the Department of Public Lands was not satisfied with his upkeep of the Botanic Gardens, it was decided to ask for his retirement at 60. Hill, described by some as stubborn and impractical to deal with, was incensed. He immediately claimed full paid leave of absence for twelve months (having not had annual leave for twenty-six years), plus a gratuity for the upkeep of five

horses. He retired on a full pension on 28 February 1881.

In retirement, Hill experimented with fruit trees. Predeceased by his wife and daughter, he died on 4 February 1904 at his home, Canonbie Lea, Eight Miles Plains, south of Brisbane. He was buried with Presbyterian forms in Toowong cemetery.

A. Meston, *Geographic History of Queensland* (Brisb, 1895); Report of the Board of Inquiry on Charges against Walter Hill, *V&P* (Qld), vol 2, 1881, p 963; *J of the Kew Guild*, 1904, p 206; Cairns Hist Soc, *Bulletin*, no 371, Aug 1991, no 372, Sept 1991; R. D. McKinnon, Summary of the Development of Brisbane's Botanic Gardens 1828-2003, ts, *and* Walter Hill and the Cairns Connection—A Rich Botanic History, ts, 2000 (copies held by author, Brisb).   ROSS MCKINNON

HILLIER, HENRY JAMES (1875-1958), teacher, collector and farmer, was born on 24 February 1875 at Ramsgate, Kent, England, elder of twin sons and one of five children of James Thomas Hillier, surgeon, and his wife Sarah Jane, née Thomson. Harry attended Dover College and grew up in prosperous circumstances until his father's death in 1888; while his eldest brother became a medical practitioner, Harry left school at 15.

Diagnosed with tuberculosis in 1893 and given about six months to live, Hillier came to South Australia. At Mr Gosnell's school, College Town, he met J. J. Stolz, through whose grandfather Rev. G. J. Rechner [q.v.6] Hillier went to Bethesda Lutheran mission, near Lake Eyre, staying with Rev. J. G. Reuther and his wife Pauline. To both he became almost a son. In the dry, desert air his health improved dramatically. Learning German and Dieri, he revelled in outdoor life, accompanying an overland drive of cattle from Hermannsburg to Bethesda in 1901 and, for several days, J. W Gregory's [q.v.9] 1901-02 expedition. Until 1905 he taught at the mission school.

Hillier was at Bethesda when it was the focus of scientific interest around the world, resultant upon A. W. Howitt's [q.v.4] collaboration with Otto Siebert and publications about the Dieri. A skilled artist with crayon and water-colour, he made dozens of fine drawings of Dieri shields painted with traditional designs. Reuther resigned in 1905, and Hillier returned to England. He was a committed Christian, and when his health again deteriorated he applied to the Church Missionary Society to work in the colonies.

Hillier's previous friendship with Carl Strehlow [q.v.12] brought him to Hermannsburg to work for the Lutherans instead. Arriving in May 1906, he lived in Strehlow's house, taught in the school in 1906-10 and learned

Aranda (Arrernte). He also collected artefacts, which he sold at cost price through his mother to the British Museum, the Horniman Museum, London, Cambridge University Museum of Archaeology and Anthropology and the National Museum of Antiquities of Scotland, Edinburgh. Strehlow apparently supplied the accompanying data—some was in his handwriting. Doris Blackwell claimed that Hillier supplied the British Museum with 'more than two thousand illustrations of insects and other specimens', but their whereabouts today are unknown. His painting may have influenced the young Albert Namatjira [q.v.15], then among his students, as were most of the later school of Hermannsburg water-colourists.

Pictures of Hillier showed a studious young man, reasonably good-looking and thoughtful. But he found life at Hermannsburg difficult: it was too remote, there were too few white people and the Aranda had a more fiery temperament than the Dieri. According to Strehlow, Hillier was afraid of some of the men who were not attached to the mission. There were also problems in the school: he was not a good teacher, and the children refused to obey him.

Leaving the mission in 1910, Hillier went to the Reuthers, then at Julia, near Kapunda. From 1916, as diocesan secretary and registrar for the Church of England bishop of Willochra, Gilbert White [q.v.12], he was based first at Peterborough and later at Gladstone. Resigning in July 1927, he moved to Laura, working as accountant for the local Ford car dealer, and by 1931 to Kojonup, Western Australia, where he lived as a gentleman farmer. On 3 May 1934 at Norwood, Adelaide, he married Lilian Gertrude Williams, who went with him to Western Australia. The couple returned in the early 1950s to South Australia, where his wife died in 1953. They had no children.

Hillier was always the English gentleman, very pukka in his panama, but imperious and with a tendency to petulance which made him difficult on occasions. In his final years he sat on the bench as a magistrate. He died on 7 August 1958 in Royal Adelaide Hospital after an unsuccessful operation. Despite his delicate constitution, he had outlived all his family, including his twin.

A lifelong friend of the Strehlows, whom he often visited in Adelaide, Hillier had great affection for T. G. H. Strehlow [q.v.16], his godson, who inherited some of 'Uncle Harry's' books and drawings. He never realized his full potential, probably due to his aborted education, and was important chiefly for making Carl Strehlow's work and the Western Aranda known to English museum directors, notably A. C. Haddon at the Horniman. Material from Hillier is to be found in the Australian

Museum, Sydney, and the South Australian Museum, Adelaide.

J. W. Gregory, *The Dead Heart of Australia*, (Lond, 1906); D. Blackwell and D. Lockwood, *Alice on the Line* (Adel, 1965); *Willochran*, Apr 1916, p 7, 1 July 1927, p 406; Frieda Keysser, diary, 1897-1917, and life story (in family possession, Berlin); T. G. H. Strehlow, diary, 1958, book 22 (Strehlow Research Centre, Alice Springs, NT); general correspondence file (British Museum, Lond); Bethesda box and Finke River Mission box (Lutheran archives, Adel); Univ Cambridge, Museum of Archaeology and Anthropology archives; Horniman Museum archives, Lond.   JOHN STREHLOW

HINGSTON, JAMES (1830-1902), notary public and travel writer, was born in 1830 in London, son of John Hingston, cabinet-maker, and his wife Sarah. James's elder brother was Edward Peron Hingston (d.1876), the essayist and friend and editor of the American humorist, Artemus Ward. As a 'mere lad', James became an office boy and soon moved to employment by an attorney, augmenting his meagre wages by night work in a newspaper office. In 1852 he arrived in Victoria aboard the *Cleopatra* and proceeded to the Mount Alexander goldfields, where he was largely unsuccessful. After six months he returned to Melbourne to establish a law agency and patent business in Chancery Lane, which he ran all his life, later in partnership with Alfred Ford.

An astute investor, Hingston benefited from the spectacular growth of 'marvellous Melbourne'. He became the largest single investor in Melbourne Tramway shares, which at the height of the boom in 1888 were estimated to be worth more than £250 000. After the crash of 1891-92, and despite his still considerable wealth, he referred to himself as a ruined man.

Gaining a well-earned reputation for eccentricity, Hingston never married and lived for over thirty years at the George Hotel, St Kilda, amid large piles of books and papers in his bedroom. An indefatigable reader, he knew Shakespeare's plays almost by heart and was considered one of Melbourne's great raconteurs. His impact was the more remarkable for his unconventional views and fierce disregard for the dropped 'h', signing himself 'Jay Haitch' in letters to close friends. He came to the notice of the reading public as a travel writer, contributing to a *Guide for Excursionists from Melbourne Dedicated to all in Search of Health, Recreation and Pleasure* (1868) and co-authored *Lorne: The Australian Torquay* (1879) with William Little of Ballarat.

Hingston's travels abroad dated from the mid-1870s. Returning to London he was overwhelmed by the beauties of eastern scenery in Ceylon (Sri Lanka). He left the steamer and, having discovered the pleasures of travelling light, sent his weighty portmanteaus back to Melbourne. Continuing his travels through India, the Middle East, Japan, China, Cochin-China, Malacca, Singapore and Java, he wrote a chapter of travel impressions at each destination.

The Melbourne *Argus* cautiously experimented with fortnightly publication of Hingston's articles under the title 'Travel Talk' by 'J.H.' When in 1879-80 a London publisher brought out his essays as *The Australian Abroad: Branches from the Main Routes Round the World*, in two handsome, but expensive, volumes, Hingston's reputation as a brilliant new writer was assured. William Inglis & Co., Melbourne, published a single-volume edition of *The Australian Abroad* in 1885. Hingston's witty and richly allusive meditation on travel and the human condition was an immediate success and remained a remarkable record of Asian travel.

Through the 1880s and 1890s, Hingston continued his contributions to the *Argus* but no further books appeared under his name. Sojourning in England, he died on 7 March 1902 at Littleham, Exmouth, Devon, and was buried in Kensal Green cemetery, London, with his parents and brother. His estate in Victoria was valued for probate at more than £50 000, with the Melbourne Benevolent Asylum a major beneficiary.

D. Walker, *Anxious Nation* (Brisb, 1999); *Table Talk*, 24 July 1885, p 4, 10 Apr 1902, p 3; *British A'sian*, 13 Mar 1902, p 454; *Age* (Melb), 14 Mar 1902, p 4; *Syd Mail*, 15 Mar 1902, p 657; *Bulletin*, 22 Mar 1902, p 13, 20 Aug 1930, p 2.

D. R. WALKER

HMELNITSKY, ALEXANDER (1891-1965), pianist, was born on 16 April 1891 in Kiev, Russia (Ukraine), son of Ilya Hmelnitsky, a musician. After studying music at the local conservatory, Alexander transferred to the Moscow conservatory and occasionally performed at the court of Tsar Nicholas II, accompanying a resident *czimbalom* player. Becoming musical director for the dancer Anna Pavlova, Hmelnitsky played the piano and conducted a ballet orchestra on her tours. He was a founding member of the Moscow Trio, which toured extensively and accompanied Pavlova. During World War I, serving in the Russian army, he lost the sight in one eye. He married Ludmila Estrin, a professional cellist, on 30 April 1917 in Moscow.

After the Bolshevik Revolution, the Hmelnitskys and Alexander's friend the pianist Paul Vinogradov escaped through China to Hong Kong. Alexander opened a music academy in Shanghai. Late in 1919 he and Ludmila

moved to Java, the Netherlands East Indies (Indonesia), where their eldest son IGOR (1920-1987) was born on 27 December 1920. After the birth of a second son, the family arrived in Sydney on 27 September 1925 and Ludmila's parents followed.

Vinogradov had preceded them. He and Hmelnitsky taught at a private conservatorium of music and made piano rolls for G. H. Horton, who owned Mastertouch. They also made gramophone records, recording some material as duets, including Rossini, Weber, Beethoven, Mendelssohn, and Tchaikovsky overtures, Schubert's *Unfinished Symphony* and Sarasate's *Zigeunerweisen*. Among Hmelnitsky's solo recordings were works by Chopin, Rachmaninov, Liszt and Debussy and items by Kreisler, Moszkowski, Raff, Scott and Bendel. Vinogradov had been a friend of Scriabin's, and music by Russian masters was a feature of the repertoire, including pieces by Liadov. Hmelnitsky was among the first to perform such works in Sydney. From 1929 he was the music director for radio station 2FC.

In February 1930 the Hmelnitskys went back to Java where a third son was born. The two elder boys returned to Sydney in August 1938 and Ludmila and the youngest child in May 1941; Alexander followed in February 1942 and resumed teaching, based at the W. H. Paling [q.v.5] studios. Alexander and Ludmila were naturalized in 1948 and lived at Neutral Bay, where he enjoyed fishing at Kurraba Point. As a teacher, Alexander brought to Sydney the broad sweep and big sound of the Russian Romantic school and the classic methods and strict training of the Moscow conservatory. His pupils included his son Igor, Maureen Jones, Laurie Davies, Robert Kolben, Elizabeth Hunt, Roy Cross and Rachel Valler. He was one of the first pianists in Australia to play the music and transcriptions of Leopold Godowsky, whom he venerated. Late in life, when he was semi-retired and almost blind, his family helped him to memorize one of the fearsomely difficult Bach-Godowsky sonatas.

An interviewer in 1954 described Hmelnitsky, known familiarly as 'the professor', as short, slim and energetic with thick, brown hair, greying slightly. His English had a strong accent—the family spoke only Russian at home. The couple retired to Wentworth Falls, in the Blue Mountains, where they lost home and possessions in a bushfire on 2 December 1957. Alexander died on 25 January 1965 at Katoomba and was buried in Rookwood cemetery with Russian Orthodox rites. His wife and three sons, all of whom were musicians, survived him.

Igor, who was 5 ft 11 ins (180 cm) tall, thin, with fair hair and greenish eyes and a moustache, had served in the Royal Netherlands Air Force during World War II. Back in

Sydney, he continued the grand Romantic pianistic tradition, performing Chopin sonatas and the Bach-Busoni *Chaconne*. In 1972-85 he taught at the New South Wales State Conservatorium of Music, undertook extensive medical studies—to assist his music teaching —and performed for the Australian Broadcasting Commission. He was a staunch champion of the composer Raymond Hanson [q.v.14], whose challenging piano works he played widely. Igor died of cancer on 27 September 1987 at St Vincent's Hospital, Darlinghurst; his fifth wife and four children survived him.

W. Bebbington (ed), *Oxford Companion to Australian Music* (Melb, 1997); *SMH*, 12 December 1925 p 9, 5 March 1940, p 10, 2 May 1954, p 70, 3 Feb 1965, p 2; *Sun* (Syd), 31 March 1959, p 15; Alexander and Ludmila Hmelnitsky—Series A261, item 1925/259, Series A12508, item 53/139, and Series A435, item 1948/4/276, Igor Hmelnitsky—Series A12508, item 53/142 (NAA, Canb); Series ST 1233/1, item N3375 (NAA, Syd); personal information.

LARRY SITSKY

HODGE, MARGARET EMILY (1858-1938), and NEWCOMB, HARRIET CHRISTINA (1854-1942), feminists and educators, were friends and business partners. Margaret was born on 8 January 1858 at Campden Hill, Kensington, London, fifth daughter and one of seven children of William Barwick Hodge, actuary, and his wife Penelope Sarah, née Smith. Educated at home, Margaret gained a higher local certificate from the University of Cambridge and in 1879 enrolled at Maria Grey Training College for Teachers, Bishopsgate, where she later became a lecturer and met Newcomb. Hodge also took an interest in social work and lectured at the London Working Women's College.

Harriet was born on 20 May 1854 at Bow, London, elder daughter of William Newcomb, accountant, and his wife Harriet Sandell, née Walker. Educated at home, where she studied for the Cambridge teachers' certificate, she lectured at Maria Grey College in 1887-97.

Encouraged by a Hodge relation, Walter Scott [q.v.11], the two women came to Sydney in September 1897 intending to work among the poor. They joined the Teachers' Association of New South Wales; in 1898 Hodge was one of two women elected to the association's council, and Newcomb became a committee member of the Kindergarten Union of New South Wales. Together, they drew up training courses for primary and secondary teachers. The secondary courses were given at Women's College, within the University of Sydney— where Hodge was honorary lecturer in the theory and practice of education (1899-1903)

—and practical work was undertaken at approved schools.

In January 1900 Hodge and Newcomb opened their own demonstration and training school for girls, at Shirley, Edgecliff Road, Sydney, where the two friends also lived. They aimed to 'give the pupils an education which shall develop individual power'. Book-study was 'but a means to this end'. Newcomb, who had 'a genius for organization', was principal and taught French; her students consistently gained Alliance Française prizes. Hodge was a gifted teacher of English, German and particularly history, and a follower of Froebel and later Montessori. A high moral tone obtained, and a liberal approach to religion. With an initial enrolment of four, they had attracted 100 students by the end of 1900. Newcomb introduced Ling's Swedish drill; Shirley was among the first girls' schools with a regular cricket team.

Involved in wider educational and feminist activities, Hodge and Newcomb each read papers to the Australasian Association for the Advancement of Science and spoke out at teachers' association meetings. Hodge also worked with Rose Scott [q.v.11] on behalf of female prisoners and joined the Council of the Womanhood Suffrage League. Newcomb addressed the Sydney Ladies' Sanitary Association and the National Council of Women.

In 1902 Hodge became ill and returned to England. Congratulating Rose Scott on the attainment of women's suffrage, she wrote, 'I think we ought to form a society for educating women to use their votes' and *in absentia* was elected a vice-president of the new Women's Political and Educational League. By 1903 she was back at Shirley, which continued to expand. She and Vida Goldstein [q.v.9] gave papers at the 1904 N.C.W. congress, and in 1907 Hodge became a vice-president of the newly formed New South Wales branch of the Peace Society. In 1903 Newcomb was a founding vice-president of the Society for Child Study. She also lectured on the principles and practice of kindergarten work.

After undergoing 'the Weir Mitchell rest cure', Hodge resumed teaching in 1907. But her uncertain health was a deciding factor in their relinquishing of Shirley. Both left for Britain in October 1908, visiting educational institutions in Japan and the United States of America *en route*. In London they settled in a flat at Maida Vale (later they lived at Golders Green), keeping in touch with former Shirley students such as Kathleen Ussher and Eunice Graham, née Mort, and becoming unofficial representatives for the Australian women's suffrage movement. One of many projects was lecturing on Australia to prospective migrants, using lantern slides provided by the Australian High Commission. In June

1910 they organized an Australian contingent to march in the suffrage procession of 10 000 women. Newcomb worked a banner with a map of Australia and the message 'Women vote throughout Australia'.

Newcomb was founding honorary secretary of the Australian and New Zealand Women Voters' Association (London), established in 1911. In 1912-13 she and Hodge revisited Australia and went to New Zealand, when steps were taken to form 'an Imperial woman suffrage union'. The forerunner of the British Dominions Woman Suffrage Union—with Newcomb as honorary secretary and Hodge honorary treasurer, later honorary press secretary—it aimed to secure for women in the Dominions the same political rights as men and to arouse women to a fuller consciousness of their duties and responsibilities as citizens.

In Melbourne in April 1913 Hodge and Newcomb supported Goldstein's campaign for the Federal seat of Kooyong. They spoke, as well, in Brisbane, Adelaide, Sydney and Perth. During a month in South Africa on her way home, Hodge reported holding public and private meetings. In 1914 she sailed with Dorothy Pethick to New York, where she lectured on suffrage in Australia, then spoke at Chicago—where she met Miles Franklin [q.v.8]—and Toronto, Canada. That year she and Newcomb organized the first conference of the B.D.W.S.U. in London.

For Hodge the outbreak of World War I precipitated another nervous breakdown. Newcomb was occupied with relief work, in particular the distribution of clothing sent from Sydney by Dr Mary Booth's [q.v.7] Babies' Kit Society for the Allies' Babies. In 1916-18 she was on the London committee of the Scottish Women's Hospitals for Foreign Service. By 1916 Hodge had recovered and helped to organize the B.D.W.S.U.'s second conference. She was elected to the Women's Freedom League executive in 1918, having been 'the hardworking literature secretary for many years'. In 1919 as a Labour candidate Hodge was elected an urban district councillor for Hendon. This threw her into a new round of activities and, perhaps inevitably, illness followed. She failed to be re-elected in 1922 and spent three months with Newcomb in Italy from December. By 1925 the B.D.W.S.U. had evolved into the British Commonwealth League of Women. Though the two pioneers remained associated, active suffrage work passed to a new generation.

To Franklin, 'Dear Margaret Hodge' was 'dotty' and woolly-headed; to a former pupil Catherine Mackerras, Hodge was 'large, eccentric, untidy ... a natural radical', although 'she believed heart and soul in the British Empire'. Mackerras saw her during World War I: 'Her blue-stocking appearance

wilder than ever—hairpins fell out as she lectured'. Miss Newcomb was 'small, precise, spinsterly in manner and appearance, fundamentally conventional' with carefully articulated speech and a frail appearance.

Increasingly Hodge, incapacitated with lameness, suffered bouts of depression The two women lived separately from 1927 but met continually. Newcomb mourned the loss of nearly all of her friend's 'glorious vivacity, I can truly say *brilliance* which was so marked in the old days'. After some time living with her siblings, Hodge spent her last years in a nursing home at Finchley, London, where she died on 13 August 1938.

Newcomb remained active, complaining only of a 'leaky memory'. In her later years she was influenced by Rudolf Steiner and sustained by anthroposophy. For her, 'interest in everything seems naturally to grow as one ascends the mountain of life'. She was still a vice-president of the B.C.L. in 1939. Following the outbreak of World War II Newcomb moved to Watford, where she died on 15 April 1942 and was cremated. Former pupils and friends set up a memorial fund, which merged into the Newcomb-Hodge Fellowship in 1950 'to foster the study of the aims and principles of true education' through an essay prize in the University of Sydney's Department of Education.

The New School (Girls) and Kindergarten (nd pamphlet held in Shirley school, miscellaneous papers, ML); R. B. Docker, *Harriet Christina Newcomb and Margaret Emily Hodge* (Syd, 1950); C. Mackerras, *Divided Heart* (Syd, 1991); B. Fletcher, *The Care of Education* (Syd, 1992); A. Woollacott, *To Try Her Fortune in London* (Oxford, 2001); *Aust Teacher*, no 27, Apr 1898, p 7, no 31, June 1899, p 2, no 32, Sept 1899, p 5; *Shirley*, no 2, July 1907, p 5; *NZ Herald*, 18 Feb 1913; Newcomb-Hodge fellowship papers *and* Shirley school papers *and* Rose Scott correspondence *and* Miles Franklin papers (ML); Bessie Rischbieth papers (NL); Scottish Women's Hospitals for Foreign Service, London cte minutes, 1916-19 (Mitchell Lib, Glasgow, Scotland); Women's Freedom League (UK), Annual conference proceedings, 1918, pp 17, 20 & 172 (ts, Women's Library, Lond).

MARGARET BETTISON

HODGSON, CAROLINE (1851-1908), better known as 'Madame Brussels', brothel proprietor, was born at Potsdam, Prussia, in 1851, one of at least two daughters of John Lohman and his wife Frederica, née Schultze. On 18 February 1871 in the register office, district of St George, Hanover Square, London, Caroline married Studholme George Hodgson (c.1836-1893), eldest son of a Hampshire landowner. The couple soon departed for Melbourne, arriving in July 1871. In October 1872 Studholme joined the Victorian police force.

Upon his posting to Mansfield two years later, if not before, the couple separated, and seem not to have been reunited until the end of his life. Despite, or perhaps because of, their years apart, Caroline retained affection for Hodgson and after his death regularly marked its anniversary in newspaper 'In Memoriam' columns.

By 1874 she was keeping a brothel and going by her sobriquet, the origins of which are unknown. For thirty-three years Madame Brussels ran houses of ill fame around the top of Lonsdale Street. Her principal establishment and residence, 32-34 Lonsdale Street, was a high-class, extravagantly furnished bordello, operating as something of a libidinous gentlemen's club. Hodgson drew on her connections for business and legal advice, and probably financial support and police protection. She was legally represented by the politician-lawyers David Gaunson and (Sir) Samuel Gillott [qq.v.4,9]; the latter's political career was ended when his role as mortgagor of her properties was revealed in 1906. In one sense operating on the margins of nineteenth-century Melbourne society, in another she was inextricably connected to its centre.

The most celebrated madam of her day, Hodgson was revered by some, for representing Melbourne's roguish character, reviled by others, for despoiling the heart of a 'great Christian city'. She had considerable organizational and entrepreneurial skills, and a greater chance to use them than most women of the period. With the passage of time, she became an icon of Melbourne's racy past. Some have claimed that she was involved with the disappearance of the Victorian parliamentary mace in 1891. While it was rumoured to have been taken to a bawdy house by drunken politicians to be used in 'low travesties of parliamentary procedure', Hodgson's name was never mentioned contemporaneously in connection with it. In her youth she was sensationally described as a 'magnificent pink, white and golden maned animal'. Later she was a 'spectacled middle aged woman', more like 'a benevolent midwife than the keeper of a notorious brothel'.

Hodgson visited Germany in 1894 and on her return married a fellow German, Jacob Pohl, on 10 April 1895 at St Patrick's Catholic Cathedral, Melbourne. The couple spent little time together and divorced in 1906. Earlier she had been romantically connected with the composer and music critic Alfred Plumpton (1848-1902). He was reputed to have promoted her establishment and to have fathered a daughter by her. While no birth certificate can be found, Caroline's will did mention an adopted daughter, Irene Hodgson.

At the turn of the century, moves to curtail prostitution increased and the Lonsdale Street area was gradually cleared of brothels—

Madame Brussels's was closed in 1907. By then she was suffering from diabetes and chronic pancreatitis, which led to her death on 12 July 1908 at her home and former brothel in Melbourne. She was buried beside her first husband in St Kilda cemetery. Her estate was sworn for probate at £4828.

C. Pearl, *Wild Men of Sydney* (Lond, 1958); K. Dunstan, *Wowsers* (Syd, 1968); G. Davison, D. Dunstan and C. McConville (eds), *The Outcasts of Melbourne* (Syd, 1985); R. Wright, *Who Stole the Mace* (Melb, 1991); *Truth* (Melb), 31 Oct 1903, p 5, 10 Mar 1906, p 5, 1 Dec 1906, p 4, 8 Dec 1906, p 4, 20 Apr 1907, p 3; C. McConville, Outcast Melbourne: Social Deviance in the City 1880-1914 (M.A. thesis, Univ Melb, 1974); P. Bentley, Edifices of Venereal Renown and Gilded Palaces of Sin: Madame Brussels, a Life on the Margins in Mid to Late Nineteenth Century Melbourne (B.A. Hons thesis, Monash Univ, 1993); A712, item 1896/C889 (NAA, Canb).
PHILIP BENTLEY

HOGARTH, JULIUS (1820-1879), sculptor, engraver and silversmith, was born on 24 December 1820 in Copenhagen, son of Jorgen Christian Hougaard and his wife Charlotte Kathrine, née Lauden. Julius reputedly trained under the Danish neo-classical sculptor Bertel Thorvaldsen. On 18 November 1842 at Trinitatis Church, Copenhagen, Julius married Christiane Ulrike Galle; they had one son and later divorced.

Hougaard reached Sydney in the *César Godeffroy* on 11 December 1852; Conrad Erichsen, a Norwegian engraver, was another passenger. Failing to make their fortunes on the goldfields, they became silversmiths and jewellers in Sydney, possibly first with Adolphus Blau. By March 1854 Julius had Anglicized his name and Hogarth, Erichsen & Co., jewellers and watchmakers, was in business in George Street. Talented artists, both created small sculptures in gold and silver of miners and Aborigines. Hogarth won attention with a three-inch (7.6 cm) high figure of a miner for J. L. Montefiore [q.v.5], and in 1854 exhibited figures of gold diggers at the Australian Museum in the preview of exhibits for the Paris International Exhibition next year. In 1856 Hogarth was naturalized. On 18 November 1858 at the Scots Church, Sydney, he married 16-year-old Charlotte Elizabeth, daughter of the bookseller James Tegg [q.v.2]. They had seven children, one dying in infancy. Hogarth's first wife remarried in Denmark in 1859.

The workshop of Hogarth, Erichsen & Co. produced major testimonial pieces and sporting trophies incorporating Australian flora and fauna motifs. In 1855 subscribers put up £700 for a gold cup presented next year to the railway contractor William Randle, designed by William Dexter [q.v.4 Caroline Dexter] and John Smedley—'the most superb achievement of art yet executed in this colony', according to the *Sydney Morning Herald*. The firm also made the 100-guinea, silver Liverpool Cup, which Randle presented in 1856. It combined local and racing motifs: a kangaroo and emu, a native fig-tree with an Aborigine climbing up after possums, a racehorse and a jockey. As early as about 1857 Hogarth and his partner produced a range of silver-mounted emu eggs.

Heavy, well-crafted 'botanical' jewellery was his specialty, as well as presentation pieces in silver and gold, often combined with other local materials, which had a market as testimonials to visitors or public figures, such as governors, leaving the colony. The expensive raw materials, however, tied up capital in inventory. In January 1861 the business was declared insolvent and the partnership dissolved. Nevertheless, Hogarth exhibited 'strikingly Australian' gold statuettes at the 1862 London International Exhibition. Bankrupted again in May 1864, he none the less made the colony's gift for the Prince of Wales's marriage to Princess Alexandra of Denmark—a massive, gold casket, combining the influence of Thorvaldsen with Australian motifs. Hogarth then moved to Melbourne, where in 1867 he was bankrupted a third time. He produced work for other silversmiths, jewellers and medallists, including Thomas Stokes, and engraved medals for agricultural associations. His first son Hagbarth, a baker, migrated from Denmark to Victoria in 1876.

Superb casting and a fine sculptural quality marked Hogarth's work. He introduced a range of naturalistically presented Australian flora and fauna and human figures, and worked with artists such as Knud Bull, Alexander Habbe and Thomas Balcombe. Returning to Sydney with some of his family about 1878, Hogarth set up shop at Newtown, but died of chronic liver disease on 5 March 1879 at his Chippendale residence; he was buried in Rookwood cemetery. His wife and their three sons and three daughters and the son of his first marriage survived him. Although much was melted down for the bullion content, some of Hogarth's work survives. Pieces attributed to him are in the Powerhouse Museum, Sydney, the National Gallery of Victoria, Melbourne, the Queensland Art Gallery, Brisbane, and the National Library of Australia, Canberra.

A. Andrews, *Australasian Tokens and Coins* (Syd, 1921), p 113; *Austn Antique & Fine Art Dealers' Fair* (Syd, 1966); L. J. Carlisle, *Australian Commemorative Medals and Medalets from 1788* (Syd, 1983); J. B. Hawkins, *19th Century Australian Silver*, 1 (Woodbridge, UK, 1990), p 130; J. Wade, 'Julius Hogarth', *Gold & Civilisation* (Canb, 2001) and 'Fanny Richardson's Brooch', *NLA News*, Oct 2003, p 3; *Austn Business Collectors Annual*, 1987/88, p 194; *World of Antiques and Art*, June-Dec 2000, p 12; *Australiana*, 22, no 2, 2000, p 36, 22, no 3, 2000, p 68; *SMH*, 18 Apr 1856, p 5, 2 Sept 1856, p 4, 19 Sept 1856, p 5.

JOHN WADE

HOOD, COLLIN (c.1836-1914), stockman and Aboriginal leader, was born near Hexham in south-western Victoria, son of 'King Blackwood' and Mary. A man of the Djabwurung people, he was given the name Merang and grew up with knowledge of traditional life. His totem was *jallan*, the whip snake. Squatters used his Aboriginal name for a local pastoral run, and on Merrang, particularly after it was acquired by Robert Hood's [q.v.9] family in 1856, he became a trusted and respected employee: station records show that he was paid as a European. Like many Aboriginal workers he was given his employer's surname.

Collin married NORA Villiers (c.1836-1871), an Aboriginal woman, also known as Ageebonyee, daughter of Ningi Burning and Nango Burn, on 1 November 1855 in a Christian service. They were to have six children. Born at Korrewarra, and baptized at Warrnambool on 24 June 1853, Nora had been a domestic servant and was exceptional in that she could read and write English. Robert Hood described her as 'highly civilised', and to the Presbyterian minister William Hamilton she was one of two Aboriginal women he had met 'possessing a greater amount of religious knowledge than many of our white population'. In 1863 the missionary J. G. Paton [q.v.5] called unannounced at her hut in the Aboriginal camp at Hexham, to find her reading the *Presbyterian Messenger*, with the Bible at hand. Impressed, he spoke about her and read her letters at his Melbourne farewell meeting, when he argued for greater efforts to 'give the Gospel to the Aborigines'.

In 1860 Collin and Nora had been among the first to ask for an individual grant of land when the Victorian government introduced a policy of providing for the dispossessed Aborigines. It appears that the land was granted but the Hoods later lost it. They moved to Framlingham Aboriginal station when it opened in 1865. Nora died on 28 March 1871 in Melbourne and was buried in the new cemetery there. On 6 August 1872 at Framlingham Collin married with Congregational forms Louisa Lutton, née King (or Tappoke), widowed daughter of 'King George' and Mary. Born near Mount Rouse, Louisa was a servant with three surviving children from her previous marriage; she and Collin were to have four children. His experience and the fact that he worked 'willingly and more constantly than most men' persuaded the manager of

Framlingham in the early 1880s to appoint him stockman there.

Collin emerged as a spokesman for his community after the Board for the Protection of the Aborigines decided on 7 August 1889 to close Framlingham. The Aboriginal station's inhabitants and their friends, including the politician (later premier) John Murray, protested, and the chief secretary Alfred Deakin [qq.v.10,8] visited Framlingham in November. Collin was one of two Aborigines who addressed him. The area had been their 'hunting grounds', he said, and 'they hoped to be allowed to live there for the remaining years of their lives' and 'if removed to other places would not agree'. Deakin was unable to sway the board, however, whose acting general inspector Rev. Friedrich Hagenauer [q.v.4] had visited Framlingham and reported: 'A few of the blacks ... have been crammed in the idea of getting a few hundred acres of land from the reserve either as a hunting ground or small farms, and their leader Collin Hood, seems very earnest in his request'. But, he assured the board, few of the Aborigines were locals, some had already left and the rest would soon follow.

To correct the impression that the residents were not locals and therefore had no special attachment to the locality, the pastoralist Robert Hood asked Collin to make 'a list of the pure blacks at present at Framlingham, their names and birth places'. Prepared by Collin's daughter, this was published in a Warrnambool newspaper. Of thirty-nine 'pure blacks' and four 'half-castes', only 'one pure black man' was born outside the district.

On 23 September 1890 Murray heard that the reserve was about to be transferred to the Council of Agricultural Education. He raised in parliament the injustice of what was about to occur and used details provided by Collin to arouse sympathy. In October Deakin announced that 500 acres (202 ha) were to be retained for the Aborigines. Murray's support was decisive, but nothing could have been achieved without the refusal of the Aborigines to move, and Hood had been vital in firming their resolve.

Louise died in 1890. Though entitled to stay on the reserve, next year Hood was living at Hexham. By 1897, in a period of economic depression, he was at Ramahyuck Aboriginal station in eastern Victoria, probably to be near his family. On 17 March 1898 at Lake Tyers he married Helen Rivers, née Johnson, a 23-year-old, widowed Kurnai woman. Hood died on 3 May 1914 and was buried at Lake Tyers with Anglican rites. His wife, their four sons and one daughter, and a daughter by his second wife survived him. Hood's actions enabled the community to survive, which led to Framlingham being, with Lake Tyers, the only former Victorian Aboriginal station

communities to receive title to land in 1971 and to the successful 1970s and 1980s land rights claim to Framlingham Forest.

J. Critchett, *Untold Stories* (Melb, 1998); J. Paton (ed), *John G. Paton, D.D., Missionary to the New Hebrides* (Lond, 1894); A. Campbell (comp), *Victorian Aborigines: John Bulmer's Recollections 1855-1908* (Melb, 1994); *Warrnambool Standard*, 2 Nov 1889, 29 Nov 1889; B313, item 57, B314, B335, item 1, B1272 (NAA, Melb); VPRS 3992, N13183 1889 (PRO, Vic); Merrang pastoral records (held by Hood family, Merrang, Vic).   JAN CRITCHETT

HORNE, JOSEPH MORTIMER; *see* RAINE

HORROCKS, JOHN AINSWORTH (1818-1846), pastoralist and explorer, was born on 22 March 1818 at Penwortham Lodge, near Preston, Lancashire, England, eldest son and one of eight children of Peter Horrocks, gentleman, and his wife Clara, née Jupp. John was educated at Chester and in London, then by a tutor when the family moved to Boulogne, France, in 1831. Sent to a school in Paris two years later, he ran away to Vienna, where the family had settled. He arrived in South Australia in 1839—on his twenty-first birthday—with his 16-year-old brother Eustace, who later returned to Britain. John was 6 ft 2 ins (189 cm) tall dark haired with blue eyes, and possessed a rugged constitution. He brought with him a family servant, a blacksmith, a shepherd, four merino rams, sheepdogs, tools, sufficient clothing for five years and a church bell.

Unlike many, Horrocks would not wait in Adelaide for the completion of land surveys. On the advice of Edward John Eyre [q.v.1], he explored land near the Hutt River, north of Adelaide, and established Penwortham village. Other pastoralists followed him into the area. In 1841 the long-awaited special survey gained a frustrated Horrocks title to only some of the fertile land he had been occupying. Nevertheless, he built up a flock of 9000 sheep and is believed to have established the first vineyard in the Clare district. In 1842, following the death of his father, he went back to Britain, but returned to South Australia early in 1844 when his affairs faced financial difficulties.

After Horrocks resolved these problems, bored with farming he rented out most of his properties. 'I want a more stirring life', he wrote, and proposed an expedition to search for new agricultural lands near Lake Torrens. An appeal for government assistance was unsuccessful but over £140 was raised by private subscription. Horrocks's own contribution included the first camel in Australia.

Leaving Penwortham on 29 July 1846 for a planned four-month absence, the party of six —including the artist S. T. Gill [q.v.1] and Jimmy Moorhouse, an Aboriginal goatherd —travelled with the camel, two carts, six horses and twelve goats. On 16-19 August the expedition crossed the Flinders Ranges via Horrocks Pass. Horrocks found that the camel was temperamental, biting both humans and goats, but it would carry up to 350 pounds (158.7 kg), vital for anticipated treks through waterless country. The horses had been without water for two days when on 21 August the party reached Depot Creek, an old campsite of Eyre's.

From here several exploratory trips were made. On 1 September Horrocks was preparing to shoot a bird on the shores of Lake Dutton. The kneeling camel moved while Horrocks was reloading his gun, catching the cock. The resultant discharge removed the middle fingers of his right hand and a row of teeth. He was taken back to Penwortham, arriving on 19 September. Having ordered the camel to be shot, Horrocks died of his wounds on 23 September and was buried in land at Penwortham that he had given to the Church of England for a church. He had not married.

While often remembered as the man who was shot by his own camel, Horrocks had pioneered use of the animals in Australian exploration, and had earlier opened up the Clare valley for settlement. He was portrayed in some of Gill's numerous water-colours and sketches held in the Art Gallery of South Australia and other institutions. The State Library of South Australia has copies of a sketch and a painting of Horrocks produced by his brother-in-law Colonel Temple from a contemporary photograph.

G. C. Morphett, *John Ainsworth Horrocks* (Adel, 1946); G. A. Pearce, *John Ainsworth Horrocks of Penwortham* (Watervale, SA, 1986); *PRGSSA*, 1899, p 83, 1904-5, pp 36-48; *SA Register*, 1 July 1846, p 2, 4 July 1846, p 2, 15 July 1846, p 3, 18 July 1846, 12 Sept 1846, 30 Sept 1846, 3 Oct 1846, 10 Oct 1846; *Advertiser* (Adel), 29 May 1888, p 6; Horrocks family papers, PRG 966 (SLSA).   JON CHITTLEBOROUGH

HORSEMAN, MARIE COMPSTON (1911-1974), cartoonist and illustrator, was born on 9 December 1911 near Rochester, Victoria, daughter of Frederick Ernest Horseman, farmer, and his wife Katherine Marie Compston, née Miller, migrants from Yorkshire, England. Mollie grew up in Melbourne. Her parents having amicably separated, in 1924 her mother took her to Sheffield, England, and on to Germany. While Katherine managed a canteen for the British Army on the Rhine, Mollie was enrolled at a finishing school for young ladies. Speaking no German, she communicated mainly by drawing fellow students (and pictures of castles on the Rhine).

On returning to Australia two years later she cheekily advertised as a 'German-speaking governess' and was briefly employed by Norman Lindsay [q.v.10] and his wife Rose [q.v.]. At (East) Sydney Technical College she was one of a brilliant crop of late 1920s female students influenced by Rayner Hoff's [q.v.9] vitalist, 'life force' ideas to create sculptures, paintings and (especially) cartoons unprecedented in their uninhibited sexuality. Mollie later called Lindsay and Hoff two of the three great influences on her life—a rather backhanded compliment as it was made in *Man* magazine, renowned for its salacious cartoons, many drawn by her.

Financial problems forced Mollie to leave the college before completing her diploma. In 1929 she joined *Smith's Weekly* with Joan Morrison (1911-1969), who had been born in Kent, England, and was a sculpture graduate from the same college. The editor Frank Marien reportedly put them in a room with a 'KEEP OUT' sign on the door. They called themselves 'the Smith's Sisters' and occasionally drew cartoons jointly. 'Joan and Molly, the "Smith's" sisters, are asked to do a strip' (21 July 1934) consists of five punning frames ending with them resigning, offended by the lewd suggestion. *Smith's* was unique in offering a living wage to about a dozen cartoonists and promoting their names, personae and creations in such pseudo-autobiographical group cartoons and caricatures, many wittily captioned by Ken Slessor [q.v.16].

Horseman and Morrison were the first Australian women to be celebrated for their adult cartoons. Tall, blonde and bouncy, Mollie was invariably depicted as towering over the entire art staff ('We had to bend her to get her into the picture'), including a self-caricature of 15 April 1933. Like most of her colleagues she adapted urban stereotypes from *Punch*, *Lilliput* and *Esquire* but usually gave them a local focus:

What was the party at Darlinghurst like last night?
They sang 'God Save the Furniture'
(8 September 1934)

or an exuberant character bereft of malice or morals:

AUNT: 'Why did your friend look so worried?'
NIECE: 'She can't remember at whose cocktail party she left the baby'
(27 October 1934).

Morrison, in contrast, was noted for her drawings of beautiful, long-legged young women.

On 2 September 1931 at North Sydney registry office Horseman married William

Longford Power, an articled clerk. They had a son, Roderick, before divorcing. On 8 June 1938 at Mosman Presbyterian Church she married Nelson Illingworth, company representative, grandson of the sculptor Nelson Illingworth [q.v.9]. There were one son and three daughters of the marriage, which also ended in divorce. The family lived in Brisbane in the early 1940s, with Mollie freelancing. She painted murals on two railway carriages used by the Queensland government as travelling dental clinics, drew 'Fatto', 'Dora' and 'Tootles' for otherwise all-male comic books published by Frank Johnson in Sydney and contributed cartoons to *Man*, *Woman's Mirror* and *Rydge's Business Journal*.

From 1946 she worked for the Sydney production unit of the Brisbane *Courier Mail*. After Jean Cullen suicided, in the early 1950s Mollie took over her new comic strip about the teenager 'Pam' in the *Sunday Mail* and gave it a distinctively Australian character. Her best-known work, it ran for over eleven years and was widely syndicated. From 1957 she lived at Avalon with the children, drawing 'Pam' and other comics and cartoons and fashion and children's book illustrations. She painted nymphs, shepherds and other rococo fantasies for special evenings at Romano's [q.v.11] nightclub. In the early 1960s she was staff artist on *Everybody's* magazine. Her numerous illustrations (either anonymous or signed 'Vanessa') included a weekly, full-page colour cartoon of the sexy *Man* type and the serial 'Girl Crusoe' (1964), a cheerful parody of the popular 'good girl cheesecake' comic. At the local jazz club on Saturday nights she played the lagerphone ('an Australian contrivance of bottle tops and broomsticks').

Horseman worked professionally for over forty years by enthusiastically embracing every opportunity. In 1963 *Everybody's* called her 'Australia's only woman cartoonist'. She was certainly the most visible. At their annual ball in 1956, her colleagues in the Australian Black and White Artists' Club 'smocked' her (presented her with an artist's smock decorated by fellow members), and she was later voted Sydney Savage Club 'Cartoonist of the Year'. In 1964 she was the only woman in a group photograph of forty-three professional cartoonists and one of nine women among 140 cartoonists in the survey exhibition *Fifty Years of Australian Cartooning*.

In 1967-69 she was back in Brisbane, illustrating books for Jacaranda Press, chiefly school readers. Then she settled in an old cottage in the Blue Mountains at Glenbrook, New South Wales, and continued freelance work, painting landscapes in oils as a hobby. In 1973 she was hit by a car. This accident led to a stroke that deprived her of speech and the use of her right hand. She taught herself to draw with her left and produced small abstracts with coloured pens. Horseman died on 7 May 1974 in the Blue Mountains Hospital, Katoomba, and was buried in the churchyard of St Thomas's Church of England, Mulgoa. The son of her first marriage, and one son and two daughters of her second, survived her.

R. P. Power, 'Marie Compston (Mollie) Horseman', in J. Kerr (ed), *Heritage: The National Women's Art Book* (Syd, 1995).   JOAN KERR*

HORSFALL, JOHN CAMPBELL (1912-1976), economist and newspaper editor, was born on 26 February 1912 at Daylesford, Victoria, third child of Victorian-born parents Francis Arthur Horsfall, shire engineer, and his wife Campbell Isabel, née Donaldson. Jack (as his name was registered at birth) was educated at Wesley College, Melbourne, then Ormond [q.v.5] College, University of Melbourne (B.A., 1933). Majoring in economics, he won several scholarships and studied under (Sir) Douglas Copland and L. F. Giblin [qq.v.13,8]. In 1933 he won a scholarship to Trinity College, Cambridge (B.A., 1935; M.A., 1941), where his teachers included D. H. Robertson and Colin Clark. A champion sprinter, Horsfall held the Australian 220-yard record (21.3 seconds in 1933) and competed in the 1934 Empire games.

After short-term jobs in Whitehall, London, at the Imperial Economic Committee, he worked in a stockbroker's office, undertaking statistical research on the account of J. M. (Lord) Keynes, and as a journalist for the *Investor's Chronicle*. When he joined the London Scottish Regiment, the Gordon Highlanders, on 17 October 1938, he was 5 ft 10 ins (178 cm) tall, weighed 149 lbs (67.6 kg) and had blue eyes and brown hair. On the outbreak of World War II he was 'embodied' in September 1939 and commissioned in the Royal Fusiliers in March 1940.

Fluent in French, German and Italian, Horsfall transferred to the Intelligence Corps in August 1942. According to his later account, he headed counter intelligence in the Greek revolution of 1944-45. In January 1945 he was mentioned in dispatches for his work in Italy, interrogating Italian prisoners. He served in Palestine, was promoted acting lieutenant colonel in September 1945 and completed his service on 27 June 1946 with the honorary rank of major. His marriage on 14 October 1939 in the parish church, Stanwell, Middlesex, to Mary Elwyn Gibson was dissolved, and on 12 July 1944 at the register office, Westminster, London, he married Joan Cellier.

After the war Horsfall joined the *Economist* news magazine in London as a journalist. In July 1950 R. A. G. Henderson [q.v.18] recruited

Horsfall as a senior finance writer for the *Sydney Morning Herald*. Henderson thought he had 'a bright likeable personality and I imagine a capacity to cultivate and establish contacts'. Within a year of his return to Australia, Horsfall was assigned to establish a weekly finance paper, to be published each Thursday by John Fairfax & Sons [qq.v.4,8] and to head off a challenge by its rival, Associated Newspapers Ltd.

The first edition of the *Australian Financial Review* appeared on 16 August 1951. Its early success was enhanced by its coverage in September of the 1951 Menzies [q.v.15] government's 'horror budget'. Horsfall produced robust and informative newspapers, but worked extremely long hours and struggled with his own finances. Six months after the inaugural edition, he resigned in a dispute with the company over pay and returned to England. Footloose, Horsfall came back to Australia in mid-1952 to work as the Melbourne correspondent of the *Financial Review* until April 1953. His marriage to Joan ended in divorce next year. On 29 July 1955 at the Register Office, Kensington, London, Horsfall married Denise Patricia Redvers-Mutton. The couple came to Australia with their two sons in 1959.

In the 1960s Horsfall worked as finance editor and writer on (Sir) Frank Packer's [q.v.15] *Bulletin* and with Maxwell Newton on the *Sunday Observer*. Though blind for the last seven years of his life as a result of diabetes, Horsfall continued his writing, which included his informed and coolly analytical *The Liberal Era* (Melbourne, 1973). He died of a cerebrovascular accident on 29 August 1976 at Heidelberg Repatriation Hospital, Melbourne, and was cremated with Anglican rites. His wife and their two sons, and the daughter and son of his second marriage, survived him.

G. Souter, *Company of Heralds* (Melb, 1981); *Austn Financial Review*, 31 Aug 1976, p 9; *SMH*, 1 Sept 1976, p 11; G. Noonan, The Establishment of the Australian Financial Review, 1951-1970, and its Impact on Public Policy (M.A. thesis, Univ of Syd, 2002); service file (Army Personnel Centre, Glasgow, Scotland); J. Fairfax group archives, Sydney; information from Mrs D. Horsfall, Melb.

GERARD NOONAN

HOWARD, SIR HENRY RUDOLPH (1890-1970), businessman and lord mayor, was born on 20 April 1890 at Sale, Manchester, England, son of Frederick Joseph Howard, solicitor's clerk, and his wife Mary Jane, née Harris. Educated at Sale School and Manchester Technical School, where he received some accounting training, Harry joined the Manchester Gas Co. as a clerk. In July 1912, after his health deteriorated, he migrated to Sydney with his widowed mother, brother and sister.

The family settled at Mosman. A keen chorister, Howard met his future wife Beatrice Thelma May Tilburn in the choir of Mosman Congregational Church, where they were married on 7 February 1920. Music continued to be a vital part of their lives. They moved to Perth in 1924, and Howard became manager for William W. Wyper, who held the Australian agency for Edison and sold phonograms and Ediphone dictating machines. The firm, Phonographs Ltd, became an institution in the city. A partner from 1934, Howard successfully diversified into household electrical goods. Following a merger in 1957, the company became known as Vox Adeon Howard. With the introduction of television to Perth in 1959 the business boomed—by 1960 the company had twelve branches and dominated electrical retailing in the city.

Howard was sometime president of the Perth Rotary Club, the Perth Chamber of Commerce, the Federated Chambers of Commerce and the Royal Automobile Club of Western Australia, as well as chairman of the Radio Traders' Association and honorary consul for Finland. From 1954 to 1968 he was chairman of the Congregational Union of Western Australia. In 1955, with the support of Perth's business community, he was elected lord mayor at his second attempt. Decent and circumspect, with conservative values and a keen sense of decorum (he habitually wore a dark, three-piece suit and a homburg hat), he brought considerable dignity to the position. A good public speaker, he never lost his strong, north-country English accent.

Chairman of the British Empire and Commonwealth Games organizing council, in 1956 Howard—and his town clerk Allan Green—made a successful bid for the 1962 Empire and Commonwealth Games to be held in Perth. His support for the building of an Olympic Pool in Kings Park, an area of bushland that had been preserved by Sir John Forrest [q.v.8], caused huge community debate. Two attempts to carry legislation permitting the pool failed, and to Howard's irritation he was nicknamed 'Pip' (Pool in the Park). A lover of roses, he created further controversy—and was satirized in a poem by Randolph Stow, 'The Utopia of Lord Mayor Howard'—when he was said to have instigated the replacement of eucalyptus trees by rose bushes along Kings Park Road.

Howard was knighted in 1961. Early next year, it was proposed that the lights of Perth be left on all night for the American astronaut John Glenn during his first orbit of Earth. The State government supported the suggestion but Howard, doubting that the lights could be seen from space, said that it was 'morally wrong for public money to be wasted'. Condemned by the press, he was further embarrassed when a visiting American millionaire offered to pay the city's light bill. In a unanimous vote, the City Council then agreed to leave on all the lights of the city for the night. Glenn thanked the people of Perth from his spacecraft, *Apollo*, giving the forthcoming games a tremendous boost, and Perth was tagged 'City of Light'.

Invited to New York to take part in the ticker tape parade for Glenn, Sir Harry accepted, again attracting critics who cited his initial stance on the lights issue. Undeterred, he set off for New York, his trip financed by the *Journal-American* and Qantas. Wearing full mayoral regalia, he and his wife were in the third car in the procession, following Glenn in the first car and Vice-President Lyndon Johnson in the second.

Sir Harry was appointed K.B.E. in 1963, and travelled to London to receive the accolade from the Queen. In 1964 he lost the lord mayoralty. He died on 11 August 1970 in hospital at West Perth and was cremated with Congregational forms; his wife and their two sons survived him.

J. Gregory, *City of Light* (Perth, 2003); *Daily News* (Perth), 25 Jan 1962, p 1, 29 May 1967, p 15, 11 Aug 1970, pp 1 & 3; *West Australian*, 20 Feb 1962, p 1, 23 Feb 1962, p 2, 12 Aug 1970, pp 6, 12; *Sunday Times* (Perth), 4 Mar 1962; J. Bannister, taped interview with Keith Howard (1999, Perth City L); K. Howard, 'A Pool in the Park. Why Not?' (research paper, 1984), held by author; Howard papers (BL); information from Mr K. Howard, Crawley, Perth.

JENNY GREGORY

HOWARDE, CATHERINE CLARISSA (KATE) (1864-1939), actor, theatrical entrepreneur, playwright and cinema pioneer, was born on 28 July 1864 at North Woolwich, London, daughter of Edward George Jones, labourer, and his wife Harriett Hannah, née Payne. The family migrated to New Zealand, where Edward became a dealer. Kate claimed to have published stories in the *Evening Post* (Wellington) in the 1870s, written a pantomime when aged 10 and managed her own theatrical company at 17. Describing herself as an actress, she married William Henry de Saxe, musician, on 28 April 1884 in the registrar's office, Christchurch. Their only child Florence Adrienne was born at Christchurch on 5 December 1884, and de Saxe soon departed.

Adopting the stage name 'Kate Howarde', by the late 1890s she based her company in Australia and toured extensively through Australasia, performing mainly in country halls and tents. Kate wrote much of the material, including sketches, songs and pantomimes, and claimed to have also written several serious plays, including *When the Tide Rises* and *Under the Southern Cross*. The troupe included her two younger brothers, Louis and Albert Howarde, and one of her two sisters ('Billie', who later married Harry Craig, also in the company).

The Craigs kept the group touring in Australia when Kate went overseas. In 1906 she travelled to San Francisco, United States of America, then to New York and London; it may have been during this trip that she married Elton Black, who had been with the company from about 1904 and returned to Australia with Kate in 1909. From 1914 to late 1917, at a time when suburban theatrical companies were not common, Howarde successfully presented weekly-change repertory at the National Theatre, Balmain, Sydney. The fare included Kate's own melodramas, *The White Slave Traffic* (1914) and *Why Girls Leave Home* (1914).

She separated from Black about 1918, just before her greatest success—the bucolic comedy *Possum Paddock*, 'written, produced and presented by Kate Howarde'—which toured country areas before opening in Sydney at the Theatre Royal on 6 September 1919. Often compared with *On Our Selection*, it told of the financial and romantic problems of a bush family, mixed sentiment with farce and produced hilarity in the audience. The play's reception encouraged Kate to turn it into a film, which she co-directed with Charles Villiers—making her the first woman to direct a feature film in Australia. Many of the original cast participated, including Kate as the widow Nella Carsley, while her daughter, using the stage name 'Leslie Adrien', took the female romantic lead, originally played by Rose Rooney. The film was released successfully at the Lyric Theatre, Sydney, in January 1921.

The success of both play and film was sufficient to finance a ten-month tour for the whole company in 1922 to South Africa, the U.S.A. and Great Britain. On return, they resumed country tours, presenting revivals of *Possum Paddock* as well as imported plays and others written or adapted by Kate herself, with occasional city seasons. Kate's second bucolic comedy, *Gum Tree Gully* (1924), was only a moderate success, but by then she had moved on to more dramatic works, such as *The Limit* (1921), *The Bush Outlaw* (1923), *Find Me a Wife* (1923) and *Common Humanity* (1927). She presented *The Judgment of Jean Calvert* in Sydney in 1935.

Catherine Clarissa Black died of cerebral thrombosis on 18 February 1939 at the home of her daughter at Kensington, Sydney, and was buried with Anglican rites in Randwick cemetery. Despite the dramatic licence of some media reports, she was of importance to Australian theatrical and film history as a pioneering female writer and producer, and for bringing live theatre to generations of rural audiences.

Theatre Mag, 1 Nov 1920; *Aust Woman's Mirror*, 15 Jan 1929, pp 12 & 45; *SMH*, 20 Feb 1939, p 13; B. Garlick, Australian Travelling Theatre 1890-1935: A Study in Popular Entertainment and National Ideology (Ph.D. thesis, Univ Qld, 1994); theatre programme collections (SLV and Performing Arts Museum, Melb); A/1336, items 12661, 16973, 7819, 9746, and 25752 (NAA, Canb).   INA BERTRAND

HOWE, ANN (c.1802-1842), newspaper proprietor, was born in Sydney, daughter of Sarah Bird, a successful convict entrepreneur and publican, and John Morris, also a former convict. On 17 December 1821 at St Phillip's Church of England Ann Bird married Robert, the London-born son of George Howe [qq.v.1]. Robert had that year inherited his father's printing and publishing business and ownership of the *Sydney Gazette*, the colony's semi-official newspaper. He was also granted his father's appointment as government printer and the associated lucrative government contracts.

Ann and Robert Howe were part of the emerging colonial middle-class society of early Sydney. Worth £10 000, George Howe's estate represented a sizeable inheritance, although it was partly tied up in a protracted legal battle with the children of his marriage to Sarah Wills, widow of the wealthy merchant Edward Wills. Reflecting their growing wealth and respectability, the Howes had a purpose-built shop and printing office and a spacious and elegant residence, reputedly designed by Francis Greenway [q.v.1].

Following a dissolute youth, Robert was a now devout Methodist. Ann agreed to raise his child Robert Charles (1820-1875) by the convict Elizabeth Lees. Ann bore four children to Robert in a turbulent marriage: at one time she was cut out of his will and then reinstated. After his death by drowning in 1829 she took an active and public role in running the *Sydney Gazette*. She later described how the executors of the Howe estate—the merchant Richard Jones and Rev. Ralph Mansfield [qq.v.2], Robert's former business partner and editor of the *Sydney Gazette*—ran the business down to such an extent that they were about to sell it for a meagre price to the owners of the newly established *Sydney Herald*. With Jones's reluctant support, Ann stepped in and took over management of the newspaper.

As proprietor, she aligned the *Sydney Gazette* with the reformist, liberal administration of Governor Bourke [q.v.1]. In doing so, she antagonized a powerful group of wealthy merchants and landowners, the 'exclusives', who argued that political and civil rights in the penal colony should be restricted to those not tainted by convict ancestry. Ann appointed as editor a ticket-of-leave convict William Augustus Watt, who wrote stinging articles exposing the slave-owning mentality and practices of many of the colony's wealthy landowners. In particular, he drew attention to the activities of a group in the Hunter Valley including James Mudie [q.v.2], a bitter opponent of Bourke's. Brought before the Sydney bench on trumped-up charges, Watt was removed by the governor to Port Macquarie, where the Howe estate had a land grant on the Macleay River.

In 1836 Ann petitioned Bourke for permission to marry Watt. Mudie attempted to prevent the marriage by producing evidence that Watt was a notoriously bad character who had both a wife abandoned in Scotland and a child from a liaison with a convict woman in the Female Factory. Bourke ruled that the charges were malicious, and the couple married on 9 February 1836 at St Thomas's Church of England, Port Macquarie. That year Jones used his position as executor and guarantor of outstanding loans to trigger a foreclosure and transfer ownership of the newspaper from Ann to Robert Howe's eldest son (Robert Charles).

Watt drowned at Port Macquarie in 1837. On 9 April 1840 at St Philip's Church of England, Sydney, Ann(e) married Thomas Armitage Salmon, a butcher and a widower. The couple lived in George Street, Sydney. Ann Salmon died on 17 November 1842 and was buried after a service in St Philip's. Using her newspaper to support Bourke's reforms and the 'emancipist' cause, she had played a prominent role during a turbulent period in the colony's development from a penal settlement.

R. B. Walker, *The Newspaper Press in New South Wales, 1803-1920* (Syd, 1976); P. Clarke, *Pen Portraits* (Syd, 1988); G. Robb, *George Howe* (Melb, 2003); *SMH*, 18 Nov 1842, p 3; F. Rogers, The Amazing Ann Bird (ms, 1980, copy on ADB file).
                                              SANDY BLAIR

HUGHES, JOHN (1825-1885), grocer, property developer and Catholic benefactor, was born on 24 June 1825 at Drumshambo, Leitrim, Ireland, eldest son of six children of Thomas Hughes, grocer, and his wife Maria, née Cogan. The family arrived in Sydney as bounty immigrants in the *Crusader* on 15 January 1840. Educated from July to December that year at Sydney College under W. T. Cape [q.v.1 W. Cape], John was apprenticed to John Stirling, a grocer. After working for T. & R.

Coveny, of Market Street, he obtained a position with Samuel Peek in George Street before going into business on his own about 1851 on the corner of Market and George streets. Prospering, he married Irish-born Susan Sharkey at St Mary's Catholic Cathedral on 2 July 1856. They were to have eight children.

Selling out his retail grocery in 1862 Hughes began as a wholesale merchant and importer, first in Clarence, later in York, Street. Again he was successful and in 1871 retired to attend to pastoral pursuits, purchasing Narromine station, near Dubbo, and other properties. He also invested in land and developed city business sites such as the warehouse he erected for Messrs Young & Lark in Castlereagh Street. In 1866 and 1871 he had been defeated in elections for the Fitzroy Ward in the Sydney Municipal Council. Selling his pastoral interests, in 1879-81 he and his family travelled in the United States of America and Europe.

Appointed a justice of the peace in 1867, Hughes attended zealously to his duties, sitting for many years as magistrate in the police courts of Sydney. He was both a pillar of the Catholic Church and a loyal citizen, in 1868 refusing to serve on the St Patrick's Day regatta committee with a man who had declined to toast the Queen's health. Hughes generously supported Catholic charities and was notable for his contribution, both as a committee member and benefactor, to the rebuilding of St Mary's Cathedral, where he worshipped. The new building was dedicated in 1882. In addition he was largely responsible for bringing the Sisters of the Society of the Sacred Heart of Jesus to Sydney that year, funding their establishment of a convent at Rose Bay. He also donated the site for St Canice's Church, Elizabeth Bay; marble altars for St Ignatius' College, Riverview, and St Columbkille's Church, Woolloomooloo; the baptismal font at St Patrick's Church and marble fonts in St Mary's Cathedral; and helped to establish scholarships in honour of Archbishop Vaughan [q.v.6] at St Ignatius'.

Having purchased land at Elizabeth Bay in 1869, over the next five years Hughes built an elegant residence, which he named Kincoppal (Erse for sea-horse) after a rock formation in the harbour nearby. In 1882 the Pope appointed him knight of the Order of St Gregory; he was later promoted knight commander but before receiving the brief died at his home on 29 June 1885. Hughes was buried in Waverley cemetery after a requiem mass at St Mary's Cathedral. He was survived by his wife, two sons and four daughters, two of whom became sisters of the Sacred Heart; Kincoppal was bequeathed to the elder, Maria (1858-1951). There in 1909 the order set up a school of which she became superior. Hughes's sons (Sir) Thomas and John [qq.v.9]

and their descendants were prominent in law and politics in Sydney in the next century. After the Elizabeth Bay property was redeveloped, Kincoppal and Rose Bay convents of the Sacred Heart were amalgamated at Rose Bay in 1971.

Australian Men of Mark, 1 (Syd, 1889); P. Frost, *The Kincoppal Story* (Syd, 1973); *V&P* (LA, NSW), 1868-69, 1, p 906; *Syd Gazette*, 16 Jan 1840, p 2; *Freeman's J*, 4 July 1885, p 15; information from Mrs A. Stevens, Waverton, Syd.   CHRIS CUNNEEN

HUGHES, THOMAS (1866-1944), outlaw, was born on 25 October 1866 at sea in the *Corona*, *en route* to Western Australia, eldest son of an enrolled pensioner guard, Thomas Hughes, and his wife Catherine, née McEvoy. After his father's death in 1880, Tom was employed on the government railways, possibly at Northampton. In 1884 he was indentured for two years to the Dempster family of Esperance as a pastoral worker, but broke his bond in 1885 and returned to Fremantle. Unemployed, he was suspected of several petty thefts.

On 17 April 1887 two policemen went to investigate the theft of tools and a case of dynamite from a quarry at North Fremantle. Encountering Hughes, they stopped him. He tried to escape and in the ensuing scuffle produced a revolver and wounded Constable Joseph O'Connell before decamping. When O'Connell died, a warrant was issued with a reward of £200 for the capture of Hughes who was described as 'rather stout and between 5 ft 10 inches and 5 ft 11 inches tall'. A capable bushman, Hughes remained at large in the country outside Perth for eleven weeks until finally caught by three policemen. After a gunfight, in which Hughes was wounded, he was captured, telling one constable that he would die like a man. On 5 October 1887, charged with manslaughter he was sentenced to penal servitude for life. Six weeks later he bashed a warder and absconded from Fremantle prison. He was soon caught and received thirty-six lashes for the assault and three years in irons for a burglary committed during his liberty.

Despite the disapproval of the press, Hughes won considerable sympathy among the Fremantle working class. His defiance of the authorities reminded some of Ned Kelly [q.v.5]. Others saw tragedy because Hughes and O'Connell were schoolfellows and both sons of pensioner guards. The reduction of the charge against him to manslaughter may have been a reaction to popular opinion. He was released from prison on a ticket-of-leave in 1896, granted conditional release in April 1898 and was given permission to carry firearms later that month. He then moved to the Pinjarra district, where he remained for the rest of his life and stayed out of trouble. Old residents remember him as eccentric but harmless. He cultivated an orchard and, on his regular visits to report to the local police station, sometimes brought in a little gold that he had panned at an unknown site in the Darling Range.

On 16 October 1902 Hughes married Alice McLevie at St John's Church of England, Pinjarra; they had a daughter and a son. Hughes was admitted into the Hospital for the Insane at Claremont in old age and died there on 10 December 1944; he was buried in the Anglican section of Karrakatta cemetery. Nobody remembered that he had figured for a brief period as Western Australia's most notorious outlaw in the generation between convict transportation and the 1890s gold rush.

Newsbeat (Perth), Dec 1993, p 9; *West Australian*, 20 Apr 1887, p 2, 22 Apr 1887, p 3, 5 May 1887, p 3, 18 July 1887, p 3; *WA Catholic Record*, 21 Apr 1887, p 3; Fremantle Prison registers, CONS 1156/F3-F4 (SRWA); information from Mr R. Richards, Applecross, Perth.

G. C. BOLTON

HUGO, WILLIAM MARKS (c.1828-1904), missioner and founder of the Bushmen's Club, was born at East Ham, Essex, England, son of Trevanion Pyle Hugo and his wife Mary Anne, née Marks. The writer Victor Hugo was a distant relation. William went to sea when young and was a purser's steward in 1842. After service in the Crimean War he worked for three years in a store at New Haven, Connecticut, United States of America. He read much. Outspoken, and with the civil war looming, he moved to Kingston, Ontario, Canada, where his elder brother lived. Relations there judged him a 'brilliant genius'; his nephew noted his 'breezy manner, rather engaging personality, and general look of brightness and smartness'.

In 1861 Hugo left for Liverpool, England, and then travelled to Queensland, where he experienced a religious conversion. Concealing his past and known only as 'William', for some years he tramped the outback as a missionary; on prodigious journeys in South Australia and beyond he carried only a swag and a little water, relying on others for sustenance and shelter. He occasionally rested at the Mount Remarkable station of J. H. Angas who, with his father George Fife Angas [qq.v.3,1], had supported a bush missionary society and William's work.

By 1866 a ravaging northern drought accelerated the need to succour bush workers, who were often victims of their own excesses and were preyed upon between jobs. Hugo

pressed for a 'bushmen's home', like a seamen's home, as a quiet, sober refuge. Opposition came from those who saw it as a squatters' movement, but his canvassing, bushmen's subscriptions and philanthropic support enabled the home to open in Whitmore Square, Adelaide, in May 1870. The Bushmen's Club included dormitories, reading room and labour office. Initially, Hugo was unpaid as superintendent. Charges were moderate, notices read: 'Swearing, drunkenness, and gambling strictly prohibited', and amusements inside and games outside were provided. In 1871 the Angases helped towards outright purchase and, with a new dormitory proposed, the government voted £500.

Despite the emergence of a new pastoral regime, requiring less labour, within two years the home had 700 members and a savings bank branch; another dormitory, government subsidies, a post office and dog kennels became features. Hugo published a *History of the First Bushmen's Club in the Australian Colonies* in 1872. Next year he advocated an inebriates' retreat for Adelaide and in 1876 published rules for health. After he married 18-year-old Mary Hanna Fisher on 23 January 1877 at St Paul's Church of England, Adelaide, he accepted a club salary. A new central building opened in 1879. But lack of funds hampered the home, and in 1880 his 'pale, care-worn face of rather massive features' wore a resigned expression. Religious observances had been discontinued; government subsidies stopped. The club, not in Adelaide's centre and affected by mining rushes, declined. In January 1899, the Salvation Army having bought the premises, Hugo reflected that bushmen were fewer and changed in type.

In 1885 his lengthy work, *The Origin and Antiquity of Freemasonry*, was published in Adelaide. He died of gastroenteritis on 7 February 1904 at his Goodwood home and was buried in West Terrace cemetery. His wife, son and daughter survived him.

R. and F. Hill, *What We Saw in Australia* (Lond, 1875); H. Hussey, *More Than Half a Century of Colonial Life and Christian Experience* (Adel, 1897); H. T. Burgess, *John Howard Angas* (Adel, 1905); J. B. Hirst, *Adelaide and the Country 1870-1917* (Melb, 1973); *Observer* (Adel), 19 Dec 1874, p 6, 1 Jan 1876, p 11, 8 Jan 1876, p 8, 22 July 1876, p 6, 12 June 1880, p 978, 26 June 1880, p 1077, 7 Jan 1899, p 29; *SA Register*, 20 Dec 1884, p 5, 23 Dec 1885, p 7, 23 Dec 1886, p 4, 13 Feb 1922, p 8, 15 Feb 1922, p 9, 17 Feb 1922, p 9, 6 July 1922, p 8; information from Mr V. E. Hugo, Brighton, Adel.

R. M. GIBBS

HUON DE KERMADEC, JEAN-MICHEL (1748-1793), mariner, was born on 12 September 1748 in the Manoir du Tromeur, Bohars, near Brest, Finistère, France, son of Jean-Guillaume Huon de Kermadec and his wife Anne, née du Mescam. Jean-Michel joined the navy as a *garde de marine* in May 1766 and was promoted *enseigne de vaisseau* in 1773. During the American war of independence he took part in the battle of Ushant (1778) and served in the *Diadème* at the capture of Grenada and the siege of Savannah (1779); in 1781 he was appointed (chevalier) to the Order of Saint Louis.

In 1785 Huon joined the *Résolution* at Brest as second-in-command to Bruny d'Entrecasteaux [q.v.1] and took part in the ship's voyage of exploration to China. Huon gained his first command, the *Rhône*, in 1789 and on 11 April that year became a member of the Académie de la Marine. He again served under d'Entrecasteaux in the *Patriote* in 1790-91, then took command of the *Espérance*, as part of d'Entrecasteaux's expedition in search of La Pérouse [q.v.2], which cleared the harbour of Brest on 28 September 1791. At sea the following day Huon was advised of his promotion to *capitaine de vaisseau*. After visiting Tenerife and the Cape of Good Hope and surveying the islands of Amsterdam and Saint Paul, d'Entrecasteaux decided to investigate reports that the inhabitants of the Admiralty Islands were 'adorned with French uniforms and marine sword belts' and to approach these islands 'by passing south of New Holland'. On 23 April 1792 the two vessels arrived at and named Recherche Bay in Van Diemen's Land, where fresh water was found. Their sojourn lasted until 28 May.

The expedition then sailed north to the Isle of Pines, along the west coast of New Caledonia to New Ireland, to the Admiralty Islands and then to Ambon without finding any trace of La Pérouse. From the Netherlands East Indies, they headed for south-western New Holland and, after negotiating the hazardous 'Archipelago of the Recherche', reached and named Esperance Bay, Western Australia, on 9 December. The French remained anchored off the coast until 17 December.

With reserves of water critically low by January 1793, Huon persuaded d'Entrecasteaux to sail directly to Van Diemen's Land, where they could be assured of replenishment, thereby losing the opportunity to determine the existence of a strait south of New Holland. On 21 January the expedition returned to Recherche Bay. This second visit to Tasmania, which lasted until 27 February, was characterized by friendly contact with the indigenous inhabitants. It was also significant for the discovery of the Derwent estuary. The *Recherche* and *Espérance* sailed on to Tongatapu and then Balade in New Caledonia where Huon de Kermadec died of tuberculosis on 6 May 1793. He was buried on the offshore island of Poudioué (Cook's [q.v.1] Observatory Island).

A well-read and cultured man, who sketched and played the flute, Huon left precise instructions that his substantial library should be distributed among his fellow officers. He was unmarried. D'Entrecasteaux named the Huon River in Tasmania and the Kermadec Islands, north-east of New Zealand after him. The Kermadec Trench and Kermadec Ridge in the Pacific also honour his name as does, indirectly, the magnificent Huon pine (*Lagarostrabus franklinii*) in Tasmania.

E. P. E. de Rossel (ed), *Voyage de D'Entrecasteaux, Envoyé à la Recherche de la Pérouse* (Paris, 1808); M. Dupont, *D'Entrecasteaux: Rien que la Mer un Peu de Gloire* (Paris, 1983); H. Richard, *Le Voyage de D'Entrecasteaux à la Recherche de Lapérouse* (Paris, 1986); F. Horner, *Looking for La Pérouse* (Melb, 1995); E. and M. Duyker (eds and translators), *Bruny D'Entrecasteaux: Voyage to Australia & the Pacific 1791-1793* (Melb, 2001); E. Duyker, *Citizen Labillardière: A Naturalist's Life in Revolution and Exploration (1755-1834)* (Melb, 2003); information from Mr P. Huon de Kermadec, Versailles, and Dr P. Huon de Kermadec, Landerneau, France.

EDWARD DUYKER

HYDE, WILLIAM GARNETT (1918-1976), musician, teacher and businessman, was born on 12 November 1918 at Carlton, Melbourne, son of Victorian-born parents Arthur Hyde, mechanic, and his wife Pearl, née Fowler. The family moved to Moonee Ponds, where Arthur worked as a cleaner and Billy was educated in the local primary and central schools, leaving at the age of 15 to become a storeman at J. L. Law [q.v.] and J. K. Pearson's Pelaco shirt factory.

From the age of 11, Hyde had been involved with drums, and his first work in the music business was with a local suburban band, the 'Night Owls', after which he joined Fred Hocking at the Casino at Brunswick. He was a self-taught musician. Learning on the job from other players, and imbued with a natural talent combined with great self-discipline, he became an expert sight-reader, capable of performing symphonic scores. His greatest ability, however, was with the swing drumming style of the dance band era. By his mid-twenties he had held the drum chair at many of Melbourne's leading dance halls, such as the Trocadero, Leonda and the Belvedere. An early manifestation of his entrepreneurial gift was evident during World War II, when it was impossible to obtain musical instruments.

Billy co-founded Sphinx Drums. Improvis-ation was necessary. Material shortages led to the drum shells being moulded from off-cuts from plywood used for the manufacture of the Mosquito bomber and torpedo boats. By 1946 Sphinx Drums was meeting orders for the Australian Army.

At Ascot Vale Presbyterian Church on 19 January 1942 Billy married Jean Urie Maple-stone, a typist. That year he began teaching drums, at home. After the war there was an acute shortage of all forms of percussion instruments, and both his students and fellow musicians began to look to him as a supplier. As well, he developed his internationally known 'natural rebound' practice pad, which has served generations of percussionists since.

In 1950-65 Hyde was staff drummer for the Australian Broadcasting Commission in Mel-bourne. His musical activities were remark-ably diverse. He became 'first call drummer' for many radio and television shows, as a studio session musician and backing visiting international stars such as Shirley Bassey and Sammy Davis junior. He also worked as per-cussionist with both the Australian Symphony and Melbourne Symphony orchestras. In 1962, in partnership with his son Garry and nephew Barry Quinn, the Billy Hyde Drum Clinic was formed in response to demands for tuition and instrument supplies. Based at Flemington, next to the family home, this developed into a nationwide business.

Billy Hyde received his widest public recog-nition as drummer and singer with the GTV-9 orchestra on the 'In Melbourne Tonight' show (1964-71). His banter with Graham Kennedy became an established part of the nightly entertainment. But his musical peers were to remember his 'jazz chops' (involving improvis-ation, interaction and anticipation). As Brian Rangott, former musical director at GTV-9, noted: 'He had the ability to listen. Especially accompanying solos, he'd be right there echo-ing figures, catching your phrasing, always swinging; there was no one during his era with his ability'.

Outgoing, of a generous spirit towards fel-low musicians and a natural entertainer, Hyde was also a devoted family man, with his wife and two children closely involved in his busi-ness. As if to balance his hectic schedule he chose solitary activities for recreation and built his own yacht; he was a devoted fisher-man all his life. Hyde died from a brain tumour on 27 December 1976 at Brunswick and was cremated. His wife, son and daughter sur-vived him.

Paul Matcott, 'Billy Hyde Drum Clinic', in *Sonics* (Syd, NSW), Oct 1980; *Age* (Melb), 29 Dec 1976, p 2; family papers held by Mrs Jean Hyde, Flemington, Melb.   AL WATSON

HYNES, SARAH (1859-1938), botanist and teacher, was born on 30 September 1859 at Danzig, Prussia (Gdańsk, Poland), one of three children of William John Hynes (1831-1909), a master mariner born on Gibraltar, and his wife Eliza Adeline, née Bell. Educated at Edinburgh Ladies' College, at Upton House, St John's Wood, London, and at Chichester College, Sussex, Sarah received a botanical certificate from South Kensington Museum, Science and Art Department. She came to Sydney about 1884 when her father became managing director of the Australasian Steam Navigation Co. At the University of Sydney (B.A., 1891) she studied physics, chemistry, natural history, botany, zoology and math-ematics, majoring in botany. In 1892 she was the first woman to join the Linnean Society of New South Wales. She was also a member of the fund-raising committee for the building of Women's College, at the university.

Hynes began teaching at Sydney Technical College in July 1897. A supporter of the Sydney Technological (Powerhouse) Museum, she and Georgina King [q.v.] helped to supply fresh flowers for its botanical display. In this way she formed an acquaintance with the director Joseph Henry Maiden [q.v.10] and in 1898 accepted a position as botanical assistant at the museum, becoming the first woman to hold a government appointment in science in New South Wales. When Maiden became director of the Botanic Gardens she trans-ferred to the herbarium there, where she identified, classified, catalogued, preserved and displayed specimens for public education and private investigation, having responsi-bility for class teaching also.

Within a few months, however, Hynes clashed with her male superiors, beginning with a demand for a higher grading and salary (awarded in 1901) and continuing over display decisions and the use of equipment. In 1905 she was suspended when the Public Service Board levied thirty-nine charges of insubordi-nation against her. In one, she was accused of using the 'unladylike' expression 'a lowdown, dirty larrikin trick'. She denied that this was 'unladylike'. The charges were disproved and Hynes was reinstated, but a similar suspen-sion and inquiry in 1910 led to her transfer to the Department of Public Instruction.

Praised by Maiden for her valuable aid in the preface to his *Forest Flora*, her botanical work led William Fitzgerald to name a species of acacia (*Acacia hynesiana*) after her in 1912. In 1913 she taught at schools in Cleveland Street and at Petersham, and from 1916 to her retirement in 1923 at St George Girls' High School, where 'Sally Hynes' was affectionately remembered by students for her enthusiasm and support.

Hynes held strong feminist and political opinions; her expression of these, in person and in writing, was forthright and piquant. Continuing her father's active connexion with the National Association, she was prominent in the Randwick branch of the National and later the United Australia associations. Sarah Hynes was honorary organizer of the campaign in 1921 to request the Federal government to purchase her friend Ellis Rowan's [q.v.11] paintings.

Said to have been in the 1920s one of the earliest women to drive a Citroën car in Sydney, she never married but all her adult life cared for an older, mentally disabled sister. Hynes was a founder and in 1933 senior vice-president of the Forum Club, Sydney. In 1934 she was appointed M.B.E. She died on 27 May 1938 at her Randwick home and was buried in the Anglican section of Waverley cemetery.

N. J. Kyle (ed), *Women as Educators in Nineteenth and Twentieth Century Australia* (Wollongong, NSW, 1989); *Aust Town and Country J*, 28 July 1909, p 39, 11 Jan 1911, p 32; *Daily Telegraph* (Syd), 13 Sept 1916, p 6; *United Aust Review*, 21 July 1933, p 21; *SMH*, 13 Dec 1923, p 4, 1 Jan 1934, p 8, 14 Jan 1937, p 20; *Smith's Weekly*, 13 Jan 1934, p 20; Powerhouse Museum (Syd) archives.

CLAIRE HOOKER

I

INGLIS, WILLIAM (1832 1896), auctioneer and stock agent, was born on 8 March 1832 in Sydney, eldest son of Scottish Presbyterian parents Thomas Inglis (1791-1874), merchant, and his wife Catherine, née Ross. Thomas had arrived in Sydney with his wife in 1830 as agent of the Australian Co. of Edinburgh and received a land grant, Craigend, at The Oaks in the Camden-Picton area. After five years in whaling pursuits and time on the Ovens goldfield in Victoria, William returned to Craigend, where on 3 March 1858 he married with Anglican rites Flora McKinnon from a neighbouring property, Montpelier. Their eldest son JOHN THOMAS (1859-1914) was born on 22 March 1859.

In 1867 William Inglis and Joseph, brother of Edward Butler [q.v.3], began an auctioneering and produce agency at 793 George Street, Sydney. Butler left the partnership after ten years, and in 1882 William began a 'horse bazaar' between Castlereagh and Pitt streets. Horse sales were held on the ground floor and the vehicles and harness areas were above, accessible by a ramp. (The local test of a draught horse was to pull a one-ton load from Sussex Street up Druitt Street to Inglis's bazaar.)

William Inglis always conducted auctions wearing a top hat, which became his trademark. A justice of the peace, he stood unsuccessfully as a protectionist candidate for Balmain in February 1899. In July 1895 he was banqueted in Sydney by a large number of his friends and customers and presented with a framed illuminated address. He died at his residence, Annesley, Balmain Road, Leichhardt, on 12 January 1896, survived by his wife, nine sons and three daughters, and was buried with Congregational forms in Rookwood cemetery. His estate was sworn for probate at under £38 724.

His son John, who had been taken into the partnership in 1884 and had married Australia Renwick in Sydney in 1885, took control of William Inglis & Son. In 1905 the firm bought the goodwill of T. S. Clibborn's [q.v.3] bloodstock business, carrying out its earliest yearling sales at that firm; in 1906 it first conducted its own sale at Tom Payten's [q.v.11] property, Newmarket, at Randwick. John died on 26 September 1914. His son ARTHUR REGINALD (1890-1957), known as Reg, who had been born on 10 February 1890 at Drummoyne, became managing director. Newmarket was purchased in 1918 and was gradually expanded to provide stable accommodation for about 600 horses. In 1921 the firm became a limited company, and in 1934,

after buying out a competitor, Henry Chisholm & Co. Pty Ltd, it became the undisputed leader in bloodstock auctioneering in Australia. Reg died on 10 December 1957. The family auctioneering tradition continued: his son John (b.1917) followed, and a nephew, Reginald Stewart Inglis (b.1952), succeeded him. The catalogue of William Inglis & Co. Pty Ltd became renowned for its detail and integrity, and its yearling sale at Randwick during Easter was one of the most important in Australasia.

William Inglis's second son WILLIAM (1864-1935), born on 24 August 1864, worked for his father for ten years before starting business on his own in the 1890s as an auctioneer and produce merchant in Sydney. He married South African-born Annie Elizabeth Gavey in 1894; they were later divorced. He took over Craigend in 1920 and married Linda Annie Sharp that year. Predeceased by her, William junior died on 10 November 1935; a son by his first marriage and a son and daughter by his second survived him. Craigend was still farmed by his family 170 years after the original grant.

HRA, series 1, vol 16; D. M. Barrie, *The Australian Bloodhorse* (Syd, 1956); *T&CJ*, 20 July 1895, pp 1, 11, 18 Jan 1896, p 18; *SMH*, 4 Feb 1889, p 8, 13 Jan 1896, p 4, 15 Jan 1896, p 5, 11 Nov 1935, p 8; *Sun-Herald*, 29 Dec 1974, p 30; *H&H Hoofs & Horns*, Summer 2005, p 36; information from Mr C. Inglis, The Oaks, NSW.   G. P. WALSH

IRVINE, ALICE CHRISTINA (1879-1940), domestic science teacher and cookery book author, was born on 12 May 1879 at Mathinna, Tasmania, third daughter of Peter Irvine, mine manager, and his wife Flora, née McLaurin. Educated at Mangana State School, Alice began her teaching career on 1 April 1897 as a paid monitor at Mathinna School. She was transferred in March 1898 to West Zeehan State School and in 1902 to Burnie, where the head teacher described her as 'a most powerful and painstaking teacher' and an inspector commended her 'great skill and ... most unremitting labour'. She was promoted to class IV teacher in 1904.

In 1906 she was a cookery student-teacher at the Melbourne Training College. On her return she was sent to Launceston, where she was briefly at Glen Dhu and then Charles Street, before being appointed head of the cookery school at Wellington Square in November 1907. Irvine was at the Hobart cookery school in 1914-15, then held her former position at Launceston until the end of 1925. During this period a new cookery school was established as part of Launceston High School, the move from Wellington Square occurring in May 1921. She was granted leave to attend the Emily MacPherson College of Domestic Economy in Melbourne for a year in 1926.

Back in Tasmania, Irvine was mistress of domestic science in charge of the State High School's cookery school in Hobart (1927) and then at the Domestic Arts School, housed in the Central School in Murray Street, from 1928 to her death. She also supervised cookery schools throughout the State and trained student-teachers in domestic science subjects. In July 1928 she received departmental permission 'to deliver six weekly lectures on Cookery through the Wireless'; in February 1930 the department notified her that there was 'no objection' to her becoming a member of the National Council of Women. Two years later she received permission 'to assist the Hydro-Electric Department by giving demonstrations in connection with the use of electric stoves'. A determined and dominant woman, Irvine was physically large as well as pro-fessionally imposing. She pioneered domestic science teaching in Tasmania, creating a forceful pattern and a lasting tradition that was followed by other domestic science teachers.

Irvine's *Central Cookery Book* (1930) became the definitive text for cookery teaching in Tasmanian schools. By its sixteenth edition (1991), it was more than simply a basic text for schools and was widely used in homes throughout the State; as the preface stated, 'it has become an institution'. One devotee wrote in 2002 that Irvine's dishes were 'models of simplicity and testimony to the days when no ingredient foreign to solid English fare was allowed within oven range'. Miss Irvine died of cancer on 12 November 1940 in St John's Hospital, South Hobart, and was buried in the general cemetery at Fingal. Over sixty years later she was still well known in Tasmania for her cookery book, the ubiquitous *Central*.

Educational Record, 15 Jan 1940, p 24; *Examiner*, 13 Nov 1940, p 2; *Mercury* (Hob), 14 Nov 1940, p 9, 1 June 2002, p 27; ED 2/20 (1896-1904), ED 13/106, 121, 191, 243, 268, 273, 285/1, 289, 294, 300, 304, 309, 318, ED 10/1054 1926 (TA); information from Dr J. Haward, Hawley, Tas.   E. A. McLEOD

J

JAMES, ELIZABETH BRITOMARTE (1867-1943), political reformer, was born on 1 June 1867 at Durban Lead near Ballarat, Victoria, eldest of nine children of English-born parents Ebenezer James, blacksmith, and his wife Clara Elizabeth, neé Maisey. Experience gained from assisting her father, who became chaplain of the missions to seamen in Port Melbourne and at Williamstown, and from visiting the poor, taught her compassion for the wives of workmen. She developed a fearless and straightforward manner, a single-minded belief in the philanthropic and patriotic duty of women of her class and a commitment to temperance and to equality and civil rights for all women.

On 25 May 1889 at Port Melbourne Britomarte married with Wesleyan forms her cousin George Henry James, a 36-year-old schoolteacher and military instructor. They lived in country regions of Victoria, before settling in Melbourne in 1908. During World War I Mrs James joined her two sons Cecil and George, who had enlisted in England. In London she worked as a journalist before qualifying as an administrator in Queen Mary's Army Auxiliary Corps. Drafted to Nottingham in charge of field cookery, she later commanded No.1 Unit of the Q.M.A.A.C. in France. She returned to Australia with her invalided sons and founded the Imperial Ex-service Women's Association.

On Cecil's soldier settlement block in the Mallee, Britomarte James observed the plight of settlers' wives and joined the women's section of the Victorian Farmers' Union; back in the city in 1921, she became president of the women's metropolitan branch. As 'Progress' she wrote a column for the *Farmers' Advocate*, focusing on women's interests and the work of such organizations as the National Council of Women and publicizing the inadequacy of the refreshment service on country trains. An advocate of increased funding for cottage hospitals, by 1930 she was a life governor of the Women's, St Vincent's and Austin hospitals.

At the V.F.U. women's section conference at Geelong in September 1921, James had spoken on 'Women's Place in Australian Politics'. She used her column to advance the candidature of 'progressive' women. Next year she offered herself to the women's section as a candidate for the Australian Senate but was rebuffed. With Eleanor Glencross [q.v.9], in August 1922 James was a founder of the Victorian Women Citizens' Movement. She was also a vice-president of the Housewives' Association.

In August 1927 James was unsuccessful as a V.W.C.M. candidate for South Melbourne City Council. Although she continued in the V.F.U. women's section and led the metropolitan branch until 1932, her main forum became the V.W.C.M., of which she was president in 1929-33, thereby being *ex officio* on the board of the Australian Federation of Women Voters. A founder and president of the State branch of the Australian Wattle League, she was also a member of the Victorian Town Planning Association.

James had been a delegate to the inaugural meetings of the British Commonwealth League in London in 1925 and also attended a League of Nations session in Geneva. She was a foundation member of the Big Brother Movement to bring British lads to Australia, as well as a member of the selection panel of the Educated Women Workers' Migration Scheme. These worked in Australia through the Victorian New Settlers' League, of which she was a committee member. On her return to Melbourne she was appointed a justice of the peace. James attended the first Pan Pacific Women's Conference, Honolulu, in 1928 and next year she and Edith Jones [q.v.] participated in the conference of associations interested in the welfare of Aborigines, convened in Melbourne by C. L. A. Abbott [q.v.13].

Under James's leadership, the V.W.C.M. held fortnightly luncheons with speakers and lobbied parliament on women's rights. She retired as president in October 1933, but was founder and president of the Victoria Centenary Club. Despite declining health, she continued to sit on the bench in the South Melbourne court, controversially refusing to leave when 'unsavoury' matters came before her. She also served on the campaign committee set up by the V.W.C.M. in 1935 to educate public opinion on the need for women in parliament. Her successor as president Julia Rapke [q.v.16] described James as 'a born administrator', impatient with those who expressed doubt or put complicating ideas in her way, but noted her 'high-mindedness', 'unfailing tact' and generosity. She sometimes appeared arrogant, an impression reinforced by her 'un-Australian, Oxford-like accent', a 'stately' and imperious demeanour, her 'air of hauteur', the ebony stick she carried and the lorgnette she employed with devastating effect on her critics.

James was appointed O.B.E. on 9 June 1938. Continuing interests included the newly formed Women Justices' Association, the

English Speaking Union and the National Theatre Movement, of which she was vice-president. After her husband's death in 1938, she accompanied the musician Ruby Davy [q.v.8] to London to introduce her into English musical circles. James's health deteriorated and she returned to Melbourne in December next year. She died on 6 November 1943 in Kareela Private Hospital, Auburn, and was buried in Springvale cemetery. Her sons survived her.

Who's Who in the World of Women, 1 (Melb, 1930); F. Paisley, *Loving Protection?* (Melb, 2000); *White Ribbon Signal*, 8 July 1929, p 103; J. Smart, 'A Mission to the Home: The Housewives' Association, the Woman's Christian Temperance Union and Protestant Christianity, 1920-40', *Aust Feminist Studies*, 13, no 28, Oct 1998, p 215; *Argus* (Melb), 21 Oct 1933, p 10, 8 Feb 1935, p 5; H. Gunn, 'For the Man on the Land': Rural Women and the Victorian National Party, 1917-1996 (Ph.D. thesis, LaTrobe Univ, 1996); Julia Rapke papers *and* Bessie Rischbieth papers (NL).   JUDITH SMART

JAMIESON, JAMES (1840-1916), medical practitioner, university teacher and health officer, was born on 5 June 1840 at Beith, Ayrshire, Scotland, youngest of seven children of William Jamieson, furniture manufacturer, and his wife Anne, née Scott. Educated at the local parish school and at an academy at Glasgow, James knew French and German and from 1858 studied medicine at the University of Glasgow (M.D., 1862; C.M., 1863), where Joseph Lister, the pioneer of antisepsis, taught surgery.

After travelling to Australia and New Zealand as a ship's doctor, Jamieson worked as a general practitioner back in Scotland and held part-time appointments as a parochial medical officer and public vaccinator. In 1868 he moved to Warrnambool, Victoria, where his brother William was a businessman. James started a practice and was health officer to the municipality and honorary medical officer at the hospital. Next year he was registered and the first of his many contributions to the press, 'Is alcohol a food?', appeared in the *Colonial Monthly*. In 1874 at Warrnambool he married Jane Pringle Hood with Presbyterian forms. They were to have five children.

When opinion was still uncertain about the origin and means of transmission of infectious disease, Jamieson promoted germ theory, better hygiene and the use of disinfectants. He believed also in quarantine for epidemic diseases and the compulsory isolation of the sick. His essay 'On the Parasitic Theory of Disease', an up-to-date summary of the work of Pasteur, Lister and others, published in the *Australian Medical Journal* in 1876, helped to swing professional opinion in favour of germ

theory. A 'popular' version was published in the *Melbourne Review* in July 1877. An inaugural member in 1875 of the influential Australian Health Society founded by Martha Turner [q.v.6], he contributed extensively to the society's lecture programme, organization and publications.

In 1877 Jamieson moved to Melbourne. He was honorary physician in the outpatient department of the Melbourne Hospital in 1879-84, then joined the senior staff at the Alfred Hospital, retiring in 1908. In 1885 he succeeded T. M. Girdlestone [q.v.] as health officer of the City of Melbourne amidst a developing sanitary crisis. Jamieson's reports to the health committee and the town clerk Edmund FitzGibbbon [q.v.4] included perceptive discussions of the public health and changing social conditions in the city and inner suburbs. His *Typhoid Fever in Melbourne* (1887) appeared in one of the two worst years for the incidence of this disease. Economic depression in the 1890s, large-scale sanitary engineering and reform of public health administration helped to resolve the crisis, reducing local government's role. Subsequently he worked effectively with the chief medical officer D. A. Gresswell [q.v.9] to have tubercular cattle removed from the milk supply in the 1890s. Jamieson retired in 1912, the city's last part-time health officer.

He had lectured at the University of Melbourne (M.D. *ad eundem gradum*, 1878) in obstetrics and diseases of women and children in 1879-87, and in the theory and practice of medicine in 1887-1908. According to K. F. Russell, Jamieson had a 'Scottish thoroughness at the bedside in his own inimitable way', and was at his best teaching clinical medicine—upon his retirement his students endowed a prize in this subject. He has sometimes been depicted as anti-feminist, for wanting women taught in separate classes, but his daughter Margaret graduated (M.B., 1906; B.S., 1907), and practised at Euroa.

Jamieson publicized what could be done to reduce maternal and infant morbidity and mortality through the control of perinatal infection in the mother and proper feeding of the children. In his writings, he made effective use of official statistics to argue for action to control typhoid, tuberculosis, puerperal fever and high infant mortality, with his *Contributions to the Vital Statistics of Australia* (1882) an example. His other outlets included the *Australian Medical Journal* (editor 1883-87), *Melbourne Review*, *Victorian Review*, *Daily Telegraph*, *Argus*, *Age* and *Australasian*.

Active in the Royal and the Medical societies of Victoria, Jamieson served a term as president of each, but was not part of the medical establishment. He never joined the Melbourne Club and was a critic of sanitary conditions and practices at the Melbourne Hospital. His opposition to the system of election of senior staff to hospitals was well known. It was a scandal that when he taught midwifery at the university he had no access to the wards or patients of the Lying-In Hospital, as he could not get elected to the staff. In 1890 he took leave and travelled to Britain and Europe, attending the International Medical Congress in Berlin, as did Pasteur and Koch.

A photograph taken in later life showed 'Wee Jimmy' as balding and bespectacled, but dapper and alert, in bow tie, waistcoat and jacket. From 1907 he progressively divested himself of public and professional responsibilities. Jamieson died on 1 August 1916 and was buried in Kew cemetery. His wife, one son and two daughters survived him.

K. S. Inglis, *Hospital and Community* (Melb, 1958); A. M. Mitchell, *The Hospital South of the Yarra* (Melb, 1977); K. F. Russell, *The Melbourne Medical School 1862-1962* (Melb, 1977); H. Attwood and R. W. Home (eds), *Patients, Practitioners and Techniques* (Melb, 1984); G. Davison et al, *The Outcasts of Melbourne* (Syd, 1985); G. Forth and P. Yule, *A History of the Warrnambool and District Base Hospital* (Syd, 2002); *MJA*, 9 Sept 1916, p 218; *Table Talk*, 3 Mar 1904, p 11; *Leader* (Melb), 21 Mar 1908; City of Melb archives.   DAVID DUNSTAN

JARVIS, GEORGE (c.1790-1825), slave, freedman and servant, was born probably in southern India. He and another child were purchased, for a total of 170 rupees, in the slave market at Cochin in January 1795 on behalf of Lachlan Macquarie [q.v.2] and his first wife Jane. The smaller boy was named after Jane's brother George Jarvis, the other Hector, presumably in memory of Macquarie's elder brother. Both children joined the Macquaries' domestic staff at Calicut, on the Malabar coast. After Jane's death in 1796 Lachlan emancipated her slaves in the West Indies and enrolled George and Hector in the parish school at Bombay. From February to May 1799 they attended him at Seringapatam, Mysore, during a military campaign. On a visit to Calcutta in 1799, however, Hector disappeared and was presumed to have been kidnapped. George accompanied Macquarie to Egypt in 1801 and in October, after the defeat of the French, was sent to Scotland to receive further schooling, while Macquarie returned to India. The provisions of Scottish and English law removed any doubts about his status: no longer Macquarie's slave, George was to be his valet.

Summoned at short notice from Scotland to become head servant, in April 1805 George sailed with Macquarie from London for Bombay. From August he enjoyed comfortable lodgings at Government House while Macquarie served as private military secretary to the governor. At this time Macquarie described him as his 'smart Portuguese boy'. In 1807 the two embarked for Britain via Persia, Russia and Denmark. They landed at Great Yarmouth, Norfolk, in October after an epic journey by land and sea of 6400 miles (10 300 km); it had taken them nearly seven months.

Macquarie married Elizabeth Campbell in Devon on 3 November, probably with George in attendance, then was posted to Perth, Scotland, before being appointed governor of New South Wales. George, an integral member of the vice-regal party, sailed on board the *Dromedary* in May 1809, with at least four other domestic servants recruited in Britain. For nearly twelve years he was an eyewitness to colonial life, as well as an observer of the stream of visitors to Government House, both in Sydney and at Parramatta. He accompanied the governor on at least six tours of inspection: to Van Diemen's Land (1811 and 1820), across the Blue Mountains to Bathurst (1815), to Newcastle (1812 and 1818) and to Lake George (1820).

On 22 March 1820 at St Philip's Church of England, Sydney, George married 30-year-old Mary Jelly who, sentenced to seven years transportation, had reached Sydney on 20 January 1820 and had served as a chambermaid at Government House. Their first child was born in December but died within six days. On 1 September 1821 the governor granted Mary an absolute pardon, allowing her to accompany George in the *Surry* in February 1822 when the Macquaries returned to Britain. On 5 May, at the port of St Salvadore, Brazil, she gave birth to a daughter, Elizabeth.

From December 1822 to July 1823 George visited France (Paris, Lyons, Nice), Italy (Genoa, Florence, Rome, Naples, Venice, Milan) and Geneva, Switzerland, with the Macquaries. He accompanied Lachlan to London in April 1824. When his master fell ill in June George summoned the doctor, was present at the old viceroy's deathbed on 1 July, then with Charles Macquarie escorted the coffin by sea to Mull, Scotland.

After the burial, George and his family remained at Jarvisfield. Macquarie, in his will, had provided a £25 annuity for him 'during his natural life', and had declared that should he 'prefer living on my Estate in Mull after my decease ... he may be allowed to do so on my farm of Gruline and that he shall be comfortably fed, clothed and lodged there at the expence of my Heirs and successors during his natural life independent of the annuity herein already allowed him'. George did not long enjoy his benefactor's generosity. He died in January 1825, aged about 35, and was buried at Jarvisfield; his wife and daughter survived him. Mary Jarvis lived on Mull for the rest of her life. She died on 5 November 1855 and was buried in Tobermory churchyard. Elizabeth Dewar, née Jarvis, died at Tobermory in 1894; the Macquarie Trust, established for her and her descendants by Elizabeth Macquarie in 1829, continued to operate in 2004.

Valuation Roll for the County of Argyll, for the Year 1893-94; M. H. Ellis, *Lachlan Macquarie* (Syd, 1965); L. Cohen, *Elizabeth Macquarie* (Syd, 1979); J. Ritchie, *Lachlan Macquarie* (Melb, 1986); *Oban Times*, 22 June 1940; Lauchlan Maclaine, Journals, 1824-1836 (Record Office, Gloucestershire, UK); Henry Nisbet, Letter Book (Argyll Bute Archives, UK); McGarvie Memorandum Book, 1829-1832 *and* Macquarie papers (ML); Macquarie family letters (NL); information from Mrs M. Douglas, Aros, Isle of Mull.   ROBIN WALSH

JAUNCEY, GEORGE ERIC MACDONNELL (1888-1947), physicist, was born on 21 September 1888 at Norwood, Adelaide, second child of George Jauncey, an accountant from England, and his Adelaide-born wife Agnes Binnie, née Davis. The economist and author Leslie Jauncey [q.v.9] was a younger brother. Two of his five siblings died in infancy, and his father died when Eric was 11.

After primary and early secondary education at public schools, he won scholarships to Prince Alfred College, where he completed the higher public examination in 1906 with outstanding results in physics, chemistry and mathematics. At the University of Adelaide (B.Sc., 1910; D.Sc., 1922), Jauncey held a cadetship in the physics laboratory, which provided tuition fees and a small living allowance. Taught mathematics and physics by (Sir) William Henry Bragg [q.v.7] in 1907 and 1908, he obtained first-class honours in physics.

In 1911-12 Jauncey held an 1851 Exhibition science research bursary at Adelaide under (Sir) Kerr Grant [q.v.9], and in 1912-13 an 1851 Exhibition scholarship with Bragg at the University of Leeds, England, where he studied X-ray absorption and scattering, heard of Bragg's particle theory of X-rays and observed his early pioneering research on X-ray spectroscopy and crystallography. Jauncey's scholarship was not extended when Bragg reported that he was 'an enthusiastic, persevering student [but] I cannot say that he has originality or exceptional merit'. On 16 January 1913 at Idle, Yorkshire, he married with Congregational forms Ethel Sarah ('Effie') Turner of Adelaide.

From 1913 to 1918 Jauncey successively held positions as demonstrator or instructor in physics at the University of Toronto, Canada, and at Lehigh University (M.Sc.,

1916), Pennsylvania, and the University of Missouri, Columbia, in the United States of America. He attempted to return to Australia in 1917 but was refused a passport because of pacifist comments he had made in private letters, which were intercepted by censors. The Australian government made his views known to the U.S. authorities, they were published in the American press and in December 1917 Jauncey was forced to resign his university post. Unemployed for some months, he eventually found work with the socialist-inclined National Non-partisan League in St Paul, Minnesota, and wrote several articles on the Australian experience with state-owned enterprises. During the influenza pandemic of 1918-19 he was seriously ill and again out of work for several months. In December 1919 he returned to university teaching, to a temporary position at Iowa State College, Ames. Repeated appeals by Jauncey to be allowed to work, teach and raise his family in his own country were refused, despite Grant's support.

In 1920 Arthur Compton was appointed head of the physics department at Washington University, St Louis, Missouri. Jauncey was one of his early appointments and built a successful career at the university as instructor and then assistant, associate and eventually professor of physics. Compton had long thought that the scattering of X-rays could be explained by classical electrodynamic theory, until late in 1922 he suddenly and successfully adopted a quantum interpretation. It was Jauncey who, from his familiarity with Bragg's ideas, prompted Compton to pursue this explanation, for which Compton shared the 1927 Nobel prize in Physics.

Continuing to study X-rays and their interactions with matter, Jauncey was awarded a doctorate by the University of Adelaide in 1922 for some of this work. He had, to an unusual degree, expertise in both experimental and theoretical physics, and published nearly a hundred research papers, many in the premier American journal, *The Physical Review*, of which he became an associate editor. Having regained his passport, in 1926 he returned briefly to Adelaide and lectured in Australia.

An excellent and dedicated teacher, Jauncey was the author of the widely used undergraduate text *Modern Physics* (1932, 1937, 1948) and a sympathetic supervisor of postgraduate students. When a severe illness curtailed his experimental research, he turned to the history of physics, publishing several articles.

Jauncey died of chronic rheumatic heart disease on 19 May 1947 at St Louis, Missouri, and was cremated. His wife and daughter survived him. At a memorial service, colleagues spoke movingly of his major contributions to

American physics, his scientific objectivity and integrity, his humanity and his modesty and courage. Contributions to a memorial fund enabled Jauncey prizes in physics to be awarded at Washington University from 1948 to 1961.

R. H. Stuewer, *The Compton Effect* (New York, 1975); R. W. Home, *Physics in Australia to 1945* (Melb, 1990); *American J of Physics*, 15, no 5, 1947, p 434; *JHSSA*, no 13, 1985, p 100; J. Jenkin, 'G. E. M. Jauncey and the Compton Effect', *Physics in Perspective*, 4, 2002, p 320; Royal Commission for the Exhibition of 1851 (Imperial College archives, Lond); Univ Adelaide archives; Washington Univ archives, St Louis, Missouri, US; Jauncey, G. E. M. —permission to return from USA, A1 1923/26495 (NAA).   JOHN JENKIN
R. W. HOME

JENKINS, JOSEPH (1818-1898), labourer, swagman and diarist, was born on 27 February 1818 at Blaenplwyf farm, Llanfihangel Ystrad parish, Cardiganshire, Wales, son of Jenkin Jenkins, farmer, and his wife Elinor. Joseph was educated locally and from an early age took an interest in poetry (which he wrote in Welsh and English), literature, philosophy and current affairs. His marriage to Elizabeth (Betty) Evans, daughter of a relatively wealthy farm owner, on 31 July 1846 at the parish church, Aberayron, enabled him to move away from his parents and acquire the tenancy of Trecefel farm near Tregaron; there were nine children of the marriage. During the next twenty-two years he became an innovative and successful farmer and an influential figure, involved in local politics and in the building of the Manchester and Milford railway (opened 1867) through the area. He was a Unitarian but, with no such place of worship nearby, was warden at St Caron's parish church.

On 8 December 1868 Jenkins impulsively departed for Victoria, reaching Melbourne in March 1869. A man of appreciable intellect and learning, he was a tormented figure and suffered from profound mood swings, believing he had been cursed from birth. It seems he had left home to escape deteriorating personal circumstances, notably worsening relations with his wife as a result of his excessive drinking and neglect of the farm. Loss of local standing, following an injudicious political stance during the 1868 general election, also contributed. He travelled the colony as an itinerant agricultural labourer, mainly in the Ballarat, Castlemaine, Maldon and Inglewood areas. From 1884 onwards he lived at Maldon, working as a drain cleaner under contract to the local council. He continued to write poetry, winning numerous prizes at the Ballarat Eisteddfod.

Jenkins's noteworthiness stemmed from the rich documentation of his experiences and thoughts that has survived. In 1839 he had begun to keep a journal in order to improve his English, maintaining it daily until his death. The diaries (complete from 1845) and the acute observations, poetry and commentary they contained have become justifiably celebrated. Those he kept in Australia provided a unique and memorable primary source for the social, cultural and labour history of colonial Victoria. Notably, he discussed farming practices and the plight of agricultural labourers, a cause for which he campaigned in local newspapers. He also included much material on his fellow Welsh in the colony, other nationalities and indigenous people.

In November 1894, with his health failing, Jenkins decided to return home, arriving at Trecefel in March 1895. He died there on 26 September 1898, survived by his wife and seven children. Jenkins's Australian diaries are held in the State Library of Victoria; extracts were published as the *Diary of a Welsh Swagman 1869-1894* (Melbourne, 1975). In 1994 a fountain in his honour was erected at Maldon in recognition of 'his monumental contribution to the life of a rural worker in Victoria as recorded in his diaries'.

L. Lloyd, *Australians from Wales* (Caernarfon, Wales, 1988); B. Phillips, *Rhwng Dau Fyd: Y Swagman O Geredigion* (Aberystwyth, Wales, 1998) and *Pity the Swagman* (Aberystwyth, Wales, 2002); *Planet* (Wales), no 61, 1987, p 72.   BILL JONES

JOHNSON, DALRYMPLE MOUNT-GARRETT; *see* DALRYMPLE

JOHNSON, GEORGE RAYMOND (1840-1898), architect and surveyor, was born on 7 February 1840 at Southgate, in the Edmonton district, Middlesex, England, one of eight children of William Johnson, carpenter, later a contractor at Derby, and his wife Fanny, née Noon. George was articled to George Hall, architect to the Midlands Railway Co., and then worked in London. Before leaving for Queensland, on 24 July 1862 he married Emma Louisa Wood at the parish church, St George the Martyr, Holborn.

In Brisbane Johnson joined John Townsend Godfrey as a house- and ship-builder and claimed experience in both London and New York. In 1863 they had contracts for the Toowoomba Gaol, Woogaroo Asylum and Woogaroo Congregational Church, but the partnership was insolvent by April 1864. In 1865 Johnson was at Bowen and next year was licensee of the Criterion Hotel, Townsville.

Again in financial difficulties, in 1867 he moved to Melbourne, where he began modestly, building cottages, villas and small hotels; he may have gained clients through Masonic connexions, though many commissions came from competitions. His earliest works included cottages for the Old Colonists' Association (1869), Fitzroy, the Eastern Arcade (1872), Bourke Street, the New German Club (1878), Adelaide, and the Austin [q.v. Elizabeth] Hospital for Incurables (1881), Melbourne.

His town halls (still in use in 2003) mostly had landmark towers and the distinctive and powerful designs that sustained Johnson's reputation. They were at Hotham (North Melbourne, 1875), Collingwood (1885), Fitzroy (1887, an addition to the first part by W. J. Ellis) and Northcote (1888), in Melbourne, and at Daylesford (1882), Maryborough (1887) and Kilmore (1893). These were all classical designs with bold and rich character from Johnson's mannerist palette, an idiom in which he was a master. Another of his dominating classical works, featuring giant Corinthian pilasters, was the Metropolitan Meat Market (1879), North Melbourne.

He was a prolific architect of theatres, long since demolished or radically altered, including the Prince of Wales Opera House (1872), the Cyclorama (1888) and the Bijou Theatre (1889), Melbourne, the Theatre Royal (1878), Adelaide, the Criterion Theatre (1886), Sydney, and the early plans for Her Majesty's opera houses in Sydney (1883) and Brisbane (1884). Johnson's greatest contemporary acclaim came from his design for the extensive and wonderful Centennial Exhibition complex (1887), which he added with sensitive deference to the northern side of the earlier Exhibition Building (1880), by Reed [q.v.6] & Barnes.

Johnson's success created some professional enmity, and he had disputes with the Victorian Institute of Architects. He served on Hawthorn Borough Council in 1870-73. On 2 December 1882 he was seriously injured in a railway accident at Hawthorn for which he received £2481 in compensation.

During the financial depression of the early 1890s, Johnson sought opportunities elsewhere. In Western Australia he worked on the Theatre Royal (1896), Perth. While returning to Melbourne in the *Pilbarra*, he took ill and died of septicaemia on 25 November 1898 at sea. Intestate, he left an estate of £150. His wife, three sons and four daughters survived him. One son, Harry Melbourne Golding Johnson (1867-1931), became an architect.

Victoria and its Metropolis, 2 (Melb, 1888); D. Watson and J. McKay, *Queensland Architects of the 19th Century* (Brisb, 1994); Institute of Architects (Vic), council minutes 1872-90 (SLV); M. Lewis, Australian Architectural Index (Architecture L, Univ Melb); Johnson family papers (held by Mr P. Johnson, Melb).   GEORGE TIBBITS
                                        PETER JOHNSON

JOHNSTON, FRANCIS CHARLES ('MASSA') (1880-1953), bandmaster, was born on 30 December 1880 in Sydney, son of David Johnston, a Scottish-born engineer (and bagpiper), and his wife Isabella, née Kiernan, from Ireland. At an early age Frank went to Melbourne where he attended St Ignatius' School, Richmond. There in the school band he came under the influence of James Hore, who had qualified at the Royal Military School of Music, Kneller Hall, Twickenham, Middlesex, England, and pioneered brass bands in Victoria. Johnston was infected by 'the romance' of the German bandsmen playing in the streets of Melbourne and, while still only a boy, his love of southern African-American music earned him the nickname 'Massa'.

Having learnt to play the tenor horn, Johnston later added the cornet and euphonium to his repertoire; he often rose at 5 a.m. to practise in a nearby quarry. He joined Richmond City Band in 1900, the year the South Street competitions at Ballarat first included band music; in 1903 he won the euphonium section with a score of ninety-nine. That year he began a fifty-year association with the Collingwood Citizens' Band. By 1906 he was conductor, and his skill in band training matured rapidly: by 1908 he had taken the band to victory in the A-grade competition, the first of many at State and national level under his leadership.

On 16 October 1909 at St John's Catholic Church, Clifton Hill, Johnston married Agnes Frances Armstrong. As the brass band movement grew in popularity, he embarked on a full-time career as a band trainer. In 1920 he succeeded the trumpeter Edward T. Code, father of E. P. Code [q.v.8], as conductor of the Victorian Police Band. Then in 1922 Johnston took over the Metropolitan Fire Brigade Band. A hard taskmaster who attracted loyal and devoted players, he could convey exactly the tone colour and style he wanted and instil the discipline of playing while marching in perfect time. Under his tutelage 'Melbourne's musical firemen' not only graced every major public occasion in their own city, they also visited every capital in Australia, where they 'set the town on fire' each time. With their 'mellow brilliance of tone and exceptional elasticity of rhythm' they were 'arguably the finest all brass combination produced' in Australia.

Johnston's busy conducting schedule included the St Kilda Citizens' Band from 1921 and the Footscray City Band from 1934. His passion extended to school bands where instruments were provided for working-class children. A sustained campaign bore fruit in 1930 with the establishment of a state schools contest supported by the William Gillies bequest. As conductor of the Hyde Street, Footscray, school band Johnston was invincible. His skill in quickly bringing young, inexperienced players up to A-grade standard had been remarked upon from his earliest days. Notwithstanding success in over 600 championships, the legacy of this 'genius in brass band music' might best be measured by the number of players who passed through his hands to become the core of Melbourne's post-war bands.

A solidly built man of medium height with a habit of chewing his thumb, at 68 Johnson was still running three laps of the South Melbourne oval every morning to maintain the fitness necessary for his rigorous conducting schedule. The Fire Brigade Band was disbanded due to changed conditions of employment in 1950. Ill health forced him into semi-retirement in 1951 after the Collingwood band once again won the Australian Championships.

Massa Johnston had played in and led brass bands that farewelled Australian soldiers from the Boer War to World War II, and entertained crowds at Melbourne Cup carnivals and football finals for half a century. He died on 17 January 1953 at St Kilda and was buried with Catholic rites in Warringal cemetery, Heidelberg. His wife, four sons and one daughter Helen Taylor, a fine pianist and composer who became a band adjudicator, survived him.

In Those Days: Collingwood Remembered (Melb, 1983); S. Wilde, *Life Under the Bells* (Melb, 1991); T. Herbert (ed), *The Brass Band Movement in the 19th and 20th Centuries* (Milton Keynes, UK, 1991); G. M. Hibbins, *A Short History of Collingwood* (Melb, 1997); J. Greaves and C. Earl, *Legends in Brass* (Kangaroo Flat, Vic, 2001); *A'sian Bandsman*, 4, no 6, June-July 1958, p 20; *VHM*, 36, no 1, Feb 1965, p 30; *Argus* (Melb), 13 Dec 1947, Weekend Mag, p 2; *Age* (Melb), 19 Jan 1953, p 3; information from Messrs C. Killingbeck, South Yarra, J. Thomas, St Andrews, F. Thomas, Blackburn, R. Thomas, Bairnsdale, and K. Roberts, McLeod, Vic.

CAROLYN RASMUSSEN

JOHNSTON, KERR (1812-1887), seamen's mission chaplain, was born on 26 August 1812 at Greenock, Renfrew, Scotland, sixth son of William Johnston, printer and publisher, and his wife Elizabeth, formerly Thomson. After his schooling, Kerr learned bookbinding in his father's business and became a member of the George Street Congregational Church, Greenock. In 1837-40, supporting himself by his trade, he took classes at the University of Glasgow and studied at Glasgow Theological Academy under Dr Ralph Wardlaw, a prominent Scottish opponent of religious establishments. Ordained on 23 January 1842, Johnston became minister of Mill Street Congregational Church, Perth. He married Eliza Denovan Gowan, daughter of a shipbuilder, on 4 August 1842 in the parish church, Berwick-on-Tweed, England. In 1847 he moved to Birdhopecraig, Northumberland. Having come to doubt the validity of infant baptism, he was baptized by his brother Robert, a Baptist minister, in Well Lane Chapel, Beverley, Yorkshire, on 9 April 1848. Johnston then became pastor of Bethel Baptist Chapel, Shipley. Late in 1852 he migrated to Australia and became pastor of the Harrington Street Particular Baptist Church in Hobart Town in May 1853.

Johnson had arrived in Van Diemen's Land in time to take part in the abortive campaign against state aid to religion, denouncing 'the unholy compact' between church and state as well as the proposal to subsidize truth and error indiscriminately. He entered wholeheartedly into evangelical inter-denominational events and agencies such as the Bible Society and the temperance movement and, it is claimed, attended the 'wild man' William Buckley [q.v.1] on his deathbed. Johnston's particular interest was the Hobart Bethel Union Seamen's Mission, a branch of the agency that George Fife Angas [q.v.1] helped to found. Johnston left Hobart in February 1857 to set up a mission to seamen in Melbourne.

There were several retired captains and merchants as well as Bishop Charles Perry [q.v.5] supported the proposal, and the Victorian Bethel Union enjoyed the patronage of the governor and the United States consul. The colonial government provided a hulk, a former American clipper, for use as 'a floating Bethel'. Painted yellow, with 'Bethel Sailors Church' inscribed on each side, the *Emily* flew the blue Bethel flag emblazoned with a white star and dove with olive branch. A chapel with a blue-draped pulpit was created in the hold. For two and a half years, the Johnston family, with eight children, three servants and livestock, also lived in the vessel, moored between Williamstown and Sandridge (Port Melbourne).

The seamen's mission, essentially non-denominational but emphatically Protestant, opened in the Bethel ship on 1 July 1857; Perry delivered the sermon. Subsequently known as the Victorian Seamen's Mission, it moved ashore at Sandridge early in 1860, using a boatshed as a temporary chapel until the Mariners' Church opened in November. As well as preaching there, Johnston visited ships to distribute Bibles and evangelical tracts, particularly temperance literature, and sometimes preached to small groups. Occasionally he met with 'some Romish opposition'. Once criticized by a Church of England minister as a sectarian, he defended his position as a teacher of essential Christianity, asserting that the mission aimed to disseminate the Gospel among sailors 'apart from sectional differences'.

Johnston joined the Evangelical Alliance when it formed in Melbourne and regretted its demise in the 1860s. The interest of the Protestant churches in the mission soon waned, though he worked tirelessly, building the seamen's mission into a significant agency. He retired in December 1885 with a gift of £100 from the committee. Johnston died on 9 October 1887 at his home in Kew and was buried with Congregational forms in Melbourne general cemetery. His wife and seven of their ten children survived him; a daughter (Janet) married Daniel Matthews [q.v.5], missionary to Aborigines, and a son (Kerr) became a Methodist minister in Canada.

A. E. Brown, *Garnered Sheaves* (Melb, 1935); N. Cato, *Mister Maloga* (Brisb, 1976); W. D. McNaughton, *The Scottish Congregational Ministry 1794-1993* (Glasgow, Scotland, 1993); Victorian Seamen's Mission, *Annual Report*, 1846, 1875; *Southern Cross* (Melb), 19 Dec 1885, 14 Oct 1887; *Argus* (Melb), 2 July 1857, p 5, 19 Nov 1860, p 5, 25 Feb 1864, p 5, 29 Feb 1864, p 7; Janet Matthews' diaries and memoirs in Norman family papers, PRG 422 (SLSA).   WALTER PHILLIPS

JOLLY, ALEXANDER STEWART (1887-1957), architect, was born on 18 July 1887 at Wardell, near Lismore, New South Wales, fourth of six children of Scottish-born parents James Jolly, carpenter, and his wife Jessie Spence, née Stewart. About 1895 Jessie took the children to Scotland for a two-year visit to their father's birthplace at Muthill, Perthshire. After schooling at Lismore, Alexander gained experience in craftsmanship with his father's building firm, Brown & Jolly. The company contracted for some of the Lismore buildings of architects Wardell & Denning, and about 1908 he began his architectural training in their Sydney office.

On 27 June 1912 at Scots Church, Sydney, Alexander married Kathleen Wilhelmina, daughter of Rev. William Marcus Dill Macky [q.v.8]. Back at Lismore, Jolly set up in sole practice and in 1914 entered into partnership with F. J. Board; St Bartholomew's Church of England, Alstonville, was their major project (1912-16).

Moving to Sydney in mid-1918, Jolly practised in the city and built Cremorne House (1919), 7 Cranbrooke Avenue, which was an early and leading example of the California Bungalow style. He was successful but in the early 1920s ill health forced him to retire prematurely. A lover of the natural environment, he joined A. E. Dashwood, an estate agent, in land speculation in the developing Avalon area. Jolly was a keen salesman and lived on the land for sale, in a small cabin or tent, until all lots had been sold. This experience of local bushland brought a reawakening of his architectural inspiration and, consequently, a few clients. After being commissioned to design a building, Jolly continued his habit of living on the site, directing and often helping with construction. A lone proponent of organic architecture on steep bushland, his uncompromising buildings, using earthy colours and textures, appeared to grow out of the surrounds. Loggan Rock (1930) and Careel House (1931), both at Careel Head, and the Elephant House (1935), Taylor's Point, highlighted his personal philosophy.

Land and building development faltered in the Depression, and financial setbacks led Jolly to alcoholism. Determined to show his family that he could overcome his addiction, he resolutely chopped off the top of his little finger with an axe, vowing never to drink again. He found comfort in writing nature poetry (unpublished) and children's books. His *Spirit of the Bush* and *Adrift at Sea* were published in 1932.

In the late 1930s Jolly joined Dashwood in successful land dealing on the New South Wales south coast. Nineteen buildings, sixteen of which were for residential use, had been completed when World War II began. Lean, slightly stooped, 5 ft 11 ins (180.3 cm) tall, with grey eyes, Jolly enlisted in the Militia on 18 December 1941 and was posted to the 7th Garrison Battalion. He was discharged on 2 November 1943. He did not return to architecture.

A skilled draughtsman and sensitive artist, Jolly, through poor health, an impractical nature and over-generosity, failed to achieve personal recognition or financial success, but found fulfilment in his unconventional architecture. He died of myocardial infarction on 17 April 1957 at his Wollstonecraft home and was cremated. His wife, son and three daughters survived him.

R. Irving (comp), *The History & Design of the Australian House* (Melb, 1985); J. Roberts (ed), *Avalon: Landscape and Harmony* (Syd, 1999); D. Anderson, Alexander Stewart Jolly, His Life and Works (B.Arch thesis, Univ NSW, 1969); B884 item N387021 (NAA).   PETER REYNOLDS
DOUGLAS ANDERSON

JONES, EDITH EMILY (c.1875-1952), community worker and Aboriginal rights advocate, was born in Clapham, London, daughter of a middle-class father named Brown. Becoming a secondary school teacher, Edith was lecturing at Glamorgan Pupil Teachers' College in southern Wales when she met Rev. John Jones (1875-1942), a Church of England clergyman, whom she married in June 1904 at Clapham, London. He had been born on 17 January 1875 in Wales. They were to have two sons.

In 1904 the couple travelled to Australia where John became head of the Church of England mission on Thursday Island, as well as vicar and tutor of Bishop's College there. By 1910 they were back in England, and he was secretary of the Society for the Propagation of the Gospel at Southwark, London. Their sons remained in an English boarding school when in 1912 John was appointed general secretary (chairman from 1917) of the Australian Board of Missions, based in Sydney. The Joneses toured Australia promoting mission work with Aborigines. Edith's energetic approach to social and political reform soon led her to form the first branches of the women's auxiliary of the mission board, and she campaigned successfully for women's greater involvement through their direct appointment to the board. In 1913 she met one of her predecessors at Thursday Island, deaconess Florence Buchanan [q.v.7], and honoured her life in a book, published in London in 1921.

A member of the girls' department of the Young Women's Christian Association, Jones served on the executive of the National Council of Women and as a member of its social hygiene committee. She and her husband moved to the East St Kilda vicarage in Melbourne in the 1920s and she was appointed a justice of the peace in the Victorian Children's Court. Joining the Victorian Women Citizens' Movement in the early 1920s, Jones became its second president and nominated as its candidate for the Federal seat of Fawkner in 1925, but withdrew due to opposition from churchwardens at St Kilda. Her growing expertise on Aboriginal issues was recognized by the Australian government in 1929 when she gave evidence on Aboriginal status and conditions to a royal commission on the constitution. She advocated Federal control of Aboriginal affairs and the rights of Aboriginal women. Through organizations affiliated with the Australian Federation of Women Voters, Mrs Jones joined an international network engaged in progressive reform. She attended the London-based British Commonwealth League conferences from their inception in 1925, and was appointed to its executive in 1930.

A photograph of her in 1925 showed a good-looking, fine-featured woman with bobbed hair and elegant dress. After returning to England in 1929, when her husband became rector of Marlborough, Jones presented over the following years a series of conference papers highly critical of race policy in Australia. Through the Anti-Slavery and Aborigines' Protection Society, she formed a special committee in 1932 to provide a focal point for international campaigns for Aboriginal rights, and in the 1930s she and John were outspoken delegates to the B.C.L. calling for Aboriginal citizenship, land, health and welfare reform. John died on 13 May 1942 at Hove, Sussex. Edith died on 24 November 1952 at Bromley, Kent.

M. M. Bennett, *The Australian Aboriginal as a Human Being* (Lond, 1930); M. Lake, *Getting Equal* (Syd, 1999); F. Paisley, *Loving Protection?* (Melb, 2000); *Woman's World*, 1 Jan 1925, p 66; *Farmers' Advocate*, 27 Feb 1925; *Age* (Melb), 28 Sept 1928, p 7; *Dawn* (Perth), 16 Aug 1929, p 4, 21 Aug 1929, p 4, 20 Aug 1930, p 7; Anti-slavery and Aborigines' Protection Society papers (Rhodes House, Oxford, Eng); Bessie Rischbeith papers (NL).

FIONA PAISLEY

JONES, HORATIO THOMAS (1870-1949), engineer, inventor and recluse, was born on 5 June 1870 at Naracoorte, South Australia, fifth child and posthumous son of Horatio Thomas Jones (d. November 1869), an insolvent storekeeper, and his wife Mary, née Cattanach, from Scotland. Mary Jones and her four surviving children soon moved to Victoria. She died at South Yarra in 1886. Before he was 20 Horatio had produced some inventions, including a model of a self-adjusting windmill, displayed at the Juvenile Industrial Exhibition in Melbourne on 28 March 1888, which won a silver medal. He served an apprenticeship for three years in a metal trade with the Atlas Co.

Described as an engineer, 5 ft 8 ins (173 cm) tall, weighing 10 st. 2 lb. (64 kg), with dark complexion, brown eyes, dark hair and a scarred face, he enlisted in the Australian Imperial Force on 17 May 1915, putting his age down to 43. He was allotted to the 23rd Battalion and landed at Gallipoli in August. In March next year he transferred to the 2nd Pioneers Battalion but after months in hospital was invalided to Australia in May. He was discharged in Melbourne on 23 November 1916 as totally and permanently incapacitated with cardiac problems and rheumatic fever.

In June 1916 Jones had reportedly persuaded his fiancée Caroline Hearst to end their engagement and return to the United States of America, as he feared he would not live much longer. He never married. Purchasing land at Tecoma in the Dandenongs, about 1920 he built for himself and his sisters Christina and Annie an extraordinary, two-storeyed house from bush timber, flattened 4-gallon (18-litre) kerosene tins and fencing wire. He created his own set of tools, levers and rollers, some of which remain in the building.

The house was an unusually grand and rare example of shanty construction in the early twentieth century. In contrast to the tin exterior, the elegant interior with antique furniture and fine furnishings illustrated the comfortable lifestyle maintained by the family under adverse conditions. The Union Jack hung over his four-poster bed. Jones's creativity and adaptiveness were also displayed in his inventions, which included a patent rabbit exterminator and a water wheel that generated power from the creek on the property.

Family legend paints Jones as a dashing man, who entertained the poet C. J. Dennis and the artist (Sir) Arthur Streeton [qq.v.8,12] at the property, but others remember him as a shy recluse. Predeceased by his sisters Annie (in December 1937) and Christina (in October 1945), Horatio died on 28 June 1949 at Heidelberg Repatriation Hospital, and was buried in the Presbyterian section of Ferntree Gully cemetery. The National Trust of Australia classified his house in 1985, and it was added to the Register of Historic Buildings in 1993 and to the Register of the National Estate in 1996.

Shell Times, May 1985, p 5; *Aust Country Style*, Oct 1994, p 49; *Age* (Melb), 12 Sept 1985, p 1, 16 Mar 1989, p 3, 12 Sept 1992, p 2, 8 Oct 1994, 'Travel Vic', p 3; *Mountain District Free Press*, 18 Sept 1985; Allom Lovell & Associates, Horatio's House, 16 Blackwood Street, Tecoma, draft conservation management plan, Feb 2002 (Heritage Vic, Melb); Horatio Jones House file no. 5622, National Trust of Aust (Vic), (East Melb).   CELESTINA SAGAZIO

JONES, JOHN; *see* ST LEON

JONES, WILLIAM (c.1842-1906), Aboriginal circus acrobat, was born near Dubbo, New South Wales, son of a labourer named William and Mary Ann, an Aboriginal woman. One of the first Aborigines to be employed in Australian circuses, Billy was noted as an infant performer in Henry Burton's [q.v.3] company at Bathurst as early as August 1851. A 'manly little fellow of exquisite proportions', he leaped on and off his cream-coloured pony 'with pleasure in all directions; sometimes running by his side when at full speed, and vaulting with surprising nimbleness on his back'. Dubbed 'Little Nugget' and 'Master Parello Frank' (after a British African entertainer Pablo Fanque), Billy performed in John Jones's [q.v. Matthew St Leon] equestrian troupe in John Malcolm's circus in Sydney in

May 1852. Jones taught him more acrobatic and equestrian acts, to dance a sailor's hornpipe and to walk the tight rope.

Travelling the goldfields and the backblocks of south-eastern Australia, Billy spent his youth with Jones's company, and adopted his mentor's surname. In outback towns, he drew the attention of the public by ascending and descending a rope stretched from a tree stump to the centre pole of the circus. Visiting Hobart Town with W. H. Foley's Californian Circus in 1866, he walked a rope stretched from the top of the circus pole to the Theatre Royal on the other side of Argyle Street, at a height of about fifty feet (15 m) to the cheers of people below. His marvellous versatility and agility remained undiminished despite advancing age and weight that reached as much as fifteen stone (95 kg). In 1873 with Bird & Taylor's Great American Circus at Kapunda, South Australia, he somersaulted his 'aldermanic corporation' so rapidly it was 'almost impossible to tell his head from his feet'. With St Leon's Circus in Brisbane in 1882 he gave 'a very neat display ... with balls and knives with great rapidity, and without the slightest mistake'.

The last years of his circus career were spent with the FitzGerald brothers' circus as a horse-trainer and ringmaster. He could still captivate audiences as late as 1896 with his leap over twenty horses. Dan FitzGerald wrote that Jones possessed the mind and energy to plan and execute the organization of a great circus. He knew every bit of harness and property, every strap and buckle, rope, seat and pole in the FitzGerald circus, and could train both its horses and its human performers in their various circus tricks. He possessed an 'extensive and peculiar' knowledge of Australia and its roads and an enormous store of anecdotes of Australian circus life. A 'stout, dark man with curly black hair', and 'very smart', he retired from his circus career in the early 1900s to become a coach-driver on the Mount Morgan road, Queensland. He was brought out of retirement in 1905 to appear one last time with FitzGeralds' in Sydney as 'Old William Jones'.

Jones had a son Frederick by his first wife Mary. In Sydney on 21 July 1893, describing himself as a widower, William Edwin Jones married with Congregational forms 21-year-old Maggie Long. They had no children. Jones spent the last months of his life as a watchman at Redfern. In straitened circumstances, he died of endocarditis on 1 July 1906 at Sydney Hospital. His wife and son survived him.

T&CJ, 3 Aug 1904, p 34; *Referee*, 11 July 1906, p 12; *Bathurst Free Press*, 6 Aug 1851, p 2, 24 Sept 1851, p 4; *SMH*, 19 May 1852, p 1; *Geelong Advertiser*, 7 Feb 1853, p 2; *Ovens & Murray Advertiser*, 22 Mar 1859, p 2; *Mercury*, 7 June 1866, p 2, 14 Feb

1884, p 2; *Kapunda Herald*, 25 Apr 1873, p 2; *Wagga Wagga Express*, 26 Jan 1876; *Brisb Courier*, 6 May 1882, p 5; *Bulletin*, 23 May 1896, p 8; Dan Fitzgerald papers (ML).   MARK VALENTINE ST LEON

JOYNER, FREDERICK ALLEN (1863-1945), solicitor, photographer and plant breeder, was born on 29 December 1863 at Wellington Square, North Adelaide, second of eight children of Edwin Vaughan Joyner, clerk, and his wife Harriet, née Allen. Following an education at North Adelaide Grammar School (Whinham College) and the University of Adelaide (LL.B., 1883), Frederick practised as a city solicitor for fifty years. On 25 September 1889 in North Adelaide, he married Annie Adelaide, sixth daughter of the city's leading stationer and bookseller Edgar Smith Wigg.

Joyner and his family lived in North Adelaide, where his neighbours G. D. Delprat [q.v.8], of Broken Hill Proprietary Co. Ltd, and Ernest Gall, a professional photographer, influenced him, as his involvement in mining ventures and photography showed. Another friend was H. P. Gill [q.v.9], later honorary curator of the Museums and Art Gallery of South Australia. Joyner wrote critiques of art exhibitions and was influential in preventing the acquisition of certain paintings by the art gallery board in 1908 and 1914. In 1899 he had been one of four men who financed Hans Heysen's [q.v.9] five years of study in Europe —in return for title to everything painted in that time. From then Joyner was the artist's friend and legal adviser.

The earliest phase of Joyner's photographic work involved narrative studies of children, portraits and lantern slides, to illustrate his lectures on subjects ranging from bees to photographic techniques. He had joined the South Australian Photographic Society by at least 1896 and was president several times and auditor until its demise in 1912. His work and that of other members was exhibited overseas. John Kauffmann [q.v.9], a professional photographer and fellow society member, introduced him to the new pictorial style of photography about 1898. In 1905-14 Joyner wrote a photographic column under the pen name of 'Diaphragm' for the monthly *Faulding's Medical Journal*. His venture into coloured photography in 1906 showed his awareness of the latest technology, as did his library.

The next stage of Joyner's photography consisted of hundreds of flower and vegetable studies relevant to his plant breeding, which he practised at his summer residence, Karkoo, in the Adelaide Hills. There he developed new types of daisy, sweet pea, lettuce and potato and an odourless onion. Under the pen-name

'Primrose', he wrote and illustrated gardening columns for local papers and for the weekly *Gardening Bulletin*, which he edited from 1917. In 1927 with Heysen he visited the Flinders Ranges: both were inspired by the light and grandeur of the area. Joyner's last stage of photographic art consisted almost entirely of Flinders Ranges scenes, pre-dating Harold Cazneaux [q.v.7] by seven years. In 1930 the Art Gallery of South Australia bought some of his photographs.

Joyner's achievements suggested that he lived up to the motto on the Joyner coat-of-arms, granted in 1591, *Non Dormio*. He died after a long illness on 10 December 1945 at St Margaret's Hospital, Payneham, survived by his wife, son and daughter. His estate was sworn for probate at £17 521.

On his son's death in 1979, several hundred of Joyner's photographs were acquired by the A.G.S.A. and an exhibition of his work and equipment was held in 1981. The State Library of South Australia, which held in excess of 2500 glass plate negatives, printed all of these and mounted them in thirty, leather-bound volumes. These were part of an October 1990 exhibition at the library. The National Gallery of Australia, Canberra, and other Australian galleries also hold examples of his work.

C. Thiele, *Heysen of Hahndorf* (Adel, 1968); *Real Visions: The Life and Work of F. A. Joyner*, exhibition cat (Adel, 1981); *E. S. Wigg and His Successors* (Adel, 1992); *A'sian Photo-review*, Sept 1894; *Register* (Adel), 8 July 1914, p 11, 10 July 1914, p 13; *Leader* (Melb), 13 Jan 1917, p 12; Ernest Gall papers (SLSA); family papers.   JEAN WATERHOUSE

JUDD, ERNEST EDWARD JOB PULLIN (1883-1959), bookseller and socialist, was born on 9 April 1883 at Scrubbing Plain, near Forbes, New South Wales, elder son of Ernest Augustus Judd, labourer, and his wife Alice Florence, née Stevens; both parents had been born in the colony. Ernie frequented W. H. McNamara's [q.v.10] bookshop and the Sydney Domain, and about 1907 he joined and became treasurer of the Socialist Labor Party, followers of Daniel de Leon in the United States of America, who in 1908 split from the Industrial Workers of the World. Judd, however, remained connected to the I.W.W. Club in Sydney.

As an independent, he contested Wollongong in the State elections of 1913 and King in 1917. He was a delegate of the Municipal Workers' Union to the Labor Council of New South Wales during World War I, an opponent of conscription and, with H. E. Boote and P. S. Brookfield [qq.v.7], a critic of the trial of members of the I.W.W. in 1916. Appointed by the Labor Council as investigator into the case, he worked vigorously for their release.

Judd was prominent in the second conscription referendum campaign and secured a scoop when he published W. A. Holman's [q.v.9] *Secret Memorandum*, which advocated dismissal of single men to encourage recruiting.

Among Judd's publications were *The War and the Sydney Labor Council* (1917) and *Judd's Speech From the Dock* (1919). He was unsuccessful as a Senate candidate in May 1917, securing 11 983 votes. Next year the Commonwealth proceeded against him for making statements prejudicial to recruiting and in 1919 he was prosecuted under the War Precautions Act. He faced heavy costs and fines, though he turned such trials into political drama. In his *Case for the O.B.U.* (1919), he urged the replacing of 'Class Governments' by an 'Industrial Parliament' and attacked the Australian Labor Party. In March 1919 Labor's John Storey repudiated 'Jock' Garden [qq.v.12,8] and Judd as 'limelighters and notoriety hunters'. Judd began his own publishing company and was proprietor of 'The Best Bookshop', 140 Castlereagh Street, Sydney, advertising free-thought and birth-control literature in *Liberator*, the secularist newspaper.

In 1920 Judd was a powerful public speaker, still full haired and of imposing appearance. A police report noted that when he mounted the platform in the Domain, 'audiences around the A.L.P. and other Socialist platforms made a beeline' for him. The release of ten of the I.W.W. in 1920, after a second royal commission, appointed by the Storey government, was perhaps the peak of his reputation. But at State elections that year, standing for Sydney, he secured only 282 votes.

Judd refused invitations to a unity conference of Sydney socialists in March 1921, denouncing the Communist Party as 'a front for capitalist spies'. When, in May, ex-soldiers and right-wing demonstrators beset him in the Domain, Judd drew a revolver; he was convicted of carrying a firearm and with offensive behaviour. In August in the Domain he debated A. D. Kay [q.v.9] on 'The Individual versus Socialism'; facetious for Kay, it was serious for Judd.

As general secretary of the S.L.P. from 1920, he experienced increasing difficulty in disciplining the industrial organizer A. W. Wilson—who described him as 'a filthy minded ... scurvy rascal ... with a yellow streak'. Later Judd also fell out with Arnold Peterson, who had succeeded de Leon as head of the American party. Demoralized by declining support, Judd became possessive about party funds. His political court battles resumed. In 1926 he was convicted for failing to vote in the 1925 Senate elections. Using the *Revolutionary Socialist* newspaper, he attacked R. J. Heffron and supported Tom Mutch [qq.v.14,10] in the seat of Botany at the 1927 and 1930 State elections. After failing to win North Sydney in the Federal election of 1929, Judd sued the *Barrier Daily Truth* for remarks during the campaign, but was awarded only a farthing damages. Heffron sued him over his propaganda in Botany.

In 1931 Judd published *How to end Capitalism and Inaugurate Socialism* and, with A. P. Warren, *Why War is Near*. From the mid-1930s Judd's vision of human improvement declined; unkempt, he lived in the past. In Ian Turner's judgement, hobbled by old dogmas, he became 'a cantankerous stump orator, preaching the truths of De Leonism to a dwindling handful of the converted'. He never married. In 1929 he was still living in Albion Street, Sydney, but later lodged at Bondi Junction. Judd was described as a labourer when he died on 20 August 1959 in Rydalmere mental hospital. He was cremated without religious rites.

I. Turner, *Sydney's Burning* (Melb, 1967); F. Farrell, *International Socialism and Australian Labour* (Syd, 1981); F. Cain, *The Wobblies at War* (Melb, 1993); *SMH*, 7 Mar 1919, p 7, 29 Apr 1919, p 9, 3 June 1919, p 5, 10 Dec 1919, p 11, 9 May 1921, p 10, 24 May 1921, p 6, 13 Sept 1921, p 7, 7 Oct 1927, p 14, 3 June 1929, p 10; A. W. Wilson, All for the Cause (ms, LaTL).   FRANK FARRELL*

JUDE, SIR NORMAN LANE (1905-1975), politician, was born on 7 April 1905 at Handsworth, Staffordshire, England, son of Archibald Alexander Jude, engineering draftsman, and his wife Edith Susan, née Lane—who died at Norman's birth. Raised by relations, he boarded at Stamford School, Lincolnshire, in 1917-23, becoming prefect, sergeant major in the Officer Training Corps and captain of Rugby; a kick to the head in a game left him deaf in one ear.

In 1924 he migrated to South Australia, entering Roseworthy Agricultural College, where he played cricket and Australian Rules football. Graduating in 1926 with a diploma of agriculture, Jude was a cellar-hand in the Reynell [q.v.6] wineries, Reynella, briefly a farm hand at the Murray mouth from 1929, then manager of a dairy near Meningie. He travelled to Adelaide on his motorbike to play hockey, and was selected for the State side. On 6 August 1935 at Christ Church, North Adelaide, he married Nancy Margaret, daughter of a pastoralist, K. D. Bowman of Poltalloch station, whose death in 1932 had left her independently wealthy. After visiting England, the couple purchased Carolside, a sheep run near Naracoorte, in 1936.

Jude served on the district committee of the Stockowners' Association, the governing council of the Chamber of Rural Industries and the Naracoorte hospital board, and was also president of the local branch of the National Fitness Council and a physical training instructor at the boys' club. He helped to form and was later president of the south-eastern fire fighting association, belonged to the Volunteer Defence Corps and supported the Australian Red Cross Society. He was a member of the South Australian Jockey Club.

In April 1944 he won Southern District for the Liberal and Country League in the Legislative Council elections. Though supporting the premier (Sir) Thomas Playford, he called the wheat stabilization bill a 'Moscow system' that would destroy growers' freedoms, and dubbed the State land tax unworthy of 'the most solid Liberal Government in Australia'. When Playford increased his cabinet in late 1953 Jude, a surprise inclusion, was allocated local government, rail and the new portfolio of roads. The family moved to Adelaide. In 1957 Robin Hill, at Collinswood, became their home; managers ran Carolside until it was sold in 1973.

Facing enormous challenges in a city which was to almost double in size in the two post-war decades, Jude was of little assistance to Adelaide's first town planner Stuart Hart, failing to act on his recommendations or to champion legislation to halt the excesses of speculative land sales. The poorly maintained rail system continued to decline, although some new lines were opened. From the mid-1950s, 'Red Hens' on metropolitan and 'Blue Birds' on country lines began the transformation from steam to diesel locomotion. Diesel buses had replaced trams on all but the Glenelg line by 1958, while trolley-buses ceased in 1963.

Convinced of the need for good arterial roads, Jude encouraged efficiencies in rail freight and refused to impose harsh restrictions on road hauliers. In 1954 he visited New Zealand to inspect its strict weight and speed limits and in 1962 attended a meeting of the International Road Federation in Madrid. With the Highways Department enjoying perhaps its most optimistic and dynamic period,

in 1960 Jude, his wife and a senior engineer spent four months in Europe and the United States of America examining road construction and traffic control. The sealing, widening and upgrading of roads continued; in 1962-64 a third bridge over the Murray was built, at Blanchetown. The South Eastern freeway was begun, its route through Arbury Park—(Sir) Alexander Downer's property—causing an imbroglio which Jude mediated with some success.

Jude's relatively humble origins may have delayed his membership of the Adelaide Club; he was elected in 1962. Playford's government fell in March 1965 and Jude was knighted in June. He became a director of the pastoral firm, Bennett & Fisher, in which he was a major shareholder, and in 1967 president of the Australian-American Association in South Australia. Excluded from Steele Hall's cabinet of 1968, he railed against reforms ending the rural gerrymander. In June 1971 he resigned.

Sir Norman kept up his interests in road transport, sports administration, his pastoral property and investments. He revisited the U.S.A. in 1974. Fond of cigars, wines and spirits, he suffered from a duodenal ulcer. Jude died of cancer on 18 February 1975 at his home. His wife, three daughters and one son survived him. After a state funeral at St Andrew's Church, Walkerville, he was buried in Centennial Park cemetery. His estate was sworn for probate at $159 884.

A. B. Cox, *Local Government in South Australia* (Adel, 1964); H. Stretton, *Ideas for Australian Cities* (Adel, 1970); N. Blewett and D. Jaensch, *Playford to Dunstan* (Melb, 1971); B. Carroll, *Getting Around Town* (Syd, 1980); P. Donovan, *Highways: A History of the South Australian Highways Department* (Adel, 1991); Roseworthy Agr College, *Student*, XXIII, Dec 1924, p 15, XXIV, i, July 1925, p 21, XXIV, ii, Jan 1926, p 18, Dec 1938, pp 80 & 86, Dec 1955, p 61; *Highway* (Adel), 13, no 2, Apr 1975, p 1; *Advertiser* (Adel), 12 June 1965, pp 1 & 3, 8 June 1971, p 16, 19 Feb 1975, p 4; Jude diary and papers (held by Mrs F. Sidey, Westbourne Park, SA).

JENNY TILBY STOCK

K

KAAWIRN KUUNAWARN ('HISSING SWAN') (c.1820-1889), Aboriginal leader, also known as 'KING DAVID', chief of the Kirrae wurrung, or 'Davie', was born at Lake Connewarren, Victoria, son of Carrowan, head of the Conewurt (Gunaward) clan. The youngster was later named after the noise the swans made when he robbed their nests.

A young adult when Europeans moved into the area, Kaawirn Kuunawarn became clan leader on his father's death in May 1841. A shepherd and general worker for James Dawson [q.v.4] and Patrick Mitchell on Kangatong station from about 1845, except for short absences to attend to tribal business, he was employed on wages under a written agreement. Dawson wrote that 'the services were performed with the strictest fidelity'. Aborigines continued to observe their own customs. In early 1859 'Davey Kinconnawanen' and others were charged with the murder of an Aborigine, Smiley Austin, but the case did not proceed to trial because 'no evidence had been or was likely to be obtained'.

King David moved to Framlingham Aboriginal station when it opened in 1865. His first wife having died about 1868, on 14 May 1879 at Coranderrk Aboriginal Station he married with Anglican rites Mary Phillips ('Queen Mary'), widow of 'King Billy' of Ballarat, who had one son. Alcohol was sometimes a problem at Framlingham, but King David was not mentioned in this regard, except for an incident in 1885. After striking his wife when he and others were intoxicated, he was brought before the Warrnambool Bench, but the case was dismissed at the station manager's request when the men promised to sign a total abstinence pledge.

King David was one of the chief informants for—and a photograph of him appeared in—Dawson's *Australian Aborigines: The Languages and Customs of Several Tribes of Aborigines in the Western District of Victoria, Australia* (1881). The author wrote that information was obtained from the 'united testimony of several very intelligent aborigines'. Of this group, it was 'the sedate old chief' who, if any levity were shown, 'reproved the wag and restored . . . attention to the matter on hand'.

Impressive looking, with white hair, moustache and beard, his image was often reproduced in the nineteenth century, featuring in an album of Victorian kings and on *cartes de visite*. He was also photographed by J. Harvey of Belfast (Port Fairy). King David was the obvious choice when Dawson sought someone to pose before the obelisk in Camperdown cemetery over the grave of Wombeetch Puyuun ('Camperdown George') in memory of the extinct tribes of the area. The resulting photographs were used in articles in the *Australasian Sketcher* (7 April 1886) and the *Australian Town and Country Journal* (7 August 1886).

King David was also the inspiration for the main Aboriginal character in Louis Bayer's opera about colonial life, *Muutchaka or The Last of his Tribe*, an individual who showed all the superior qualities of human nature that the composer believed to be widespread among the Aborigines before the destructive effects of European invasion. The opera was first staged at Camperdown in May 1887 and has been produced at least twenty-nine times since.

On 4 September 1889 the Board for the Protection of the Aborigines reaffirmed its decision to close Framlingham Aboriginal station, despite the desire of the Aborigines to stay on at least part of the land. Predeceased by his daughter, Kaawirn Kuunawarn died there on 24 September. William Goodall, Framlingham's manager, notified Dawson by telegram: 'Old Davie (Hissing Swan) dead. Idea of his leaving home killed him. Buried on Thursday'. Dawson reproduced the wording in the *Camperdown Chronicle*, adding: 'my faithful friend of forty years, as honest a man as ever breathed, sacrificed to the greed of a race of men, who, not satisfied with having deprived him and his friends of their hunting grounds, now seek to turn them, in their old age, out of their established homes and associations'. To the *Hamilton Spectator*'s Warrnambool correspondent, however, Davie was a 'very violent old rascal . . . and a few broken heads were saved, to his womenkind especially, when the gin-soddened, possum-gorging old warrior was laid *hors de combat*'. Appalled at this final 'kick at the dying lion', Dawson responded that King David had been an exemplary worker on Kangatong for over twenty years and that there was little need to defend his character, given that 'his enemies and slanderers' were 'straining every nerve' to rob the Aborigines of the little they had left.

J. Critchett, *Untold Stories* (Melb, 1998); *Camperdown Chronicle*, 26 Sept 1889, p 2, 8 Oct 1889, p 3, 15 Oct 1889, p 2; *Hamilton Spectator*, 5 Oct 1889, p 4; VPRS 12, unit 12, item 7, VPRS 937, unit 32, bundle 6, 1859 (PRO, Vic); information from the late Dr D. Barwick.   JAN CRITCHETT

KAYE, RUTH EMILIE; *see* SAVILLE-KENT

KEEN, JOSEPH (1819-1892), curry-powder maker, was born on 11 January 1819 at Reading, Berkshire, England, eldest child of Joseph Keen and his wife Sarah, née Clement. Young Joseph married Johannah Sergent, a dressmaker from London, and in October 1841 they sailed for Australia. A bounty passenger, Joseph was engaged as a carpenter upon reaching Sydney early in 1842. Johannah died in April 1843 and was buried in the Congregational burying grounds. Joseph then left for Van Diemen's Land, arriving in Hobart Town on 21 December. On 20 March 1847 at St John's Church, New Town, describing himself as a cabinet-maker, he married 19-year-old Annie (Nancy) Burrows (Borrows) (1828-1915), a cook from Barnsley, England, who had arrived in the colony with her parents in 1842. The Keens were to have nine daughters and seven sons.

Joseph and Annie settled at Browns River, Kingston, south of Hobart, where they established a general store and a small manufacturing outlet. From their store, Joseph also worked as the district's postmaster from 1853. In addition, he and Annie ran a bakery, which their fourth son Walter helped to manage, and a grocery, where the sauces and condiments that were made on the premises were sold. Within a decade Keen had produced award-winning sauces and condiments and was advertising his curry powder throughout the colony. He received a medal for his spice mix at the 1866 Inter-Colonial Exhibition in Melbourne, and in 1879 a spicy sauce of his received an honourable mention at the Sydney International Exhibition.

Joseph died on 30 March 1892 at Sandy Bay, Hobart. Annie continued manufacturing the products and working as a storekeeper until about 1903, also taking over her husband's role as postmaster for a further two years. She died on 18 December 1915 at Margate and was buried with Joseph in St Clement's Anglican cemetery, Kingston.

Many of their children had married and settled at Kingston, close to their parents. Their sixth daughter Louisa and her husband Horace Watson took over the curry-powder business. Horace purchased land in the foothills of Mount Wellington, overlooking Hobart, and in 1905 transformed it into a large advertising sign. Heavy stones were collected from the site, painted white and used to form the words 'Keen's Curry' in letters some fifty feet (15 m) high. Public uproar resulted, but Horace won the right to use it as an advertising sign. In June 1926 the familiar landmark briefly changed to read 'Hell's Curse' as a university prank, and students altered it again in 1962 to promote a theatre production. In 1994 the landmark read 'No Cable Car' as a protest against a proposed development. After every change the sign was restored and in 2005 was still in place.

Joseph's product, Keen's Curry Powder, well known in Tasmania for more than a century, became an Australian household name after 1954, when the formula and rights were sold to the company Reckitt & Colman Australia Ltd, which had long been the manufacturers of a different product, Keen's mustard.

J. Edwards, *Out of the Blue* (Syd, 1982); *Zeehan & Dundas Herald*, 20 July 1905, p 4; *Illustrated Tas Mail*, 23 June 1926, p 36; *Mercury*, 27 Jan 1984, p 2, 23 Mar 1992, p 1, 24 Apr 1995, p 6, 11 Dec 1998, p 7; *Sunday Tasmanian*, 6 Jul 2003, p 3; information from Mr D. Wilson, Hob.   LYNN DAVIES

KELLY, ALEXANDER CHARLES (1811-1877), winegrower and medical practitioner, was born on 5 June 1811 at Leith, Scotland, son of John Kelly, agent of the British Linen Co.'s Bank, and his wife Margaret, née Porteus. Alexander was educated in France and Scotland, and studied medicine at the University of Edinburgh (M.D., 1832). After practising briefly in Scotland, he became a surgeon aboard the East India Co. ship *Kellie Castle*; he kept a vividly written and illustrated journal of the voyage from England to Bengal in 1833.

Later, Kelly visited Canada, where he became interested in the problems of popular education, then returned to Scotland and practised medicine at or near Dunbar. Perhaps inspired by his brother Thomas Bell Kelly, who had migrated to South Australia in 1839, he followed, arriving in the *Baboo* on 11 March 1840. Kelly was enrolled as the twelfth name in the medical register of South Australia and set up at Port Adelaide. In June 1842 he was made resident dispenser at Adelaide Hospital. He bought 80 acres (32.4 ha) of land west of Morphett Vale, south of Adelaide; the official title was dated 21 August 1843, although he probably occupied the land earlier. Here he built his home, Trinity, and planted his first vineyard, about 1845.

On 1 November 1854 Kelly married Annie Frances Worthington, in the Church of Scotland, Morphett Vale. He drew on the writings of French and other European authorities, which he translated and commented on, for his first book, *The Vine in Australia* (Melbourne, 1861); it introduced wine chemistry and modern science to Australian wine-growers and was so popular that it was reprinted next year. His *Wine-growing in Australia* (Adelaide, 1867) followed. Kelly's two influential books did much to establish Australian technical expertise in viniculture.

In November 1862 he and five of Adelaide's businessmen—(Sir) Thomas and Alexander

Lang Elder, (Sir) Samuel Davenport, Robert Barr Smith and (Sir) Edward Stirling [qq.v.4,6]—formed the Tintara Vineyard Co., with Kelly as manager. Next year he sold Trinity to concentrate on clearing the 213 acres (86.3 ha) of heavily timbered country near McLaren Vale which the trustees had bought in December 1862, and on planting vines, building cellars and, eventually, making mainly table wine. In 1871 Tintara shareholders sent him to London to search for new markets. The difficulties of an English market more accustomed to the strong, coarse wines of Spain and Portugal, financial depression in the colony and inter-colonial tariffs that disadvantaged South Australian wines contributed to the demise of the company. In September 1877 it was announced that Thomas Hardy [q.v.4] had purchased the vineyard, with 27 000 gallons (122 742 litres) of wine. The land was not transferred to Hardy until June 1878.

In 1868 Kelly had given articulate evidence before a parliamentary select committee on education reflecting his long-standing interest in the subject. A photographic portrait of him later in life showed a clear, kindly, open face with silvery hair and a full white beard. In 1876 he retired to his home at Norwood, where he died of bronchitis on 9 October 1877. He was buried in Clayton Chapel cemetery, Kensington, survived by his wife, three daughters and two sons, one of whom (John) was involved in the wine industry. An obituarist noted Kelly's 'obliging disposition . . . his kindness to people in straitened circumstances . . . high character, benevolence, and kindly genial manner'.

D. Hall and V. Hankel, intro to A. C. Kelly, *Winegrowing in Australia* (Syd, 1980) and *The Vine in Australia* (Syd, 1980); *PP* (SA), 1868-69, vol 2, paper no 56; *Advertiser* (Adel), 10 Sept 1877, p 5, 11 Oct 1877, p 4; *SA Register*, 3 Nov 1877, p 13; Kelly papers (SLSA). VALMAI A. HANKEL

KELLY, ELLEN (c.1832-1923), matriarch and mother of Ned Kelly [q.v.5], was born in County Antrim, Ireland, fourth of eleven children of James Quinn, farmer, and his wife Mary, née McCluskey. Ellen had an adventurous spirit that rebelled against any confinement and led her often to play truant from school and roam the countryside—a practice that left her able to read but not to write, and with a lifelong affinity for horses and the land. The Quinns, then numbering ten, reached Port Phillip as assisted migrants in July 1841.

After a period of menial work in Melbourne, James took the family north to rented farmland at Brunswick, then in 1849 a further 30 miles (48.3 km) to Wallan. Lively and slim with black hair and grey eyes, and an expert horsewoman, Ellen caught the eye of 30-year-old John 'Red' Kelly, an Irishman who had been transported to Van Diemen's Land for theft in 1841. Defying her father, Ellen took up with Red, and fell pregnant to him in May 1850. They married on 18 November at St Francis's Catholic Church, Melbourne, and moved into their own cottage on the Quinns' Wallan property.

Their first-born, a girl, survived only briefly. In 1853 Red set off alone to the goldfields, where he made enough to buy a farm near Beveridge. Ellen had a daughter Anne and in December 1854 a son, who was named Edward after Red's brother. The extensive Quinn and Kelly clans tended to skirt the fringes of the law, and for Ellen and Red financial difficulties, several moves, further births and mounting police attention set a definitive pattern. Red began drinking heavily. In 1865 he stole a calf and served four months in gaol. The following year he died, an alcoholic, of oedema, leaving Ellen with seven children aged from 18 months to 13 years.

As she struggled to raise her children on inferior farmland, she became notorious for her sometimes-violent temper, resulting in several court appearances. After moving her family into the far north-east of Victoria to stay near relations, she leased a selection of 88 acres (35.6 ha) there and sold 'sly grog' to make ends meet. The bushranger Harry Power [q.v.5] became a family friend, introducing 14-year-old Ned to the life of a bandit. In 1869 Ellen took a lover, Bill Frost, and became pregnant, he promising marriage. The baby—her ninth—was born in March 1870, but Frost did not keep his word. Trouble with the law increased, with several of Ellen's siblings and offspring suffering periods of imprisonment.

Late in 1872, with Ned in prison, she met George King, a 23-year-old Californian horse-thief, and once more fell pregnant. On 19 February 1874 they married at Benalla with Primitive Methodist forms. She had three children by King. Alice, the last, was born in April 1878, six months after King abruptly deserted them, and only days before Constable Fitzpatrick arrived at the Kelly home to arrest Ellen's son Dan for horse-theft. Set upon by Ellen (wielding a spade) and probably Ned, Fitzpatrick brought charges of attempted murder; she was sentenced to three years in prison.

A model prisoner, Ellen was allowed, after Dan's death and Ned's capture, to visit Ned in the prison hospital and later in the cells, seeing him for the last time on the eve of his execution. According to tradition, she said, 'Mind you die like a Kelly, son'. Released in February 1881, Ellen returned home to scenes of incipient civil rebellion; the authorities feared a pro-Kelly uprising. Constable Robert Graham, however, gained her confidence and persuaded her to calm her sympathizers. She settled down to become, for the first time in her life, a respectable community identity—although she was never able to rise to even modest prosperity.

Her daughters Maggie and Kate died in the late 1890s, leaving Ellen to raise three of her grandchildren, helped by her son James. He continued to live with her, caring for her in her old age. She died on 27 March 1923 at Greta West and was buried in Greta cemetery with Catholic rites. Of her twelve children, a son and daughter of her first marriage and a son and two daughters of her second survived her.

J. McQuilton, *The Kelly Outbreak 1878-1880* (Melb, 1979); M. Lake and F. Kelly, *Double Time* (Melb, 1985); I. Jones, *Ned Kelly: A Short Life* (Melb, 1995); N. Kelly, *The Jerilderie Letter* (Melb, 2001).   JACQUELINE ZARA WILSON

KENNEDY, MARTIN VICTOR (1895-1952), journalist and author, was born on 11 August 1895 at Eaglehawk, near Bendigo, Victoria, third child of Victorian-born parents Martin William Kennedy, miner, and his wife Mary Jane, née Turner. Always known as Victor, he was educated to the age of 14 at the local state school, attended art classes at the Bendigo School of Mines, and learned shorthand. He also became secretary of the Bendigo West Labor League. As a freelance journalist, he wrote for the local newspapers. His first book of verse, *The Unknown Anzac and Other Poems*, was published at Bendigo in 1917.

After working as a reporter for the *Shepparton Advertiser*, Kennedy obtained a position on the *Geraldton Guardian* in Western Australia. Disliking the owner's politics, he quit the paper and became editor of the rival *Geraldton Express*. He then returned to freelance work and, while on leave back in Victoria on 20 November 1926 at the Methodist parsonage, Bendigo, married Dorothy Emily Fidge, also known by her pen-name 'Claire'.

From 1926 to 1931 Kennedy edited the *Cairns Post*, Queensland. While there, he wrote a life of the businessman A. J. Draper [q.v.8] and several travel books promoting North Queensland, and published his second book of verse, *Farthest North* (1928). He also contributed verse and paragraphs to the Sydney *Bulletin*. Retrenched from the *Cairns Post*, he established and edited the short-lived but lively literary periodical *Northern Affairs*. His illness, resulting from recurring kidney stone problems, and the Depression killed the magazine, however, and, seeking better medical treatment, he moved to Brisbane, once more freelancing.

Befriended by James Devanny, James Picot [qq.v.13,15] and other local poets and writers, Kennedy became secretary of the Queensland Authors and Artists Association. For five years from December 1935 he was a junior reporter on the *Gympie Post*. He then moved to New South Wales and worked on the *Tweed Daily*, Casino, the *Richmond River Express*, Murwillumbah, and the *Newcastle Sun*, before being appointed editor of the *Sunraysia Daily*, Mildura, Victoria, in the early 1940s.

Kennedy was attracted to the Jindyworobak Movement. He edited its 1942 anthology; the previous year it had published his *Flaunted Banners*, an essay on literary values. During World War II he surveyed Australian poets for an unpublished book on 'Whither Australian Poetry'.

Late in 1944 Kennedy obtained a sub-editor's position on the Melbourne *Argus*. The move allowed him to be work closely with Rex Ingamells [q.v.14] in promoting the Jindyworobak ideals. He was also a keen member of the Bread and Cheese Club, succeeding J. K. Moir [q.v.15] as its knight grand cheese in 1950. He continued to publish books of verse. In the late 1940s he began a biography of Bernard O'Dowd [q.v.11]. He had O'Dowd's close co-operation and was awarded a Commonwealth Literary Fund grant of £500 to finish the book in January 1952. However, he died of cancer that month—on 14 January—in hospital at South Melbourne and was cremated. His wife and their two daughters and one son survived him. The O'Dowd biography, finished by Nettie Palmer [q.v.11], was published under their joint names in 1954.

Kennedy was congenial, well liked and admired for his dedicated commitment to promoting Australian literature. He was president of the Australian Literature Society at the time of his death. His verse conveyed a love of his country and of things Australian.

Fellows All: The Chronicles of the Bread and Cheese Club Melbourne (Melb, 1943); *Southerly*, 13, no 2, 1952, p 115; *Journalist*, Jan 1952, p 3; *Argus* (Melb), 15 Jan 1952, p 11; Kennedy papers (LaTL); Kennedy unpublished essays (NL).

JOHN ARNOLD

KENNY, MICHAEL (1808?-1892), farmer, was born probably on 24 December 1808 at Six-mile Bridge, County Clare, Ireland. He later claimed that in 1829, imbued with patriotism, he was involved in nominating the Liberal Daniel O'Connell for his election to the British House of Commons. On 5 November 1841 Kenny sailed in the *Brankimmor*, reaching Launceston, Van Diemen's Land, on 6 April 1842.

Moving to Port Phillip to meet a brother and two sisters, he stripped wattle bark in

Gippsland, sailed to Hobart Town and walked back to Launceston, carrying 'a double-barrelled gun on my shoulder, always ready and willing to take any employment'. He and a brother then settled at Morphett Vale, South Australia, finding work by grubbing, fencing, reaping and threshing. Each then purchased an 80-acre (32.4 ha) section in the hundred of Noarlunga for £80. On 22 October 1848 at Morphett Vale Catholic church Michael married Irish-born Bridget Ayrene (Herreen), née Purtle, a widow with four children. They were to have six children between 1849 and 1863. Kenny was a leading sportsman and in a race won a silver cup, which arrived from England two years later. His wife and children stayed in South Australia when he went to the Ballarat diggings for nine months in 1852. He claimed to have been involved in the Eureka rebellion.

In 1856 the Kennys moved to 600 acres (abut 240 ha) at Shea-oak Log, purchased for £1 2s. 6d. per acre with the proceeds of his prospecting. They also owned and ran the Freeling Railway Hotel, which became a focus for local meetings. Kenny founded and became secretary of the Light Farmers' Club. Dissatisfied with the railway rates for the carriage of wheat, he put heavily loaded teams on the roads. The consequent damage persuaded Governor Daly [q.v.4] to meet a deputation of 150 farmers; as a result uniform railway freight on all goods was introduced. Kenny was active in discussions leading to the South Australian Waste Lands Amendment (Strangways [q.v.6]) Act of 1869, which encouraged closer settlement and the spread of agriculture.

About 1870 Kenny and several sons selected land in the hundred of Melville, southern Yorke Peninsula, under the Strangways Act. Crop yields began to decline with reduced soil fertility, however, and in 1876 the family sailed from Edithburgh to Waterloo Bay (Elliston), on the western coast of South Australia. In September Kenny took up a wheat and sheep property at Colton, about 120 miles (nearly 200 km) beyond Port Lincoln; he named it Balla McKenny (home of the Kennys). Grain was shipped from Port Kenny, on Venus Bay.

Kenny and his family were staunch Catholics, associated with building the churches at Morphett Vale and Colton. His contribution to the Irish National Federation of South Australia, particularly through assisting early colonists to South Australia, was recognized by presentation of a gold medal. He died on 11 May 1892 at Colton, survived by his wife and their four sons and one daughter. His son Patrick took over Balla McKenny.

Cyclopedia of South Australia, 2 (Adel, 1909); K. Kenny, *The Descendants of Brigid Purtle & Daniel*

Herreen 1840-1847 and Brigid Herreen (nee Purtle) and Michael Kenny 1847-1892 (np, 1979); *Observer* (Adel), 19 Feb 1887, p 35, 21 May 1892, p 37.

JOHN C. RADCLIFFE

KENT, CONSTANCE; see SAVILLE-KENT

KENT, WILLIAM SAVILLE; see SAVILLE-KENT

KERMADEC, JEAN-MICHEL HUON DE; see HUON

KERR, BEATRICE MAUDE (1887-1971), swimmer and entertainer, was born on 30 November 1887 at Williamstown, Melbourne, eldest child of Alexander Robert Kerr, bookkeeper, and his wife Eliza Sophia, née Clark. Beatrice was raised at Albert Park, where at an early age she and her sister and three brothers were taught to swim by their mother.

Kerr's early competitive swimming career was at Geelong, and in Melbourne at Brighton and Albert Park; in 1905 she won two medals in Victorian championships (100 yards and 120 yards) and a gold bangle for the Australasian amateur championship. In a twenty-week season that year, she completed 366 swimming and diving performances at Princes Court, Melbourne. She was a strong rival to Annette Kellermann [q.v.9], who on 25 February 1905 judged the diving at Brighton Baths when Kerr took first place. During a six-week tour to Adelaide, Kalgoorlie and Coolgardie, Western Australia, and Perth next year, Kerr won five open championships, entered forty-three races and won forty-three prizes. Her sister and her brother-in-law, who was her manager, accompanied her.

To consolidate her career, Kerr sailed from Perth for London in the *Commonwealth* on 3 May 1906. *En route*, the ship called at Durban, South Africa, where she gave a performance of fast and ornamental swimming and diving. A handbill printed for the occasion referred to her as 'Australia's Champion Lady Swimmer and Diver'. This title was popularized in promotional literature for her many tours throughout England in the following five years. She issued a public challenge to Kellermann in February 1906 and renewed it after her arrival in England in September that year, but Kellermann did not respond.

Kerr had a busy schedule of performances during each English swimming season—from Easter to October. Additional theatrical swimming events, such as 'The Treasure Ship', during the winter months, at venues including the

Olympia, Liverpool, and the Manchester and London hippodromes, earned her between £9 and £14 a week. At Bradford in September 1906 she attracted record attendances, with many people being turned away. They came to see her demonstrate such swimming techniques as the trudgeon stroke and the 'revolving waterwheel' and give diving displays, which included somersaults, high diving, blindfold backjumps, kneeling dives and tricks such as the 'Flying Honey Pot'. They also came to see her in daring swimsuits, which were not made for fast times—her spangled costume weighed over five pounds (2.3 kg).

With a turning style said to be similar to Barney Kieran's [q.v.9], Kerr had a fastest time of 1 minute 21.4 seconds for 100 yards and 27.5 minutes for the mile. Unlike her contemporaries Kellermann, Sarah 'Fanny' Durack [q.v.8] and Mina Wylie, she neither held world records nor swam in the Olympic Games. Nevertheless, her skill as a swimmer and entertainer inspired many young women to take to the water.

Returning to Australia in October 1911, Beatrice married Griffith Ellis Williams, a Welsh-born dispenser, on 3 April 1912 at the Presbyterian Church, Redfern, Sydney, and retired from professional swimming. The Williams family lived at Bondi and took a keen interest in the development of the beach there. A park at North Bondi was named after the family. Predeceased by her husband, Beatrice Williams died on 3 August 1971 at Aqua Vista Convalescent Hospital, Coogee, and was buried with Anglican rites in Waverley cemetery. Her only son survived her.

A. Woollacott, *To Try Her Fortune in London* (NY, 2001); J. Nelson, 'Beatrice Kerr: Australia's Champion Lady Swimmer and Diver', *Heritage Aust*, 9, no 4, Summer 1990, p 24; *Table Talk*, 16 Feb 1905, p 12, 12 Oct 1905, p 19; *Argus* (Melb), 17 Feb 1906, p 17; *Advertiser* (Adel), 20 Feb 1906, p 7, 26 Feb 1906, p 10; *Manchester Evening Chronicle (Eng)*, 18 Sept 1906; *Bradford Daily Argus* (Eng), 29 Sept 1906; *Halifax Courier* (Eng), 29 Sept 1906; family information.
                                          JUDY NELSON

KING, GEORGINA (1845-1932), amateur geologist and anthropologist, was born on 6 June 1845 at Fremantle, Western Australia, second daughter of Rev. George King [q.v.5], a Church of England clergyman from Ireland, and his wife Jane, née Mathewson. Georgina's brother was (Sir) Kelso King [q.v.9]. In 1847 the family moved to Sydney. Largely taught by her father, a fellow of St Paul's College within the university, she read new works on evolution and natural history; her interest in geology was encouraged by the family physician George Bennett [q.v.1], a naturalist. In the 1870s Georgina looked after a nephew and niece at Springwood until 1881 when she visited Britain and Europe. She numbered Rose Scott [q.v.11] among her closest friends; both were early members of the Women's Literary Society, founded in 1889, and Georgina was an original member of the Women's Club.

In 1888 she had attended the inaugural meeting of the Australasian Association for the Advancement of Science and there met and entertained distinguished scientists. She later corresponded with R. L. Jack in Queensland and (Sir) Frederick McCoy [qq.v.4,5] in Victoria, whose outdated beliefs about geology agreed with what she had read and remembered from her youth. This support emboldened her to publicize her 'Tertiary Period Catastrophism' theory, which she expected would revolutionize Australian science. Her ideas, which were grand, romantic and wrong, centred on a vision in which volcanic action, shaped by the mystical powers of heat, electricity and magnetism, had created all valuable mineral deposits and all modern geological structures from the Jenolan Caves to the Niagara Falls. She was deeply hurt when a paper to be read on her behalf (women were not eligible to attend) was rejected by the Royal Society of New South Wales in 1892. She believed that Professor (Sir) Edgeworth David and E. F. Pittman [qq.v.8,11] had repudiated her work in order to pass off her ideas as their own. To retaliate, she published her papers in the *Sydney Morning Herald* and wrote to major organizations and scientists—from the University of Sydney to T. H. Huxley [q.v.1]—to plead her cause. As she became more isolated and eccentric, her claims became more extravagant, including that Einstein had 'stolen' her ideas about relativity and that diamonds were originally marine organisms. She increasingly cast herself as a persecuted genius.

In the early twentieth century King turned to publishing papers on anthropological subjects, drawing on her father's publications and extending her geological theories to explain the evolution of the Aborigines. Her works were admired by amateur anthropologists who were also in dispute with university professionals. Elected a fellow of the Royal Anthropological Society of Australasia, she published several articles in its journal, *Science of Man*. From 1913 she corresponded with Daisy Bates [q.v.7], whom she financially supported and with whom she developed a close friendship. Both were frustrated that established scientists failed to acknowledge and praise their work.

A 'keen observer of natural phenomena and a collector of specimens of interest', King donated many to the Australian and the Technological (Powerhouse) museums, Sydney. She wrote numerous letters on diverse subjects to the daily newspapers, and during

World War I worked for the Australian Red Cross Society. Later she made golliwogs for patients at the Royal Alexandra Hospital for Children.

Her father and Bennett having advised her not to marry if she wished to develop her talent, she reputedly refused a proposal of marriage from Sir Ferdinand von Mueller [q.v.5], to whom she sent botanical specimens. Towards the end of her life she wrote: 'I was one of those pioneer women who have had a hard time, but I was making things easier for women coming after me'. Georgina King died on 7 June 1932 at her Darling Point home and was cremated.

Hist Records Aust Science, 11, no 3, 1997, p 340; U. Bygott, 'Georgina King—Amateur Geologist and Anthropologist—1845-1932', Univ Syd Archives, *Record*, Jan 1982, p 11; D. F. Branagan, 'Georgina King: Geological Prophet or Lost?', Univ Syd Archives, *Record*, Sept 1982, p 4; *SMH*, 11 June 1932, p 18; C. Hooker, Not a Job in the Ordinary Sense: Women and Science in Australia 1788-1960 (Ph.D. thesis, Univ Syd, 2001); file 8764 (Univ Syd Archives); G. King papers (ML). URSULA BYGOTT
CLAIRE HOOKER

KING DAVID; *see* KAAWIRN KUUNAWARN

KING JOHN; *see* MULLAWIRRABURKA

KIRTLEY, JOHN THOMAS (1897-1967), printer and patriot, was born on 3 September 1897 at Marrickville, Sydney, second child of Louis Russell Kirtley, a Sydney-born engineer, and his wife Elizabeth, née Dixon, from Ireland. John's parents were in the hotel trade and, after his father died in 1918, his mother—a Catholic—retained an interest in several hotels. Educated at East St Leonards Public School and St Aloysius' College, North Sydney, Kirtley worked as a stockbroker's clerk with Martyn & Brownhill. He was a keen reader and book-collector, and developed a desire to print his own fine books. A meeting with Jack, son of Norman Lindsay [q.v.10], in a Sydney bookshop in the early 1920s led to the foundation of his press.

Kirtley taught himself the rudiments of printing on a Chandler and Price platen press. His first publication was a collection of Jack's verse, *Fauns and Ladies* (1923). Limited to 210 copies, with woodcuts by Norman Lindsay, the book appeared under the imprint of 'The Handpress of J. T. Kirtley', as did Kenneth Slessor's [q.v.16] first book, *Thief of the Moon* (1924). Two further books of verse followed: Raymond McGrath's *Seven Songs of Meadow Lane* and *Seven Poems* by Dora Wilcox [q.v.10 W. G. Moore].

Kirtley's next publication was a deluxe, limited edition of Aristophanes's *Lysistrata*, translated by Jack Lindsay. A large folio, it was printed on a Golding platen Kirtley had bought especially. Concerned about his stockbroker employers' reaction to the book's subject matter, Kirtley issued it under the imprint of the Fanfrolico Press, a name suggested by Norman Lindsay's bawdy collection of tales relating to the Duke of Fanfrolico in the imaginary court of Micomicon. Kirtley and Jack Lindsay decided to transfer the press to London. Arriving in May 1926, Kirtley took an office in Bloomsbury Square. Another edition of *Lysistrata* was followed by Slessor's *Earth Visitors* and a deluxe edition of *The Complete Works of Gaius Petronius*, translated by Lindsay.

In mid-1927 Kirtley handed the business over to Lindsay and returned to Australia via the United States of America. He managed hotels for his mother in Sydney, but the business failed. On 30 April 1929 at St Stephen's Presbyterian Church, Phillip Street, he married Isabel Young, a clerk. The marriage broke up shortly after the birth of their son in 1930 and the couple divorced in 1941. Kirtley lived with his mother at Woy Woy, planning to write fiction, then worked intermittently for P. R. Stephensen [q.v.12].

Because of this association, Kirtley was linked to the right-wing, nationalist Australia First Movement during World War II. He was not a formal member of the movement, but some intemperate personal letters and possession of the movement's publications led to his arrest on 10 March 1942 and his internment for almost two years. The experience, with its forced separation from his teenage son, embittered him.

After the war Kirtley briefly edited a musical magazine and then managed a chicken farm. About 1948 he moved to Victoria, living in a house at Ferntree Gully owned by J. K. Moir [q.v.15], who encouraged him to establish the Mountainside Press. The effort of printing R. D. FitzGerald's *Heemskerck Shoals* (1949), one of the finest books ever produced in Australia, was too much for the perfectionist Kirtley. Except for a few ephemeral pieces, he abandoned printing and moved closer to the city.

On 10 January 1955 at the Unitarian Church, East Melbourne, he married Jean Rich, a ledger-keeper. Through Moir, he obtained a clerical position with Payne's Bon Marche department store. *People* magazine described him as 'a chubby little man' who enjoyed punting on the horses. In the late 1950s, encouraged by Harry Chaplin, a Sydney book-collector, Kirtley wrote a detailed and at times vituperative history of the Fanfrolico Press; the State Library of Queensland holds the unpublished manuscript. He died of coronary artery disease on 27 August 1967 at Camberwell and was cremated with Anglican rites. His wife and son survived him. Kirtley deserves to be remembered as a fine printer rather than as a puzzled patriot.

B. Muirden, *The Puzzled Patriots* (Melb, 1968); J. Lindsay, *Life Rarely Tells* (Melb, 1982); G. Farmer, *A True Printer* (Syd, 1990); *People*, 2 Aug 1950, p 33; C421, items 12 and 55 (NAA, Syd); J. Arnold, History of the Fanfrolico Press (ms, held by author); J. K. Moir collection (SLV); Kirtley papers (OL).

JOHN ARNOLD

KITCHEN, JOHN AMBROSE (1835-1922), businessman, was born in February 1835 at Watlington, Oxfordshire, England, second son of John Kitchen (1799-1890), grocer, and his wife Ruth, née Freeman. Raised at Reading, Berkshire, John Ambrose became a solicitor's clerk there, but after his mother's death and his father's business failure the family migrated to Victoria in 1854.

Arriving ahead of his father and two brothers (Philip and Theophilus), Kitchen sold newspapers and second-hand books at the Caledonian diggings. He prospected unsuccessfully at Mount Blackwood, before returning to Melbourne, where his father was managing a candle factory. The family began making tallow candles from butchers' scraps in the backyard of their Emerald Hill (South Melbourne) house. Ordered out as an offensive trade, the business removed to Sandridge (Port Melbourne) in 1858. On 11 December 1860 at the registry office, Melbourne, Kitchen married Scottish-born Catherine Miller Sandeman (d.1874).

Fire destroyed the company's premises in 1860, but they were quickly rebuilt and a Melbourne office was opened. In 1870 the Kitchens bought Gossage Bros' soap and candle factory at Footscray, to which they transferred their boiling-down operations. Manufacture of stearine candles commenced in 1871, when the Berry [q.v.3] government increased the protective tariff. The driving force in the subsequent expansion of J. Kitchen & Sons was John Ambrose, who established a factory in Wellington, New Zealand (1876), and bought out competitors at Sandhurst (Bendigo) in 1878, Echuca (1887) and Wangaratta (1887). By the early 1880s the firm employed some 300 workers in Melbourne. The merger with the Apollo Stearine Candle Co. made it the pre-eminent soap and candle manufacturer in the eastern mainland colonies, with a factory in Brisbane and a half-interest in the Sydney Soap & Candle Co.

Baptized a Wesleyan Methodist, Kitchen joined the Plymouth Brethren in Victoria, but by 1870 belonged to the Church of England. On 3 September 1875 at Kew he married with Congregational forms 21-year-old, Irish-born Gertrude Walker. Having left his Sandridge cottage for Kew in 1868, in 1876 he acquired the mansion Elsinore. Kitchen also developed an apple orchard at Pakenham from the late 1870s, set up the Melbourne Coffee Taverns Co. with William McLean and (Sir) Matthew Davies [qq.v.5,4 Sir John] in 1878 and co-founded the Royal Bank of Australasia (1888). Financed by the Commercial Bank of Australia, Kitchen speculated in real estate during the 1880s. After the bank crashes, he made a secret composition for his £167 507 debt in July 1892, resigned briefly from the board of J. Kitchen & Sons, and moved to a modest, eight-room villa in East Malvern. All company property was mortgaged when the banks threatened foreclosure, and in 1894 the New Zealand business was sold.

Kitchen's company had expanded to Western Australia and South Australia by 1902, and in 1907 began producing copra oil from a plantation at Milne Bay, Papua. Velvet soap was introduced as a brand name by 1906 and Solvol by 1915. The firm was employing 1000 workers across Australia when it merged with the British firm Lever Bros in 1914; the Australian subsidiary, however, remained under Kitchen family control.

John Ambrose died on 24 May 1922 at Malvern and was buried in Kew cemetery, survived by his wife and their two sons and by three sons and four daughters of his first marriage. His estate was valued for probate at £46 014, and he made substantial bequests to charities. One son, Frederick William (1879-1940), succeeded him as managing director and another, John Hambleton (1862-1925), managed the Sydney company. Lever had fully acquired the business by 1924; in 1976 John Kitchen & Sons was renamed Unichema, and Lever and Kitchen soaps became Lever Rexona.

G. D. Meudell, *The Pleasant Career of a Spendthrift* (Lond, 1929); M. Cannon, *The Land Boomers* (Melb, 1966); G. Serle, *The Rush to be Rich* (Melb, 1971); *PP* (Vic), 1883, vol 4, paper no 50, 1894, vol 2, paper no 37, 1895-96, vol 2, paper no 3; *PP* (Cwlth), 1906, vol 4; *Industrial Aust and Mining Standard*, 31 Oct 1918, p 684; *Unilever Aust Reporter*, Sept 1956; *VHJ*, 64, no 1, Apr 1993, p 46; *Argus* (Melb), 25 May 1922, p 6.

DAMIAN VELTRI

KITE, JIM; *see* ERLIKILYIKA

KLEEMAN, RICHARD DANIEL (1875-1932), physicist, was born on 20 January 1875 at Rowlands Flat, South Australia, eldest of nine children of native-born parents of

German-Lutheran ancestry Christoph Daniel Kleemann, farmer, and his wife Johanna Elenore, née Munchenberg. At 13 Richard left school to work on the family farm. In 1893 he was apprenticed to a cooper at Yalumba winery, then practised that trade at Chateau Tanunda distillery until 1901. Meanwhile, he also read mathematics and physics privately with help from his Lutheran pastor. In 1897 he began sending short papers to Professor (Sir) William H. Bragg [q.v.7] who, impressed, arranged for his special admission to the University of Adelaide (B.Sc., 1905; D.Sc., 1908). In 1901-03 Kleeman (as he generally spelt his name) passed compulsory mathematics and physics subjects for the ordinary degree, before obtaining first-class honours in physics.

An evening lecturer and demonstrator in physics at the university in 1904-05, he also assisted Bragg in his pioneering studies of radioactivity: Bragg included him as joint author on three papers. As a result Kleeman was awarded an 1851 Exhibition research scholarship to study science in 1905-08 in England at the University of Cambridge (B.A., 1907). At the conclusion of this time Ernest (Lord) Rutherford reported that Kleeman had published 'five important papers' after 'unusually good work'. In 1908 he shared the Emmanuel College Sudbury-Hardyman prize for his dissertation and was awarded his Adelaide doctorate. Kleeman held a Mackinnon studentship of the Royal Society, London, in 1909-11 and shared the Clark Maxwell scholarship at the Cavendish Laboratory in 1910-13, enabling him to continue his research at Cambridge. Renewing his association with Bragg at Leeds, in 1909 he produced two papers on the ionization of gases. In England Kleeman published prolifically on radioactivity and the interaction of its several radiations with matter and on the subject of his later, major work, *A Kinetic Theory of Gases and Liquids* (New York, 1920).

In 1908-09 and 1912-13 Kleeman applied for professorial positions in several countries but was unsuccessful. He was bitterly disappointed not to win the foundation chair of mathematics and physics at the University of Western Australia. In 1911 he visited Australia on holiday, and on 11 July 1912 at the parish church, Woburn Square, London, he married Bertha Pauline Martin of Adelaide. They had two children, only one of whom survived to adulthood. In November 1914 Kleeman travelled to the United States of America. He was 5 ft 5 ins (165 cm) tall, with brown hair and brown eyes. Bertha followed in June 1915. Richard became an assistant professor (1914-20) and associate professor (1920-27) of physics at Union College, Schenectady, New York. From 1919 until 1927 he was also a consulting physicist at the General Electric Co. of New York.

Kleeman's early years in America were spent preparing his 1920 book. Thereafter he elaborated and developed themes discussed there, focusing initially on the electrical and magnetic properties of atoms and molecules in gases and liquids. In 1927 he left the college and devoted himself to private research, undertaking theoretical studies of the properties of substances at the absolute zero of temperature. He died of pneumonia on 10 October 1932 in the Presbyterian Hospital, Manhattan, New York, and was buried in Mount Hope cemetery. His wife and one son survived him.

R. E. Teusner, *Kleeman Family History* (Adel, 1969); R. W. Home, *Physics in Australia to 1945* (Melb, 1990); *JHSSA*, no 13, 1985, p 100; *Advertiser* (Adel), 16 Nov 1932, p 16; Kleeman student card (Emmanuel College Library, Cambridge, UK); Kleeman faculty file (Schaffer Library, Union College, Schenectady, New York); Royal Commission for the Exhibition of 1851 (Imperial College Archives, Lond); Univ Adelaide Archives; Bragg-Kleeman correspondence in Bragg papers (Royal Institution, Lond); Rutherford-Kleeman correspondence in Rutherford papers (Cambridge Univ Library, UK).

JOHN JENKIN
R. W. HOME

KLEINSCHMIDT, CLARA; *see* SERENA

KNIGHT, GEORGE WILLIAM (1831-1923) architect, engineer and horticulturist, was born in 1831 in London, son of John Knight, builder and stone merchant, of Limehouse. George was educated at Professor Fitzgerald's school and trained as an architect and engineer. His love of horticulture was already evident at 18, when he built a conservatory adjoining his parents' dining room. Aged 21, he commenced work under Henry Martin, a marine and railway engineer. On 31 December 1853 in the parish church, Stepney, London, he married Elizabeth Patience Middleton (d.1901). They were to have eleven children.

Reaching Melbourne in the *Sureswift* in 1857, with Elizabeth and two children, possibly to join his brother John George [q.v.5], who was engaged in building Parliament House, George became an engineer on the Williamstown and Sandhurst (Bendigo) railways, being responsible for the bridge over Jacksons Creek at Sunbury. He applied for a crown grant of land at Riddells Creek, near Sunbury, where he established a vineyard. It was not profitable and by 1870 he was working as an architect at Sandhurst. After two years, and with a growing family, he became city building surveyor, a position he held for fourteen years. The work was arduous, as he was also city valuator, city inspector, inspector of nuisances, inspector of cattle for slaughter, inspector of abattoirs and health inspector. In 1874 he attracted criticism from councillors for taking on additional building work, which he denied. When the demands of the position became too great, he was appointed city and building surveyor at a salary of £400. Knight was accused of neglecting his official duties in favour of his plant nurseries. Counter claims that councillors were undermining his authority by interfering in council contracts united the council against him. In 1886 he resigned in the face of imminent dismissal.

With his children, Knight developed four extensive nurseries in the Bendigo area, transforming barren, mining-affected land into horticultural showplaces. At his Rosenberg Nursery, Back Creek, he grew one of the world's largest rose trees, Cloth of Gold, 14 ft (4.2 m) high, 43 ft (13.1 m) in breadth and 64 ft (19.5 m) long. He had an enduring enthusiasm for palms (a row at his Epsom nursery became a local landmark) and grew more than 400 types of orchid, including New Guinea varieties. Knight's most striking vine-breeding success was a large and delicious table grape, evolved from the Waltham Cross variety. Exhibited at the Centennial International Exhibition of 1888-89 and admired by vice-regal visitors, it became known as the Centennial grape. A fellow of the Royal Horticultural Society, England, Knight served as a judge in many horticultural shows.

Ever vigilant concerning public matters, he was publicly acknowledged in 1888 for forcing the Bendigo Gas Co. to reduce its prices to consumers. Knight was a founding member of the committee formed in 1891 for the advancement of the Bendigo district, and twenty years later was elected to the municipal council on the strength of his opposition to the reticulation of sewerage. He lost his seat in 1914. In the 1921 State election he stood unsuccessfully for Bendigo East. In March 1922 the city's legal profession acknowledged his fifty-two years as a justice of the peace and magistrate, claimed to be the longest service on the bench in Victoria.

A picturesque figure in old age, with grey locks and venerable yet keen aspect, Knight retained the optimistic outlook of youth to the end. He died on 3 August 1923 at Bendigo, and was buried in the local cemetery with Anglican rites. Five daughters and one son survived him.

W. B. Kimberley, *Bendigo and Vicinity* (Melb, 1895); D. Dunstan, *Better than Pommard!* (Melb, 1994); *Bendigo Advertiser*, 25 Oct 1873, p 2, 28 Mar 1888, p 2, 21 Feb 1891, 31 Mar 1922, p 8, 4 Aug 1923, p 11; Bendigo Council, correspondence, 1886.

MIKE BUTCHER
DAVID DUNSTAN

KNORR, FRANCES LYDIA ALICE (1867-1894), baby-farmer, was born on 6 November 1867 at Hoxton New Town, Middlesex, England, second daughter of William Sutton Thwaites, tailor, and his wife Frances Janet, née Robin. William became a respectable hat-maker at Chelsea, London. After at least one affair with a military man, young Frances (known as 'Minnie') migrated to Australia, reaching Sydney in the *Abyssinia* in 1887. Initially in domestic service, she became a waitress and on 2 November 1889 at St Philip's Church of England married Rudolph Knorr, a German-born waiter (and swindler). They moved to Melbourne. After the birth of their daughter in 1892, during the financial depression, Rudi was sentenced to a gaol term in Adelaide for selling off the family's partially paid-for furniture.

Left to fend for herself and her child, Frances tried her hand at dressmaking but when this venture failed she stole money and went back to Melbourne. There she took up with Edward Thompson, a fishmonger's assistant. When he left her, she turned to 'baby farming'—taking care of usually illegitimate children. Many such children died in circumstances that led to the belief that they had been murdered or neglected. Mrs Knorr moved around Melbourne frequently, and when Rudi was released the couple returned to Sydney. Following the discovery of the corpses of three infants in premises at Brunswick, Melbourne, that she had occupied, she was arrested and, after giving birth to a second child on 4 September 1893, brought back to Melbourne, where she was tried for murder.

The circumstantial case against Knorr maintained that she was not only promiscuous and deceitful but also a ruthless racketeer. A more sympathetic reading of the evidence was that she was an unstable young woman eking out a precarious existence in difficult times. She had cared for some infants, and returned one to its mother. In other cases she passed on children to other women, paying them a lower fee. She made no great profit from any of these enterprises.

The Crown used against her a letter she wrote to Thompson, attempting to persuade him to obtain false evidence on her behalf, and she was convicted on 1 December 1893 of the wilful murder of a female child. Rudi's plea for clemency to the governor claimed that his wife was an epileptic, given to severe fits that sometimes led to irrational impulses and long bouts of staring blankly into space. Despite a petition from the 'Women of Victoria', who prayed that 'the killing of any woman by any body of men does not accord with the moral sense of the community', Frances Knorr was hanged at Pentridge gaol on 15 January 1894.

She went to her death singing 'Abide with Me'. Her final words were said to have been, 'The Lord is with me, I do not fear what man can do unto me, for I have peace, perfect peace'. In her own hand, but not her idiom, she left a letter advising the premier how better to regulate baby-farming so as to protect infant life. She was one of only five women hanged in Victoria.

J. Allen, *Sex & Secrets* (Melb, 1990); K. Greenwood (ed), *The Thing She Loves* (Syd, 1996); K. Laster, 'Frances Knorr: "She Killed Babies, Didn't She?"', in M. Lake and F. Kelly (eds), *Double Time* (Melb, 1985) *and* 'Arbitrary Chivalry: Women and Capital Punishment in Victoria, 1842-1967', in D. Philips and S. Davies (eds), *A Nation of Rogues?* (Melb, 1994) *and* 'Infanticide: A Litmus Test for Feminist Criminological Theory', *Aust and NZ J of Criminology*, 22, no 3, Sept 1989, p 151; series 264, unit 22, series 30, unit 953, file 583/1893 (PRO, Vic); *Argus* (Melb), 28 Nov 1893, p 5, 29 Nov 1893, p 4, 30 Nov 1893, p 4, 1 Dec 1893, p 5, 2 Dec 1893, p 9, 8 Jan 1894, p 5, 15 Jan 1894, p 5, 16 Jan 1894, p 5; *Weekly Times* (Melb), 20 Jan 1894, p 21; *People*, 24 Feb 1954, p 20.   KATHY LASTER

KOCH, WILHELM RUDOLPH WALDEMAR (1874-1952), architect, was born on 13 September 1874 at Richmond, Melbourne, second of nine surviving children of John Augustus Bernard Koch [q.v.9], a German-born architect, and his wife, Anna, née Puttmann, from Switzerland. Rudolph completed his education at Melbourne Church of England Grammar School in 1891, and probably began training in his father's office.

By 1898 Koch was employed as an architectural draughtsman by the Tasmanian Smelting Co., at Zeehan, Tasmania, and by 1900 he was a qualified architect. He designed the School of Mines, Zeehan, which opened in 1903. On 14 October that year at the Lutheran church, East Melbourne, he married Elinor Burton and the couple moved to Ulverstone, Tasmania. His early work included Furner's Hotel there and the Grand Hotel, Devonport. By 1905 he had set up in Hobart. A fellow (1906) of the Royal Victorian Institute of Architects and licentiate (1912) of the Royal Institute of British Architects, he advertised as a surveyor and sanitary engineer (1906), town planner (1918) and road engineer (1921). He was a founding member and president (1913-14, 1925-26) of the Tasmanian Institute of Architects. Influenced by the Garden City movement, he helped to establish the Southern Tasmanian Town Planning Association in 1915. He also lectured on architectural history at Hobart Technical College.

Koch designed Richmond Town Hall (opened 1908) and won design competitions for the Children's Hospital (1908) and the Hobart Teachers' College (Philip Smith Hall, 1909). He was the supervising architect for alterations (1912) to the Theatre Royal, Hobart. His other Hobart designs include the A. G. Webster building (1906), Liverpool Street, Tasma House, Collins Street, the university engineering building and St James the Apostle Church, New Town, where the family worshipped.

Domestic architecture by Koch ranged from the important Federation style house, 11 Lord Street (1917), to the modest extension (1924) to a gardener's cottage, Maning Ave, both at Sandy Bay. He designed 15 Stoke Street, New Town, for his family in 1916. Koch was honorary architect for Hobart Sanatorium and executive vice-president from 1914; his plan for the site at New Town showed awareness of modern hospital design and the need for a landscaped setting for a tuberculosis sanatorium (1906, with additions 1910, 1919, 1922).

In 1929 Koch left private practice when he was appointed building surveyor for Hobart City Council. He helped to revise the Building Act (1932), containing comprehensive by-laws on hoardings—which he abhorred. Under the Public Health and Factories Act (1934), he personally inspected all new buildings in the city, an increasingly busy task as Hobart emerged from the Depression. Retiring in 1937, he returned to Melbourne in 1947.

Koch was president (1911-12) of the local Australian Natives' Association, a founder, sometime secretary, of the Tasmanian branch of the Old Melburnians, and a member (captain 1925-26) of the A.N.A. and the Tasmanian rifle clubs. He was a past master of the Tasmanian Union Masonic Lodge and a member of the Buckingham Bowling Club, Hobart. Later he joined the Malvern Club, Melbourne. While he had a somewhat daunting public persona, he was a convivial companion and a warmhearted family man who loved music and the poetry of 'Banjo' Paterson [q.v.11]. He actively encouraged the first creative efforts of his grandson the novelist Christopher Koch. Predeceased by his wife, Koch died as the result of a motor accident on 25 August 1952 in hospital in Melbourne and was cremated. Two sons and a daughter survived him.

Theatre Royal: Grand Re-opening Souvenir Programme, Sat. Jan 13th, 1912; D. Henslowe, *Our Heritage of Anglican Churches in Tasmania* (Hob, 1978); C. Craig, *More Old Tasmanian Prints* (Launc, Tas, 1984); M. Roe, *Life Over Death* (Hob, 1999); D. McNeill and L. Woolley, *Architecture From the Edge* (Hob, 2002); City of Hobart, *Mayor's Annual Report*, 1922, 1929-36; *Advocate* (Burnie), 4 Feb 1903, p 2, 24 Feb 1903, p 2; *Tas Mail*, 14 Feb 1903, p 22, 9 Feb 1911, p 9, 21 Mar 1928, p 14; *Mercury* (Hob), 26 Aug 1952, p 12.   GILLIAN WINTER
                                              CHRISTOPHER KOCH

KOLIOS, NICHOLAS (1885-1927), fruit-grower and writer, was born in 1885 at the small port town of Chesme, near Smyrna (Izmir), Turkey, son of Greek parents Konstantinos Kolios, farmer, and his wife Vassiliki. Nicholas received a better than elementary education at the French *lycée* on the island of Rhodes, then secured a banking position in Turkey. Having established himself as a merchant and importer, on 15 September 1914 at Mersina he married Kyriaki (Sunday) Athanasiadis, also from Chesme. At the onset of the Greco-Turkish War in 1921 he and his family fled to the island of Chios (Khios). Late in 1922, with a cousin, Kolios migrated to Victoria. His family, including four children followed two years later; another daughter was born in Australia.

A short, lean, well-groomed man with a neat moustache, Kolios worked as a draper at Bairnsdale and later in Melbourne. In July 1923 he became a journalist with the Greek language weekly *Ethniki Salpinx* (*National Bugle*), in Melbourne, touring Greek communities in Sydney and Brisbane as the paper's representative. Three months later, after obtaining financial support from Greek food caterers and retailers, he purchased the publication, but sold it in July next year due to financial difficulties, aggravated perhaps by his propensity for gambling. As well as his news articles, Kolios had published in the paper a number of poems and short stories, focusing mostly on the life of Greeks in Australia, and on issues concerning the Greeks who had become refugees through the exchange of minorities after the Greco-Turkish war. Later, he contributed poems to another Greek newspaper, *To Ethniko Vema* (*National Tribune*).

Early in 1924 Kolios purchased a 100-acre (40.5 ha) lot near Mildura. With an uncle Petros Zymaris and two other partners, he camped on the property and pruned fruit trees, dressed vines and picked grapes on other blocks. He and his colleagues quickly recognized the inferiority of Mildura sultanas to those produced at Smyrna. The 'hot dip' curing process employed at Mildura (with grapes immersed in a solution of heated caustic soda prior to sun drying on racks) resulted in leathery skins. In exchange for a partly arable 42-acre (17 ha) block, £500 and the loan of cultivation equipment, Kolios gave the Australian Dried Fruits Association details of the process used in Smyrna. With the arrival of another uncle Alexander Zymaris and a Smyrniot vigneron Aristotle George, Kolios's confidence surged, accelerating his ambition beyond the initial contract (which was simply to demonstrate the technique on his group's new vineyard) to one of gaining commercial viability. The 'cold dip' process (immersing grapes in a correctly proportioned emulsion of potassium carbonate and olive oil) and spraying to avoid mildew and insects before being left to dry in the sun were quickly embraced by Mildura growers. The coveted world quality five-crown grade for dried sultanas was thus attained, and at the Toronto exhibition, Canada (1927), the success was internationally recognized.

Salinity affected his group's block, however, and there were disputes between the partners. Disappointed and disillusioned, Kolios left with his family for Melbourne in mid-1927. Failure in another business venture with two other Greeks proved personally bitter and deeply corrosive. He committed suicide on 8 September 1927 by drowning in Port Phillip Bay and was buried with Greek Orthodox rites in Fawkner cemetery. His wife and their two daughters and three sons survived him.

E. Hill, *Water into Gold* (Syd, 1937); H. Gilchrist, *Australians and Greeks*, 2 (Syd, 1977); G. Kanarakis, *Greek Voices in Australia* (Syd, 1987); J. Jupp (ed), *The Australian People* (Cambridge, UK, 2001), p 391; *Sunraysia Daily*, 19 Jan 1924, p 1; *Argus* (Melb), 8 Oct 1926, p 13; M. P. Tsounis, Greek Communities in Australia (Ph.D. thesis, Univ Adel, 1971); correspondence and interview transcripts held by author, Macquarie Univ.   LEONARD JANISZEWSKI

KORNER, JOHANNA (1891-1969), beauty salon proprietor, was born on 21 July 1891 at Fogaras, Hungary (Romania), daughter of Alfred Adler, photographer, and his wife Helena, née Springer. Following the example of an aunt, Johanna trained as a beautician in Paris, Vienna and Berlin. She married Jeno (Eugene) Korner, a lawyer, on 3 November 1916 at Vac (Brasson).

In 1936 Johanna was running a beauty salon in Budapest, said to be one of several owned by the family. Her son George Gabriel (1918-2002), a cosmetic chemist, was already involved in the business. With Hungary an ally of Germany, during World War II George was forced into a Jewish labour battalion and sent to the Russian front. Surviving the German retreat from Moscow, he made his way back to Budapest. By 1943 the family had fled to France and Madame Korner had established a business in the Place Pigalle. She considered moving her business to Beirut, but George, who came to Australia in February 1951, persuaded his parents to join him. They reached Sydney in September 1955, their married daughter having preceded them. Although David Jones's [q.v.2] department store had hosted an Elizabeth Arden salon from 1936 and regularly had visits from overseas experts in the use of cosmetics, Australian women knew little of skin nourishing creams or beauty treatments.

George had already commenced business in his mother's name, with the first Madame Korner Beauty Salon opening in the fashionable St James Building, Elizabeth Street, Sydney, in 1953. Early clients were from European backgrounds, but as the business prospered and more salons opened, Australian-born women benefited too. The salons introduced a more intense regime of skin care to many women who previously had used only soap and water. In 1954 George opened a beauty training school to teach his mother's methods and in 1956 launched the Madame Korner Skin Care range of products for use in professional salons and at home.

The core of the beauty school curriculum was Johanna's philosophical and ethical ideas. She believed that beauty could be achieved with thoroughness and patience, and that all clients should be treated with the same respect and given the same service. Trainees were instructed to be honest with clients and to refrain from extravagant promises, to acquire a thorough knowledge of cosmetology, to believe in the profession sincerely and to practise it conscientiously.

Eugene died on 4 March 1965 in Sydney. Johanna died from the effects of barbiturate and bromine poisoning, self-administered, on 30 March 1969 at her home at Double Bay, Sydney, and was buried in the Jewish section of Rookwood cemetery. Her son and daughter survived her. In 1987 George established a student scholarship at Sydney Technical College in his mother's memory, and in 2005 the Madame Korner Beauty Salons continued to be run by Johanna's descendants.

SMH, 21 Feb 1936, p 4, 17 Mar 1936, p 4, 4 May 1948, p 5, 13 Sept 1979, p 13, 16 Sept 2002, p 40; *Eastern Herald* (Syd), 24 Oct 1991, p 16, 20 Feb 1992, p 12; *Sun-Herald* (Syd), 18 Oct 1998, 'Sunday Life', p 13; SP1122, item N1960/33450 (NAA, Syd); inquest records, 94/1970 (SRNSW).

RACHEL GRAHAME

KREITMAYER, MAXIMILIAN LUDWIG (1830-1906), waxworks proprietor, was born on 31 December 1830 in Munich, Bavaria, son of Maximilian Ludwig Kreitmayer, artist. After studying anatomy in Munich, young Max visited Britain for further study and worked as a medical modeller at St Bartholomew's Hospital, London. Describing himself as an artist, he married Eliza Spong on 2 July 1856 in the parish church, Leeds, Yorkshire. They were to have four children.

Attracted by the gold rush, Kreitmayer reached Melbourne in December that year; Eliza joined him in February 1858. Not having much success at the diggings, in 1859 he opened an anatomical museum, a popular, if unrespectable, form of 'instructive' entertainment, which included wax models of sexual organs decayed by venereal disease. He toured the goldfields with his collection of anatomical items and by 1862 had opened a museum in Bourke Street, Melbourne. The collection was shown to segregated audiences, his wife lecturing to the women. He also opened anatomical and waxworks museums in Sydney, Adelaide and Hobart.

In 1862 Kreitmayer sold his collection of anatomical models to the government of Chile, for the Santiago medical school. He exhibited another collection at L. L. Smith's [q.v.6] Polytechnic Institute, then in mid-1863 went into partnership with a phrenologist, Philemon Sohier, and his wife Ellen, proprietors of Madame Sohier's Waxworks of Melbourne and Sydney. Kreitmayer managed the Sydney business. On 31 January 1868 in Sydney, a widower, he married with Anglican rites English-born Emily Anne Waite, who had arrived in Melbourne in 1860, and had apparently already borne him three children.

Returning to Melbourne in 1869, Kreitmayer became proprietor of that city's sole waxworks. The Victorian government commissioned him to make figures for international exhibitions. Notable among these were figures of Aborigines for the Paris (1878) and Indian and Colonial (1886) exhibitions. Kreitmayer's waxworks museum came to be regarded by some as a 'gallery of reference'. It included historical and newsworthy figures such as the royal family, Dreyfus, Sarah Bernhardt and Melba [q.v.10]. The Chamber of Horrors also portrayed a Kelly [q.v.5, E. Kelly] gang tableau (1880), the Deeming murders (1892) and Jimmy Governor [qq.v.8, 9] and his victims (1900).

Kreitmayer ran the Bourke Street entertainment until shortly before his death but also employed managers and other wax modellers. His manager Phil Stuart had a theatrical background, and from the 1880s the waxworks included vaudeville and music hall acts such as magicians, ventriloquists and chorus girls.

Emily died in 1879. On 29 March 1884, claiming to be a bachelor, Kreitmayer married Harriet Mary Watts at Launceston, Tasmania. He was elected to Collingwood council in 1887 and was mayor in 1893. He lost in mining ventures, however, and his business suffered a downturn during the 1890s, causing his insolvency in 1898. By 1903, with Harriet's financial help, the waxworks' yearly takings were more than £1000.

Kreitmayer died on 1 June 1906 at Collingwood and was buried in Melbourne general cemetery with Anglican rites. His wife and their son and daughter, and two sons and two daughters of his second marriage survived him. Despite his somewhat Bohemian life, he was remembered as 'a man of most loveable disposition'. His widow (d.1934) continued the business, incorporating a cinema in the building. Her projectionist was F. W. Thring [q.v.12], who married Max and Harriett's daughter Olive.

Our Local Men of the Times (Melb, 1889); *MJA*, 4 Feb 1956, p 164; M. Colligan, 'Anatomical Wax Museums in Melbourne 1861-1887', *Aust Cultural History*, no 13, 1994, p 52, *and* 'Waxworks shows and some of their proprietors in Australia, 1850s-1910s', *Australasian Drama Studies*, no 34, Apr 1999, p 87; *South Australian*, 15 July 1862; *Bell's Life in Sydney*, 16 Aug 1862, p 2; *Argus* (Melb), 25 May 1869, p 6, 20 June 1910, p 5, 10 June 1939, 'Weekend Mag', p 3; *Australasian*, 5 June 1886, p 1098, 9 June 1906, p 1350; *Age* (Melb), 2 June 1906, p 11; insolvency files, VPRS 765/P, unit 283, file 90/3390 (PRO, Vic).   MIMI COLLIGAN

KROEMER, VICTOR EUGENE (1883-1930), printer, socialist, clairvoyant and healer, was born on 5 November 1883 at Tanunda, South Australia, fifth of seven children of John Stephen Anthony Kroemer, storekeeper, and his wife Alice Jane, née Trotter. Both parents had been born in South Australia. Leaving school and entering the printing trade at the age of 12, Victor undertook a course of intensive evening reading of 'religious, scientific and philosophical literature' in the Public Library, Museum and Art Gallery in Adelaide. He joined various literary and religious organizations, but his membership of a young men's class at a Baptist Sunday School ended when his freethought ideas became known to the superintendent. Although, as a youth, Victor often found himself 'surrounded by a bluish or violet light', it was not until later that he 'discovered the nature of that force'. From about 1901 he was secretary of the Christian Metaphysical Society and a member of the Clarion Fellowship, a socialist group, several of whose members combined political radicalism with mental science and 'new thought' healing.

Moving to Victoria in 1903, Kroemer worked as a printer on the *Bendigo Independent*. In 1905, while he was living in Melbourne, 'there came to him . . . an outpouring of the force of which later he was destined to achieve such conscious mastery'. He developed a healing technique that drew on this force but, in the meantime, he was an active member of the Social Questions Committee, a Fabian-style organization formed in 1905 by Tom Mann [q.v.10]. Next year Kroemer joined the Victorian Socialist Party; he wrote regularly for its newspaper, the *Socialist*, ran the party's Sunday School, became a Theosophist and practised vegetarianism.

In August 1907 the tall, handsome Kroemer represented the newly formed Socialist Federation of Australasia at the seventh congress of the Second International at Stuttgart, Germany. During a debate on migration, at a gathering including most of the world's leading socialists, he allegedly claimed clairvoyant knowledge that the world revolution would commence in South Australia. The Reuters correspondent called the speech 'an extraordinary mixture of blasphemy and inconsequence', while H. M. Hyndman, a British delegate, wrote to an Australian socialist demanding to know why Australia had chosen such a stupid dreamer as its representative!

Early in 1908 in Paris Kroemer married Lillian Hammett Dyer. Later that year he was back in London. The couple's three children were born in England. While working for various newspapers and publishers, Victor mixed in Theosophical, spiritualist and new thought circles. In 1912 he attended a Theosophical convention at Adyar, India, the headquarters of the society, and then travelled to Colombo, where he briefly managed the Buddhist Press.

Next year Kroemer and his family moved to Australia. He worked as a journalist on the *Daily Herald* in Adelaide and for four years as general secretary of the Workers' Educational Association of South Australia, which he had helped to found. After the outbreak of World War I, he established an occult class in Adelaide that sought to understand 'the inner meaning of the World Crisis'. He published a transcription of the teachings of a seer called 'Althea' as *Why This World Crisis?* (Adelaide, c.1915); it interpreted the war as a consequence of a lack of harmony in the solar system and of the success of Lucifer, the God of Jupiter, in gaining control of the Kaiser.

Kroemer began treating patients as a new thought healer 'in a small way' in Adelaide from 1916. He expanded his practice in the following decade and published *The Rise of Democracy* (1919), and in the 1920s he and Lillian went to Sydney where, as 'Victor Cromer', he ran the Spiritual Healing Institute. He died of appendicitis and peritonitis on 2 February 1930 in Edward Rivett's [q.v.11] Cabarisha Private Hospital, Castlecrag, and was cremated with Anglican rites. His wife and their son and twin daughters survived him.

B. Walker, *Solidarity Forever* (Melb, 1972); J. Roe, *Beyond Belief* (Syd, 1986); *Herald* (Adel), 23 May 1903, p 1, 4 July 1903, p 7; *Socialist*, 22 June 1907; *Argus* (Melb), 26 Aug 1907, p 7; *Federal Independent*, 1 Apr 1930, pp 1-3.
                                        FRANK BONGIORNO

KUBATJI; *see* CUBADGEE

KYTE, AMBROSE HENRY SPENCER (c.1822-1868), merchant, property investor and politician, was born at Nenagh, Tipperary, Ireland, son of Stephen Kyte and his wife Margaret, née Mitchell. Arriving in Melbourne in January 1840, Ambrose worked as a brewer's labourer. On 20 November 1842 at St James's Church of England he married Irish-born Sarah Ann Finnin. They had five children.

Unemployed in 1843 and with meagre earnings next year, Kyte saved enough during 1845 to open a hay and corn store in Bourke Street, later expanding into general merchandise and investing in urban properties. Among these was the Theatre Royal, where he was often seen leaning against an entrance column, estimating crowd numbers and the evening's receipts. By 1857 Kyte's annual rental income, estimated to have reached £15 000, was sufficient to enable him to retire from business. He became founding chairman (1859) of Melbourne's second private gas company, based at Collingwood and Fitzroy.

Dark-haired, thin-lipped and taciturn, Kyte was frugal and shrewd, taking pride in not 'making many mistakes, where money-making is the question'. He told of forcing payment from an unwilling debtor at pistol point and of once having his arm set in plaster, so that he could disown a signature on a document he did not wish to honour. He avoided the religious quarrels that disfigured the early years of Port Phillip. Apparently secure in his wealth, and known for numerous acts of private generosity, Kyte turned to public philanthropy. He funded prizes for the advancement of agriculture, the encouragement of marksmanship and the discovery of a goldfield near the Snowy River. His promise of £1000 towards the financing of the Burke and Wills [qq.v.3,6] expedition, provided the public subscribed another £2000, was crucial in bringing the enterprise to fruition. Although these benefactions were made anonymously, the identity of the donor was soon public knowledge, suggesting that Kyte enjoyed 'the double praise of liberality and of doing good by stealth'.

Kyte also had ambitions to participate directly in public life. In 1861 he was elected to the Legislative Assembly for East Melbourne as a Protectionist, campaigning for secular education, the further opening up of land for selectors and 'a stiff tax on absentee proprietors'. He referred to squatters as 'greedy . . . hungry and undeserving men'. Defeated in 1865, Kyte was re-elected in 1866 at a by-election for Richmond. He contributed little to parliamentary debate, but behind the scenes he was said to have been a willing and active participant in the parliamentary corruption initiated by Hugh Glass [q.v.4]. Despite his public views, Kyte disbursed funds raised by Glass and other squatters for the purpose of encouraging the passage of a bill to recompense the holders of land certificates. Glass later claimed to have had little knowledge of how Kyte spent the money given to him.

Struggling against financial reverses and said to be 'very much aggravated by nervous agitation', Kyte died intestate of pneumonia on 16 November 1868 at his Carlton home. He was buried in Melbourne general cemetery with Anglican rites. His wife, a son and two daughters survived him, inheriting real property valued at £10 000.

Subsequently a select committee inquiring into allegations that some parliamentarians had been bribed found Kyte a convenient scapegoat. The full extent of his culpability, however, could not be determined. The solicitor administering his estate declared that 'Mr Kyte's accounts were of the most complicated and intricate description anyone could conceive, kept entirely by himself; and it would be impossible for anyone to form the most distant notion of what his transactions were'.

M. Kiddle, *Men of Yesterday* (Melb, 1961); C. E. Sayers, *David Syme* (Melb, 1965); H. Love, *The Golden Age of Australian Opera* (Syd, 1981); T. Bonyhady, *Burke & Wills* (Syd, 1991); R. Wright, *A People's Counsel* (Melb, 1992); Report from the Select Committee on Complaints, *V&P* (LA, Vic), 1869, vol 2, paper no D3; *Age* (Melb), 17 Nov 1868, p 2; *Argus* (Melb), 17 Nov 1868, p 5; *Leader* (Melb), 21 Nov 1868, p 912; *Australasian*, 21 Nov 1868, pp 657, 659; *Truth* (Melb), 30 June 1917, p 3.

GEOFF BROWNE

L

LAKE, SERENA (1842-1902), evangelist and suffragist, was born on 28 October 1842 at Shebbear, Devon, England, daughter of Samuel Thorne, a farmer who became printer and publisher for the Bible Christian denomination, and his wife Mary, née O'Bryan, an evangelist whose father had founded that church. Serena was well read, lively and vivacious. At 17 she 'felt the Master's call' and first preached. From 1861 in Devon and Cornwall's Bible Christian circuits the 'sweet girl gospeller' drew crowds and converts, attracted by her persuasive, vivid oratory, unclouded faith and 'compassion for souls'. In 1865 she accompanied her brother to Queensland, worked among Primitive Methodists, then established a mission, at the English Bible Christian Conference's request, in 1866. Invited to Melbourne next year, she gave valuable assistance evangelizing there and throughout Victoria: she regularly preached three Sunday sermons.

In 1870 South Australian Bible Christians, including the lawyer (Sir) Samuel Way and medical practitioner Allan Campbell [qq.v.12, 7] invited Miss Thorne to Adelaide. On 22 May, at the first of her thirteen, crowded, Town Hall Sunday services, over 2000 listened to her sermon 'with breathless attention'; hundreds were turned away. She preached, too, in suburban churches and in the country. On night visits to Adelaide prostitutes, she influenced some 'poor fallen sisters' to enter the Female Refuge.

Serena's life changed at country Auburn when a former Shebbear admirer, the Bible Christian minister Octavius Lake, proposed marriage. Torn between love and duty, she finally accepted when he vowed approval of female preachers: they married in Way's house on 2 March 1871. Serrie had seven children: only one survived early childhood. She preached and helped the needy in her husband's country and suburban circuits. On Yorke Peninsula, among familiar Cornish settlers, in 1877 and 1879 she opened new churches.

Because she believed sexual equality to be 'the original design of the Creator', Mrs Lake supported women's suffrage and in July 1888, having seconded the motion founding the South Australian Women's Suffrage League, was elected to its council. She combined logical argument, wit and evangelical passion, sharing platforms with suffrage leaders, including Mary Lee [q.v.10]. In August 1889 Mrs Lake was appointed 'colonial organiser and suffrage superintendent' of the Woman's Christian Temperance Union and shaped the union's commitment to women's suffrage.

Living at Kapunda and later Gladstone, she drove her buggy long distances across country and travelled by train to Broken Hill, New South Wales, opening some thirty-eight new local unions in the country and Adelaide, gaining hundreds of members, male associates and suffrage petition signatures. Her efforts epitomized the contemporary influence of evangelical religion. Confident that women 'possessing that sword—the ballot' would curb the 'abominable liquor traffic', she campaigned also on temperance society platforms. In 1891 she was appointed a W.C.T.U. life vice-president.

In May 1892 Serena eloquently moved adoption of the suffrage league's annual report. Subsequently, however, she apparently devoted herself to evangelical and humanitarian causes. In June 1891, in step with the 'forward movement' to win poor city-dwellers 'for Christ', she had been mainly responsible for initiating the Bible Christian Woman's Missionary Board, of which she was foundation president and, from October 1892, superintendent of evangelists. Following an operation for cancer, she died of peritonitis on 9 July 1902 in Adelaide Hospital and was buried in Payneham cemetery. Her husband and daughter survived her.

A. Hunt, *This Side of Heaven* (Adel, 1985); M. Harry, *A Century of Service* (Adel, 1986); B. Dickey (ed), *The Australian Dictionary of Evangelical Biography* (Syd, 1994); WCTU (SA), *Annual Convention Minutes*, 1889-92; WCTU Executive Committee, *Minutes*, 1891; *Bible Christian Mag* (UK), 1866, p 284, 1869, p 289, 1870, p 434, 1902, p 620; *Alliance and Temperance News*, July 1890, p 7; *SA Bible Christian Monthly*, 1891, pp 309, 351, 1892, p 144; *Aust Christian Cwlth*, 25 July 1902; *SA Register*, 21 July 1888, p 6; *Observer* (Adel), 21 May 1892, p 33, 12 July 1902, p 34; S. Thorne, diary (Uniting Church History Centre, Black Forest, Adel).

HELEN JONES

LAMBRICK, AMELIA (1864-1956), public servant and social reformer, was born on 23 March 1864 in North Melbourne, eldest of five children of Erasmus Pascoe Lambrick, a carrier born in Cornwall, England, and his wife Amelia, née Bertram, from Norfolk. Amelia entered the Victorian public service in 1886 and, after holding various positions in the Postmaster General's Department, worked in the Customs Department, under Victorian then Federal control, for thirty-seven years.

Lecturing was the chief way that she advocated her particular brand of social reform. Lambrick was a member of the Theosophical

Society, the Woman's Christian Temperance Union, the Women's International League for Peace and Freedom, the Henry George [q.v.4] Club and the Victorian Citizens' Movement. She spoke in the suburbs for Vida Goldstein's [q.v.9] 1910 campaign for election to the Senate, and wrote for the *Socialist* under the pseudonym 'Hypatia'. In 1926 she represented the Australian section at the W.I.L.P.F. congress in Dublin, and during the 1920s and 1930s travelled and lectured extensively overseas. She was president of the Victorian branch of the W.I.L.P.F. from 1932 to 1936 and of the East Malvern branch of the auxiliary of the Austin [q.v.1] Hospital for Incurables (1934). A contributor to *Peace*, the booklet produced in conjunction with the 1937 Australian Peace Congress, she remained involved with the International Peace Campaign.

Lambrick's 'wellspring came from theosophy'. In a similar vein to the Greek Hypatia who brought spiritualism to Platonism, perhaps Lambrick's favourite lectures were those on the great Indian spiritual leaders, Gandhi, Kagawa, Tagore and Krishnamurti. She never failed to insist that belief in 'universal brotherhood' was a key to peaceful relations, greater equality and better governance. 'Peace', she announced in 1937, 'stands for truth, justice, brotherhood, and these are the foundations of all true civilisation'. Frustrated by the hypocrisy of the Christian Church and the prevalence of rhetoric rather than 'knowledge' in democracies around the world, she felt that socialism and communism were understandable responses to the 'appalling' unequal distribution of wealth, but hoped that 'true democracy' would prevail. In the more just society for which she worked, individuals would not necessarily be perfectly equal, but they would not be discriminated against on grounds of race, class, gender or creed. She closely studied events in the Pacific, regularly lecturing on the Soviet Union and China, and objected strongly to the White Australia policy, arguing that 'we have insisted on our superiority in such a way that we have made ourselves ridiculous'.

An 'impressive woman', Lambrick was upright and tall, with a fiery knowledge of a broad range of subjects, a gentle voice and 'a certain sweetness in her expression'. She was a good platform speaker and 'guaranteed to draw questions'. Her hobbies were reading and gardening. Lambrick's family remembered her as 'something of a crank and a life-long nonconforming eccentric', but were 'still proud of her intelligence and wit'. She died on 27 September 1956 at her home at East Malvern, and was cremated. She had not married, but was survived by her sister-in-law and niece.

Who's Who in the World of Women (Melb, 1934); E. M. Moore, *The Quest for Peace* (Melb, 1949?); A.

Curthoys, S. Eade and P. Spearritt (eds), *Women and Work* (Canb, 1975); J. Roe, *Beyond Belief* (Syd, 1986); C. Rasmussen, *The Lesser Evil?* (Melb, 1992); J. M. Bloomfield, *That Dangerous and Persuasive Woman: Vida Goldstein* (Melb, 1993); J. Damousi, *Women Come Rally* (Melb, 1994); *Labour History*, no 29, 1975, p ix; WILPF papers (Univ Melb L); information from Mrs L. Hamilton, North Balwyn, Melb.

AMANDA RASMUSSEN

LANGFORD, CLEMENTS (1853-1930), master builder, was born on 25 March 1853 at Portsea, Hampshire, England, son of George Langford, brewer, and his wife Betsey Dyer, née Clements. The family arrived in Tasmania in March 1864 and moved to Melbourne in 1868. After working with auctioneers Beauchamp & Rock, Clements was apprenticed to the builder David Mitchell [q.v.5] in 1869 and won first prize for architectural drawing at the Richmond School of Design in 1874. In 1877-78 he worked as a carpenter and owned a house at Richmond and in 1879-88 a nearby grocery.

On 20 December 1882 at St Stephen's Church of England, Richmond—where he became senior church-warden—Langford married Sarah Ann Coverlid, a teacher. The couple lived in a house newly built by Langford, had eight children and in 1902 moved to a larger residence (named Netley after a Portsmouth locality) which he had built, also at Richmond. From 1887 he had a holiday house at Sorrento.

In 1881 Langford had formed a partnership with Robert Hutchison, and they set up as builders and contractors in Bridge Road, Richmond. From 1886 he continued the business in his sole name. Having insufficient capital structure to be vulnerable to the building boom collapse of the 1890s, the firm was involved in several major projects, by 1909 employing 300. Incorporated as Clements Langford Pty Ltd in May 1923, by 1930 it encompassed 'shop and office fitters, plumbers, painters [and] decorators', and boasted large joinery, timber-machining and plumbers' shops. Langford undertook an eclectic range of contracts including premises for Makower, McBeath [q.v.10] & Co. Pty Ltd, additions to the university medical school, the Bryant & May factory, Centreway, Hoyts' Theatre in Bourke Street, the Melbourne Sports Depot, the Myer [q.v.10] Emporium, Scott's Hotel, the Comedy Theatre, Dall & Welch's store, the Safe Deposit Building, the Adelaide Steamship Co. building, the Dunlop factory at Montague, the Australian Mutual Provident Society's new Melbourne office and the Herald Building.

Sarah died in 1916. On 10 December 1919 at St Philip's Church, Collingwood, Clements married Gertrude Saunders, a maltster's daughter. They lived at Riversmount, Camberwell, which Langford built to D. F. Stevenson's design. The firm worked with leading architects, and itself contributed the design element in many jobs, such as the alterations to Langford's beloved St Stephen's, Richmond. The culmination of his career as builder and churchman was the erection of the St Paul's Cathedral spires, which he commenced in 1926, following a 1925 trip to England, and whose completion he bequeathed to his son George.

Langford's other business interests included directorships of suppliers of building materials such as cement, bricks and timber. He was president (1913-14) and long-time treasurer of the Melbourne Master Builders' Association, president of the Master Builders' Federation of Victoria and an executive member of the Victorian Employers' Federation.

A Freemason and Rotarian, in 1927 he became a lay canon of St Paul's Cathedral. Langford was handsome and of strong appearance, 'a tough employer, a driver'—and the owner of a Rolls Royce motorcar—but with a reputation for generosity to the church and needy employees. He died on 6 February 1930 at Sorrento and, after services at St Stephen's and at St Paul's, was buried in Boroondara cemetery. His wife and the five sons and three daughters of his first marriage survived him, inheriting an estate sworn for probate at £181 632. A mosaic portrait of Langford is in St Stephen's, Richmond.

J. Smith (ed), *The Cyclopedia of Victoria*, 1, (Melb, 1903); M. T. Shaw, *Builders of Melbourne* (Melb, 1972); G. Wenzel, *Pater: Builder of the Spires* (Melb, 1998); *V&P* (LA, Vic), 1909, vol 1, paper no D5; *Building and Construction & Cazaly's Contract Reporter*, 10 Feb 1930, 3 Mar 1930, 4 Aug 1930; *Herald* (Melb), 6 Feb 1930, p 1; *Argus* (Melb), 7 Feb 1930, p 6; Clements Langford Pty Ltd papers (Univ Melb Archives).   MARK RICHMOND

LAW, JAMES LINDSAY GORDON (1881-1963), shirt manufacturer, was born on 21 January 1881 at Ballarat, Victoria, eighth child of Scottish migrants James Law, contractor, and his wife Margaret, née Bartholomew. James senior was killed in an accident in Tasmania when the youngster, known as 'Lin', was only 6. He was educated in state schools at Ballarat but left at 11 and was subsequently tutored by his eldest sister, a schoolteacher. His first job was with Banks & Co. at Ballarat in 1892. After working from 1896 as a salesman with Paterson, Laing & (J.M.) Bruce [q.v.3] in Flinders Lane, Melbourne, in 1904 he met his future partner JAMES KERR PEARSON (1881-1950).

Born on 31 July 1881 at Glasgow, Scotland, son of James Pearson, drapery warehouseman, and his wife Mary-Ann, née Kerr, Pearson had come to Victoria in 1902. Employed by Richard Allen Pty Ltd, he then worked as a traveller with Kornblum & Co. In 1905 he founded a company manufacturing shirts, and Law became a partner in 1906. From 1911 Pearson & Law was a limited company in Gertrude Street, Fitzroy; in 1917 it became Pelaco Ltd (from the first two letters of each owner's surname). Law was managing director from 1911 until the early 1950s. Pearson was joint managing director from 1917.

On 12 January 1915 in St Mary's Catholic Cathedral, Sydney, Law married Elsie Russell, a saleswoman. The couple lived most of their married life at Brighton, Melbourne, and had four children. He was very much a family man. Although nominally a Methodist, he was not religious. Pearson, a Presbyterian, had married Amy Harriet, sister of E. C. Dyason [q.v.8], at All Saints' Church of England pro-Cathedral, Bendigo, on 24 May 1910.

A member of the Victorian Chamber of Manufacturers, Law was sometime president of its clothing trades section and of the Commercial Travellers Club and vice-president of the Australian Industries Protection League. He was the employers' representative on the Victorian Shirt Wages Board during both world wars and a key witness for the employers in the Commonwealth Arbitration Court in the 1920s.

Best known for his innovative approach to the management of clothing production, Law elaborated his philosophies in a series of articles in the *Australasian Manufacturer* (1916-17); he included 'scientific management' principles derived from Frederick Winslow Taylor, and paternalist approaches to industrial relations. Law was an avid reader of relevant literature and, after World War I, spent five months in the United States of America observing production methods. In the Pelaco factory he employed Taylor's ideas on subdivision of labour and supervision of workers as well as Henry Ford's standardization of products. He was also influenced by the industrial efficiency movement, using physical conditions of work and length of work periods to maximize the productivity of the workforce. The outcome was a modern, well lit and ventilated factory, equipped with recreation and lunch rooms, a piano, and radios provided for the use of workers.

Pelaco was one of the first companies in Australia to employ an industrial psychologist, and published a regular factory newsletter, *Pelacograms*, to inspire a sense of community and pride. Law believed passionately in piece rates as a solution to 'the problem of labour': 'Capital must awaken to the fact that it does not matter how high a man's wage is so long as he earns it, and Labour must awaken to the fact that if he receives a high wage it must be earned'. The practice of employing large numbers of juvenile females on piece rates brought him into conflict with both the Clothing Trades Union and the Commonwealth Court of Conciliation and Arbitration, especially in the 1920s when he became a leading anti-union campaigner in the Victorian Chamber of Manufacturers.

Of average height, 5 ft 8 ins (173 cm) tall, Law was good-looking, clean cut, a forceful character and a fighter. Nevertheless, he wished to be seen as a fair man: despite designing his workrooms on the open-plan model to allow maximum supervision, he refused to wear rubber-soled shoes for fear that workers would think he was sneaking up on them. In his youth he rowed with Albert Park Rowing Club. He had joined the Victorian Scottish Regiment during the South African War but did not serve overseas. From the early 1920s he belonged to Melbourne Rotary Club and Victoria Golf Club. In later life he played tennis at home and enjoyed gardening and motoring. He was also a member of the Athenaeum and Melbourne Scots clubs.

Pearson too enjoyed golf and tennis and belonged to the Athenaeum club. He died on 2 October 1950 at Richmond, leaving an estate sworn for probate at £92 967. His wife, two daughters and three sons survived him. Law died on 18 February 1963 in a private hospital at Fitzroy and was cremated. His wife, one daughter and three sons survived him. His estate was sworn at £22 701. The company's mass advertising—with captions 'Mine Tinkit They Fit!', under an image of an Aboriginal man 'Pelaco Bill' [q.v.15 Mulga Fred], and 'It is indeed a lovely shirt, sir!', with the product held by the model Bambi Smith—made a lasting impression on Australian consumers.

R. Frances, *The Politics of Work* (Melb, 1993); *A'sian Manufacturer*, 28 Oct 1916, 24 Mar 1917, 2 June 1917; *Triad* (Syd), no 2, 1916, p 57, no 3, 1916, p 46; family papers (held by Mr J. Law, Glen Iris, Vic). RAELENE FRANCES

LAZENBY, GEORGE (1807-1895), cabinetmaker, builder and town clerk, was born in October 1807 at Spaldington, East Yorkshire, England. After his family moved to Leeds George was apprenticed to a cabinet-maker. The youngster was musical and played the cello and the violin. Taking ship in his brother's vessel for his health, he visited Western Australia about 1831 and saw opportunities there. Soon after, he returned to Britain and became engaged to Mary Ann Wells.

Reaching the Swan River colony in January 1833 in the *Cygnet*, with George Shenton [q.v.2] and others, Lazenby commenced business as a cabinet-maker and builder. He married Mary Ann on 1 January 1839, shortly after she had arrived to join him. They had ten children. Mary Ann reputedly ran a school in Perth in the 1870s. In Murray Street Lazenby built a house for himself, followed by twelve cottages to rent and later a store. A member of Perth Road Committee in 1842-44, he was sometime chairman of the Swan River Mechanics' Institute and in 1855 of the Public Institutions Society.

There was no ordained Methodist minister in the colony in its first six years. Lazenby became a lay preacher—he was known to habitually look at the ceiling while preaching —and in 1834 formed the first Methodist fellowship class. He was a generous supporter of his denomination, contributing to the cost, serving on the management committees and supervising the building of at least four chapels; he was also a founder of the Sunday School. In a colony controlled primarily by 'Church' (of England) there was some stigma attached to being 'Chapel'. The Wesleyans, however, formed a close-knit group. Lazenby employed other Methodists, the most notable being an apprentice, Benjamin Mason, and the pianoforte-maker Joseph Hamblin, a consummate craftsman who worked for him until 1847.

Attempting to establish an export market for local timber, Lazenby took samples of furniture made from jarrah to England aboard the *Victoria* in 1845. Hamblin's wife and son sailed with him, while Hamblin remained to run Lazenby's business. Returning to Perth in 1846, Lazenby was appointed clerk of works to the Perth Town Trust in 1850. In this capacity he was in charge of refurbishing Government House. He ceased business in 1856 and in 1862 became foreman of works for the government, supervising the erection of the barracks and the colonial hospital.

In 1869 Lazenby became supervisor and town clerk for Perth City Council. Criticized for inefficiency in 1875, he resigned but, after an apology, was persuaded to withdraw the resignation. A sympathizer pointed out that as well as being supervisor, he was 'Clerk of the Council, Clerk of the Market, Caretaker of the Town Hall, Inspector of Nuisances, Inspector of Weights and Measures, Receiver of Allotments belonging to the Council, keeps labourers' accounts and pays their wages daily'. A secretary was appointed to assist him and he remained in office until 1881.

At Cardup, near Byford, in the 1860s he built a two-storey house and a flourmill, dammed a brook, bred cattle, pigs and horses, opened a clay pit and burnt bricks. His son Joseph worked the property in the 1860s. In 1877-78 Lazenby and his wife again visited Britain. Mary Ann died in 1886. Hale and hearty until his last weeks, Lazenby died on 9 June 1895 in Perth. One son and six daughters, including Hannah, who married W. S. Hall [q.v.4], survived him.

C. T. Stannage, *The People of Perth* (Perth, 1979); R. E. Turner, *Foundations not Made by Hands* (Perth, 1984); WA Hist Society, *Journals and Proceedings*, 2, pt 13, 1933, p 1; *West Australian*, 10 June 1895, p 3, 11 June 1895, p 5. DOROTHY ERICKSON

LEIGH, WILLIAM AUGUSTINE (1802-1873), benefactor, was born on 4 November 1802 at Roby Hall, near Liverpool, England, only child of William Leigh, merchant, and his wife Catherine, heiress and daughter of Sir Richard Robinson, Bart. Young William was educated at Eton, then at Brasenose College, Oxford, without taking a degree. After extensive European travel, on 30 April 1828 he married Caroline, fifth daughter of Sir John Geers Cotterell, Bart. Of the Leighs' four children, one son died in infancy and two daughters died young.

Leigh lived at Roby Hall, then at Aston Hall in Staffordshire, of which county he was a justice of the peace and deputy-lieutenant. Always of a pious disposition, he supported the Society for the Propagation of the Gospel and became a committee member of the South Australian Church Society, formed in 1834 to raise money to build churches and rectories and support United Church of England and Ireland clergymen in the first British colony in which they would not be funded from the public revenue.

In June 1837, through his Adelaide agent (Sir) John Morphett [q.v.2], Leigh bought seven town acres (0.41 ha) and several country sections in the colony. Morphett made them all income producing. In 1840 Leigh donated two town acres between Hindley and Currie streets, bordering what was named Leigh Street, to the S.P.G., with a written declaration of his intention to add 400 acres (161.87 ha) of rural land for a glebe and £2000 to build a church and parsonage on it. Pending this development, the society held Leigh's £2000 in trust. In the early 1840s the rents from the Leigh Street properties provided three-quarters of the Church of England's South Australian income.

Meanwhile, Leigh became interested in the Oxford Movement and in March 1844 joined the Catholic Church. He thereupon asked the S.P.G. that the bulk of the land and money not yet appropriated for Church of England purposes be made available to Francis Murphy [q.v.2], Adelaide's first Catholic bishop. The society agreed. Murphy received 500 acres (202.34 ha) on the Little Parra River and four acres (1.62 ha) in West Adelaide. After build-

ing St Patrick's Church and a residence for himself, the bishop had enough cash left to invest in the Burra copper mine. Leigh had thus rescued two denominations from penury, lessening the dominance that dissenters would otherwise have asserted in South Australia.

Another beneficiary of Leigh's generosity was William Ullathorne [q.v.2], bishop of Birmingham, who started the myth, magnified in Monsignor Frederick Byrne's [q.v.7] *History of the Catholic Church in South Australia* (1896), that Leigh had wanted the Leigh Street acres transferred too, and was 'displeased' when they were not. Though vigorously rebutted—on the evidence of Leigh's correspondence with the S.P.G.—the legend was continued by Labor politician W. J. Denny [q.v.8] and long persisted.

In 1844 the Leigh family moved to Gloucestershire where, consulting the architects Augustus Pugin and Charles Hansom, Leigh had built Woodchester mansion and a church in Woodchester Park. Pope Pius IX, with whom he had had an audience as a young man, appointed him to the Order of St Gregory the Great (grand cross). Leigh died of congestive heart failure on 4 January 1873 at Nymphsfield, survived by his wife and one son and leaving personalty sworn at under £9000. A photograph showed a serious, dignified man, characteristic of his times and social milieu. His portrait in oils was painted in Rome by Caralleri in 1827.

G. H. Jose, *The Church of England in South Australia* (Adel, 1937); J. Gallow, *A Literary and Biographical History, or Bibliographical Dictionary of the English Catholics*, 4, (NY, 1968); B. Condon (ed), *Letters and Documents Supporting Historical Studies of the Catholic Church in Australia* (Adel, 1984); J. Tregenza, *Collegiate School of St Peter Adelaide* (Adel, 1996); *PD* (SA), 13 Nov 1929, p 2008; *Adelaide Church News*, 21 May 1897; Leigh papers (ML); Church of England newsclipping books, SRG 94/10 (SLSA). MARGARET M. PRESS

LESCHEN, HEINRICH ADOLPH (c.1836-1916), gymnastics teacher, was born at Rendsburg, in the Danish duchy of Holstein (Germany), fourth child of Polish-born Christian Heinrich Leschen (1792-1867), who had changed his name from Leszczynski and become a naturalized Dane. After attending the University of Kiel, Schleswig, where he was influenced by the ideas of the charismatic educationist Friedrich Jahn, Adolph trained as a schoolteacher and belonged to a student gymnastics group.

Migrating with his father, older brother and sister in the *Peter Godeffroy*, Leschen reached South Australia in September 1857. He first tried farming, then established the German

School in Wakefield Street, Adelaide, and was also employed at the Adelaide Gymnasium in King William Street, teaching German gymnastics. On 25 February 1862 at the Lutheran Church in Light Square he married Johanna Christina Dithmer. Leschen was naturalized in October. In 1864 he set up his own *Deutschen Turnverein* (gymnastics club), in Flinders Street, which attracted some influential men in Adelaide. When the future chief justice (Sir) Samuel Way [q.v.12], a member of one of Leschen's classes, joined the State Education Board in 1874 he argued for the inclusion of gymnastics in South Australian schools.

Way was responsible for Leschen teaching gymnastics in South Australian model schools during the term of J. L. Parsons [q.v.11] as minister of education from 1881 to 1884. Leschen continued to give demonstrations in many state schools and private colleges and encouraged physical education as an important aspect of a holistic curriculum. His popular annual displays of mass gymnastics at the Jubilee Exhibition Building, in North Terrace, did much to encourage local belief in the combination of character-building, English sports with systematic, European gymnastics as an ideal physical education. In an article in 1884, '*Mens Sana in Corpore Sano*', he wrote: 'Whatever can be said in favour of cricket, football and other games, they do not strengthen and develop the body like the systematic training of gymnastics'.

Employed as gymnastics and German master at the Collegiate School of Saint Peter in 1879-91, Leschen was also a part-time teacher at Prince Alfred College in 1881-92. Both colleges built gymnasiums—replicas of the model *turnhalle* of the Adelaide *Turnverein*. Prince Alfred College *Chronicle* in 1885 claimed that 'few schools in the colonies ... possess so fine a gymnasium ... and so efficient a teacher as Mr Leschen'. He and his third son Hugo (1868-1926), who in 1891-92 studied gymnastics in Germany, pioneered medical massage (physiotherapy) in South Australia in the 1890s, both being employed at the Adelaide Hospital and working in close co-operation with Professor Archibald Watson [q.v.12].

Retiring from his school activities in 1892, Leschen continued teaching German gymnastics at the Adelaide *Turnverein* until 1909. Hugo, an enthusiastic volunteer soldier and sometime major in the cadet corps, succeeded his father as instructor at Prince Alfred College (where he had been educated) and from 1893 continued the annual demonstrations at the exhibition building. By 1900 more than 1500 of his pupils, from various schools, took part in these spectacular displays. Adolph Leschen died on 2 April 1916 in a rest home at Dulwich, survived by his wife and their five sons. An obituarist in the Adelaide *Register* acknowledged him as 'one of South Australia's best known identities' who 'may rightly be termed the father of gymnastics in the State'.

D. M. Horner, *Prince Alfred College Cadet Unit* (Adel, 1964); J. A. Daly, *Elysian Fields* (Adel, 1982) and 'Adolph Leschen: The "Father of Gymnastics" in South Australia', *JHSSA*, no 10, 1982, p 92; R. M. Gibbs, *A History of Prince Alfred College* (Adel, 1984); *Prince Alfred College Chronicle*, 2, no 7, Oct 1885; *Register* (Adel), 18 Apr 1892, p 5, 26 May 1914, p 10, 3 Apr 1916, p 6, 25 Oct 1926, p 13; *Observer* (Adel), 11 Feb 1899, p 41; *Advertiser* (Adel), 3 Apr 1916, p 6; A. Leschen, diary (SRSA).

JOHN A. DALY

LEVVY, FRANCES DEBORAH (1831-1924), animal protection advocate, was born on 14 November 1831 at Penrith, New South Wales, fourth child of Barnett Levey [q.v.2], a Jewish watchmaker and theatre director, and his wife Sarah Emma, née Wilson. Both parents had come free to the colony from London. Barnett died in 1837, and his impoverished widow educated their four children in the country. They became devoutly Christian. Later, Frances and her mother may have lived with the elder daughter Emma (1826-1885), who in 1847 married Dr George Thomas Clarke of Hill View, Penrith. By 1873, when Sarah died, both Emma and Frances had adopted the surname Levvy.

George Clarke died in 1874, and his widow and her sister moved to Newtown in Sydney. Later Frances lived at Woollahara until she purchased Yulah Cottage at Waverley. On 4 January 1884 she became involved with the cause that was to shape and fill the rest of her life: she and Emma founded Australia's first Band of Mercy, to teach children kindness to animals. Frances was reported (1889) as aiming to make children more alert 'to save something, to stop stone throwing at old people, and to induce men to desist from being cruel to the dumb animals under their charge'. Miss Levvy worked energetically to expand her organization. By 1897 she claimed 446 bands with membership numbering 26 000. Permitted to establish bands within New South Wales public schools, she was paid £50 per annum by the Department of Public Instruction. Each year she visited up to sixty schools, organizing and judging an essay competition that elicited hundreds of entries. She also engaged in voluminous correspondence with leaders of bands outside Sydney.

In December 1886 Levvy helped to found and was honorary secretary of a women's branch of the Royal Society for the Prevention of Cruelty to Animals. During the 1890s, however, one of her inspectors was convicted of extortion. This led to a humiliating public rejection by the British R.S.P.C.A. in 1896, and Levvy's organization became the Women's

Society for the Prevention of Cruelty to Animals. In 1899 its committee presented her with a purse of sovereigns. She resisted amalgamation with the Animals' Protection Society of New South Wales in 1902.

Levvy's greatest capacity was for writing, and her major achievement was her editorship of the *Band of Mercy and Humane Journal of New South Wales*. Each month from July 1887 until August 1923 she presented a publication, of remarkably even quality, for both children and adults. The magazine reported the activities of the bands and the W.S.P.C.A. on behalf of animals, such as deputations for a lethal chamber for the painless destruction of stray dogs and fund-raising for a horse ambulance. Submitted articles were subjected to her energetic editorial comment, while she wrote many of the poems and stories herself. Full of passionate concern for animals and reflecting her deeply held religious convictions, the magazine was a rare record of a moderate animal protectionist's personal philosophy and life.

Levvy also belonged to the Girls' Friendly Society and the Church of England Temperance Society. She donated money to the London Society, an organization for promoting Christianity among Jews. In her later years she was blind, bedridden and almost deaf, but continued her magazine. She died on 29 November 1924 at Waverley and was buried in the Anglican cemetery at Randwick. Sir Joseph Carruthers [q.v.7], former minister for education, and the R.S.P.C.A. honoured her with the establishment of the Frances Levvy essay competition. Her will asked that she be buried with oil paintings of her beloved sister.

H. Radi (ed), *200 Australian Women* (Syd, 1988); *Church of England Record*, 21 Nov 1884, p 163, 27 Feb 1885, p 261, 1 Jan 1887, p 5, 18 Jan 1890, p 6; *Band of Mercy and Humane Jnl of NSW*, 14 Sept 1896, p 101, 27 Sept 1911, p 10; *R.S.P.C.A. Jnl*, 7, no 2, 20 Dec 1924, p 10; *SMH*, 18 Nov 1885, p 6; *Daily Telegraph* (Syd), 16 Dec 1889, p 3; J. MacCulloch, Creatures of Culture: The Animal Protection and Preservation Movements in Sydney, 1880-1930 (Ph.D. thesis, Univ Syd, 1994).   J. MacCulloch

LEWIS, GEORGE BENJAMIN WILLIAM (1818-1906), circus owner and theatrical entrepreneur, was born on 19 November 1818 in London, and baptized in St Clement Dane's Church of England, Westminster, son of William Lewis and his wife Susan. George joined Ducrow's circus as a child and became a gymnast and ringmaster in Hengler's circus. After touring Europe in 1849-51, he claimed to have earned £30 000. With this fortune he came to Victoria late in 1853, reaching Geelong accompanied by a 14-year-old boy called Tom, his pupil and part of a 'Risley' gymnastic act. Late next year, in partnership with the American hotelkeeper Thomas Mooney, Lewis opened Astley's Amphitheatre, Spring Street, Melbourne, a brick and timber structure for equestrian drama and circus. This venture failed and the building later became the first Princess Theatre.

After moderate success touring the goldfields with his circus, Lewis took his company to China in 1859. Back in Melbourne the troupe appeared at Coppin's [q.v.3] Cremorne Gardens. Abandoning equestrian shows in 1863, he formed a dramatic company, which toured British communities in Asia. At Shanghai in 1864 he married Rose Edouin Bryer (1844-1925), an English-born actress known as Rose Edouin. From a talented theatrical family, she had been born on 29 January 1844 at Brighthelmston (Brighton), Sussex, and had performed in Victoria with the American comedian Joseph Jefferson [q.v.4]. There were to be at least seven children of the marriage.

From 1867 the Lewises opened seasonal dismountable theatres on the Calcutta maidan, India. Until early 1876 the couple and their company commuted from Australia to China and India, playing Shakespeare and melodramas such as *East Lynne*. Rose played roles ranging from Romeo to Lady Macbeth. Their last season (1875-76) featured J. C. Williamson and Maggie Moore [qq.v.6,5]. Returning to Melbourne, in November 1876 Lewis became the first lessee of the Academy of Music (Bijou Theatre), Bourke Street. By 1878 he had both the Bijou and the Opera House, with Rose as 'directress'. Their connection with the Bijou ended in 1885. During the 1880s Mrs Lewis opened a school of elocution and formed a company of juveniles who starred in her productions of *H.M.S. Pinafore* in Melbourne and Sydney. In the same decade the couple leased theatres in Sydney and in New Zealand. Lewis's success was reflected by his investment in Melbourne property; he owned several houses in St Kilda Road. By the late 1880s they were living in semi-retirement.

Lewis lost heavily in the depression of the 1890s. Rose returned to the stage and in 1892 had success in London at her brother Willie Edouin's Strand Theatre. In Australia again after a tour of South Africa, she continued her school which, with her stage appearances in Sydney, Melbourne, Adelaide and Launceston, Tasmania—where she played Hamlet —became the couple's main source of income. In 1905 Melbourne's theatre community, led by Williamson, noticed that 'G.B.W.' had fallen on hard times and held a benefit for him. Lewis was described in old age as tall, 'straight as a dart', with a 'beautiful speaking voice'. He died on 18 July 1906 in the Alfred Hospital and was buried in Melbourne cemetery. His wife and one son survived him. Rose returned to the London stage, playing character roles such as the nurse in *Romeo and Juliet*, and died on 24 August 1925 at Harrogate, Yorkshire.

Vic Theatres Trust, *Newsletter*, May 1998; M. Colligan, 'Circus in the Theatre: Astley's Amphitheatre, Melbourne 1854-1857', *A'sian Drama Studies*, no 35, Oct 1999, p 31; *Argus* (Melb), 22 Sept 1854, 28 Sept 1854, p 5, 22 Jan 1869, p 5, 31 Oct 1869; *Times* (Lond), 27 Nov 1855, p 10, 25 Aug 1925, p 12; *Englishman* (Calcutta), 18 Sept 1867, p 3, 23 Nov 1875, p 4, 29 Jan 1876, p 1; *Australasian*, 18 Sept 1869, p 370, 6 Dec 1873, p 723, 21 July 1906, p 146; *Leader* (Melb), 28 Feb 1885; *SMH*, 29 Oct 1898, p 4; *Punch* (Melb), 1 June 1905, pp 714 & 731; *Age* (Melb), 19 July 1906, p 5.   MIMI COLLIGAN

LIGHTFOOT, LOUISA MARY (1902-1979), dancer, choreographer and impresario, was born on 22 May 1902 at Yangerry, near Warrnambool, Victoria, fourth child and third daughter of Victorian-born parents Charles Lightfoot, schoolteacher, and his wife Mary, née Graham. Louise was always fond of dancing, but could see no way to practise it as a profession. At the Catholic Ladies' College, East Melbourne, she won exhibitions in drawing and mathematics, and in 1920 her father sent her to study architecture at the University of Melbourne. She passed her final subjects in the diploma of architecture in 1923, the only woman to have then done so.

Lightfoot was tall, slender and graceful, striking in profile, beautiful rather than pretty. While still a student, she began a four-year apprenticeship in the innovative architectural office of Walter Burley Griffin and Marion Mahony Griffin [qq.v.9] in Melbourne. Late in 1924 the Griffins moved to Castlecrag, Sydney, a new suburb intended as an ideal community in anthroposophic harmony with nature and culture. Lightfoot went too, as companion and reluctant cook for Marion, as well as draughtswoman and designer in the Sydney office where, in Walter's words, she showed 'resourcefulness and trustworthiness, as well as artistic comprehension and diligence'.

Encouraged by Marion Griffin, Lightfoot began to study 'Eurythmic' Greek dancing, and found it 'a little dull'. On Anna Pavlova's first tour of Australia in 1926, Louise found her fusion of classical technique and romantic emotion a 'revelation'. Through the tour Lightfoot met the character dancer Misha Burlakov and persuaded him to teach her the Russian mazurka; later she wrote that her 'real happiness started' when she danced with him in peasant costume and red leather boots.

She studied enough classical ballet to begin giving classes for children. In October 1928 she left the Griffins. She and Burlakov worked together preparing folk-dances for charity performances and amateur opera. After classes in the technique of Mary Wigman, Lightfoot added dances in that starkly modern style. By 1931 the 'Lightfoot-Burlakov Classic Dance School' became the 'First Australian Ballet' for a staging of *Coppélia* in the Savoy Theatre, choreographed by Lightfoot from a score and production notes discovered in the J. C. Williamson [q.v.6] library.

Lightfoot choreographed and produced several ballets a year in the 1930s, sometimes from her memory of productions seen in Australia, often from descriptions in books and magazines. She also composed original ballets, including a set of abstract compositions 'in the modern expressive style', performed to percussion, and *The Fruits of Forgetfulness*, inspired by the paintings of Gaugin, set to a locally written *avant-garde* score. Pupils remembered her as aloof, a strict disciplinarian and an inspired choreographer.

In 1937 she and Burlakov visited London and Paris, securing the rights to perform a number of new ballets including Diaghilev's *The Blue God*. Lightfoot took classes with experts in modern, Spanish and Hindu dance; she was particularly impressed by the performance of the Indian Uday Shankar troupe and told the *Woman's Weekly* that she intended to create a new Indian ballet on her return to Australia. A two-week stopover in India extended to five months as she travelled to Kalamandalam in Kerala, where she began her study of the complex traditions of Kathakali dance.

After returning to Sydney early in 1938 and producing her own 'authentic' version of *The Blue God*, Lightfoot dissolved her partnership with Burlakov and went back to India. In the next half-decade she lived in Kerala and Tamil Nadu, learning the different techniques of the sacred dance styles Kathakali and Bharata Natya, keeping herself by teaching classical ballet to children of the Raj. She became a great publicist of Indian dance (despised or ignored by Indian high culture), organized tours by dancing troupes in South India and Ceylon (Sri Lanka), worked with the filmmaker K. Subramanyam at Madras (Chennai) and published widely in the Indian press.

In 1947 Lightfoot brought the young Kathakali dancer Shivaram to Australia and trained a group of Australian dancers to work with him. Next year they introduced Kathakali dance to the British stage. In 1949 for the Australian National Theatre she presented Shivaram in a ballet of her own design, *Indra Vijayam*, and in 1950 he again toured successfully. Performances in Japan, the United States of America and Canada more often took the form of lecture-demonstrations in universities and galleries, with Lightfoot providing commentary. Shivaram made a series of visits to Australia, the last in 1976.

In 1951 Lightfoot had gone to the mountain state of Manipur to learn a third tradition of sacred dance. Here she discovered and popularized a form older than the Hindu traditions. She published a monograph, *Dance-Rituals of Manipur* (New Delhi, 1958); her recording of songs and ritual music was released in the American Ethnic Folkways series in 1960 as *Ritual Music of Manipur*. Lightfoot organized Australian, Japanese and North American tours for dancers and drummers from Manipur and Kerala.

From the late 1950s she worked with Shivaram to establish an Indian dance school in San Francisco, U.S.A. From 1965 she lived and worked at the yoga ashram of Swami Vishnudevananda in Montreal, Canada. Lightfoot never married. In 1968 she retired to Oakleigh, Victoria, where she continued to train dancers in the Indian styles. She died on 18 May 1979 at Malvern and was buried in new Cheltenham cemetery. The Cochin *Indian Express* lamented the death of 'Kathakali's Australian mother'.

E. H. Pask, *Enter the Colonies Dancing* (Melb, 1979) and *Ballet in Australia* (Melb, 1982); J. Turnbull and P. Y. Navaretti (eds), *The Griffins in Australia and India* (Melb, 1998); *Dancing Times*, Mar 1939, p 742; *Brolga*, no 2, June 1995, p 7, no 15, Dec 2001, pp 22 & 26; *Dance Australia*, no 94, Feb/Mar 1998, p 40; *Sruti*, May 2001; A. Card, History in Motion, Ph.D. thesis, Univ of Syd, 1999, pp 119-30; L. Lightfoot, Memories of the Burley Griffins (ts, folio 4, Anthroposophy collection, Willoughby Library, Syd); Lightfoot dance collection (Monash Univ School of Music Archive).

MARY LOUISE LIGHTFOOT
MARIAN QUARTLY

LINDSAY, ROSE (1885-1978), artist's model, printmaker and author, was born on 5 July 1885 at Gosford, New South Wales, and registered as Rosa, third of nine children of English-born parents John Francis Soady, labourer, and his wife Rosanna, née Gale. Although Catholic, her parents kept religion out of their family's daily lives. Rose was raised in bushland near the Lane Cove River, in the Sydney suburb of Longueville.

Distinguished by her fine, pale skin, deep-set almond eyes, rosebud lips and luscious dark hair, Rose was an artist's model *par excellence*. Never nymph-like, her body possessed a muscular force suggesting her confident character. In 1902 Julian Rossi Ashton introduced her to the artist Norman Lindsay [qq.v.7,10]. She became Lindsay's principal model, and then secret lover. His marriage ended and he moved to London in 1909; next year she joined him.

Rose modelled for Sydney Long, Dattilo Rubbo, Sydney Ure Smith, Harold Cazneaux [qq.v.10,11,7] and Ashton, among others, as well as for hundreds of Lindsay's drawings, etchings and paintings. She posed for his 'Crucified Venus'—a pen-and-ink drawing shown at the Society of Artists' exhibition in Melbourne in 1913—in which a firm, sensuous body was nailed to the crucifix. More shocking to some was the furrowed brow of the figure, displaying a pained, even ecstatic, expression. Scandalized reactions from church figures and the press led the Melbourne committee to remove the work from public view. This incurred the wrath of Ashton, president of the Society of Artists, who threatened to withdraw all the New South Wales paintings from the exhibit. 'Venus' was rehung within the week.

Late in 1912 Rose and Norman had purchased a house and built a studio near Springwood, in the Blue Mountains, which was visited by such well-known figures as 'Banjo' Paterson, Henry Lawson, Dame Nellie Melba and Miles Franklin [qq.v.11,10,8]. On 14 January 1920 at Hawthorn, Strathfield, Rose married Norman with Presbyterian forms. His divorce was made absolute two weeks later. Their children Janet and Helen were born in 1920 and 1922 respectively. Committed to Norman as both his muse and collaborator, Rose spent many hours at the etching press, perfecting her printmaking skills. In addition, she efficiently managed his career, while working on her own creative interests.

Rayner Hoff [q.v.9] in 1926 sculpted a statue of Rose striking a signature pose—with defiant throw of the neck, arched spine, and the back of her hand resting provocatively on her hip; significantly, she was depicted wearing her wedding ring. Rose and Norman travelled to the United States of America and England in 1931-32. In 1940 Rose accompanied a collection of Norman's water-colours, pen-drawings, etchings and oils to the U.S.A. A fire in a freight train destroyed nearly all these works and next year, distraught, Rose returned to Springwood.

From about 1958 she lived with her daughter Janet at Hunters Hill, Sydney. In her late seventies Rose began to write. *Ma and Pa* (1963) was the first of her two volumes of autobiography. The second was *Model Wife* (1967). They were reprinted in 2001 as *Rose Lindsay: A Model Life*, edited by Lin Bloomfield. Her books, which revealed a particular interest in bodies, adolescent and adult, recounted how she balanced the demands of home and children with managing an often difficult marital relationship. The books also contributed significantly to the Lindsay legend.

Norman died in 1969. In February 1973 the property at Springwood was purchased by the National Trust of Australia and opened to the public as the Norman Lindsay Gallery and Museum. Rose Lindsay died on 23 May 1978 at the Caroline Chisholm [q.v.1] Nursing Home, Lane Cove, and was cremated. Her two daughters survived her. She was fondly remembered for her dry wit and vivacious temperament.

J. Hetherington, *Norman Lindsay* (Melb, 1973); *Norman Lindsay, Master Craftsman Etcher: Rose Lindsay, Master Etching Printmaker*, exhibition catalogue (Syd, 1974); *SMH*, 24 Nov 1969, p 6, 24 May 1978, p 8; H. de Berg, taped interview with R. Lindsay (1965, NL).   ANA CARDEN-COYNE

LING, MARY (1865-1953), writer and parliamentary candidate, was born on 6 January 1865 on a farm north of Braidwood, New South Wales, fifth child of English migrants George Bentley and his wife Mary Ann, née Moore. Mary's father tried his hand at farming, gold digging and dairying. Although she attended three small bush schools, she and her two younger brothers were educated mainly by their mother. Her parents subscribed to religious and secular journals and joined the Braidwood Mechanics' Institute library.

Mary later recalled the physical freedom of her childhood in the bush, the hard labour of farm work and regular Methodist religious observance in an affectionate family. She first visited Sydney in 1879 with her sister to see the Sydney International Exhibition. When their money ran out, for six months they worked as domestic servants, a humiliating experience. By next year the family had settled at Marrickville, and Mary became a nursemaid in the household of Colonel Charles F. Roberts [q.v.6]. Later she established a dressmaking business at Homebush. On 3 September 1889 at the Salvation Army barracks, Burwood, she married with Wesleyan Methodist forms Henry Hill Ling, a postal clerk. The marriage was childless. She and Henry separated in 1897 and divorced in 1906.

A niece later described Mary as 'a compulsive writer of poems, short stories, fact and fiction, using all her resources to buy pen and paper'. A novel she had written was rejected by London publishers about 1890. *A Woman of Mars; or, Australia's Enfranchised Woman* by 'Mary Ann Moore-Bentley' was published in Sydney in 1901. A committed follower of Henry George [q.v.4], she joined the Sydney Single Tax League, formed that year, addressed its Georgian evening in December 1902 and promoted his views in her *Sketched from Life* (self-published 1903). One of eight women appointed to the league's executive council, she attended only two meetings.

Women in New South Wales were to vote for the first time in December 1903 (for the Commonwealth elections). Mary joined the newly formed Women's Social and Political League and stood for the Senate—as Mary Ann Moore Bentley—but failed to gain the league's support. She spoke at Granville Town Hall and addressed open-air meetings in the Hawkesbury area and at Bathurst and Lithgow. Introducing herself as 'the working woman's candidate', she said she was 'a democrat first', who believed that 'Australian democracy will yet lead the world'. The only tax should be that on land values. She supported free trade, advocated the abolition of State parliaments and proposed the establishment of a state bank. Her books were sold at her meetings to defray expenses. In Sydney she spoke on street corners, on hotel balconies and in the Domain. Appearing first on the ballot paper (under Bentley), she received 18 924 votes, some 400 more than the State's only other female Senate candidate, Mrs Martel [q.v.], and 166 793 votes short of being elected in third position.

By 1906 Mary was living at Bangor, near Menai, in 'a small ... two-roomed hut'. Relations with her brothers—her nearest neighbours—grew increasingly strained. She continued to write, the subject matter becoming increasingly esoteric. In January 1917 her *Psychological Interpretation of the Gospel* was published in Boston, United States of America. Mary sailed to America later that year, hoping to obtain a publisher for 'An Original Hypothesis of the Origin of Life'. The following February, alone in a New York boarding house, she sought assistance to return to Australia and was repatriated at government expense, reaching Sydney on 7 May 1918. She blamed the U.S.A.'s 'Secret Service' and 'misrepresentation' by the Australian government (because of her anti-conscription activities) for her failure in America.

Tall and slender, Ling was described as 'a woman of pleasing presence'; she retired to the isolation of Menai, at intervals issuing in typescript children's stories and poems and an attempt at a fortnightly journal, 'Something to Amuse'. Her last ten years were spent in the Mental Hospital, Stockton, Newcastle, where she died on 1 September 1953. She was buried in Stockton cemetery with Methodist forms. *Journey to Durran Durra 1852-1885*, by Mary Moore-Bentley, her memoir written about 1935, was published in 1983.

Evening News (Syd), 19 Dec 1902, p 3, 16 Mar 1906, p 4; *Daily Telegraph* (Syd), 16 Oct 1903, p 5, 6 Nov 1903, p 6; *SMH*, 17 Oct 1903, p 11; *Windsor and Richmond Gazette*, 31 Oct 1903, p 9, 7 Nov 1903, pp 3, 9, 13; *Bathurst Daily Times*, 6 Nov 1903, p 2;

Hawkesbury Herald, 6 Nov 1903, p 7; *Nepean Times*, 7 Nov 1903, p 4; *Lithgow Mercury*, 10 Nov 1903, p 2; A1, item 1919/1567, A11804, items 1918/304 and 1919/59 (NAA, Canb); Freetrade and Land Values League, Minutes, 1901-05 (ML).

MARGARET BETTISON

LLOYD, JESSIE MARY (1883-1960), temperance campaigner, was born on 13 June 1883 at Wolverhampton, Staffordshire, England, daughter of Harry Hunt, iron-plate worker, and his wife Louisa, née Griffiths. The family migrated to Melbourne in the *Lusitania* in May 1884. On 24 October 1905 at St Hilary's Church of England, East Kew, Jessie married Robert Griffiths, a company manager also from Wolverhampton. They had three children before Robert died in 1916. On 22 August 1923 at the Methodist Church, Kew, Jessie married Rev. George Samuel Lloyd, a Methodist minister and a widower with one surviving child; he was stationed at Stawell.

Jessie had joined the Woman's Christian Temperance Union as a young woman. Her activities focused particularly on educating children about the importance of teetotalism for the health and the welfare of society. One important W.C.T.U. programme for children was the elocution contest, in which they would recite poems or prose on the subject of temperance. Mrs Lloyd (most often known as Griffiths Lloyd) was the Australasian superintendent of this department in 1921-30 and served on W.C.T.U. education committees that aimed to teach children teetotalism through the schools and W.C.T.U.-endorsed literature. She wrote regular articles for the Victorian *White Ribbon Signal* and contributed often to its home hints page, believing that the best way to produce a generation of teetotallers was by reaching out to the mothers.

In addition, Lloyd served as recording secretary to the Victorian W.C.T.U. in 1913-15 and in 1920-23. She was vice-president (1929) and in 1930-33 president. By then, the organization had a membership of almost 10 000, and it held the ambitious aim of procuring the prohibition of alcohol in Australia. A State poll taken in 1930, at which forty-three per cent of electors had voted for a dry Victoria, gave hope that this would eventually be possible. In 1933 she was elected vice-president of the Australasian (later the National) W.C.T.U. and was president from 1936.

After stepping down as president in 1945, Lloyd continued her work of promoting alcohol awareness in mothers' groups, especially in working-class areas. As superintendent of the Victorian W.C.T.U.'s peace and arbitration department, she co-operated with other peace and church organizations in petitioning the government for progressive disarmament. The W.C.T.U. delegate at the 1957 convention for the Australian Association for Peace, on her return she persuaded the executive to protest to the British government against atomic testing on Australian territory. In her later years she campaigned for regulations for food and hygiene. Lloyd was not a single-issue campaigner and did not see alcohol as the only scourge of humanity: at the National W.C.T.U. convention of 1960 she stated that the greatest problem of the day was inadequate food for the world's people.

Recognized for her fine oratorical skills and her musical talents, she played the piano accompaniment at meetings and, with Mrs H. C. Herbert, compiled a W.C.T.U. songbook. Predeceased by her husband, Mrs Lloyd died at her home at Blackburn on 24 October 1960, and her body was donated to the anatomy department of the University of Melbourne; a service was held at Blackburn Methodist Church. Two daughters and a son from her first marriage survived her and inherited her estate, sworn for probate at £10 719.

I. McCorkindale (ed), *Pioneer Pathways* (Melb, 1948); J. Pargeter, *For God, Home and Humanity* (Adel, 1995); WCTU (Vic), *Annual Report*, 1920-60; *White Ribbon Signal*, Nov 1960.

ANNA E. BLAINEY

LOCK, MARIA (c.1805-1878), Aboriginal landowner, was born at Richmond Bottoms, on the eastern floodplain of the Hawkesbury River, daughter of Yarramundi, 'Chief of the Richmond Tribes'. The family belonged to the Boorooberongal clan of the D(h)arug people. On 28 December 1814 Yarramundi's clan attended the inaugural annual conference hosted for the Aborigines by Governor Macquarie [q.v.2]. On the same date Maria was admitted to the Native Institution, for tuition by William and Elizabeth Shelley [q.v.2].

In 1819 the *Sydney Gazette* reported that an Aboriginal girl of 14 had won first prize in the anniversary school examination, ahead of twenty children from the Native Institution and almost 100 European students. That girl was probably Maria, who was reported by teachers to be well in advance of other students.

At the end of 1822 Maria was being 'maternally treated' by Anne, the wife of Rev. Thomas Hassall [q.v.1], and living in their household at Parramatta when she married Dicky, a son of Bennelong [q.v.1] and a member of the Richmond clan through his mother. He too had been in the Native Institution, but had moved to the household of the Wesleyan missioner William Walker [q.v.2], and was baptized Thomas Walker Coke. Within weeks of his marriage he became ill and died. He was buried on 1 February 1823 at St John's Church of England, Parramatta, where on 26 January 1824 Maria married Robert Lock (1800-1854), an illiterate, convict carpenter who had been assigned to work on the construction of the new Native Institution buildings at Black Town (Blacktown) in 1823. The marriage was the first officially sanctioned union between a convict and an Aboriginal woman, and Robert was assigned to her. The Locks settled on a small farm at the Native Institution, but later moved to the employ of Rev. Robert Cartwright [q.v.1] at Liverpool.

The legacy of Maria's education became evident in March 1831, when she petitioned Governor Darling [q.v.1] for her deceased brother Colcy's (Colcbcc) [q.v.1, Colebe] grant at Blacktown, opposite the Native Institution. She asserted that she and her husband were entitled to earn 'an honest livelihood, and provide a comfortable home for themselves, and their increasing family'. In 1831 forty acres (16.2 ha) 'as near to your present residence as suitable vacant land can be found' were granted to Robert on Maria's behalf, but Cartwright frustrated this claim, as he felt it was injurious to the established buildings on his adjoining allotment. Maria persisted, and in 1833 another forty acres was granted to her at Liverpool in Robert's name. She received Colebee's thirty-acre (12.1 ha) grant in 1843.

The Locks returned to Blacktown in 1844, acquiring a further thirty acres there. Of their ten children born between 1827 and 1844, nine survived to adultood. Robert died in 1854. Maria died on 6 June 1878 at Windsor and was buried beside Robert at St Bartholomew's Church of England, Prospect. Her burial registration, which read 'Last of the Aboriginals from Blacktown', wrongly gave her birth date as 1794. Her lands at Liverpool and Blacktown were divided equally among her surviving children, and were occupied by her descendants until about 1920, by which time the freehold land was considered to be an Aboriginal reserve (Plumpton) and was revoked by the Aborigines Protection Board. Dozens of families in 2005 trace their descent through Maria to Yarramundi and to his father Gomebeeree, an unbroken link stretching back to the 1740s.

J. Brook and J. L. Kohen, *The Parramatta Native Institution and the Black Town* (Syd, 1991); J. Kohen, *The Darug and their Neighbours* (Syd, 1993); *Syd Gazette*, 31 Dec 1814, p 2, 17 Apr 1819, p 2; *Hobart Town Gazette and Van Diemen's Land Advertiser*, 15 Mar 1823, p 2; J. Kohen, From the Mountains to the Sea: Genealogies in the Sydney Area (ms, 2002, held by author, Macq Univ); Missionary papers, Bonwick transcripts 50, vol 127, p 480 (ML); Colonial Secretary's Correspondence re land: petition Maria Lock 14 Mar 1831, 2/7908 (SRNSW).

NAOMI PARRY

LOGIC (c.1855-1903), stockman and tracker, whose Aboriginal name was Pinba, was probably a Dieri man, born in the far north-east of South Australia. By the mid-1870s he was working as a stockman on stations in the Lake Eyre basin and across the border in Queensland. While riding the boundaries of Tinga Tingana station on the Strzelecki Creek in March 1878, Logic and his partner, a European stockman named Cornelius Mulhall, began to argue. As the dispute escalated, Mulhall stockwhipped Logic and shot him in the back, whereupon he stabbed Mulhall to death.

Logic escaped arrest by fleeing across the Stoney Desert to the Diamantina River region in Queensland. Later he returned to Strzelecki Creek and in October 1880 was recognized and arrested. Next February in the Supreme Court, Adelaide, Logic was tried for murder. Despite supportive character evidence from a number of European pastoral workers, he was found guilty of manslaughter and sentenced to fourteen years hard labour. Prison records described him as 5 ft 5 ins (165 cm) tall and stocky, weighing 11 st. 7 lb. (73 kg), married with two children. As one of his upper teeth was missing, he had probably gone through the early stages of initiation. He was a model inmate of Yatala Labour Prison, with no breaches of discipline recorded against him. In October 1885 a petition seeking a remission of his sentence was being prepared for Governor Sir William Robinson [q.v.6]. But Logic pre-empted the decision. On the evening of 15 October, while working in the prison quarry, he and another prisoner set explosive charges in the rock-face. Once the job was complete, his companion ran back to the work-gang but Logic used the confusion of the blast to escape.

As he made his way north, back to his country, local farmers helped him, providing food and water, boots, a butcher's knife and a blanket. Settlers 'gave bread, meat and tea cheerfully, and tobacco is not grudged either'. It was even reported that he was given a brown tweed suit. Logic's case became a *cause célèbre*, with letters of support daily appearing in the press and editorials suggesting that the chase be given up. On 10 December he was recaptured with the aid of Aboriginal trackers near Parachilna in the southern Flinders Ranges. Support for his cause grew. As he was transported to Adelaide by train, crowds gathered at stations *en route* to glimpse him. Letters to the press continued to call for his release, and petitions were organized asking the governor to exercise his prerogative of mercy.

The extraordinary campaign succeeded. Just before Christmas 1885 by order of the governor, advised by the Downer [q.v.8] government, Logic was released. He was put on a train to Port Augusta and sent on to Beltana, completing his trek home to Tinga Tingana station on foot. He remained in the Innamincka area and occasionally worked as a tracker for the police. Logic died on 23 December 1903 at Innamincka. The Adelaide *Observer* published a short obituary under the heading 'Death of a Notorious Blackfellow'.

R. Foster, 'Logic's Unexpected Celebrity', in J. Simpson and L. Hercus (eds), *History in Portraits* (Canb, 1998); *Observer* (Adel), 9 Jan 1904, 'Country supplement', p 1, 16 Jan 1904, p 25.

ROBERT FOSTER

LORD, MARIA (c.1780-1859), convict and entrepreneur, was born in England, daughter of Robert Riseley and his wife Mary. Tried on 9 August 1802 at Surrey Assizes for stealing from a dwelling house, Maria was transported for seven years, reaching Sydney in the *Experiment* on 24 June 1804.

On 25 June next year she gave birth to a daughter; the father was recorded as John Thompson, but the child was raised as Caroline Maria Lord. John Pascoe Fawkner claimed that Edward Lord [qq.v.1,2], a well-connected Welsh marine officer who had arrived in Van Diemen's Land in 1804, had chosen Maria Risley from a line-up of convict women at the Female Factory at Parramatta. She was in Hobart Town by 22 December 1805. Until she was pardoned in 1808, Maria seems to have been assigned to Lord as his convict servant, although shortly after her arrival she opened a store with goods brought from Sydney. A daughter was born in 1806 but died after two days, and another was born in 1808; both were named Elizabeth Riseley. Maria married Lord in Hobart on 8 October that year, after she had been granted a free pardon. Five more children followed between 1810 and 1819.

In 1810 David Collins [q.v.1] died in office, and Edward was briefly acting lieutenant-governor. He then sailed to England, resigned his commission and returned with his own ship stocked with £30 000 worth of goods. Maria and their children had remained in Sydney—a son was baptized there in March 1812. Edward reached Sydney next March, and the family resumed business and trading interests in Hobart Town.

While Edward concentrated on acquiring land and capital, Maria expanded her retail interests, forming partnerships with her brother John Risley, who arrived in the colony in 1819. From 1816 Edward travelled regularly to England, often with one or more of his children, who were left there with relations or in schools. During his absence, Maria acted as his agent and ran and extended his business, various well-stocked properties and two hotels. By 1820 she reputedly controlled over a third of colonial resources, holding monopolies for the supply of wheat and meat and a portion of the profitable rum trade. Socially, she was recognized as the wife of one of the colony's richest men.

In August 1823 Dr Samuel Hood replaced Maria as her husband's agent and she announced that she was retiring and leaving for England; however, she moved only to the country, near Longford. Hood advertised in July 1824 that he was not authorized to pay her debts. In October Edward returned to Hobart Town, where he successfully charged Charles Rowcroft, who had been frequently in the company of Maria, with criminal conversation. Immediately after the trial, Lord went back to England, taking his youngest daughter with him. Rowcroft also left the colony. Back in Hobart Town, in 1825 Maria opened a retail shop and a butchery. Edward reappeared briefly in 1828; his convict servant Ann Fry named him as the father of her child. He had also established another family, with five children, in England.

Maria continued in business on a smaller scale, and also ran a boarding house in the 1830s. She later moved to Bothwell, where she operated a trading store. She died there on 22 July 1859.

A. Alexander, *Governors' Ladies* (Hob, 1987); H. Radi (ed), *200 Australian Women* (Syd, 1988); P. Tardiff, *Notorious Strumpets and Dangerous Girls* (Syd, 1990); K. Daniels, *Convict Women* (Syd, 1998); Tas Hist Research Assn, *Papers and Procs*, 20, no 2, June 1973, p 98; D. Snowden, Women and Work in Van Diemen's Land (B.A. Hons thesis, Univ Tas, 1982).

DIANNE SNOWDEN

LORD, ROBERT PERCY (1878-1938), sheep breeder, was born on 28 January 1878 at Gympie, Queensland, eldest of eight children of Alfred Percy Lord (d.1927), farmer, later bank manager, and his wife Catherine Annie Louise, née Hillcoat. Alfred's grandfather was Simeon Lord [q.v.2]. Educated at Mr Marks's school, Brisbane, and in 1893 at Brisbane Grammar School, Robert entered pastoral work when his father bought Kiah Lake, near Berridale, New South Wales, in 1894. Later Robert and other family members managed or owned properties in the Narrabri and Wee Waa district.

In 1906 A. P. Lord bought Victoria Downs, 30 000 acres (12 000 ha), near Morven in south-western Queensland. Robert became manager, then a partner with his brothers and in 1922 sole owner. At Beecroft, Sydney, on 10 July 1907 he had married with Presbyterian forms Nelsie Charlotte Wicks. They had four daughters. Nelsie died in childbirth in 1916. On 8 February 1921 at St James's

Church of England, Toowoomba, Queensland, Robert married Ethel Violet Sefton.

Lord led the establishment of a stud merino flock on Victoria Downs in 1911. The foundation stock, of Peppin [q.v.5] blood, was from T. Millear's Deniliquin Stud Park, with some additional rams from Wanganella Estate. Later Lord also bought rams from E. E. I. Body's Bundemar and F. B. S. Falkiner's [qq.v.7,8] Haddon Rig studs. He steadily reiterated his goal: to produce sheep that had plain bodies, large frames, strong backs and hardy constitutions, bred in Queensland for Queensland conditions. Victoria Downs wool was predominantly of medium fibre, but Lord was content for some to be of stronger type. The Lord brothers also set up a stud of Shorthorn cattle, with purchases of stock from about 1917 to 1921. Eventually, however, the Shorthorn stud could not maintain its place against studs in the southern Darling Downs and coastal regions.

Through the later 1920s and the 1930s Victoria Downs was regularly described as Queensland's leading merino stud. Its rams were normally priced top or second at annual ram sales in Queensland, competing against New South Wales studs. Land legislation in 1927 gave concessions that promoted the establishment of larger stud flocks in Queensland. Contemporary discussion could well have used Lord's station as a model.

When the Queensland Merino Stud Sheepbreeders' Association was formed in 1934, Lord was elected its president unopposed. The dedication and optimism of his remarks in the association's *Foundation Souvenir Book* (1935) offset his down-to-earth listing—at the first annual meeting—of their problems: drought, blowflies, 'dogs' and taxes.

Lord was often a vice-president or councillor of public bodies centred on Charleville, such as the Murweh Shire Council, Central Warrego Pastoral and Agricultural Association and Warrego Graziers' Association. He led the renaissance of the Morven Cottage Hospital under the Bush Nursing Association in 1929. With a neat figure, moustached, he was an enthusiastic sportsman, particularly enjoying cricket. Visitors described the friendly hospitality and good humour of the 'bright household' at Victoria Downs.

Robert Lord died of a cerebrovascular accident on 29 January 1938 in Sydney and was buried in the Anglican cemetery at Manly. His wife and children survived him. A championship trophy at the Queensland State Sheep Show was named after him. Descendants, the Roberts family, still held Victoria Downs in 2005.

M. J. Fox, *The History of Queensland*, 2 (Brisb, 1921); *Queensland Merino Stud Sheepbreeders' Association Souvenir Book* (1935 and 1983); M. Roberts (ed), *Morven* (Morven, Qld, 1987); C. Massy, *The Australian Merino* (Melb, 1990); *Dalgety's Review*, July 1911, p 57; *Pastoral Review*, Feb 1921, p 160, June 1930, p 537, Feb 1938, p 131; *Graziers' Review*, Feb 1923, p 1153; *Qld Country Life*, 3 Feb 1938, p 4.

S. J. ROUTH

LORENZINI, AUGUSTO LEOPOLDO FRANCESCO (1852-1921), artist and decorator, was born on 3 August 1852 in Rome, son of Giovachino Lorenzini, engineer, and his wife Santa, née Tinbastari. Augusto's education, including art training, was in Rome and there in 1873 he married 18-year-old Maria Boleta. Late in 1879, after a sojourn in Paris, Lorenzini travelled to London where he established himself as a decorative artist and teacher of decorative fine art with a studio in Newman Street, off Oxford Street. He took on some specialist commissions for the house painting and decorating firm of Thomas Bates & Co. and was known among the staff there as 'Tangerini', almost certainly a reference to his red hair.

In 1883 the Lorenzinis left London for Sydney, possibly induced to emigrate by Charles James Roberts [q.v.6], publican and politician. Soon after his arrival in September in the *Orient*, Lorenzini began work on a major commission for Roberts: the painted decoration of his Potts Point mansion, Chatsworth, featuring on the ballroom ceiling a large-scale, allegorical painting of Amphitrite. With a flyer announcing 'Augusto Lorenzini, Italian artist decorator' he quickly became part of a small but highly visible circle of Italian artists and artisans in Sydney. He joined the Art Society of New South Wales in 1884 and worked in a studio in Phillip Street with the sculptor Tomaso Sani [q.v.6].

In the 1880s and early 1890s Lorenzini's commissions in Sydney, mostly carried out in the High Renaissance style of Raphael, ranged across commercial, ecclesiastical and domestic work. They included the decoration of Gunsler's Café, Pitt Street, the Roberts Hotel on the corner of George and Market streets, the Garrick Theatre, Castlereagh Street, new ceiling and wall decorations for the head office of the London Chartered Bank, George Street, a ceiling and organ front for the Wesleyan church at Waverley and a design for the painted decoration for St Mary's Catholic Church at Concord.

He was awarded a first order of merit for his mural art decorations in the New South Wales court at the 1888 Melbourne Centennial International Exhibition, but his plan to establish an 'Industrial Studio of Art' came to nothing, despite the publication of a detailed prospectus in February 1886. A less ambitious 'advanced art decoration class' had recently been established by Parnell Johnson at Sydney

Technical College. Lorenzini tried unsuccessfully to persuade the college that the existing evening classes in art instruction were useful to intending tradesmen such as carpenters and masons but inadequate to provide the necessary knowledge for those who wanted to make their future living as art decorators.

In the early 1890s Lorenzini formed a shortlived partnership with Giuseppe, brother of the painter Giulio Anivitti [q.v.3]. Unable to survive the deepening economic depression in the mid-1890s, Lorenzini retreated to his orchard at Dural. When he applied for a certificate of naturalization in September 1904, he described himself as art decorator and orchardist. He was declared insolvent in 1914 and he was still involved in legal wrangles when he died of cardiac failure on 29 July 1921 at Dural. The *Cumberland Argus*, reporting the death and subsequent inquest, expressed sorrow for a 'highly respectable man'. The coroner described him as 'a man with a big head of hair'; neighbours remembered him for his artist's beret. Lorenzini's wife, and a nephew who had migrated from Italy in 1905, survived him.

J. Plummer, *A Mayoral Year* (Syd, 1885); S. Carlin and M. Martin, *Augusto Lorenzini* (Syd, 2001); *A'sian Decorator and Painter*, 1 Mar 1917, p 144; *Cumberland Argus and Fruitgrowers' Advocate*, 17 Aug 1921, p 1; M. Martin, 'Augusto Lorenzini: Unravelling an Auction Room Mystery', *World of Antiques & Art*, no 61, July-Dec 2001, p 116, *and* 'Augusto Lorenzini: Italian Artist Decorator in Victorian Sydney', *Italian Hist Soc Jnl*, 8, no 2, July-Dec 2002, p 4; Lorenzini archive (Historic Houses Trust of NSW, Conservation Resource Centre, Syd); A1, item 1904/8160 (NAA, Canb); insolvency file no 19823, 10/23720 (SRNSW).

MEGAN MARTIN

LOWE, WILLIAM (1874-1936), clothing retailer, was born on 30 August 1874 at Clara, Tullamore, King's County (Offaly), Ireland, son of Stephen Lowe, grocer, and his wife Maria, née Hays. With £7 in his pocket, in 1889 Bill migrated to Melbourne, where he learned the trade of tailor. In 1893 he moved to Sydney to work with the department store of Mark Foy [q.v.4] and then with Gowings [q.v.].

By 1898 Lowe had saved enough out of his earnings to open his own shop in Oxford Street with two employees. The profits for a time were limited. However, he began to specialize in hats and then added a tailoring and clothing department. He promoted the early closing and Saturday half-holiday movements; the latter was achieved in 1910. In 1903 he had opened a large store in George Street, which became the headquarters of a chain of shops purveying men's and boys' wear. The clothes were made to measure, and numerous tailors and seamstresses occupied the upper floors of the George Street building. He quickly adapted to the trend towards readymade clothing.

On 26 January 1899 at St Peter's Church of England, Melbourne, Lowe had married Victorian-born Grace Alison Ferguson. They had five children. Although given to saving intensely, Lowe was a showman. Tall, neatly moustached, with a bright and cheerful personality, he was noted for his sartorial elegance and was often considered 'the best dressed man' at the Royal Easter Show. This and other actions were designed purely to promote custom for his stores. One advertisement he placed in the window of the George Street store read: 'Bill Lowe's trousers are coming down ... come and see his goat'. It drew a crowd and attention to his stores, before the police ordered the poster to be removed. In 1923, described as 'one of the captains of industry', he controlled a business with a turnover of £500 000 annually and a thousand employees.

Lowe was the first city retailer to establish a branch at Parramatta, in 1932. It proved a success and was soon followed by a number of others including one at Newcastle, until with ten shops Lowe's became the largest chain of men's and boys' wear stores in New South Wales. With branches in the Haymarket, in Oxford Street and at Circular Quay as well as frontages on both George and Pitt streets, the firm could advertise 'Stores all over town'. They had a sharper, more insistent presence than those of their more traditional rivals, Gowing and Sir James Murdoch [q.v.10].

A member of the Civic and Millions clubs, Lowe also held debentures in the New South Wales Masonic Club and the Bonnie Doon Golf Club, Arncliffe. One of his hobbies was surfing. He died of pernicious anaemia and pneumonia on 13 August 1936 at his residence, Exeter Hall, Double Bay, survived by his wife, two daughters and two sons. Lowe was buried in the Anglican cemetery at South Head, Sydney. His estate was sworn for probate at £46 907. From the 1950s the company changed hands several times and no longer had any connection with the family. Lowe's practice of acquiring the freehold of the property occupied by his shops limited his flexibility to shift outlets as shopping traffic altered; it also led to properties becoming undervalued for shopping purposes and thereby attracting developers, especially from the late 1970s. In 2005 the firm still advertised that 'you can get it at Lowes'!

Sydneyites As We See 'Em 1913-14-15 (Syd, 1915); *Rydge's Business J*, 1 Nov 1930, p 977; *Sun-Herald* (Syd), 8 Apr 1979, p 140; *Daily Telegraph* (Syd), 12 Dec 1921, p 5, 22 Dec 1923, p 13; *SMH*, 14 Aug 1936, p 12, 15 Aug 1936, p 23; *Aust Worker*, 19 Aug 1936, p 14.

JOHN PERKINS

LOWIN, PAUL (1892-1961), businessman and philanthropist, was born on 22 September 1892 at Jägerndorf, Silesia, Austria-Hungary (Krnov, Moravia, Czech Republic), younger of two sons of Jewish parents Edmund Löwin, manufacturer, and his wife Laura, née Goldberger. In a statement to a Sydney court in 1940, Lowin testified that he had been a soldier in the Austro-Hungarian army during World War I. In 1915, he asserted, he was captured by the Russians and was held prisoner at Odessa and for three years in Siberia, where his left kidney was removed, which adversely affected his health thereafter. He also claimed that he went home via Vladivostok in 1919, worked in his father's factory and married in 1926, and that his wife died giving birth to their son in 1931.

Official Austrian records show, however, that Löwin lived in Vienna from September 1918 until March 1935, occasionally visiting Paris, Berlin, Jägerndorf and Prague. Although in 1918 he described himself as Jewish, by 1930 he no longer specified a religious affiliation. Documents recorded his profession as opera singer (one specifying 'at the *Volksoper*') and he was invariably described as unmarried. His name was also given as 'Liban' or 'Löwin-Liban'.

According to Lowin's subsequent account, he worked as a journalist in Prague before moving to Cairo in 1936, partly for health reasons, as a reporter for a Prague newspaper and a publicist for Czech merchandise. After the German annexation of the Sudetenland in October 1938 his brother was forced to flee from Krnov and later died in a concentration camp. Paul was offered a position as a foreign correspondent in Australia and reached Sydney on 16 August 1939 in the *Strathnaver*. He was described as 5 ft 6 ins (168 cm) tall, with grey eyes and black hair.

Lowin initially worked freelance for newspapers in England and the United States of America. By 1941 he was a textile manufacturer, trading as the Swedish Handweaving Co. in George Street. The business was successful, as were his property investments largely in the eastern suburbs. As part of an application for naturalization, in 1948 his solicitor wrote that Lowin planned to visit Czechoslovakia 'to reclaim his family property and purchase machinery for his business'. His application had been delayed by the Department of Immigration, principally because of his conviction in May 1940 on a possibly trumped-up charge of sexual assault on a 15-year-old boy in a public lavatory in the Sydney Domain. Lowin was naturalized on 6 April 1948. By then he owned and lived in a flat at Elizabeth Bay, and had a house and business interests in Vienna.

After his arrival, Lowin had become friendly with the expatriate Viennese conductor Henry Krips, with whom he took singing lessons—although Kurt Prerauer [q.v.16] had a poor opinion of his musicianship. Lowin was also involved in German-speaking theatre in Sydney during the early 1940s. Frau Krips recalled him as 'full of ideas and cultural ambition; rather colourful'. He often brought back from Europe recordings and musical scores that were unavailable in Australia and would use them in musical *soirées* in his flat, holding court to a group of artistically inclined young men and his large and affable black dog. Some of his protégés (including James Murdoch and Denis Condon) would play significant roles in Sydney's intellectual life. He loved opera and *Lieder*, like his friends who founded Musica Viva, his tastes were conservative, favouring Wagner, Verdi and Richard Strauss in particular. Lowin was homosexual and was very fond of the beach, especially Bondi, and its culture of youthful, muscular beauty.

By mid-1953 Lowin had returned permanently to Vienna, although he retained property in Sydney, which he revisited on several occasions. He sold out of his business about 1956. Lowin died in Vienna General Hospital (Allgemeines Krankenhaus) on 7 October 1961; apparently only a nephew in London survived him. The death registration recorded his occupation as 'Korrespondent' and his religion as Roman Catholic. His estate in New South Wales was estimated to be almost £20 000; by the finalization of complex legal issues in 1988, the nett value was in excess of $340 000. After personal bequests, the will established the Paul Lowin prize for the composition of an orchestral piece or a song cycle in alternate years. The richest for music composition in Australia, the prize was first awarded in 1991.

Austn Jewish Times, 12 Aug 1988, p 13; *SMH*, 7 May 1963, p 1, 8 May 1963, p 16, 8 Nov 1972, p 26, 30 July 1991, p 12; series SP11/2 *and* series A442, item 1952/14/1897 (NAA, Canb); 10/38500, item 363/1940, 10/6164, item 1385/58, and Sydney Qtr Sessions, 30/31 May 1940, 6/2091 (SRNSW); information from Perpetual Trustees Ltd and Messrs K. W. Tribe, D. Condon and S. Maher, Sydney, and J. Murdoch, Bali.   JOHN CARMODY

LUCAS, MARY ANN (c.1826-1900), community worker and temperance advocate, was born in Yorkshire, England, daughter of William Branfoot, gardener. She came to Sydney about 1846 and on 9 May 1848 at Chippendale Wesleyan Chapel married Robert Jeremiah Martin, a shopkeeper. They had two children before he died in 1853. Following her marriage to GEORGE LUCAS (1813-1900), shingler, on 12 April 1853 at Pitt Street Free

Presbyterian Church, she began her career as a community worker.

Born on 4 March 1813 in the Trafalgar Hotel, Sydney, son of William Lucas, publican, and his wife Sarah, despite his father's business, George had joined the Total Abstinence Society—the first in the colony—in 1835. He became a builder, reputedly one of the earliest to use slates as a building material. In 1867 he founded the Sons of Temperance and began a teetotal Brass Band. George and Mary's fourth child RUTH (1859-1953), born on 26 December 1859 in Sydney, also became a prominent temperance worker.

George had helped to convene an early anti-transportation meeting in Sydney, and was a supporter of (Sir) Henry Parkes [q.v.5] whom, with his long, white hair and beard, he was later said to resemble. Lucas was an advocate of Parkes's Public Schools Act (1866), in support of which Mary personally collected over 14 000 signatures. The family residence and business were in Francis Street, Hyde Park, where, in rented premises, Mary founded a night refuge for homeless men in 1867. She and George carried on this work at their own expense for two years until they handed over to a committee, although the refuge continued under their patronage until 1898, with both Mary and George active until 1893. In the same street, in a tent on adjacent vacant land, Mary started the first Band of Hope, to focus on temperance teaching to children.

On 18 March 1871 Mary was appointed matron and George superintendent of the Industrial School for Girls and Reformatory, which was relocated from Newcastle to Cockatoo Island and renamed Biloela to remove the convict taint. Adjacent to the Fitzroy Dry Dock and the institution for wayward boys—the ship *Vernon*—the site was badly chosen, having inadequate access and a lack of fresh water. Mrs Lucas introduced training schemes in laundry and domestic skills and dressmaking to assist the girls to become more employable. After-dinner activities included religious instruction, reading and draughts. From the age of 12 Ruth helped Mary to teach crochet and wool work; items were sold and the proceeds handed to the girls.

Although acknowledged to be kindly, George was unable to cope with the bawdy, unseemly behaviour of the girls and the lack of support from staff. An inquiry by the Public Charities Commission (1871-73) elicited strong criticism of the Lucas administration. Despite their good intentions and their pioneering and Christian philanthropic work, Mary and George requested a formal release from duties in December 1873. The reformatory continued until 1888, with a trained teacher in charge, and then reverted to a gaol.

In Sydney in September 1882 Mary attended the first meeting in New South Wales of the Woman's Christian Temperance Union and was immediately elected to the executive. She subsequently held many offices, becoming secretary for unfermented wine and in 1896 Australasian superintendent, and remaining on the executive until her death. Ruth worked with her mother in the Band of Hope until 1888, when she became active in the worldwide W.C.T.U., devoting herself primarily to children. A member (later colonial superintendent) of the first committee for scientific temperance examination, she provided prize money and silver medals as well as certificates to those who did not gain a prize. In 1892 Ruth became joint editor of the official organ of the W.C.T.U. of New South Wales, *White Ribbon Signal*, to which she also contributed articles. She helped to increase membership, became renowned as a public speaker, organized the Sydney 'Y' Union (Young W.C.T.U.) and became its president. When in 1893 Jessie Ackermann [q.v.] was obliged to return to the United States of America, Ruth acted as her private secretary, confidently took charge of her work and became her representative in Australia.

George died in Sydney on 30 April 1900. A late photograph of Mary showed a portly, white-haired, Victorian matriarch. She died on 6 July 1900 at their home in George Street, Canterbury, and was buried with Congregational forms in Rookwood cemetery. A daughter and a son of her first marriage, and four sons and two daughters of her second, survived her.

Ruth did not marry; her image is that of a forthright and dedicated person. She later lived at Kurrajong and Neutral Bay. She died on 27 March 1953 in hospital at Ryde, and was buried in Woronora cemetery with Anglican rites. The aim of the Lucases, like that of the W.C.T.U. itself, was ever the suppression of intemperance and 'the social, intellectual, and moral elevation of the people'.

Golden Records: Pathfinders of Woman's Christian Temperance Union of N.S.W. (Syd, 1926); K. Daniels and M. Murnane (comps), *Uphill all the Way* (Brisb, 1980); J. S. Kerr, *Cockatoo Island: Penal and Institutional Remains* (Syd, 1984*); WCTU of NSW Jubilee Convention, 1882-1932* (ML); *White Ribbon Signal* Supplement: Report of World's Biennial Convention, 1895 (ML); *V&P* (LA, NSW), 1873-74, vol 6, p 133; *Town and Country J*, 31 Mar 1894, p 19; *Daily Telegraph* (Syd), 2 April 1894, p 5, 2 May 1900, p 9; Colonial Secretary, in correspondence, 1873, reel no 9526 (SRNSW).

VILMA PAGE

LYNCH, WILLIAM (c.1839-1913), Aboriginal community elder, was born near Bannaby (Bonamby) station, south of Wombeyan

Caves, New South Wales, reputedly the son of Maurice Lynch (c.1819-1888), an Irish-born, convict shoemaker and bagpipe-repairer, and a Gundungurra mother whose name was not recorded. In his boyhood, Billy moved with his family to the Hartley district, where his attendance at a blanket distribution at the courthouse is recorded on 3 May 1841, his Aboriginal name given as Mawiack.

For some years he worked as a guide and police tracker in western New South Wales and near the Lachlan River, later as a shepherd on Dalziel's Rosevale property in the Kanimbla Valley. Between 1862 and 1875 he and his wife Rose Anna Fisher—who was also known as Fanny Page and had been born about 1850 at Hartley—had six children: William, Emily, Fanny, Joseph, Rosie and James. The youngsters were also given Gundungurra names.

In 1887 Joseph applied for a conditional purchase of a 40-acre (16 ha) lot on the Cox River, where the family lived for the next ten years. Peter and Jane O'Reilly, early settlers of the Megalong and Kanimbla valleys, knew them well. The O'Reillys' son Bernard [q.v.11] included a number of reminiscences of Billy's family in his memoir, *Cullenbenbong* (Brisbane, 1944).

The Lynchs participated in the community life of the Megalong Valley and the developing town of Katoomba. Billy tracked down lost tourists and sold bush honey, rabbits and possum-skin rugs in the town. In 1889 it was reported, probably sarcastically, that he planned to open a delicatessen for travellers on the Six Foot Track. He and his sons played in the all-Aboriginal cricket team, Coxs River, against the valley's settlers' team. In 1896 a journalist from the *Sydney Mail* described Lynch as 'an active clear headed intelligent veteran of Parkesian [q.v.5 Sir Henry Parkes] appearance'. The published interview was a poignant record of environmental and social changes in the Blue Mountains.

As settlement of the Blue Mountains valleys intensified, the Gundungurra people found access to traditional food sources difficult, and they became more reliant on the settler economy. From 1893 a fringe encampment had developed around the Nellies Glen shale mine, where there was casual work. The mine's closure in 1897 led to a migration of Aboriginal families to Katoomba, where they settled in an unoccupied gully in the upper part of Kedumba Falls Creek. Lynch, then the oldest and most respected Aboriginal person in the region, probably played an important role in helping to establish a viable Aboriginal community in the gully, relatively independent of control by the Aborigines Protection Board. Fanny died in 1900.

The Katoomba gully settlement was accepted and respected by the non-Aboriginal people of the town. William Lynch died there of 'senile decay' on 13 November 1913. After a Catholic service, his body was transported by bullock cart to an ancient, Aboriginal burial area in the Megalong Valley. Here he was buried upright in the traditional Gundungurra manner, on a spur overlooking Megalong Creek. This acceptance by Lynch of the burial rites of two cultures symbolized his life of reconciliation and adaptation in a world that changed dramatically in his lifetime. Survived by two sons and two daughters, he also had twenty-two surviving grandchildren, and by 2005 there were hundreds of proud descendants.

J. Smith, 'The Gundungorra Aboriginals' in M. Shaw, *Historic Megalong Valley* (Syd, 1988) and 'Katoomba's Fringe Dwellers' in E. Stockton (ed), *Blue Mountains Dreaming* (Syd, 1993); *Sydney Mail*, 12 Dec 1896, p 1250; *Blue Mountains Echo*, 21 Nov 1913, p 3; family papers held by Mrs M. Jordan, Moonee Ponds, Melb.   JIM SMITH

LYNG, JENS SØRENSEN (1868-1941), public servant, soldier and author, was born on 16 April 1868 at Hasle, near Aarhus, Denmark, son of Søren Jensen Lyng, farmer, and his wife Maren, née Hansen. On finishing school, Jens joined the Royal Danish Standing Army and was commissioned second lieutenant. With dim prospects of promotion, he migrated to Melbourne in 1891, but retained his Danish commission until he was naturalized in Australia in 1900.

After working as labourer, land-clearer and shearer, Lyng was secretary to Baron von Mueller [q.v.5]. Enthusiastically involved in Melbourne's Scandinavian communities, Lyng became secretary of the Danish Society in 1896, assisted the pastors of the United Scandinavian Lutheran Church in social and welfare work and edited the congregation's biannual magazine. Aware that the three communities were too small to form viable individual organizations, Lyng espoused the pan-Scandinavian movement. To promote this aim, in 1896 he founded a monthly newspaper, *Norden*, which he produced single-handed; he remained editor until 1906.

On 28 October 1897 in his Richmond home Lyng had married with Scandinavian Lutheran rites Victorian-born Mary Eleanor Gertrude Burrowes. They had four children. In 1906 he bought a farm at Kinglake, continuing to work in Melbourne during the week and visiting his family at weekends. These experiences formed the background to his novel, *Teddy Wilkin's Trials* (Melbourne, 1910).

In 1909 Lyng joined the naval works branch of the Department of Defence as a draughtsman. Later he worked on the 1911 census. He was commissioned lieutenant in the Senior

Cadets, Commonwealth Military Cadet Corps, in 1912. At the outbreak of World War I, because of his knowledge of German—as well as Danish, Swedish and Norwegian—he was appointed to the Australian Naval and Military Expeditionary Force on 11 September 1914. He joined the commander of the force, Colonel William Holmes [q.v.9], as interpreter and participated in the first phase of the occupation of German New Guinea. On 26 September he took charge of the Government Printing Office, Rabaul. Lyng was printer, publisher and editor of the official, fortnightly *Government Gazette* and a monthly paper, the *Rabaul Record*. He also censored letters written to the stranded German planters. Promoted captain in April 1916, in May 1918 he was appointed district officer at Madang in Kaiser Wilhelmsland. His New Guinea experiences led to two books: *Our New Possession* (Melbourne, 1919) and *Island Films* (Sydney, 1925). Lyng's A.N.M.E.F. appointment was terminated in Melbourne on 11 September 1918; he returned to the Commonwealth Public Service as a censor of foreign mail and in 1920 transferred to the Bureau of Census and Statistics, where he was appointed chief draughtsman.

In 1922 Lyng helped to form the Scandinavian Progress Association, which in 1925 was recognized as a branch of the New Settlers' League of Australia. A keen promoter of Danish immigration, in 1923 he approached the Victorian government for the grant of a suitable tract of land for farms. He went to Denmark to promote his scheme, but it collapsed because of the poor Danish response. During this time he was the (William) Harbison-(George) Higinbotham [q.v.4] scholar at the University of Melbourne and worked on his *Non-Britishers in Australia* (1927). Always deeply involved in the affairs of the Danish Club in Melbourne, Lyng was briefly its president in 1928.

When the Bureau of Census and Statistics transferred to Canberra the family moved to the national capital. Promoted to librarian and draughtsman in the bureau in May 1929, Lyng retired in August 1932 and returned in 1937 to Victoria. Throughout his life he had collected material on—and written in both Danish and English about—Scandinavians in the antipodes, and his major work, *The Scandinavians in Australia, New Zealand and the Western Pacific*, was published in Melbourne in 1939. Predeceased by his wife in 1940, Lyng died on 25 October 1941 at Birchip and was cremated. Two sons and a daughter survived him.

S. S. Mackenzie, *The Australians at Rabaul* (Syd, 1927); O. Koivukangas and J. S. Martin, *The Scandinavians in Australia* (Melb, 1986); J. S. Martin, *The Danish Club Dannebrog in Melbourne 1889-1989* (Melb, 1989); *Norden*, 26 May 1906, 10 Dec 1910, 25 Aug 1917, 26 Nov 1921, 11 Nov 1922, 14 Apr 1923, 1 Sept 1923, 28 July 1928, 8 July 1939; A712, item 1900/M10269 (NAA, Canb); information from Dr I. O'Donnell, Brighton, Melb.

JOHN STANLEY MARTIN

M

MacCALLUM, DORETTE (DOROTHEA) MARGARETHE (1863-1952), community worker, was born in 1863 at Elbstorf, Hanover, Prussia (Germany), one of eight children of Lorenz Peters, farmer and grazier. In 1881 she was teaching German and French at Aberystwyth, Wales, where she met (Sir) Mungo William MacCallum [q.v.10]; they married on 28 June 1882 at Elbstorf. On his appointment to the University of Sydney in 1886, as foundation professor of modern languages and literature, MacCallum, with his wife and their two children, sailed for Australia, reaching Sydney in February 1887. A son born next year died in infancy.

Dorette became involved in all aspects of university life. An intelligent woman with good organizing ability and appropriate social skills, she was also an excellent cook and hostess. These attributes were to enhance her role as wife of a professor who would later hold office as vice-chancellor and chancellor. A grandson later described her as tall and ungainly, with smooth hair, broad brow, wide-set eyes and Saxon features.

Louisa Macdonald [q.v.10] noted in 1895 that the MacCallums were a devoted couple 'so happy yet so full of interest in matters not immediately concerning themselves'. In 1895 Louisa became godmother to their fourth child Walter [q.v.15]. All the surviving MacCallum children were well educated and graduates of the University of Sydney. The eldest, Mungo Lorenz (d.1933), a lawyer and journalist, was a Rhodes scholar.

Dorette showed a keen interest in the work and activities of the female undergraduates and later the graduate body. In 1891 she helped to set up the Sydney University Women's Society (University Settlement), of which she was vice-president in 1891-92 and 1895-1903 and president in 1925-32. It was largely due to her foresight, and the generous financial assistance provided by her and her daughter Isabella Lightoller (d.1940), that a property at Chippendale was purchased in 1925 as a permanent home for the settlement.

When the Sydney University Women's Union was formed in 1909-10, Mrs MacCallum was among those wives of the university staff who took out life membership to help the young members financially. She was patroness from 1931. Various sporting activities received her help: she provided prizes for tennis competitions and in 1910, when the university's three women's sports clubs formed a single association, she became its president.

Present at the founding meeting of the National Council of Women in 1895, she became active in many aspects of its work, holding the presidency in 1919-27. Among her interests were the Infants' Home at Ashfield and the Sydney Day Nursery and Nursery Schools Association. As president of the latter in 1924-38 and prominent in the establishment of its nursery training college in 1932, she was also associated with the Royal Society for the Welfare of Mothers and Babies and the New South Wales Society for Crippled Children. She was, as well, a council member of Sydney Church of England Girls' Grammar schools at Darlinghurst and Moss Vale.

Lady MacCallum was a spirited and formidable woman. Family members, especially the younger generation, at times disagreed with her strong views. Her grandson, who wrote of her 'iron hand', believed that she 'thought in German till the end of her life'. Predeceased by her husband, she died on 4 July 1952 in hospital at Rose Bay and was cremated. An Anglican memorial service was held in St Andrew's Cathedral, Sydney. One son survived her. Her portrait by E. A. Harvey was presented to the University Settlement in 1933.

M. MacCallum, *Plankton's Luck* (Melb, 1986); R. Williams, *The Settlement* (Syd, 1988); C. Turney et al, *Australia's First*, 1 (Syd, 1991); J. Roberts, *Maybanke Anderson* (Syd, 1993); J. Beaumont and W. Vere Hole, *Letters from Louisa* (Syd, 1996); S. Lilienthal, *Newtown Tarts* (Syd, 1997); *Union Recorder*, 10 July 1952, p 141; *SMH*, 10 Feb 1926, p 8, 25 Nov 1927, p 4, 17 Dec 1927, p 4, 28 Nov 1933, p 44, 9 June 1938, p 20.   URSULA BYGOTT

McCLEMANS, WILLIAM JOSEPH (1874-1960), clergyman and educationist, was born on 15 December 1874 at Crossakiel, County Meath, Ireland, son of Hugh McClemans of the Royal Irish Constabulary, and his wife Mary, née Cromer. Educated at Elphin Cathedral Grammar School, Roscommon, and Trinity College, Dublin (B.A., 1897), William graduated with honours in Greek.

After migrating to Western Australia, he was ordained deacon (1899) and priest (1900) by the Church of England bishop C. O. L. Riley [q.v.11]. Energetic and popular, McClemans was curate (1899-1901) of Greenbushes and rector of Day Dawn, on the Murchison goldfields (1901-02), Geraldton (1902-05) and Boulder (1905-07), building a church at each of his posts except Geraldton. At Christchurch, Geraldton, on 3 January 1905 he married Ada Lucy Walker, a nurse. In 1907 he became rector of an important suburban parish, Christ Church, Claremont, and in 1912 canon of St George's Cathedral. He became a prominent public figure, forthright and respected for his intellect and oratorical skills. Perceiving the need for a private school for boys not sufficiently advanced or too young for the established secondary schools, McClemans founded Christ Church Preparatory School in premises adjacent to his rectory. From a modest start with one classroom and nine dayboys, Christ Church survived early difficulties to become a grammar school covering all secondary years. By 1960 it had grown into the largest private school in Western Australia, with 669 boys on the roll. McClemans was also influential in the decision by the Church of England to purchase the small, private school of Charles Harper, which became Guildford Grammar School.

Although a married man with five young daughters, McClemans thought it his duty to serve as a chaplain during World War I. When commissioned in the Australian Imperial Force on 30 October 1915, he was 6 ft 1 ins (185 cm) tall and weighed 13 stone (82.5 kg). Discharged on 18 April 1917, he returned to Claremont deeply affected by his experiences on the front, and increasingly sought consolation in alcohol. Late in 1922 he was obliged to resign as rector. Separated from his wife— they divorced in 1929—and family, he spent twenty years farming on several different blocks, acquired through the Soldier Settlement Scheme, in the Lake Hinds and West Kondut area, north-west of Wongan Hills, 125 miles (200 km) north of Perth. This was a significant period of withdrawal from the social life he had known, though he found support from friends in the area. His inexperience and the 1930s Depression led to his efforts at farming being ultimately unsuccessful.

Circumstances improved when McClemans married with Methodist forms Susie Violet Forrest, the niece of Sir John Forrest [q.v.8], on 19 May 1943 at Claremont. Though estranged from many of his family, he re-established contact with some of them in his declining years. After the death of his wife in 1950 McClemans lived at York, then Gosnells and finally Subiaco, where he died, after a long illness, on 17 April 1960. He was buried in Karrakatta cemetery, survived by five daughters of his first marriage, of whom Sheila (Kenworthy) became the first woman to enter legal practice in Perth and Dorothy (Sanders) was a popular novelist.

A. and D. Muir, *Family History of William and Margaret Forrest* (Manjimup, WA, 1982); P. Sharpe and L. O'Hara, *A Goodly Heritage* (Perth, 1992); G. C. Bolton and J. Gregory, *Claremont* (Nedlands, 1998); L. Davies, *Sheila* (Syd, 2000); *West Australian*, 22 Apr 1960, p 10.   R. J. S. BARRETT-LENNARD
G. C. BOLTON

McDERMOTT, GEORGE (c.1895-1972), Aboriginal stockman, linguist and collector of traditions, was born near Nockatunga, Queensland, son of Nellie Murray, a Wangkumara woman born in 1880, and a white man named McDermott, who was working as a tank-sinker. Nellie's people came from the Lake Eyre basin in the 'corner country', and their territory included areas around the Wilson River in south-western Queensland. When George's father died, H. M. L. (Edgar) Hughes of Nocundra employed the boy at Nockatunga station. The cook there taught him to read, and he went on droving trips to Cockburn near Broken Hill, New South Wales. He also worked on other stations, including a period as head stockman at Naryilco, near Quilpie, Queensland.

In 1920 George's mother and her husband Larry Gilmore were working for Hughes at Nockatunga station; she remained there until 1954. In the 1920s, however, most of the Wangkumara from Queensland moved to Tibooburra, New South Wales, where, about 1920, George married Ruby Ebsworth. Of the 200 people living at the old camping ground there in the 1930s, about half were Wangkumara. In the late 1930s the Aborigines Protection Board moved them all to Brewarrina in three large trucks. Numbers at the Brewarrina reserve increased further after Angledool station closed. A number of elderly Wangkumara died in the first year, so some people decided to walk back to Tibooburra. They got as far as Wanaaring before a flooded river stopped them. Many Aboriginal people later moved to Bourke and Wilcannia for work.

About 1940 McDermott attended a ceremonial gathering at Innamincka, South Australia, where he went through an initiation ceremony. From Wangkumara elders he learned many songs, stories and traditions and became highly regarded for his knowledge and as a 'clever man'. He later blamed alcohol for his previous loss of language and other cultural knowledge. His expertise was shared with George Dutton [q.v.14] and George Harrison when they met to quiz each other about their traditional knowledge. On a trip to Wanaaring, New South Wales, he found his mother living there, and stayed with her until she died in 1959.

Some time in the 1960s, McDermott moved to Bourke, where he lived at the Aboriginal reserve. The linguist Luise Hercus recorded 'language' words from him there in 1968. When another linguist Max Kamien went to Bourke in 1971, he found that four of the six fluent speakers of Aboriginal languages spoke Wangkumara. Kamien recorded Wangkumara vocabulary, songs and myths from McDermott, helping to keep the language alive. Predeceased by his wife, McDermott died on 11 November 1972 at Bourke District

Hospital, and was buried in the local cemetery with Anglican rites. His daughter survived him. A Wangkumara dictionary, based on the knowledge of McDermott and others, edited by Carol Robertson, was published in 1985.

B. Hardy, *Lament for the Barkindji* (Adel, 1976); M. Kamien, *The Dark People of Bourke* (Canb, 1978); D. Horton (ed), *The Encyclopaedia of Aboriginal Australia*, 2 (Canb, 1994); *JRHSQ*, 14, no 3, Aug 1990, p 113; L. A. Hercus, Aboriginal Informants for Linguistic Research and Station Scenes *and* taped interviews with G. McDermott, 1969 (AIATSIS); M. Kamien, taped interview with G. McDermott (1971, AIATSIS); A/58553, A/58912, HOM/B58 (QSA).   JONATHAN RICHARDS

MacDONALD, PETER FITZALLAN (1830-1919), pastoralist, entrepreneur and politician, was born on 4 September 1830 at Campbelltown, New South Wales, fourth son and one of twelve children of Alexander Macdonald, an Edinburgh-born emancipist farmer, and his wife Sarah, daughter of the prosperous ex-convict John Warby [q.v.2]; A. C. Macdonald [q.v.5] was an older brother. A younger brother John Graham Macdonald (1834-1918), also an early Queensland explorer and landholder, sometime partner of (Sir) John Robertson and Robert Towns [qq.v.6], was later a police magistrate at Bowen and Townsville. Educated in 1840-42 at The King's School, Parramatta, Peter gained farming experience before achieving moderate success on the Victorian goldfields and later overseeing and managing Ingleby station, near Geelong.

At Rockhampton, Queensland, in 1857 MacDonald joined the Canoona goldfields rush, but soon embarked on a series of pastoral explorations with squatters and Aboriginal guides along the Mackenzie, Isaacs, Connor and Nogoa rivers. One such expedition in 1858 almost cost him his life and led to chronic health problems. His aim was to take up as many leases as possible, retain and stock such properties as Marmadilla, near Springsure, Columbura, on the Mackenzie, Fernlees, near Tilpal, and Lake Larmouth and Yaamba, his headquarters, on the Fitzroy near Rockhampton, and sell the rest. One property, Cullinlaringo, which he sold to Horatio Wills [q.v.2] in 1860, was the scene next year of a massacre by Aborigines. MacDonald was one of the party who avenged the slaughter, 'and it was generally recognised ... that the work was well done'.

MacDonald returned to Geelong to marry with Church of Scotland forms Julia Ayrey on 1 January 1861; she was the orphaned daughter of a wealthy Western District pastoralist.

There were seven children of the marriage. Elected to the Queensland Legislative Assembly for Blackall in November 1873, he was a progressive squatter, supporting (Sir) Samuel Griffith [q.v.9], secular education, liberal land legislation for viable selectors and a port at Broadsound. MacDonald made much of his contribution as a pioneer confronting 'a new treacherous enemy in the Aborigines, an unknown climate, and adverse seasons while burying himself in the bush for the best years of his life'. He maintained that 'he was so identified with the district that he could not promote its interests without promoting his own and he could not serve himself without serving the electors'.

In 1869 MacDonald had sued the Crown for damages resulting from its resumption of western leaseholds and river frontages that he had taken up. The Great Northern Run case dragged on until 1880 when it was settled for £22 700 in MacDonald's favour. He was hotly attacked for using parliament to further his own interests rather than those of his constituents. By August 1876 he acknowledged, 'I am sick of Parliamentary affairs and must resign at the end of the session'. He did not recontest the seat in November 1878 and failed to win North Rockhampton in 1888.

Taking a trenchant position against the rising tide of labour, in 1890 and 1891 MacDonald attempted to thwart the shearers' union by employing selectors' sons and Chinese, commenting, however, that 'the latter are easily scared and it might be very humiliating and financially disastrous if a body of Union men hunted my shearers out of the shed'. His mining ventures lost money, but his pastoral investments were supplemented by town properties including hotels throughout Queensland, as well as the Rockhampton *Northern Argus* daily newspaper and meat works at Lakes Creek. These enterprises saved him when 90 per cent of his stock died in the drought of 1899-1904.

In middle age MacDonald was 6 ft 2 ins (188 cm) tall, well built, weighing 15 stone (95 kg), with determined eyes, a long, narrow, Scots face fringed by a full white beard and no moustache. Early privations and hypochondria led to frequent illness, assuaged by draughts of strychnine and opium. Increasingly conservative in the last thirty years of his life, meticulous, stern and distrustful, 'P.F.' was a 'hard man' to his family and servants. Financing several central Queensland political campaigns for 'Liberty' and 'Progress' against 'Anarchy, lawlessness and confiscation', he spent much time reviving his pastoral holdings and successfully jousting with the authorities over his tax assessments.

MacDonald died on 19 June 1919 at Morningside, his Rockhampton residence, and was buried in Yaamba cemetery. His wife, two sons and two daughters survived him. Literate and productive but not insightful, patriarchal but not paternal, political but neither persuasive nor effective, MacDonald was essentially a loner. Yet he was a successful pastoral pioneer and an early and sustained contributor to the development of Rockhampton and its hinterland.

J. T. S. Bird, *The Early History of Rockhampton* (Rockhampton, Qld, 1964); L. McDonald, *Rockhampton: A History of the City* (Brisb, 1981); A. E. Hermann, *Development of Rockhampton*, 1 (Rockhampton, Qld, 2003); M. Vale (comp), *Warby: My Excellent Guide* (nd); *PD* (Qld), vol 18, 30 June 1875, p 607; *Morning Bulletin* (Rockhampton, Qld), 11 Nov 1873, p 3, 18 Nov 1873, p 2, 20 Nov 1873, p 2, 12 May 1888, p 8, 11 May 1888, pp 4 & 5, 15 May 1888, p 5, 19 June 1919, p 1, 23 June 1919, p 7, 20 Nov 1873, p 6; *Northern Argus* (Rockhampton, Qld), 18 Nov 1873, p 1; *Daily Record* (Rockhampton, Qld), 19 June 1919, p 4; B. Cosgrove, Peter Fitzallan MacDonald: A Life Apart (M.A. thesis, Univ Central Qld, 1994); P. F. MacDonald letterbooks and diaries, Rockhampton Municipal Library; Yaamba pastoral records, Fryar L, Univ of Qld, Brisb.

D. B. WATERSON

McGAHEY, SUSAN BELL (1862-1919), hospital matron and reformer, was born in 1862 at Stewartstown, County Tyrone, Ireland, one of six children of Robert McGahey, farmer, and his wife Annie. In the early 1870s the family moved to England. Susan trained in 1884-87 at London Hospital under Florence Nightingale's friend Eva Luckes. After completing her general training and obtaining an obstetric certificate, McGahey travelled to Sydney at the suggestion of a friend, Charlotte Thomas, whose husband David established Manly Cottage Hospital.

Following a highly successful term as the first matron (1890-91) of Carrington Convalescent Hospital, Camden, in July 1891 McGahey was appointed matron at (Royal) Prince Alfred Hospital, Sydney, specifically to reform the nursing department. Over the next thirteen years, McGahey made nurse training more rigorous and systematic, employed wardsmaids to take over the heavy cleaning previously done by probationers, appointed senior nurses to newly established administrative positions and founded the Prince Alfred Trained Nurses' Reunion. These reforms raised the status of nursing at the hospital and brought McGahey international acclaim.

More contentious was McGahey's introduction of a fourth, postgraduate year for nurses, the first of its kind in Australia, and her proposal that a preliminary training school be established at R.P.A.H. The powerful chairman of the board, Professor (Sir) Thomas Anderson Stuart [q.v.12], dismantled the first and refused approval for the second. He later argued that these changes, while of benefit to nurses, disadvantaged the hospital. Following months of difficult negotiations McGahey resigned, citing ill health. She left the hospital in January 1904 and opened a small private hospital, Charlemount, at Potts Point, as a training school for nurses, which she operated for the next decade.

McGahey's interest in reforming nursing had made her one of the most prominent matrons in New South Wales. She corresponded with Ethel Bedford Fenwick and Isla Stewart, leaders of the movement to professionalize nursing in Britain, and was elected an honorary member of the Matrons' Council of Great Britain and Ireland. In 1899 she helped to found the Australasian Trained Nurses' Association, the voluntary self-regulatory organization that set uniform standards for training and registered trained nurses and training hospitals until state registration in 1924. McGahey held the most senior nursing position in the A.T.N.A., that of founding honorary secretary; she was a member of its council until 1912 and founding editor of its journal, the *Australasian Nurses' Journal.* She represented the association at the first International Council of Nurses Congress at Buffalo, United States of America, in 1901.

In 1904 McGahey was elected president of the I.C.N., in recognition of her achievements. When enthusiastically accepting the presidency, she made no mention of the ill health referred to when she resigned from R.P.A.H. On the contrary, she looked forward to taking an active interest in nursing reform. Lacking an official position in a leading hospital, however, and located so far from the U.S.A. and Britain, she was ineffective as president of the I.C.N. She attended no meetings nor, as far as is known, did she make any recommendations.

McGahey did not marry. She died of cancer on 16 November 1919 at Carlingford and was buried in Rookwood cemetery with Anglican rites. In 1922 a memorial tablet to her was unveiled and a yearly prize inaugurated in her name at R.P.A.H.

Prince Alfred Hospital, *Annual Report*, 1891-1904; *A'sian Nurses' J*, Jan 1904, p 132, 15 Dec 1919, p 407, 15 Jan 1923, p 11; *Nursing Record & Hospital World*, 21 Aug 1901, p 147; *Prince Alfred Hospital Gazette*, 24 Sept 1904, 30 Mar 1904; Royal London Hospital, Register of Probationers, no 2, 1884-88 (London Hospital archives); Prince Alfred Hospital, Board of Directors reports, 1891-1904 *and* Matron's reports to the House Committee, 1893-1904 (RPAH archives); A'sian Trained Nurses' Assn, Council meetings and records, 1899-1923 (ML); International Council of Nurses, Minutes and records, 1899-1909 (ICN archives, Geneva).   SUE FORSYTH

McGILLIVRAY, DONALD (1855-1921), horsebreaker, was born in 1855 on a sheep station at Dartmoor, Victoria, second of six children of Scottish-born parents James McGillivray, grazier, and his wife Mary, née McIntosh. Donald was brought up on his father's property, Maaoupe Park, near Penola, South Australia, where he was privately educated by J. W. Ashley, B.A., from the University of Glasgow. At 18 he managed Murrabinna station, near Kingston, for Messrs Hutchison & Dunn and, after experimenting on wild, unbroken horses, was soon dealing with large mobs of 'walers' for the Indian remount trade. He once handled 202 unbroken colts in three weeks. Six feet (183 cm) tall, weighing 14 stone (89 kg), McGillivray was 'active, muscular and proportionately well built'. On 1 September 1880 at Robe he married with Presbyterian forms Elizabeth ('Bessie') Hayes. They had five daughters.

Horse-breaking methods received much attention in Australia. The ideas of J. S. Rarey (1827-1866), demonstrated in Sydney and Melbourne in 1858, were in advance of previous practices and were taken up by such noted horsemen as Cuthbert Fetherstonhaugh and E. M. Curr [qq.v.4,3]. In 1884 'Professor' H. Sample came to Australia from the United States of America and taught what he claimed was an improvement on Rarey's method. After watching a Sample demonstration in Melbourne, McGillivray was 'so surprised at … the small amount of knowledge to be gained from him for two guineas' that he decided to teach his own method for half the price. For the next fifteen years he gave demonstrations and advice on all aspects of horse management throughout eastern Australia. He estimated that he taught 'upwards of 24,000 pupils' and styled himself 'Professor McGillivray'.

In his treatise, *Australian Horses from Paddock to Park* (Sydney, 1902), he denounced the prevalent 'station method' where horses were broken in by 'hauling about', often in a brutal fashion. While he built on Rarey's and Sample's methods he also criticized them. He reckoned they were at their weakest at the most difficult stage of breaking in, catching the horse, although he owed more to Rarey than he cared to admit. Among the many devices he invented were a 'patent halter', a crush pen, a safety buggy strap and 'McGillivray's Rarey Strap'. Once asked by a 'smart alec' to reveal his secret equine recipe for two shillings and six pence, he wrote out: 'Oil of common sense, two drachms; oil of kindness, two drachms; clear, cool courage, two drachms; clear grit, two drachms; mix and apply in a small yard'!

In 1904 McGillivray, who also practised as a veterinary surgeon, moved to a property, Merrigong, south of Nimmitabel, New South Wales. His wife died next year. On 28 May 1908 at Grenfell, described as an auctioneer of Wagga Wagga, he married Jessie West. Returning to Mount Gambier, he became well known in sporting circles and followed the hounds with the Mount Gambier Hunt Club. In World War I McGillivray became one those described by A. B. Paterson [q.v.11] as 'Methusaliers': on 24 September 1915, claiming to be 45, he enlisted in the Australian Imperial Force and joined the First Australian Remount Unit. After service as a veterinary surgeon in Egypt, he was discharged in Australia on 18 October 1916. He died of cancer on 14 August 1921 at Mount Gambier; two days later a mounted party formed part of the cortège to the Presbyterian cemetery, where he was buried. His wife and their daughter, and three daughters of his first marriage, survived him.

G. Walsh, *Pioneering Days* (Syd, 1993); *Pastoral Review*, Mar 1904, p 21, Sept 1921, p 708; *J of the Aust War Memorial*, Oct 1982, p 9; *South-Eastern Star* (Mount Gambier), 15 Aug 1921, p 3; B2455/1 1944195 (NAA); information from Dr L. MacGillivray, Fullerton, SA.
                                                            G. P. WALSH

McINTOSH, SAMUEL (1867-1939), irrigation administrator and horticulturist, was born on 11 December 1867 at Findon, Adelaide, eldest child of Daniel McIntosh, labourer and later farmer, and his wife Mary, née Allison (d.1874). Sam's parents had migrated from Ayrshire, Scotland in 1866. Following education at St Clair, Woodville, Houghton and Telowie, he worked on his father's mixed farm at Tickera, upper Yorke Peninsula, helping to prepare the land for cultivation by scrub rolling and water carting. Here on his father's orchard he saw at first hand the benefits of irrigation from the Beetaloo reticulation system. He also joined the Independent Order of Odd Fellows Manchester Unity lodge at Tickera and became secretary and presiding officer.

In June 1891 McIntosh went to Renmark on the River Murray and found employment with Chaffey Brothers [qq.v.7] Ltd, at five shillings and sixpence per day, as a planter, grader and ganger, before being appointed head ganger in the planting section. Next year, offered the opportunity to gain experience in California with one of the Chaffeys' experts, he preferred to stay at Renmark, where he was foreman of the gang grading and irrigating the channels on the river blocks until mid-1898. During this time he learned much about management of his workers and assessing the fertility of the soil for cultivation.

To stem the flow of South Australians following William Lane [q.v.9] to Paraguay, in March 1894 the first village settlements on the river were started. On the instruction of the Chaffeys, McIntosh assisted Lyrup settlers by planting the first vineyard and laying out irrigation channels. As chairman of directors of the Ral Ral Prospecting Co., he went to Western Australia in 1895 but soon returned to the river settlements. At the end of that year Chaffey Bros went into liquidation, owing huge amounts in wages to its employees and holding thousands of acres of unsold land. Appointed chairman of the employees' committee, McIntosh settled at Renmark and ran an orchard and ornamental tree nursery. He assisted with the report to the South Australian parliamentary sub-committee on Chaffey Bros' affairs. As a consequence, the commissioner of crown lands made McIntosh expert for village settlements, at an annual salary of £200; his role was to advise and instruct settlers in better horticultural methods, in the hope that their settlements could become self-sufficient, while keeping the government informed of their progress and problems.

On 10 September 1896 at Kadina, Yorke Peninsula, Samuel married with Congregational forms Constance Effie Taylor. They went to live at Overland Corner on the Murray, where McIntosh established the earliest experimental river irrigation plot in the colony. He was also appointed assistant inspector of fisheries and had the use of the first motor launch on the river. Several years later he recommended the establishment of a floating fish hatchery, but the radical concept was not followed through. McIntosh gained the confidence of the village settlers, his diplomacy with his government employers enabling many local problems to be solved. His reports helped a South Australian royal commission (1899-1900) to wind up six unsuccessful village settlements, with bad debts written off and village lands being let under perpetual lease.

In December 1900 McIntosh moved his family to Waikerie, where he started a river irrigation experimental orchard and vineyard. His position was renamed village settlement inspector; this was reduced in scope in 1903 when the Markaranka Irrigation Co. offered him the part-time position of general manager and he moved to North West Bend. He was also appointed manager of Holder settlement and irrigation administrator for the New Era Fruitgrowing Co.

McIntosh resigned his various appointments in 1906 to become chairman of government irrigation boards and manager of the Murray Bridge experimental farm, in addition to river fisheries and village settlements. In January 1910 he inaugurated the Government Irrigation Department in South Australia, becoming officer-in-charge of irrigation and reclamation works the following July, at a salary of £450 per year; in March 1911 he was appointed director of irrigation. Next month he left for Europe and North America on behalf of the South Australian government, primarily to observe irrigation practices. He brought back valuable information to be assessed for suitability for local irrigation needs.

During and after World War I McIntosh was involved in the State government's plans to establish returned soldiers on blocks along the Murray, using his knowledge of river conditions, soil and suitable crop types. In 1923 a three-man irrigation commission replaced him; McIntosh was one of its members but resigned in October 1926. At the age of 58 he established a fruit block at Berri on his own property, Moy, with his son Douglas.

With all his official appointments, McIntosh still managed to find time to become involved in local organizations. A member of the Morgan District Council and the first Renmark Literary and Debating Society and Model Parliament, he founded the Murray Bridge Fathers' Association and Agricultural Bureau and the Murray River Progress Association. In 1901 he had been appointed a justice of the peace. He also served as chieftain of the Murray Bridge Caledonian Society; his sporting interests included the Murray Bridge and South Australian rowing clubs.

Detailed diaries that McIntosh kept from about 1895 to 1935 recorded his visits to river settlements, the work he oversaw there, his plans for improvements, meetings attended, notes regarding equipment used and crops planted and his overseas trip in 1911. They revealed the dedication with which he undertook all his projects, his official appointments and associated activities. He also wrote articles, including 'Lucern cultivation and management' (*Bulletin* of the Department of Agriculture, 1910) and 'Irrigation in South Australia' (*Journal of Agriculture of South Australia*, 1914).

Predeceased by two sons, McIntosh died on 21 February 1939 at Berri and was buried with Anglican rites; the attendance at the funeral was the largest in the district to that time. His wife and their three daughters and one son survived him. There were many tributes in the local newspaper to his personality, ability and outstanding contribution to the establishment of irrigation work along the Murray.

H. J. Finnis, *Village Settlements on the River Murray* (Adel, 1959); A. Jones, *Lyrup Village* (Lyrup, SA, 1994); Berri Jubilee Historical Committee, *River Reflections* (Berri, SA, 1986); *Riverlander*, no 377, Aug 1982, p 5; *Sunraysia Daily*, 18 Oct 1920, p 1; *Advertiser* (Adel), 22 Feb 1939, p 24; *Murray Pioneer*, 23 Feb 1939, p 11; McIntosh papers (SLSA).   NEIL THOMAS

McKEDDIE, JOHN EDWIN (1902-1980), army officer and stockbroker, was born on 25 November 1902 at Meeniyan, Victoria, youngest of six children of John McKeddie, a storekeeper who came from Scotland, and his Victorian-born wife Margaret Jane, née Witherden. Educated at Melbourne High School, Jack obtained employment in the Bank of New South Wales. In 1929 he entered the stockbroking firm of Eric J. Morgan. Having served in the militia, he enlisted in the Australian Imperial Force on 25 May 1940 as a gunner. He was commissioned lieutenant on 15 October. Next day at the Cairns [q.v.3] Memorial Church, East Melbourne, he married with Presbyterian forms Doris Muriel McFadyen (1896-1988), a saleswoman; they were to remain childless. For many years Doris was in charge of the fashion department of the Myer [qq.v.10,15] Emporium Ltd, travelling regularly to Paris, Berlin, Rome and New York.

In November 1940 McKeddie sailed for the Middle East with the 2/12th Field Regiment. Detached to headquarters, 9th Division, in January 1941, he was appointed aide-de-camp to Major General (Sir) Leslie Morshead [q.v.15] in March and served with him during the siege of Tobruk, Libya, in April-October. McKeddie advised Morshead that the 2/12th Field Regiment was more suitable than the 2/7th to be sent to Tobruk as it had experience on the 60-pounder (27 kg) guns available there, and so the 2/12th became the only Australian field regiment to take part in the siege. Rejoining his unit in October 1941, McKeddie saw action at Tel el Eisa, Egypt, in July 1942 and at El Alamein in October-November, returning to Australia in February 1943.

After training in Queensland, the 2/12th reached Papua in August and from September was involved in the battles for Lae and Finschhafen, New Guinea. On 1 October McKeddie was forward observation officer with a company of the 2/13th Battalion during an attack near Kakakog. He won the Military Cross for 'coolness and devotion to duty' in bringing accurate fire on the enemy despite being under heavy fire from three sides. Next month he was with the 26th Brigade as it advanced towards Sattelberg. On the night of 2/3 December he was forward observation officer with the 2/23rd Battalion when it was heavily counter-attacked near Kuanko village. He occupied his observation post while under enfilade machine-gun fire, and 'his efficient direction of fire was largely responsible for breaking up the enemy attack'. He was awarded a Bar to his M.C.

Following the pursuit of the Japanese to Sio, the 2/12th Field Regiment sailed to Australia in February 1944. McKeddie had been promoted captain that month. Having twice been in hospital with malaria, he was attached to headquarters, Royal Australian Artillery, 9th Division, from November to January 1945. He was posted to the Land Headquarters Tactical School, Beenleigh, Queensland, in February. Rejoining his unit in April, he reached Morotai in May. In May-August the 2/12th supported the 24th Brigade in operations on Labuan and in British North Borneo. He returned to Australia in September, transferring to the Reserve of Officers on the 19th.

On 8 November 1945 McKeddie bought a seat on the Stock Exchange of Melbourne and became a partner (senior partner 1952) of Eric J. Morgan & Co. Vice-president of his regimental association in 1947-51, he became a trustee of the association's Patriotic Relief Fund, a position he held until his death. He was a member of the Legacy Club of Melbourne from 1953 (president 1959), a member and trustee of the Rats of Tobruk Association and president of the Nurses Memorial Centre in 1966-71. In March 1971 he sold his seat on the stock exchange and retired.

Having rowed with Banks Rowing Club as a young man, McKeddie was patron of the Old Oarsmen's Association of Victoria and a member of the Victorian Club and Amateur Sports Club. He belonged to the Atheneum and Naval and Military clubs; a Freemason, he was a foundation member of Lodge Henley. Survived by his wife, McKeddie died on 3 November 1980 at Prahran and was cremated. His estate was sworn for probate at $207 206.

D. Dexter, *The New Guinea Offensives* (Canb, 1961); M. Parsons, *Gunfire!* (Melb, 1991); B883, item VX17668 (NAA, Canb); PR84/122 (AWM); information from Mr M Parsons, Cheltenham, Mr N. Morgan, Toorak, and Mr D. Growns, Melb, and Miss M. Bowman, Mornington, Vic.

JOLYON HORNER

MACLEAN, WILLIAM EUSTACE (1884-1964), engineer, was born on 4 October 1884 in Sydney, son of Hector Roderick Maclean, a London-born musician, and his wife Margaret, née McKay. Educated at Fort Street Model School, William studied fitting and turning and technical drawing at Sydney Technical College and by his own account attended the University of Sydney without completing a degree. He worked as a surveyor, draftsman and engineer in private firms, the Department of Public Works and the New South Wales Government Railways and Tramways.

Moving to Canada in 1911, Maclean was employed on power-station construction, surveys and designs. In 1915-16 in Russia he was general superintendent of a team of 520

Canadians, building the Kola to Kandalashka section of the Murmansk war emergency railway. Back in Canada, on 30 November 1918 he married Lilian Agnes Balcombe. Learning of a hydro-electric scheme being built in Tasmania, he wrote to (Sir) John Butters [q.v.7], general manager of the Hydro-Electric Department, to ask about employment prospects, describing himself as 'a first class instrument man and draftsman [with] a thorough knowledge of present-day construction methods' and supplying references. Butters replied: 'You will commence at a salary of £375 if you match your papers'.

Next year Maclean joined the H.E.D. as an assistant engineer, surveying the hydroelectric power potential of the Huon River system and at Lake Rolleston. Twelve months later, his wife having tired of life in the bush, he applied for a position in head office. Instead, Butters gave him a pay rise and sent him as resident engineer to the southern end of the Great Lake, on Tasmania's bleak central plateau, to supervise construction of a massive, multiple-arch dam at Miena. His superior later wrote that Maclean had 'great executive ability, a vigorous constitution and a personality that commands respect and a hearty cooperation'. In 1922, shortly before the dam was completed, Maclean went back to Canada because of his pregnant wife's ill health. He also worked in the United States of America and England, before returning to Sydney in 1927 as managing director of International Combustion (Australasia) Ltd. He was responsible for power developments at Newcastle, Collie (Western Australia) and Wonthaggi (Victoria).

Following the death in office of Harry Curtis [q.v.], Maclean was appointed chief of the Hydro Electric Commission, Tasmania, on 4 September 1933. As commissioner, he built the Tarraleah power station (opened in February 1938), on the Upper Derwent, to increase power for Tasmanian industries, including pulp and paper mills. Later that year he spent five months in Europe and North America to study dam construction and make contact with aluminium-producing interests.

By then Maclean was at increasingly bitter odds with some of his senior staff, notably two with higher academic qualifications than his. In 1940 a public inquiry found that some of his actions indicated 'a desire to control the undertaking alone'. The premier (Sir) Robert Cosgrove [q.v.13] introduced a bill in line with the inquiry's report, threatening to end Maclean's tenure, but he fought back, and emerged in August 1941 with a renewed, five-year contract. Maclean then had his internal critics dismissed, but problems continued as wartime stringency impeded further development, and the commissioner disagreed with Cosgrove's emphasis on extending services to rural areas. There was little doubt that when the five years expired the government would seek a successor with higher qualifications and a more dynamic style. Maclean did not reapply, and (Sir) Allan Knight succeeded him.

Appointed justice of the peace in February 1940, Maclean was coroner at the Kingston court in 1951-63. He belonged to the Tasmanian Club and Hobart Rotary Club, and his hobby was golf. A Freemason, he was a member of the Tasmanian Union Lodge, Hobart, and sometime master of Bothwell Tasmanian Union Lodge. Maclean died on 17 February 1964 in Royal Hobart Hospital and was cremated. His wife and their two daughters survived him.

R. Lupton, *Lifeblood: Tasmania's Hydro Power* (Syd, 2000?); *Mercury* (Hob), 26 July 1933, p 6, 16 May 1938, p 6, 19 Feb 1964, p 5.

ROGER LUPTON

McLEOD, BILLY; *see* TULABA

McLEOD, HANNAH (1857-1912), hospital matron, was born on 25 August 1857 at Redfern, Sydney, fourth child and second daughter of English-born parents William Browne McLeod, master mariner, and his wife Eleanor Fowler, née Phillips. Hannah was educated in Sydney. She began as a probationer at Newcastle General Hospital on 1 July 1891, and in 1893 was appointed by (Sir) James Graham and Dr Andrew Watson Munro [qq.v.4,10] to take charge of a two-bed hospital in Hay Street, which they had started for 'genteel poor' women of Sydney. This became the Women's Hospital (commonly known as 'Crown Street' after it moved there in 1897); she was to be foundation matron for nineteen years.

While working as matron, McLeod trained as a midwife, taking lectures and coaching from Graham and Munro. Having obtained her midwifery certificate in 1897, she assumed responsibility for training midwives. She worked tirelessly to make 'Crown Street' a respected and significant women's hospital and midwifery training school. Short in stature, of frail physique, weak in health and frequently suffering pain, she nevertheless demonstrated indomitable energy and spirit and strict discipline; she was highly regarded by the medical and nursing professions and in the community.

Inaugurating a systematic approach to an outdoor system of midwifery nursing, McLeod began a district nursing service. She later reported that the out-patient maternity duties of the nurses were decidedly hard, involving calls at all hours of the day and night. After midnight, they travelled on foot or in rough carts or conveyances. The greatest respect was shown to Matron McLeod and her nurses, even in the poorest parts of the city. The police kindly took care of them in the doubtful neighbourhoods. Thus they were able to move about 'the lanes of Sydney and its environs, to save lives and conserve the health of mothers and infants'.

Both an able administrator and a practical woman, in the first years of the hospital's existence Matron McLeod had to attend to the cooking and washing and walk to nearby markets to purchase supplies, accompanied by an employee with a wheelbarrow. She was an early member of the Australasian Trained Nurses' Association, founded in 1899. In 1901 she patented a baby cot. She did not marry. Hannah McLeod died of pneumonia on 24 October 1912 at Crown Street hospital and was buried in St Thomas's Church of England cemetery, North Sydney. In a published 'appreciation', her colleagues recalled that 'this smart, thin woman-in-white' had a living interest in the entire field of nursing, was expert alike in surgical and obstetric nursing, and devoted, truthful and ingenuous almost to a fault, but that her qualities at the bedside were the finest lessons she imparted to her pupils.

W. Adcock, *With Courage & Devotion* (Syd, 1984); B. Schultz, *A Tapestry of Service*, 1 (Melb, 1991); *The Women's Hospital (Crown Street) 1893-1983* (Syd, 1994); *SMH*, 21 Oct 1912, p 8; *T&CJ*, 6 Nov 1912, p 34; *A'sian Nurses' J*, 16 Dec 1912, p 400; History of Three Crown Street Matrons Interwoven with North Sydney (ms, 1974, North Sydney Hist Soc).   BETTY CAPPER

MACLURCAN, HANNAH (1860-1936), hotelier, was born on 17 October 1860 at Tambaroora, near Hill End, New South Wales, fourth child of Jacob Aaron Phillips, a London-born Jewish storekeeper and later hotelier, and his first wife Susan, née Moses (d.1866), from Scotland. The family had moved to Queensland by 1866. Hannah later told her children that her father put her in the kitchen of his hotel at Townsville at an early age, and she gradually worked through the dining room to the office so she knew the organization thoroughly. He sent her, aged 15, to manage his Club Hotel at Toowoomba.

On 25 March 1880 in her father's house in Brisbane Hannah married with Presbyterian forms Robert Watson Wigham, an English-born banker. They had two daughters. In 1883, while returning from England in the *Roma*, they were caught in the tidal wave caused by the eruption of Krakatoa. 'We sailed through the debris of the explosion—sea covered with pumice stone, floating bodies, human and animal', she wrote later. On 2 July 1887 in the manse, Leichhardt Street, Brisbane, Hannah, now a widow, married Donald Boulton Maclurcan, a retired master mariner, from Devon, England, also a hotelier. With him she managed the Criterion and later the Queen's hotels at Townsville. Two children were born in the next two years. She published her first book, *Mrs Maclurcan's Cookery Book: A Collection of Practical Recipes, Specially Suitable for Australia*, at Townsville (1898), helping the printer to set the type, which she bought herself, and reprinting when it sold out in a couple of weeks. There was also a London edition, a copy of which was presented to Queen Victoria, and later editions were published in Sydney and Melbourne. In all there were twenty editions of *Mrs Maclurcan's Cookery Book*, with revisions and enlargements from time to time, the last appearing in 1930.

In England again, she published *The 20th Century Cookery Book: A Thousand Practical Recipes for Everyday Use* (1901). That year Hannah and her husband took over, from Mrs Mary Hayes, the lease of the Wentworth Hotel on Church Hill, near Wynyard Square, Sydney, in time to capitalize on the visit of the Duke and Duchess of York in May and June 1901. The lease for £735 per annum was for an establishment which, though licensed, functioned mainly as a boarding-house with thirty-two bedrooms let at 28 shillings per week each. Donald Maclurcan died in 1903, and the lease and licence were transferred to his widow. Though Hannah could and did take over the kitchen when necessary, she began transforming the Wentworth into a grand hotel. In 1912 a limited company was set up with Hannah as managing director. The freehold of the property was acquired and two more floors were added, increasing the number of bedrooms to eighty-three. In 1920, after the acquisition of adjoining property, 'a palatial ballroom' decorated 'in the style of the Georgian period' and capable of accommodating a thousand dancers and diners was built. To publicize the hotel, in addition to her books, Hannah contributed a cookery column to the society magazine *The Ladies Sphere*. She encouraged art exhibitions, charity functions and fashionable weddings at the hotel. The Wentworth ballroom, 'one of the finest in the Southern hemisphere', was said to be a favourite haunt of the Prince of Wales when he was in Sydney in 1920.

Her hotel was renowned for its fine cuisine, especially the cold buffet luncheons served in the Palm Court, 'Sydney's Premier Café'. She was perhaps the first Australian celebrity cook writer (and perhaps also the earliest to be accused of passing off others' recipes as her own). Mrs Maclurcan's cookery books showed some evidence of her Queensland origins, with occasional recipes using tropical fruit and seafood, but by the 1920s they reflected the stodgy depths to which Australian middle-class cooking had descended.

She shamelessly courted titled and celebrity visitors and generated publicity through her glossy, in-house *Wentworth Magazine*, edited by Winifred Hamilton and illustrated with pictures of wedding receptions and other significant events taken by leading society photographers. As well there were Mrs Maclurcan's much promoted antiques with which the hotel was furnished, her famous floral arrangements, her cars and her collection of Pekinese dogs. The magazine fostered such writers as Mabel Forrest [q.v.], (Dame) Mary Gilmore, Nettie Palmer, Jessie Litchfield [qq.v.9,11,10], Marjorie and Roderic Quinn [q.v.11] and Camden Morrisby, and gave space to poetry and theatre and book reviews. By 1928 the Wentworth had its own parking station with space for 400 cars a day and a 'modern car laundry and filling station' under the management of G. Underwood Grimes. Next year a 'chic and delectable little stall' selling curios, lingerie, hosiery and 'toiletry trifles a man may have forgotten to pack' was established in the lounge. The Depression, however, brought a decline in occupation rates and a reduction in the tariff as well as the demise of the *Wentworth Magazine*.

'Madame' retired as hotel manager in 1932. Her place was taken by her son Charles Dansie Maclurcan (1889-1957) who, although an electrical engineer (he used the flat roof of the hotel for his pioneering experiments in wireless transmission), had been a director since 1916. Her daughter Evelyn Clara (b.1888), Mrs Postle, also served on the board. Hannah continued as managing director.

As a retreat from the hotel, she acquired Bilgola, the house built originally as a weekender by W. B. Dalley [q.v.4] at Bilgola Beach, and there lived in style. She travelled to the United States of America most years to study developments in hotel management and add to her collection of curios and antiques. On 17 August 1931 at St Nicholas's Church of England, Mordialloc, Melbourne, she married English-born Robert Lee. His occupation was described as 'gentleman', hers as 'domestic duties'. She died on 27 September 1936 in St Vincent's Hospital and was cremated. Her husband, two daughters of her first marriage and the son and daughter of her second survived her.

Illustrated Souvenir Programme of the Visit of T.R.H., the Duke and Duchess of York (Syd, 1901); C. D. Maclurcan, *The Story of the Wentworth Hotel* (Syd, 1946); S. Addison, *A Good Plain Cook* (Brisb, 1985); B. R. Austin (comp), *A Bibliography of Australian Cookery Books Published Prior to 1941* (Melb, 1987); H. Radi (ed), *200 Australian Women* (Syd, 1988); B. Kennedy, *Sydney's Own: 25 Years of the Sheraton Wentworth* (Syd, 1991); *Wentworth Mag*, July 1925, Dec 1930; *Daily Telegraph* (Syd), 6 Apr 1932, p 4.   BEVERLEY KINGSTON

MCMAHON, JAMES (1838-1914), carrier, was born on 31 May 1838 in County Clare, Ireland, eldest son of John McMahon, labourer and carter, and his wife Catherine, née Cunningham. Having little education, if any, Jimmy migrated to Sydney with his family when he was 9; three siblings were born in New South Wales.

For his first job when aged 13, with a baker, McMahon was paid seven shillings a week. He was next employed by a wine and spirit merchant, then for six years by Patrick Murphy, a carrier, acquiring a basic knowledge of the industry. After two years with J. P. Elliot & Co. at Woolloomooloo, McMahon launched his own business, by buying a horse and harness and renting a dilapidated dray. He worked for a time in Queensland, first in partnership with George Fox, then joined the firm Woods, Shortland & Adair, master carriers and forwarding agents. Next McMahon contracted for the cartage of copper from the Peak Downs copper fields, near Clermont, to Broadsound. Returning to Sydney, from 1864 he held an exclusive contract with the New South Wales railways, delivering to the warehouses all wool received at the Darling Harbour rail siding. This exclusivity, with his other transport clients, provided him with a platform to acquire wealth, which he used to purchase real estate in the city and suburbs and extensive grazing properties. On Amaroo, at Molong, he raised sheep and agisted his horses. He also owned Bumbaldry at Cowra and land at Mount Druitt.

At St Mary's Catholic Cathedral on 6 June 1864 McMahon married Mary Coyle, a housemaid, who had been born in County Fermanagh, Ireland. They had seven children: the eldest James Patrick (1868-1951) helped his father to manage the business; the twins Ernest and Joseph were employed as outriders (foremen on horseback); Thomas and John managed country properties, William was a solicitor; and Agnes, under the protection of a trusted male escort, collected his rents—it took her five days of every week to perform this task.

Although McMahon was of medium height, he had a large frame, and was renowned as a wrestler and weightlifter. This served him well as an employer of a large body of horse drivers and labourers. He became known as 'Butty', allegedly for his propensity to settle disputes by head-butting his antagonists. During the 1890 maritime strike he used force to subdue his own employees: he boasted that when strikers endeavoured to prevent him from leaving his yard he gained passage by assaulting them, resulting in three being sent to (Royal) Prince Alfred Hospital. Harassed outside his yard during the strike by the Trolley, Draymen and Carters' Union secretary and Louis Carlo, a picket from the Wharf Labourers' Union, McMahon lost his temper, rushed at Carlo and struck him on the head with a stave from a cask. The picket ended up in hospital. In 1890-92 McMahon was the first president of the Master Carriers' Association of New South Wales, and in 1900-11 served a second term. As president, he was in continual conflict with W. M. Hughes [q.v.9], an organizer for and later president of the carters' union.

In the creation of his real estate holdings McMahon was single-minded. When he completed a dwelling, he insisted that one of his drivers reside in it, thus guaranteeing him the rent (deducted from the employee's wages). Similarly, he acquired hotels adjacent to his yards, so that his drivers would drink in them, allowing him to recover some of their earnings. In 1906 he had 400 horses and employed 253 men. By 1914, with 250 teams and 550 horses—said to be the biggest fleet in the southern hemisphere—he reputedly transported 750 000 bales of wool annually. According to the *Bulletin*, 'the richer he got the more prodigious grew his girth'. He lived at Redfern, where he also had four yards and stables and, wearing a trilby, was a familiar figure driving his buggy.

McMahon died on 17 November 1914 at his home and after a requiem mass was buried in the Catholic section of Rookwood cemetery. His wife and children survived him, inheriting an estate sworn for probate at £236 325. Some property was apparently omitted, however, and the *Bulletin* described him, probably accurately, as a 'reputed millionaire'. James, a notable Rugby Union footballer in his youth, succeeded his father as owner of the transport business, which he converted to motor vehicles; he was president of the Master Carriers' Association in 1925-35. Butty's grandson William was prime minister of Australia in 1970-72.

Aust Country Life, 1 Aug 1906, p 21; *Freight Carriers*, May-June 1980, p 2; *SMH*, 16 Sept 1890, p 5, 17 Nov 1914, p 8; *Catholic Press* (Syd), 19 Nov 1914, p 23; *Daily Telegraph* (Syd), 19 Nov 1914, p 6, 6 Feb 1922, p 4; *Bulletin*, 26 Nov 1914, p 16; *Smith's Weekly*, 17 May 1920, p 14; Inventory of assets, 16 April 1915 (SRNSW).   ANTHONY NORMAN

MACMAHON, PHILIP JOHN (1857-1911), horticulturist, author and public servant, was born on 13 December 1857 at Sandyford, Dublin, eldest son of Peter MacMahon, estate agent and gardener at Jamestown House, and his wife Maria, née Riley. After attending school locally at Black Rock, Philip acquired some technical education and travelled in Europe before being employed in the large nursery firm Dickson & Sons, in Cheshire, England. The Earl of Denbigh recommended him to Sir Joseph Hooker [q.v.4] who offered Philip a studentship at the Royal Botanic Gardens, Kew, in 1881.

In March 1882 MacMahon was appointed curator at the Hull Botanic Gardens, where in five years he achieved success with the gardens and with a public education programme he instigated on botany and horticulture. Inspired by an interest in tropical agriculture, he accepted a position in India, which proved of short duration when he became ill. Making his way to Victoria in July 1888, MacMahon became a journalist with the *Daily Telegraph*, Melbourne, writing on botany, horticulture, economics and science. A chance meeting with a Queensland parliamentary delegation led to an offer of the directorship of the Botanic Gardens, Brisbane.

Arriving in April 1889, MacMahon devoted long hours and his full capacities to revitalizing the gardens, only to face severe inundation during the 1893 flood. Over a century later some of his remodelling and rebuilding remained evident. With enthusiastic encouragement, but scant resources, the government adopted his suggestions to use the labour of the unemployed and for incorporating landfill from railway excavations. Although mainly relying on native plants, the curator called upon associates throughout the world to introduce exotic species, while he shared Queensland seed material with his correspondents.

Endeavouring to popularize botany, MacMahon lectured extensively to large audiences and instructed school children in gardening. The supplying of trees to schools for Arbor Day, which he instituted in 1890, continued his involvement in educating all generations. In addition to providing a place of relaxation for city dwellers and visitors, he established a pharmaceutical garden to provide research facilities for chemists and doctors. In 1904 MacMahon was appointed director of forests and continued his lifelong interest in propagating trees and timber conservation. He published a comprehensively illustrated text, *The Merchantable Timbers of Queensland* (Brisbane, 1905).

MacMahon's professional reports and writings exhibited a lyrical quality amid precise practical information, while his love of language and literature found an outlet in his chairmanship of the Queensland Irish Association literary group. The charm and courtesy of this small, dapper, bewhiskered man were renowned and appreciated.

On 20 January 1909 at St Joseph's Catholic Church, Woollahra, Sydney, MacMahon married 29-year-old Ethel Alicia Hendy-Pooley, a teacher born at Madras, India. She was expecting their child when her husband died of dengue fever and heart failure on 12 April 1911 at Maryborough. He was buried there, survived by his wife and by a son born four months later. At the time of his death, MacMahon was working on an inventory of the quality and quantity of some 5800 square miles (1.5 million ha) of state forests and timber reserves. His personal books, acquired by the government for £31, and scant pension provided little for his family.

Queensland, 1900: A Narrative of Her Past, Together with Biographies of Her Leading Men (Brisb, 1900); J. Harrison, 'An Irish Horticulturist in Queensland: The Philip MacMahon Story', *JRHSQ*, 16, no 1, Feb 1996, p 31; *Maryborough Chronicle*, 13 Apr 1911; staff card, SRS 1189/2, item 134 (QSA); information from the late Deirdre MacMahon, Dublin.   JENNIFER HARRISON

MacNAMARA, FRANCIS (c.1810-1861+), convict, known as 'Frank the Poet', was possibly from County Clare, Ireland, although he was reported at his trial at Kilkenny in January 1832 to be 'a real Corkonian' in his speech. His writings show that he had a good education in English literature and was familiar with the Irish Bardic tradition and its poetic forms. MacNamara was entered in the convict records as both Protestant and Catholic and with different places of origin and occupations. Sentenced to seven years transportation for smashing a shop window and stealing a piece of cloth, he entertained the court to an extempore epigram expressing his happiness at being sent to 'Botany Bay'. Aboard the convict transport *Eliza* he composed 'a mock heroic poem' about his trial; this did not prevent him from incurring a flogging for 'bad conduct'.

Reaching Sydney on 6 September 1832, MacNamara was assigned to John Jones, but within three months was put in an ironed gang for an undisclosed offence. During the next eight years he received fourteen floggings (650 lashes) and served three and a half years in road gangs, thirteen days of solitary confinement and three months on the treadmill. Early in 1838 he was assigned to the Australian Agricultural Co. at Calala on the Peel River, before being moved to Stroud and in 1839 to the company's coalmines at Newcastle. Apparently refusing to work underground, he was transferred to an ironed gang at Woolloomooloo and from there to Parramatta, then to Berrima to work on road making. For escaping and carrying arms stolen from their guards, he and four others

were sentenced to seven months transportation to Van Diemen's Land in July 1842.

Apart from being punished for leading a successful go-slow protest, MacNamara did not get into trouble at Port Arthur. He received his ticket-of-leave in January 1847, his conditional pardon late that year and his full pardon in July 1849. Moving to Melbourne, he subsequently vanished from the record apart from an appearance in 1861 at the Mudgee goldfields in New South Wales where he made a genealogy for a local innkeeper and an illuminated copy of Burns's 'Man was Made to Mourn'. An 1868 description by Marcus Clarke [q.v.3] of an Irish poet in one of the 'low' Melbourne pubs sounds very like MacNamara, but there is no record of what became of him.

There is dispute over how many of the verses that circulated orally and were written down by other people late in the nineteenth century were composed by 'Frank the Poet'. Incontestably, he wrote his *magnum opus*, 'The Convict's Tour to Hell', while working as a shepherd at Stroud in October 1839, and subsequently at Newcastle composed three petitions to the authorities, in verse. Other works which can be more or less confidently attributed to him were: 'Dialogue Between Two Hibernians in Botany Bay', 'Labouring with the Hoe', 'The Seizure of the Cypress Brig', 'The Ballad of Martin Cash', the celebrated 'The Convict's Lament' (also known as 'Moreton Bay') and some epigrams. While possessing an extensive knowledge of classical literary allusions, he was also an extempore versifier. His poems and songs had instant appeal to the convict population for their spirited opposition to the 'System' and were enthusiastically rendered around the evening campfire wherever convicts gathered.

J. Meredith and R. Whalan, *Frank the Poet* (Melb, 1979); B. Reece, 'Frank the Poet' in B. Reece (ed), *Exiles from Erin* (Lond, 1991).   R. H. W. REECE

McRAE, TOMMY (c.1835-1901), Aboriginal artist, whose Aboriginal names have been recorded as Yackaduna or Warra-euea, was probably from the Kwatkwat people, whose country stretched south of the Murray River near the junction of the Goulburn River in Victoria. He lived in or close to the Upper Murray all his life; one early twentieth-century report described him as 'a well-known identity throughout the country from Albury to Yarrawonga'. On the evidence of his art and at least one contemporary account, his early years were spent in a relatively undisturbed, traditional lifestyle. During his life he witnessed (and recorded in drawings) the establishment of pastoral settler society in his country.

Like many of his contemporaries, Tommy became a labourer for the pastoralists who opened up sheep stations in northern Victoria. He was also reputedly a stockman for Andrew Hume, who developed Brocklesby station at Corowa, New South Wales, between 1849 and 1857. The earliest written reference to McRae described him as 'an Australian Aboriginal of David Reid's [q.v.6] station on the Upper Murray'. Until 1865 Reid's property was at Barnawartha, although he had earlier held other runs in the region, including Yackandandah. McRae's first drawings were collected between 1861 and 1864 at Barnawartha by the sculptor Theresa Walker. They were described as the work of 'Tommy Barnes'. The artist possibly adopted the name of an employer, the Wodonga pastoralist David Barnes.

At Wahgunyah in the 1860s McRae met Roderick Kilborn, a Canadian vigneron and telegraph-master, who later became a patron and protector when the artist settled on the shores of Lake Moodemere at Wahgunyah, probably in the early 1880s. The minutes of the Victorian Board for the Protection of the Aborigines for 1885 listed McRae, his wife Lily, four children and his brother and sister-in-law living at Lake Moodemere. During these years McRae made and sold books of drawings, raised poultry and fished for Murray cod. His family also made possum-skin rugs. He acquired a reputation for his pen-and-ink drawings, several books of which were collected by travellers who sought him out and paid him for his work. European settlers admired McRae, a dedicated non-drinker, for his industry; one described him as 'an astute financier', and he was able to buy a horse and buggy.

His books of drawings mostly recorded traditional Aboriginal life, such as ceremonies and scenes of hunting and fishing. He depicted individuals and animals (predominantly silhouetted) in landscapes composed of sparse trees and earth; the scenes were often accompanied by annotations. A number of sketches included squatters and Chinese. In several books he chronicled the life of William Buckley [q.v.1], the 'wild white man'. McRae focused on the subject's integration into Aboriginal society rather than on the aspect that so captivated European artists—Buckley's emergence from years of living with indigenous people. During the 1890s McRae continued to make and sell drawings. Between 1890 and 1897, however, all of his children were taken from him under government regulations and sent to various reserves in Victoria. He turned to Kilborn to prevent these seizures but without success.

In 1897 McRae and another Aboriginal man, John Friday, sued a photographer, Thomas Cleary, in Corowa court for failing to pay the £10 he had promised if he were allowed to photograph Aboriginal people at Lake Moodemere. Cleary claimed that the photographs had not turned out, and the case was dismissed. Nevertheless, the action was evidence of the artist's strength of character.

McRae died on 15 October 1901 and was buried in the Carlyle cemetery at Wahgunyah. His drawings are held in several public collections in Australia, including the National Museum of Australia and the National Gallery of Australia, Canberra, the State libraries of Victoria and New South Wales and the Melbourne Museum.

A. Sayers, *Aboriginal Artists of the Nineteenth Century* (Melb, 1994); *Aboriginal History*, 5, no 1, June 1981, p 80; *Corowa Free Press*, 14 May 1886, p 4, 25 Oct 1901, p 3; *Argus Camera Supplement*, 8 June 1929, p 4.   ANDREW SAYERS

MADAME BRUSSELLS; *see* HODGSON

MAHOMED, GOOL BADSHA; *see* ABDULLAH

MAKIN, JOHN (1845-1893), drayman, and his wife SARAH JANE (1845-1918), midwife, became notorious as 'baby farmers'. John was born on 14 February 1845 at Dapto, New South Wales, fourth of eleven children of William Samuel Makin, farmer, and his wife Ellen Selena, née Bolton. Sarah was born on 20 December 1845 in Sydney, only daughter and elder child of former convict Emanuel Sutcliffe, miller, and his Irish-born wife Ellen, née Murphy. On 29 April 1865 Sarah married with Presbyterian forms Charles Edwards, a mariner, in Sydney. They had a daughter. On 27 August 1871 Sarah Jane Edwards, a 'spinster', married, with Free Church of England rites, John Makin, a drayman for a brewery; both were literate. They had five sons and five daughters.

After John suffered an accident, the Makins made a meagre living by taking care of illegitimate babies. Commonly John answered an advertisement, negotiated payment of £3 to £5 and signed 'papers' exonerating the putative father from further responsibility. The mortality rate for babies separated from their mothers was so high that public institutions were reluctant to admit them. Makin, either from fear of destitution or recklessly, accepted babies whom other carers avoided. The family moved frequently, sometimes owing rent.

The Makins came to police attention in October 1892 when workmen uncovered the bodies of two children at 25 Burren Street, Macdonaldtown. John, Sarah and their teenage daughters swore that there had been only one infant in their care while there and it had been returned to its parents. A coronial jury returned open verdicts. But four more bodies were found at Burren Street and police dug in eleven backyards where the Makins had lived since 1890, recovering thirteen bodies in all.

Inquests into the causes of deaths of the infants proceeded in November 1892 in a blaze of publicity. Unable to identify bodies or establish causes of death—there was no evidence of violence or poison—on 28 November a jury returned open verdicts in four cases, but identified one body as that of the illegitimate child of Minnie Davis and Horace Bottamley and recommended a manslaughter charge against the Makins. Exceptionally, Bottamley and Davis had made weekly payments and visited every Saturday night. They were 'quite satisfied' with their baby's treatment. When the child had fallen ill, Makin sent Bottamley a telegram and the baby was taken to a doctor. The parents saw the body beautifully laid out and accepted Makin's offer to arrange burial.

Next month inquests were held into the deaths of four more of the infants, one of whom was Horace Murray, born on 30 May 1892, the illegitimate son of Amber Murray, who advertised for someone to adopt the baby. After Makin accepted £3, his daughter Blanche collected the baby on 27 June, two days before the family departed suddenly for Burren Street. A fellow prisoner testified that John had confided to him that no doctor could find poison but 'they will have me for perjury and illegally burying'. On 21 December a coronial jury returned a verdict of murder in the case of Amber Murray's child.

In March 1893 John and Sarah Makin were tried for the murder of Horace Murray or, if identification failed, of an unknown infant at 109 George Street, Redfern, on 29 June 1892. Neither defendant took the stand. Disregarding testimony of disfiguring sores, the trial judge when addressing the jury spoke of a 'healthy' infant dead within two days. The jury found both defendants guilty of murdering an unknown infant, but recommended mercy for Sarah.

On appeal, defence objection to wrongful admission of the testimony from other mothers (which established the Makins' reputation as 'baby farmers') was dismissed, on the grounds that it was impossible to suppose that such testimony had any influence on the verdict of the jury. An appeal to the Judicial Committee of the Privy Council also failed—the committee would not set aside a jury's decision, the jury having had the 'advantage' of seeing and hearing witnesses. The Dibbs [q.v.4] government rejected a plea for clemency. John then signed a statement that the body was not Amber Murray's son, claiming that it 'was buried in the yard four to five weeks before we got her child'. John Makin was hanged on 15 August 1893 at Sydney gaol.

Sarah's sentence was commuted to penal servitude for life, which she served at Bathurst and in Sydney. Her daughters petitioned for early release in 1907 and again in 1911. On 29 April that year she was discharged from the State Reformatory for Women at Long Bay to the care of her daughter Florence on the grounds of her great age and declining health. She nursed her eldest daughter through a fatal illness, then lived with her son-in-law. 'Mother Makin', as she had been known during her notoriety, died on 13 September 1918 at Marrickville and was buried with Anglican rites in Rookwood cemetery. Three sons and four daughters survived her.

G. C. Addison, *A Digest of Criminal and Magistrates' Cases Decided in New South Wales from 1840 to 30 June 1894* (Syd, 1895); C. Herben, *From Burren Street to the Gallows* (Syd, 1997); *Jnls* (LC, NSW), vol 50, pt 1, p 541; *SMH*, 5 Nov 1892, p 10, 15 Nov 1892, p 3, 16 Nov 1892, p 3, 29 Nov 1892, p 3, 22 Dec 1892, p 4, 7 Mar 1893, p 3, 10 Mar 1893, p 3, 24 Mar 1893, p 2, 31 Mar 1893, p 3; *Bulletin*, 12 Nov 1892, p 7, 19 Nov 1892, p 4.   HEATHER RADI

MARION DUFRESNE, MARC-JOSEPH (1724-1772), mariner, was baptized on 22 May 1724 at St Malo, Brittany, France, youngest of eight children of Julien Marion Dufresne (1681-1739), a wealthy shipowner and merchant, and his wife Marie Seraphique, née Le Fer de la Lande. Marc (also known as Macé and mistakenly by some historians as 'Marie-Joseph' and 'Nicolas-Thomas'), probably educated by a private tutor, first went to sea at the age of 17. During the war of the Austrian Succession (1744-47), he proved a brilliant young privateer and, commanding the *Prince de Conty*, helped to rescue 'Bonnie' Prince Charles Stuart from the west coast of Scotland in September 1746.

Marion Dufresne spent three months as a prisoner of war in England in 1747. Returning to France, he was employed by the French East India Co. and voyaged to Africa, China, India and the Netherlands East Indies. On 20 April 1756 at the Church of St Louis, Lorient, Brittany, he married Julie Bernardine Guilmaut de Beaulieu; they apparently had no children. After military service during the Seven Years War, in 1761 he took the astronomer Alexandre Gui Pingré to the Indian Ocean to observe the transit of Venus, and organized an expedition to the Seychelles in 1768 before settling on the Isle de France (Mauritius).

In 1770 the Polynesian Aotourou (who had journeyed to France with Bougainville) arrived at the island with orders that a passage to his native Tahiti should be arranged for him. Marion Dufresne volunteered to convey Aotourou home and to explore southern waters on the way. Largely financing the voyage himself, he purchased the *Marquis de Castries*, gained the use of the *Mascarin*, and left the Isle de France on 18 October 1771. An outbreak of smallpox resulted in Aotourou dying at Port Dauphin, Madagascar. Undeterred, Marion Dufresne proceeded to the Cape of Good Hope for provisions and headed east. On 13 January 1772 he sighted the Prince Edward Islands, one of which was later named in his honour by Captain Cook [q.v.1]. On 14 January his vessels collided, one being left with a splintered bowsprit and no foremast. Despite the damage he maintained an easterly course, and on 21 January the Crozet Islands were seen and claimed for France.

In need of fresh water and timber to remast the *Marquis de Castries*, Marion Dufresne set a course for Van Diemen's Land. On 3 March 1772 his sailors sighted the coast, near High Rocky Point. Rounding the island's most southerly point on 5 March, the vessels anchored off Cape Frederick Hendrick—in waters now called Marion Bay and North Bay —close to where Abel Tasman [q.v.2] had anchored 130 years before. Marion Dufresne led a party ashore in two boats on 7 March 1772; they were the first French explorers to reach any part of Australia and apparently the first Europeans to encounter the Aborigines of Van Diemen's Land. Initially relations were cordial. When a third boat approached, however, a shower of stones was thrown and Marion Dufresne ordered a retreat. Following another hail of hatchets and stones, which wounded him and several of his party, he ordered a volley of shots to frighten off the attackers. He then sought another landing place but was again showered with missiles. One of his crew being speared in the leg, Marion Dufresne gave the order to fire and give chase. This time at least one Aborigine was killed.

Disappointed in his search for timber and fresh water, after six days he made for the Bay of Islands, New Zealand, where he attempted to remast his vessel. At Te Hue on 12 June 1772 Maoris killed him and twenty-four of his crew. His family was bankrupted by the expedition, which returned to the Isle de France in April 1773. Marion Dufresne's journal has been lost, but that of his second-in-command Julien Crozet, published as *Nouveau voyage à la mer du sud* (Paris, 1783), and manuscript accounts of the expedition provide valuable evidence about indigenous Tasmanian and early Maori life.

Extracts from Journals Relating to the Visit to New Zealand in May-July 1772 of the French Ships 'Mascarin' and 'Marquis de Castries' Under the Command of M.-J. Marion du Fresne (Wellington, NZ, 1985); *Dictionary of NZ Biog*, 1 (Wellington, NZ, 1990); E. Duyker (ed), *The Discovery of Tasmania* (Hob, 1992); E. Duyker, *An Officer of the Blue: Marc-Joseph Marion Dufresne, South Sea Explorer, 1724-1772* (Melb, 1994).　　EDWARD DUYKER

MARKS, JAMES (1834-1915), architect and builder, was born in December 1834 at Yeovil, Somerset, England, son of Paul Marks, ropemaker. James entered the building industry in 1850 as office boy for Joseph and Charles Rigby at Bristol, later working for them as a carpenter on the Central Somerset Railway. His close study of Peter Nicholson's *New Complete Builder* was recognized by the contractors Kirk & Parry, who entrusted him with a complex contract at Portsmouth Harbour. Marks was living at Gosport when he married Elizabeth Marsh on 22 August 1858 at the parish church at Alverstoke, Southampton. They were to have nine children. He worked with the architects and builders Joseph Bull & Sons and other firms on mansions and model farm buildings until he embarked for Queensland.

When Marks arrived with his family in May 1866 the colony was in recession. At Dalby he engaged in 'sundry works' until 1868 and was then contracted by the pastoralists G. H. Davenport and C. B. Fisher [q.v.4] to construct farm buildings 'unequalled in Queensland' at Headington Hill. He later designed and built numerous homesteads and farm buildings. Moving to Toowoomba in 1874, he continued to work as a contractor until he was declared insolvent in 1879. He recovered quickly.

After managing a timber yard, Marks set up as an architect at Toowoomba in 1880. He also became a successful businessman, purchasing in 1884 the timber yards he formerly managed and developing them into the sawmillers Filshie, Broadfoot & Co. His practice on the Darling Downs was broad ranging, including residential, commercial, industrial and institutional buildings. A devout Presbyterian, he provided plans for Toowoomba's first Presbyterian church, St John's, and he later designed St Stephen's Church, also at Toowoomba. In addition, Marks was the architect for St Patrick's Catholic Cathedral, Toowoomba, having won a competition for the commission in 1883. In the late 1880s his eldest son Henry James (1870-1939) trained with him. The firm became James Marks & Son in 1892—the second son Reginald John (1877-1918) was to join the practice after James's retirement.

Marks's reputation and technical competence was complemented by Harry's inventive ingenuity and flair. Unlike James's mostly conventional work, Harry's was unconventional, uninhibited and idiosyncratic; many of the firm's admired buildings (such as St James's church hall, additions to the Toowoomba Maltings and Alexandra Hall) were his designs. Evident in these were construction and climatic innovations that Harry patented, including his Austral windows, which were widely used in the United States of America in the 1920s. Harry also designed St Luke's church hall (1901), featuring Byzantine-like cupolas, cruciform decoration and ventilating gables. According to Janet Hogan, 'the clerestory lighting, the heavy timber detailing to the entrance portico and the triple casement windows with the curious balance of flat head and ornate sill all contribute to form a ... fascinating structure'.

With Elizabeth, in 1900 James travelled to Europe, where they visited the Paris Exhibition. In 1906 he retired. He was active in local affairs, having failed to win East Ward in the 1896 municipal elections, and was a foundation member of the Pioneer Club. Predeceased by his wife, Marks died on 29 October 1915 at Toowoomba, and was buried with Presbyterian forms in Toowoomba cemetery. Four daughters and two sons survived him.

J. Hogan, *Building Queensland's Heritage* (Melb, 1978); D. Watson and J. McKay, *Queensland Architects of the 19th Century* (Brisb, 1994); *Darling Downs Gazette*, 5 Feb 1896, 21 May 1900, 30 Oct 1915; M. Papi, James Marks and Sons, Architects, Toowoomba—An Architectural Study (B.Arch. thesis, Qld Univ Technology, 1987); interview with U. Webb *and* J. Marks memoir and architectural plans (Local History Collection, Toowoomba City Library, Qld).   DON WATSON

MARSH, JACK (c.1874-1916), Aboriginal cricketer, was born at Yulgilbar, in the Clarence River district, New South Wales, one of the Bunjdalung people. He possibly derived his surname from Francis Henry Marsh, whose property, Camira, was separated from Yulgilbar by the Richmond Range. Jack first made his mark as a professional runner. Influenced by the example of Charlie Samuels [q.v.], he followed his elder brother Larry to Sydney in 1893. A sprinter and hurdler, Jack had a number of important wins and competed in Victoria and Queensland. Like a number of Aboriginal runners, however, he was exploited by his trainer and was suspended for 'running stiff' in Sydney in 1895.

Marsh began playing cricket in the Moore Park competition, then with South Sydney in 1897-98 and (following a merger) with the Sydney District Club. A right-arm, fast bowler, he famously clean bowled Victor Trumper [q.v.12] for one in a colonial trial match in November 1900. Marsh was strongly supported by the Sydney club's secretary, Alf Dent, and was a brilliant performer in grade cricket, topping the bowling aggregates from 1901 to 1904, but became the victim of the hysteria over throwing that was then raging in both Australia and England. In his only full first-class season in 1900-01 he was leading the Australian bowling averages, with 21 wickets at 17.38 from three games, when Victorian umpire Bob Crockett no-balled him seventeen times for throwing in the first innings of his fourth match, against Victoria, in Sydney. This cast a cloud of suspicion over Marsh's subsequent career and enabled the selector Monty Noble [q.v.11] to ignore frequent calls to pick him for subsequent interstate games.

At the centre of a controversial incident involving the English captain Archie MacLaren, Marsh was forced to withdraw from a match at Bathurst in 1902. Two years later he played against (Sir) Pelham Warner's visiting English team at Bathurst and took 5 for 55, bowling a mixture of pace and medium-paced off-cutters, but again his action was considered suspect. In later years Marsh possibly experimented with the googly, and commentators such as the journalist J. C. Davis and player-writer Leslie Poidevin [q.v.11] rated him in the same class as Australian bowlers Charles Turner and Frederick Spofforth [qq.v.6] and England's Sydney Barnes. In six matches for New South Wales in 1901-03 Marsh took 34 wickets at 21.47. Warren Bardsley [q.v.7] wrote in his recollections that the reason Marsh had been 'kept ... out of big cricket was his color'.

Poidevin described Marsh, as 'a well set-up, perfectly built ... man, with an ebony-black, smooth, clear shining skin and twinkling black eyes' who 'is quite good looking'. He was 5 ft 7 ins (170 cm) tall. Photographs of the fashionably moustached athlete, dressed in a suit, supported Davis's description: 'he loved to be decked out well, not gaudily, but neatly and sylishly'. Marsh's cricket ended in Sydney in 1905. Next year he ran against Arthur Postle at a carnival organized by John Wren [qq.v.11,12] in Melbourne. Marsh joined Alexander's Hippodrome Company, touring the country in a sideshow, and then probably became an itinerant worker.

Gaoled for assault in Melbourne in 1909, he blamed drink for his behaviour. He died on 26 May 1916 at Orange, New South Wales, from injuries received when he was attacked outside the billiards saloon of the Royal Hotel. His two assailants were charged with manslaughter but acquitted. A documentary film about Marsh was produced in 1987.

C. Tatz, *Obstacle Race* (Syd, 1995); *The Oxford Companion to Australian Cricket* (Melb, 1996); B. Whimpress, *Passport to Nowhere* (Syd, 1999); M. Bonnell, *How Many More are Coming?* (Syd, 2003); P. Derriman, 'Death in Orange', *SMH*, 12 Jan 1985, 'Good Weekend', p 23.

BERNARD WHIMPRESS

MARSHALL, RICHARD (1838-1923), farmer and wheat-breeder, was born in 1838 at Hartland, Devonshire, England, son of Richard Marshall, and was educated at local schools and Shebbear College. Young Richard reached Melbourne in the *George Marshall* at the age of 16, and worked in a market garden at Geelong. In 1854 he joined his brother John at Yankallila, South Australia, and later farmed in a partnership with John Way at Second Valley. On 13 September 1860 at the Bible Christian Chapel, Bald Hills, Yankallila, Marshall married Mary Ann Watson. They were to have ten children. Marshall farmed at Rapid Bay, but disposed of the property to go to the diggings at Sandhurst (Bendigo), Victoria. After two and a half years, he returned to farm for three years at Lovely Valley, near Myponga, where he suffered successive crop failures. In 1865 he moved to Wasleys, renting 246 acres (99.6 ha), but lost his first crop there to red rust (*Puccinia graminis*), and suffered further losses in 1866-67. However, he successfully established his property, Hope Farm, ultimately expanding it to 3800 acres (1537.8 ha). His farming encompassed cereal growing, dairying and sheep raising.

After his losses from rust, Marshall began to improve disease resistance, selecting plants from available wheat varieties in 1868, notably Purple Straw. In 1880 Richard Schomburgk [q.v.6] imported Du Toit's (otherwise known as Early Baart) from South Africa. From this, James Ward, a farmer of Nelshaby, near Port Pirie, selected Ward's Prolific. Marshall likewise experimented with wheats he imported from France, Germany, England, Russia and the United States of America: in July 1892 he had 180 varieties growing in plots at Hope Farm, including 100 new ones. As well as rust resistance, he sought other selection characteristics, including likelihood of grain shakeout when ripe, quality and yield of grain, stooling, and strength and length of straw.

The Intercolonial Rust in Wheat Conference in 1896 recommended a change from the still widely grown Purple Straw. By 1910 this was almost totally replaced by Marshall's No. 3, probably a natural cross between Ward's Prolific and Purple Straw. Marshall's variously selected and cross-bred varieties—such as the Majestic, Gallant, Silver King (a white-grained selection from Marshall's No. 3), Phyllis' Marvel and Dart's Improver—were distributed among farmers about the same time as those of W. J. Farrer [q.v.8]. Marshall's most successful variety, Yandilla King, which was widely available from 1907, was derived from a cross between his Silver King and Farrer's Yandilla and was a 'half-sister' to Farrer's well-known Federation. Until the 1920s, Marshall's No. 3 and Yandilla King remained standards of yield among later-maturing varieties throughout Australia.

Marshall was a member of the District Council of Mudla Wirra North for seven years (chairman 1876-80) and a long-serving committee member of the Gawler Agricultural Society. He retired from active farming in 1899 to his Adelaide residence, Hartland, 73 Frederick Street, Unley. Two of his sons continued to farm at Wasleys, while the other two established farms at Lameroo and Cootamundra. In 1901 Marshall was appointed a member of the Central Agricultural Bureau, continuing with its successor, the South Australian Council of Agriculture until 1905. In 1904 he received an illuminated address from the Agricultural Bureau of South Australia in recognition of his work.

Marshall's first wife died in 1905. On 3 July 1906 at Southwark, Adelaide, he married Elizabeth Richards. In the last years of his life he was blind. He died at home on 5 August 1923 and was buried in West Terrace cemetery, leaving an estate sworn for probate at £29 700. His wife, and four sons and five daughters of his first marriage survived him. Although his work has been overshadowed by that of Farrer, Marshall left 'an indelible record on the scroll of Australian wheat breeders'.

H. T. Burgess (ed), *The Cyclopedia of South Australia*, 2 (Adel, 1909); H. Wenholz, *The Improvement of Australian Wheat* (Syd, 1937); R. D. Watt, *The Romance of the Australian Land Industries* (Syd, 1955); E. Dunsdorfs, *The Australian Wheat-growing Industry 1788-1948* (Melb, 1956); A. Lazenby and E. M. Matheson (eds), *Australian Field Crops*, 1 (Syd, 1975); *Observer* (Adel), 11 Aug 1923, p 38.

JOHN C. RADCLIFFE

MARSHALL, THOMAS HENRY (c.1862-1909), publican and politician, was born probably at Bailup, west of Toodyay, Western Australia, son of Edward Marshall, ex-convict timberworker, and his wife Louisa, née Harris. In 1883-86 Harry worked as a clerk and shop assistant in South Australia. On 7 April 1886 at Trinity Church of England, Adelaide, he married Clara Wilhelmina Ohlmeyer. Returning to Western Australia, between 1886 and 1894 he was successively a baker, an import merchant and a publican at Fremantle.

Marshall served on the Fremantle Municipal Council (1888-91, 1893-94), acted as secretary of the Lumpers' Association (founded 1890) and the Liberal Association, and was a committee member of the Fremantle Rowing Club and an official of the (Australian Rules) football club. Gaoled for twenty four hours in 1891, following involvement in a riot at Fremantle oval, he was welcomed by a brass band on his release. That year his wife died in Adelaide; on 19 October 1892 Marshall married Jane Ann McLean at Fremantle Congregational Church.

When the Legislative Council became elective in July 1894, Marshall nominated for one of the three West Province seats. In the same month the Supreme Court of Western Australia upheld a fine of £750 against him for breaches of the customs regulations, involving a strong suspicion of forgery. Because of his detention by a sheriff's officer he was unable to make the customary speech to the electors. Enough voters thought him victimized to ensure his election to the conservative, property-owning council. The *West Australian* was scandalized: Marshall's return was 'a reproach to the entire colony' which 'brought a sense of intolerable shame to every respectable person in the community'. He was the first son of an ex-convict to enter Western Australia's parliament. But his performance was brief and unremarkable. Declaring himself a staunch supporter of Sir John Forrest's [q.v.8] government, he spoke seldom and only on Fremantle matters. Late in 1894 he went to the Murchison goldfields as licensee of the Excelsior Hotel, Cue. In June 1895 he was declared bankrupt, probably because of his fine, and his seat became vacant after a constitutional debate in the Legislative Council.

At Cue Marshall founded the Excelsior brewery and a cordial manufactory and again showed himself a keen sportsman, being patron of the local cycling club and president of the Central Murchison Football Association. His popularity was apparently unaffected by his imprisonment for twelve months in 1898 for larceny of part of an aerated water machine. He served on Cue Municipal Council in 1906-09 and on the local water board. In 1908 he moved to nearby Day Dawn, as licensee of the Great Fingall and Day Dawn hotels, and was still on the municipal council when he died of gastroenteritis on 28 December 1909. He was buried in Cue cemetery with Anglican rites, and was survived by his wife and their three sons, and by two daughters and one son of his first marriage. An early example of sporting populism in Western Australia, Marshall probably found himself out of his depth in parliament and contented himself with energetic community activities and larrikin entrepreneurship.

C. T. Stannage (ed), *A New History of Western Australia* (Perth, 1981); D. Black and G. Bolton, *Biographical Register of the Members of the Parliament of Western Australia*, 1 (Perth, 2001); *Western Mail*, 7 July 1894, p 10; *West Australian*, 17 July 1894, p 3, 18 July 1894, p 4; *Geraldton Express*, 27 May 1898, p 3; *Murchison Times*, 30 Dec 1909, p 3.

G. C. BOLTON

MARTEL, ELLEN (NELLIE) ALMA (1855-1940), suffragist, elocutionist and parliamentary candidate, was born on 30 September 1855 at Beacon, Saint Agnes, Cornwall, England, seventh of thirteen children of John Charleston, hammer-man, and his wife Elizabeth, née Williams. An older brother migrated to South Australia in 1869, followed in 1878 by a married sister. Nellie came to Australia the next year and reached Sydney from Adelaide in January 1880. On 4 April 1885 at Christ Church Cathedral, Newcastle, she married with Anglican rites Charles Martel, a widower from Guernsey. He worked as a photographer and invested successfully in real estate. They lived in Sydney before sailing to Britain in 1889. On her first visit to London she was shocked by the 'emaciated faces, stooping shoulders and halting steps' of the men working in sweatshops. In Cornwall she was a witness at her sister's marriage to Alfred Goninan [q.v.14].

The Martels also visited France and Italy. They returned to Sydney in 1891, the year of the formation of the Womanhood Suffrage League, of which they both became early members. In 1894 Mrs Martel was elected to its council and organizing committee. Her brother D. M. Charleston [q.v.7], a South Australian politician, spoke at meetings of the league in 1892, 1894 and 1895. That year she was on the finance committee and was secretary of a committee to take charge of petitions. She was recording secretary until 1901; during that time 14 718 signatures collected by the league for the enfranchisement of women were presented to the New South Wales parliament. She was one of five signatories to the league's petition presented to the Australasian Federal Convention, Adelaide, in March 1897.

A talented elocutionist with a 'rich contralto' voice and a quick wit, she took part in the W.S.L. debates and lectures and gave recitations. By 1896 the Martels held monthly 'At Homes' at the Hotel Arcadia, with musical and elocutionary items to which they both contributed. They were honorary secretaries of the *Cercle Littéraire Français*. Nellie was a member of the Victoria Salon, and recited at the inaugural 'At Home' of the new Victoria Club in November 1896. In September 1901 the first public meeting of the Women's Progressive Association of New South Wales was held, with Nellie president and Annie Golding [q.v.9] secretary. The formation of the group was a reaction to Rose Scott's [q.v.11] domination of the W.S.L., but its aim was to assist reform, especially with regard to working women.

In September 1893 Charles had been bankrupted, due to a failed business venture; he obtained a certificate of discharge in March 1894. Responding 'with courage and determination and a good business head', Nellie taught elocution from her Paddington home —she had paid off its mortgage by 1900 when she advertised as a teacher at a studio in George Street. In 1902 she gave a recital in the Centenary Hall under vice-regal patronage.

At a conference of the Temperance Alliance in March 1903 Mrs Martel supported local option without compensation. In June she spoke at the first social meeting of the Women's Social and Political League. Next month, at a meeting held at her new studio in Margaret Street, she was elected president of the Women's Liberal and Reform Association. In early October she was elected to the finance committee of the Australian Freetrade League.

With women in New South Wales voting for the first time in December 1903 (in the Commonwealth elections), Mrs Martel advised them 'to organise and record their vote, not for the use of fiscalism or sectarianism, but for the good of humanity'. She requested support from the W.S.P.L. as a Senate candidate. When the Freetrade League selected three male candidates, the women's league decided that 'the time is not yet ripe for women representatives'. She then announced that she would stand as a free trade candidate for the Senate and nominated as Nellie Alma Martel.

Auburn-haired, fashionably dressed and fond of jewellery, Martel was a 'fluent and somewhat demonstrative speaker' with a determined jaw. She campaigned at Newcastle, Tamworth, Lambton and Maitland, speaking in halls and from balconies for up to an hour and a half. Though standing to represent her sex and to promote domestic and social legislation, she disapproved of women in parliament if they had home ties (Charles was in a nursing home after a breakdown and she was childless). Opposed to the Political Labor League because of its caucus structure and support of the minimum wage, she advocated equal pay for women, arguing that men would then be employed in preference to females and 'every man would be able to [marry] and keep his wife at home'. This would solve the problem of the falling birthrate.

Martel supported free trade; the encouragement of private industries; irrigation to combat drought; and the teaching of foreign languages as part of the commercial education of young men. She objected to the country 'being full of Chinese and other foreigners', but believed Australia should be 'open to every British subject'. In the last nine days of electioneering she addressed open-air audiences nightly (except on Sunday) in Sydney and the suburbs, closing her campaign on election eve at North Sydney. She gained 18 502 votes, coming eleventh of the twelve candidates.

Charles, now convalescing, sailed for England in 1904. Alarmed by news of his erratic behaviour, Nellie followed on 27 July—they were a devoted couple. Louisa Lawson's [q.v.10] the *Dawn* continued to carry articles about her: a lengthy interview in Natal, South Africa, an interview in the London *Daily News*, a letter about her activities in London. There she achieved notoriety as a woman who had not only voted but also stood for parliament. By May 1905 she had joined Mrs Pankhurst's Women's Social and Political Union. On 12 May she was at the House of Commons for the debate on a women's enfranchisement bill. After delaying tactics resulted in an adjournment, some 300 women held a meeting nearby, where Martel read aloud a petition of protest. Early in 1906 the W.S.P.U. formed a central London committee, of which she was a member and a few months later an organizer. Next year the W.S.P.U. published Martel's pamphlet, *The Women's Vote in Australia*. In January 1908 she accompanied Pankhurst to Devon, where they successfully campaigned against a candidate who did not support women's enfranchisement. Later that year, however, she left the W.S.P.U.

In 1918 Nellie's 'strenuous advocacy' of the coalition Unionist candidate in Sunderland assisted his re-election. That year she hosted Christmas Day festivities for six Australian soldiers at her home in Ladbroke Gardens, Notting Hill, London. Charles died in 1935. Nellie died at home on 11 August 1940. Her estate was valued at £3057.

A. Rosen, *Rise Up, Women!* (Lond, 1974); A. Oldfield, *Woman Suffrage in Australia* (Melb, 1992); *Daily Telegraph* (Syd), 11 Feb 1892, p 4, 23 Jan 1894, p 6, 30 Oct 1903, p 11, 6 Nov 1903, p 6, 19 Nov 1903, p 6; *Evening News* (Syd), 28 Aug 1896, p 3, 8 Oct 1896, p 5, 21 Oct 1896, p 2, 30 Oct 1896, p 7, 5 Nov 1896, p 5, 27 Nov 1896, p 2, 25 Mar 1898, p 7, 30 Sept 1898, p 3; *Dawn*, Oct 1900, p 8, Nov 1901, p 8, Jan 1903, p 12, Mar 1903, p 8, May 1903, p 7, July 1903, p 23, Aug 1903, p 14, Oct 1903, p 14, Sept 1904, p 6, Nov 1904, p 6, June 1905, p 5, July 1905, p 7; *SMH*, 30 Oct 1903, p 8; *Newcastle Morning Herald*, 27 Nov 1903, p 6, 28 Nov 1903, p 5, 30 Nov 1903, p 5; *Tamworth Observer*, 5 Dec 1903, p 4; Womanhood Suffrage League papers (ML); bankruptcy file, C. Martel, item 10/22892 (SRNSW); information from Mrs I. Hurley, Chatswood, Syd.

MARGARET BETTISON

MARTIN, ANNA MONTGOMERIE (1841-1918), teacher, was born on 8 November 1841 at Dale End, Birmingham, England, third of eight children of Unitarians Edward Montgomrey Martin, chemist, and his wife Ann, née Thornton, teacher. Annie attended school at Highgate, Birmingham, where she was instructed by an aunt. In 1850 the family migrated to Adelaide. Taught by Caroline Emily Clark [q.v.3] at Hazelwood, Burnside, Annie was 'bookish, good tempered and willing', despite a despotic father. In 1859-61 she was in England, visiting her extended family, schools, a workhouse, lunatic asylum and gaol. She noted that 'many nice women are old maids in England ... there is so much interesting work for women ... Sunday Schools ... Ragged Schools'.

Returning to Adelaide, Annie became engaged to Henry Septimus, brother of her sister Lucy's husband Howard Clark [q.v.3]. Henry was a vigneron and founder of Stonyfell vineyard. After Lucy died in 1863 and Henry died from tuberculosis in 1864, Annie began teaching in her own home. Later she moved to city premises. She was 'an excellent teacher, being very successful in inducing her pupils to like their work & to pursue it with vigour'. Child welfare also concerned her.

Martin's schools were in different places, always small and, as she was a Unitarian, never fashionable. Her methods were unconventional—no set homework and no cramming, although excellence was recognized with prizes. As she walked from her parents' home at Norwood to her school she collected students and told them, as a serial, stories by Sir Walter Scott. She 'felt the heat badly, wore her hair short ... and sometimes just dipped her head into a bucket of water, shook her hair like a dog, and continued teaching'.

Annie Martin closed her school in 1874 and taught elsewhere. She spoke and taught French, German and Italian and also taught Latin and Greek. After a visit to Britain and Europe in 1883-84 she re-established her school in Adelaide. Daughters of former pupils came to her and soon she was preparing girls for university. A few, such as Helen Mayo [q.v.10], left because of a lack of discipline. Female students at the University of Adelaide who had been taught by Martin included Laura Fowler, the first woman to graduate in medicine (1891), and Annie's niece Caroline Clark, who graduated M.A. (1901) and later took over Miss Martin's school. The novelist Catherine Martin [q.v.10] was Annie's sister-in-law.

A foundation councillor of the Women's Suffrage League, Miss Martin was a member of its delegation to the premier in 1891. She later joined the Women's League, founded in 1895 by her former student Lucy Morice [q.v.10] to educate women to take part in politics and interest themselves 'in questions relating to women and children'. Martin had unorthodox views about the extension of deep drainage in Adelaide, and in 1893 read to the Australasian Association for the Advancement of Science a paper opposing it on environmental grounds. Inheriting a small legacy after her mother's death, she retired in 1901 and left Adelaide for Europe, settling after years of travel at Viterbo, Italy. Martin died of dysentery on 9 August 1918 in Rome and was cremated. Annual prizes and medals, established in her memory by her former scholars and administered by the Senior Secondary Assessment Board of South Australia, are in 2005 still presented to leading students at public examinations in French and history.

C. H. Spence, *State Children in Australia* (Adel, 1907); H. Jones, *Nothing Seemed Impossible* (Brisb, 1985) and *In Her Own Name* (Adel, 1986); *The Hatbox Letters* (Adel, 1999); *Observer* (Adel), 24 Aug 1918, p 13; family information.   ANNE HARDY

MARTIN, WILLIAM WALKER (c.1860-1942), cyclist, was born in Dublin, second child and only son of Lynam Martin, farmer and lumber contractor, and his wife Jane, née Tuttle. The family migrated to the United States of America when Bill was 3, and lived in Maine for six years before moving to Lawrence, Massachusetts. Leaving school at 14, Martin found work as an assistant to traders in exotic goods, travelling to Europe, South America and Africa. Back in the U.S.A., for three years he was a professional footrunner in the mid-west, then took up cycling as an amateur in Nebraska in 1885. Turning professional in 1890, he broke his right thigh in a fall during a race at Detroit, Michigan, next year. Thereafter, one leg was shorter than the other and he walked with a pronounced limp. At Madison Square Garden, New York, in 1891 Martin won a six-day race described as the long-distance championship of the world, earning £1000 in gold for the victory. In December 1894 he won both the 10-mile and 25-mile world championships.

Competing in Europe in 1895 Martin won forty races. Next year, attracted by the prize money, Martin made the first of a number of visits to Australia, during a 'boom' in professional cycling, and won the Austral one-mile championship at the Melbourne Cricket Ground. At a similar meeting there in 1899, he won eight of nine events on the first day, the 10-mile scratch race on the second and the mile handicap and 5-mile scratch race on the last.

Martin's popular appeal owed as much to his personality as to his achievements. He acquired a variety of nicknames, including the 'Castiron Man', but was best known as 'Plugger' or 'Plugger Bill', which reflected his racing style—steady and grinding. Fair-haired, stocky, with powerful thigh muscles, he was quick-tempered and handy with his fists. He was also financially canny, with a fine instinct for publicity, giving the crowd 'its money's worth because he was never out of trouble'.

In 1896 Martin had been suspended for two months after an assault on another cyclist in Adelaide. In Sydney next year, he responded to abuse from a spectator by jumping off his bicycle, pursuing the man through the crowd and beating him. He again ran into trouble during the 1897 Adelaide carnival. After being fined over a series of misconduct charges, Martin scratched himself from subsequent events. Acting on legal advice, however, he rode in two races, playing up to the record crowd. A few days later, he administered a thrashing to a member of the committee that had banned him the previous year. For this he was sentenced to fourteen days gaol.

Between 1895 and 1901 Martin rode in every Australian colony, and was said to have won 249 races. His most famous victory came in the classic Austral Wheel Race, in Melbourne in December 1901, a 2-mile handicap. In excellent physical condition, he rode a remarkable race from scratch to win by 15 yards. Enormous sums were wagered on the event, and there were rumours of bribery and intimidation. Following an inquiry, one rider was suspended for pacemaking on Martin's behalf, but no other action was taken. In 1907, relying on testimony from Martin's trainer, the magazine *Lone Hand* claimed that John Wren [q.v.12] had fixed the race:

> bribes were laid out in piles of notes and sovereigns upon Martin's bed at the Albion Hotel, Melbourne. One by one the cyclists were admitted to the bedroom, and Martin, who had a loaded revolver beside him, addressed each successive visitor by name in a loud voice, and stated the terms of their contract.

Of his nineteen opponents in the Austral, the journal alleged that all bar two or three 'ran dead'. 'Plugger' acknowledged that Wren had backed him to win £7000.

Martin continued racing in New Zealand and in the U.S.A. before retiring in 1903. On 21 November that year, at Holy Trinity Church of England, Balaclava, Victoria, he married Victorian-born Alice Eva West; she was 19. Between 1900 and 1909 he ran hotels in Melbourne city and at Prahran and Collingwood before departing for New Zealand. His final public appearance on the cycling track was in 1933 in a veterans' event at the M.C.G. Martin lived in Western Australia for the last six years of his life, but his family remained in New Zealand. He tried prospecting at Marble Bar and Sandstone; his last job was as an optical goods traveller. He died on 28 March 1942 in Perth Hospital and was buried in Karrakatta cemetery, survived by his wife and their three daughters and two sons.

'Plugger Bill's' Biography (Melb, 1902); H. Grivell, *Australian Cycling in the Golden Days* (Adel, 1954?); N. Lindsay, *Bohemians of the Bulletin* (Syd, 1965); K. Dunstan, *The Confessions of a Bicycle Nut* (Melb, 1999); *Bulletin*, 19 Jan 1901, p 15; *Argus* (Melb), Dec 1901, p 5, 31 Mar 1942, p 6; *Sportsman*, 17 Dec 1901, p 2; *Truth* (Melb), 16 Sept 1905, p 2; *Lone Hand*, 1 May 1907, p 86; *West Australian*, 14 Aug 1936, p 10; *Daily News* (Perth), 30 Mar 1942, p 6; *SMH*, 31 Mar 1942, p 8.   GEOFF BROWNE

MATRA, JAMES MARIO (1746?-1806), sailor and diplomat, was born James Magra, probably in the second half of 1746 in New York, son of James Magra and his wife Elizabeth. A member of a prominent Corsican family, Magra senior had migrated to Dublin in the early 1730s and changed his name from Matra. He perhaps studied medicine in Ireland and moved to New York before 1740. By his death in April 1774, Dr Magra had become prosperous, with large property holdings; however, the family lost its wealth in the American Revolution.

According to Evan Nepean [q.v.2], the under secretary at the Home Office, who knew him well, young Magra was educated in England. He entered the Royal Navy as 'Captain's Servant' in May 1761 and served in European waters until the end of the Seven Years War. In July 1764, having returned to New York, he became a midshipman in the *Hawke*. This and other ships in which he later served undertook peacetime patrols on the eastern coast of North America and around the British Isles.

On 25 July 1768 Magra joined the *Endeavour* and sailed on James Cook's [q.v.1] first great voyage of Pacific exploration. In May 1770, when midway up the coast of New South Wales, suspecting that Magra was implicated in the drunken cropping of his clerk's ears, Cook suspended the midshipman from duty, noting that he was 'one of those gentlemen, frequently found on board Kings Ships, that can very well be spared, or to speake more planer good for nothing'. During this voyage, Magra became acquainted with (Sir) Joseph Banks [q.v.1], and their friendship lasted until his death. The *Endeavour* returned to England in July 1771. Circumstantial evidence has identified Magra as the anonymous author of *A Journal of a Voyage round the World*, which appeared two months later, and which offered some details of Cook's voyage not found in other accounts.

In 1775 Magra petitioned the King to 'take the name and bear the Arms of Mario Matra', so as to obtain a Corsican inheritance. He followed a penurious career in minor diplomatic posts on the fringes of Europe, becoming consul at Tenerife (1772-75), then embassy secretary in Constantinople (1778-80).

Matra became a leading proponent of the idea of establishing a convict colony at Botany Bay. He presented his schemes for settlement to the Portland and Pitt administrations in 1783 and 1784. One of the very few Europeans then alive who had actually visited New South Wales, he testified to the House of Commons committee enquiring into the resumption of transportation in May 1785.

As Nepean's 'Memo of matters to be brought before Cabinet', about December 1784, indicated, when Pitt's ministers considered 'The Erecting a Settlement upon the Coast of New South Wales which is intended as an Assylum for some of the American Loyalists, who are now ready to depart and also as a place for the Transportation of *Young* Offenders who[se] crimes have not been of the most heinous nature', they were considering Matra's plan. His proposal to colonize New South Wales accorded well with the government's interests in disposing of the convicts, in building strategic resources in the Pacific Ocean and in establishing a trading network linking Asia and the Americas to Europe.

Disappointed in his hopes for a post in his proposed colony, in July 1786 Matra accepted the appointment of consul at Tangier, Morocco, where he was to remain (with some respites at Gibraltar when the plague ravaged North Africa) until his death. His later life exemplified the common lot of American Loyalists who, displaced and poverty-stricken, had to eke out precarious existences. 'I occupy but a small place on this Globe', he wrote plaintively in 1781, '& yet there is not room on it for me'.

In his letters from North Africa, Matra reported informatively on the geography and peoples of the region. He supplied Banks with curiosities; and he assisted travellers sent by the Association for the Exploration of the Interior Parts of Africa. Through the long years of war with revolutionary France, he saw that the British had the food supplies they needed to maintain their garrison at Gibraltar and to keep their Mediterranean squadron at sea.

In October 1793 Matra married Henrietta Maxwell, daughter of the army victualling agent at Gibraltar. They had no children. Matra died on 29 March 1806 at Tangier, survived by his wife.

A. Frost, *The Precarious Life of James Mario Matra* (Melb, 1995), and for bib.   ALAN FROST

MAWSON, FRANCISCA ADRIANA (PAQUITA) (1891-1974), community worker and writer, was born on 19 August 1891 at Acton, London, sixth of seven children of Dutch-born parents Guillaume Daniel Delprat [q.v.8], engineer, and his wife Henrietta Marie Wilhelmine Sophia, née Jas. Paquita spent the first eight years of her life in Andalusia, Spain, where her father was working as a mining engineer. In 1898 Delprat moved to Broken Hill, New South Wales, where he had joined the Broken Hill Pty Co. Next year, his wife and five of their children arrived from Europe.

Paquita and some of her siblings attended the convent school at Broken Hill until, in 1902, their father bought a house in North Adelaide. The Delprat girls were enrolled at Tormore House, a progressive private school in North Adelaide, where Paquita stayed until 1908, after which she took piano and singing lessons at the Elder [q.v.4] Conservatorium of Music under the tutelage of William Silver.

At the age of 19 Paquita became engaged to (Sir) Douglas Mawson [q.v.10], geologist and explorer. They married on 31 March 1914 at Holy Trinity Church of England, Balaclava, Victoria. Their daughter Patricia was born in March 1915 in the Delprat family home in Melbourne. Paquita left the infant with Henrietta Delprat in 1916, while she journeyed through war-torn waters to join her husband at Liverpool, England, where he worked in the explosives section of the Ministry of Munitions. Lady Mawson made hospital dressings and worked as Sir Douglas's secretary in the afternoons. They moved to London in September 1917, and their second child Jessica was born there the following month. The Mawsons returned to Australia early in 1919 and built a house in the Adelaide seaside suburb of Brighton, where they spent the remainder of their married life.

Lady Mawson took active roles in the University Wives', the Lyceum and the Queen Adelaide clubs. For thirty years she was involved with the Mothers' and Babies' Health Association, including nine years as president, and travelled by train to many country areas to spread the message of good infant care. During World War II she also worked tirelessly as the convenor of the civilian relief department of the South Australian branch of the Australian Red Cross Society. She was appointed officer of the Order of Oranje-Nassau (1946), in recognition of the help she gave to Dutch refugees, and O.B.E. in 1951.

Music, her garden, their farm in the Adelaide Hills, reading (in several languages) and writing for journals and radio remained her abiding interests. She was a prolific letter writer and frequent hostess and was a strong supporter of her husband in both public and private life. Lady Mawson made her own contribution to Antarctic knowledge in writing *Mawson of the Antarctic* (London, 1964). She also wrote *A Vision of Steel*, a biography of her father (Melbourne, 1958).

For most of her life, she travelled extensively throughout Europe and America, maintaining strong connections with the Netherlands, and with her far-flung brothers and sisters and their families. A tall, striking woman, she was noted for her talent for public speaking, her quick wit and generous spirit. After Sir Douglas's death in 1958, Lady Mawson moved to Mount Lofty.

Having outlived all of her siblings, she died on 26 May 1974 and was buried beside her husband in St Jude's cemetery, Brighton. Their two daughters survived her. Lady Mawson's strong character and flair for fashion were portrayed in four surviving portraits, three of which are held privately. The other, an oil painting by her nephew Paul Delprat, belongs to the Mawson collection and in 2005 hangs in the Robert Barr Smith [q.v.6] library, University of Adelaide.

N. R. Flannery (ed), *This Everlasting Silence* (Melb, 2000); Tormore House records *and* Mawson family papers (SLSA); Delprat papers *and* Delprat and Teppema papers (NL); family papers held privately.

EMMA MCEWIN
NANCY ROBINSON FLANNERY

'MAXWELL, ERICA'; *see* PYKE, LILLIAN

MAXWELL, JOHN HENRY (1885-1954), ranger, stockman and horseman, was born on 27 January 1885 at Tuggeranong, New South Wales, son of Thomas Philip Maxwell, station hand, and Mary Wall. Jack grew up in the Queanbeyan area and was later employed by Thomas Franklin to help to manage Brindabella station, where Maxwell developed his skills as cattleman and horseman. Here, too, he met Ivy Violet Franklin, a cousin of the author Miles Franklin [q.v.8]. Ivy and Jack married with Presbyterian forms on 16 August 1911 at Queanbeyan. Following Thomas Franklin's death in 1925, the Maxwells moved to Queanbeyan.

About 1927 Maxwell was appointed by the Commonwealth government to be its first ranger in the rugged upper Cotter River valley, to help safeguard Canberra's water supply catchment. Responsible for an area of 98 842 acres (40 000 ha), he patrolled on horseback, policing the prohibition on grazing (though travelling stock were allowed through), trapping rabbits, poisoning foxes, controlling the wild horse population and burning off to reduce the bushfire threat to the developing national capital. Working mostly alone, he was joined occasionally by other mountain men.

Described by contemporaries as 'a wiry bushman' and 'a bit of a loner', Maxwell lived for two to three months at a time at the slab-walled Cotter hut, which, though basic, was comfortable by the standards of bush huts of the era. He returned to Queanbeyan and his family for only a week before setting out again. Ivy and some of their boys joined him during the summer. His attitude to the responsible position of ranger was reflected by the fact that he always wore a coat and tie when riding into and out of the catchment.

For several decades Maxwell led the summertime brumby-running forays in the mountain catchment: joined by his family and many friends, he helped to build trapyards and caught numbers of wild horses; some brumbies were sold or broken-in, others were shot. Miles Franklin's letters revealed that she occasionally joined Jack and Ivy for rides in the Brindabellas. In addition to his ranger duties, Maxwell had grazing leases in the mountains west of the Australian Capital Territory, where at Little Leura and Hardys Lease he grazed stock with other landowners. He ceased to work as upper Cotter ranger in 1953.

In many ways Maxwell was the archetypal Australian bushman. At home in the saddle, he held a store of knowledge about the mountain bushland, welcomed passing stockmen to his hut and regaled visitors with yarns. He died on 29 October 1954 at Queanbeyan and was buried in the Catholic section of Canberra cemetery. His wife and their three sons survived him. The area patrolled by Maxwell became a key element of the chain of Australian Alps national parks.

Maxwell's eldest son Douglas (1911-1958), a stockman, became inaugural ranger at Bulls Head (on the western edge of the catchment) and his third son Lachlan (1918-2001) also worked at Bulls Head before taking up a property at Yaouk. His second son Jock (1913-1985), who like Lachlan served in World War II, became a stock and station agent and auctioneer at Queanbeyan and was a close friend and inspiration to the poets David Campbell [q.v.13] and Douglas Stewart.

M. Higgins, *Voices from the Hills* (Canb, 1990) and *Brumby Running in Namadgi* (Canb, 1993); *Canb Times*, 31 Aug 2000, p 11.

MATTHEW HIGGINS

MAY, FREDERICK (1921-1976), professor of Italian, was born on 3 August 1921 at Kensington, London, son of John May, labourer, later a builder, and his wife Elizabeth Ann, née Owens. Raised in the home of Italian opera singers, to whom his mother was in service, and bilingual from the age of 3, Frederick received a free place at the Quintin School and a junior county scholarship to complete his Higher School Certificate in 1939. After holding a summer scholarship at Perugia, Italy, in 1939, he entered Birkbeck College, University of London (B.A., 1947), in June 1940. On 23 November that year at the parish church, Kingsbury, Middlesex, he married Heather Constance Armstrong, a typist.

Registering as a conscientious objector on religious grounds in World War II, May (and his wife) trained and did volunteer work with the Friends' War Relief Service in Devon. With the birth of his eldest son in 1943, he took paid employment, first as a hospital porter at Cambridge and then, during the V1 and V2 raids, as a theatre orderly at Middlesex Hospital, London. He resumed his evening studies at Birkbeck, then at Bedford and University colleges, graduating with first-class honours.

Active in student politics, university theatre and adult education, May was recruited in 1949 by the Italian department, University of Leeds, first as lecturer then as senior lecturer and head of department. Despite suffering from tuberculosis in 1954, he worked to build his department and to perform the works of Italian dramatists in the Student Theatre Group and the Civic Arts Guild. He translated over fifty plays, directed, jousted with the Lord Chamberlain over censorship, and tirelessly promoted the work of Pirandello, who had become his principal interest.

Appointed to the chair of Italian at the University of Sydney, May reached Australia with his family in January 1964. Even before his personal library arrived by sea, and his copy of Nabokov's *Lolita* was confiscated, he had become involved in the growing Australian debate over censorship, condemning the law as 'a wilful and noxious intrusion upon man's right to read what he will when he will'.

Soon after his arrival at the university, May recruited postgraduate students and introduced a course structure whereby beginners could reach honours standard in four rather than five years. His curriculum was extraordinarily broad and demanding, encompassing literature, philology and drama from the thirteenth century to the *neoavanguardia*.

With his horn-rimmed spectacles, broken tooth, beard, lank hair, string bag and apple, May was one of the university's great eccentric characters, who left much administration to the forces of nature and time. Although he claimed to prefer seminars and tutorials, students from all faculties would come to hear him lecture in mellifluous tones on Italian literature—and indeed on any subject that crossed his fertile mind.

From 1969 May had been suffering from diabetes and failing eyesight, exacerbated by stress. Despite these infirmities, in 1970 he turned to radio broadcasting and to reading poetry with Winsome Evans's Renaissance Players. With his diabetes poorly controlled, May developed pneumonia and died at his Roseville home on 11 January 1976; he was cremated. He was survived by his wife and their four sons and by a fifth son by Fiona Garrood. The Frederick May Foundation (1976-99) at the University of Sydney, established in his memory, promoted the study of Italian language and culture.

The Department of Italian and the Frederick May Foundation for Italian Studies (Syd, 1980); *Aust Left Review*, no 3, 1966, p 8; May papers (Univ of Sydney Archives).
NERIDA NEWBIGIN

MAYNE, PATRICK (c.1824-1865), butcher, businessman and alderman, and MARY (1826?-1889), businesswoman, were husband and wife. Born at Cookstown, County Tyrone, Ireland, son of Isaac Mayne and his wife Rose, née Mullen, Patrick came to New South Wales in the *Percy* in 1841. By 1846 he was at Moreton Bay, working as a butcher at the boiling down works, Kangaroo Point. On 9 April 1849 in Brisbane he married with Catholic rites Mary McIntosh. A Protestant, Mary had been born possibly on 16 August 1826 at Kilkishen, near Ennis, County Clare, Ireland, daughter of William McIntosh, soldier, and his wife Mary, née Nash; she had migrated to Sydney in the *Champion* in February 1842. Patrick and Mary had six children.

Mayne purchased the goodwill of a butchery in Queen Street, Brisbane, in September 1849, built a substantial enterprise, based on his shop and on rental properties including hotels, shops and houses, and speculated in land. He went surety for numerous publicans and engaged in money lending. To finance his expansion he borrowed heavily and in September 1860 consolidated his loans through a mortgage to the Bank of New South Wales for £3300. A leading Catholic businessman, he contributed to the building of St Stephen's Cathedral. Although he reportedly had little formal schooling, Patrick appreciated the value of education, as did Mary. Three of their children went to Catholic schools, but Patrick also supported the state system and in 1859 contributed £100 to the building of the National School.

In October that year Mayne was elected to the first municipal council in Brisbane. He was an alderman and a member of the finance committee for each year, except 1862, until his death, and of the incorporation committee in 1863. In February 1861 he declined to accept nomination as mayor, perhaps influenced by the anti-Irish and class prejudices that had followed his appointment in February 1860 to the Board of National Education. A moderate, Mayne was concerned with practical matters such as water, sewerage, the levelling of streets and setting rates. He opposed jobbery and endeavoured to ensure that council rates were paid and appropriately spent.

Mayne could be provoked to violence and at times clashed with the law. In 1852 he had intervened when a police constable used excessive force in taking a drunk to the watch house, and in June 1855 he was fined for contempt of court when, following the trial of John and Anne Clune for assaulting William Collard, he asked Collard if he had got his blood money. John Cameron, a contemporary, acknowledged that Mayne's manners could be rough, but described him as a kindly man who privately assisted those in need.

Long-standing rumours about Patrick, the mental illness of one of his children (Isaac) and perhaps another (Rosey), and other matters were collected by Rosamond Siemon in *The Mayne Inheritance* (Brisbane, 1997). This claimed that at the Bush Inn at Kangaroo Point on 26 March 1848 Patrick had murdered Robert Cox, a sawyer and ex-convict, robbing him of some £350, and that it was this money that had allowed Mayne to establish himself in business in September 1849. The book alleged that he framed William Fyfe—who was tried, convicted and executed for the crime. It also asserted that Mayne suffered from a hereditary form of insanity and that some days before his death he confessed to the murder to his priest. Such claims, however, are open to challenge.

Mayne died on 17 August 1865 in Queen Street, Brisbane. His funeral was the largest to that date in the city. His wife, three sons and two daughters survived him. Mary took over the butcher shop, paid rent to his estate and traded in her own name. An executor of the Mayne estate, she managed its business interests and lent it money to ensure that, despite the commercial downturn, it remained solvent without the need to sell core assets. Although Patrick had appointed trustees, Mary largely controlled the management of the estate. She did not hesitate to use the law to protect her interests and, late in 1869, following a dispute over her meat contract, initiated a claim against the government that was finally settled out of court in February 1870. Her own sharp business practices resulted in others seeking redress from the law.

From November 1865 Mary began buying land in her own name and in March 1878 paid £2450 for Moorlands to become the family home. She had closed the butchery in 1871, but maintained other business interests, including the management of the estate's valuable city and suburban land. Mary Mayne

died of coronary heart disease on 4 September 1889 at Toowong, leaving an estate valued at £15 810. Just before her death she had converted to Catholicism. She was buried in the family tomb in Toowong cemetery. Both Patrick and Mary were commemorated in stained-glass windows in St Stephen's Cathedral, Brisbane.

None of the children married. The last surviving siblings, Dr James O'Neill Mayne (1861-1939) and his sister Mary Emelia (1858-1940) [qq.v.10], financed the purchase in 1926-29 of the site for the University of Queensland, at St Lucia, donated rural land at Mogill for the university, and upon their deaths willed the income from their estates to its medical school.

G. Greenwood and J. Laverty, *Brisbane 1859-1959* (Brisb, 1959); B. E. Turner, 'The Burden of Proof', *Procs of the Univ of Qld Hist Research Group*, no 13, 2002, p 29, and 'Was Isaac Mayne an Insane Murderer?', *Jnl of the Roy Hist Soc of Qld*, vol 18, no 8, Nov 2003, p 337, and 'Mary Mayne', *Univ of Qld Hist Procs*, no 14, 2003, pp 105 & 117, and 'Patrick Mayne's Butcher Shops', *Jnl of the Roy Hist Soc of Qld*, vol 18, no 10, Apr 2004, p 432; *Qld Review*, vol 11, no 1, 2004; *Moreton Bay Courier*, 1 Apr 1848, p 2, 8 Mar 1860, p 2, 21 Aug 1865, p 2; *SMH*, 8 June 1848, p 3; *Brisb Courier*, 19 Feb 1870, p 4; *Telegraph* (Brisb), 13 Mar 1895, p 6; Colonial Secretary's Office, Register of letters received, 1870, 70/389 (QSA); R v William Fyfe, Supreme Crt, Brisb, 9/6345 *and* Notebook of Stephen, C.J., Criminal Crt, 5 June 1848, Supreme Crt, NSW, CGS 7696 2/7014 (SRNSW).   BERNADETTE TURNER

MAYRHOFER, GUIDO SAVERIO CARLO (1898-1968), medical practitioner, was born on 1 March 1898 in Perth, eldest of six children of Alberto Fortunato Mayrhofer, a merchant and picture-framer from Naples, Italy, and his Victorian-born wife Mabel Emma, née Allpress. Educated at the Christian Brothers' College, Perth, Guido won a government exhibition in 1914 to the University of Western Australia (B.A., 1917) and graduated with first-class honours in Greek and Latin. He then studied medicine at the University of Melbourne (M.B., B.S., 1923). Successively junior resident at the Perth Public (Royal Perth) and Children's (Princess Margaret) hospitals, he retained honorary clinical appointments with both institutions and by 1953 was honorary consultant physician to the Princess Margaret Hospital.

In 1927 Mayrhofer had joined a partnership with Dr D. R. C. Tregonning at Claremont; he remained in general practice there for more than four decades but never lost his interest in the broad conspectus of medical science. On 10 July 1937 at Claremont Presbyterian Church he married Elsa Pauline Shearer, a teacher. Described as 'somewhat slow and deliberate in manner, and painstaking to the nth degree', though with 'a tendency to un-punctuality', he was a competent diagnos-tician, never hesitating to refer and, therefore, a highly trusted family physician. He was a much-appreciated medical officer for the town of Claremont and for twenty eight years doctor and friend to St George's College.

His investigative qualities led Mayrhofer to pursue exacting epidemiological research by collecting case histories from his patients and collating selected specimens for examination in the State public health laboratory. Reputedly he was 'the first doctor in general practice in Australia to take the time' to help establish the overall pattern of virus infection in the com-munity. Welcoming the establishment of a medical school in Western Australia (1958), he regularly attended clinical meetings at Royal Perth Hospital to keep abreast of cur-rent procedures. He soon formed a working relationship with such faculty members as professors Neville Stanley and Eric Saint.

Mayrhofer was of average height, balding and with a twinkle in his dark eyes; his mildly absent-minded demeanour belied his inner strength. Well read, a philosopher and talented violinist, he was vice-president of the Royal Schools of Music (Western Australia) and a member the Perth Chamber Music Club. He regularly played in a string quartet whose performances were praised by music critic Albert Kornweibel [q.v.15]. Mayrhofer died of myocardial infarction on 28 February 1968 in hospital at Subiaco and was cremated. His wife and their two daughters survived him. In June 1969 the (Royal) Australian Col-lege of General Practitioners—of which he had been an active promoter in Western Aus-tralia and a founding member—posthumously awarded him the Francis Hardey Faulding [q.v.4] memorial research prize and bronze medal for his work *Some Observations on Virus Diseases in General Practice* (1967).

Daily News (Perth), 29 Feb 1968, p 12; *Critic* (Perth), 10 Apr 1968, p 79; *West Australian*, 12 June 1969; information from Mrs J. Hassell, Dalkeith, Perth.   WENDY BIRMAN

MAZURE, LÉON EDMOND (1860?-1939), winemaker, was born probably on 30 October 1860 at Villeneuve, Coulommiers, Seine *et* Marne, France, son of Alphonse Mazure, and educated at the Christian Brothers' College, Nogent, Burgundy. Edmond's father and uncle were vignerons, and he acquired some knowledge of winemaking. When he was about 18 he went to the celebrated vineyard Clos Vougeot for some nine months before acquiring experience in Spain, at vineyards in the Xeres district and in Catalonia.

At Barcelona an opportunity for adventure presented itself, and Mazure joined the Marquis de Rays' [q.v.6] expedition to New Ireland (1880). The party arrived at its desti-nation but, disappointed with their prospects and their treatment, he and two others left in an open boat. They were wrecked on the coast of New Ireland, however, and after a fortnight of vicissitudes were picked up by a German ship and taken to New Britain. Mazure re-mained there for about twelve months trading for a German firm and, after recovering from an attack of fever, started to return to France.

While waiting in Sydney for a vessel, Mazure learned that (Sir) Samuel Davenport [q.v.4] required a vigneron at Beaumont, South Australia, and secured the position, arriving about 1884. He stayed for eighteen months, then took charge of C. B. Young's Kanmantoo vineyard for a similar period. Mazure was naturalized in 1885. On 16 May that year at the registrar general's office, Adelaide, he married Philomine Henriette, sister of Joseph Gelly, winemaker at Beaumont and later Chateau Tanunda; there were to be five children of the marriage.

At the jubilee exhibition in Adelaide in 1888, Mazure was in charge of the cellars; his job involved the classification of about 1000 different kinds of Australian and European wines for the jury. Engaged by (Sir) Josiah Symon [q.v.12] as manager of the Auldana vineyard, in 1899 he was taken into partner-ship and, when the enterprise became a limited company in 1903, became managing director. In May 1900 he was appointed honorary commissioner to enquire into the European wine industry, visiting Spain, Por-tugal and every wine district of France. In 1909 he again returned to Europe for the Franco-British Exhibition in London.

Mazure was among the first vignerons in South Australia to make champagne on a large scale (in 1896), to preserve olives and to intro-duce *levures* into the making of wine. In 1887-1912, while at Auldana, he was awarded eighty-three first prizes, seventy-one seconds and twelve thirds by the Royal Agricultural and Horticultural Society at the Adelaide wine shows. For three years in succession Auldana hock, chablis and sherry gained the cham-pion ten-guinea cup against all Australia. A councillor of the South Australian Vignerons' Association, Mazure became a wine and prun-ing judge, initiated a pruning competition for boys under 18, and took out several patents for ideas including the Mazure corkscrew, a corking machine and a windmill bird scarer. He was a member of the Adelaide Stock Exchange and was appointed a justice of the peace in 1901.

In 1909 Mazure bought part of Home Park and called it La Pérouse. Between 1914 and 1921 he won a further fifteen first prizes and ten seconds at the Adelaide wine shows, under his own or his wife's name. By 1920 he had built substantial cellars on the corner of Government and Penfold roads, and employed Hurtle Walker [q.v.12], whom he had trained at Auldana. Under the Romalo label, Walker carried on the *méthode champenoise* as did his son Norman later under the Seaview label. Mazure had created the original St Henri claret by 1890, followed by the St George and the St Henri special. The winemaker John Wilson claimed in August 1993 that Mazure also created the unique style of Australian sparkling burgundy in 1895.

Retiring to Victor Harbor in the early 1920s, Mazure established a roller-skating rink, a dance hall and a coffee shop in his casino on the foreshore. Photographs showed a well-dressed man, chubby-faced, with a waxed moustache and dark hair. He had blue eyes, smoked small cigars and was proficient in traditional French-style cooking. His grandchildren reported that he was strict but compassionate. Mazure died on 29 April 1939 at Albert Park and was buried in the Cheltenham cemetery, Adelaide. His wife, three sons and one daughter survived him.

E. Whitington, *The South Australian Vintage 1903* (Adel, 1903); H. T. Burgess (ed), *Cyclopedia of South Australia*, 2 (Adel, 1909); S. Williams et al (eds), *The Regenerative Spirit*, 2 (Adel, 2004), p 86; *Austn Vigneron and Fruit-Growers J*, 2 July 1894, p 52; *Wine and Spirit News and Australian Vigneron*, 25 Mar 1915, p 120; *Austn & NZ Wine Industry Jnl*, 8, no 3, Aug 1993, p 207; *Advertiser* (Adel), 1 May 1939, p 14; J. Ludbrook and Associates, Hurtle Walker of Romalo, notes (1964, held by author); Royal Agricultural and Horticultural Society (SA), Wine Show results, 1887-1912, 1914-21.

MERRILY HALLSWORTH

MEANY, JAMES (1879-1953), Catholic priest, was born on 17 May 1879 at Knockasnuff, Blarney, County Cork, Ireland, son of John Meany, farmer and publican, and his wife Margaret, née Cronin. Educated at the National School, Blarney, Presentation Brothers' College, Cork, and St Colman's College, Fermoy, James was ordained at All Hallows' College, Dublin, on 24 June 1904.

Arriving in Sydney in November that year, Meany was a curate at parishes at Leichhardt and Concord and then at St Mary's Cathedral. Quiet, practical and hard working, he was appointed diocesan inspector of schools in 1910. In his diplomatic but insistent annual reports, he urged schools to ensure that pupils completed their primary education by the age of 14 so that they would be free to attend secondary school, and emphasized the need for more boys' schools and male religious teachers.

In 1919 Meany became parish priest at Drummoyne, a position he retained until his death. Commissioned to build a new church, he promised 'give me but a few weeks and I'll get matters going'. Archbishop Michael Kelly [q.v.9] appointed him a parish priest consultor and diocesan assessor in 1920 and a member of the advisory committee (later chairman) of Sancta Sophia College, within the University of Sydney, in 1925. Meany retained a personal interest in the students, even helping them in their choice of songs for musicals.

Meany attended the International Eucharistic Congress at Chicago, United States of America, in 1926 as he was secretary of the organizing committee for the 1928 congress, to be held in Sydney. In 1927 he began renting time on radio 2UE to publicize the congress and to allow Rev. Dr Leslie Rumble [q.v.16] to broadcast on Sundays explaining Catholic doctrine. Meany raised the finances to allow Kelly to form the Catholic Broadcasting Co. Ltd, which obtained a licence for radio 2SM in 1931. The station broadcast sessions on the doctrine and history of the Church, special religious events, appeals for charities and Rumble's popular 'question box'. Becoming managing director, Meany liaised with the postmaster-general, co-ordinated charity drives and ran the extended Good Friday and Christmas Day sessions. Kelly was impressed by the station's efficiency; in 1946 it earned a net profit of £4015.

In 1929 Meany had been created a domestic prelate with the title of monsignor. Appointed a director of the *Catholic Press* in 1935, he found the paper moribund and in 1942 oversaw its amalgamation with the *Freeman's Journal* to create the *Catholic Weekly*, the official organ of the Sydney diocese. In 1949 he became chairman of the Catholic Press Newspaper Co. Edited by James Kelleher [q.v.14], the *Catholic Weekly* was a modern, pictorial tabloid, featuring local and international news, statements from Cardinal (Sir) Norman Gilroy [q.v.14], and pages for women and children. It campaigned for state aid for Catholic schools and implacably opposed communism. By 1950 sales had doubled compared with the combined circulation of the weekly's predecessors.

Constantly called upon to fulfil administrative roles, Monsignor Meany was chancellor of the archdiocese in 1937-44 and a diocesan consultor from 1942. He was a scratch golfer. On its formation in 1939 he accepted the presidency of St Michael's Golf Club, Little Bay, then helped to put the club on a sound financial footing. In 1941 he was appointed chaplain of the Catholic Club and subsequently joined the board of the Catholic Club Land & Building Co. He also attended screenings at the Commonwealth Film Censor's Office and represented Catholic schools on

271

the National Fitness Council and the Repatriation Department's Soldiers' Children's Education Board.

A courteous and dignified man who won the devotion of all who worked under him, Meany had to relinquish some duties in the late 1940s as his health was failing. Nevertheless, about 1950 Gilroy asked him to help to conduct a secret investigation into the activities of the Catholic Social Studies Movement. When his doctor advised him to take a six-month break in 1951, Meany remained on the boards of radio 2SM and the *Catholic Weekly*.

'To me God is a pure spirit, incorporeal, but try as I may I fail to conceive the immaterial without in some way giving it material form', Meany had explained in 1936. However, he came to feel some ambivalence about his secular responsibilities. In 1950 he suggested to Gilroy that *monsignori* should wear their robes at all times; he was a poor example and 'the worst offender', having convinced himself that in the hurly-burly of his commercial work 'the purple' was an embarrassment to others.

On 23 June 1953 Meany died in his radio 2SM office, Sydney. After a requiem mass—presided over by Gilroy and broadcast on 2SM—at St Mark's, Drummoyne, the church he had built, Meany was buried in Rookwood cemetery. His estate, sworn for probate at £12 372, was left largely for Catholic school children at Drummoyne.

B. Duncan, *Crusade or Conspiracy?* (Syd, 2001); *Freeman's J*, 6 Nov 1919, p 22; *Catholic Weekly*, 5 Mar 1942, p 4, 29 June 1950, p 3, 25 June 1953, p 1; 2 July 1953, pp 7 & 24, 8 Oct 2000, p 14; *Daily Telegraph* (Syd), 5 Apr 1940, p 1; *Newspaper News*, 1 July 1953, p 28; Meany file (Sydney Catholic Archdiocesan Archives); information from Br J. J. Luttrell, Syd; Aust Broadcasting Control Board, MP 522/1, 2SM (NAA).   BRIDGET GRIFFEN-FOLEY

MEEKIN, DAVID TERENCE (1888-1966), boxer and showman, was born on 31 December 1888 at Attunga Springs, Tamworth, New South Wales, and registered as David Thomas, fifth son and seventh child of William Meekin, an English-born labourer, and his wife Mary, née Wright, from Ireland. Dave boxed at school, then professionally while working as a rural labourer. Giving his occupation as traveller, he married Florence Mary Brown on 7 November 1914 at St Peter's Catholic Church, Surry Hills, Sydney. He hardened into a welterweight and middleweight fighter in Brisbane main events, and claimed to have won titles in California, South Africa and—as 'Champion of the Orient'—in Manila, before retiring in 1923.

As a boy, Meekin had wanted to be a 'showie' after attending country shows, and his boxing career drew him further into the world of performance. His trip to Africa, a continent he later described as 'wonderful and mysterious', heightened his interest in the exotic. He entered sideshow alley in the 1920s with a boxing tent, but failed to survive as Jimmy Sharman [q.v.11] and others monopolized the lucrative big shows. Meekin and Bronte ('Snowy') Hodge struck success at the Royal Easter Show, Sydney, exhibiting Goliath, a monstrous bull. Their advance publicity was so effective that they set a showman's record by covering their costs on the first day. Meekin then successfully showed 'Abdullah the Indian Magician' and ran successful equine 'in-out' shows, exhibiting 'Pom Pom the World's Smallest Horse', 'Wee Jimmy, the World's Smallest Racehorse', shod with gold-plated shoes, and 'Ajax, the Biggest Horse in the World', allegedly owned by the Sultan of Arabia. While the first two were genuinely small, the last was a 'con', the horse being an ex-baker's hack. Meekin also worked as a lion tamer, once being mauled on the arm. Thinking that too dangerous, he exhibited Chinese giants, Filipino firewalkers and 'Jang', a Borneo boy with a tail. Meekin helped to found the Showmen's Guild of Australasia in 1938.

Travelling extensively in Africa, he made contact with Pygmies and learned their language. In the late 1920s he assumed the rights to exhibit Ubangi Chilliwingi, also known as 'Maria Peters', a Pygmy woman from Cape Province touring the Australian show circuit. Their professional association over a generation established a Pygmy troupe that became famous and made the pair, especially Meekin, very wealthy. Meekin accompanied Ubangi and the troupe back to Africa each year, after their visas expired, and then resigned those available. In a reciprocal paternalism, he called Ubangi 'Bubby' and she referred to him as 'Baba' or 'Daddy'. Meekin, despite his homburg and tailored suits, assumed the title 'Africaneer' on his letterhead, promising to search 'the Universe for Strange People, Freaks and Novelties for the Entertainment of Show Patrons'. Other showmen revered his exploits and thought him honourable, and there is little evidence to the contrary. Television and modern attitudes, however, made his Pygmy show outmoded by the 1960s. In retirement he lived at Kings Cross, Sydney.

Predeceased by his wife, Meekin died on 19 March 1966 in hospital at North Sydney and was buried with Anglican rites in Woronora cemetery. His daughter Beryl, a Tivoli performer, survived him; she persuaded the Department of Immigration to allow Ubangi to live with her on the Gold Coast, Queensland.

A. Badger, *The Boy from Buninyong* (Melb, 1993); R. Broome with A. Jackomos, *Sideshow Alley* (Syd, 1998); *Aust Women's Weekly*, 29 Mar 1947, p 19; *Outdoor Showman*, Nov-Dec 1949, p 29, June 1951, p 5, Sept 1951, p 4, May 1966, p 16, Nov 1966, p 21; *Argus* (Melb), 21 May 1917, p 4; *People*, 17 Apr 1957, p 27; Maria Peters file, J25, item 1975/11361 (NAA, Brisb).   RICHARD BROOME

MELOCCO, PIETRO OLIVO (1883-1961), ANTONIO NICHOLAS (1886-1946) and GALLIANO EUGENIO (1897-1971), mosaic manufacturers, were born at Toppo, Udine, Friuli, in northern Italy, sons of Giovanni Battista Melocco, dairy farmer, and his wife Teresa, née Fabris. Born on 18 March 1883, Pietro was sent at the age of 10 to the United States of America to live with his father's three brothers in New York. He trained as a mosaic artist and marble worker under their tutelage and at the Cooper Union technical college in New York. In August 1904 he became an American citizen. He later claimed that he had been disillusioned by corruption in the New York building industry, and a lantern slide show about Sydney inspired him to take his skills to Australia. After returning briefly to Italy he reached Sydney in the *Gneisenau* on 6 May 1908 and went to live at Forest Lodge.

Peter (as he was known in Australia) worked with G. E. Crane & Son for six months, then set up his own workshop at Redfern. Learning that Cardinal Moran [q.v.10] was importing mosaics from Italy for the floor of the chapel of Irish saints at St Mary's Cathedral, in 1910 Melocco submitted designs for half the quoted price. Moran agreed to employ him on the condition that shamrocks be included.

Antonio, born on 17 December 1886, and Galliano, born on 6 March 1897, came to Sydney in the *Seidlitz* in June 1910. A skilled artist and craftsman who had trained in mosaic work in Paris, Tony worked alongside Peter in St Mary's. Galli finished his schooling as a boarder at Knox College before becoming a marine engineer and working in vessels trading to New Zealand and Canada. On 24 December 1920 at the Sacred Heart Church, Mosman, Peter married with Catholic rites Giuseppa Vittoria Asioli, a Sydney-born seamstress. He was naturalized in February 1925. On a visit to Italy, Tony married Victoria Pellarossa, a schoolteacher, on 19 June 1922 at San Giorgio, Udine. In 1928 he too was naturalized.

The 1920s were a boom time for the Meloccos, whose work was included in many of Sydney's picture theatres, including the Capitol. Melocco Bros Ltd was registered in 1925, becoming Melocco Bros Pty Ltd in 1927; the firm had moved to Annandale the previous year and employed up to two hundred people. The brothers' mother and sisters had migrated from Italy and settled in a residence at Annandale built for the family by Peter.

Galli, who had been naturalized in 1923, joined the family business in 1926 and opened a division in Brisbane in the late 1920s. At Fortitude Valley on 29 October 1932 he married Eva Letitia Maud Bell, a stenographer, and next year returned to Sydney with her and their first child. Galli was responsible for building up the construction and concrete aspects of the business. In 1941 he introduced ready mixed concrete to Australia. His children were raised in the Presbyterian Church of their mother's family. Peter and Tony sent their children to Catholic schools. Although knowledgeable about Celtic art and renowned for his association with St Mary's Cathedral, Peter was not devout—on Sundays he waited outside church while his family attended Mass.

In 1928, as part of his work for the Government Savings Bank of New South Wales in Martin Place (now occupied by the Commonwealth Bank of Australia), Tony had used the Italian technique of scagliola—an imitation marble made from keen cement—which became the Meloccos' trade secret. After travelling in Italy and the U.S.A. investigating the process, he spent many hours refining it in the Sydney workshop. From 1930 the brothers also ran Road Construction Ltd. During the Depression their businesses were vilified in *Smith's Weekly* for allegedly denying work to Australians. The Meloccos claimed, however, that they insisted on their mainly Friulani Italian employees speaking English and that their preference was based on skills rather than ethnicity. Despite his respectability as a businessman and board member of the Royal Prince Alfred Hospital, Peter was interned on the outbreak of war with Italy, on 11 June 1940, partly because of his membership of the Italian Chamber of Commerce in Sydney. After a few days in Long Bay gaol and five weeks in an internment camp at Orange, he was released on 14 July, reputedly after the intervention of Kim Beasley senior and Arthur Calwell [q.v.13]. Tony's son Albert served with the Australian Imperial Force.

The postwar construction boom in Sydney benefited the Meloccos, whose marble and terrazzo work also featured in corporate construction in Canberra. Tony suffered from Parkinson's disease and died of cerebrovascular disease on 27 June 1946 in a private hospital at Normanhurst. His wife and their son and daughter survived him. Peter and his craftsmen completed work on the mosaic floor of the crypt of St Mary's Cathedral in 1958. He died on 18 July 1961 at his Vaucluse home and was buried in Rookwood cemetery with Catholic rites. His wife and their son and two daughters survived him. That year the company became a subsidiary of Blue Metal Industries Ltd, of which Galli became a director. He died on 26 December 1971 in hospital at Hornsby and was buried with Catholic rites in the Garden of Calvary cemetery, Rouse Hill. His wife and their son and daughter survived him.

It has been estimated that about 90 per cent of the marble, scagliola and terrazzo work in Sydney between 1910 and 1965 was undertaken by the Meloccos and their studio. They designed and crafted the interior of Boomerang, Elizabeth Bay, and were responsible for the mosaic work in the Anzac Memorial, Hyde Park. The frieze and mosaic in the ticket office at Central Station, the Tasman [q.v.2] map mosaic floor in the vestibule of the State Library of New South Wales and decorations in the State Theatre are some of their other best-known surviving work.

Melocco Brothers Fiftieth Anniversary Calendar (ML); C. Kevin and R. Pesman, *A History of Italian Settlement in New South Wales* (Syd, 1999); P. Genovesi and W. Musolino (eds), *In Search of the Australian Italian into the New Millennium* (Melb, 2000), p 377; *Italian Hist Soc Jnl*, 10, no 1, Jan-June 2002, p 4; series A1, items 1923/8262, 1924/27314 and 1928/6394, series A367, item C78210, series A12217, items L3955 and L8392 (NAA); information from Mrs L. Hannam, Roseville, Mrs A. Trenoweth, Haberfield, Mr J. Melocco, Castlecrag, and Mr G. Melocco, Pennant Hills, Syd.

CATHERINE KEVIN

MENDIS, PUNCHI HEWA (1883-1965), merchant, jeweller and pearler, was born on 12 September 1883 at Magalle, Galle, Ceylon (Sri Lanka), second of four children of Sadiris Punchihewa, merchant, and his wife Nikkonona Warusavithane. After primary schooling, Mendis received a British education to grade 4 at Richmond College, Magalle.

A number of Singhalese in northern Australia had come from Galle province, and in 1896 Mendis arrived at Thursday Island at the invitation of an uncle, Mendis de Silva, who was already there but had intended the arrangements for Mendis's older brother Marshall Punchihewa. Nevertheless, the youngster obtained employment with Alexander Corran [q.v.13] as a reporter for the *Torres Strait Pilot*; he covered the 1899 cyclone that decimated the pearling fleet and cost over 300 lives and the 1905 fire that destroyed nineteen shops. In 1904 he had begun a retail business as agent for S. Hoffnung [q.v.4] & Co., whose torches and batteries were in great demand.

Next year he rented the See Kee building in Douglas Street and eventually became local agent for some prominent Brisbane wholesalers. He learned photography and attached a studio and dark room, and a printery that produced the Church of England *Parish Gazette*.

Known in Australia as Punchi Hewa Mendis, he also acquired skills in valuing and cleaning pearls and by 1913 had become a licensed pearl trader, achieving great success in a period of booming prices. In 1913 a store was opened at his hometown, Magalle, where a Punchihewa club acted as a friendly society for the clan. Marshall started a jewellery business at Yokohama, Japan, which was destroyed by the 1923 earthquake. The brothers had pioneered the first experimental consignment of trochus shell from Australia to Japan in 1915. This became a lucrative industry that buoyed the Australian pearl fishery through a number of upheavals.

In 1915 Mendis returned to Magalle to marry Mercy de Silva, from a family that ran a jewellery emporium based in Singapore. Mercy, a woman of independent means, never came to Australia, where the migration of Asian women contravened official policy. They had two sons, Siripala (b.1919) and Nissanka (1926-1989), before Mercy died in childbirth in 1932. After their mother's death, both boys were brought to Australia to attend All Souls' School, Charters Towers, before joining the Mendis business, which by then was acting as agent for Thomas Brown, (Sir John) Chandler [q.v.13], Kodak and others, and ran the only newsagency on the island. Mendis also partnered J. C. Harman in a pearling fleet. It was confiscated, however, with all pearling luggers, during World War II.

Becoming a prominent resident of Thursday Island, Mendis had affectionate links with the white elite, including the bishop of Carpentaria and Corran, the mayor, and family links with the Asian-born population, forged by clan members whose immigration he had sponsored, including Peter Warnakulasuriya, who became part of the local Ahmat family. In 1940 Mendis expanded his business to Darwin, then thriving with preparations for war. He commenced construction of a large building (now demolished), which became the headquarters of General MacArthur's [q.v.15] staff and survived bombing to become a police station. During the civilian evacuation of Darwin, Mendis moved to Brisbane where he purchased the Tillse shop in Adelaide Street. In 1942 he responded to Prime Minister Chifley's [q.v.13] appeal by purchasing £60 000 in war bonds to support the war effort. In 1944 he acquired a farm at Manly, to shelter his extended family, among them a number evacuated from Thursday Island. He returned to the island, its business centre wrecked by the allied armies, in 1946, rebuilt several shops and resumed pearl and shell trading to the United States of America. But the island's golden age had passed.

When Mendis became a justice of the peace in Queensland in 1946, then a rare appointment for citizens of Asian descent, as a devout Buddhist he swore on the Tripitaka instead of the Bible. He judiciously abstained from alcohol and spoke Singhalese to his sons. Every few years he revisited Ceylon. He lived and breathed his work, keeping shop hours from 9 a.m. to 11 p.m., seven days a week during the lay-up season, when the community's numbers were swelled by the considerable floating population from the luggers. He died on 8 September 1965 and was buried with Buddhist rites on Thursday Island, which he considered his home. His sons survived him. Mendis Road at Berrimah, Darwin, was named after him. Although the Thursday Island store was sold in 1974, in 2003 it was still popularly known as the 'Mendis Shop'.

A. C. C. Lock, *Destination Barrier Reef* (Melb, 1955); J. C. H. Foley, *Timeless Isle* (Thursday Island, Qld, 1982); W. S. Weerasooria, *Links Between Sri Lanka and Australia* (Colombo, Sri Lanka, 1988); R. Ganter, *The Pearl-Shellers of Torres Strait* (Melb, 1994); *People*, 9 Apr 1952, p 30; *Courier-Mail*, 29 Aug 1958, p 7, 13 Sept 1960, p 12.   REGINA GANTER

MERANG; *see* HOOD

MERCER, HENRY FREDERICK (1872-1949), clergyman and rogue, was born on 30 March 1872 at Barrow-in-Furness, Lancashire, England, son of Thomas Atherton Mercer, accountant, and his wife Mary, née Darricott. Educated at Giggleswick Grammar School, Henry entered Christ's College, Cambridge, in 1890, but remained only five terms. In 1893-94 he attended St John's College, Highbury (the London College of Divinity), and passed the Cambridge preliminary for theology in 1895. Made deacon that year, he served curacies in London and Hertfordshire. On 12 May 1896 at St Saviour's Church, Bristol, he married Eleanor Kate Hill. He was ordained priest by the Bishop of St Alban's on 27 September 1896, and appointed to St Cuthbert's, Hampstead. The Mercers' daughter was born in 1897.

In 1899-1906 Mercer was metropolitan secretary of the Church Army in London then a student at Western University, London, Ontario, Canada, from which he graduated B.A. (1906) (and later falsely claimed to have an M.A.). On 7 February 1907 he was appointed to St Columb's Church of England, Hawthorn, Melbourne, and in 1909 was given special responsibilities for men's work.

Mercer's wife died in 1908. On 2 August 1909 at All Saints' Church, Geelong, he married Victorian-born Jean Miller Tannock.

Mercer's reputation for bringing men back to the Church attracted the attention of Bishop C. O. L. Riley [q.v.11] of Western Australia, who installed him as dean of Perth on 15 April 1912. A good-looking man, fair-haired, 5 ft 10 ins (178 cm) in height and weighing about 11 stone (69.9 kg), he initially made a favourable impression. His stress on practical preaching and moral instruction matched Riley's interests well, and he lost no time in introducing special services for men, supplemented by a mid-week social club (disbanded 1916) combining gymnastics with moral concerns such as opposition to gambling and promotion of temperance. These activities proved successful, though, according to the *Truth* newspaper, Mercer's observations on the temptations that men should avoid were 'so vaguely and delicately worded that any man might take his maiden aunt without fear of increasing the lady's stock of worldly wisdom'.

Meanwhile, serious doubts had developed about Mercer's character, and Riley and the cathedral chapter came to believe they had been misinformed about his credentials. Moreover, by July 1916 the dean had contracted debts of over £2000, which were eventually paid by leading laymen, including Septimus Burt [q.v.7]. A *Truth* columnist observed that 'Dean Mercenary was more a fool than a rogue'. Granted leave of absence on 8 September, he used the occasion to expand his earlier Citizen Military Force connexions to be appointed, on 28 September, chaplain (voyage only) in the Australian Imperial Force.

Mercer left Fremantle on 9 November 1916 in the troopship *Argyllshire*. Reaching England in January 1917 he was chaplain at No.2 Auxiliary Australian Hospital, Southall, London. He resigned as dean of Perth on 1 March and his A.I.F. commission in May. His wife and daughter returned to Melbourne where, in 1919, they unsuccessfully applied to the Department of Repatriation for a free passage to England. The family was never reunited. Jean Mercer was to die at Armadale, Melbourne, in 1947.

Mercer was a temporary lieutenant in the Royal Naval Volunteer Reserve from August 1917 and captain in the Royal Air Force in 1918-19. By 1921 he was teaching in an English school at Calcutta, India, styling himself 'Dr H. F. Mercer (late Captain A.I.F.)'. He was gaoled at Zürich, Switzerland, for twenty days in 1927 for failing to pay his hotel bill. In England between 1930 and 1948 he was imprisoned on five other occasions for periods of from six to eighteen months, for charges of minor fraud. From 1930 a woman said to be twenty years younger accompanied him; police attributed his problems mainly to 'the intemperate habits of the woman he calls his wife'. Mercer died on 22 February 1949 in Wandsworth Prison Hospital. An inquest returned a verdict of death by natural causes, the prison doctor testifying that 'he seemed to be a happy man and very cheerful up to within half an hour of his death'.

WA Church News, 1 Mar 1912, p 61; *Western Mail*, 23 Mar 1912, p 16, 20 Apr 1912, p 19, 6 July 1912, p 42; *West Australian*, 18 Apr 1912, p 4, 22 Apr 1912, p 9; *Truth* (Perth), 13 July 1912, p 42, 27 Jan 1917, p 4; *Age* (Melb), 7 Dec 1933, p 4; *Sunday Sun* (Syd), 22 Sept 1946, 'Fact & Opinion', p 1; *Wandsworth Borough News*, 11 Mar 1949, p 3; B2455, item Mercer, Henry Frederick (NAA, Canb); C. O. L. Riley, diary (BL).   JOHN TONKIN

MERLIN, HENRY BEAUFOY (1830?-1873), photographer, was born probably in 1830 in London, son of Frederick Merlin (Murlin), chemist, and his wife Ann Harriett, daughter of Lieutenant Benjamin Beaufoy, R.N. Henry Murlin, who was possibly a copyist for a London pantomime by Horace Mayhew in 1847, arrived in Sydney from London with his mother on 8 December 1848 as a steerage passenger. Ann Murlin married Henry John Forster in 1851; Mrs Forster was later described as an 'artist in wax flowers'.

In 1853 Henry was granted three licences for marionette performances and from April to May was based in the former Olympic Circus, Castlereagh Street, advertising as the Royal Marionette Theatre, which he claimed was the company of that name that had opened in London in 1852. The programme included animated scenes as well as marionettes. When the show transferred to Maitland in May he began using the name 'Henry Muriel', sometimes with a middle initial 'B'. He was granted licences in 1855, for a display of scenes of the Crimea, Russia, in June 1856 and February 1857, for theatres in which he acted at Maitland and Newcastle, and in May 1857 for a display of 'panoramas' in Sydney. In 1858 he gave a lecture to accompany Guy and Merlin's Grand Indian Panorama in Sydney as Henry Merlin and was so listed on the 1859-60 East Sydney electoral roll.

Back in London, on 27 January 1863 in the parish church of St Mary, Stratford, Bow, Henry Beaufoy Merlin married Louisa Eleanor Foster (b.1844). By 1866, and henceforth known as 'Beaufoy Merlin', he was in Victoria working as a travelling photographer, using the wet-plate or collodion method for glass negatives, under the name American and Australasian Photographic Co., although lacking any provable American connexion. In 1869 he presented the governor of Victoria

with his photographs of the Western District. He advertised his arrival in Sydney in September next year, claiming to have worked extensively in Victoria as well as at Yass, Braidwood, Queanbeyan, Goulburn and Parramatta in New South Wales. His assistant Charles Bayliss, then aged about 16, had travelled with him.

In late 1871 Merlin sailed as official photographer on the eclipse expedition to northern Queensland, reporting on the journey and its disappointing outcome for the *Australian Town and Country Journal* (6 January 1872). By the end of March the A. & A. Photographic Co. had established itself at Hill End. There Merlin met the German-born goldminer B. O. Holtermann [q.v.4], and a studio was built for the A. & A. Co. on a block Holtermann owned. After three months of photographing at Hill End and Tambaroora, Merlin's company travelled to Gulgong where they set about making images of practically every building, with owners, tenants and passers-by, achieving an unrivalled documentation of a town of that time. At Hill End on 19 October Merlin, again photographing house-to-house, recorded the unearthing of 'Holtermann's nugget'. He wrote an account of Holtermann's life for the *Town and Country Journal* (2 November 1872).

In December Merlin was at Bathurst when he learned that he had been selected to photograph settled areas of New South Wales and Victoria for the Holtermann Exposition, which would publicize the colonies overseas. On a tour of the central west, he took pictures at Bathurst, Orange, Dubbo and smaller towns, and wrote an extensive account of the journey for the *Town and Country Journal* (19 April, 5 July and 27 September 1872). By August next year he had returned to Sydney, where he took further photographs; his wife appeared in pictures of picnic groups. For the *Town and Country Journal* (9 August 1873) he also wrote a vivid, second-hand account of Captain Moresby's [q.v.5] expeditions to New Guinea.

Merlin died of pneumonia on 27 September 1873 at his home in Abercrombie Street, Leichhardt, Sydney. His wife and their two daughters and two sons survived him. His age was given as 43. He was buried in the Anglican section of Balmain cemetery (Pioneers' Park, Leichhardt). Bayliss and Holtermann continued the photographic work. Merlin, however, had been responsible for most of the Holtermann collection of photographs that was later acquired by the Mitchell [q.v.5] Library, Sydney.

Beaufoy Merlin's work reflected his mastery of a difficult technique and talent for composition. His unique record of the people and buildings of Hill End and Gulgong in 1872 is of extraordinary value to historians. The Macleay [q.v.5] Museum, University of

Sydney, holds twenty-two cartes-de-visite taken by him in 1872.

K. Burke, *Gold and Silver* (Melb, 1973); A. Davies and P. Stanbury, *The Mechanical Eye in Australia* (Melb, 1985); M. Colligan, *Canvas Documentaries* (Melb, 2002); R. Bradshaw, 'The Merlin of the South', *A'sian Drama Studies*, no 7, Oct 1985, p 82.

RICHARD BRADSHAW

METTERS, FREDERICK (1858-1937), and SPRING, HENRY LANGDON (1864-1937), stove manufacturers, were business partners. Metters was born on 14 May 1858 in Melbourne, eighth child of James Metters, a Cornish-born bricklayer, and his wife Susan, née Flux, from the Isle of Wight. Fred probably worked for his father, who by 1869 was employed as a stove setter.

After moving to Adelaide, on 8 October 1883 Fred married Frances Fisher at Clayton Congregational Church, Kensington. The family lived in Melbourne for some years in the 1880s. Back in Adelaide from 1890, next year he founded his stove-making company. Holding patents for cooking ovens, a firebox for ovens and a cooking apparatus—which won a prize at the Royal Agricultural and Horticultural Society's Show in 1899—he advertised himself as a 'Maker of Kitchen Ranges and Patent Improved Ovens' and a 'Coppersmith and Galvaniser'. To promote sales of his 'top-fire' fuel stove, he toured South Australia, demonstrating it at country shows. In 1894 he opened a branch in Perth where, at 68 Hay Street, he obtained premises being leased to Henry Spring.

Henry had been born on 25 September 1864 at Hackney, London, son of Henry Spring, merchant's clerk, later insurance broker, and his wife Marion, née Ballment. After working for ten years in a stockbroker's office in London, Spring sailed for South Africa and at the age of 25 joined the British South African Police. His health affected by malaria, about 1892 he migrated to Victoria, where he ran a country store and a travelling caravan. He then moved to Western Australia and operated a carrying business between Perth and Fremantle. On 6 November 1895 in St George's Cathedral, Perth, he married with Anglican rites Ellen Orianna Daw, from Adelaide. The previous year Spring had started as a clerk in Metters & Co. He quickly became its driving force and in 1898 was made a partner. After Metters sold his interest to Spring in 1907, Metters Ltd was formed in Adelaide with Spring as managing director. The nominal capital of the company in 1911 was £200 000.

Spring's younger brother ROBERT ALEXANDER (1873-1971), born at Woodford, Essex, had reached Perth in 1897 and was assistant to the manager of the factory there. In 1902 he established a Metters foundry in Sydney, and was its first manager. On 29 August next year, at St Philip's Church of England, he married Ellen's sister Josephine Constance Daw.

The firm advertised (1909) as 'stove and range makers, ironfounders, engineers, coppersmiths, sheetmetal workers' and undertook to provide windmills, pumps, troughing and irrigation requirements. A new, illustrated catalogue (c.1910) showed ornamental castings, ventilating friezes, crestings, finials, verandah drops and memorial tablets. In 1911 new or rebuilt factories on larger blocks of land appeared in Adelaide and at Subiaco, Perth, and in 1913 new premises were erected in Elizabeth Street, Sydney. Henry Spring oversaw an expansion as the company produced gas and fuel stoves, other domestic appliances and agricultural machinery, including water tanks. During World War I large quantities of cooking equipment were provided for the armed services. In 1918 Metters Ltd bought the business of R. Foreman & Sons, Hobart, makers of porcelain-enamelled baths, the manufacture of which was brought to Sydney. Capital in the company increased again in 1924 to £1 000 000. When a controlling interest was acquired in Porcelain Enamellers, New Zealand, Metters (N.Z.) Ltd was formed in 1926.

Three former employees of Metters Ltd had begun the K.F.B. Foundry in Sydney in 1916; competition became keen and in 1927 the two businesses amalgamated, each keeping its old trade identity while a holding company, General Industries Ltd, was formed. Henry Spring became the chairman of directors of the holding company while retaining control of Metters Ltd. Soon a factory was built at Footscray, Melbourne.

Henry was a councillor for many years of the Metal Trades Employers' Association and had pastoral interests in Western Australia; he was said to have been among the first to introduce motor transport of cattle and sheep. Living at Mosman, Sydney, he was interested in motorcars and motorboats and was a founder of Mosman Golf Club. He died on 21 April 1937 in St Luke's Hospital, Elizabeth Bay, and was cremated, survived by his wife, three sons and one daughter. His estate was sworn for probate at £17 698.

Metters lived comfortably in a grand house at Rose Park, South Australia, from 1911 to 1922; thereafter he lived with his sons at Waikerie and Gumeracha. He was a tall, solid, full-faced man, broad-minded and determined, who neither smoked nor played any sport and did not attend church. Predeceased by his wife, he died intestate on 25 September 1937 in Ru Rua private hospital, North Adelaide, and was buried in West Terrace cemetery. His three sons and three daughters survived him.

He had already divided his assets among his sons, none of whom entered the business.

Robert Spring, a plump, cheerful man with a jocund smile, became managing director of Metters Ltd after his brother's death. In World War II the firm produced land mines and pontoon bridges. Plagued by strikes, in 1952 Spring announced a pact with 1300 workers at the big factory at Alexandria, Sydney, which he hoped would end labour disputes. He retired from the company in 1956. Robert was a life member of the Royal Zoological Society and a member of the Metal Trades Employers' Federation. Predeceased by his wife, he died in his home at Clifton Gardens on 15 April 1971 and was buried in Northern Suburbs cemetery. Two sons and a daughter survived him.

In 1974 Email Ltd purchased the company. Perhaps the best remembered of all Metters products was the two-coloured (cream and green), enamel 'Early Kooka' stove—featuring a kookaburra with a captured worm—which was first made in 1937, the year in which both Fred Metters and Henry Spring had died.

The Story of Metters (1965); *Daily Telegraph* (Syd), 25 Sept 1922, p 3; *SMH*, 9 July 1927, p 17, 22 Apr 1937, p 17, 2 Mar 1952, p 2, 20 Apr 1971, p 14; *National Times*, 24-30 Oct 1982, p 15; information from Mr H. Metters, Ascot Park, Adel.

JOYCE GIBBERD

MICKEY OF ULLADULLA (c.1820-1891), Aboriginal artist, was born on the south coast of New South Wales, a member of the Dhurga people. The first written record of him was a note on some of his drawings in the collection of the Mitchell [q.v.5] Library, Sydney:

Drawn by 'Mickie'
An old crippled blackfellow
of Nelligen, Clyde River NSW
1875

Later drawings, dating from the 1880s, were annotated with inscriptions describing the artist's location as Ulladulla.

By the 1840s, Aboriginal men at Ulladulla were employed by settlers in reaping, tree felling and trading in native fauna. Women were employed in such pursuits as digging potatoes and husking maize. As the south coast industries developed, Aboriginal labour was used on farms, in sawmills and on wharves. The principal activity, however, was fishing. Mickey's drawings recorded some of these activities. In one, a man supporting himself on two sticks (almost certainly a depiction of the artist) was shown selling brooms.

Most of his drawings were made in the 1880s at Ulladulla. Many appear to have been pairs: one part depicting the corroboree, the other depicting fishing activities. He devel-oped a pattern for these sketches. Those of corroborees included a row of spectators along the lower edge of the composition, while centrally placed, in European dress, was the man with crutches, the artist himself. In his fishing scenes, specific vessels were depicted, such as the boats given to the Ulladulla community by the Aborigines Protection Board and the *Peterborough*, a steamer that made a weekly trip between Ulladulla and Sydney in the 1880s and 1890s.

Mickey's medium was a mixture of pencil, water-colour and coloured crayons. Like his fellow Aboriginal artists of the nineteenth century Tommy McRae [q.v.] and William Barak [q.v.3], he had a particular relationship with members of the European community, who provided materials and who ensured the preservation of the works. Mickey's patron was Mary Ann Gambell, the wife of the Ulladulla lighthouse keeper, who lived close to the Aboriginal Reserve at Ulladulla and had a reputation as a friend of indigenous people.

Mickey of Ulladulla died on 13 October 1891. He may have succumbed to the virulent strain of influenza that caused a minor epidemic in the town in October and November that year. A brief report of his death in the local newspaper described him as 'gifted with some of the qualities of an artist. He produced some very fine pencil sketches, and indeed showed ability in that direction.' In 1893 the Board for the Protection of Aborigines and two local officials (George Ilett of Milton and John Rainsford) showed five of Mickey's drawings at the World's Columbian Exposition, Chicago, United States of America. Ilett was awarded a bronze medal for exhibiting work that was described as 'unique and valuable as a specimen of primitive art, being uninfluenced by the white man'. Mickey of Ulladulla's drawings are in many public collections including the Australian Institute of Aboriginal and Torres Strait Islander Studies, the National Library of Australia and the National Gallery of Australia, all in Canberra, and the State Library of New South Wales, Sydney.

A. Sayers, *Aboriginal Artists of the Nineteenth Century* (Melb, 1994); *Ulladulla and Milton Times*, 17 Oct 1891, p 2.   ANDREW SAYERS

MILLER, FRANCIS BOWYER (1828-1887), assayer, was born on 18 December 1828 at Edgbaston, Warwickshire, England, youngest son of William Miller, brewer, and his wife Frances Bowyer, née Vaux, a writer of children's books. Both parents were Quakers, and the Miller and Vaux families were active in agitation against the slave trade. Francis was educated at King Edward's Grammar

School, Birmingham, and King's College, London. In 1849 he joined a British Admiralty expedition to the Bight of Benin, Africa, to see if lagoons there could be used by British gunboats in the suppression of the slave trade. Returning to England about 1850, he worked with a mining company in Cornwall for twelve months then became an assistant to his brother William, professor of chemistry at King's College and non-resident assayer to the Royal Mint and the Bank of England.

In November 1853 Francis Miller and W. S. Jevons [q.v.4] were appointed to the newly established Sydney branch of the Royal Mint, partly on William Miller's recommendation. Offered a retainer of £100 per annum, they were expected to establish their own assay offices and to undertake work for private banks and individuals as well as for the mint on piece rates. By the time the mint opened in May 1855, however, he and Jevons had become full-time public servants with no need to take private work. On 11 January 1854 in the Parish Church of St Clement Danes, Westminster, Miller had married Alicia, only daughter of Maurice Fitzgerald O'Connell, R.N. Two months later the Millers sailed with their servant for Sydney in the *Granite City*. They were to have four children.

On arrival in Sydney, Miller set up an assay office in Bligh Street. In November 1859 he became a member of the Philosophical (later Royal) Society of New South Wales, before which, in July 1860, he read a paper on the detection of spurious gold, concerned in particular with a species of fake gold 'nuggets' that had deceived many Sydney storekeepers. Rachel Henning [q.v.4], to whom he showed a sample 'nugget' at Bathurst in July 1861, found him to be 'rather a clever, agreeable man'.

Miller's crowning scientific achievement was his development of a process of refining and toughening gold by means of chlorine gas. He patented this process in London in June 1867 and registered it as an invention before the New South Wales Legislative Assembly in November. Twelve months later his paper describing the process was read before the Chemical Society, London, and by December 1869, when Miller read another paper on the subject before the Royal Society of New South Wales, his method had been successfully put into operation at the Sydney Mint and by the Bank of New Zealand at Auckland, New Zealand.

In 1870 Miller was transferred to the new Melbourne branch of the Royal Mint, and was paid £2000 for the sole Victorian rights to the gold-refining process. He sold the 'remarkably handsome Gothic villa and grounds' that he had built on the waterfront at Double Bay and relocated his family to the Melbourne suburb of Kew. By then Miller's method had been introduced into mints in England, the United States of America and Norway and he had travelled to England and the U.S.A. to advise on the process.

Superintendent of the bullion office at the Melbourne Mint from 1877, in 1884 he was briefly acting deputy master. Chronic Bright's disease forced him to take sick leave from June 1887 and he died in his home at Kew on 17 September 1887, survived by his wife, two sons and one daughter. He was buried with Anglican rites in Boroondara cemetery. At the time of his death he was a member of the Philosophical Society of Philadelphia, a fellow of the Chemical Society of London and of the Institute of Chemistry of Great Britain and a corresponding member of the Royal Society of New South Wales. In 2005 the Miller process was still used worldwide to treat molten gold.

W. S. Jevons, *Money and the Mechanism of Exchange* (Lond, 1875); H. M. Humphreys (comp), *Men of the Time in Australia: Victorian Series* (Melb, 1882); H. E. Forrest, *A History of the Forrest Family of Birmingham & Shrewsbury, with their connection with the Miller, Vaux and Jefferys families* (Wellington, UK, 1923); D. Adams (ed), *The Letters of Rachel Henning* (Melb, 1969); NSW Parliament, Legislative Assembly, *Letters of Registration of Inventions Under 16 Victoria*, no 26, no 163, 7 Nov 1867; M. Martin, 'Mr Miller of the Mint', *Insites*, no 35, Winter 2003, p 4; *SMH*, 19 July 1860, p 4; *Argus* (Melb), 24 Sept 1887, p 9.　　　MEGAN MARTIN

MILLS, HELENA MABEL CHECKLEY; *see* FORREST

MILNE, AGNES ANDERSON (1851-1919), factory inspector, was born on 1 December 1851 at Lambeth Walk, London, second daughter of William Inglis, carpenter, and his wife Lydia, née King. The family migrated to South Australia in the *Caroline* in 1855 and settled at Hindmarsh. On leaving school, Agnes worked as a shirtmaker in a small workshop until her marriage to Henry Milne, a saddler, on 10 April 1873 at Hindmarsh Congregational Church. They had four children, none surviving infancy. Henry died in 1883 and Agnes attempted to continue his business. When this failed, she returned to shirtmaking and became a skilled cutter. By 1892 she was proprietor of a workshop employing five girls.

Strong Christian principles motivated Milne. As a young woman she taught in Hindmarsh Congregational Church Sabbath school, later transferring to the Church of Christ. A foundation member in 1889 of the South Australian branch of the Woman's Christian Temperance Union, she was president of the union at Bowden for twenty-six years, head of various departments within the colonial executive and a delegate to several W.C.T.U. national conferences. She was a woman of strong character and opinions, and in photographs somewhat severe in appearance.

Milne became a member of the first executive of the Working Women's Trades Union, set up in 1889, and a delegate to the United Trades and Labor Council. She joined forces with social reformers such as Mary Lee and Augusta Zadow [qq.v.10,12], differing from those ladies, however, because she was herself a working woman, involved at the grassroots level with the clothing trade. At a commission of inquiry into shops and factories in 1892, she gave evidence of excessively low rates of pay and cases of exploitation; as a result of the inquiry a Factories Act was passed in 1894. She also wrote letters to newspapers and lobbied to publicize the miserable conditions of many female workers.

On 22 July 1896, following the death of Zadow, Milne was appointed South Australia's second female factory inspector. In this post she attempted to ensure that premises were registered, clean and well lit and had adequate sanitary provisions, water and space for employees, and that hours worked were not excessive and machinery was safe. Milne took time to canvass support for workers not covered by the Act, writing a series of articles on 'Women's work and wages' in the *Journal of Agriculture and Industry* (1899). She gave evidence to another parliamentary inquiry in 1904. Passionate in her commitment to eliminating sweated labour, she became personally involved in many cases. She organized help from her own resources and approached parliamentary leaders and social reformers regarding the formation of an Anti-Sweating League (1900). Lady Tennyson [q.v.], the governor's wife, described Milne as 'a very interesting, sensible woman'.

Initially, Milne had the support of her superiors for her campaign against sweating, but the department became more bureaucratic as legislative controls were extended to cover all aspects of factory, workshop and home employment. Her reforming zeal and tendency to act independently began to be criticized. On 30 April 1907 she resigned to take over management of the South Australian Co-operative Clothing Factory, owned and run by and for women, which she had been largely responsible for establishing. In time this venture foundered through competition from larger firms. Shortly before the company went into liquidation in 1913, Milne retired to a small house (once her mother's) next to the Hindmarsh school, and set up shop selling sweets and hot lunches to the school children.

On 22 December 1916 at Holy Trinity Church, Adelaide, she married Hartley Wright Edwards, a contractor. Agnes Edwards died of cancer on 10 August 1919 at her home and was buried in Hindmarsh cemetery. Her husband survived her.

A. Hasluck, *Audrey Tennyson's Vice-regal Days* (Canb, 1978); E. Pearson, *Women in Bustles or People in History?* (Adel, 1976); Report of the Shops and Factories Commission, *PP* (SA), 1892, vol 2, paper no 37, p 109; P. L. Fletcher, 'An Adelaide Woman of Interest: Agnes Milne, Inspector of Factories, 1896-1906', *JHSSA*, no 15, 1987, p 54 *and* The Working Woman's Champion, Agnes Anderson Milne 1850-1919 (B.A. Hons thesis, Flinders Univ, 1986); *Labour Hist*, no 87, Nov 2004, p 11; *Advertiser* (Adel), 15 May 1893, p 7; *Daily Herald* (Adel), 14 June 1913, p 13; *Chronicle* (Adel), 27 Sept 1919, p 17.

PHILIPPA. L. FLETCHER*

MITCHELL, ERNEST LUND (1876-1959), photographer and farmer, was born on 9 August 1876 at Horton, Yorkshire, England, second child of Oliver Mitchell, wool and waste dealer, and his wife Eliza, née Lund. Ernest came to Melbourne with his parents and sisters in October 1884 because of his father's asthma. The family later went to Sydney before returning to Yorkshire about 1891, where Ernest was apprenticed to his uncle Percy Lund, owner of a printing firm at Bradford. Mitchell migrated to Sydney with friends in the *Frederich Der Große*, arriving on 31 December 1899, by which time he owned good cameras and was a skilled photographer.

Travelling around rural New South Wales, Mitchell sold rubber and worked as a photographer while concurrently following his interests in prospecting. About this time he married Helena 'Lena' Louise; they were to have no children. In 1906-07 Ernest was a partner in Emu Studio at Lismore then went to North Queensland where he met Ion Idriess [q.v.9]. By 1909 he had moved to Western Australia and in the next two years photographed the State extensively. In 1911 he undertook his only international expedition—to Java. He established a studio at 364 Murray Street, Perth, about 1913.

Mitchell's photographs dominated the Western Australian commercial and official markets from 1909 until the late 1920s. He undertook private commissions and was engaged by commercial clients, such as the *Western Mail*, and several State government departments. After winning a gold medal at the Samarang Exhibition, Java, in 1914, he was appointed official photographer to the governor of Western Australia. Mitchell's images of landscapes, towns, primary industry and Aboriginal people in the Kimberleys and the Pilbara and at the Moore River Mission were widely reproduced in government publications. His pictures received an international audience as part of the official pearling display at the British Empire Exhibition at Wembley in 1924, and one was published in the 1929 edition of *The Encyclopaedia Britannica*.

Through reproduction in official Immigration and General Information Department publications, Mitchell's work helped to shape international perceptions of Australia and Western Australia. By 1914 his photographs were incorporated into collections of the Western Australian government printer and the London offices of the agent-general and the Australian High Commission, and were widely distributed through picture agencies. They were used in geography and history texts, adventure narratives, pictorial atlases and encyclopaedias, official advertisements to migrants in England, lantern slide shows and picture postcards. His pictures of Aboriginal people also featured in adventure stories, including books by Idriess. Always a son of the British Empire, Mitchell remembered his photograph of the train derailment during the 1920 visit of the Prince of Wales as one of the high points of his career.

Mitchell was a tall, fine-figured man, with a moustache. A Freemason, in 1900 he had joined Lodge Cambrian No.10 in Sydney and in 1918 Swan Lodge in Perth. He was a member of the Perth-based Commercial Travellers' Club, and used political and pastoral connections to further his photographic career and agricultural interests. In 1926, in partnership with a shearing contractor, Robert Strachan, he purchased land at Carnamah. Within a year, Strachan and Strachan's wife were dead and Mitchell was left with unanticipated debt at the beginning of the Depression. As his photographic trade was in decline, he closed his studio in 1931 and moved with his wife to the farm, where he remained until 1946. Having little knowledge of agriculture, he relied on an Italian migrant, Phillip Di Masi, and his family to manage the property. Snapshots of this period painted a picture of poverty, contrasting with his previous commercial photographs used to advertise the State.

Mitchell returned to Perth in 1946 and lived at Claremont. He regularly corresponded with family members in England, whom he never met, but did not succeed in returning to Britain as he wished. Survived by his wife, he died on 3 January 1959 in hospital at Claremont and was cremated with Anglican rites. The State Library of Western Australia holds some of his glass negatives, and his prints are widely distributed in private and public collections; some are also held in the Royal Geographical Society in London and archives of picture agencies in England.

J. Sassoon, An Archaeology of Memory: A Biography of Photographs Taken by E. L. Mitchell 1908-1930 (Ph.D. thesis, Univ WA, 2001); E. L. Mitchell papers (BL); Mitchell family papers (AJCP, M2760).   JOANNA SASSOON

MITFORD, EUSTACE REVELEY (1811-1869), satirist, was christened on 25 May 1811 at St Pancras, London, son of John Mitford, barrister, and his first wife Sara, née Woodward. Eustace was proud of his family, especially his great-uncle John Freeman Mitford, first Baron Redesdale. Later Eustace claimed to have joined the navy and to have served in Spain against the Carlists. He married Eliza Sanders on 7 November 1834 at Ledbury, Hereford; they had eleven children.

Migrating to South Australia in 1839, Mitford bought and farmed eighty acres (32.4 ha) near the Sturt River. He also tried droving and mineral exploration. Usually in debt to family and friends, he was gaoled briefly for insolvency in 1856. In 1861, claiming to be the 'real discoverer', he challenged (Sir) Walter Hughes's [q.v.4] right to the rich copper deposits at Moonta. He pressed his claim, without success, through a select committee in 1863 and a petition to Queen Victoria in 1869.

Mitford continued to live at Edwardstown, but found his true vocation in 1867 when he began publishing in Adelaide a weekly journal, *Pasquin: Pastoral, Mineral and Agricultural Advocate*. It reviewed plays and books and campaigned on behalf of the oppressed—such as prisoners and destitute children—but its chief aim was to 'aggravate our subscribers in every possible way', and Mitford had a sure eye for what would annoy South Australians most. Introducing the grape was 'a great mistake'. Democracy was another: 'democracy and dishonesty, universal suffrage and universal pillage ... are synonymous terms and inseparable results'. Adelaide's architecture was 'mediaeval Clapham Common Gothic with a tendency to the Old Bailey Tuscan'. The colonists were wrong to sack the 'conscientious' Judge Boothby [q.v.3]. Their hero Surveyor-General Goyder [q.v.4], who gave the copper to Hughes, was hopelessly incompetent. Wakefield [q.v.2] was 'an ignoramus', and £1 an acre for land was ruining the colony.

Satire resists description. Here is Mitford at his lethal best:

People in England are profoundly astonished to hear that the land has not cost the Government or the country a single farthing—that, in fact well, to put it as mildly as possible—that we stole it!—took possession, you understand, in the Queen's name—just as they used aforetime to burn alive respectable ladies and gentlemen in the name of the Deity—and that when the native rangers attempted to remove the sheep found trespassing on their lands, we shot them like dogs, also in the name of the Queen—and then sent missionaries— very nice men, in white chokers—to inform them of a beautiful new kind of religion, which strictly prohibited theft and murder, or to covet a blackfellow's land or his lubra or his waddy, his boomerang or his beer, or anything that is his, or any other man's. Of course the blacks were deeply impressed with the sanctity and consistent justice of a religion, which was to save their souls, but played the very devil with their bodies, their lands, and their kangaroos. We make as much fuss about permitting settlers to occupy this land as if we had a right to it.

Mitford died of a chest infection on 24 October 1869 at Edwardstown, leaving an intestate estate valued at less than £80, and was buried in the Anglican cemetery at St Mary's. His wife, three daughters and six sons survived him; the journal, *Pasquin*, ceased after his death.

P. Depasquale, *A Critical History of South Australian Literature 1836-1930* (Adel, 1978); M. Middleton, Mitford's Marion (ms, c.1990, held by Marion Hist Soc); Report of the Select Committee of the House of Assembly on the Tipara Mineral Claims, *PP* (SA), 1863, vol 2, paper no 51; *SA Register*, 18 Oct 1863, p 3, 25 Oct 1869, p 2; *Bunyip*, 30 Oct 1869, p 2; *Adelaide Punch*, 25 Oct 1879, p 6.

PAT STRETTON

MOBOURNE, ERNEST (c.1862-1918), rural worker and Aboriginal leader, was born at Ettrick, near Heywood, Victoria, son of Jackie (Johnnie) Mobourne and his wife Eliza, both Aborigines. On 24 January 1893 at Lake Condah mission station Ernest married MARGARET (c.1872-1917), who had been born on Glenisla station, near Balmoral, daughter of Aboriginal parents Robert Turner and Janet Callaghan. Ernest and Margaret had grown up on Lake Condah mission, established in 1867, and were well educated at its school. They had four sons, who died while young, and a daughter Ethel. From 1892 Ernest began to question the paternalism and authoritarian style of Rev. J. H. Stähle [q.v.], the station's manager.

In 1897 Ernest wrote to the parliamentarian John Murray [q.v.10] about mismanagement at Lake Condah. Falling out with Stähle, in May 1899 Mobourne moved to nearby Dunmore, where a number of 'half-caste' Aborigines, forced by government policy out of the station, had established themselves. To Stähle's dismay, other 'full blacks' followed. A police constable, sent to remove the 'pure-blood Aborigines' from Dunmore, reported that Ernest was 'without doubt a *Bush Lawyer* and the others recognise him as a sort of King or leader'. Ernest appealed to the Board for the Protection of the Aborigines not to allow force to be used against him, as he was 'earning a living' and 'much happier than I would be living on the Station'. By September 1899, however, the Mobournes were back at Condah.

Stähle was soon objecting that they wanted to roam the countryside 'in defiance of law and order'; he asked that they be moved to another station and their rations stopped. Ernest and Maggie responded by writing to the *Hamilton Spectator* and to the board and lodging a written complaint against Stähle with a justice of the peace. They were sent under an Order in Council to Lake Tyers station in Gippsland in March 1900, only returning to Lake Condah in 1903 through the intervention of the governor, to whom Ernest had written for help. In July 1907 Maggie eloped with Henry Albert, a 'half-caste'.

That year the B.P.A. decided to close Lake Condah and Ramahyuck stations. Lake Condah Aborigines fought to thwart these plans, and Ernest played a leading role, petitioning the government and appealing to the ratepayers of the district for help—348 people signed the petition. Although Ramahyuck was closed, the protest saved Lake Condah mission, which was allowed to continue for a further decade.

Maggie returned to Ernest in December 1910. Stähle watched in disapproval as she came and went over the next few years, staying some months with Henry Albert, returning to the station when Henry left for shearing or other work, then living with him again when he returned home. Matters were further complicated by the birth in November 1911 of a daughter, Dorothy ('Dolly'), fathered by Henry but raised as a Mobourne. When the Mobournes, upset by the behaviour of the station teacher, told Stähle that they planned to leave, he warned that they would be prevented from taking their daughter Ethel, who was still at school, and wrote to the board: 'these educated blacks are much more difficult to deal with than the old blacks were'. The Mobournes stayed.

Maggie and her baby Dolly were removed to Lake Tyers in January 1914. In August Ernest and Ethel were allowed to visit Maggie. Thereafter, despite constant requests, the board refused to allow him or his family to return to Lake Condah. In March 1916 he again wrote to the governor, bitterly complaining about his family's treatment by the B.P.A. and its secretary, W. J. Ditchburn:

Why are we kept prisoners here and not permitted to return to our friends and our home? This country is free and we understand we are under the British flag, but it seems we [are] slaves in Mr Ditchburn's sight.

Maggie spent a month in hospital in Melbourne in 1916. She died on 30 May 1917 at Lake Tyers and was buried in the cemetery there. After her death Ernest was once more refused permission to go home to Condah.

Sociable and well liked, a fighter for justice, he was remembered by Joe Sharrock, a neighbour, as a 'happy sort. Orator, could speak good English, and once made a speech to the Governor. Very bald.' In his last years Ernest was a leader in Lake Tyers Aboriginal community, acting as a lay preacher and conducting services, with Ethel as organist. He died on 16 May 1918 at Bairnsdale District Hospital, and was buried in the local cemetery, survived by his daughter and by Maggie's daughter by Henry Albert.

J. Critchett, *Untold Stories* (Melb, 1998); series B337, item 507, series B313, item 138 (NAA, Melb); series 1096, unit 51, S3275A, 1903, *and* series 3992, unit 1457, B5755 in file A5318 of 1907 (PRO, Vic); *Portland Guardian*, 11 May 1961, p 4.

JAN CRITCHETT

MOBSBY, HENRY WILLIAM (1860-1933), and WILLS, FREDERICK CHARLES (1870-1955), were artists and photographers and motion picture pioneers. Mobsby was born on 17 August 1860 at Hove, Sussex, England, son of William Mobsby, watchman, and his wife Sarah, née Humphrys. Educated at Hampton Place school, Henry trained in art, design, chemistry and commercial practice at the School of Arts, Brighton, and in London. In 1883 he accompanied the artist I. W. Jenner [q.v.9] to Queensland. Mobsby married Jenner's eldest daughter Mary Ellen on 10 September 1884 at the general registry office, Brisbane, and for some years taught decorative art at Brisbane Technical College.

Wills was born on 14 November 1870 at Torquay, Devon, England, son of Charles Rundle Wills, tailor, and his wife Elizabeth Sarah, née Mountstephen. Frederick came to Australia about 1889 and by the mid-1890s was an artist, living at Croydon, Sydney. On 26 April 1895 at the district registrar's office, Waverley, he married English-born Edith Emily Walker. They were to have five children.

Appointed to the Queensland Department of Agriculture and Stock as its first official artist and photographer on 13 March 1897, Wills moved to Brisbane with his family. His duties initially involved illustrating plant life and farming scenes for the new *Queensland Agricultural Journal* and specimens for the Botanic Gardens. He also produced photographic enlargements and lantern slides to advertise the colony's primary industries and resources. Actively involved with the Queensland Amateur Photographic Society, he frequently contributed to Australian photographic magazines.

The prospect of the Greater Britain Exhibition in London in 1899 induced the Queensland government to agree to Wills's proposal to supplement its displays with motion pictures, 'lantern slides ... prepared on the Lumière Cinematographe principle'. The Chief Secretary's Department agreed to finance the motion picture venture for a year from October 1898. In December Wills was sent to Sydney to obtain a Lumière cinematograph and the expertise to operate it. Photographic suppliers Baker & Rouse imported the equipment, and Wills made five successful trial films in Sydney.

On Wills's return to Brisbane in March 1899, Mobsby was appointed as his assistant. By October 1899 Wills and Mobsby had produced some thirty, one-minute films during various 'still' photography excursions around Queensland. These illustrated agricultural processes and also covered topical events. Among the earliest was the arrival of Governor Lamington [q.v.9] for the opening of parliament on 18 May 1899. The next evening, Wills exhibited 'some very good specimens of locally taken cinematograph pictures' at the Queensland Amateur Photographic Society. Between June and August 1899 Mobsby took the cinematograph to the Torres Strait on a tour led by the home secretary Justin Foxton [q.v.8], but the productions lacked the technical and artistic assurance of Wills's.

Most of the films made by Wills and Mobsby were shot in the spring of 1899 and illustrated wheat harvesting on the Darling Downs, sugar harvesting at Nambour and aspects of stock management. These were the first Australian industrial documentary films and are among the world's earliest films of the type. Many of the sixty-second rolls were constructed in sequences of two- and three-camera set-ups and intended for screening in a logical order to construct a narrative of the processes shown. 'When a subject takes more than one film', Wills casually observed in 1900, 'they are joined with the aid of amyl acetate with some of the celluloid dissolved in it'. He made the earliest surviving Australian films exhibiting sequential editing techniques.

'There is artistic taste needed in the choice and management of subject as much, and perhaps more, than in ordinary photography', he wrote in 1900. Yet Wills was at pains to point out that a cinematographer was 'by no means a wizard, but, to use a familiar expression "a real hard grafter"'. He claimed that 'out of thirty negative and thirty positive films which I have exposed only two negatives and one positive have been spoilt. It behoves one to be careful when each film costs 22/6d.'

The series was also important for such images as those of Kanaka labourers at work in the cane fields in conditions resembling slavery. Wills and Mobsby also filmed the Queensland cabinet boarding the government paddle steamer *Lucinda* for a ministerial banquet. Their last and most impressive films recorded Queensland troops bound for the

South African War, the only known surviving footage of such departures. Shot in Brisbane between 28 and 31 October, this marked the end of the film experiment. The chief secretary's twelve months of funding had elapsed.

The only recorded complete showing of the films was a private one in the Department of Agriculture boardroom on 17 November 1899. By the time they reached Britain in 1900 (too late for the exhibition) the Lumière 35 mm stock, with round sprocket holes, had fallen victim to technological change and the films would not fit newer projectors. The films also met resistance from George Randall [q.v.], Queensland's immigration lecturer, who avoided using a Lumière projector even after one was provided. Randall had not been consulted and considered that these motion picture novelties would attract 'the flotsam and jetsam of the cities' rather than 'the good men from the villages'.

Though Wills gave a 'Paper on Cinematography' to the Queensland Amateur Photographic Society on 15 June 1900, he was never to resume moving film production. In 1903, after continued disputes over limits to the quantity and quality of pictorial content in the *Queensland Agricultural Journal*, he resigned his government post. For two years he operated a photographic studio in George Street, Brisbane, before taking his family to Toowoomba where he ran a photographic equipment business and studio as an agent of Baker & Rouse. He published a series of postcard views of Toowoomba, gave art classes on Saturdays and was president of the Toowoomba Photographic Society. Nevertheless, in 1914 he and his family left for Sydney. His name appeared on *Souvenir of Brisbane*, a pictorial guide to the city published that year by the New South Wales Bookstall Co. His last known photographic assignment was a portrait of a 5-year-old at Croydon in 1938.

Mobsby had taken over as official artist and photographer for the Department of Agriculture in 1904 and remained until his retirement in 1930. He had scant direct involvement in subsequent Queensland government film production, preferring to commission others, such as the Salvation Army limelight department's former cameraman Sid Cook, to undertake the filmmaking. Mobsby's contemporary reputation stemmed from his scenic photography and exhibition design. A fellow of both the Royal Geographical Society and the Royal Society of Artists, London, he regularly designed and organized Queensland's exhibits for the annual shows in southern capitals and at the Royal National Exhibition in Brisbane. His photography gained international distinction, and he officially represented Queensland at the Franco-British Exhibition, London, in 1908, the Panama-Pacific Exhibition, San

Francisco, in 1915, the British Empire Exhibition, Wembley, in 1924 and the South Pacific Exhibition, Dunedin, in 1925-26.

In December 1905 Mobsby's 11-year-old son Arthur Timewell drowned; each year thereafter, the Mobsby memorial medal was awarded to the Indooroopilly State School student who achieved the highest percentage in the year 8 scholarship public examination. A keen Freemason, Mobsby was a member of the Lodge, Indooroopilly, No.155, United Grand Lodge of Queensland. He died on 9 April 1933 at his home in Station Road, Indooroopilly, and was buried in Toowong cemetery. His wife and their daughter survived him.

Predeceased by his wife, Wills died on 8 August 1955 at his son-in-law's sheep property, Beethoven, Rowena, New South Wales, and was buried with Anglican rites at Collarenebri. Two sons and a daughter survived him. That year the Lumière cinematograph and the Wills and Mobsby films were transferred from the Department of Agriculture to the Queensland Museum to await their belated first public exhibition on 15 September 1993.

P. J. Skerman et al, *Guiding Queensland Agriculture 1887-1987* (Brisb, 1988); C. Long and P. Laughren, 'World's First Government Film Production' in K. Berryman (ed), *Screening the Past* (Canb, 1995), and 'Australia's First Films: Facts and Fables', *Cinema Papers*, no 96, Dec 1993, p 32, and *Queensland's First Films, 1895-1910* (video, 1996); T. Barker (comp), *Frederick Charles Wills* (Brisb, 2000); J. K. Brown, Versions of Reality: The Production and Function of Photographs in Colonial Queensland 1880-1900 (Ph.D. thesis, Univ Qld, 1985); Randall papers (Fryer Lib, Univ Qld).

PAT LAUGHREN

MOFFATT, LAWRENCE FRANCIS (1897-1966), Aboriginal leader and labourer, was born on 11 November 1897 at Ramahyuck, Gippsland, Victoria, and registered as Francis Lawrence, son of Aboriginal parents Edward Moffatt, a labourer from the Monaro district in southern New South Wales, and his wife Florence, née Foster, a local Kurnai woman. On 21 February 1924 at Lake Tyers Aboriginal station Laurie married Regina Harrison with Anglican rites. They were to have eight children.

Throughout his life Moffatt moved on and off Lake Tyers station, leaving to work in nearby towns and returning to be with his family. At various times he worked near Lakes Entrance, at a sawmill at Healesville and at Yallourn. This freedom was a right he always exercised, much to the frustration of the station managers at Lake Tyers, and it was central to his demands for Aborigines. He called for the reduction of the station manager's powers, to enable residents to leave the station or relatives and friends to visit without being required to obtain permission or risk being charged with trespass.

On 15 June 1940 Moffatt enlisted in the Australian Military Forces, lowering his age by four years. He served as a private in the 23rd Battalion at Albury, New South Wales, and was discharged at Caulfield, Melbourne, on 22 March 1941, after which he returned to Lake Tyers. As a campaigner for Aboriginal rights, Moffatt was most active during the 1950s and 1960s. He had a knack of capturing media attention. At the opening of the inaugural Moomba Festival in 1955, he slipped through the barricades and joined the governor on stage. He said he brought greetings from his people.

At a time when the government pursued a policy of assimilation and threatened to close down the remaining Aboriginal stations, including Lake Tyers, Moffatt argued for self-determination and self-reliance. He criticized a system whereby 'the Government gives us charity instead of letting us do something for ourselves'. Residents of Lake Tyers wanted to run the station as a co-operative and proposed several schemes, including farming, fishing and a timber mill. He explained: 'We feel it is a way in which we can become financially and economically secure without splitting up and moving away from our families ... We love the land here and don't want to lose it'.

In 1963, and again in 1965, Moffatt led Lake Tyers residents as they marched on Parliament House, Melbourne. He addressed a public meeting organized by the Aborigines Advancement League and spoke to members of the Trades Hall Council. Elected to the Council for Aboriginal Rights in 1961, he was vice-president in the mid-1960s. In 1965 he attended the Federal Council for the Advancement of Aborigines and Torres Strait Islanders conference and spoke of the situation at Lake Tyers. Moffatt also entertained delegates at the conference's cultural evening—he had been a member of the Lake Tyers Gum Leaf Band in the 1920s.

By 1966 Lake Tyers had been gazetted as a permanent reserve, and in 1971 4000 acres (1620 ha) of land were handed over to the Lake Tyers Aboriginal Trust. Predeceased by his wife, Moffatt died of pneumonia on 24 August 1966 at Traralgon and was buried in Lake Tyers cemetery. Three daughters and three sons survived him. In the annual report of the Council for Aboriginal Rights, an obituarist described him as 'the epitome of a great ideal':

A man of great personal charm, with a sense of humour and a sense of dignity ... absolutely dedicated and persistent in his endeavours to influence *all* with whom he came in contact, that Aborigines were entitled to the dignity of Group Identity.

The McLean Report, *PP* (Vic), 1956-58, vol 2, paper no 14; *Truth* (Melb), 25 Aug 1962, p 9; *Herald* (Melb), 22 May 1963, p 11, 16 Mar 1965, p 7; *Age* (Melb), 17 Mar 1965, p 2, 18 Mar 1965, p 2; *Sun-News Pictorial* (Melb), 17 Mar 1965, p 13; Lake Tyers correspondence files, B356 (NAA, Melb); Council for Aboriginal Rights papers (LaTL).

JOANNE BACH

MOKARE (c.1800-1831), Aboriginal guide, also known as Mawcarrie, Markew or Makkare, was a Nyungar man of the Minang people, whose territory centred on King George Sound on the south-western coast of Western Australia. He had a married sister and two known brothers, Mollian (d.1829), who may have been known as Yallapoli, and Nakina, also a significant figure of the times. In 1830 Mokare's betrothed was still a child. Reports about him and his band covered six years of pre-settlement European contact, when successive garrison commandants acknowledged Aboriginal traditional rights and respected their customs. There was no competition for resources or violent conflicts over women and property. Mokare and his people were neither a threat nor a source of labour.

Probably he was the charismatic 'Jack' who proved of great assistance to the visiting Captain P. P. King [q.v.2] in 1821. Mokare was first sketched and named by Louis de Sainson, an artist with the French expedition under Dumont D'Urville, who was at King George Sound in October 1826. Later that year a British garrison under the command of Edmund Lockyer [q.v.2] was established there. Mokare became the companion of the surgeon-assistant J. S. Nind, who described him in 1829 as 'Mawcarri, a Native Black, who has now resided with me many months'. The informant for the first anthropological study of the Aborigines of Western Australia, his name appeared as Mawcurrie in Nind's paper, read to the Royal Geographical Society in London.

In Commandant Collett Barker's [q.v.1] daily journal, maintained from 18 January 1830 to 26 March 1831, Mokare was recorded as visiting frequently, describing the customs and beliefs of his people, arbitrating misunderstandings and reporting tribal disputes and the effects of an influenza epidemic that killed many of his people in 1830. In December 1829 he had served as guide to T. B. Wilson's [q.v.2] overland expedition, during which Mount Barker and Mount Lindsay were named as well as the rivers Hay, Denmark and Wilson. Two months later Mokare was again the guide for Barker's expedition over much of the same country.

Captain F. C. Irwin [q.v.2], commanding a detachment of the 63rd Regiment at the Swan River Colony, invited Mokare to visit Perth as his guest, but on the eve of his departure Lieut-Governor Stirling [q.v.2] spoke against it. Mokare agreed to accompany Barker to Sydney in March 1831. As the garrison made ready to leave, however, Mokare withdrew to the bush and Barker was fatally speared.

In the early letters of Alexander Collie [q.v.1], the resident magistrate, Nakina and Mokare were named as his house guests, and the latter as interpreter and guide during an expedition to the Porongorups in April 1831. The brothers were Collie's informants for an essay on the Aborigines of King George Sound published in the *Perth Gazette* in July-August 1834. The article described the illness of Mokare and his death on 26 June 1831. The Aborigines and Europeans had assembled at Collie's house and walked to a site selected by Nakina where the Europeans dug a grave to Nakina's specifications. Mokare was laid to rest; his cloak and personal artefacts adorned the grave as those assembled cried and wailed. A short time later, the Aborigines left the settlement for a period of mourning. When Collie was dying in 1835, he asked to be buried alongside Mokare. The graves were disturbed during construction of Albany Town Hall in the twentieth century, and some remains, presumed to be Collie's, were interred in the pioneers' cemetery, Albany. A memorial on Mount Barker commemorates his 1831 expedition and Mokare's role in it.

J. D. D'Urville, *Voyage de la Corvette L'Astrolabe: ... Atlas*, 1 (Paris, 1833), plate 8; J. Cross (ed), *Journals of Several Expeditions Made in Western Australia During the Years 1829, 1830, 1831, and 1832* (Lond, 1833), p 14; D. J. Mulvaney and J. P. White (eds), *Australians to 1788* (Syd, 1987); J. Mulvaney and N. Green, *Commandant of Solitude* (Melb, 1992); *J of the Royal Geographical Soc of Lond*, 1, 1832, p 21.   NEVILLE GREEN

MOORE-BENTLEY, MARY ANN; *see* LING

MOOWATTIN, DANIEL (c.1791-1816), Aboriginal guide, was born in the Parramatta district, New South Wales, and adopted as an infant by Richard Partridge, alias 'Rice', the colony's notorious hangman. Rev. Samuel Marsden [q.v.2] described Daniel as 'a very fine youth'. Moowattin, meaning 'bush path', was probably a name received in initiation. Aged about 14, he became a helper for George Caley, the botanist employed by Sir Joseph Banks [qq.v.1]. Daniel was Caley's interpreter, bush guide, plant- and leaf-getter, bird-trapper, servant and companion on botanizing expeditions around Sydney. He lived in Caley's cottage near Government House, Parramatta. Caley marked eucalyptus leaves, gumnuts and flowers as 'got by Dan'.

In 1805 Daniel sailed with Caley to Norfolk Island and Van Diemen's Land. Back in Sydney in 1807, while searching for a koala south-west of the settlement, Daniel found a high waterfall which Caley named and sketched as the 'Cataract of Carrung-Gurring on the River Moowat'tin'. 'Moowattin River' appeared in Plate 1 of Matthew Flinders's [q.v.1] *Atlas of Terra Australis* (London, 1814). It was later renamed the Cataract River and the cataract the Appin Falls. In 1808, when Caley heard a false rumour that Moowattin had been speared and killed, he wrote to Banks: 'The native I have been speaking of is the most civilized, of any that I know ... and is the best interpreter of the more inland natives' language of any that I have met with ... I can place that confidence in him that I cannot in any other—all except him are afraid to go beyond the limits of the space which they inhabit with me'.

Moowattin sailed with Caley to England in H.M.S. *Hindoostan* in 1810. During one year in London he was supported by Banks and, dressed in the 'pink of fashion', he frequented theatres and public houses and smoked his pipe in the evening at a Chelsea coffee house. In conversation he always said that the fine shops and houses of the city were 'not equal to the woods' in his own country. He took to drink, which angered Caley so much that on 11 February 1811 he struck him forcefully, breaking his own thumb. Caley remained in England when Dan sailed for Sydney in the *Mary of London* with the nurseryman George Suttor [q.v.2]. After two weeks at Suttor's Baulkham Hills farm, Moowattin sold a shot-gun given to him by the botanist Robert Brown [q.v.1], bought some peach cider and ran off into the bush.

'Daniel Mow-watty or Mowwatting', employed as a labourer at the farm of James Bellamy at Pennant Hills, was tried in September 1816 for the rape and robbery of Hannah Russell, daughter of a convict settler. In court, Marsden, Gregory Blaxland [q.v.1] and others testified that Daniel understood the difference between good and evil. Found guilty, he was hanged on 1 November 1816 probably at the Rocks, Sydney, the first Aborigine to be legally executed in Australia. Some of the specimens he collected for Caley are in the National Herbarium, Royal Botanic Gardens, Sydney.

G. Caley, *Reflections on the Colony of New South Wales* (Melb, 1966); N. Gunson (ed), *Australian Reminiscences and Papers of L. E. Threlkeld, Mission-*

ary to the Aborigines, 1824-1859 (Canb, 1974); Chambers' Edinburgh J, 1832, p 199; Hist Records of NSW, vol 5, p 299; Sydney Gazette, 23 May 1812, p 3, 28 Sept 1816, p 1; 12 Oct 1816, p 2; G. Caley, diary, 1811-17 (Botany L, Natural Hist Museum, Lond); G. Suttor, Memoirs, and Banks papers and Lachlan Macquarie diary A773, 1 November 1816, p 295 (ML).   KEITH VINCENT SMITH

MORGAN, ANNA EUPHEMIA (1874-1935), Aboriginal leader, was born on 7 October 1874 at Ebenezer station, a Moravian mission in north-western Victoria, daughter of Aboriginal parents Nathan Bowden, labourer, and his wife Margaret, née Murray. At the age of 11 Anna was placed in domestic service and worked in the Wimmera area. In her early twenties she moved to New South Wales, near Cumeroogunga (Cummeragunja) Aboriginal reserve, where she was a servant. Here she met CALEB MORGAN (c.1874-1943), a labourer. They married with Baptist forms on 1 May 1899 at Echuca and were to have three children.

The son of Alfred Morgan, tracker, and his wife Caroline, née Malcolm, Caleb had been born on Coranderrk station, Victoria. His father had given evidence before an 1881 inquiry into Coranderrk and, like many other residents of that reserve, moved his family north to the Maloga mission and, later, across the Murray River to Cummeroogunga. In 1888 farm blocks were allocated to the residents of Cummeroogunga, enabling them to become self-sufficient. Caleb had thirty acres (12 ha) of this land. However, the Aborigines Protection Board (New South Wales) revoked the agreement in 1907, with the result that profits were to be directed to the board and the residents were to become farm labourers for the government. Those who refused to accept these conditions were branded agitators and expelled from the station. If they refused to leave, they were charged with trespass. Caleb was among those expelled, and the Morgans departed immediately, leaving many of their possessions behind. When they returned to collect them several months later, Caleb was charged with trespass and gaoled for fourteen days.

The family then moved to Wagga Wagga where Caleb worked as a farm labourer. In 1927 they went back to Victoria, first to Swan Hill and then to Coldstream, several miles from Coranderrk. In 1930 the Morgans applied to the Board for the Protection of the Aborigines for assistance. Refused on the basis of their classification as 'half-castes', they applied to the Sustenance Department for rations. Again they were refused. Anna then applied for a Commonwealth pension but was unsuccessful due to her classification as an Aborigine.

Following this experience, Anna became active in her campaign for equal rights for Aboriginal people. She published an article in Labor Call in September 1934: 'Under the Black Flag' told the story of a life constrained by government regulations, and articulated demands for justice and equality. 'We have not the same liberty as the white man, nor do we expect the same justice', she said. In an occasional series on Melbourne radio station 3LO, as 'Ghingobin' ('the name my mother called me'), she told stories that had been passed on by her grandmother. She was able to use her public prominence to draw attention to her political messages.

A member of the fledgling Australian Aborigines' League, she took part in a delegation to the Minister for the Interior in January 1935, pleading for education for Aboriginal women: 'If we get the same education as the white girl we could stand alongside white people'. She also addressed a meeting of the International Women's Day Committee that month. Anna Morgan died of acute renal infection on 1 August 1935 at Coldstream and was buried in the new Melbourne general cemetery, Fawkner. A daughter survived her, as did Caleb, who died on 18 May 1943 in Melbourne and was buried in Fawkner cemetery.

T. S. Epstein and D. H. Penny (eds), Opportunity and Response (Lond, 1972); H. Goodall, Invasion to Embassy (Syd, 1996); Herald (Melb), 24 Jan 1935, pp 1, 10; Board for the Protection of Aborigines, correspondence files and Chief Secretary, in-letters (PRO, Vic); Board for the Protection of Aborigines, correspondence files, B313 (NAA).

JOANNE BACH

MORGAN, DANIEL (c.1830-1865), bushranger, was probably Jack Fuller, born at Appin, New South Wales, the illegitimate son of Mary Owen and George Fuller, and attended the Catholic school at Campbelltown. Although he was suspected of stock theft from the late 1840s, his known criminal record began when, under the name 'John Smith', occupation jockey, he was sentenced to twelve years hard labour for highway robbery at Castlemaine, Victoria, on 10 June 1854. Released from the hulk Success on a ticket-of-leave in June 1860 for good behaviour, he failed to report to the police in the Ovens police district.

Now known as 'Down-the-River Jack', he found work as a horse-breaker and station hand. In August that year he stole a prized horse belonging to the Evans family, who held the Whitfield run in the upper King River valley. Evan Evans, with fellow squatter Edmond Bond, tracked him to his camp. Jack was badly wounded but escaped into the eastern

Riverina and western slopes of New South Wales. This would become his base, although he frequently crossed into north-eastern Victoria, a pattern common among those involved in the cross-border, stolen-stock trade.

From mid-1863 'Daniel Morgan, alias Billy the Native', was identified in several major episodes that involved robbery under arms and included the bailing up of Henry Baylis [q.v.3], a police magistrate, near Urana. A reward of £200 was posted for him, dead or alive, although he had yet to be firmly identified as a murderer. The turning point came during a raid on Round Hill station on 19 June 1864 when he shot the overseer John McLean, who died three days later. On 24 June Morgan shot and killed Sergeant David Maginnity near Tumbarumba. The reward reached £1000. In September police searching for the bushranger were fired upon, and Sergeant Smyth died of wounds. Morgan later claimed that he had shot the sergeant.

Morgan frequently targeted the region's squatters, especially those who were believed to be hard masters, and delighted in humiliating them. During raids, he insisted that employees be fed and given drink. At Burrumbuttock the owner Thomas Gibson was forced to write cheques for his employees totalling some £400. Erratic, Morgan was often nervous, and his moods could swing rapidly from an almost courtly treatment of prisoners to threats, rage and violence—hence his sobriquet 'Mad Dan'. Although he was sometimes assisted by companions during his hold-ups, accomplices differed from robbery to robbery and he often worked alone. An imposing man, over 5 ft 10 ins (178 cm) in height, Morgan had dark hair worn in ringlets, a full, dark beard, hazel eyes and a long, hooked nose which some claimed made him look like a ferocious bird of prey.

Between January and March 1865 Morgan seemed ubiquitous. He was credited with no less than six major robberies of coaches and pastoral stations and the attempted murder of a stock-keeper at Wallandbool. In March the government of New South Wales introduced the Felons Apprehension Act, which made him an outlaw. Next month Morgan crossed the Murray to settle his old score with Evans and Bond. Reaching Whitfield on 7 April, he bailed up the head station. Evan Evans was not there. Morgan headed north and held up traffic on the Sydney Road between Benalla and Glenrowan. On the evening of 8 April he bailed up the Macpherson homestead at Peechelba, north of Wangaratta, unaware that the station's co-owner George Rutherford lived less than a quarter of a mile (0.4 km) away. Alice Keenan, the Macphersons' nurse, carried news to Rutherford, who rounded up his workforce, selected and armed five trustworthy men and sent them to watch at Peechelba homestead. Police and armed vigilantes augmented the party.

Next morning, as the bushranger walked towards the stockyards to select a horse to continue his flight, he was shot from behind by John Wendlan. Morgan died at about 1.45 p.m. on 9 April 1865. Locks were cut from his hair, his body was publicly displayed at Wangaratta, his beard was flayed from his face as a souvenir and his head severed, to be forwarded to the professor of anatomy at the University of Melbourne. He was buried on 14 April in Wangaratta cemetery.

Morgan's time at large owed much to his bush skills, an inept and undermanned police force and an effective 'telegraph' of sympathizers and supporters among the shepherds and stockmen in the region. There was also an element of fear: he had no hesitation in shooting two men he believed were police informants. He passed into folklore, however, as the 'travellers' friend'.

G. E. Boxall, *History of the Australian Bushrangers* (Syd, 1935); B. Wannan, *Australian Bushranging* (Adel, 1963); M. Carnegie, *Morgan the Bold Bushranger* (Syd, 1975); C. White, *History of Australian Bushranging*, 2 (Melb, 1981); P. C. Smith, *Tracking Down the Bushrangers* (Syd, 1982); E. F. Penzig, *Morgan the Murderer* (Katoomba, 1989); *Victoria Police Gazette*, 5 Apr 1865; *Albury Banner*, 11 Apr 1865, p 6; *Argus* (Melb), 11 Apr 1865, p 6; *Empire* (Syd), 11 Apr 1865, p 5, 14 Apr 1865, p 5; *SMH*, 11 Apr 1865, p 5, 12 Apr 1865, p 5; *Ovens and Murray Advertiser*, 13 Apr 1865, p 2; *Sydney Mail*, 15 Apr 1865, pp 4, 5.
                                                    JOHN McQUILTON

MORGAN, VALENTINE (1876?-1952), publicist, was born probably in 1876 at Albert Park, Melbourne, third of five children of William Morgan, an English-born journalist, and his wife Annie, née Browne (d.1880), from Sydney. As a boy Val sold the *Record* at Melbourne football matches. He later sold advertising space on billboards around sports grounds as well as in the *Record* and in programmes issued by local police, fire brigades and metropolitan councils. Morgan was an advertising agent, living at Albert Park, when he married Emmeline Jolly on 25 May 1895 in Melbourne, with the rites of the Christian Church, an undenominational assembly. As 'Val Morgan Advertising Contractor' he had begun operations in Melbourne in 1894. The business was a proprietary company by the 1920s. For several decades he held the contract for advertising all the social events of the Victoria Police, such as their football and athletics clubs and their brass band.

In 1914 Morgan began to produce and distribute cinema advertising slides and from 1921 moving picture films (produced at first by Australasian Films Pty Ltd) for advertising on cinema screens. In 1916 he purchased the business that issued *Moulton's Street Directory*. The publication became *Morgan's Street Directory* and ran to more than fifty issues up to the late 1970s. The company had a reputation for professionalism not common in the advertising industry at that time. In 1930 Industrial Printing & Publicity Pty Ltd (a company set up by various trade unions) took over the licence for Melbourne radio-station 3KZ, and a few months later leased the station to Morgan, who established two interrelated companies: 3KZ Broadcasting and 3KZ Advertising. After his three sons entered the business Val Morgan & Sons Pty Ltd was registered in 1933. As the company's activities prospered it grew to be the largest cinema advertising company in Victoria and spread to South Australia and Western Australia.

Retaining a lively interest in sports, Morgan was a member of three Melbourne racing clubs as well as South Melbourne Football Club. He lived at Brighton. After working in his office on the morning of 11 July 1952 he collapsed and died later that day in Bank Place, Melbourne. His wife, two of their three sons and a daughter survived him. He was buried with Catholic rites in St Kilda cemetery.

His eldest son William Valentine carried on as managing director of both the family's advertising company and 3KZ Advertising, while the youngest son Sydney was managing director of 3KZ Broadcasting. Val Morgan Advertising gradually absorbed its rivals, reducing the number of cinema advertising firms in Australia from thirteen to two, and becoming the largest such company in the country. In 1987, when the enterprise was under the direction of the founder's grandson Valentine Charles Morgan, the family sold its interest in the firm, which in 2005 continued to provide cinema advertisements in Australia and overseas.

A'sian Manufacturer, 27 Mar 1920, p 18, 4 June 1921; *Everyone's*, 1 Oct 1924, p 3; *Smith's Weekly*, 16 Jan 1937; *Film Weekly*, 17 July 1952, p 6; *A'sian Exhibitor*, 17 July 1952, p 3; *A'sian Cinema*, 11-18 Nov 1983, p 20; *SMH*, 12 July 1952, p 5; *Argus* (Melb), 12 July 1952, p 11; *Age* (Melb), 14 July 1952, p 2; *Sunday Age*, 25 June 1985, p 19.

INA BERTRAND

MORRICE, NELLIE CONSTANCE (1881-1963), nurse and administrator, was born on 31 March 1881 at Ealing Forest, near Berrima, New South Wales, seventh of eleven children of Australian-born parents David Morrice, grazier, and his wife Sarah Mary, née Hale. On 27 November 1903 Nellie began training at Royal Prince Alfred Hospital, Sydney. She qualified as a staff nurse (1906) and gained her four-year certificate in April 1907, passing

'with credit', with experience as a theatre nurse and instruments nurse, and a dispensary certificate. After a midwifery course at the Royal Hospital for Women, she nursed privately in 1907-09 and was senior sister at the Pines Private Hospital, Randwick. Returning to R.P.A.H., she was acting sister-in-charge of the Alexandra and Mary Roberts wards in 1912.

Sister Morrice had joined the Australian Army Nursing Service in May 1910. She enlisted in the Australian Imperial Force on 21 November 1914, was appointed a staff nurse and embarked in the *Kyarra* on 28 November. After serving as head sister, No.1 Australian General Hospital, Heliopolis, Egypt, she was detached to No.1 Australian Auxiliary Hospital and then No.3 A.G.H., both in England. Early in 1917 she was posted to the British Expeditionary Force in France; she later rejoined No.3 A.G.H. at Abbeville. On 3 June 1918 Morrice was awarded the Royal Red Cross (2nd class) 'for valuable services with the Armies in France and Flanders'. She returned to Sydney, and her appointment ended on 15 January 1919. She later wrote that four of her brothers also served in World War I. Photographs of her in military nursing sister's uniform showed a tall woman, direct and forward looking, with a hint of the smile of a controlled and confident person.

After the war Morrice was matron of Georges Heights Military Hospital (No.21 A.A.H.), Mosman, then sub-matron at the Prince of Wales Hospital, Randwick. In June 1924 she was appointed secretary to the New South Wales (Lady Dudley's [q.v.8]) Bush Nursing Association, which focused on midwifery and the care of infants. Morrice was responsible for finances, subscriptions, donations and the preparation and presentation of annual reports. She also visited every centre to establish personal relationships with the nurses and observe where services were needed. In 1926 she represented New South Wales at an interstate bush nursing conference and passed on the policy of Tresillian mothercraft training and details of the 'Sylvia' ambulance stretcher (patented by Sister Elizabeth Kenny [q.v.9]), which Morrice had observed in use in France. Several Country Women's Association branches donated these units and provided cars to tow them. Her extensive travelling soon led to the appointment of a full-time assistant secretary. In June 1934 Morrice was appointed M.B.E. By 1938 her staff included a publicity officer and an inspector and organizer. She was by then visiting some sixty nurses.

World War II presented the B.N.A. with additional problems such as a shortage of nurses and petrol rationing, but Morrice managed to gain an extra 100 gallons (455 litres) of fuel per month. The need for midwifery was reducing, however, as the Hospitals Commission linked bush nursing hospitals into the district hospital system. In 1948 she retired, having worked as secretary for twenty-four of the then thirty-seven years of the B.N.A. She was elected a life member 'by virtue of her service and devotion' and lived in retirement at Chatswood. Miss Morrice died at home on 11 April 1963 and was cremated with Anglican rites.

NSW Bush Nursing Assn, *Annual Report*, 1924-48; *SMH*, 29 Aug 1918, p 8, 5 June 1934, p 9; Matron's reports, 1904-18 (Museum of Nursing, Royal Prince Alfred Hospital, Syd); Aust Trained Nurses' Assn, Register of members, 1904-1917 (ML); AWM41/1013, AWM43/A612, 2DRL/0764, 3DRL/2000 and 2074 (AWM). VILMA PAGE

MORWOOD, JAMES ERIC (1901-1974), electrical engineer, was born on 27 May 1901 at Toowong, Brisbane, son of Harry Morwood, commercial traveller, and his wife Elsie, née Bilbrough. James's English-born parents later took up dairy farming at Yalangur, on the Darling Downs, where he was educated at local primary schools and Toowoomba Grammar School (dux, 1918). Morwood won a State government open scholarship to the University of Queensland (B.E., 1923; M.E., 1931); he was 880 yards sprint champion in 1921, and graduated in mechanical and electrical engineering, with first-class honours and the university medal. The generation of electricity and its application to traction, particularly in tramways, attracted his early interest and remained prominent throughout his career.

In June 1923 Morwood became a junior engineer in the Countess Street power station of the Brisbane Tramways Trust. He resigned on 2 July 1925 to take up a Walter and Eliza Hall [qq.v.9] travelling fellowship, which he proposed to use to study overseas developments in electricity generation and electric traction. He sailed from Brisbane on 15 August, bound for London, but a seamen's strike delayed his departure from Australia and, with the approval of the Hall trustees, he spent two months studying the electrification of Sydney suburban railways and of Victorian railways and industries. Morwood reached London on 27 November and visited railway, tramway and electricity supply organizations and engineering laboratories in Britain, Europe and the United States of America. Back in Brisbane, on 29 August 1927 he joined the construction workforce at the Brisbane City Council's New Farm power station, where he was later appointed efficiency engineer.

At New Farm on 15 September 1928 Morwood married with Anglican rites Myrtle Florence Lilley, a high school teacher of English and French. He became chief engineer at New Farm power station in 1948 and in 1951 was appointed deputy chief engineer of the council's department of electricity, which included the Brisbane suburban electricity distribution system as well as the power station and the tramway system. Prominent in the development of Tennyson power station, on 1 July 1955 he became chief engineer and manager of the council's electricity department. In 1963 the State government sought rationalization of electricity supply in southeastern Queensland. Morwood played an important role in the negotiations, which led to the transfer of New Farm and Tennyson power stations to the Southern Electric Authority of Queensland and of the inner city distribution system of S.E.A.Q. to the council. He retired in 1966.

Active in the Institution of Engineers, Australia, Morwood was a committee member of its Brisbane division from 1940 to 1955 and chairman in 1945-46—when he was *ex-officio* a board member of the faculty of engineering, University of Queensland. He also at various times lectured at the university and at the Central Technical College, and was Queensland representative of the Institution of Electrical Engineers (London). Morwood enjoyed tennis and, from the 1950s, bowls; he also belonged to the Johnsonian Club and Brisbane and Caloundra Rotary clubs. He died on 25 May 1974 at Caloundra and was cremated. His wife and their daughter and three sons survived him.

G. Cossins (ed), *Eminent Queensland Engineers*, 2 (Brisb, 1999); Faculty of Engineering, Univ Qld, Report to the Senate, 1931 (Univ Qld archives); J. E. Morwood personal file (Brisb City Council archives); biography of J. E. Morwood (Qld Energy Museum archives, Brisb). D. R. MERCER

MOSELEY, JOHN (c.1850-1938) and PERCIVAL (c.1880-1942), Aboriginal farmers, were father and son. John was born at Rollands Plains, New South Wales, in the Macleay River valley, the territory of the Dhan-gadi. His father was said to be a prominent local pastoralist, and his mother Elizabeth, née Bullock, an Aborigine. Moseley's *bagar* (totem) was the Jewfish at Crescent Head. About 1878 he married Elizabeth Jane Robinson. They had twelve children, Percy being born near Kempsey about 1880.

John's skill as a tracker led to service with the local police. By 1884, with his wife and five of his children and his half brother Jimmy Linwood (c.1850-1935), he was farming corn on a gazetted Aboriginal reserve on the Fattorinni Islands, having cleared the land of bushes and vines. After the big flood of 1892, the Moseleys moved to Burnt Bridge, Euroka Creek, clearing the land once more and, like most European smallholders, growing maize. In 1900, when Aboriginal children were excluded from Euroka Public School, John (who signed with a mark), Percy and others petitioned for a provisional Aboriginal school, which was set up in 1905 at Burnt Bridge. Percy was a labourer when he married with Presbyterian forms Rachel Sapphira Russell in the mission hall, Purfleet, on 3 November 1909.

Under the Aborigines Protection Act (1909, amended 1915), the Aborigines Protection Board was given a responsibility of care for Aborigines. The A.P.B. policy was to establish stations run by European managers but many Aborigines were reluctant to reside on them. Established reserves were often revoked, and the land sold or leased to non-Aboriginal farmers. By 1914 Percy and Rachel were farming at Ballengarra, near Port Macquarie. When the land they occupied was leased to a white farmer in 1915, Percy protested, refusing to accept 'out of pocket expenses' to move to Rollands Plains. He visited Sydney to put his case to the A.P.B. Unsuccessful, he nevertheless returned to Ballengarra. While living on the nearby reserve, in an arrangement with the new lessee, he share-farmed part of the land he formerly occupied. From 1919, five of the nine reserves in the Macleay valley were revoked and previously autonomous Aboriginal people came under the control of A.P.B. managers. The lease of Fattorinni Islands was revoked on 20 March 1925. In October that year, in their own language, John Moseley and Jimmy Linwood addressed a meeting at Kempsey showground as part of the Australian Aborigines Progressive Association's campaign for Aboriginal rights.

About 1930 Percy and Rachel joined John and other family members on the farm at Euroka Creek. In 1937 the A.P.B. secured gazettal of a large block adjoining the Moseley farm for Burnt Bridge Aboriginal station. Aborigines from various communities were accommodated there without adequate housing or a satisfactory water supply. The Moseleys refused to move, and on 30 June the manager arrived at their cottages and the school and began to demolish the buildings. Percy nailed up the gate to stop him returning, so the manager called the police and with their assistance removed the family's water tank. The *Macleay Chronicle* published John's letter:

I made a protest ... and ... was told that I own nothing ... not even the land which I spent the best part of my life working and improving for the past forty-five years ... I served my State with honesty. The very thing I took pride in, the Police Force, two days ago made me feel as small as a slug under an elephant foot.

When the manager began to erect a fence across what Percy regarded as the family's land, he chopped it down and reputedly fired a shotgun to warn off the workers. After Michael Sawtell's [q.v.] intervention, and the visit to Sydney of one of John's sons, the board directed that the old man was 'not to be removed' without authorization.

John Moseley died on 3 July 1938 at Burnt Bridge and was buried with Methodist forms in the Anglican cemetery, East Kempsey. One daughter and two sons survived him. Percy persisted with his claim to the land. The manager's response was to threaten expulsion. Although Percy was refused title to the property, he was granted permissive occupancy of eighty acres (32.4 ha) of the old reserve in June 1939. His continued protests provoked further threats of expulsion. Percy Moseley died of acute pyelonephritis on 10 May 1942 in the Macleay District Hospital, West Kempsey, and was buried with Anglican rites at East Kempsey. Childless, he was survived by his wife.

B. Morris, *Domesticating Resistance* (Oxford, UK, 1989); H. Goodall, *Invasion to Embassy* (Syd, 1996); *Macleay Chronicle*, 26 May 1937, p 5, 7 July 1937, p 4; Aborigines Protection Board, minutes, reel 2792, 6 July 1934, 12 Sept 1934, 7 July 1937, 5 Aug 1937, 14 June 1939, *and* Premier's Dept, correspondence, A37/193, reel 1862, *and* school files, 5/15854, Euroka, 5/15182.1, Burnt Bridge (SRNSW).

BARRY MORRIS

MOSES, JOHN (1861-1945), commercial traveller and bush troubadour, was born on 12 January 1861 at George Street, Sydney, son of John Moses, a London-born storekeeper of Jewish ancestry, and his second wife Mary Ann, née Shea, who was native-born. As a small boy Jack used to drive the family cow up through the streets from the Haymarket to graze in Hyde Park. He spent most of his working life as a salesman in wine and whisky. Based in Sydney, from about 1888 he travelled widely, following the agricultural show circuit of New South Wales and other colonies as a salesman for city wine merchants. At the Presbyterian manse, Ashfield, on 18 June 1900 he married 23-year-old Lucy Florence Nightingale (d.1932).

A popular reciter and teller of yarns at smoke concerts, Moses was everywhere welcomed, largely because of his 'unfailing good nature' and 'unquenchable cheerfulness and optimism'. In Hobart in the 1900s Frank Morton [q.v.10] heard him 'reciting bush-verse better than I had heard any other man recite it before. It was "Saltbush Bill".' The *Bulletin Book of Humorous Verse and Recitations* (1920) was dedicated to him. One of his favourite authors was Henry Lawson [q.v.10] who in the poem 'Joseph's Dreams and Reuben's Brethren' (1909) referred to him: 'My best friend was a Yid'. Moses recalled their friendship in *Henry Lawson by His Mates* (Sydney, 1931). In 1925 the secretary of the Royal Agricultural Society of New South Wales organized a luncheon for him at which he was presented with a cheque for 'a substantial amount'. Later Moses was patron of the Showmen's Guild of Australasia.

For many years Jack Moses contributed to the *Bulletin*, the *Sydney Mail*, *Smith's Weekly* and other journals. He published *Beyond the City Gates* (Sydney, 1923), a volume of sketches and bush verse 'rich in quiet chuckles and friendly reminiscences'. The book included 'Nine Miles from Gundagai', his well-known version of the teamsters' song; his refrain 'the dog sits on the tucker box' inspired the bronze statue by F. P. Rusconi [q.v.11] which was unveiled at the teamsters' camping place, five miles (8 km) outside Gundagai, by Prime Minister J. A. Lyons [q.v.10] on 28 November 1932. Moses's mistaken mileage has caused continuing confusion. Occasionally he wrote in a more serious vein: his 'Lock the Lachlan', a plea for water conservation, also appeared in the book. A second collection, *Nine Miles from Gundagai*, came out in 1938; Moses gave the proceeds of both books to the Australian Red Cross Society during World War II.

J. R. Tyrrell [q.v.12] thought he 'was very much like a happy leprechaun ... and a kinder-hearted little chap or a more enthusiastic barracker for his native Australia never existed'. He loved giving presents; he sometimes slipped a complimentary copy of one of his books into a case of wine for a client, and kept Lawson supplied with hats. Although a member of the 'Bondi Icebergs'—who regularly swam all the year round—he never went in, to which he attributed his longevity.

Towards the end of his life Moses lived in the Hotel Arcadia, Pitt Street, Sydney. He was so pleased with the cartoonist John Frith's depiction of him for the *Bulletin* as his own 'dog on the tuckerbox' that he had the drawing done 'as one of the bundle of postcards he always carried in his pockets'. Still scribbling rhymes shortly before his death, he claimed to be 'the last of the bush troubadours'. Moses died on 10 July 1945 in Royal Prince Alfred Hospital, Camperdown, and was buried with Anglican rites in South Head cemetery. His son survived him.

J. R. Tyrrell, *Old Books, Old Friends, Old Sydney* (Syd, 1952); *SMH*, 15 Apr 1925, p 13, 11 July 1945, p 2; *Gundagai Independent*, 1 Dec 1932, p 1, 12 July 1945, p 1, 16 July 1945, p 3; *Bulletin*, 18 July 1945, p 9.
MARTHA RUTLEDGE

MOTT, GEORGE HENRY (1831-1906), newspaper editor and proprietor, was born on 13 May 1831 at Hammersmith, London, son of Isaac Henry Robert Motte, a medical practitioner, and his wife Rebecca, née Jackson. After attending Hammersmith Grammar School, George worked with a firm of brokers. On 18 December 1852 at St Andrew's Church, Holborn, he married Allegra Haidee Charnock, against the wishes of her father, a barrister. They referred to their marriage as 'a runaway match'—two weeks later they sailed for Australia as unassisted migrants, reaching Melbourne with George's younger brother Arthur in the *Elizabeth Wilthen* in June 1853.

Mott (as he was known in Australia) was employed in the office of the *Argus* and then moved to the *Melbourne Morning Herald*, becoming in 1854 its correspondent at Castlemaine. Next year he bought an interest in a Beechworth newspaper and in October 1856 established the *Border Post* at Albury, New South Wales. In 1859 he founded the successful Murray Valley Vineyard Co., but he was primarily interested in newspapers and, by 1863, was printing with different mastheads at Chiltern and Beechworth in Victoria, while remaining proprietor and editor of his paper at Albury.

In 1869 Mott sold his interests, intending to move to Fiji as a provisional director of the Polynesia Co. South Pacific, but was deterred by news of a massacre of settlers there. He acquired the *Hamilton Spectator* instead. In Melbourne from 1885 to 1894 he was managing director of Gordon & Gotch [q.v.4] Ltd. He lived at Kew and in 1888 started the *Kew Mercury*, in which he published his 'Reminiscences of a Victorian Journalist' in 1895. Next year he retired.

Mott succeeded in establishing newspapers that were credible movers of information and opinion, using them to argue for local causes and the better provision of local services. In and around Albury he established the cross-border district as a print community. A lively speaker, he was secretary of the Customs Abolition and the North East Railway leagues, an early champion of a federated Australia—with Albury as 'the Federal City'—and a persistent advocate for what became the route of the railway between Sydney and Melbourne. In 1868 he had failed to win the parliamentary seat of Murray Boroughs, but became mayor of Albury for a year. At Hamilton he agitated for the extension of the railway and formed the gas company. He served on Kew Borough Council for four years.

In October 1856 Mott had been prominent in the unsuccessful campaign—which he claimed to have initiated—for the Riverina district to become a separate colony. He won the support of Rev. John Dunmore Lang [q.v.2], who had championed the separation of the Port Phillip and the Moreton Bay districts. Mott argued that it was 'a physical impossibility for us to be properly governed from a centre so distant as Sydney', but preferred separation to annexation with Victoria in energetic campaigns in 1863-64 and 1866-67.

Allegra died in 1905 and George on 7 January 1906. Both died at Kew and were buried in the Anglican cemetery there. Of their fourteen children, five sons and three daughters survived them. Their sons established newspapers in Western Australia, regional Victoria and in suburban Melbourne; Hamilton [q.v.10] started the *Border Morning Mail* (Albury) which, as the *Border Mail*, was still in the hands of his descendants a century later.

The Story of a Runaway Match (Melb, 1894); C. A. Mott, *The Runaway Family* (Wodonga, Vic, 1980); R. Kilpatrick, *Country Conscience* (Canb, 2000); L. Frappell, *Lords of the Saltbush Plains* (Melb, 2003); *Border Post*, 7 Jan 1863, p 2, 30 Mar 1863, p 2, 20 Jan 1869, p 2; *Border Morning Mail*, 9 Jan 1906, p 3; Mott papers (Border Morning Mail archives, Wodonga, Vic).   BRUCE PENNAY

MOULE-PROBERT, JOHN; *see* PROBERT

MOWBRAY, PHILIP HENRY MITCHELL (c.1845-1903), swagman, writer and eccentric, was born at Tullibody, 'under the Ochil Hills', in Clackmannanshire, Scotland, son of James Mowbray, distiller, and his wife Mary, née Rodger. Phil was educated in Edinburgh, for a year at Stirling Academy, and at schools at Coldstream, Berwickshire, and on Jersey in the Channel Islands. Though 'meant for a meenister' or 'doctor', at 16 he entered the Royal Military Academy, Woolwich, England. After graduating he served with the Royal Artillery in India, with Sir Charles Napier's force in Abyssinia in 1868 and next year at Gibraltar.

Leaving the artillery, apparently under a cloud, according to his own account, Mowbray spent 1870-71 in the United States of America as a schoolmaster, draftsman and Mississippi riverboat deckhand and in 1872 came to Australia as a remittance man. Carrying his swag, he worked as a miner, drover, horse-breaker, shearers' cook, surveyor, schoolmaster, night watchman and cherry picker—all the time 'corresponding with any newspapers that wanted copy and many that did not'. After hearing of an old Scots shepherd who was a fount of helpful information, he adopted the pseudonym 'Scotty the Wrinkler' and contributed stories —and paragraphs for its 'Aboriginalities' page —to the *Bulletin* (Sydney). At his camp, 'The Hollow Log', on the Murrumbidgee River, near Narrandera, New South Wales, he was a generous host to itinerant workers, tramps and 'ne'er-do-weels'.

Scotty also wrote *The Swag: The Unofficial Flute of the Sundowners and other Colonial Vagrants; with which is enfurcated the Bush Marconi and the Whaler's Telegraph* (Melbourne, 1900). This oddity contained a letter, signed 'Phil Mowbray, Whaler Journalist', to Lord Hopetoun [q.v.9] welcoming him as governor-general on behalf of swagmen— 'those who carry their all on their backs to the doors of employers'—but pointing out that they had not been invited to the events in connection with the inauguration of the Commonwealth. It also solicited Hopetoun's patronage for swagmen, as 'We, the proletariat, consider that we are as powerful and intelligent a political factor ... as many more prominent organisations'.

In May 1902 Mowbray wrote to J. M. Creed [q.v.3], an expert on the care and treatment of inebriates, telling him that 'unless you get *some* of my sort to let you know how, and why, and where they drink', all initiatives on the drink problem were doomed. He told Creed he was also an expert on rabbits, cooking, education, 'Murrumbidgee Whaling', soldiering and the unemployed!

Moubray (as his name was sometimes spelt) was unmarried, but 'dearly loved the lassies'. Nuggety, balding, with a full beard and somewhat distracted expression, he was a kindly cynic who abhorred cant and humbug. Well educated, he did not wear his learning lightly, but as a raconteur he had few equals in the outback. Whatever he was hiding from no one ever knew, but once when complimented on his retentive memory he replied: 'It's my curse. I wish I could forget everything'. Friend to every battler on the gypsy road, he had two great loves: the free life of the bush and animals. His love of animals hastened his end: he caught hydatids from his dog and died after an operation for cystitis on 2 November 1903 in Narrandera hospital. He was buried in the local Presbyterian cemetery. Henry Lawson's [q.v.10] poem, 'The Passing of Scotty', appeared in the *Bulletin* a week later.

J. M. Creed, *My Recollections of Australia and Elsewhere 1842-1914* (Lond, 1916); G. Walsh, *The Bush and the Never Never* (Rockhampton, Qld, 2004); *T&CJ*, 16 Dec 1898, p 44; *A.A.A.: All About Australians*, Dec 1904, p 10; *Bulletin*, 27 June 1891, p 23, 25 July 1891, p 23, 21 Nov 1891, p 18, 5 Nov 1903, p 30, 12 Nov 1903, p 17, 26 Nov 1903, p 15, 7 Nov 1956, p 13; *Aust Worker*, 12 Jan 1927, p 13.   G. P. WALSH

MOWLE, MARY BRAIDWOOD (1827-1857), diarist, was born on 3 August 1827 at Durham, England, first child of Scottish-born naval surgeon Thomas Braidwood Wilson [q.v.2] and his wife Jane, née Thompson. Mary arrived in Sydney on 24 June 1836 in the *Strathfieldsaye*, in which her father made his ninth and final voyage as surgeon superintendent in convict ships. Her mother died following childbirth in 1838. On her father's land grant at Braidwood Mary was brought up as the daughter of a large landowner. When she visited Sydney, she was regarded as the 'nicest' girl in society circles.

Mary Wilson's circumstances changed dramatically in the drought and depression of the early 1840s when her father was declared bankrupt. On 11 November 1843 he committed suicide while mentally deranged. Left a penniless orphan at 16, she went to live with her father's brother George Wilson at Mount Seymour, Oatlands, Van Diemen's Land. On 12 May 1845 at Oatlands she married with Anglican rites Stewart Marjoribanks Mowle, a protégé of (Sir) Terence Murray [q.v.2] of Yarralumla, New South Wales. The Mowles lived at first at Murray's outstation at Mannus, near Tumbarumba, then at a farm known as Klensendorlffe's on the Limestone Plains (Canberra), where Mowle combined unsuccessful farming on his own behalf with employment as overseer for Murray. At the end of 1850, with three children, Mary began a diary, which she kept for five months, and which presented a wide-ranging picture of rural family life in mid-nineteenth-century Australia. Her life veered from the extremes of being short of food for her children to attending the best social events in the district, the balls and race meetings that had been part of her youth. Keeping the diary was an emotional consolation as important as playing the piano, which she described as her 'chief solace'.

In 1852 Stewart Mowle was appointed sub-collector of customs at Eden and there, on 1 January 1853, she began a new diary. It provides the most intimate glimpse that has survived of life in the mid-nineteenth century in a small but important seaport. She detailed ships' movements, the arrival and departure of south coast and Monaro families, and whaling operations at Twofold Bay, as well as the day-to-day work involved in raising and educating a young family, the hazards of childbirth and childhood illnesses and the social interchanges in a small community.

The Mowles left Eden in 1855 when Stewart was transferred to the Customs House, Sydney. Mary's sixth child was born on 31 August 1857. Two weeks later at Balmain, on 15 September, Mary died from the complications of childbirth. Her husband, two sons and three daughters survived her. She was buried in the Presbyterian section of the Devonshire Street cemetery, Sydney.

Mary's diaries have particular interest in having been written by a woman who—in remarkably direct language—expressed feelings of fury and frustration, but also of pride and resilience. The originals are held in the National Library of Australia, Canberra, and copies in the Mitchell [q.v.5] Library, Sydney.

P. Clarke, *A Colonial Woman: The Life and Times of Mary Braidwood Mowle 1827-1857* (Syd, 1986), and for bib.   PATRICIA CLARKE

MOYNIHAN, CORNELIUS (1862-1915), poet and librarian, was born on 10 June 1862 in County Kerry, Ireland, second child and elder son of Denis Moynihan, dairyman, and his wife Margaret, née McGillicuddy. In 1868 the family migrated to Brisbane, where they took up two acres (0.8 ha) in an area known as The Dip, in North Brisbane (later Ascot and Hamilton), and built a house, Oakvale, later noted for its musical evenings and dancing parties. Denis and his family prospered.

In 1880 Con Moynihan brought out a slim volume, *Miscellaneous Poems*—mainly love lyrics and epigrams in an archly urbane style —under the pen-name 'Vivian'. Over the next thirty years he published poems prolifically in all of the Brisbane and several of the provincial Queensland newspapers. A selection of these began to circulate in 1910 in a type-script volume, 'The Bunyip of Wendouree', which contained satires on the Queensland political scandals of the 1890s, as well as poems on Aboriginal, sentimental-Irish and personal themes.

Moynihan had been appointed assistant librarian at the Queensland parliament in 1884. The position, which he held until his death, gave him ready access to the pioneering work of (Sir) Baldwin Spencer and F. J. Gillen [qq.v.12,9] on the central Australian Aborigines, and to the reports of the protector of Aborigines Archibald Meston [q.v.5]. These were sources for his book, *The Feast of the Bunya*, an 'Aboriginal ballad', published in 1901 and presented to the Duke and Duchess of York on the occasion of their visit to Brisbane that year. It gave a narrative account of the three-yearly pilgrimage of the local tribes to Mobolon, the highest point of the Bunya Mountains, to feast on the bunyas and conduct intertribal business. The poem also contained digressions on the Kilcoy poisonings of 1842, the murder of the Fraser family at Hornet Bank in 1857, and the celebrated 'recovery' of the escaped convicts David Bracewell and James Davis [qq.v.1] from Aboriginal communities.

Three years later Moynihan's Irish-Australian interests were to the fore in an epic of a more classical kind: two thousand hexameters in rhyming couplets (the model was Pope's translation of the *Iliad*) on the Battle of the Eureka Stockade. The poem was technically very accomplished, but Ward, Lock & Co. of Melbourne rejected 'Eureka' for publication, its subject matter considered too parochial for English or American readers. His last published book, *The German Armageddon* (Brisbane, 1915), was a collection of short jingoistic poems about Australia's role in World War I.

Moynihan died of pulmonary haemorrhage from tuberculosis while swimming in the sea at Sandgate, Brisbane, on 14 November 1915. A motion of sympathy, moved in parliament by the premier T. J. Ryan [q.v.11], referred to his 'very considerable talent as an author' and his 'genial and sunny disposition'. Unmarried, he bequeathed half his estate of over £1000 to Sarah, the mother of Brian Penton [q.v.15], and half of the remainder to her second son Wilfred, who had, however, died in 1902, and this portion also reverted to Sarah. These arrangements gave substance to Penton's reported claim that Moynihan, who had been the landlord and a close friend of the Penton family and shared a house with them for five years about 1900, was his natural father.

H. A. Kellow, *Queensland Poets* (Lond, 1930); J. H. Hornibrook, *Bibliography of Queensland Verse* (Brisb, 1953); P. Buckridge, *The Scandalous Penton* (Brisb, 1994); *PD* (LA, Qld), 16 Nov 1915, vol 121, p 2097; C. Moynihan, The Bunyip of Wendouree and Other Poems (ts, 1910, Univ Qld L) *and* Eureka (ms, 1904, Qld Parliamentary L)

PATRICK BUCKRIDGE

MULLAWIRRABURKA (c.1811-1845), Aboriginal leader, also known as Kertamero, 'King John' and 'Onkaparinga Jack', belonged to the Kaurna people, the traditional occupants of the Adelaide Plains. Born in the Willunga area, south of Adelaide, he was aged about 25 when the first colonists arrived in 1836. His Kaurna name, which translated literally as 'Dry Forest Old Man' (from *Mullawirra*, the gum forest on the eastern side of the Aldinga Plain, and *burka*, an old man) indicated that he was a ritual leader of considerable importance.

Mullawirraburka was a skilful warrior, his fighting prowess enabling him to acquire four wives—Koa Warrarto (Maria), Yerrarto (Jane), Kertanya and Kauwadla—more than any other Kaurna man at that time. About 5 ft 8 ins (173 cm) tall, he was, according to one settler, a 'finely-built fellow'; another referred to his 'very powerful frame and commanding appearance'. Articulate and intelligent, he was regarded by settlers and the authorities as one of the chiefs or leading men of the local Aboriginal people. Although a number of other Kaurna individuals were identified in the historical records, Mullawirraburka was the most prominent.

After the colonial authorities established the 'Native Location' on the banks of the River Torrens in 1838, Mullawirraburka took up semi-permanent residence there and developed a close relationship with Christian Teichelmann and Clamor Schürmann [qq.v.], Lutheran missionaries based there. Mullawirraburka quickly learned to speak English and was one of several Kaurna men who taught the missionaries the local language. He spent many hours with them, discussing spiritual matters but, like most Kaurna people, he would not accept the Christian teachings; his 'attachment to the superstitions in which he was brought up' was 'invincible', according to one account.

Appointed honorary police constable by the governor in 1838, Mullawirraburka acted as an intermediary between the Kaurna and the settlers, and was regarded by the authorities as the spokesman for his people. He seems to have done his best to keep the peace between his people and the colonists. He was, however, quick to defend his land when rival Aboriginal groups, such as those from Moorundie on the River Murray, visited Adelaide, attracted by the availability of food, tobacco and other goods.

Mullawirraburka died, probably of tuberculosis, on 2 January 1845 in Adelaide, survived by two sons and a daughter. His body was subsequently smoke-dried, in accordance with the custom of southern Kaurna clans, and later buried at Noarlunga, south of Adelaide. A newspaper obituarist observed:

He was always decent and peaceable with respect to the Europeans, and would occasionally submit to labour, but nothing could overcome his habits of vagrancy, or love for wandering in the bush, far away from the haunts of civilized man.

At the time of his death, two of his wives and six of his nine children were already dead, victims, like many other Kaurna people, of introduced diseases and poor living conditions in the wake of their dispossession from their lands by the white settlers. In a sketch by W. H. Leigh, reproduced in 1839, Mullawirraburka was depicted wearing a skin cloak, with hair in long ringlets and a thick beard. A wax portrait by Theresa Walker, held in the Art Gallery of South Australia, showed him with thick, curly hair and a neat beard.

T. J. Gara, 'The Life and Times of Mullawirraburka ("King John") of the Adelaide Tribe', in

J. Simpson and L. Hercus (eds), *History in Portraits* (Canb, 1998); *SA Register*, 6 Jan 1845, p 3.

TOM GARA

MULLENS, JOSIAH (1826-1915), stock-broker, was born on 4 July 1826 in London, one of seven children of Richard Mullens, a clerk in the Court of Chancery, and his wife Anne, née Mather. After attending school, Josiah began work with Drummond's Bank and later became clerk-in-charge of the bank's stock exchange department. In November 1852 he reached Melbourne in the *City of Poonah*, then went to Sydney. Through his family connexions, and in particular the Congregational Church, he obtained employment with G. A. Lloyd [q.v.5], gold merchant, and was later appointed gold buyer for the firm. On 18 February 1854 at the Independent Chapel, Pitt Street, Josiah married with Congregational forms Mary Ann Broome (d.1904), from London. They had six children.

On 3 January 1860 Josiah set up his own stockbroking firm. The only other Sydney broker then was (Sir) Edmund Barton's [q.v.7] father William. Elected an alderman of Balmain council in 1869, Mullens was mayor next year. When the Sydney Stock Exchange was established in May 1871, he became a founding member. The mining boom of 1872 brought major challenges to the new exchange. There was a dramatic increase in membership from 22 to 131. Most new entrants were inexperienced in share trading, and some were recent arrivals who lacked the ability to give sound investment advice.

By 1874 Mullens had become Sydney's most respected and successful stockbroker, dealing only in high-quality shares and New South Wales government securities. With a reputation for integrity and financial acumen, he was the obvious choice of the members as second chairman of the exchange upon the death that year of W. F. Cape. Under Mullens, the exchange developed policies for controlling the listing and trading in shares, established the call system of trading and restored its reputation, for which he was largely responsible. His record term ended in 1889, Joseph Palmer [q.v.11] succeeding him. Mullens's son Arthur had joined the firm in 1887; after a trip to Egypt and Britain in 1889, Josiah retired from stockbroking in 1892. He was a director of the Joint Stock Bank briefly in 1893 and of the Sydney Exchange Co. (the Royal Exchange) for some twenty years from that year.

Mullens was of 'studious and retiring habits'. His hobby was Egyptology and archaeology, and he took a deep interest in the Palestine Exploration Society and the discoveries in Babylonia and elsewhere. He was appointed vice-president of the Australian branch of the Egyptian Exploration Fund and was elected a fellow of the Royal Geographical Society of London. In 1861 he drew the attention of Professor John Woolley [q.v.6] to the availability of a facsimile edition of the *Codex Sinaiticus*, which was obtained for the University of Sydney library. Mullens was also a committee member of the university's Nicholson [q.v.2] Museum of Antiquities. A connoisseur of the fine arts, he was a vice-president of the National Art Gallery, Sydney. He was elected to the Royal Society of New South Wales in 1877 and frequently attended its meetings.

A 'staunch Nonconformist', Mullens took a leading part in the Congregational Church and was deacon and Sunday School teacher at Balmain and from 1875 at Burwood. He was interested in higher biblical criticism and familiar with current philosophical and theological literature. A founder of Camden Theological College, he was treasurer and a member of the college council until failing health compelled him to retire. He also fostered from its beginning the Congregational ministers' retirement fund.

Mullens died on 21 October 1915 in his home at Burwood and was buried in Rookwood cemetery with Congregational forms. Three daughters and one son survived him. His estate was sworn for probate at £26 501. Mullens had been the most influential stockbroker in the first fifty years of the Sydney Stock Exchange, of which his son Arthur and great-grandson Frank were also to become chairmen.

S. Salsbury and K. Sweeney, *The Bull, the Bear and the Kangaroo* (Syd, 1988) and *Sydney Stockbrokers* (Syd, 1992); *Congregationalist* (Syd), 10 Nov 1915, p 5; Roy Soc NSW, *J and Procs*, 50, 1916, p 6; *Univ Syd Gazette*, Apr 1970, p 293; *Daily Telegraph* (Syd), 22 Oct 1889, p 7, 22 Oct 1915, p 9; *Aust Independent* (Syd), 1 Nov 1889, pp 10 & 20, 15 Dec 1889, p 235; *SMH*, 22 Oct 1915, p 6, 23 Nov 1915, p 7; information from Mr F. H. Mullens, McMahon's Point, Syd.

JIM BAIN

MÜLLER, FLORENS THEODOR REINHARD (1825-1881), botanist and poet, was born on 26 December 1825 at Dresden, Saxony, son of Georg Heinrich Müller, administrative officer in the Saxon Office of Justice. Theodor was well educated and had some background in botany. He arrived in South Australia in 1849, probably aboard the *Australia* in September, and worked as a butcher in Adelaide before moving to Victoria in 1852 as a gold digger.

After mining at Bendigo, Müller moved to Back Creek in 1854 and later to goldfields in the Pyrenees. By 1857 he was quartz mining at Maryborough, where he remained until 1861. Müller helped to form German clubs at Maryborough and Back Creek, serving as secretary of both, and was also founding secretary of the short-lived Castlemaine German Club when he moved there in 1861 to work in the nursery and seed shop of Charles Lenne and Edward Nicolai. In September 1862 Müller moved to Melbourne, where he obtained a temporary position as assistant at the Botanic Gardens on 8 October and became active in the Melbourne *Turnverein* (gymnastics club). In July 1863 he was elected secretary of the newly formed central committee of the German Associations in Victoria.

Müller was best known in Victoria as a poet and writer in German. His 1857 poem, 'Der Digger', established his reputation among locals of German origin and was so popular that it was reprinted in 1859 and 1864. At least twenty of his other poems were published in German newspapers in Melbourne, many of them commemorating German meetings, anniversaries and other events held in Victoria. He was awarded a prize for his prologue, *Gut Heil!*, recited at the first general German gymnastic and song festival, held at Cremorne Gardens in November 1862. He also wrote two short novels, *German Jack* and *Der Gefundene*, which were serialized in *Victoria Deutsche Presse* and published together as *Australische Buschgeschichten* in 1860 by F. Gelbrecht. Several of his short articles and essays appeared in various Melbourne German-language newspapers.

On 30 April 1869 Müller resigned from the gardens. Returning to Dresden, he worked at the Natural History Museum and at the Royal Polytechnikum as *custos* of the botanical collection when it was transferred there from the museum. After his return to Saxony, he married Clara Bornowska; the couple had a foster child, Helena Bornowska. In Germany, Müller published some short articles on Australia, a novel, *Australische Kolonisten oder Heute so—Morgan so!* (1878), and a book on hunting, *Jagden in Australien* (1878). He died on 4 March 1881 at Dresden and was buried in Trinitätskirche cemetery; his wife and daughter survived him. Müller's poems and writings were sentimental and patriotic, but had a definite Australian flavour and appealed to the mass of Germans living in Victoria in the 1860s.

J. Fletcher in M. Clyne et al (eds), *Antipodische Aufklärungen: Festschrift für Leslie Bodi* (Frankfurt, Germany, 1987), p 87; A. Corkhill, *Antipodean Encounters* (Bern, Switzerland, 1990); T. A. Darragh, 'Theodor Müller, Victoria's German Poet', Bibliographical Society of Aust and NZ, *Bulletin*, 18, nos 2-3, 1994, p 118; *Dresdener Anzeiger*, 5 Mar 1881, p 14.

THOMAS A. DARRAGH

MUNRO (MUNROE), JAMES (c.1779-1845?), convict, seaman and storekeeper, was convicted at the Old Bailey, London, in January 1799 of stealing twenty yards (18 m) of printed calico from a haberdasher in Oxford Street. Aged 20, he was sentenced to transportation for seven years and reached Sydney in the convict transport *Royal Admiral* on 22 November 1800. He was probably exposed to religious teaching *en route*, as twelve missionaries from the London Missionary Society were also on board. In the 1806 Sydney muster roll he was described as a boatswain, free by servitude, and he sailed on a number of voyages from Sydney from 1809.

Munro's navigational skills stood him in good stead in the dangerous waters around the Furneaux Group, Bass Strait, where he settled (on Preservation Island) about 1820. By 1824 he had a good vegetable garden, fowls, pigs, goats and sheep. Two years later an observer described his establishment as 'a little village, situated under a Cluster of Trees. It has a very pretty appearance.' He also grew wheat and barley, and bred rabbits. He sold his produce to vessels, traded in mutton birds, bartered his vegetables with sealers and acted as a storekeeper for their seal skins. Known as 'King of the Sealers' or 'Governor of the Straits', he was distinguished by his 'crack-jaw dictionary words and wise looks'.

Following his letter to the superintendent of police at Launceston reporting the arrival of prisoners on the island, in 1825 Munro was appointed a constable in the straits, with a special brief to watch for escaped convicts. When G. A. Robinson [q.v.2] came to the region in 1830 to establish an Aboriginal settlement, he attempted unsuccessfully to remove Munro—whom he accused of having previously abducted indigenous women from the mainland. Next year Munro went to Hobart Town to frustrate Robinson's attempts to deprive the sealers of their Aboriginal consorts. Munro has been called 'an exception among the sealers, who were rogues almost to a man'. Looking for contentment on Preservation Island, he was a religious man who wanted 'to make peace with his maker', received religious tracts, read the Bible to local children and taught an Aboriginal woman to say her prayers.

Robinson described Munro as being 5 ft 5 ins (165 cm) tall, with light hair and a fair complexion. A water-colour (1831) by Henry Laing depicted his establishment on Preservation Island. Six Tasmanian Aboriginal women, a native of New Holland and a New Zealand woman lived with him at various times, and Munro for the most part treated them well.

Munro died in December 1844 or January 1845 on Preservation Island and was buried near his dwelling. The *Hobart Town Courier*, in an obituary headed 'The Tasmanian Crusoe', praised his hospitality and many acts of kindness. According to the *Courier*, he left three children by an Aboriginal woman, although other accounts of his issue varied. Louisa Briggs [q.v.] was reputedly his grand-daughter. Mount Munro and Munro Bay on Cape Barren Island were named after him.

N. J. Plomley (ed), *Friendly Mission* (Hob, 1966) and *Weep in Silence* (Hob, 1987); A. C. Begg and N. C. Begg, *The World of John Boultbee* (Christchurch, NZ, 1979); D. Barwick et al (eds), *Metaphors of Interpretation* (Canb, 1985), p 185; Tas Hist Research Assn, *Papers and Procs*, 37, nos 2 & 3, June-Sept 1990, p 37; Old Bailey Sessions Papers 1788-99, no 99, p 105, reel FM4/7163 (ML).

BARBARA VALENTINE

MUSKETT, PHILIP EDWARD (1857-1909), medical practitioner and health reformer, was born on 5 February 1857 at Collingwood, Melbourne, son of English-born, Particular Baptist parents Charles Muskett, bookseller, and his wife Phoebe, née Charlwood. Educated at Melbourne Model School and at Wesley College, where he won a Draper [q.v.1] scholarship, in 1877 Philip enrolled in medicine at the University of Melbourne, passing several subjects, but not graduating. He undertook further medical studies at Glasgow and Edinburgh, Scotland, and became a licentiate of the royal colleges of Physicians and of Surgeons, Edinburgh, in 1880. After spending some time in London, he returned to Australia and became a medical officer at (Royal) Melbourne Hospital.

In 1882 Muskett moved to Sydney, taking up a position at Sydney Hospital. Within a year he became surgeon superintendent of the steam immigration service, medical superintendent of the quarantine station and honorary surgeon at Sydney Hospital. He went into private practice in 1885 and, since about a third of his patients were children, focused on infant health and welfare, taking up contemporary concerns about infant mortality rates—in his *Australian Appeal* (1892)—and the incidence of rickets. In 1888 he brought out the first of four editions of a small book on the feeding and management of Australian infants and also a more comprehensive guide to *The Health and Diet of Children in Australia*. In 1891 came his more scientific *Prescribing and Treatment in the Diseases of Children*. He served as secretary to the New South Wales section of four intercolonial medical congresses in the 1880s and 1890s. In addition, he was medical officer and honorary surgeon to the New South Wales League of Wheelmen, the Royal Agricultural Society of New South Wales and the Civil Ambulance and Transport Brigade. Remembered by the bookseller James Tyrrell [q.v.12] as a keen bibliophile, he was president and chairman of the Sydney School of Arts debating society and a founder of the New South Wales Literary and Debating Society's Union. Muskett discussed the need for more technical education (including compulsory cookery lessons for girls) in his public lectures on health, published in 1899 as *The Diet of Australian School Children and Technical Education*.

In *The Art of Living in Australia* (London, 1893), which included recipes by Harriet Wicken [q.v.], he extended to the population his arguments about feeding children as a whole, advocating radical changes in the diet of Australians. He abhorred their love of meat, tobacco and tea and their lack of interest in vegetables and fruit apart from cabbage and potatoes. Girls and women, he thought, risked their health and childbearing abilities through consuming excessive amounts of tea, bread and butter. Coffee he thought preferable to tea and Australian wine the ideal beverage with meals. More fish and oysters should be substituted for meat. He advocated fresh air, regular exercise, woollen undergarments and pyjamas rather than bed gowns, and advised the use of floss silk as well as powder for teeth. *The Book of Diet* (Melbourne, 1898), based on his lectures at the recently established Hawkesbury Agricultural College and the School of Arts, was a guide to vegetables, fruit, salads and alcoholic beverages, many of them unfamiliar, with suggestions for their preparation and consumption.

Muskett's last major project, an *Illustrated Australian Medical Guide* (1903 and 1909), with drawings by D. H. Souter [q.v.12], took three years to write, ran to two volumes and over a thousand pages, and cost three guineas. His straightforward and clear discussion of female diseases and anatomy in 'the female organs of generation', published as a separate pamphlet in 1903 with Souter's coloured illustrations, including a very pregnant woman, made him a pioneer sex educator. His last work, *The Attainment of Health* (1909), was a detailed guide to foods to eat or avoid for specific complaints and diseases.

His books were eloquent, idiosyncratic and repetitive on some of his pet themes. They contained numerous digressions and quotations from philosophers (Montesquieu an understandable favourite), novelists, poets, and authorities, well known and obscure. He was one of the first writers in Australia to realize and cultivate the demand for scientific but easily comprehensible information on childcare, diet and health especially related to local climatic conditions.

A bachelor, Muskett relaxed by writing and walking. Despite his rigorous regimen, he became ill in August 1909 and died of heart failure on 25 August in his rooms at 143 Elizabeth Street, Hyde Park, where he lived with his sister Alice [q.v.10], an artist and writer. He was buried with Anglican rites in Waverley cemetery. In his will Muskett left money for a biennial essay prize on any of his favourite subjects; however, his sister, who had already established an art prize in his memory, disregarded his instructions. Most of the money disappeared in subsequent litigation. Muskett was rediscovered by the 'lifestyle' enthusiasts of the 1980s, and in 1993 a prize for writing on gastronomy was named after him.

J. Tyrrell, *Old Books, Old Friends, Old Sydney* (1952); B. Santich, *What the Doctors Ordered* (Melb, 1995); *A'sian Medical Gazette*, 20 Sept 1909, p 520, *SMH*, 26 Aug 1909, p 6; *T&CJ*, 1 Sept 1909, p 53; J. Vickers, A Study of Equity Suits and the Judiciary as a reflection of N.S.W. Society's Values (M.A. Hons thesis, Univ NSW, 2002).

STEPHEN GARTON
BEVERLEY KINGSTON

MUSQUITO (c.1780-1825), Aboriginal resistance leader and tracker, also known as Mosquito, Musquetta, Bush Muschetta or Muskito, was probably an Eora (Gai-Mariagal) man, born on the north shore of Port Jackson, New South Wales. In 1805 he participated in raids on settlers' properties in the Hawkesbury and Georges River districts. After the *Sydney Gazette* reported that, in good English, he had expressed his determination to continue his 'rapacities', General Orders issued on 9 June 1805 authorized his arrest to prevent further mischief. Local Aborigines agreed to capture him, and he was apprehended by them and gaoled at Parramatta in July, but not charged. Next month Governor King [q.v.2] exiled Musquito and 'Bull Dog', 'principals in the recent outrages', to Norfolk Island, where Musquito remained for eight years.

In January 1813 Musquito was evacuated aboard the *Minstrel* for Port Dalrymple (Launceston), Van Diemen's Land. Next year his brother Phillip, in New South Wales, gained Macquarie's [q.v.2] consent for him to be sent back to Sydney, but Musquito remained in Van Diemen's Land. In 1817 Lieutenant-Governor Sorell [q.v.2] praised his service as a tracker of bushrangers and approved his return to 'his Native Place', but this never eventuated.

Contemporary commentators blamed Musquito for influencing the island's 'sable natives' to violent retribution, and colonial historians John West and James Bonwick [qq.v.2, 3] greatly embellished his character and deeds. According to them, he was transported to Van Diemen's Land for the gruesome murder of a pregnant Aboriginal woman and mutilated, murdered and prostituted his women before corrupting the local Aborigines.

By February 1818 he was a servant of Edward Lord [q.v.2]. In October he helped to track and kill the bushranger Michael Howe [q.v.1]. Henry Melville [q.v.2] later recounted Musquito's statement that Sorell's broken promise, and ostracism by convicts, drove him into the bush, where he formed the 'tame gang', which Rev. William Horton met at Pittwater in 1823. Horton conversed with him, and described him as possessing superior skill and muscular strength to that of his companions. Musquito subsequently became antagonistic towards settlers, and joined the 'wild' Oyster Bay tribe. His knowledge of the English language and customs and his expertise in guerrilla warfare were assets to people who, frustrated, resorted to aggression. With 'Black Jack', the band killed several stockkeepers in raids on the east coast in November 1823 and in 1824.

In August 1824 Musquito was wounded and captured by an Aboriginal boy named Teague. After his recovery, Musquito and Jack were charged with aiding and abetting the murder of a stockkeeper, and tried without oaths in the Supreme Court, Hobart Town, in December 1824. Musquito was convicted on dubious evidence, Jack on a second charge; both were hanged on 25 February 1825. Melville considered the trial and executions to constitute a 'most extraordinary precedent'. Gilbert Robertson [q.v.2] felt the hangings incited further violence. It remained unclear whether Musquito committed any murders. The indigenous resistance leader was the subject of a series of paintings by the Aboriginal artist Lin Onus in 1978-82.

Another Port Jackson Aboriginal known as Musquito, an associate of Bennelong's [q.v.1], had been drawn by Nicolas Martin-Petit of the Baudin [q.v.1] expedition in 1802 and was killed in a battle early in 1806.

Hist Records of Aust, series I, vol 5, pp 306-7, 497; J. Bonwick, *The Last of the Tasmanians* (Lond, 1870); H. Melville, *The History of Van Diemen's Land*, pt 1 (Syd, 1959); E. Fry (ed), *Rebels and Radicals* (Syd, 1983); *Sydney Gazette*, 19 May 1805, p 2, 30 June 1805, p 2, 7 July 1805, p 2, 4 Aug 1805, p 2, 12 Jan 1806, p 1, 19 Jan 1806, p 2, 2 Feb 1806, p 2; *Hobart Town Gazette*, 14 Feb 1818, 6 July 1824, 6 Aug 1824, 3 Dec 1824, 25 Feb 1825; Rev Horton, Wesleyan Missionary papers, 3 June 1823, BT 52, vol 4, p 1268, *and* Sorell dispatches, 20 Oct 1818, CY 1096, p 91 (ML); Colonial Secretary correspondence, King, 8 Aug 1805, reel 6040, p 41, *and* T. Campbell to Lt Gov Davey, reel 6004, p 251 (SRNSW); Mosquito correspondence file, *and* CSO 1/177/4306, *and* Gilbert Robertson's journal, CBE 1/1 (TA).

NAOMI PARRY

N

NAGLE, JACOB (1761-1841), sailor, was born on 15 September 1761 at Reading, in the American colony of Pennsylvania, one of four children of George Nagle (1735-1789), a blacksmith of German descent, and his wife Rebecca, née Rogers. George was sheriff of Berks County in 1770-75. In the American War of Independence he was an officer in George Washington's Continental Army and in 1776 took Jacob with him to barracks in Philadelphia. The youngster joined the army in August 1777 and fought in the battle of Brandywine in September. After the winter of 1777-78, spent at Valley Forge, he and his father left the army and the family moved to Philadelphia where George ran a tavern that was popular with seamen.

Enlisting in the Continental Navy early in 1780, Jacob was briefly attached to the *Saratoga* before joining the sixteen-gun privateering brig *Fair American*. In November 1781 he was serving in the *Trojan* when that vessel was captured while making repairs at sea after a storm and the crew taken on board H.M.S. *Royal Oak*. Imprisoned on St Christopher, Leeward and Windward Islands, in the Caribbean, Nagle was freed by the French after authorities surrendered in January 1782. He joined a French ship but was soon gaoled for helping a British sailor, and then escaped. Nagle eventually became a seaman in the Royal Navy after an exchange of prisoners in May and served in H.M.S. *Lucia* and two other ships until he was selected to serve aboard H.M.S. *Sirius* in March 1787.

With the First Fleet, Nagle reached Sydney in January 1788 and as part of Captain Phillip's [q.v.2] boat party explored the harbour and the Hawkesbury River. In October he sailed in *Sirius* via Cape Horn to Cape Town to replenish dwindling supplies, thus circumnavigating the world. Back in Sydney, he was an eyewitness to the spearing of Phillip by Aborigines in 1790. In March that year Phillip, facing food shortages again, sent *Sirius* and *Supply* to Norfolk Island with a third of the convicts and two companies of marines. Nagle was still with *Sirius*, which, off Norfolk Island, was swept onto a reef and lost. In February 1791 *Supply* arrived from Batavia with a rented Dutch ship, *Waaksamheyd*, in which Nagle sailed back to Sydney and then on to England in March, being paid off at Portsmouth on 4 May 1792.

Nagle married a 'lively, hansome girl' in London in 1795; she and their children died of fever in Lisbon in 1802, the year he left the Royal Navy. Thereafter he crewed in merchant ships voyaging to South America, India and South East Asia and traversing the Mediterranean, before returning to the United States of America in 1822 and retiring in 1825. He moved around frequently, from Maryland to Ohio then to Pennsylvania, working as a ledgerkeeper. Penniless and seeking a military pension, he lived in a boarding house for his last years. Nagle died on 17 February 1841 at Canton, Ohio.

His manuscript journal 1775-1802 (compiled probably after 1829), a version of which was acquired by the State Library of New South Wales in 1995, is valuable as a rare source of information on the first European settlement in Sydney and of events on Norfolk Island during his enforced stay. Opinionated, self-confident, by turns severe and ribald, Nagle told a rollicking tale.

J. Dann (ed), *The Nagle Journal* (NY, 1988); M. Gillen, *The Founders of Australia* (Syd, 1989).

ARTHUR EASTON

NARELLE, MARIE (1870-1941), singer, was born on 28 January 1870 at Combaning station, near Temora, New South Wales, fourth child of native-born parents of Irish lineage, John Ryan, goldminer, and his wife Catherine, née Comans, daughter of the occupier of Combaning. Registered as Catherine Mary, the child was known as Molly. She was educated locally and at the Presentation convent (Mount Erin), Wagga Wagga, where she learned music and singing. After an itinerant life mainly around southern New South Wales, the family settled at Candelo, near Bega. Molly had already gained a reputation singing at concerts for local charities. On 29 January 1891 at St Mary's Cathedral, Sydney, she married with Catholic rites Matthew Aloysius Callaghan, an attorney's clerk. A drunkard, he left her about 1894 with three small children to support. Finding few opportunities in Sydney, she became a music teacher at Candelo, visiting her scattered pupils on horseback and by horse and sulky.

After Bishop Joseph Higgins [q.v.9] heard Molly singing at Cobargo Catholic Church and offered introductions in Sydney, she took a studio in W. H. Paling's [q.v.5] building in George Street. She studied first at St Vincent's Convent, Potts Point, with Mary Ellen Christian (Sister Mary Paul of the Cross), who had taught Melba [q.v.10] and had been a student of the renowned Manuel Garcia (1805-1906) of the Royal Academy of Music. Later, Molly studied in Sydney under Roberto Hazon [q.v.9] and Signor Steffani.

Molly Callaghan adopted the stage name 'Marie Narelle', reputedly taking the surname from an Aboriginal 'Queen of the Moruya tribe' as a 'sort of talisman'. In 1898-1902 she gave concerts in New South Wales, Queensland and Tasmania, managed by the flautist John Lemmone [q.v.10], some in association with the contralto Eva Mylott (1875-1920). Irish and Scottish ballads were Narelle's specialty, but she sang operatic arias and oratorio as well. During the tours, Mrs William Bourke, a cousin, cared for Narelle's children. Invited by the visiting Irish politician William O'Brien to sing in Ireland at the close of the Cork Exhibition, she left Australia in July 1902. Narelle was acclaimed in Ireland, where Michael Davitt, the socialist, opined that it 'took an Australian to teach the Irish to render their own songs', and gave the then unknown tenor John McCormack (1885-1945) a place on her programme. In London she renewed lessons with Steffani and studied Gaelic. On 8 June 1903 she shared the platform at the Royal Albert Hall with (Dame) Clara Butt and Ada Crossley [q.v.8].

Narelle and McCormack went to the United States of America in the Irish cultural delegation to the St Louis World Fair; for seven months from April 1904 they were the principal artists in the 'Blarney Castle Theatre' at the fair's Irish village exhibit. Following many American engagements, and having made wax cylinder recordings for T. A. Edison, in June 1906 she returned to the Australian concert circuit; she also sang in New Zealand then went back to Europe.

During another Australian tour in 1909, including Western Australia, Narelle obtained a divorce from Callaghan in Sydney on 2 June. Next year she settled in New York and in 1911 gave recitals throughout the U.S.A. with McCormack. On 9 December at the West End Presbyterian Church, Manhattan, she married Harry Allen Currie, a Canadian-born electrical engineer. The couple lived in New York, where her hospitality to Australian soldiers passing through the U.S.A. in World War I was famous.

Narelle made her last Australian tour in 1925-26, revisiting the New South Wales scenes of her youthful successes, including Temora, Candelo and Boorowa—'the Tipperary of Australia'. After her husband's death in 1934, she moved to England. Reconciled with the Catholic Church, Catherine Mary Narelle Currie died on 26 January 1941 at Clevecot, Chipping Norton, Oxfordshire, England, and was buried in Holy Trinity churchyard. She was survived by her son Reginald and daughters Kathleen, a pianist

who had sometimes accompanied her, and Rita, a coloratura soprano. When the churchyard was resumed for a children's playground, Marie Narelle's headstone was sent to Australia and re-erected in the grounds of the Temora Rural Museum in 1980.

'The Australian Queen of Irish Song' was noted for a voice 'not unlike Melba's', for her marvellous diction in four languages and for the passion with which she performed. Commenting on the pre-eminence of Australian singers such as Melba and Crossley, she held that, rather than physical influences like climate, it was 'the Australian personality that has made the Australian voice. We are a natural people ... free in all we do and say and think and it is that freedom, I believe, that makes us good singers.'

B. and F. Mackenzie, *Singers of Australia* (Melb, 1967); H. V. Lloyd, *Boorowa* (Syd, 1990); W. Bebbington (ed), *The Oxford Companion to Australian Music* (Melb, 1997); *Sydney Mail*, 9 Sept 1899, p 637; *Catholic Press*, 29 Mar 1902, p 14, 28 Dec 1905, p 5; *Freeman's Journal*, 23 June 1906, p 14; *Bulletin*, 17 Feb 1921, p 42; *SMH*, 30 Oct 1925, p 6; Narelle material, ScreenSound, Canb; information from Mr R. Maslin, Temora, NSW.   G. P. WALSH

NEWCOMB, HARRIET CHRISTINA; *see* HODGE, MARGARET

NGABIDJ, GRANT (c.1904-1977), Aboriginal stockman, was a Kadjerong man who was born near Cow Creek, between Brolga Spring and the north-eastern coast of Western Australia. The black-mouthed and striped tiger snake, *danggamang*, and the water goanna, *yelaugiing*, were his conception totems and *marrimarri*, the pelican, his subsection totem, from which came the name Wilmirr, given to him by his mother. His people moved across their traditional area between the Keep River (Northern Territory) and the Cambridge Gulf. As a child of about 3 at Grant Creek, with his elder sister and mother, he was separated from the rest of their group. While they were being taken away on horseback, he later recalled, he heard the sound of gunfire behind them. The shooting was that of many men of Ngabidj's group, who had been chained to a tree. Although not mentioned in the records, the killings were known in the oral tradition of the Miriwoong and Kadjerong.

Ngabidj was taken to Ningbing cattle station, where he was reared and introduced to droving and stock work. All his life he remained deeply involved in the traditional world and the spiritual life of his people. He visited relations over long distances in Miriwoong and Kadjerong country and as far west as the Forrest River, participated in ceremonies and fought in clan battles.

In his youth Ngabidj was a tough man—he had cicatrices from collarbone to navel. He killed at least two Aboriginal men. One homicide, about 1924, was an act of impulse in an inter-group skirmish. The other in 1929, in the company of his countrymen Waddi Boyoi and Joe Nurunggin, was a payback against a man named Toby, an outsider from the Halls Creek area, who had become involved with Boyoi's wife and then threatened him. Ngabidj and Boyoi were arrested in June 1929, but the hearing in the Supreme Court at Wyndham two years later resulted in a verdict of not guilty. The two defendants were released, and Ngabidj walked to Forrest River Mission.

About August 1926 he became betrothed to Kalwik, and in the 1930s they lived at Ningbing station. Following the death of Kalwik by 1932 and of another wife Daarrn some two years later, Ngabidj married Daisy Djanduin about 1940. After World War II he worked as a stockman at Carlton Hill station. In 1962 in Wyndham and Perth hospitals he was treated for tuberculosis. By 1969 he had moved with Djanduin to the Aboriginal reserve at Kununurra, where he recorded his life history on tape in 1973-74. Ngabidj's memories told of his having had 'comparatively more violent experiences at first hand under white cattle-station management than many of his contemporaries'. However, such crimes—some at levels described as 'massacres' but more usually isolated killings—were also reported by other Miriwoong and Kadjerong people. Highly respected in the community, Ngabidj died on 1 July 1977 at Kununurra. His wife and at least one son survived him.

B. C. Shaw (ed), *My Country of the Pelican Dreaming* (Canb, 1981); D. Horton (ed), *The Encyclopaedia of Aboriginal Australia*, 2 (Canb, 1994).   BRUCE SHAW

NICHOLLS, WORTHY WORTHINGTON GEORGE (c.1808-1849), workman, carrier and socialist, claimed to have born in a London slum. After a training 'under the fear of the Lord and a broomstick', George later avowed that he was bundled into a workhouse when aged 3, was taken out at 5, and at 7 was sold by his mother, a drinker and card player, for £10. He also claimed that he started work in a factory, had eight years service in a sweep's cellar and was imprisoned when struggling for a free press. Through radical politics he became known to Robert Gouger [q.v.1], whom he followed to Adelaide. Nicholls

was described as a bricklayer when he arrived in the *Navarino* with his wife Maria and three children in December 1837. 'Complete with black beard, red shirt and immoral habits', he quickly became notorious locally as a self-avowed socialist with atheistic views.

The press chronicled Nicholls's progress, beginning as a builder and earning the nickname 'Pisé' for his improved method of *pisé* building. He offered to work for goods or labour in kind and undertook to supply freehold plots and cottages to those with few means, but refused to meet his wife's debts. Tribulations followed. Turning to water carting, Nicholls suffered abuse from fellow carters, and only by compromising his religious views could he swear the oath and bind other carters to keep the peace. He proclaimed himself the most ill-used person ever in a British colony; when a drunken mob invaded his house he escaped in his shirt through the roof. Forced to carry arms, he attributed his misfortune to 'a mere report, that I am what I am not, namely an *infidel*'. In 1843 he opened a boarding house in Hindley Street for 'sober and orderly' guests, while offering other property for sale, including his water cart and horse, Old Windsor Castle, 'warranted to draw 2 tons' weight, and anything else in reason, except an inference'.

Despite announcing his return to England, Nicholls remained in Adelaide as a carrier, water carter and advocate of reform. He recommended a refuge for destitutes; he warned about polluting the Torrens River but equivocated about letting conditionally pardoned convicts pollute South Australia. At a meeting in 1842 he condemned Governor (Sir) George Grey [q.v.1] and the biased press. Editors often pilloried him as an ignorant socialist, though his replies, supporting the universal rights of man, were not those of an ignorant man. His public performances, when he attacked land jobbery, mining magnates and workers' disadvantages, were usually denounced. In 1846 he won praise for introducing a fast passenger cart from his boarding house to Burra, but by 1848 his life had become frenzied. He proclaimed his Owenite views more fervently in advertisements, which he often embellished with verse, and in public meetings, where few took him seriously.

Nicholls's home was a refuge for the downtrodden and his charitable acts were recognized, but first his wife and then a widow-companion left him. He suicided by taking drink and an overdose of laudanum on 13 December 1849 at Black Forest, leaving his wife and seven children unprovided for. His vision of a better society for small capitalists and workers had not been unreasoned, yet gained few adherents in a colony that championed outward rectitude and personal gain.

D. Pike, *Paradise of Dissent* (Melb, 1957); *J of the Hist Soc of SA*, no 8, 1980, p 84; *SA Gazette and Colonial Register*, 21 July 1838, p 3, 18 Aug 1838, p 2, 9 Mar 1839, p 5, 13 Sept 1845, p 4; *SA Register*, 11 Mar 1843, p 3, 4 Mar 1848, p 2, 11 Mar 1848, p 1, 24 June 1848, p 2, 22 July 1848, pp 2 & 3, 29 Nov 1848, p 4, 16 Dec 1848, p 2, 15 Dec 1849, p 2; *Southern Australian*, 28 Mar 1843, p 2, 14 Dec 1849, p 2, 18 Dec 1849, p 2, 21 Dec 1849, p 3; *Observer* (Adel), 2 Dec 1843, p 1, 9 Dec 1843, p 1, 16 Dec 1843, p 2, 23 Dec 1843, p 1, 25 May 1844, p 5, 21 Dec 1844, p 5, 12 Apr 1845, p 5, 28 Mar 1846, p 5, 19 Sept 1846, p 1; *News* (Adel), 21 Oct 1957, pp 18 & 19.

R. M. GIBBS

NICOLAY, MARY ANN (1850-1939), Nightingale nurse and hospital matron, was born on 2 August 1850, probably at Chelsea, London, fifth of eight children of Rev. Charles Grenfell Nicolay [q.v.5], sometime librarian of King's College Hospital (which had a nursing school), and his wife Mary Ann, née Raven. Educated at Clifton High School, Bristol, young Mary Ann became a pupil-teacher. She joined the Nightingale School of Nursing at St Thomas's Hospital, London, on 13 March 1876, later recalling long days, cleaning as well as nursing, and writing notes for checking by Miss Nightingale. She left in March 1877 for the National Nursing Association, with 'good' to 'moderate' assessments—except for her truthfulness, which was 'unreliable'.

In 1878 Mary Ann, her mother and siblings joined her father in Western Australia. After about a year she went back to Britain, where she possibly worked in a hospital at Newport, Monmouth. Returning to Western Australia about 1888, she stayed with her widowed father at Fremantle. In 1890 she was appointed matron at Perth Colonial Hospital. She re-signed after six months but stayed in office for the rest of the year. From 1891 Nicolay undertook private nursing. Her professional care was not cheap: ten guineas a month for midwifery cases, one guinea a day to nurse patients who had survived a major operation. By 1897 she was running a private hospital in North Perth. Although the main beneficiary of her father's will, she was never wealthy.

In March 1900, sponsored by the public, Sister Nicolay conducted ten nurses to the South African War in the steamer *Salamis*, despite criticism for taking scarce, trained personnel from local hospitals. Some of the group found their way into South African hospitals, but Nicolay returned to Western Australia; next year she was employed again at Perth hospital. From February 1902 she was inspecting and relieving matron, Perth, a post that also involved travel to government hospitals as far distant as Broome and Albany. She retired in 1917 but returned to Perth Hospital in 1919 during the influenza epidemic. In 1921 she was awarded honorary life membership of the Australasian Trained Nurses' Association; she was also a member of the Royal British Nursing Association.

Nicolay was credited with establishing a training regime for probationers and remembered as a disciplinarian. She brought modern nursing ideals to Western Australia and exerted a moral influence over the profession by her often-advertised links with the heroine Nightingale. She was also a strict Anglican churchwoman, as was her friend Jane Isabella Gill, matron of Perth Hospital to 1928, whom she visited every week to take lunch with in the nurses' dining room. In 1935, opening the Preliminary Training School for Nurses in Murray Street, she dedicated a grandfather clock to Gill's memory.

A short, plump and cheerful public figure, Nicolay always wore the blue, outdoor uniform of a Nightingale nurse, including bonnet with ribbons tied under her chin, and a belt that was said to be fastened with a St Thomas's buckle. She travelled twice weekly from her rooms in Subiaco to the Literary Institute to keep up with current publications. In April 1936 she spoke at the opening of the Florence Nightingale Club. Next year she was awarded the Coronation medal. She published several accounts embellishing her legend, including reminiscences in the *Magazine* (April 1930). Miss Nicolay died on 15 October 1939 in (Royal) Perth Hospital and was buried in Karrakatta cemetery.

D. Popham (ed), *Reflections* (Perth, 1978); G. C. Bolton and P. Joske, *History of Royal Perth Hospital* (Perth, 1982); V. Bullough et al (eds), *Florence Nightingale and Her Era* (NY, 1990); J. Bassett, *Guns & Brooches* (Melb, 1992); *J of WA Nurses*, 19 May 1936, p 14, 17 Oct 1939, p 13; *WA Church News*, Nov 1939, p 6; *Royal Perth Hospital Journal*, Nov 1954, p 21, May 1955, p 93, F. M. Nicolay, A General History of Nursing in Perth, Western Australia (thesis, Graylands Teaching College, Perth, 1964); Nightingale Training School records, H01/ST/NTS/C/1/2 (London Metropolitan Archives); F. G. Nicolay, Diaries and Reminiscences (BL).

MICHAL BOSWORTH

NIMMO, ROBERT HAROLD (1893-1966), soldier and peacekeeper, was born on 22 November 1893 at Oak Park station, near Einasleigh, far north Queensland, fifth of nine children of James Russel Nimmo (d.1905), a Scottish-born grazier, and his Victorian-born wife Mary Ann Eleanor, née Lethbridge. Harold—as he was known within his family—was educated in 1904-11 at The Southport School, where he won academic and sporting honours. On 7 March 1912 he entered the Royal Military College, Duntroon, Federal

Capital Territory, in the second intake. Here he acquired the nickname 'Putt'. In November 1914 his class graduated fourteen months early for service in World War I. He was later retrospectively awarded the sword of honour as top student.

Joining the 5th Light Horse Regiment, Australian Imperial Force, in Egypt in February 1915, Lieutenant Nimmo landed on Gallipoli as a troop commander on 20 May. He saw extensive fighting (the official history later noted his courage and leadership on 28 June). Appointed regimental adjutant, he was evacuated to Britain with enteric fever in late August. He returned to Egypt in May 1916 and served throughout the Palestine campaign in a variety of staff and squadron command appointments with the 5th Light Horse, the 1st and 2nd Light Horse brigades, and the British 160th Infantry Brigade. Rising to major in July 1917, he was mentioned in dispatches and returned to Australia in February 1919.

Nimmo resumed service in the Permanent Military Forces and from 1920 instructed at Duntroon. On 25 June 1921 at St John's Church of England, Darlinghurst, Sydney, he married Joan Margaret 'Peggy' Cunningham, from the grazing family that owned Lanyon station, F.C.T.; they had one son and one daughter. From 1925 Nimmo held staff appointments in Melbourne. He represented Australia in hockey in 1927, 1930 and 1932, and played hockey, Rugby, cricket, tennis and polo for Victoria. A lieutenant colonel at Headquarters, 1st Cavalry Division, Sydney, on the outbreak of World War II, Nimmo, like most other senior cavalry officers, was kept in Australia to help develop a modern armoured capability.

In March 1940 Peggy died in a fall at The Gap. The army transferred a devastated Nimmo to Brisbane. On 10 February 1942 at the Church of All Saints, Woollahra, Sydney, he married 26-year-old Mary Dundas Page, from Queensland. They had two children. His elder son James was killed while serving with the Royal Australian Air Force in 1944.

Nimmo was promoted colonel in September 1941 and brigadier in January 1942. In 1942 and 1943 he commanded the 4th Cavalry Brigade, 1st Armoured Brigade and 1st Motor Brigade. In 1943-45 he was brigadier, general staff, successively of 3rd Australian Corps, 2nd Australian Army and Northern Territory Force, before commanding 4th Australian Base Area in New Guinea and serving at Headquarters, 1st Australian Army, at Lae.

At the war's end Nimmo assumed command of the 34th Infantry Brigade on Morotai, the first formation of the incipient Australian Regular Army, as it waited to take part in the occupation of Japan. In January 1946 he impressed many, including the soldiers themselves, with his calm handling of the 'Morotai incident' when troops came close to mutiny over delays and public criticism. The next month he led the brigade to Japan. Three months later he returned to Australia and was promoted major general as general officer commanding Northern Command in Brisbane. Appointed C.B.E. in 1950, he retired from the army in November.

Late that year, following Sir Owen Dixon's [q.v.14] ultimately unsuccessful efforts at mediating a settlement in Kashmir, the United Nations had sought an Australian to serve as chief military observer of the U.N. Military Observer Group in India and Pakistan. With his broad experience and calm and resolute personality, Nimmo was chosen. He arrived in Kashmir in November 1950, and was joined three months later by his wife. Their children also spent time in Kashmir. The observer group's role was to monitor the ceasefire line between Indian and Pakistani forces, much of it in rugged mountains. Nimmo acquired a reputation as a hard-working and efficient administrator. He was an ideal military observer, 'a model of firmness, tact, and silence', as one onlooker wrote. He regularly visited local commanders along the line. He also earned the parties' respect with his sporting prowess, playing polo into his sixties.

With dark hair and a trim moustache, Nimmo was remembered by one who served under him in 1945-46 as a handsome officer of compact stature, unflappable and popular. In 1954, at the United Nations' suggestion, Nimmo was promoted honorary lieutenant general. He led U.N.M.O.G.I.P. until his death, the longest ever command of a United Nations operation. Following the 1965 war between India and Pakistan, he also raised and initially commanded the U.N. India-Pakistan Observation Mission outside Kashmir. Nimmo died in his sleep, of a heart attack, on 4 January 1966 at Rawalpindi, Pakistan, and was buried in the Anzac section of Mount Gravatt cemetery, Brisbane, with full military and U.N. honours; senior representatives of both India and Pakistan attended his funeral. His wife and their son and daughter, and the daughter of his first marriage, survived him.

C. E. W. Bean, *The Story of ANZAC*, 2 (Canb, 1944); T. A. G. Hungerford, *A Knockabout with a Slouch Hat* (Perth, 1985); *Old Southportians Review*, Jan 1964, June 1966; *SMH*, 15 Mar 1940, p 11, 5 Jan 1966, p 3, 14 Jan 1966, p 14; *Courier-Mail* (Brisb), 5 Jan 1966, p 1; *Canb Times*, 5 Jan 1966, p 1; A1868, items 681/27/2 and 854/10/18/3, A5009, item A7/3/2/3, and A5954, item 2277/4 (NAA); Nimmo letters (RMC Duntroon Archives, Canb); information from Mrs A. Truman, Dangar Island, NSW, Mr R. Nimmo, New York, and the late Brigadier W. R. Artis, Lt Gen Sir Mervyn Brogan and Maj Gen R. N. L. Hopkins.   NEIL JAMES
PETER LONDEY

NISBET, ALWYN TOM HAYS (1892-1953), radiologist, was born on 5 February 1892 at Townsville, Queensland, second of five children of Walter Blake Nisbet (1861-1920), medical practitioner, born at Durham, England, and his wife Mildred Janet, née Booth, from Northamptonshire. Walter was a pioneer Queensland radiologist who used X-rays in the South African War; inspired by this, Tom studied medicine at the University of Sydney (M.B., 1915; Ch.M., 1916). Commissioned in the Australian Imperial Force on 1 March 1916, he was 5 ft 8½ ins (174 cm) tall and weighed 136 lbs (61.7 kg). He left for England on 1 May in the *Marathon* as captain, 9th Field Ambulance, Australian Army Medical Corps, and began his lifetime involvement in radiology.

On 13 September that year, at the parish church, Durrington, Wiltshire, Nisbet married Eva Buchanan Lambert. He served with the 3rd and 5th Australian General and the 2nd Australian Auxiliary hospitals, and gained a diploma in sanitary science from the University of Cambridge in 1919. Returning to Australia in June, he was discharged in Brisbane on 4 August. Nisbet was acting medical officer of health at Townsville from 1919, then held appointments as honorary senior radiologist at the Mater Hospital in Brisbane, the Hospital for Sick Children, the Department of Repatriation and Ipswich Hospital. In 1926 he undertook postgraduate work overseas, and from 1928 was director of the Queensland Cancer Clinic.

In 1929 Nisbet moved to Sydney and into private practice with Leila Keatinge, one of the first Australian female radiologists. In addition, he held honorary positions as both diagnostic and therapeutic radiologist at Royal Prince Alfred, Royal North Shore and Sydney hospitals, and the Department of Repatriation. He published two journal articles on X-ray therapy. On 25 September 1929, now divorced, he married Dorothy Irene McGill at the district registrar's office, Paddington.

Both a visionary and an activist, from the 1920s Nisbet was the 'guiding light' in motivating the radiologists to create an Australasian specialist organization. The Australian and New Zealand Association of Radiologists was formed in 1935; he became its first president, holding this position until 1947. During this time he nurtured the infant association, holding meetings in his consulting rooms and in his home. With an engaging personality and hugely energetic, he then threw himself with the same driving enthusiasm into fulfilling his vision of an autonomous Australasian college, outside the umbrella of the English body. This was achieved in 1949. Ill health prevented Nisbet from becoming the first president of the College of Radiologists (Australia and New Zealand), and internal politics denied him the

honour of giving the first Roentgen oration as promised; the annual Nisbet symposium (continuing in 2004 as a lecture) was instituted to commemorate him.

Nisbet had gained his diploma in radiology from the University of Sydney in 1942. In 1950 he was made an honorary fellow of the Faculty of Radiologists (England). A widower, he married Eileen Gladys Stephenson at the district registrar's office, Chatswood, on 27 September 1950. Nisbet died of coronary heart disease on 5 November 1953 at the Mater Misericordiae Hospital, Crows Nest, and was cremated with Anglican rites. His wife, the son and two daughters of his first marriage, and four daughters of his second, survived him.

J. Ryan et al, *Australasian Radiology: A History* (Syd, 1996); A. Tate, *Shadows and Substance* (Syd, 1999); *A'sian Radiology*, 14, no 2, May 1970, p 126, *and* 25th anniversary issue (The Silver Book), 1982, pp 28 & 38; A. T. Nisbet, ms, *and* H. Ham, Memoirs of a Senior Radiologist, ms, 1991 (Royal Aust and NZ College of Radiologists' archives, Syd); service records (NAA).   AUDREY TATE

NIVEN, FRANCIS WILSON (1831-1905), lithographic printer and mariner, was born on 15 July 1831 in Dublin, son of Ninian Niven, a gardener of Scottish extraction, and his wife Agnes, née Craig. Francis was educated at respectable schools in Dublin. At the age of 13 he went to sea and was apprenticed to John Sargent, captain of the *Stebonheath*. Niven's mariner's register ticket, issued in Dublin on 11 November 1847, described him: hair light, eyes blue, complexion fair, height 'growing'. While at sea he illustrated sea stories and made model ships. Following voyages to Victoria in 1851 and 1853, having gained the rank of first mate (1852), he was discharged in London on 15 June 1854. He married Elizabeth Close at St Mary's Church, Edge Hill, West Derby, on 6 July that year, and the couple migrated to Victoria shortly afterwards in search of gold. They were to have eight children.

After prospecting with limited success, Niven decided upon the occupation of printing, specifically lithography, because it suited the artistic disposition he had inherited from his father. He purchased presses for £40 from Alfred Ronalds, a nurseryman at Ballarat who had formerly been a lithographer at Geelong. Niven taught himself to use this equipment with the aid of Ure's *Dictionary of Arts*. His first known commercial work was assisting with illustrations on *Ballarat Punch* in 1857. In the 1860s he trained with the lithographic artist Hermann Deutsch in his Bridge Road office. They produced many prints of Ballarat scenes. Between 1863 and 1865 Deutsch sold him the business. Innovation in lithography was a significant part of the firm's success, and in 1873 Niven imported one of the earliest known commercial steam lithographic presses in Australia. He took an interest in nature printing, which led to the development of the 'Crisp Photo' process, with Henry Crisp's assistance, for colour lithography.

F. W. Niven & Co. became a large provincial printing business at Ballarat, at its peak employing seventy hands and having some £7000 worth of machinery. The firm began a publishing campaign in the 1870s that brought it international recognition for elegantly produced books such as W. B. Withers's [q.v.6] *History of Ballarat* (1887) and *The Cyclopedia of Victoria* (1903-05). Some of this success was attributed to H. W. H. Irvine [q.v.9], who was manager in the 1880s. Niven and his son Henry Ninian (1862-1925), who was later to become manager and partner, patented 'an improved gelatine printing plate' on 7 July 1891. About 1893 they relocated part of their operations to Melbourne, for which a new building was erected in Flinders Street. With this move came a shift in concentration from lithographic work to jobbing and publishing. The Ballarat plant in Lydiard Street became Ballarat Litho & Printing Co. Pty Ltd in 1905.

Remembered within the printing trade as a fair employer concerned for the welfare of the workers, Niven took an interest in public affairs: at Ballarat he was president of the Chamber of Commerce, a member of the art gallery committee, president of the Amateur Photographic Society and a supporter of charitable institutions. Photographs showed him clean-shaven with flourishing sideburns. He died on 3 December 1905 in East Melbourne, survived by his wife, three daughters and two sons. He was buried in the new cemetery, Ballarat; members of the printing trade from both Ballarat and Melbourne attended. Niven's estate was sworn for probate at £4137.

W. B. Kimberly (ed), *Ballarat and Vicinity* (Ballarat, Vic, 1894); *Cyclopedia of Victoria*, 3 (Melb, 1905); S. J. Herrin, *The Development of Printing in Nineteenth-century Ballarat* (Melb, 2000); *Cowans* (Melb), Dec 1905, p 14; *A'sian Typographical J*, Jan 1906, p 13; *Argus* (Melb), 4 Dec 1905, p 5; *Ballarat Star*, 5 Dec 1905, p 2; *Ballarat Courier*, 7 Dec 1905, p 5; *Leader* (Melb), 9 Dec 1905, p 43; F. W. Niven papers (Univ Melb Archives); F. W. Niven & Co. records (SLV). STEPHEN HERRIN

NORTH, FRANCIS ROGER (1894-1978), solicitor and soldier, was born on 13 April 1894 at Fairnie Lawn, near Ipswich, Queensland, second son of Robert Dundas North, a Queensland-born grazier of Northern Irish ancestry, and his wife Blanch Sarah, née Thomson, from Cheshire, England. Frank

attended Bowen House School, Brisbane, from 1904 and The Southport School in 1908-12. At the latter he played in the first football and cricket teams and was captain of tennis; he was to be president of the Old Southportonians' Association in 1922-23. On leaving school he was articled to William Hart, of Flower & Hart, solicitors, Brisbane, and in 1912 joined the 8th Oxley Regiment, Citizen Military Forces, being commissioned in June 1914.

On 3 June 1915 North enlisted as a private in the Australian Imperial Force. He was 5 ft 7 ins (170 cm) tall and weighed 144 lbs (65.3 kg). Commissioned on 24 August, next month he sailed for Egypt in the *Ayrshire* and on 21 November joined the 15th Battalion on Gallipoli. He transferred to the 47th Battalion in February 1916, rose to captain on 1 June and soon left for France. North fought at Gueudecourt and Pozières. On 11 April 1917 he was wounded in the leg during the battle of Bullecourt. After three months in hospital, he returned to Australia, having been twice mentioned in dispatches.

When North recovered, he refused the offer of demobilization or a post in Australia and asked to be sent back to his unit on the Western Front. He arrived on 28 March 1918 and was promoted temporary major twelve days later. From May he served with the 46th Battalion. For his inspirational command of two companies in an attack at Sailly-le-Sec, France, on 8 July he won the Military Cross. At Le Hamel on 8 August he displayed 'conspicuous gallantry and brilliant leadership of his company'. Recommended for the Distinguished Service Order, he was awarded a Bar to his Military Cross. Later in August, again severely wounded, he was admitted to hospital in London. His appointment terminated in Brisbane on 21 October 1919 when he held the honorary rank of major. At this time he also received the Efficiency Medal. As a result of his war injuries, he walked with a slight limp and the hearing in his right ear was affected.

North rejoined Flower & Hart and was admitted as a solicitor on 7 December 1921. He moved to Townsville in May 1923 and joined the firm of Roberts, Leu & Barnett (later Roberts, Leu & North). On 17 April 1929 at St James's Cathedral, Townsville, he married with Anglican rites Margaret May Craddock. North was closely involved in community, local government, church, returned soldiers', military and sports activities. He was chancellor of the Anglican diocese of North Queensland (1927-71) and Carpentaria (1929-71). An alderman of Townsville City Council in 1936-39, he was foundation president (1948-67) of Townsville Citizens Association.

Having served as a legal officer in the C.M.F. in 1920-23, North was given command of the 31st Battalion, the Kennedy Regiment, Townsville, on 1 December 1924. Promoted lieutenant colonel in 1927, he led the regiment, except for four years, until 1940. Taking up full-time duty, from September he commanded the 11th Infantry Brigade with the rank of temporary brigadier. He served briefly in Brisbane as commander of the 7th Infantry Brigade in April-May 1942 and as investigating officer following the 'Battle for Brisbane' riot in November. That year he was appointed C.B. He had returned to Townsville in June to command No. 1 (North Queensland) Lines of Communication (Sub-Area). Ceasing full-time duty on 26 November 1945, he retired from the C.M.F. in 1951 as honorary brigadier but continued as honorary colonel of the Kennedy Regiment until 1959.

In 1953 North was appointed to the Royal Order of Vasa for his twenty-year service as honorary vice-consul for Sweden. Despite his bad leg, he played tennis for Townsville and was an 'A' grade cricketer and foundation president in 1927 of the North Queensland Golf Association. A successful racing greyhound, Brigadier North, was named after him. North retired from his law practice at the end of 1974 and moved to Brisbane. Predeceased by his wife in 1971, he died on 1 November 1978 in Greenslopes Repatriation Hospital and was cremated. Two daughters survived him.

T. P. Chataway, *History of the 15th Battalion* (Brisb, 1948); *The Story of Scartwater* (Brisb, 1956); E. C. Rowland, *The Tropics for Christ* (Townsville, Qld, 1960); T. M. Hawkins, *The Queensland Great Public Schools* (Brisb, 1965); A. Smith, *Roberts Leu and North* (Townsville, Qld, 1986); *Reveille*, 1 Apr 1933, p 36; *Crossed Boomerangs*, 5, 1971, pp 191 & 192; B2455, item North F R, B883, item QX50080 (NAA, Canb); M. Eastgate, A Man Among Men: The Life of Francis Roger North (ms, copy held by author); North family papers (held by author).

MARIANNE EASTGATE

NOTT, LESLIE CECIL JOSHUA (1895-1963), comptroller-general of prisons, was born on 5 April 1895 at Cobbora, near Wellington, New South Wales, twelfth and youngest child of English-born parents James Nott, farmer, and his wife Elizabeth Ann, née Thompson. Educated locally and at Mudgee High School, Leslie entered the Department of Prisons in 1913 as an administrative clerk at Bathurst gaol. Competent and diligent, in 1923 he was promoted chief clerk at the central state penitentiary at Long Bay, Sydney. On 31 March that year at St Barnabas's Church of England, South Bathurst, he married Minnie Gaynor Doswell, a dressmaker.

Transferred to the comptroller-general's office in 1925, Nott was chief clerk there in 1931-36. He was inspector of prisons from 1936, gaining a comprehensive knowledge of prison conditions across the State, and was promoted deputy comptroller in 1941. In 1943 he was responsible for setting up for the prison system's incorrigibles the small, retractable wing, based on a Canadian model, at Grafton Gaol. The wing acquired a brutal and draconian image and was widely known by prisoners as 'the Bloodhouse'; here 'any sense of defiance' was 'well and truly knocked out of them'—a place to which they feared to be transferred. This revealed the harsher side of Nott's penal ideology for prisoners whom he believed to be incapable of rehabilitation. His ideas for redeemable prisoners were more humane and progressive.

Obviously being groomed for higher office, in April 1947 Nott was sent to examine the prison systems of Britain and North America. On his return in July he presented a neatly analytic and well-received report that became a blueprint for the future. He argued that the foundation of an effective prison system was a highly structured 'discipline', in contrast to the outdated Victorian notion of moral reformation. Nott proposed four 'pillars': accurate classification of prisoners according to age and criminal history; provision of trade training in prisons to allow inmates to acquire work skills so that they could earn an honest living on release; expansion and articulation of academic and general education for prisoners; and the introduction of structured leisure and recreational activities to develop and maintain good morale. He emphasized the need to develop policies of supervised after-care, to complete successful rehabilitation into society. While none of these ideas were new, they were systematically organized in Nott's proposed scheme.

On his promotion in 1949 to comptroller-general of prisons, Nott introduced his declared policies, but was hampered by lack of resources. He was particularly impressed by the casework services that he had observed at first hand in American prisons. In 1951 he appointed two parole officers, whose work was primarily limited to inmates of prisons in the various forms Nott had defined and refined: penitentiaries, training centres and afforestation camps. Their prime task was classification on arrival, which was carried out at Long Bay. While Nott recognized the diversity of the prison population, he believed most were 'good prisoners' and a few 'bad' or habitual for whom nothing could be done. He restructured prisons as maximum, medium and minimum, with graduated forms of discipline and differing educational and training opportunities.

Nott was appointed O.B.E. in June 1954. Next year the film division of the Department of the Interior produced a documentary highlighting his achievements in the prison system. Before Nott ceased duty in 1956, a reporter described 'the kindly, almost shy man with the rugged face as he sat ... behind his blue serge-covered desk and stoked his pipe'. He retired on 30 June that year. As comptroller-general, Nott had modernized the State's geographically vast system, with its average prison population of around 5000. The Laurel Hill Afforestation Camp was renamed the Leslie Nott Afforestation Camp in his honour in 1958. After retirement he remained active as a member of the Parole Board. A Freemason, he belonged to Maroubra lodge No. 725, United Grand Lodge of New South Wales. Nott died of myocardial infarction on 23 October 1963 in hospital at Little Bay and was cremated. His wife and their son and daughter survived him.

T. Vinson, *Wilful Obstruction* (Syd, 1982); R. Hay, *Catch Me If You Can* (Syd, 1992); J. Ramsland, *With Just But Relentless Discipline* (Syd, 1996); *Annual Report of the Comptroller-General of Prisons* (NSW), 1947-56; *MJA*, 13 Aug 1955, p 249; *Austn J of Social Work*, 12, no 2, Dec 1959, p 14; *Sun-Herald* (Syd), 8 Apr 1956, p 28.   JOHN RAMSLAND

NOWLAND, EVELYN GRACE IONE (1887-1974), nurse and trade unionist, was born on 10 November 1887 at Penrith, New South Wales, second of four children of Edward Joseph Byrnes Clare Nowland, a carriage-builder from Cape Town, South Africa, and his wife Marie Louisa, née Maguire, from Mudgee. Ione undertook training at the Sydney Hospital, passing her final examinations in September 1915 and registering with the Australasian Trained Nurses' Association in May next year. On 24 May 1917 she enlisted in the Australian Imperial Force. She served in the Australian Army Nursing Service as a staff nurse in military hospitals at Salonika, Greece, from August 1917. In October next year Nowland was evacuated to Cairo with nervous debility and in December was invalided to Australia. She was discharged on 31 May 1919. On 27 March 1920 at St Philip's Church of England, Sydney, she married William Charles O'Toole, a surveyor. The childless marriage ended in divorce, and Nowland resumed her maiden name.

In 1925 the State minister for health appointed her assistant to the registrar of the newly established Nurses' Registration Board, set up under the Nurses Registration Act (1924). With the assistance of a number of inspectors, Nowland was responsible for inspecting training schools. Appalled by the conditions under which nurses lived and worked in many hospitals, in 1931 she agreed to a request from Jessie Street [q.v.16] to help to form a nurses' union in New South Wales.

The move was prompted, in part, by legislation of the Lang [q.v.9] Labor government to make union membership a compulsory condition of employment. Fearful that they could be required to join a conglomerate union, nurses saw the formation of an exclusive union as a preferable alternative. On 27 March 1931 Nowland called the founding meeting and became the first president of the New South Wales Nurses' Association, with Georgina Johnstone [q.v.15 McCready] as secretary.

Nowland demonstrated confidence and courage when she accepted this role while holding a senior government position. One of the first tasks was to obtain an award governing wages and conditions. She guided the union's case through the Industrial Commission. Her profession was by no means united in this endeavour. The A.T.N.A., which had been established in 1899 as a credentialling association, disapproved of legal regulation of nurses' conditions and opposed the N.S.W.N.A.'s case in the Industrial Commission. Nevertheless, the initial award was granted in 1936, and for the first time there was uniformity of pay and conditions for nurses in public and private hospitals in the State. Soon after, Nowland resigned as president and for some years apparently worked as a private nurse in Sydney's northern suburbs.

Described as 'a trim figure', 5 ft 5¾ in (167 cm) tall with brown eyes and in her youth short brown hair, she was outspoken and always definite about her beliefs. Nowland died on 4 November 1974 in a convalescent home at Roseville and was cremated. The trade union she had helped to establish was still flourishing in 2005.

M. Dickenson, *An Unsentimental Union* (Syd, 1993); H. Radi (ed), *Jessie Street* (Syd, 1990); *A'sian Nurses' J*, Apr 1920, p 124; file no TU696 (NSW Industrial Registry, Syd); Ione Nowland service record (NAA).   MARY DICKENSON

NUNAN (NOONAN), JOSEPH DENIS (1842-1885), patriot, convict and architect, was born in February 1842 at Rathcormack, County Cork, Ireland, one of at least three sons of Denis Noonan, carpenter, and his wife Joanne, née Murphy. Trained by their father in his trade, on completion of their apprenticeships Joseph and his brother Frank established their own firm and became successful contractors, with buildings in Cork and County Kerry.

In 1864 Joseph joined the Irish Republican Brotherhood, better known as the Fenian

Brotherhood. In February 1867 he was identified as being with two other Fenians, one of whom had shot and wounded a constable. Noonan fled to England, where he was arrested on 30 April. During the return journey he escaped from the train but was recaptured and taken to Ireland. He was tried on a charge under the Treason-Felony Act at the Kerry Summer Assizes, Tralee, on 25 July. Mercy was recommended, and on 8 August Noonan was sentenced to seven years penal servitude.

One of some sixty-two Fenians and more than two hundred other convicts transported to Western Australia in the *Hougoumont*, he helped to organize musical and dramatic entertainments during the voyage and contributed to a newspaper, 'The Wild Goose'. He wrote a humorous account of his escape, recapture and trial, entitled 'A Leap for Liberty', for the first issue. Arriving on 10 January 1868, the prisoners were taken to the convict establishment at Fremantle. 'Joseph Noonan 9837' was described as 5 ft 8 ins (173 cm) tall, with brown hair, blue eyes and long face, fresh complexion and healthy appearance. Distinguishing marks were noted as a cut on the ball of his thumb, two teeth protruding from his palate and a boil on his left thigh.

Pardoned (as Joseph Nunan) in May 1869 as a result of the Gladstone government's new conciliatory approach to Ireland, he chose to remain in Western Australia and undertook to further his knowledge of architecture. That year he and fellow Fenian and builder Hugh Brophy, from Dublin, formed a highly successful partnership as general contractors, carpenters and joiners. They won a number of important contracts for the Catholic Church, the government and private enterprise, hiring ticket-of-leave men to undertake stone cutting, carpentry and labouring. Buildings included Walter Padbury's [q.v.5] store and residence at Guildford and the Greenough Flats police station. Reputedly Nunan was also involved in planning Perth Town Hall. In October 1871 the firm successfully completed the convent for the Sisters of Mercy in Perth. St Patrick's Church in York, 'a gem of pure Gothic architecture', has been claimed as the finest example of Nunan's work. All the buildings named still survived in 2005. Brophy left the partnership and went to Melbourne in 1872.

On 21 June 1871 at St Mary's Catholic Cathedral, Perth, Nunan had married Anne Marie Farrelly, from a respected family. He continued to be involved with Fenian affairs, was one of the nominated trustees of the relief fund set up to assist unreleased Fenians, and attracted unjustified criticism for allegedly failing to advance funds to assist escaping prisoners. Contracting tuberculosis, Nunan wished to return to Ireland but died on 18 May 1885 at his home in Howick Street, Perth, and was buried in East Perth cemetery with Catholic rites.

R. Erickson (ed), *The Brand on His Coat* (Perth, 1983); Austn Irish Heritage Assn of WA, *J*, 5, no 4, Summer, 1997, p 44; *Studies in WA History*, 20, 2000, p 59; *WA Catholic Record*, 21 May 1885, p 5; *Times* (Lond), 30 July 1867, p 11; 31 July 1867, p 10, 13 Aug 1867, p 9; convict records, AN358, Acc 1156 (SRWA); Wild Goose copies, Acc 1675A (SRWA) and MSS 1542 (ML).
                                          ROBYN TAYLOR

NUTTALL, JAMES CHARLES (1872-1934), artist and journalist, was born on 6 September 1872, at Fitzroy, Melbourne, eldest child and only son of English-born parents James Charles Nuttall, house-painter and decorator, and his wife Caroline, née Dean. Charles was encouraged by his parents to pursue a career in art and, probably after a period with the family firm, enrolled at the National Gallery school of design in 1895.

Under the drawing master Frederick McCubbin [q.v.10], Nuttall's draughtsmanship developed into a confident, brisk, linear style. Constrained by colour blindness, however, he chose a career as an illustrator, establishing himself at studios in Collins Street where he produced drawings, cartoons, and magazine and book illustrations. His place in the male, Bohemian art community was captured in Percy Lindsay's [q.v.10] 'Smoke Night, Victorian Artists Society' (c.1896), which comprised medallion portraits of Nuttall and others including John Mather, Walter Withers [qq.v.10,12] and McCubbin. Nuttall belonged to the Melbourne Savage Club and was secretary of the Black and White Club (1900) before its affiliation with the Victorian Artists Society. He considered himself and his colleagues 'professional humorists', but he also produced postcards, drawings and etchings in the portrait, landscape and figurative genres.

Nuttall received a major commission in 1901 from a Melbourne business syndicate, the Historical Picture Association. His large monochromatic, sepia painting, 'The First Federal Parliament of Australia, May 1901', contained 343 recognizable portraits of the dignitaries present at the historic opening ceremony. The Paris engraving firm *Goupil et Cie* reproduced this 'fine and faithful impression' as a large photogravure edition. Well marketed —'No Australian Home will be complete without a Copy'—the print hung in homes, lobbies and State schools throughout the country, inspiring patriotism and reminding Australians of the birth of their nation. The importance of Nuttall's picture declined as the century progressed and was further eclipsed when Queen Elizabeth II returned Tom Roberts's [q.v.11] epic painting of the same subject to Australia in 1960.

Slightly built and amiable, with a keen sense of humour and adventure, Nuttall was politically conservative, Anglican and strongly nationalist. During four years in the United States of America from 1905, he was successful as a staff artist on the *New York Herald* and contributed to *Life, Scribner's Magazine*, the *Century, Harper's Bazaar* and children's serial journals. His pictorial journalism was semi-autobiographical, and after his return to Australia in 1910 he made use of anecdotes and sketches from his travels through Europe, North Africa and Egypt in various publications. These included Melbourne *Punch, Table Talk*, the Sydney *Bulletin, New Idea*, the boys' weekly paper *Pals*, the British *Daily Graphic*, and such books as *Representative Australians* (1902), school editions of R. M. Ballantyne's *Coral Island* (1910-22) and *Melba's Gift Book of Australian Art and Literature* (1915). On 4 December 1918 at St John's Church of England, Toorak, he married Leila Mary Blackbourn. They had no children.

In the late 1920s and 1930s Nuttall worked for the Melbourne radio-station 3LO, and his programmes 'World at Large' and 'Thought for the Day' covered many contemporary issues, including employment during the Depression. Nuttall died of a cerebral haemorrhage on 28 November 1934 at his home at South Yarra, and was buried in Boroondara general cemetery, Kew, in his wife's family grave. She survived him. His art is represented in State, national and private collections, and his painting of the first Federal parliament is displayed in the Royal Exhibition Building, Melbourne.

W. Moore, *Studio Sketches* (Melb, 1906); D. M. Dow, *Melbourne Savages* (Melb, 1947); U. Prunster, *The Legendary Lindsays* (Syd, 1995); D. Dunstan, *Victorian Icon* (Melb, 1996); A. Colquhoun (ed), *The Year Book of Victorian Art 1922-3*; *New Idea*, 6 Jan 1911, p 1; *Pals*, 26 Mar 1921, p 409; *Age* (Melb), 22 June 1903, p 4, 20 Dec 1986, 'Sat Extra' p 2; *Argus* (Melb), 29 Nov 1934, p 10; information from Mrs A. Traill Nash, Balwyn, Melb.   SHERIDAN PALMER

NUYTS, PIETER (1598-1655), company official and mariner, was born in 1598 at Middelburg, the Netherlands, son of Laurens Nuyts (Nuijts), textile merchant, and his wife Elisabeth. Educated at the University of Leiden from 1613, Pieter became well versed in the classics, the Bible and law. He returned to Middelburg and his father's business, married Cornelia Jacot on 26 April 1620 and had two sons. Nuyts invested heavily in land, hoping for profits and status and to see the

world. He also secured a position with the Verenigde Oost Indische Compagnie (Dutch East India Co.), where his education and practical experience gained him rapid promotion. He decided to move to Batavia, Netherlands East Indies (Indonesia), the company's main centre.

Leaving his pregnant wife and his son Pieter to follow later, Nuyts and his son Laurens left Vlissingen in the *Gulden Seepaert* (Golden Seahorse), captained by Francois Thijssen, on 22 May 1626. After rounding the Cape of Good Hope, they sighted the Australian coast near Cape Leeuwin (Western Australia) on 26 January 1627. In 1622 Jan Pieterszoon Coen, governor-general of the East Indies, had ordered a thorough investigation of the South Land. Sailing east along the southern coast for more than 800 nautical miles (1482 km), Thijssen mapped and named the region 't Land van Pieter Nuyts, after the highest ranking officer on board, and the islands of St Francis and St Pieter (Peter). This voyage resulted in the first definite chart of the southern coast (from what was to be Albany to Ceduna) and the first knowledge of what became South Australia. Later French and English explorers praised the accuracy of the Dutch map.

Turning back and then heading north, on 10 April 1627 Nuyts reached Batavia, where the V.O.C. directors were so impressed by his connexions that on 30 April he was appointed ambassador to Japan. He left with Laurens on 12 May, instructed to restore and improve relations between the V.O.C. and Japan, but failed and settled at Formosa (Taiwan), where on 28 June he became governor. His wife and son Pieter having died after arriving in Batavia, Nuyts married a Formosan and had numerous affairs (requiring an interpreter under his bed to translate amorous conversation). Arrogant, haughty and dedicated to his own financial interests, he was recalled, leaving his son Laurens imprisoned in Japan, where he died on 29 December 1630. Having reached Batavia on 11 October 1629, Pieter Nuyts was heavily fined and, after several inquiries, suspended and arrested on 9 May 1630.

Released on 5 July 1636, Nuyts left for the Netherlands in December 1637. There he married Anna van Driel on 1 January 1640 but she died nine months later while giving birth to a son. A landowner near the city of Hulst, Nuyts became a member of its council. He was thrice mayor of Hulster Ambacht and twice of Hulst. On 26 April 1649 he married Agnes Granier. He died on 11 December 1655, survived by his wife and by the son, also named Pieter, of his previous marriage. After the funeral Nuyts was found to have collected more taxes than was shown in the council's books. His son repaid them.

In 1717 Jean Pierre Purry, who had been working for the V.O.C., proposed the establishment of a Dutch colony in Nuytsland, but it did not eventuate. Jonathan Swift may have chosen the islands of St Francis and St Peter as models for Lilliput and Blefescu in *Gulliver's Travels* (1726). In 1802 Matthew Flinders [q.v.1] named Nuyts's Reef, Cape Nuyts and Nuyts Archipelago. Later still, the Western Australian Christmas Tree was named *Nuytsia floribunda*.

P. A. Leupe, *Stukken Betrekkelijk Pieter Nuyts, Gouverneur van Taqueran 1631-1634* (Holland, 1853); C. Fenner, *The First Discoverers of South Australia* (Adel, 1926?); W. P. Coolhaas, *Jan Pietersz Coen*, 7 (Holland, 1953); J. Fletcher, *Pieter Nuyts and his 'Album Amicorum'* (Melb, 1974); *Bijdragen en Mededelingen van het Historisch Genootschap*, vol 66, 1955, p 27; *Zeews Tijdschrift*, no 6, 1993, p 234, no 3, 2000, p 15.   NIC KLAASSEN

NYHAN, CARMEL (1893-1962), trade union organizer, was born on 8 July 1893 at Kellys Creek, Grenfell, New South Wales, fourth of at least five children of Irish-born James Nyhan, farmer, and his wife Ellen Mary, née Clifford, from Victoria. The family moved to Western Australia during Carmel's childhood. She was employed as a shop assistant at Boan [q.v.7] Ltd's store in Perth before the Nyhans went to Sydney in the 1920s. Carmel worked as a shop assistant at Grace [q.v.9] Bros Ltd, Broadway, then joined the staff of the Shop Assistants' and Warehouse Employees' Federation of Australia (the 'shoppies') as an office assistant. She was later promoted to organizer of women, becoming one of the first women to be thus employed by an Australian trade union, for which she worked for forty-one years. A staunch advocate of reforms for female employees, she fought for improved ventilation and lighting and roomy lunchrooms as well as for earlier closing of shops. She was elected employees' representative on the Confectioners' Wages Board in 1926.

Described as 'a fine platform speaker', Nyhan was the first woman to be president of the organizing committee of the six-hour day demonstration (1933). From October 1937 to January 1939 she ran the 'Women's Page' in the *Shop Assistant*, the quarterly journal of the union. The page focused on female members' engagements and weddings and department store social functions, but also addressed questions such as long shopping hours, low wages and poor employment conditions. The secretary Ernie O'Dea [q.v.15] tightly managed the shop assistants' union, however, and individual organizers were rarely mentioned by name in publicity.

A member of the North Randwick branch of the Australian Labor Party, Nyhan was a long-serving delegate of her union to the A.L.P. State Conference and the Labor Council of New South Wales and an executive officer of the Trades Hall Association and the Labor Day Committee for thirty-five years. In addition, she was an employee representative on the New South Wales Retail Industry Conciliation Committee, which considered award applications under the Industrial Arbitration Act of 1901. She was a member of the Council of Action for Equal Pay, founded in 1937 by Muriel Heagney [q.v.9] and others under the auspices of the State branch of the Federated Clerks' Union. The report of the C.A.E.P.'s first annual general meeting in the *Shop Assistant* acknowledged the political climate that made it necessary for the shop assistants' union to participate in the C.A.E.P. but demonstrated the lack of real commitment to any broad-based, progressive political action for equal pay for women.

Nyhan lived for many years at Randwick and never married. She gave her hobbies as swimming and travel, but was devoted to her work. In the course of her duties as an organizer, she was struck by a motor vehicle when crossing the Pacific Highway at Turramurra on 14 June 1962. She died that day in hospital at Hornsby from the injuries, and was buried with Catholic rites in Randwick cemetery. A plaque in the foyer of the Trades Hall, Sydney, commemorated her.

Labor Daily Year Book, 1933, p 173; *Aust Women's Weekly*, 7 Oct 1933, p 3; *Shop Assistant*, Oct 1938, p 10, Aug 1962, p 4; *Labor Daily*, 13 Jan 1927, p 7; *SMH*, 10 Mar 1933, p 3, 2 Oct 1933, p 11, 23 Apr 1956, p 3; information from Mr. J. Johnson, Maroubra, Syd.   JANE TIMBRELL

O

O'MALLEY WOOD, WILLIAM HENRY; *see* WOOD

O'NEILL, EUGENE PATRICK (1874-1953), sanitary-carter and trade unionist, was born on 19 June 1874 at Wentworth, New South Wales, seventh of nine children of Irish-born parents James Francis O'Neill, brickmaker and rural contractor, and his wife Catherine, née Reilly, who was illiterate. Following Catholic schooling at Wentworth, Paddy went dam sinking and bullock driving with his father, who died a year after the family moved to Broken Hill in 1894. Paddy worked in shearing sheds, then joined his brothers as a mineworker on the Broken Hill line of lode. On 28 September 1899 at All Saints' Catholic Church, South Broken Hill, he married Mary Anne Gearon, from South Australia. They had six children.

Joining the Amalgamated Miners' Association, O'Neill represented the union on the local section of the Australian Labor Federation and on the Barrier Labor Federation. In 1908 he became secretary of the South Broken Hill branch of the A.M.A. His outlook was informed by Catholic social conservatism and an aversion to the militancy that characterized the 1909 Broken Hill lockout, while his experience gave him a lifelong preference for direct bargaining over arbitration and transformed him into an astute union leader and formidable negotiator.

In April 1913 O'Neill became a sanitary-cart driver with the Broken Hill Municipal Council. In 1922 he helped to form a local branch of the Municipal Employees' Union and was its president, then secretary from 1924. He also represented the M.E.U. on both the craft-union-dominated Broken Hill Trades and Labor Council and the Barrier District Assembly of the Australian Labor Party.

O'Neill's most decisive contribution to Broken Hill unionism, however, was his involvement in the formation of a new, all-inclusive and powerful local peak union body. Within weeks of his election as president of the local trades and labour council in January 1923, that body was transformed into the Barrier Industrial and Political Council, with O'Neill as its leader. In October, after years of sectional tension between the A.M.A. and the local craft unions, the miners, who in 1921 had restyled their union as the Workers' Industrial Union of Australia, voted to affiliate with the new body, which in November 1924, at O'Neill's urging, assumed its enduring title, the Barrier Industrial Council.

Under O'Neill's leadership, the B.I.C. oversaw the town's near-complete withdrawal from the State and Federal arbitration systems and the signing in 1925 of the first of what would become a stable regime of triennial collective agreements for local mine workers. Between 1925 and 1931 O'Neill also oversaw a successful drive to unionize local town employees, but the campaign was informed by a patriarchal moral economy that systematically excluded married women from paid employment in the town sector. O'Neill was also a staunch localist, and when the W.I.U.A. closed its books to outsiders in the early 1930s, he lent the initiative the B.I.C.'s full support. The 1935 mines agreement, which O'Neill finalized jointly with the new Mining Managers' Association president Andrew Fairweather [q.v.14], provided the foundations of long-term material prosperity for Broken Hill mine workers. O'Neill continued to work as a sanitary-cart driver. His style as union leader was blunt but effective, with impromptu negotiations frequently conducted from the seat of his dunny cart.

O'Neill survived a series of internal challenges, most notably from communist-inspired job committees. While illness caused his occasional absence from the industrial scene from 1943, it was not until 1949, two years after his wife's death, that he relinquished the B.I.C. presidency. Next year he retired from paid employment with the Broken Hill Municipal Council.

Throughout his working life, O'Neill was active in local Catholic, Labor Party and sporting circles. Big and powerful, he had been in demand as an 'anchor man' for tug-of-war teams in his youth. He later helped to introduce greyhound racing to the area. Lauded in his retirement as the 'uncrowned king of Broken Hill', O'Neill died on 24 May 1953 in hospital at Broken Hill, and was buried in the local cemetery following a requiem Mass in Sacred Heart Cathedral. Four daughters and one son survived him.

Conveyor, May 1952, p 4, June 1952, p 22; *J of Industrial Relations*, 38, no 3, Sept 1996, p 377; *Labour History*, no 78, May 2000, p 116, no 80, 2001, p 41; *Labour & Industry*, 11, no 1, Aug 2000, p 69; *Economic and Labour Relations Review*, 12, no 1, June 2001, p 61; *Barrier Daily Truth*, 17 Dec 1926, p 5, 7 Sept 1933, p 5; 25 May 1953, p 1; B. Maughan, Review of Industrial Negotiations, 1920-1946 (ts, 1947, Charles Rasp Memorial Library, Broken Hill, NSW); Broken Hill Trades and Labour Council,

Minutes, 1922-23, Barrier Industrial and Political Council, Minutes 1923-24, Barrier Industrial Council, Minutes, 1924-49 (held Trades Hall, Broken Hill).

JOHN SHIELDS
BRADON ELLEM

ORR, ELIZABETH (1860-1945), hospital and army matron, was born on 8 September 1860 in the Hamilton district, Tasmania, youngest of at least seven children of Irish-born assisted migrants Robert Orr, farmer, and his wife Jane, née McGuffin. Lizzie's parents had probably arrived from Scotland in 1855. After attending school in Hobart, she returned home, spending all available time with her horses and becoming an excellent rider. In 1881 she began nursing training at (Royal) Hobart General Hospital. On qualifying she entered a lifetime in the profession she regarded as a gift and a vocation. Her working life began as a country nurse visiting patients on horseback. In 1891-99 she was a sister at Hobart hospital.

As Tasmania did not send nurses to the South African War, those wishing to serve proceeded at their own discretion and expense. Reaching South Africa in January 1900, Orr joined Queen Alexandra's Imperial Military Nursing Service Reserve. She served in military hospitals until 1902. On 19 June 1903, from Johannesburg, she joined the Australasian Trained Nurses' Association and later became a life member. Continuing to nurse privately in South Africa, she was matron of hospitals in the civil service until April 1913, then spent a year in England. Back in Australia she opened a private hospital at Maitland, New South Wales.

On the outbreak of World War I Orr returned to England in August 1914 and, putting her age down thirteen years, rejoined the Q.A.I.M.N.S.R. on 10 October. She was posted to the 21st British General Hospital in Egypt. For eighteen months she was matron of transports in the Mediterranean, Gallipoli and Salonika areas, including duties in troop-ships and hospital ships. She later served in hospital ships in the Persian Gulf. In April 1916 she attended the first Anzac service in Cairo. Three months later she was present at the funeral of Lord Kitchener whom she knew personally, admired greatly and spoke of often in later life. As a matron with the 2500-bed 60th British General Hospital at De-el-Belah, in tents on sand, Orr served through the Palestine campaign. With deteriorating health due to malaria, she was invalided to England in March 1919, 'still weak' and looking 'older than her reputed age'. In January she had been awarded the Royal Red Cross. She was also twice mentioned in dispatches.

After recuperation Orr returned to duty at Royal Herbert Military Hospital, Woolwich. Her appointment having ended on 9 January 1920, she embarked from Liverpool for Tasmania, where she became matron of Vaucluse Infectious Diseases Hospital. Six feet (183 cm) tall, self-possessed and dignified, she was a stern disciplinarian. On retiring in 1931 she took an extended vacation in England before entering Lasswade Rest Home, Hobart.

An inaugural member of the Nurses' Club, Hobart, from 1922, Orr was also president, later patroness, of the Returned Army Sisters' Association. She never missed an Anzac Day service, remarking that she had 'seven medals and a good chest to put them on'. Miss Orr died on 30 April 1945 in Lasswade home and was cremated with Anglican rites following a funeral service at St David's Cathedral, attended by dignitaries and representatives of service and nurse organizations; her ashes were scattered in Bass Strait. Her medals were subsequently displayed in the Graduate Nurses Museum within the Royal Hobart Hospital.

V. Veale, *Women to Remember* (Launc, Tas, 1981); J. Bassett, *Guns and Brooches* (Melb, 1992), *A'sian Nurses' J*, 15 Jan 1917, p 10; *Mercury* (Hob), 2 May 1945, p 14, 3 May 1945, p 7, 26 July 1997, p 76; A'sian Trained Nurses' Assn, Register, 1904, 1914, 1917 (ML); information from Mr J. Jones, Richmond, Tas; service file WO 399/6371 (PRO, Lond).

ROSEMARY MACINTYRE

O'SHEA PETERSEN; *see* PETERSEN

P

PACKHAM, CHARLES HENRY (1842-1909), orchardist and pear breeder, was born on 14 September 1842 at Toongabbie, New South Wales, second of nine children of English-born parents Henry Packham, milkman, and his second wife Ann, née Unicombe, the widow of William Eggins. In 1848 the family moved to Larras Lake, near Molong, leased 15 acres (6 ha), and grew wheat. Ten years later Henry selected 240 acres (97 ha) known as Quickbourne, nearer to Molong.

Charles married Mary Robards with Wesleyan forms on 23 November 1863 in the bride's home near Orange. The couple, who were to have nine children, first lived in a wattle and daub house, Little Quickbourne. Charles helped his father with a carrying business (from Forbes to Sydney and back) and worked as a shepherd on a neighbouring property, Garra. In 1874 he purchased a part of it, known as Cherry Hill. He was a petitioner for the establishment of a school at Garra in 1877. Next year he selected an additional two blocks, totalling 106 acres (43 ha), which he named Clifton, where he grazed sheep. Later he added an adjacent 55 acres (22 ha). A brick house was built on Clifton, where he had a general farm and an orchard. Here he started his interest in crossbreeding fruit to create a pear of a greater commercial value. He kept an apiary and used bees for pollination. In 1889 Packham won a prize for pears at the Sydney Royal Show; he later exhibited his skill as an orchardist with a pear tree about three feet (90 cm) high, bearing fruit, a triumph of grafting.

Packham achieved his great success in 1896 with the crossing of the Uvedale St Germain (Bell) with a Williams. Samples were sent to the Department of Agriculture, which reported favourably, and many orders were taken. W. J. Allen, the department's expert, named the fruit Packham's Triumph, claiming it to be the finest he had tasted. Light green in colour, well shaped with a short neck and a clear skin, the fruit stored well after picking in March, making it a healthy winter treat and suitable for trans-seasonal export. Soon Packham's Late was developed, with some small success. By 1909 there were 20 000 seedlings at Garra. Many requests came for trees, and these were propagated and distributed to government experiment farms as far away as Tasmania, and later marketed to nurserymen.

Active in the Methodist church, Garra, Packham was 'quiet and unassuming' and a lifetime teetotaller, wearing the temperance society's blue ribbon on his jacket to indicate this. He died of acute dysentery on 20 March 1909 at his home and was buried in the Methodist cemetery, Garra. His wife, four sons and four daughters survived him. The food authority Stephanie Alexander wrote in 1996 that the Packham's Triumph was 'still one of the principal cultivated pears grown in Australia and the best-selling variety in the world'. Packham's original Triumph tree was destroyed about 1915, and later all the seedlings were grubbed out because of the prevalence of pests. In 2004 there was no longer an orchard at Clifton, only some decorative fruit trees, but members of the Packham family still farmed near Molong.

B. L. Higginson, *The Packham Family* (1988); S. Alexander, *The Cook's Companion* (Melb, 1996); information from the Packham family, Molong, NSW.

ROSSLYN FINN

PANGIERAN; *see* CUPER, MARY ELLEN

PARKER, KATHARINE (1886-1971), pianist and composer, was born on 28 March 1886 at Parknook, Cressy, Tasmania, and registered as Catherine, third of seven children of Erskine James Rainy Parker, sheep farmer, and his wife Florence Agnes, née Leary. Inheriting her mother's musical talent, Kitty studied in Melbourne at the University Conservatorium from 1904, graduating with a diploma of music in 1906. Next year she won a gold medal, for 'piano solo over 20', at the Australian Exhibition of Women's Work in Melbourne. After a farewell concert at Launceston, Tasmania, early in 1909 she went to London, to further her career and study with Percy Grainger [q.v.9]. Later that year, with fellow Tasmanians, Parker took part in a musical evening in honour of the newly appointed governor of Tasmania Sir Harry Barron [q.v.7].

Grainger described Parker as the most gifted piano pupil he ever had. 'She did everything by nature (or out of the good teaching she had at the Melbourne University Conservatorium) and I felt a fool trying to teach her.' Through Grainger, she met the English tenor Hubert Mortimer Eisdell, whom she married on 16 June 1910 at St Mark's Church, Hamilton Terrace, London. They had one son Michael (1912-1986). In 1911 she made her London concert début as a soloist. Her first compositions were published in 1913, but Hubert's career overshadowed hers. In 1920 the couple made a concert tour of Australia, their talents combining to be 'one in perfect harmony with the other'. At their final Australian concert at Launceston, Eisdell sang two of his wife's compositions.

Back in England, by 1930 the two had separated, and two years later Hubert left alone for Canada where he remarried. Kitty remained in England. Her musical activities were affected by her personal misfortunes, and she did not resume composing. In 1930, however, she had sent to Grainger *Four Musical Sketches*, which included the piece for which she is best known, *Down Longford Way*, written in 1928, which Grainger orchestrated in 1935. Her music was published under the name Katharine Parker, some pieces by Boosey & Hawkes, others by Augener. Resuming her career as an accompanist, she toured Las Palmas and Tenerife in 1935 and Berlin in 1936 and 1937.

In London in World War II Kitty Eisdell drove an ambulance. Losing touch with the musical world, she experienced poor health and suffered depression. Her son had gone to Australia in 1935. After the war, during which he served in the Australian Imperial Force and was wounded, he resumed working as an announcer with the Australian Broadcasting Commission in Sydney.

Advised to find a dry climate to counter the effects of tuberculosis, Kitty returned to Australia in January 1947. The next two years were spent in various locations—with her son in Sydney, in Melbourne, in Tasmania, where she broadcast for the A.B.C., and in Sydney again. In 1950 she accepted a position with a radio station at Launceston and also began taking pupils there and in surrounding districts. Although she continued to give lessons at Launceston, ill health ended her teaching elsewhere and she did scarcely any composing.

A tiny person, she had a lively personality and a zest for life. From 1960 she lived with her sister Reike, also a musician, at Elizabeth Bay, Sydney. 'Katherine Erskine Eisdell' died on 28 March 1971 in the Sacred Heart Hospice, Darlinghurst, and was cremated with Catholic rites. Her son survived her. A manuscript memoir by Kitty Eisdell is held by the Grainger Museum, University of Melbourne.

K. S. Inglis, *This is the ABC* (Syd, 1983); E. Dorum, *Percy Grainger* (Melb, 1986); *Weekly Courier* (Launc), 24 Dec 1908, p 28, 26 Aug 1909, 22 June 1911, p 28, 11 Dec 1913, p 2, 15 July 1920, pp 27 & 29, 28 Oct 1920, pp 27 & 37; information from Ian Munro, Toronto, NSW, and Peter Bridley, Lindisfarne, Tas.   MARGARET GLOVER

PARNELL, MELINA FLORENCE (1870-1944), teacher and school proprietor, was born on 2 July 1870 at Bow, London, one of six children of Frederick Charles Parnell, a watchmaker, and his wife Melina Sarah, née Blake. Young Melina was raised in London and at Luton, Bedfordshire, where her grandfather was Baptist parson. Although she wished to attend university, her father wanted 'no blue stockings' in the family, nor for his daughters to engage in any worldly occupation. Her uncle, an organist at the City Temple, paid for music lessons at the Guildhall School of Music, where she won many prizes. A talented painter and musician, with a fine singing voice, she was a qualified music teacher, with credentials from the University of Cambridge and the College of Preceptors.

About 1887 the family migrated to Victoria for the health of one of the children. In the 1890s depression Melina worked by making buttonholes on blouses and taught in Victoria and at Burradoo Park, near Bowral, New South Wales; there she later became headmistress. When the owner of the school died, Parnell returned to England, where she taught and worked as a governess. The rest of the family went to Western Australia. At her mother's request, about 1897 she took a position at Amy Best's [q.v.3] Central High School for Girls in Perth. In 1904 Parnell bought the Claremont Ladies' College and Kindergarten and renamed it the Girls' High School.

Parnell's experience of the changes in girls' education in England benefited girls' education in Western Australia. She understood the demand for a more rigorous approach but also the need for her 'First Class Establishment' to appeal to middle-class parents who did not necessarily intend their daughters to work after leaving school but required them to be given an education suited to their class. She disapproved of the appearance of class in the school and disliked uniforms and examinations. After a pupil wore a white fox fur to church she agreed to the introduction of uniforms. Examinations were also introduced because they enhanced the school's reputation.

With the addition of boarding facilities in 1906 and a permanent home on the river at Claremont, Parnell's school prospered, partly because it catered for girls from all over the State, from kindergarten through to university entrance. From 1908 it was recognized as a private school at which Education Department secondary scholarships were tenable. She was the only representative of a private school for girls to sit on the examination board of the University of Western Australia when it was established in 1913, and was also a foundation member of the Girls' Secondary School's Association in 1915. Former G.H.S. and other private school pupils were employed as teachers, and her past students also taught in other schools or established their own. In 1926 Parnell retired; she sold the school to the Church of England, and by 1930 it had become St Hilda's Church of England Girls' School.

Devoted to her family and siblings, she cared for two nieces after their mother died when they were aged 3 and 6 respectively. Having retired to her home at West Leederville, in 1933 she accompanied her nieces to England, where she remained for some years before returning to Perth. Miss Parnell died on 30 August 1944 at West Leederville and was buried in the Anglican section of Karrakatta cemetery.

WA Church News, May 1905; *Morning Herald*, (Perth), 21 Dec 1908, p 3; *West Australian*, 15 Dec 1911, p 8; St Hilda's Anglican Girls' School archives, Perth; family information.   NOREEN RIORDAN

PARRY, WILLIAM HENRY (1855-1936), wheelwright, HENRY GRIFFITH (1886-1971), nurseryman, orchardist and quarry manager, and PERCY JOSEPH (1901-1986), nurseryman, were father and sons. William was born on 17 March 1855 at Lower Mangrove, near Gosford, New South Wales, one of ten children of Griffith William Parry, farmer and carpenter, and his wife Sarah Jane, née Watkins. Describing himself as a carpenter, William married Frances Alice Miller at St Luke's Church of England, Burwood, Sydney, on 8 April 1885. They had twelve children. Although he moved around the colony to work as an engine driver, by 1890 William had returned to Gosford and established a wheelwright's shop in Erina Street. Something of an entrepreneur, he had previously built an assembly hall with 'a marvellous floor for dancing' near the corner of Mann and Erina streets. The first Gosford Wildflower Show was held there in September 1885, with ferns, staghorns, palms, rock lilies, waratahs and native roses wrenched from the soil with their roots or cut from the bush to produce 'the finest display of wildflowers and ferns ever exhibited in the colony'.

With Parry family encouragement, the Gosford wildflower show became an institution. In 1890 its main attractions were two bangalow palms, one with a (dead) diamond python curled round its trunk, the other graced by a (live) native bear (koala) with a bow of red ribbon round its neck. Following the Parrys' example, similar shows became popular as fund raisers in and around Sydney in the late nineteenth century, but they did considerable damage in the bush, especially near Gosford because so much of the material came from there, leading to the New South Wales Wild Flowers and Native Plants Act of 1927, which banned the indiscriminate picking and sale of wildflowers. William began

acquiring citrus orchards, and was described as a farmer when he died on 1 January 1936 at Erina Street. He was buried in Bradys Gully cemetery, Gosford. Five sons and four daughters survived him.

Henry, the eldest son, was born on 22 January 1886 at Ulmarra on the Clarence River but grew up at Gosford. There he involved himself in the rising citrus industry and established a wholesale and retail fruit shop, with refreshment rooms attached, at the corner of Mann and Erina streets, near his father's wheelwright shop. His sisters Lena, Ethel and Bella were involved as staff members. With his brother Charles he also established a nursery behind the fruit shop providing, among other things, citrus trees, especially oranges, for the expanding local industry. By 1905 Henry had selected land at Kariong, an area noted for its wildflowers, to secure supplies from the existing Christmas bush for the Sydney cut flower market. On 2 June 1928 at Christ Church, Gosford, Henry married 25-year-old Amy Elizabeth, daughter of George Margin, a cordial manufacturer.

Henry became general manager of Gosford Quarries in 1926, and installed the latest machinery. Building and monumental stone was quarried at sites in and around Gosford, mainly for shipment to Sydney. The company came to employ about 100 men. He continued as managing director after his brother-in-law A. K. Margin succeeded him as manager in 1966. Henry was prominent in local branches of such organizations as the St John Ambulance Association, the Girl Guides Association and in the orchid society and the garden club. He died on 12 December 1971 in the district hospital, Gosford, and was buried in the Anglican cemetery, Point Clare. His wife and their daughter survived him. Henry Parry Drive, which by the 1990s curled through new Gosford suburbs, was formerly an access road to a quarry site closed in 1975.

William's eighth child, Percy, had been born on 12 October 1901 at Gosford. Having worked before and after school with his brother Henry in the nursery at Gosford and on the land at Kariong, he became interested in breeding native plants and shrubs. In 1925 he bought the Kariong land, now known as Floralands, from Henry and began a programme to preserve the native flora by propagation and cultivation. He claimed a 95 per cent success rate with the waratah seeds he collected and planted, and he began to grow waratahs, Christmas bush with consistent colour, Christmas bells, eriostemon and other native species that would flower reliably and sustainably for commercial purposes. On 30 October 1929 at Christ Church, Gosford, he married Olive Kari Olsen, a public school teacher. They had seven children, and Olive became a partner in his work at Floralands.

In 1942-44 Percy served part time in the Volunteer Defence Corps.

As a result of pressure from conservation groups, in the 1940s it was proposed to ban the picking and selling of all wildflowers. Percy wrote to J. J. Cahill [q.v.13], the responsible minister, and after an examination of the work at Floralands in 1945 a system of licensing the sale of native flowers as recommended by Parry was introduced. He then had 113 acres (45.7 ha), four acres (1.6 ha) devoted entirely to Christmas bush, and approximately a thousand mature waratah plants, each of which produced up to forty blooms a year. By the 1960s when the Society for Growing Australian Plants was established, Parry's years of observation and experiment became an invaluable resource for the society. Olive was an early office-holder. They were generous with seeds and plants to those interested in cultivating Australian native plants, and displays were regularly packed and dispatched as requested in Australia and from overseas. The waratahs and pink bottlebrush (a Parry hybrid) that decorated the dining room in 1968 when the Australian parliament entertained President Lyndon B. Johnson came from Floralands.

Percy and Olive were both appointed O.A.M. on Australia Day 1981 for their service to the preservation and cultivation of native flora. Percy died on 25 May 1986 at his home at Kariong, and was buried in the Anglican cemetery, Point Clare. His wife (d.1987), three sons and three daughters survived him. Floralands has since been consumed by a housing estate, with not a Christmas bush nor a waratah anywhere in sight.

G. Dundon, *The Third Old Gosford and District in Pictures* (Gosford, NSW, 1980); P. Nixon, *The Waratah* (Syd, 1987); *Agnes Fagan's Diary 1885* (Gosford, NSW, 1991); *PD* (NSW), 28 Feb 1945, p 2184; *Native Plants for NSW*, 21, no 3, June/July 1986, p 3; *Gosford Star*, 15 Dec 1971, p 18; *T&CJ*, 27 Sept 1890, p 40.   BEVERLEY KINGSTON

PEARSON, JAMES KERR; *see* LAW

PEEVAY; *see* EUMARRAH

PELZER, AUGUST WILLIAM (c.1862-1934), landscape gardener, was born in the German free state of Bremen, son of John Henry Christian Pelzer. Trained in horticulture and landscape gardening at the Royal Horticultural College at Geisenheim, Nassau, young Pelzer gained an apprenticeship in I. C. Schmidt's nursery at Erfurt, Saxony, and

served as a council landscape gardener in Borsig's Garden, Berlin, and Baur's Park, Hamburg. While employed in the nursery of F. Sanders & Co. at St Albans, Hertfordshire, England, he gained first-hand experience of London's gardens and parks. About 1886 he reached Adelaide, joining members of the extended Pelzer family who had arrived in the 1840s and 1850s.

Pelzer worked first on the garden of the (R. C.) Baker [q.v.7] family at Morialta, before establishing a working relationship with the nursery of Charles Newman (Neumann) & Sons. Through Newman he designed and planted large suburban gardens for several prominent Adelaide families, including that of J. V. O'Loghlin [q.v.11]. On 8 March 1899 Pelzer married with Presbyterian forms Lucie Bothe in the bride's residence, Walkerville. He was naturalized in February 1903, and the couple lived at Wayville from 1909.

In July 1899 Pelzer, characterized as possessing stern features and a distinguished moustache, had become Adelaide city gardener (later curator of the parks and gardens). Upon appointment he stated that he had 'a good twenty years' work … to bring the 2000 acres [809 ha] of Parks under control up to the standard of sightliness which the most favoured spots possess at the present'. He created many fine avenues of trees and numerous parks and gardens, in formal and informal European and gardenesque styles, using both native and exotic species. He indirectly credited John Ednie Brown's [q.v.3] 'master plan' in his *Report on the System of Planting for the Adelaide Park Lands* (1880). These areas included Creswell, Brougham, Kingston, Osmond, Prince Henry and Pennington gardens, Rundle and Elder parks, Victoria Square and the other city squares, and the establishment of the city's nursery to test-trial and acclimatize potential street-tree species—all actions proposed by Brown.

After World War I Pelzer advised on the design of the Soldiers' Memorial Gardens, Victor Harbor. He often served as a judge for gardening competitions, including those of the (Melbourne) *Herald* and the Adelaide Royal Show. In 1927, as the main speaker at a major conference on tree-planting at Ballarat, Victoria, he surveyed practices and successes in Adelaide, claiming that Oriental Planes (*Platanus orientalis*) and 'English' Ash (*Fraxinus excelsior* 'Aura') had proved the most reliable trees in Adelaide. He was correct about the former, wrong about the latter. The *Herald* described him as 'one of the leading authorities on arboriculture, floriculture and landscape gardening in Australia'. After retiring in 1932 he served as an official adviser to the council.

Pelzer died on 27 August 1934 at Wayville and was buried in North Road cemetery,

Adelaide, leaving an estate sworn for probate at £3767. His wife, son and daughter survived him. An obituarist in the *Advertiser* wrote of Pelzer: 'Many of Adelaide's municipal gardens were laid out under his supervision, and will remain a lasting tribute to his skill and artistic sense'.

P. Morton, *After Light* (Adel, 1996); Swanbury Penglase Architects, *Adelaide Oval Conservation Study* (Adel, 2001); R. Aitken and M. Looker (eds), *The Oxford Companion to Australian Gardens* (Melb, 2002); D. S. Jones, *Adelaide Park Lands Cultural Landscape Assessment* (Adel, 2004) and 'Designing the Adelaide Parklands in the 1880s: The Proposals of John Ednie Brown', *Studies in the History of Gardens and Designed Landscapes*, no 26, 1998, p 287; *Herald* (Adel), 30 Mar 1929, p 17; *Advertiser* (Adel), 28 Aug 1934, p 9, 29 Aug 1934, p 17, 5 June 1999 (Weekend), p 6; G. Ruckert, Descendants of Johann Heinrich Leopold Pelzer (ms, 1990, held privately).   DAVID S. JONES

PEMULWUY (c.1750–1802), Aboriginal warrior, was born near what was later named Botany Bay, on the northern side of the Georges River, New South Wales. His name (also spelt as Pemulwhy, Pemulwoy or other variations) was derived from the Darug (Dharug) word *pemul*, meaning earth. Europeans also rendered his name as 'Bimblewove' and 'Bumbleway'. He spoke a dialect of the Darug language and had a blemish in his left eye. According to Colebe [q.v.1], his left foot had been clubbed, suggesting he was a *carradhy* (clever man). In December 1790 Pemulwuy speared John McIntyre, Governor Phillip's [q.v.2] gamekeeper, who later died of the wound. The spear was barbed with small pieces of red stone, confirming that Pemulwuy belonged to one of the 'woods tribes' or Bediagal (Bidjigal) clan. A bungled retaliatory expedition failed to find any Aborigines.

From 1792 Pemulwuy led raids on settlers at Prospect, Toongabbie, Georges River, Parramatta, Brickfield Hill and the Hawkesbury River. In December next year David Collins [q.v.1] reported an attack by Aborigines who 'were of the Hunter's or Woodman's tribe, people who seldom came among us, and who consequently were little known'. He also reported that 'Pe-mul-wy, a wood native, and many strangers, came in' to an initiation ceremony held at *yoo-lahng* (Farm Cove) on 25 January 1795. Collins thought him 'a most active enemy to the settlers, plundering them of their property, and endangering their personal safety'. Raids were made for food, particularly corn, or as 'payback' for atrocities: Collins suggested that most of the attacks were the result of the settlers' 'own misconduct', including the kidnapping of Aboriginal children.

To check at once 'these dangerous depredators', military force was used against Pemulwuy and his people. Captain Paterson [q.v.2] directed that soldiers be sent from Parramatta, with instructions to destroy 'as many as they could meet' of the Bediagal. In March 1797 Pemulwuy led a raid on the government farm at Toongabbie. Settlers formed a punitive party and tracked him to the outskirts of Parramatta. He was wounded (by John Caesar [q.v.]), receiving seven pieces of buckshot in his head and body. Extremely ill, he was taken to the hospital. Yet, late in April that year, when the governor met several parties of natives near Botany Bay, Pemulwuy was among them. Having 'perfectly recovered from his wounds', he had 'escaped from the hospital with an iron about his leg. He saw and spoke with one of the gentlemen of the party; enquiring of him whether the governor was angry, and seemed pleased at being told that he was not.'

Pemulwuy's close escapes resulted in the Darug believing that firearms could not kill him. In Collins's words: 'Through this fancied security, he was said to be at the head of every party that attacked the maize grounds'. On 1 May 1801 Governor King [q.v.2] issued a government and general order that Aborigines near Parramatta, Georges River and Prospect could be shot on sight, and in November a proclamation outlawed Pemulwuy and offered a reward for his death or capture.

Pemulwuy was shot dead about 1 June 1802 by Henry Hacking [q.v.1]. George Suttor described the subsequent events: 'his head was cut off, which was, I believe, sent to England'. On 5 June King wrote to Sir Joseph Banks [q.v.1] that although he regarded Pemulwuy as 'a terrible pest to the colony, he was a brave and independent character'. He further wrote: 'Understanding that the possession of a New Hollander's head is among the desiderata, I have put it in spirits and forwarded it by the Speedy'. The head has not been found in an English repository to date.

Pemulwuy's son TEDBURY (d.1810), known as Tjedboro, also threatened colonists. He became attached to John Macarthur [q.v.2], who allowed him to come and go at Elizabeth Farm. After Governor Bligh [q.v.1] was placed under military arrest in 1808, Tedbury, armed with a bundle of spears, went to Macarthur's cottage in Sydney and reportedly said that he had come to spear the governor. Next year he and Bundle attempted to rob a traveller on the Parramatta road, and he also took part in an attack on the farm of a settler at Georges River. In 1810 Tedbury was shot by Edward Luttrell at Hobartville, Richmond, and died of his wounds. He had a wife and possibly a son Tommy Dadbury, who was living with the Wianamattagal clan at Penrith in 1837.

Historians argue about the nature and extent of Aboriginal resistance to European settlement of Australia, but if one person can be identified who clearly carried out armed warfare against the settlers of early Sydney it was Pemulwuy. He has become a heroic figure to Aborigines, and Eric Willmot published a novel about him in 1987.

D. Collins, *An Account of the English Colony of New South Wales*, 1-2 (Lond, 1798-1802); J. L. Kohen, 'The Dharug of the Western Cumberland Plain: Ethnography and Demography', in B. Meehan and R. Jones (eds), *Archaeology with Ethnography* (Canb, 1988); J. L. Kohen, *The Darug and their Neighbours* (Syd, 1993); Return of Aboriginal natives, 4/1133.3 and 37/7370 (SRNSW); *Hist Records of NSW*, vol 4; *Newsletter of the Royal Aust Hist Soc*, Jan 1970, p 3; *SMH*, 1 2 Nov 2003, p 38; S. Smith, Journal, 20 July 1802 *and* G. Suttor, Memoirs (ML); information from Mr K. V. Smith, Macquarie Univ, Syd.

J. L. KOHEN

PEPPER, NATHANIEL (c.1841-1877), Aboriginal evangelist and teacher, was born in the Wimmera district of Victoria, one of at least five children of Billey (Toney) and Iabbe (Linna); Billey was a leader of the Gromiluk group and the Wotjoballuk clan of the Wergaia people. In 1845 two Irishmen John Pepper and George Belcher selected Coonanga Mamool in Gromiluk territory, Pepper taking the western side of Lake Hindmarsh. The Wotjoballuk worked for the new owners.

The occupation had taken its toll on local people, and the Moravian missionaries Friedrich Hagenauer [q.v.4] and Friedrich Spieseke agreed to start a mission. On 17 January 1859 they opened a school at Lake Hindmarsh and established Ebenezer mission, near the Wimmera River. One of the first pupils was a youth referred to as 'Pepper' by Hagenauer, who also recorded that the boy's father was chief. A talented student, Pepper was soon able to read the New Testament and conduct morning classes. Outside the mission, he taught the Wotjoballuk in their own language.

On 12 August 1860 Pepper was baptized, choosing the name of Nathaniel (Nathanael). The missionaries broadcast his baptism widely, declaring that he worked as a true and faithful evangelist. Hagenauer toured Melbourne and Geelong, telling of the conversion and showing pencil sketches of Nathaniel and examples of his writing books. Pepper's conversion was deep and powerful. By 1862 he had early signs of tuberculosis, but he continued working on the farm and preaching to his people.

On 21 May 1863 at Ebenezer he married with Moravian rites Rachel Warndekan, an 18-year-old, Christian Aboriginal girl from King

Georges Sound, Western Australia. Twelve months later they had a son who died soon after his birth. Pepper was appointed a missionary assistant in 1865 with a salary of £12 per annum. Over the following years his illness caused the loss of a lung. Although he recovered, Rachel had contracted the disease. She died in March 1869.

That year Pepper followed Hagenauer to Ramahyuck, Gippsland, where he taught the children and preached to the adults. He also conducted church services at Ramahyuck and in local churches. On 17 February 1870 he married Louise Arbuckle. She was 16, an Aboriginal Christian girl of the Bratowoloong people. He was 5 ft 6 ins (168 cm) tall, and at this time his weight was down to 128 lb (58 kg). A sketch of him in European clothing showed a good-looking man with a neat moustache and beard. He worked as a carpenter and farmer at Ramahyuck. His kindness and sympathy towards the sick, his charity and readiness to help, 'made him beloved among the blacks as well as among white people'.

The Peppers lived with their children in a cottage not far from the mission church, but by 1876 his health had deteriorated and he was seriously ill. He died on 7 March 1877 at Ramahyuck and was buried in the churchyard there with the whole congregation taking part in the funeral service. His wife and their three sons and one daughter survived him. Nathaniel's descendant Phillip Pepper (d.1985) was a leader of his people a century later.

R. B. Smyth, *The Aborigines of Victoria* (Melb, 1876); F. A. Hagenauer, *Mission Work Among the Aborigines of Victoria* (Melb, 1880?) and *Further Facts Relating to the Moravian Mission* (Melb, 1861-67); S. Robertson, *The Bell Sounds Pleasantly* (Melb, 1977); P. Pepper with T. De Araugo, *The Kurnai of Gippsland* (Melb, 1985), and *You Are What You Make Yourself to Be* (Melb, 1989); T. S. De Araugo, The Wotjoballuk of the Wimmera District (ms, held by author); G. Belcher, diaries (LaTL); J. Bulmer collection (National Museum of Vic); information from the late Mr P. Pepper.

TESS DE ARAUGO

PERKINS, CHARLES COLLIER (1906-1961), farmer and politician, was born on 5 August 1906 at Moonee Ponds, Melbourne, eldest of four children of Australian-born parents Charles Henry Perkins, farmer, and his wife Gwendoline, née Collier. Young Charlie was educated at Rainbow State School, in the Wimmera, and Geelong Church of England Grammar School. He arrived by rail in Western Australia in 1929, with a team of Clydesdale horses—destined to lead future grand parades at the Royal Agricultural Show in Perth.

Acquiring a wheat and sheep property at Belka, close to the goldfields pipeline, Perkins became involved in and often chaired organizations such as the Bruce Rock Agricultural Society, the Primary Producers' Association and its York zone wheat council, and the Clydesdale Horse Society (Western Australia). He was also a parish synodsman and a lay reader at St Peter's Church of England. With Kingsley Laffer, he established the Bruce Rock Literary and Debating Society in 1933, and he persuaded the Road Board to set up a free lending library. On 25 August 1938 at St George's Cathedral, Perth, he married Kathleen Jennings Laffer, a typist.

Perkins was vice-president of the P.P.A. in July 1944 when it split to form the Country and Democratic League. He was a trustee for the Western Australian wheatgrowers' £5671 subvention for the Nelungaloo wheat case, which was eventually rejected by the Privy Council, and a director of Wesfarmers Ltd and deputy director of Westralian Farmers Co-operative Ltd. As a member of the University of Western Australia's senate, he was nominated to the Adult Education Board in 1946. Perkins constantly advocated a statewide lending library service and in 1953 was a foundation member of the Library Board of Western Australia. He was also a founder of Wollaston [q.v.2] Theological College.

Afflicted by rheumatoid arthritis in childhood, Perkins was rejected for military service in 1939. Instead, he succeeded (Sir) Charles Latham [q.v.10] in the Legislative Assembly in 1942 as Country Party member for York; from 1950 he represented Roe. Perkins was chairman of committees in 1947-53. As minister for transport, police, labour and native welfare, from April 1959 to November 1961, Perkins faced taxing challenges. He was soon no stranger to change and controversy; his numerous ministerial responsibilities inspired Paul Rigby's cartoons in the *Daily News* and led to thousands of miles of travel to interstate conferences and remote Aboriginal communities.

Perkins's duties included the co-ordination of transport, traffic control and safety, and he sought Federal funds to improve road systems and upgrade country transport. He oversaw the introduction of seatbelts and parking meters and supported the National Safety Council's instructional centre at Mount Lawley. As minister for labour he introduced safety legislation for construction sites. Illegal betting was a major police issue and, after the Ligertwood [q.v.15] royal commission into betting (1959), Perkins strengthened the powers of the Totalisator Agency Board. Promoting a 'New Deal' for Aborigines, he endeavoured to improve their health and education. State housing was provided for some Aboriginal families; special trade courses were devised for adolescents, and hostels to accommodate schoolchildren were con-

structed at outback places like Yalgoo, Cue and Onslow. The proposed relocation of the Allawah Grove community was the most contentious issue during his incumbency as minister of native welfare.

Of average height, with a tanned complexion and receding hair, Charlie Perkins was genial, generous and approachable. He died of myocardial infarction on 7 November 1961 at his home at Wembley. After a state funeral service at St George's Cathedral, he was cremated. His wife and their two sons and two daughters survived him. His estate was valued for probate at £41 165.

J. K. Ewers, *Bruce Rock* (Bruce Rock, WA, 1959); *PD* (WA), 9 Dec 1942, p 1951, 1 Aug 1950, p 30, 8 Nov 1961, p 2413; *West Australian*, 3 Apr 1959, p 1; 30 Apr 1959, p 1, 20 June 1959, p 2, 23 May 1960, p 4, 8 Nov 1961, pp 1 & 7, 9 Nov 1961, p 16, 10 Nov 1961, p 2, 7 July 1962, p 9; *West Anglican*, Dec 1961, p 10; *Corian*, Dec 1961, p 262; *Merredin Mercury*, 2 Oct 1963, p 14; Allawah Grove community records (BL); information and cuttings from Mrs K. MacDonald, South Perth.   WENDY BIRMAN

PERRY, FRANCES (1814-1892), community worker, was born on 16 June 1814 and baptized on 21 July at the Fish Street Independent Chapel, Kingston-upon-Hull, Yorkshire, England, youngest of ten children of Samuel Cooper, merchant, and his wife Dorothy, née Priestley. Through her brother John at the University of Cambridge, Fanny met Charles Perry [q.v.5], curate at Newtown, a Cambridge parish. Fanny married Charles on 14 October 1841 at Kirk Ella parish church, Yorkshire. They were to have no children. Perry accepted the new bishopric of Melbourne in 1847.

The couple left England in October in the *Stag*, the voyage a rehearsal for life in a colonial diocese: the bishop led services and taught his clergy Greek, while Mrs Perry took Scripture classes for the women and practised her benevolence on the steerage passengers. Immediately upon arrival at Port Phillip on 23 January 1848, the Perrys began their task, to advance the Church of England in Victoria in both public and private spheres. Mrs Perry made mixed impressions on the local establishment. Mary, wife of (Sir) William Stawell [q.v.6], recalled her as 'a lively good little woman, nothing very particular as a companion, and has a good deal of English wit or kitten liveliness'.

In addition to genteel expectations, Mrs Perry coped with physically exhausting work as her husband's personal assistant, copying out sermons and accompanying him on long journeys to visit his clergy. She disliked some duties, especially tea meetings: 'I cannot help considering them useful things, but I get dreadfully tired, and shirk them whenever I can'. Nevertheless, her colourful letters, published under the pseudonym 'Richard Perry' as *Contributions to an Amateur Magazine in Prose and Verse* (London, 1857), revealed a detailed interest in the people and landscapes she encountered. She had little time for Aboriginal people, making only brief comments about native police or the 'very troublesome' inhabitants of Gippsland. Nor were they a focus of her charity. She took leading roles in the Governesses' Home, the Carlton Refuge, and the Melbourne Orphan Asylum. Her chief work, however, was as head of the committee that founded the Melbourne Lying-in (Royal Women's) Hospital; she was first president from 1856 to 1874. Here she espoused moral and domestic purity, monitoring the marital status of patients and regularly inspecting the wards.

While Mrs Perry's philanthropy pushed her into the public realm, she always deferred to male authority and confined herself solely to women's welfare. As one contemporary put it, 'she did not pose as a theologian or as a logician, nor did she, after the modern fashion, stand up to make a speech'.

The Perrys left Melbourne on 26 April 1874 and retired to Regents Park, London, although Fanny maintained her correspondence with colonial acquaintances and a keen interest in church affairs. After Charles died in 1891, she moved near her brother John, vicar of Kendal. She died exactly one year after her husband, on 2 December 1892, at Mrs Clay's house, Miller Bridge, Loughrigg, Westmorland. Her memory was preserved in Melbourne with the opening of Frances Perry House in 1979 at the Royal Women's Hospital.

G. Goodman, *The Church in Victoria During the Episcopate of the Right Reverend Charles Perry* (Lond, 1892); M. F. E. Stawell, *My Recollections* (Lond, 1911); H. McRae (ed), *Georgiana's Journal* (Syd, 1966); A. de Q. Robin, *Charles Perry* (Perth, 1967); A. de Q. Robin (ed), *Australian Sketches* (Melb, 1984); P. Grimshaw, *Women, Christianity and the Australian Colonies* (Melb 1988); P. Sherlock, '"This Episcopal Hotel and Boarding House": Bishops' Wives in Colonial Australia and New Zealand', in M. Crotty and D. Scobie (eds), *Raiding Clio's Closet* (Melb, 1997), p 32; *Church of England Messenger*, 6 Jan 1893; *Argus* (Melb), 29 Sept 1934, p 12.

PETER SHERLOCK

PETERSEN, ALICIA TERESA JANE O'SHEA (1862-1923), social activist and political candidate, was born on 2 July 1862 at Broadmarsh, Tasmania, daughter of Hugh McShane, farmer, and his wife Jane, née Wood. Alice became a machinist in the clothing industry. On 28 May 1884 in St Joseph's Catholic Church, Hobart, she married Patrick O'Shea, a draper and widower with a son. Patrick died in 1886 leaving her to care for her stepson with a small annuity and a house in Wilmot Terrace (Harrington Street), Hobart, in which she lived until her death; there on 16 December 1891 she married with Catholic rites William (Hjalma) Petersen (d.1912), a mining investor from Gotland, Sweden. She had no children by either marriage.

Alicia joined the Tasmanian Workers' Political League, which her cousin John Earle [q.v.8], later Labor premier of Tasmania, founded in 1903. That year she came to public attention when, as '(Mrs) A. O'Shea-Petersen', she placed an open letter in the daily press offering herself as a Senate candidate in the Federal election. She proposed the abolition of State governors and the replacement of each State parliament by a locally elected body based on economic and social interests. A protectionist, she agreed with the White Australia policy and favoured old age pensions, equal pay for equal work and arbitration to prevent strikes. Aware that she was breaking new ground as a woman candidate, she said, 'I will ask no favour for a woman that I am not prepared to give to a man'. Within a week of this announcement she had withdrawn her candidacy, but she continued to be active throughout the campaign.

O'Shea Petersen attended parliament whenever it was in session. From about 1905 she was a member of the Tasmanian Women's Political Association. While expressing sympathy with Labor women, she remained committed to the non-party stance espoused by the T.W.P.A. During 1906, in the campaign to secure a royal commission on sweating, as a delegate of the Catholic organization Ladies of Charity, Mrs O'Shea Petersen emerged as a prominent speaker for the Citizens' Social and Moral Reform League, established by the Anglican bishop J. E. Mercer [q.v.10]. She founded in 1909, and was later life president of, a local branch of a friendly society for women, the Australasian Women's Association (from 1916 affiliated with the Australian Natives' Association). Also active in the Women's Health Association and the National Council of Women, she helped to establish the Bush Nursing and Child Welfare (Health) associations. Her belief in personal self-improvement was expressed practically in 1914 by gaining the certificate of sanitation from the Royal Sanitary Institute, London.

In 1913 O'Shea Petersen became the first woman to stand for parliament in Tasmania when she contested the Federal seat of Denison. Although she sought election to represent the interests of women and children, she held broader political views, which the press trivialized or ignored. She was accused of accepting funds from both political parties, and the National and Labor parties brought female organizers from Victoria to campaign against her. She received 261 of the 17 043 votes polled. During World War I she supported the women's anti-conscription campaign of Vida Goldstein [q.v.9] during the latter's 1917 visit. A member of the Criminal Law Reform Association (established in 1921), with Frances Edwards she campaigned to raise the age of consent. She was also on the State council of the Workers' Educational Association.

O'Shea Petersen was a frequent contributor to the press; her letters were 'always to the point, sometimes caustic and occasionally humorous'. Women obtained the right to stand for State parliament in Tasmania in 1922 and in June that year she was a candidate for Denison in the House of Assembly. Ill with cancer, she was unable to campaign and placed a notice in the press asking voters to judge her on her twenty years work. She gained only 0.6 per cent of the vote. O'Shea Petersen died on 22 January 1923 at her home.

H. Radi (ed), *200 Australian Women* (Syd, 1988); S. Petrow, *The Furies of Hobart* (Hob, 1993) and *Sanatorium of the South?* (Hob, 1995); M. Roe, *The State of Tasmania* (Hob, 2001); V. F. Pearce, '"A Few Viragos on a Stump": The Womanhood Suffrage Campaign in Tasmania 1880-1920', Tas Hist Research Assn, *Papers and Procs*, 32, no 4, Dec 1985, p 151, and The Lowest Common Denominator —Children, State and Society, Tasmania, 1896-1920 (B.A. Hons thesis, Univ Tas, 1984); *Examiner* (Launc), 2 Dec 1903, p 1, 23 Jan 1923, p 7; *Mercury* (Hob), 28 Aug 1906, p 6, 18 Aug 1909, p 8, 3 June 1922, p 9, 23 Jan 1923, pp 4 & 5; *Daily Post* (Hob), 1 May 1913; *World* (Hob), 23 Jan 1923, p 4; *Weekly Courier* (Launc), 25 Jan 1923, p 33.

VICKI PEARCE

PETTIGREW, WILLIAM (1825-1906), sawmiller, politician and diarist, was born on 25 August 1825 at Burton Farm, near Ayr, Scotland, second child and eldest son of Robert Pettigrew, a prosperous farmer and businessman, and his second wife Mary, née McWhinnie. William was educated at the parish school at Tarbolton. After his father's death and the family's move to Newton-upon-Ayr, he attended Ayr Academy in 1836-41.

Pettigrew worked first as a farmer, then trained as a surveyor. Unemployed in the recession of 1847-48, he migrated to Australia in the *Fortitude* as agent for Rev. J. D. Lang [q.v.2], reaching Moreton Bay in January 1849. Disappointed in Lang's promises of work as a surveyor, Pettigrew was employed for the next three years by Stephen Simpson [q.v.2], to farm at Woogaroo. With Simpson he defined the boundaries of the sheep runs of the Moreton Bay District, and also assisted James Warner with surveys at Moggill, Ipswich, Yeerongpilly, Mount Gravatt and Cleveland.

In 1853 Pettigrew established Brisbane's first steam sawmill in William Street on the riverbank and operated it until 1900, rebuilding after fires in 1855 and 1874. During the 1850s he supported moves to end convict transportation, encourage free immigration, achieve separation from New South Wales and establish Brisbane as a municipality. From 1862 to 1865, while looking for timber, he explored and mapped the coast north of Moreton Bay and began to acquire lands and forests and a fleet of steam and sailing ships. In partnership with the Sim family, he operated Dundathu sawmill on the Mary River and the Union (Urara) sawmill at Maryborough. On 18 February 1859 in Brisbane he married with Congregational forms Amelia Davis, née Boughay, a London-born widow with three children. They had two daughters and a son.

To draw timber from the forests at Tin Can Bay, in 1873 Pettigrew and Sim constructed the Cooloola railway, probably the colony's earliest privately owned line, and commissioned John Walker & Co. of Maryborough to build the first steam locomotive in Queensland, the *Mary Ann*. An inventive, self-taught engineer and architect, Pettigrew designed machines, ships and bridges as well as railways and sawmills. He served as an alderman on the Brisbane Municipal Council in 1863-66, 1868-73 and 1878-85, as mayor in 1870-71, and in 1880-83 also as a member of the first Caboolture Divisional Board (chairman, 1881). Appointed to the Legislative Council in 1877, he was a liberal and in parliament promoted railways and improved sanitation, and advocated forest conservancy. He resigned in 1894.

Pettigrew was a member of the North Brisbane School of Arts, the National (Agricultural and Industrial) Association and the Philosophical Society (Royal Society from 1883) of Queensland, and a founder of the Caledonian Association. A justice of the peace from 1864, he served as a magistrate, a member of boards of health and a trustee of the Paddington and Toowong cemeteries. He helped to establish an insurance company and was involved in the building society movement. Devoutly religious, Pettigrew was an elder and trustee in Presbyterian congregations and helped to establish a theological college, Divinity Hall, and the *Queensland Evangelical Standard* newspaper. In 1891 he built his sixth sawmill, at Maroochydore; but in 1893 his businesses were hit by flood, fire and economic depression, and he was bankrupted in 1898.

A short, wiry, energetic man, with blue eyes, sharp features, light brown hair and a bushy beard, Pettigrew was a visionary and an individualist, noted for a determination that sometimes bordered on stubbornness.

Five of his lectures were published in the *Transactions of the Philosophical Society of Queensland*, and 'The Habitat and Peculiarities of Some of Our Timbers' (1878) was also issued as a booklet. Predeceased by his wife in 1893, he died on 28 October 1906 at Bowen and was buried in the local cemetery. His three children and one stepdaughter survived him. Pettigrew's diaries and papers have provided useful primary material on the history of colonial Queensland.

T. W. H. Leavitt, *Australian Representative Men* (Brisb, 1888), pp 196-7; D. B. Waterson, *A Biographical Register of the Queensland Parliament 1860-1929* (Canb, 1972); *Queenslander*, 12 June 1897, p 1289, 7 Aug 1909, p 19; *Brisb Courier*, 4 July 1908, p 12, 25 Aug 1928, p 23; M. Eckoff, The Late Hon. William Pettigrew, MLC (ts, 1961, OL); Pettigrew papers (Royal Hist Soc of Qld, and Mr A. Pettigrew, Brisb); information from Mr A. Pettigrew, Brisb, Mr K. Pettigrew and Mrs J. Smallhorn, Toowoomba, and Mr D. Hardgrave and Mr G. Pettigrew, Sunshine Coast, Qld.   ELAINE BROWN

PEYSER, DORA (1904-1970), social worker and nurse, was born on 22 February 1904 in Berlin, second of four children of Alfred Peyser, a specialist physician, and his wife Sofie, née Frankel. Dora grew up in a liberal Jewish household in central Berlin. After her secondary education, she completed a kindergarten course and volunteered at the Pestalozzi-Froebel Haus. She then undertook a child-nursing course at the Hugo Neumanns Kinderhaus and studied social work from 1925 at the social school for women (Soziale Frauenschule). In 1927-34 she worked as an assistant to the school's founder Alice Salomon, a pioneer social work educator and theorist. Recommended by Salomon, she gained entry to Berlin University (Ph.D., 1934), graduating *magna cum laude*.

A disciple of Salomon's, Peyser was a member of her coterie of gifted Jewish social workers. Her thesis *Hilfe als Soziologisches Phaenomen (Assistance as a Group Phenomenon)* was published in Germany and received favourable reviews but was withdrawn after Hitler's anti-Jewish legislation. With increasing anti-Semitism in Germany, Salomon arranged, through an Australian colleague Aileen Fitzpatrick [q.v.14], director of the New South Wales Board of Social Study and Training in Sydney, for Peyser to continue welfare research in Australia.

Allowed a special entry visa for one year, she reached Melbourne in the *Bendigo* on 5 November 1934 and moved to Sydney in May 1935. She was supported by the Jewish Council for Women, New South Wales, and lived in a room at Edgecliff. To supplement her income, she taught German at the University of Sydney for two terms and at Hopewood House, Darling Point. In 1937 her 16-year-old brother Thomas, who was sponsored by the Jewish Welfare Society, joined her; their parents later escaped to Sweden. Dora worked as secretary for the society and helped refugees—meeting them at the boat, finding accommodation and sponsorship, and communicating with authorities in Australia and overseas.

Meanwhile, she conducted her research into the development of social services in Australia and completed a two-part paper, 'The History of Welfare Work in Sydney 1788-1900', published in the *Journal of the Royal Australian Historical Society* (1939). Despite her qualifications, she was unable to find employment in professional social work; her heavily accented English prevented her using her knowledge and skills. Undaunted, she opted to train in Melbourne as a nurse. In addition to obtaining a double nursing certificate there, she completed a course at the Tresillian Mothercraft Training Centre in Sydney and worked with the District Nursing Association at Glebe. She was naturalized on 9 February 1940.

Peyser lived at the nurses' headquarters in Boyce Street, Glebe, and also rented a small room nearby, which she used as a study. In 1951 and 1952 she was a part-time lecturer in the social studies department at the university. Encouraged by Australian social workers Norma Parker and Kate Ogilvie, she revised and published her thesis as *The Strong and the Weak* (Sydney, 1951), an examination of the sociological interpretation of social assistance. Forced to retire from nursing about 1961 due to the onset of Parkinson's disease, she moved to a flat in North Sydney and lived on an invalid pension until, increasingly debilitated, she was admitted to Greenwich Hospital in 1962.

Short, with dark hair and brown eyes, Peyser was outspoken, with a forthright manner. She could be intimidating but also generous, organizing activities for refugee children, taking them bushwalking and introducing them to art, literature and philosophy. She worshipped at the Temple Emanuel, Woollahra, where she sang with an *a capella* group. She also played the guitar.

Her Australian publications, although pioneering efforts, failed to generate further literature on social work practice. Although unable to work in her chosen field, she was not resentful of her treatment in her adopted country. Rather, she regarded nursing as a 'wonderful learning experience', which gave her the opportunity to achieve her goal by working in the welfare system. She died of complications from Parkinson's disease on 15 February 1970 at Princess Juliana Hospital, Turramurra. She donated her body to

Sydney University for scientific research and was cremated.

L. Cohen, *Beginning With Esther* (Syd, 1987); *Daily Telegraph* (Syd), 3 Nov 1934, p 10; *SMH*, 5 Dec 1934, p 7, 10 Dec 1934, p 4; A435, item 1945/4/1225, C123/1, item 4888, B13, item 1934/20174 (NAA); Dept Social Work files (Univ Syd Archives); information from Alice-Salomon-Fachhochschule fur Sozialarbeit and Socialpadogogick, Berlin, and the late Mr T. Peyser.   KERRY REGAN

PHILLIPS, JOYCE EILEEN; *see* EYRE

PINBA; *see* LOGIC

POHL, CAROLINE; *see* HODGSON

POLTPALINGADA   BOOBOOROWIE (c.1830-1901), Aboriginal fringe-dweller, better known as 'Tommy Walker', was a Ngarrindjeri man, reputedly born on the shores of Lake Albert in the upper south-east of South Australia, son of a man who was reportedly killed in a tribal fight with Kaurna people. Poltpalingada worked for settlers, and may have travelled to the Victorian goldfields in the 1850s.

Unlike many of his countrymen who gravitated to Point McLeay Mission (Raukkan) after its establishment in 1859, he was more often a visitor than a resident, spending most of his life travelling among a network of fringe camps that emerged as European settlement displaced Aboriginal people from their country. He was one who, by choice or circumstance, spurned the restrictions of mission life for a precarious freedom that often brought trouble with the law. By the 1870s his constant companion was Mary. After she died in 1892 he was usually in the company of Ada Walker (Niledalli). Photographs and sketches depicted him with a full white beard and grey felt top hat, wearing a ragged jacket or tail-coat, and barefooted. He was also the subject of several portraits by the Adelaide artist Oscar Friström [q.v.8].

By the 1890s, perhaps for no other reason than force of personality, Walker became prominent among the community of fringe-dwellers in Adelaide. The press often reported on his activities and his numerous appearances in court, usually on charges of being drunk and disorderly, using insulting language or begging alms. These accounts revealed a man with a sharp wit and acid tongue. At times, his begging resembled a sort of street theatre in which he would parody the magistrate bringing down his sentence and imposing a fine. His activities inspired cartoons and doggerel.

One of many stories about Walker, recalled by Aboriginal people at Point McLeay mission, was that when in church the communion cup was passed to him, Tommy seized and drained it, crying eagerly, 'Fill 'im up again!' A renowned mimic, he spoke good English and scorned being addressed in pidgin. 'His goings out and comings in were watched with great interest, most especially by juveniles ... "It's a funny thing", he exclaimed on one occasion, "that a gentleman can't walk along the footpath without a crowd of kids after him".'

In May 1901 he went to Adelaide with Aborigines from Encounter Bay to see the visiting Duke of York. 'Pollapalingda—known as Tommy Walker' died on 4 July 1901 in Adelaide Hospital. The Adelaide Stock Exchange paid for his headstone in West Terrace cemetery. But he was not laid to rest. In 1903 it was revealed that the coroner Dr W. Ramsay Smith [q.v.11] had removed his skeleton before the burial and sent it, along with other 'anthropological specimens', to the University of Edinburgh. In an era when evolutionary anthropology was in the ascendant, a board of inquiry found that the coroner's actions had been 'indiscreet' and that he had allowed his 'zeal in the cause of science to outrun his judgment'.

R. Foster, 'Tommy Walker Walk up Here ...', in J. Simpson and L. Hercus (eds), *History in Portraits* (Syd, 1988).   ROBERT FOSTER

POTTER, JOHN OAKDEN; *see* CRAWFORD

POTTIE, ELIZA (1837-1907), evangelist, pacifist and reformer, was born on 14 December 1837 at Belfast, Ireland, second child and eldest daughter of William Bell Allen [q.v.3], soap and candle manufacturer, and his wife Ruth, née Johnston, late Sayers, a devout Quaker. William came to Sydney in 1841 and the family followed in 1844. Eliza married John Pottie [q.v.5], veterinary surgeon, on 13 March 1862 at Woollahra Congregational Church. They had ten children between 1863 and 1882, four dying in infancy.

By the 1880s Eliza Pottie was an active executive member of at least seventeen organizations supporting her Quaker, evangelical Christian beliefs and commitment to social reform for women and children. She and her husband were both officeholders of the Sydney City Mission, and she supported her brother Alfred Allen's [q.v.3] efforts to reduce working hours for female shop assistants.

Initially she joined committees supporting children's orphanages but later she supported cottage homes by having children from such institutions holiday in her home. A founding member of the Young Women's Christian Association in Sydney in 1880—having attempted to establish such a body in the late 1870s—she supported refuges for destitute women and sat on the first committee of the Sydney Female Mission Home. She helped to set up the Ladies' Sanitary Association (president 1892-1901) to educate women about public hygiene.

Pottie's causes were those of the Woman's Christian Temperance Union. She joined its Sydney branch in December 1882, was vice-president from 1883 and head of its peace and arbitration department until her death, her Quaker pacifism unequivocal. She was a vocal supporter of votes for women, in 1890 becoming president of the W.C.T.U.-sponsored (Women's) Franchise League. After five months she resigned and the league dissolved because of opposition to the temperance link. In 1891 she became a founding council member of the Womanhood Suffrage League but soon resigned over criticism of the institution of marriage by fellow member Eliza, wife of Julian Rossi Ashton [q.v.7]. Pottie represented the W.C.T.U. at the meeting that created the National Council of Women in 1896.

Having regularly visited aged, destitute women in the government asylums, first at Hyde Park, later at Newington, in 1886 she was appointed to the ladies' committee of the Asylums Inquiry Board. Pottie's blunt and impassioned evidence about the brutal ill treatment and neglect of Newington inmates was reflected in the majority report and led to improved management. During the 1890s depression, she helped to organize the Quaker Relief Committee and in 1896 was treasurer of Dr Emily Ryder's Fund for Indian child wives.

As an individual, Pottie evangelized and distributed charitable relief to women and children, regularly visiting women in institutions and the La Perouse Aboriginal settlement. She published her poems in the press and contributed letters to the newspapers on social issues, in 1884 sparking controversy by writing to the Brisbane *Courier* objecting to the harsh treatment of suspected prostitutes under the Queensland Contagious Diseases Act. She used the 1888 centenary of settlement to call for prison reform, urging that the anniversary be celebrated by an amnesty for deserving prisoners and a prohibition on manacles.

Photographs showed a stern-faced woman who 'always adhered to the style of dress worn by the Quakers'. Pottie was a capable public speaker and frequently participated in deputations to politicians. A passionate and energetic worker in the public sphere for women's causes, she was also remembered by her grandchildren as a loving matriarch. She died on 14 November 1907 in her home at Manly and was buried in Waverley cemetery. Her husband, two daughters and three sons survived her.

Golden Records: Pathfinders of Woman's Christian Temperance Union of N.S.W. (Syd, 1926); C. Stevenson, *With Unhurried Pace* (Syd, 1973); J. Godden, 'Eliza Pottie' in H. Radi (ed), *200 Australian Women* (Syd, 1988), p 35, *and* Philanthropy and the Women's Sphere (Ph.D. thesis, Macquarie Univ, 1983); *Brisb Courier*, 26 July 1884, pp 4 & 5, 15 Aug 1884, p 6; *SMH*, 3 Dec 1887, p 6, 18 Nov 1907, p 6; *Daily Telegraph* (Syd), 13 June 1891, p 10; *Sydney City Mission Herald*, 1 Jan 1898, 1 Jan 1908, 1 Sept 1908, 2 Nov 1914; Cottage Home for Destitute Children (NSW), *Annual Report*, 1884; WCTU (NSW), *Annual Report*, 1894-95; Sydney City Mission, *Annual Report*, 1908; information from Mrs J. M. Ible, Kirrawee, and Mr G. Allen, Normanhurst, Syd.

JUDITH GODDEN

POUND, CHARLES JOSEPH (1866-1946), microscopist, was born on 29 May 1866 at Harrow, Middlesex, England, son of Joseph Pound, grocer's assistant, and his wife Martha Susannah, née Wingrove. Educated at council schools, Charles trained in laboratory technology at King's College, London, under specialists in disciplines that included microscopy, physiology and the new science of bacteriology (microbiology). On 25 December 1888 at St Mark's Church, Clerkenwell, he married Elizabeth Ann Leader; they had three children.

In September 1888 King's College established Britain's first bacteriology laboratory where Pound was appointed principal assistant to F. M. Crookshank, professor of bacteriology and comparative anatomy. Pound also studied briefly at the Pasteur Institute, Paris, learning the new technology of making vaccines. In 1892 Professor (Sir) Thomas Anderson Stuart [q.v.12] invited him to establish a bacteriology laboratory in the medical school at the University of Sydney. Learning on arrival that the laboratory was yet to be built, he became bacteriological laboratory assistant with the New South Wales Department of Health, then on 2 December 1893 director of the Queensland Stock Institute in Brisbane—the first laboratory in that colony dedicated to investigating disease of any kind, animal or human.

In September 1894 Pound investigated 'red-water disease of cattle' in the gulf district. Guided by the findings of scientists in the United States of America investigating 'Texas fever', Pound reported that redwater fever was confined to bovines and that the disease was readily transmissible by ticks. J. S. Hunt, a scientist and surgeon at Hughenden, took stained blood smears and preserved specimens of cattle tick to the U.S.A. and confirmed the co-identity of Australian redwater disease and Texas fever, as well as of the genus of the tick vector *Boophilus*. He also documented the American bureau's inoculation techniques using 'recovered blood'—from beasts recovered from Texas fever—containing protective antibodies.

In 1895 Pound and Hunt carried out inoculation trials against redwater disease. Pound then embarked on an energetic campaign of educating stockowners, demonstrating how to collect recovered blood by jugular venipuncture, defibrinate it and inoculate this vaccine into at-risk cattle. To deliver multiple injections, he modified an apparatus—the 'Pound syringe'—and arranged for commercial suppliers to make these instruments available to stockowners. Pound gave numerous lectures on the cattle tick and tick fever, exhorting farmers on the need for protective inoculation of susceptible herds. He published articles in Queensland and overseas, and by 1901 his work had saved hundreds of thousands of cattle.

In the absence of a health department, Pound also carried out unofficial laboratory diagnoses for medical practitioners. He persuaded the government to erect new research laboratories, occupied in 1899 and named the Bacteriological Institute; administration was transferred to the health division of the Home Secretary's Department, and Pound was appointed government bacteriologist. The only scientist in Australia producing tuberculin, used in diagnosing human and bovine tuberculosis, he also carried out medical and diagnostic work on leprosy.

In March 1900, examining rats caught in the Brisbane docks, Pound found plague organisms of *Pasteurella* (*Yersinia*) *pestis* in the stomachs of fleas carried by infected rodents. He subsequently confirmed the diagnosis of the first plague patient in Brisbane. During this outbreak, a laboratory assistant accused him of wrongful dismissal, which led to a full-scale inquiry. Then a Brisbane physician brought a court action claiming that Pound had defamed him by disputing his diagnosis that a patient had died of plague. Both cases gained wide publicity, but Pound emerged with his reputation intact. In 1897, however, he had aroused the ire of Henry Tryon [q.v.12], the government entomologist, for criticizing the rabbit commission's pronouncement that chicken cholera did not exist in Australia. Pound had shown that it did and had published the results of his experiments, but such instances earned him the displeasure of medical and scientific men and gained him the reputation of being unprofessional. In 1910 Dr John J. D. Harris was appointed the first medical director of the Bacteriological Institute, which was renamed the Laboratory of Microbiology and Pathology and transferred to the new Health Department. Pound took charge of the new Stock Experiment Station at Yeerongpilly, retaining his title of government bacteriologist. He retired on 31 July 1932.

When photographed in 1896 Pound sported a handlebar moustache; later he was clean-shaven. He enjoyed bowls and yachting and belonged to the Johnsonian and Royal Queensland Yacht clubs. Predeceased by his wife in 1930, Pound died on 25 September 1946 at Yeronga and was cremated with Anglican rites. One son and one daughter survived him. In 1999 the Department of Primary Industries opened the C. J. Pound Laboratory at the Tick Fever Research Centre, Wacol, in honour of a man who was described by one newspaper as the 'boffin' who 'saved the cattle industry'.

Queensland 1900: A Narrative of Her Past (Brisb, 1900); R. Patrick, *A History of Health & Medicine in Queensland 1824-1960* (Brisb, 1987); B. M. Angus, *Tick Fever and the Cattle Tick in Australia 1829-1996* (Brisb, 1998); Qld Stockbrokers' Assn, *Annual Report*, 1899; *Australian Tropiculturist and Stockbreeder*, 1, no 5, 1 July 1895, p 132; *Sunday Sun* (Brisb), 17 July 1988, 'Magazine', p 4; Dept of Agriculture & Stock packet, AGS/N237 (QSA).

BEVERLEY M. ANGUS

PRIMROSE, MAUD VIOLET FLORINDA (1872-1954), nurse, was born on 31 July 1872 at Bendigo, Victoria, daughter of Robert Primrose, a Scottish-born mining legal manager, and his wife Maria Louise ('Maisie'), née Walsh, from London. Maud grew up on a farming property at Kerang with her sister Lilian. After nursing training at Wagga Wagga General Hospital, New South Wales, by her early twenties Maud had qualified as a trained nurse and in dispensing and massage. Despite her youth, she was appointed matron, a post she held for seven years before returning to Victoria.

While working for a Melbourne doctor, Primrose promoted nursing as a profession, becoming involved in the (Royal) Victorian Trained Nurses' Association, formed in 1901. She was later made a life member of this association and of the Victorian Nursing Council. In 1909 she established and became honorary organizing secretary of the Visiting Trained Nurses' Association of Victoria, valuing the greater independence and initiative of visiting, compared with a fixed salary position. Her dynamism was often remarked upon and she was not afraid of controversy. As well as cycling to her patients, she was one of the first women in Melbourne to hold a motorcar driver's licence. Her growing interest in maternal and infant health led her to New Zealand about 1913 to undertake specialized training for a year from the Plunket Society at Dunedin, under the distinctive regime of (Sir) Frederic Truby King at Karitane.

Back in Melbourne, Primrose threw herself into what became her major life's work, the promotion of the Truby King method of caring for babies. With the support of her mentor Dr J. W. Springthorpe [q.v.12], between 1916 and 1920 she helped to establish the Society for the Health of Women and Children of Victoria—Plunket System. A rival to the Victorian Baby Health Centres Association, the first Truby King or Plunket infant welfare clinic opened at Coburg in 1919. Several other clinics followed, and specially trained mothercraft nurses also worked in private homes and gave advice in department stores. Trained at the Tweddle [q.v.12] Hospital for Babies and School of Mothercraft from 1921, the nurses were formally named 'Primrose nurses'. In subsequent years the lively debates over the most appropriate regime for feeding and managing babies, particularly over the protein content of artificial milk formula, made infant welfare more like 'infant warfare'. Primrose founded the Truby King Mothercraft League of South Australia in October 1934, then returned to Victoria to run a hospital again at Kerang. Her influence continued in the mid-1930s through her articles on infant care in the *New Idea* and the *Housewife*, and radio broadcasts, 'The 3UZ Truby King Mother Craft Circle'.

Reports of Primrose's initiative as a pioneer nurse suggested her strength and determination, but her gentleness, mischievous nature, and personal warmth and affection for children belied the rigidity and discipline of the Truby King system. An attractive, strong woman, she was known as 'Sandy' by some family members because of her reddish hair. She also spent some time with her sister Lily and her family at their property near Balranald, New South Wales.

In Melbourne Miss Primrose lived quietly with her close friend and companion Gertrude Millar at Camberwell, and was involved in activities at her local Church of England. She died on 16 July 1954 in the Austin [q.v.] Hospital, Heidelberg, and was buried in Box Hill cemetery. A newspaper death notice inserted by patients and staff of Ward 9 at the Austin referred to their 'sweet memories', in tribute to a controversial and passionate advocate for mothers' and children's health.

Who's Who in the World of Women (Melb, 1934); M. King, *Truby King* (Lond, 1948); K. M. Reiger, *The Disenchantment of the Home* (Melb, 1985); P. Mein Smith, *Mothers and King Baby* (Lond, 1997); *Southern Sphere*, 1 Feb 1911, p 18; *Weekly Times* (Melb), 10 Feb 1912, p 10; Society for the Health of Women and Children in Vic, Minutes (Tweddle Hospital, Footscray, Melb); information from Ms D. Primrose, Geelong, Vic, and Mrs M. Telford, Melb.

KERREEN M. REIGER

PROBERT, JOHN WILLIAM (1893-1945), soldier and farmer, was born on 15 November 1893 at Elsternwick, Melbourne, only child of Victorian-born parents Charles Moule Verdon Probert, gentleman, and his wife Maud Mary, née Woodward. John's parents divorced in 1901; Charles remarried in 1905. Educated briefly at Cumloden school, East St Kilda, and Melbourne Church of England Grammar School, John left home in 1910 and soon fell foul of the law. Fined £2 in May for 'borrowing' a camera at Castlemaine, he caught a train to Sydney, was arrested for breaching the Influx of Criminals Prevention Act (1903) and sentenced in July to six months imprisonment. His sentence was remitted four weeks later, and he immediately joined the crew of the windjammer *Marian Woodside*, bound for Chile, to redeem himself. Shortly after returning in March 1911, however, he was fined for evading a cab fare and in May, convicted of obtaining clothes by false pretences, was sentenced to twelve months hard labour in Goulburn gaol.

Released in July 1912, Probert sailed for England and in September enlisted in the Rifle Brigade, British Army. Serving in the brigade's 1st Battalion when World War I broke out, he arrived in France on 23 August 1914. He was wounded during the battle of Le Cateau on the 26th and captured by the Germans. Held in a prisoner-of-war camp at Döberitz, near Berlin, he escaped in September 1917 after receiving news that his father was seriously ill. He made his way to Stettin (Szczecin), hid in a Swedish ship's coal bunker and emerged more than a week later at Malmö, Sweden. There he learned that his father had died. For his gallantry Probert was awarded the Military Medal.

Back in England, he transferred to the Royal Flying Corps in October 1917. Probert qualified as a pilot and was commissioned in the Royal Air Force on 1 November 1918. On Armistice Day he crashed his S.E.5a while performing celebratory aerobatics. Next month he sustained serious facial injuries in another aircraft accident. After recovering, he was repatriated to Australia and placed on the Unemployed List on 14 June 1919.

In 1924 Probert leased, under the soldier-settlement scheme, 1555 acres (629 ha) near Rankins Springs, New South Wales. At St Nicholas's Church of England, Coogee, Sydney, on 8 June 1925 he married Minnie Cook. He worked hard to establish his wheat-farm, but conditions were harsh; his wife left him in 1927, taking their son. Divorced in

April 1933, he married 26-year-old Nora Gwendoline Peach on 14 June that year at St Alban's Church of England, Griffith. Although prospects improved after he turned his attention to sheep, the cumulative effects of the Depression and drought forced the Proberts off the land in 1938. Early in 1939 he opened a small farmers' produce store at Griffith.

Appointed pilot officer, Royal Australian Air Force Reserve, on 1 February 1939, Probert was called up for full-time duty on 2 September, but six days later was discharged medically unfit. On 30 April 1940, understating his age, he enlisted in the Australian Imperial Force. Promoted to acting warrant officer, class two, in June, he was posted to the intelligence section, I Corps headquarters. He arrived in the Middle East in September, but was sent home in November and discharged in January 1941 'not on account of misconduct'. His correct age had perhaps been discovered.

Adopting the surname Moule-Probert, which he had used for a time while serving in the R.A.F., he re-enlisted in the A.I.F. in April 1941. He reached Singapore in August and became a driver in the 2/15th Field Regiment. The unit moved to Malaya in September, went into action against the advancing Japanese forces in mid-January 1942 and withdrew to Singapore at the end of the month. On 15 February the island fell, and Moule-Probert once again became a prisoner of war. As part of 'B' Force, he was shipped to Sandakan, British North Borneo. There, more than 2400 Australian and British prisoners were overworked, starved, beaten and denied medical supplies. Only six survived. Moule-Probert died on 10 May 1945. The cause of death was recorded as malaria. Survived by his wife and their two sons, and by the son of his first marriage, he is commemorated on the Labuan Memorial, Sabah, Malaysia, for servicemen with no known graves.

J. B. Kiddle (comp), *War Services of Old Melburnians 1914-1918* (Melb, 1923); L. R. Silver, *Sandakan* (Burra Creek, NSW, 1988); S. and J. Probert, *Prisoner of Two Wars* (Adel, 2001); AWM 43, item A707, *and* AWM 140 (AWM); A9300, item PROBERT J W M, *and* B883, item NX10894 (NAA, Canb); WO 339/128673 *and* AIR 76/413 (PRO, Lond).

JOLYON HORNER

PROESCHEL, FREDERICK (1809-1870), map-maker and publisher, was born on 11 March 1809 at Colmar, Haut Rhin, France, son of Jacques Proeschel, rope-maker, and his wife Madeleine, née Trautt. In 1832 Frederick married Christine Marguerite Hafler, with whom he had at least two children. By 1833 he was living in Paris carrying on his trade as an upholsterer. In the 1840s he experimented with various materials in the manufacture of bedding, including designing mattresses with springs. Proeschel also invented a method of making moisture-resistant bricks, for which he received a silver medal in 1841 and a cash prize of 400 francs in 1843 from the Société d'Encouragement pour l'Industrie Nationale. After suffering substantial losses in the revolution of 1848, he migrated to the United States of America, but departed in 1852 aboard the *William Frontingham*, reaching Melbourne—probably without his family—in December.

By the end of July 1853 Proeschel had set up an English, French and German (he was fluent in all three languages) information and labour agency in Little Bourke Street and published a map showing routes to the gold diggings. A map of Melbourne quickly followed, then maps of Collingwood, Richmond, North Melbourne and Geelong in 1855. For a fee, he would number houses, in 1859 taking credit 'for the foundation of a good numbering of houses in Geelong, Collingwood, Richmond and North Melbourne'. His first map of Victoria was issued in 1856. These early productions were fairly crude lithographs but in 1859 he issued a more sophisticated engraved map of Victoria, updated as new information came to hand and issued in several editions. He also published maps of Hobart Town and Launceston, of New South Wales, South Australia and another one of Melbourne, as well as of the routes to the Snowy River goldfields.

Proeschel was extraordinarily successful in selling his maps, which he promoted by brochures, once by a lottery and by publishing the lists of subscribers around the edges of the maps. In 1863 he issued his *Atlas of Australasia*, based on his earlier maps of the eastern Australian colonies, together with new material. He was unlikely to have recouped his outlay of over £3000 on this expensive undertaking, though the atlas was widely acclaimed in reviews. Apart from his map-making, he experimented in separating gold from quartz, but did not produce any useful process. He also embarked on an atlas to show exploration of the world in the 400 years previous to the 1860s, but this was never finished. In May 1860 he became a member of the Royal Society of Victoria.

Proeschel left Melbourne for London in February 1864 to promote his work there, apparently unsuccessfully, and soon returned to Paris. There his attempts to promote his atlas through the Ministère de l'Instruction Publique and his requests for support for the atlas of exploration had no success. In the late 1860s he published pamphlets in Paris on cholera and investment. He died on 1 May 1870 at his residence in Paris leaving an estate valued at a mere 40 francs. During his eleven years in Victoria Proeschel was its only private map publisher, who enjoyed considerable success by applying the methods of canvassing throughout the colony and other parts of Australia for selling maps.

T. A. Darragh, 'Frederick Proeschel, Colonial Map Maker', *Bibliographical Soc of Aust and NZ Bulletin*, 15, nos 3 and 4, 1991, *and* 'Commercial Map Publishing in Nineteenth Century Melbourne', Austn Map Circle, *The Globe*, no 37, 1992, p 74.

THOMAS A. DARRAGH

PUGLIESE, CAROLINE FRANCES (1865-1940), theatre proprietor, and HUMBERT JAMES (1884-1955), film producer and shop proprietor, were mother and son. Caroline was born on 17 February 1865 at Five Dock, Sydney, second daughter of James Donaldson, an Irish-born gardener, and his wife Mary, née Vidler, from England. On 16 October 1883 at St John's Church of England, Ashfield, Caroline married Antonio Pugliese (1853-1916), a labourer from Viggiano, Basilicata, Italy, who had arrived in New South Wales about 1881 and had two children by an earlier marriage. Antonio was soon working as a watchmaker and jeweller in Sydney; reputedly, he was later a successful racehorse owner and trainer. The eldest of their seven children was born on 14 February 1884 at Park Street and registered as Umberto. He later claimed to have been connected with the moving picture business 'ever since a mere boy'.

Described as a cinematograph operator, Humbert married Elsie Beatrice Harvey, a vocalist, on 22 December 1910. The family had taken over the 'somewhat despised' Alhambra Theatre in George Street, Haymarket, a few years earlier. A music hall from 1884, then a waxworks venue, it was never in the theatrical mainstream. Here the Puglieses began to show the new cinematograph. In 1916 Raymond Longford [q.v.10], having no other outlet for his *Maori Maid's Love*, described it as 'an obscure theatre'.

'Pugliese Enterprises' ran the Alhambra, the Star cinema at Bondi and a cinema at Leichhardt. It was a family business, with Caroline controlling the purse strings and other members (such as Humbert's sister Rita) acting as projectionists and ticket collectors. They tried to make each presentation an 'occasion' for patrons, whether at a film screening or a variety show. Sunday night concerts at the Alhambra were popular, while at the Star cinema, twice a week, the Pugliese family, from mama to grandchildren, sat in a reserved section. Humbert, a handsome man with a flourishing moustache, was described as a 'charmer', floating down the aisle of the cinema, saying, 'This way Madam, careful Madam, comfortable Madam'. By 1922 the Star had been sold and the Alhambra, under different ownership, was known as the Melba.

The Pugliese family had been involved in the production of three early Australian films. Caroline was the driving force behind, and wrote the script for, *The Church and the Woman*, produced by Humbert and directed by Longford, which opened at the Theatre Royal on 13 October 1917 to good reviews. It was then the subject of a plagiarism suit that helped publicity but delayed its release in Melbourne until 1921. Judgement had been given against Humbert, and if he wanted the film exhibited he had no choice but to come to a financial agreement with the plaintiff, Edward Finn.

The Waybacks, billed as 'Australia's Sweetest Comedy', produced by Humbert, opened at the Sydney Town Hall on 18 May 1918 and was an instant success, continuing to be distributed in 1925. His third film, the old stage hit *Struck Oil*, was directed by Franklyn Barrett [q.v.7] and, like the others, shot mainly in exteriors; it opened at Sydney Town Hall in October 1920. Featuring an ageing star—Maggie Moore [q.v.5]—it was not a success. The Pugliese family, which had always experienced difficulty competing with Australian Films Ltd's monopoly, abandoned film production.

In 1920 Humbert, a 'theatre ticket collector', had petitioned in the Supreme Court for an order for restitution of conjugal rights—his wife had refused to live with him, citing his strong dependence on his mother. Elsie died in 1925. On 7 May 1932 in St Jude's Church of England, Randwick, Humbert married Mary Margaret 'Mabs' Wilson, née McGuirk, a divorcée. In partnership with her, he became a shoe-shop proprietor, owning a chain of high-quality shops known as 'Mabs McGuirk', in such city addresses as Elizabeth and King streets and the Imperial Arcade.

Caroline Pugliese died on 4 May 1940 at Arden Street, Coogee, and was buried in Randwick cemetery. Three sons and four daughters survived her. Humbert died on 28 May 1955 at Royal Prince Alfred Hospital, Camperdown, and was buried in the family vault at Randwick. His wife survived him, as did his son by his first marriage.

A. Pike and R. Cooper, *Australian Film 1900-1977* (Melb, 1980); *Lone Hand*, 1 July 1918, p 352; *Historical Waverley*, vol 7, 1983 (whole issue); *Sun* (Syd), 8 Sept 1958, p 23.

BILL CROWLEY

PYKE, LILLIAN MAXWELL (1881-1927), author, was born on 25 August 1881 at Belfast (Port Fairy), Victoria, tenth child and one of three daughters of Robert Moseley Heath, a draper from Totnes, Devon, England, and his wife Susannah Ellen, née Wilson, of Kent. Lillian was described as both a teacher and a journalist before her marriage with Presbyterian forms to Richard Dimond Pyke on 7 April 1906 at Canterbury Road, Toorak; he was an accountant working in Brisbane and formerly of Collingwood. They moved to Queensland where he was employed as accountant in a railway construction camp at Monkland, near Gympie. Her first child was born there in 1907, followed by two more children in 1908 and 1912. Richard Pyke shot himself in the head on 4 December 1914, aged 37. Lillian returned to Melbourne with her children. In order to support and educate them she returned to writing.

Between 1916 and 1927 as Lillian Pyke she wrote sixteen books classified as children's books, though they were better suited to adolescents. As 'Erica Maxwell', she wrote three novels for adults, one of which, *A Wife by Proxy* (1926), contained Esperanto themes, was translated into Esperanto, and published in 1930 as *Anstataria Edzino*. Under the influence of her brother-in-law J. G. Pyke, who was president of the Esperanto Society, Melbourne, in 1913-29, she had become involved in the movement.

As well she produced a *Guide to Australian Etiquette*, which she quickly adapted from an outdated English text. It was first published probably in 1919 and reissued in 1931, then twice after her death in 1945, and with a modernized text in 1960. She also edited various collections of stories, abridged and adapted Ethel Turner's [q.v.12] *Miss Bobbie* 'for the use of schools', and produced several illustrated alphabet books. In all, her output averaged a little more than two books a year for eleven years.

Most of her stories for both children and adults came out of her experience of Queensland railway construction camps or her involvement in education, and had an improving intention. *Camp Kiddies* (1919) was almost a memoir illustrated with photographs. The boys' stories were set in the fictional St Virgil's, based on Wesley College, Melbourne, where her son became a student in 1920. She dedicated *Jack of St Virgil's* (1917) to L. A. Adamson [q.v.7], the headmaster of Wesley, 'to whose teaching I am indebted for whatever understanding of "the public school spirit" I may have acquired and whose kindly assistance and influence have enabled me to keep in touch with school life'. The books contained strong themes of fair play and heroism, but also adventure, often involving engineering, explosives and skullduggery afar off. The girls' stories were also based on a fictional girls school, Riverview, and probably owed much to the interests of her daughters (whose names occasionally occur in her stories), though they too contained adventures not unlike those of the boys. One explored the relatively new Girl Guide movement. Another of her children's stories was an early fictional account of the First Fleet and the settlement at Port Jackson. Several drew on an imagined Pacific Island called Vilatonga from which the 'Prince' and his sister both went to school in Victoria.

Pyke died of chronic renal disease on 31 August 1927 at St Andrew's Hospital, Brighton, and was buried in Box Hill cemetery after a service at Sleight's Mortuary Chapel conducted by the Rev. Charles Strong [q.v.6]. Her daughter Joyce graduated with a B.A. from the University of Melbourne, and son Laurence followed with a B.Sc. and a Rhodes scholarship. From 1952 to 1960 he was head of Newington College, Stanmore, Sydney, and later dean of graduate studies at the University of Melbourne. He died in July 1987.

H. M. Saxby, *Offered to Children: A History of Australian Children's Literature 1841-1941* (Syd, 1998); *Queenslander*, 28 Mar 1925, p 43, 15 Sept 1927, p 19; *A'sian* (Melb), 10 Sept 1927, p 741.

BEVERLEY KINGSTON

Q

QUONG, ROSE MAUD (1879-1972), performer and writer, was born on 15 August 1879 in East Melbourne, eldest of four children of Chun Quong, a merchant from Canton (Guangzhou), China, and his Victorian-born wife Annie, née Moy Quong. Rose's parents encouraged their children's education, and she attended University High School. Late in 1896 she passed the matriculation examination at the University of Melbourne in nine subjects, including Latin, algebra and physics, and planned to study medicine. From June 1897, however, Quong was a public servant. She was working as a telephone switch operator in Melbourne for the Postmaster General's Department in 1901. By 1919 she had become a clerk in the Auditor General's Office, central staff, naval and military branch.

Yet her heart lay with the theatre. When questioned by a journalist late in life as to why she never married, she responded: 'I never met anyone I've been interested in. Perhaps I've been too much of an actress. Perhaps I've always acted life'. In the 1890s an Englishman, Mr Chisley, had taught her to read Shakespeare and poetry. After winning a prize in the elocution competition run by the Australian Natives' Association in 1903 she made her name on the local amateur stage and helped to found the Mermaid Play Society (Melbourne Repertory Players), informally connected with the university. Quong served on the company's executive and acted in works ranging from ancient Greek drama to a play by John Masefield.

In 1924 Quong won a scholarship to study drama in London at the academy of Rosina Filippi. At first Quong felt ambivalent about presenting herself professionally as Chinese. When it became clear that she was not going to succeed as a Shakespearean or general actress, her friends urged her towards a specialized career, that of exotic or Oriental reciter, actress and performer. In December 1924 and January 1925 several British newspapers interviewed her. By September 1925 she had met Arthur Waley, whose translations of Chinese poetry she read at the Writers' Club next month. She was also in demand for private receptions. In November that year, when she recited and commented on Chinese poetry on radio for the British Broadcasting Corporation, the *British Australian and New Zealander* celebrated her success. In 1929 she appeared with Laurence (Lord) Olivier and the Chinese American actress Anna May Wong in *The Circle of Chalk*, a play by the German dramatist Klabund, based on Chinese legend. She again appeared in the play in 1931.

The Australian community in London embraced Quong. By 1932 she had launched her 'Circle', a regular event on alternate Sunday evenings at which she would lecture on Chinese themes and recite poetry, probably in her own flat. She travelled frequently, addressing the Leeds Women's Luncheon Club late in 1932. Of medium height and build, she adopted an Oriental style of hair and dress to accentuate her Chinese appearance. For a lecture to the Belfast Alpha Club in October, she dressed in 'a Chinese costume of bright green trousers embroidered in gold and a kimono-like top in soft yellow patterned with snakes' and discussed the position of women in China, the 'Bandit problem' and Chinese language, poems and stories. In February 1934 she embarked on an eleven-month trip to the United States of America.

At the end of 1935 Quong returned to the U.S.A. for another extensive lecture tour, and next year she made her only visit to China, where she was reported as having lectured in Mandarin, which she had learned in London. She studied Chinese culture and literature avidly, and by 1938 had become a welcome guest at the Chinese embassy in London. By then she had adopted the role of cultural interpreter between East and West. This stance underlay the books she later published, *Chinese Wit, Wisdom and Written Characters* (New York, 1944) and *Chinese Ghost and Love Stories* (New York, 1946), the latter a work of translation. From January 1939 she lived permanently in New York, continuing to travel and lecture and to run a 'Circle'.

Despite successes, such as appearing in the Broadway production of the Rodgers and Hammerstein musical *Flower Drum Song* in 1958-59, Quong worked hard, lived modestly and frequently delivered lectures. She also used the name Rose Lanu Quong. In 1971 she appeared as herself (an aged Chinese astrologer) in a Canadian film, *Eliza's Horoscope*. She died on 14 December 1972 in Midtown Hospital, New York, and was buried in Rosedale cemetery, Linden, New Jersey.

British Australasian and New Zealander, 15 Jan 1925, p 5, 3 Dec 1925, p 14, 8 Dec 1932, p 12, 19 Oct 1933, p 10, 4 Mar 1937, p 14; *Manhattan Tribune*, 13 May 1972, p 7; Quong papers (Balch Inst for Ethnic Studies, Hist Society of Pennsylvania, US).

ANGELA WOOLLACOTT

R

RADCLIFFE, PHILIP WALKER (1884-1956), teacher and lecturer, was born on 16 June 1884 at Goodna, Queensland, second of five children of Oliver Radcliffe, an Australian-born teacher and later chief inspector of schools, and his wife Janet Wilson, née Walker, from Scotland. After attending Breakfast Creek State School, where his father was head teacher, Philip won a coveted state scholarship and entered Brisbane Grammar School in 1897. He passed the Sydney junior public examination and in 1900 became a pupil-teacher at Sherwood State School, Brisbane. In the minimum time, he completed the requirements to become a classified teacher in 1903.

On 7 May 1904 Radcliffe married Grace Kidston Macfarlane at the district registrar's office, Toowong. After working briefly in one-teacher schools at Plainview and then Thargomindah, he returned to Brisbane and was an assistant teacher at Milton, then Manly. He enlisted in the Australian Imperial Force on 18 January 1916, was promoted to acting lance sergeant with the 8th Training Battalion in England then, reverting to private, served with the 31st Battalion in France. In September 1917 he was wounded in action, and was discharged in Brisbane on 6 July 1918. He returned to teaching at Manly and then Taringa. In 1919 Radcliffe taught in the high school section of the Central Technical College. He moved in 1921 to the recently opened State High School, South Brisbane. A talented teacher, he received outstanding inspectors' reports.

Although enrolled at the University of Queensland in English I, Latin I, logic and psychology I in 1913, Radcliffe did not sit the examinations until 1919. The requirements for promotion to teacher class I satisfied, his formal education ceased. His personal library attested to his abiding love of literature—Greek, Latin, English and Australian. He was also a brilliant mathematician. Colleagues and students always found him a gracious, knowledgeable and generous mentor. In May 1933 he was appointed lecturer at the Queensland Teachers' Training College, later becoming senior lecturer and occasionally acting principal.

'Raddie' was remembered as a short, slighty humped man with closely cropped grey hair and nicotine-stained (crooked) teeth, brown hair and hazel eyes, clad usually in an ill-fitting, crumpled suit. He lacked self-importance ('Please stay seated. I'm not royalty'), and addressed staff and students alike with unhurried courtesy. Whether the enquirer was seeking help on teaching the use of the apostrophe to 10-year-olds or translating a passage of classical Greek, serious attention was assured. In his English classes at the college many students discovered for the first time that a poem might be memorized for pleasure, not simply to pass an examination. He often introduced poetry that was not widely known. His delivery was unaffectedly eloquent ('no Elocution please').

Radcliffe was responsible for the first Queensland school radio broadcasts by the Australian Broadcasting Commission in 1937. He also compiled the splendid *Queensland School Reader* for different grades, containing much literary content—prose and poetry alternating—which encouraged many children to learn to read and to love reading. In World War II he served part time as a lieutenant in the Volunteer Defence Corps. He retired from the teachers' college in 1954. Radcliffe died on 11 March 1956 in Brisbane General Hospital and was cremated with Anglican rites. His wife, two sons and a daughter survived him. In 2004 facsimile copies of his *Readers* were still being printed and sold to former students.

S. Pechey and P. Thomas, *Telling Tales* (Brisb, 1992); N. Kyle et al, *A Class of its Own* (Brisb, 1999); Friends of Antiquity, Univ Qld, *NOVA*, 1, no 4, 2002, p 6; P. W. Radcliffe, staff card, Education Dept (QSA); B2455, item Radcliffe P. W., *and* B884, item Q200379 (NAA, Canb).

DORIS H. SWAN
GEOFFREY SWAN

RADECKI, JOHN (1865-1955), stained-glass designer, was born on 2 August 1865 at Łódź, Russia (Poland), son of Pavel Radecki, coalminer, and his wife Victoria, née Bednarkiewicz. Jan trained at a German art school at Poznan (Posen). With his parents and four siblings he migrated to Australia, reaching Sydney in January 1882. The family settled at Wollongong, where his father and he worked in the coalmines. His parents had two more children in Australia. Moving to Sydney in 1883, Jan attended art classes. He boarded with the Saunders family from England at Oxford Street, Paddington, and on 17 May 1888 married their daughter Emma at the local district registrar's office. Living at Hurstville, John (as he was now known) was naturalized in November 1904.

From 1885 Radecki had been employed by Frederick Ashwin, who taught him to work with glass. In the 1890s the two men

332

had crafted stained-glass windows entitled 'Sermon on the Mount' (St Paul's Church, Cobbitty) and 'Nativity' (St Jude's, Randwick). Other works included a window at Yanco Agricultural College, produced in 1902 by F. Ashwin & Co. reputedly to Radecki's design, and the chancel window (1903) in St Clement's, Mosman. His first, major independent work was the 'Te Deum' window in Christ Church St Laurence, Sydney, in 1906. Ashwin and Radecki also collaborated on windows in St James's, Forest Lodge, and St John's, Campbelltown.

Following Ashwin's death in 1909, Radecki became chief designer for J. Ashwin & Co, in partnership with Frederick's brother John; he was proprietor of the company from John Ashwin's death in 1920 until 1954. The largest glassmaking establishment in Sydney, with a high reputation, the firm created the chapel windows for St Scholastica's Convent, Glebe, in the early 1930s. Radecki's work included windows in such churches as St John the Evangelist's, Campbelltown, St Patrick's, Kogarah, St Joseph's, Rockdale, St Matthew's, Manly, and Our Lady of Dolours', North Goulburn, Scots Kirk, Hamilton, Newcastle, and the Presbyterian Church, Wollongong.

A church committee member during the building in 1928 of St Declan's Catholic Church, Penshurst, Radecki designed, produced and donated the stained-glass windows there, including a memorial window dedicated to his wife, who had died in 1919. On 8 January 1921 at the Church of Christ, Hurstville, Radecki married Sydney-born Jean Hughes (d.1944).

During the 1920s J. Ashwin & Co. produced the stained glass for the impressive, vaulted ceiling of what became the Commonwealth Savings Bank in Martin Place to designs by Radecki. These had an Australian character, illustrating 'the basic sources of wealth': sheep and cattle grazing, agriculture, mining, shipping and building; stockmen, carpenters, gold panning, farming and wharf labourers were shown alongside a typical banking scene. A window for the reading room of the Mitchell [q.v.5] Library, signed 'John Radecki, Sydney 1941', depicted the printer William Caxton with the first book printed in English.

Radecki's strengths were a natural aptitude for figure drawing and composition, an eye for colour, which he used as a compositional device, an outstanding knowledge of his medium and facility with techniques in glass painting. His recreational passion was playing chess. He died on 10 May 1955 in his home at Hurstville, and was buried with Catholic rites in Woronora cemetery. The six daughters and three sons of his first marriage survived him. His daughter Winifred Siedlecky continued the company until the building's owners demolished the premises in Dixon Street in 1961.

J. Zimmer, *Stained Glass in Australia* (Melb, 1984); B. E. Meagher, *An Outline History of St. Declan's Parish Penshurst, N.S.W.* (Syd, 1985); B. Sherry, *Australia's Historic Stained Glass* (Syd, 1991); J. Foster and J. Shailer, *The Treasure of St Scholastica's* (Syd, 2002); *Commonwealth Home*, 1 Feb 1929, p 20; *Aust Women's Weekly*, 7 Sept 1946, p 26; D. Giedraityte, Stained and Painted Glass in the Sydney Area, c.1830-c.1920 (M.A. thesis, Syd Univ, 1982); series A1, item 1904/9087 (NAA, Canb); information from Radecki family, Sr J. Foster, Glebe, and Dr S. Siedlecky, Balmoral, Syd.

LOUISE ANEMAAT

RAINE, TOM RAINE (1858-1929), real-estate agent, was born on 20 June 1858 at Frederick Valley, near Orange, New South Wales, second of three sons of Edmund William Worsley Raine, a Sydney-born miller, and his wife Augusta Eliza, née Dunlop, who came from Ireland. The boy was named after his adventurous grandfather Thomas Raine, a friend and business partner of W. C. Wentworth [qq.v.2]. After the death of young Tom's brothers in infancy and that of their father in 1863, Augusta ran the mill and educated her son at home. They lived on a farm leased from the Wentworth family. Raine learned early the value of hard work.

In the early 1880s Fitzwilliam Wentworth recommended Raine to J. R. Hill [q.v.4], manager of the extensive Wentworth and (Daniel) Cooper [q.v.1] estates, who offered him the position of agent for the Cooper estate. The young man's mentors were Hill and JOSEPH MORTIMER HORNE (1842-1927), who had been agent for the Wentworth estate for some years. Born on 22 June 1842 at Huntley, Aberdeen, Scotland, eighth of nine children of George Horn(e), merchant, and his wife Helen, née Milne, Joseph had met W. C. Wentworth's son D'Arcy in Britain, reached Sydney in 1871 and lived for some fourteen years in Vaucluse House. In 1883 Raine and Horne became partners, setting up as land agents—managing properties, collecting rents, making valuations, and buying and selling on commission. Horne married with Anglican rites Annie Marrietta Clutterbuck, a Nightingale nurse from England, on 5 August 1886 at Christ Church St Laurence, Sydney.

At St John's Church of England, Ashfield, on 4 February 1889 Raine married Jean Vardon Ralston. On 31 October 1894 he was badly burned when the train in which he was travelling was involved in a collision at Redfern station. He needed six months treatment in Sydney Hospital and daily attention to his burns for the rest of his life.

As the firm became better known, business grew. In 1898 Raine replaced Sir Daniel Cooper [q.v.3] as trustee of the Hunter Baillie estate and took the place of Hill as trustee of the Cooper estate. The Raine family moved in 1899 from Ashfield to Guyong, at Double Bay, which the architect Ernest Scott had designed. That year Horne retired from the business, but he continued to manage the Wentworth estate until 1920. He died on 28 November 1927 at Croydon and was buried with Brethren forms in Rookwood cemetery. His wife survived him.

Raine's business life had begun with his excellent connexions but was transformed into success by his ability, energy and personal charm. He sought to improve the standing of agents by insisting that no member of his firm should deal in real estate on his own behalf. In 1929 the *Bulletin* described him as 'a small, mercurial, smiling man who loved life and his fellow-men'. His hobbies were shooting, fishing and golf, and he belonged to the Australian Jockey and the Royal Sydney Golf clubs as well as to the Australian Club in Sydney and the Wellington in London. He was a life governor of Sydney, Royal Prince Alfred, the Royal South Sydney and Royal North Shore hospitals and of the Royal Alexandra Hospital for Children. During World War I Jean Raine was president of the Belgian Babies' Kit Society, which sent clothing to the needy wives of British and Allied soldiers and sailors.

His health failing, Raine decided to provide for the future of his family and the firm. Raine & Horne was incorporated as an unlisted public company on 1 February 1928. Raine died on 2 May 1929 in a private hospital and was buried in Waverley cemetery. His wife and their five daughters and three sons survived him. In 2004 his company, chaired by his grandson, had more than 450 franchise offices throughout Australia and Asia, affiliated offices in Europe and an annual turnover exceeding $9 billion.

E. Warburton, *Private Property* (Syd, 1998); *SMH*, 1 Nov 1894, pp 5 & 6, 29 Nov 1927, p 12, 3 May 1929, p 14, 1 Mar 1983, pp 11 & 12; *Daily Telegraph* (Syd), 23 June 1915, p 6; *Bulletin*, 8 May 1929, p 14; Minutes of the Real Estate Auctioneers & Agents Assn of NSW, 1910-29 (Real Estate Inst of NSW archives, Rushcutters Bay, Syd); Raine & Horne, Board minutes, 1928-29 (held by Raine & Horne, Syd); A. O. Sullivan, The Raine and Horne Story (ms, held by author, Woollahra, Syd); information from Mr M. R. Horne, Syd.

A. O. SULLIVAN

RANDALL, GEORGE (1843-1930), confectionery manufacturer, migration officer and orchardist, was born on 9 February 1843 at Hertford, England, son of Richard Randall, tailor, and his wife Eliza, née Webb. Educated at the Cowper Testimonial National School and then privately, George worked initially in domestic service. He married Naomi Jackson on 20 May 1868 in the parish church, Anwick, Lincolnshire, and the couple immediately left for Queensland in the *Planet*. Randall kept a shipboard diary describing the four-month voyage.

After seven years hard work, he acquired premises in Stanley Street, South Brisbane, where he manufactured confectionery and jams, sold under the Superior brand. In 1877 the couple and their two sons went to England. Randall's enthusiasm for Queensland was obvious in newspaper correspondence and his unsolicited but popular lectures. Returning to Brisbane, the Randalls lived at Panshanger, a mansion in Merivale Street, near the factory. As the business succeeded, the family methodically acquired extensive real estate.

In July 1881, when (Sir) Arthur Palmer [q.v.5] appointed him as lecturer and emigration agent in England, Randall confounded the government by not requesting a salary. From October that year, with untiring energy, he visited nearly every county, concentrating on the farming districts of Norfolk, Lincolnshire and western Yorkshire. His optimistic reports in English and Queensland newspapers encouraged agricultural labourers experiencing depressed conditions to migrate. George returned to his family in February 1884 but immediately was reappointed at a salary of £500. He toured the colony before resuming duties in England in March 1885. When Queensland experienced further economic difficulties late in 1889, once more the slight figure with his neat beard returned to Brisbane.

The government re-employed Randall from January 1890, when he again toured Queensland. His third English term, this time accompanied by his family, lasted for four years from July 1891. Following the withdrawal of free and assisted passages, Randall concentrated on recruiting smallholders at agricultural shows where he displayed samples of familiar crops prospering in sub-tropical conditions. Although he advocated village settlement and co-operative communities recently made possible by Queensland legislation, these projects did not attract English support. In 1896 he bought an orchard at Birkdale. Randall's fourth appointment to woo settlers covered six years from January 1897. Returned colonists were seconded to promote Queensland, enabling Randall to concentrate on exhibitions and farming fairs, where he also acted as a commercial agent. Free and nominated migration was renewed in 1899, and he resumed his lectures.

When Randall rejoined his family at Birkdale late in 1902, large-scale recruitment seemed finished. His total absorption with migration to Queensland extended to writing poems, booklets and pamphlets. While some initiatives were considered expensive, he encouraged several thousand individuals, particularly farmers, to migrate during twenty-one years efficient service.

Randall's elder son RICHARD JOHN (1869-1906), artist, had been born on 5 February 1869 in South Brisbane. After studies in Brisbane and England he returned in 1899 to become a talented and prolific painter, particularly of landscapes but with some portraiture. After Richard's death from a cerebral tumour on 15 October 1906, George vigorously supported his son's reputation by memorial publications, the gift of his works to the City of South Brisbane and the maintenance of his studio there (later relocated and restored) as a public asset.

Predeceased by his wife and both sons, George Randall died on 5 July 1930 in hospital in Brisbane and was buried in Cleveland cemetery with Anglican rites. His estate, sworn for probate at £12 386, was left to six young grandchildren.

J. K. Brown and M. Maynard, *Fine Art Exhibitions in Brisbane 1884-1916* (Brisb, 1980); *Brisb Courier*, 20 Oct 1906, p 10; *Queenslander*, 10 July 1930, p 54; J. Keys, George Randall's Role in Queensland Immigration Policy, 1881-1902 (B.A. Hons thesis, Univ Qld, 1966); Randall collection (Univ Qld L); G. Randall, Diary, 1868 (NL); J. Walton, George Randall—Emigration Agent Extraordinary (ms, held by Dr J. Walton, Mount Tamborine, Qld).

JENNIFER HARRISON

REDE, MARY LEMAN; *see* GRIMSTONE

REES, ELIZABETH LAURIE (1865-1939), temperance activist and social reformer, was born on 18 December 1865 at Grosvenor Square, Mayfair, London, second of seven children of Thomas Johnston, a journeyman coachmaker and later motor-body builder from Edinburgh, Scotland, and his wife Margaret, neé Kirkcaldy. The family migrated to Sydney when Bessie was 5, then moved to Victoria about 1875. On 26 October 1892 in Melbourne she married with Baptist forms Evan Rees (1860-1935), a successful, Welsh born grocer. They had five children and lived in North Carlton, then at Bryn-y-mor, Hampton.

Evan and Bessie were dedicated Baptists, members of both the Collins Street 'mother' church and their local congregation. Sec-retary of the North Carlton church for twenty-six years, Evan was sometime president of the Baptist Union of Victoria. Bessie was a founder and for many years president of the Baptist Bouverie Street kindergarten and served on the executive of the Free Kindergarten Union. She was the 'strongest original advocate' for the Victorian Baptist Women's Association, which she organized with Cecilia Downing [q.v.14] in 1924; she was its vice-president in 1925-27 and 1936-37 and president in 1928-30. In 1928 she attended the fourth Baptist World Congress at Toronto, Canada, and led one of the sessions of worship there. She was elected secretary of the new Australian Baptist Women's Board in 1935.

Rees's public work focused primarily on the Woman's Christian Temperance Union, which she had joined when young. Having served as a branch officer and member of the State executive, soon after her youngest child started school she reluctantly accepted nomination as general secretary of the Victorian branch upon the retirement of its founder Maria Kirk [q.v.9] in 1913. Rees continued in that role until 1933. She was, as well, superintendent of the school of methods (leadership and meeting procedure) in 1924-33, national treasurer (1924-30) and corresponding secretary (1930-36). From 1933 to 1936 she was State president, then resumed the position of secretary in addition to being elected national general secretary. She was also national superintendent of the literature department (1933-39). Rees was made a life member of the World's W.C.T.U. in 1923 and life president of the Victorian branch in 1938.

In 1921 she had organized and led a deputation of women's groups to ask the attorney-general 'that women be appointed among the justices of the peace as in most if not all of the other States'. Appropriately, she was sworn in as one of the first six female justices in Victoria on 17 February 1927 and three years later was appointed special magistrate to the children's court. At the Maternity Bonus Conference (Melbourne, 1923), hers had been the resolution chosen as the most concise statement of the majority decision. Feminist principle and morals combined in the leading role she took in the campaign against beauty contests in 1927: Rees moved the resolution objecting to girls being 'parade[d] like prize cattle ... for the purposes of gain'. Next year she was a delegate to the W.W.C.T.U. convention at Lausanne, Switzerland, and one of the few selected to address the conference.

Rees represented the W.C.T.U. on the League of Nations Union executive in Victoria from 1928 and at a meeting in October 1930 convened by the Victorian Women Citizens' Movement to organize a world peace demonstration. Also active in the National Council of Women, the Women's Centenary Committee and the Local Option League, she was the W.C.T.U. delegate on such bodies as the Travellers' Aid Society, the Children's Cinema Council, the Slum Abolition League and the Pan Pacific Women's Association. She was awarded King George V's jubilee medal in 1935. In 1937, to support women in favour of temperance principles as candidates for State parliament, she helped to set up the League of Women Electors.

Perhaps Rees's most important achievement, however, was her editorship of the *White Ribbon Signal* from its inception as the national voice of the W.C.T.U. in 1931 to 1939. She was responsible for the radically progressive tone and content of the journal on matters of race, international peace and social reform. In her last issue, published after her death, the editorial argued that Aboriginal people were 'physically, mentally, socially and spiritually … capable of a development which can equal our own', and advised white people to 'think black'.

Rees died on 19 March 1939 at Auburn and was buried with Baptist forms in Melbourne general cemetery. Her two daughters and three sons survived her. Friends and colleagues praised her unostentatious manner, hard work, temperate speech, 'good humoured tolerance', 'clear sight and sound thought'.

Who's Who in the World of Women, 1 (Melb, 1930); I. McCorkindale, *Pioneer Pathways* (Melb, 1948); J. Pargetter, *'For God, Home and Humanity'* (Adel, 1995); *White Ribbon Signal*, 1 Nov 1918, p 187, 1 Jan 1922, p 14, 8 Apr 1923, p 144, 8 May 1923, p 85, 8 June 1924, p 91, 8 Mar 1927, pp 35 & 42, 8 Aug 1927, p 115, 8 Mar 1928, p 40, 9 July 1928, p 103, 8 Oct 1928, p 147, 8 Nov 1930, p 167, 8 Dec 1930, p 179, 2 Dec 1935, p 235, 1 Dec 1936, p 229, 1 Apr 1939, p 63, 1 May 1939, p 92; *Vic Baptist Witness*, 5 Jan 1939, p 8, 5 Apr 1939, p 15, 5 Nov 1949, p 6; Baptist Union of Vic archives, Melb.

JUDITH SMART

RICHARDS, THOMAS JAMES (1882-1935), footballer, soldier and commercial traveller, was born on 29 April 1882 at Rose Valley, Vegetable Creek (Emmaville), New South Wales, fourth of six children of John Richards, a Cornish-born miner, and his wife Mary Ann, née Davis, from Victoria. The family moved to Charters Towers, Queensland, in 1883. After attending the local central state school, Tom worked in the mines. In 1897 a visiting New South Wales Rugby Union team fired his ambition 'for the glory and the glamour of a footballer's life'. He joined the local Waratahs team in 1898 and next year began a successful career with the Natives club.

In 1902 Richards represented Charters Towers against other towns. He played in Brisbane for the Northern District and Country 'B' (1903) and for Queensland 'Next Fifteen' against New South Wales (1905). He and other family members then followed his father to Johannesburg, South Africa, where Tom played for the Mines club and represented Transvaal in the Currie Cup. Ruled ineligible for South Africa's tour of Britain, he nevertheless sailed for England, where he played for Bristol in 1906-07 and represented Gloucestershire; one match was against the South Africans. Hearing of plans for an Australian team to visit Britain, he returned home in July 1907; performances for Queensland next year ensured his selection for the team. Modest and unassuming, he was a handsome athlete, with brown eyes and brown hair, 6 ft (183 cm) tall, weighing 13 stone (82.5 kg).

In Britain, France and North America with the Wallabies, 'Rusty' Richards played mostly in the breakaway position. Big, fast, versatile and opportunistic, with a natural brain for Rugby, he set up chances to score but was alert to fall back in defence. He played against Wales and England, and for the gold-medal-winning Australian team at the London Olympic Games in 1908.

Richards returned to Australia in March 1909. To the *Referee*'s 'Cynic', he differed from the average colonial footballer in his intimate knowledge of world Rugby and capacity to discuss the game. That year Richards captained and coached Charters Towers and North Queensland against the Newtown club, from Sydney. He sailed to South Africa during the visit of a British team in 1910 and in Johannesburg was invited to join the tourists, half of whose players were injured. He played in twelve games, including two Tests for Britain versus South Africa.

Back in Sydney in June 1911, Richards played for Manly and for a Metropolitan XV; though unqualified, he also played for Queensland against Metropolitan. In 1912 he toured North America as vice-captain of the Waratahs and was in the Australian team for the 'All-America' Test. He then went to England and in February 1913 to the south of France with an East Midlands team. He helped to train France for its match against Wales in Paris, then played for Toulouse. Briefly he lived at Biarritz. In August 1913, again in Sydney, he retired from football and wrote for the *Sydney Morning Herald*, the *Referee* and other newspapers.

Giving his occupation as 'traveller', Richards enlisted in the Australian Imperial Force on 26 August 1914 and in October sailed for Egypt with the 1st Field Ambulance. Landing at Gallipoli on the morning of 25 April 1915, he served as a stretcher-bearer, and was mentioned in divisional orders in July for 'acts of gallantry'. He returned to Egypt in January 1916 and in March left for the Western Front. On 25 November Corporal Richards was commissioned second lieutenant and on 2 December transferred to the 1st Infantry Battalion. In May 1917 near Bullecourt he led a nineteen-man bombing party; he was promoted lieutenant in June and awarded the Military Cross in August. He was evacuated to England twice in 1917 and again in May 1918, with his back and shoulders damaged by a bomb blast. Having spent some four months in South Africa *en route*, in February 1919 he returned to Sydney where his A.I.F. appointment was terminated on 3 November. For two years he was in charge of the employment section, Department of Repatriation, Sydney, before becoming a travelling salesman in electrical goods and then for the Perdriau [q.v.11] Rubber Co. Ltd.

On 27 August 1921 at St Stephen's Presbyterian Church, Sydney, and also on 25 March 1922 at Punt Road Methodist Church, Melbourne, he married Lillian Effie Jane Haley, née Sandow, a widow. They lived at Manly in Sydney and had two children but, with Richards often working away, soon separated. Mostly isolated and lonely and in worsening health, he wrote a series of articles for the *Sydney Mail*. In April 1935 he moved to Brisbane and the family reunited. Richards died of tuberculosis on 25 September that year at the Repatriation Hospital, Rosemount, and was cremated with Baptist forms. His wife and their son and daughter survived him. His elder brother Edward William (Bill) (1880-1928) had also played Rugby for Australia. In 2001 the trophy for Rugby Tests between Australia and the British and Irish Lions was named the Tom Richards Cup to honour the only player to have represented both sides.

J. Pollard, *Australian Rugby* (Syd, 1994); M. Howell & L. Xie, *Wallaby Greats* (Auckland, NZ, 1996); G. Crowden, *Gold, Mud and Guts* (Syd, 2001); *Town & Country Jnl*, 16 Apr 1919, p 5; *Courier-Mail* (Brisb), 26 Sept 1935, p 10; service record (NAA, Canb).   DON WILKEY

RICHARDSON, ROBERT PEMBERTON (c.1827-1900), stock and station and estate agent, was born at Liverpool, England, son of David Richardson, wool merchant, and his wife Isabella. Trained to follow in his father's footsteps, Robert decided to migrate and reached Sydney in 1850. He joined T. S. Mort [q.v.5] & Co., auctioneers and wool brokers, and was soon sales representative. On 25 August that year at All Saints Church of England, Sutton Forest, he married Scottish-born Violet Alston (1830-1893). Their first

home, of which there were many in succeeding years, was Prospect Cottage, Newtown, Sydney. It was a long and happy marriage that produced nine children.

At the end of 1857 Richardson left Mort & Co to set up his own business at 235 George Street, specializing in stock and station sales and country estates. He began with a clerk (John Little) and an office boy (Alec Gregg), both of whom spent their lives with the firm and eventually became partners.

EDWARD THOMAS JONES WRENCH (1828-1893) had been born on 11 January 1828 in London, son of Edward Wrench, optician, and his wife Anne. On 25 January 1851 in the parish church of St Andrew, Holborn, he married Mary Ann Smith. Next year the couple arrived in Sydney, and Wrench joined the Australian Joint Stock Bank, rising in a few years to general manager. He resigned when it was found that a swindle had been perpetrated without his knowledge. His friend Richardson, who had an unassailable reputation in the Sydney business world, stood by him and offered him a partnership in 1860.

Richardson & Wrench prospered during the 1860s, playing a substantial role in the pastoral occupation of Queensland. Their wool stores at Circular Quay, Sydney, were 'the best lighted and most convenient warehouses for the exhibition and sale of wool in this city', and vast quantities of wool, hides and skins were stored there for transhipment. Meanwhile, their reputation as real estate agents grew. By the 1880s they had become a major force in the development of suburban Sydney, with trains and once even the vessel *Lady Rawson* hired to transport prospective buyers to sales.

As well as having a keen eye for wool and real estate, Richardson was a natural salesman. He was also a strict Presbyterian who set great store by the strength and loyalty of his family. Within the firm he was punctilious and demanding, but fair in his treatment of both customers and employees. His character, it was said, was marked by 'sagacity and promptness'. Wrench handled the firm's finance and administration with meticulous efficiency. Patient and methodical, his was also the more gregarious personality, well known in Sydney social circles. His wife died in 1876, and on 3 June 1879 he married Theresa Clementine Throckmorton, née Horne, a widow with five children.

Richardson retired in 1875 but became bored and in 1881 returned to the business, which next year was lucky enough to secure the exchange number 1 when a telephone service was introduced in Sydney. Since none of Richardson's sons was interested in entering the firm, and Wrench was childless, in 1889 the partners, including A. W. S. Gregg and his brother James (Little had retired in

1885), decided to convert to a public company. Although he remained a shareholder, Richardson declined to become a director. On 27 March 1892, however, he agreed to join the board and on 5 April replaced the ailing Wrench as chairman. In part this was a consequence of the crisis caused by the disastrous Gibbs, Shallard & Co.'s fire on 2 October 1890, when Richardson & Wrench Ltd's offices were partially destroyed, but it also reflected the worsening economy and the end of that boom in suburban real estate. The fire led to the creation of Martin Place and the rebuilding of much of that part of the city. Richardson & Wrench also survived as a public company. Its fire-damaged records, including an impeccably kept series of contract books from 1858 to 1936 that have proved invaluable to historians tracing the history of Sydney property, were transferred to the Mitchell [q.v.5] Library in the 1960s.

Wrench died on 26 October 1893 at his home, Glenora, Edgecliff Road, Woollahra, and was buried with Anglican rites in Ashfield cemetery. His estate was sworn for probate at £14 764. Richardson finally retired in April 1900 and died on 23 May that year at Drummoyne, survived by three daughters and two sons. The funeral and burial in Waverley cemetery was 'of the simplest character' in accordance with his wishes. His estate was sworn for probate at £30 475.

A. Barnard, *Visions and Profits* (Melb, 1961); *Richardson and Wrench's Pastoral and General Advertiser*, 22 June 1864; *SMH*, 27 Oct 1893, p 1, 26 May 1900, p 9; R. G. Rabone, The History of Richardson & Wrench Ltd (ms, ML).

BEVERLEY KINGSTON

RIDGEWAY, SIDNEY WILLIAM (1895-1959), Aboriginal labourer, was born on 12 October 1895 at Karuah, New South Wales, youngest of three sons of William Ridgeway, fisherman, and his wife Charlotte, née Russell; William and Charlotte were of Worimi descent, and were referred to by missionaries as 'King' and 'Queen'. Sidney was educated at the half-time Aliceton (Karuah) Public School. In 1902 William was a petitioner for its restoration to full-time status; in 1907 white parents secured the exclusion of Aboriginal children, so Sid's formal education ended before he was 12.

The families of Ridgeway brothers and cousins at Port Stephens lived by fishing and growing crops, moving between Aboriginal reserves at Sawyers Point (Karuah) and Soldiers Point; they were drawn partly by seasonal factors but also as converts of the Aborigines Inland Mission of Australia. When contacted by Retta Long [q.v.15] about 1904, they already knew some hymns. Ridgeways

became staunch supporters of the A.I.M. Its tiny church at Karuah was built entirely by Aboriginal labour, Sid helping to decorate it with woodcarving.

When Dan Ridgeway attempted to enrol Aboriginal children at Karuah school in 1914, again white parents blocked admission Mrs Long's badgering of the authorities on their behalf resulted in the appointment of an untrained teacher to a segregated provisional school. The family lost access to land at Soldiers Point in 1916, when the reserve was resumed. In 1925 Sid was a foundation executive member of the Australian Aboriginal Progressive Association, set up by Fred Maynard [q.v.15]. The association demanded 'sufficient good land in fee simple to maintain a family' and removal of the Aboriginal Protection Board's authority over children. Its programme expanded to include replacement of the board's reserve managers by educated Aborigines, care for 'incapables' and a royal commission.

In Sydney on 26 November 1927 at Chatswood Baptist Church Sid married CORRA Robertson (1892-1975), who had been born at Mudgee, daughter of William Robertson and his wife Nancy, née Phillips. There were two sons of the marriage, one dying in infancy. A cousin of Maynard's, Corra had been given into the care of A.I.M. missionaries at Singleton as an infant and from about 1916 was in domestic service with the Watson family at Ashfield. Believing a proper education was essential for Aboriginal success, Corra persuaded Sid to move to Sydney, where he worked as a builder's labourer and later at Chullora railways workshops. Aboriginal descent being no bar to public schools in Sydney, though it remained so at Karuah, the Ridgeways' surviving son proceeded to the leaving certificate and later ran a trucking business. Corra was a strict Baptist and an A.I.M. supporter. Her sweet singing graced many of its meetings.

Mrs Long believed Aborigines should take responsibility for training their own people. Having acquired land for a Native Workers Training College at Pindimar on Port Stephens, in 1937 she set up the Australian Aboriginal Missionary Movement, with Mr and Mrs Sid Ridgeway of Chullora as its 'central officers'. The A.A.M.M. was an autonomous Aboriginal organization for funding the training of and paying stipends to Aboriginal evangelists. By 1939 it had fourteen branches and had raised £1311. The intention of channelling the money through the Ridgeways to where need was greatest broke down with the mission's expansion interstate, and from 1941 co-ordination of the A.A.M.M. was centred at the training college.

The Ridgeways were well regarded at Chullora (Greenacre). Sid became a reader at the Church of Christ, Bankstown, and played cricket for North Bankstown. He died of cerebral thrombosis on 29 August 1959 at his home and was buried in the Independent section of Rookwood cemetery; his wife and son survived him. Corra died on 25 April 1975 at Lidcombe Hospital.

W. Scott, *The Port Stephens Blacks* (Dungog, NSW, 1929); H. Goodall, *Invasion to Embassy* (Syd, 1996); *NSW Aborigines' Advocate*, 31 Oct 1904, p 3; *Our AIM*, July 1916, p 4, 30 June 1919, p 3, 31 Dec 1919, p 7, 20 Dec 1923, p 9, 23 Jan 1928, p 4, 15 May 1937, p 11, 15 Mar 1938, p 4; *Voice of the North*, 14 Apr 1925, p 17, 10 Dec 1925, p 18, 10 June 1927, p 18; *Austn Evangel*, 2, no 11, Dec 1931, p 8, 21, no 7, 1952, p 3; NSW Aborigines' Welfare Bd, *Dawn*, Nov 1959, p 21; *Aboriginal History*, 14, nos 1-2, 1990, p 1; *Newcastle Morning Herald*, 2 July 1927, p 6; school files, 5/14638.2, 5/16423.2 (SRNSW); information from Mr K. B. Ridgeway, Bluff Point, NSW.

HEATHER RADI

RIGBY, HANNAH (c.1794-1853), embroiderer, servant and convict, was born in Lancashire, England. Convicted of larceny at the Quarter Sessions at Liverpool on 2 October 1821, 26-year-old Hannah was sentenced to transportation for seven years. She reached Port Jackson on 27 February 1823 in the *Lord Sidmouth*. Her occupation was embroiderer, she was fair with a freckled complexion, brownish-red hair and brown eyes, and she stood 5 ft 1¾ ins (157 cm) tall.

In Sydney Hannah had a son, Robert Frederick, born on 6 June 1824, by Robert Crawford, who had come free in the *Royal George* in 1821 and who later became principal clerk in the Colonial Secretary's Office. At St John's Church of England, Parramatta, on 3 January 1825 she married George Page, who had been transported in the *Shipley*. Apprehended for absconding from service in September 1826, she was confined to the Female Factory for three months. Her absence was probably connected with Page's trial, as in May 1826 he had been found guilty of stealing from a ship and on 19 September was sent to Moreton Bay for seven years. Hannah Rigby was described in the 1828 census as a sempstress, free by servitude, living at Newcastle with two sons, Robert aged 5 and Samuel aged three months. That year she obtained her certificate of freedom.

On 16 February 1830 Rigby appeared at the Maitland Quarter Sessions, charged with stealing with force and arms thirty yards of ribbon valued at £1 belonging to Frederick Boucher. Although her accomplice received only a short prison term, Rigby was sentenced to transportation to a penal settlement for seven years. Her two sons accompanied her to Sydney gaol. On 16 October she boarded the *Isabella* with seven other female convicts, bound for Moreton Bay, where they joined eighteen women prisoners already resident there among more than a thousand males.

In Brisbane, Rigby was in hospital for a few days in February 1831 with a fever. On 27 September 1832 she gave birth to a third son, James, whose father was probably her husband—and fellow prisoner—George Page. At the expiration of her colonial sentence on 16 February 1837, she was sent back to Sydney. Her certificate of freedom, issued on 6 March 1837, indicated she had rejoined Page who had returned to Sydney in 1833. Less than three months later she was yet again before the courts, this time convicted for stealing two hats. Once more she was sentenced to seven years and was returned to Moreton Bay on 26 October in the *Isabella*.

Although the other female convicts were sent back to Sydney in 1839 when the Moreton Bay penal settlement was closed, Rigby remained in Brisbane. By this time she was the servant of the assistant colonial surgeon David Ballow [q.v.1], one of the civilians maintaining the establishment for free settlers who were to arrive from March 1842. In July 1840 Ballow requested the commandant Lieutenant Owen Gorman to petition for a remission of sentence for her, indicating that her conduct had been exemplary and she had never given him any cause for distrust or complaint.

A free woman once more, Rigby decided to remain at the settlement. She resided in a hut near Queen Street. Having danced vigorously at wedding festivities five nights earlier, on 10 October 1853 she succumbed to apoplexy. An inquest held at the Donnybrook Hotel returned a verdict of death by visitation of God. She was buried in St John's church graveyard. Although her age was estimated at 77, she was nearer to 59. Hannah Rigby had served three sentences of transportation and was the only Moreton Bay female convict who stayed in the district after gaining her freedom.

Moreton Bay Courier, 15 Oct 1853, p 2; permission to marry, 4/3513, p 64, reel 6014, and *Lord Sidmouth* indent, 4/4008, fiche 649, p 261, and Sydney Gaol Book, 4/6429, p 85, reel 850 (SRNSW); HOS 1/2, pp 21 & 33, *and* Chronological Register of Convicts at Moreton Bay, no 2200 (QSA); AJCP reel 2766, piece no 22, and reel 3201, piece no 44.

JENNIFER HARRISON

RISLEY, MARIA; *see* LORD, MARIA

ROBERTSON, HELEN LOTHAN (1848-1937), tailoress and trade unionist, was born in 1848 at Glasgow, Scotland, daughter of Joseph Biggs, carpenter, and his wife Elizabeth, née Baird. The family came to Victoria in 1853. At 14 Helen 'started with her needle at the trade'; clothing machinists were then paid 10 shillings to 12s. 6d. per week, about half the rate for unskilled male labourers. On 15 April 1870 at Fitzroy she married with Presbyterian forms Scottish-born James Stewart Robertson, carpenter. In the next eleven years they had six children, three of whom died in childhood. She probably combined home duties with outwork, the endemic, lowest paid form of employment in the garment industry.

Mrs Robertson was reputedly involved in trade union activity as early as 1874. In 1880 she led Melbourne tailoresses in their campaigns against oppressive work practices, or 'sweating', in the garment industry. That year she and some workmates established the Tailoresses' Association. They made little headway against recalcitrant employers and the resistance of tailoresses anxious about being blacklisted, but eventually convened a meeting and approached the Trades Hall Committee, which was reluctant to support them. After agitation against sweating in the printing and retail industries led to a royal commission in 1882 the working conditions of female workers attracted wider public sympathy.

Confident in the support of the *Age* newspaper and reforming Liberals, on 10 December 1882 Robertson and her colleagues led a deputation, sponsored by the Tailors' Union, to the Trades Hall to protest at wage cuts in a leading clothing factory. The T.H.C., anxious to expand its role in co-ordinating industrial disputes, responded by establishing the Tailoresses' Union on 11 December, with an all-male executive and a committee of seven women, including Robertson. Public support for the women's plight was such that the *Age* raised £1000 in the first week of an appeal for funds. Trades Hall officers drew up and negotiated a 'catalogue of claims' that was largely accepted by most protectionist employers by March 1883. The royal commission heard evidence from Robertson and other tailoresses in August that year. The 1885 Factory Act, inspired by the commission's report, included some improvements, despite Legislative Council amendments.

By the late 1880s Robertson and her comrades had expanded the role of women unionists to such an extent that the newly established Trades Hall Council agreed to the construction of a Female Operatives' Hall, with Robertson a member of the foundation committee. However, the economic collapse affected the clothing trade so severely that by 1890 the Tailoresses' Union membership had fallen to a mere hundred. Virtually moribund for most of the decade, like many unions, in

1906 it merged with the Tailors' Society to become the Tailors' and Tailoresses' Union. Despite this dramatic decline, Robertson and a few others carried on the struggle. In 1896 they had obtained their first Wages Board. She had begun her long-standing membership of the Eight Hours' Committee in 1894.

Following the formation of the Federated Clothing Trades Union (1907) she continued as a member of the Victorian branch executive until 1925 and served a term as vice-president. A photograph showed her as big, strong and resolute. Her husband had died in 1901. Revered as a pioneer of female trade unionism in Australia, Robertson progressively withdrew from the public sphere in the late 1920s. She died on 22 June 1937 at Collingwood and was buried in Melbourne general cemetery. Two daughters and a son survived her.

G. Serle, *The Rush to Be Rich* (Melb, 1970); M. McMurchy et al, *For Love or Money* (Melb, 1983); B. Ellem, *In Women's Hands* (Syd, 1989); *Clothing Trades Gazette*, 15 May 1922, p 6; *Recorder* (Melb), no 120, Feb 1983, p 9; *Labour History*, no 44, May 1983, p 27; *Age* (Melb), 24 June 1937, p 12; *Labor Call*, 1 July 1937.   PETER LOVE

ROGERS, MARY CATHERINE (1872-1932), community and political worker, was born on 2 August 1872 in Melbourne, fifth child of Irish-born parents John Skeahan, a labourer and later a produce dealer, and his wife Margaret, née Welsh. Brought up at East Richmond, Mary attended a local Catholic school. On 28 November 1900 at St Ignatius's Catholic Church, Richmond, she married Patrick Denis Rogers, an upholsterer. Their five children were born between 1901 and 1909; one died in infancy. Patrick, a stalwart of the Working Men's College, sometime president of the Furniture Trades Union and a committee member for the eight-hour day celebration, died in 1910. While rearing her children, Mary was employed as a cleaner and became active in the Australian Labor Party and in community welfare work.

Appointed secretary (later president) of the Women Office Cleaners' Union, then vice-president of the Miscellaneous Workers' Union, Rogers became organizer for the Victorian branch of the A.L.P. in 1918. She was secretary of the party's North Richmond branch for several years and a member of the Richmond Benevolent Society. On 5 November 1920 she was elected to Richmond City Council at a by-election, becoming the first female councillor in Victoria and the second in Australia (after Susan Benny [q.v.7]). That year she was appointed to a board of enquiry into neglected children. Her aim was to improve the sanitary and living conditions of the poor at Richmond. She also worked to have baby clinics established and for municipal control of the milk supply. In 1922 she was re-elected unopposed. At a Yarra Bank public meeting in April 1924, Rogers protested against the government's decision to execute the convicted murderer Angus Murray. She was a member of the council's finance and legislative committee in 1925, but was defeated in municipal elections in August. Among the first women to be appointed justices of the peace in Victoria—in February 1927—she was a special magistrate at the Children's Court at Richmond.

At the Trades Hall Council in July 1923, with Mrs Nelle Rickie, Rogers had moved a resolution calling for equal pay for the sexes. Sometime president of the Labor Women's Organizing Committee, from 1925 to 1932 she was its active and energetic secretary. For two years she was a member of the central executive of the Victorian branch of the A.L.P. In addition, she was honorary secretary of the Richmond auxiliary of St Vincent's Hospital, a member of the State's Central Unemployment Relief Committee and of the royal commission on children's welfare, vice-president of the Victorian Baby Health Centres, a member of the board of the Heatherton Sanitorium and of the council of the Richmond Technical School, secretary of the welfare committee of the Catholic Women's Social Guild and president of the Carmel crèche.

It was said of Rogers that she 'worked on countless committees to countless beneficent ends' and showed 'force of character, devotion to principle, and great organising ability'. She died of cancer on 25 September 1932 at Richmond. Three daughters and one son survived her. At her burial in Boroondara cemetery, Kew, with Catholic rites, trades union and Labor officials were prominent, and Arthur Calwell [q.v.13] was a pallbearer.

F. Fraser and N. Palmer (eds), *Centenary Gift Book* (Melb, 1934); B. Walker, *Solidarity Forever!* (Melb, 1972); A. V. Smith, *Women in Australian Parliaments and Local Governments* (Syd, 1975); K. Daniels et al, *Women in Australia*, 2 (Canb, 1977); *Richmond Austn*, 3 Sept 1910, p 3; *Argus* (Melb), 6 Nov 1920, p 18, 16 Feb 1927, p 21, 26 Sept 1932, p 1, 28 Sept 1932, p 6; *Lone Hand*, 1 Dec 1920, p 29; *Melb Punch*, 2 Dec 1920, p 2; *Sun-News Pictorial* (Melb), 13 Sept 1922, p 10; *Advocate* (Melb), 29 Sept 1932, p 15; *Richmond, Hawthorn and Camberwell Weekly*, 30 Sept 1932, p 3; *Richmond Guardian*, 1 Oct 1932, p 2; *Aust Worker*, 5 Oct 1932, p 1; information from Mr G. Clancy, Kilmore, Vic.

CHRIS CUNNEEN
KIM TORNEY

ROHU, ADA JANE; *see* TOST

ROMA, DIAMANTINA; *see* BOWEN

ROOKE, JESSIE SPINK (1845-1906), suffragist and temperance reformer, was born on 10 September 1845 in London, daughter of William Walker, bookkeeper, and his wife Catherine, née Scollay. By 1867 Jessie was living in Melbourne. On 3 January that year at Fitzroy she married with Presbyterian forms Peter Charles Reid, a warehouseman from New Zealand. After he died, she married with Presbyterian forms Charles Rooke, a medical practitioner, on 14 August 1883 at Germanton (Holbrook), New South Wales. Born at Weymouth, England, he was a widower with two sons.

In Sydney Mrs Rooke was prominent in the British Women's Bible and Prayer Union and the Marrickville branch of the Woman's Christian Temperance Union. Moving to Tasmania in the early 1890s, she became involved in the Burnie W.C.T.U., of which she was elected president (1894); from 1898 she was a vigorous president of the Tasmanian branch. The W.C.T.U. became the focus of the women's suffrage movement in Tasmania. Mrs Rooke travelled extensively, speaking publicly and gathering signatures petitioning parliament to legislate for the vote for women. The first campaign in 1896 resulted in some 2000 signatures, and a similar number was secured in 1897. Legislative Council opposition defeated bills to amend the Tasmanian suffrage in both years, but Rooke reassured her members that their efforts in public and in their drawing-room meetings kept the issue prominent. The unions obtained a further 5500 signatures to support a referendum bill in 1898, and suffrage remained an important issue until the Electoral Act of 1903 enfranchised Tasmanian women.

Rooke was heavily involved in the National Council of Women, established in 1899, which worked closely with the W.C.T.U. in the suffrage campaign. As a W.C.T.U. delegate in 1902 to the International Council of Women Conference in Washington, she worked with Vida Goldstein [q.v.9] in supporting the campaign of the United Council of Women's Suffrage for Federal adult suffrage. Succeeding Elizabeth Nicholls [q.v.11], of South Australia, as Australasian president of the W.C.T.U. in 1903, that year Rooke founded the Tasmanian Women's Suffrage Association, which attracted a membership beyond those interested mainly in moral and temperance issues. After the vote was achieved, the association continued as a non-party organization 'to interest women in all laws relating to women and children', educate members on wider political questions and encourage women to enrol. It urged women to use their right to vote in Federal elections as 'the highest expression of citizenship'. For the December 1903 Federal election, Rooke joined the support group for James Brickhill in the Darwin electorate. She was president of the Women's Political Association (probably the successor of the W.S.A.) at Launceston in 1905-06.

Espousing the sanctity of marriage, the privacy of the home and the need to give assistance to the poor, she was an excellent and forceful speaker, despite some fragility in health. Jessie Rooke was a self-denying worker and a good mediator, highly respected by her fellow workers. She died of congestive heart failure on 4 January 1906 at South Burnie and was buried in Wivenhoe (Burnie) cemetery. Her husband apparently destroyed her papers shortly after her death.

M. Roe, *The State of Tasmania* (Hob, 2001); *White Ribbon Signal*, 1 Feb 1906, p 1, 1 Mar 1906, p 4; Tas Hist and Research Assn, *Papers and Procs*, 32, no 4, 1985, p 151; *Tas Mail*, 28 Mar 1903, p 9, 19 Sept 1903, p 9, 26 Sept 1903, p 9, 3 Oct 1903, p 9, 24 Oct 1903, p 9, 31 Oct 1903, p 9, 13 Jan 1906, p 9; *Mercury* (Hob), 18 Sept 1903, p 4, 19 Sept 1903, p 3; *Daily Telegraph* (Launc), 14 Dec 1903, p 5; A. Alexander, The Public Role of Women in Tasmania (Ph.D. thesis, Univ Tas, 1989); NS 337/66, 2 Nov 1894, NS 337/88, 11 Feb 1906 (TSA).   FAYE GARDAM

ROSS, COLIN CAMPBELL EADIE (1892-1922), convicted murderer, was born on 11 October 1892 at North Fitzroy, Melbourne, third of five children of Thomas Ross, groom, and his wife Elizabeth Campbell, née Eadie. By the late 1890s the Ross family was living at Maidstone. After Thomas left for Western Australia, never to return, Elizabeth struggled to raise her children.

Reputedly a quiet, even docile, child, Colin was educated at Braybrook State School, then was employed in a local quarry where he became a diligent and thrifty worker and one of the best jumper-men. He was forced by an appendectomy to abandon quarrying and was a general labourer from 1915 until 1920, when he joined his family in running the Donnybrook Hotel. Crossed in love in March 1920, Ross attempted to persuade the woman in question to marry him, and was fined for carrying an unlicensed firearm and placed on a good behaviour bond for using threatening words. In April 1921 he became licensee of the Australian Wine Café in the Eastern Arcade, Melbourne, and the saloon soon acquired an unsavoury reputation as a haunt of criminals and prostitutes. In October he was charged with involvement in robbing and shooting a customer. He was acquitted, but allowed his saloon licence to expire on 31 December 1921.

Early that morning the raped, strangled and naked body of 12-year-old Alma Tirtschke was found in a right-of-way off nearby Gun Alley. The press, notably the *Herald* under (Sir) Keith Murdoch [q.v.10], fanned public outrage, pressured police for an arrest and matched the government's initial reward, which was quickly raised from £250 to £1000. Ross, one of many people routinely interviewed, was arrested and remanded. The police, relying on the information of dubious characters, including the fortune-teller 'Madame Ghurka' [q.v. Julia Gibson], claimed that Ross had confessed to violating and choking the girl. The *Herald* prejudiced his trial by publishing his photograph and printing the names and addresses of the jury. George Maxwell, appearing for Ross with T. C. Brennan [qq.v.10,7], described the Crown witnesses as 'disreputables', mercenaries whose evidence was contradictory and untrustworthy. But a government analyst matched the auburn hair of the victim with hairs on blankets from the wine saloon. Ross had an alibi, but his courtroom behaviour, at first nonchalant, then truculent and finally angry, weakened the defence case. After a five-day trial the jury returned a verdict of guilty. Justice W. J. Schutt [q.v.11] sentenced Ross to death. 'My life', Ross averred, 'has been sworn away by desperate people'.

Appeals to the Victorian Full Court and to the High Court of Australia failed. The Executive Council confirmed the death penalty and, notwithstanding deputations and petitions, leave to appeal to the Privy Council was refused. Ross composed himself with dignity for his quiet but resolute statement from the scaffold:

> I am now face to face with my Maker, and I swear by Almighty God that I am an innocent man. I never saw the child. I never committed the crime, and I don't know who did. I never confessed to anyone. I ask God to forgive those who have sworn my life away, and I pray God to have mercy on my poor darling mother, and my family.

He was hanged on 24 April 1922 at Melbourne Gaol.

The Ross family and their sympathizers formed the Colin Ross Vindication Committee, and Brennan published a measured rebuttal of the Crown case. Murdoch and the *Herald* never lived down their shameless exploitation of the crime: opposition journalists dubbed the new *Herald & Weekly Times* headquarters on Flinders Street 'the Colin Ross Memorial'. The case has divided crime writers. Some have presented Ross as a monster who got his deserts, others as a scapegoat who fell victim to press hysteria, police chicanery and public outrage. His trial, the first in which scientific comparisons of human hair produced a conviction, led to anonymity for jurors. In his farewell letter to his family, Ross wrote that 'the day is coming when my innocence will be proved'. After experts re-examined the hair samples in 1998 and concluded that they did not match, a case began to quash Ross's conviction.

T. C. Brennan, *The Gun Alley Tragedy* (Melb, 1923); A. Downer, *Crime Chemist* (Lond, 1965); *InForMed*, 5, no 3, Sept 2000, p 11; *Age* (Melb), 8 Mar 1920, p 6, 13 Jan 1922, p 7, 14 Jan 1922, p 11, 25 Apr 1922, p 6, 5 Mar 2000, p 1, 7 Mar 2000, p 16, 12 Mar 2000, 'News', p 3; *Herald* (Melb), 22 Oct 1921, p 6, 10 Apr 1922, p 1, 13 Apr 1922, p 1, 20 Apr 1922, p 7, 21 Apr 1922, p 8, 24 Apr 1922, p 1; *Argus* (Melb), 24 Oct 1921, p 10, 1 Nov 1921, p 5, 24 Nov 1921, p 10, 13 Jan 1922, p 7, 14 Jan 1922, p 21; *Independent* (Footscray), 14 Jan 1922, p 2; *Truth* (Melb), 5 Nov 1921, p 3, 19 Nov 1921, p 2, 26 Nov 1921, p 7, 7 Jan 1922, p 3, 14 Jan 1922, p 6, 28 Jan 1922, p 5, 25 Feb 1922, p 5, 4 Mar 1922, p 6, 11 Mar 1922, p 5, 18 Mar 1922, p 5, 25 Mar 1922, p 5, 1 Apr 1922, p 6, 8 Apr 1922, p 6, 15 Apr 1922, p 3, 22 Apr 1922, p 5, 29 Apr 1922, p 5; *Smith's Weekly*, 4 Mar 1922, p 3; *People*, 15 Mar 1950, p 38; VPRS 30/P, unit 1953 (PRO, Vic).

JOHN LACK
KEVIN MORGAN

ROSS, HEDWIG (1900-1971), teacher and socialist, was born on 17 September 1900, at Palmerston North, New Zealand, daughter of German-born settlers Friedrich Gustav Weitzel (d.1917), a brass-founder later farmer, and his wife Maria, née Benninghoven; three children had been born in Sydney in 1888-91. By 1912 the family had moved to Wellington. Hettie attended Wellington Girls' College from 1914 and then Victoria University College (B.A., N.Z., 1920), where she 'was a wonderfully brilliant student' according to the future prime minister Peter Fraser. She majored in Latin, English and philosophy.

Weitzel enrolled at Wellington Training College in 1921. That year she joined the Socialist Party and subsequently was a founding member of the Communist Party of New Zealand. In these circles she met Fintan Patrick Walsh (born Patrick Tuohy), a handsome seaman and firebrand atheist influenced by the Industrial Workers of the World, who probably became her lover. On 19 August 1921 Weitzel was convicted and fined for selling seditious literature—the *Communist*, an Australian newspaper—and consequently was dismissed from the training college. That year Hettie's mother and two siblings migrated to the United States of America.

Experiencing difficulty in obtaining a passport to join them, in February 1922 Weitzel moved to Sydney—which she described as 'this rotten city'—where she immersed herself in the Communist Party of Australia, edited a broadsheet, the *Young Communist*

(which lasted for nine issues), and spoke at and chaired meetings in the Domain on Sundays and in Bathurst Street on Friday and Sunday evenings. She also taught at a Communist Sunday school that drew the hostility of the minister for justice T. J. Ley [q.v.10]. Despite her retaliation in the *Communist*, from February 1923 the Department of Public Instruction employed her at Bondi Domestic Public School before she was transferred to Maitland West Girls' High School. She married Hector Ross, builders' labourer, another Communist Sunday school teacher, in the Paddington registry office in Sydney on 15 December 1923. Nonetheless, she started the new school year at Newcastle, where she stayed until her transfer to Gladesville Public School in September 1925. She gained a diploma of education in 1926 at the University of Sydney. In the summer of 1924-25 she and Hector went to New Zealand to help to reorganize the ailing local communist party.

During her first decade in Australia Hettie was on the central committee of the C.P.A., responsible for the party's women's committee. She edited the *Working Woman* (*Women Today*) and, during the absence of Hector in the Soviet Union, edited (in his stead) the *Workers Weekly*, the official organ of the party. In 1926 when the C.P.A. felt the need for a separate women's association, Hettie was the acknowledged leader of the Militant Women's Group and was most responsible for the pamphlets *Hands off China* (1927) and *Women's Path to Freedom*. 'The Rosses are heroes', Esmonde Higgins [q.v.14] wrote to Harry Pollitt in England.

After nearly three years at Canterbury Domestic Public School in Sydney, Hettie resigned in April 1928. She did not return to teaching until she was employed at Cleveland Street Boys' Intermediate High School in August 1929 whence she was transferred to the Cowra Intermediate School in central western New South Wales. Her marriage was childless and ended in divorce in 1931. That year at a special meeting of the Cowra Parents and Citizens' Association, she was one of two teachers charged with being closely identified with communism. Amid the subsequent clamour she was transferred to North Sydney Intermediate High School. The recently formed Educational Workers' League supported her cause, and she subsequently became one of the league's active members and a close associate of S. P. Lewis [q.v.15].

Hettie taught at various schools in Sydney and maintained her membership of the C.P.A., but her time was increasingly committed to the Women Assistant Teachers' Association within the New South Wales Teachers' Federation. She was 'for ever at Federation House, not only to attend endless meetings, but to put the cases of those people who thought they had been unfairly treated'. During the Depression she led campaigns against salary reductions and the Married Women's Dismissal Act and chaired the Equal Pay Committee from 1936. For twelve years she represented the W.A.T.A. on the federation's council and was the council's delegate to the Labor Council of New South Wales; for ten years she was on the executive of the Teachers' Federation and for seven years she was a vice-president. She retired in 1956. That year Ross began corresponding with the New Zealand poet and Chinese resident Rewi Alley. In 1957 she visited China.

Described by Audrey Johnson as a 'Jenny Wren with sparkling eyes', Hettie Ross battled Parkinson's disease in the last years of her life. She died on 26 October 1971 at Mortdale, Sydney, and was cremated.

Dictionary of New Zealand Biography, vol 4 (Auckland, NZ); G. Phelan, *Women in Action in the Federation* (Syd, 1981); A. Johnson, *Bread & Roses* (Syd, 1990); C. Macdonald et al (eds), *The Book of New Zealand Women* (Wellington, NZ, 1991); G. Hunt, *Black Prince* (Auckland, NZ, 2004); *PD* (NZ), 1921, vol 191, 28 Oct 1921, p 953; *Australian Studies*, no 17, Apr 1992, p 25; M. Sullivan, 'Hetty Ross Formerly Hedwig Weitzel', *Hecate*, 22, no 1, 1996, p 127; Conrad Bollinger papers, folder 442, MS-Papers-2151, *and* Rewi Alley papers, outwards correspondence, Read–Ross, MS-Papers-6533, items 244 & 250 (Alexander Turnbull Lib, Wellington, NZ); A402, item W286, A6119, item 269, A8911, item 172 (NAA, Canb).   MARTIN SULLIVAN

ROSS, JOSEPH (c.1836-1909) and THOMAS (1866-1936), glassmakers, were father and son. Joseph was born at Sunderland, Durham, England, son of Scottish-born parents. On 7 December 1859 in Edinburgh he married Christina Frazer (c.1841-1914), from Wick. They were to have four children born in Scotland and another ten in Australia. Joseph became a glassblower and about 1865 migrated with his family to Rockhampton, Queensland. In Sydney next year J. A. Brown employed him as a bottle maker. By 1871 Ross occupied his own premises in Australia Street, Camperdown, later named the Perseverance Glass Works. Here his workforce made bottles although, as he was a staunch Methodist and supporter of the temperance movement, apparently not for brewers, distillers and vintners.

In the early 1880s Ross subscribed to the Protection and Political Reform League and was an inaugural committee member (1885) of the Chamber of Manufactures of New South Wales. Next year he helped to create the Protection Union of New South Wales. In 1887 he was a founding director of the Australian

Newspaper Co. Ltd, which launched the protectionist newspaper the *Australian Star*, and a delegate to the first intercolonial conference of Chambers of Manufactures, in Adelaide. Next year he attended a subsequent conference in Melbourne.

Neighbours at times hauled Ross into court under the Smoke Nuisances Protection Act. In 1885 he had been brought before a parliamentary select committee, established by free traders to enquire into allegations that the protectionist Ninian Melville [q.v.5] had corruptly helped Ross to sell land at Newtown to the Department of Railways at an inflated valuation. The committee found the charge 'not proven'.

Glassblowing was a family trade. Christina, at least early in the marriage, made the clay pots and crucibles within which the molten alloy was smelted. Four sons entered the business. When young, the daughters swept the works and shovelled coke into the furnaces; one married a glassblower. In 1894 Ross sold his factory to the Australian Drug Co., which tore it down to end competition with the company's North Botany (Mascot) bottle works. Ross agreed to stay out of business for ten years, but within three months his sons John and Alexander, as Ross Bros, had opened new kilns in Bray Street, Erskineville. Joseph and Christina moved next door to this factory, and at times Christina was listed as its owner. Joseph's photograph showed a bold and mischievous face, with a fair curly beard and flourishing moustache. He died at home on 23 July 1909 and was buried in the Methodist section of Rookwood cemetery. His wife, five sons and two daughters survived him. Christina died on 14 June 1914.

Their fifth child Thomas had been born at Dixon Street on 18 August 1866, said to have been the night his father first fashioned a bottle in Sydney. Tom was business manager of the Perseverance works from an early age. On 23 January 1895 at St Paul's Church of England, Redfern, he married Ann Elizabeth Tye, née Mason, a widow. After 1894, instead of joining John and Alexander in Ross Bros, he managed glassworks at Alexandria, where he became associated with the Scottish-born master glassblower David Vance (c.1852-1931). Vance had arrived in Sydney about 1886 with his wife Catherine, née Hutton, whom he had married on 24 April 1885 at Glasgow. He worked for the Australian Drug Co. at its North Botany bottle works and then acquired two small glass-foundries at Waterloo. By 1904 he was in partnership with Thomas Ross. Their Alexandria Glass Works was known particularly for fruit preserving jars and whisky bottles.

A Freemason and a justice of the peace, Thomas had learned his politics in the tight little world of Camperdown and Newtown and followed his father as a committee member of the Chamber of Manufactures. In 1908-09 he was mayor of Waterloo. He was recruited by (Sir) James Joynton Smith [q.v.11] as senior vice-president and government nominee on the board of South Sydney Hospital in 1909. His wife Elizabeth joined the board in January 1913. In 1910 Thomas failed to win Liberal pre-selection for the State seat of Botany.

Australian Glass Manufacturers Co. Ltd bought out Vance & Ross in 1915, paying the partners £24 000 in cash. As well, Vance received 9000 A.G.M. shares and Ross 7000. The Alexandria plant was demolished. Ross, in poor health for some years, retired to Burraneer Bay, Cronulla, naming his home Bottles. In the 1920s Vance moved to Glen Nevis, next door, where he died on 25 August 1931. An ardent promoter of Empire Day, Ross had celebrated the end of World War I by creating a large mosaic of three flags from coloured bottle glass set in concrete at his front gate, in honour of and relief at the survival of his sons Flight Lieutenant Frederick and Lance Corporal Thomas (who had won the Military Medal) and of a nephew. Thomas Ross senior died at his home on 27 December 1936, survived by his wife and their two sons.

Both sons worked for the A.G.M. subsidiary Crown Crystal Glass Pty Ltd, set up in 1926 to make cut glass, lighting ware and Pyrex. Young Tom became commercial manager. A stocky, hard-faced man, he presided over the works' cricket team, its golf days and its annual ball and represented the company in court against the trade unions. In 1955, however, the board tried to force his resignation, perhaps because of his ill health, and when he refused dismissed him. He died at his Bellevue Hill home on 18 February 1963. Legends he and his father had elaborated about their family as pioneer glassmakers, into which they had adopted Vance, were accepted by A.G.M. (later Australian Consolidated Industries Ltd) without question as part of its corporate history.

W. Chubb (ed), *Jubilee Souvenir of the Municipality of Newtown* (Syd, 1912), p 200; C. R. Hall, *The Manufacturers* (Syd, 1971); *V&P* (LA, NSW), 1883, vol 1, p 127, vol 3, p 1013, 1885-86, vol 1, p 60, vol 2, pp 113 & 117; *PD* (LA, NSW), vol 18, 11 Dec 1885, p 449, 28 Jan 1886, p 603, 24 Feb 1886, p 868; South Sydney Hospital, *Annual Report*, 1910-18; *Manufacturers' Jnl*, 15 July 1910, p 170; Royal Austn Hist Soc, *History*, no 77, Sept 2003, p 7; *Newtown Chronicle*, 29 Sept 1894; *Daily Telegraph* (Syd), 24 July 1909, p 9, 12 Oct 1910, p 8; *SMH*, 24 July 1909, p 12, 16 June 1914, p 8, 26 Aug 1931, p 13; *Town & Country Jnl*, 24 June 1914, p 28; *Hurstville Propeller*, 31 Dec 1936, p 1; Austn Drug Co records, Minute Book, 10 Nov 1893-1 Nov 1894 *and* ACI records (ML).
BARRIE DYSTER

ROSSI, DAISY MARY (1879-1974), artist and writer, was born on 18 January 1879 at Upper Wakefield, South Australia, fourth of eight children of William Rossi, a civil servant of Italian parentage, and his English-born wife Julia Emma, née Walter, an amateur artist and singer. Daisy spent her childhood at Auburn and Mount Barker until the family moved in 1900 to Adelaide, where she studied at the School of Design with Harry Gill [q.v.9] and Archibald Collin and took lessons with Madame Berthe Mouchette. Under 4 ft 11 ins (150 cms) tall, brown-eyed, vivacious and forthright, she was later described by 'Eva Bright' (possibly a pen name for herself) as 'a tiny little Dresden shepherdess ... with Cinderella's slippers peeping out ... "like mice beneath her petticoat" ... [and] the smallest hand ever seen on a grown woman'.

Moving to Perth in 1905 to join her brother Guy, she studied with the painter and theosophist Florence Fuller. Daisy Rossi's work was shown in the Australian Exhibition of Women's Work in Victoria in 1907. From 1905 to 1913 she exhibited paintings and designs for interiors and furnishings with the Western Australian Society of Arts. Funded by commissioned portraits, including one of her future husband the architect George Thomas Temple Poole, and another of her friend Bessie Rischbieth [qq.v.11], she went to London where she studied at the Grosvenor School of Modern Art under Walter Donne. After visiting Paris, in 1911 she returned to set up a studio at 300 Hay Street, Perth, also teaching at Fremantle Technical School and working as an interior designer.

Now painting in a more vigorous style, with a lighter palette and freer brush strokes, Rossi looked at Western Australian wildflowers with new eyes and started to paint them in their natural surroundings. She hoped to create a body of work that could be hung in a dedicated building, such as Marianne North's at Kew, England. She was commissioned to undertake a series for Savoy House in London, but the installation was abandoned during World War I; Sir John Winthrop Hackett [q.v.9] donated two of the panels to the Art Gallery of Western Australia. Rossi exhibited in Adelaide, Perth and Sydney and at the British Empire Exhibition, Wembley, London, in 1924.

With an 'intense wish to make art, and the influence of art, felt', Rossi had become one of the first female members of the Town Planning Association in 1917 and arranged salons—gatherings of artists, writers and men and women of affairs—at her studio. On 23 December 1918 at the bishop's chapel, Perth, with Anglican rites she married Temple Poole, a widower. They lived at Tagel, Crawley, on the edge of Kings Park 'surrounded by bush'; she had a daughter, Iseult, in 1920. In 1926 a fire destroyed Daisy's studio and her European works, and she ceased to paint, because of her failing eyesight, her social commitments and her husband's health. The family moved to Darlington in the Darling Ranges; after George's death in 1934 she and Iseult lived in South Perth.

Writing for publications as Daisy Rossi, Daisy Temple Poole and 'Mary Temple', she also lectured, made radio broadcasts and continued to teach art. An improvement in her eyesight about 1960 enabled her to resume painting. Some later works were subsequently donated to the National Trust of Australia (Western Australia). In 1966 she moved to Victoria to live with her daughter, who survived her when she died on 4 August 1974 at North Geelong. She was cremated with Methodist forms.

L. W. Matters, *Australasians Who Count in London* (Lond, 1913); J. Gooding, *Western Australian Art and Artists 1900-1950* (Perth, 1987); T. Snell, *Cinderella on the Beach* (Perth, 1991); J. Kerr (ed), *Heritage: The National Women's Art Book* (Syd, 1995); J. Altmann and J. Prott, *Out of the Sitting-room* (Perth, 1999); S. Daffen, *The Daisy Rossi Wild-flower Story* (Perth, 199?); *Woman's Budget*, 22 June 1923, p 3; National Trust of Aust (WA), *Trust News*, Dec 1996, p 8; *Sunday Times* (Perth), 8 July 1917, p 22; C. Bennett, 'Rossi'—Artist and Citizen in Early Twentieth Century Perth (B.A. Hons thesis, Univ of WA, 1998).   DOROTHY ERICKSON

RUSSELL, DELIA CONSTANCE (1870-1938), community worker, was born on 5 April 1870 at Emerald Hill, Victoria, eldest of four children of James Donaldson Law, an accountant born in British Guiana, and his wife Alice Annie, née Meeson, from England. When her father was promoted to general manager of the Bank of Victoria in 1889, the itinerant life of a bank officer's daughter gave way to a settled existence at Camberwell, Melbourne, and an education at Grace Park Ladies' College. Delia trained as a pianist with Alberto Zelman [q.v.6], was interested in various music societies, and began a long association with the Melbourne Symphony Orchestra. On 7 October 1893 at St John's Church of England, Camberwell, she married Percy Joseph Russell [q.v.11], a solicitor who became mayor of Hawthorn that year.

Delia Russell's social activities, motoring and six overseas visits were made possible by wealth, servants and boarding school for her only child, a son born in 1904. But she also demonstrated formidable organizing capacities. In her second term as mayoress (1904-05) she arranged many financially successful social events. She was a founder of the Talbot Epileptic Colony, Clayton, and a member of its executive for twenty-five years.

As a fiercely patriotic mayoress of Hawthorn again in 1915-17, Mrs Percy Russell established the St Kilda Road Red Cross Kitchen. From a small group with a budget of £10 a week working from the town hall to provide dainties for wounded soldiers in two hospitals grew a mass volunteer catering enterprise located in a purpose-built Department of Defence facility providing more than 6000 evening meals a month to eighteen hospitals, and special meals three days a week to four others. For this work she was appointed O.B.E. in 1920. She continued her association with the Australian Red Cross Society after the war, becoming a member of the State council and convenor of the Junior Red Cross in Victoria. An executive member of the National Council of Women, she was also active in the English Speaking Union.

In 1929 Russell was appointed a justice of the peace and a special magistrate of the Children's Court, and assumed an executive position with the Playgrounds Association. Her voluntary work with the (Royal) Women's Hospital, Melbourne, begun in 1919 (president 1933-34), expanded as she served on numerous committees dealing with matters as diverse as selecting royal wedding presents and raising funds to the training and discipline of nurses and major building works. She urged the appointment of an almoner for the hospital and became vice-president of the Victorian Institute of Almoners.

Russell gained notoriety from her connexion with the Housewives' Association of Victoria. In March 1929 she was elected president; she argued that it was of no use talking about the poor or the want of employment unless 'we get down to practical matters and try to make it possible for them to live better on a smaller wage'. Initially very successful, she ran foul of the executive, which next year publicly repudiated her over her support for temperance by education rather than prohibition, the ownership of the journal the *Housewife*, and constitutional issues. The ensuing acrimonious power struggle was played out in the press and split the organization. As the 'beloved leader' of the breakaway Victorian Housewives' Association she was vindicated in court and retained a loyal following in all her varied activities.

In 1930 *Table Talk* described Delia Russell as 'tall, slim and graceful' with 'big, animated eyes'. While she advocated that women should move from 'a chattel to man's equal', her activities reinforced gender and class differences. Never robust, she died of liver cirrhosis on 16 February 1938 at her home, Cliveden Mansions, East Melbourne, and was buried in Boroondara cemetery, Kew. Her husband and son survived her. The family holds a portrait of her by George Coates [q.v.8].

Who's Who in the World of Women (Melb, 1930 and 1934 edns); *Justice of the Peace*, 7 Feb 1921, p 7; *Hawthorn, Kew and Camberwell Citizen*, 25 Aug 1916, 1 Sept 1916; *Table Talk*, 20 Feb 1930, p 13; *Housewife*, 1, no 1, Sept 1929, p 3, and no 2, Oct 1929, p 2; *Argus* (Melb), 17 Feb 1938, p 2; R. Oldfield, The Early Years of the Housewives Association of Victoria 1915-1930 (B.A. Hons thesis, Monash Univ, 1989); J. Biddington, From a Chattel to Man's Equal? (ms, 2002, Boroondara Library, Melb); VPRS 932/P/0000, unit 414, no 7700 (PRO, Vic); Housewives Assn of Vic, Minute Books (LaTL); Royal Women's Hospital archives, Melb; family papers (held by author, North Carlton, Melb).

JUDITH BIDDINGTON

RUSSELL, EDWARD FITZGERALD (1867-1943), trade unionist, was born on 27 June 1867 at Rocky Lead, near Daylesford, Victoria, second child of Henry Russell, an Irish-born teacher, and his wife Maria Louisa, née Doyle, from England. Edward was a compositor when he married Catherine McCoy (1872-1939), a domestic servant, on 24 October 1890 at St Mary's Catholic Church, Dandenong. They had six children. By 1894 the family had moved to Port Melbourne where Edward continued in the printing trade until 1899.

Russell was working as a labourer in 1902 and as a candlemaker in 1904 and 1906. These were difficult years for the family, and he tried his hand as a casual dockhand. In 1907 Kate recalled that he would 'earn 10s. one week, 15s. the next, £1 the next and some weeks more, and some weeks nothing at all'. When he moved to John Kitchen's [q.v.] soap factory, work as a vat man was 'heavy and labourious' but more regular. On only thirty-six shillings per week, it cost her all her husband earned to live and they got by with a little monetary assistance from an aged parent.

In August 1907 Russell was appointed secretary to the Victorian Agricultural Implement Makers' Society. He had no experience in this industry, but was a member of the Victorian Socialist Party, which had strong links with the union. Within a month Russell conducted the society's case in the Commonwealth Court of Conciliation and Arbitration opposing H. V. McKay [q.v.10]. When Justice Higgins [q.v.9] called for evidence on the cost of living, Russell had to rely on that of assembled trade union leaders and of a few union members' wives, including Kate. In his Harvester judgement, which established the concept of a living wage for a worker and his family, Higgins drew on the evidence of Kate Russell and her battles to economize. Next

year, however, the judgement was set aside by the High Court of Australia, Russell had to seek wage increases through wages boards and the union was deeply in debt for its legal fees.

After experiencing frustrating delays in the wages boards, in January 1911 the agricultural implement makers' society declared that all workers in the industry must join the union. McKay led the employers in a lock-out. After a bitter and sometimes violent eight weeks, during which free labour was recruited, Russell was forced to compromise and his members went back to work with only minimal wage increases.

Formerly a member of the Labor Party, in 1907 Russell failed to win in Port Melbourne municipal elections as a revolutionary socialist. Rejoining Labor, he was municipal councillor for Port Melbourne in 1912-14 and mayor in 1913. A sometime member of the Industrial Workers of the World, he was Labor candidate for East Gippsland in the Legislative Assembly in 1911 and for Echuca in the House of Representatives in 1919. For the conscription referenda of 1916-17 he helped to organize the 'no' campaign in South Australia. He was president of the Trades Hall Council, Melbourne, in 1918-19.

From 1911, leading a bankrupt trade union, Russell avoided industrial action. By 1925 the union had regained sufficient strength to attempt to win wage increases through the arbitration court, but Justice Sir John Quick [q.v.11] rejected his case. Next year Russell failed to convince the court that, because technological change had intensified the pace of work, hours should be reduced. By the late 1920s, unemployment among his members forced Russell to join the manufacturers in demanding increased tariffs on machinery. With mass unemployment among implement makers, in 1930 the finances of the union were again in a parlous state. In January his salary was reduced by £1 per week, and his son Roy, who worked for him, was made an honorary assistant. The financial position of the union did not improve, and in February 1933 Russell resigned.

Becoming embroiled in a bitter row with his former colleagues, he and his son claimed almost £500 in back pay, while the union executive accused Russell of misappropriating union property. In April 1936 Roy addressed the union on behalf of his father. Stating that his father was destitute, he threatened to take the matter to the press. The executive agreed to pay off the debt at £1 per week and to settle for the balance when the union was in stronger financial position.

Russell became a secretary for local friendly societies and other bodies and was treasurer of the Melbourne Technical College council.

A Freemason, he was past master of the Cruffel Lodge, Yarraville. Russell died on 14 August 1943 at his home at Footscray and was buried with his wife in Dandenong cemetery. Two daughters and one son survived him.

F. Bongiorno, *The People's Party* (Melb, 1996); C. Fahey and J. Lack, '"We Have to Train Men From Labourers": The Agricultural Implement Trade 1918-1945', *Jnl of Industrial Relations*, 42, no 4, Dec 2000, p 551, *and* '"A Kind of Elysium Where Nobody Has Anything Difficult to Do": H. B. Higgins, H. V. McKay and the Agricultural Implement Makers, 1901-26', *Labour History*, no 80, May 2001, p 99; *Argus* (Melb), 20 Aug 1914, p 6; *Age* (Melb), 16 Aug 1943, p 3; Agricultural Implement Makers, Minutes, 1906-36 (Univ Melb Archives); B1958/3, items NN1925 and 22/1925, and series C2274 (NAA).

CHARLES FAHEY

RUSSELL, JANE FOSS; *see* BARFF

RYAN, CATHERINE MARY; *see* NARELLE, MARIE

S

ST LEON, MATTHEW (1826?-1903), acrobat, equestrian and circus proprietor, was born in London, possibly the John Coney who was baptized at St George's Hanover Square in 1826. He was aged about 8 when the parish apprenticed him to a chimney sweep at Westminster. Known as John Conley or Connelly, he learned to read at a Sunday School by memorizing passages from the Bible, and to write his name. His usefulness as a sweep's climbing boy diminishing with adolescence, he adapted his agility to tumbling, and performed in London streets. At Astley's Amphitheatre, across the Thames, he learned the circus arts. When implicated in a theft, he was tried (under the assumed name 'John Jones') at the Old Bailey on 24 October 1842. Transported to Van Diemen's Land, he received a ticket-of-leave in July 1847.

Jones was one of 'four wonderful acrobats' in Australia's first successful circus, opened by Robert Avis Radford, an expert horseman, at Launceston in December 1847. Here Jones polished his acrobatic skills and developed into a fine equestrian. At St George's Church of England, Battery Point, Hobart, on 21 December 1848 he married Margaret Monaghan (c.1833-1897), an educated, Dublin-born woman. With an Irish ropewalker, Edward Hughes (known professionally as 'Edward La Rosiere'), Jones opened the Royal Australian Equestrian Circus at Malcolm's Adelphi Hotel, York Street, Sydney, on 15 October 1850. Joining Henry Burton [q.v.3] the following year, Jones travelled to the Bathurst goldfields. At Sofala in September 1851 he formed his own circus, one of his performers being an Aboriginal boy, later known as William Jones [q.v.]. In the gold rushes, Jones's National Circus travelled through south-eastern Australia. At Ballarat, diggers commandeered his tent for a meeting before the Eureka Stockade. By 1858 members of the Wirth family [q.v.12], German musicians, had become bandsmen with his circus.

At Barry Sullivan's [q.v.6] Theatre Royal, Melbourne, on 27 January 1865 Jones and his three young sons were billed as 'The St Leon Troupe', gymnasts from the Gymnase Imperiale, Paris. Jones subsequently took the professional name 'Matthew St Leon'. Eventually the family retained that surname. St Leon's Circus first appeared at Kilmore in May 1875 and grew rapidly in size and reputation; by 1883 its cavalcade of '150 men and horses', brightly painted wagons, menagerie of wild animals and glittering band carriage extended over half a mile (0.8 km) in length.

St Leon boasted more than £5000 in receipts from a Sydney summer season in 1883-84, when he was acclaimed as 'one of the cleverest equestrians' to have visited the city. In 1885-86 a second circus, headed by his sons Augustus (c.1851-1924) and Alfred (1859-1909), toured New Zealand. In 1889, after floods affected business, 'Matthew Jones' was declared insolvent and forced to liquidate his 'splendidly appointed' circus and land holdings in Melbourne.

Described as 'a sterling character, straightforward and honest', with bright eyes and a mild disposition, barely 5 ft (152 cm) tall, St Leon was an 'exceedingly dapper little gentleman'. He enjoyed a cigarette but 'never drank [or] swore'. At the height of his success, he had kept his wife and their two daughters 'in plush' in Melbourne, where the women were active in the Salvation Army. 'John Leon Jones' died on 14 April 1903 in his daughter's home at Oakleigh and was buried in Springvale cemetery; the Wirth brothers' circus band played a requiem at his graveside. Four sons and two daughters survived him.

Matthew St Leon's sons and their children carried the name into vaudeville, theatre and film, as well as circus, in the twentieth century. With their families, Gus and Alf worked the circus and vaudeville circuits of the United States of America in the early 1900s. Another son Walter (c.1856-1943) and his family combined with Ashton's [q.v.7] circus in 1906-07. Soon after, Gus and his family, including the Honeys [q.v.14], returned to Australia to start the Great United Circus, which toured from 1909 until 1941. Gus's son Philip (1890-1957), an equestrian, later joined the May Wirth [q.v.12] troupe. Gus died on 16 October 1924 in hospital at Junee, New South Wales, and was buried in the Church of England section of Liverpool cemetery. Descendants of Gus and Walter were active in circus in Australia and the U.S.A. in the 1960s.

Cornwall Chronicle (Launc), 29 Dec 1847, p 3; *SMH*, 15 Oct 1850, p 1, 5 Jan 1884, p 2; *Bulletin*, 5 Jan 1884, p 9, 16 May 1903, p 30, 9 July 1914, p 9; *Wangaratta Dispatch*, 10 Jan 1885, p 2; *Lorgnette*, 20 July 1889, p 5, 24 Aug 1889, p 6; *Age* (Melb), 14 Apr 1903, p 5; *Punch* (Melb), 23 Apr 1903, p 516; *Chicago Inl*, 11 Sept 1908; *New York Clipper*, 27 Feb 1909, p 70; *San Francisco Call*, 24 Dec 1913; *Moving Picture World*, 8 Nov 1913, p 593; *Wyckoff News* (USA), 23 Nov 1939; CRIM 4/208 (PRO, Lond); St Leon papers (ML); information from the late Mr R. Harvey, the late Brigadier T. H. Lynn.

MARK VALENTINE ST LEON

SAMPSON, NOEL EDGAR (1901-1976), headmaster and union leader, was born on 19 November 1901 in Perth, second son of Henry Charles Sampson, a Victorian-born police constable, later a public servant, and his wife Sara Ellen, née O'Brien, from New South Wales. After attending Highgate State School Noel won an entrance to Perth Modern School in 1913 and completed his leaving certificate in 1917. His teaching career began as a monitor at East Perth Primary School and then at Perth Boys' School, to which he returned in 1923 after two years at Claremont Teachers' Training College. He studied part time at the University of Western Australia (B.Sc., 1924; B.A., 1931; Dip.Ed., 1932), majoring first in mathematics then in English. In 1926 he won the University prize in logic and philosophy.

In 1927 Sampson returned to the teachers' college, first as a junior lecturer and later a senior lecturer, remaining there until 1936. During the three years (1931-33) that the college was closed because of the Depression, he taught science and geography at Perth Modern School. Appointed inspector of primary schools in 1936, he succeeded Joseph Parsons [q.v.11] as headmaster of Perth Modern School in 1940. On 30 December next year at St George's Cathedral Sampson married with Anglican rites 47-year-old Hughina Bell; she was also a teacher and vice-president (1937-39) of the Western Australian State Teachers' Union.

Sampson had joined the teachers' union in 1925 and become a vice-president in 1926 and president in 1933-35. While president, and also acting as secretary, he led the union in a major dispute regaining pay and working conditions lost during the Depression. From 1940 to 1948 he was inspector of country schools as well as principal of the Modern School. After his inspectorial appointment ended, he rejoined the union and was its president for a record term between 1951 and 1966. Under his leadership the union worked towards equal pay for women (achieved soon after his retirement), improved the inspectorial system and had formal promotional procedures established, winning equal representation with the government on the new Government School Teachers' Tribunal. Sampson acted for the union on the tribunal from 1961 until his retirement in 1967. He had thrice acted as president of the Australian Teachers' Federation, twice representing that body at the World Confederation of Organizations of the Teaching Profession.

Under Sampson, Perth Modern School maintained its record of high academic achievement and output of distinguished students, including R. J. L. Hawke, later prime minister. Through the teachers' union, he opposed the restructuring by which from 1959 selective entry to Perth Modern School ended and it became just one of a number of comprehensive, district-based government secondary schools in the Perth metropolitan area. He resigned as headmaster in 1963. 'Sammy' was remembered as a remote figure with many nervous mannerisms—such as fiddling with his pocket—while addressing the school during assemblies. He died on 21 September 1976 at Sir Charles Gairdner Hospital, and was cremated with Catholic rites. His wife survived him; they were childless.

West Australian, 25 Sept 1976, p 14; *W. A. Teachers' Jnl*, 3 May 1934; *Western Teacher*, 7 Oct 1976, pp 3 & 12; V. Horner, The Influence of the State School Teachers' Union of Western Australia on the Policies of the Education Department of Western Australia 1898-1960 (M.Ed. thesis, Univ WA, 1961).   DAVID BLACK

SAMUELS, CHARLES (c.1864-1912), Aboriginal athlete, was born at Jimbour station, southern Queensland, and named Sambo Combo, one of three children of Combo and Mary Ann, Kamilaroi people from north-western New South Wales. He later became known as Charles Samuels because his older brother George was also successfully involved in pedestrianism (professional running). Growing up with the local Bunyinni people (part of the Barunggam group) and close to the sons of (Sir) Joshua Bell [q.v.3], owner of Jimbour station, Charlie worked as a stockrider and general hand. His talent for running led to involvement in such local professional circuits as Toowoomba. In 1885, accompanied by his 'owner and trainer' William Robertson, he competed unsuccessfully in a handicap event at Botany, Sydney. He returned in August next year and easily won the Botany handicap at the Sir Joseph Banks Hotel grounds.

His achievements at Sydney venues in the next few years led to his being acclaimed as an Australian champion and among the best exponents of sprinting 'the world has ever seen' over distances up to 300 yards (274 m). Samuels was 5 ft 7 ins (170 cm) tall. To a *Referee* reporter, he seemed built for speed, light in the upper body but with 'tremendous hips and thighs, and a long tapering calf'; his 'beautiful action was ... the secret of his pace, as he was a lovely balanced runner'. He was also praised for his courage and determination. His times were consistently 'inside even time' (better than ten yards per second) with his best performance recorded over 134 yards at '9 yards inside even time' (12.5 seconds) at Botany in 1888, which was dubbed as an Australian record. Timings were suspect, but he was reported to have run 100 yards in 9.1 seconds. Samuels also competed in four match races against Harry Hutchens, the English champion, winning three; although popular with the public, they led to allegations about 'gate money and betting considerations'.

Samuels was described as 'a splendid tempered man', who would give his last dollar away, and 'the last Australian champion'— many believing that as Aborigines were doomed his like would not be seen again. Rife with bribery and corruption, however, pedestrianism was barely surviving by 1892, as amateur athletics and other sports gained greater popularity. When not in training, Samuels fought occasionally at Larry Foley's [q.v.4] White Horse Hotel. His success as a runner led to handicaps that restricted both his winnings and the financial rewards for his managers, who increasingly left him on his own. Tensions and frustrations emerged. Although he was associated with drinking, fighting and some 'stiff' (fixed) racing, he retained public admiration. He lived for a time at a camp at Centennial Park, then moved to La Perouse Aboriginal reserve at Botany. There he was reported in 1894 to have a grievance against the police regarding his rights. In 1896 he was admitted into the Hospital for the Insane, Callan Park, with a 'form of mental disorder (Melancholia)' caused by 'ill health & love affairs'.

In January next year, wasted, and viewed as a nuisance, Samuels was sent back to Queensland at the Aborigines Protection Board's expense. He returned to Jimbour station but, made unwelcome by the new owners, led a wandering life and was seen at some local running events. In 1905 he and his wife Maggie and two daughters were staying in Brisbane, and Samuels was reported to be drinking and threatening relatives. On 17 May the family was transferred to Barambah Aboriginal reserve. Maggie died of consumption on 13 October in Maryborough hospital. Both children contracted the disease and died in January 1906. Samuels for the most part continued to live and work on the settlement. He had a second family but an infant child died in 1911. Predeceased a few days earlier by his wife Lizzie, Samuels died of pulmonary tuberculosis on 13 October 1912 at Barambah.

Tom Petrie's Reminiscences of Early Queensland (Brisb, 1904); *Qld Chief Protector's Report*, 1904/05, p 18; *Referee* (Syd), 5 Dec 1888, p 7, 21 Aug 1889, p 3, 28 May 1890, p 3, 1 Nov 1893, p 3, 2 May 1894, p 3, 6 Nov 1912, p 9; *Sun* (Syd), 24 Nov 1981, p 42; G. C. Blades, *Australian Aborigines, Cricket and Pedestrianism: Culture and Conflict, 1880-1910* (B.A. Hons thesis, Univ Qld, 1985); Callan Park, Fol 95, no 3776 (SRNSW); A/58675, A/58676 (QSA).

GENEVIEVE BLADES
KEN EDWARDS

SASSE, HERMANN OTTO ERICH (1895-1976), Lutheran pastor and theologian, was born on 17 July 1895 at Sonnewalde, Lower Lusatia (Lausitz), Germany, eldest of five children of Hermann Sasse, pharmacist, and his wife Maria, née Berger. Young Hermann began reading theology and ancient philology at the University of Berlin in 1913. He later maintained that war was his tutor in practical theology: in World War I he was one of only six from his battalion to survive trench warfare in Flanders.

Ordained on 13 June 1920 in St Matthew's Church, Berlin, Sasse worked in several Brandenburg parishes and in 1923 took the licentiate in theology (Berlin); in 1926 as an exchange student at Hartford seminary, Connecticut, United States of America, he obtained a master's degree. On 11 September 1928 in St Nicolai's Church, Oranienburg, Germany, he married Charlotte Margarete Naumann (d.1964). They had three children. During the Depression, Sasse was *Sozialpfarrer* (pastor with social duties) ministering especially to factory workers in Berlin.

A participant in the ecumenical movement, Sasse was also a delegate and interpreter at the first world conference of the Faith and Order Movement (Lausanne, Switzerland, 1927) and attended the disarmament conference in Geneva (1932). Among the earliest to speak out against Nazism, he was an active if critical member of the Confessing Church Movement, promoted by Martin Niemoeller. In 1933 Sasse and his younger colleague Dietrich Bonhoeffer were among the small but growing church opposition to Hitler. Together they produced the Bethel Confession, which clearly addressed discrimination against the Jews. Next year Sasse left the synod that produced the Barmen Declaration, objecting that the Confessing Movement was wrongly arrogating church authority for itself. In 1933 he had accepted a professorship in church history at the University of Erlangen, Bavaria. His passport was withdrawn in 1935, but his popularity as a lecturer and protection from the dean of the faculty helped him to retain his university post through the Nazi era.

In 1948 Sasse protested at the formation of the Evangelical Church in Germany. His opposition to its policy of restoration rather than renewal and unease over state-supported university faculties of theology led him to join the Lutheran Free Church. Receiving a call to teach at Immanuel (Luther) Seminary, North Adelaide, he migrated in 1949 to South Australia, where he swung his weight behind efforts to unite Australia's divided Lutheran churches. He devoted his energy and his teaching and writing skills to this cause, and was deeply involved in formulating new agreed doctrinal bases; the church union occurred in 1966. Involved in the German Lutheran community in Adelaide and Melbourne, he assisted many immigrants with pastoral advice and care.

Sasse retained his wider connections and perspectives—he was known as 'Mr Lutheran' in the U.S.A. A correspondence including regular doctrinal and pastoral 'Letters to Lutheran Pastors' across the globe was supported by continuous research, particularly in Scripture as Word of God, and the Eucharist. His reputation for strongly defended conservative stances was balanced by lively personal contacts across denominational boundaries. He involved himself in the Australian Roman Catholic-Lutheran dialogue from its inception. Retiring from the seminary in 1969, in 1972 he was appointed to the Order of Merit by the Federal Republic of Germany.

Among Sasse's 479 publications were *Here We Stand*, published in translation in Minneapolis, U.S.A., in 1946, and *This is My Body* (Minneapolis, 1959), written in English. He died on 9 August 1976 in a fire at his home in North Adelaide and was buried in Centennial Park cemetery. Two sons survived him. An obituarist described Sasse as 'Australia's most distinguished acquisition from the Continental theological scene'.

F. W. Hopf (ed), *Sacra Scriptura* (Erlangen, 1981); K. Beyschlag, *Die Erlanger Theologie* (Erlangen, 1993); R. Feuerhahn, *Hermann Sasse: A Bibliography* (Lond, 1995); *Lutheran Theological Jnl*, 2, nos 2-3, Aug-Dec 1968, p 61, 29, no 1, May 1995, p 11; *Colloquium*, 9, no 1, Oct 1976, p 36; *Lutherische Kirche in der Welt*, 42, 1995, p 71.

MAURICE SCHILD

SATURDAY; *see* WINDRADYNE

SAVILLE-KENT, WILLIAM (1845-1908), fisheries scientist and author, was born on 10 July 1845 at Sidmouth, Devon, England, youngest of ten children of Samuel Savill Kent, sub-inspector of factories, and his first wife Mary Ann, neé Windus. William was educated in boarding schools at Bath, Worcester and Gloucester. His early life was disturbed by his father's infidelity, his mother's death in 1852, and the conviction in 1865 of his sister CONSTANCE KENT (1844-1944) for the murder of their infant half-brother in what was alleged to be an act of revenge against a former governess, now their stepmother. Despite her age, and being convicted solely on her doubtful confession, Constance was to serve twenty years in prison. There were three other half-siblings.

After study at King's College (University of London) and at the Royal School of Mines under T. H. Huxley [q.v.1], William became a naturalist and from 1868 worked at the British Museum. In 1870 he received a grant from the Royal Society to conduct a dredging survey off Portugal. Recognizing the potential for experimental marine biology of the public aquaria then being constructed in a number of British cities, in 1872-73 he was resident naturalist at the Brighton Aquarium, Sussex. His ambition was to establish a national marine research laboratory. Although he floated a company, he was forced to leave its development to others. At the Manchester Aquarium (1873-76) he developed an interest in aquaculture. He also worked in aquaria on Jersey, in London and Norfolk and, from 1879, back at Brighton.

On 11 June 1872 at St Matthias's Church, Stoke Newington, London, he had married Elizabeth Susannah Bennett (d.1875). On 5 January 1876 at the parish church, Prestwich, Lancaster, he married Mary Ann Livesay, giving his surname as Saville Kent. Later he added a hyphen. A fellow (1869) of the Royal Zoological Society, London, in 1873 he was elected a fellow of the Linnean Society of London.

Following Saville-Kent's work at the Great International Fisheries Exhibition in London in 1883, Huxley recommended him to the Tasmanian government to restore badly depleted oyster beds. Appointed superintendent and inspector of fisheries, William arrived at Launceston with his wife and a half-sister on 15 July 1884. In the following decade he produced the first comprehensive and scientific surveys of Australian fisheries and their potential for development, covering not only the biological aspects of the stocks but also fisheries laws, the economics of the industry and the marketing of the catch. The first to require fishing vessels to be registered, he rebuilt the oyster beds in Tasmania through the establishment of government reserves, the introduction of minimum-size regulations and the leasing of areas in which to apply modern culture methods, but fell out with members of a commission charged with acclimatizing salmon and trout in Tasmania's rivers. When his Tasmanian appointment was not renewed, he applied the same techniques in Victoria (1887-88), Queensland (commissioner of fisheries, 1889-92) and Western Australia (commissioner of fisheries, 1893-95) for both edible and pearl oyster fisheries. He also examined and reported on fish, bêche-de-mer, corals, sponges, dugong and turtles during this period.

Although sceptical about attempts to acclimatize salmon in Tasmania, Saville-Kent introduced trout into Western Australia and attempted to acclimatize other freshwater sporting fish from eastern Australia. He planned to export high-quality Australian species into British waters. The author of many scientific papers and reports, he wrote three major books: *A Manual of the Infusoria* (three volumes, London, 1880-82), *The Great Barrier Reef* (London, 1893) and *The Naturalist in Australia* (London, 1897).

William's personal life seemed strongly shaped by women, including friends in Australia, such as Louisa Ann Meredith and Ellis Rowan [qq.v.5,11]. In 1886, following her release from prison, he had met his sister Constance in England and brought her to Tasmania. She adopted the name 'Ruth Emilie Kaye' and, after accompanying her brother to Victoria and Queensland, worked as a nurse in Melbourne, then in Perth and finally in Sydney, where she became matron first of Prince Henry Hospital and then at Parramatta Industrial School for Girls. She died on 10 April 1944 in Sydney.

Saville-Kent and his wife lived in England in 1892-93 and from 1896 to 1904. He now put his ideas into commercial effect. In 1904 he worked for Lever Bros in a pearl culture experiment based in the Cook Islands. Forming a company back in England in 1905, next year he began to culture pearls in tropical Australia, at Somerset, Torres Strait. He was probably the first to succeed in producing both blister and spherical pearls of commercial quality—a necklace believed to have been made with his pearls has recently attracted specialist attention.

As private research, Saville-Kent devoted much attention to corals and sponges and lizards. These objects of his interest shared his residences. In mid-1908, in poor health, he returned to England and on 11 October, following surgery, he died in hospital at Bournemouth. His wife survived him; they were childless. Saville-Kent was a pioneer of scientific management of Australian fisheries. His grave in All Saints' churchyard, Milford-on-Sea, Hampshire, is decorated with corals.

B. Taylor, *Cruelly Murdered* (Lond, 1979); A. J. Harrison, *Savant of the Australian Seas* (Hob, 1997); *ODNB* (2004); *Austn Gemmologist*, 15, no 5, Feb 1984, p 155; *Protist* (Germany), vol 153, no 4, 2002, p 413.   A. J. HARRISON

SAWTELL, OLAF (MICHAEL) (1883-1971), socialist agitator and Emersonian, was born on 20 August 1883 in Adelaide, second son of Charles Sawtell, optician, and his Swedish-born wife Florence Arabella, previously Hooper, née Stockenstrom. Educated at the Collegiate School of St Peter, where he won the McCulloch history scholarship (1898), in 1899 Mick chose adventure as a drover's boy

with (Sir) Sidney Kidman [q.v.9] over further study.

By 1900 Sawtell was at Annandale station, on the Georgina River in Queensland. He then worked the Birdsville Track, with forays into the Simpson Desert to reclaim stray cattle. Exhilarated by the life and delighting in campfire culture, he also learned much from Aboriginal boys his age, the knowledge resulting in lifelong respect for Aboriginal spirituality.

On Kidman's recommendation, in 1904 Sawtell left for Western Australia, where he was employed on Obagooma station, north-east of Derby. In the Northern Territory by 1907, he tried tin-mining and lived for a time at Humpty Doo, undertaking droving trips for a Darwin butcher and taking a six-month 'study holiday' at Borroloola. Here he read his way through the outpost's remarkable library and encountered the writings of the American transcendentalist Ralph Waldo Emerson, his guiding light thereafter.

In 1908, droving cattle overland from Darwin to Derby, where he had taken out a lease at Trent Creek, Sawtell happened upon Robert Blatchford's *Merrie England* (1895) and was converted to socialism. He engaged in 'poddy dodging' (cattle rustling) and read Plato's *Republic* and theosophical books delivered monthly by a missionary. Despite learning the dialect of the 'Munjongs' (local Aborigines), their cattle spearing and grass burning drove him out, and in 1910 he headed south, calling on Daisy Bates [q.v.7] at Carnarvon *en route*. Now an itinerant labourer, in Perth he attended meetings of the Theosophical Society and joined the Socialist Party. From 1914, with Montague Miller [q.v.10], he was a stalwart of the Industrial Workers of the World.

A persuasive speaker, Sawtell urged workers that sound organization, direct action and education would usher in the co-operative commonwealth by peaceable means. After some success as an organizer on the goldfields, in October 1916 at Gascoyne, during the first conscription referendum campaign, he was arrested with Miller and others for seditious conspiracy. On a separate charge of 'threatening with intent', Sawtell was gaoled for six months in 1917.

Released, Sawtell moved to Broken Hill, New South Wales, as a paid organizer for the I.W.W. In August he was arrested for belonging to an illegal organization and sentenced to six months hard labour, subsequently attracting a twelve-month sentence at Deniliquin in December for having led a demonstration at the North Mine. Sawtell served seven of eleven months of the sentence in solitary confinement at Parramatta, then returned to Perth early in 1919. Boycotted by employers, he devoted himself to advocacy of the One

Big Union. By August he was in Adelaide as an organizer for the South Australia Socialist Party. There he helped to establish a new version of the I.W.W. and, on 2 September 1919 at the registrar-general's office, he married Elizabeth Pole, a teacher, with whom he had corresponded while in gaol.

The marriage ended in divorce. After writing *Job Control, or the Industrial Basis of the New Society* (Adelaide, c.1920) he was a self-described 'bush worker cum socialist organiser'. He argued against the violence of the Bolshevik Revolution with the Melbourne communist Guido Baracchi [q.v.13] in 1921 and later contributed to Sydney newspapers. Another pamphlet, *An Apocalypse of Labor: A New Interpretation of an Old Movement*, and his prose poem *The Wisdom of a Vagabond* were published in Sydney in 1926, when his address was William Street Post Office, Kings Cross. By 1929 he was working in a Sydney paint factory.

In 1930 Sawtell experienced romance with an English-born chiropodist, Elsie Vanda Grant, née Idenden, whom he was to marry on 2 May 1964 at the registrar-general's office, Sydney. They opened a health food shop in the Victoria Arcade, where Sawtell long presided over the Emerson Society. He spoke in the Domain and was arrested during a demonstration against war and fascism in 1934. The appeal of socialism, however, had faded. He now advocated reason and Emersonian individualism. Reading more widely than ever, he practised vegetarianism and yoga and, as a student of the Vedanta, in 1938 joined the Theosophical Society—he resigned in 1949, rejoined in 1957 and his membership lapsed in 1960. Numerous contributions to theosophical publications in 1936-49 indicated a prior association with Sydney's breakaway Independent Theosophical Society.

Sawtell regarded the Aboriginal cause as a 'stern social duty'. He introduced Jack Patten to P. R. Stephensen [qq.v.11,12] and as president of the committee of Aboriginal Citizen Rights, formed in 1938, mobilized support for reform in New South Wales. In 1940, when the Aborigines Welfare Board replaced the discredited Aborigines Protection Board, he campaigned with Pearl Gibbs for Aboriginal representation and later joined the A.W.B. himself. Serving some twenty years as a government nominee, he went 'walkabout' annually to obtain information, and claimed to have directed 60 000 letters about pension rights to (Sir) Robert Menzies [q.v.15]. Resented and criticized as an opponent of detribalization, which he deemed destructive of crucial Aboriginal beliefs, Sawtell resigned in 1962, having opposed lifting the ban on the sale of alcohol and believing that the board had outlived its usefulness. He has since been seen as paternalist, but his experience and dedication were exceptional, and as a friend of Albert Namatjira [q.v.15] he knew there could be no quick fix.

During World War II Sawtell lectured for the Army Education Service and to disaffected leftists at the Hasty Tasty Café, Darlinghurst Road. In later life, he was a prodigious contributor of letters and articles to the press, made radio broadcasts, and in 1946 participated in an Australian Broadcasting Commission forum of the air opposing British weapons tests in Australia as 'evil business'. Short, sprightly and fresh voiced, he lectured several nights a week to community organizations, his favourite topics being Emerson, the Aborigines and, after meeting the engineer J. J. C. Bradfield [q.v.7] in 1938, water for the inland. He lectured throughout the State on 'The Ideal for Australia'—Lake Eyre as a great food-producing area and Alice Springs as the national capital.

Towards the end Sawtell felt the only hope of converting his fellow Australians to his theories was 'a costly catastrophe'. His tenacity was admired nonetheless. An idealist rather than an eccentric, he died on 1 October 1971 at Kings Cross, Sydney, and was cremated with Catholic rites. Childless, he was survived by his wife. His will specified that, instead of flowers, donations be made to the Foundation for Aboriginal Affairs.

I. Turner, *Sydney's Burning* (Melb, 1967); J. Horner, *Vote Ferguson for Aboriginal Freedom* (Syd, 1974); J. Roe, *Beyond Belief* (Syd, 1986); F. Cain, *The Wobblies at War* (Melb, 1993); V. Burgmann, *Revolutionary Industrial Unionism* (Melb, 1995); H. Goodall, *Invasion to Embassy* (Syd, 1996); Amalgamated Engineering Union, *Monthly Jnl*, Sept 1948, p 19, Jan 1955, p 16, June 1955, p 19; *New Dawn*, Jan 1972, p 13; *SMH*, 26 Dec 1928, p 4, 20 Apr 1929, p 13, 7 June 1960, p 1, 22 Sept 1961, p 4, 2 Oct 1971, p 8; *Sun* (Syd), 11 Jan 1961, p 9; *Daily Mirror* (Syd), 15 Nov 1971, p 26; D. Huggonson, Michael Sawtell (ts, 1995, copy on ADB file); oral history interview with M. Sawtell (nd, ML); Union Index of Theosophical Articles (Theosophical Society Archives, Syd); St Peter's College, Adel, archives.

JILL ROE

SCHÜRMANN, CLAMOR WILHELM; *see* TEICHELMANN

SCHUTT, HELEN MACPHERSON (1874-1951), philanthropist, was born on 17 April 1874 at Darnick, Melrose, Roxburgh, Scotland, only child of Robert Smith, a Scottish-born timber merchant from Melbourne, and his Australian-born wife Jane Priscilla, née Macpherson. Jane's father, the Scottish-born pastoralist John, father of J. A. MacPherson [q.v.5], was an early landholder in Limestone

Plains (Canberra) with large holdings in Victoria's Western District. Helen's paternal grandfather John Smith was an architect, sculptor and builder at Darnick, best known for his work on the writer Sir Walter Scott's home, Abbotsford. Her father and six of his brothers came to Australia in the 1850s, establishing themselves in timber businesses in Melbourne and at Ballarat, as well as in Hobart and Sydney, and in property dealing.

Brought to Melbourne in September 1874, Helen lived at Fitzroy with her parents until she was 7, when she accompanied them on their travels in Australia, Britain and Europe. Educated partly at boarding schools in Scotland, and for two years in Hanover, Germany, in 1889 she returned to Melbourne, where she attended Presbyterian Ladies' College as a day girl for one year, taking 'Music from the best master, German, Elocution and Dancing'.

On 11 December 1901 at Toorak Presbyterian Church Helen married William John Schutt [q.v.11], a barrister. A glittering occasion, the wedding was widely reported in the press. The couple lived at Toorak in a villa that was a wedding gift from Helen's parents. William became a Supreme Court judge in 1919. Beautiful and elegant—a passport photograph showed a fine-boned, slender woman with a direct gaze—Helen supported a number of charitable causes, including the missions to seamen, the Royal District Nursing Service and the Royal Society for the Prevention of Cruelty to Animals. On 24 December 1923 the Schutts left Melbourne. William disembarked in Colombo while Helen went on to London. She never returned to Australia. Although he lived in Melbourne, from 1924 to his death (at sea) in 1933, William occasionally travelled with Helen in England and Europe, their presence noted in the social pages of the *British Australasian*.

After 1933 Helen sent, from Europe, occasional postcards, paid the school fees of young family members in Australia and apparently divided her time between the south of France and Switzerland. On 19 April 1951, while staying at the Hotel Majestic at Cannes, France, she died of pneumonia. She was childless. For reasons so far unexplained, she was buried in a pauper's grave at Marseilles. Her body was later exhumed and her remains cremated.

From an estate sworn for probate at £406 121, Helen Schutt left some £275 000 to establish a perpetual charitable trust for the benefit of Victorians, originally known as the Helen M. Schutt Trust. In 2001, to mark the fiftieth anniversary of her benefaction and the contribution made by both the Macphersons and the Smiths, the name was changed to the Helen Macpherson Smith Trust and an obelisk was erected at the Melbourne general cemetery to honour her memory. By June 2004, $50 million had been given to Victorian charitable institutions.

J. Sandilands, *Helen Macpherson Schutt, Philanthropist, 17 April 1874-19 April 1951* (Melb, 2001); Helen Macpherson Smith Trust records (Melb).

JANE SANDILANDS

SEEKAMP, HENRY (c.1829-1864), newspaper editor and nationalist, and CLARA MARIA (c.1819-1908), actress and newspaper editor, were born in England and Dublin respectively. Henry claimed to have an 'Arts Bachelor'. He came to Victoria in August 1852, among the earliest gold-seekers. A dapper little man with a fierce temper, he launched Ballarat's first newspaper, the *Ballarat Times, Buninyong and Creswick Advertiser*, in March 1854.

His journal proclaimed a radical and civic-minded programme, and Seekamp became a forceful advocate of reform of the goldfields administration, votes for diggers, and improvements in education and local government. He served on a committee for a national school and convened a meeting in September 1854 to found a hospital for sick and destitute diggers. Raffaello Carboni [q.v.3] described him as a 'short, thick, rare sort of man' who hated humbug and 'yabber yabber'. Soon Clara Maria Du Val (Duval), née Lodge, infatuated Seekamp. An Irish actress with three children by George William (Claud) Du Val, a teacher of languages, Clara had arrived in Victoria about 1847 and conducted a theatrical company. She had taken Seekamp's name by early 1854.

The *Ballarat Times* became the mouthpiece of the diggers in their protests at government corruption. In November 1854 Seekamp proclaimed the Ballarat Reform League to be the 'germ of Australian independence'. On the morning after the battle at Eureka, police raided the newspaper office, arrested Seekamp and confiscated all copies of his newspaper. He was incarcerated with those who had been captured after the battle, including his reporter John Manning.

On 23 January 1855 Seekamp was tried in the Supreme Court in Melbourne for seditious libel. The jury found him guilty, but recommended mercy. He was sentenced to six months gaol, starting on 26 March, reduced to three months following the presentation of a monster petition to Governor Hotham [q.v.4] from the citizens of Ballarat on 29 May. During his time in custody, Clara became editor and she kept the newspaper, briefly known as the *Ballarat Times and Southern Cross*, afloat. Henry was released on 28 June 1855, the only man to serve a prison term as a result of the Eureka Stockade.

Seekamp gained further notoriety in February 1856 when he turned his vitriolic pen upon the Irish-born actress Lola Montez [q.v.5], accusing her of immorality. They took to each other with whips in the main street of Ballarat, and accused each other of assault and libel, creating a public sensation. The court cases were dismissed, but public sympathy went to Lola, and the fiery editor lost much of his popularity.

In October 1856 the Seekamps sold their newspaper and left Ballarat. Henry headed north, to Sydney and then to Queensland. He died of 'natural causes accelerated by intemperance' at the Drummond diggings, Clermont, on 19 January 1864. His age was shown as 35 and his occupation as journalist. Clara remained in Melbourne and died on 22 January 1908. She was buried in the Church of England section of Melbourne general cemetery with her son Oliver (d.1884). Another son survived her. The two leading Melbourne papers carried obituaries and praised her intellect and determination. Carboni best characterized Henry Seekamp, writing that 'his energy never abated, though the whole legion of Victorian red-tape wanted to dry his inkstand'.

W. B. Withers, *History of Ballarat* (Ballarat, Vic, 1870); R. Carboni, *The Eureka Stockade* (Melb, 1975); W. Bate, *Lucky City* (Melb, 1978); I. MacFarlane (comp), *Eureka: From the Official Records* (Melb, 1995); *Ballarat Times*, 18 Nov 1854, p 2; *Argus* (Melb), 24 Jan 1855, p 5, 27 Jan 1855, p 5, 27 Mar 1855, p 5, 25 Jan 1908, p 15; *Herald* (Melb), 9 Feb 1864, p 2; *Age* (Melb), 25 Jan 1908, p 10; Henry Seekamp (ts, nd, Ballarat Public Library); VPRS30/P, unit 40, case no 23 (PRO, Vic).

ANNE BEGGS SUNTER

SEERY, EVA MARY (1874-1937), political organizer, was born on 27 February 1874 at Tangmangaroo, near Yass, New South Wales, second daughter of six children of Edwin Joseph Dempsey, farmer, sometime hotel-keeper and goldminer, and his wife Mary, née Kelly. Her sister SOPHIA BEATRICE (1872-1946) had been born on 31 May 1872, also at Tangmangaroo. The family later moved to Temora then to West Wyalong. The two sisters became dressmakers and joined the Labor League in the Grenfell electorate as the only female members in 1889. Sophy married John Seery (1870-1925), a miner, on 26 November 1898 at Wyalong with Catholic rites. On 23 May 1900 at St Mary's Catholic Church, West Wyalong, Eva married John's brother Joseph Michael Seery (1875-1956), a gaol warder at East Maitland.

About 1903 Eva and Joseph came to Sydney. Eva joined the Waverley Labor League and made her first public campaign speech in August next year. In 1906 she helped to form the Surry Hills league, from which she was a delegate to the party conference for many years. She was a founding member of the Labor Women's Central Organising Committee in September 1904. In 1909 she replaced Mrs Bethel [q.v.] as secretary, a position she held till 1922. Not in paid employment herself, she campaigned for the rights of low-paid women workers and in 1913 became president of the Domestic Workers Union. She was a member of the boards of the Lady Edeline (Strickland) Hospital for Children and in 1914 of the Stannumville settlement, known as 'Canvas Town' or 'Calico City', at Daceyville.

Of medium height with dark hair and blue eyes, Mrs Seery was an impressive speaker with a 'well modulated' voice. At the tumultuous Labor conferences before World War I, often to interjections and catcalls, she and other women called for child endowment, better working conditions for women, equal pay and the right to serve on juries, enter the legal profession, sit on the municipal councils and stand for parliament. In 1911 she strenuously refuted accusations that the L.W.C.O.C. attempted to pack the conference by organizing its membership to fill up union delegations. She asked at the 1914 conference that women be included among the increased numbers being proposed for the Legislative Council and in 1916 sought regulation of employment agencies, which were charging women up to £1 to find domestic work.

In 1916, with Kate Dwyer, May Matthews [qq.v.8,10] and Mary Beddie, Eva unsuccessfully stood for Labor pre-selection for the Senate. She helped to form and became joint secretary of the short-lived Labor Women's Council, which sought to enhance the role of Labor women beyond canvassing for male candidates. In 1917 she failed to win the House of Representatives seat of Robertson, gaining nearly 44 per cent—she and Henrietta Greville [q.v.9] were the first women to be endorsed as Federal Labor candidates in New South Wales.

Eva spoke extensively throughout the State opposing conscription in the referenda campaigns of 1916 and 1917. At the 1919 Commonwealth Political Labor Conference she opposed the socialist objective. Among the first sixty-one women appointed justices of the peace on 13 May 1921, she became an active member, and president, of the Women Justices' Association. She was a Labor Party executive member in 1913, 1914, 1919, 1920 and 1922. The survival of the L.W.C.O.C. was largely due to the political and organizing skills of Eva and of Kate Dwyer.

Sophy and her husband John had campaigned for W. A. Holman [q.v.9] in the Grenfell electorate. On coming to Sydney about 1910 Sophy become active in the labor leagues and the L.W.C.O.C. and briefly ran Balconies Restaurant at Bondi before moving to Surry Hills. Later John was supervisor of the Emu Farms Prison farm. In 1914, like her sister, Sophy was on the party's central executive. She was appointed a justice of the peace in July 1921 and later lived at Coogee. Sophy died on 7 December 1946 at Coogee, survived by three daughters and a son.

Following appointments to Parramatta (1918), Maitland (1919) and Bathurst (1922), Joseph Seery was appointed superintendent of Long Bay gaol and state reformatory for women in 1925. The couple moved to the residence in the grounds, which became the venue for Eva's many women's gatherings. At Jack Lang's [q.v.9] meetings she would interject in support of him. Later she supported R. J. Heffron's [q.v.14] Industrial Labor Party. During the Depression she took bread and vegetables to the people in the shantytowns across the road from the gaol, at nearby La Perouse (Happy Valley) and at Matraville. She was a great supporter of St Aidan's school, Maroubra, which many of her grandchildren attended. At the 1930 A.L.P. Women's State Conference she presented a paper on 'The Delinquent Girl'.

Eva Seery died of diabetes on 22 May 1937 at Long Bay gaol and was buried in Botany cemetery after a requiem Mass at St Andrew's Catholic Church, Malabar, with a guard of honour from the penitentiary. She left an estate sworn for probate at £592. Her husband, who later remarried, and their three daughters survived her.

Truth (Syd), 29 Jan 1911, p 11; *Sun* (Syd), 21 Feb 1911, p 8; *SMH*, 2 Dec 1914, p 7, 13 Apr 1916, p 6, 19 Apr 1917, p 7, 23 May 1937, p 11; *Austn Worker*, 28 Oct 1915, p 9, 4 May 1916, p 13, 18 May 1916, p 20, 25 May 1916, p 20, 19 Apr 1917, p 5, 26 June 1919, p 7, 26 May 1937, p 10; *Labor News*, 19 June 1920, p 1; *Catholic Press* (Syd), 3 Sept 1925, p 16; *Bulletin*, 26 May 1937, p 34; ALP (NSW), Executive report, 1913, 1914, 1930-31 (ML); information from Ms K. Deverell, Dept of History, Univ NSW, and Mrs J. Gibbons, Lavender Bay, NSW.

SUE TRACEY

SENNITT, JOHN PAUL (1851-1922), engineer and ice and ice-cream manufacturer, was born on 12 January 1851 at Stretham, Cambridgeshire, England, son of David Sennitt, wheelwright and carpenter, and his wife Martha, née Paul. John was apprenticed to an engineer and later moved to South Africa where he worked as a refrigeration engineer. On 24 November 1875 at Port Elizabeth, Cape Colony, he married Harriett Coulbeck (1852-1941). Sennitt established refrigerating works at Durban, Natal. The family, including five children (two had died in infancy) reached Melbourne in 1888; two more children were born in Australia.

Sennitt was employed as engineer to the Victorian Cold Accumulator Co. Pty Ltd in La Trobe Street. The business was transferred in 1894 to 'centrally-situated, prominent and commodious premises'—a big, white building looming large on the south bank of the Yarra, between Princes and Queens bridges. About 1896 he took over the enterprise with the financier and former hardware merchant Edward Keep; in 1899 Sennitt acquired the firm, in partnership with his eldest son William John Coulbeck Sennitt, although the premises and land were retained by Keep (d.1901).

On the company's incorporation in 1906 as J. P Sennitt & Son Pty Ltd, the Keep estate retained a controlling interest. John Sennitt was employed (at a salary of £6 10s. per week) as manager, to 'do the outside work of the company that is to say by calling upon existing customers … getting new customers … and endeavouring to develop in every way the business … as Ice Manufacturers and Cold Storers'. William was employed as engineer (on £4 per week). The businesses of cold storage and ice-making grew rapidly. Expansion and the acquisition of substantial new plant resulted in a dramatic reduction in the cost of ice to the consumer—from 5s. per hundredweight in 1894 to 1s. 6d. in 1904. About that year the company began to manufacture ice-cream.

In 1901 John had been elected for Fawkner Ward to South Melbourne City Council and appointed a justice of the peace. He sat from time to time in the local Court of Petty Sessions, was elected a council member of the Honorary Justices' Association and was a Freemason in the Admiral Collingwood lodge. His youngest son Alfred Josiah was killed in action in France on 1 September 1918.

Photographed in 1912, Sennitt appeared severe and moustached, with a cleft chin. He died at his Middle Park home on 8 April 1922 and was buried in Coburg cemetery. His wife, four daughters and one son survived him. He left no estate for probate purposes, 'only an old desk with one drawer full of worthless mining scrip and another full of IOUs from friends'. The Sennitt family acquired the Keep estate's interest and the business remained a private company with William as managing director. In the early 1930s, when the firm proclaimed itself the 'oldest-established manufacturer in Victoria of Quality Ice Cream', he introduced the popular polar bear trademark. A huge neon sign on the roof of the South Melbourne factory showed a moving bear vigorously licking an ice-cream cone. William died on 29 January 1940 at Malvern. The ice-cream part of the business was acquired by

Unilever in 1961 and merged with Street's [q.v.]. Soon after, the Sennitt brand and its polar bear disappeared.

Cyclopediu of Victoria, 1 (Melb, 1903); *Jubilee History of the City of South Melbourne* (Melb, 1905); *500 Victorians* (Melb, 1934); M. Cozzolino and G. F. Rutherford, *Symbols of Australia* (Mclb, 1987); *Justice of the Peace* (Melb), Dec 1912, p 142; *A'sian Confectioner and Soda Fountain Jnl*, 23 Mar 1939, p 45, 24 Feb 1940, p 64, 27 Dec 1947, p 754; *A'sian*, 2 Jan 1904, p 28; *Argus* (Melb), 10 Apr 1922, p 1, 30 Jan 1940, p 7; information from Mr D. K. Sennitt, Mount Martha, Vic, Mr H. Price, Toorak, and Mr M. Cozzolino, Heidelberg, Melb.

ANDREW J. RAY

SERENA, CLARA (1890-1972), contralto, was born on 9 June 1890 at Lobethal, South Australia, and registered as Clara Serena Hulda, daughter of Lutheran parents Hermann Franz Kleinschmidt, farmer, and his wife Ida Wilhelmine Mathilde, née Seiler. Hermann's father Friedrich Wilhelm had migrated from the German free city of Bremen in 1836. When Clara was aged 14, the pastoralist Peter Waite [q.v.6] recognized her potential, took her into his family and established the 'Serena Trust' to provide for her education. She received tuition with Guli Hack at the Elder [q.v.4] Conservatorium of Music, Adelaide. Waite's daughter Elizabeth became her friend and acted as chaperone when Kleinschmidt won a conservatorium scholarship in 1908 to the Royal College of Music, London, where J. H. Blower and Albert Visetti were her teachers. She qualified in 1911 with a diploma with credit, and after further study in Italy and Germany she took the name 'Clara Serena' in 1913.

Returning to Adelaide at the outbreak of World War I, Serena sang in concerts for the British (Australian) Red Cross Society. To Peter Waite's chagrin, she married her accompanist Albert Roy Mellish (1886-1970) on 3 November 1917 at Chalmers Presbyterian Church. Waite thereafter refused to have any contact with her, an instruction that extended to his children as well, but was disobeyed by his daughter Elizabeth MacMeikan, who when she died in 1931 left a generous annuity to her beloved Clara.

In 1918 the *Australian Musical News* described Serena's voice as 'even and mellow' and commented that her 'splendid physique and admirable breathing enable her to deliver her highest notes with thrilling volume and richness'. She returned to London in 1922 and next year made her operatic début there. In January 1924 she created the title role in Rutland Boughton's *Alkestis* at Covent Garden and in 1926 appeared in Vienna, Berlin and Paris. During seasons of opera at Covent Garden in 1928, 1929 and 1931 her roles included Amneris, Delilah, Erda and Waltraute. She joined the British National Opera Co. in 1937. Conductors she appeared with included Sir Thomas Beecham, Sir Henry Wood, (Sir) Adrian Boult and (Sir) John Barblrolli. In 1939 negotiations for an American tour were foiled by the outbreak of World War II, and she retired. Roy Mellish worked at Australia House until the end of the war, then came back to South Australia. Clara remained at Eastbourne, Sussex, until 1951 when she also returned to Adelaide.

During her career she was befriended by both Dame Nellie Melba and Ada Crossley [qq.v.10,8]. A fine dramatic contralto, Serena had a range of three octaves extending to a top B flat. Her linguistic ability enabled her to sing fluently in many languages, and on the concert platform she exuded charm, dignity and an absence of mannerisms. Her tall, graceful stature and magnificent physique enabled her to withstand the rigorous training needed to reach the peak of her career. Also accomplished as an oratorio artist, especially in Handel's *Messiah* and Mendelssohn's *Elijah*, she recorded for Vocalion and Columbia Records.

Roy and Clara had no children. She lived in her later years in Adelaide. Clara Serena Mellish died on 11 August 1972 at Aldersgate Village, Felixstow. Photographs of her in the roles of Delilah and Amneris and a collection of her stage jewellery are held in the Performing Arts Collection of South Australia, Adelaide.

J. Glennon, *Australian Music and Musicians* (Adel, 1968); B. and F. Mackenzie, *Singers of Australia* (Melb, 1967); *The Times* (Lond), 5 Mar 1913, p 1, 11 July 1928, p 14, 12 Sept 1937, p 10; *Australian Musical News*, 1 June 1915, p 350, 1 Mar 1918, p 224, 1 May 1923, p VII; *Observer* (Adel), 29 Apr 1922, p 28, 6 Jan 1923, p 32, 12 Jan 1924, p 37, 13 June 1925, p 63; *Chronicle* (Adel), 10 Mar 1932, p 40; *Sunday Mail* (Adel), 26 June 1965, p 30; *Advertiser* (Adel), 16 Aug 1972, p 27; G. Hogg, Clara Kleinschmidt, commemorative program, Urrbrae House, 5 June 1993 (held by Performing Arts Collection of SA, Adel).   JO PEOPLES

SHEEHY, SIR CHRISTOPHER (1894-1960), dairy industry administrator, was born on Christmas Day 1894 at Gympie, Queensland, third of six children of Irish-born parents Jeremiah Sheehy, goldminer, and his wife Kate, née O'Driscoll. Educated at the Christian Brothers' College, Gympie, Christopher studied accountancy in Brisbane and joined the Department of Agriculture and Stock as a clerk on 9 January 1911. On 7 February 1920 at St Patrick's Catholic Church, Fortitude Valley, Brisbane, he married Ruby Maria

Bridget Barlow, a Sydney-born clerk. She was to be a powerful force in the family.

Sheehy worked with the Queensland Wheat Board (secretary from 1920) and the Queensland Council of Agriculture (secretary from December 1926 to December 1938), and commenced his long association with the dairy industry in 1923 when he was secretary to a special committee of investigation. Dairying was suited to land development and soldier settlement, but the smallholdings carried an average of only twenty-five cows in 1922; this figure was to double by 1956 (and to increase six-fold by 2000).

In 1928 Sheehy became secretary of the Queensland Butter Board, a position he combined with that of State secretary (1928-34) for the (Thomas) 'Paterson [q.v.11] Plan', which levied butter production to pay a bounty on the exported product. In 1937 he became general manager of the Commonwealth Dairy Produce Equalisation Committee Ltd, retaining the post until his death. A voluntary arrangement, the scheme compensated butter factories with a favourable export ratio. The committee needed to accommodate the warring factions of producers from different regions and of processors, retailers, exporters and regulatory authorities. Its success rested greatly on Sheehy's personal skills—his instant empathy when making new acquaintances, fluency, diligence, grip of detail and tough negotiating stands—and on the support of chairmen such as James Purcell and Thomas Flood Plunkett [qq.v.11,16]. Sheehy suffered from headaches after the removal of an abscess and his medication exacerbated a duodenal ulcer; therefore, he abstained from alcohol and tobacco, but drank dry ginger ale into the night with his colleagues.

Manpower shortages and drought meant that dairy output decreased during World War II when Australia had special obligations to Britain and to feeding troops. The Commonwealth government appointed Sheehy controller of dairy products under the New Food Plan in 1943, and he worked to enhance production of powdered and condensed milk and cheese until the scheme terminated in 1946. For this he did not accept a salary. He helped to obtain substantial government subsidies and to maintain price support. As chairman of the Australian Dairy Produce Board from 1952 he continued an involvement in the British purchase of Australian surplus butter, the maintenance of quality control and the acquisition of new markets. He made several overseas trips to study the sale of dairy foods.

Sheehy was a kindly man and mentor to young dairy technologists. Appointed O.B.E. in January 1951 and knighted in June 1959, Sir Christopher was reappointed chairman of the A.D.P.B. in June 1960. He died of a ruptured duodenal ulcer on 31 August that year

in hospital in Brisbane. After a requiem Mass in St Stephen's Catholic Cathedral, he was buried in Nudgee cemetery. His wife, son and two daughters survived him.

History of Queensland Dairying (Brisb, 1923); R. J. J. Twohill, *Epitome of Dairying Industry Organisations in Australia* (Syd, 1956); N. T. Drane and H. R. Edwards (eds), *The Australian Dairy Industry* (Melb, 1961); *Butter Fat and Solids*, 2, no 4, Dec 1960, p 175; *Qld Country Life*, 1 Sept 1960, p 4; *Courier-Mail*, 13 June 1959, p 1, 1 Sept 1960, p 7; information from Mr E. B. Gilbert, Mt Eliza, Mr L. Muller, East Bentleigh, Vic, Mr S. J. Routh, Brisb, Mr P. Rowley, Mt Pleasant, Miss K. Sheehy, Southport, and Mrs P. M. Woulfe, Hollywell, Qld.

L. R. HUMPHREYS

SIEBENHAAR, WILLEM (1863-1936), writer, public servant and socialist, was born on 28 July 1863 in The Hague, son of Christiaan Siebenhaar, a sergeant-major in the Netherlands army, and his wife Geertruida Johanna, née Frölich. Willem graduated from the University of Delft in 1882, having studied philology and literature. The Christian anarchist and socialist Ferdinand Domela Nieuwenhuis (1846-1919) possibly influenced him. Siebenhaar left in 1884 to work as a teacher in England.

Seeking a freer political environment, he reached Western Australia in the *Ormuz* in June 1891. Siebenhaar taught briefly at Perth High School, became a clerk in the Land Titles Department on 1 January 1892 and was naturalized in November 1894. On 7 March 1899, while on leave in Britain, he married Lydia Bruce Dixon in the Church of St Peter and St Paul, Bromley, Kent. He probably met the Russian anarchist Prince Petr Alekseevich Kropotkin (1842-1921), who lived a few streets from the Dixon family at Bromley. Willem and Lydia honeymooned in Italy. Back in Perth, Siebenhaar helped to form the Civil Service Association and was elected vice-president in 1904. Compiler and sub-editor of the *Western Australian Yearbook* until October 1906, he was deputy government statistician and deputy registrar-general from 1908. He enjoyed the support of his immediate superiors, but was not favoured by Liberal governments, doubtless because of his socialist views.

About 1895 Siebenhaar had begun translating the *Ongeluckige Voyagie* (1647), Jan Jansz's account of the 1629 *Batavia* shipwreck and mutiny on the Western Australian coast. Siebenhaar's 'Abrolhos Tragedy', published in the *Western Mail* in 1897, later inspired the work of a number of Western Australian historians, writers and marine archaeologists. He also wrote poetry, including a patriotic collection (with Alfred Chandler), *Sentinel Sonnets*, a eulogy to Montague Miller [q.v.10] and an unpublished narrative poem, 'The Further Pilgrimage', and contributed articles to newspapers and magazines in Western Australia and overseas. In 1910 he founded and co-edited the short-lived literary magazine *Leeuwin*.

Interested in chess from the age of 15, Siebenhaar had won a divided 3rd prize in the Dutch Chess Federation's annual tournament in 1881. He continued this pastime in Perth and became the unofficial Western Australian champion following a match with Ernest Hack in 1892; he took over Hack's chess column in the *Western Mail*. In 1894 he lost his honorary champion's title but remained an active player. Suffering from ill health, he again visited Britain and attended the Scheveningen chess tournament in the Netherlands in 1913.

In October 1916, during the bitter conscription debate, the State government suspended Siebenhaar and H. M. Leighton, a clerk in the Registrar-General's Department who was president of the Anti-Conscription League. A press release described Siebenhaar as a 'German' in the civil service, linked to the Industrial Workers of the World and a vocal anti-conscriptionist and Labor Party identity. Both men were accused of improper or disloyal conduct. An inquiry was set up to establish whether he had manifested sympathy with the 'illegal methods' of the I.W.W. and had collected money to provide a legal defence for his friend Miller, who had been arrested. The latter charge Siebenhaar readily admitted. The inquiry examined his character and political views, including those expressed in his long narrative poem 'Dorothea' (1909). Though exonerated—he had in fact raised money for the Allied war effort—and restored to his civil service position with all salary arrears paid, he remained bitter about his treatment.

A libertarian socialist and theosophist, Siebenhaar was also an advocate of women's suffrage. Friends knew him as 'Seeby'. His romantic and polemical literary style was anathema to Western Australian 'shirt-sleeve' poets such as 'Dryblower' [q.v.10 E. G. Murphy], with whom he had conducted a running debate. He retired from the public service for health reasons as from July 1924, but only worked until 28 February, leaving Australia shortly thereafter to settle in Findon, Sussex, England. In 1927 he published an English translation of Eduard Douwes Dekker's *Max Havelaar*. This included a preface by D. H. Lawrence, whom Siebenhaar had met in Western Australia in 1922 and who reputedly based a character in his novel *Kangaroo* ('Willie Struthers', a left-wing organizer) partly on him.

Three weeks after being struck by a motorcar, Siebenhaar died of chronic kidney disease and complications on 29 December 1936 at Littlehampton, West Sussex. His wife survived him.

J. S. Battye, *The Cyclopedia of Western Australia*, 1 (Perth, 1912); H. Drake-Brockman, *Voyage to Disaster* (Syd, 1963); R. Darroch, *D. H. Lawrence in Australia* (Melb, 1981); E. Duyker, *The Dutch in Australia* (Melb, 1987); N. Segal, *Who and What Was Siebenhaar* (Perth, 1988); *Bromley Record* (Lond), Apr 1899, May 1899; *Austn Chess Lore*, vol 1, 1981, p 38, vol 3, 1984, p 55; *Austn Literary Studies*, 21, no 1, 2003, p 3; W Siebenhaar personal file, Colonial Sec's Office, 2033 1919, Cons 752 AN24/2 and Premier's Dept, 865/30 AN2/10 Acc 1704 (SRWA).

NAOMI SEGAL
EDWARD DUYKER

SIEVWRIGHT, CHARLES WIGHTMAN (1800-1855), soldier and protector of Aborigines, was born on 31 March 1800 in Edinburgh, third of seven children of Andrew Sievwright, a solicitor and merchant burgess, and his wife Ann, née Robertson. When Charles was 15, £400 was paid to gain him a commission as an ensign in a Scottish infantry regiment. He served for twenty years in the army, half the time in Britain and half in the Mediterranean, without being involved in combat. On 3 April 1822 he married Christina Watt in the Episcopal church, Stirling, Scotland. They had seven children. 'A fine, soldierlike man, muscular and strong, straight as a ramrod', Sievwright was forced to sell his commission to pay off gambling debts in 1837 and returned to London from Malta, where he had been a captain in the Royal Fusiliers. Well-connected friends helped him to gain a post in Australia as assistant to G. A. Robinson [q.v.2], recently appointed chief protector of Aborigines in the Port Phillip District.

Reaching Sydney in the *Lord Eildon* in November 1838, Sievwright moved with his family to live in tents among the Aborigines near the tiny settlement of Geelong. With responsibility for the whole of what would later become the Western District of Victoria, he was charged with protecting the Aborigines 'from cruelty, oppression and injustice' and 'from encroachments upon their property'.

From his first official report, he was complaining to Robinson about Aboriginal deaths, as their traditional sources of food and clothing were depleted. Sievwright also began what would become a lengthy series of investigations into massacres of Aborigines. His determination to seek prosecutions for mass murder—in one case of up to eighty people —helped to make him 'the most unpopular man that ever breathed' among his countrymen. Inaction by the authorities in Melbourne and Sydney were constant themes of his reports. The deterioration in his relations with the white community soon extended as far as Superintendent Charles La Trobe and Governor Sir George Gipps [qq.v.2,1].

Despite his limited ability to address their needs, Sievwright won considerable respect from the Aborigines who lived with him at several camps—as many as 270 at a time—most having had little or no previous contact with Europeans. With sporadic supplies, he attempted unprecedented food-for-work schemes, hoping to replace some of the lost traditional food with crops grown by the Aborigines themselves. But guerrilla attacks by Aborigines and stock thefts continued, and the squatters and the press blamed him for failing to stop them. When the colonial administration received Sievwright's report outlining the murder of three unarmed Aboriginal women and a child by a group of white men, he was suspended without pay in 1842 for alleged incompetence. Simultaneously, there were references to disharmony within his family. Gipps and La Trobe, nervous about the possible reaction in London to Sievwright's claims that the protectorate had not been given a fair trial, ignored his demands for an official inquiry.

Following confimation of his dismissal, Sievwright returned to Britain in November 1845 to clear his name, leaving his family in poverty. A limited investigation by the Colonial Office in 1847, largely comprising statements from his detractors, found his dismissal justified. As late as mid-1849 he was still campaigning in London for a full inquiry. Having gone both deaf and blind, he never again saw the family he left behind in Australia. Sievwright died of rheumatic heart disease on 10 September 1855 in Belgrave, London, and was buried in a common grave in Brompton cemetery. Christina had died in 1854 in Melbourne. Seven children in Australia survived him. A miniature oil on ivory portrait of Sievwright (c.1825), held privately in Victoria, shows him as a young man with curly, red hair, dressed as a Royal Fusiliers officer.

L. Arkley, *The Hated Protector* (Melb, 2000), and for bib.   LINDSEY ARKLEY

SIGGINS, SELINA SARAH ELIZABETH; *see* ANDERSON

SIMOS, ZACHARIAS THEODORE (1897-1976), confectioner and café proprietor, was born on 15 August 1897 at Kousounari, Kythera (Cerigo), Greece, eldest of four children of Theodore Zachariou Simos, farmer and cooper, and his wife Areanthe, née Theodorakakis. In 1912 Zacharias migrated to Sydney with several other Kytheran boys in the *Omrah*, disembarking on 13 May with little money and minimal English. In the following four years he worked in Greek cafés in Sydney and at Tenterfield, before setting up business at Windsor, where he served ham and eggs next door to a skating rink and sold fruit and vegetables door-to-door.

In 1916, having improved his English and saved sufficient funds, Simos established himself as a confectioner at Katoomba, in the Blue Mountains, and opened a shop that would later become the Paragon café. In 1921, when he was naturalized, he was 5 ft 8 ins (173 cm) tall with dark hair and dark eyes. That year he bought a commercial property at 110-114 Katoomba Street and three years later purchased the café premises he had been leasing at 65 Katoomba Street. 'Jack' Simos set about turning the Paragon into a high-class refreshment room. The popular Katoomba landmark Orphan Rock became his trademark, an image of the 'stand-alone' excellence to which he aspired. In 1925 Simos employed H. & E. Sidgreaves, the shop-fitting firm responsible for the design of Washington H. Soul's [q.v.6 Caleb Soul] Sydney pharmacies, to convert the interior of the café premises on classical lines. A soda fountain, of the finest Moruya marble, and booths of Queensland maple were installed and the timber-panelled walls decorated with alabaster friezes depicting classical Greek figures.

In 1929 Simos returned to Kythera and spent a year in Europe observing trends in confectionery manufacture and café culture. He also arranged to import new ingredients and learned about presentation and packaging. On Kythera he met and courted Mary Panaretos (1912-2001). She had been born on 20 June 1912 at Elkton, Maryland, United States of America, where her parents were café proprietors who regularly spent the summer months on Kythera. Mary and Zacharias married there on 30 January 1930 and reached Katoomba later that year. Mary became identified with the Paragon; generous and cultured, she was always on hand to welcome visitors and press chocolates into the hands of children.

Simos immediately began planning two large extensions at the rear of his café, designed by the architect H. E. White [q.v.12]: the banquet hall (1934), influenced by pre-Columbian decoration, was followed by the blue room (1936), in 'ocean liner' style, with mirrored walls and sprung dance floor. The Paragon gained a wide reputation. Its ice-creams—originally hand-churned and frozen with American ammonia freezing machines—and sundaes blended with syrups and fruit ingredients, often specially imported, and the Art Deco ambience attracted devoted customers. With the help of his brothers Peter and George, bread, cakes and pastries were manufactured on the premises, as well as chocolates and other confectionery sold in exquisitely designed and coloured boxes.

In the early 1940s Simos built a house, Olympus, in Cliff Drive, near Echo Point, Katoomba, which was the principal family residence; he also maintained a home in Sydney at Centennial Park. He devoted many hours to his garden—the Paragon always had fresh flowers—loved music, played the violin and was a keen fisherman and backgammon player. Enjoying travel, he visited Europe, the U.S.A. and Kythera several times. He was a foundation member of Katoomba Rotary Club, which for many years held its meetings in the Paragon.

Simos's rise from penniless immigrant to successful businessman stemmed from his innate business sense, capacity for hard work and sense of community responsibility. He died on 15 November 1976 in Royal Prince Alfred Hospital, Sydney, and was buried in Randwick cemetery following a funeral at St George's Greek Orthodox Church, Rose Bay. His wife, who carried on as manager of the Paragon until 1987, and their two daughters and one son, a Supreme Court judge, survived him. The café was sold in 2000. Mary Simos died on 15 May 2001 at Rose Bay and was buried beside her husband. The café had been listed by the National Trust in New South Wales in 1975 and placed on the Australian Heritage Commission's 1977 Register of the National Estate. Despite concessions to changing times, the Paragon's interiors in 2005 still reflected the era in which they were created.

A'sian Confectioner, 22 July 1930, p 54; *Bulletin*, 5 Apr 1969, p 35, 8 May 1971, p 67; *Blue Mountains Advertiser*, 12 Aug 1971, p 4, 25 Nov 1976, p 10; *Blue Mountains Echo*, 1 May 1985, p 3, 19 June 1985, p 4, 7 Oct 1986, p 17; *SMH*, 4 Feb 1995, p 5, 22 May 2001, p 32; A1, item 1921/22059 (NAA, Canb); Katoomba Municipal Council, rate records, 1889-1947 (Blue Mountains City Library, Springwood, NSW); Blue Mountains heritage inventory sheets relating to Paragon Café (Blue Mountains City Council, Katoomba, NSW).   JOHN LOW

SIMPSON, PERCY (1789-1877), surveyor, engineer and administrator, was born on 5 March 1789 in Canada, son of Major Noah Simpson of the 31st Regiment of Foot, and reputedly christened Pierce. Young Simpson was commissioned in the 1st Garrison Battalion in 1809. In 1812 he became a lieutenant in the Royal Corsican Rangers as well as judge-advocate then governor (1812-16) of the Ionian Island of Paxos. On 1 October 1819 at Ballymascanlan, County Louth, Ireland, he married Hester Elizabeth McNeill (d.1875).

The family migrated to New South Wales in the *Mangles* in November 1822 with sufficient capital for a grant, cattle, convict servants and six months rations. As a relation of Major John Ovens, Simpson had immediate entrée to Governor Brisbane [qq.v.2,1], who persuaded him to become commandant of an experimental agricultural settlement for 'educated convicts' in the Wellington valley, northwest of Bathurst. Simpson later described his responsibilities as unlike those of any other in the colony: commandant, chaplain, commissary and engineer, he was paid on productivity rather than a set salary. The system of payment was flawed; for the rest of his life he petitioned against the financial loss he incurred.

In June 1828 Simpson was appointed an assistant surveyor of roads and bridges and a magistrate, responsible for the construction of the technically challenging Great North Road through difficult terrain from Wisemans Ferry. Based on MacAdam's principles, the buttresses, culverts and drains were built by convict road gangs, often working in irons, under Simpson's overall direction. The work, his part of which was completed in 1832, was tangible evidence of his engineering skills.

Declared insolvent late in 1830, Simpson found his government employment under threat and argued that the Wellington valley issue was the cause, rather than 'speculation and extravagance'. Governor Bourke [q.v.1] intervened to prevent his dismissal, reporting that Simpson had paid his debts (he sold his army commission for £700), was of good character and had no access to public funds. In 1832 he moved to Parramatta, where he built Oatlands House, Dundas (which he was later forced to sell). The same year he declined to supervise the construction of the Western Road, as he was unwilling to impose the rigours of another isolated posting on his delicate wife and his large, young family. In 1833 he was reappointed assistant surveyor and became a commissioner of crown lands.

Simpson's ability to manage convict labour and his administrative and engineering skills were recognized by successive governors who valued his 'zeal, assiduity and ability, as well as respectability of demeanor in private life'. Mitchell knew of 'no other officer in the Colony to whom I could with better expectation as to the results, intrust any work connected with the formation of roads, bridges and streets'. The difficult line from Lapstone Hill to Mitchell's pass, bridges at Wollombi, Lansdowne and Duck Creek, and the Queen's Wharf—designed by David Lennox [q.v.2]— were all examples of Simpson's skill.

In 1836 responsibility for road works was transferred from the surveyor-general to the Royal Engineers. Now a civilian with no formal training as a surveyor, Simpson was placed in charge of the depot office of the County of Cumberland Road Department, based at Parramatta. Governor Gipps [q.v.1] abolished this position in February 1839 and appointed Simpson police magistrate at Patrick's Plains (Singleton), where the family lived until the appointment was terminated in 1842. Next year Simpson went to Britain to pursue his Wellington valley claim with the government. He also sought a loan from relations to support his family. For six years he worked with two railway companies in Ireland.

Returning to Sydney in March 1850, now a civil engineer, Simpson was involved in the design and construction of Parramatta Dam on Hunts Creek, which was built to a radical new circular (arch) design. In the late 1850s and 1860s he served as Parramatta district registrar. He died on 25 September 1877 in Sydney and was buried with Hester in Balmain cemetery. Three sons and three daughters survived him, including (Sir) George Bowen Simpson [q.v.6]. Edward Percy Simpson, Helen De Guerry Simpson and Edward Telford Simpson [qq.v.11,16] were Percy's descendants. His works on a disused section of the Great North Road and Parramatta dam have been listed by the Australian Heritage Council (1978) and by the Heritage Council of New South Wales (1989). Part of his house, Oatlands, still survived in 2004.

Hist Records of Aust, series 1, vol 13, p 402; *V&P* (LC, NSW), 1859-60, vol 4, p 1257; Royal Aust Hist Soc, *Jnl and Procs*, vol 6, 1920, p 201; *Australian*, 2 July 1828, p 3, 10 Mar 1837, p 2, 3 Aug 1842, p 2; *Empire*, 26 June 1852, p 1135; *SMH*, 28 June 1852, p 3, 29 June 1852, p 3; *United Service*, Apr 1992, p 29; C. Liston, N.S.W. Under Governor Brisbane 1821-1825 (Ph.D. thesis, Univ Syd, 1980); G. Karskens, 'The Grandest Improvement in the Colony', M.A. thesis, Univ Syd, 1986; WO 25/744, f 24r and 24v (PRO, Lond); Governor's despatches, vol 53, p 1037, A1242, and 1830-31, p 1349, A1267-13, (ML); Colonial Secretary, letters received, 1832, 4/2140, p 13 (SRNSW).   BEVERLEY JOHNSON

SISLEY, BARBARA (1878-1945), teacher of speech and drama, was born on 19 March 1878 at Streatham, London, one of three daughters of Thomas Alexander Sisley, civil service clerk, and his wife Susan, née Sisley. Barbara was educated at Queen's College, Tufnell Park, and about 1899 came to Melbourne, where her father taught elocution. She attended Manuel College, Hawthorn, and, having been trained by her father, began working as a professional actress, touring Australia with George Rignold [q.v.6 Rignall] and the Robert Brough [q.v.3] comedy company. A friend later recalled her as 'long legged, eager' with 'pretty brown eyes' and a deep voice.

Arriving in Brisbane in 1916, Sisley became one of the first professional instructors in speech and drama to work there. She began teaching 'Speech Training and Dramatic Art' in a private studio and at such Brisbane girls' schools as St Margaret's, Stuartholme convent and Somerville House. Her interest in encouraging women to participate in drama influenced the establishment of several theatre companies. She trained Rhoda Felgate, Jean Trundle and Daphne Roemermann, who became significant figures in Brisbane's theatrical life and teaching institutions.

Sisley helped to establish the Young Women's Christian Association Drama Group during World War I and, in the early 1920s, the Brisbane Shakespeare Society, encouraging her students to perform extracts from plays at its monthly meetings. They also produced a complete play annually. She organized performances by her younger students under the banner of the Barbara Sisley Juveniles, and was a foundation member of the Dickens [q.v.4] Fellowship, formed in 1921. Each year the group studied a different novel by Dickens and held a reading competition that encouraged people to perform short extracts.

In 1923 Sisley returned to England to study with Elsie Fogarty. Inspired by the work that she saw in repertory theatre companies, and armed with new teaching techniques, she decided to form the Brisbane Repertory Theatre Society in 1925. Her primary role was as a director, but she was also an executive member of the organization and occasionally acted. Sisley remained the artistic head of Brisbane Repertory until her death. She produced fifty-seven of the 125 plays performed. She also organized tours of repertory productions to regional areas, including Ipswich, Toowoomba, Stanthorpe, Rockhampton and Townsville. One of her main objectives was to encourage the production of Australian plays and to this end she ran playwriting competitions. The most famous winning entry, George Landen Dann's [q.v.13] *In Beauty it is Finished*, scandalized Brisbane's theatregoers in 1931 by dealing frankly with issues of Aboriginality and prostitution. Sisley was a founding member of the Speech and Drama Teachers' Association and its inaugural vice-president in 1939.

Sisley died on 18 November 1945 in Brisbane hospital, after having been struck by a taxi in Adelaide Street, and was cremated with Anglican rites. She had not married. Brisbane Repertory produced Dann's *Caroline Chisholm* [q.v.1] in 1946 as a tribute. In 1947 the Speech and Drama Teachers' Association of Queensland established the Barbara Sisley scholarships for the best students in the State in public speech and drama examinations. Traditionally the awards were presented at the annual Barbara Sisley recital. The Brisbane Repertory Company was still operating in 2004 under the name La Boite.

T. D'Arcy and D. Roemermann (eds), *The Turning Years* (Brisb, 1989); J. M. Cook, *Ponder the Path of Thy Feet* (Brisb, 1992).   DELYSE RYAN

SMITH, CHRISTINA (1809?-1893), teacher and missionary, was born probably on 25 July 1809 at Glenlyon, Perthshire, Scotland, one of nine children of devout Presbyterian parents James Menzies, tenant farmer, and his wife Catherine McNaughton. About 1832 Christina married Finlay Stewart. After her husband's death she migrated to Victoria with two brothers and her son Duncan Stewart (1833-1913), reaching Port Phillip in the *David Clark* on 27 October 1839.

Christina worked for five months as a housekeeper for Rev. William Waterfield and nursed her ill brother. On 19 October 1841 she married with Presbyterian forms James Smith (1796-1860), a minister's son who had emigrated from Scotland in 1840 and was teaching at a day school in Collins Street Congregational Church vestry. They had eight children. In 1845 the Smiths moved to Rivoli Bay south (Greytown), an isolated port in south-eastern South Australia, where Christina was the sole European woman. James worked variously as postmaster, agent for the South Australian Co. and as storekeeper for his brother-in-law Captain Emanuel Underwood, a coastal trader. According to her son Duncan, her husband did not treat Christina well.

Convinced that Aborigines were victims of European aggression, disease and land depredation, Christina 'yearned to be used by God' in ministering to 'the miserable remnant' of the formerly numerous and powerful Booandik (Buandig) people, whose territory ranged from the mouth of the Glenelg River to Beachport. At their request, as their numbers were rapidly diminishing Smith began recording their customs, legends and social relationships for the 'antiquary, historian and philologist'. Duncan compiled a Booandik vocabulary and was appointed interpreter in 1853, having acted in the position since he was 14. In that capacity, he attended legal proceedings throughout the district and in Adelaide.

In 1854 the family moved to a small farm near Mount Gambier. Despite her frail physique, Christina supplemented their income by undertaking physically demanding work on nearby sheep runs. Next year the Smiths opened a night school where they nurtured Aboriginal orphans and taught adults of mixed race until James's death on 4 January 1860. In 1864 Mrs Smith published as a pamphlet a memoir of Wergon, an Aboriginal Christian convert, and in 1865 *Caroline and her Family*. That year, with funding from Lady Burdett-Coutts provided through Bishop Short [q.v.6], Mrs Smith achieved her long-held dream of establishing a school and home for local Aboriginal children, in Commercial Street West, Mount Gambier. Her pupils learned prayers and hymns and completed religious exercises based on Scripture. Proof of her claim that Aborigines were not 'too low intellectually or morally to be either Christianised or civilised', students left her school literate and prepared for service locally. Due to an epidemic and loss of support, however, only four students remained in 1867, and the school closed in 1868 to become a home for Aborigines.

In 1880 as Mrs James Smith she published *The Booandik Tribe of South Australian Aborigines*, an account of their rites of passage, songs and language, with brief biographies of fourteen converts. An influential ethnography, blending scholarly observation with personal narrative, it was a unique window onto an Aboriginal-settler frontier. In 1881 she contributed to the work of A. W. Howitt [q.v.4]. Christina Smith died on 28 April 1893 at Mount Gambier and was buried in Lake Terrace cemetery. Duncan Stewart, and three sons and three daughters of her second marriage, survived her. In 1994 the Mount Gambier building in which she had established her school was classified for its heritage value.

H. Carthew, *Rivoli Bay* (Millicent, SA, 1974); T. McCourt and H. Mincham (comps), *Two Notable South Australians* (Beachport, SA, 1977); B. Dickey (ed), *The Australian Dictionary of Evangelical Biography* (Syd, 1994); W. Prest (ed), *The Wakefield Companion to South Australian History* (Adel, 2001); *Mt Gambier Heritage Survey* (1994); *Austn Feminist Studies*, 16, no 34, Mar 2001, pp 83 & 91; *Border Watch*, 29 Apr 1893, p 2; *South-Eastern Star*, 2 May 1893, p 2; *Observer* (Adel), 6 May 1893, p 15; C. Smith, diary *and* D. Stewart, diary (SLSA).

LEITH G. MACGILLIVRAY

SMITH, HELEN MACPHERSON; *see* SCHUTT

SMITH, MARIA ANN ('GRANNY') (1799-1870), orchardist, was baptized on 5 January 1800 in the rural parish church of St Peter and St Paul, Peasmarsh, Sussex, England, daughter of John Sherwood, farm labourer, and his wife Hannah, née Wright. Maria followed her parents into farm service. On 8 August 1819 in the parish church at Ebony, Kent, she married Thomas Smith (1799-1876), a farm labourer from Beckley. Both bride and groom signed with a mark. The Smiths lived at Beckley for the next nineteen years, during which time Maria bore eight children, three of whom died in infancy. With several other farming families from Peasmarsh, Beckley and surrounding villages in eastern Sussex and western Kent, the family migrated to New South Wales under the government bounty scheme. They reached Sydney in the *Lady Nugent* on 27 November 1838.

Thomas found employment with a settler in the well-established fruit-growing district of Kissing Point (Ryde); he and Maria remained in the district for the rest of their lives. Their youngest and only Australian-born child William was baptized at St Anne's Church of England, Ryde, in May 1842. In the mid-1850s Thomas bought two blocks of land for an orchard, totalling about 24 acres (9.7 ha) on the edge of the Field of Mars common (Eastwood).

Descendants of Thomas and Maria ('Granny') Smith have from time to time disputed the circumstances of the Granny Smith apple's discovery, but the earliest and most authoritative account of its origin appeared in the *Farmer and Settler* in June 1924, in an article by the Dundas orchardist and local historian Herbert Rumsey [q.v.11]. Rumsey interviewed two fruit-growers who had known Maria. One remembered that in 1868 he and his father had been invited by her to examine a seedling apple growing by a creek on her property and that she had explained that the seedling had developed from the remains of some French crab-apples grown in Tasmania. According to this recollection, Mrs Smith herself then began to work a few of these seedling trees and soon afterwards Edward Gallard, a local orchardist, planted out a large number of them, from which he marketed a crop annually until his death in 1914.

Maria Smith had died on 9 March 1870 at Ryde and was buried in St Anne's churchyard. Her husband, three sons and two daughters survived her. The apple was not a commercial variety in her lifetime but its cultivation was sustained by local orchardists, including Gallard—who purchased part of the Smith farm after Thomas's death in 1876. By 1891-92 'Granny Smith's seedlings' had begun to win prizes in the cooking-apple class and several local growers were exhibiting the apples. In 1895 Granny Smith's seedlings were planted on a large scale at the Government Experimental Station at Bathurst. That year the variety was included in the Department of Agriculture's list of fruits suitable for export and began its long and successful commercial life.

J. Spurway and M. Martin, *Granny Smith & Her Apple* (leaflet, Ryde, 1992); J. T. Spurway (ed), *Australian Biographical and Genealogical Record: Series 1, 1788-1841* (Syd, 1992); *Farmer and Settler* (Syd), 20 June 1924, p 13; *Agricultural Gazette of NSW*, 1 Oct 1924, p 758; *Descent*, 4, pt 1, 1968, p 14.

MEGAN MARTIN

SMITH, MATTHEW SKINNER (1836-1887), commissioner of police, was born on 30 August 1836 in England, one of at least two sons of Matthew Smith, an army officer who eventually rose to the rank of lieutenant general. Young Matthew was commissioned as an ensign in the 44th Regiment of Foot on 7 June 1854. After serving with distinction in the Crimean War (1854-56) and the China expedition of 1860, he was promoted lieutenant and captain by merit, rather than by purchase, and held two responsible administrative positions during the 1860s. In 1867 he left the army and married Elizabeth Nolan on 4 July in the parish church, River, Kent. Next year he moved to Western Australia in the expectation of becoming private secretary to Colonel John Bruce [q.v.3], who hoped to be appointed governor. Bruce was not selected, however, and Smith was employed as a bank clerk.

On the retirement of Gustavus Hare, Smith (recommended by Bruce) was appointed chief of police with the rank of superintendent on 9 May 1871. Finding the police force disorganized and held in low regard, Smith coped with public criticism and financial cuts, and fended off attempts to exert greater political control. A methodical and hard-working administrator with a reserved manner, he treated its members with tact and consideration and reformed the force from the ground up.

Smith's major achievements included founding the criminal investigation (1873) and mounted (1875) sections, reorganizing police districts, introducing probationary constables and 'favourable record' systems, and amalgamating the Imperial Water Police into the force. In 1876 he approved the publication of the first *Police Gazette*, which was to become one of the oldest continuing official publications in Western Australia. The escape from Fremantle of six Fenian convicts in April that year in the American whaler *Catalpa* did not reflect on his efficiency; Governor (Sir) William Robinson [q.v.6] commended his 'energy and discretion' in the matter.

Beginning a tradition of using the police annual reports to comment on social and judicial issues of the day, Smith analysed alcohol abuse, which he identified as a health—rather than a law enforcement—problem and recommended the founding of an 'inebriates asylum'. He discounted capital punishment as a fair method of dealing with tribal killings and took steps to prevent the exploitation of Aborigines in the pearling industry. As well, he warned the government of the likely impact of mineral discoveries and of a consequent need to establish a police presence in mining centres. By the early 1880s the public image of the police force had improved dramatically, and Smith was one of the most respected public officials in the colony. He had connexions with the colonial elite and was a founder and vice-president of the Weld [q.v.6] Club. In 1880 he obtained the additional post of commandant of the enrolled pensioner guard.

Smith took leave of absence to become acting colonial secretary in 1885 and was appointed to the Legislative Council next year. The office of commissioner of police was re-established for his benefit, and he returned to duty in the police force on 13 January 1887. Smith died of gastric bleeding on 18 April that year, while visiting Albany, where he was buried. His wife survived him; the marriage was childless.

R. M. Lawrence, *Police Review 1829-1979* (Perth, 1979); K. Amos, *The Fenians in Australia 1865-1880* (Syd, 1988); M. Bentley, *Grandfather was a Policeman* (Perth, 1993); P. Conole, *Protect & Serve* (Perth, 2002).   PETER CONOLE

SMITH, RICHARD BOWYER (1837-1919), blacksmith and inventor of the stump-jump plough, was born on 2 September 1837 in London, eldest child of Smith Owen Smith, carpenter, and his wife Mary Ann, née Lee. They were to have twelve children, of whom six died in infancy. Accompanying his parents as an infant aboard the *Trusty*, Richard reached South Australia on 15 May 1838.

Owen Smith set up as a builder in Adelaide, but the family lived for a few years in Victoria; CLARENCE HERBERT (1865-1901), the ninth child, was born on 10 August 1865 at Alma. Back in South Australia, Richard was apprenticed to James Gardner Ramsey, an agricultural implement manufacturer at Mount Barker, then went into trade as a blacksmith and carpenter at Port Wakefield. On 23 May 1863 at Kensington, Adelaide, he married with Wesleyan forms Margaret Smith. They had eight children. In 1872 Clarence was apprenticed to Richard as a blacksmith and machinist.

Following an initial trial, Richard, then in business with Clarence at Kalkabury (Arthurton) on Yorke Peninsula, exhibited two prize-winning versions of a stone- and stump-jumping plough at the agricultural show at Moonta in November 1876. The *Farmers' Weekly Messenger* accurately forecast that Smith's invention had the potential to 'cause a complete revolution in tilling uncleared land'. The mechanism allowed the shares to glide over stumps which otherwise required grubbing, a laborious and costly process. He failed, however, adequately to secure his rights under the Patents Act of 1877 and prosperity eluded him. Late in 1877 he was granted the first licence of the Arthurton Hotel. Although he and Clarence made design improvements to the plough, Richard was struggling to make a living from his trade until (Sir) Robert Dalrymple Ross [q.v.6] took up his cause. In February 1882, as president of the Royal Agricultural and Horticultural Society of South Australia, Ross led a delegation to the commissioner of crown lands, recommending that Smith be awarded a grant of land. In the face of rival claims, on 5 September 1882 parliament acknowledged Richard Bowyer Smith as the inventor of the stump jumping plough, rewarding him with a bonus of £500 rather than a land grant. In 1884 he moved with his family to Western Australia, where he exhibited the plough in 1885 but was unable to realize a profitable return on sales.

Clarence had married Emma Sarah Beck in the Congregational manse, Maitland, South Australia, on 26 June 1879. That year he briefly held title to a 228-acre (92.3 ha) section, in the Hundred of Tiparra, on which the stump-jump plough had first been demonstrated. In 1880 he established agricultural machinery works at Ardrossan, attractive for its shipping facilities. He died of renal disease on 25 July 1901 at Ardrossan, having prepared his young sons Alma Owen and (Clarence) Glen to take over the thriving business. When the local community proposed a memorial to Clarence senior, Richard took umbrage, perhaps resentful of his brother's success. He denied that Clarence had played any part in the invention or development of the stump-jump plough, despite the earliest drawings and several subsequent patents bearing Clarence's name. The Ardrossan firm Clarence H. Smith Ltd, incorporated in 1913, did not weather the 1930s Depression. Relocated to Port Adelaide (1935) it went into receivership.

In Western Australia Richard managed a hotel at Beverley, was a member of the Beverley Road Board (1893-95), and operated railway refreshment rooms in 1895-99 before taking up a farming lease at Beverley of 181½ acres (73.5 ha), relinquished in 1911. At a foundry there he resumed making agricultural implements, then established a workshop at Highgate, Perth, in 1912. He was remembered as a dapper man who frequently dressed in a 'frock coat and striped trousers, patent leather boots and spats'. Smith died on 4 February 1919 at Subiaco and was buried in Karakatta cemetery with Anglican rites. His wife, three daughters and four sons survived him. The Smith brothers' plough was one of the most important Australian inventions of the nineteenth century; by the mid-twentieth century twenty-four-farrow heavy disc ploughs were in use, essentially working on the same principle.

H. T. Burgess (ed), *The Cyclopedia of South Australia*, 2 (Adel, 1909); B. E. Neumann, *The Smith Brothers and the Stump Jump Plough* (1976); G. McLaren and W. Cooper, *Beverley: Our Journey Through Time* (Beverley, WA, 2002); *Procs of the Royal Agricultural and Horticultural Society of SA*, 1881-82, p 29; *Farmers' Weekly Messenger* (Kapunda, SA), 17 Nov 1876, p 2; *Yorke's Peninsula Advertiser*, 13 July 1880, p 2, 2 Aug 1901, p 3; *Observer* (Adel), 18 Feb 1882, p 27, 1 July 1882, p 9, 10 June 1899, p 3, 3 Aug 1901, p 9, 14 Sept 1901, p 9; *Inquirer and Commercial News* (Perth), 14 Jan 1885, p 9, 2 Sept 1885, p 3, 23 Sept 1885, p 3; *SA Chronicle*, 22 Jan 1948, pp 18 & 23; *Wallaroo Times*, 21 June 1882, p 2, 13 Sept 1882, p 2; *PD* (SA), 5 Sept 1882, p 843; Clarence H. Smith collection, National Trust Museum, Ardrossan, SA; C. H. Smith papers, PRG 432 (SLSA); GRS 513/5/P/46/1913 (SRSA).

ROGER ANDRÉ

SOUTH, WILLIAM GARNET (1855-1923), police officer and chief protector of Aborigines, was born on 8 August 1855 at Dry Creek (Modbury), Adelaide, one of ten children of Henry James South, farmer, and his wife Margaret, née Moncrieff. William's early years were spent at Modbury, where he was educated at a local school established by Scottish Presbyterians.

On 27 July 1877 South joined the South Australian mounted police force. He married Fanny Stevens on 2 October 1882 at St Luke's Church of England, Adelaide. They had four children. After serving at Melrose, Blinman, Farina, Barrows Creek, Port Augusta, Yarrowie and Peake, he was appointed to Alice Springs in March 1888 as officer in charge and warden of the goldfields. Here he became acquainted with Francis Gillen, (Sir Walter) Baldwin Spencer and (Sir) Edward Stirling [qq.v.9,12,6]. South displayed greater consideration for Aboriginal people than many of his fellow policemen, and in 1891 he co-operated with Gillen in the arrest of Constable Willshire [q.v.12] for shooting two Aboriginal men at Tempe Downs station. In 1895 South was removed from Alice Springs because of his involvement in the ownership of a liquor store and mining shares. This did not affect his career, however, as he was stationed at the police barracks, Adelaide, from 1898 and promoted senior constable in 1907.

South was appointed protector of Aborigines on 1 March 1908, and chief protector in 1911. He defined part of his role as to 'provide shelter, food and clothing' to the 'full descent' Aborigines so that they would be 'comfortable and happy for the remainder of their lives'. Nevertheless, he considered as most important the necessity to train and educate the 'half-caste' Aboriginal children so that they could be 'merged' into the white community. By late 1910 a system of removing such children living in Aboriginal camps was established, using the mechanisms of the State Children's Council. In 1911 the Aborigines Act, 'to make better provision for the Protection and Control of the Aboriginal Inhabitants of South Australia', was passed. A royal commission in 1913 recommended that mission stations be taken over by the government. During the later part of his term, South sought to obtain legislation that would enable children to be removed from the former mission stations. This was to culminate in the 1923 Aborigines (Training of Children) Act.

Described by the *Advertiser* as 'a friend to the natives', South did display concern for Aborigines as individuals. But he believed in the inevitable extinction of Aborigines, except for those who had inherited 'characteristics of the white blood' that endowed them with the potential to be absorbed into the general population. Fanny died in 1908, and on 12 February 1909 in St Paul's Church, Port Adelaide, he married Sophia Lalor, née Reid, a widow with five children. He was a member of the board of management of the South Australian Police Widows' and Orphans' Association.

Short and lean, South had sharp facial features and a trim beard. He belonged to the Hope Valley Lodge, Grand United Order of Oddfellows. South died of heart disease on 27 May 1923 in hospital at North Adelaide. His wife and three sons of his first marriage survived him; a son had been killed in action in World War I.

H. T. Burgess (ed), *The Cyclopedia of South Australia*, 2 (Adel, 1909), p 760; J. Mulvaney et al, *From the Frontier* (Syd, 2000); Report of the Pastoral Lands Commission, *PP* (SA), no 33, 1891, vol 3; Progress Report of the Royal Commission on the Aborigines, *PP* (SA), no 26, 1913, vol 2; *Public Service Review*, (Adel), Feb 1908, June 1923; *Register* (Adel), 1 July 1910, p 7; *Advertiser* (Adel), 28 May 1923, p 12; Protector of Aborigines, Annual Report, 1911-23, 52/1, and Commissioner of Police correspondence files 5/2/1894/568, and item 52/1/1912/28, (SRSA); W. South, service record (SA Police Historical Society, Thebarton, Adel).

NORM LALOR

SPRING, HENRY LANGDON and ROBERT ALEXANDER; *see* METTERS

SPRINGFIELD, MABEL ANGELINA (1892-1966), swimmer and coach, was born on 10 March 1892 at Mooloolah, near Landsborough, Queensland, second youngest of seven children of English-born parents Frank Springfield, carpenter, and his wife Angelina Bianca Clementina, née Koch. Frank worked for the Queensland railways and the children were educated at Mooloolah State School before they moved to Brisbane.

Mabel's siblings earned reputations in swimming, cycling and sailing. Frank (junior) swam in the London Olympic Games (1908) as the first Queensland competitor to represent Australia, Ernest was a Queensland cycling and sailing champion, and Sidney competed in the Inter-Allied Games following the cessation of World War I. Mabel excelled at swimming. Competing from an early age, she participated in the first women's State championship run by the Queensland Ladies' Amateur Swimming Association in 1906. She was a long-term State representative and won the Queensland championship for successive years. While overshadowed by Fanny Durack [q.v.8] and Mina Wylie, Springfield qualified to compete in two Olympic Games (1920 and 1924) but on both occasions, probably for financial reasons, she was thwarted. Her ambition was not achieved until the 1928 Amsterdam Olympics when she was selected as the chaperon for the female competitors. Required to pay her own way, Springfield looked after four athletes during their travelling, training and competition.

In Amsterdam, Springfield discovered the importance of coaching to European athletes and swimmers. On her return home, she approached the Brisbane City Council to start teaching and coaching swimming at the Booroodabin (Valley) Baths, initially in an honorary capacity. As a result of many requests she became a professional teacher and coach. Mostly based at the Booroodabin Baths, she travelled to pools at private, government, primary and secondary schools where she taught swimming. Springfield was mentor to many female athletes and considered a very astute breaststroke coach. She trained a number of State representatives. Her most famous protégée was dual Olympian Nancy Lyons. As successful as Springfield was in both teaching and coaching, her livelihood could not be met by these pursuits exclusively. Pools were not heated during the colder months, so Springfield supplemented her income by running a catering business as well as making dresses and costumes. Her career reflected the slow development of swimming coaching as a profession, but she distinguished herself as one of the first female coaches in an era when the field was predominantly a male domain.

Maintaining her aquatic business became more difficult as pool managers, who leased public pools, also began teaching and coaching swimmers, but she kept a link with the sport until her death. She never married. On 26 November 1966 Mabel Springfield died in Royal Brisbane Hospital from injuries received in a car accident when returning from her family's holiday house at Coolum. She was cremated with Anglican rites.

H. Gordon, *Australia and the Olympic Games* (Brisb, 1994); *Telegraph* (Brisb), 4 Oct 1947, p 7, 4 June 1982, p 13; family information.

MURRAY G. PHILLIPS

STÄHLE, JOHANN HEINRICH (1840-1915), missionary, was born in 1840 at Alpirsbach, in the German kingdom of Würrtemberg, son of Johann Heinrich Stähle, manufacturer, and his wife Katherina Elizabeth, née Trion. Young Johann served on the medical staff of the Prussian Army in the Franco-Prussian War (1870-71) then entered the seminary of the Moravian Church to train as a missionary. He was ordained in 1871 and married Marie Magdelene Stainer, a Moravian sister.

The Stähles reached Melbourne from England in the *Essex* in May 1872 and took charge of the school at the Ebenezer Aboriginal mission in the Wimmera, then under the management of F. W. Spieseke. In October Marie died giving birth to a daughter, who also died a month later. These deaths may have contributed to Stähle's decision to leave the mission, although his then deficiency in English (expressed in a letter back to Germany) probably made teaching difficult. He was appointed manager at the government mission at Coranderrk near Melbourne early in 1874. On 19 November that year at Chalmer's Presbyterian Church, Melbourne, he married with Lutheran rites Mary Anne McLean, a governess from Scotland, then also living at Coranderrk.

In 1875 Stähle accepted an offer from the Church of England to take charge of its Aboriginal mission at Lake Condah in the Western District of Victoria. His second marriage, to a non-Moravian, apparently led to a withdrawal of Moravian recognition of his ordination. Refusing to be reordained as an Anglican, he was thus limited as a minister, not being permitted to conduct Holy Communion. He managed Lake Condah for most of its existence. As for most mission managers of this period, reports of his conduct at Lake Condah ran to extremes: that he was beloved by the Aborigines, or hated and resisted. He was certainly authoritarian, causing rebellious reaction from such Aborigines as Ernest Mobourne [q.v.]. As early as 1876 one resident charged him with assault; the charge was dismissed but Stähle sought more power to discipline his charges. Yet, after the 1886 Aborigines Protection Law Amendment Act, which required that all Aborigines who were not 'full blood' leave the missions, he attempted to gain land grants for those required to leave Lake

Condah and criticized government policy. The number of residents declined greatly after the 1886 Act (as was the intention), and the last years of his supervision witnessed the mission's decay.

Stähle was naturalized in January 1898. He and his wife resigned when the mission closed in June 1913 and lived on a pension at Portland. John Henry Stähle, as he was by now generally known, died there on 23 August 1915 and was buried in the local cemetery with Anglican rites. His estate was sworn for probate at £5676. His wife and their three daughters and four sons survived him.

K. Cole, *The Lake Condah Aboriginal Mission* (Bendigo, Vic, 1984); B. Dickey (ed), *The Australian Dictionary of Evangelical Biography* (Syd, 1994); J. Critchett, *Untold Stories* (Melb, 1998); B. Edwards, *Moravian Aboriginal Missions in Australia 1850-1919* (Adel, 1999); C. W. Schooling papers (SLV); A712, item 1897/F12740 (NAA, Melb); Moravian archives (AIATSIS, Canb).   ROBERT KENNY

STANLEY, ANNIE CREO (1865-1940), trade union leader, was born on 16 October 1865 at Clermont, Queensland, and registered as 'Nanny', eldest child of Dublin-born (William) Michael Stanley, hospital attendant later umbrella-maker, and his wife Hannah Maria, née Benbow, from Wales; the couple had married in New Zealand. Creo spent her childhood in Sydney, where her father was a shopkeeper at Redfern, then pursued an acting career until suffering a lung ailment. On 29 March 1888 at the district registrar's office, Redfern, she married English-born Bronterre Washington Dooley, a carriage-builder and socialist. He deserted her and she reverted to her maiden name; they were divorced in March 1893. Dooley became a Labor politician in Western Australia.

When the Female Employees' Union was formed in Sydney on 20 July 1891 Stanley was elected its first secretary. The union was intended as 'a centre of action for working women' generally, but Stanley focused on recruiting barmaids, waitresses and laundresses, for whom unions already existed. This led to a demarcation dispute with the Barmaids and Waitresses' Union, which the Trades and Labor Council attempted to mediate. The council actively supported Stanley's organizing in laundries, and in August 1891 she became embroiled in a strike at the Pyrmont Steam Laundry over the dismissal of a union member.

On 3 September Stanley became the first female delegate to the T.L.C. She declared that she was not afraid of any man in the council nor any press representative, drawing loud cheering from some delegates—one of whom, however, objected to female representation.

The *Daily Telegraph* described her as 'dressed in semi-masculine attire—starched shirt, a high collar, white tie and open jacket, a small travelling cap set on a bunch of closely-cropped hair'. Revealing the extent of prejudice, the *Bulletin* declared that she 'should take up the manly custom of smoking a pipe'. A photograph showed a wide-eyed, determined young woman.

Stanley gained financial support from the council's affiliates for the strikers and for the establishment in October of a co-operative laundry at Redfern to employ them. When the laundry could not employ all the women, some complained to the T.L.C., which established a committee of inquiry into allegations against Stanley of mismanagement of strike funds. She and her supporters refused to co-operate, but she resigned as F.E.U. secretary at the beginning of 1892. An investigation by the union exonerated her from the 'malicious slander' and expelled four members who had laid complaints. As well, the T.L.C. cleared her.

Stanley also championed female members of the Amalgamated Tobacco Workers' Association, who complained that male union members were preventing them from working. After denials from the union concerned, the council lamely decided to ignore the issue, since it was 'an internal union matter'.

In 1891 Stanley had agitated for the adoption of female suffrage as Labor Party policy. She also advocated the formation of co-operatives in needlework and millinery, but failed to gain sufficient union backing to establish a co-operative laundry in Melbourne. In the Sydney laundry she pursued a 'communistic' ideal, as she described it: the women lived and laboured 'in harmony without the intervention of unnecessary authority, and dividing equally among themselves weekly the net profits resulting from their labours'. She was an active member of the Australian Socialist League. In 1893 she refused to act as an organizer for William Lane's [q.v.9] New Australia expedition in Paraguay.

From about 1892 Stanley lived with the A.S.L. secretary E. J. Brady [q.v.7]. After his divorce, Stanley and Brady married on 12 June 1895 at Smithfield registry office, but soon separated. Reputedly, she refused to give him a divorce. By 1903 'Annie Brady' was living at Granville. From about 1906—as Mrs A. Stanley —she ran a grocer's shop there, sharing the address for the rest of her life with Alvilde Christine Nielson, a milliner. Annie Creo Brady died childless on 30 November 1940 in her home at Granville and was buried in the Catholic section of Rookwood cemetery.

Female Employees' Union, *Rules and Regulations* (Syd, 1891); B. James, *Anarchism and State Violence in Sydney and Melbourne 1886-1896* (Newcastle, NSW, 1986); R. Markey, *The Making of the Labor*

Party in New South Wales 1880-1900 (Syd, 1988);
Labour History, no 36, May 1979, p 18; *SMH*, 3 Oct
1887, p 5; *Daily Telegraph* (Syd), 4 Sept 1891, p 4;
Bulletin, 5 Sept 1891, p 19; *Austn Workman*, 26 Sept
1891, p 3, 7 Nov 1891, p 1, 2 Apr 1892, p 1, 29 June
1895, p 3; Syd Trades and Labour Council, General
Meeting Minutes, 1891-92 (ML); information from
Mr L. F. Gooley, Blaxland, NSW.   RAY MARKEY

STEFFANONI, LEWIS (1835-1880), illumi-
nator and embroiderer, and SOPHIA ELIZA-
BETH (1873-1906), artist, were father and
daughter. Lewis was born on 14 September
1835 at Holborn, London, son of Luigi
Guiseppe Steffanoni, upholsterer, reputedly
an Italian nobleman, and his second wife
Sophia Elizabeth, née Samweis, who was
Jewish and German-born. The family business
at Holborn catered to the upper and middle
classes with gilding and coats of arms in gold
bullion embroidery. Lewis made badges and
flags for the Royal Navy. He migrated and
reached Sydney on 9 November 1852 in the
City of Poonah, travelling first class—with
forty-eight needlewomen in steerage.

Living at Mrs Murphy's boarding house
at the Rocks, Steffanoni ran his own business producing illuminations, testimonials,
addresses and gold, silver and silk embroidery while working as a clerk in the advertising department of the *Sydney Morning Herald*.
When the wedding of the Prince of Wales was
celebrated in Sydney in 1863, Steffanoni
painted transparencies for the five front windows of the *Herald* building. Portraits of the
royal couple and Britannia were backlit by 600
candles, and cauldrons on the roof spouted
flames—one of the outstanding 'manifestations of loyalty in the city'. He painted many
such transparencies as well as oil and water-
colour landscapes and seascapes, including
'the Weatherboard Falls', which he exhibited
at the 1870 Intercolonial Exhibition in Sydney.

On 15 April 1869 at Pitt Street Congregational Church Steffanoni married John
Fairfax's [q.v.4] niece Sarah Ann Reading
(1844-1916), who had been born at Warwick,
England. Sarah's widowed mother took Lewis
into partnership in the family import business,
which became Reading, Son & Steffanoni.
The firm made regalia, flags, badges, vestments and trappings for regiments, yacht
clubs and Masonic and ecclesiastical organizations, as well as governors' uniforms and
numerous elaborate illuminated addresses.
Sophia was born on 8 May 1873 at Pitt Street,
second daughter and third of five children.

At a meeting to form a New South Wales
Academy of Art in April 1871, Steffanoni became the third member after Edward Reeve
and E. L. Montefiore [qq.v.6,5] and joined a
general committee to draw up the rules,
which opened full membership to women.
Steffanoni served on the council of the academy in 1871-76, designed the catalogues for
the first two exhibitions and collected the
paintings at the shop for each exhibition until
1875. He worked towards establishing an art
training school; two Italian instructors Achille
Simonetti and Giulio Anivitti [qq.v.6,3] were
appointed. In September 1871 Steffanoni introduced (Sir) James Reading Fairfax [q.v.8],
his cousin by marriage, to the council of the
academy to fill a vacancy. This led to the Fairfax family's long philanthropic association
with the National Art Gallery of New South
Wales. An alcoholic, Steffanoni died of epilepsy on 29 May 1880 at Wynyard Square,
Sydney, and was buried in Rookwood cemetery. His wife, two sons and three daughters
survived him.

With five children under 9, Sarah Steffanoni
took over the failing business, concentrated
on embroidery and operated from a rented
house, where she also took in boarders.
Sophie went to Fort Street Model School. In
1886 her embroidery was exhibited at the
Colonial and Indian Exhibition in London.
She attended Sydney Girls' High School in
1887-88, a contemporary of Ethel Burwell
[q.v.12 Turner] and Louise Mack [q.v.10],
then joined the family business as full-time
designer and embroiderer. In 1891 she won
the prize for water-colour painting at the
National Juvenile Industrial Exhibition. At the
World's Columbian Exposition in Chicago,
United States of America, in 1893 she exhibited an Australian Coat of Arms in gold bullion, winning a medal. (This piece was to be
exhibited posthumously at the Australian
Exhibition of Women's Work in Melbourne
in 1907.) In 1891-93 she probably attended
the Art Society School, where Tom Roberts
[q.v.11] was a tutor, and was a private student
of W. Lister Lister [q.v.10].

From 1895 to 1903 Sophie's pictures featured regularly in the annual exhibitions of
the Royal Art Society. She spent several summers painting in Tasmania with Kate Cowle—
who later married Gustav Weindorfer—and
in Melbourne with Jane Sutherland [qq.v.12].
In 1901 Sophie's work in the R.A.S.'s Federation Exhibition received favourable reviews:
'In her sea pieces this artist is always attractive; the glint of sunlit waves and spray, the
turgid, rough water, the rich-hued rocks, the
distant cliffs, the wonderful skies are all
painted with a hand that never errs'. By 1903
her reputation was established and her painting, 'Paradise Hill, Blackheath', was depicted
in the *Sydney Mail* with others by Fred Leist,
Sydney Long, George Collingridge, Dattilo
Rubbo [qq.v.10,8,11] and Lister. In the early
1900s ill health confined her to her home in
North Sydney, where she died of pulmonary
tuberculosis on 1 November 1906. She was

buried with Congregational forms in Rookwood cemetery.

Sophie's mother Sarah ran the family embroidery business until her death in 1916, when it was taken over by Sophie's sister Alice (1875-1956). The Mitchell [q.v.5] Library, Sydney, holds an illuminated address made by Lewis Steffanoni, apparently the only one of many to survive. The family holds most of Sophie's paintings.

J. Kerr (ed), *The Dictionary of Australian Artists* (Melb, 1992) and *Heritage: The National Women's Art Book* (Syd, 1995); A. Butterfield, 'Lewis Steffanon—1835-1880', *Australian Antique Collector*, Jan-June 1992, p 59, *and* 'Sophie Staffanoni (1873-1906—Sydney Woman Impressionist', *Austn & NZ Jnl of Art*, 2, no 1, 2001, p 27; *Sydney Mail*, 8 Apr 1903, p 859; family information.

ANNETTE BUTTERFIELD

STEVENSON, MARGARET (c.1807-1874), poet and satirist, was born at Chester, Cheshire, England, only child of John G. Gorton (d.1835), journalist, and his wife Margaret, née Hutton. Young Margaret grew up in a literary family. Her father was a writer and translator, and under his editorship the *Globe* (London) became a vigorous Whig opponent of the Tory *Morning Times*. With a classical education in Paris, she became fluent in French, Italian and German and an accomplished pianist, helped her father with his *General Biographical Dictionary* (London, 1828) and was music critic for the *Globe*. Among her friends was Kate Hogarth, future wife of Charles Dickens [q.v.4].

Margaret married George Stevenson [q.v.2], a *Globe* journalist, on 12 May 1836 at St George's Church, Hanover Square. The Stevensons and Margaret's mother sailed for South Australia in the *Buffalo* with Governor Hindmarsh [q.v.1], arriving in December 1836. As editor of the *South Australian Gazette and Colonial Register*, George was a trenchant critic of official policy, encouraged by his wife. In Douglas Pike's [q.v.16] words, with their intellectual capital and advantageous social network, the colony had gained 'a formidable couple almost impossible to overawe'. Together they wrote a diary from 1836 to 1837 containing Margaret's early, elegant prose impressions of South Australia.

George and Margaret settled on land between Finniss and Melbourne streets, North Adelaide, and built Lytton Lodge, later known as 'Buffalo Cottage', where they had a celebrated garden. They also established a plant nursery (Leawood Gardens), managed by Margaret's mother, in the Adelaide Hills and a small inn nearby. Margaret was a prolific private versifier, sometimes in French and Italian. Some poems were addressed to her husband. Two from 1838 compared European with indigenous societies. She frequently satirized Adelaide's politics and its pretensions. In her husband's newspaper, under the pseudonym of 'A Colonist', she made scathing attacks on (Sir) James Hurtle Fisher [q.v.1], accusing him of private profiteering. Though Fisher sued for libel, he was awarded only £2 on one occasion and a shilling on two other occasions.

Under the same pseudonym, in 1838 Margaret ran literate weekly columns for women. Drawing on her classical background, she quoted from anecdotes, moral fables and brief biographies of classical Greek and European masters and from newspapers as wide-ranging as the *Edinburgh Review*, *Liverpool Mail*, *Blackwood's Magazine* and the *Spectator*. In 1838 she wrote a dramatic piece for Twelfth Night, using classical characters whom she identified with local worthies.

Between 1839 and 1849 she gave birth to three children. George became insolvent in 1852. After her mother died that year and her husband in 1856, Margaret became increasingly isolated and alienated, although she managed to educate her children well. Her last extant poem was written in 1860. By 1864 she had moved to Norwood. She died of congestive heart failure on 28 September 1874 in her daughter's home at Glenelg and was buried beside her husband in St Matthew's churchyard, Kensington. Her daughter and one son survived her. Stevenson's unpublished verse was circumscribed by contemporary romantic conventions and her satire was localized, not always sharp, but fearless. Some of her poems praised music, others lamented the life of an upper-class woman, transplanted to a colonial, cultural wilderness, utterly remote from the congenial, literary world of her upbringing.

D. Pike, *Paradise of Dissent* (Melb, 1957); M. Stevenson, letter, 6 Nov 1856, PRG 527/5/174, *and* V. de Mole papers (SLSA).

LEITH G. MACGILLIVRAY

STREET, EDWIN (1891-1975), ice cream manufacturer, was born on 8 August 1891 at Corrimal, New South Wales, youngest of ten children of Staffordshire-born parents James Street, miner, and his wife Ann, née Cooper. By 1914 Ted and his brothers had established a farm at Leeton. There he met Daisy Olive Grigg, a farmer's daughter from Western Australia, whom he was to marry in the Leeton Methodist Church on 7 June 1921. They had no children.

On 29 June 1916 at Kiama, Street had enlisted as a private in the Australian Imperial Force and served in the 45th Battalion in

France from 1917. Twice wounded, after demobilization in July 1919 he returned to Corrimal where he established a grocer's shop and in 1920 began hand churning frozen custards. Increasing production by attaching a one-horsepower engine to the churn, he began selling his ice cream to other local shops. By the 1930s reliable mechanical refrigeration systems offered the opportunity for expansion. Street seized the chance, purchasing the Corrimal Ice Works in 1934—the year Streets Ice Cream Ltd was registered in Sydney—and establishing the Illawarra Delicacy Co. On weekends he travelled extensively in the region promoting his product, marketed as 'The Cream of the Coast'. Although concentrating on vanilla ice cream (from quart-size bricks to twenty-two-gallon containers), Street also sought a more popular market through 'penny pinkies'—ice creams in a cone sold from travelling carts.

In 1939 Street set up a distribution depot at Bexley to capture a slice of the lucrative Sydney market. World War II stalled further expansion plans but in 1946 he established a factory at Turella, Sydney, and that year brought out his first popular stick ice cream, 'The Heart'. Fired by his fierce rivalry with Frederick Peters [q.v.11], Street moved quickly to become a bigger player in the industry, buying Lynam's Ice Cream Co. in 1950 and a year later establishing a second factory at Moruya. In 1953 the business was listed as a public company, with Street as managing director. Despite early boardroom struggles and difficult economic times, he was able to plough profits back into the business. This gave the enterprise a firm base and the capacity to expand into other parts of New South Wales, with depots at Gosford, Wagga Wagga, Goulburn, Queanbeyan and Nowra. Street established long-term supply contracts with Dairy Farmers Ltd and worked hard to break Peters' tight hold over local distribution networks. Street's famous 'Paddle Pop' was launched in 1953, selling ninety million by the end of the century, per capita the largest selling ice cream in the world.

Hard working, innovative, domineering and argumentative, Street nonetheless inspired great loyalty. He was square jawed, brown eyed and dark haired and, despite his growing wealth, retained the common touch. Driven to work in a Holden 'ute', and shunning ostentation, Street devoted himself to business and continued to live at Corrimal. His wife was of similar disposition, working long hours in the factory, taking an intense interest in the welfare of the female factory workers and rarely bothering to lighten domestic chores with modern household appliances.

By the late 1950s Streets was sufficiently profitable to attract the attention of larger firms. In 1960 Kraft Foods Ltd, Unilever Aus-tralia Pty Ltd and the old rival Peters put in offers to buy the company. Although Peters made a higher bid, Street sold out to Unilever for nearly £4 million. In new hands Streets became a market leader in the 1960s, pioneering such household names as 'Splice', 'Gaytime', 'Cornetto' and 'Blue Ribbon Ice Cream'.

Ted and Daisy retired to Narooma, becoming prominent local philanthropists. Street was appointed O.B.E. in 1970. A sometimes combative and demanding benefactor, he nonetheless made substantial donations to build public swimming pools at Corrimal, Batemans Bay, Dapto, Moruya and Narooma, and a skating rink and tennis courts at Narooma. The couple also generously funded retirement and nursing homes for the aged on the South Coast, including the Daisy Street Lodge Retirement Home. The Australian Red Cross Society, Narooma ambulance station and Legacy were also the beneficiaries of their largesse. Although they travelled widely, they liked nothing better than visiting schools to tell their story of Streets ice cream. They also supported research into Parkinson's disease at Prince Henry Hospital, Little Bay, where Street died on 10 August 1975, survived by his wife. Daisy continued their tradition of giving school children at Narooma a free Streets ice cream each year. She died in 1990.

Unifoods Pty Ltd, *First Choice*, no 1, Dec 1995, p 3; *Observer* (Syd), 19 Mar 1960, p 37; *Examiner* (South Coast, NSW), 4 July 1968, p 5; *Canberra Times*, 3 Sept 1975, p 12; *Illawarra Mercury*, 1 Dec 1990, p 12; *Sunday Telegraph* (Syd), 2 Dec 1990, p 26; *SMH*, 21 Aug 1999, 'Good Weekend', p 13; Moruya and Narooma Hist societies' files; Unilever archives, Syd.   STEPHEN GARTON

STYANT BROWNE, FRANK; *see* BROWNE

SULLIVAN, PATRICK PETER (1885-1933), cartoonist and animated film producer, was born on 22 February 1885 at Ivy Street, Paddington, second son of Patrick Sullivan, a cab proprietor from Ireland, and his Sydney-born wife Margaret, née Hayes. Young Pat was educated by the Marist Brothers at St Benedict's School, Chippendale, and St Mary's Cathedral Boys' High School, Woolloomooloo. His father thought that the boy's early interest in drawing was unlikely to make him a living. Pat worked as a gatekeeper at Toohey's [q.v.6] brewery, Surry Hills, and reputedly attended classes at the Art Society of New South Wales.

Sullivan contributed occasional cartoons and illustrations to the *Worker* and the *Gadfly* (as 'P. O'Sullivan') before sailing to London in 1909 to further his ambitions. He worked for a time on the comic strip 'Ally Sloper' but, his earnings meagre, tried music-hall work, failed as a motion picture exhibitor and was reduced to being an animal handler in trans-Atlantic ships. Reaching New York by early 1910, he boxed for prize money.

In 1911 Sullivan obtained a position with a successful cartoonist William Marriner of the McClure newspaper syndicate, creating his own short-lived comic strips, 'Willing Waldo' and 'Old Pop Perkins'. On Marriner's death in October 1914, Sullivan joined the pioneering and successful film animation studio run by Raoul Barre. Although laid off after nine months because of unsatisfactory work, Sullivan managed to open his own animated cartoon studio and won contracts for advertising and entertainment shorts. By 1916 his studio staff were turning out films under his name. He adapted a Marriner 'Sambo' strip as a 'Sammy Johnsin' animated cartoon and produced Charlie Chaplin film cartoons. About this time he hired Otto Messmer, a talented comic-strip artist.

In 1917 Sullivan was convicted of the rape of a 14-year-old girl. While he was on bail he married Marjorie Gallagher on 21 May in the municipal building, Manhattan; she wrote to the Justice Department pleading for leniency. During nine months in gaol Sullivan practised his cartooning on postcards and envelopes sent to his lawyer.

Upon release, Sullivan revived his studio and was rejoined by Messmer. Sullivan widely asserted that he and his wife had invented a black cat as a film character, featured in his short animated films *The Tail of Thomas Kat* (1917) and *Feline Follies* (1919). Nearly fifty years later, however, Messmer claimed that it was he who had devised the cat. Descended from 'Sammy Johnsin' and drawn with Chaplinesque humour, the cat had become 'Felix' by the fourth film, changing from a four-legged to a two-legged character. Under the title 'Pat Sullivan's Felix the Cat', contracts were secured to provide a cartoon a month to cinemas. A change of distributor in 1921 saw Felix in 60 per cent of cinemas in North America.

Felix cartoons were aimed at adults, incorporating skits on cubism and flappers. The films—and from 1923 the published comic strips—spread to Europe and in 1924, when the Sullivans toured England, Felix was so famous that entrepreneurs were producing pirated dolls and toys. Sullivan managed to obtain a share of the royalties. An up-and-coming animator, Walt Disney, copied Felix with a character named Julius. Forced to withdraw, Disney created a new character, Mickey Mouse, which soon put a dent in Sullivan's business.

Sullivan had quietly visited Australia in 1920. On another trip to Sydney with his wife in December 1925 he was given a civic reception at which T. D. Mutch [q.v.10], minister for education, revealed that he and the cartoonist had roomed together when boys. Sullivan also came back to Sydney briefly in 1927. Felix cartoons were still exhibiting well between 1926 and 1928, when Disney released his first 'talkie' Mickey Mouse cartoon. By 1931 Disney productions had eclipsed Felix, but Sullivan stuck with his one and only successful formula. Chronic alcoholism probably prevented him from matching Disney's inventiveness, and the dubbing of sound onto silent Felix cartoons proved decidedly second-rate.

In March 1932 Marjorie fell to her death from the Sullivans' second-floor apartment in New York. She had lived in an increasingly strained marriage. Sullivan suffered from syphilis and his mental faculties declined. He died of pneumonia and alcoholism on 15 February 1933 in Sharman Square Hospital, New York, and was buried in Cathedral cemetery, Scranton, Pennsylvania. The cartoon character continued as a print comic strip and after World War II in children's picture books, always billed as 'Pat Sullivan's Felix the Cat', a title continued by Sullivan's nephew, also Patrick Sullivan.

J. Canemaker, *Felix: The Twisted Tale of the World's Most Famous Cat* (NY, 1991); *SMH*, 7 Dec 1925, p 5, 15 Apr 1954, p 9, 27 Dec 1955, p 6, 2 Apr 1988, 'Good Weekend', p 30; *NY Times*, 16 Feb 1933, p 19; *The Times* (Lond), 17 Feb 1933, p 14; *Bulletin*, 19 Nov 1991, p 133; Felix the Cat, 'Rewind', ABC TV, 31 Oct 2004; information from Ms J. Nelson, ML, Syd.   PETER SPEARRITT
                                       JOHN YOUNG

SUMMERFIELD, ROSE ANNA (1864-1922), feminist and labour leader, was born on 18 April 1864 at Middleton Creek, Victoria, third child of John Stone, a Polish-born miner, and his wife Mary, née Dargan, from Ireland. Rose's precocious radical consciousness was stirred by the Australasian Secularist Association in the mid-1880s and the influence of Joseph Symes [q.v.6]. By 1886 she was active in the A.S.A. in Melbourne as a Sunday School teacher. On 23 March that year at Fitzroy she married with the rites of the Free Church of England a fellow freethinker, Henry Lewis Summerfield, a 55-year-old English-born widower and tailor. They moved to Sydney and settled at Waverley; a son was born in 1887.

Rose's secularism developed into an impassioned mix of socialism, temperance and women's rights. Described as 'a rattling lecturer and organiser—full of fire and energy', with a strong face and intense gaze—she spread 'the gospel of discontent' from the early 1890s. She wrote for the *Democrat*, the *Liberator* and the *Northern People*, 'any paper that was battling for something better'. As 'Rose Hummer', she regularly contributed to the *Hummer* and its successor, the (Sydney) *Worker*. In a July 1892 lecture, 'Master and Man', for the Australian Socialist League, Rose expressed an urgent alienation and idealism, preaching working-class agitation for 'emancipation' before their masters subjected them to the status of 'almond-eyed slaves'.

By August 1892 Rose had emerged as the leading organizer of female workers in Sydney. With the encouragement of W. G. Spence [q.v.6], she established a women's division of the nascent Australian Workers' Union. She also conducted a labour exchange for female workers in Castlereagh Street and proselytized across country New South Wales. These activities collapsed as a result of the 1890s depression and bank crashes. In October 1892 she felt compelled to reject an appeal from the Trades and Labor Council of New South Wales to organize women in the clothing trades, although in January-March 1893 she assisted John 'Chummy' Fleming [q.v.8] to organize Melbourne bootmakers, part of an unsuccessful effort to spread the A.W.U. campaign to Victoria.

Urging working-class women to their 'duty to ask for the vote', Rose turned her energies to the Womanhood Suffrage League of New South Wales. She established the league's Waverley branch and served as a member of its governing council in 1893-94. Also active in the temperance cause, in 1896 she was on the executive of the Metropolitan District Lodge No.2 and the Hearts of Oak Lodge No.188, Waverley, of the Independent Order of Good Templars. She lectured on 'Woman's Place in the Temperance Movement' in January.

Henry had died in 1890. On 22 September 1897 at the registrar's office, Waverley, Rose married John Cadogan, a shearers' cook and mine manager. Disillusioned with Australian workers and Labor politics, she resigned from the A.S.L. in 1897, and bitterly lamented workmen who were 'gulled' by the 'mighty bribe' of suffrage. William Lane's [q.v.9] New Australia co-operative settlement in Paraguay promised socialism, equal rights for women, temperance and racial exclusion; the Cadogans sailed from Sydney in April 1899, farewelled by 'every section of the reform movement'.

Paraguay, however, only intensified Rose's alienation. By 1901 she felt outcast among the 'ignorant and superstitious' locals. In 1908 the Cadogans left New Australia to become shopkeepers at nearby Yataity. By 1915 she pined for the scent of wattle, a longing cruelly denied by the loss of the family's savings in a bank failure only months before they finalized arrangements to return to Australia in 1920. Despite her despair of the Paraguayans, she worked among them for many years, treating malaria and hookworm with herbal cures.

Predeceased by the son of her first marriage, Rose died of cancer on 14 April 1922 at Villa Rica, Paraguay. Her husband survived her, as did their four sons, one of whom (Leon) inherited his mother's passion for social justice, expressed in anthropological research and campaigns for the rights of indigenous Paraguayans. Rose Cadogan, a pioneer of emancipation, was buried in the Las Ovejas cemetery at New Australia.

G. Souter, *A Peculiar People* (Syd, 1968); V. Burgmann, *'In Our Time'* (Syd, 1985); A. Whitehead, *Paradise Mislaid* (Brisb, 1997); *Labour Hist*, no 87, Nov 2004, p 65; *Liberator* (Melb), 14 Feb 1886, p 184, 21 Mar 1886, pp 267 & 272, 11 Apr 1886, p 313; *Hummer* (Syd), 23 Apr 1892, p 3, 30 July 1892, p 3, 13 Aug 1892, p 2, 3 Sept 1892, p 3; *Worker* (Syd), 8 Oct 1892, p 2, 29 Oct 1892, p 3, 4 Mar 1893, p 4, 29 Jan 1898, p 7, 19 Feb 1898, p 8, 1 Apr 1899, p 3, 23 Nov 1901, p 1; *Shearers' and General Laborers' Record*, 15 Mar 1893; *Austn Temperance World and Good Templar Record*, 2 Mar 1896, p 3, 1 Apr 1896, p 3; *Common Cause* (Syd), 28 July 1922, p 12.

MARK HEARN

SUTTON, SAMUEL JOHN (1836-1906), businessman and politician, was born on 19 April 1836 in Hobart Town, eldest of fourteen children of free immigrants Samuel Sutton, writer, and his wife Sarah, née Fielder. Samuel senior had reached Van Diemen's Land in the *Charles Eaton* in June 1834 and Sarah in the *Strathfieldsay* in August that year. By 1843 the family had moved to Launceston, where Samuel John was educated and where his father worked as a clerk and later a butcher.

About 1862 young Sutton set up as a baker and confectioner in Wellington Street, moving in 1873 to Brisbane Street. On 4 March 1862 he married Annie York with Independent rites at the bride's residence, Launceston. She died in March 1876. On 9 August that year at Talina, Glenore, Westbury, he married with Wesleyan Methodist forms Jane Ann French, a farmer's daughter, who died in June 1877. His third marriage, with Congregational forms, was to Emma Eliza Farmilo on 4 March 1880 at the Memorial Church, Hobart; they had seven children.

In 1880-81, aware of the growing demand for quality facilities for accommodation and entertainment, Samuel built to high standards the Launceston (Metropole) Coffee Palace at 75 Brisbane Street. The success of this temperance hotel brought him prominence. He was a member (sometime president) of the Chamber of Commerce and an alderman of Launceston Municipal Council from 1885 to 1905 (mayor, 1890-92 and 1898). Sutton contested North Launceston in July 1886, represented South Launceston in the House of Assembly from May 1891, failed to win Launceston in January 1897 and March 1900, but was elected for that seat in October 1901. In April 1903 he failed to win East Launceston.

More progressive in outlook than many fellow aldermen, Sutton was the driving force behind the erection in Launceston of the Albert Hall, the Queen Victoria Museum and Art Gallery and the Victoria Baths. He supported the electrification of the city, slum clearance and improvement of the drainage and water schemes. A highlight of his civic career was the successful organization of the Tasmanian International Exhibition in 1891-92 at Launceston; he was chairman of the commissioners. Appointed a justice of the peace in 1892, Sutton was chairman of Launceston Benevolent Society, member of the Prisoners' Aid and Rescue Society and treasurer of the London dock labourers' fund (1889). He was closely connected with the Tamar Street Congregational Church and superintendent of its Sunday School.

A big, hard-working man, who made the most of his opportunities, with an active and practical interest in his religion, Sutton enjoyed life and was generous and hospitable. He was a total abstainer from alcohol—though he enjoyed a pipe—and he believed that he should provide the public with wholesome entertainment and recreational activities in lieu of drinking. In 1900 he sold his Coffee Palace, but continued his philanthropic and civil work from Fairlawn, his Elphin Road villa, where he died of heart disease on 7 September 1906; his wife, two sons and three daughters survived him. Sutton was buried in Launceston general cemetery, but was later re-interred in Carr Villa cemetery. His coffee palace was demolished in 1976.

Daily Telegraph (Launc), 20 Aug 1881, p 3, 8 Sept 1906, p 3; *Examiner* (Launc), 26 Nov 1891, p 3, 8 Sept 1906, p 7; Launceston City Council archives (Queen Vic Museum and Art Gallery, Launc).

GWENDA M. WEBB

SWEETAPPLE, THEODORA MAUDE (1872-1972), nurse, was born on 25 May 1872 at Port Adelaide, tenth child and fifth daughter of English-born parents William Deane Sweetapple, shipping agent, and his wife Anna Mapleson, née Mitchell. After the death of Dora's father in 1875 her mother conducted a school where Dora received her early education.

In November 1891 Sweetapple became a trainee nurse at the Adelaide Children's Hospital. On completing the course late in 1893 she returned to Port Adelaide where, at the suggestion of the local Church of England rector, she began nursing the sick poor in their own homes. In November 1894 she was the second nurse appointed to the staff of the newly established District Trained Nursing Society. Sweetapple often travelled on foot to her patients' homes, but in the widely scattered Port Adelaide district she appreciated free use of the local horse tram. Later a bicycle offered more independent transport. To visit patients on the further side of the Port River, a boatman rowed her over. In 1896 she made 1612 visits to 157 patients for which she received an annual salary of £30 and a further £55 for board.

After a strenuous five years Sweetapple resigned to take up a new challenge in community health nursing. In 1899 the medical officer for the Adelaide City Council, Thomas Borthwick, obtained the council's approval to appoint a nurse to work among families in the narrow back streets of the city. Theodora Sweetapple was appointed as 'city trained nurse'. Her first concern was with families in which cases of infectious disease, including tuberculosis and typhoid fever, had been reported. In addition to visiting and supervising disinfection in the home, she gave talks on elementary hygiene to meetings of women in the city. In his reports the medical officer commended Sweetapple for her quiet, tactful, methodical approach to her work. Studies in disinfection led to the award to her in 1900 of the certificate of the Institute of Hygiene and Bacteriology, Adelaide. In 1907 she gained a qualification from the Royal Sanitary Institute, London, as inspector of nuisances.

When a South Australian branch of the Australasian Trained Nurses' Association was formed in 1905, Sweetapple was one of the founding members. Upon retirement as city trained nurse in 1906 she became co-proprietor of a private hospital at Victor Harbor with her close friend Mabel Gill, with whom she had trained at the Adelaide Children's Hospital. In 1913 the two women went to Britain where they remained during World War I and had nursing appointments with the Queen's Institute of District Nursing and the Order of St John of Jerusalem.

Returning to Adelaide in 1919, Sweetapple and Gill ran a nursing home at Henley Beach for three years, then moved to Stirling, in the Adelaide Hills, and for the next twelve years conducted a boarding house. Ten years later they moved back to Adelaide. After the death of her friend in 1965 Sweetapple was admitted to Resthaven infirmary, Leabrook. She died on 9 October 1972 and was cremated. Her estate was sworn for probate at $32 882.

Nursing in South Australia (Adel, 1939), p 370; J. Durdin, *They Became Nurses* (Syd, 1991); T. Morton, *After Light* (Adel, 1996); Mayor's Report, 1898-1899, 1902 (Adel City Council Archives); District Trained Nursing Society, *Annual Report*, 1896-97 *and* Minutes of General Meeting, 19 Oct 1894 (Royal District Nursing Soc, Glenunga, Adel); family papers (held by Mr G. Sweetapple, Unley Park, Adel).

JOAN DURDIN

T

TARENORERER (c.1800-1831), Aboriginal leader, known as WALYER by the sealers of Bass Strait, was born near Emu Bay, Van Diemen's Land, a woman of the Tommeginne people. In her teens she was abducted by Aborigines of the Port Sorell region and sold to white sealers on the Bass Strait Islands. She became proficient in speaking English and took particular notice of the use and operation of firearms.

In 1828 Tarenorerer returned to her country in the north of Tasmania, where she gathered a group of men and women from many bands to initiate warfare against the invaders. Training her warriors in the use of firearms, she ordered them to strike the *luta tawin* (white men) when they were at their most vulnerable, between the time that their guns were discharged and before they were able to reload. She also instructed them to kill the Europeans' sheep and bullocks. Seeking to apprehend her, G. A. Robinson [q.v.2] was told by sealers that Tarenorerer, whom he called an 'Amazon', would stand on a hill to organize the attack, abuse the settlers and dare them to come and be speared. She was reported to have said 'she liked a *luta tawin* as she did a black snake'. Robinson pursued her, but she eluded him and in September 1830 his party narrowly escaped being attacked by her warriors.

Challenged by Aboriginal rivals in battle, she escaped to Port Sorell with her brothers Linnetower and Line-ne-like-kayver and two sisters but was taken by sealers to the Hunter Islands and then placed on Bird Island to catch seals and mutton birds. Known as 'Mary Anne', she was given to John Williams ('Norfolk Island Jack') and lived with him and other men and Aboriginal women on Forsyth Island, in the Furneaux group. In December 1830 she plotted to kill one of the sealers but was foiled by Robinson's agents and taken to Swan Island, where her identity was revealed after she was given away by her dog Whiskey and by other Aboriginal women. Robinson was elated at a capture that he saw as 'a matter of considerable importance to the peace and tranquility of those districts where she and her formidable coadjutors had made themselves so conspicuous in their wanton and barbarous aggression'. It was, he thought, a 'most fortunate thing that this woman is apprehended and stopped in her murderous career ... The dire atrocities she would have occasioned would be the most dreadful that can possibly be conceived.'

Tarenorerer was isolated because Robinson feared she would incite revolt. In February 1831 he noted in his diary that in his opinion, 'nearly all the mischief perpetrated upon the different settlements' had been traced to Tarenorerer's warriors. He believed that she was responsible for killing other Aborigines. Moved with the others to Gun Carriage (Vansittart) Island, Tarenorerer became ill and died of influenza on 5 June 1831. She had fought on behalf of her people with bravery and tenacity in a war for which there are no memorials.

N. J. B. Plomley, *Friendly Mission* (Hob, 1966); D. Lowe, *Forgotten Rebels* (Melb, 1994); H. Felton, *Adapting & Resisting*, book 6 of *Living With the Land* (Hob, 1991); L. Ryan, *The Aboriginal Tasmanians* (Syd, 1996); Tas Hist Research Assn, *Papers and Procs*, 5, no 4, 1957, p 73, and 23, no 2, June 1976, p 26.

VICKI MAIKUTENA MATSON-GREEN

TEICHELMANN, CHRISTIAN GOTTLIEB (1807-1888), and SCHÜRMANN, CLAMOR WILHELM (1815-1893), were Lutheran missionaries and pastors. Teichelmann was born on 15 December 1807 at Dahme, in the German kingdom of Saxony, one of eight children of Friedrich August Teichelmann, master cloth-maker, and his wife Johanna Rosina, née Böttcher. After attending school until the age of 14, he was apprenticed to a carpenter then spent four years travelling as a carpenter's assistant in Saxony and Prussia.

In 1829 Teichelmann travelled to Berlin and took private tuition in algebra, arithmetic and geometry as preparation for acceptance into the Royal Building Trades School, which he attended in 1830-31. During these years he came into contact with pupils from Jaenicke's Missionsschule, and his early wish for missionary service was reawakened. He entered the school in September 1831.

Schürmann had been born on 7 June 1815 in Schledehausen, near Osnabrück, Hanover, youngest son of Johann Adam Schürmann and his wife Maria Elisabeth, née Ebcker. His father died when Clamor Wilhelm was aged 1 and his mother when he was 11. After his elementary education he applied to enter Jaenicke's Missionsschule, Berlin, to follow his brother Johann Adam, later a missionary at Benares, India, and was accepted on 23 July 1832.

The students were taught Latin, English, Greek and Hebrew as well as foreign geography, world history, church history and theology. A call was received from the Society for the Propagation of the Gospel in Foreign Parts for missionaries to serve in India. Both declined, however, due to the requirement that they sign the Thirty-Nine Articles of the Church of England and be ordained in that denomination. Meanwhile, the Evangelical Lutheran Mission Society of Dresden had been approached by Pastor A. L. C. Kavel and George Fife Angas [qq.v.2,1] about missionaries for South Australia. On 1 September 1836 Teichelmann and Schürmann entered the society's seminary, where they received additional tuition, including Hebrew and Greek, and were ordained as Lutheran pastors on 4 February 1838. They reached Adelaide on 12 October in the *Pestonjee Bomanjee*, which also carried Governor Gawler [q.v.1].

With little financial support, the two missionaries soon established the first school for Aborigines in South Australia, initially in the open air, then at Piltawodli (possum house) near Adelaide gaol. Teichelmann and Schürmann published *Outlines of a Grammar: Vocabulary and Phraseology of the Aboriginal Language of South Australia, Spoken by the Natives in and for Some Distance around Adelaide* (1840), including some 2000 words of what is now known as the Kaurna language. Their work became an invaluable resource for modern Kaurna language reclamation.

Perhaps a more rigid and intractable personality than his younger colleague, Teichelmann was, like him, a gifted and diligent student of indigenous language who forthrightly voiced the sufferings of the Aboriginal people of Adelaide. Gawler paid tribute to this work and respected the two as 'serious, intelligent, persevering Christian men'. In 1840, with the arrival of two further missionaries from Dresden, Teichelmann was appointed government interpreter, while Samuel Klose took over the running of the school (which closed in 1845). Teichelmann published *Aboriginals of South Australia: Illustrative and Explanatory Note of the Manners, Customs, Habits and Superstitions of the Natives of South Australia* in 1841. In November 1842 he moved to Happy Valley and attempted to establish a mission farm, Ebenezer, with the aim of inducing indigenous people to settle and work the land but, lacking funding, the venture failed.

On Christmas Day 1843 in Adelaide Teichelmann married with Church of Scotland forms 21-year-old Margaret Nicholson. They had fourteen children. In 1846 the family moved back to Adelaide and next year to a farm near Morphett Vale. To supplement his income, Teichelmann commuted fortnightly to Adelaide as guest pastor to the new Lutheran congregation, Old Trinity. In 1856 he accepted a call to the Lutheran congregation of Salem, and founded congregations at Callington and Monarto. Here he revisited his early language work and compiled a manuscript of his Kaurna vocabulary and grammatical notes

(1857), which he sent to Sir George Grey [q.v.1] in South Africa.

Teichelmann remained active in church life, contributing to the discussion on the resumption of mission work at Lake Killalpaninna in 1866. He retired to farm at Haywood Park, Stansbury, Yorke Peninsula, where he died on 31 May 1888. His wife, six sons and four daughters survived him.

In September 1840 Schürmann had taken up a government position as deputy-protector of Aborigines at Port Lincoln. As interpreter he often accompanied police investigations and travelled to Adelaide for court proceedings, but had difficulty harmonizing this work with his missionary activities. By the end of that year he had collected 500 words of the Parnkalla (Banggarla) language. He repeatedly requested government support for an agricultural settlement and school for the Aboriginal population away from the influence of European settlers. In 1843 he was recalled to Adelaide as court interpreter and next year published a dictionary of 2000 entries, *A Vocabulary of the Parnkalla Language, Spoken by the Natives Inhabiting the Western Shores of Spencer's Gulf*. Back at Port Lincoln in 1844, Schürmann wrote:

It is bad enough that a great part of the colonists are inimical to the natives; it is worse that the law, as it stands at present, does not extend its protection to them, but it is too bad when the press lends its influence to their destruction.

He published *The Aboriginal Tribes of Port Lincoln* in 1846.

Next year Schürmann moved to work with the Dresden missionary H. A. E. Meyer at Encounter Bay. He purchased land to farm and, on 11 February 1847, in the schoolhouse there married with Lutheran rites Wilhelmine Charlotte Maschmedt, like him from Osnabrück. They had nine children. After the Encounter Bay mission attempt was abandoned, Schürmann returned to Port Lincoln in December 1848 as Aboriginal interpreter and in 1850 opened a school, with instruction in the Parnkalla language, at nearby Wallala. In 1852 funding was withdrawn and pupils were transferred to the Native Training Institution at Poonindie, established by Archdeacon Mathew Hale [q.v.4] with a similar vision for educating and christianizing the Aboriginal community, but with no learning or teaching in indigenous languages.

Rejecting again the offer of Church of England ordination, in 1853 Schürmann followed a call to Portland, Victoria, to minister to a German congregation. He also travelled extensively throughout the Wimmera, serving German settlers. From 1883 he was editor of the *Kirchenbote* and in 1885 became president of the Victorian district of the Evangelical Lutheran Synod of Australia.

Schürmann was small in stature with a ruddy complexion and a genial disposition. He was a gifted linguist and a compassionate and dedicated missionary, and his documentation of the indigenous languages in the Adelaide and Port Lincoln areas was an enduring legacy. Predeceased by his wife in 1891, Schürmann died on 3 March 1893 while attending synod at Bethany, South Australia; he was buried in West Terrace cemetery, Adelaide, and later reinterred in South Hamilton cemetery. Four sons survived him.

Fr Hesekiel (ed), *Darstellung der Ordinationsfeier von zwei nach Sudaustralien Bestimmten Missionaren in der St. Bartholomaikirche zu Altenburg am 5. Sonntage nach Epiphanias 1838* (Altenburg, 1838); T. Hebart, *Die Vereinigte Evangelisch-Lutherische Kirche in Australien* (Adel, 1938); J. F. O'Donnell, *The Teichelmann Family in Australia* (Adel, 1974); A. Brauer, *Under the Southern Cross* (Adel, 1985); E. A. Schurmann, *I'd Rather Dig Potatoes* (Adel, 1987); J. Harris, *One Blood* (Syd, 1994); R. Amery, *Warrabarna Kaurna!* (Lisse, Netherlands, 2000); C. Rathjen, 'A Difficult and Boring Task', *Jnl of Friends of Lutheran Archives*, no 8, 1998, p 59; *Observer* (Adel), 9 June 1888, p 1087, 11 Mar 1893, p 30; Teichelmann and Schürmann files (Lutheran archives, Adel).   HEIDI KNEEBONE

TEMPLE POOLE, DAISY; *see* ROSSI

TENNYSON, AUDREY GEORGIANA FLORENCE (1854-1916), letter-writer, hospital founder and vice-regal wife, was born on 19 August 1854 at Tillington, Sussex, England, fourth child and only daughter of Charles John Boyle, clerk of the Legislative Council in the Cape Colony, and his wife Zacyntha Antonia Lorenzina, née Moore. Both parents were scions of the Irish Protestant ascendancy. Audrey was brought up in Cape Town and from 1856 to 1860 in Mauritius, where her father was director of the railway department, before her mother took the children back to Britain for better schooling. In 1868-82 Audrey nursed her invalid father. Reading to him, she became knowledgeable about literature and current affairs. Dark-haired and blue-eyed, she had 'the loveliest smile' and 'a look of great distinction'. On 25 June 1884 in King Henry VII's chapel at Westminster Abbey, London, she married Hallam Tennyson [q.v.12], son of the poet laureate Alfred, first Baron Tennyson.

Hallam succeeded to the peerage in 1892. With happy recollections of colonial life, Audrey encouraged him to accept when he was offered the governorship of South Australia. She and their three sons accompanied him to Adelaide in April 1899. Lady Tennyson wrote weekly to her possessive and dominating 'Darling own Mother', and 262 of her letters, some more than sixty foolscap pages long, are now in the National Library of Australia, Canberra. They provide an important and fascinating record of the family's experiences and activities, and perceptive accounts of people from all walks of life. A substantial selection, edited by Dame Alexandra Hasluck, was published as *Audrey Tennyson's Vice-Regal Days* (Canberra, 1978).

Loving Australia, Lady Tennyson was much more than an observer. Though often plagued by headaches, she looked for 'the bright side of things' and was unremitting in carrying out, with style, the public duties expected of a governor's wife. She encouraged charity workers and other volunteers striving to enhance the quality of life. Appalled to find that female outworkers in the garment industry were being paid $1\frac{1}{2}$d. to make shirts, which department stores sold for twenty times that amount, she urged the premiers Charles Kingston and (Sir) Frederick Holder [qq.v.9] to greater zeal in establishing tribunals to improve sempstresses' pay and conditions, and supported Agnes Milne [q.v.], the factory inspector battling sweatshop owners.

Tennyson's outstanding contribution was to found South Australia's first maternity hospital. Concerned especially about the plight of women in the outback, she wanted them to have, after delivery, the benefit of 'rest & quiet & the best trained nursing & food' until they were fit to cope at home without female or professional assistance. Many city women warmed to the plan, but Holder refused any government money. Tennyson secured the gift of an acre (0.4 ha) at suburban Rose Park from the South Australian Co. and a cheque for £500 from Robert Barr Smith [q.v.6] to launch a public appeal in December 1900.

Most of the medical profession opposed her project. For attending home births, doctors billed even the poor several guineas. Tennyson—annoyed to find that the wealthiest practitioners were so 'furious at the idea of losing a few fees' that they remained indifferent to the needs of countrywomen and wrote to newspapers criticizing her scheme—pressed on. She oversaw the design and construction of the building down to the last detail. Her supporters wanted the hospital named in her honour. She insisted on its being a memorial to Queen Victoria. The Queen's Home (later the Queen Victoria Maternity Hospital) was opened in May 1902.

In July that year, when Lord Hopetoun's [q.v.9] resignation made Hallam the administrator of the government of the Commonwealth, the Tennysons left to occupy the governor-general's residences in Melbourne and Sydney. Lady Tennyson strove not to do anything to clash with or win popularity from the State governors' wives. She adhered to this when her husband accepted appointment as governor-general, for a year from January 1903, remained busy, and revisited Adelaide to promote her hospital's development. To her mother's relief, Lady Tennyson and her boys left Australia in mid-December 1903.

Back in England she and Hallam lived at Farringford, Freshwater, Isle of Wight. After her youngest son Harold was killed in action in World War I, Lady Tennyson threw herself into work as commandant of a Red Cross hospital, which she had established in 1914 at Freshwater. She died of pneumonia on 7 December 1916 at her home and was buried at Freshwater. Her husband and two sons survived her. A portrait (1899) by Briton Rivière is in the National Library of Australia. After the Queen Victoria Hospital was amalgamated with the Children's Hospital at North Adelaide in 1995, Tennyson's building and extensions were sold; escaping conversion to an abortion clinic, they have been remodelled as luxury apartments.

A. Thwaites, *Emily Tennyson* (Lond, 1996); P. A. Howell, *South Australia and Federation* (Adel, 2002); *Quadrant*, Oct 1978, p 50; Tennyson papers (NL); Obituaries box (Tennyson Research Centre, Lincolnshire County Council, Eng).

P. A. HOWELL

TEPPER, JOHANN GOTTLIEB OTTO (1841-1923), botanist, schoolteacher and entomologist, was born on 19 April 1841 at Neutomischel (Nowy Tomysl), Posen, Prussia (Poznan, Poland), one of eight children of Joh Christoph Tepper, baker and later farmer, and his wife Johanna Wilhelmina, née Protsch. The family migrated for religious reasons, reaching Port Adelaide in the *Gellert* in December 1847. Schooled at Hoffnungsthal, Otto left at 14 to farm in nearby Lyndoch valley and spent four years as a shearer in the Mount Bryan district. He was described as a storeman when he was naturalized on 5 April 1865 at Tanunda.

After completing examinations to become a public school teacher, Tepper was appointed to New Mecklenburg (Gomersal) in the Barossa Valley in December 1867. On 22 April that year at Redbank he had married Jane Brock with Presbyterian forms. They were divorced in 1874. He taught at Two Wells (1869), Monarto (1872-73), Nuriootpa (1873-78), Ardrossan (1878-81) and Clarendon (1881-83). Between 1873 and 1883 he wrote a series of natural history papers about Nuriootpa, 'Notable Native Plants about Ardrossan' and '*Die flora von Clarendon*',

the latter for a German scientific magazine, *Botanisches Centralblatt*.

In March 1883 Tepper was appointed natural history collector at the South Australian Museum; in 1888 he was promoted to entomologist, numismatist and librarian there. Many of his entomological papers were later to appear in the *Garden and Field* and in the *Transactions of the Royal Society of South Australia*, which society he joined in 1878; he was an honorary fellow from 1912, and was sometime chairman of its field naturalists' section. In 1879 he became a fellow of the Linnean Society of London and a life member of the Society of Science Letters and Art (London), receiving their medal in 1898.

A capable artist, Tepper sketched South Australian countryside scenes and the orchids of the colony. With his friend Ralph Tate [q.v.6] he was partly responsible for the reservation of Flinders Chase on Kangaroo Island as a national park. In 1880 he suggested that native plants 'deserve a place in our gardens and parks'. Tepper's efforts to secure a plot of trees, marking the site of a settlement near Lyndoch in 1839, led to its later acquisition by the District Council of Barossa. He was an associate, later committee member, of the Society for the Protection of Birds (Adelaide branch), formed in 1894, and a member of the South Australian Gardeners' Society for over thirty years. Short, with a full beard, he was described as 'a very kindly gentleman with a trusting nature'. H. M. Hale wrote that Tepper was a heavy pipe smoker, his room at the museum redolent of 'a not unpleasant mixture of naphthalene and tobacco'. An ardent collector of books, papers, stamps and coins, he was a prolific contributor to magazines, journals and newspapers.

Tepper retired from the museum in 1911. While reclining in his favourite Morris chair, he died on 16 February 1923 at Norwood. His son and two daughters survived him, inheriting an estate sworn for probate at £2165. Several plants and fungi have been named after him, including *Dodonaea tepperi, Helichrysum tepperi* and *Stylidium tepperianum* (endemic to Kangaroo Island). He described 164 insect species and some were named after him. Tepper's sketchbook was donated by his grandson to the South Australian Museum; the State Library of South Australia and the Field Naturalists' Society hold copies of his orchid drawings.

D. N. Kraehenbuehl, 'The Life and Works of J. G. O. Tepper, F.L.S., and his Association with the Field Naturalists' Section of the Royal Society of South Australia', *SA Naturalist*, 44, no 2, Dec 1969, p 23; *Garden and Field*, Sept 1907, p 11; *Adel Chronicle*, 24 Feb 1923, p 47; Tepper papers (SLSA); family information.

DARRELL N. KRAEHENBUEHL

THOMAS, MARY (1787-1875), diarist and poet, was born on 30 August 1787 at Southampton, England, daughter of George Harris, innkeeper and merchant, and his wife Mary, née Batchelor. Young Mary married Robert Thomas [q.v.6], law stationer, on 8 January 1818 at Holy Rood Church, Southampton. Of their six children, one died young. Published in London in 1831, Mary's *Serious Poems* were written 'with the sole view to the instruction and amusement of my own family'. With four of their children—Frances, William Kyffin [q.v.6], Mary and Helen—she embarked with her husband for South Australia in the *Africaine*, arriving at Holdfast Bay in November 1836. She was reunited there with her eldest son Robert George, an apprentice in Colonel Light's [q.v.2] survey team. Mary was present when the inauguration of the first Council of Government was proclaimed on 28 December and at the printing, in a reed hut, of the proclamation document by her husband Robert, the government printer.

He and George Stevenson [q.v.2] established R. Thomas & Co. to publish the *South Australian Gazette and Colonial Register.* The first issue appeared in London in June 1836 and the first Adelaide edition in June 1837. Mary was considered 'to have taken so active and useful a part in the journalistic department of the colony's first newspaper that she might have been classed as one of the firm'. She wrote 'many meritorious contributions' to the press in the colony's foundation years. Her involvement ceased when the paper, due to insolvency, passed to James Allen during the depression of 1842. Later, her son William regained part proprietorship.

Mary Thomas's letters between 1855 and 1860 to her daughter Helen Mantegani on the Victorian goldfields gave an intimate and detailed account of colonial domestic life. For thirty years, until 1872, Mary managed her family's thirteen properties—houses, cottages and a leased hotel. She was generous and compassionate, her family's mainstay both emotionally in times of stress and bereavement and financially in times of economic difficulty. As well, she provided succour to others in need. Her husband and her eldest daughter Frances (1818-1855), wife of J. M. Skipper [q.v.6], predeceased her. Mary Thomas died on 10 February 1875, at her home, Rantregynwyn Cottage, Adelaide. Two sons and two daughters survived her.

In 1867 she had transcribed her diary of the voyage out and the first weeks of settlement, expanding these with reminiscences. Thirteen of her letters 'home', written between 1838 and 1842, were ultimately returned to Adelaide. Evan Kyffin Thomas, a proprietor of the *Register*, edited the first version of *The Diary and Letters of Mary Thomas* in 1915 and a second in 1925. They provided a lively and valuable record of the first six years of settlement. Descendants hold a watercolour copy of a portrait (c.1834) of her by her daughter and a manuscript book of other poems, also written before emigration. None of Mary's verses written in the colony has survived.

SA Register, 6 Aug 1842, p 2, 13 Feb 1875, p 5; Index of insolvencies, 63/1842 (srsa); Mantegani and Thomas family papers (slsa); information from Mrs J. K. Willington, St Georges, Adel.

BETH DUNCAN

THOMPSON, JOSEPH (c.1784-1839), mariner, pearler and pastoralist, was born probably in England. By 1809 he was sealing in the Auckland Islands, south of New Zealand, in the *Perseverance*. He participated in the attack on Te Pahi's island, Bay of Islands, on 26 March 1810, when whaling crews revenged the Maori leader's alleged part in killing the crew of the *Boyd* in Whangaroa harbour. Thompson was on board *Perseverance* when Macquarie Island was discovered in July that year, and by August 1812 was chief officer.

From 1811 he worked for William and Robert Campbell [qq.v.1] and others on Pacific voyages for seals, whales, pearls, sandalwood, arrowroot, molasses and bêche-de-mer. On 13 January 1812 in St Matthew's Church of England, Windsor, Thompson married Isabella Wood. He was master of the *Trial* in 1814-16. In charge of sealers at Macquarie Island, he recorded in a journal the effects of earthquakes between October 1815 and April 1816. From late 1816 to 1822 he commanded the *Active* for the Church Missionary Society. Although he chiefly supplied missionaries' needs in New Zealand and the Pacific, the society was not averse to trade, and Thompson ranged widely, his cargo including pine spars, timber planks, salt pork and coconut oil from Tahiti.

About July 1822 he took over the *Midas*. Thompson habitually included Tahitians and Maoris among his crew. With Peter Dillon, Richard Siddins [qq.v.1,2] and others, he formed the Sydney Bethel Union to provide regular church services for sailors in port, and in 1823 made the *Midas* available for divine worship. In 1827 he sat on a committee to examine the *Fame* as a possible permanent chapel. He was also involved in the Benevolent Society of New South Wales.

In 1824, with the majority shareholder in the *Midas* Thomas Icely [q.v.2], Thompson sailed for London, where they contacted investors for a proposed Pacific Pearl Fishery Co., which was floated in April 1825. The enterprise advertised its dependence on 'the application of science' by using modern equipment, including a diving bell, and the leadership of Thompson, 'an experienced and able person' with extensive local knowledge. The naturalist Samuel Stutchbury [q.v.6] documented the expedition around the world. Leaving Gravesend in August 1825 in two ships, it made important scientific observations and obtained pearls from Hao Atoll in the Tuamotus. One vessel, the *Sir George Osborne*, completed the voyage at Dartmouth in May 1827.

Thompson, however, had not gone back to London but sailed on the second ship, the *Rolla*, from Tahiti directly to New South Wales. Reaching Sydney on 21 February 1827 he quit seafaring. His wife died next year, leaving him to care for two daughters and three sons, two of whom attended Captain John Beveridge's Mercantile and Naval Academy. In 1829-30 Thompson imported goods and traded from his home, particularly offering charts of the Pacific region. He was elected to the committee of the Church Missionary Society in 1829 and in March 1831 supported the subscription to commemorate Laurence Halloran [q.v.1]. On 14 June 1831 in St Phillip's Church of England he married Catharine Ann Dean, a widow, whose eleven children had all died. In 1833 he established Biggan station in the Monaro district. Next year the Thompsons moved to Liverpool. About 1837 he began to suffer mental illness, disturbing the services at St Luke's Church. Rev. Richard Taylor recorded that Thompson 'had in early life I fear been a dishonourable character ... his children are undutiful and a constant anxiety ... and he ... always in a passion, swearing, drinking and keeping company with a bad woman'.

Thompson died after a long and painful illness on 24 September 1839 in his cottage and was buried at Christ Church St Laurence, Sydney. His son William leased Biggan in 1850.

S. Stutchbury, *Science in a Sea of Commerce* (Syd, 1996); *Syd Gazette*, 1 June 1816, p 2, 15 June 1816, p 2, 2 Jan 1819, p 2, 9 Jan 1819, p 2, 6 Feb 1819, p 4, 19 June 1823, p 2, 15 July 1824, p 2, 8 Dec 1825, p 2, 24 Feb 1827, pp 2 & 3, 3 Oct 1839, p 3; *Times* (Lond), 31 Mar 1825, p 2; *Australian* (Syd), 29 Dec 1825, p 3, 13 Nov 1835, p 2, 19 June 1838, 'supp', p 2; Church Missionary Society archives, Lond; Cooper & Levey ledger book (Univ Syd Lib); Richard Taylor's journal (Alexander Turnbull Lib, Wellington, NZ); ML catalogue under J. Thompson (ML).

D. F. BRANAGAN

THORNE, SERENA; *see* LAKE

THWAITES, MINNIE; *see* KNORR, FRANCES

TIMBERY, EMMA (c.1842-1916), Aboriginal shellworker, was born at Liverpool, New South Wales, daughter of Hubert Walden, farmer, and his wife Betsy, an Aboriginal woman. Emma, a Dharawal speaker, was sometimes given her stepfather's surname, Lond or Lownds. On 31 May 1864 at Botany she married George ('Trimmer') Timbery (c.1839-1920), an Aboriginal fisherman, who had been born in the Illawarra. They had eleven children.

George fished regularly between Botany Bay and the Illawarra area. By 1882 the Timberys lived at La Perouse, where Aboriginal women earned extra income by gathering wildflowers and making shell baskets, for sale in Sydney and the suburbs. Emma was particularly accomplished at this craft. Shellwork had probably been introduced by missionaries who had spent time in the Pacific —it apparently had no basis in traditional Aboriginal art forms. In addition to their baskets, Aboriginal women at La Perouse became well known for shell-adorned, heart-shaped boxes, baby shoes and boomerangs. While the work was a social activity, carried out in the company of other women, each shellworker had an individual style. Emma regularly displayed and sold her handiwork at the Royal Easter Show in Sydney; in 1910 it was included in an exhibition of Australian manufactures in London. One Sydney newspaper reported that it was 'almost fought for'.

From her conversion in the early 1890s, Emma worked closely with missionaries at the La Perouse Aboriginal settlement, from whom she learned to read a little. In 1894 the La Perouse Aborigines' Christian Endeavour Society was formed, and Emma became its vice-president next year. Through their Christian work, she and the missionary Retta Dixon [q.v.15 Long] became 'friends and comrades'. When Dixon was installed as missionary at La Perouse in 1897, Emma, in front of a large crowd, promised Retta's father and friends to be a mother to her. The two women often travelled together, visiting other Aboriginal settlements along the south coast to 'spread the word'. Emma made a valued contribution to the early work of the La Perouse (United) Aborigines Mission.

A photograph of Emma taken in 1895 showed a small woman with a gentle yet determined gaze. That year the six acres (2.4 ha) occupied by the La Perouse Aboriginal settlement was gazetted as a reserve for its residents' exclusive use. As the community matriarch, Emma became popularly known as 'Queen', or 'Granny' Timbery (sometimes spelt Timbury). She died on 26 November 1916 at La Perouse, survived by her husband and by three sons and one daughter. Emma was buried in Botany cemetery, 'in the presence of a large company of mourners', with her funeral expenses paid for by a 'white friend', indicating her close association with missionaries and their supporters. A tribute in the *Australian Aborigines Advocate* noted that 'many wreaths and other floral tributes were sent along, and numerous letters of sympathy from white and dark friends', George Timbery died at Berry on 21 December 1920.

Emma's grandson Joseph (1912-1978) won repute as a boomerang maker, and demonstrated his throwing skill on the Eiffel Tower in Paris and for Queen Elizabeth II on her visit to Sydney in 1954. The family workshop became the Bidjigal Aboriginal Corporation, based at Huskisson, Jervis Bay. Three fig trees at La Perouse Aboriginal reserve were dedicated in 1986 to the memory of Emma Timbery. The tradition of shellworking continued to be practised by many of her female descendents, including her great-granddaughter Esme Russell, née Timbery.

E. J. Telfer, *Amongst Australian Aborigines* (Syd, 1939); *La Perouse: The Place, the People and the Sea* (Canb, 1987); J. Kerr (ed), *Heritage: The National Women's Art Book* (Syd, 1995), p 449; S. Kleinert and M. Neale (eds), *The Oxford Companion to Aboriginal Art and Culture* (Melb, 2000); *Austn Aborigines Advocate*, 28 Feb 1910, p 4, 30 Nov 1916, p 4; M. Nugent, Revisiting La Perouse (Ph.D. thesis, Univ of Technology, Syd), 2001); La Perouse Aboriginal Community oral history collection, MRS 278/1-9 (Powerhouse Museum, Syd); Timbery family papers (held by Mrs B. Beller, Matraville, Syd).

MARIA NUGENT

TJALKABOTA, MOSES (c.1869-1954), Aboriginal evangelist, was born at Laprapuntja, east of Hermannsburg, South Australia (Ntaria, Northern Territory), fourth of five children of Tjita and Aranaljika; he and his family were western Arrarnta (Arrernte) speakers. He was called Tjalkabota (lump of meat) by his father, and chose the name Mose (German for Moses) at his baptism at the Lutheran mission, Hermannsburg, on Christmas Day 1890, when his age was stated to be 12. His recollection of the Irpmankara massacre (about 1875), however, suggested that he was older. His childhood followed the traditional nomadic patterns of his people.

Moses, his parents and others in his group thought that white men were 'black men who had died, and then returned as spirits to the place where they had died long ago'. When the missionaries made overtures for the children to go to school, Moses's parents at first hid him but relented, and he began attending classes. The children were taught the Christian faith through Bible stories, as well as reading, writing and arithmetic. Moses also worked in the mission garden and as a shepherd. About 1891 his father and mother urged him to leave Hermannsburg:

Boy, if you continue here, your head will implode, and you will dry up. Then the wind will blow you away to the sand hills like a dried-up cicada, and we will be unable to find you.

But when his parents returned to Laprapuntja, Moses stayed working at the mission, where in 1903 he married Sofia Ingkamala, an Arrarnta-speaking woman. Having suffered a heat stroke that affected his eyesight, by 1905 he became blind and began to assist with the formal instruction of people desiring to be baptized.

Moses worked as a catechist and lay preacher at Hermannsburg until, on a visit to Horseshoe Bend, he arrived at Henbury station, where he was persuaded to stay and teach the word of God. So began his immensely influential Gospel ministry, in the course of which he visited Aborigines living at Deep Well, Alice Well, Horseshoe Bend, Idracowra, Jay Creek, Alice Springs, Undoolya, Arltunga and other places. He travelled by donkey, camel, buggy, on foot and occasionally on the back of a truck.

Mostly, Moses was welcomed. In a few places, however, his message that the men should put their trust in Jesus and give up their tjurunga (sacred objects) met with polite rejection. He recorded one such dialogue with a man called Njetjaka:

I am the tjurunga called Ilbangura and I have the songs and decorations. Look, at the un-created home of the kangaroo at Krenka, we have many more tjurunga, and more powerful ceremonies. I said, 'You men are unbelievers'. They said, 'We have another one that we believe in. You at Ntaria believe in one God, but we have another one'.

Moses used the methodology by which novices were instructed about their tjurunga, telling the story with Bible pictures, and teaching hymns and the Commandments, and prayers by rote. He had a prodigious memory and could recite whole chapters of the Bible.

'Blind Moses' assisted the missionary C. F. T. Strehlow [q.v.12] with his translation of the New Testament into Western Arrarnta and later the anthropologist T. G. H. Strehlow [q.v.16]. In his last ten years Moses preached and taught children at Jay Creek, near Alice Springs, and dictated a valuable account of his life. Predeceased by his five children, Moses died on 6 July 1954 at Hermannsburg and was buried there with Lutheran rites. His wife and three grandchildren survived him.

B. Dickey (ed), *The Australian Dictionary of Evangelical Biography* (Syd, 1994), p 386; P. G. E.

Albrecht, *From Mission to Church* (Adel, 2002), pp 237-300; *Lutheran Herald*, 16 Feb 1925, p 52, 24 July 1954, p 215.   PAUL ALBRECHT

TONGA, ANTONIUS TUI (c.1850-1905), Pacific Islander community leader and farmer, was born probably on the island of Bau (Mbau), Fiji. By about 1876 he had arrived at Mackay, the main sugar-growing area in Queensland. In 1880, although described as under indentures, he was an overseer on Pleystowe plantation. On 14 June that year in Holy Trinity Church of England, Mackay, as 'Tui Thacambau' he married Lelia, a servant, from Myes (Emae) Island in the New Hebrides (Vanuatu). He claimed that his parents were Tui Thacambau (Cakobau), King of Fiji, and his wife Temonia, who may have been one of the two wives Cakobau divorced in 1857.

Between 1880 and 1885 Tui Tonga acted as an *agent provocateur* and in 1890 as interpreter for the police, helping to obtain convictions of hoteliers and shopkeepers for selling alcohol and firearms to Islanders. On 16 November 1885, again at Holy Trinity Church, and again claiming to be the son of the King of Fiji, 'Tuie Tonga', a widower, married Fanny from Aoba (Vanuatu). He gave his occupation as 'warder', and from that year he worked in the dispensary of the government hospital for Islanders.

By 1892 Tui Tonga was living with Lilian, a woman from Malaita, Solomon Islands, and their son. On 21 January that year he shot Lily and attempted to kill himself. Found guilty of murder, on 25 May he was condemned to death. Over two hundred of Mackay's leading citizens petitioned the governor for leniency, claiming that he had been temporarily insane through jealousy at the time of the murder. The presiding judge noted that 'the Prisoner was a highly educated man speaking several European languages' and that if he had been white the jury would probably have found him not guilty. On 10 June the sentence was commuted to fifteen years penal servitude. Tui Tonga was discharged from St Helena prison, Brisbane, on 18 June 1897, with the remainder of his sentence remitted conditionally. Records described him then as a 47-year-old Catholic, with black hair and black eyes and with two stars tattooed on his right shoulder and a fern leaf, tree and fish on his right arm; he was 5 ft 8 ins (173 cm) tall and weighed 10 st. 4 lb. (65 kg)

Tui Tonga returned to Mackay, where he operated a boarding house for Islanders and a farm. On 22 February 1901 at St Joseph's Catholic Church, Townsville, now styling himself Antonius Tuietonga, he married Agnes Davison Brown, a Scottish-born domestic ser-

vant, stating that he had was the son of Daniel Tuietonga, labourer, and his wife Mary, née Mitchell. In November that year he founded at Mackay the Pacific Islanders' Association, to fight against the mass deportation ordered by the Australian government's Pacific Island Labourers Act (1901). The campaign spread in the southern Queensland and northern New South Wales sugar districts and helped to lead to a royal commission into the use of imported labour in the sugar industry, which eventually caused the Commonwealth government to ease its policy to deport all Islanders.

Tui Tonga died of heart disease on 30 December 1905 at his Mackay farm and was buried with Catholic rites in the local cemetery. His 5-year-old daughter, and a son by an earlier marriage, survived him.

C. Moore, *Kanaka: A History of Melanesian Mackay* (Port Moresby, PNG, 1985) and '"Goodbye, Queensland, Good-bye, White Australia; Goodbye Christians": Australia's South Sea Islander Community Deportation, 1901-1908', *New Federalist*, no 4, Dec 2000, p 22; D. Routledge, *Matanitu* (Suva, Fiji, 1985); *Jnl of Pacific History*, 11, pts 1-2, 1976, p 28; *Mackay Mercury*, 27 Mar 1880, 22 May 1880, 21 May 1884, 4 June 1884, 14 June 1884, 4 Apr 1885, 24 Apr 1890, 23 Jan 1892, 4 Feb 1892, 7 June 1892, 16 Nov 1901, 18 Jan 1906; Mackay Deposition Books, A/38111-2, May 1884-Apr 1885 *and* PRI 2/7 p 369 *and* EXE 6 1892/43 *and* A/18577 (QSA); information from Drs A. Thornley, Sydney, M. Tuimaleali'ifano, Suva, Fiji, and J. Spurway, Christchurch, New Zealand, and Rev T. Baleiwaqa, Canb.
                                                    CLIVE R. MOORE

TOODWICK; *see* BROUGHTON

TORRES, FULGENTIUS (1861-1914), Benedictine abbot, was born on 24 June 1861 at Ibiza, Balearic Islands, Spain, and named Antonio, son of Don Juan Torres y Torres and his wife Dona Manuela Mayans, of Formentera. Educated at the University of Barcelona (B.A., 1877; B.Sc., 1880) and the ecclesiastical seminary, Vich, he entered the Benedictine monastery of Montserrat in 1885 and took the name Fulgentius; he made his first vows on 21 June 1886, was ordained priest on 5 June 1887 and made his solemn profession on 13 July 1889. Torres helped to revitalize Montserrat as a training centre for overseas missions, opening a mission at Mindanao in the Philippine Islands in 1895. In 1898 he became rector of the Church of Montserrat, Naples, Italy, where he met Rosendo Salvado [q.v.2], who chose him to be his successor as abbot of New Norcia, Western Australia.

Reaching Fremantle in the *Weimar* on 9 April 1901 with eleven recruits, Torres was welcomed by, among others, Paul Piramino, an Aboriginal organist and conductor of a brass sextet. Erudite, acute and practical, Torres brought a creative, reforming energy to the colonial settlement and Aboriginal mission, transforming it into a monastic township with a distinctly European architectural heritage. He was confirmed as abbot on 26 December 1902 and was naturalized in May 1904.

Responding to the diocesan needs of Bishop Gibney [q.v.8] of Perth, Torres also ministered to the developing wheat-belt east to Southern Cross and north to the diocese of Geraldton. At New Norcia Torres provided boarding schools for the children of farming families, designed new accommodation for the Aboriginal boarders, greatly expanded the monastery and added a campanile to the abbey church. After a personal reconnaissance, he established the Pago Mission (1908) on Napier Broome Bay, the forerunner of the Drysdale River Mission (Kalumburu).

In Rome in May 1910 Torres was consecrated administrator apostolic of Kimberley and titular bishop of Dorilea. Voyages to the north by Torres in 1906, 1908 and 1911 were feats of physical endurance. In 1908 the return journey alone took two months, with considerable privation. Initially the Kimberley Aborigines resisted the isolated missionaries and their lay employees, including other Aborigines. A major attack in September 1913 led the State government to direct that the Drysdale River mission be abandoned; Torres did not resile.

In the south, Torres recruited artisans, both lay and religious, for the decorative work that is a feature of the monastic township at New Norcia. In 1904 he commissioned Teresian Sisters from Spain for the Aboriginal Girls' Orphanage. He invited Sisters of St Joseph from Sydney to Southern Cross (1905) and then to run the secondary college of St Gertrude at New Norcia (1908); he also enlisted Marist Brothers for St Ildephonsus College (1913). In addition, he obtained Presentation Sisters from Geraldton for the Goomalling convent (1914) and clergy for diocesan duties. Stephen Moreno [q.v.15] was among monastic recruits.

Torres revised the monks' timetable, including meditation times. The ageing veterans from Salvado's time preferred the clatter of battered tinplates and pannikins in the refectory to the clink of porcelain tableware, embossed with the Benedictine motto 'PAX', as introduced by the new leader. Reputedly, (Sir) Walter Murdoch [q.v.10] delighted in visiting New Norcia and conversing with Torres, whose philosophical arguments, elegant posture and piercing eyes were 'enough to enkindle a dormant soul; but to me he was an electric shock'. Torres died of peritonitis on 5 October 1914 in hospital at Subiaco, Perth, and was buried at New Norcia. An edition of his translated *Diaries* (1901-14) was published in 1987. The Benedictine Monastery precinct is on the Register of the National Estate.

J. Flood, *New Norcia* (Lond, 1908); J. S. Battye, *The Cyclopedia of Western Australia*, 2 (Perth, 1913), p 948; A. Catalan, *Drysdale River Mission* (New Norcia, WA, 1935); E. Perez, *Kalumburu* (New Norcia, WA, 1958); D. F. Bourke, *The History of the Catholic Church in Western Australia* (Perth, 1979); S. Lennon, *The Story of New Norcia* (New Norcia, WA, 1979); New Norcia archives, WA.

CLEMENT MULCAHY

TOST, JANE CATHARINE (c.1817-1889), and ROHU, ADA JANE (1848-1928), taxidermists and shopkeepers, were mother and daughter. Jane and her brother (Edwin) Henry (1812-1878) were born probably in London, children of John Herbert Ward, bird breeder, and his wife Catherine, and both took up taxidermy. On 1 April 1839 at St Anne's Church, Westminster, Jane married Charles Gottleibe Tost, a Prussian-born pianoforte maker. They were to have six children. In the 1840s and 1850s Jane was employed at the British Museum, preparing specimens under John Gould's [q.v.1] direction, and may have also worked in Belgium.

Charles and Jane Tost and their children sailed from Liverpool in the *Indian Queen* and on 22 January 1856 reached Tasmania, where Jane took up a position stuffing and mounting specimens for the Royal Society of Tasmania at the Hobart Town Museum. They moved to Sydney in 1860, Jane offering her services as a naturalist from the family home in Bridge Street. In 1864 she became taxidermist at the Australian Museum, earning £10 a month, the same wage as her male counterparts: she was one of Australia's earliest female museum staff members. Her employment ended in 1869 when her husband, who also worked at the museum as a taxidermist and carpenter, clashed with the curator Gerard Krefft [q.v.5]. An inquiry found that Krefft, who was later dismissed, had attempted to frame Charles for theft by depositing museum property at the Tosts' home. According to family tradition, Charles returned to England.

The Tosts' third child Jane Catherine (known as Ada Jane) had been born on 16 March 1848 in London. After a career on the stage of the Queen Victoria Theatre in Sydney, on 8 October 1868 at Woolloomooloo she married with Wesleyan forms James Richardson Coates, a dealer in earthenware, glass and china. They had three children. In 1872 Ada's husband and brother were killed fighting a fire at the Prince of Wales Theatre.

With money from a benefit fund, Jane and Ada opened 'Tost & Coates Berlin Wool Depot and Taxidermists' at 60 William Street, catering to a growing middle-class taste for fancy work and stuffed animals in interior decoration, as well as to scientific collectors and museums. Following Ada's marriage on 12 September 1878 at St Peter's Church of England, Woolloomooloo, to Henry Stewart Boventure Rohu, a Scottish-born upholsterer and curio collector, the firm became Tost & Rohu. Ada and Henry had six children, and the shop supported a large extended family. The business grew, selling an eclectic mix of furs, stuffed animals, and Aboriginal and Islander artefacts.

Jane and Ada promoted their business by exhibiting examples of work at international exhibitions. In over forty years from 1860, together they won more than twenty medals. Their exhibits, ranging from a stuffed black swan to a wallaby fur muff, were prized not only for the skill displayed but also for the ingenious adaptation of the taxidermist's art to Australia's fauna. They were part of a larger group of women engaged in the taxidermy trade: in 1892 the New South Wales women's work committee for the World's Columbian Exposition, Chicago, 1893, claimed that 'a good deal of the bird and animal stuffing, done in Sydney, [was] performed by females'. Predeceased by her husband, Jane Tost died on 24 April 1889, and was buried in the Church of England section of Rookwood cemetery. Two sons and a daughter survived her. Ada carried on their remarkable shop, which in 1896 moved to larger premises at 10 Moore Street (Martin Place). An advertisement in the 1910s revealed an astonishing assemblage, much like that later described by the bookseller James Tyrrell [q.v.12]—'armour, spears, boomerangs, teapots, native dresses, ancient muskets, tiger skins, birds' feathers [and] stuffed animals'.

Predeceased by her husband, Ada Rohu died on 28 July 1928 at Newtown and was buried in Rookwood cemetery. Two sons and one daughter of her first marriage, and four daughters and a son of her second, survived her. Tyrrell purchased the business in the 1920s, delighting in the fact that it was known as 'the queerest shop in Sydney'. An exhibition about the work of Tost and Rohu was held at the Macleay [q.v.5] Museum, University of Sydney, in 1996. The one confirmed example of Jane Tost's work, a squirrel, is in the collection of the Australian Museum, Sydney.

J. R. Tyrrell, *Old Books, Old Friends, Old Sydney* (Syd, 1952); J. Kerr (ed), *Heritage: The National Women's Art Book* (Syd, 1996), pp 183 & 464; M. Sear, '"Curious and Peculiar"? Women Taxidermists in Colonial Australia', J. Kerr and J. Holder (eds), *Past Present* (Syd, 1999), *and* Unworded Proclamations: Exhibitions of Women's Work in Colonial Australia (Ph.D. thesis, Univ Syd, 2000);

Tost and Coates Benefit papers (ML); Aust Museum Archives, Syd; Royal Soc of Tas Archives, Hobart.

MARTHA SEAR

TRIPP, EDWARD CLAVELL (1900-1979), political organizer, was born on 25 September 1900 at Acton, London, son of Clavell John Francis Tripp (d.1908), a cigar merchant who was involved in the Liberal movement, and his wife Violet Mary, née Vinall. Ted was placed in a boarding-school and took the University of Cambridge junior entrance examinations, but his mother arranged an engineering apprenticeship for him. During World War I he worked in the locomotive shop of the Metropolitan Railways in London and was radicalized by the Russian Revolution in 1917. He later claimed that his desire to read Marx's *Das Kapital* was thwarted only by his inability to afford its purchase price.

About 1924 Tripp came to Western Australia, then moved to Townsville, Queensland, where he worked as a fitter in the government railways and joined the militant Australian Railways Union and the State branch of the Communist Party of Australia. He attended the 1927 party conference, and in May 1929 stood for the Legislative Assembly seat of Mundingburra as an Independent (Communist) candidate. Later that year, after visiting Britain and Germany, he travelled to Moscow, where under his party pseudonym 'Clayton' he was a student at the International Lenin School. His experience predisposed him to Trotskyism, although student sympathizers of Bukharin at the university were already disappearing and Trotsky was *persona non grata*. He was back in Australia by August 1930.

In January next year Tripp became the first C.P.A. candidate for the House of Representatives when he contested a by-election for the seat of Parkes, New South Wales; in December 1931 he stood for Darling. Appointed full-time national organizer of the Friends of the Soviet Union late in 1930, he lectured widely and set up successful branches in several States. In June 1932 he stood for the seat of King in the Legislative Assembly. He was, however, already out of favour with the party leadership and in July next year was removed from his F.O.S.U. post. In June 1934, described as 'a Right opportunist', he was expelled from the party. Next month he joined the Sydney Trotskyists—the Balmain branch of the Workers' Party of Australia.

Tripp's conversion to Trotskyism was at first strategic, but soon became more theoretical. Subjected to C.P.A. harassment while working at the ammunition factory, he became the Workers' Party secretary in 1935, edited the journal, the *Militant*, and spoke regularly in the Domain. In 1937, falling out with the local Trotskyist leadership, he led a rival group, the League for Revolutionary Democracy (Independent Communist League), and edited the journal *Proletarian Review*.

In 1938 Tripp moved to Melbourne, married Ruby May Bullock, a Queensland-born waitress, on 30 July at Erskine Presbyterian Church, Carlton, and ceased political organizing. He worked as a fitter at the Footscray munitions factory until 1965 and was a militant shop steward in the Federated Ironworkers' Association. In 1945 he was appointed tutor at the Victorian Labor College, teaching Marxism to trade unionists at the Trades Hall, and about 1956 succeeded May Brodney [q.v.13] as the college's secretary, retaining the position until his death. A small man, large headed, retaining traces of an English accent, he possessed considerable gravity. In 1978, in a final gesture of solidarity with the Trotskyist movement, he joined the Socialist Workers' Party. Tripp died on 21 September 1979 at Footscray and was cremated. His wife and their daughter survived him.

S. Macintyre, *The Reds* (Syd, 1998); H. Greenland, *Red Hot* (Syd, 1998); *Labor College Review* (Melb), vol 10, no 10, Nov 1979, p 10, vol 10, no 11, Feb 1980, p 5; P. Beilharz, 'Trotskyism in Australia—Notes from a Talk with Ted Tripp', *Labour History*, no 62, May 1992, p 133; *Workers Weekly* (Syd), 28 Nov 1930, p 4, 30 Jan 1931, p 6, 14 Aug 1931, p 2, 13 July 1932, p 4; *SMH*, 26 Oct 1932, p 11; *Militant* (Syd), no 10, July 1934, pp 1 & 6, 10 Jan 1938, p 3; *Direct Action*, 26 Oct 1978, p 8, 30 Nov 1978, p 10; *A'sian Spartacist*, no 60, Dec 1978, p 2; interview with E. Tripp, 1961, N57/109 (Noel Butlin Archives, ANU); A6119, item 3529 (NAA); Tripp collection (Univ Melb Archives).   PETER BEILHARZ

TROUETTE, JEAN-PIERRE (c.1833-1885), vigneron, was born at Estampes, Gers, south-western France, son of Pierre Trouette, farmer, and his wife Marie Jeanne, née Sorbet. As a young man, Jean-Pierre went to Montevideo, probably to avoid army service. After three years in Uruguay he travelled to Adelaide in 1853 and, while working in the mines at Burra, heard of the gold discoveries in Victoria.

At Daylesford he met Ann Marie Blampied (c.1825-1905) and her brother Emile (c.1837-1914) from Meurthe-et-Moselle, Lorraine, north-eastern France, who had reached Melbourne in 1853. Jean-Pierre married Anne on 9 April 1856 at St Monica's Chapel, Heidelberg, with Catholic rites. In 1858 the Trouettes and Emile Blampied took over a vegetable garden on Concongella Creek, Great Western, and purchased twenty-seven acres (10.9 ha) freehold about 1862, the year Trouette was naturalized. Sludge and gravel were cleared

and fruit and vegetables sold to miners at Lamplough, Redbank and Landsborough. In 1863 half an acre (0.2 ha) of vines was planted for fresh fruit. By 1866 the vineyard consisted of more than fifteen acres (6.1 ha) with enough grapes to make table wines. At the Intercolonial Exhibition in Melbourne that year connoisseurs noticed Trouette's well-made wines. His varieties included 'White Nice', chasselas, riesling and esparte (mourvedre). A prize-winning red wine in 1867 was 'clean and full, yet delicate of flavour'. The complex took the name St Peter's. Other vignerons followed their example at Great Western, notably the brothers Best [q.v.3].

In 1873 Emile Blampied married Louise, daughter of Louis Metzger, an Alsatian-born winemaker from nearby Doctors Creek. By 1878 the partnership had 200 acres (80.9 ha) with orchards and forty-five acres (18.2 ha) under vine, with cellar storage and a two-storey building; the vineyard would later reach 110 acres (44.5 ha), and the Trouette children Nicholas and Marie were groomed to take over the enterprise, which employed six people and thirty extras at vintage. Jean-Pierre was a shire councillor at Stawell and sold wine there, although he complained that publicans undercut him with 'doctored' material.

Trouette was a talented viticulturist and winemaker. Old World experience helped him, but he was resourceful as well; close planting was abandoned early. The soil that he considered unremarkable, a mixture of clay and loam, produced the finest grapes. More important was the climate, as good as the South of France without its devastating storms. Champagne method sparkling wine appeared in 1882.

St Peter's was famous for its vintage and holiday festivities, attracting travellers from Ballarat, Melbourne and Geelong. Hubert de Castella [q.v.3] visited on the Queen's birthday in 1882, when food, wine, toasts, singing and dancing were enjoyed well into the night. Madame Trouette was 'tall and strong', wearing traditional Lorraine dress, only 'a little bowed by her toil'; her brother Emile, 'large and handsome', had a face 'which inspires confidence from the first', and Jean-Pierre was 'hospitable to the last'.

Trouette died of pulmonary tuberculosis on 24 November 1885 at Great Western, and was buried in the local cemetery. His wife, son and daughter survived him, inheriting an estate sworn for probate at £7461. Next year, however, Nicholas and another worker were asphyxiated in an underground wine tank. The cumulative effects of personal loss, crop failures, bad seasons and economic depression led to the sale of the property in 1894 to purchasers with no interest in winemaking. The Blampieds, whose share had been a third, moved to Nhill. St Peter's vineyard and winery did not survive but winemaking, which the French migrants had pioneered at Great Western, flourished.

H. de Castella, *John Bull's Vineyard* (Melb, 1886); R. Kingston, *Good Country for a Grant* (Stawell, Vic 1989); L. R. Francis, *100 Years of Wine Making* (1965); A. Kuehne, *Grapes and Gold* (1980); D. Dunstan, *Better Than Pommard!* (Melb, 1994); *Austn Brewer's Jnl*, 20 Mar 1886, p 128; *Ararat and Pleasant Creek Advertiser*, 19 Feb 1867, p 2, 2 July 1867, p 3, 12 Nov 1867, p 2, 25 Dec 1868, p 2, 6 Aug 1869, p 4, 26 May 1882, p 2, 5 Jan 1906, p 2.

DAVID DUNSTAN

TROUP, GILBERT REYNOLDS (1896-1962), anaesthetist, was born on 4 February 1896 at Christchurch, New Zealand, son of Irish-born parents James Troup, iron founder, and his wife Elizabeth Beda, née De Pass. Educated at Melbourne Church of England Grammar School from 1910, Gilbert studied accountancy and worked as a tea planter in Ceylon (Sri Lanka) before completing a medical degree at the University of Melbourne (M.B., B.S., 1922); he lived at Ormond [q.v.5] College and was president of the Medical Students' Society.

Moving to Western Australia, Troup was resident medical officer at (Royal) Perth Hospital. He commenced private practice as a consultant physician at Subiaco, where, at St Andrew's Church of England on 24 March 1924, he married Brisbane-born Ethel Winifred May, daughter of (Sir) Charles Powers [q.v.11], a judge of the High Court of Australia. In 1929 Troup visited Britain and became a member (1930) of the Royal College of Physicians. Returning to Perth, he was a pioneer of modern anaesthesia in Australia, introducing techniques that improved surgical procedures and the well-being of patients. He was a foundation member (sometime president) of the Australian Society of Anaesthetists. At the Mayo Clinic, Rochester, Minnesota, United States of America, in 1935 he was introduced to cyclopropane, an anaesthetic that led to major improvements to the science.

In 1938 Troup was elected a fellow of the Royal Australian College of Physicians. On 4 April 1940 he was appointed temporary major, Australian Army Medical Corps (Militia). Seconded to the Australian Imperial Force on 1 July 1941 as a lieutenant colonel, he held senior posts with the 2nd/12th Australian General Hospital, including two months in Ceylon, and the 110th Military Hospital, Hollywood, Perth, before transferring to the Reserve of Officers on 11 February 1944 and returning to civilian practice. Next year he recognized the potential of the arrow poison, curare, especially for lung surgery. He was honorary physician at Royal Perth Hospital and senior anaesthetist at the Repatriation General Hospital, Hollywood. In 1956 he was anaesthetist in the first thoracic surgical team to visit Papua and New Guinea.

Although Troup practised for most of his life in Perth, his influence was felt throughout the country and he regularly visited Melbourne and Sydney. His achievements in the operating theatre were the more remarkable because he had an elbow disability, caused by an accident when young. To offset this, he designed a simpler device for the insertion of a tube down a patient's throat, which proved to be valuable to many anaesthetists and helped to pioneer one-lung anaesthesia. Colleagues noted his humility, patience, attention to detail and unfailing courtesy. He was particularly helpful to young anaesthetists. Troup enjoyed carpentry (in which he showed great skill) and fishing.

A sufferer from rheumatoid arthritis, towards the end of his life he saw his own electrocardiograph on a new machine being tested, and recognized signs of heart disease. Troup continued working, however, until a few days before he died of a cerebral haemorrhage on 14 August 1962 in hospital in Perth. He was cremated, survived by his wife and their two daughters. Two annual prizes honour him: one for a final year medical student in anaesthetics at the University of Western Australia, the other for outstanding work by a specialist registrar in training in the field that Troup had helped to found in Australia.

MJA, 30 Mar 1963, p 584; B883, item WX11140, B884, item W237659, and MP508/1, item 21/710/40 (NAA, Canb); information from Dr T. Nichols and Mr A. White, Perth.   JOHN MCILWRAITH

TUCKIAR; *SEE* DHAKIYARR

TULABA (c.1832-1886), Aboriginal leader and anthropological informant, was born near Bruthen, East Gippsland, Victoria, son of Bembinkel, of the Bruthen clan of the Brabiralung division of the Kurnai people, and an Aboriginal woman Mary McLeod. Bembinkel was a brother of Bruthen-munji, one of the last fully traditional senior Brabiralung elders, who died about 1862. Before the first stage of his initiation Tulaba (also spelt as Toolabar) was called Burrumbulk; he possibly never proceeded to his final initiation stage. He was also known as Karlbagwran and later as 'Billy McLeod'; his nickname 'Taenjill' meant incessant talker.

When he was a boy, Tulaba was taken by the pastoralists Archibald and John McLeod and raised on their properties, within his traditional territory. An able horseman and drover, he visited Melbourne in 1861 to guide the missionary J. Bulmer to Lake Tyers. During the 1860s Aborigines were pressured to settle at Lake Tyers and Ramahyuck missions, but except for sporadic visits, probably when unemployed, Tulaba avoided mission life.

In 1866 A. W. Howitt [q.v.4] settled at East-wood on the Mitchell River near Bairnsdale, successfully growing hops. He provided a bark hut for Tulaba, his first wife Kitty (Thanaberrang) and infant Anne (d.1873), his sole issue. When Kitty died he married Mary Bruthen (1819?-1884), a Bairnsdale clan widow. The couple became identified with Eastwood, Mary as domestic help and informant through Howitt's wife and Tulaba as foreman of the enthusiastic indigenous hop-pickers. Summer harvesting provided congenial communal opportunities, within regional kinship networks. Outside the hops season, Tulaba stripped stringy bark.

Because the McLeods never interfered with Aboriginal ritual life and Howitt positively encouraged it, modified traditional ceremonies continued on settlement fringes. From about 1870 the latter's burgeoning anthropological interests concentrated upon Tulaba, who spoke English. This relationship preceded Howitt's association with Lorimer Fison [q.v.4] and L. H. Morgan. Tulaba accorded Howitt kinship status, calling him 'brother' while Howitt called Tulaba's wife Mary 'wife', a device promoting reciprocity. For information provided, Tulaba expected food, clothing or payment; no initiation ceremony was involved.

Becoming the most prominent of Howitt's more than twenty Gippsland informants, in 1873 Tulaba supplied the key enabling Howitt's comprehension of the kinship system: following difficulty with abstractions, Howitt imaginatively asked him to arrange matchsticks to indicate the generational relationships and terminology of named individuals centred around him. This mode of interrogation became Howitt's standard. He compiled a circular genealogy to enable investigation of 'terms of consanguinity and affinity', printed in 1874 by the Board for the Protection of the Aborigines. The genealogical table that was provided used Tulaba as the exemplar, so 500 copies citing his model circulated around Australia.

In 1884 Tulaba was active in the jeraeil, a male, regional initiation ceremony sponsored by Howitt, which had last been held under Bruthen-munji's control during the 1850s. This revival of traditional ceremonies caused the missionaries concern, for religious reasons and because people deserted the missions and their work. It also worried Tulaba, who challenged Howitt's right to witness secret rituals, but Howitt overcame his scruples.

Bearded and adaptable, Tulaba was slightly built, 5 ft 3 ins (160 cm) tall, weighing 130 lb. (59 kg). He died of cancer on 16 October 1886 at Lake Tyers mission where he was buried with Anglican rites.

R. B. Smyth, *The Aborigines of Victoria* (Melb, 1878); L. Fison and A. W. Howitt, *Kamilaroi and Kurnai* (Melb, 1880); M. H. Walker, *Come Wind, Come Weather* (Melb, 1971); P. Pepper with T. De Araugo, *The Kurnai of Gippsland* (Melb, 1985), B. Attwood, *The Making of the Aborigines* (Syd, 1989); D. J. Mulvaney, 'The Anthropologist as Tribal Elder', *Mankind* (Syd), 7, no 3, 1970, p 205; Howitt papers (Museum Vic); Fison collection (St Mark's Lib, Canb).   D. J. MULVANEY

U

UMARRA(H); *see* EUMARRAH

UNAIPON, JAMES (c.1835-1907), Aboriginal leader, was born at Piwingang, a Murray River lagoon (west of present-day Tailem Bend), South Australia. His clan was the Wunyalkundi, of the Potawolin language group, part of the Ngarrindjeri confederation. The black swan, *Kungari*, was his totem. During the boy's childhood his family moved to nearby Wellington, which became a focus for Ngarrindjeri and European interaction in the 1840s. As a youth, he absorbed his people's traditions through initiation, ceremony and tribal fighting, losing an eye in a spear fight. Bearded and 5 ft 7 ins (170 cm) in height, he was taller than most Ngarrindjeri.

Initially he adopted the name James McPherson, after a Wellington publican for whom he probably worked. In 1861 he was baptized by the Scottish Free Church missionary James Reid as his first Christian convert. Taught by Reid (whose surname he then adopted), he became one of the first Ngarrindjeri to read and write. The two James Reids sailed in the missionary's small boat to Aboriginal camps along the Murray, in the lakes and to the Coorong, South Australia. After Reid drowned in Lake Albert in July 1863, George Taplin [q.v.6] considered training the missionary's assistant as his own evangelist. Arriving at Raukkan, Point McLeay Mission in 1864, intending to 'work and improve himself in reading, writing', James became known as Ngnunaitpon, his Potawolin name, later anglicized as Unaipon.

Taplin's attempts to erase traditional initiation, sorcery and burial rites faced dogged resistance from tribal elders, and Unaipon's support was influential. The missionary allowed him to begin 'scripture readership' among lakeside camps, supplying him with a boat for this purpose in 1869 and paying him a wage. The results were mixed, as Taplin's moral code was rigid and Unaipon's privileged status was often resented. But Taplin later described him as 'a steady Christian ... a nucleus around which those who were impressed by divine truth would rally'. Unaipon's marriage on 27 July 1866 to Nymbulda, a Karatindjeri clanswoman and daughter of the traditional Yaraldi leader Pullum ('King Peter'), was the mission's first Christian wedding. The union, a victory for Taplin, cemented James's status in his adopted community. He and Nymbulda were to have nine children, the fourth being David Unaipon [q.v.12]. Their surviving children all attended the mission school.

Aside from his evangelical role, James had special status. Reid's sponsor Henrietta Smith of Dunesk, Scotland, corresponded with Unaipon, whom she regarded as her own convert. Having earlier purchased land for South Australian Aborigines, she transferred this interest to Point McLeay mission in the late 1860s. She also paid for a small stone cottage for Unaipon and a writing desk, and vested a lifetime annuity of £100 in his name. In translating Christian gospels into the Potawolin language and as an ethnographic informant, Taplin relied heavily upon Unaipon, whose contributions underpinned the former's publications.

In 1871 Unaipon was appointed the first Ngarrindjeri church deacon, assisting Taplin to administer the sacrament. His advocacy of literacy—as much as the traditional *tendi* (inter-clan forum)—helped to underpin the increasing demand by Ngarrindjeri church councillors for a greater role in mission affairs. Until 1879 Unaipon continued to undertake lengthy evangelical tours to outlying Ngarrindjeri camps, walking 120 miles (200 km) or more. He also worked in the mission school as an assistant teacher, cook and librarian, and as shepherd, boatman, labourer and rabbiter until ill health forced his retirement in the late 1880s. He then became reliant upon the small annual interest from his annuity. When the mission's funds were embezzled in 1892 the authorities agreed to pay him an equivalent allowance.

Like other Ngarrindjeri, Unaipon took his family to the Coorong by canoe during school holidays. Periodically he also canoed back to Wellington. In 1895, following tension with mission authorities over dwindling privileges for 'full-blood natives', he returned to camp life and moved to Goolwa, supporting his family by selling game. In 1898 he applied unsuccessfully to lease land near Wellington, where he had hoped to spend his final years. A respected leader of his people, he died at Point McLeay on 24 October 1907. His wife and two sons survived him.

G. Taplin, *The Narrinyeri* (Adel, 1874) and *The Folklore, Manners, Customs, and Languages of the South Australian Aborigines* (Adel, 1879) and Journal (SLSA); G. Jenkin, *Conquest of the Ngarrindjeri* (Adel, 1979); R. Linn, *A Diverse Land* (Meningie, SA, 1988); R. M. and C. H. Berndt, *A World That Was* (Melb, 1993); Aborigines' Friends' Association papers, SRG 139 (SLSA); Frederick Taplin letter-books, SA Museum Archives.   PHILIP JONES

V

VIRTUE, WILLIAM WRIGHT (1863-1926), engineer and Christian Scientist, was born on 27 March 1863 at Glasgow, Scotland, second of four children of George Wright Virtue, iron moulder, and his wife Hannah Roy, née Graham. Only William and one sister survived childhood. Studying chemistry at the Glasgow Mechanics Institution in 1875-78, William won medals in first and second year, and topped the class every year. A mechanical engineer and resident of Springburn, north Glasgow, on 23 June 1886 he married Harriet McDougal at Mount Florida, east of Glasgow, according to the forms of the New Jerusalem (Swedenborgian) Church. Their son was born in Scotland in 1888. Doubtless due to family associations with the mining entrepreneur and Swedenborgian John Moffat [q.v.10], the Virtues migrated to Queensland, where a daughter was born in 1890. Next year they moved to Burwood, Sydney; another daughter was born there in September 1891.

The move was the making of Virtue. Moffat had become interested in shearing machines, and Virtue's engineering skills enabled their joint registration of several patents for improvements in 1891-94. By 1893 Virtue was Sydney co-director and manager of the Moffat-Virtue Sheep Shearing Machine Co. From 1908, following a capital-raising and diversification restructure by Moffat, Virtue was general manager of Moffat-Virtue Ltd and the Federal Sheep Shearing Co., Sydney, where he earned the respect of staff. In 1911 all the entrants in the first sheep-shearing competition at the Sydney Royal Show chose the company's machines. By 1914 'Moffat-Virtue' was a household name in rural Australia.

Virtue's work involved considerable overseas travel, to the United States of America in 1898, and to Britain and the U.S.A. in 1901 and 1909. A student of 'spiritual science', in Boston in 1898 he encountered Christian Science, with 'never-to-be-forgotten' experiences at the Mother Church, and sent literature home to Harriet, a semi-invalid. On 3 June 1899, having sought instruction from Julia Bartlett, a Mary Baker Eddy loyalist, he joined the Mother Church and became an accredited practitioner, as did Harriet, who went on a separate trip to Boston in 1899.

The Virtues were among the earliest Christian Science practitioners in Australia. The first *Science and Health* reading group and Christian Science meetings in Sydney were held in their home. In June 1899 William was also the first Australian contributor to the Boston-produced *Christian Science Sentinel*. In September 1900 he presided over a meeting in the city to establish a Christian Science Society, which became First Church, Sydney, in December 1902, with William and Harriet first and second readers.

The Virtues moved to Neutral Bay about 1900, then to Cremorne. Sometime after his wife's death from cancer in 1915, William married his cousin Bessie Graham Stirling. Retiring as managing director of Moffat-Virtue in 1922, he retained a directorship but returned to Scotland. Virtue died on 18 September 1926 at Glenfarg, Perthshire. He was survived by his three children in Australia and by his wife. His estate was sworn for probate in New South Wales at £4994.

R. S. Kerr, *John Moffat of Irvinebank* (Brisb, 2000); J. Roe, '"Testimonies from the Field": The Coming of Christian Science to Australia, c1890-1910', *Jnl of Religious History*, 22, no 3, Oct 1998, p 304; G. Walsh, *Pioneering Days* (Syd, 1993); First Church, Syd, Minute Book, 1898-1905; Church records (Mary Baker Eddy Lib, Boston, US); *SMH*, 24 Sept 1909, p 6; information from Mrs B. Thomas, Burwood, Vic.

JILL ROE

VON STIEGLITZ, KARL RAWDON (1893-1967), pastoralist and antiquarian, was born on 19 August 1893 at Andora, a holding near Evandale, Tasmania, second son of four children of John Charles von Stieglitz, pastoralist and politician, and his second wife Lilian Brooke Vere, née Stead. The family was originally from Pomerania, Saxony, but had moved to County Armagh in Ireland, then to Van Diemen's Land in 1829. F. L. von Stieglitz [q.v.2] was John's uncle. Karl was educated at home by tutors, because bouts of rheumatic fever prevented regular school attendance, and later in England.

In March 1917 he reputedly enlisted in the Australian Imperial Force and was allotted to the Australian Medical Corps but was discharged in November on health grounds. Remaining in New South Wales, von Stieglitz studied for two years at Hawkesbury Agricultural College, Richmond, and married Eileen Bessie Helsham at St Peter's Church of England, Richmond, on 19 June 1920. Returning to Andora, he top-dressed the soil, sowed subterranean clover pasture, developed a Corriedale stud flock and planted more trees than he felled. His innovations did not extend to mechanization, however, as he retained draught horses until after World War II. Karl became active in the local community. In 1952 he was appointed O.B.E. in recognition of his involvement in local government, the

Church of England, the Boy Scouts' Association, Freemasonry, Evandale Agricultural Show and the Royal Society of Tasmania.

Von Stieglitz was best known for his contributions to local history, inspired by an enthusiasm for his pioneer pastoral ancestors, a visit to Britain in 1906-07 and his belief in the primacy of the landowning class. His thirty-eight works, which covered pastoral history, bushrangers and churches, could best be described as a pageant of pioneer families. The books lacked a chronological or thematic framework, included unverified stories and had a concept of pastoralists as the motive force for change. He had a roseate view of convict assignees as old lags, and regarded Aborigines as simple and inoffensive until roused to revenge. His charm and pastoral background, however, gave him access to oral reminiscences and previously unused family material such as letters, manuscripts and photographs. In epilogues and interludes he showed a poetic streak and an Arcadian appreciation of the environment. According to the Launceston *Examiner*, his books, radio broadcasts, lectures and excursions, brought history 'alive'. He donated the proceeds from his writings to charity.

His works coincided with a burgeoning interest in the State's heritage, previous Tasmanian history having been concerned mainly with celebratory accounts of major institutions such as independent schools and churches. He exemplified the antiquarian imagination, based on intimate knowledge of local sites and sources.

Von Stieglitz died on 26 March 1967 during a service in St Andrew's Church of England, Evandale, and was buried in that churchyard. His wife and their son and daughter survived him. The Launceston branch of the National Trust of Australia established a memorial lecture in honour of him and his fellow stalwarts Isabella Mead and Roy Smith.

The Tasmanian Cyclopedia (Hob, 1931); T. Griffiths, *Hunters and Collectors* (Melb, 1996); *Austn Women's Weekly*, 22 Oct 1975, p 30; *Examiner* (Launc), 27 Mar 1967, p 3, 29 Mar 1967, p 7, 10 July 1973, p 9; *Mercury* (Hob), 1 Jan 1952, p 3, 27 Mar 1967, p 6; information from Mr D. von Stieglitz, and Miss E. Florence, Evandale, Tas.   TIM JETSON

W

WADE, ABDUL (1866–1928+), Afghan camel merchant and businessman, was born on 18 January 1866 at Coonah (Kunar), Afghanistan, to parents from the Ghilzai tribe. His name may have been Wahid or Wadi. Although he claimed to have reached Western Australia in 1879, he probably arrived in the mid-1880s when gold was discovered in the Kimberley region. He and his cousin Gunny Khan were working for the camel merchants Faiz and Tagh Mahomet [q.v.10] in northern South Australia by 1892.

Next year Wade began importing camels and recruiting Afghan cameleers for the recently formed Bourke Camel Carrying Co., New South Wales. An Afghan settlement, with a mosque as its central focus, developed on the outskirts of Bourke, where Wade had his house. In 1895 he was appointed manager and overseer of the company. With the firm's secretary George Tull, he made several trips to Karachi, India (Pakistan), to purchase camels and recruit drivers; in one year in the late 1890s he reputedly landed 750 camels at Port Augusta, South Australia—some 500 in one shipment. The company served western New South Wales and Queensland, including the copper fields of Mount Garnet, Chillagoe and Mungana and the OK mines. A depot was established at Cloncurry, where Sayed Omar, the ghantown's religious leader, was Wade's agent. Dressed like an English gentleman and riding a white camel, Wade was sometimes seen on the copper fields supervising his men.

On 10 June 1895 in Perth he married Dublin-born Emily Ozadelle, née Murcutt, a widow with one son. They had three sons, one of whom died in infancy, and four daughters. The drought of 1901-02 benefited Wade's business. In 1903 he purchased Wangamanna station, a grazing property thirty-five miles (56 km) east of Wanaaring, New South Wales. That year he and Tull again sailed for Karachi for an additional 350 camels and some sixty men. Faced with paying their wages on landing at Port Augusta, however, Wade abandoned about sixteen men. Gunny Khan sought help from the police, but Wade offered only basic food rations until they found other employment.

With part of this shipment, Wade established a camel breeding and carrying business at Wangamanna station, where the Afghan settlement had a mosque. His men were put to work carrying in the district as well as harvesting and bagging salt from the property's lakes and transporting it to Bourke to be sent by rail to Sydney. Wade's monopoly of the cartage business in the Warrego region sometimes led to violent clashes with European teamsters.

Wade was a flamboyant and stylish entrepreneur, with a passion for horse racing on the country circuits. His employees treated him with such respect that he was known locally as an 'Afghan prince'. He issued a challenge for a race from Bourke to Wanaaring and back, between himself, riding a camel, and a European on horseback. The race resulted in victory for Wade, his rival's horse having died from exhaustion at the halfway mark. He liked to be seen in restaurants, clubs and hotels.

In 1902 Wade was naturalized. Next year he bought Northwood House, designed by Edmund Blacket [q.v.3], on the Lane Cove River, Sydney, and adjacent property, which he subdivided. According to local legend, he sometimes landed camels at Northwood wharf. His son attended The King's School, Parramatta, in 1910-11, and his daughters were educated at private schools. By 1917 he had sold his Lane Cove land, having reputedly lost Northwood House in a poker game, and moved to Chatswood. He later had property at Redfern.

Although Wade attempted to move as a successful gentleman among Europeans, he was ridiculed for his 'Afghan-ness': a ballad recounted how he purchased a new saddle in Sydney but gave it away when persuaded that it was made from pig skin, taboo to Muslim beliefs. Another tale lampooned his commitment to religious butchery restrictions: he would reportedly instruct the Gumbalie Hotel, near Bourke, to provide a live chicken which he would kill and bleed *halal*; he would then eat a previously cooked chicken for lunch.

Recognizing that camels were not suited to conditions in monsoonal regions, in 1905 Wade had purchased five steam traction engines in Sydney for £7000. These were intended to service the booming copper mines of North Queensland, employing European labour to operate the machines. In 1914-15 he offered his Australian camels and his contacts in Afghanistan to the Australian government for service in the Imperial Camel Corps against the Turks; the offer was apparently not accepted. Following the introduction of motorized transport into the outback in the 1920s, and the passage of the Camel Destruction Act (1925) in South Australia, Wade sold Wangamanna station. Many camels from its neglected stud escaped into the bush or were shot.

In October 1923 Wade had left for Afghanistan. Next year he surrendered his

Australian passport. His wife died in Sydney in 1926. Wade was said to be living in England in 1928. His children remained in Sydney, including his son Abdul Hamid (1900-1982), a taxi-driver who served in the Royal Australian Navy in World War II.

G. C. Bolton, *A Thousand Miles Away* (Brisb, 1963); C. Stevens, *Tin Mosques & Ghantowns* (Melb, 1989); *The History of Bourke*, vol 10 (Bourke, NSW, 1985), p 155; *SMH*, 7 Nov 1987, 'Good Weekend', p 48; A1, item 1925/3882, A6770, item Wade, A. H. (NAA, Canb); Alan Barton collection (Public Lib, Bourke, NSW); information from Ms C. Johnston, Gymea Bay, NSW.   CHRISTINE STEVENS

'WAIF WANDER'; *see* FORTUNE

WAITE, GEORGE (1860-1941), trade union leader, was born on 27 September 1860 at Old Quartz Hill, Moonlight Flat, Victoria, third son of William Wait(e), an English-born miner, and his wife Agnes, née Blythe, from Scotland. On 4 September 1880 George married Emily Jane Hill at the Wesleyan parsonage, Tamworth, New South Wales, giving his occupation as labourer. They had six children. A self-confessed follower of Thomas Paine, he held socialist beliefs and was strongly influenced by libertarian ideals.

In 1886, living at St Leonards, Sydney, Waite was president of the North Shore branch of the Brickmakers, Brickmakers' Labourers and Pipemakers Union. He joined the Australian Socialist League in the 1890s and was a delegate for the Amalgamated Navvies and General Labourers' Union to the Trades and Labor Council of New South Wales, where he campaigned against sub-contractors on government works and Sunday employment. In 1891-92 he was active within the St Leonards Labor Electoral League.

Waite then moved to the 2100-acre (850 ha) Pitt Town Co-operative Settlement, near Windsor, established under the Labour Settlements Act of June 1893 in response to demands for measures to reduce unemployment. Of the 500 settlers (100 married men with families), few had experience of farming and bush work, being mainly unemployed city workers. The socialist-dominated Board of Control had initially appointed an agricultural expert to act as superintendent, but dismissed him after three months for habitual drunkenness and appointed Waite as superintendent —although opponents later alleged that he could not tell a pumpkin from a melon.

When the settlement split, about twenty-five families wishing to continue on co-operative lines while some seventy-five demanded subdivision into individual blocks, Waite, an ardent co-operationist, resigned. He agreed to reappointment, however, after his replacement succumbed to alcoholism. The *Australian Workman* insisted that being 'of more than ordinary intelligence, honesty, and ability', he was the best man on the settlement for the post of superintendent. The 'individualist' party was so enraged at his reappointment in December 1894 that police were called to restore order. In June 1896 the government evicted the few remaining settlers, and the settlement became a casual labour farm.

That year Waite moved to Broken Hill then to Western Australia. In 1897 he was selected as Labor candidate for the North-East Coolgardie electorate. Early in the twentieth century he became vice-president of the Boulder Labor Party, organizer of the regular workers' lectures held in the Workers' Hall and an agitator on behalf of the unemployed 'to relieve suffering humanity and better the conditions of Labor on these fields'.

During the early 1900s Waite also spent time back in Sydney, where he was active in the United Laborers' Protective Society from January 1900. Living again in North Sydney from about 1905, he served as an official (sometime assistant secretary) of the U.L.P.S. from 1910 to 1924. A supporter of the Industrial Workers of the World, he was a member of the Sydney I.W.W. club and a propagandist for the local Detroit faction in 1908-17, serving on the State executive committee in 1913. He was acting secretary of the Lithgow Unionists Strike Prisoners' Release Committee in 1912 and active in the Anti-Coercion and Political Freedom League in 1914. In 1916 he was honorary secretary of the committee campaigning for the release of Tom Barker [q v 7] and Louis Klausen, and chaired anti-conscription meetings. By 1919 he was prominent in the Social Democratic League of New South Wales and, in 1921, the Self-Determination for Ireland League of Australia.

A U.L.P.S. delegate to the Labor Council of New South Wales, by 1921 Waite was an opponent of Jock Garden [q.v.8] and the council's left-wing executive, which retaliated by expelling him. The U.L.P.S. withdrew its affiliation to the council, upholding Waite's objections to Bolshevism and to its Australian supporters, whom he depicted, in his pamphlet *A Labor Man's Appeal to Labor* (c.1922), as authoritarian extremists 'endeavouring to bring about a bloody revolution'.

Waite supported Sir Joseph Hector Carruthers's [q.v.7] 'Million Farms' campaign of the early 1920s, claiming in *Waite's Warning to Workers* (1922) that these farms would find work for all the unemployed. He also justified his support on racist and nationalist grounds in his *White Australians* (c.1922). Although active in A. C. Willis's [q.v.12] Australian Industrial Christian Fellowship in 1923 and a supporter of the J. T. Lang [q.v.9] group within the Labor Party in 1924, by 1925 he was associated with Aubrey Barclay's [q.v.] rightwing journal, *Sane Democracy*, and hostile towards Lang's government. In December that year he resigned as assistant secretary of the U.L.P.S. Campaigning against the 1925 seamen's strike, he claimed in *Unionism Degraded* (c.1925) that industrial strife would 'hamper the progress of white Australia'. Waite became a prolific letter writer to the *Sydney Morning Herald*. In 1926 and in 1930 he made world tours, during the latter visiting the Soviet Union. He remained active in the Sane Democracy League until May 1939.

Predeceased by his wife, Waite died on 16 September 1941 in Trescol Private Hospital, North Sydney, and was cremated with Anglican rites. Three sons survived him.

V. Burgmann, *'In Our Time'* (Syd, 1985) and *Revolutionary Industrial Unionism* (Melb, 1995); *Labour History*, no 18, May 1970, p 19; *SMH*, 8 June 1891, p 5, 9 June 1891, p 8, 7 May 1921, p 13, 27 May 1921, p 8, 17 Aug 1921, p 12, 14 Dec 1925, p 11, 25 Nov 1926, p 12, 9 Sept 1930, p 10, 6 June 1932, p 8; *Austn Workman*, 14 May 1894, p 6, 16 June 1894, p 1; *Westralian Worker*, 24 June 1904, p 2; *Austn Worker*, 19 May 1926, p 1; *Sane Democracy* (Syd), Dec 1937, p 12; C. Priday, Sane Democracy in New South Wales 1920 to 1940 (B.A. Hons thesis, Macquarie Univ, 1975); P. Sheldon, Maintaining Control (Ph.D. thesis, Univ of Wollongong, 1989); Waite papers (ML).   VERITY BURGMANN

WALCOTT, RICHARD HENRY (1870-1936), mineralogist and museum curator, was born on 30 September 1870 at Dunedin, New Zealand, son of James Alexander Walcott, merchant, and his wife Catherine, née Russell. After three years study at the University of Otago, Henry obtained a diploma (1891) as associate of the School of Mines. In 1892 he attended more university classes 'simply for the love of it, and a desire to improve my knowledge'. Walcott was appointed mineralogist at the Industrial and Technological Museum in Melbourne on 5 January 1893; his enthusiastic referees included Professor G. H. F. Ulrich [q.v.6], the museum's first mineralogist. After Cosmo Newbery [q.v.5] died in 1895, Walcott succeeded him as the museum's senior officer. On 28 September 1898 at St George's Church of England, Malvern, he married Jane Elizabeth Moore.

When the Industrial and Technological Museum was closed to make room for the collections of the National Museum of Victoria in 1900, Walcott was transferred there with the geological and mineralogical collection, on which he continued to work. He added care of the ethnological section to his duties and worked closely with (Sir Walter) Baldwin Spencer [q.v.12] in the development and display of that collection. Among his publications was a paper describing Victorian meteorites and one with Spencer on the origin of cuts on bones of extinct Australian marsupials. Although taking primary responsibility for the Pacific collection, he also accompanied Spencer on some field trips and contributed geological expertise to analysis and dating of the findings.

Throughout this period Walcott's assiduous work behind the scenes to have the Industrial and Technological Museum reopened attracted the influential support of George Swinburne and (Sir) John Monash [qq.v.12, 10] on the eve of World War I. He resumed full-time duties as curator in 1914 to prepare for the museum's reopening, which occurred on 17 May next year. Characterized by systematic presentation of exhibits drawn from various branches of engineering, applied science, industry and agriculture, the museum (later Science Museum of Victoria) earned considerable praise in the 1920s. Much of its content was skilfully garnered by Walcott through donations and, as sole professional officer, there were few tasks he did not undertake himself.

A fellow of the Royal Geological Society, London, in 1897 he was elected a member of the Royal Society of Victoria, on whose council he served from 1900 until 1916, when he began to devote himself exclusively to the museum. Walcott was a 'tall, slim man with a moustache who looked at the world, quietly and unassumingly, through thick glasses'; his deep intellectual curiosity and commitment to public education through effective museum displays stood him in good stead through the institution's fluctuating fortunes until he retired in 1935.

Predeceased by his wife, Walcott died of hypertension and heart failure on 9 October 1936 at Caulfield and was buried in St Kilda cemetery. A daughter survived him. His estate was sworn for probate at £9518; he bequeathed funds in trust for the education of his daughter's children, but 'not in any school of Roman Catholic denomination'. The Science Museum of Victoria was incorporated into the Museum of Victoria in 1983.

W. Perry, *The Science Museum of Victoria* (Melb, 1972); D. J. Mulvaney and J. H. Calaby, *'So Much that is New'* (Melb, 1985); C. Rasmussen, *A Museum for the People* (Melb, 2001); Industrial and Technological Museum, *Annual Report*, 1908, 1914, 1926; *Argus* (Melb), 28 Sept 1935, p 22; Royal Soc of Vic, Council Minutes, 10 Aug 1933, 14 Sept 1933 (SLV).   CAROLYN RASMUSSEN

WALKER, JANET (1850-1940), costumier and teacher, was born on 10 June 1850 at Neilston, Renfrewshire, Scotland, daughter of Andrew Robertson, librarian, and his wife Jane, née Gemmell. In 1863 Janet (known as 'Jessie') migrated with her family to Queensland. Tutored by Brunton Stephens [q.v.6], on 1 February 1872 she was appointed assistant teacher on probation at Brisbane Girls' Normal School.

In August 1875 Jessie was transferred to the new West End State School to head the girls' department. Gerard Anderson, district inspector for the Board of Education, described her as 'a lively, energetic, and intelligent person, with very good ideas of school-keeping … The pupil teachers are far behind her in animation.' She resigned on 31 December 1876 and on 16 January next year she married with Presbyterian forms James Laughland Walker (d.1924), a Scottish-born draper. Between 1878 and 1882 they had four children; two daughters died in infancy.

Mrs Walker began business as a dressmaker in Queen Street in 1882. She moved to larger premises in Adelaide Street in 1886 and back to Queen Street in 1918. In October 1884 a female journalist from the *Queenslander* visited her rooms, as well as those of her colleagues Miss Margaret Caldwell and Miss Margaret Scott. From 1887 to 1901 the local press acknowledged Walker's designs worn at eighty-four weddings, fourteen balls and six receptions, and described thirty sets of trousseau garments made in her atelier. 'Her clients included most of the well known society ladies of the time.'

Gowns made by Walker reflected her skill as a designer and her high standard of workmanship. These qualities enabled her to operate the largest private dressmaking establishment in colonial Brisbane. By the end of 1898 she employed 120 staff, the majority of whom worked in her atelier. She did not pay her apprentices during their first year, but never expected them to work overtime. Her remaining employees were paid the minimum wage, overtime and bonuses during busy periods. She trained her staff well, and several later set up their own businesses.

Walker and Margaret Caldwell, who had become her partner, matched the competitive services offered by larger drapery stores by opening a 'Ladies' Emporium' in September 1896. The business was so successful that the premises were remodelled three times before 1900. In 1897 a showroom was also established on the ground level of the *Courier* building, Queen and Edward streets. Walker offered customers both made-to-measure and ready-made garments. To ensure individuality, much of the fabric was imported in dress lengths, with just enough lace and trimming to embellish them. A large mail order clientele was established in rural Queensland and New South Wales. Several gowns worn at the opening of the Commonwealth Parliament in Melbourne in 1901 and at the reception at Government House, Brisbane, for the Duke and Duchess of Cornwall and York, were attributed to her new workrooms.

In July 1904 Walker was granted a patent for an improved dressmaker's stand, known as the 'plastic bust', which could be manipulated to produce a replica of a customer's body shape. The design was sold to the House of Worth and Madame Paquin in Paris and to the House of Redfern, London. In 1905 she successfully floated the Plastic Bust Co. while in London. A talented and skilled costumier, Mrs Walker operated her business until she retired in 1938. She died on 27 November 1940 at Toowong and was buried with other family members in South Brisbane cemetery. One of her two sons survived her. Some of her gowns are held by the Queensland Museum, Brisbane.

Report with Minutes of Evidence Taken Before the Shops, Factories and Workshops Commission, *V&P* (Qld), 1891, vol 2, p 1201; *Flashes of Society & Sport* (Qld), 19 July 1900, p 12; *Queenslander*, 11 Oct 1884, p 587; *Qld Figaro*, 2 Feb 1889, p 352; Board of Education (Qld), Inspector's Reports, 1875, EDB/N5, *and* Register of Teachers, 1860-76, entry 275, *and* EDU/V13, vol 1, p 97, reel Z7590 (QSA).

MICHAEL MARENDY

WALKER, TOMMY; *see* POLTPALINGADA

WALLACE, THEODOSIA ADA (1872-1953), journalist, was born on 18 August 1872 at Jolimont, East Melbourne, daughter of English-born parents Alexander Britton, journalist and historian, and his wife Ada, née Willoughby. Theodosia's education began at the Misses Budds' kindergarten school and, when the family moved to Sydney, about 1885, continued at home; by 1890 the Brittons lived at Ravensworth, Woolloomooloo. The same tutors taught Theodosia and her two brothers, and she took private music lessons from Madame Charbonnet Kellermann, mother of Annette [q.v.9]. Matriculating in March 1888, Theodosia studied English, Latin, Greek, mathematics, chemistry and physics at the University of Sydney (B.A., 1891). In 1900 she was honorary secretary of the University Women's Association.

Theodosia's father, grandfather, two uncles and a cousin were journalists, and after teaching briefly she switched to a long life of writing. At the age of 20 she wrote a social column for the Melbourne *Argus* and *Australasian* as 'Biddy B.A.' She also contributed to the *Sydney Morning Herald* and later joined its staff, writing mainly on temperance and feminist subjects, such as the passing of the Married Women's Property Act, free kindergartens and changes to the laws on prostitution. The *Herald* started a weekly feature, 'A Page for Women', in September 1905 and Theodosia was appointed editor, under the general editorship of Thomas Heney [q.v.9]. The first issue contained jottings on fashion ('Snuff brown chiffon is one of the newest materials for evening gowns'), gardening, table decoration, shopping in Paris, Australians in England and women artists in Sydney, and advice by Ethel Turner [q.v.12] on suitable literature for young girls. On its second appearance the page was more attractive, with an artwork title piece and fashion drawings. The page increased the *Herald*'s circulation by 700 copies in the first week and 1400 in the second, but numbers reverted to former levels thereafter.

On 28 December 1905 at St John's Church of England, Darlinghurst, Theodosia married Irish-born Albert Edward Noble Wallace (1872-1928), accountant and civil servant, sometime Queensland and New South Wales chess champion; they had met through her chess-enthusiast brother Alexander. Theodosia left the *Herald* before her first child was born in 1907; a second was born in 1908. She wrote *The Etiquette of Australia* (1909), which went into three editions by 1922.

In 1914 the *Australian Woman's Weekly* described Wallace as a 'most practical-looking, learned, and to-the-manner-born journalist'. She worked for various newspapers, such as the weekly *Bystander*, where for £3 a week she supplied most of the letterpress, and wrote syndicated letters for the *Orange Leader* and a Dubbo newspaper. In the *Newcastle Herald*, under the pseudonym 'INO', her weekly column 'An Idle Woman's Diary' ran from 1920. She was the first head of the Country Press Association's press-cutting service, working there for about thirty years. In the 1920s her poem, 'My love for you', set to the music of Lillian Mitchell, was published by W. H. Paling [q.v.5] & Co. Wallace wrote for the *Sydney Morning Herald* in 1934 about bell-ringing in Sydney churches, describing the 'ear-filling sound' as having 'something satisfying to the soul in it'.

A founding member of the Society of Women Writers, she attended a meeting convened in September 1925 to form an organization that would draw together women writers and newspaper artists, including Zara Aronson and (Dame) Mary Gilmore [qq.v.7,9]; Wallace was elected to the first executive committee, and became a vice-president in the 1940s. She died on 1 October 1953 at her Double Bay home and was buried in Rookwood cemetery. Her son and daughter survived her.

G. Souter, *Company of Heralds* (Syd, 1981); P. Clarke, *Pen Portraits* (Syd, 1988); *Austn Women's Weekly*, 26 Sept 1914, p 6; *SMH*, 2 May 1900, p 8, 24 Nov 1934, p 11; Society of Women Writers, Minute Book, 7 Sept 1925 (ML); correspondence with Mrs A. Farr, 1981 (held on ADB file).

ROBYN ARROWSMITH

WALLIS, ALEXANDER ROBERT (1848-1928), agricultural expert, was born in 1848 in Ghazipur, India, second son of Rev. Alexander Wellington Wallis, in the service of the East India Co., and his wife Eliza, née Wootton. From 1856 young Alexander attended Lancing College, Sussex, England, the Royal Agricultural College, Cirencester, and Stuttgart Polytechnic, Würrtemberg (Germany), with the ambition of becoming an 'agricultural professional' rather than a farmer or land agent. He reputedly rejected the offer of the foundation chair of agriculture at Cornell University, Ithaca, New York; instead, he reached Melbourne in the *Anglesey* on 21 June 1871 to become the agricultural journalist for the *Australasian*.

Under the byline 'Ackermann', Wallis established himself as an agricultural authority. In June 1872 he served on a royal commission on Victoria's first outbreak of foot and mouth disease. On 9 November that year he won an essay competition to become secretary of a newly formed department of agriculture. Located within, but supposedly separate from, the chaotic Department of Crown Lands and Survey, the new department lacked resources and professional respect; disputes with lands department officials, in part a product of Wallis's acerbic personality, proved especially vexing. He was dapper, moustached, hardworking and assertive.

Shortages of funds, staff and support were countered by his unrelenting quest for professional, scientific agriculture. Informed by a blend of certitude and impatience, Wallis rode around the colony—judging shows, encouraging innovation, mounting exhibitions, gathering data and hectoring farmers. He rationalized the colony's many agricultural societies by manipulating the distribution of grants-in-aid, created an agricultural library and published annual reports (1873-75) replete with technical papers. Successive governments increased his responsibilities. He was associated with James Harrison's [q.v.1] demonstrations in pioneering the frozen meat industry. Agricultural chemistry, industries and education and forestry management were added to his duties, and in 1877 Wallis was instructed to establish and oversee a model farm at Dookie. He could not meet such excessive expectations, and in the late 1870s there was press and parliamentary criticism of the department, comprising just himself and the chemist W. E. Ivey.

On 15 December 1874 at Holy Trinity Church, East Melbourne, Wallis had married with Anglican rites Harriet Stephen Walsh, née Hughes, a widow with five children; she, too, had been born in India. From 1877 Wallis was asked to eradicate *Phylloxera* from vineyards in the Geelong district. While his methods proved successful, compensation levels awarded to vignerons whose vines had to be destroyed were questioned. In February 1882 minister Charles Young appointed a board of inquiry to investigate matters in dispute between himself and Wallis, the most notable being that Wallis had interfered in compensation judgements, an accusation that he vehemently denied. Although the board exonerated him, on 25 March 1882 his position was 'dispensed with'.

After dabbling in pastoral investment in Western Australia and Victoria, and in importing, in 1887 Wallis migrated with Harriet to New Zealand. She died in Melbourne in 1889. At St John's Church, Invercargill, on 4 January 1893 he married 24-year-old, Irish-born Frederica Theresa Stronge. Wallis managed the Morton Mains estate near Edendale, Southland, until 1894 when he purchased the Woodstock estate. In 1900 he founded the sawmilling firm A. R. Wallis Ltd at Invercargill. He was a justice of the peace. Wallis died on 15 May 1928 at Dunedin and was buried at Andersons Bay cemetery. Frederica and their two sons survived him.

The Cyclopedia of New Zealand, 4 (Christchurch, NZ, 1905); R. Wright, *"Dispensed With": A. R. Wallis, First Secretary for Agriculture in Victoria 1872-1882* (Melb, 1982), and for bib; *Reports of the Secretary for Agriculture* (Vic), 1873-75; *Otago Daily Times*, 17 May 1928; *Pastoral Review*, 16 Aug 1928, p 810.

R. WRIGHT

WALYER; *see* TARENORERER

WARING, CHARLOTTE; *see* BARTON

WARNER, JAMES (1814-1891), surveyor, was born on 12 March 1814 in London, son of James Warner, master mariner. Young James followed his father into the merchant navy and became second officer in the *Runnymede*, trading between London and China and to Port Jackson. Resigning his commission, Warner reached Sydney in the *Persian* on 25 August 1835. By 1837 he was junior clerk, third class, in the Surveyor-General's Depart-

ment. He became an assistant surveyor in 1839. Posted to the Moreton Bay district, under the supervision of Robert Dixon [q.v.1] he cleared the trees on the Herbert Taylor Range for a trigonometrical station, leaving a single tree as a surveyors' marker. The feature, for many years called One Tree Hill, was later named Mount Coot-tha.

On 18 November 1839 at Moreton Bay Warner married with Anglican rites Clara Lindo, née Brandon, a widow with three children. Next year, when assisting Dixon to survey the coastline between Cape Moreton and the Richmond River, he was 'wrecked with loss of personal property, and considerable risk of life'. He continued to survey towns and rural selections near Brisbane. In 1846 he was sent to trace the River Boyne from its source and to mark latitude 26°, the southern boundary of the short-lived colony of North Australia, centred on Port Curtis.

The rigours of the outdoor life began to tell on Warner's health; he suffered from rheumatism, pleurisy and impaired sight and his work output decreased. When the surveyor-general Sir Thomas Mitchell [q.v.2] asked him in April 1852 to quit, he refused, but on 1 June next year he retired on a pension of £70. He continued to work, privately subdividing land for houses and farms and acting as a contract surveyor for the government, and expanded his business to include property management and home design.

In January 1861 Warner produced, for sale, a large coloured map of Brisbane, which he exhibited at the Town Hall. It ran to a second edition in 1871. Economic conditions forced him into insolvency in March 1870. Upon the formation of the Queensland Institute of Surveyors in 1875, he was its first secretary and treasurer.

When he lived at Kangaroo Point in the 1850s, 'a dance at Warner's was the best in Brisbane'. A man of deep religious convictions, he gave land for the building of St Mark's Church at Lutwyche, to which area he later moved. He was 'full of genial fun and jokes', but could 'read aloud the Bible to youthful hearers with a pathos and heartfelt intonation which some Archbishop might envy'. A keen gardener, with an extensive knowledge of botany, he received a silver medal at the 1861 International Exhibition, London, for a display of coffee beans grown in his own garden. He was also a cricketer and sailor.

In 1885, in recognition of his service to the colony, Warner was appointed sergeant-at-arms to the Queensland Legislative Assembly. He died on 6 May 1891 at his home, Runnymede, in Brisbane and was buried below Mount Coot-tha in Toowong cemetery. His wife had predeceased him; their five daughters and one of their two sons survived him.

D. Watson and J. McKay, *Queensland Architects of the 19th Century* (Brisb, 1994); D. Gray-Woods, *With Compass Chain and Courage* (Brisb, 1997); *Moreton Bay Courier*, 27 Oct 1855, pp 1 & 3; *Qld Guardian*, 7 Jan 1861, p 2; *Brisb Courier*, 14 Dec 1871, p 1, 5 July 1876, p 3, 7 May 1891, p 3; C0201/465 (SRNSW).

W. S. KITSON

WATSON, ANDREW DOUGALD (1885-1962), Antarctic explorer and headmaster, was born on 27 June 1885 at New Lambton, New South Wales, fourth son of nine children of Scottish-born parents William Watson, miner, and his wife Jane, née Thomson. After primary schooling at Newcastle, Andrew attended Maitland Boys' High School. A pupil-teacher at Hamilton (1901) and New Lambton (1902), he gained a scholarship to Fort Street Training School, Sydney, in 1905. Next year he was a temporary teacher at Paddington and Lithgow and in 1907 at Forest Lodge, Crystal Street and Newtown, Sydney. In 1908 he received a scholarship, initially in arts, to the University of Sydney (B.Sc., 1913), where he studied geology, chemistry and biology.

Watson represented New South Wales at baseball in 1907-11 and in 1914 when he played against visiting teams from the United States of America. He was a first-grade cricketer for the university in 1910-11 and North Sydney in 1918-19 and also an outstanding golfer. Later his pastimes included woodwork, fishing and bowls.

Joining (Sir) Douglas Mawson's [q.v.10] 1911-14 Australasian Antarctic Expedition as a geologist and photographer, Watson spent almost a year in 1912-13 in the group of eight led by Frank Wild, at the Queen Mary Land or Western Base. There he trained the party's dogs and dug a shaft to study the glacial ice. He also studied glacial effects on the landscape and accessible rock such as the Hippo Nunatak. In the summer expeditions, Wild, A. L. Kennedy, C. T. Harrisson and Watson explored to the east, but broken ice hindered their mapping of the coast. A promontory on David Island was named Watson Bluff. In December Watson was rescued from a crevasse: 'in an instant I found myself dangling at rope's end, fully fifteen feet, into a yawning chasm, with sheer walls'. A subsequent lecture on the expedition was published in the *Journal* of the Royal Australian Historical Society in 1937. In 1946 he was president of the Antarctic Club of former explorers.

On 8 May 1913 at St Stephen's Presbyterian Church, Sydney, Watson married Esther Enid Godfrey, to whom he had become engaged before leaving for the Antarctic. He lectured in geology at the University of Adelaide in 1913, then returned to the New South Wales Department of Public Instruction next year as a science teacher at Sydney Boys' High School. A long period followed at North Sydney Boys' High School, first as science master and then as deputy headmaster. He was headmaster at Glen Innes (1933-35), Bowral (1935-37), Canberra (1938-45) and Homebush Boys' (1946-49) high schools. Respected by staff and students, Watson set the tone in his schools. About 6 ft (183 cm) tall and of solid build, he wore spectacles and an academic gown at school. He was 'a very dignified man', courteous and quietly spoken but aloof and austere. A Canberra High School colleague commented, 'Andy went southward ho with Mawson and he hasn't thawed out yet'. Watson died on 9 January 1962 at Cremorne, Sydney, and was cremated. His wife and son survived him.

D. Mawson, *The Home of the Blizzard* (Lond, 1915); *Jubilee Yarralumlan* (Canb, 1988), p 1; *Sun-Herald*, 18 Feb 1979, p 160; Watson papers, (ML); information from Ms J Grimsley, Yarralumla, ACT, Mr P. Watson, Brisb, and Dr A. D. Watson, Glebe, Syd.

BARRY PRICE

WATSON, JAMES THOMAS (1872-1938), mining engineer, was born on 24 July 1872 at Ballarat, Victoria, eldest of five sons of Scottish-born parents William Watson (d.1881), engineer, and his wife Johanna, née Holland. James began working in mines about 1885, and took a course in coal-mining and mine surveying at the Newcastle branch of Sydney Technical College. He earned his colliery manager's certificate in 1898, managed the Stockton and Gunnedah collieries for two years, and taught coal-mining and mining surveying at Newcastle Technical College from May 1901. On 3 November 1898 at North Lambton he had married with Particular Baptist forms Elizabeth Pickering, an English-born waitress. They had six children.

Appointed government inspector of collieries at Wollongong in August 1902, Watson zealously prosecuted managers who breached regulations. After the Mount Kembla mine explosion of 1902, when ninety-six miners died, he played a large part in the enquiry in which the manager William Rogers became a scapegoat for the disaster; Watson also chaired a panel that drew up stringent new safety regulations.

In 1907 he became manager of the Paparoa colliery, New Zealand, and in 1910 of the Corrimal colliery, Wollongong, New South Wales. A 'man of considerable note in the coal world' by 1912, Watson was retained by the Chillagoe Co. Ltd to report on their coal prospects at Mount Mulligan in North Queensland. Appointed superintending engineer of the new mine when it opened in 1914, he installed the latest mining plant. On 19 September 1921 an underground explosion killed seventy-six miners; it was the third-worst industrial disaster in Australian history. Watson bravely led the rescue efforts until he collapsed.

Defending himself before the subsequent royal commission, Watson claimed that he was superintending engineer—a title unknown in Queensland mining law—and had not been involved in the management of the mine. The underground manager and his deputies were all dead; the commissioners found that these men had all tolerated gross breaches of safety regulations, but rejected Watson's evidence and placed the responsibility for the disaster squarely on him. The irony increased when in 1922 the Royal Humane Society of Australasia presented him with its (Sir William John) Clarke [q.v.3] silver medal, for his courage in the disaster aftermath. Watson left Mount Mulligan early in 1923 and never worked in the mining industry again. He wrote several articles over the next few years seeking to blame others for the disaster. After working as manager of the Inkerman Irrigation Area, Queensland, from about 1927 to 1932, he became a consulting engineer in Brisbane, at one time working for the Queensland Department of Main Roads. He retired in 1937.

There is little doubt that Watson was unfairly treated by the royal commission, which was a cynical political exercise, dominated by friends of the premier E. G. Theodore [q.v.12]. The commission conspicuously avoided comment on the failings of Chillagoe Ltd and the Queensland Mines Department. At the time, the government was secretly negotiating to purchase the Mungana mines near Chillagoe —a fraudulent transaction that would end Theodore's political career. The hasty Mount Mulligan enquiry was preoccupied with averting bad publicity, and neither satisfactorily explained the cause of the disaster nor convincingly established Watson's culpability.

A big impressive man, grim-faced in later years, Watson was a founding member of the Institution of Engineers Australia and remained active in his profession until he died of cancer on 19 January 1938 at Coopers Plains, Queensland. His wife, four daughters and one son survived him. He was cremated with Presbyterian forms.

Mount Mulligan Colliery Disaster (Brisb, 1922); P. Bell, *'If Anything, Too Safe'* (Townsville, Qld, 1996); S. Piggin and H. Lee, *The Mt Kembla Disaster* (Syd, 1992); *Jnl of the Institution of Engineers Aust*, 11, Dec 1939, p 440; *Cairns Post*, 25 Sept 1912; A1007/1, item 1905/48 (NAA); information from the Royal Humane Soc of A'sia, Melb, and Mr R. Beveridge, Canb.   PETER BELL

WAUGH, JULIAN BARBARA (1857-1938), political and community worker, was born on 9 June 1857 at Balmain, Sydney, and registered as Julianna, third daughter of twelve children of Ewen Wallace Cameron [q.v.3], a French-born merchant, and his wife Sophia Usher, née Nail, from Mauritius. Julian's grandfather was Lieutenant Colonel Charles Cameron [q.v.1]. As a child, she spent some time in France. On 27 February 1879 at St Mary's Church of England, Balmain, she married John Waugh (1852-1928), a clerk, later a bank manager. The couple moved to Parramatta, where Julian brought up two children, played croquet and was president of the local croquet club.

Mrs Waugh participated in the Australian Exhibition of Women's Work, held in Melbourne in 1907. In 1909-10 she was mayoress of Parramatta when John was mayor. An active member of the Women's Liberal (Reform) League of New South Wales, in 1909 she seconded a resolution to support the effort 'to contribute to a Dreadnought [for] the Mother-Country'; the motion was carried —'the women all springing to their feet and displaying the utmost enthusiasm'. In 1913-18 Waugh was president of the league, which she believed voiced 'the women's point of view' on legislation affecting women and children. She was a fund-raiser for the Royal Prince Alfred Hospital, of which she was an honorary life governor from 1911.

During World War I Waugh was the embodiment of 'patriotic feminism', supporting the war effort without reservation and embracing the opportunities for public activism that the conflict offered to women of her class. At the invitation of Eveline, the wife of Governor Sir Gerald Strickland [q.v.12], she convened the meeting of patriotic women at the Victoria Club that originated the Travelling Kitchen Fund, of which she became president; it presented seven kitchens to the Australian military forces. Active in collecting comforts, she spoke extensively in public, encouraging recruiting, the early closing of hotels and the 'Yes' vote in the conscription referenda. With a strong personality and a handsome appearance, 'Mrs John Waugh' was described in a 1915 newspaper series on 'Our Public Women' and photographed wearing a tiara.

After the formation of the National Party in 1917, she was an indefatigable member of its State council. She was also a council member of the United Australia Party and was prominent in its Mosman branch; she retired as president of the latter in December 1932. Other associations to which she belonged included the Queen Victoria Club (president, 1913-20), the National Council of Women of New South Wales (executive member), the Fresh Air League (council member), the Boy Scouts' Association, the Women's Reform League (general president), the Citizens'

Association, the Maternal Mortality Committee and the Twilight House. Although she supported the National Service League, her inherent conservatism led her to oppose anything that would 'interfere in any way with industrial conditions'. During a visit to Britain in 1921 she was invited by the Women's Guild of Empire to represent Australian women at the Cenotaph in London. In 1928 she was a delegate to the first Pan-Pacific Women's Conference, Honolulu.

Waugh was appointed M.B.E. in June 1934. She died on 2 January 1938 at her home, Waughope, at Mosman, and was cremated. Her daughter and son survived her.

T. Kass et al, *Parramatta: A Past Revealed* (Syd, 1996); *United Aust Review*, 20 Dec 1932, p 21; *Women's World*, 1 July 1934; *Daily Telegraph* (Syd), 17 Mar 1909, p 6, 24 Mar 1909, p 7, 6 Oct 1915, p 6; *Sun* (Syd), 15 Oct 1916, p 14; *SMH*, 3 Jan 1938, p 4.

JOAN BEAUMONT

WAY KEE (c.1824-1892), storekeeper, was born in Canton (Guangzhou), China, son of Toy Yue, a merchant, of the Dongguan (Doong Goong) clan, and claimed to have come to Sydney about 1853. He had commenced business in the Rocks by 1871 and five years later leased 164-68 Lower George Street, where he demolished the existing buildings and built three new stores, two of which he rented out. Typical of the ten or eleven elite Chinese merchants who ran regional trading networks through their businesses in Lower George Street, Way Kee imported Chinese goods for sale in Australia, including through country stores at Bourke, Bega and Hillston and at Stanthorpe, Queensland, remitting some £7000 to £8000 in gold to Hong Kong in 1891. During the 1880s he rented a market garden at Lane Cove, Sydney, from a local policeman for £30 a year, employing four men.

Way Kee's influential position entailed obligations, such as serving from 1857 to 1889 as treasurer of the Koon Yee Tong, an association that returned the bodies of the deceased to their homes in China. Poorer Chinese gardeners and hawkers entrusted him with their savings; if they were in trouble with the police, he would bail them out. Through his firm he sponsored Chinese migrants, housed new arrivals, provided information and assistance —especially with bureaucratic procedures— and channelled job-seekers to the market gardens or country towns. A grandson, Ah Wah (War Moo), arrived from China in 1881 and later became his partner.

Although anti-Chinese feeling was strong, wealthy merchants were often able to maintain their independence. Way Kee spoke no English, and stated through an interpreter: 'I very seldom go out. I am in the store all day'. He returned to China four times, marrying on four occasions. He brought his fourth wife Jung See to Sydney, with Ah Wah's wife, in 1891. Like other merchants, at times he sought to subvert restrictive immigration regulations. In June 1890 seven stowaways were detected aboard the *Changsha*, three destined for Way Kee's business.

A cultural intermediary, Way Kee traded with local European firms, including those of Christopher Newton and Sigmond Hoffnung [q.v.4], and developed personal contacts with customs and wharf officials. Like Quong Tart [q.v.5] and other successful Sydney merchants, he was a generous philanthropist, who campaigned against the 'vices' of the lower classes of overseas Chinese, such as opium smoking. He gave evidence to the 1891 royal commission on alleged Chinese gambling and immorality.

Way Kee died of heart disease on 15 August 1892 at his home in Sydney. Following a Christian service conducted by the Rev. Young Choy, his funeral procession through the city, attended by a crowd of about 3000 Chinese representing all major clan associations, was a notable and colourful event. A mile (1.6 km) in length, with elaborate banners and two brass bands, it moved from his house along George Street to the Town Hall, then north to Smith's Wharf. Here a shrine had been erected for a Chinese ceremony before his body was placed aboard the *Tsinan* for return to China. His wife, and five sons of his first marriage, survived him.

S. Fitzgerald, *Red Tape, Gold Scissors* (Syd, 1996); J. Lydon, *Many Inventions* (Melb, 1999); Report of the Royal Commission on Alleged Chinese Gambling and Immorality, *V&P* (LA, Qld), 1891-92, vol 8, p 467; *SMH*, 5 Sept 1892, p 4; *Daily Telegraph* (Syd), 5 Sept 1892, p 4.

JANE LYDON

WEBSTER, EDWARD (1866-1928), schoolteacher and co-founder of the Gould [q.v.1] League of Bird Lovers, was born on 8 January 1866 at Richmond, New South Wales, fifth child of William Webster, an English-born engine-driver, and his wife Isabella, née Farquhar, from Scotland. Attending Cleveland Street Public School, Redfern, from the age of 4, by 1880 Edward was a pupil-teacher at Camden Public School. After a one-year course at the Fort Street Training School, in January 1886 he was appointed to Goulburn and then worked at Birchgrove, Sydney, and Croydon. Next year he was sent to half-time country schools at Browns Creek and Wallendibby, then at Murrambego and Wallendibby. From Tenderden (1889) and Glen Innes (1890) he was promoted to Young in 1893.

At Pitt Street Presbyterian Church, Sydney, on Boxing Day 1893 Webster married Dolleina Ross. In 1895 he was posted to Burke Ward Public School, Broken Hill, where 365 children endured crowded and unsuitable conditions. He had some success in securing new schoolrooms, but the Websters' infant daughter died in 1897 from an illness that the doctor believed was 'largely influenced by the climate and local conditions'. Advised to leave the town for his health and that of his young son, he was sent to Bondi, Sydney, in 1898, then to Majors Creek. In October 1905 he became head teacher at Wellington, where he showed an enthusiasm for school drill and threw himself into the life of the town, becoming the choirmaster for a local choir of sixty voices.

In 1910 Webster's deputy Walter Finigan (1885-1976) drew his attention to the creation in Victoria of the Gould League of Bird Lovers —suggested by a teacher, Jessie McMichael —and the celebration of Bird Day in October 1909. The idea followed from the Junior Audubon Society in the United States of America but in Australia honoured John Gould. On 22 October 1910 Webster and Finigan called a meeting at Wellington and established the Gould League of Bird Lovers in New South Wales. The chief inspector James Dawson ensured that the school system supported it. Children contributed a penny for a certificate and pledged to protect birds, mainly by not collecting their eggs. The movement spread to all States; New South Wales, however, with 10 000 members by 1917 and over 130 000 by the 1930s, had the largest membership. Webster was on the State committee while Finigan, promoted to Sydney, remained the league's secretary for several years.

Confident and ambitious, Webster applied in 1909 and 1910 for appointment as an inspector; although he was unsuccessful, he was promoted to the top teaching grade at the end of 1910 and moved to Sydney in 1913. He became headmaster at Darlinghurst and then at Cleveland Street Intermediate High School, where he remained until his death. With L. H. Allen [q.v.7], he contributed to a study, 'An Experiment in Imaginative Writing', published in the *Records of the Education Society* (Sydney, 1918). In 1928 Webster published *The New Syllabus English Grammar for Primary Schools*. He also conducted large choirs of school children in Sydney Town Hall.

Applying for promotion in 1910, Webster had expressed conventional views about the British heritage, religion and morality, but called for patriotism based on a respect for Australian nature. He regretted the lack of efforts to improve flannel flowers or 'that queen among bush flowers, the waratah', and believed that schools should work to 'eradi-cate the idea that nature is for exploitation for material gain'. Webster died of cancer on 24 March 1928 at his home at Manly and was buried in Rookwood cemetery. His wife, three sons and two daughters survived him.

C. Barrett, *The Bird Man* (Melb, 1938); *SMH*, 26 Mar 1928, p 12, 13 Sept 1928, p 8, 3 Nov 1928, pp 12 & 18; teachers' records and information from school history section *and* M. McPherson, History of Burke Ward Public School, 1994, (NSW Dept of Education); Wellington school files (SRNSW).

BRUCE MITCHELL

WEIGEL, JOHANNA WILHELMINE (1847-1940), paper-pattern manufacturer, was born in 1847 in Poland; her father's surname was Astmann. As a young woman she went to the United States of America and in New York worked as a designer at McCalls, a leading paper-pattern establishment, where she met August Louis William Oscar Robert Carl Weigel (1844-1915), an engineer who had been born in the German dukedom of Brunswick. In 1876 she and Oscar married in New York; they travelled to Melbourne for their honeymoon, arriving in March 1877 in the *Mysore*, intending to stay for six months.

By her own account, after many requests from friends who admired her dress sense Johanna Weigel started to cut patterns from her own clothes and give them away. The easy-to-follow instructions for measuring, cutting and sewing made the patterns popular, and their increasing success led her and Oscar to start their fashion business in 1877 in premises in Lennox Street, Richmond. They imported all their printing machines and tissue paper and soon established offices in central Melbourne and Sydney and agencies throughout Australia and New Zealand.

In 1880 they started *Weigel's Journal of Fashion*, a monthly subscription journal that claimed to be the first fashion magazine to be designed, published and printed in Australia. It included illustrated fashion articles, housekeeping hints and serialized fiction. The impact of her patterns and journal on women and their families, particularly in country areas, was considerable. Miles Franklin [q.v.8] later wrote that her mother was a regular subscriber to the *Journal*:

It was an 'elegancy' to which she clung through the leanest lean years ... Mother always dressed herself and us by Madame W's paper patterns Madame Weigel was to me a figure of legend as Mrs Beeton or 'The Ingoldsby Legends'.

In 1893 Oscar (and therefore his wife) was naturalized. In 1890 they had built Drusilla, a two-storeyed house with twenty-six rooms on twenty-seven acres (11 ha), at the foot of

Mount Macedon, where they developed a substantial garden. The house burned down in July 1903. They subsequently moved to South Melbourne. The Weigels were frequent contributors to charity, much of their philanthropy being anonymous. On 7 February 1915 Oscar died at Los Angeles while he and Johanna were on a business trip. Johanna returned to Australia in April with Oscar's ashes. His estate in Victoria was sworn for probate at £32 740.

After her retirement from active association with the business, Weigel travelled extensively overseas. In U.S. shipping records, she was described as blonde, blue-eyed and 5 ft 2 ins (158 cm) tall. For the last twelve years of her life she and her friend and companion Sarah Neilson lived at the Oriental Hotel in Collins Street, Melbourne. Madame Weigel died on 10 January 1940 and was cremated. When Oscar had died during World War I there were difficulties in transferring money to Germany. The same problem arose with her estate, which was sworn for probate at £71 844. In addition to legacies for family and for friends in the U.S.A., England and Australia and for her former cook, she bequeathed £20 000 to be invested in the Oscar Weigel Charitable Trust with the income to provide exhibitions for engineering students. A committee of the heads of faculties of engineering at the University of Melbourne and Monash University and the Victorian State College awards Oscar Weigel exhibitions to outstanding students each year. The residue of her estate was left to the employees of Madame Weigel Pty Ltd, which continued until at least the 1960s. On the death of the last surviving employee in 1972 the final distribution of her estate was made to five hospitals named in her will.

Madame Weigel's Jnl of Fashion, 1 Feb 1940, p 487; *Argus* (Melb), 28 Apr 1915, p 8, 11 Jan 1940, p 11; *Herald* (Melb), 10 Jan 1940, p 4; *Age* (Melb), 11 Jan 1940, p 3; A3201, item TE1762 (NAA, Canb); Miles Franklin papers, MSS 364, notebooks, vol 3, p 461 (ML); J. Weigel biog file (LaTL).

DEIRDRE MORRIS

WEITZEL, HEDWIG; *see* ROSS, HEDWIG

WELLS, CHARLES FREDERICK (1918-1975), seaman and journalist, was born on 4 August 1918 in Hobart, the son of Violet Wells and Charles Frederick Saunders, a war pensioner. By 1940 Fred Wells was living in Sydney with his mother and working as a coal lumper.

Enlisting in the Australian Imperial Force on 15 March that year, Wells served in the 2/33rd Battalion in the Middle East and New Guinea. His army career was unexceptional until January 1942 when he gave up his rank of acting sergeant at his own request. Then followed three years of personal turmoil. He was absent without leave on many occasions, including a period of six weeks triggered by the decision of a medical board that he was fit for duty in April 1943. After a time in detention, he rejoined his battalion for the fighting at Milne Bay in New Guinea. There he caught malaria and became deaf in the left ear. After being admitted to the 113th Australian General Hospital, Concord, Sydney, suffering from anxiety, he was discharged with a 40 per cent disability pension on 28 February 1945.

Wells went to sea. Joining the Communist Party of Australia and the Seamen's Union of Australia in 1945, he was a prominent industrial militant for the next fifteen years. A dark-complexioned, nuggety man of medium build, 5 ft 8 ins (173 cm) tall, with tattoos on his upper arms, he was proud of his strength, fond of alcohol and not reluctant to use physical force for political ends. By 1951 he had been arrested in three street demonstrations. He also became a trusted lieutenant of the C.P.A., as a leader of the Australian delegation to the 1951 World Youth Festival in Berlin and as a relieving official in the communist-controlled seamen's union. He attended the eighteenth national conference of the party in 1958.

The C.P.A. leadership worried, however, about Wells's irresponsibility and hoped that his marriage to a fellow party member, Philippa Marion Hilda Schapper, a teacher, on 29 August 1953 at Doncaster, Melbourne, would keep him sober. In 1960, soon after confessing to Eric Aarons that he had suffered a breakdown in the army, he left the ships and the Communist party, and entered the psychiatric ward of the Repatriation Hospital, Concord. A journalist on the *Bulletin* (Sydney) between 1963 and 1965, he became industrial roundsman for the *Sydney Morning Herald* from 1965.

Wells suffered no further periods of instability, which suggested that his new career as a journalist liberated an intelligent man from the dulling effects of physical labour and political dogma. Recognition of his intellectual capacity and his knowledge of industrial relations came quickly. He wrote two chapters on the Communist party for a university text on Australian politics, edited by Henry Mayer. Wells was the first honorary secretary of the Sydney branch of the Labour History Society in 1963.

Exposures of communist policy and organization were his specialty. When Wells's pamphlet on the communist-inspired Sydney peace congress, *The Peace Racket* (Sydney, 1964), was sent under a plain wrapper to school principals, his former associates knew that he was receiving help from the Australian Security Intelligence Organisation. He was an informant, reporting to a case officer responsible for liaising with journalists. His A.S.I.O. file reveals that opposing factions in the Communist party fed him information during the late 1960s. Using his own knowledge, his extensive circle of contacts, and analyses from A.S.I.O., his articles were authoritative commentaries on communist industrial and cultural activities in these years.

In May 1975 Wells travelled to Western Australia to report on the conference of the Australian Council of Trade Unions. He died of 'meprobate poisoning self ingested but not with the intention of taking his own life' on 22 May 1975 in the Transit Inn, Perth, and was cremated in Sydney. His wife and their two sons survived him.

D. McKnight, *Australia's Spies and their Secrets* (Syd, 1994); *Labour History*, no 7, Nov 1964, p 57; coronial file, 12879/75 (Crown Law Dept, Perth); B883, item NX10188, A6119, items 911 and 2957 (NAA, Canb); information from Mr E. Aarons, Ms G. O'Brien, Mr J. Mundey, and Mr G. Souter, Syd.

T. H. IRVING

WERTHEIM, HUGO (1854-1919), merchant and manufacturer, was born on 12 July 1854 at Lispenhausen, in the German electorate of Hesse-Kassel, son of Meyer Wertheim and his wife Minna, née Heinemann. Tall and dark, Hugo reached Melbourne in the *Great Britain* in October 1875. Soon he was advertising, from premises at 39 Flinders Lane East, as agent for his father's cousin Joseph Wertheim, a well-established manufacturer of sewing machines. On 27 February 1882 Hugo was naturalized. Back in Germany, he married Joseph Wertheim's daughter Sophie Emilie (1864-1953) on 30 August 1885 at Frankfurt and the couple came to Melbourne. Thereafter, he frequently returned to Europe. In the 1880s he built a 17-bedroomed mansion, Gotha (later Hadleigh Hall, demolished 1935), at South Yarra, where such musicians as the visiting Paderewski played.

In a short time, with extensive advertising, Hugo established a substantial business, selling sewing machines, bicycles, pianos and other mechanical devices, under brands such as Wertheim, Electra, Planet, Griffin and Hapsburg. He also mounted elaborate displays at agricultural shows and in 1901 at the Pan American Exposition, Buffalo, United States of America. O. C. Beale [q.v.7] worked with him before setting up his own piano business in New South Wales. Hugo continued to own 25 per cent of one of Beale's companies, which became Wertheim's Queensland business.

In 1908 at a cost of some £75 000, Wertheim opened a large, innovative piano factory at Richmond, Melbourne, intending to produce 2000 pianos and player pianos annually, predominantly using Australian materials. In laying the foundation stone, Prime Minister Alfred Deakin [q.v.8], observed that 'few men with such opportunities for a life of ease would have embarked on such an enterprise ... the first in Victoria to commence making pianos'. Theodore Fink [q.v.8] remarked that Wertheim had left behind the controversial position of an importer and grown into the patriotic position of a manufacturer. Premier Sir Thomas Bent [q.v.3], to reported cheers, said that he had found him as good a Briton as any in promoting industry.

World War I, however, caused difficulties for Wertheim. Australian military intelligence files showed that he and his family were reported numerous times as spies or 'pro-German'. Beginning in 1914, various wild assertions were investigated and found groundless. Wertheim's second son Rupert Carl (1892-1933), known as 'Soss' (for German sausage), served in France with the Australian Imperial Force and was thrice mentioned in dispatches; in September 1917 he interrogated captured Germans, deriving information that averted a German counter-attack.

Hugo died of chronic hepatitis on 11 July 1919 at his home at South Yarra and left an estate in Victoria valued for probate at £51 539. His wife, two daughters and three sons survived him; Herbert Joseph (1886-1972), the eldest, continued the business. Rupert became a sharebroker; he represented Victoria in inter-State tennis in 1913-27 and Australia in Davis Cup matches against Czechoslovakia in 1922. The piano factory closed in 1935, becoming a Heinz food processing plant and, in 1955, GTV Channel 9 studios and offices.

J. Smith (ed), *Cyclopedia of Victoria* (Melb, 1903); J. B. Kiddle, *War Services of Old Melburnians 1914-1918* (Melb, 1923?); *Liber Melburniensis* (Melb, 1937 and 1965); C. E. W. Bean, *The A.I.F. in France*, 1917, (Syd, 1938), p 774; *Richmond Australian* (Melb), 9 Oct 1880, p 4; *Weekly Times* (Melb), 2 Nov 1901, p 12, 3 Sept 1910, p 30, 10 Sept 1910, p 27; *Leader* (Melb), 12 Sept 1903, p 35; *Argus* (Melb), 22 Oct 1908, p 4, 19 June 1935, p 6; *Richmond Guardian*, 24 Oct 1908, p 2; *Punch* (Melb), 17 July 1919, p 89; information from Mr W. R. Fanning, Malvern, and Mrs S. Chambers, Ashwood, Vic.

ANDREW J. RAY

WEST, THOMAS (1773-1858), convict and landowner, was born on 4 June 1773 at Hooe, Sussex, England, fifth of nine children of John West, farmer, and his wife Margaret. Thomas was a carpenter at Canterbury when he married Martha Goodwin on 8 July 1793 at

St Nicholas's Church, New Romney. At the Sussex Assizes, Horsham, on 17 March 1800 he was convicted of burglary and sentenced to transportation for life. He reached Sydney in the *Earl Cornwallis* in June 1801. His wife —who later remarried—remained in England; one of their sons (Thomas d.1856) migrated as a free settler in 1821.

West formed a liaison with Mary Rugg (c.1769-1865), a convict; they had a daughter in 1805 and a son OBED (1807-1891), who was born on 4 December 1807. Employed in the government lumberyard, Thomas showed entrepreneurial skills by making coffins and reputedly hanging the peal of bells in St Phillip's Church. In June 1810 he successfully petitioned Governor Macquarie [q.v.2] for permission to erect a watermill in Lacrozia Valley, on land that he named Barcom Glen, surrounded by Darlinghurst, Paddington and Rushcutters Bay. No document of title was issued, however, and the boundaries were vague: the deputy surveyor James Meehan's [q.v.2] 1816 survey indicated only some forty acres (16 ha), but West extended his fences towards Old South Head Road.

On Christmas Eve 1813 West received a conditional pardon and the gift of a cow from the government herd. Dairying, an orchard and quarrying were added to his growing commercial activities. By 1824 he owned 120 head of cattle. Needing pasture for them, he received from Governor Brisbane [q.v.1] a ticket of occupation for 160 acres (65 ha) in the Picton district for which he received title in July 1835. His holdings further increased that year when he obtained a 1280-acre (518 ha) grant, near The Oaks, as an offset from the Crown for quarrying on Barcom Glen.

West's powerful neighbours in Sydney included Alexander McLeay and (Sir) Thomas Mitchell [qq.v.2]. Discussions on the boundaries, particularly with Mitchell, were unproductive and court action resulted. *R.* v. *West* opened in the Supreme Court in October 1831, before Mr Justice John Stephen [q.v.2] and a special jury of landholders. West relied on his twenty-one-year unbroken possession of the land as proof of title. The case was seen as emancipist against exclusivist, especially as he was represented by W. C. Wentworth [q.v.2]. The jury returned a verdict of 'No intrusion'—a victory for West.

The *Australian*, co-edited by Wentworth, reported the win as 'foiling Mr. McLeay and his favourites ... the sharks are outwitted'. Following a review of the case by crown law officers, however, the Supreme Court agreed to hear the case again. A compromise, in which West offered to accept a new western boundary, was rejected. In October 1832 the case was retried, with Wentworth again appearing for him. The jury found he had committed a minor trespass on about five acres (2 ha) but held good title to seventy-one acres (29 ha). Although Barcom Glen's boundaries and title had been established, it was not until 1844 that the title deeds were issued.

Determined by nature, short in stature, and thickset, particularly in later life, West was the quintessential 'John Bull' type. His right index finger was missing, a sign of a life spent in physical toil. Thomas died on 21 September 1858 at Burwood and was buried in St John's churchyard, Ashfield. Mary and their two children survived him.

Obed had worked closely with his father in family business affairs from an early age. On 23 December 1831 at St James's Church, Sydney, he married with Anglican rites Jane Margaret Lindsey (d.1875), daughter of a convict. Obed extended the family's land holdings to include tracts, both for farming and speculation, on Sydney's northern peninsula, and goldmining at Hill End. He was 6 ft 4 ins (193 cm) tall and weighed 16 stone (101.6 kg), and won a gold medal for rifle shooting. Late in his life he published articles about his detailed memories of early Sydney in the *Sydney Morning Herald*. Obed died on 24 August 1891 at Barcom Glen, Paddington, and was buried in Randwick cemetery. His four sons and eight of his nine daughters survived him, inheriting an estate sworn for probate at £74 389; the ninety-nine-year leases of his land at fixed rentals, however, created a legacy of legal complexities for his beneficiaries.

B. T. Dowd, *Thomas West Convict Transportee, 1801 and his Barcom Glen Grant Lacrozia Valley, Darlinghurst* (Syd, 1974); E. W. Marriott, *Thomas West of Barcom Glen* (Bowral, NSW, 1982) and *The Memoirs of Obed West* (Bowral, NSW, 1988); G. L. Curnow, Thomas West, the Yeoman of Barcom Glen (B.A. Hons essay, ANU, 1974).   GREG CURNOW*

WESTWOOD, WILLIAM ('JACKEY JACKEY') (1820-1846), convict and bushranger, was born on 7 August 1820 and baptized on 27 August at the church of St Mary the Virgin, Manuden, Essex, England, one of several children of James Westwood, labourer, and his wife Ann. William learned to read and write and became an errand boy. He had previously served twelve months for highway robbery when he was tried on 3 January 1837 at the Essex Quarter Sessions, Colchester, for stealing a coat. Sentenced to transportation for fourteen years, he reached Sydney on 9 July 1837 in the *Mangles*. He had a ruddy complexion, brown hair, dark grey eyes and various scars.

Assigned to Phillip Parker King [q.v.2], Westwood was sent to his station, Gidley, near Bungendore, where the overseer ill-treated him and provided insufficient food and clothing. On 19 April 1838 Westwood was sentenced to six months imprisonment for stealing wheat. Sent back to his master, he escaped but was quickly recaptured and received fifty lashes on 4 February 1839. From September 1840 Westwood 'was out 7 Months in the bush under Arms'. Known as 'Jackey Jackey', he roamed the Southern District, eluding capture by retreating to mountain hideouts and riding long distances in a very short time. He stole horses, money, clothes, provisions and arms, but never hurt his victims and was courteous towards women. On one occasion he held up the mail, took £200 and spent a month in Sydney, staying at a hotel in George Street. Old hands remembered him as 'the gentleman bushranger'.

At Berrima on 15 April 1841, Westwood was tried for robbery with firearms and stealing a mare, and was sentenced to transportation for life. Although in chains, he escaped from the Stonequarry (Picton) lock-up on the way to Sydney and hid up a tree. The *Australian* commented that the 'cool intrepidity and daring of this man is astonishing ... he is moreover well-dressed, assumes all disguises'. Recaptured in mid-July, he was held in the prison on Cockatoo Island, Port Jackson, until transported to Van Diemen's Land in the *Marian Watson*.

Reaching Hobart Town on 8 March 1842, Westwood was sent to Port Arthur. He twice absconded that year and twice received 100 lashes. On a third occasion he escaped from Port Arthur—this time by swimming across the channel; his companions were eaten by sharks. On 7 November 1843 he was sentenced to twelve months imprisonment with hard labour, with three months in solitary confinement. Next year W. T. Champ [q.v.3], the new commandant, promoted Westwood to his boat crew. After the crew had rescued two men from drowning, the lieutenant-governor approved of the removal of Westwood from Port Arthur in May 1845 to serve six months probation at Glenorchy. Habit was too strong: on 4 September 1845 he was tried in the Hobart Supreme Court for robbery, 'being armed whilst illegally at large'. As he had not harmed anyone, the death sentence was commuted to transportation for life to Norfolk Island.

Instructed by the British government to impose strict discipline, Joseph Childs [q.v.1], commandant of Norfolk Island, ordered the secret removal of the prisoners' 'tins and knives, and other utensils for cooking their food'. The next morning, 1 July 1846, Westwood led a mutiny and killed an overseer and three constables before being overpowered by the military. In the condemned cell he was befriended by the religious instructor Thomas Rogers [q.v.2] who encouraged him to write (or dictate) an account of his life—Rogers, as 'Peutetre', published it in the *Australasian* in

1879. Sentenced to death with twelve others, Westwood was hanged on 13 October 1846. Although he was in communion with the Church of England, he was buried in unhallowed ground. Westwood had written to his parents, sending them a lock of his hair, and also to a clergyman: 'Sir, out of the bitter cup of misery I have drank from my 16th year,—ten long years—and the sweetest draught is that which takes away the misery of a living death; ... all will then be quiet—no tyrant will then disturb my repose, I hope'.

G. E. Boxall, *The Story of the Australian Bushrangers* (Lond, 1899); R. Nixon Dalton, *Colonial Era Cemetery of Norfolk Island* (Syd, 1974); G. Dick, *The Bushranger of Bungendore* (Bungendore, NSW, 1979); 'Correspondence on the Subject of Convict Discipline and Transportation', *PP* (Great Britain), 1847, vol 48, p 174; *Canb Hist Jnl*, Sept 1975, p 92; *Australasian*, 20 Apr 1841, p 2, 27 May 1841, p 2; 1 Feb 1879, p 134, 8 Feb 1879, p 166, 15 Feb 1879, p 199, 22 Feb 1879, p 231; *Hobart Town Courier*, 2 Sept 1842, p 3, 6 Sept 1845, p 3; *Hobart Town Advertiser*, 7 Oct 1843, p 3, 6 Sept 1845, p 3; *Britannia* (Hob), 5 Nov 1846, p 3, 4 Apr 1847, p 4, 29 Apr 1847, p 4; CSO 20/2/64, CSO 22/19/779, ff 1-5, and Con 55/1, p 597, no 3035 (TSA); Index to NSW Convicts 1788-1843, fiche 727, p 95.

MARTHA RUTLEDGE

WICKEN, HARRIETT FRANCES (1847-1937), cookery writer, was born on 31 December 1847 at Lambeth, England, daughter of Joseph Smith, ironmonger, and his wife Harriett, née Pugh. On 24 November 1865 at the parish church of St Mary, Lambeth, as Harriette she married George Charles Wicken, a builder of Tulse Hill. A son, PERCY GEORGE (1866-1952), was followed by four more sons and two daughters. George Wicken died of phthisis in 1873 and apparently only two sons, Percy and Arthur, survived to adulthood. Soon after it opened in 1874, Harriette acquired a diploma from the National Training School for Cookery, South Kensington, and became a cookery lecturer and demonstrator. In 1885 her *Kingswood Cookery Book*, based on her classes, was published in London.

In 1884 Percy migrated to Victoria and Harriet (as she now spelled her name) followed him with Arthur in September 1886. Befriended by Lady Loch, wife of the governor Sir Henry Loch [q.v.5], Harriet gave cooking classes at Warrnambool. Having arranged an Australian edition of her cookery book, she moved to Sydney where she was appointed lecturer in charge of the department of domestic economy at Sydney Technical College, Ultimo. On 2 September 1889 she presented to (Sir) Joseph Carruthers [q.v.7], minister of public instruction, a copy of the revised, enlarged Australian edition of the *Kingswood Cookery Book*, in which she set out to teach a modern scientific domestic economy to Australian housekeepers. A new edition, now dedicated, with permission, to the Countess of Jersey [q.v.9], to be used as a text by her cooking classes, appeared in 1891 with a companion handbook of domestic economy, *The Australian Home*, which was dedicated to Carruthers 'in recognition of his eminent services in the cause of technical education'.

To *The Art of Living in Australia* (Sydney, 1893), written by her Macquarie Street neighbour and diet reformer, Dr Philip Muskett [q.v.], she contributed a section of about 300 recipes. Though in sympathy with his campaign to encourage Australians to eat more fish and less meat, and to be more adventurous in the use of fruit and vegetables, her recipes were not really suited to Muskett's purpose. In other small cookbooks that appeared during the 1890s she stressed simplicity and her favourite 'dainty' recipes, though most merely adapted traditional English styles. For lighter food she advocated the use of an ice chest, which she thought a more desirable but less common piece of household equipment in Australia than either a sewing machine or a piano.

Percy gained a diploma from Hawkesbury Agricultural College in 1892 and joined the college staff as chief experimentalist. Muskett lectured to his students. The chokos, okra, eggplants and madagasca beans recorded in Percy's annual reports began to appear also in Harriet's vegetable dishes.

After 1896 Harriet no longer taught at the technical college, but her students—like Amy Schauer [q.v.11]—began to staff the new schools of domestic economy throughout the education system. Harriet continued to demonstrate cooking with gas, which became one of her specialties. She also continued to produce small cookery books to order, such as *The Cook's Compass* (Sydney, 1890) to promote the Sydney grocers J. G. Hanks & Co., and *Fish Dainties* (Melbourne, 1892) for the Melbourne Mutual Provedoring Co., or as seasonal gestures, for example *Recipes of Lenten Dishes* (1896).

In 1898 Arthur died in Sydney of phthisis. In 1900 Percy married and moved to Perth as officer in charge of the information bureau, Western Australian Agricultural Department. Harriet also went to Perth and taught for some time at Perth High School. The sixth and last edition of her *Kingswood Cookery Book* appeared in 1913.

When she died on 27 October 1937 at The Haven, Leederville, Percy was her only surviving relation. She was buried in the Anglican section of Karrakatta cemetery. On her death certificate her father had become a 'merchant' and her name had reverted to Harriett. Percy died on 23 July 1952 at Subiaco. Judging from her books, Harriet Wicken was brisk, con-

fident, practical and very neat, even dainty, keenly aware of the value of influence, and shameless at using it. She saw Australia as part of 'Greater Britain' and, though she became devoted to 'Australia's fair daughters', she remained the complete Englishwoman.

The Official Guide to Western Australia (Perth, 1909), p 103; B. R. Austin (comp), *A Bibliography of Australian Cookery Books Published Prior to 1941* (Melb, 1987); C. Bannerman, *A Friend in the Kitchen* (Syd, 1996); Wicken card file (ML).

BEVERLEY KINGSTON

WILLASON, THOMAS PARKING (1882?-1939), Methodist minister, was born possibly on 19 April 1882 in London, son of Thomas Willason, an Irish Catholic. Migrating to New Zealand, probably as a stowaway in 1895, young Thomas was apprenticed to a butcher. He made several voyages around the world, qualifying as a first mate in sail. Converted to membership of the Methodist Church at a Wellington evangelistic mission, he began a lifelong friendship with Samuel Forsyth [q.v.8] and from 1905 trained at W. Lockhart Morton's Bible college, Belair, South Australia.

Employed by the Methodist Church from 1908, Willason was ordained in 1914 and, after serving at Saddleworth, Port Broughton and Wallaroo, was appointed superintendent of the Port Adelaide Central Methodist Mission in 1924. On 9 April 1914 at the Methodist Church, Henley Beach, he had married Ethel May Goldring, a nurse. She contributed her managerial and nursing skills to the mission's work. They had three children.

With a Jew's harp and fine tenor voice, Willason brought evangelistic urgency to the struggling mission. His unconventional background eased his acceptance. Alongside standard Methodist church activities—youth clubs, happy hours, Sunday night services—he convened open-air meetings and talks at the wharfies' morning smokos, and hired local cinemas for meetings. A Freemason, he exploited his Masonic connexions.

Willason's fortnightly columns in the *Australian Christian Commonwealth* sought funds for the mission's growing relief work. He also wrote with passionate conviction against the 'bolshevik menace' that threatened the workers of Adelaide. Willason believed that 'we are fighting the battles of the Lord against a dangerous and unscrupulous enemy' and wrote of 'the devilishness of the organisation represented by such devilish looking men'. For him, Christ was 'the only man who can set the times right'.

At one public meeting, convened with the authority of the Waterside Workers' Union, Willason defended himself, the mission and

Christianity. He subsequently described 'how the communistic leader got up and roared like a bull of Bashan', but the crowd 'yelled him down'. There were many in Adelaide who sided with Willason and religion, who acknowledged the hard work that the mission was doing and who would not have either it or the missioner blackguarded just for wanting to offer help in a time of trouble. Few of these people ever became regular churchgoers, but their support reflected a significant working-class religiosity.

Aided by Ethel Marsden (a social worker known as a 'Sister of the People'), volunteer supporters and his own wife, Willason over-saw a rapid growth in food and clothing assist-ance to starving families. A soup kitchen served thousands of meals in 1931-32. A free kindergarten helped families to survive. Willason explored the idea of a residential col-ony for unemployed men similar to Forsyth's Kuitpo Industrial Colony, but nothing came of it. The most notable practical scheme was a fishing fleet. By 1931, nine small boats crewed by men who had been jobless and equipped by local business houses and gifts from the public were plying the waters of the Gulf of St Vincent. With support from the philan-thropists Tom Barr Smith and Sir Langdon Bonython [q.v.11,7], Willason purchased a steam-powered trawler, with refrigeration chambers for six tons of fish, which worked the Great Australian Bight, giving employ-ment to another dozen men. The project brought publicity to the mission and enabled the Methodist Church to show it was re-sponding to the desperate poverty of the Depression.

The intense physical and emotional strug-gle for survival at Port Adelaide sapping his strength, Willason took several long breaks seeking relief from heart problems, including a trip to Dunedin, New Zealand. In 1935, despite widespread local protests, he was posted to Archer Street, North Adelaide. Later he moved to Parkside Methodist Church. Willason died of myocardial infarction on 26 July 1939 in hospital at North Adelaide and was buried in Cheltenham cemetery. His wife, a son and a daughter survived him. The Port Adelaide Mission has continued as a major welfare services provider.

B. Dickey and E. Martin, *Building Community* (Adel, 1999); *Austn Christian Commonwealth*, 12 Oct 1928, 7 Nov 1930, 21 Nov 1930, 4 Aug 1939; *Advertiser* (Adel), 27 July 1939, p 20.

BRIAN DICKEY

WILLIAMS, BEATRICE MAUD; *see* KERR

WILLS, FREDERICK CHARLES; *see* MOBSBY

WILSON, JOHN (1882-1967), consulting engineer, was born on 5 July 1882 at Gilnahirk, Belfast, Ireland, son of Samuel Wilson, farmer, and his wife Jane Edgar, née Malcolm. John was educated at Tullycarnett School and Campbell College, Down, and at Kelvin House School and the Municipal Technical Institute, Belfast. In 1897 he became a clerk in the engineer's office, Northern Counties Com-mittee, Belfast. From 1903 he studied engin-eering at Queens College, Belfast (B.E., 1907 Royal University of Ireland) while working at the Engineer's Office of the Midland Railway Co. in Dublin. Wilson migrated to Queensland in 1909 to join the engineering branch of the Department of Railways as a survey drafts-man. He was assistant engineer at Rock-hampton planning and designing lines, before spending a year at Dalby supervising day labour construction. For the next ten years he was resident engineer-in-charge of day labour construction of railway branch lines in various parts of the State.

In January 1922, from forty-five applicants, Wilson was appointed assistant engineer with the newly formed Main Roads Board; some months later he became engineer to the board. The construction of main roads was largely placed in the hands of local authorities, few of which employed full-time engineers. After a year Wilson resigned and during the next forty-four years was a successful consult-ing engineer, engaged principally in local authority works in south-eastern Queensland. At first he helped with the design and super-vision of roads and associated bridges that, by 1942, totalled 1000 miles (1609.3 km). As econ-omic conditions improved, he extended his services to urban water supplies and sani-tation, including complete sewerage schemes for Bundaberg and Warwick with a Mel-bourne firm. On 14 December 1942 at St Andrew's Presbyterian church, Brisbane, he married Muriel Florence Geater, an English-born nurse.

From 1943 Wilson was the senior member of John Wilson & Partners, whose work expanded to provide virtually full engineer-ing services to small local authorities, and branched into town planning. Outstanding projects included major water supply schemes for the joint Pine Rivers Shire and Redcliffe City as well as Redland Shire, each involving a significant dam. As local author-ities grew and prospered, most appointed full-time engineers, but retained Wilson's firm as consultants for major investigation and design work.

An associate of the Institution of Civil En-gineers (London) from 1920 (member 1928), Wilson was elected an associate of the Insti-tution of Engineers, Australia, and then mem-ber in 1926; he was chairman of the Brisbane division in 1931-32 and president of the

Institution of Engineers, Australia, in 1939. He served on the Board of Professional Engineers of Queensland from 1932 until 1956.

An able and efficient engineer, scholarly and well read, Wilson had a profound understanding of people. His integrity was his password. He remained in active practice until shortly before he died on 15 February 1967 in Royal Brisbane Hospital; he was buried in Bald Hills cemetery. His wife and their two daughters survived him.

G. Cossins (ed), *Eminent Queensland Engineers*, 2 (Brisb, 1999); M. F. Wilson, John Wilson, July 5th, 1882-Feb 15th, 1967 (ms, 1973, copy held Engineering Heritage Aust (Qld), Brisb); N27821 (QSA); J. Wilson papers (held by Justice M. Wilson, Indooroopilly); information from Mrs M. Wilson and Mrs E. Axelsen, Kenmore, Justice M. Wilson and Ms S. L. Hardy of John Wilson and Partners, Brisb.

GEOFFREY COSSINS

WIMBLE, FREDERICK THOMAS (1846-1936), ink-maker, type-founder, printers' furnisher and politician, was born on 28 November 1846 at Clerkenwell, London, thirteenth child and one of two sons of Benjamin Wimble, a second-generation ink-maker associated with Cambridge University Press, and his wife Elizabeth, née Smith. In 1867 the consumptive youth migrated for his health, reaching Melbourne in the *Anglesey* on 29 June.

Wimble had brought out printing materials valued at £150 and a £30 bank draft to establish himself with support from his father who forwarded further plant and raw materials. Attached to the firm of J. Spencer, Wimble produced his first ink on 4 May 1868, claiming that his blue ink made the *Melbourne Star* in that year the first newspaper published with a local supply. His provision of red ink for a South Australian postage stamp in 1869 led to contracts from other colonies. On 13 March 1872 in the manse of the Scots Church, Melbourne, he married Harriett Gascoigne, née Howard, a milliner and draper; she was a widow with two children. There were to be three children of the marriage, which ended in divorce. In 1876 Wimble travelled to the United States of America and Britain, securing agencies for printing equipment. Returning to Australia in 1878, he moved the headquarters of F. T. Wimble & Co. to Sydney, from where he furnished the printing trades throughout Australia and New Zealand.

In 1883 Wimble left the business to his partners and, hoping to become 'a sugar baron', moved to Cairns, Queensland, where he speculated in land, founded the *Cairns Post* in 1883 and was elected an alderman. He then reputedly spent £7000 in a successful campaign to be returned to the Legislative Assembly as a Liberal member for Cairns on 5 May 1888. On 16 August 1890 in Brisbane he married with Presbyterian forms London-born Marian Sarah Benjamin (d.1933). When Wimble's printers' furnishing business opened in Brisbane, he rejoined the firm and presided over the branch. With business affected by the economic depression, he did not recontest his seat in parliament in April 1893, but returned to Sydney 'with nothing left but my good name'. Obtaining a loan and resuming control of his company, he expanded, with a plant at Mascot as well as offices and warehouse showrooms in Clarence Street and branches in each mainland capital. From 1895 he promoted the firm's wares through *Wimble's Reminder*, which developed into a handsome new series that was to run from 1906 until 1957. A periodical-cum-catalogue, it championed process engraving and colour printing, the possibilities of which he displayed in a lavish edition in July 1927. In 1920 he had registered F. T. Wimble & Co. Ltd as a public company.

Wimble conducted a type foundry with overseas-designed faces that were renamed as Extended Tasmanian Gothic or Wentworth Bold. These nativist attractors were an earnest of his devotion to protectionism. 'Books fit to be read here must be printed here', he declared in 1927. 'When you are reading a Novel note where it is printed.' In keeping with the New Protectionism, he supported what he called 'legitimate unionism', but exhorted his tradesmen to lead the fight against 'the madness of Moscow'.

A Freemason, Wimble belonged to Lodge Austral, No. 194, United Grand Lodge of New South Wales. As a hobby, he took up poultry farming at Wimbleford, Bankstown. He published his autobiography, *Climbing the Ladder,* in 1924. Still chairman of his company, Wimble died on 3 January 1936 in his Artarmon home and was cremated. One daughter and two sons of his first marriage and the son and two daughters of his second survived him. A printing museum at New England Regional Art Museum, Armidale, commemorates his business, which continued with his name until 1991, but under outside managements.

The History of the House of Wimble in Australia (supplement to *Wimbles Reminder*, no 84, 4 May 1928); R. Kirkpatrick, *Sworn to No Master* (Toowoomba, Qld, 1984); *Queenslander*, 17 May 1928, p 22; *Argus* (Melb), 4 Jan 1936, p 20; *SMH*, 4 Jan 1936, pp 13 & 16; F. T. Wimble & Co. Ltd records (Powerhouse Museum, Syd).

HUMPHREY MCQUEEN

WINDRADYNE (c.1800-1829), Aboriginal resistance leader, also known as SATURDAY, was a northern Wiradjuri man of the upper Macquarie River region in central-western New South Wales. Emerging as a key protagonist in a period of Aboriginal-settler conflict later known as the 'Bathurst Wars', in December 1823 'Saturday' was named as an instigator of clashes between Aborigines and settlers that culminated in the death of two convict stockmen at Kings Plains. He was arrested and imprisoned at Bathurst for one month; it was reported that six men and a severe beating with a musket were needed to secure him.

After some of the most violent frontier incidents of the period, including the killing of seven stockmen in the Wyagdon Ranges north of Bathurst and the murder of Aboriginal women and children by settler-vigilantes near Raineville in May 1824, Governor Brisbane [q.v.1] placed the western district under martial law on 14 August. The local military was increased to seventy-five troops, and magistrates were permitted to administer summary justice. Windradyne's apparent involvement in the murder of European stockmen resulted in a reward of 500 acres (202.3 ha) being offered for his capture. The crisis subsided quickly, although the failure to capture Windradyne delayed the repeal of martial law until 11 December. Two weeks later he and a large number of his people crossed the mountains to Parramatta to attend the annual feast there, where he was formally pardoned by Brisbane.

The *Sydney Gazette* described Saturday as 'without doubt, the most manly black native we have ever beheld ... much stouter and more proportionable limbed' than most Aborigines, with 'a noble looking countenance, and piercing eye ... calculated to impress the beholder'. Another observer thought him 'a very fine figure, very muscular ... a good model for the figure of Apollo'. His sobriety and affection for his family and kinsmen were considered remarkable.

Apparently remaining camped in the domain at Parramatta for some time after the 1824 feast, Windradyne then returned to Bathurst. He declined to attend Governor Darling's [q.v.1] feast the following year. In later years, he was intermittently reported as being involved in raids on maize crops or in clashes with settlers around Lake George. In 1828 an Aboriginal man being led to his execution for the murder of a stockman at Georges Plains attempted vainly to pin the crime on the 'notorious Saturday'. Mortally wounded in a tribal fight on the Macquarie River, Windradyne died a few hours later on 21 March 1829 at Bathurst hospital, and was buried at Bathurst.

Windradyne had been closely associated with George Suttor and his son William Henry [qq.v.2,6], who were strong advocates on behalf of Aborigines during and after the period of martial law. Both lamented his passing in the Sydney press in April 1829. One of William Henry Suttor junior's *Australian Stories Retold* (1887) placed Windradyne at the scene of the Wyagdon attacks in May 1824 and described how his warriors had spared the life of the author's father.

Another Suttor tradition, aired shortly after World War II, disputed earlier accounts of Windradyne's death and burial, claiming that he had in fact departed from Bathurst hospital to join his people at nearby Brucedale and that he died on the property. In 1954 the Bathurst District Historical Society erected a monument beside a Wiradjuri burial mound at Brucedale, attaching a bronze plaque commemorating 'The resting place of Windradene, alias "Saturday", last chief of the Aborigines: first a terror, but later a friend to the settlers ... A true patriot.' His death date was erroneously given as 1835.

In the late twentieth century Windradyne was transformed from a local figure to a character of national importance as a resistance hero. A suburb at Bathurst and a student accommodation village at Charles Sturt University, Wagga Wagga, were named after him. In May 2000 his presumed resting place was put under a voluntary conservation order, the occasion celebrated by Wiradjuri descendants and the Suttor family, continuing a 180-year-old friendship and creating a potent symbol of reconciliation.

Hist Records of Aust, series 1, vol 11, p 410; W. H. Suttor, *Australian Stories Retold and Sketches of Country Life* (Bathurst, NSW, 1887); T. Salisbury and P. J. Gresser, *Windradyne of the Wiradjuri* (Syd, 1971); M. Coe, *Windradyne: A Wiradjuri Koorie* (Canb, 1989); *Sydney Gazette*, 8 Jan 1824, p 2, 30 Dec 1824, p 2, 20 May 1826, p 3, 2 Jan 1828, p 3, 21 Apr 1829. p 3; *Australian*, 19 Jan 1826, p 3, 4 Oct 1826; *Sydney Monitor*, 18 Apr 1829, p 2; *SMH*, 27 May 2000, p 9.   DAVID ANDREW ROBERTS

WINTLE, SAMUEL HENRY (1830-1909), scholar, publicist and poet, was born on 16 September 1830 in Hobart Town, elder son of Samuel James Wintle, a shoemaker and tanner who had arrived in Van Diemen's Land in 1823, and his wife Ann Mary, née Magill. Samuel James's brother Henry, known as Melville [q.v.2], changed his surname, possibly as a journalistic *nom de plume* but also perhaps because of his brother's modest place in society. In 1839 the family moved to Sydney, where young Samuel's sister Mary Harriet Gedye (1834-1876) later became a well-known artist. Wintle's scientific education, probably acquired in Sydney, was 'limited and faulty' and his understanding of basic geological concepts and methods 'weak'.

After the death of his father in 1854 Wintle returned to Hobart.

Hailed as the first 'native mechanic' to address the Mechanics' Institute (of which he was a keen supporter), in June 1860 Wintle delivered a paper that reconciled geology with religion. In 1863 he was elected to the Royal Society of Tasmania, to which he read several papers. Cultivating leaders in the field of geology, including Rev. W. B. Clarke and (Sir) Frederick McCoy [qq.v.3,5], to whom he sent specimens, in the 1860s and 1870s Wintle published numerous articles (particularly concerning fossils, coal, tin, iron and gold) in newspapers and journals in Tasmania and other colonies. At least one appeared in the *Journal* of the Geological Society of London, having been forwarded by Sir Roderick Murchison. The articles were not received uncritically, nor was his florid prose style admired by the *Hobart Town Punch*. In 1866 Wintle exhibited geological specimens at the Melbourne Intercolonial Exhibition and next year he advertised collections of geological specimens and a geological panorama of Hobart.

According to James Bonwick [q.v.3], Wintle 'laboured freely and nobly in the cause of science', and similar tributes were paid by R. M. Johnston and by Julian Tenison-Woods [qq.v.9,6] who, in 1873, named a Table Cape fossil in Wintle's honour. The 'agreeable local geologist' Mr Wanfel in Bonwick's novel *The Tasmanian Lily* (London, 1873) was probably a portrait of Wintle. During the 1870s he explored the north-east of the colony, probably as a mining prospector and promoter, achieving some financial success.

As a social commentator, Wintle was also controversial. His letter in the *Tasmanian Times*, concerning the visit of Prince Alfred, Duke of Edinburgh [q.v.4], in 1867, attracted derision. One of the few Tasmanians to publish comments on the serialized novel *His Natural Life* (1870-71), he criticized the author Marcus Clarke [q.v.3] for bringing the police force into disrepute. A collection of Wintle's poems, *Fragments of Fern Fronds* (Launceston, 1870), was dedicated to Governor Du Cane [q.v.4]; in 1880 his *Wayside Sketches in Tasmania* was published in Melbourne.

Elected a fellow of the Linnean Society, London, in 1880, Wintle listed his interests as entomology and geology. He failed in an application for the curatorship of the Royal Society of Tasmania's museum in 1883 and moved to Melbourne, where he continued to publish articles, including seven in the *Victorian Naturalist*. He visited Tasmania periodically, where he had acquired property, emulating his uncle Richard Cleburne [q.v.1]. Wintle, who did not marry, died on 3 January 1909 in East Melbourne and was buried with Methodist forms in Springvale cemetery.

Tasmanian Messenger, July 1860, p 358; *Mercury* (Hob), 20 Mar 1861, p 3, 23 Dec 1871, p 3, 6 Jan 1872, p 2; information from Dr M. R. Banks, Sandy Bay, Hob.   GILLIAN WINTER

WOINARSKI, GERTRUDE; *see* ZICHY-WOINARSKI

WOLFF, SIR ALBERT ASHER (1899-1977), chief justice and lieutenant-governor, was born on 30 April 1899 at Geraldton, Western Australia, and registered as Asher Albert, only son and second of four children of Simon Wolff (d.1914), a Russian-born jeweller, and his wife Bertha Clara, née Shrimski, from London. From an orthodox Jewish family, Albert was educated at Geraldton State and Perth Boys' schools and won a scholarship to Perth Modern School. After serving articles in a legal firm, he was admitted to the Supreme Court on 20 October 1921 and practised at Goomalling and in Perth until appointed crown prosecutor in 1926. On 17 April 1924 at the district registrar's office, Perth, he had married Ida Violet Jackson (d.1953), a schoolteacher.

Wolff prosecuted constables J. G. St Jack and R. H. Regan for murder following the 1926 Kimberley massacre; they were acquitted. In 1929 he was promoted crown solicitor and parliamentary draftsman and won repute for his drafting skills. Taking silk in 1936, he was appointed to the Supreme Court bench in 1938 and became senior puisne justice in 1954. He was praised for his 'clear concise judgement with underlying legal and social reasoning' in *Adamson* v. *the Motor Vehicle Insurance Trust* (1956), involving the liability of a lunatic for tort. In February 1959 he succeeded Sir John Dwyer [q.v.14] as chief justice and became deputy president of the State Arbitration Court; he was appointed K.C.M.G. in June. Sir Albert was lieutenant-governor of Western Australia from 1968 to 1974.

In the Supreme Court, Wolff attempted to reduce administrative red tape. Some thought him dour, but his ability and courtesy were respected. He was a firm supporter of an independent Bar after it was founded in 1961. Although a professed advocate of law reform and clarification of parliamentary statutes, he consistently supported final appeal to the Privy Council and disagreed with a bill of rights as proposed by the Federal attorney-general Lionel Murphy. Seldom errant in his judgements, Wolff believed in stern retribution or 'a short, sharp salutary lesson'. He was also committed to capital punishment. One of his most contentious criminal cases was the 1961 murder trial of the deaf mute Darryl Raymond Beamish. Wolff pronounced the death sentence, which was later commuted to life imprisonment. After the emergence of fresh evidence, in 2005 the conviction was quashed.

Presiding (1937-38) over a royal commission into youth unemployment and the apprenticeship system, Wolff had recommended improving literacy at the primary level, raising the school leaving age to 15 and reviewing policy and funding for technical education. By singling out the building industry for inadequate training regulations he hastened the passage of the Builders' Registration Act (1939). Wolff's comprehensive 1941 royal commission report on the administration of the University of Western Australia concentrated on financial and administrative matters, although he was critical of academic standards and 'student wastage'. He recommended the appointment of a full-time vice-chancellor and the reconstitution of the senate and convocation, and foreshadowed the introduction of fees. He also served on royal commissions in 1946 (when he criticized the government's purchase of twenty-five unsatisfactory Garratt locomotives) and in 1965 (when he investigated parliamentary salaries). He retired as chief justice on 30 April 1969.

Wolff was a trustee of the Public Library, Museum and Art Gallery of Western Australia from 1947. As president of the trustees (1954-58), he was thought by some to be conservative, autocratic and uninspired. He was a stubborn litigant against the council at Mosman Park, where he lived. Dark, thickset and of average height, in public he was formal; he wore carpet slippers and a carpenter's apron at home—he was a keen and competent cabinetmaker—and proudly drove a 1964 Silver Cloud Rolls Royce. He was a member of the Weld [q.v.6] Club.

At St Mary's Cathedral, Sydney, on 8 February 1956 Wolff had married with Catholic rites Mary Godwin (d.1974). Sir Albert died on 27 October 1977 at the Home of Peace, Subiaco, and was buried in the Jewish Orthodox section of Karrakatta cemetery after a State funeral. The son and daughter of his first marriage survived him.

F. Alexander, *Campus at Crawley* (Melb, 1963); P. Brett, *The Beamish Case* (Melb, 1966); M. A. White, *The Community and Post-school Education* (Perth, 1981); *Austn Law Jnl*, vol 11, 1937-38, p 563, vol 33, 1959-60, p 216, vol 43, 1969, p 251; Law Society of WA, *Brief*, 4, no 6, Dec 1977, p 62; *West Australian*, 7 Dec 1956, p 5, 30 Apr 1969, p 9, 7 May 1974, p 3, 28 Oct 1977, p 1, 1 Nov 1977, p 15, 28 Jan 1995, 'Big Weekend', p 2, 10 June 2000, p 1; *Independent* (Perth), 27 Apr 1969.
WENDY BIRMAN

WOOD, MALVINA EVALYN (1893-1976), librarian and college warden, was born on 1 August 1893 at Guildford, Western Australia, eldest child and only daughter of John Wood, soldier and railway porter, and his wife Sarah Josephine, née Cross. Malvina was educated at various schools and the University of Western Australia (B.A., 1927; M.A., 1943), and took a correspondence library course from the University of London. She became an associate of the Library Association of the United Kingdom in 1933.

Having joined the staff of the Museum and Art Gallery of Western Australia as a typist and librarian in 1910, by 1919 Wood had become an administrative assistant to J. S. Battye [q.v.7] in the public library, which had amalgamated with the museum and art gallery in 1911. She was appointed the first full-time librarian of the University of Western Australia in 1927. Hampered by low status, poor funding and inadequate accommodation, which she consistently strove to upgrade, it was not until 1956 that she was granted status equivalent to a senior lecturer. Nevertheless, supported by competent staff she developed the library from its rudimentary beginnings into a collection and services that were capable of supporting a fast-growing university.

Under a grant from the Carnegie Corporation of New York, Wood visited American and European libraries in 1935; in 1954 she spent a year on study leave in Britain. She was an *ex officio* member of the university's Adult Education Board, publications committee, library committee and medical library committee and the board of management of the University Press. One of the six people who initiated the Western Australian branch of the Australian Institute of Librarians (a forerunner of the Australian Library and Information Association), she was its founding president and general councillor in 1937-58. From 1944 the branch actively supported, among other things, the Free Library Movement and promoted the establishment in 1952 of the Library Board of Western Australia, on which she served as a member in 1952-54 and 1955-59; she acted as honorary secretary until 1 April 1953. In her capacity as university librarian she promoted co-operation between the two organizations. Joining the Women Graduates Association of Western Australia (Australian Federation of University Women) in 1927, she was an executive member (1938-39), vice-president (1939-40), president (1940-41), past-president (1941-42) and its representative on the Western Australian Joint Equal Pay Committee (1941-43).

In 1928 the association had formed a university women's college fund committee, of which Wood was founding honorary secretary (1928-37), trustee (1931-58) and honorary treasurer (1937-58). From the commencement of the

Women's (later St Catherine's) College in 1946 until 1959 she held the positions of senior resident, then acting warden and later honorary warden, with free accommodation and meals but no remuneration. She was a council member of the Women's College in 1946-60 and a fellow of St Catherine's College from 1970.

Thickset, meticulous and earnest, Miss Wood was caring towards her staff and students and highly respected. She did not marry, but had a long liaison with a male friend; he died in 1947. She died on 17 September 1976 in a nursing home at Mosman Park and was cremated with Anglican rites. She had invested in the stock market and left an estate of some $250 000, of which St Catherine's College was the main beneficiary. This has been used for scholarships, building extensions and amenities commemorating her name. Her portrait by Romola Morrow hangs in the (Sir Alexander) Reid [q.v.16] Library, University of Western Australia.

F. Alexander, *Campus at Crawley* (Melb, 1963); N. Stewart, *St Catherine's College* (Perth, 1978); *Gazette of the Univ of WA*, Mar 1960, p 9; Univ of WA, *University News*, Oct 1976, p 11; Austn Institute of Librarians (WA) records *and* WA Assn of Univ Women, Minutes, 1923-59, *and* Women's College Fund Committee, Minutes, 1928-56, *and* Univ Women's College Auxiliary, Minutes, 1956-59 (BL); information from Mrs J. Grime, Pinjarra, Perth.

M. MEDCALF

WOOD, WILLIAM HENRY O'MALLEY (1856-1941), surveyor and banker, was born on 15 June 1856 at his family's station, Brundah, near Grenfell, New South Wales, fifth of fourteen children of John Butler Wood, a native-born pastoralist, and his wife Elizabeth, née Mylecharane, born at sea *en route* to Australia. William was an unhappy boarder at Sydney Grammar School in 1866-68. After returning to Brundah, he worked as a farmer, drover and storekeeper and adopted the surname 'O'Malley Wood' to distinguish himself from other William Woods.

Joining the Department of Lands, O'Malley Wood undertook two years of fieldwork and learned surveying under John Kinloch before passing the surveyors' admission examination in December 1875. On 23 January 1878 he married Susannah Sarah Kemp at St Thomas's Church of England, North Sydney. Working in various regions of New South Wales, he became a district surveyor; he was chairman of the land board at Tamworth from 1890 and later at Forbes. In 1902 he was appointed chairman of the Advances to Settlers Board. The board was incorporated into the Government Savings Bank of New South Wales in 1907; O'Malley Wood was appointed one of two commissioners under a president. He was a member of the royal commission on decentralisation in railway transit in 1910-11.

In 1921, following the advances department's conversion into the rural bank department, O'Malley Wood became president of the G.S.B. During his term the bank's deposits grew from £50 million to £74 million and the branches increased from 142 to 192, becoming the second largest savings bank in the British Empire, behind the British Post Office Savings Bank. In 1928 a new, lavish building was opened on the corner of Martin Place and Elizabeth Street, Sydney. In December that year O'Malley Wood retired.

Encouraged by comments of the Nationalist leader (Sir) Thomas Bavin [q.v.7] during the State elections in October 1930, a run on the bank began early next year. With the government unable to help and the G.S.B.'s board failing to ration withdrawals, the bank ceased trading on 22 April 1931. O'Malley Wood was brought back to help to plan a new scheme for the bank; in August he became one of five new commissioners. Next month he again became president and the bank resumed trading. Although the Commonwealth Savings Bank of Australia had earlier refused an amalgamation, the success of the reopened bank encouraged discussions between the G.S.B.'s vice-president Sir John Butters and the Commonwealth Savings Bank's Sir Robert Gibson [qq.v.7,8], leading to a combined institution commencing operations on 15 December 1931.

In June 1933 O'Malley Wood was made chairman of the Rural (State) Bank of New South Wales, which was established by the Stevens [q.v.12] government to incorporate the G.S.B.'s rural banking and advances for homes departments. Although precluded from savings bank activities, the new bank rapidly expanded. A site for a new head office was purchased in Martin Place and twenty-three rural branches, employing 520 officers, were opened before he retired again in April 1934. (Sir) Roy McKerihan [q.v.15] succeeded him. In the most difficult of economic times during the Depression and in the face of opposition from some of Sydney's financial experts, O'Malley Wood had remained dedicated to maintaining a functioning government banking system in New South Wales.

A tall, muscular man, optimistic and tenacious, he was self-taught in a range of commercial and agricultural matters. His chief relaxation was woodcarving and cabinetmaking and he had a small farm in the Lachlan district for much of his career. His wife died in 1932. On 18 March 1933 at St Andrew's Church of England, Roseville, he married Lilla Emmaline Raines, née Bertram (1885-1960), a divorcee with two children. Predeceased by the son of his first marriage, O'Malley Wood died on 5 August 1941 at his home at Vaucluse and was buried in Northern Suburbs cemetery. His wife survived him. She was president of the 2/1st and 2/2nd Pioneer Ladies of Australia, a leader of the Australian Women's Movement against Socialisation (1947-60) and sometime president of the Feminist Club of New South Wales.

N. Griffiths, *A History of the Government Savings Bank of N.S.W.* (Syd, 1930); G. C. Harvey, *The Origins, Evolution and Establishment of the Rural Bank of New South Wales 1899-1979* (1980); J. B. Wood, *Squatter* (2000); F. Cain, *Jack Lang and the Great Depression in Australia in the 1930s* (Melb, 2005); *SMH*, 19 May 1920, p 10, 31 Oct 1927, p 10, 5 Dec 1928, p 21, 14 Dec 1928, p 13, 26 Aug 1931, p 11, 8 Sept 1931, p 9, 30 June 1933, p 11, 7 Aug 1941, p 11, 23 May 1960, p 28; *Smith's Weekly*, 16 Dec 1922, p 2, 23 Aug 1941, p 15; Rural Bank of NSW, *Annual Report*, 1934; K. A. Polden, The Government Savings Bank of NSW 1871-1931 (M.A. thesis, Macquarie Univ, 1970).   FRANK CAIN

WOOTTON, RICHARD RAWSON (1867-1946), horse-trainer, FRANCIS LEONARD (1893-1940), jockey, and STANLEY THOMAS (1895-1986), horse-trainer, were father and sons. Richard was born on 31 March 1867 at Taree, New South Wales, second of ten children of William Wootton, bootmaker, and his wife Jane, née Rawson, from New York. William, whose parents had been convicts, became a hotelier at Taree, an alderman and a dairy farmer; he also trained some horses. Dick began his career on local tracks and at 19 won the Manning River Cup with Bay Fly. He moved to Sydney as an owner and trainer and lived at Forest Lodge. On 19 December 1893 at St Andrew's Cathedral he married with Anglican rites 19-year-old Catherine Gertrude Johnson, a blacksmith's daughter.

On the pony tracks and proprietary courses in Sydney Dick Wootton soon won repute as a trainer and punter. His eldest son Frank was born on 14 December 1893 at Glebe; Stanley was born on 26 June 1895 at Surry Hills. In 1902 Dick won the Australian Jockey Club's Metropolitan Handicap at Randwick with Queen of Sheba. The boys had a miserable childhood as their father, determined that they should become jockeys, reputedly did not permit them to have a decent meal. Frank rode track work and training gallops at the age of 9 was thought by his father to be ready to race; but the A.J.C.'s minimum age for a registered jockey was 14. Dick moved his family and a string of horses to South Africa, where this age limit did not apply.

Settling in the Transvaal, Wootton trained at Germanston racecourse. Frank won his first race in October 1903 and left school; by 1906 his tally was seventeen. That year the Woottons returned to Sydney, where Dick quickly re-established himself by winning the 1906 Tattersall's Club Cup with Fabric. Frustrated by the wait for Frank's licence to ride, within six months the family departed for England. Dick acquired a training establishment at Treadwell House, Epsom, Surrey, but maintained his links with Australia—he brought over a kangaroo and an emu. Kate died giving birth to their fifth child in 1909.

Wootton's training methods, use of lightweight and apprenticed jockeys and careful placement of runners attracted owners, such as (Sir) Edward Hulton, who brought in superior horses. Beginning in 1906 with fourteen winners, in 1913 Wootton topped the English trainers' premiership with sixty-six, and expanded his training establishment at Epsom. The English Derby, however, always eluded him: in 1913 his horse Shogun, with Frank up, was checked in one of the wildest Derbys on record. Wootton had a reputation for punting plunges and well-planned coups. When accused of fixing races by the bookmaker Robert Sievier [q.v.11] in his publication *Winning Post*, Wootton issued a pamphlet attacking Sievier, who unsuccessfully sued him for libel. The litigation continued, however.

Frank's riding technique and experience led, in 1909, to his becoming the first Australian to top the English jockey's premiership, with a tally of 165. Known as the 'Wonderboy', he also headed the jockeys' list in 1910-12 and won many classic races, riding on a retainer for wealthy owners, such as Hulton and Lord Derby. Frank rode seven winners at the St Leger meeting at Doncaster in 1908 and at Ascot week in 1912, and ten at the Goodwood carnival in 1911. Increasing weight reduced his opportunities, however, and he had effectively retired by his visit to Sydney in January 1914.

Stanley, more interested in stable management, soon also surrendered his jockey's licence. With reduced racing in Britain during World War I, Dick continued training at Treadwell House. Frank enlisted in the army, served in Palestine and Mesopotamia and was mentioned in dispatches. Lieutenant Stanley Wootton joined the 17th Battalion, Royal Fusiliers. On the night of 7 July 1916 he won the Military Cross for rescuing a fellow officer during the Battle of the Somme, France.

When his sons returned from the war, Dick left Treadwell House in their hands and by 1921 had returned to Sydney. He established R. Wootton Pty Ltd, hotel and picture theatre proprietors and property owners; his holdings included the Doncaster Hotel, Randwick, the Doncaster and Vocalist theatres, and residential real estate at Kensington, Randwick and in the city. Wootton also bought a property, Kicatoo, at Condoblin, and developed his interes t in breeding. Now wealthy, he raced his horses for recreation; his Zuleika won the Villiers Stakes at Randwick in 1927. He was appointed a judge of thoroughbred entries at the Sydney Royal Show. On 2 February 1931 at St Jude's Church of England, Randwick, he married Frances Young.

Having first won a jumping event while serving in Baghdad, after his war service Frank began a new career as a National Hunt Club jockey and trainer. Riding at 12 stone (76 kg), he retained his balanced riding technique and judgement and in 1921 won the Imperial Hunt Club Cup on Noce d'Argent, trained by Stanley. He was known for his dashing style and the risks he took. Back in Sydney from 1933, he suffered ill health, perhaps partly due to serious falls and to the exacting regime and weight wasting of his youth. He had not married. On 6 April 1940 at Central Police Court, Sydney, he was convicted of drunkenness. Later that day he died in Long Bay gaol of traumatic epilepsy and was buried with Catholic rites in Botany cemetery.

Dick died on 26 June 1946 at Randwick and was buried in the Anglican cemetery there. His wife and their three daughters survived him, as did two sons and two daughters of his first marriage.

Stan maintained a strict establishment at Epsom and remained a successful trainer of horses and jockeys until 1962. He had married Kathleen Griffiths on 15 January 1938 at St Joseph's Catholic Church, Epsom. They separated during World War II. One of the wealthiest and most powerful turf figures in England, Stan Wootton made frequent visits to Australia. From the mid-1950s he was notable as a breeder and owner in New South Wales; he invested in stud properties and sent out selected horses including the famous sire Star Kingdom, who stood at Baramul stud and produced a notable thoroughbred bloodline in Australia; his progeny included the stallions Todman, Biscay and Bletchingly the Derby winners Sky High and Sky Line and the first five winners of the Sydney Turf Club's Golden Slipper Stakes. In Sydney, Wootton's wins as the owner included the Golden Slipper with Todman in 1957 and the Australian Jockey Club's Epsom Handicap with Noholme in 1959.

Stan Wootton died on 21 March 1986 at Epsom, England, and was buried in the cemetery there. His wife and their daughter Catherine Remond, a successful thoroughbred breeder in Australia, survived him.

D. Hickey, *Gentlemen of the Australian Turf* (Syd, 1986); N. Penton, *A Racing Heart* (Syd, 1987); B. Eacott, *The Wootton Family* (2003); *Austn Jockey Club Racing Calendar*, Dec 1991; *Sydney Mail*, 28 Jan 1914, p 33; *SMH*, 8 Apr 1940, p 15, 15 Apr 1961, 'Weekend Mag', p 12, 11 Apr 2003, 'The Form', p 15.
J. A. RYAN

WRENCH, EDWARD THOMAS JONES; *see* RICHARDSON

WRIGHT, EDMUND WILLIAM (1824-1888), architect, engineer and businessman, was born on 4 April 1824 at Fulham, London, son of Stephen Amand Wright, master of ordnance at the Tower of London, and his wife Lucy Elizabeth, née Tomkins. Articled to the borough surveyor of Bermondsey, Edmund trained as an architect, surveyor and engineer, then found public employment as a clerk of works at Yarmouth dockyard and subsequently in Bermuda. While working in Montreal, Canada, he suffered exposure to the weather, which left him lame for life. In 1849 he became the third of six siblings who migrated to South Australia, where he worked with his brother Edward as a land agent and broker but also advertised his services as an architect and engineer.

When the architect Henry Stuckey died in June 1851, Wright took over his business, avowedly to assist the widow Agnes Jane, née Rippingville, and her newborn daughter. He persuaded the trustees of the Collegiate School of St Peter to roof the school's main building in galvanized iron, rather than slate, and supervised some work on the first stage of Bishop's Court, North Adelaide. In March 1852 he joined the exodus to the Victorian goldfields. Returning six months later, Wright was appointed Adelaide's city surveyor and, on 23 October that year, married Mrs Stuckey at Christ Church, North Adelaide, with Anglican rites. They had four children. Wright resumed private practice in February 1853, designing houses, business premises and churches, including an imposing but sombre one for the Anglicans at Kapunda. In 1856 he won a competition to design a building for the North Adelaide Masonic and Public Hall Association. Work stopped when the front part of this structure, let to the North Adelaide Institute, was opened in 1858. In 1863 it was sold and became a private residence, Belmont, to which another architect added extra rooms. Wright's 'Roman Doric' facade still enhanced Brougham Place in 2005.

In a paper in 1859 to the short-lived South Australian Society of Architects, Engineers and Surveyors, Wright argued that the province's climate lent itself to the use of Italian-style architecture rather than forms from northern Europe. He advocated flat roofs, large rooms with lofty ceilings and narrow windows, all aimed at coolness. His Adelaide office for the Union Bank of Australia (1858, demolished 1925) and the large houses Athelney (1858), College Park and The Olives (1864), Glenelg, reflected these theories. Wright was elected an alderman on Adelaide City Council in 1857. He became mayor in 1859 but resigned eleven months later, for which he was fined £10. The previous year he had won a competition to design a new town hall, but the council could not raise the money to build it.

From the early 1860s Wright was busy with non-architectural work, becoming South Australian manager of the Imperial Fire Assurance Co., chairman of the Mt Craig Mining Co. and a director of other companies. He planted a vineyard near Penfold's [q.v.5] at Magill, purchased an adjoining cellar and winery and was a founding member and major shareholder in the South Australian United Vineyards Association. In the 1870s he became engineer for, and a shareholder in, the Adelaide & Suburban Tramways Co., which eventually built and operated the city's first horse-drawn tram services.

To keep his architectural practice going, Wright had entered a series of partnerships with men better trained and, in some cases more experienced, than himself. The first (from 1861) was another Londoner, Edward John Woods, the architect of the splendid Kent Town Wesleyan Methodist (Uniting) Church. In 1863 they gained first prize (£50) in a fresh competition for a more modest Adelaide town hall. This time the councillors found the money, but demanded such substantial modifications to the ground-plan and elevations that they made it 'for all purposes' a different design. Wright accepted the changes and was paid to superintend the work. Opened in 1866, the Town Hall has served Adelaide well. More controversy greeted Wright & Woods's prize-winning design (1865) for the General Post Office. The postmaster general (Sir) Charles Todd [q.v.6] and the colonial architect R. G. Thomas secured major alterations before its first stage was opened in 1872.

Wright and Woods designed the most beautiful of Adelaide's early commercial buildings—the National Bank and adjoining premises for Wright's insurance company (both 1867, demolished 1968). He also designed many banks in country towns, houses —notably Princess Royal (1864), near Burra, and Kingsmead (1865) next door to Belmont —and, with the brothers Edward and George Hamilton, the grand, baroque Congregational Church in North Adelaide. Woods left the partnership in 1869, to work full time on the Anglicans' St Peter's Cathedral, and was replaced by by J. H. Reed. J. G. Beavor joined at the end of the 1870s. The reconstituted firm produced the Bank of Adelaide (1880), the palatial Paringa Hall (1882) for J. F. Cudmore [q.v.8] at Somerton, Cabra Dominican Convent (1886), which provided an extreme example of Wright's preference for narrow windows, and major structures later demolished, including the Adelaide office of the Bank of New South Wales (1888).

Wright and the Melbourne architect Lloyd Tayler [q.v.6] had won competitions to design new houses of parliament for Adelaide and a new head office for the Bank of South Australia. Tayler did the creative work. Wright oversaw construction. Work on the foundations of Parliament House commenced in 1877 but stopped a few months later as the project became embroiled in disputes. The first third of the building, providing new accommodation for the House of Assembly, was erected on new footings in 1883-89, under the supervision of Woods, who had made extensive alterations to the plans. Tayler and Wright had better success with their Renaissance-style Bank of South Australia. Costing £63 000 to erect in 1875-78, it was the noblest commercial building erected in colonial Adelaide.

In his last years Wright was the colony's senior practising architect but he lost heavily on mining investments that he had been making since 1860. He died of obstruction of the bowel on 5 August 1888 in North Adelaide and was buried in the North Road cemetery, Nailsworth. His wife, their son and daughter, and a stepdaughter survived him.

Since 1971 Wright's reputation has become larger than it was in life. That year the owners of the Bank of South Australia's last head office sold it to a company that planned to replace it with a nineteen-storeyed office block. Some 67 000 people petitioned against the building's demolition and a public appeal raised $250 000. The bank's champions found that a local resident had shared in the design and, when the Dunstan government agreed to buy and restore the building, it was renamed Edmund Wright House—an injustice to the principal architect Tayler. Enthusiasts began tracing all work attributed to Wright, sometimes giving him sole credit where little or none was his due. The sculptor John Dowie dubbed him 'the Christopher Wren of Adelaide', but most of Wright's partners were gifted professionals who merited a large share of the honour accorded him.

W. H. Bagot, *Some Nineteenth Century Adelaide Architects* (Adel, 1958); E. J. R. Morgan and S. H. Gilbert, *Early Adelaide Architecture 1836 to 1886* (Melb, 1969); M. Burden, *Lost Adelaide* (Melb, 1983); M. Page, *Sculptors in Space* (Adel, 1986); P. Stretton, *The Life and Times of Old Parliament House* (Adel, 1988); S. Marsden et al (eds), *Heritage of the City of Adelaide* (Adel, 1990); *Advertiser* (Adel), 22 Mar 1971, p 3, 25 Mar 1971, pp 2 & 3.

P. A. HOWELL

WROBLEWSKI, CHARLES ADAM MARIE (c.1855-1936), editor, chemist, geologist and merchant, was born at Grodno, Lithuania, Russia (Belarus), third of four sons of Dr Felix Jan Wróblewski, a scholarly landowner, and his wife Zofia, née Jelska. Karol's maternal grandmother was Amelia, daughter of Prince Alexander Michal Sapieha—marshal and chancellor of the Grand Duchy of Lithuania under the last king of Poland Stanislaw August Poniatowski. Educated in Russian Poland, Charles also spent twenty years in France.

In 1884 Wroblewski graduated as a chemist, reputedly from a university in Vienna. By 1885 he was employed as an analytical chemist with the royal commission on water conservation in New South Wales. Travelling widely in the colony, he worked at such locations as Rooty Hill, Warren and Mungindi. In June next year he returned to Sydney, where he analysed water samples and completed maps. In 1888 he was employed by the Monte Cristo Pyes Creek Silver Mining Ltd. During the shearers' strike in 1890 Wroblewski was a special constable and was thanked by Sir Henry Parkes's [q.v.5] government for his services. He was briefly a merchant in Sydney, then had a farm near Liverpool. At St Patrick's Catholic Church on 21 November 1891 Wroblewski married 18-year-old Daisy Marie Consolation, only daughter of Jean Emile Serisier [q.v.6], a French-born storekeeper and vigneron. They had three children.

On 30 April 1892 Wroblewski launched the French-language weekly *Le Courrier Australien*; its subtitle described it as *Journal Cosmopolitain du Samedi. Politique, Litterature, Sciences, Beaux Arts, Commerce, Mode, etc.* The journal's predecessor, *L'Oceanien*, had failed because of its limited readership.

Wroblewski, therefore, appealed not only to the French settlers but also to Australian students of French. He aimed to create an entertaining publication that would not be affiliated with a particular party or a propagator of subversive ideas. Furthermore, he promised to defend the interests of the French and other nationalities living in Australia, and secured contributions from good writers and prominent personalities, including a column by a professor.

Wroblewski also owned a printing business and on 20 March 1893 he launched another newspaper in Sydney, the *Deutsch-Australische Post*, for the German-speaking public. Transferring *Le Courrier Australien* to Léon Magrin in November 1896, he took his family to Victoria, where he established an importing firm. In 1903 he moved his business to Perth and founded the City & Suburban Advertising Co., later run by his son Charles. During World War I Wroblewski returned to Sydney and is said to have become an interpreter for the military, using his knowledge of seven languages. His elder son Leo Emile served in the Australian Imperial Force and was killed in France in 1918. Later Wroblewski retired to Melbourne. He died on 24 July 1936 at St Kilda and was cremated. His wife, daughter and one son survived him. *Le Courrier Australien* continued, and in 2005 was Australia's oldest surviving foreign-language newspaper.

A. P. L. Stuer, *The French in Australia* (Canb, 1982); L. Paszkowski, *Poles in Australia and Oceania 1790-1940* (Syd, 1987); *Jnl of the Royal Austn Hist Society*, 61, pt 1, Mar 1975, p 26; *Le Courrier Australien*, 3 Sept 1943, p 1, 11 Sept 1953, p 4, 28 Apr 1972, p 1; PP14/1, item 1/2/131 (NAA, Perth).

BOGUMILA ZONGOLLOWICZ

Y

YATES, ARTHUR (1861-1926), seedsman, was born on 10 May 1861 at Stretford, Lancashire, England, one of six sons of Samuel Yates, seed merchant, and his wife Mary, née McMullen. Arthur's grandfather George Yates had started as a grocer and seed merchant in 1826. Three years later he opened a separate seed shop and put his eldest son Samuel, aged 15, in charge. Within a few years Samuel's firm outstripped that of his father; in 1855 he joined his father in partnership and in 1888 acquired the whole business. All Samuel's sons joined the firm.

An asthmatic with a weak chest, Arthur was sent to New Zealand for his health, arriving on 23 December 1879 in the *Auckland*. He worked on the land near Otago for two years before opening a small seed shop in Victoria Street West, Auckland, in 1883. He also travelled on horseback selling seeds and taking orders from farmers.

In 1886 Yates visited Australia and on his return sent a commercial traveller to Sydney to take orders for seeds, and leased premises in Sussex Street. After his younger brother Ernest joined him in New Zealand in 1887, Arthur decided to move to Sydney, where the climate suited him better, leaving Ernest to manage the New Zealand business. Arthur visited England in 1888; on 13 November that year in the parish church, Wellington, Shropshire, he married Caroline Mary Davies (d.1918). After a honeymoon in Italy the couple came to Australia.

In 1893 Yates launched his profitable range of packet seeds for suburban home gardeners in Australia. Two years later he set about writing a gardening book. This became *Yates' Gardening Guide for Australia and New Zealand: Hints for Amateurs*, directing its instructions to home gardeners rather than to professionals, as many previous gardening books had done. The ninety-page *Guide* had black and white illustrations. It became an annual publication and contained information on new seeds and varieties as well as the planning and management of gardens and care of shrubs, flowers and vegetables. Still produced more than a century later, it has been the most useful and popular of the relatively inexpensive garden books available.

Yates's seed business had soon become the largest such firm in the colonies. He built an office and warehouse in Sussex Street in 1896, travelled to Europe in search of quality seeds and established seed farms elsewhere in Australia. About 1907 the two brothers decided to operate separate enterprises, Arthur in Australia and Ernest in New Zealand; both businesses were named Arthur Yates & Co. and each maintained close links with their father's business at Manchester. Arthur Yates & Co. Ltd was incorporated in New South Wales in 1910. Arthur's sons Harold, Arthur, Guy and Philip all joined the firm. As was then the custom, his daughters Vera and Maud did not.

Yates lived at Didsbury, Shaftesbury Road, Burwood, worked for St Paul's Church of England and liberally supported the Boys' Home, Millewa, at Ashfield, and the Farm Home, Windsor. He died of cancer on 30 July 1926 at his home, survived by his six children, and was buried in Enfield cemetery. His estate was sworn for probate at £48 686. The firm operated as a family company until 1951 when it became Yates Seeds Ltd. Later it merged with Hortico to become Arthur Yates & Co. and in 2001 Yates Ltd, which in 2003 was purchased by Orica Ltd for $45 million.

Yates Garden Guide: Centennial Edition 1895-1995 (Syd, 1995); R. Aitken and M. Looker, *The Oxford Companion to Australian Gardens* (Melb, 2002); *Carcoar Chronicle*, 10 Apr 1908, p 4; *SMH*, 2 Aug 1926, p 12, 4 Sept 1926, p 19; *Daily Telegraph* (Syd), 3 Aug 1926, p 8; *Australian*, 27 Oct 2001, p 36; *Austn Financial Review*, 25 Sept 2003, p 19; *Business Review Weekly*, 30 Oct 2003, p 11; W. H. Ifould statutory declaration re origin of Yarraura Spencer Sweet Peas (ML).   VICTOR CRITTENDEN

Z

ZICHY-WOINARSKI, GERTRUDE MARY (1874-1955), community welfare worker, was born on 2 March 1874 at Ballarat, Victoria, sixth child of English-born parents Henry Brind, chemist, and his wife Hester Barnet, née Goodfellow. On 17 April 1895 at Christ Church Cathedral, Ballarat, Gertrude married with Anglican rites Victorian-born Victor Joseph Emanuel Zichy-Woinarski, a physician and surgeon of Hungarian and Polish descent. They had four children.

Elected a member of the Melbourne Ladies' Benevolent Society when aged 26, Gertrude became a 'district visitor' and worked for many years in North Melbourne. In August 1913 she was elected a vice-president of the society. Following the death of a son in 1919 and of her husband in 1921, she assumed an increasingly prominent and active role in the M.L.B.S. and from June 1926 was honorary secretary. Politicians, parliamentary committees and the Australian Broadcasting Commission frequently sought her opinion on social welfare issues. In 1929 the former premier G. M. Prendergast [q.v.11] praised her 'immense service' and claimed: 'This lady can be fully trusted and the workers have confidence in her'.

Her involvement with the benevolent society coincided with a period of modernization of social welfare. Despite being politically conservative, in a time of changes in practice and ideology during the 1930s Zichy-Woinarski demonstrated her willingness to work towards ideals associated with modern welfare. She represented the M.L.B.S. on the committee that in 1929 formed the Victorian Institution of Almoners. That year she helped to form the Central Council of Victorian Benevolent Societies, of which she became secretary. In 1930 she was asked by Jessie Henderson and Stanley Greig Smith [qq.v.9,16] to assist in the development of a movement to assist unemployed and homeless girls.

During the Depression, Zichy-Woinarski was involved with the State Relief Committee and in 1933 became secretary of the Melbourne Public Assistance Committee, which distributed government sustenance payments. From 1939 she was secretary of the Victorian Association of Benevolent Societies, which amalgamated with the Central Council of Benevolent Societies. In 1942 she was approached to serve on the advisory board of women on the Evacuation Committee, established by the government to research and plan the co-ordination of children's evacuation during World War II.

Zichy-Woinarski worked with journalist Edith Abbott to write *Women Who Helped Pioneers* (Melbourne, 1945), a history of the M.L.B.S. Late in 1945, having resigned from her various roles as secretary, she threw herself into other causes. Despite suffering a heart attack next year, she took little leave from her work and was determined to establish a home for older homeless women. Her commitment helped to establish in 1948 Ravenswood, which became a major focus of the benevolent society beyond the 1950s when its role in welfare provision changed dramatically.

Having received King George V's jubilee medal (1935), in 1954 Zichy-Woinarski was appointed M.B.E. She continued attending meetings of the benevolent society up until her death on 4 November 1955 in hospital at Mordialloc. She was cremated. Two sons and one daughter, Beryl Asche, who was also an office-holder in the M.L.B.S., survived her. Gertrude's daughter-in-law, Elsie Zichy-Woinarski, a trained hospital almoner, was also active on the society's committee.

Melbourne Ladies' Benevolent Society, *Annual Report*, 1920-39; J. Bush, Crisis of Moral Authority: The Ladies Benevolent Societies in the Victorian Welfare Field, 1920-1939 (Ph.D. thesis, ANU, 2002); Melbourne Ladies' Benevolent Society, Minutes, 1900-56 (SLV); information from Mr B. Zichy-Woinarsky, Melb.   JANINE BUSH

ZÖLLNER, SIMON (1821-1880), manufacturer, was born in 1821 at Posen, Prussia (Poznan, Poland), son of Marcus Zöllner, merchant, and his London-born wife Rosalie, née Indig. Simon reached Sydney from Hamburg in the *Cesar Godeffroy* on 11 December 1852 as one of 230 migrants. By 1853 he was working as a merchant at Sofala, but was living in Sydney when he was naturalized in August 1855. In partnership with Louis Heitz and Henry Lippman, he began business as a tin plate manufacturer at 381 George Street, as Zöllner & Henry. At St James's Church of England, King Street, on 15 August 1857 he married London-born Anne Maria Thurston (d.1915). They had six children.

Heitz had left the partnership in October 1855 and Lippman departed about 1860. In the meantime, the company had turned its attention to the galvanizing process, patented in France in 1837, whereby iron was coated with molten zinc to prevent corrosion. Zöllner's business thrived and in the 1860s he secured larger premises, including a new factory in Dixon Street and a wholesale warehouse and office in York Street. By 1870 his Sydney Galvanizing Works employed fifty-two men and boys and worked up fifteen to eighteen tons of black sheet-iron a week into galvanized tubs, buckets, tanks, sheep troughs, guttering and ridging in addition to tinware products, including cans, pannikins, candlesticks, candle moulds, pitchers and teapots. A particular specialty was the manufacture of household and blacksmiths' bellows.

Zöllner, with other Sydney businessmen, including Ebenezer Vickery and John Frazer [qq.v.6,4], was a leading shareholder in the Fitzroy Ironworks Co. at Mittagong. Beginning in 1864, its blast furnace supplied iron for the Gundagai bridge and Vickery's new premises in Pitt Street, Sydney, but its operations proved uneconomical and in 1873 Zöllner and others sold their interests to the Fitzroy Bessemer Steel Hematite Iron & Coal Co. Ltd, incorporated in England.

Zöllner died of pneumonia on 17 October 1880 at his Potts Point home, survived by his wife and their two sons and two daughters, and was buried in the Anglican section of Rookwood cemetery. His estate was sworn for probate at £8860.

His eldest son MARTIN LEO (1858-1900), born on 25 June 1858 in Sydney, took over the business, which he expanded and modernized. The works, stores and office were moved to 443-445 Kent Street. By 1888 a new patent process for tinwork had been acquired and three large presses and a stamper were in constant use, the dies for the latter being made on the premises. Zöllner's products were renowned for their finish and durability and were particularly favoured by country storekeepers. The firm had a considerable market throughout Australasia and won awards at intercolonial and international exhibitions from 1869.

Leo Zöllner lived at Carmyle, West Street, Petersham, and was a member of the Sydney Rowing Club. On 28 April 1890 at St Michael's Church of England, Sydney, he married Maude Hoctor. Following the outbreak of the South African War, he sailed to Cape Town and by 28 February 1900 had joined Kitchener's Horse, a unit largely composed of men from many countries. Serving with 'G' Squadron, Trooper Zöllner was killed on 27 April 1900 at Thaba Nchu, east of Bloemfontein, in the Orange Free State. His wife and three children survived him. About 1923 S. Zollner & Co., which had become Zollner Ltd and moved to Dowling Street, Waterloo, was taken over by Briton Ltd.

The Industrial Progress of New South Wales (Syd, 1871); W. F. Morrison, The Aldine Centennial History of New South Wales, 2 (Syd, 1888); G. J. R. Linge, Industrial Awakening (Canb, 1979); T&CJ, 30 Mar 1872, p 401; Newcastle Morning Herald, 10 Jan 1901, p 5; The Times (Lond), 8 Apr 1903, p 4; 4/3272, item 3913 and naturalization records, register 1, pp 388 & 658 (reel 129) (SRNSW); information from Mr A. W. Zollner, Ayr, Qld.   G. P. WALSH

Name Index

To *Australian Dictionary of Biography* Volumes 1 to 16 and *Supplement*

This index includes the names of all major and minor (small-capped) entries appearing in volumes 1 to 16 of the *Australian Dictionary of Biography* as well as in this *Supplement*, together with the names of other persons about whom significant biographical data is contained in the text. The index is not, however, a concordance, and names with only limited biographical detail have been omitted because of lack of space.

Life dates have been used to distinguish between identical names. Where full life dates were not available, abbreviated life dates or *floruit* dates have been used. Cross-references have been used to help the reader with pseudonyms, aliases and commonly used names. Space precluded the cross-referencing of all married women to their maiden names, except in those cases where information in the text related to activities carried out under more than one name.

The numbers following the names indicate the volume number, or Supp (for Supplement), followed by the page number. Thus, 1.1 indicates volume 1, page 1, and Supp.418 indicates Supplement, page 418.

Aikenhead, James, 1.3
Ainslie, James Percival, 13.16
Ainsworth, Alfred Bower, 7.21
Ainsworth, George Frederick, 7.21
Aird, John Allan, 13.17
Airey, Henry Parke, 7.22
Airey, Peter, 7.23
Aiston, George, 13.18
Aitken, George Lewis, 7.24
Aitken, James, 7.24
Aitken, John, 1.4
Akehurst, Arthur Purssell, Supp.6
Akeroyd, Arthur Gordon, 13.19
Akhurst, Daphne Jessie, 7.25
Alanson, Alfred Godwin, 7.26
Albert, Jacques, 7.27
Albert, Michel François (Frank), 7.27
Albiston, Arthur Edward, 7.28
Albiston, Walter, 7.29
Alcock, Alfred Upton, 7.30
Alcock, Henry, 7.30
Alcock, Randal James, 7.31
Alcorn, Cyril David, 13.19
Alcorn, Ivan Wells, 13.19
Alden, John, 13.20
Alder, Milton Cromwell, 13.21
Alderman, Sir Harry Graham, 13.22
Alderman, Walter William, 7.32
Alderson, Sir Harold George, 13.22
Alderson, William Maddison, 3.20
Alexander, Albert Ernest, 13.23
Alexander, Frederick Matthias, 7.32
Alexander, Lilian Helen, Supp.7
Alexander, Maurice, 3.20
Alexander, Samuel, 7.33
Algeranoff, Harcourt, 13.24
Allan, Andrew, 7.34
Allan, Catherine Mabel Joyce, 13.25
Allan, David, 1.5
Allan, Frances Elizabeth, 13.26
Allan, George Leavis, 3.21
Allan, Herbert Trangmar, 13.27
Allan, James Thomas, 3.22
Allan, John, 7.34
Allan, Margaret Theadora, 13.28
Allan, Norman Thomas William, 13.28
Allan, Percy, 7.36
Allan, Robert Marshall, 7.37
Allan, Stella May, 7.39
Allan, William, 3.23
Allard, Sir George Mason, 7.40
Allardyce, Sir William Lamond, 7.40
Allcot, John Charles, 13.29
Allen, Alfred, 3.26
Allen, Alfred Weaver, Supp.7
Allen, Arthur Denis Wigram, 13.30
Allen, Arthur Max, 13.31
Allen, Arthur Samuel, 13.32
Allen, Sir Carleton Kemp, 7.44
Allen, George, 1.5
Allen, George Thomas, 7.41
Allen, Sir George Wigram, 3.24
Allen, Sir Harry Brookes, 7.42
Allen, Horace William, 7.45

Allen, Joseph Francis, 7.44
Allen, Leslie Holdsworth, 7.44
Allen, Mary Cecil, 7.46
Allen, William (1790?-1856), 1.7
Allen, William (1847-1919), 7.44
Allen, William Bell, 3.25
Allen, Sir William Guildford, 13.33
Allen, William Johnston, 3.26
Alleyne, Haynes Gibbes, 3.26
Allingham, Christopher, 3.27
Allison, Francis, 1.7
Allison, Sir William John, 13.34
Allison, William Race, 1.7
Allman, Edith Dora, 13.35
Allman, Francis, 1.8
Allman, George Faunce, 13.35
Allnutt, Albert George, 13.36
Allnutt, Marion Ellen Lea, 13.36
Allport, Henry, 13.37
Allport, Joseph, 1.9
Allport, Morton, 3.28
Allport, Morton John Cecil, 13.37
Allsop, Raymond Cottam, 13.38
Allum, Mahomet, 7.47
Allwood, Robert, 1.10
Allworth, Edith, 16.376
Alngindabu, (Lucy McGinness), 13.39
Alsop, Rodney Howard, 7.47
Alston, James, 7.48
Alston, Mary, 7.49
Alt, Augustus Theodore Henry, 1.11
Alwyn, Phyllis Ethel von, 9.100
Alyandabu, see Alngindabu
Amadio, John (Bell), 7.49
Ambrose, Theodore, 7.50
Amess, Samuel, 3.29
Amies, Sir Arthur Barton Pilgrim, 13.39
Amies, Geraldine Christein Wilhelmina,
 Lady, 13.39
Amiet, William Albert, 13.40
Amos, Adam, 1.12
Ampt, Gustav Adolph, 7.51
Ancher, Sydney Edward Cambrian, 13.41
Andersen, Clifford Werlin, 13.42
Anderson, Alfred William, 13.43
Anderson, Alice Elizabeth Foley, Supp.8
Anderson, Andrew Canning, 13.44
Anderson, Austin Thomas, 13.46
Anderson, Charles, 7.51
Anderson, Sir David Murray, 7.52
Anderson, Sir Donald George, 13.45
Anderson, Ernest Augustus, 7.53
Anderson, Ethel Campbell Louise, 13.46
Anderson, Sir Francis, 7.53
Anderson, Frank Struan, 13.47
Anderson, George, 13.48
Anderson, George Herbert, 13.48
Anderson, Harry Ross, 13.49
Anderson, Henry Charles Lennox, 7.55
Anderson, Hugh, 1.14
Anderson, James Outram, 13.50
Anderson, Jean Cairns, Lady, 7.63
Anderson, John (1790-1858), 1.13
Anderson, John (1893-1962), 7.56

Cameron, Charles, 1.196
Cameron, Cyril St Clair, 7.535
Cameron, Donald (1780-1857), 3.336
Cameron, Donald (1814-1890), 3.337
Cameron, Donald (1838-1916), 3.337
Cameron, Donald (1877-1950), 7.531
Cameron, Donald Alastair, 13.348
Cameron, Sir Donald Charles, 7.532
Cameron, Donald James, 7.533
Cameron, Donald Norman, 7.535
Cameron, Elizabeth (Bessy), Supp.59
Cameron, Ewen Hugh, 3.338
Cameron, Ewen Wallace, 3.339
Cameron, Sir Gordon Roy, 13.349
Cameron, James (1827-1905), 3.340
Cameron, James (1846-1922), 7.536
Cameron, John, 7.537
Cameron, Keith Addison, 13.350
Cameron, Mary Isabella, 3.337
Cameron, Maud Martha, 15.361
Cameron, Robert George, Supp.60
Cameron, Samuel Sherwen, 7.539
Camfield, Julius Henry, 7.539
Camidge, Charles Edward, 7.540
Camm, Daniel Thomas, 13.351
Camm, Philip John, 13.351
Campbell, Alan Walter, 13.351
Campbell, Alexander (1805-1890), 1.197
Campbell, Alexander (1812-1891), 3.341
Campbell, Alexander James, 3.342
Campbell, Alexander Petrie, 13.352
Campbell, Alfred Walter, 7.541
Campbell, Allan, 7.542
Campbell, Archibald George, 7.543
Campbell, Archibald James, 7.543
Campbell, Archibald Stewart, 13.353
Campbell, Arthur Lang, 13.353
Campbell, Charles (1810-1888), 1.198
Campbell, Charles (1840-1905), Supp.61
Campbell, Charles William, 7.550
Campbell, Colin, 3.343
Campbell, Colin Wallace, 13.354
Campbell, David Alexander Stewart, 13.355
Campbell, David Watt Ian, 13.356
Campbell, Donald (1813-1868), 7.551
Campbell, Donald (1886-1945), 7.544
Campbell, Edward (d.1931), 7.544
Campbell, Edward (1883-1944), 7.544
Campbell, Elizabeth (Bessie), 7.545
Campbell, Envidale Savage Norman, 3.344
Campbell, Eric, 7.546
Campbell, Francis Rawdon Hastings, 3.345
Campbell, Frederick Alexander, 7.547
Campbell, Gerald Ross, 7.548
Campbell, Sir Harold Alfred Maurice, 13.357
Campbell, James, 7.549
Campbell, James Lang, 7.550
Campbell, John (1802-1886), 1.199
Campbell, John (Tinker) (d.1876), 1.201
Campbell, John Alan, 7.551
Campbell, John Archibald, 7.551
Campbell, John Dunmore, 7.549
Campbell, John Fauna, 7.552
Campbell, John Thomas, 1.199

Campbell, John William Wallace, Supp.62
Campbell, Joseph, Supp.63
Campbell, Oswald Rose, 3.346
Campbell, Persia Gwendoline Crawford,
  13.358
Campbell, Pieter Laurentz, 1.201
Campbell, Robert (1769-1846), 1.202
Campbell, Robert (1789-1851), 1.206
Campbell, Robert (1804-1859), 1.206
Campbell, Robert Richmond, 13.360
Campbell, Sir Thomas Cockburn, see
  Cockburn-Campbell
Campbell, Thomas Draper, 13.361
Campbell, Thomas Irving, 7.552
Campbell, Walter Scott, 7.553
Campbell, William, 3.347
Campbell, William Douglas, 1.208
Campbell Praed, Mrs, see Praed, Rosa
  Caroline
Campion, Frederick Henry, 7.554
Campion, Sir William Robert, 7.555
Candler, Samuel Curtis, Supp.63
Cani, John, 3.348
Cann, George, 7.555
Cann, John Henry, 7.555
Cann, William Henry, 7.556
Cannan, James Harold, 13.362
Cannan, Kearsey, 3.349
Canning, Alfred Wernam, 7.557
Cantamessa, Ettore Giuseppe, 13.363
Canterbury, John Henry Thomas Manners-
  Sutton, Viscount, 3.350
Cantor, Maurice Emanuel Henry, 13.364
Cape, William, 1.209
Cape, William Timothy, 1.209
Carandini, Cristofero Palmerston, see
  Palmerston, Christie
Carandini, Jerome, 3.351
Carandini, Marie, 3.351
Carandini, Rosina, see Palmer, Rosina Martha
  Hosanah
Carbasse, Louise, see Lovely
Carboni, Raffaello, 3.352
Card, Mary, 7.558
Cardell-Oliver, Dame Annie Florence Gillies,
  13.365
Cardell Oliver, Arthur, 13.365
Cardigan, see Wolfe, Herbert Austin
Cardus, Sir John Frederick Neville, 13.366
Cardwell, Edward, 1st Viscount, 3.354
Carew-Smyth, Ponsonby May, 7.558
Carey, George Jackson, 3.354
Carey, John Randal, 7.559
Carington, Rupert Clement George, 7.560
Carington Smith, Jack, 13.367
Carlile, Sir Edward, 7.561
Carlile McDonnell, Ethel, see McDonnell,
  Ethel
Carlton, James Andrew, 7.561
Carmichael, Ambrose Campbell, 7.562
Carmichael, Grace Elizabeth Jennings, 7.564
Carmichael, Henry, 1.210
Carmichael, Sir Thomas David Gibson,
  Baron, 7.564

Johnstone, John Edward, 14.577
Johnstone, John Lorimer Gibson, 9.503
Johnstone, Robert, *see* Johnston, Robert
  Mackenzie
Johnstone, Robert Arthur, 4.486
Johnstone, Thomas, 4.487
Johnstone, William Raphael, 14.578
Jollie-Smith, *see* Smith, Christian Brynhild
  Ochiltree Jollie
Jolly, Alexander Stewart, Supp.205
Jolly, Norman William, 9.504
Jolly, William Alfred, 9.504
Jones, Alfred James, 9.505
Jones, Allan Murray, 9.506
Jones, Arthur, 14.579
Jones, Auber George, 4.488
Jones, Charles Edwin, 4.488
Jones, Sir Charles Lloyd, 9.507
Jones, David, 2.23
Jones, Sir David Fletcher, 14.579
Jones, Doris Egerton, 9.508
Jones, Edith Emily, Supp.205
Jones, Ernest, 9.509
Jones, Frederic Wood, 9.510
Jones, Harold Edward, 9.512
Jones, Harriet, *see* Knowles, Harriet
Jones, Sir Henry, 9.513
Jones, Hooper Josse Brewster, 9.514
Jones, Horatio Thomas, Supp.206
Jones, Inigo Owen, 9.515
Jones, John (1826?-1903), *see* St Leon,
  Matthew
Jones, John (1875-1942), Supp.206
Jones, John Alexander Stammers, 9.518
Jones, John Percy, 9.516
Jones, Joseph, 4.489
Jones, Kathleen Annie Gilman, 9.517
Jones, Leslie John Roberts, 9.518
Jones, Mary, *see* Morgan, Molly
Jones, Nina Eva Vida, 9.518
Jones, Norman Edward Thomas, 14.581
Jones, Owen, 3.117
Jones, Sir Philip Sydney, 4.490
Jones, Ralph, 14.584
Jones, Rees Rutland, 9.519
Jones, Reginald Stuart, 14.584
Jones, Richard (1786-1852), 2.24
Jones, Richard (1816-1892), 2.25
Jones, Thomas Gilbert Henry, 14.585
Jones, Thomas Henry, 14.586
Jones, William (c.1842-1906), Supp.207
Jones, William (1842-1907), 9.520
Jones, William Ernest, 9.520
Jonsson, Nils Josef, 9.521
Jordan, Sir Frederick Richard, 9.522
Jordan, Henry, 4.491
Jorgenson, Jorgen, 2.26
Jorgensen, Justus, 14.587
Joris, Joannes Julius Alphonsus, 14.588
Jose, Arthur Wilberforce, 9.523
Jose, George Herbert, 9.524
Jose, Sir Ivan Bede, 14.588
Joseland, Richard George Howard, 9.524
Joseph, Samuel Aaron, 4.492

Josephson, Jacob, 4.492
Josephson, Joshua Frey, 4.492
Joshua, Robert, 14.589
Joske, Enid, 14.590
Joubert, Didier Numa, 4.493
Joubert, Jules François de Sales, 4.493
Jowett, Edmund, 9.525
Joy, Jean, 13.559
Joyce, Alfred, 2.28
Joyce, Anthony Walter, 14.591
Joyce, Donovan Maxwell, 14.592
Joyce, Edmund Michael, 9.526
Joyce, George, 2.28
Joyner, Frederick Allen, Supp.208
Joynton-Smith, James John, *see* Smith, Sir
  James John Joynton
Juan, John, 14.593
Judd, Ernest Edward Job Pullin, Supp.208
Jude, Sir Norman Lane, Supp.209
Judkins, George Alfred, 9.527
Judkins, William Henry, 9.527
Jukes, Joseph Beete, 2.29
Julius, Sir George Alfred, 9.528
Julius, Max Nordau, 14.593
Jull, Martin Edward, 9.529
Jull, Roberta Henrietta Margaritta, 9.530
Jury, Charles Rischbieth, 14.594
Kaawirn Kuunawarn, Supp.211
Kaberry, Phyllis Mary, 14.596
Kable, Henry, 2.31
Kable, John, 2.32
Kabu, Tommy, 14.597
Kaeppel, Carl Henry, 9.532
Kaleski, Robert Lucian Stanislaus, 9.532
Kane, Benjamin Francis, 5.1
Kane, Henry Plow, 2.32
Kapiu, Gagai, *see* Gagai, Kapiu Masi
Karloan (Kaloni), Albert, 14.597
Kashiwagi, Taira, 9.533
Kater, Sir Gregory Blaxland, 14.598
Kater, Henry Edward, 5.1
Kater, Norman Murchison (Mick), 14.598
Kater, Sir Norman William, 9.534
Kates, Francis Benjamin, 5.2
Kauffmann, John, 9.535
Kauper, Henry Alexis, 9.536
Kavanagh, Edward John, 9.537
Kavanagh, John Patrick Marcus, 14.600
Kavanaugh, Robert Murray, 14.600
Kavel, August Ludwig Christian, 2.33
Kay, Alick Dudley, 9.538
Kay, Joseph Henry, 2.34
Kay, Margaret, 14.601
Kay, William Elphinstone, 9.538
Kay, William Porden, 2.34
Kaye, Ruth Emilie, *see* Kent, Constance
Kaylock, Susie Olive, 14.602
Kayser, Heinrich Wilhelm Ferdinand, 5.3
Kean, Charles John, 5.4
Kean, Ellen, 5.4
Keane, Edward Vivien Harvey, 5.4
Keane, Francis Charles Patrick, 14.602
Keane, Richard Valentine, 14.603
Keaney, Paul Francis, 9.540

Morgan, William Matheson, 15.407
Morgans, Alfred Edward, 10.586
Moriarty, Abram Orpen, 5.289
Moriarty, Barbara (Biddy) Ierne, 15.408
Moriarty, Daniel, 10.586
Moriarty, Edward Orpen, 5.291
Moriarty, Merion Marshall, 5.290
Moriarty, William, 2.259
Morice, James Percy, 10.587
Morice, Louise (Lucy), 10.587
Morison, Alexander, 5.291
Morisset, James Thomas, 2.260
Morley, William, 10.588
Moroney, James Vincent, 15.409
Moroney, Timothy, 10.589
Morphett, Sir John, 2.261
Morphew, Essie Adele, *see* Ackland, Essie
  Adele
Morres, Elsie Frances, 10.590
Morrice, Nellie Constance, Supp.289
Morrill, James, 2.262
Morris, Albert, 10.591
Morris, Augustus, 5.292
Morris, Basil Moorhouse, 15.410
Morris, Edward Ellis, 5.293
Morris, Emanuel Sydney, 15.411
Morris, Ethel Ida, 15.415
Morris, George Francis, 5.294
Morris, Isack, 15.412
Morris, Sir John Demetrius, 15.412
Morris, Sir John Newman, *see* Newman-
  Morris
Morris, Sir Kenneth James, 15.414
Morris, Myra Evelyn, 10.591
Morris, Robert Newton, 5.295
Morris, William Perry French, 15.415
Morrison, Alexander, 5.295
Morrison, Allan Arthur, 15.417
Morrison, Askin, 5.297
Morrison, Charles Norman, 10.592
Morrison, Edward Charles, 10.593
Morrison, Eliza Fraser, *see* Mitchell, Eliza
  Fraser, Lady
Morrison, Frank Richard, 15.417
Morrison, George, 5.298
Morrison, George Ernest, 10.593
Morrison, Joan, Supp.186
Morrison, Philip Crosbie, 15.418
Morrison, Sibyl Enid Vera Munro, 10.596
Morrison, William Shepherd, *see* Dunrossil
Morrow, Sir Arthur William, 15.420
Morrow, James, 5.298
Morrow, James Cairns, 15.422
Morehead, Sir Leslie James, 15.423
Mort, Eirene, 10.596
Mort, Thomas Sutcliffe, 5.299
Mortimer, Rex Alfred, 15.425
Mortlock, Dorothy Elizabeth, 15.426
Mortlock, John Andrew Tennant, 15.426
Mortlock, William Ranson, 5.301
Mortlock, William Tennant, 5.302
Morton, Alexander, 10.597
Morton, Frank, 10.598
Morton, William Lockhart, 5.302

Morwood, James Eric, Supp.290
Moseley, Henry Doyle, 15.427
Moseley, John, Supp.290
Moseley, Percival, Supp.290
Moses, John, Supp.291
Moses, Margaret Veronica, 15.428
Mosman, Archibald, 2.263
Mosman, George, 2.263
Mosman, Hugh, 5.303
Moss, Alice Frances Mabel (May), 10.599
Moss, William, 5.303
Moss, William Lionel, 15.429
Moten, Murray John, 15.429
Mott, George Henry, 10.599, Supp.292
Mott, Hamilton Charnock, 10.599
Moubray, Thomas, 5.304
Mould, John Stuart, 15.430
Moulden, Beaumont Arnold, 10.600
Moulden, Deborah, *see* Hackett, Deborah
  Vernon, Lady
Moulden, Sir Frank Beaumont, 10.600
Moulds, Constance, 10.601
Moule-Probert, John, *see* Probert, John
  William
Moulton, James Egan, 5.305
Mountford, Charles Pearcy, 15.431
Mountgarrett, Jacob, 2.264
Mouton, Jean Baptiste Octave, 10.602
Mowbray, Philip Henry Mitchell, Supp.293
Mowle, Mary Braidwood, Supp.294
Mowll, Dorothy Anne, 15.433
Mowll, Howard West Kilvinton, 15.433
Moyes, Alban George (Johnny), 15.434
Moyes, John Stoward, 15.434
Moyes, Morton Henry, 10.602
Moynihan, Cornelius, Supp.294
Moysey, Annie, 15.436
Mudie, Ian Mayelston, 15.437
Mudie, James, 2.264
Muecke, Carl Wilhelm Ludwig, 5.306
Muecke, Hugo Carl Emil, 10.604
Mueller, Baron Sir Ferdinand Jakob Heinrich
  von, 5.306
Muir, Alan Holmes (Bonnie), 15.438
Muir, Thomas, 2.266
Muirden, William, 10.604
Mulga Fred, 15.438
Mulgrave, Peter Archer, 2.267
Mullagh, Johnny, 5.308
Mullaly, John Charles, 10.605
Mullan, John, 10.606
Mullawirraburka, Supp.295
Mullen, Leslie Miltiades, 10.607
Mullen, Samuel, 5.309
Mullens, Josiah, Supp.296
Mullens, Phyllis Katherine Fraser, 15.439
Müller, Florens Theodor Reinhard, Supp.296
Muller, Frederick, 10.607
Mulley, Daniel Stern, 15.440
Mulligan, James Venture, 5.310
Mullins, John Lane, 10.608
Mulquin, Katherine, 10.609
Mulvany, Edward Joseph, 10.610
Mumaring, *see* Bindi, Daisy

Toutcher, Richard Frederick, 12.246
Tovell, Raymond Walter, 16.405
Town, Andrew, 6.294
Towner, Edgar Thomas, 12.247
Townley, Athol Gordon, 16.406
Towns, Robert, 6.294
Townsend, Albert Rinder, 16.408
Townsend, Alfred Richard, 12.248
Townsend, George Wilfred Lambert, 12.249
Townsend, Harry Orton, 16.408
Townsend, William, 6.296
Townson, John, 2.536
Townson, Robert, 2.537
Tozer, Sir Horace, 12.250
Tracey, Eliza, 12.250
Tracy, Richard Thomas, 6.297
Traeger, Alfred Hermann, 12.251
Traill, Jessie Constance Alicia, 12.252
Traill, John Charles Merriman, 12.252
Traill, William Henry, 6.298
Train, George Francis, 6.299
Tranter, Charles Herbert, 12.253
Treacy, Patrick Ambrose, 6.300
Treasure, Harry Louis, 12.254
Treflé, John Louis, 12.254
Tregurtha, Edward Primrose, 2.538
Treloar, George Devine, 12.255
Treloar, John Linton, 12.256
Trenerry, Horace Hurtle, 12.257
Trenwith, William Arthur, 12.258
Trethowan, Sir Arthur King, 12.260
Trethowan, Hubert Charles, 12.261
Trevascus, William Charles, 12.261
Treweek, Elsy, see Collier, Elsie Louise
Triaca, Camillo, 12.262
Tribolet, Donald Hamilton, 16.409
Trickett, Edward, 6.301
Trickett, Joseph, 6.302
Trickett, Oliver, 12.262
Trickett, William Joseph, 6.302
Trigg, Henry, 2.539
Triggs, Arthur Bryant, 12.263
Tripp, Edward Clavell, Supp.385
Tritton, Harold Percy Croydon (Duke), 12.264
Tritton, Lydia Ellen, 16.409
Troedel, Johannes Theodor Charles, 6.302
Trollope, Anthony, 6.303
Trompf, Percival Albert, 12.264
Trooper Bluegum, see Hogue, Oliver
Trott, Albert Edwin, 12.265
Trott, George Henry Stevens, 12.265
Trouette, Jean-Pierre, Supp.386
Troup, Gilbert Reynolds, Supp.387
Trout, Sir Herbert Leon, 16.410
Trouton, Frederick Henry, 6.304
Trower, Gerard, 12.266
Troy, Patrick Laurence, 16.411
Truchanas, Olegas, 16.412
Truebridge, Benjamin Arthur, 16.413
Trugernanner (Truganini), 6.305
Truman, Ernest Edwin Philip, 12.266
Truman, John, 12.267
Trumble, Hugh, 12.268

Trumble, Hugh Compson, 16.414
Trumble, Thomas, 12.269
Trumper, Victor Thomas, 12.269
Trundle, Jean Amalie, 16.415
Truscott, Keith William, 16.415
Truscott, William John, 12.272
Tryon, Sir George, 6.305
Tryon, Henry, 12.272
Tubb, Frederick Harold, 12.273
Tuck, Marie Anne, 12.274
Tucker, Albert Edwin Elworthy Lee, 6.306
Tucker, Charles, 12.274
Tucker, Gerard Kennedy, 12.275
Tucker, Graham Shardalow Lee, 16.416
Tucker, Horace Finn, 12.275
Tucker, James, 2.539
Tucker, Percy John Robert, 16.417
Tucker, Thomas George, 12.277
Tucker, Tudor St George, 12.278
Tuckett, Francis Curtis, 12.279
Tuckett, Francis John, 12.279
Tuckett, Joseph Helton, 12.280
Tuckett, Lewis, 12.279
Tuckett, Philip Samuel, 12.280
Tuckfield, Francis, 2.540
Tuckfield, William John, 12.280
Tuckiar, see Dhakiyarr
Tuckson, John Anthony, 16.418
Tudawali, Robert, 16.419
Tudor, Francis Gwynne, 12.281
Tufnell, Edward Wyndham, 6.307
Tulaba, Supp.387
Tulk, Augustus Henry, 6.308
Tullipan, Ronald William, 16.420
Tulloch, Eric William, 12.282
Tully, Joan, 16.420
Tully, William Alcock, 6.309
Tunbridge, Walter Howard, 12.283
Tunn, John Patrick, 12.284
Tunnecliffe, Thomas, 12.284
Turley, Joseph Henry Lewis (Harry), 12.285
Turnbull, Adam, 2.541
Turnbull, Archibald, 12.286
Turnbull, Ernest, 12.287
Turnbull, Gilbert Munro, 12.287
Turnbull, Keith Hector, 16.421
Turnbull, Stanley Clive Perry, 16.422
Turnbull, Sir Winton George, 16.423
Turner, Alfred Allatson, 6.310
Turner, Alfred Jefferis, 12.288
Turner, Charles Thomas Biass, 6.310
Turner, Dora Jeannette, 12.289
Turner, Ethel Mary, 12.290
Turner, Fred, 12.292
Turner, Sir George, 12.293
Turner, Henry Gyles, 6.311
Turner, Ian Alexander Hamilton, 16.424
Turner, James Alfred, 12.296
Turner, James Francis, 6.313
Turner, John William, 12.296
Turner, Lilian Wattnall, 12.290
Turner, Martha, 6.314
Turner, Walter James, 12.297
Turner, Walter James Redfern, 12.297